The Civil Litigation Process
Cases and Materials
Seventh Edition

GENERAL EDITOR

Janet Walker
Osgoode Hall Law School
York University

FOUNDING EDITOR

Garry D. Watson, QC
Osgoode Hall Law School
York University

SENIOR EDITOR

Timothy Pinos
Cassels, Brock & Blackwell, LLP
Toronto

EDITORS

Jane Bailey
Faculty of Law
University of Ottawa

Colleen M. Hanycz
Brescia University College
University of Western Ontario

Andrew Pirie
Faculty of Law
University of Victoria

Barbara Billingsley
Faculty of Law
University of Alberta

Erik S. Knutsen
Faculty of Law
Queen's University

Sean Rehaag
Osgoode Hall Law School
York University

Trevor C.W. Farrow
Osgoode Hall Law School
York University

Ronalda Murphy
Dalhousie Law School
Dalhousie University

Lorne Sossin
Faculty of Law
University of Toronto

2010
EMOND MONTGOMERY PUBLICATIONS LIMITED
TORONTO, CANADA

Emond Montgomery Publications Limited
60 Shaftesbury Avenue
Toronto ON M4T 1A3
http://www.emp.ca

Printed in Canada.

We acknowledge the financial support of the Government of Canada through the Book Publishing Industry Development Program (BPIDP) for our publishing activities.

Acquisitions editor: Peggy Buchan
Marketing manager: Christine Davidson
Sales manager: James W. Black
Production editor: Cindy Fujimoto
Permissions editor: Jennifer Blackmore
Copy editor: Paula Pike
Indexer: Michael Bunn

Library and Archives Canada Cataloguing in Publication

The civil litigation process : cases and materials / Janet Walker ... [et al.]. — 7th ed.

Fourth ed. published under title: Civil litigation, cases and materials.
Earlier eds. published under title: Canadian civil procedure.
Includes index.
ISBN 978-1-55239-342-0

1. Civil procedure—Canada—Cases. 2. Actions and defenses—Canada—Cases.
I. Walker, Janet (Janet Elizabeth)

KE8349.C55 2010   347.71'05   C2009-907150-9
KF8839.ZA2C48 2010

Acknowledgments

American Society of Comparative Law   Robert D. Cooter and Wolfgang Fikentscher, "Indian Common Law: The Role of Custom in American Indian Tribal Courts" (1998), 46 *American Journal of Comparative Law* 287.

Bancroft-Whitney   Louisell and Wally, *Modern California Discovery*, 2nd ed. (San Francisco: Bancroft-Whitney, 1972), 1-6.

Blackwell Publishing   American Law Institute, *Restatement of the Law (Second), Judgments* (Philadelphia: American Law Institute, © 1982), 196-97. Reprinted with permission. All rights reserved.

Blackwell Publishing   William L.F. Felstiner, "The Emergence and Transformation of Disputes: Naming, Blaming, Claiming" (1980-81), 15 *Law & Society Review* 631.

Blackwell Publishing   Carrie J. Menkel-Meadow, "The Many Ways of Mediation" (1995), 11 *Negotiation Journal* 217, at 228-30.

Branch McMaster   Ward Branch, *If It Ain't Broke, Don't Fix It! Does B.C. Need a New Costs Regime for Class Actions?* (Vancouver: Branch McMaster, 2003). Available online: http://www.branchmacmaster.com/storage/articles/civil_lit_conference.pdf.

Canada Law Book   John Morden, "An Overview of the Rules of Civil Procedure in Ontario" (1984), 5 *The Advocates' Quarterly* 257.

Canada Law Book   Janet Walker, "Coordinating Multijurisdiction Class Actions Through Existing Certification Processes" (2005), 41 *Canadian Business Law Journal* 112.

Canada Law Book   Janet Walker, "Recognizing Multijurisdiction Class Action Judgments Within Canada: Key Questions—Suggested Answers" (2005), 46 *Canadian Business Law Journal* 450.

Canada Law Book   Garry D. Watson, "Joinder of Defendants Sued in the Alternative: Solicitors as Co-Defendants" (1981), 2 *The Advocates' Quarterly* 365.

Canadian Bar Association   H. Landerkin and A. Pirie, "Judges as Mediators: What's the Problem with Judicial Dispute Resolution in Canada?" (2003), 82 *Canadian Bar Review* 249.

Canadian Bar Association   Garry D. Watson, "Amendment of Proceedings After Limitation Periods" (1975), 53 *Canadian Bar Review* 237, at 276-78.

Canadian Bar Association   Garry D. Watson, "Duplicative Litigation: Issue Estoppel Abuse of Process and the Death of Mutuality" (1990), 69 *Canadian Bar Review* 623.

Carswell   Lorne D. Sossin, *Boundaries of Judicial Review: The Law of Justiciability in Canada* (Toronto: Carswell, 1999), 202-6. Reprinted and adapted by permission of Carswell, a division of Thomson Reuters Canada Limited.

Carswell   Samuel D. Stevens, "Access to Civil Justice for Aboriginal People" in A. Hutchinson, ed., *Access to Civil Justice* (Scarborough, ON: Carswell, 1990), 203-35 and 212-13. Reprinted by permission of Carswell, a division of Thomson Reuters Canada Limited.

Carswell   Garry D. Watson and Craig Perkins, "Purpose of Examination for Discovery" in Holmested and Watson, *Ontario Civil Procedure (Rule 31/7)* (Scarborough, ON: Carswell, 1984). Reprinted by permission of Carswell, a division of Thomson Reuters Canada Limited.

Carswell   Marvin A. Zuker, *Small Claims Court Practice* (Scarborough, ON: Carswell, 1998), 2-3, 6, and 20-21. Reprinted by permission of Carswell, a division of Thomson Reuters Canada Limited.

Duke University School of Law   Edward H. Cooper, "Class Action Advice in the Form of Questions" (2001), 11 *Duke Journal of Comparative and International Law* 215.

Duke University School of Law   Garry D. Watson, "Class Actions: The Canadian Experience" (2001), 11 *Duke Journal of Comparative & International Law* 269.

The Harvard Law Review Association   Abram Chayes, "The Role of the Judge in Public Law Litigation" (1976), 28 *Harvard Law Review Association* 128. Copyright 1976 by the Harvard Law Review Association.

International Association of Procedural Law   Garry Watson and P.H. Lindblom, "Courts and Lawyers Facing Complex Litigation Problems" in Role and Organization of Judges and Lawyers in Contemporary Societies (9th World Conference on Procedural Law, Coimbra-Lisboa, September 1991), 1 *General Reports* 165.

Irwin Law Inc.   Cara Zwibel, "Settling for Less—Problems and Proposals in the Settlement of Class Actions" (2004), 1 *Canadian Class Action Review* 2, 165. Reprinted by permission of the publisher.

Erik S. Knutsen   Erik S. Knutsen, "Secret Settlements in Canada" (article forthcoming, 2009).

Law Society of Upper Canada   Rosalie Abella, *The Law Society of Upper Canada Professionalism Revisited.* Available online: http://www.ontariocourts.on.ca/coa/en/ps/speeches/professionalism.htm. Reproduction is not an official version of the material reproduced and is not made in affiliation with or with the endorsement of the Ontario courts.

Law Society of Upper Canada   Constance Backhouse, "Gender and Race in the Construction of 'Legal Professionalism': Historical Perspectives." Available online: http://www.lsuc.on.ca/news/pdf/constance_backhouse_gender_and_race.pdf.

LexisNexis Canada Inc.   Alan W. Bryant, Sidney N. Lederman, and Michelle K. Fuerst, *Sopinka, Lederman, and Bryant: The Law of Evidence in Canada*, 3rd ed. (Toronto: LexisNexis, 2009), 950-51 and 957-59.

NYU Press   Oscar Chase, *Law, Culture and Ritual: Disputing Systems in Cross-Cultural Context* (New York: New York University Press, 2005), 1-2.

Osgoode Hall Law Journal   Neil Brooks, "The Judge and the Adversary System" in A. Linden, ed., *The Canadian Judiciary* (Toronto: Osgoode Hall Law School, 1976), 90-116.

Osgoode Hall Law Journal   Trevor Farrow, "Sustainable Professionalism" (2008), 46 *Osgoode Hall Law Journal* 51, at 53-55, 57, 83-87, and 96-100.

Osgoode Hall Law Journal   Frederick Zemans and Patrick Monahan, *From Crisis to Reform: A New Legal Aid Plan for Ontario* (revised and updated) (Toronto: Osgoode Hall Law School, 1996).

Ottawa Law Journal   Jennifer L. Schulz, "Mediator Liability in Canada: An Examination of Emerging American and Canadian Jurisprudence" (2001), 32 *Ottawa Law Review* 269.

Oxford University Press   W.A. Bogart, *Courts and Country: The Limits of Litigation and the Social and Political Life of Canada* (Don Mills, ON: Oxford University Press Canada, © 1994), 107-24. Reprinted by permission of the publisher.

Oxford University Press   H. Patrick Glenn, *Legal Traditions of the World*, 3rd ed. (Don Mills, ON: Oxford University Press Canada, © 2007), 225-31. Reprinted by permission.

Queens Law Journal   J. Watson Hamilton, "Protecting Confidentiality in Mandatory Mediation: Lessons from Ontario and Saskatchewan" (1999), 24 *Queen's Law Journal* 561, at 569-75.

Queen's Printer of Ontario   Marion Boyd, *Dispute Resolution in Family Law: Protecting Choice, Promoting Inclusion* (Toronto: Queen's Printer for Ontario, © 2004), 13-19. Reproduced with permission.

Queen's Printer of Ontario   Ontario Civil Justice Review, *Civil Justice Review, First Report* (Toronto: Queen's Printer for Ontario, © 1995). Reproduced with permission.

Queen's Printer of Ontario   Ontario Law Reform Commission, "Barriers to Access to Civil Justice for Disadvantaged Groups" in *Rethinking Civil Justice: Research Studies for the Civil Justice Review* (Toronto: Queen's Printer for Ontario, © 1996), 637, at 663-74. Reproduced with permission.

Queen's Printer of Ontario   Ontario Law Reform Commission, *Report on the Law of Standing* (Toronto: Queen's Printer for Ontario, © 1989), at 87-89. Reproduced with permission.

Queen's Printer of Ontario   Ontario Legal Aid Review, *Blueprint for Publicly Funded Legal Services: Report of the Ontario Legal Aid Review* (Toronto: Queen's Printer for Ontario, © 1997), 67-74. Available online: http://www.attorneygeneral.jus.gov.on.ca/english/about/pubs/olar/toc.asp. Reproduced with permission.

Queen's Printer of Ontario   Michael Trebilcock, *Report of the Legal Aid Review* (Toronto: Queen's Printer for Ontario, © 2008), 106-110. Reproduced with permission.

Routledge   Allan C. Hutchinson, "Legal Ethics for a Fragmented Society: Between Professional and Personal" (1997), 5 *International Journal of the Legal Profession* 175. Available online at: http://www.tandf.co.uk/journals.

Russell Sage Foundation   Marc Galanter, "Adjudication, Litigation and Related Phenomena" in Leon Lipson and Stanton Wheeler, eds., *Law and Social Sciences* (New York: Russell Sage Foundation, 112 East 64th Street, New York, NY 10021, © 1986), 152, at 152-60. Reprinted with permission.

Stanford Law Review   Kenneth E. Scott, "Two Models of the Civil Process" (1975), 27 *Stanford Law Review* 937.

Statistics Canada   Statistics Canada, "Comparative Statistics on Legal Aid in Canada: 2000-01," adapted from the Statistics Canada publication: *Legal Aid in Canada: Resource and Caseload Statistics 2002/03*, catalogue no. 85F0015, February 2004.

Statistics Canada   Statistics Canada, "Comparative Statistics on Legal Aid in Canada: 2002-03," adapted from the Statistics Canada publication: *Legal Aid in Canada: Resource and Caseload Statistics 2002/03*, catalogue no. 85F0015, February 2004.

Stevens   Sir Jack I.H. Jacob, *The Fabric of English Civil Justice* (London: Stevens, 1987), 5-19.

Sweet and Maxwell   Colleen Hanycz, "More Access to Less Justice: Efficiency, Proportionality and Costs in Canadian Civil Justice Reform" (2008), 27 *Civil Justice Quarterly* 98.

Sweet and Maxwell   W.A. Bogart, "Developments in the Canadian Law of Standing" (1984), *Civil Justice Quarterly* 340-42.

Texas Technical Law Review   Duncan Kennedy, "The Responsibility of Lawyers for the Justice of Their Causes" (1987), 18 *Texas Technical Law Review* 1157, at 1157-58.

UCLA Law Review   Carrie Menkel-Meadow, "For and Against Settlement: Uses and Abuses of the Mandatory Settlement Conference" (1985), 33 *UCLA Law Review* 485, at 486-511.

Uniform Law Conference of Canada   Uniform Law Conference of Canada, *Report of the Uniform Law Conference of Canada's Committee on the National Class and Related Interjurisdictional Issues: Background, Analysis, and Recommendations* (Ottawa: Uniform Law Conference of Canada, 2005). Available online: http://www.ulcc.ca/en/poam2/National_Class_Actions_Rep_En.pdf.

University of Chicago Law School   J.H. Langbein, "The German Advantage in Civil Procedure" (1985), 52 *University of Chicago Law Review* 823-66.

University of Windsor, Faculty of Law   Rod MacDonald, "Access to Justice and Law Reform" (1990), 10 *Windsor Yearbook of Access to Justice* 287.

Janet Walker   Janet Walker, *The Constitution of Canada and the Conflict of Laws* (Thesis: 2001), 85-87. Available online: http://osgoode.yorku.ca/osgmedia.nsf/research/walker_janet.

Washington University Law Review   Thomas O. Main, "The Procedural Foundation of Substantive Law" (2010), 87 *Washington University Law Review* (article forthcoming). Printed by permission.

Garry Watson and Tim Pinos   Garry Watson and Tim Pinos, "A Note on Counterclaims and Set-Off" (2004).

The Yale Law Journal Company, Inc.   Rob Atkinson, "How the Butler Was Made To Do It: The Perverted Professionalism of The Remains of the Day" (1995), 105 *Yale Law Journal* 177, at 181-94. Reprinted by permission of The Yale Law Journal Company, Inc.

The Yale Law Journal Company, Inc.   Owen M. Fiss, "Against Settlement" (1984), 93 *Yale Law Journal* 1073, at 1075-90. Reprinted by permission of The Yale Law Journal Company, Inc.

Table of Contents

Preface to the Seventh Edition

When we began preparing this edition of *The Civil Litigation Process*, it seemed like only yesterday that we were putting the finishing touches on the last edition. And yet, when we took stock of the changes in the law and the approach that Canadians are taking to dispute resolution, we were amazed. The interest in reform and improvement of the traditional forms and forums for resolving disputes seemed to be matched only by the desire to embrace a plurality of perspectives on the process and to pioneer a range of options to meet the needs of those affected. While the basic structure of the book has not changed, we have added a number of new topics and materials—on Indigenous dispute resolution, constitutional rights to legal services, expert witnesses, and national class actions, to mention just a few—and we have made adjustments to the focus and sequence of many of the topics of continuing interest.

Despite an ever-richer array of issues to address, we have been mindful of the need to make the book manageable in size and user-friendly. We have worked hard to trim each excerpt and each section of notes and questions as much as we could; and we look forward to launching a companion website to carry many of the materials that we simply could not include. We are grateful to the staff of Emond Montgomery for all that they have done to support our collaboration throughout, to ensure the quality of the editing, to construct the various tables and indexes, and to make the presentation even more attractive and easy to read. We hope that this will be an edition that you will really enjoy.

As in previous editions, the preparation of the seventh edition has brought changes to the team of co-authors. Allan Hutchinson has joined the ranks of our distinguished authors emeriti and we are pleased to welcome three new authors: Barbara Billingsley, Erik S. Knutsen, and Sean Rehaag. Having consolidated our representation from several of Canada's jurisdictions, we look forward to welcoming authors from other jurisdictions in future editions.

We are proud to say that this has been a truly collaborative enterprise. From the detailed discussions of proposed outlines for each of the chapters, to the co-authoring of many of the chapters, to the careful review and extensive commentary on draft chapters by other members of our team, the book has benefited from a lively exchange of views throughout the process. Nevertheless, special credit should be given to those who were primarily responsible for the preparation of the various chapters as follows: chapter 1, Janet Walker; chapter 2, Sean Rehaag and Erik S. Knutsen; chapter 3, Barbara Billingsley, Janet Walker, and Erik S. Knutsen; chapter 4, Lorne Sossin; chapter 5, Erik S. Knutsen, Lorne Sossin, and Ronalda Murphy; chapter 6, Barbara Billingsley and Trevor C.W. Farrow; chapter 7, Jane

Bailey; chapter 8, Ronalda Murphy; chapter 9, Timothy Pinos; chapter 10, Colleen M. Hanycz, Andrew Pirie, and Erik S. Knutsen; and chapter 11, Garry D. Watson and Janet Walker.

Despite the many updates that we have made in the current edition to reflect recent developments in the law and the evolving approach the teaching and learning of procedural law, we are greatly indebted to the strong tradition of teachers and scholars of procedural law in Canada, a number of whom have been co-authors of previous editions of this work. It is with the highest regard that we dedicate this edition to the editors and contributors to previous editions, including:

Stephen Borins
Neil J. Williams
Allan C. Hutchinson
W.A. Bogart
Robert J. Sharpe
Janet E. Mosher
Kent Roach

Janet Walker
November 2009

Table of Cases

Civil Litigation in Context

I. INTRODUCTION

Most subjects studied in Canadian law schools focus on substantive law and legal standards. By studying statutes, judicial decisions, and academic commentary we can understand the nature of the obligations owed by persons and authorities to one another in society. However, to understand how these obligations operate and how they evolve, we need to understand procedural law. As the *Canadian Encyclopedia* explains, "Procedural law brings substantive law to life and enables rights and duties to be enforced and defended."

Chapter 1 places civil litigation in context and introduces some of the fundamental aspects of civil justice. This basic information will provide the grounding needed to understand the more advanced practical and theoretical issues that are addressed in the other chapters. This chapter places civil litigation into three contexts.

1. *The common law.* The first context is historical and theoretical. We examine the role that procedure played in the birth of common law and that procedure continues to play in its ongoing development. We explore the contrast between the traditional description of procedure as mere "adjectival law" and the important ways in which procedure shapes the evolution of substantive rights and obligations. We also consider the evolving social and political bases for this tension in the relationship between procedural law and substantive law.

1

2. *The adversary system.* The second context is comparative and cross-cultural. We examine the common law tradition of resolving civil disputes through the "adversary system" and how this contrasts with other means of resolving disputes, notably the "inquisitorial system" of the civil law tradition and aboriginal dispute resolution processes. The historical and practical implications of resolving disputes through the adversary system can be seen in every aspect of civil procedure. The materials in this section trace the main features of the adversary system, contrasting it with the inquisitorial system and indigenous dispute resolution, and then exploring the extent to which the distinctions between them are becoming blurred. Finally, the main steps in a civil proceeding are described in a brief overview. Obviously, many important details are left to be pursued in the chapters that follow. However, this section provides a concise account of the main elements of civil litigation so that it is possible to get a sense of the "forest" before learning the about the particular "trees" and their role in the civil dispute ecosystem.

3. *Litigation and dispute resolution.* The third context is pragmatic and sociological. We examine the role played by civil litigation as one form of dispute resolution among others in the broad spectrum of conflict resolution. We explore the way that the adversary system, which ostensibly seeks binding third-party decision-making, increasingly supports other means of resolving disputes and drives civil justice reform. Lawyers must now understand the many options open to them to meet their clients' needs.

II. PROCEDURE AND THE COMMON LAW

The study of procedural law focuses on the processes by which civil disputes are resolved. This is important because the rights and obligations of persons to one another in society are not entirely self-enforcing. Understanding procedural law helps to ensure the efficacy of substantive rights. Understanding procedural law is important also because the way in which disputes are resolved can influence the nature of the legal standards themselves. For example, in the common law, where the law is developed partly through case law, the way in which cases come to be decided can have a profound effect on the development of the law.

To be sure, some parts of the law are also developed and articulated through legislative initiatives and not through the legal process. The political process of making law is studied in courses on public law. And, it is also true that the obligations of persons to society at large, as reflected in administrative law and criminal law, are vindicated and advanced in specialized procedures that are studied in other courses. But when we speak of "common law procedure," we generally mean the process by which law is made through the resolution of civil disputes.

A. The Procedural Roots of the Common Law

In the following excerpt, Professor Patrick Glenn describes the historical circumstances under which the common law was born and how it emerged as a law that was essentially procedural in nature.

H. Patrick Glenn, *Legal Traditions of the World*
3rd ed. (Oxford: OUP, 2007), at 225-31 (footnotes omitted)

... [T]he best explanation for the existence of a common law tradition is the historical accident, or chance, of the military conquest of England by the Normans. ...

The Norman, francophone heads of state of England put together the basic ingredients of the common law in about a century and a half after the conquest of 1066. If you put yourself in their place, and think what you would have done in the circumstances, you might have brought about the same results. ...

The only avenue for a Norman legal order, common to the realm, was through a loyal judiciary. This immediately marks off a common law tradition from all others. There was here no loyal chthonic people, no available revelation, no corpus of learned indigenous doctrine. So, as monarch, you could not rely on God, the people, or your own legislation. You needed a corps of loyal adjudicators, able to bring a newer, more efficient, and modern king's peace to the different parts of the realm. ...

... [A] process of "judicialization" of royal disposition of complaints to the crown occurred. First everyone came to the king, and his council, who then began referring things to the chancellor, who then began to ensure that things were properly looked at by some type of judge. ...

The common law grew slowly in the plenitude of laws and legal institutions of medieval England. It did so by the accretion of learning around the royal commands, given by the chancellor, for the resolution of individual disputes. Each writ gave rise to a particular procedure to be followed, appropriate for the type of dispute. If you are not a common law lawyer, and even for many who are, the writs and forms of action are a world filled with darkness, complexity and more recently, boredom. They are slowly losing their grip. But you can't really understand a common law tradition without understanding their broad outlines and function. They were all there was; outside the writs, there was no common law, no way to state a case or get before a judge. They also allowed the judge to attain, and maintain, priority of place in the hierarchy of common law institutions.

A writ took the form of instructions from the Crown to a royal officer (usually the sheriff, hence the classic expression, "The King to the sheriff, greetings ...") indicating what the sheriff had to do to advance investigation of a dispute. It might command the sheriff to require a defendant to appear and show cause; to seize property unless the defendant justified the keeping of it; to empanel a jury; and so on. Maitland described each writ, with its accompanying form of action, as a "pigeon-hole." A plaintiff had to choose amongst them; there was no changing in mid-litigation (even if the case was filled with surprises) and it might well be that no writ was available. "Where there is no remedy there is no wrong." So the common law came to be composed of a series of procedural routes (usually referred to as remedies) to get before a jury and state one's case. The jury enjoyed a monopoly on what we today call substantive decision-making. The system of writs (there were about 50 of them by the middle of the thirteenth century; six centuries later only another 25 or so had been added) profoundly influenced contemporary common law procedure and the judicial role, as well as substantive law.

In contemporary language the common law was therefore a law of procedure; whatever substantive law existed was hidden by it, "secreted" in its "interstices," in the language of Maine. The procedure was, and is, unique in the world and may be today the most distinctive feature of the common law. Chthonic law had no trials, and little procedure; roman law used no jury; neither talmudic nor islamic used (much) representation, and parties were expected to collaborate more than contest; in contemporary civil law it is the judge who investigates. In the common law world all came together to produce something radically different. The judge's function was not to decide the case; that was left to the jury. Yet the judge had things to decide, notably whether the case which emerged fell within the chosen writ; otherwise the court was without jurisdiction (choice of writ was not only binding, it contained all the royal authority which had been granted). Originally the jury know all about the case (local knowledge, local law), so the task of the lawyers was to argue about whether the verdict they wanted from the jury fell within the writ ("pleading to issue"). When witnesses eventually came to be necessary, the lawyers continued to plead to issue, and not brought forth the facts they needed, within the writ. The judge had no responsibility of finding "objective" fact; nor did the lawyers. There was no external law stating with precision the facts to which it applied. Since the members of the jury had day jobs, and were usually illiterate, the argument and proof had to be made orally, in what came to be known as a trial (as in the old trial by ordeal, but now radically made over). The trial is a dramatic event, and one in which the judge plays a commanding, but distant, role, as befitting a source of law. Freed from the burden of finding fact, advised on law and fact by the barristers (themselves historically benefiting from judge-like treatment, long enjoying immunity of function, though no longer), the judge could concentrate on the general contours of the writs, the general contours of the law. Judicial rulings, by a very small number of royal judges the working out of Westminster on circuit, eventually came to define the ambit of the writs, encrusting themselves slowly, with no notion of stare decisis, on the skeletal language of the royal commands. There were only first-instance judges, not courts of appeal. The judges worked out for themselves what was to be allowed. It was better not to suggest that they had erred. And the jury, of course, could not. ...

If you made it through all that your writ required, and the jury believed you, you would win your case. So it is possible to say that the procedure implied a substantive law, on the merits it was simply that no one other than the jury knew what it was. They were the law-finders, playing a fundamental, mediating role between local, unwritten law and central, royal courts. The writs were fundamental, however, since they determined when you could get to the jury, and they became the best available indicators of a secreted, substantive, common law. They indicated when a truthful, aggrieved party might obtain relief; they intimated obligation. Gradually the great writs began to fill entire fields of human activity, which other lawyers (civilian, islamic, talmudic, hindu) recognized as fields of substantive law.

NOTES AND QUESTIONS

1. Professor Glenn describes how the "justice" available from the Royal Courts was spread throughout the country by judges on circuit who evaluated the arguments of lawyers as to whether a claim could be pleaded to a jury in accordance with a prescribed form. While this system made available relief for harm to those who would otherwise need to ob-

tain it through force (and those who might not be able to obtain it by force) it was far from perfect, as is suggested by the notion that a person with a claim that could not be fit into one of the pigeonholes could not be granted a remedy. Today's rules of procedure continue to include rules enabling parties to move to "strike out a pleading on the ground that it discloses no reasonable cause of action ..." (for example, Ont. Rule 21.01(b)). What approach do you think should be taken to the determination of such a motion based on today's standards? What do we mean today by "a reasonable cause of action"?

2. Much of the contents of the current *Rules of Civil Procedure* are concerned with the "pre-trial" phase of the litigation. In this respect, the rules might be viewed as the direct descendants of the procedures described by Professor Glenn for determining whether you could get your case before a jury. However, things have changed. Many of the rules currently contain a general principle of interpretation that requires them to be "liberally construed to secure the just, most expeditious, and least expensive determination of every civil proceeding *on its merits.*" Why do you think that the rules would now emphasize that matters should be determined on their merits, and not disposed of on the basis of whether they fit within the prescribed procedure?

B. The Procedural Foundation of Substantive Law

The foundation of the common law might be described as concerned with questions of *how* an aggrieved person might obtain a remedy more than *what* a person's rights and obligations might be. Nevertheless, Professor John Jolowicz observed in his book *On Civil Procedure* (1999) that even if much of the study of procedural law and its reform is concerned with the "how" of law and legal reform, we must not overlook the "what" and the "why" of procedure. This is because the study of procedural law can provide special insights into the way in which the law has developed and how it will develop in the years ahead.

In the next excerpt Professor Main picks up the story where Professor Glenn left off and describes how substantive law, which was once thought to be "secreted in the interstices of procedure" came to be segregated from procedure and elevated as the product of the democratic process, relegating procedure to the role of mere "adjectival" law.

Thomas O. Main, "The Procedural Foundation of Substantive Law"
(2009), 87 *Wash. UL Rev.* (forthcoming) (footnotes omitted)

The history of Anglo-American law, which is typically dated from 1066, is approaching the end of its first millennium. Interestingly, however, the categories of substance and procedure appear only in the last quarter of that historical narrative. One scholar has traced the development of a substance–procedure dichotomy to the waning years of the 18th century:

> The dichotomy was fathered by Jeremy Bentham in a 1782 work entitled *Of Laws in General*, *sub nom* the distinction between substantive law and adjective law. Bentham there makes clear that he believes he is drawing a new distinction in the descriptive organization and analysis of the concept of law, and an examination of the leading pre-Bentham sources on English legal theory supports his claim.

As Professor Risinger observes, Bentham located a substance–procedure dichotomy within an extremely elaborate conceptual analysis of the phenomenon of law. And the originality of the dichotomy was a major point of the entire structure of *Of Laws in General.*

In previous work I have credited (or blamed, as the case may be) Sir William Blackstone for introducing categories of substance and procedure. In his famous *Commentaries on the Laws of England*, Blackstone, using what he called a "solid, scientific method," restated the entire corpus of English law in the form of *substantive* rules. In so doing, he appears to have differentiated substantive rights from the procedural mechanisms to prosecute the wrong, announcing in his *Commentaries*:

> I shall, first, define the several injuries cognizable by the courts of common law, with the respective remedies applicable to each particular injury; and shall, secondly, describe the method of pursuing and obtaining these remedies in the several courts.

Blackstone died in 1780, so we do not have the benefit of his response to the claims of originality that fill Bentham's 1782 book. But there is no doubt that Bentham was very familiar with his former professor's work. Bentham was a persistent and often savage critic of Blackstone, and may have been loath to share credit for introducing the substance–procedure paradigm.

More important than attributing the paradigm to a single source is understanding the context of its emergence. Specifically, why would the categories of substance and procedure (or "adjective law") emerge in the 18th century, rather than earlier in the many centuries of English jurisprudence? The answer is that, until then, substance and procedure were inextricably intertwined in both the Law courts and in the Equity courts.

First, the Law courts had centuries of experience with writs, forms of action, and single issue pleading. That system boasted a network of highly technical pleading and practice rules that determined the course and outcome of litigation. These rules earned common law the dubious distinction as "the most exact, if not the most occult, of the sciences." Importantly, these procedural forms "were the terms in which the law existed and in which lawyers thought." Accordingly what we might today refer to as a substantive law of, say, torts, could only be explained through the actions of trespass, case trover. "[O]ne could say next to nothing about actions in general, while one could discourse at great length about the mode in which an action of this or that sort was to be pursued and defended." The *substantive* law was subsumed within the *procedural* form. Hence the familiar words of Sir Henry Maine that English "substantive law has at first the look of being gradually secreted in the interstices of procedure."

Meanwhile, in the traditional courts of Equity, there were no procedural rules and, instead, an all-encompassing substantive mandate. There were no writs, forms of action, nor emphasis upon the formation of a single issue. Indeed, animated by the juristic principles of discretion, natural justice, fairness and good conscience, the essence of a jurisprudence of Equity was somewhat inconsistent with the establishment of formal procedural rules. Hence the characterization of Equity as "loose and liberal, large and vague." A broad *substantive* mandate dominated the jurisprudence of Equity in much the same way that *procedure* captured the jurisprudence applied in the Law courts. But in neither Law nor Equity was there meaningful appreciation of the separability of substance and procedure.

For centuries in England the separate systems of Law and Equity had been both rivals and partners. But by the middle of the 18th century, a profound transformation was underway; among other changes, both systems were incorporating key components of the other. Law was absorbing many of the best practices of Equity. Meanwhile, Equity was becoming systematized by rules and processes.

Very importantly, the words substance and procedure offered a vocabulary for explaining this phenomenon. With each system looking increasingly like the other, "differences between the systems were viewed as merely procedural." Blackstone wrote:

> Such then being the parity of law and reason which governs both species of courts, wherein (it may be asked) does their essential difference consist? It principally consists in the different modes of administering justice in each; in the mode of proof, the mode of trial, and the mode of relief.

The perception that parallel court systems were applying substantially similar substantive rules of law under different procedural schemata led inevitably to the ultimate merger of law and equity. The merger of law and equity, on one hand, and the emergence of a substance–procedure duality, on the other, thus presented interlocking narratives: a purely *procedural* merger of Law and Equity purported to leave the grand *substantive* jurisprudence of both systems intact. Put another way: the words substance and procedure helped explain how the merger of law and equity could be an ambitious yet also safe reform.

It is no coincidence that the categories of substance and procedure surfaced during the Enlightenment, when scientists and philosophers sought to understand all of the world around them by categorizing it. The capacity to distinguish between and among things became an integral part of intelligibility. And the Enlightenment epistemology produced particularly binarist thinking such as subject/object, culture/nature, mind/matter, and rational/irrational. A substance/procedure antinomy likewise resonated, especially for Blackstone, a law professor at Oxford who wrote his *Commentaries* for instructional purposes (as opposed to law reform).

But rather than remaining in the ivory tower for maturation and refinement, the categories of substance and procedure were put to immediate use—as foundational legal infrastructure. Quite unfortunately, consciousness of the substance–procedure antinomy happened to coincide with the formation of new systems and courts and methodologies in the nascent United States of America. This apparent distinction between matters substantive and procedural offered a tempting and accessible conceptual structure for a system of jurisprudence that was being built from scratch. The First Congress, for example, passed a statute providing that the new federal courts would, in cases at law, generally follow the "modes of process" of the state in which the court sat. The Second Congress prescribed a distinctive court procedure for equity cases. Other statutes recognizing a substance–procedure distinction soon followed.

This process of codification converted a substance–procedure antinomy into a substance–procedure dichotomy. Before this conversion, substance and procedure represented conceptual opposites—substantive laws detailed the rights and responsibilities of the parties, and procedures prescribed the vindication of those rights and the fulfillment of those responsibilities. That antinomy revealed the diverse purposes and functions that for centuries had been seamlessly integrated (in concept as well as nomenclature) in a corpus of laws. Antinomy is an especially apt descriptor of the relationship between substance and procedure because these concepts are not only counter-terms or antonyms, but are also paradoxically yoked: each is extraordinarily difficult to define without also defining the other. Yet the substance–procedure antinomy invited a more nuanced and sophisticated appreciation for laws' multiple intentions and meanings.

But the law did not codify this new consciousness; it codified a dichotomy. As a dichotomy, substance and procedure were still conceptual opposites; but dichotomies are characterized by mutually exclusive and mutually exhaustive categories. The exclusive disjunction had severe consequences: lost was the conceptual possibility for laws that belonged in both categories or in neither category. As antinomy the counter-terms substance and procedure were more localized, open-ended, and did not contain this sense of closure; laws could be both substantive and procedural, or could be neither substantive nor procedural. But with codification as a dichotomy, this heterogeneity was lost.

Further, a dichotomy is not simply a neutral division of an otherwise all-encompassing descriptive field. "Dichotomous thinking necessarily hierarchizes and ranks the two polarized terms so that one becomes the privileged term and the other its suppressed, subordinated, negative counterpart." Indeed, the inferiority of procedure to substance is a familiar refrain. In the 18th century, Bentham degraded procedure—suggesting even the term adjectival law implied too much influence for procedure. Then in the nineteenth century, David Dudley Field undertook to refine the machinery of procedure. At the turn of the twentieth century Thomas Shelton analogized procedure to "a clean pipe, unclogged artery, clear viaduct, or bridge." Decades later, Charles Clark drafted rules to be a handmaid rather than a mistress. And as a contemporary example, one of my colleagues, a property professor, teaches his students that procedure is like the player piano to substantive law's musical compositions. That substance and procedure are frequently defined with metaphors may be some evidence that the terms lack innate definition. ...

. . .

... The argument that procedure is substantive presents in two basic forms. The classic version is that procedure has substantive qualities because it affects the outcome of cases. A more contemporary version is that procedural reformers have a substantive agenda. Both versions are verifiable.

No procedural decision can be completely neutral in the sense that it does not affect substance. If procedures are to serve any purpose at all, they will affect litigation behavior, and create new winners and new losers. When the discovery rules were adopted in 1938 they were expected to make a trial less about sport and ambush, and more about truth and evidence. This presupposed that those rules would change the results in many cases. In this vein, procedure is *substantive* in that it is *not unimportant*, as the subordinate role assigned to it by the substance–procedure dichotomy would suggest.

Procedural rules can also change how certain substantive laws are (or are not) enforced. To this end, scholars have analyzed the substantive capacity of numerous procedural devices and doctrines including, among many others, pleadings, sanctions, summary judgment, joinder, evidence (e.g., ... discovery, case management, bifurcation, and class actions). The bulk of this literature has documented how so-called procedural reforms have intentionally, relentlessly, and quite successfully weakened civil rights and discrimination laws. Other substantive areas that have been examined in some depth include antitrust, corporate law and securities regulation, racketeering, and environmental protection.

The perception that procedure is relatively insignificant can be exploited. Indeed, "[s]ometimes substantive decisions are disguised as process." This subterfuge is dangerous because procedural reforms can have the effect of denying substantive rights without the transparency, safeguards and accountability that attend public and legislative decision-making. And procedural laws can be applied retroactively. ...

All this is a familiar story. And only the broadest summary of this literature is necessary to remind that procedural means can achieve substantive ends, whether or not intended. ...

... [S]ubstantive law is neither *aprocedural* nor *trans-procedural*, but rather is constructed with a specific procedural apparatus in mind to vindicate the rights created or the responsibilities assigned by that substantive law. Whether consciously or subconsciously, the drafters of substantive law embed an associated procedure.

Substantive law relies on procedure to effectuate the substantive mandate. Substantive law without any procedure at all would be a vain and hollow thing. Although some substantive laws may be merely aspirational or symbolic, it is surely true that generally speaking "[t]he best laws in the world are meaningless unless they can be meaningfully enforced." To borrow a useful phrase often invoked in another procedural context, substantive law without procedural law would be a "castle in the air." As castles in the air are seldom built, substantive law would seldom be constructed without some procedure to vindicate that law. Because substantive law requires procedure, it is not aprocedural.

Nor is substantive law trans-procedural. Substantive law would be trans-procedural only if the rights established and responsibilities assigned in the substantive law could be fulfilled and realized in any procedural system.

C. How the Rules Are Made

If the historical roots of the common law are essentially procedural and procedural law plays a key role in the development of substantive law, then it is important to understand how the rules themselves are made, or more precisely, who has the authority to make the rules.

This question has a particular significance for legal systems that are based on the idea of the separation of powers. For example, in the United States, the concern over the way in which rules of civil procedure could affect substantive law gave rise to a federal enactment called the *Rules Enabling Act*. Professor Main describes the way in which the "antinomous" relationship between procedure and substance was operationalized as a dichotomy in the formative years of the American legal system. Under the *Rules Enabling Act*, 28 USC § 2072, the judicial branch of government is empowered to make rules of procedure, provided that "such rules shall not abridge, enlarge or modify any substantive right." This restriction was designed to protect the exclusive authority of the legislative branch to make substantive law. As a result, the separation of powers that underlies the American system of government produces what Professor Main regards as an inherently unstable relationship between substance and procedure in the legal system. Professor Main argues that this relationship is inherently unstable because substantive law is necessarily developed and applied in a particular procedural context. However, the issue was a live one long before that. Here is what one American scholar had to say nearly a century ago, before the *Rules Enabling Act* was passed in a comparison between English and American rulemaking:

> In no province does the familiar constitutional doctrine of the separation of powers break down more completely than in the special field of the law of civil procedure occupied by what we know as the rules of practice. The substantive law of the State may lay down with the greatest precision the rights of an individual, and how far their infringement will be repaired by legal remedy, but to the person wronged the question of how and when he can obtain his remedy is equally important. Suitors are not satisfied with syllogisms; they are more interested in the results. It is therefore necessary to provide a means by which the litigant can, with proper expedition and directness, pass through contention and obtain the satisfaction he desires. Upon what department of State should that duty be placed? Is the function of prescribing rules of procedure executive, judicial, or legislative? In so far as it pertains to the carrying out and practical enforcement of substantive law, it is an executive duty; in so far as it aids judges to arrive at the true issues in controversy, it is judicial; and in so far as it has a binding effect on the conduct of the parties, it is of a legislative nature. Undoubtedly, it partakes of all three of the attributes enumerated. It appears, therefore, that no one of the three branches of our Government is, by the theory of the Constitution or the character of the duty, so peculiarly fitted for this work that the other two must be excluded from consideration. In such a position, the guiding principle becomes one of expediency.
>
> ... [W]hy is it that the great nations on the opposite side of the Atlantic who rule themselves by legal principles developed out of a common law have come to such different conclusions. ... Although practically all of the United States are committed to the plan of issuing practice rules from their State capitols by way of legislative fiat, the people of England place in the hands of their judges the power to mold the practice of the courts. ... The motives behind these strikingly different conclusions are, in some measure, capable of historical explanation. The courts of Pennsylvania were, from their very beginning, tribunals not of a superior power, but of the people themselves. ... The English courts, on the other hand, were not the people's but the King's.

(Samuel Rosenbaum, *The Rule-Making Authority in the English Supreme Court* (Littleton, CO: Rothman, 1917), at 1-3.)

NOTES AND QUESTIONS

1. Despite the fact that expediency resulted in the passing of the *Rules Enabling Act*, authorizing the rules to be made by a body other than one with authority delegated by legislation, difficulty remained in that, as argued by Professor Main, it would be impossible to formulate a system of procedural rules that constitutes a genuinely neutral framework for the resolution of disputes, even if this was thought to be necessary or desirable. In the article excerpted above, Professor Main goes on to canvass the extent to which each substantive

legal regime needs its own procedural regimen, and to what extent this implies that we must return to the old forms of action on which the common law was originally based. Would that be desirable? Would it be possible?

2. In the United States the segregation of procedure from substance has been considered important because if rules are neutral then they can be formulated by bodies of experts who need not be elected. If, however, rules embody substantive values, there is a concern to ensure that the rules of procedure are the product of the democratic process, or at least, those who make them are answerable to it.

By contrast, the Civil Rules Committee in Ontario, which develops and revises the rules of procedure, is composed of judges and lawyers as follows: chief justice and associate chief justice of Ontario; the chief justice and associate chief justice of the Superior Court of Justice; the chief justice of the Ontario Court of Justice or his or her designee; two judges of the Court of Appeal; eight judges of the Superior Court of Justice; one judge who was assigned to the Provincial Court (Civil Division) on the first day of October 1989; the attorney general or his or her designee; one law officer of the Crown; two persons employed in the administration of the courts; four lawyers appointed by the Law Society, one lawyer appointed by the chief justice of Ontario; and four lawyers appointed by the chief justice of the Superior Court. Section 66(2) of the Ontario *Courts of Justice Act* specifically empowers the Civil Rules Committee to make rules, "even thought they alter ... the substantive law." When do you think it is possible or appropriate for the Rules Committee, in the course of making rules, to alter substantive law?

3. When several Canadian provinces took steps to provide for a modern form of class actions, they each decided to pass new legislation rather than to proceed by making new rules or amending existing legislation. In the *Report of the Attorney General's Advisory Committee on Class Action Reform* (Ontario, 1990), that committee recommended that any provision for class action be made in an act, rather than through rules changes. In doing so, the committee referred to the following factors:

> The procedure represents a significant development in the administration of justice in Ontario. It has been the subject of controversy and debate. The recommended reforms call for the removal of substantive obstacles to class proceedings. ...
>
> The new procedure requires a specificity and, in some cases, a priority over other litigation which the *Rules of Civil Procedure* are unaccustomed and inappropriate in providing.

Despite the pattern of introducing class actions through legislative initiatives, the Supreme Court of Canada held in *Western Canadian Shopping Centres Inc. v. Dutton*, 2001 SCC 46 that class actions could proceed in provinces in which no legislation existed.

In a more dramatic example of this debate, the issue was addressed directly in the Australian state of Victoria. Following the failure of the legislature to take up the recommendation of the Law Reform Commission to introduce class actions, the rules were simply amended to include such a scheme by the body responsible for amending the rules, which was comprised of judges. In the first case to come before the courts on the new rules, the defendant argued that this exceeded the rule-making power of the judges. The rules-based scheme was narrowly upheld on appeal in *Schutt Flying Academy (Aust) Pty Ltd. v. Mobil Oil Australia Ltd.*, [2000] VSCA 103, but soon after, the legislature introduced legislation for class actions.

4. In addition to the question of who has authority to pass a particular law, there are two other situations in which we commonly need to distinguish between procedural and substantive laws. The first situation arises when the law has changed between the time a cause of action arose and the time the rights of the parties are being determined. It is often said that a person's substantive rights can be "vested" and that substantive laws can operate only in a prospective fashion, but a person has no vested right in procedure and procedural laws can be applied retrospectively, unless they themselves provide otherwise.

Second, even if foreign law applies to the substance of a dispute, the court will still apply local procedural rules because that is the only way it can operate. The Supreme Court of Canada reasoned in *Tolofson v. Jensen*, [1994] 4 SCR 1022 that the kinds of laws that are characterized as procedural should be confined to those that are essential to the administrative efficacy of the proceedings. Difficult questions of characterization continue. For example, is a statutory cap on damages a matter of procedure because it impacts on the quantification of damages, which, it is thought, can only be done in accordance with the law of the forum, or a matter of substance as an imposition of local public policy? See *Somers v. Fournier* (2002), 60 OR (3d) 225, 214 DLR (4th) 611 (CA).

III. THE ADVERSARY SYSTEM

From a slightly different angle, it might be said that regardless of whether our preoccupation in the common law with procedure is distinctive, the nature of common law procedure is distinctive. The nature of our procedures for resolving civil disputes can tell us much about our culture. Professor Oscar Chase explains this by comparing the common law trial with other dispute processes in other cultures. In the following brief excerpt from his cross-cultural analysis of disputing systems, Professor Chase describes a truth-seeking process that is strikingly different from that used in American courts. In doing so, he seeks to "free us even somewhat of the preconception that there is only one right way to find truth and justice, which just happens to be ours, [so that] we can better uncover the cultural underpinnings of our own dispute resolution practices."

**Oscar Chase, *Law, Culture and Ritual: Disputing
Systems in Cross-Cultural Context***
(New York: NYU Press, 2005), at 1-2 (footnotes omitted)

… Any society's approved way of handling disputes is the result of conscious and unconscious choices that are made within the constraints of the knowledge, beliefs, and social structure available to it.

Among the Central African Azande, the *benge* oracle would be consulted. A small portion of poison would be fed to a baby chick as the question was put to the oracle: "If the plaintiff tells the truth, let the chicken die, let the chicken die, let the chicken die. …" The chick lived (or died). The oracle had spoken. In another time and place (the United States) a judge orders that a jury be consulted. A group of strangers is summoned to a special hall, used only for airing disputes. They hear from the plaintiff, the defendant, and the conflicting witnesses. The strangers retire to a private room and caucus. They return with the verdict. In yet another time and place (most of Continental Europe and Latin America), the facts are determined by a specially trained judge whose decision is based primarily on documents and who may not even allow contesting parties to testify. Every one of these methods is defended in the place it is (or was) used as the best way of getting at the truth about an ultimately unknowable past. ...

Dispute processes are in large part a reflection of the culture in which they are embedded: they are not an autonomous system that is predominantly the product of insulated specialists and experts. More, they are institutions through which social and cultural life is maintained, challenged, and altered, or as the same idea has been expressed, "constituted" or "constructed."

NOTES AND QUESTIONS

1. By juxtaposing the consultation of the *benge* oracle with the deliberations of a common law jury and with those of a civilian judge, Professor Chase highlights the variety of means for establishing the facts upon which the rights and obligations of the parties to a dispute will be determined. Similarly striking contrasts may also be found in dispute resolution systems *within* traditions. For example, while jury trials and judicial deliberations are regular features of Western legal traditions, the consultation of oracles was also a well-known practice in ancient Greece; and while the consultation of the *benge* oracle may seem simple, many indigenous cultures have highly sophisticated consensus-based processes; and a number of important determinations are currently made in Western societies on the basis of pure chance, such as conscription for military service.

2. In what might seem a somewhat less dramatic comparison, the adversary system may be contrasted to the approach to civil litigation that prevails in civil law countries, and with the approach taken in Native communities in North America. It may then be reconsidered in the light of increasing interest in public-interest litigation. Finally, the adversary system may be viewed as a basis for the main elements of civil procedure.

A. The Basic Premises

Sir Jack I.H. Jacob, *The Fabric of English Civil Justice*
(London: Stevens, 1987), at 5-19 (footnotes omitted)

The Adversary System

The fundamental, characteristic feature of English civil justice is commonly referred to as the adversary system. This, system has been the traditional, cardinal basis for the conduct of civil procedure in England since about the middle of the thirteenth century, and it is well settled and deeply rooted. It was not the creation of statute nor was it implanted as the result of a doctrinal choice of other methods of procedure but rather it grew and developed out of the soil, responding in a practical way to the social, political and cultural needs of the people. It was probably the product which stemmed from the fortuitous conjunction in 1215 of the promise in Magna Carta of the right to "trial by peers" and of the prohibition by the Lateran Council forbidding the clergy to take part in trials by ordeal. It followed the adoption on a general basis of the method of trial by jury by the Superior Common Law Courts, which at about that time replaced other modes of trial, such as trial by battle, by oath or compurgation and by ordeal. It enabled the English legal system to escape the new procedure by "inquisition" introduced by Pope Innocent III. It affords strong evidence of the historical continuity of the system of English civil justice, which has been capable of surviving great political, social and constitutional crises and of absorbing and adapting radical and fundamental changes in procedure. It also under-scores the extensive and widespread influence of English civil justice, for almost all the countries in which English law was introduced have continued to operate their civil pro-cedure, with appropriate modifications to meet their separate national and local condi-tions and social aspirations, on the model of the English adversary system.

The main alternative method of conducting civil procedure is that prevailing in the civil law countries of Europe which is called "the inquisitorial system." In both the adver-sary and the inquisitorial systems, there is a division of functions between the Court on the one hand and the parties on the other. This division of functions, however, is the very reverse in the adversary system from the way in which it operates in the inquisitorial system. The fundamental divergence between the two systems is that under the English adversary system the court plays an inactive, passive, non-interventionist part whereas under the civil law inquisitorial system, the court plays an active, authoritative, interven-tionist role; and, correspondingly, under the adversary system, the parties play a major, dominating, independent role to persuade the court to adjudicate or otherwise resolve the dispute in their favour whereas under the inquisitorial system, they play a minor, tentative, supportive role to enable the court to perform its function to inquire into and determine the dispute.

Both systems assume the contradictory or adversarial character of the civil proceed-ings they are called upon to deal with, namely, that the opposing parties are in contro-versy, in conflict, in combat about the dispute between them, but they employ essentially different ways for their adjudication, resolution or other disposal. These different ways derive from fundamentally different conceptual criteria and perhaps also different social, cultural and political tenets of what civil procedure is about, what courts are for and how they should operate. Under the adversary system, the basic assumptions are that civil disputes are a matter of private concern of the parties involved, and may even be regard-ed as their private property, though their determination by the courts may have wider, more far-reaching, even public repercussions, and that the parties are themselves the best judges of how to pursue and serve their own interests in the conduct and control of their respective cases, free from the directions of or intervention by the court. On the other hand, under the inquisitorial system, the basic assumptions are that civil procedure is a branch of public law, so that a right of action is seen as a public law right over and above the private substantive right of the party asserting it, and that once the jurisdiction of the court is invoked in relation to a private dispute, there arises an immediate public interest, and the court then comes under a state duty forthwith to take that dispute under its con-trol, to charter its future content and conduct, to search for the underlying truth, to bring the dispute to a conclusion by conciliation if possible or otherwise by adjudication. Each system is naturally content with its own machinery of civil justice, subject to improving its methods and techniques. It may perhaps be permissible to speculate whether on the merits of a given case, based on substantially similar facts, the conclusion of the dispute arrived at in the Courts of both systems would be substantially the same.

1. Role of the Court

When dealing with the expected behaviour of a judge Pollock and Maitland contrasted the conduct of a man of science, carrying out research in his laboratory and using all appropriate methods for the solution of problems and the discovery of truth, with the role of the umpire in English games, who does not invent tests for the powers of the two sides but is there merely to see that the rules of the game are observed. They concluded that the strong inclination of English procedure was toward the second of these ideas, and they added, referring to the cricket match,

> The judges sit in Court, not in order that they may discover the truth, but in order that they may answer the question, "How's that." The English judge will, if he can, play the umpire rather than the inquisitor.

The inactive, passive and non-interventionist role of the court in English civil justice operates throughout the whole range of civil proceedings. This generalised role of the English court is, however, subject to important exceptions in which the court is under the duty or is empowered to act of its own motion and thus to be active and if necessary to ascertain "the truth." Apart from these exceptional circumstances, the court takes no initiative at any stage of the proceedings; it has no power or duty to determine what are the issues or questions in dispute between the parties, save as may appear from the pleadings or other statements of the parties. The court has no investigative process of its own; it cannot appoint a court expert, nor call for the report of an expert or require experiments or observations to be made, save at the request of a party. It does not itself examine, still less cross-examine, the parties or their witnesses, for to do so, as Lord Greene pointed out, the judge would be descending "into the arena and is liable to have his vision clouded by the dust of conflict or as Lord Denning expressed it, he would, "drop the mantle of a Judge and assume the role of the advocate." The judge has no power to call a witness, whom neither party desires to call, though he may recall a witness for further examination. The court has no power or duty to promote a settlement or compromise between the parties. It relies on the advocates to cite or refer to the applicable law and it does not normally carry out its own researches in this respect. In short, the English court takes no active part in the initiation, conduct, preparation or presentation of a civil case before or at the trial or on appeal.

Nevertheless, although the English court maintains its inactive role, it does not remain negative or remote during the actual hearing or trial of the proceedings. On the contrary, at all stages of the proceedings before or at the trial or on appeal, at the actual trial or hearing, the English court plays a dominating, positive and interventionist role. The conduct of the proceedings then comes under the direct, immediate and overall control of the court which thus plays a pointed and practical role by the dialectical process of asking searching questions calling for immediate answers about any matters arising in the proceedings. This open intervention for the search for the truth, within the parameters of the proceedings as they are constituted, helps greatly to clarify, amplify or correct any points or questions raised by the parties or the court.

It should also be emphasised that the passive role of the English court greatly enhances the standing, influence and authority of the judiciary at all levels and may well account for the high respect and esteem in which they are held, as well as their comparatively small numbers.

2. Role of the Parties

By contrast, under the adversary system, the passive role of the court becomes the active role of the parties and their lawyers. The roles are in fact reversed, and the responsibility for the initiation, conduct, preparation and presentation of civil proceedings is shifted from the court to the parties, mainly of course the legal practitioners. This has the effect of greatly increasing the duties and obligations of the lawyers in the civil judicial process and also the dependence of the litigants themselves as well as the courts on their skill, competence and integrity.

Under the principle of what is called "party control," but subject to compliance with the rules, practices and orders of the court, and so far as the lawyers are concerned subject to their duties and responsibilities as officers of the court and their obligations under the disciplinary code of their respective professional bodies, the parties retain the initiative at all stages of civil proceedings. They can agree to extend time limits which they are required to observe under the rules or orders of the court. They are free by their pleadings or other requisite statements to delimit the issues or questions of fact or law, which they desire the court to determine and the court is bound to confine itself only to those issues or questions and no others. They interview the parties and their witnesses, including experts, take statements from them and they can call at the trial only those witnesses they, choose and in the order they choose, though they have the responsibility of ensuring their attendance at the trial. Under the principle of "party prosecution," the parties may move a case forward rapidly or slowly, though if there is prolonged and inexcusable delay extending beyond the applicable limitation period which is prejudicial to the defendant the action may be dismissed for want of prosecution. It is up to each of the parties to apply to the court to compel his opponent to comply with the rules or orders of the court or to apply for the appropriate sanction either by way of costs or by way of dismissing the action or striking out the defence, as may be, if there is a breach or failure to comply with the rules or orders of the court. At the trial, the parties have the primary responsibility of examining and cross-examining the witnesses. Under the principle of "party autonomy," parties are entitled at all stages of the proceedings (save in the case of claims by or on behalf of minors or mental patients) to settle their cases on any terms they choose without the approval of the court.

In short, it is the duty and responsibility of the lawyers of the parties, both of the solicitor who is employed by the litigant whose main responsibilities are to initiate and prepare the case and of the barrister who is engaged by the solicitor and whose main responsibilities are to present and conduct the case at the stages of pre-trial and trial and on appeal, to ensure that the case of the client is fully and effectively begun or defended and framed, prepared and presented. They are also entitled, within the limits of professional propriety, to take advantage of any weaknesses or mistakes of the opposite party. As Lord Denning expressed it in martial terms,

> In litigation as in war. If one side makes a mistake, the other can take advantage of it. No holds are barred.

Under the adversary system there is room for the employment of surprise and technicalities as weapons in the conduct of the litigation. Indeed, throughout the whole litigation process, the parties and their lawyers are at arms' length and in general it is contrary to professional usage for the lawyers of either party to inform or alert the lawyer of the opposite party that he may be committing a fatal error.

3. Failings and Changes

By exalting the role of the parties and their lawyers, the English adversary system has the effect of setting the parties against each other as opponents or antagonists, or even as foes or enemies, who must be vanquished in the forensic combat. The lawyers on both sides engage in what is called "a battle of wits"; they take each other on as "legal gladiators" in the litigation arena. Yet in spite of, or perhaps because of this feature, the adversary system is much admired, particularly by practitioners who operate it and the judiciary who apply it; and indeed, there is much to commend it, especially as it should be regarded and evaluated, not in isolation as a separate system, but as the framework for the functioning of the other· fundamental principles of English civil justice. My own belief is that it reflects and responds to English cultural values, and conforms more closely with the English character of independence and "fair play," and that therefore the common people of England would prefer to retain, it rather than to adopt the inquisitorial system, its counterpart on the European continent. They would, I believe, prefer that the conduct of their civil disputes should be under the control of the lawyers of their own choice rather than be managed by the judges, however eminent and independent, who are in no way answerable to them.

Nevertheless, the English adversary system has many inherent failings, which are manifested in practice more often than is generally realised. Since it is the lawyers who choose when and what procedural steps should be taken or resisted, which they think would best serve their respective interests, it is a hit and miss system, sometimes producing the right result and sometimes not. The adversary system inevitably creates avoidable delays and increases both the labour and the costs. It introduces an element of sportsmanship or gamesmanship into the conduct of civil proceedings, and it develops the propensity on the part of the lawyers to indulge in procedural technical manoeuvres. For the proper functioning of the adversary system, a basic assumption is that the opposite parties command equal resources and can engage lawyers having equal skill, expertise and competence, but in practice this assumption is not fulfilled in a much larger volume and variety of cases than is generally imagined; and indeed, the adversary system accentuates the inequality in terms of resources and legal advice and representation between the parties. Under the adversary system, some lawyers at any rate fall below, a few very much below, the standard of skill, competence and integrity expected of them by their respective professions, with the result that many claims and defences are defeated, often without a decision on the merits, and are thrown on the dust-heap of lost causes. The true casualties of the adversary system are the litigants themselves, who are frustrated in their search for justice, and the notion that a litigant who is defeated by the negligence of his own lawyer will seek redress against him by going to another lawyer is more fanciful than real. Lastly, it may be said that, in the interplay between the court and the parties and their lawyers, the adversary system envelops the machinery of civil justice with a kind of mystique, even mysticism, which alienates people and inhibits them from resorting to the courts for the resolution or determination of their disputes.

In view of these and other failings and defects of the adversary system, it is clearly necessary that urgent steps be taken to improve its machinery. The obvious solution which springs to mind, that the English adversary system should be replaced by the Continental inquisitorial system, is wholly misconceived both in principle and in practice. As a matter of principle, the proposal to reverse the roles of the court and the parties does not take into account some imponderable intangibles, such as the cultural texture of society, the habits and practices of the legal profession, the needs, values and aspirations of the people, their inarticulated concept of how civil justice should be administered, especially the overriding social need for public justice, so that justice can be seen to be done. As a matter of practice, such a proposal does not take into account the overwhelming difficulties which would be experienced by the practitioners and the judiciary if they were required to change their methods, practices and habits to conform with the inquisitorial system. Moreover, such a proposal would be impracticable since the fundamental difference between the common law system and the continental system in the administration of civil justice lies much deeper, for it lies in the way in which the judiciary is chosen, appointed and promoted. In the continental systems of law, the judiciary at all levels is largely, though of course not entirely, comprised of career judges, that is, lawyers trained, after passing their educational qualifications, to be judges, and they follow a judicial career and are promoted to higher judicial office according to the career structure of the judiciary without ever having been engaged in the actual day-to-day practice of the law. On the other hand, in the common law systems, the judiciary is largely, but of course not entirely, chosen from among practising lawyers and there are no career judges. This difference in the composition of the judiciary between the continental and common law systems, is, I suggest, a decisive reason for dismissing altogether the idea that we can or should replace the adversary system by the inquisitorial system of civil justice.

On the other hand, in remodelling and refashioning the adversary system, I suggest it would be useful to look for guidance to the principle underlying the inquisitorial system, namely, that once the jurisdiction of the court has been invoked, the court should become invested with the public duty and interest to ensure the proper conduct, content and progress of the proceedings. Such increased power of the court, to be more active and responsible, would also help to promote equality in procedure, especially where one party is not legally or even competently represented. The active role of the court would enable it to monitor the progress of the proceedings, to control their future conduct, to formulate the real issues or questions between the parties, to determine that there has been full disclosure of documents between them, to ensure the exchange of experts' reports and if and when this power is introduced the exchange of the statements of the witnesses of the parties, to increase the powers of the court to act of its own motion as, for example, to appoint a court expert and to enable the trial court to call a witness not called by the parties. Above all, the court should be under a duty at all stages to endeavour by conciliation to promote the settlement or compromise of the proceedings. In these and other ways, the adversary systems would be able to cast-off its present failings and defects and respond more positively to producing a more effective and efficient machinery of civil justice.

NOTES AND QUESTIONS

Sir Jack Jacobs's classic description of the adversary system captures many of the themes that are discussed throughout this book. To what extent does the sense of procedural fairness reflected in this excerpt coincide with your own? Are there any points on which you disagree? To what extent do you think that they might be attributed to differences between the English legal system and that in the common law provinces of Canada? To what extent might they be attributed to the passage of time and changing attitudes toward civil litigation?

In the following excerpt, Neil Brooks examines one central difference between the adversary system and continental procedure—that of the role of the judge.

Neil Brooks, "The Judge and the Adversary System"
in A. Linden, ed., *The Canadian Judiciary* (Toronto: Osgoode Hall Law School,
York University, 1976), at 90-116 (footnotes omitted)

The adversary system, as that term is used by many proceduralists and as it will be used in this paper, embodies two distinct principles. The issues resolved by these two principles raise the two most basic questions that confront any adjudicative procedural system. The first issue is what should the respective functions of the parties and the judge be with reference to the initiation and content of the adjudication. The adversary system rests on the principle of party-autonomy. That is to say, that the parties have the right to pursue or dispose of their legal rights and remedies as they wish. The second issue is what should the respective functions of the parties and the judge be with reference to the progress of a dispute through the procedural system once initiated and defined. The adversary system rests on the principle of party prosecution. This principle holds that the parties have the primary responsibility to choose without interference from the judge the manner in which they go forward with their case and the proofs they will present for the judge's consideration in adjudicating the dispute.

A. Party-Autonomy

The principle of party-autonomy has two aspects. First, it limits the judge's function to disputes which have been presented to him. A judge plays a role only when a conflict has arisen between two or more parties, and at least one of them seeks the assistance of the judge in resolving the dispute. John Chipman Gray, in defining a judge, summarized this principle: "A judge of an organized body is a man appointed by that body to determine duties and the corresponding rights upon the application of persons claiming those rights." The authors of a casebook on civil procedure described the principle more pro- saically: "Courts ought not to function as self-propelled vehicles of justice and right like King Arthur's knights in Good Humor trucks." Lon Fuller quotes a socialist critic of bourgeois law who caricatured this premise of the adversary system by asserting that courts in such a system "are like defective clocks; they have to be shaken to set them go- ing." Fuller noted that, "[h]e of course added the point that the shaking costs money."

The second aspect of party-autonomy is that the parties have the sole responsibility for defining the dispute that they would like adjudicated. Thus, if the parties want the judge to decide one dispute, he will not insist on resolving another even though he per- ceives that other issue to be the real cause of the conflict between the parties.

Both aspects of party-autonomy are subject to qualifications. While the judge cannot initiate proceedings, he can prevent the parties from initiating certain proceedings. The courts have an important social function to perform by resolving disputes. Thus the judge can prevent parties from using the litigation process to resolve hypothetical or moot problems. He can judicially notice all facts he considers beyond reasonable dispute and thus prevent the parties from consuming the time of the court by presenting evi- dence on clear factual issues. He can also prevent misuse of the process by a judicial screening of cases, he can give judgment on the pleadings or give a summary judgment. Indeed he is assisted in controlling the use of the court's process by counsel for the par- ties. Lawyers have a professional responsibility to ensure that the claims and defences they put forward have merit and are related to a real conflict.

The limits of the principle of party-autonomy can, of course, only be defined by refer- ence to the reasons why it is regarded as being an essential principle of the Anglo- American procedural system. Two justifications sometimes put forward fail to appreciate that party-autonomy is only a principle which defines the respective roles of the parties and the judge. In civil cases, it has been said that the principle of party-autonomy—that the judge only operates when the parties present him with a dispute to resolve—rests on the judgment that "the social interest in securing general observance of the rules of pri- vate law is sufficiently served by leaving their enforcement to the self-interest of the par- ties more or less directly affected." However, while this reason might explain why the state need not become involved in the enforcement of the civil law, it does not go directly to the issue of the roles of the parties and the judge in initiating actions. In many areas where there is an important public interest in the enforcement of the civil law, as in the enforcement of the criminal law, the state, through an administrative agency, might initi- ate actions enforcing the law. And yet, since it is not the judge who initiates such actions, the principle of party-autonomy would be satisfied.

· · ·

[T]he above reasons given for the principle of party-autonomy stem from the miscon- ception of what the principle demands. The principle does not require that the state re- frain from initiating civil actions. It merely requires that the judge not initiate them. Fleming James more correctly stated the rationale when he noted, "… the adversary sys- tem and party-(autonomy) may well exist in areas extensively regulated by government in what is deemed to be the public interest. Their existence stems not from laissez-faire or a philosophy of individualism but rather from a notion of the proper allocation of function between the parties to a dispute (one of whom may be the government) and the tribunal which is to decide it, under any economic or social order, at least in a free society." Professor Lon Fuller also argued that the principle that an arbiter should not act on his own motion in initiating a case rests not on a political philosophy, but on a judgment that it increased the effectiveness of adjudication: "... it is generally impossible to keep even the bare initiation of proceedings untainted by preconceptions about what happened and what its consequences should be. In this sense, initiation of the proceedings by the arbiter impairs the integrity of adjudication by reducing the effectiveness of the litigant's participation through proofs and arguments."

B. Party-Prosecution

This principle holds that the parties have the right and the responsibility to choose the manner in which they will go forward with their case and the proof they will present to support it. The judge's role is to passively evaluate the merits of the case as and when it is presented to him.

In the remainder of this paper I will explore the reasons why the principle of party-prosecution is adhered to at trial, and offer some general comments on the parameters that these reasons place upon the judge's intervention in the conduct of the case. The conclusion that I reach is that viewed in this way the adversary system does not impose as severe restraints on the judge's intervention as is often assumed, and that in appropriate cases the judge should, if he deems it necessary, play a much larger role in the conduct of the case. My argument will be a plea for more judicial activism in controlling the conduct of the trial.

The principle of party-prosecution at trial rests, in the main, upon two broad empirical assumptions. Firstly, that the legitimacy of adjudication as a means of social ordering is enhanced if it is conducted according to an adversarial presentation. Secondly, that more accurate fact-finding is likely to result if parties motivated by self-interest are given the responsibilities of investigating facts and presenting arguments, and if the decision-maker remains passive.

2. The Adversary System Increases the Acceptability of Adjudication

Every means of social ordering used by the state must be acceptable not only to those immediately affected by its particular sanctions but also to all those governed by the state. This need for legitimacy is particularly paramount in a free society with respect to adjudication since a judge's decision might be perceived, in some sense at least, to be undemocratic.

Legitimacy or acceptability is a derivative value. That is to say, a decision-making process will be acceptable to the extent that it meets all the criteria that people expect of that decision-making process. With respect to adjudication these expectations undoubtedly include such considerations as expediency, finality, inexpensiveness, and the operation of privacy and other social values. To the extent that the adversary system furthers these values it will render the adjudicative process more acceptable than would some other procedural device for finding the facts. But aside from these considerations, which are necessary attributes of any acceptable adjudicative proceeding, it is often argued that the adversary system has unique characteristics which render it in judicial trials a more acceptable procedure in our society than other methods of fact-finding. The reasons for the acceptability of the adversary system, if indeed it is more acceptable than other methods of fact-finding, must rest ultimately upon complex questions of political theory and psychology. I can only be suggestive here, in part repeating what others have speculated. Four reasons might be given as to why the adversary system is a more acceptable method of fact-finding in judicial trials than any other method.

A. Relationship to the Prevalent Political and Economic Theory

The adversary system yields greater satisfaction to the litigants and others because it is a procedure that is consistent with the prevalent social and political ideology of western society. An assertion made in the editorial page of a bar association journal illustrates this argument: "If you believe in the Anglo-Saxon common law tradition, that the individual is the important unit of our society, and the state exists to serve him, then it seems that the adversary system is preferable. If you hold a corporate view of society, that is to say, that the community is the important unit, and that the citizen must be primarily considered as a part of the corporate unit, then it seems you should champion the inquisitorial system. ..."

Jerome Frank is well known for linking the adversary system with economic theory. In his writings he repeatedly associated it with classic, laissez-faire, economic theory and unbridled individualism. Surprisingly, however, only recently has scholarship emerged in the English language which attempts to seriously study the influence of political and economic theory on judicial procedure. Naively, perhaps, the assumption has been made that procedure is value-free. Scholars who have turned their attention to this question in recent years seem to agree that at least at a very general and theoretical level there are connections between ideology and procedural choices. The connection may not be direct, nor empirically demonstrable. However, at least arguably, the adversary system can be seen as reflecting the political and economic ideology of classic English liberalism in three ways: by its emphasis upon self-interest and individual initiative; by its apparent distrust of the state; and, by the significance it attaches to the participation of the parties.

The adversary system legitimizes, indeed necessitates, a self-interest role for the parties. Thus one of its premises would appear to be consistent with the premise of the capitalist system of economic organization that if each individual strives to promote his self-interest an optimum allocation of resources will result. ...

If this is one of the justifications for the adversary system then not many people today would likely perceive of it as placing very serious constraints on the judge's intervention in the trial. Laissez-faire theory is no longer taken as being determinative in the economic and social fields. It would be incongruous if its basic postulate was still the premise used to define the respective roles of the parties and the judge in a judicial trial.

A basic socialist value is a strong emphasis on collectivism. The interests of the state and the individual are assumed to coincide, state power is not distrusted. On the other hand, liberal political philosophy is premised on a distrust of the state and public officials. The adversary system can thus be viewed in a liberal state as a means of decentralizing power, and as an attempt to prevent abuses of political power. ...

Again, assuming this to be a premise of the adversary system, it would not appear to require that the judge be totally passive in the conduct of the trial. Indeed since in most cases he has the responsibility for the ultimate disposition of the case it would be incongruous to attempt to prohibit him from intervening in the proof-taking under the belief that his power was being constrained. This premise of the adversary system might have more relevance in defining the limits of party-autonomy.

Finally, the adversary system can be seen as being consistent with our prevalent political philosophy because it affords the parties the opportunity to participate in the making of decisions that affect their interests. Both psychological and theoretical literature in political philosophy support the view that the most acceptable type of decision in a democracy is personal choice. However, since it is clearly impossible to realize personal choice in many situations the best alternative is a system that assures to those affected by the decision some participation in the decisional process. A procedural system in which the judge assumes the primary responsibility for eliciting the proof, but permits the parties to assist in the proof-taking, would provide the parties a measure of participation in the decision-making process. However, Fuller argues that the adversary system "heightens the significance of ... participation" and thus "lifts adjudication toward its optimum expression." For this reason, he concludes that the adversary system is an essential characteristic of the adjudicative process.

The extent to which the judge's intervention in the trial, either in clarifying evidence or in calling for new evidence, impairs the parties' sense of participation is obviously an extremely complex question that cannot be explored in any detail here. In some instances, however, it might clearly be a consideration that leads the judge to the conclusion that he should not intervene. But in other situations his intervention in the form of asking questions might actually increase the meaningfulness of the parties' participation. Everyone has different cognitive needs and if the judge makes these needs known to the parties then it will make their participation more meaningful—obviously their participation will be meaningless unless the judge's understanding of the case is the meaning that they are attempting to convey to him. Also, even if the judge were to call additional proof, so long as he gives the parties the opportunity to test such proof and call rebutting proof their participation in the decision-making process would appear to remain meaningful.

B. Cathartic Effect

Particularly in civil suits the adversary system might be a more acceptable procedure for fact-finding than the inquisitorial system because it satisfies the psychology of the litigants by legitimizing a courtroom duel which is a sublimation of more direct forms of hostile aggression. It has been suggested that there are psychological benefits in the "battle atmosphere" of adversary litigation. Charles Curtis in his book *It's Your Law* summarized this argument. He said:

> The law takes the position that we ought to be satisfied if the parties are; and it believes that
> the best way to get this done is to encourage them to fight it out, and dissolve their differ-

ences in dissention. We are still a combative people not yet so civilized and sophisticated as to forget that combat is one way to justice.

The use of the adversary system to satisfy the primeval competitive urges of the litigants might be suggested by its genealogy. The ancestry of the trial is of course the blood feud, trial by battle and individual or class acts of revenge. This justification for the adversary system is also apparent in the frequent analogy of the judicial trial to a sporting event. It leads lawyers to talk of tactics and strategy and to refer to the judge as an umpire. This view of the adversary process is most clearly perceived if the trial is regarded as a "game," using that word in the sense that it is used by game theorists. The "sporting theory of justice" describes the rules of the game. There has been a social disturbance and the game is played only to gain some relief or satisfaction.

The adversary system viewed as part of a game perhaps explains the system's acceptance of the result when a party loses on a technicality, even if his loss was due to a violation of one of the technical rules of evidence or procedure which regulate the game. If justice is equated to the satisfaction of the litigants then the adversary system, which is directly responsible for this satisfaction, becomes an end in itself. The true facts of the case are less important than how well the parties play the game. Reasoning from this premise, Charles Curtis concluded:

> Justice is something larger and more intimate than truth. Truth is only one of the ingredients of justice. Its whole is the satisfaction of those concerned. ... The administration of justice is no more designed to elicit the truth than the scientific approach is designed to extract justice from the atom.

If this justification for the adversary system is correct then the judge's role in the trial would be a limited one. However, the basic premise of the argument is disputable. As one author posed the question: "Is the battle atmosphere of trial proceedings truly cathartic, in the sense of relieving tensions and aggressions that would otherwise find more destructive outlets, or does it instill an aggressive approach to problems that is incompatible with the need to compromise and co-operate in the vast majority of interpersonal contacts?" Unfortunately, no serious effort has been made to resolve this question by asking the ultimate consumers of the system—the litigants. Basing a judgment on common experience, however, most people would probably agree with Professor Garlan who wrote at the height of the legal realist movement, referring to the jurisprudential theory of what he called "sporting fairness":

> The game has become too brutal, too destructive of human life, too exhaustive to those who win, and too fatal for those who lose. Living begins to look more like a struggle, than a game. The participant's sense of humor and sense of balance are worn, and the sporting morale is breaking up into a fighting morale. The sides are too unequal for successful competition, and, in the eyes of the defeated, the game looks more like exploitation than competition.

While we know very little about the psychology of litigants, I suspect that most of them do not view social conflicts as social events. They come to court expecting justice, and unless the rules of substantive law are perverse, that means they expect their dispute to be resolved according to the law. A theory about the judge's role that begins by assuming that rules of evidence and procedure are simply rules of competition is therefore deficient.

C. Role of Counsel

A third aspect of the adversary system that might render it more acceptable than the inquisitorial system is the role played by counsel. It has been hypothesized that "[i]f parties perceive their adversary attorneys as having interests convergent with their own, they may begin to experience the comforting strength of belonging to a coalition the total purpose of which is to gain a favorable verdict at the expense of the opposing party." Also the lawyer will be a person who, in some sense, shares in the litigant's defeat. Certain institutional characteristics of the adversary system encourage this coalition and the apparent identity of interest between the adversary lawyer and his client. However, assuming this to be true, intervention in the trial proceedings by the trial judge is unlikely to destroy in any way this coalition or this sense of shared purpose.

D. Appearance of Impartiality

Finally, the adversary system might be more acceptable than an inquisitorial system because it gives the tribunal the appearance of impartiality. Proponents of the Anglo-American procedural system attach great importance to the appearance of impartiality. While its importance cannot be denied, the intelligent control of the conduct of the trial need not leave a judge open to the charge of partiality. The possible appearance of impartiality is a matter a judge should consider when intervening, and to that extent it limits his intervention. For instance, if a judge calls a witness he must ensure that the parties have an opportunity to test the testimony of the witness and to call rebutting evidence or he might be open to the charge that he is shaping the record. If a witness is evasive in answering questions the judge must ensure that he does not appear hostile towards the witness. However, if the judge intervenes in a fair and dispassionate manner this consideration should not seriously impair his ability to intervene when he thinks it is necessary.

3. The Adversary System Increases the Accuracy of Fact-Finding

A second justification given for the adversary system [in addition to increasing the acceptability of adjudication] is that it is a better fact-finding mechanism than the inquisitorial system. That is to say, given all the interests that must be balanced in a procedural system, more accurate factual judgments about past events are likely to be achieved using the adversary system than using some other system. This justification rests, in turn, upon two premises. The first premise is that the adversary system will result in a more thorough investigation of the facts than the inquisitorial system. The second premise is that under the adversarial system the trier of fact is more likely to reach the correct decision because during the proceedings he will not acquire a bias towards one conclusion or the other. He will be able to remain completely disinterested in the outcome until all the proof has been elicited and the arguments made. In order to define the role of the judge in the adversary system these two premises must be explored in detail.

A. Parties Motivated by Self-Interest Are Likely To Be Most Diligent in Presenting and Critically Evaluating All the Evidence

The first premise of this justification for the adversary system is that in an adversary proceeding the judge will, when he makes his decision, be more informed as to the facts than a similarly situated judge in an inquisitorial system. This is so, it is argued, because parties who are given a free hand in pursuing their perceived self-interest are more likely than an official motivated only by official duty to transmit to the judge all evidence favourable to their case and to critically test all unfavourable evidence presented to him. Empirical studies have attempted to test whether this premise is correct. However, for purposes of defining the judge's role in the adversary system the premise must be accepted as true.

The parties do not have complete control over the presentation and testing of proof and this premise of the adversary system does not require them to have such control. Control is given to the parties to promote accurate fact-finding and to further achieve this end the parties are constrained in the conduct of their case by rules of procedure and evidence. The need for these rules arises because if this premise of the adversary system is to achieve its objective a number of factors must be present in the litigation of particular disputes. The rules are intended, in part, to ensure that these factors are present. If these factors are not present in a particular case the adversary system will not achieve its goal of accurate fact-finding; or if it is to achieve this end in their absence the judge may have to regulate his conduct accordingly. Thus the judge, in defining his role, must be sensitive to the presence or absence of these factors. For purposes of clarity I will discuss these factors as assumptions of the premise that the adversary system is an accurate fact-finding mechanism because parties motivated by self-interest will present and critically test all relevant evidence.

Assumption 1: The Parties Are Initially Motivated

The first assumption that this premise of the adversary system makes is that the parties are initially motivated to seek out all the evidence favorable to their case. This obviously depends upon both parties being equally interested in the outcome of the case, that is, equally interested in pursuing their respective rights and remedies and in opposing the rights of the other party. If this is not the case, if one of the parties is not motivated to oppose the other party's case, the requisite factual investigation and presentation of proof will not take place.

Assumption 2: The Parties Will Sustain Their Motivation

A second assumption of this premise of the adversary system is that throughout the proceedings both parties will sustain their motivation to present all the evidence. A number of rules of evidence have been developed to encourage parties to diligently pursue all the evidence favorable to their side; at least these rules can, in part, be understood by reference to this need. …

A further rule of evidence that has the effect of encouraging the parties to independently investigate all evidence in their favour is the solicitor–client privilege—at least that part of it that the Americans call the work product rule. This rule, in general, prevents one lawyer or litigant from demanding disclosure, particularly before trial, of the other litigant's trial briefs, witness statements and related materials prepared or collected for use in the litigation. If a litigant could compel such disclosure there would be a great temptation for each litigant to rely on the other to do the investigations and to gather the necessary information. Eventually, litigants would become more and more reluctant to make an independent effort to collect information and to prepare arguments for trial. ...

As well as forming the basis of a number of rules of evidence and procedure this assumption of party-prosecution has a more direct implication in defining the judge's role. In a system that relies on party prosecution the judge cannot intervene to such an extent in the trial that the parties begin to rely upon him to search out all the facts favourable to their case and thus become less diligent themselves in seeking out the facts. ...

Assumption 3: The Parties Have Equal Capacity, Skill and Resources

Party-prosecution, as a principle of the adversary system, rests on a third assumption: that each party has the ability, skill, and resources to search out the evidence favorable to his or her case and to present it to the court. Do the parties always have the capacity or ability to obtain access to all facts favorable to their case? The adversary system encourages parties to assume a self-interested role. While casting the parties into this role it ensures that they will be diligent in presenting evidence favorable to their cause, it also legitimizes or at least would appear to sanction their suppressing evidence that is unfavorable to their case. This temptation laid before the parties is regarded by many as the greatest obstacle to accurate fact-finding in the adversary system. ... There is little a judge in any system can do to prevent the parties from suppressing or falsifying evidence. A number of rules of evidence and procedure, however, attempt to provide both parties with access to as much evidence as possible. While these rules do not bear directly on the judge's role they are important in increasing our understanding of the adversary system and thus at least indirectly the judge's role in it.

First, rules of pre-trial discovery assist the parties in obtaining evidence. In civil cases, these rules generally permit a party to question the other prior to the trial about his knowledge of the facts in the case. It has been argued that pre-trial discovery is inconsistent with the adversary system. However, this argument confuses means with ends. If one begins the analysis by looking for reasons for the adversary system, the better view would appear to be that of Professor Goldstein who concluded that discovery "has as its object the harnessing of the full creative potential of the adversary process, bringing each party to trial as aware of what he must meet as his finances and his lawyer's energy and intelligence permit." ...

Finally, to ensure that the party's strong sense of self-interest and stake in the trial does not result in the degeneration of the trial into fraud and deceit, interposed between the litigant and the process is a lawyer; a person who will, to a large extent, conduct the proceedings and who has a responsibility not only to the litigant, his client, but also to the process. While the exact nature of the lawyer's responsibility to the process is the subject of dispute, there is agreement that he has a responsibility in most cases to protect the process from evidence he knows to be falsified.

For this assumption of the adversary system to be operative both parties must also have equal resources to investigate and collect facts favorable to their case, and both must be of equal skill in presenting these facts and in testing the facts presented that are unfavorable to their case. If the adversaries do not have equal representation—if for instance the accused in a criminal trial is unable to avail himself of effective counsel—this premise, upon which the adversary system rests, will be impaired. But even when both parties are represented by counsel, the quality of the representation will obviously seldom be equal. What is the role of the judge if one party is not represented or if her representation is inadequate? In such a situation the adversary system will fail to achieve its objective. The judge should not hesitate to intervene. Whatever dangers arise when a judge intervenes in such a situation, they are outweighed by the serious danger that is present if he does not intervene.

A final aspect of this assumption of the adversary system is the necessity that both parties have the resources to carry out a thorough investigation of the facts. This, of course, is seldom the case. …

Assumption 4: The Parties Will Be Given the Opportunity To Test Adverse Evidence

Party-prosecution assumes that each party will have the opportunity and the ability to thoroughly test the evidence unfavorable to his case. It assumes, also, that this testing of adverse evidence must be done by an adversary cross-examination as opposed to a dispassionate inquisitorial examination. Opinions on the utility of cross-examination are sharply divided. …

Assumption 5: All Interests Affected Are Represented

Finally, the principle of party-prosecution assumes that all interests affected by the adjudication are represented by the parties. The adversary system depends upon the parties to bring forward the information upon which the judge will rely in reaching his decision. In reaching a decision the judge must reconcile all the competing interests affected by his decision. If he does not receive information about some of these interests because they are interests of no immediate concern to the parties before him the adversary system will be a defective method of fact-finding for that decision. …

Another area in which the adversaries will not represent all the interests might be described broadly, if not with some circularity, as being the area of public interest law, such as environmental, consumer protection law. Again, in these areas, the wise judge might well call upon the intervention of third parties to represent those interests not represented by the immediate parties to the particular dispute. At the appellant level this is commonly done by means of asking for or inviting amicus curiae factums. …

4. The Adversary System Counteracts Bias in Decision-Making

The second reason often given as to why the adversary system leads to more accurate fact-finding than an inquisitorial system is that the adversary system permits the judge to remain unbiased as between the parties throughout the proceedings. Bias is a word used in a wide variety of senses, many of which shade into each other. In this context, where important consequences are being drawn from the concept, it is particularly important to be clear about its meaning.

Bias in this context does not mean, as it commonly means in other contexts, a preconceived point of view about issues of law or policy, a personal prejudice against certain types of parties, or bias in the sense of being personally interested in the outcome of the case. No fact-finding mechanism can remove these types of biases. It refers to a bias or prejudgment that is acquired by a decision-maker because of the mechanism of fact-finding used. If the judge takes an active part in proof-taking, it could be argued he might acquire a bias towards one party or the other for one of the following reasons:

1. If the judge questions a witness and the witness is evasive, disrespectful, hostile, or in some way does not live up to the expectations of the judge, the judge may become antagonistic towards that witness and therefore tend to discredit his testimony.

2. If the judge in proof-taking is responsible for having some important evidence revealed, he may tend to give too much weight to that evidence, either because he is overly impressed with the skilful manner in which the evidence was presented, or because it is important to him that his intervention is seen to have served a useful purpose.

3. The judge may, in his investigation, become so concerned about a detail of the case that the balance of the evidence will escape his careful attention. This is perhaps the kind of consideration that judges are concerned about when they assert that their ability to evaluate the credibility of a witness is impaired if they themselves become too involved in examining a witness. That is to say, as an investigator preoccupied with his own line of thought, the judge may unconsciously fail to explore important points, may amass so much detail that obvious truths are obscured, or may not carefully observe all of the diverse matters, such as demeanor evidence, that he should take into consideration in evaluating the probative value of testimonial proof.

4. A fourth source of bias that is not present in the adversary system, but which one might argue is present in the inquisitorial system, is the bias that is acquired when the judge is presented with a file of the evidence before the case is heard by him. In an inquisitorial system the judge will of course have had to study the documents contained in the file with some care if he is to be efficient in carrying out the proof-taking at trial. There is an obvious danger that the information supplied in the file will bias the judge towards one side or the other. As Glanville Williams noted, "Our reaction to the French system is that it creates a danger that the point of view of the prosecution will communicate itself to the judge before the case has been heard."

5. Finally, it has been contended that the adversary system is an unbiasing fact-finding technique because it counteracts what psychologists call decision-maker bias. Decision-maker bias is acquired when a decision-maker himself investigates the facts upon which he is to rest his judgment. It arises because of the need when one begins to investigate facts to form certain tentative hypotheses about the reality that one is called upon to reconstruct. More or less imperceptibly, these

preconceptions influence the course of the investigation. As well, facts which confirm the original hypothesis will make a strong imprint upon the mind, while facts that run counter to it are received with diverted attention. This bias, which arises from the process of fact-finding, is avoided in the adversary system, it is argued. It is avoided because, in the adversary system, the judge, since he is not responsible for the investigation, is able to avoid any judgment of the case until he has heard all the evidence.

While all of these kinds of bias may be present in an adversary proceeding, none of them should limit to any great extent, within the framework of our present trial, the judge's intelligent intervention in the case. A recognition of their presence should permit the judge to conduct the proceedings in a fashion that minimizes the dangers that might arise.

NOTES AND QUESTIONS

1. These classic descriptions of the principles underlying the adversary system were written many years ago. In subsequent chapters we will consider to what extent they may have changed. To what extent do you think changes to the system might impact on the role of lawyers?

2. The Ontario *Rules of Professional Conduct* describe the lawyer's role as advocate as "openly and necessarily partisan. Accordingly, the lawyer is not obliged ... to assist an adversary or advance matters derogatory to the client's case." See rule 10, commentary 13. However, pursuant to rule 4.01(2)(h), while one need not generally assist one's adversary, one is obliged to inform the tribunal about relevant binding authority, even if it harms one's case and one's opponent has not raised the matter. What are the implications of these rules for a quest to ascertain the "truth"?

B. Civilian and Indigenous Counterparts

This section compares procedures in the common law world with procedures in other legal traditions. In particular, the common law adversarial approach to civil procedure will be compared with the inquisitorial approach to civil procedure found in many civil law jurisdictions. Next, comparisons will be made to procedures found in certain indigenous legal traditions.

An inquisitorial system of adjudication places the responsibility for the development of the factual and legal issues of the case largely on the court, rather than on the parties. For example, the court assumes the main responsibility for gathering information relevant to the case. The judge decides which witnesses must testify and takes the lead in questioning them and determining what, if any, further information need be sought in the case. The implications that the inquisitorial system has for the contours of civil procedure are canvassed in the following article by John H. Langbein.

J.H. Langbein, "The German Advantage in Civil Procedure"
(1985), 52 *University of Chicago Law Review* 823, at 823-54 (footnotes omitted)

Our lawyer-dominated system of civil procedure has often been criticized both for its incentives to distort evidence and for the expense and complexity of its modes of discovery and trial. The shortcomings inhere in a system that leaves to partisans the work of gathering and producing the factual material upon which adjudication depends.

We have comforted ourselves with the thought that a lawyerless system would be worse. The excesses of American adversary justice would seem to pale by comparison with a literally nonadversarial system—one in which litigants would be remitted to faceless bureaucratic adjudicators and denied the safeguards that flow from lawyerly intermediation.

The German advantage. The main theme of this article is drawn from Continental civil procedure, exemplified for me by the system that I know reasonably well, the West German. My theme is that, by assigning judges rather than lawyers to investigate the facts, the Germans avoid the most troublesome aspects of our practice. But I shall emphasize that the familiar contrast between our adversarial procedure and the supposedly nonadversarial procedure of the Continental tradition has been grossly overdrawn.

To be sure, since the greater responsibility of the bench for fact-gathering is what distinguishes the Continental tradition, a necessary (and welcome) correlative is that counsel's role in eliciting evidence is greatly restricted. Apart from fact-gathering, however, the lawyers for the parties play major and broadly comparable roles in both the German and American systems. Both are adversary systems of civil procedure. There as here, the lawyers advance partisan positions from first pleadings to final arguments. German litigators suggest legal theories and lines of factual inquiry, they superintend and supplement judicial examination of witnesses, they urge inferences from fact, they discuss and distinguish precedent, they interpret statutes, and they formulate views of the law that further the interests of their clients. I shall urge that German experience shows that we would do better if we were greatly to restrict the adversaries' role in fact-gathering. …

I. *Overview of German Civil Procedure*

There are two fundamental differences between German and Anglo-American civil procedure, and these differences lead in turn to many others. First, the court rather than the parties' lawyers takes the main responsibility for gathering and sifting evidence, although the lawyers exercise a watchful eye over the court's work. Second, there is no distinction between pretrial and trial, between discovering evidence and presenting it. Trial is not a single continuous event. Rather, the court gathers and evaluates evidence over a series of hearings, as many as the circumstances require.

Initiation. The plaintiff's lawyer commences a lawsuit in Germany with a complaint. Like its American counterpart, the German complaint narrates the key facts, sets forth a legal theory, and asks for a remedy in damages or specific relief. Unlike an American complaint, however, the German document proposes means of proof for its main factual contentions. The major documents in the plaintiff's possession that support his claim are scheduled and often appended; other documents (for example, hospital files or government records such as police accident reports or agency files) are indicated; witnesses who are thought to know something helpful to the plaintiff's position are identified. The defendant's answer follows the same pattern. It should be emphasized, however, that neither plaintiff's nor defendant's lawyer will have conducted any significant search for witnesses or for other evidence unknown to his client. Digging for facts is primarily the work of the judge.

Judicial preparation. The judge to whom the case is entrusted examines these pleadings and appended documents. He routinely sends for relevant public records. These materials form the beginnings of the official dossier, the court file. All subsequent submissions of counsel, and all subsequent evidence-gathering, will be entered in the dossier, which is open to counsel's inspection continuously.

When the judge develops a first sense of the dispute from these materials, he will schedule a hearing and notify the lawyers. He will often invite and sometimes summon the parties as well as their lawyers to this or subsequent hearings. If the pleadings have identified witnesses whose testimony seems central, the judge may summon them to the initial hearing as well.

Hearing. The circumstances of the case dictate the course of the hearing. Sometimes the court will be able to resolve the case by discussing it with the lawyers and parties and suggesting avenues of compromise. If the case remains contentious and witness testimony needs to be taken, the court will have learned enough about the case to determine a sequence for examining witnesses.

Examining and recording. The judge serves as the examiner-in-chief. At the conclusion of his interrogation of each witness, counsel for either party may pose additional questions, but counsel are not prominent as examiners. Witness testimony is seldom recorded verbatim; rather, the judge pauses from time to time to dictate a summary of the testimony into the dossier. The lawyers sometimes suggest improvements in the wording of these summaries, in order to preserve or to emphasize nuances important to one side or the other.

Since the proceedings in a difficult case may require several hearings extending across many months, these summaries of concluded testimony—by encapsulating succinctly the results of previous hearings—allow the court to refresh itself rapidly for subsequent hearings. The summaries also serve as building blocks from which the court will ultimately fashion the findings of fact for its written judgment. If the case is appealed, these concise summaries constitute the record for the reviewing court. ...

Expertise. If an issue of technical difficulty arises on which the court or counsel wishes to obtain the views of an expert, the court—in consultation with counsel—will select the expert and define his role. (This aspect of the procedure I shall discuss particularly in Part IV below.)

Further contributions of counsel. After the court takes witness testimony or receives some other infusion of evidence, counsel have the opportunity to comment orally or in writing. Counsel use these submissions in order to suggest further proofs or to advance legal theories. Thus, nonadversarial proof-taking alternates with adversarial dialogue across as many hearings as are necessary. The process merges the investigatory function of our pretrial discovery and the evidence-presenting function of our trial. Another manifestation of the comparative efficiency of German procedure is that a witness is ordinarily examined only once. Contrast the American practice of partisan interview and preparation, pretrial deposition, preparation for trial, and examination and cross-examination at trial. These many steps take their toll in expense and irritation.

Judgment. After developing the facts and hearing the adversaries' views, the court decides the case in a written judgment that must contain full findings of fact and make reasoned application of the law.

II. Judicial Control of Sequence

From the standpoint of comparative civil procedure, the most important consequence of having judges direct fact-gathering in this episodic fashion is that German procedure functions without the sequence rules to which we are accustomed in the Anglo-American procedural world. The implications for procedural economy are large. The very concepts of "plaintiff's case" and "defendant's case" are unknown. In our system those concepts function as traffic rules for the partisan presentation of evidence to a passive and ignorant trier. By contrast, in German procedure the court ranges over the entire case, constantly looking for the jugular—for the issue of law or fact that might dispose of the case. Free of constraints that arise from party presentation of evidence, the court investigates the dispute in the fashion most likely to narrow the inquiry. A major job of counsel is to guide the search by directing the court's attention to particularly cogent lines of inquiry.

Suppose that the court has before it a contract case that involves complicated factual or legal issues about whether the contract was formed, and if so, what its precise terms were. But suppose further that the court quickly recognizes (or is led by submission of counsel to recognize) that some factual investigation might establish an affirmative defense—illegality, let us say—that would vitiate the contract. Because the court functions without sequence rules, it can postpone any consideration of issues that we would think of as the plaintiff's case—here the questions concerning the formation and the terms of the contract. Instead, the court can concentrate the entire initial inquiry on what we would regard as a defense. If, in my example, the court were to unearth enough evidence to allow it to conclude that the contract was illegal, no investigation would ever be done on the issues of formation and terms. A defensive issue that could only surface in Anglo-American procedure following full pretrial and trial ventilation of the whole of the plaintiff's case can be brought to the fore in German procedure.

Part of what makes our discovery system so complex is that, on account of our division into pretrial and trial, we have to discover for the entire case. We investigate everything that could possibly come up at trial, because once we enter the trial phase we can seldom go back and search for further evidence. By contrast, the episodic character of German fact-gathering largely eliminates the danger of surprise; if the case takes an unexpected turn, the disadvantaged litigant can count on developing his response in another hearing at a later time. Because there is no pretrial discovery phase, fact-gathering occurs only once; and because the court establishes the sequence of fact-gathering according to criteria of relevance, unnecessary investigation is minimized. In the Anglo-American procedural world we value the early-disposition mechanism, especially summary judgment, for issues of law. But for fact-laden issues, our fixed-sequence rule (plaintiff's case before defendant's case) and our single-continuous-trial rule largely foreclose it.

The episodic character of German civil procedure—Benjamin Kaplan called it the "conference method" of adjudication—has other virtues. It lessens tension and theatrics, and it encourages settlement. Countless novels, movies, plays, and broadcast serials attest to the dramatic potential of the Anglo-American trial. The contest between opposing counsel; the potential for surprise witnesses who cannot be rebutted in time; the tricks of adversary examination and cross-examination; the concentration of proof-taking and verdict into a single, continuous proceeding; the unpredictability of juries and the mysterious opacity of their conclusory verdicts—these attributes of the Anglo-American trial make for good theatre. German civil proceedings have the tone not of the theatre, but of a routine business meeting—serious rather than tense. When the court inquires and directs, it sets no stage for advocates to perform. The forensic skills of counsel can wrest no material advantage, and the appearance of a surprise witness would simply lead to the scheduling of a further hearing. In a system that cannot distinguish between dress rehearsal and opening night, there is scant occasion for stage fright.

In this business-like system of civil procedure the tradition is strong that the court promotes compromise. The judge who gathers the facts soon knows the case as well as the litigants do, and he concentrates each subsequent increment of fact-gathering on the most important issues still unresolved. As the case progresses the judge discusses it with the litigants, sometimes indicating provisional views of the likely outcome. He is, therefore, strongly positioned to encourage a litigant to abandon a case that is turning out to be weak or hopeless, or to recommend settlement. The loser-pays system of allocating the costs of litigation gives the parties further incentive to settle short of judgment.

III. Witnesses

Adversary control of fact-gathering in our procedure entails a high level of conflict between partisan advantage and orderly disclosure of the relevant information. Marvin Frankel put this point crisply when he said that "it is the rare case in which either side yearns to have the witnesses, or anyone, give *the whole truth*."

If we had deliberately set out to find a means of impairing the reliability of witness testimony, we could not have done much better than the existing system of having partisans prepare witnesses in advance of trial and examine and cross-examine them at trial. Jerome Frank described the problem a generation ago:

> [The witness] often detects what the lawyer hopes to prove at the trial. If the witness desires to have the lawyer's client win the case, he will often, unconsciously, mold his story accordingly. Telling and re-telling it to the lawyer, he will honestly believe that his story, as he narrates it in court, is true, although it importantly deviates from what he originally believed.

Thus, said Frank, "the partisan nature of trials tends to make partisans of the witnesses."

Cross-examination at trial—our only substantial safeguard against this systematic bias in the testimony that reaches our courts—is a frail and fitful palliative. Cross-examination is too often ineffective to undo the consequences of skillful coaching. Further, because

cross-examination allows so much latitude for bullying and other truth-defeating strata-
gems, it is frequently the source of fresh distortion when brought to bear against truthful
testimony. As a leading litigator boasted recently in an ABA publication: "By a carefully
planned and executed cross-examination, I can raise at least a slight question about the
accuracy of [an adverse] witness's story, or question his motives or impartiality."

When we cross the border into German civil procedure, we leave behind all traces of
this system of partisan preparation, examination, and cross-examination of witnesses.
German law distinguishes parties from witnesses. A German lawyer must necessarily
discuss the facts with his client, and based on what his client tells him and on what the
documentary record discloses, the lawyer will nominate witnesses whose testimony
might turn out to be helpful to his client. As the proofs come in, they may reveal to the
lawyer the need to nominate further witnesses for the court to examine. But the lawyer
stops at nominating; virtually never will he have occasion for out-of-court contact with
a witness. Not only would such contact be a serious ethical breach, it would be self-
defeating. "German judges are given to marked and explicit doubts about the reliability
of the testimony of witnesses who previously have discussed the case with counsel or
who have consorted unduly with a party."

No less a critic than Jerome Frank was prepared to concede that in American procedure the adversaries "sometimes do bring into court evidence which, in a dispassionate
inquiry, might be overlooked." That is a telling argument for including adversaries in the
fact-gathering process, but not for letting them run it. German civil procedure preserves
party interests in fact-gathering.

At trial, the battle of experts tends to baffle the trier, especially in jury courts. If the
experts do not cancel each other out, the advantage is likely to be with the expert whose
forensic skills are the more enticing. The system invites abusive cross-examination. Since
each expert is party-selected and party-paid, he is vulnerable to attack on credibility regardless of the merits of his testimony. A defense lawyer recently bragged about his technique of cross-examining plaintiffs' experts in tort cases. Notice that nothing in his
strategy varies with the truthfulness of the expert testimony he tries to discredit:

> A mode of attack ripe with potential is to pursue a line of questions which, by their form
> and the jury's studied observation of the witness in response, will tend to cast the expert as
> a "professional witness." By proceeding in this way, the cross-examiner will reap the benefit
> of a community attitude, certain to be present among several of the jurors, that bias can be
> purchased, almost like a commodity.

Thus, the systematic incentive in our procedure to distort expertise leads to a systematic distrust and devaluation of expertise. Short of forbidding the use of experts altogether, we probably could not have designed a procedure better suited to minimize the
influence of expertise.

The Continental tradition. European legal systems are, by contrast, expert-prone.
Expertise is frequently sought. The literature emphasizes the value attached to having
expert assistance available to the courts in an age in which litigation involves facts of
ever-greater technical difficulty. The essential insight of Continental civil procedure is
that credible expertise must be neutral expertise. Thus, the responsibility for selecting

and informing experts is placed upon the courts, although with important protections for party interests.

Selecting the expert. German courts obtain expert help in lawsuits the way Americans obtain expert help in business or personal affairs. If you need an architect, a dermatologist, or a plumber, you do not commission a pair of them to take pre-ordained and opposing positions on your problem, although you do sometimes take a second opinion. Rather, you take care to find an expert who is qualified to advise you in an objective manner; you probe his advice as best you can; and if you find his advice persuasive, you follow it.

When in the course of winnowing the issues in a lawsuit a German court determines that expertise might help resolve the case, the court selects and instructs the expert. The court may decide to seek expertise on its own motion, or at the request of one of the parties. The code of civil procedure allows the court to request nominations from the parties—indeed, the code requires the court to use any expert upon whom the parties agree—but neither practice is typical. In general, the court takes the initiative in nominating and selecting the expert. ...

Preparing the expert. The court that selects the expert instructs him, in the sense of propounding the facts that he is to assume or to investigate, and in framing the questions that the court wishes the expert to address. In formulating the expert's task, as in other important steps in the conduct of the case, the court welcomes adversary suggestions. If the expert should take a view of premises (for example, in an accident case or a building-construction dispute), counsel for both sides will accompany him.

Safeguards. The expert is ordinarily instructed to prepare a written opinion. When the court receives the report, it is circulated to the litigants. The litigants commonly file written comments, to which the expert is asked to reply. The court on its own motion may also request the expert to amplify his views. If the expert's report remains in contention, the court will schedule a hearing at which counsel for a dissatisfied litigant can confront and interrogate the expert.

The code of civil procedure reserves to the court the power to order a further report by another expert if the court should deem the first report unsatisfactory. A litigant dissatisfied with the expert may encourage the court to invoke its power to name a second expert. The code of criminal procedure has a more explicit standard for such cases, which is worth noticing because the literature suggests that courts have similar instincts in civil procedure. The court may refuse a litigant's motion to engage a further expert in a criminal case, the code says,

> if the contrary of the fact concerned has already been proved through the former expert opinion; this [authority to refuse to appoint a further expert] does not apply if the expertise of the former expert is doubted, if his report is based upon inaccurate factual presuppositions, if the report contains contradictions, or if the new expert has available means of research that appear superior to those of a former expert.

When, therefore, a litigant can persuade the court that an expert's report has been sloppy or partial, that it rests upon a view of the field that is not generally shared, or that the question referred to the expert is exceptionally difficult, the court will commission further expertise.

A litigant may also engage his own expert, much as is done in the Anglo-American procedural world, in order to rebut the court-appointed expert. The court will discount the views of a party-selected expert on account of his want of neutrality, but cases occur in which he nevertheless proves to be effective. Ordinarily, I am told, the court will not in such circumstances base its judgment directly upon the views of the party-selected expert; rather, the court will treat the rebuttal as ground for engaging a further court-appointed expert (called an *Oberexperte*, literally an "upper" or "superior" expert), whose opinion will take account of the rebuttal.

To conclude: In the use of expertise German civil procedure strikes an adroit balance between nonadversarial and adversarial values. Expertise is kept impartial, but litigants are protected against error or caprice through a variety of opportunities for consultation, confrontation, and rebuttal. …

Outside the realm of fact-gathering, German civil procedure is about as adversarial as our own. Both systems welcome the lawyerly contribution to identifying legal issues and sharpening legal analysis. German civil procedure is materially less adversarial than our own only in the fact-gathering function, where partisanship has such potential to pollute the sources of truth.

Accordingly, the proper question is not whether to have lawyers, but how to use them; not whether to have an adversarial component to civil procedure, but how to prevent adversarial excesses. If we were to incorporate the essential lesson of the German system in our own procedure, we would still have a strongly adversarial civil procedure. We would not, however, have coached witnesses and litigation-biased experts. …

Prejudgment. Perhaps the most influential justification for adversary domination of fact-gathering has been an agreement put forward by Lon Fuller: Nonadversarial procedure risks prejudgment—that is, prematurity in judgment. Fuller worried that the judge would make up his mind too soon.

> What generally occurs in practice is that at some early point a familiar pattern will seem to emerge from the evidence; an accustomed label is waiting for the case and, without awaiting further proofs, this label is promptly assigned to it. …
>
> An adversary presentation seems the only effective means for combatting this natural human tendency to judge too swiftly in terms of the familiar that which is not yet fully known. The arguments of counsel hold the case, as it were, in suspension between two opposing interpretations of it. While the proper classification of the case is thus kept unresolved, there is time to explore all of its peculiarities and nuances.

This passage obtains much of its force from the all-or-nothing contrast that so misdescribes German civil procedure. In a system like the German, which combines judicial fact-gathering with vigorous and continuing adversarial efforts in nominating lines of factual inquiry and analyzing factual and legal issues, the adversaries perform just the role that Fuller lauds, helping hold the decision in suspension while issues are framed and facts explored.

In German procedure counsel oversees and has means to prompt a flagging judicial inquiry; but quite apart from that protection, is it really true that a "familiar pattern" would otherwise beguile the judge into investigating too sparingly? If so, it seems odd that this asserted "natural human tendency" towards premature judgment does not show up in ordinary business and personal decision-making, whose patterns of inquiry resemble the fact-gathering process in German civil procedure. Since the decision-maker does his own investigating in most of life's decisions, it seems odd to despair of prematurity only when that normal mode of decision-making is found to operate in a courtroom. Accordingly, I think that Fuller overstates the danger of prematurity that inheres in allowing the decision-maker to conduct the fact-gathering; but to the extent that the danger is real, German civil procedure applies just the adversarial remedy that Fuller recommends.

Depth. Fuller's concern about prematurity shades into a different issue: how to achieve appropriate levels of depth in fact-gathering. Extra investment in search can almost always turn up further proofs that would be at least tenuously related to the case. Adversary domination of fact-gathering privatizes the decision about what level of resources to invest in the case. The litigants who are directly interested in the outcome decide how much to spend on search. In German procedure, by contrast, these partisan calculations of self-interest are subordinated, for a variety of reasons. The initiative in fact-gathering is shared with the judge; and the German system of reckoning and allocating the costs of litigation is less sensitive to the cost of incremental investigative steps than in our system where each side pays for the proofs that it orders. On the other hand, the German judge cannot refuse to investigate party-nominated proofs without reason, and this measure of party control greatly narrows the difference between the two systems.

Writing in 1958, Kaplan and his co-authors recorded their "impression" that German civil "proceedings do not in practice serve as an engine of discovery comparable in strength to the modern American methods," in part because German courts are hostile to fishing. Further, the authors worried that the technique of recording witness testimony in succinct summaries could bleach out "[f]ine factual differentiations." They found German procedure to be "far less preoccupied than the American with minute investigation of factual detail of reliability of individual witnesses."

Defenders of the American status quo may take too much comfort from these observations. A main virtue of German civil procedure, we recall, is that the principle of judicial control of sequence works to confine the scope of fact-gathering to those avenues of inquiry deemed most likely to resolve the case. Fact-gathering occurs when the unfolding logic of the case dictates that investigation of particular issues is needed. That practice does indeed contrast markedly with the inclination of American litigators "to leave no stone unturned, provided, of course, they can charge by the stone." The primary reason that German courts do less fact-gathering than American lawyers is that the Germans eliminate the waste. Likewise, when American observers notice that there is less harrying of witnesses with "those elaborate testings of credibility familiar to American courtrooms," I incline to think that the balance of advantage rests with the Germans, since so much of what passes for cross-examination in our procedure is deliberately truth-defeating. ...

VI. *Judicial Incentives*

Viewed comparatively from the Anglo-American perspective, the greater authority of the German judge over fact-gathering comes at the expense of the lawyers for the parties.

Adversary influence on fact-gathering is deliberately restrained. Furthermore, in routine civil procedure, German judges do not share power with jurors. There is no civil jury.

Because German procedure places upon the judge the responsibility for fact-gathering, the danger arises that the job will not be done well. The American system of partisan fact-gathering has the virtue of its vices: It aligns responsibility with incentive. Each side gathers and presents proofs according to its own calculation of self-interest. This privatization is an undoubted safeguard against official sloth. After all, who among us has not been treated shabbily by some lazy bureaucrat in a government department? And who would want to have that ugly character in charge of one's lawsuit?

The answer to that concern in the German tradition is straightforward: The judicial career must be designed in a fashion that creates incentives for diligence and excellence. The idea is to attract very able people to the bench, and to make their path of career advancement congruent with the legitimate interests of the litigants.

The career judiciary. The distinguishing attribute of the bench in Germany (and virtually everywhere else in Europe) is that the profession of judging is separate from the profession of lawyering. Save in exceptional circumstances, the judge is not an ex-lawyer like his Anglo-American counterpart. Rather, he begins his professional career as a judge.

American contrasts. If I were put to the choice of civil litigation under the German procedure that I have been praising in this article or under the American procedure that I have been criticizing, I might have qualms about choosing the German. The likely venue of a lawsuit of mine would be the state court in Cook County, Illinois, and I must admit that I distrust the bench of that court. The judges are selected by a process in which the criterion of professional competence is at best an incidental value. Further, while decent people do reach the Cook County bench in surprising numbers, events have shown that some of their colleagues are crooks. If my lawsuit may fall into the hands of a dullard or a thug, I become queasy about increasing his authority over the proceedings.

German-style judicial responsibility for fact-gathering cannot be lodged with the Greylord judiciary. Remodeling of civil procedure is intimately connected to improvement in the selection of judges. I do not believe that we would have to institute a German-style career judiciary in order to reform American civil procedure along German lines, although I do think that Judge Frankel was right to "question whether we are wise" to disdain the Continental model, and to "wonder now whether we might benefit from some admixture of such [career judges] to leaven or test our trial benches of elderly lawyers." The difference in quality between the state and federal trial benches in places like Cook County is sufficient to remind us that measures far short of adopting the Continental career judiciary can bring about material improvement.

NOTES AND QUESTIONS

1. How are the two fundamental questions of procedural design posed by Brooks, above—the allocation of function as between the judge and the parties for initiating and defining the dispute and for the development and presentation of proofs and arguments—resolved in the German procedural scheme?

2. Are you convinced of the German advantage in civil procedure? Is the procedural regime that Langbein describes likely to result in improved quality of testimony and greater efficiencies than a purely adversarial approach?

3. Of particular relevance to legal systems in Canada, it should be noted that Quebec, though a civil law jurisdiction, largely follows common law procedures.

The following excerpt compares the procedural traditions of indigenous legal systems in North America with those of the common law.

Robert D. Cooter and Wolfgang Fikentscher, "Indian Common Law: The Role of Custom in American Indian Tribal Courts"
(1998), 46 *American Journal of Comparative Law* 287 (footnotes omitted)

Introduction

A way of life expresses itself in norms sustained by institutions. Scholars have long studied the distinctive norms of American Indians, but no one has studied systematically whether or how tribal courts sustain these norms. Have custom and tradition worked their way into judge-made law on reservations and created distinctively Indian common law? This article provides an answer based upon interviews with judges on Indian reservations throughout the western United States. ...

We began our study with the belief that Indian common law exists when no scholar notices it. To test this belief, we conducted more than 120 interviews with tribal officials on 37 reservations in the West. We sought answers to four questions:

(1) Is there Indian common law? Specifically, does custom work its way into judge-made law on reservations?
(2) Is Indian common law specific to each tribe or generic to many tribes?
(3) How does Indian common law develop? Is the process different in tribal courts than in American state courts?
(4) Should public policy encourage or discourage the development of distinctively Indian common law?

The Anglo-American legal tradition identifies the common law as a body of substantive rules and a process. The substantive rules come from judges selectively enforcing social norms, and the common law process comes from judges systematically refining precedent. Mark Twain quipped that reports of his death were greatly exaggerated. Similarly, Tom Tso, whom we interviewed in 1990 when he was Chief Judge of the Navajo Reservation, thinks that reports of the death of Navajo common law are greatly exaggerated. He used Navajo social norms daily to decide cases. Our field research concludes that all tribal courts selectively enforce social norms and few tribal courts systematically refine precedent. These conclusions coincide with the conclusions of legal anthropologists about the general character of dispute resolution in tribes.

Unlike other minority groups in America, many Indian tribes have their own lands and governments. The U.S. Constitution recognizes tribal sovereignty. In recent years, Indian and non-Indian officials have stressed that sovereignty should be a fact, not just a slogan. If tribes exercise sovereignty, they would presumably absorb social norms into tribal laws. Thus our research reports on progress towards the realizing Indian legal sovereignty.

· · ·

In this section we refine these four questions into hypotheses.

Conquest and confinement to reservations ended most aboriginal political institutions, but customs and traditions survived. Imbedded in customs and traditions are concepts of justice and fairness relevant to legal disputes. Our first hypothesis is that Indian judges inevitably draw upon their own sense of justice and fairness in deciding cases and interpreting legislation.

The extent to which judges explicitly rely upon custom should vary systematically with the three types of courts that we distinguished above. Custom and tradition should prevail in traditional courts, such as the Peacemakers Court of the Iroquois, other traditional tribal courts, and the traditional secular courts of the Pueblos. Similarly, custom and tradition should play a central role in informal dispute resolution, such as peacemaking, mediating, and settlement negotiations. Our observations, however, concern CFR [Courts of Indian Offences] or IRA courts [courts established under the *Indian Reorganization Act*]. In these courts we anticipate heavy reliance by judges upon the sense of justice, which customs and norms shape, and modest reliance upon explicit social norms.

Turning to the second question, we hypothesize that Indian common law can be distinguished according to whether it is unique to a tribe, characteristic of groups of tribes, or common to all Indians. We will discuss briefly the causes of different levels of generality in Indian common law. Earlier we divided Indian history into three phases—autonomy and independence, conquest and submission, sovereignty and dependence. In thinking about tradition, Indians often try to reach back to the first phase for guidance. Most traditional Indians believe that their tribe originally had its law or "Way." A tribe's way of life is the sum of its customs and traditions, which are often imbedded in stories beginning with the creation of the world. The customs and traditions provide an encompassing guide to living backed by sacred sanction. The Way of the tribe should shape the tribal judge's sense of justice.

Although each tribe had its own "way," anthropologists group tribes into cultural areas in which the tribes share many attributes, such as the Great Plains, the Eastern Woodlands, the Northwest Coast, and the Pueblos of the southwest. In addition, the tribes can be divided into language groups that sometimes indicate common ancestry or cultural similarity. Law should follow culture. Consequently, we expect to find some common law specific to each tribe, and some common law shared by cultural groups.

Anthropologists have identified general differences in dispute resolution between tribes and industrial societies. Tribal people live their lives among kin, so a dispute indicates a rupture in these relationships. Dispute resolution in the tribe typically aims to repair relationships. To repair relationships, adjudicators examine the character of the parties and the history of their interaction, not just the particular event in the legal complaint. Compared to other American courts, we expect tribal courts to attend to relationships more than rules. In this respect, we anticipate similarities in the common law of all tribes.

Another reason suggests similarities among all tribes. Conquest subjugated all the tribes to similar forces. Thus the Bureau of Indian Affairs, like all bureaucracies, strives for uniformity in its practices. Different tribes may have adopted similar legal strategies to respond to similar external pressures.

Now we turn to the third question, which concerns the process by which tribal judges make law. Common law evolves in American state courts through reasoned elaboration of rules in formal proceedings. As noted, anthropological studies of dispute resolution in tribes typically observe less reliance on rules and more reliance on informal proceedings. America's aboriginal tribes did not possess writing or a professional bar. Most modern tribal courts keep few written records and conduct many trials without lawyers. We hypothesize that the common law process in tribal courts focuses more on relationships and less on rules in resolving disputes.

When making Indian common law, tribal judges confront a central problem in legal anthropology: How to distinguish customary obligations that are enforceable at law (which can be called "common law") from customary obligations that are not enforceable at law (which can be called "mere customs")? Put succinctly, the problem is to distinguish "law from custom." If a custom is law, then legal officials are obligated to enforce it, whereas if custom is not law, then legal officials require an independent justification for enforcing it. Thus disagreements about how to solve this problem involve values and policies, not mere linguistic convention for defining words. Distinguishing law from custom inevitably involves our fourth question—whether public policy should encourage the development of Indian common law.

Some theorists identify law with a formal apparatus of making rules and enforcing them, which implies that stateless societies lack law. For example, H.L.A. Hart defines law as the conjunction of "primary rules" for regulating behavior and "secondary rules" for creating, modifying, or extinguishing primary rules. Custom lacks secondary rules, so it is not recognized as law under this definition. At the opposite extreme, some theorists identify law with rules of social organization. Pospisil goes so far as to argue that each distinct unit of social organization, including the family, has its own law.

These theories are not so useful to tribal judges who must decide which customs to enforce. A more useful approach comes from the study of enduring relationships by social scientists. In economic jargon, an "efficient" rule enables people to accomplish their ends as fully as possible given the constraints on their resources, whereas an "inefficient" rule frustrates people unnecessarily. Theory and research have identified specific features of the interaction that cause efficient rules to emerge, and also deficiencies in the interaction that cause inefficient rules to emerge. Theory and empirical research suggest that people in enduring relationships tend to create efficient rules for interacting that allow them to accomplish their ends. Consequently, many customs (but not all) tend towards efficiency. In addition to efficiency, when the same activity has been repeated for years without objection or apparent harm, people often feel that they have a right to go on doing it. Consequently, many customs (but not all) tend towards fairness. Our final hypothesis asserts that aligning law with custom in tribal courts promotes efficiency and fairness.

Efficiency and fairness concern the treatment of individuals, whereas culture belongs to a society. Like some other ethnic groups in America, Indian cultures are in peril. Unlike other ethnic groups who emigrated to America, however, Indians have no homeland abroad where their original culture will persist. Consequently, the assimilation of Indians in America extinguishes cultures. Enforcing Indian customs in tribal courts can contribute to the survival of Indian cultures. This reason for promoting Indian common law stands apart from efficiency and fairness.

IV. Procedure in Tribal Law

Now we turn to the results of our field research, beginning with legal procedure and proceeding to substantive law.

A. Independent Versus Amalgamated Judiciary

The American constitution creates separate offices for judges and insulates them from politics. In contrast, aboriginal tribes in America apparently amalgamated judicial activities with other activities. Do modern tribal courts conform to the old principle of amalgamation or the new principle of independence?

The answer is complicated. Formal independence requires separating the judiciary from the legislature, executive, and electorate. At the level of the appeals courts, tribes differ with respect to the separation of judges from politics. The Navajo and Hopi reservations have independent courts of appeal, thus following the principle of separation of powers. In contrast, the tribal council acts as appeals court at Acoma, Taos, and some other reservations, thus following the principle of amalgamation. In Warm Springs, the voters directly elect a large appeals court consisting of people without training in law or experience with courts. Some tribes have joined together to share an appeals court. Other reservations have no appeals court.

Compared to appeals courts, tribal constitutions prescribe relatively uniform organization for trial courts. Except for some of Pueblos, government on each of the reservations that we visited divides power among a court (judiciary), an elected council (legislature), and an elected chairman or governor (executive). On most of the reservations that we visited, "trial judge" is a distinct job performed by someone with no other tribal office. Different reservations use different methods for selecting and replacing judges. To illustrate, the Navajo tribal council, elected by the Navajo people, appoints the seventeen Navajo judges, including the three Navajo Supreme Court judges. After a two year probation period, Navajo judges may be appointed permanently to serve until the age of seventy. This method of selection insulates the Navajo judiciary from politics. Similarly, in many Pueblos, the tribal council elects the judge or judges, who are sometimes hired from outside the tribe.

Separation of powers at the level of the trial court achieves formal independence for judges. In reality, however, the influence of the tribal council and chairman upon judges varies from one tribe to another, and from one historical period to another. Effective independence requires that politicians do not influence the decisions of judges. To achieve effective independence, the income and power of judges must not depend upon the evaluation of their decisions by politicians. Alternatively, the judiciary and politics intertwine when politicians can dismiss or promote judges in response to their decisions in cases. The extent to which officials tribal politicians can influence judges depends in part upon formal laws for removing judges, and in part upon informal traditions and personalities.

To illustrate, the Navajo Supreme Court showed its political independence during a series of recent cases triggered by crimes allegedly committed by the former chairman. In the San Carlos Apache Reservation, any judge can be dismissed for just cause by a two-thirds vote of the council. We were told, however, that judges at San Carlos are not usually dismissed when a new group assumes elected office. Some judges, such as the Chief Judge at Hopi, remain in office for many years as politicians come and go. On most reservations, however, the council can impeach or dismiss judges, and politicians sometimes use this power to force judges to resign. For example, elections in recent years at the White Mountain Apache Reservation have been bitter and many officials, including judges, have been replaced after a new chairman assumed office. Similarly, the chief judge at Warm Springs told us that he brooks no intrusion of the council into the activities of his court, but he was subsequently compelled by the council to resign.

To remain in office, tribal judges on many reservations must balance a diverse set of interests. Judges cannot appear partisan in adjudication, but neither can they appear unresponsive to the electorate or disloyal to the council and chairman. Three US Senate and House bills contemplate creating incentives for tribes to increase the independence of judges. The bills offer more money for tribal courts on reservations whose constitutions separate powers and protect judicial independence much as in the federal constitution. For tribes that follow the traditional practice of amalgamation, such an offer poses a familiar tradeoff between tribal autonomy and federal funding. Tribal politicians want federal money, but they also want to be sovereign. We cannot predict which of these contradictory tendencies will prevail in the future.

Before leaving the topic of judicial independence, we want to say something more about the character of tribal politics. To most Americans, the legitimacy of elections and the right of the majority to govern seem self-evident. In contrast, tribal elections often cause enduring bitterness and rancor. To understand why, one must understand Indian political history. The role of leaders in aboriginal government has been described as assisting people to reach a consensus. A consensus is reached when everyone sufficiently agrees with a proposal so that no one objects in public. If someone persists in public dissent, preserving a consensus requires either abandoning the proposal or having the dissenter withdraw from the group. The abrupt change from consensus methods to majority rule among the tribes in the 1930's caused much of the bitterness in tribal politics.

A critique of majority rule based on modern political theory explains why a small community might prefer government by consensus. Under majority rule, the majority can make decisions without taking into account the minority's strength of feeling. In the jargon of political theory, a majority vote reflects the ordering of preferences by individuals, but not their intensity. In contrast, rule by consensus requires the group to continue its discussions until everyone remaining in it accepts the decision. In the jargon of political theory, rule by consensus has high transaction costs and risks fragmentation or paralysis. A large nation adopts majority rule to reduce transaction costs and avoid political paralysis. A small, intimate community, however, might prefer to retain rule by consensus in order to reflect more fully the intensity of peoples' feelings. However, majority rule avoids paralysis caused by the absence of a consensus in a large, heterogeneous group.

Being accustomed to majority rule, Americans have difficulty appreciating consensus politics. In an aboriginal band where people interacted face-to-face each day, political leadership often depended upon personal prestige more than formal office. ...

. . .

B. Qualifications of Judges

Do tribal judges have the knowledge and inclination to apply tradition to cases? Once again, the situation varies from one reservation to another. Navajo law stipulates that a tribal judge must be fluent in Navajo, knowledgeable in Navajo customs, have at least two years of experience in a law-related area, and be over 30 years of age. In contrast, some reservations have no law stipulating qualifications for judges based upon age, experience, or ability to speak an Indian language. We estimate that at least half of the judges whom we interviewed were not fluent in a native language spoken on the reservation where they preside.

Some tribal judges and almost all jurors have no formal training in law. People without legal education who must make legal decisions inevitably draw upon their own sense of justice, which in turn draws upon custom and tradition. For example, we were told that Navajo jurors in wrongful death cases award damages in light of the specifics of Navajo culture, such as marital practices and family structure. Similarly, we were told that judges on the Blackfeet tribal court take specific cultural considerations into account when awarding damages.

Some of the judges were deeply rooted in the culture of the tribe where they presided in court, whereas others were outsiders. The outsiders might be Indians from other tribes, Indians returning to their own reservation after a long absence, or non-Indians. Outsiders have the advantage of not being implicated in political factions and family feuds that affect reservation politics. For example, one of the three non-Indian judges whom we met said that he was hired to restore integrity and prestige to a court previously compromised by political infighting. He predicted, accurately as it turned out, that he would finish the process and be replaced with a tribal member.

C. Procedural Provisions for Custom in Law

Tribal law everywhere distinguishes between custom as law and custom as fact. Custom as law draws its contents and strength from custom as fact. Tribal law, which cannot be identified with custom, draws much of its authority from custom. Many tribal constitutions or codes, therefore, recognize the authority of custom and some assign an explicit role to it. To illustrate, Art. VIII, Sec. 2 of the Constitution of the Pascua Yaqui Tribe of 1987 says:

> The jurisdiction of the courts shall extend to all cases in law and equity arising under this constitution and the laws, traditions, customs or enactments of the Pascua Yaqui Tribe ...

Thus the Pascua Yaqui constitution recognizes custom as a source of law, without providing any details about when or how to enforce it. Title 7, Article 204 of the Navajo Tribal Code not only recognizes custom as a source of law, but provides the courts with a process for its authoritative determination:

> Law applicable: (a) In all cases the Courts of the Navajo Nation shall apply any laws of the United States that may be applicable and any laws or customs of the Navajo Nation not prohibited by applicable federal laws. (b) Where any doubts arise as to the customs and usages of the Navajo Nation the court may request the advice of counselors familiar with these customs and usages. (c) Any matters not covered by the traditional customs and usages or laws or regulations of the Navajo Nation or by applicable federal laws and regulations, may be decided by the Courts of the Navajo Nation according to the laws of the state in which the matter in dispute may lie.

Some judges whom we interviewed, notably Chief Judge Don Costello at Warm Springs, actively seek counsel on custom as authorized in the tribal constitution. Even where explicit constitutional authorization is lacking, assembling elders to discuss custom or tradition is common practice in the Pueblos. Many courts assign cases involving custom to a particularly expert judge. The judicial expert on custom is typically an older person who grew up on the reservation and speaks its language or languages. This was the approach at the Flathead and White Mountain Apache reservations. However, the most traditional members of the tribe, including the elders who are most immersed in the old way of life, often seem to avoid connection with tribal government and do not participate in court deliberations. One person observed wryly that much unwritten law "eludes the organizers of modern tribal life."—ES.

D. Procedure in Trials

As remarked earlier, anthropological studies around the world have found that dispute resolution in tribes aims at repairing relationships. Thus judges at Laguna and Acoma described four steps to resolving a dispute along traditional lines. First, the person who commits the wrong must admit what he has done and promise not to do it again. Second, he must apologize to the victim. Third, he must pay damages to the victim, usually as compensation but sometimes as punishment. If the offender does not have enough money to pay damages, either a symbolic payment will do, or, under a new procedure being tried at Laguna, the offender works for the victim or for wages passed to the victim. Fourth, the injurer must "make it up" to the community by service. One judge illustrated the fourth point by explaining that his courtroom was decorated by somebody "who had to make good to us for what he had done." In Tesuque, a delinquent was ordered to repair a "fence that was down." On a Paiute reservation, "washing windows" was the penalty for a light offense.

Repairing a relationship requires going deeper into the dispute than the immediate cause of the disagreement. Anthropologists have found that tribal people frequently treat everything about the relationship between the parties as relevant to a dispute, including the character and feelings of the parties. In contrast, rules of procedure in federal and state courts narrow the dispute to the specific wrongdoing alleged by the plaintiff. These facts raise the question, "To what extent do tribal courts examine the relationship and character of the parties, rather than the specific act in dispute?"

Within certain limits prescribed by federal law, tribal judges are free in principle, to regulate the conduct of parties, witnesses, and experts in tribal courts. Many tribal judges take the federal rules of procedure as their model, especially in disputes involving large stakes. Given large stakes, the parties usually have counsel provided by lawyers or "legal advocates," who may prefer standard, adversarial procedures. However, we heard many complaints against the claim-isolating procedures of modern courts, which were described as "cultural impositions" that create antagonisms over "non-issues." Some tribal judges whom we surveyed seemed reluctant to follow the federal rules of evidence or Anglo-American common law rules of evidence.

Some judges and some courts explicitly follow alternative procedures in an effort to adapt procedure to local needs. To illustrate, before hearing the case, Judge Frank A. Demolli of Pojoaque Pueblo announces the following rules of Pojoaque Pueblo procedure to the parties:

1. In addition to evidence admitted according to generally accepted rules of evidence, hearsay will be given due consideration.
2. The judge may direct questions to the parties and their witnesses.
3. A party who wants to keep silent may do so. However, there will be no "counsel's privilege."
4. An appeal from the decisions of the Pojoaque Tribal Court goes to the Tribal Council, whose decisions are binding and trigger res judicata.

Judge Demolli announces these rules to the parties. We found that outside legal counsel has no difficulties in submitting to these tribal procedural rules, and welcomes the advance information.

In admitting hearsay, Pojoaque law resembles the "Rule of Free Evaluation of Evidence" found in continental law (France, Italy, Germany, etc.) more closely than the common law rule against hearsay. Other variations exist. Jicarilla Apache law takes a "middle ground" between free evaluation of proofs including hearsay, and the Federal Rules of Civil Procedure. Thus, hearsay there has "minimal weight" because evidence must be "reliable and trustworthy."—CV. By allowing the judge to direct questions to the parties and witnesses, Pojoaque law assigns a more active role to judges resembling the so-called "inquisitorial system" of continental Europe rather than the role of passive umpire assigned to judges in the common law's "adversarial system."

Some tribal judges say that they need freedom from formal procedural rules to make the legal process congenial to Indians. A Hopi legal scholar remarked to us, "We apply law holistically."—ES. Such judges proceed informally in their courts. To illustrate, the court in the Gila River Pima-Maricopa Community handles offenses committed within the family "as informally as possible." In one case, the court required the offender to hug his mother with the entire family present.—RP. An apology to the victim, along with the promise not to repeat the wrong, is commonly required of defendants.—FC.

Tribal judges often try to channel cases outside the courtroom. A Hopi judge told us that a good legal practice is to tell the litigants what his decision may be before the trial ("If you don't find a solution, I will, and it's going to be ..."—RA), and then recommend an out-of-court settlement based on village traditions. A judge in Zuni told us that if the families of the criminal and the victim in a rape case settle their dispute by mutual agreement (for example, by apology and compensation), then the court might accept the settlement rather than prosecuting the offender.—MZ.

An older way of deciding disputes apparently persists in tribal courts, sometimes resulting in formal rules different from the federal rules of procedure, and sometimes resulting in informality. As explained, tribal judges adapt procedures to make courts more congenial to Indians. In addition, outside counsel and non-members of a tribe may prefer a tribal court proceeding, because it is faster and more flexible than state or federal trials. On the other hand, and different from our experience in Pojoaque, outside attorneys sometimes have little trust in the fairness of a trial conducted on a reservation. Unfamiliarity with tribal law and procedures increases mistrust by outsiders.

E. Common Law Process?

A social norm exists in the practices of people. Anthropologists sometimes describe dispute resolution in tribes as the application of inchoate social norms. An inchoate norm is not fully explicit. Flexibility and responsiveness are advantages of inchoate social norms, which especially appeal to small, intimate communities. In contrast to "social law," Anglo-American "common law" stresses the reasoned elaboration of rules by judges. Reasoned elaboration aspires to a fully explicit statement of rules, which exist in the decisions of judges, not just the practices of people. Predictability and boundedness are advantages of common law, which especially appeal to large, diverse societies. To achieve predictability and boundedness, common law rules are promulgated authoritatively. Consequently, changing common law rules requires an official revision. In contrast, social norms are not promulgated, so they can change without an official revision. In deciding how far to formalize law, predictability and boundedness apparently trade-off with flexibility and responsiveness.

Does the development of law in tribal courts correspond more closely to the process of social law or to the process common law? The judges in all the courts that we visited expressed respect for precedent and the desire to follow past practices in current decisions. Lawyers or legal advocates argue the more important cases before the judges. However, the reasoned elaboration of rules requires institutional memory. The tribal courts that we visited sometimes record cases on cassette tapes. The tapes may be poorly organized and difficult to use. Only the most important cases are transcribed. When we asked tribal judges for files from previous cases, many judges did not have any to show us. Most tribal judges cannot consult records of rules and principles articulated in past decisions in their own courts. Some tribal judges apparently read many federal cases and some state cases, but they seldom read cases decided in tribal courts.

Courts without adequate written records must rely upon individual memory about past decisions. Face-to-face conversations and telephone calls substitute for retrieving court records when researching a case. All the judges whom we visited have participated in training programs and conferences, which provide an opportunity to exchange experiences and ideas. Some tribal judges remain in office for years, have a good memory for cases, and discuss them over many years. Through the work of such judges, Indian common law evolves orally and informally. Other tribal judges, who change jobs rapidly or remain intellectually isolated, make single decisions rather than lasting rules of law. (An interesting historical question is whether the courts of the "Five Civilized Tribes" in 19th century Oklahoma, which apparently kept good written records, had a formal common law process.)

There is one notable exception to these generalizations. The Navajos, who have the largest, most populous, and one of the richest reservations in America, also have the best funded tribal court system. The Navajo Supreme Court hears many cases each year argued by lawyers who continually refer back to its past decisions, which are published and stored in an impressive library. The Navajo judges speak about "Navajo common law" and regard themselves as participating in its elaboration and development.

Most tribal courts have some, but not all, of the features necessary for the Anglo-American common law process. Some aspects of the common law processes are at work in all of the tribal courts that we visited, but it seems to us that few—possibly only Navajo—have a formal common law process like those found in state courts. Are these facts to be interpreted as a deficiency in the tribal courts, or as a preference for social law over common law? Most tribal judges would like better funding to improve the quality of legal records. Providing tribal courts with more institutional memory would facilitate the common law processes in the tribes. Many tribal judges, however, might want to stop far short of the Anglo-American common law process. Stopping short represents, according to the preceding analysis, a choice in favor of more flexibility and responsiveness, and less predictability and boundedness.

Thus, in essence, Indian customary law develops into Indian common law, which sometimes resembles the Anglo-American common law process, sometimes not. The latter situations are certainly more frequent. Hence, there is a "folk common law" in most tribes, and it is tribe-specific.

James Zion relates Indian customary law and Indian common law in the following way:

> For the purpose of a rational discussion of Indian customary law, it is best to use the term "Indian Common Law." Indian government, law and daily life are founded upon long-standing and strong customs, and since the stated rationale for the English Common Law is that it is a product of custom, that approach maybe used for Indian law as well.
>
> Indians have every right to assert that their law stands on the same footing as the laws of the United States and Canada. It is unfortunate that the term "custom" implies something that is somehow less or of lower degree than "law."

On the whole we agree with this statement by Zion. However, we would add two remarks: (1) Common law is a process-related term referring to a source of law, while customary law concerns a part of substantive law regardless of process; and (2) the common law of an Indian tribe includes tribal legal developments in which tribal judge-made law refers to customs as being part of the law, or as being of a mere factual, not legal nature; or which is not based on custom at all but represents recent tribal judge-made law, for example in cases of consumer protection in "rent-to-own" contracts. Therefore, we prefer a definition of Indian common law that comprises tribal judge-made law, developed either in a common law process according to the Anglo-American tradition, or in a tribe specific legal process different from the Anglo-American model; but in each case including both customs of legal nature and force, judge-made law using customs as mere facts, and judge-made non-customary "new law" answering to contemporary tribal social needs. ...

...

The existence of customary law is a fact that influences many cases. For example, social norms influence the way people understand contractual obligations, property rights, and fair punishments for crimes. While social norms influence altitudes in most cases, most customs—whether Indian or Anglo-American—are unsuitable for legal enforcement. For example, most customary promises given in daily life should be enforced informally, not legally. Legal enforcement of daily promises would inject a coercive, bureaucratic element into human relationships. Promises are the source of contracts, but most promises are not contracts. In general, the common law process requires judges to enforce custom selectively.

Moreover, the foundation of any common law system is a vibrant intellectual community of legal experts. An intellectual community that emphasizes oral communication needs frequent face-to-face interaction. Tribal judges especially need conferences, seminars, and telephone calls. In contrast, the Anglo-American common law process relies relatively more on the circulation of written documents. As compared to Anglo-American common law, support of Indian common law requires a different emphasis.

Finally, tribal judges often make law by interpreting statutes. As in Anglo-American law, making law by interpreting statutes differs in important ways from making law by enforcing customs. A discussion of Indian common law must recognize that judge-made law encompasses both sources of law.

NOTES AND QUESTIONS

1. Many formal tribal courts in the United States have a long history of recognition and respect by the federal and state legal systems. In Canada, fewer indigenous communities have established similar institutions, and those that have focus mainly on criminal and regulatory matters (see, for example, the Mohawk Court of Kahnawake at http://www.kahnawake.com/org/court). There is extensive debate within aboriginal communities and by aboriginal scholars concerning the role of indigenous law and legal systems in the fraught relationship between aboriginal peoples and the Canadian state. See, for example, Professor Val Napoleon "Thinking About Indigenous Legal Orders" Research Paper for the National Centre for First Nations Governance, June 2007, available at http://www.fngovernance.org/research/val_napoleon.pdf. Professor John Borrows has considered this issue in depth, see: "Indigenous Legal Traditions in Canada" (2005), 19 *Washington Journal of Law and Policy* 167; *Recovering Canada: The Resurgence of Indigenous Law* (Toronto: University of Toronto Press, 2002); *Canada's Indigenous Constitution* (Toronto: University of Toronto Press, 2009); and *Drawing Out Law: A Spirit's Guide* (Toronto: University of Toronto Press, 2009).

2. One controversy that has arisen in the context of US tribal courts is when (if at all) these courts should exercise jurisdiction over matters that involve parties who are not members of the indigenous community in question, particularly where non-members object to being subject to the jurisdiction (see, for example, *Montana v. United States*, 450 US 544

(1981) and *Nevada v. Hicks*, 533 US 353 (2001)). In your view, when would it be appropriate for a tribal court to exercise jurisdiction in the following circumstances:

(a) a contractual dispute between a non-member employee of a business that is owned and operated on the reserve by a member;

(b) a family law dispute between a member and a non member who lived together on the reserve;

(c) a dispute over damage to property caused when a non-member federal police officer searched property on the reserve held by a member; and

(d) a land claims dispute between the indigenous community and the federal government?

3. The first part of this chapter noted that we may need different forms of dispute resolution to resolve various kinds of disputes. We are increasingly recognizing that we may need different procedures to facilitate the various objectives of civil litigation. This is discussed further in the next part of this chapter, which revisits some of the underlying principles of the adversary system in the light of particular objectives of litigation pursued in the interests of the public in contrast to individual claims.

C. The Interests of the Public

Kenneth E. Scott, "Two Models of the Civil Process"
(1975), 27 *Stanford Law Review* 937

[W]hat is the purpose of imposing civil liability on a person, and how should the rules governing civil actions be shaped toward achieving that end?

A. The Conflict Resolution Model

One possible view of the civil process is a Conflict Resolution Model that sees civil process primarily as a method of achieving peaceful settlement of private disputes. If *A* has acted in a way that injures or threatens to injure *B*, *B*'s resort to force in order to forestall the injury or obtain redress is undesirable, if for no other reason, because violence has a tendency to escalate and to injure innocent bystanders in the process. So in the interests of preserving the peace, society offers through the courts a mechanism for the impartial judgment of personal grievances, as an alternative to retaliation or forcible self-help. The services of the court system are furnished free or at nominal cost to the disputants in order to make the alternative of recourse to the courts more attractive.

This model has only weak implications for the precise content of the legal rules whereby judgment is rendered. To facilitate acceptance of the outcome and resort to the process, the rules should be seen as "fair" in terms of prevailing community values, but notions of what is fair may vary a great deal from one era or society to another. Such variations are of only secondary importance; it is more important for society that the dispute be settled peaceably than that it be settled in any particular way ...

The Conflict Resolution Model quite naturally leads to emphasis, first, on the extent to which the plaintiff has been harmed, for that is correlated with the possibility that he may resort to means of redress leading to violence, and second, on compensating him if he is determined to be in the right. Conversely, if his grievance is less intense, concern with giving him a judicial remedy is much less; if he is content to grumble and let it pass, society feels no threat. Hence this model is strongly inclined to let sleeping dogs lie. It does not welcome anyone stirring up trouble or "fomenting litigation," and it takes a dim view of officious intermeddlers. Seeking out persons who are unaware that they have a cause of action or unlikely to litigate a claim or pursue any other remedy, and persuading them to file suit, burdens the courts with matters beyond their proper function and wastes the judicial subsidy on trivia. ...

B.   The Behavior Modification Model

A Behavior Modification Model, on the other hand, sees the courts and civil process as a way of altering behavior by imposing costs on a person. Not the resolution of the immediate dispute but its effect on the future conduct of others is the heart of the matter. Consistency and predictability of outcome, therefore, assume an importance that they do not possess in the Conflict Resolution Model.

The implications of the Behavior Modification Model are at their most powerful if coupled with a view of the substantive rules of civil liability as designed to contribute to economic efficiency. If a person negligently injures another, the law of torts requires him to pay for the damages he has caused; if he breaches his agreement, contract law requires him to make whole the person who has relied on it. As a result he is led to take appropriate precautions to avoid injury and to make appropriate judgments about honoring agreements; and consequently, the social loss from such conduct is minimized. The imposition of legal liability is, in economists' jargon, a way of making a person "internalize" or take into account the costs of his actions, thereby inducing appropriate levels of care and performance toward others. But this Essay is not principally concerned with the correctness or justification of the substantive rules of civil liability. Whatever their actual merits may be, if legal rules are seen as attempts to alter public behavior in ways that have been deemed desirable, the civil sanction contributes toward that end by depriving one who violates them of his gains or by imposing on him the costs occasioned by his violation.

The Behavior Modification Model, then, focuses on the defendant, not on the plaintiff. The fact that the cost imposed on the defendant takes the form of a payment to the plaintiff is significant only in that it affords the needed incentive for the plaintiff to bring the action and activate the machinery. The real concern is to confront the defendant (and the rest of society) with the right set of costs for different behavioral choices rather than to compensate the plaintiff for his harm or effect a wealth redistribution in the name of equity.

Nonetheless, the incentive to the plaintiff is an aspect of the model's operation that may not be ignored. In particular, the plaintiff's incentive causes difficulty in the class of situations where the costs of the defendant's conduct, while large in the aggregate, are not concentrated on a few but are widely shared in amounts that are in general fairly small.

Air pollution provides familiar examples, as does the field of consumer protection. Despite subsidization of the court system (which this model would not generally call for), the private costs of litigation are still substantial. Especially in a system which does not charge the winner's attorneys' fees to the loser, few individuals will sue to recover modest amounts. And even if one person did sue, an award of merely his own damages would not impose the proper total amount of costs on the defendant.

If the Behavior Modification Model is not to prove ineffectual in cases where damages are widely spread, a way to surmount the incentive gap has to be found. The creation of an administrative agency charged with the duty of enforcing the legal rules in these situations is one solution that has been tried. But a statutory instruction is not the same as an incentive for efficient enforcement, as continuing dissatisfaction with the performance of administrative agencies has led a growing number to perceive. Furthermore, agency resources are limited by the political process; in an area in which by definition the stakes for the defendants are large while the theoretical plaintiffs are numerous and only moderately concerned, it is not difficult to predict what will be the balance of pressures exerted on the political process and the agency.

Another device that has evolved to meet this need is the private representative action. In the stockholder's derivative suit or the class action, one plaintiff may sue on behalf of, and seek a judgment in the amount of aggregated damages for, the entire group. This procedure in no way changes the size of the plaintiff's individual recovery, which is still inadequate. If the device is to function effectively, therefore, the incentive must lie elsewhere, and of course in fact it does—in the recovery of sizeable fee awards by plaintiff's counsel if successful.

. . .

These two models, like all models, are abstractions from reality; they bring together and organize certain aspects of the civil process as it exists and of our attitudes toward it. They are not the only models which could be constructed and they do not purport to capture all of a complex world. In practice, judges and decisions may reflect a blend of both models, in varying proportions. ...

Abram Chayes, "The Role of the Judge in Public Law Litigation"
(1976), 89 *Harvard Law Review* 1281 (footnotes omitted)

We are witnessing the emergence of a new model of civil litigation and, I believe, our traditional conception of adjudication and the assumptions upon which it is based provide an increasingly unhelpful, indeed misleading framework for assessing either the workability or the legitimacy of the roles of judge and court within this model.

In our received tradition, the lawsuit is a vehicle for settling disputes between private parties about private rights. The defining features of this conception of civil adjudication are:

    (1) The lawsuit is *bipolar*. Litigation is organized as a contest between two individuals or at least two unitary interests, diametrically opposed, to be decided on a winner-takes-all basis.

(2) Litigation is *retrospective*. The controversy is about an identified set of completed events: whether they occurred, and if so with what consequences for the legal relations to the parties.

(3) *Right and remedy are interdependent*. The scope of the relief is derived more or less logically from the substantive violation under the general theory that the plaintiff will get compensation measured by the harm caused by the defendant's breach of duty—in contract by giving the plaintiff the money he would have had absent the breach; in tort by paying the value of the damage caused.

(4) The lawsuit is a *self-contained* episode. The impact of the judgment is confined to the parties. If plaintiff prevails there is a simple compensatory transfer, usually of money, but occasionally the return of a thing or the performance of a definite act. If defendant prevails, a loss lies where it has fallen. In either case, entry of judgment ends the court's involvement.

(5) The process is *party-initiated* and *party-controlled*. The case is organized and the issues defined by exchanges between the parties. Responsibility for fact development is theirs. The trial judge is a neutral arbiter of their interactions who decides questions of law only if they are put in issue by an appropriate move of a party. ...

Whatever its historical validity, the traditional model is clearly invalid as a description of much current civil litigation in the federal district courts. Perhaps the dominating characteristic of modern federal litigation is that lawsuits do not arise out of disputes between private parties about private rights. Instead, the object of litigation is the vindication of constitutional or statutory policies. The shift in the legal basis of the lawsuit explains many, but not all, facets of what is going on "in fact" in federal trial courts. For this reason, although the label is not wholly satisfactory, I shall call the emerging model "public law litigation."

The characteristic features of the public law model are very different from those of the traditional model. The party structure is sprawling and amorphous, subject to change over the course of the litigation. The traditional adversary relationship is suffused and intermixed with negotiating and mediating processes at every point. The judge is the dominant figure in organizing and guiding the case, and he draws for support not only on the parties and their counsel, but on a wide range of outsiders—masters, experts, and oversight personnel. Most important, the trial judge has increasingly become the creator and manager of complex forms of ongoing relief, which have widespread effects on persons not before the court and require the judge's continuing involvement in administration and implementation. School desegregation, employment discrimination, and prisoners' or inmates' rights cases come readily to mind as avatars of this new form of litigation. But it would be mistaken to suppose that it is confined to these areas. Antitrust, securities fraud and other aspects of the conduct of corporate business, bankruptcy and reorganizations, union governance, consumer fraud, housing discrimination, electoral reapportionment, environmental management—cases in all these fields display in varying degrees the features of public law litigation.

The object of this article is first to describe somewhat more fully the public law model and its departures from the traditional conception, and second, to suggest some of its consequences for the place of law and courts in the American political and legal system.

I. The Received Tradition

The traditional conception of adjudication reflected the late nineteenth century vision of society, which assumed that the major social and economic arrangements would result from the activities of autonomous individuals. In such a setting, the courts could be seen as an adjunct to private ordering, whose primary function was the resolution of disputes about the fair implications of individual interactions. The basic conceptions governing legal liability were "intention" and "fault." Intentional arrangements, not in conflict with more or less universal attitudes like opposition to force or fraud, were entitled to be respected, and other private activities to be protected unless culpable. Government regulatory action was presumptively suspect, and was tested by what was in form a common law action against the offending official in his private person. The predominating influence of the private law model can be seen even in constitutional litigation, which, from its first appearance in *Marbury v. Madison*, was understood as an outgrowth of the judicial duty to decide otherwise-existing private disputes.

Litigation also performed another important function—clarification of the law to guide future private actions. This understanding of the legal system, together with the common law doctrine of stare decisis, focused professional and scholarly concern on adjudication at the appellate level, for only there did the process reach beyond the immediate parties to achieve a wider import through the elaboration of generally applicable legal rules. So, in the academic debate about the judicial function, the protagonist was the appellate judge (not, interestingly enough, the appellate court), and the spotlight of teaching, writing, and analysis was almost exclusively on appellate decisions. …

In contrast to the appellate court, to which the motive power in the system was allocated, the functions of the trial judge were curiously neglected in the traditional model. Presumably, the trial judge, like the multitude of private persons who were supposed to order their affairs with reference to appellate pronouncements, would be governed by those decisions in disposing smoothly and expeditiously of the mine-run of cases. …

• • •

Because the immediate impact of the judgment was confined to the parties, the traditional model was relatively relaxed about the accuracy of its factfinding. If the facts were not assumed as stated in the pleadings or on the view most favorable to one of the parties or determined on the basis of burdens or presumptions, they were remitted to a kind of black box, the jury. …

• • •

II. The Public Law Litigation Model

Sometime after 1875, the private law theory of civil adjudication became increasingly precarious in the face of a growing body of legislation designed explicitly to modify and regulate basic social and economic arrangements. At the same time, the scientific and deductive character of judicial lawmaking came under attack, as the political consequences of judicial review of that legislation became urgent.

These developments are well known and have become an accepted part of our political and intellectual history. I want to address in somewhat greater detail the correlative changes that have occurred in the procedural structure of the lawsuit. Most discussion of these procedural developments, while recognizing that change has been far-reaching, proceeds on the assumption that the new devices are no more than piecemeal "reforms" aimed at improving the functional characteristics or the efficiency of litigation conducted essentially in the traditional mode. I suggest, however, that these developments are inter-related as members of a recognizable, if changing, system and that taken together they display a new model of judicial action and the judicial role, both of which depart sharply from received conceptions.

A. The Demise of the Bipolar Structure

Joinder of parties, which was strictly limited at common law, was verbally liberalized under the codes to conform with the approach of equity calling for joinder of all parties having an "interest" in the controversy. The codes, however, did not at first produce much freedom of joinder. Instead, the courts defined the concept of "interest" narrowly to exclude those without an independent legal right to the remedy to be given in the main dispute. The definition itself illustrates the continuing power of the traditional model. The limited interpretation of the joinder provisions ultimately fell before the banners of "rationality" and "efficiency." But the important point is that the narrow joinder rule could be perceived as irrational or inefficient only because of a growing sense that the effects of the litigation were not really confined to the persons at either end of the right-remedy axis.

The familiar story of the attempted liberalization of pleadings under the codes is not dissimilar. Sweeping away the convolutions of the forms of action did not lead to the hoped-for elimination of technicality and formality in pleading. The immediate response was the construction of cause-of-action rules that turned out to be almost as intricate as the forms themselves. The power of the right-remedy connection was at work here too, but so also was the late nineteenth century impulse toward systemization, which tended to focus attention on accurate statement of legal theory. The proponents of "efficiency" argued for a more informal and flexible approach, to the end that the courts should not have to rehear the same complex of events. This argument ultimately shifted the focus of the lawsuit from legal theory to factual context—the "transaction or occurrence" from which the action arose. This in turn made it easier to view the set of events in dispute as giving rise to a range of legal consequences all of which ought to be considered together.

This more open-ended view of the subject matter of the litigation fed back upon party questions and especially intervention. Here, too, the sharp constraints dictated by the right-remedy nexus give way. And if the right to participate in litigation is no longer determined by one's claim to relief at the hands of another party or one's potential liability to satisfy the claim; it becomes hard to draw the line determining those who may participate so as to eliminate anyone who is or might be significantly (a weasel word) affected by the outcome—and the latest revision of the Federal Rules of Civil Procedure has more or less abandoned the attempt.

The question of the right to intervene is inevitably linked to the question of standing to initiate litigation in the first place. The standing issue could hardly arise at common law or under early code pleading rules, that is, under the traditional model. There the question of plaintiff's standing merged with the legal merits: On the facts pleaded, does this particular plaintiff have a right to the particular relief sought from the particular defendant from whom he is seeking it? With the erosion of the tight structural integration of the lawsuit, the pressure to expand the circle of potential plaintiffs has been inexorable. Today, the Supreme Court is struggling manfully, but with questionable success, to establish a formula for delimiting who may sue that stops short of "anybody who might be significantly affected by the situation he seeks to litigate."

"Anybody"—even "almost anybody"—can be a lot of people, particularly where the matters in issue are not relatively individualized private transactions or encounters. Thus, the stage is set for the class action. … Whatever the resolution of the current controversies surrounding class actions, I think it unlikely that the class action will ever be taught to behave in accordance with the precepts of the traditional model of adjudication. The class suit is a reflection of our growing awareness that a host of important public and private interactions—perhaps the most important in defining the conditions and opportunities of life for most people—are conducted on a routine or bureaucratized basis and can no longer be visualized as bilateral transactions between private individuals. From another angle, the class action responds to the proliferation of more or less well-organized groups in our society and the tendency to perceive interests as group interests, at least in very important aspects.

The emergence of the group as the real subject or object of the litigation not only transforms the party problem, but raises far-reaching new questions. How far can the group be extended and homogenized? To what extent and by what methods will we permit the presentation of views diverging from that of the group representative? When the judgment treads on numerous—perhaps innumerable—absentees, can the traditional doctrines of finality and preclusion hold? And in the absence of a particular client, capable of concretely defining his own interest, can we rely on the assumptions of the adversary system as a guide to the conduct and duty of the lawyer?

These questions are brought into sharp focus by the class action device. But it would be a mistake to think that they are confined to that procedural setting. The class action is only one mechanism for presenting group interests for adjudication, and the same basic questions will arise in a number of more familiar litigating contexts. Indeed, it may not be too much to say that they are pervasive in the new model.

B. The Triumph of Equity

One of the most striking procedural developments of this century is the increasing importance of equitable relief. It is perhaps too soon to reverse the traditional maxim to read that money damages will be awarded only when no suitable form of specific relief can be devised. But surely, the old sense of equitable remedies as "extraordinary" has faded.

I am not concerned here with specific performance—the compelled transfer of a piece of land or a unique thing. This remedy is structurally little different from traditional money-damages. It is a one-time, one-way transfer requiring for its enforcement no continuing involvement of the court. Injunctive relief, however, is different in kind, even when it takes the form of a simple negative order. Such an order is a presently operative prohibition, enforceable by contempt, and it is a much greater constraint on activity than the risk of future liability implicit in the damage remedy. Moreover, the injunction is continuing. Over time, the parties may resort to the court for enforcement or modification of the original order in light of changing circumstances. Finally, by issuing the injunction, the court takes public responsibility for any consequences of its decree that may adversely affect strangers to the action.

Beyond these differences, the prospective character of the relief introduces large elements of contingency and prediction into the proceedings. Instead of a dispute retrospectively oriented toward the consequences of a closed set of events, the court has a controversy about future probabilities. Equitable doctrine, naturally enough, given the intrusiveness of the injunction and the contingent nature of the harm, calls for a balancing of the interests of the parties. And if the immediate parties' interests were to be weighed and evaluated, it was not too difficult to proceed to a consideration of other interests that might be affected by the order. ...

C. The Changing Character of Factfinding

The traditional model of adjudication was primarily concerned with assessing the consequences for parties of specific past instances of conduct. This retrospective orientation is often inapposite in public law litigation, where the lawsuit generally seeks to enjoin future or threatened action, or to modify a course of conduct presently in train or a condition presently existing. In the former situation, the question whether threatened action will materialize, in what circumstances, and with what consequences can, in the nature of things, be answered only by an educated guess. In the latter case, the inquiry is only secondarily concerned with how the condition came about, and even less with the subjective attitudes of the actors, since positive regulatory goals are ordinarily defined without reference to such matters. Indeed, in dealing with the actions of large political or corporate aggregates, notions of will, intention, or fault increasingly become only metaphors.

In the remedial phases of public law litigation, factfinding is even more clearly prospective. ... [T]he contours of relief are not derived logically from the substantive wrong adjudged, as in the traditional model. The elaboration of a decree is largely a discretionary process within which the trial judge is called upon to assess and appraise the consequences of alternative programs that might correct the substantive fault. In both the liability and remedial phases, the relevant inquiry is largely the same: How can the policies of a public law best be served in a concrete case?

In public law litigation, then, factfinding is principally concerned with "legislative" rather than "adjudicative" fact. And "fact evaluation" is perhaps a more accurate term than "factfinding." The whole process begins to look like the traditional description of legislation: Attention is drawn to a "mischief," existing or threatened, and the activity of the parties and court is directed to the development of on-going measures designed to cure that mischief. Indeed, if, as is often the case, the decree sets up an affirmative regime governing the activities in controversy for the indefinite future and having binding force for persons within its ambit, then it is not very much of a stretch to see it as, pro tanto, a legislative act. ...

D. The Decree

The centerpiece of the emerging public law model is the decree. It differs in almost every relevant characteristic from relief in the traditional model of adjudication, not the least in that it is the centerpiece. The decree seeks to adjust future behavior, not to compensate for past wrong. It is deliberately fashioned rather than logically deduced from the nature of the legal harm suffered. It provides for a complex, on-going regime of performance rather than a simple, one-shot, one-way transfer. Finally, it prolongs and deepens, rather than terminates, the court's involvement with the dispute.

The decree is also an order of the court, signed by the judge and issued under his responsibility (itself a shift from the classical money judgment). But it cannot be supposed that the judge, at least in a case of any complexity, composes it out of his own head. How then is the relief formulated?

The reports provide little guidance on this question. Let me nonetheless suggest a prototype that I think finds some support in the available materials. The court will ask the parties to agree on an order or it will ask one party to prepare a draft. In the first case, a negotiation is stipulated. In the second, the dynamic leads almost inevitably in that direction. The draftsman understands that his proposed decree will be subject to comment and objection by the other side and that it must be approved by the court. He is therefore likely to submit it to his opponents in advance to see whether differences cannot be resolved. Even if the court itself should prepare the initial draft of the order, some form of negotiation will almost inevitably ensue upon submission of the draft to the parties for comment.

The negotiating process ought to minimize the need for judicial resolution of remedial issues. Each party recognizes that it must make some response to the demands of the other party, for issues left unresolved will be submitted to the court, a recourse that is always chancy and may result in a solution less acceptable than might be reached by horse-trading. Moreover, it will generally be advantageous to the demanding party to reach a solution through accommodation rather than through a judicial fiat that may be performed "in a literally compliant but substantively grudging and unsatisfactory way." Thus, the formulation of the decree in public law litigation introduces a good deal of party control over the practical outcome. Indeed, relief by way of order after a determination on the merits tends to converge with relief through a consent decree or voluntary settlement. And this in turn mitigates a major theoretical objection to affirmative relief—the danger of intruding on an elaborate and organic network of interparty relationships.

Nevertheless it cannot be supposed that this process will relieve the court entirely of responsibility for fashioning the remedy. The parties may fail to agree. Or the agreement reached may fail to comport with the requirements of substantive law as the judge sees them. Or the interests of absentees may be inadequately accommodated. In these situations, the judge will not, as in the traditional model, be able to derive his responses directly from the liability determination, since, as we have seen, the substantive law will point out only the general direction to be pursued and a few salient landmarks to be sought out or avoided. How then is the judge to prescribe an appropriate remedy?

If the parties are simply in disagreement, it seems plausible to suppose that the judge's choice among proposals advanced by the quondam negotiators will be governed by his appraisal of their good faith in seeking a way to implement the constitutional or statutory command as he has construed it. The interest in a decree that will be voluntarily obeyed can be promoted by enforcing a regime of good faith bargaining among the parties. Without detailed knowledge of the negotiations, however, any attempt to enforce such a regime can rest on little more than an uneasy base of intuition and impression. Where a proposed decree is agreed upon among the parties, but is inadequate because the interests shared by the litigants do not span the range that the court thinks must be taken into account, resubmission for further negotiation may not cure this fundamental defect. Here too, the judge will be unable to fill the gap without a detailed understanding of the issues at stake in the bargaining among the parties. ...

E. A Morphology of Public Law Litigation

The public law litigation model portrayed in this paper reverses many of the crucial characteristics and assumptions of the traditional concept of adjudication:

(1) The scope of the lawsuit is not exogenously given but is shaped primarily by the court and parties.

(2) The party structure is not rigidly bilateral but sprawling and amorphous.

(3) The fact inquiry is not historical and adjudicative but predictive and legislative.

(4) Relief is not conceived as compensation for past wrong in a form logically derived from the substantive liability and confined in its impact to the immediate parties; instead, it is forward looking, fashioned ad hoc on flexible and broadly remedial lines, often having important consequences for many persons including absentees.

(5) The remedy is not imposed but negotiated.

(6) The decree does not terminate judicial involvement in the affair: its administration requires the continuing participation of the court.

(7) The judge is not passive, his function limited to analysis and statement of governing legal rules; he is active, with responsibility not only for credible fact evaluation but for organizing and shaping the litigation to ensure a just and viable outcome.

(8) The subject matter of the lawsuit is not a dispute between private individuals about private rights, but a grievance about the operation of public policy.

In fact, one might say that, from the perspective of the traditional model, the proceeding is recognizable as a lawsuit only because it takes place in a courtroom before an official called a judge. But that is surely too sensational in tone. All of the procedural mechanisms outlined above were historically familiar in equity practice. It is not surprising that they should be adopted and strengthened as the importance of equity has grown in modern times. ...

III. A First Appraisal

* * *

In practice, all government officials, including judges, have exercised a large and messy admixture of powers, and that is as it must be. That is not to say that institutional characteristics are irrelevant in assigning governmental tasks or that judges should unreservedly be thrust directly into political battles. But such considerations should be taken as cautionary, not decisive; for despite its well rehearsed inadequacies, the judiciary may have some important institutional advantages for the tasks it is assuming:

First, and perhaps most important, is that the process is presided over by a judge. His professional tradition insulates him from narrow political pressures, but, given the operation of the federal appointive power and the demands of contemporary law practice, he is likely to have some experience of the political process and acquaintance with a fairly broad range of public policy problems. Moreover, he is governed by a professional ideal of reflective and dispassionate analysis of the problem before him and is likely to have had some experience in putting this ideal into practice.

Second, the public law model permits ad hoc applications of broad national policy in situations of limited scope. The solution can be tailored to the needs of the particular situation and flexibly administered or modified as experience develops with the regime established in the particular case.

Third, the procedure permits a relatively high degree of participation by representatives of those who will be directly affected by the decision, without establishing a liberum veto.

Fourth, the court, although traditionally thought less competent than legislatures or administrative agencies in gathering and assessing information, may have unsuspected advantages in this regard. Even the diffused adversarial structure of public law litigation furnishes strong incentives for the parties to produce information. If the party structure is sufficiently representative of the interests at stake, a considerable range of relevant information will be forthcoming. And, because of the limited scope of the proceeding, the information required can be effectively focused and specified. Information produced will not only be subject to adversary review, but as we have seen, the judge can engage his own experts to assist in evaluating the evidence. Moreover, the information that is produced will not be filtered through the rigid structures and preconceptions of bureaucracies.

Fifth, the judicial process is an effective mechanism for registering and responding to grievances generated by the operation of public programs in a regulatory state. Unlike an administrative bureaucracy or a legislature, the judiciary must respond to the complaints of the aggrieved. It is also rather well situated to perform the task of balancing the importance of competing policy interests in a specific situation. The legislature, perhaps, could balance, but it cannot address specific situations. The bureaucracy deals with specific situations, but only from a position of commitment to particular policy interests.

Sixth, the judiciary has the advantage of being non-bureaucratic. It is effective in tapping energies and resources outside itself and outside the government in the exploration of the situation and the assessment of remedies. It does not work through a rigid, multilayered hierarchy of numerous officials, but through a smallish, representative task force, assembled ad hoc, and easily dismantled when the problem is finally resolved. ...

There are also counter-instances and counter-arguments for each of the advantages of the public law model suggested above. Can the disinterestedness of the judge be sustained, for example, when he is more visibly a part of the political process? Will the consciously negotiated character of the relief ultimately erode the sense that what is being applied is law? Can the relatively unspecialized trial judge, even with the aid of the new authority and techniques being developed in public law litigation, respond adequately to the demands for legislative and predictive factfinding in the new model? Against the asserted "responsiveness" of the courts, it may be argued that the insensitivity of other agencies represents a political judgment that should be left undisturbed. And although the courts may be well situated to balance competing policy interests in the particular case, if as is often true the decree calls for a substantial commitment of resources, the court has little basis for evaluating competing claims on the public purse. Each of these considerations needs exploration in much more detail—although I would hope that the discussion would proceed on the basis of what has been happening in the cases rather than a priori. ...

IV. Some Thoughts on Legitimacy

... As the traditional model has been displaced in recent years, ... questions of judicial legitimacy and accountability have reasserted themselves. ...

For it cannot be denied that public law litigation explicitly rejects many of the constraints of judicial method and procedure in which we have characteristically sought respite from the unease. Now, I do not deny that the law, like other creative and performing arts, encompasses a recognizable (and teachable) technique; and this technique plays an important part in the development of the medium and in the criticism and evaluation of its practitioners. But in the law, as elsewhere, technical virtuosity has never been a guarantee of acceptable performance.

Moreover, an amalgam of less tangible institutional factors will continue to operate to shape judicial performance in the public law system as in the past: general expectations as to the competence and conscientiousness of federal judges; professional traditions of conduct and performance; the accepted, often tacit, canons and leeways of office. These are amorphous. They mark no sharp boundaries. ...

More fundamentally, our transformed appreciation of the whole process of making, implementing, and modifying law in a public law system points to sources other than professional method and role for the legitimacy of the new model lawsuit. As we now begin to see it, that process is plastic and fluid. Popular participation in it is not alone through the vote or by representation in the legislature. And judicial participation is not by way of sweeping and immutable statements of the law, but in the form of a continuous and rather tentative dialogue with other political elements—Congress and the executive, administrative agencies, the profession and the academics, the press and wider publics. Bentham's "judge and company" has become a conglomerate. In such a setting, the ability of a judicial pronouncement to sustain itself in the dialogue and the power of judicial action to generate assent over the long haul become the ultimate touchstones of legitimacy.

In my view, judicial action only achieves such legitimacy by responding to, indeed by stirring, the deep and durable demand for justice in our society. I confess some difficulty in seeing how this is to be accomplished by erecting the barriers of the traditional conception to turn aside, for example, attacks on exclusionary zoning and police violence, two of the ugliest remaining manifestations of official racism in American life. In practice, if not in words, the American legal tradition has always acknowledged the importance of substantive results for the legitimacy and accountability of judicial action.

NOTES AND QUESTIONS

1. While Chayes is writing in the context of procedural developments in the United States, many of the same procedural developments have occurred in various Canadian jurisdictions. In later chapters we take up several of these specific changes—for example, those related to the scope of discovery, party structure, standing, intervention, and class actions. At the same time, not all of what Chayes describes accurately reflects the Canadian context. What differences can you identify?

2. To what extent is the public law model favoured by Chayes premised on judges' receptivity to the substantive issues argued in such cases, including questions dealing with the environment, prisoners' rights, and civil rights. Given that the political complexion of the US judiciary, and in particular the Supreme Court, has been reshaped by conservative presidential appointments in recent decades, would Chayes be as optimistic concerning the public model today? What does Chayes mean, at the end of the excerpt, when he says, "In practice, if not in words, the American legal tradition has always acknowledged the importance of substantive results for the legitimacy and accountability of judicial action"?

3. Others have also written on models of civil procedure, contrasting a "behaviour modification" model (emphasizing prevention and deterrence) and a "conflict resolution" model (emphasizing retrospective compensation and dispute settlement): see, for example, Bryant Garth, "Conflicts and Dissent in Class Actions: A Suggested Perspective" (1982), 77 *Northwestern University Law Review* 492; Bruce Wildsmith, "An American Model of Civil Process in a Canadian Landscape" (1980), 6 *Dalhousie Law Journal* 71; and Per Henrik Lindblom, "Group Actions in Civil Procedure in Sweden" (published in the Swedish National Reports to the XIIIth International Congress of Comparative Law in Montreal 1990 (Uppsala, 1990)). Lindblom refers to the Swedish proceduralist Professor Ekelöf who, 50 years ago, conceived of civil procedure as having long-term effects on the morality and sense of duty of the citizens and thereby on their behaviour. By contrast, the US commentators (above) see behaviour modification as coming principally through deterrence resulting from "cost internalization"; the effects of the litigation on the defendant will or should lead others in the same position to find it economically rational to abstain from actions of a kind that might give rise to future legal actions. The goal of the competing model—the conflict-resolution model—is different, and much more modest: "It is more important for society that the dispute be settled peacefully than it be settled in any particular way" (Scott, "Two Models of the Civil Process," above). It can be argued that the conflict-resolution and behaviour-modification models are not contradictory and competing (in the same way as the "crime control model" and the "due process model" are in criminal proceedings): effective conflict resolution at the individual level leads to behaviour modification at the general

level, and vice versa. Consequently, it is argued, both models contribute to the overall function of civil procedure: the maximum realization of the values underlying the substantive law. But, in fact, the conflict resolution and behaviour modification models in civil procedure do not always walk hand-in-hand. For example, various issues (such as standing, and the role of class actions in civil procedure) may be resolved in quite different ways according to which of the two models is emphasized.

Lindblom and Watson, "Courts and Lawyers Facing Complex Litigation Problems," in the *General Report to the Meeting of the International Association of Procedural Law* (Lisbon, August 1991), make the following observations:

> Conflict resolution resulting in retrospective compensation, with an emphasis on increased access to justice for the individual acting as plaintiff, is considered all over the world as a relevant (and by some the only relevant) function of civil procedure. Behaviour modification with its emphasis on deterrence is a more controversial perspective and model. Some proceduralists, such as Professor Ekelöf, define behaviour modification as the principal function and individual conflict resolution as a by-product. But some are unwilling to accept behaviour modification as a task for civil proceedings and private law at all. The development towards "public law litigation" in the [United States] during the 60s and 70s was well tuned to the efforts to use civil litigation as a tool for behaviour modification, but "the spirit of the 80s" gives expression to the opposite view. Discussions about the function of civil procedure in general, and group actions in particular, seem to have a parallel in the political arena.

D. The Structure of a Civil Proceeding

Much of this casebook deals with the interpretation and application of the rules of civil procedure. It is helpful at this early stage to get a sense of the nature and function of such rules. As we have seen, each civil jurisdiction in Canada (provincial, territorial, and federal) has legislation that established the court system, defines its substantive jurisdiction, provides for certain basic procedural and substantive rules respecting civil actions, and, perhaps most important, provides for a procedure by which rules of civil procedure may be enacted from time to time by regulation. In Ontario, these tasks are accomplished in the *Courts of Justice Act*. For example and contrast, the same topics are dealt with in British Columbia in the *Supreme Court Act*, RSBC 1996, c. 443, the *Court of Appeal Act*, RSBC 1996, c. 77, the *Court Order Enforcement Act*, RSBC 1996, c. 78, and the *Law and Equity Act*, RSBC 1996, c. 253. In Nova Scotia, see the *Judicature Act* (1989), RSNS 240, s. 1.

Read ss. 65 and 66 of the Ontario *Courts of Justice Act*, which are typical of the statutory provisions that authorize the making of rules of civil procedure, and consider the following:

1. Why should the rules of civil procedure be enacted as regulations rather than statutes? Is it merely administrative convenience due to the fact that they are amended with great frequency?

2. In the overall legislative process, the rules of civil procedure are relatively invisible, and changes to the rules rarely attract public notice or debate. Is this an appropriate result of nature and composition of the Civil Rules Committee? Are all potentially relevant interests represented on the committee?

The rules of civil procedure are intended to be a complete code of procedure for civil proceedings. They provide a general framework for the litigation of disputes. Justice John Morden of the Ontario Court of Appeal commented as follows about the rules in "An Overview of the Rules of Civil Procedure in Ontario" (1984), 5 *Advocates Quarterly* 257:

> If I may indulge in a generality, it seems to me that there is a fairly widespread attitude among those involved in the legal process that relegates procedure to a position vastly inferior to that of substantive law and regards procedural rules somewhat as a nuisance. This is unfortunate for two reasons.
>
> First, without fair and effective procedural law there cannot be substantive justice. Professor Harold Potter did not put the matter too highly when he said: "The fight for human justice must be on a procedural plane, since procedure may determine how far the truth can come out." (*The Quest of Justice* (1951), p. 28.)
>
> Secondly, in the field of civil litigation there is no other law which will receive as much daily interpretation and application as the rules. The facts in any dispute in the litigation process are bound to differ from those in all other cases. The applicable substantive law from case to case will vary accordingly. However, there can be no variation in the basic procedural law which is applicable to every civil case. All civil cases must pass through the same procedural mould, after giving effect, of course, to the kind of proceeding in question and to the differences between cases which will make certain parts of the rules relevant to some cases and not to others. Generally, all actions are treated the same and all applications are treated the same.

Recall Professor Main's suggestion earlier that substantive legal rules are not trans-procedural. Does this mean that procedural rules cannot be, as Morden J suggests, trans-substantive? Consider this on reading the following discussion.

E. Procedural Pathways

Modern rules of civil procedure can be distinguished from the common law writs and forms of action that they displaced by the fact that they are intended for application to adjudication arising out of all forms of disputes between private parties. In contrast, common law writs were fashioned for particular kinds of disputes such as, for example, the eviction of a tenant or the tort of deceit.

Does the fact that "all civil cases must pass through the same procedural mould" have an effect on substantive law? Is it correct to assume that all litigation must be treated the same? Although the rules of civil procedure apply generally to all civil disputes, there has been an increasing tendency for procedures to be moulded to fit particular types of action. They may have their source in specific provisions of the rules or more informal practices of the court.

The rules of civil proceedings contain a significant number of supplements to or variations to the generally applicable rules for use in specific types of litigation, such as mortgage actions, proceedings for judicial review of administrative action, divorce actions, family law proceedings, and estate matters.

Procedural approaches can also be varied on the basis of the perceived complexity of litigation, which is usually roughly measured by the value of the matters in dispute, as is the case for matters to be brought in the Small Claims Court. An effort to provide a procedural pathway that is intermediate between the simple procedures of that court and the full-fledged procedures of the Superior Court of Justice may be seen in Ontario rule 76, which provides for a simplified procedure for actions where the matters in dispute are below a certain value.

In addition, the courts have used practice directions and other administrative means to create procedures for special categories of litigation. The most far-reaching example of this is the creation of the Commercial List in the Ontario Court of Justice. The *Commercial List Practice Direction* (1995), 24 OR (3d) 455 not only creates a distinct administrative structure for the handling of specified categories of commercial disputes, but also provides a number of specific procedural innovations in the handling of those disputes.

More specialized pathways for litigation raise a number of specific issues. What is the rationale for the establishment of such alternative pathways? Some are the result of historical accident, whereas others reflect a more recent decision to allocate additional resources to specific disputes (that is, the *Commercial List*). Some of these pathways are discussed in chapter 3, which deals with choices in the commencement of proceedings.

Garry D. Watson, "The Structure and Purpose of Civil Procedure"
(1996)

The term "civil procedure" is typically used to refer to the rules that have to be followed in the conduct of a particular type of dispute resolution—that is, adjudication in the courts. (Obviously there are other methods of dispute resolution—for example, negotiation and mediation—and there are also other forms of adjudication—for example, arbitration that takes place outside of court and before somebody who is usually not a judge.)

Described generally, adjudication by a judge normally involves (1) the judge hearing the evidence put forward by the parties; (2) the making of findings of fact by the judge; and (3) the judge applying the law to those facts to reach a decision. (Where the trial is by a judge and jury, the jury will make the factual findings and will apply the law, as announced by the judge, to arrive at its verdict.)

Most of the cases that you read in law school courses are appellate cases that are concerned with resolving competing arguments about what law is applicable in a particular case. However, at the trial court level, generally the fact-finding process dominates—whether it be a three-hour or three-week trial, most of the time will be taken up by the parties adducing their evidence. Typically a small percentage of the time is spent arguing about the law. Indeed, there may be little dispute between the parties about what law is applicable. Often, what divides parties is the differing view of the facts. At the trial court level, the majority of decisions turn on the facts, not on the law.

I would like to consider two different ways of viewing or explaining civil procedure. Both approaches are essentially functional—that is, designed to explore the function or purpose of civil procedure. The first is a quasi-historical perspective that argues that by adopting a particular form of adjudication—a fact-finding trial that comes at the end of the process—we have more or less conditioned what had to come earlier in the process. The second approach, a due process perspective, is more abstract and poses the question what characteristics the civil procedure process should possess in order to be "fair."

1. Historical Perspective

I suggest that to understand the structure of our civil procedure one has to understand its historical genesis, because one particular characteristic of the civil procedure process conditioned its overall basic structure. If one goes back into the 19th century, at common law all civil actions were tried by a jury, and trials had a particular character—they were "oral, continuous trials" (and this is still largely true today). They were "oral" in the sense that witnesses attended in person, were sworn, and gave their evidence orally, although documents might be proven by oral evidence and thus received into evidence. By contrast, in equity (the judicial system that competed with the common law) the fact-finder was confronted not with live, oral evidence, but with evidence that had been reduced into writing in the form of affidavits or written transcripts of examinations. This orality ("oralness") has both a purpose and a consequence. The purpose is to better enable the fact-finder to evaluate the evidence—to make a determination about the credibility of the witnesses—by being able to observe the manner in which the evidence is presented and in particular the demeanour of the witness. But an important consequence of this process (from the lawyer's perspective) is its *immediacy*. The production of the evidence and its receipt by the trier of fact takes place simultaneously, unlike the situation where, for example, evidence is being adduced by affidavit. If I am adducing a witness's evidence by affidavit, I will know what the witness's evidence is when the affidavit is sworn, which will usually be well in advance of when it is presented to the judge. More important, you (as opposing counsel) will typically see that affidavit before the hearing and before the judge hears (or sees) the evidence. Hence you know in advance of the hearing what my evidence will be (indeed, exactly what my evidence will be, assuming that I have to serve you with my affidavits before the hearing). By contrast, at an oral trial, you (as my adversary) hear my witness's actual evidence at the very same time as it is heard and received by the judge.

This brings us to the second aspect of the oral, continuous trial. At common law, trial by jury was always continuous. If you, as my adversary, were taken by surprise by the evidence you heard for the first time when my witnesses testified orally, there was no question of relieving against this surprise by granting you an adjournment—that is, stopping the trial for some days or weeks while you developed a response to the unanticipated evidence that you had just heard for the first time. The jury, a group of strangers brought together for the purpose of trying the case, could not be sent away (it was felt) and told to come back on another day to hear further evidence. So as not to inconvenience the jury, there could be no adjournments.

Although today trial by jury in civil cases is the exception rather than the rule and it is much easier for a judge sitting alone to grant an adjournment, our modern-day civil procedure continues to be shaped by the notion of the oral, continuous trial. We want the process to be fair (more of this later under due process); if there is to be an oral, continuous trial, in order for the process to be fair, the parties need to know in advance what evidence is going to be adduced at trial. Otherwise, parties can be faced with what is often referred to as "genuine surprise." By this term we usually mean that parties are confronted at trial with evidence that, had they known in advance that such evidence was going to be adduced, they would have been able to contradict by marshalling and producing evidence. We thus have developed pre-trial procedures that are designed, *inter alia*, to avoid surprise at trial by (in a sense) "scripting in advance" what will happen at the trial. We do this principally through various forms of notice giving. The issues to be litigated are defined in advance through the exchange of written allegations and responses referred to as *pleadings*—the plaintiff sets forth what he or she alleges the defendant did, and the defendant responds in writing stating whether he or she agrees with this statement or how he or she otherwise responds to these allegations. However, in developing our pre-trial procedure (at least in North America), we have gone beyond merely requiring the parties to articulate their allegations and responses well in advance of the trial. We also require parties to go a long way in terms of disclosing, before the trial, the facts and evidence they will adduce at the hearing. This process of fact disclosure is generically referred to as discovery and encompasses both the disclosure of documents and the disclosure of facts and evidence through the process of pre-trial examination for discovery (and to a lesser extent through such other discovery devices as medical examinations and orders for the inspection of property). It is now well recognized that the major objective of "discovery" is to avoid surprise at trial—that is, situations where a party is confronted with evidence for the first time at the oral hearing, which does not give the party a fair opportunity to respond to the evidence.

If you think about it, there are other ways to deal with this problem of surprise, at least if you are not wedded to the concept of an oral, continuous trial. One obvious way to deal with it would be to abandon the concept of a continuous hearing and simply adopt a rule that if a party is genuinely surprised by evidence that is adduced at trial then we will grant an adjournment—that is, sufficient time for the surprised party to marshall evidence in response to the surprising evidence. Indeed, today in cases of genuine surprise this is how the court will often react (at least if it is a trial by judge alone; in jury trials, a court is still loath to grant adjournments). However, such an approach can be inefficient and lead to increased costs that will have to be borne by somebody. Continental procedure never found itself in this "bind" of how to deal with surprise, because it never adopted the idea of an oral, continuous trial. Typically, in continental procedure, the hearing wasn't continuous but rather a series of partitive hearings with the court, for example, sitting for a day or two to take evidence and then reconvening, perhaps a month later, to hear some more evidence. This vehicle of partitive hearings allowed the parties to deal with any problem of surprise by turning up at the next hearing date prepared to counteract evidence that may have been heard at an earlier hearing date. But this was not the style of the common law. At least in conception, the trial is viewed much like a theatrical play, oral and continuous, which starts and continues until it is finished. And just like a play, the common law concluded that the trial must be scripted in advance through the devices of pleading and discovery.

So, I have argued, the oral, continuous trial necessitates the procedural notice-giving devices of pleadings and discovery. But the analysis does not stop there. Other characteristics of the trial have also conditioned or structured our civil procedure.

Provisional remedies. The common law assigns fact finding to the trial—a culminating event that comes at the end of the process and that nearly always takes a considerable time to reach (at least, in part, because the pleading and discovery phases take time). Because of this, the common law has had to allow for *provisional remedies* (for example, for interim injunctions to restrain allegedly injurious activity) before trial and before the court has an opportunity to finally rule on whether the alleged injurious activities are in fact illegal. (Such remedies, and indeed any relief that a party wishes to seek before the trial, are obtained by making a *motion* to a non-trial court. This is typically done by a document called a *notice of motion*, if necessary supported by affidavit evidence.)

If there are no facts in dispute, we do not need a trial. The trial is a forum for resolving disputed issues of fact. As explained earlier, that is why the hearing is oral—so that the fact-finder (judge or jury) can hear and see the witnesses and make findings as to their credibility. It follows logically from this proposition that if there are no genuine issues of fact to be resolved, we do not need a trial. This is the role of a *motion for summary judgment*. If one party can show early in the litigation and long before trial (despite what is said by the parties in their paper allegations—that is, the pleadings) that there is no genuine issue or dispute with regard to the facts, the court will rule that a trial is unnecessary. If the dispute between the parties is simply about applicable law, a trial is unnecessary, because the purpose of the trial is to hear oral evidence and resolve disputes about the facts. If no facts are in dispute, a non-trial court (for example, the court hearing the motion for summary judgment) is in as good a position to enunciate and apply the law as any trial court would be, and it will do so and grant a final judgment.

If a claim or defence is legally invalid, we do not need a trial. Similarly, a trial is unnecessary if a party's claim or defence is untenable or *invalid in law*. In such cases we do not need a trial (or any of the procedures that are designed to aid *factual* development—that is, discovery). Typically, in the pleading, the plaintiff will frame his or her case as broadly as possible (alleging multiple grounds of liability or multiple causes of action). If the defendant can convince the court that if the plaintiff proves everything that is set out in his or her statement of claim, he or she will lose at trial because of the applicable law, a non-trial court can dismiss the action as "failing to state a reasonable cause of action" without allowing the case to proceed to trial. Similarly, if the defence pleaded by the defendant is not a valid defence in law, it can be struck out in advance of the trial by a non-trial court.

2. Due Process Perspective

Let us now view civil procedure from a different, but still functional, perspective—that is, due process. What do we mean by this term? In certain contexts, this term has developed a technical meaning, but here it simply embodies the idea that the process of adjudication (that is, the rules for the conduct of the adjudicative process) should be "fair" to both parties. In this context, due process or fairness is simply a basic element of what we understand to be justice. If the process of adjudication is to determine the rights of the parties, we hope that the final decision will be accurate (that is, correct), but in any event the losing party should not be able to complain that the process by which the decision was arrived at was unfair.

What characteristics must the court's procedure have to satisfy this notion of fairness? Here we run into what may be considered an enigma. There is no body of *case law* that tells us what are the criteria or indicia of fairness in court proceedings. This is because we have typically addressed the issues of fairness *legislatively*, embodying our notions of fairness in the rules that have been enacted for the conduct of litigation (the rules of civil procedure). This matter rarely falls to be determined by the court in case-by-case decisions, because fairness of the procedure has been earlier addressed by the bodies that draft and enact the rules of civil procedure. Moreover, there is no constitutional or common law doctrine that *says* the procedure in court proceedings must be fair. (This is true in the Canadian context, but it is not the case in the United States. The 14th amendment to the US constitution forbids governments to deprive individuals of "life, liberty or *property*" without due process of law. Since rules of civil procedure are clearly governmental or state action, and since civil proceedings are usually about "property," in the United States ultimately all rules of civil procedure are subject to scrutiny as to whether or not they afforded the parties "due process." In Canada, as a consequence of the deliberate decision to exclude "property" from the Charter's s. 7 guarantee of fundamental justice, civil procedure is not subject to the same constitutional scrutiny as in the United States.) Of course, courts are called upon all the time to interpret these written procedural rules and what is "fair" will play an important part in that process.

In Canada, the context in which we find the courts articulating notions of fundamental justice, due process, or natural justice is in the context of administrative law. One of the basic tenets of administrative law is that the procedure followed by the governmental decision makers must be "fair." It falls to the courts (through the process known as "judicial review of administrative action") to review administrative procedures for fairness and to articulate—for administrative tribunals and decision makers—what types of procedures are fair. If the procedures followed were not fair, the proceedings under review may be invalidated or set aside. (In fact, in recent years in some jurisdictions, the minimum standards of fairness to be followed by administrative tribunals have been spelled out legislatively.)

However, as already mentioned, the procedures to be followed by courts in their adjudicative process are spelled out by subordinate legislation (that is, the Rules of Civil Procedure) that typically goes beyond the minimal levels of due process or natural justice that the courts require administrative tribunals or decision makers to follow.

What, then, are the ingredients of fairness within the court-based adjudicative process? What do you think they should be? Are the following what most people would consider to be the basic elements of procedural due process?

- *notice*—that there is a proceeding and the nature of the allegations made by the adversary;
- the concept of notice incorporates the further concept that the notice must be in writing and brought to the attention of the opposing party—that is, that the opposing party was *served* with the documents setting out the adversary's contentions;
- *the right to be heard*—the right to participate in the adjudicative process by adducing evidence as to the relevant facts and by making submissions as to what is the relevant law;
- the decision maker (the judge) will be *impartial* and not biased;
- a party will receive not only notice of the institution of the proceedings against him or her but also timely notice of any relevant step in the proceeding;

- the right not to be bound by any decision except one in which a party has an opportunity to participate through the adducing of evidence and the making of argument (third-party proceedings and issue estoppel);
- the right to a reasoned decision and to reasons for the decision;
- the right to appeal an initial adverse decision (to keep the initial decision maker "honest"); and
- the right not to be dragged through discovery and trial where there is no genuine issue for trial (summary judgment) or where the adversary's pleadings fail to start a reasonable cause of action or defence.

We can see that these "statements of rights" are becoming more tenuous or less compelling as *basic* rights than the rights initially articulated. However, one of the characteristics of civil procedure, certainly in higher courts, is that (unlike administrative law) it provides not minimal fairness, but "maximal" fairness.

NOTES AND QUESTIONS

1. The term "due process" embodies the idea that the process of adjudication (that is, the rules for the conduct of the adjudicative process) should be "fair" to both parties. Due process or fairness is simply a basic element of what we understand to be justice. If the process of adjudication is to determine the rights of the parties, we hope that the final decision will be accurate (that is, correct), but in any event the losing party should not be able to complain that the process by which the decision was arrived at was unfair.

Assume that you have been sued—that is, you are a defendant in an action commenced in court. What characteristics should the court process (that is, its civil procedure) include to satisfy your notion of fairness?

2. The following is an overview of the main stages of a civil proceeding. Many important details and issues will be covered in subsequent chapters. The goal here is to provide an overall account of a civil action in order to orient you to the more detailed and specific treatment of issues that follow in other sections of the casebook.

The overview is provided in two ways: first, by means of a concise description, and, second, by setting out the main stages in a chart. However, before contemplating litigation there are important preliminary considerations.

1. Considerations Before Commencing Litigation

When a client comes to a lawyer with a potentially litigious problem, the prudent lawyer will not immediately and automatically commence an action. Litigation is expensive, time-consuming, and, when contested, its outcome is often uncertain. Before resorting to litigation, the responsible lawyer will explore alternatives and give close consideration to a number of matters.

A lawyer will usually advise his or her client to explore the possibility of settlement before bringing an action. Often a client will have attempted to reach a private settlement before consulting a lawyer. No doubt, he or she appreciates and wants to avoid the expenses and risks of litigation. Indeed, many disputes of the kind that courts entertain never reach a lawyer's office—they are disposed of by agreement between the parties themselves. Many complaints are legitimate, and many prospective defendants, realizing that they will probably not defeat an action brought against them, capitulate or offer terms that the prospective plaintiff finds acceptable. Whether or not the client has attempted a compromise for the claim, a lawyer who is asked to act in the dispute will normally canvass the possibility of settlement before bringing an action. At the very least, the lawyer will take the step of sending a letter of demand on behalf of the client. Commencing an action is usually a measure of final resort, taken after other efforts to persuade the defendant to remedy the plaintiff's grievance have failed.

The decision to sue is influenced by a variety of factors and a lawyer should give these careful consideration before advising the client to institute proceedings. The lawyer will first need to be satisfied that the client has a reasonable prospect of winning the action. This involves two factors: first, that based on the facts as the client has stated them, there is a complaint for which the law gives a remedy. This is a question for the substantive law.

In determining whether plaintiffs have a valid cause of action, their lawyers will assume for the moment that they will be able to prove, through evidence that is admissible under the laws of evidence, the facts on which their complaints are based. They will then determine, given these facts, whether the law will recognize that a legal wrong has been done and afford their clients some form of relief, often, but not always, by way of damages. If so, they have a good cause of action. In cases raising innovative legal claims, lawyers cannot be certain that they have a good cause of action. When a client pursues an innovative claim, we will see that the defendant has an option at a preliminary stage of the litigation to ask the court to strike out the claim as disclosing "no reasonable cause of action"—that is, no cause of action known in law.

Next, if the defendant will dispute the facts at trial, the lawyer will have to conclude that the probabilities favour the court accepting the client's version of the facts. (Of course, it should be kept in mind that there is always the possibility that the defendant will not defend the action, which means that the plaintiff can obtain judgment without a trial. Also, often the mere commencement of proceedings will suffice to persuade a recalcitrant defendant to settle the claim.)

Second, the client should understand the financial consequences not only of losing but also of winning the action; there still may be considerable expenses to pay. The lawyer has a responsibility to explain these consequences (which will be examined in chapter 2, "The Economic and Professional Context") to the client before embarking on litigation.

Finally, it must be remembered that success in an action is one thing, recovering on a favourable judgment another. Success will be illusory if the defendants cannot satisfy the judgment and there is no prospect of them ever doing so. Consequently, before commencing an action and incurring the expenses involved in litigation, it will be prudent to make some inquiry as to the ability of the defendant or defendants to satisfy a judgment. There will usually be no problem if the plaintiff seeks an order from the court directing the defendant to perform some act or to refrain from committing some act. The failure or refusal of a party to obey such an order amounts to a contempt of the court's process and the court has ample power to compel compliance by fine or imprisonment. However, it is not a contempt of court to fail to satisfy a judgment for a sum of money. The defendant can be compelled to obey such a judgment only if he or she has sufficient assets within the jurisdiction.

The law provides a party who has a money judgment in his or her favour with a variety of methods of execution for reaching the assets of the other party within the jurisdiction.

The ability of the defendant to satisfy a judgment is therefore an essential matter to be considered by a plaintiff in deciding whether to commence or continue an action. However, in many tort situations, typically the automobile accident case, the prospective defendant will be insured against liability. In such circumstances the extent of the personal assets of the defendant will not be material as the insurer will satisfy the amount of any judgment against its insured to the extent of the policy limits. Finally, the client has to remember that he or she will be liable for his or her own lawyers' fees in any event; failure to recover from the defendant does not excuse payment of these costs.

Once a litigant and his or her legal advisor arrive at the decision to sue, steps must be taken to commence the legal proceedings.

2. Selecting the Appropriate Court

All plaintiffs must decide in which court they will commence their lawsuit. The choice is relatively simple in Canada, where there are courts of general civil jurisdiction, such as the Superior Court of Justice (Ontario). This court has a branch known as the Small Claims Court. Its monetary jurisdiction is prescribed by regulation, but presently its limits are $25,000.

Two basic factors will determine in which court the action is brought. The first is that the court has jurisdiction over the subject matter of the case. The Superior Court of Ontario has all the power and authority exercised historically by courts of common law and equity in Ontario and England. The plaintiffs would only be concerned with subject matter jurisdiction in limited circumstances. They might have to bring certain claims involving federal subject matter in the Federal Court of Canada and some family law disputes in a specialized family law court. Second, the plaintiffs would be concerned with any limits on the jurisdiction of the courts to award remedies such as damages.

3. Commencing the Proceeding: Actions

Until January 1985, plaintiffs commenced their action by means of a document known as a writ of summons. Using a standard form, they prepared the writ of summons (usually referred to as the "writ"), and then attended at the court office where a clerk issued the writ. To do so, the clerk collected a fee from them, affixed a seal to the original writ, assigned a number to it, dated it, and signed the name of the registrar of the court on the writ. The clerk retained a copy of the writ for the court files and returned the original to them.

An action in British Columbia is still commenced by issuing a writ of summons. The writ of summons names the plaintiffs and defendants in the action, gives the defendants notice that an action has been commenced against them, and provides directions on the steps a defendant must take to enter an appearance and defend the action. There can be advantages to commencing an action by writ of summons. In some cases, the writ of summons may be the only formal court document required because the case gets settled or the defendants default in defending. Drafting an endorsement—a concise statement of the nature of the claim and relief required—on this form document is fairly straightforward and less complicated than drafting a statement of claim. Also, if speed is required, a writ of summons can be prepared and filed quickly.

The writ of summons has been abolished in Ontario, as it has been in many other jurisdictions. Actions are now commenced by statement of claim, issued by the clerk in the same manner as described. In case of urgency, an action may be commenced by notice of action, to be followed shortly by a statement of claim. The statement of claim will contain a description of the parties to the action—the plaintiff and the defendant. This description of the parties to the action is called the "title of proceeding," formerly "style of cause."

Once the statement of claim has been issued, the plaintiff must serve a copy of the claim on the defendant by means of personal service. To do this, somebody will have to locate the defendant and hand him a copy of the claim. Where a defendant is a corporation, it will only be necessary to leave the statement of claim with an officer, director, or agent of the corporation or with a person at the corporation's place of business who appears to be in control or management. If the defendant is a municipality, board, or commission, personal service may involve leaving a copy of the statement of claim with a person in authority.

Usually, the plaintiff will engage the service of the sheriff's office or employ a private process server to carry out service. The rules also provide for certain alternatives to personal service (by mail or by leaving a copy at the defendant's residence). Should the plaintiff be unable to locate the defendant for the purpose of serving him in the manner required, or if it appears that the defendant is purposely evading service, the plaintiff can ask the court to grant permission to allow him to effect substituted service. In this way, the court will permit service in a manner other than by personal service, perhaps by an advertisement in a newspaper.

The statement of claim will contain a formal notice to the defendant explaining that, if no steps are taken to defend, judgment may be given by default.

Issues relating to the commencement of civil proceedings are discussed further in chapter 3.

Some superior courts have rules that attempt to simplify procedures where comparatively small amounts of money are involved—for example, in Ontario, $100,000 or less (see rule 76). Details vary with different courts that use this device. However, generally these procedures attempt to reduce costs and time associated with discovery (see below). The procedures also attempt to eliminate the need for a trial altogether—for example, by encouraging the use of summary judgment (see below). In addition, if a trial is required, the rights of parties may be circumscribed—for example, regarding cross-examination of witnesses in order to save time and minimize costs.

4. Commencing the Proceeding: Applications

The plaintiff may also have the option of starting proceedings by way of an application rather than an action. Applications are generally used with respect to matters where it is unlikely that there will be any material fact in dispute that requires oral evidence for its determination. As will be examined, applications differ from actions by their use of written evidence, known as affidavits. Thus, most stages of an action do not apply to application. For example, there are neither pleadings nor a trial in application.

5. *Asserting Claims and Defences: Pleadings*

How detailed should the statement of claim be? Obviously, the degree of detail could vary from a simple allegation to a detailed and complex narrative of what the plaintiff alleges took place. Thus, a plaintiff could state, "the defendant injured me and owes $50,000." On the other hand, he might give a complete account of the accident itself and elaborate in detail the evidence by which he intends to prove this account. Under our system of civil procedure, he should adopt neither of these alternatives. Rather, his statement of claim must contain only a statement in a summary form of the facts on which he relies in support of his case and a statement of the relief sought. Thus, the statement of claim will contain the plaintiff's allegation of the bare facts constituting the cause of action, but not the evidence by which he expects to be able to prove those facts. Through the vehicle of the statement of claim, the plaintiff will notify the defendant of the basis of his complaint.

Another purpose served by the statement of claim is to permit the court to determine at an early stage whether the plaintiff has a good cause of action. If the facts alleged in the statement of claim do not disclose a cause of action, the defendant is entitled to ask the court to dismiss the action. The rationale for this is that even if the plaintiff is able to prove each and every fact alleged in the statement of claim, if those facts do not constitute a cause of action, the court will not grant relief. Consequently, it would be unreasonable to require the defendant to incur the expense and inconvenience of a trial in which the defendant is bound to succeed.

After the plaintiff has delivered his statement of claim, the defendant must file his own pleading, which is known as a *statement of defence*, to avoid a default judgment. What must it contain? Like the plaintiff, the defendant must allege the facts relied on in support of the defence. In addition, defendants must also indicate which of the allegations in the statement of claim are in dispute.

After receiving the statement of defence, the plaintiff, if he wishes to respond, may deliver a further pleading known as a *reply*.

There are other pleadings that may be available to a defendant in some cases. If a defendant has sustained some damage as a result of a plaintiff's conduct, then he or she may assert a *counterclaim* against the plaintiff. This document, like the statement of claim, will allege the facts relied on, must be served on the plaintiff, and may be subject to a defence by the plaintiff in the main action. If the defendant wishes to make a related claim against a co-defendant or a person not yet party to the proceeding, or wishes to allege that a co-defendant is responsible for the plaintiff's damages, the defendant may bring a *crossclaim* or *third-party claim*.

In addition to their notice-giving function, the pleadings also serve to define the issues in the case. For instance, if the defendant denies a key fact, then that fact becomes an issue at trial that the plaintiff must prove. However, if the defendant admits a fact or facts, then these are no longer issues between them.

There is a further aspect to the issue-defining function of pleadings. When the action reaches trial, the plaintiff and the defendant are permitted to produce evidence only with regard to the allegations set forth in the pleadings. If either seeks to prove a fact that is not alleged in the pleadings, a *variance* is said to occur. The proof offered by a party must conform to the issues raised in the pleadings. At trial, parties may request permission from the judge to *amend* their pleadings to raise matters not already pleaded. Whether such permission will be granted will depend on the circumstances of the cases. Pleadings are discussed further in chapter 6.

6. *Obtaining Information Before Trial: Discovery*

The pleadings are not the only device available to plaintiff and defendant for the development of the issues in their case. Our procedural system is premised on the philosophy that each party is entitled to go to trial knowing the case that must be met. Pleadings go only part way to achieving this goal. Various *discovery* devices provide the means by which a party is able to obtain more information about the opponent's case. These devices also permit parties to gather facts or information to support or prove their own case.

The parties obtain *discovery of documents* from one another by disclosing under oath, by means of an *affidavit* of documents, all documents now, or previously, in their possession pertaining to the action.

They also have the right to conduct an *oral examination for discovery* of a representative of the other party. Our procedural system permits the parties to an action to examine one another under oath, before trial, concerning the issues in the action. On such an examination they may ask the opposing party's representative to disclose the facts on which it relies in support of its case. The questions and answers will be transcribed and made available to the parties for use at trial. If the answers given by the official at trial differ from those given on examination for discovery, the examination may be used for the purposes of impeaching credibility. Also, they may use any admissions made on examination for discovery at trial to prove their case.

Various discovery devices, such as orders to inspect property and orders requiring parties claiming personal injuries to submit to medical examinations to determine the validity and extent of injuries, are available to both plaintiffs and defendants. If parties intend to introduce medical or other expert evidence at trial, they must make a version of such evidence available to their opponent before trial. Discovery is discussed further in chapter 7.

7. *Disposition Without Trial*

Do the parties have any alternative methods of resolving their dispute in order to avoid the time, expense, and delay involved in taking the case all the way through to trial? Our system provides a number of devices that may lead to disposition without trial. There is the possibility of a *settlement* of a dispute before trial. In this regard, the Ontario *Rules of Civil Procedure* create incentives (through potential adverse costs awards) to settle matters. Usually, the prospects of settlement are best after discovery when each party knows the facts on which the opposite party relies. With this information at their disposal, parties are in a good position to negotiate a settlement.

What are the formal devices provided for disposing of a case short of trial? We have already mentioned one of them in the context of the failure of the statement of claim to state a reasonable cause of action. In such a situation, the defendant can ask the court to dismiss the action. Similarly, if the statement of defence fails to raise any matter that could in law amount to a defence, the plaintiff can apply for judgment. In circumstances where the parties agree about the facts and the only issue between them is the applicable law, parties can agree to proceed by placing a question of law before the court. By this procedure, the parties set forth their agreed statement of facts (thereby avoiding the necessity of bringing witnesses before the court), and the court decides which legal principles apply and renders judgment in the action. In other circumstances, if a party has made admissions in pleadings or on discovery that clearly entitle the opposing party to succeed in the action, that party may move for judgment.

While the above devices are infrequently invoked, many actions are disposed of without trial on the ground that there can be no doubt on the facts that one side or the other will prevail in the end. Most of these cases are simple "collection" matters where the plaintiff sues to collect the price of goods sold, services provided, or money lent. The *Rules of Civil Procedure* make provision for *summary judgment* in cases where one party can demonstrate that there is no triable issue in the case.

In British Columbia there are an increasing number of cases disposed of without trial through a process called summary trial under rule 18A. The summary trial process was developed to expedite the early resolution of many cases and overcome the restrictive interpretations placed on other summary judgment mechanisms. Based only on written materials such as affidavits and evidence on an examination for discovery, a judge hearing the application can give judgment if he or she can make the necessary factual findings and it would not be unjust to grant judgment. In *Inspiration Management v. McDermid St. Lawrence Ltd.* (1989), 36 BCLR (2d) 202 (CA), Chief Justice MacEachern said, "[W]hile every effort must be made to ensure a just result, the volumes of litigation presently before our courts, the urgency of some cases, and the cost of litigation do not always permit the luxury of a full trial with all traditional safeguards in every case, particularly if a just result can be achieved by a less expensive and more expeditious procedure. … The procedure prescribed by rule 18A may not furnish perfect justice in every case but that elusive and unattainable goal cannot always be assured even after a conventional trial." Even if judgment is not given, the summary trial process can help speed up the disposition of the case by disposing of some issues or highlighting what is the true conflict between the parties. This procedure is now available in a number of provinces.

Finally, in cases where the defendant fails to deliver a statement of defence, the plaintiff may obtain *default judgment*. Similarly, if the plaintiff fails to proceed with the action, the defendant may have the action dismissed for want of prosecution. Disposition without trial is discussed further in chapter 9.

8. *Case Management and Alternative Forms of Dispute Resolution*

There are two widely used innovations in the resolution of disputes and the conduct of litigation that can alter substantially the way parties dispose of claims—case management and alternative forms of dispute resolution (ADR).

a. Case Management

Canadian courts have moved toward a more activist role in controlling the preliminary stages of litigation. These alterations, particularly in the role played by the judiciary, are said to be motivated by the rising cost of litigation and delays in bringing proceedings to some resolution. Essentially, case management shifts much more responsibility for the pace of litigation to the court. Such supervision depends on establishing reasonable but firm time limits for various procedures and on the court policing these limits to ensure compliance by the parties. This can be effected in a variety of ways. One means, particularly when the litigation is complex, is through the use of case management conferences where, in appropriate circumstances, the court, after receiving representation from the parties, sets a schedule for the various pre-trial stages of the litigation. The court then monitors the proceeding to ensure compliance with the schedule and to achieve other efficiencies regarding the conduct of the litigation.

Finally, some BC Supreme Court justices are incorporating judicial dispute resolution (JDR) into the litigation process. JDR may be viewed as a form of case management or seen as a distinct stage in the litigation process, where judges, in settlement conferences or when requested by the parties, act as facilitators or mediators and appropriately use their considerable problem-solving skills to assist the parties to resolve their disputes without a trial. See chapter 10, Managing the Process, for a full description of JDR.

b. Other Forms of Dispute Resolution

Mediation, arbitration, and conciliation have existed for a long time, but increasing attention is being paid to them as a way of curtailing costs and delay and giving more control to the parties. Moreover, if arbitration as an independent means of resolution is selected, the parties may bypass the courts altogether.

Mediation is also increasingly used in litigation in court—that is, court-annexed mediation. This form of dispute resolution is used to enhance the possibility of resolving litigation without the expense, delay, formality, and limited terms of disposition of trial. In some instances, court-annexed mediation is an option that all parties must agree to try in an attempt to settle their differences. However, many courts are introducing mandatory court-annexed mediation: see Ontario rule 24.1. British Columbia is increasingly integrating mediation into the various stages of litigation rather than leaving it to the parties to choose it. In the Provincial Court, there is a mandatory settlement conference required where the judges are given authority to mediate disputes. In the BC Supreme Court, there is a quasi-mandatory mediation program. In almost all types of cases, if one of the parties wants to engage in mediation, they can serve a notice to mediate on the opposite party that then requires all parties to attempt a mediated settlement. The success of this program is likely to lead to a full mandatory mediation program in the future where the parties cannot proceed past a certain point in the litigation process without attempting settlement by way of mediation. Managing the process is discussed further in chapter 10.

9. *Setting the Case Down for Trial*

After the pleadings are completed and the plaintiff has conducted pre-trial discovery and brought any necessary interlocutory motions—for example, to amend the statement of claim—the plaintiff puts the case on the list for trial; the parties then wait until their case is called by the court. Increasingly, as indicated above, courts are concerned about caseload management, and they may require litigants to explain delays in getting a case to trial.

10. *Mode of Trial*

Our legal system provides for two methods of trial—by a judge alone or by a judge sitting with a jury. In trials before a judge alone, the judge decides all matters, both of law and fact. In jury trials, these functions are divided, with the jury deciding questions of fact and the judge deciding questions of law. In most actions, either party is entitled to have the case tried by a *jury*. However, there are some cases that, for historical reasons, cannot be tried by a jury.

At the commencement of the trial, the parties must select the members of the jury. In Ontario, there are 6 persons in the civil jury. (A jury in a criminal case has 12 members.) A large number of persons, selected in an impartial manner from the municipal assessment rolls, will have been ordered to report to the court house for jury duty. If it is known to the plaintiff's counsel, for example, that one of the persons called is a personal friend of the defendant, there probably will be a successful *challenge for cause* by the plaintiff's counsel. However, suppose that the defendant is a physician. If his counsel learns that one of the panel has recently had an unfortunate experience with a doctor, this will likely be insufficient to result in a successful challenge for cause. However, concerned that the juror may be prejudiced against his client, the defendants' lawyer will probably exercise one of his or her four *peremptory challenges* for which no reason need be given. Ultimately, the panel of six jurors will be chosen. In Canada, most civil actions are tried by a judge alone.

11. *The Trial*

At the trial, the plaintiff's lawyer, after the jury has been selected, makes an *opening statement*. For the benefit of the judge and jury, the nature of the case is outlined, as are the facts intended to be proved through the evidence of witnesses. The lawyer presents evidence by asking questions of each witness for the plaintiff and obtaining their answers under oath. The examination of witnesses by the lawyer for the party calling them is known as *examination-in-chief*. After the plaintiff's lawyer has examined a witness in-chief, the defendant's lawyer has the opportunity to *cross-examine* that witness. The main purposes of cross-examination are to test the veracity of the witness and to obtain answers that assist the case of the cross-examining party. Following the cross-examination, should there be any point that the plaintiff's lawyer wishes to clarify, the witness may be *re-examined*. This procedure continues until the plaintiff has called all of his or her witnesses. The questions put to the parties and other witnesses, and their answers, are recorded.

Rules of evidence apply with regard to the testimony that is permitted at trial. These rules are complex and their study forms the basis of an entire course at law school. However, at the very least, to be admissible, evidence must be relevant to the issues that the parties have raised in their pleadings. It is for the trial judge to make rulings throughout the trial with regard to the admissibility of evidence. If, for example, a lawyer is of the opinion that evidence is inadmissible, he or she must *object* to that evidence and ask the trial judge to make a ruling.

After the plaintiff's lawyer has called all of the witnesses, the case for the plaintiff is closed. At this point in the trial, the defendant's lawyer may wish to contend that the plaintiff has failed to adduce sufficient evidence to establish his or her case. In other words, there may be an application for a *non-suit*, asking the judge to dismiss the action. The trial judge will not rule on this motion unless the defendant's lawyer elects not to call any evidence. If he or she indicates an intention to call witnesses, the trial judge will reserve his or her decision on the motion until all of the evidence in the case has been completed. On the other hand, if the defendant's lawyer elects to call no evidence, the trial judge may rule on the motion for non-suit at once. However, in a jury trial, the judge will only rule on the motion after the jury has had the opportunity to consider the evidence and reach its decision.

Where the defendant's lawyer does not move for a non-suit, or has moved for a non-suit and elects to call evidence, the defendant then presents his or her case. He or she does so in exactly the same manner as the plaintiff, by calling witnesses who are examined-in-chief, cross-examined, and re-examined. After the defendant has concluded its case, the plaintiff is allowed to meet any issues raised by defence evidence by calling evidence in reply. However, the plaintiff cannot use the right to call reply evidence for the purpose of introducing evidence that should have been introduced initially but that, for some reason, was overlooked. The right of reply is restricted to meeting new issues raised by the defendant.

After all the evidence has been concluded, counsel for the parties have the opportunity to *address the jury*. In a jury trial, the jury has the duty of finding the facts; the judge has the duty of making all decisions with regard to the law. At trial, the jury must accept the directions of the judge about the law that they are to apply to the facts as they find them.

In addressing the jury, the plaintiff's lawyer will attempt to convince members that the plaintiff has discharged those *burdens* that rest on him or her. The plaintiff has the *burden of persuading* the members of the jury that they should accept the version of the event given in evidence by the plaintiff's witnesses and the plaintiff and that the conduct of the defendant amounted to negligence or a violation of some other legal standard. Thus, the plaintiff's lawyer will summarize the evidence and base argument on it in urging the jury to find for the plaintiff. In addressing the jury, it is improper for the lawyers to rely on anything other than what the witnesses have said. The defendant's lawyer will have the opportunity to address the jury after the plaintiff's lawyer has done so. He or she, too, will summarize the evidence, but will attempt to convince the members of the jury that the plaintiff has not proved his or her case.

After counsel have addressed the jury, it is the function of the trial judge to deliver his or her *charge*. The judge's major function is to instruct the jury on the law that they must apply to the facts as they find them. After concluding the charge, the jury will retire to consider the case.

After the trial judge has charged the jury, if one or more of the parties disagrees with anything that the judge has said, they may *object* to the charge. If the judge sustains the objection, the jury will be recalled and recharged on the point to which objection was made.

Although other methods of obtaining the decision of the jury are available, the most common method employed is to require the jury to answer a series of questions. The trial judge will usually render judgment in conformity with the jury's answers to the questions. However, the judge is not obliged to do so and may, at the request of one of the parties to the action, give judgment *notwithstanding the verdict of the jury*—that is, judgment not for the party in whose favour the jury found, but for the opposite party. The judge will only do this where he or she is of the opinion that there was no evidence on which the jury, acting reasonably, could have reached its verdict.

Where a judge hears the trial without a jury the procedures are simpler. The judge hears the evidence and submissions of the parties. The judge then renders oral judgment immediately or in writing after further consideration of the evidence and submissions.

12. *The Judgment, Its Enforcement, and Its Effect*

The *judgment* of the court is the final determination of the lawsuit, subject to any appeal. In many cases, the judgment will be in the form of an award of money that the defendant is required to pay. However, a money award represents only one type of judgment that may be given by the court. In an appropriate case, the court may make a declaration of rights between the parties, order the specific recovery of property, or make an order requiring or prohibiting some future activity. For example, a plaintiff or applicant might ask for a declaration that her Charter rights had been violated or even for a mandatory order of the court (an injunction).

The fact that the plaintiff has been awarded damages against a defendant is of little significance unless the plaintiff can collect the amount of the damages. The burden lies on the plaintiff to take the appropriate steps to collect his or her money. *Execution* is the common method of forcing the losing party to satisfy a money judgment in situations where he or she does not voluntarily do so. The plaintiff will obtain a *writ of execution* from the court commanding one of its officers, usually the sheriff, to seize the defendant's property and, if necessary, to sell it at a public sale and use the proceeds to satisfy the plaintiff's judgment. In a case where the plaintiff's recovery takes the form of an order (an *injunction*) requiring the defendant to do something, or to cease or refrain from doing something, the judgment is said to operate against the defendant's person. If the defendant fails to obey, the plaintiff may apply to have the defendant found in *contempt of court*, and, if so found, the defendant may be punished by a fine or imprisonment.

Costs, as provided by the tariffs contained in the rules, are usually awarded to the successful party and are included in the judgment of the court. Usually these costs represent only some of the fees (about 50 to 65 percent) that the successful party is required to pay to the lawyer plus those disbursements contained in the tariff and incurred by the lawyer. The successful party prepares a *bill of costs*. If the unsuccessful party does not agree to the amount of the bill, the other party is required to have the bill assessed before a judicial officer. If the costs are not paid voluntarily after assessment, they can be recovered by execution in the same way as a money judgment.

Subject to the right of appeal, the judgment rendered in an action is final and binding on the parties and may not be challenged in any subsequent proceeding. Their dispute is said to be *res judicata*, a thing decided, and it cannot be relitigated.

13. *The Right of Appeal and Motions*

a. Appeals

In Canada, the judicial system provides a right of appeal in almost every case. In Ontario, this right of appeal is, depending on the amount in issue or whether the decision finally disposes of the rights of the parties in the action, either to the Divisional Court or to the Court of Appeal. (In the following paragraphs, "Court of Appeal" includes Divisional Court.) A party exercises this right by filing a notice of appeal that sets forth the ground of appeal. If the defendant is the unsuccessful party and elects to appeal, he will be known as the appellant. The plaintiff will be known as the respondent. The appellant is required to file with the court a statement of fact and law that sets out the facts of the case and a brief resume of the points of law relied upon. Similarly, the respondent is given the opportunity to file a statement of fact and law in reply to that of the appellant.

The Court of Appeal can affirm the decision appealed from, reverse it, or vary it. In appropriate cases, if the appeal is allowed, the Court of Appeal may substitute for the decision of the trial judge the decision that ought to have been reached. In other cases, however, it may be necessary to direct that there be a new trial. While the powers of the Court of Appeal are broad, there are certain limitations. The major limitation is in relation to the findings of fact made at trial. Even though the Court of Appeal would have come to a different finding of fact if it had been the initial tribunal, it will not substitute its own finding for that reached at trial, if there was evidence on which the trial judge or jury could reasonably have found the facts as it did. Therefore, relatively few cases are successfully appealed on the ground that the findings of fact at trial were in error.

Rather, most appeals are based on errors of law—for example, if the trial judge incorrectly instructed the jury with regard to the applicable law. In such a case, if the trial judge was clearly wrong and thereby occasioned a miscarriage of justice, the case will likely be sent back for a new trial. However, in a non-jury case, if the trial judge misapplied the law to the facts, or applied an incorrect principle of law, the Court of Appeal will be able to apply the law correctly and substitute its own decision for that of the trial judge.

Another ground of appeal relates to the admissibility or inadmissibility of evidence. In such circumstances, where the trial judge's error with regard to the admissibility of evidence has resulted in a miscarriage of justice, the Court of Appeal will order a new trial so that the proper evidence can be considered by a new trial judge or jury.

Appeals are usually argued on the basis of a transcript of the evidence of the witnesses taken at trial. Counsel will present their oral arguments before the Court of Appeal and no witnesses are called. There is a limited right of appeal from a decision of the Divisional Court to the Court of Appeal, and appeal of civil matters to the Supreme Court of Canada is available only with leave of the Supreme Court.

b. Motions

One further area of procedure has been referred to only briefly. These are motions, which are made to the court by a party to an action before the trial itself. (There may also be certain kinds of motions in applications. Applications were described above under section III.E.4, "Commencing the Proceeding: Applications.") Such motions frequently relate to the pleadings or to discovery. They may be made to a judicial officer known as a master or prothonotary, but certain motions must be made to a judge. As mentioned previously, parties may frequently seek to amend their pleadings to include, for example, facts of which they were unaware at the time the pleadings were initially prepared and that may have subsequently been obtained, perhaps as a result of discovery. In such circumstances, the party will apply to the master for leave to amend the pleadings. Another common example of a motion results from the refusal of a party to answer certain questions on examination for discovery. In order to compel an answer, the opposite party must bring a motion before the master for that purpose and the master will decide whether the witness must answer the questions. The right of appeal from such orders is restricted and it varies depending upon whether the order made is final or interlocutory. If it were not, actions could be delayed by an inordinate number of motions followed by a series of appeals.

14. *Flowchart of an Action Under the Ontario Rules of Civil Procedure*

The flowchart in figure 1.1 depicts the steps that may be taken in an action under the Ontario *Rules of Civil Procedure*. The dark line and boxes indicate the steps that will occur in every action (that proceeds that far). The light boxes indicate motions that *may be* made, or steps that *may be* taken, but which will not necessarily occur in every case. (The actual stage at which such motions or steps may be taken can vary and in this regard the chart location merely represents what will happen in most cases.)

An asterisk (*) indicates that an interlocutory appeal under rule 62, Appeals from Interlocutory Orders, may be possible (for an illustration see the arrows leading out of box A).

Of course an action may be settled at any time, discontinued, or the defence withdrawn (rule 23, Discontinuance and Withdrawal), in which case judgment will usually be entered under rule 59, Orders (see box 7). When a motion is decided, this will result in an order that will be entered under rule 59.

IV. LITIGATION AND DISPUTE RESOLUTION

As we become more familiar with the various contexts in which litigation operates, we realize that one of the most significant contexts from a practical perspective is that litigation is just one form of dispute resolution. As we will explore further in chapter 10, Managing the Process, the relationship between these forms of dispute resolution and their capacity to resolve disputes effectively and efficiently is fluid and it is changing. These days, lawyers in private practice regularly advise clients to consider the various alternatives open to them, such as mediation and arbitration, to resolve their disputes. Commencing a civil action is only one option among several that might be pursued; these other "alternative" forms of dispute resolution are routinely employed alone, or in combination with civil litigation, to meet the needs of the parties. Indeed, although very few claims that give rise to litigation are left to be resolved by a trial and the subsequent court order, this is increasingly because members of the legal community and others have taken seriously the opportunity to resolve contentious matters in other ways.

There is an even more fundamental sense, however, in which civil litigation is shaped by the social and institutional context in which it operates. The excerpt below from an article by William Felstiner considers the steps by which a grievance emerges and is transformed into a dispute that may result in civil litigation.

Figure 1.1a

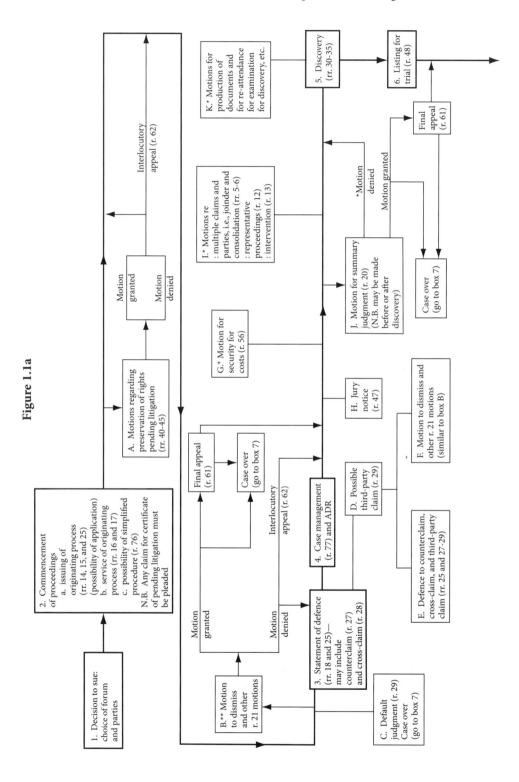

Figure 1.1b

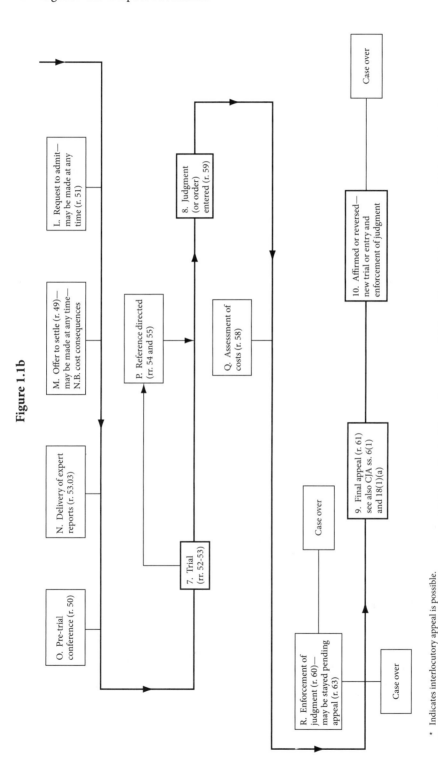

* Indicates interlocutory appeal is possible.
** Depending on its nature, a rule 21 motion may be made before or after the delivery of a statement of defence. If brought before a statement of defence is delivered and the motion is denied (either at first instance or on appeal), the defendant must then deliver a statement of defence.

A. The Formation of Disputes

**William L.F. Felstiner, "The Emergence and Transformation of Disputes:
Naming, Blaming, Claiming ..."**
(1980-81), 15 *Law and Society Review* 631 (footnotes omitted)

The sociology of law has been dominated by studies of officials and formal institutions
and their work products. This agenda has shaped the way disputes are understood and
portrayed. Institutions reify cases by reducing them to records; they embody disputes in
a concrete form that can be studied retrospectively by attending to the words used by lay
persons and officials and by examining the economic and legal context in which cases
occur. But disputes are not things: they are social constructs. Their shapes reflect whatever
definition the observer gives to the concept. Moreover, a significant portion of any
dispute exists only in the minds of the disputants.

These ideas, though certainly not novel, are important because they draw attention to
a neglected topic in the sociology of law—the emergence and transformation of disputes—the
way in which experiences become grievances, grievances become disputes,
and disputes take various shapes, follow particular dispute processing paths, and lead to
new forms of understanding. Studying the emergence and transformation of disputes
means studying a social process as it occurs. It means studying the conditions under
which injuries are perceived or go unnoticed and how people respond to the experience
of injustice and conflict. ...

Assume a population living downwind from a nuclear test site. Some portion of that
population has developed cancer as a result of the exposure and some has not. Some of
those stricken know that they are sick and some do not. In order for disputes to emerge
and remedial action to be taken, an unperceived injurious experience (unPIE, for short)
must be transformed into a perceived injurious experience (PIE). The uninformed cancer
victims must learn that they are sick. The transformation perspective directs our attention
to the differential transformation of unPIEs into PIEs. It urges us to examine, in
this case, differences in class, education, work situation, social networks, etc. between
those who become aware of their cancer and those who do not, as well as attend to the
possible manipulation of information by those responsible for the radiation. ...

The next step is the transformation of a perceived injurious experience into a grievance.
This occurs when a person attributes an injury to the fault of another individual or
social entity. By including fault within the definition of grievance, we limit the concept
to injuries viewed both as violations of norms and as remediable. The definition takes the
grievant's perspective: the injured person must feel wronged and believe that something
might be done in response to the injury, however politically or sociologically improbable
such a response might be. A grievance must be distinguished from a complaint against
no one in particular (about the weather, or perhaps inflation) and from a mere wish unaccompanied
by a sense of injury for which another is held responsible (I might like to
be more attractive). We call the transformation from perceived injurious experience to
grievance *blaming*. ...

The third transformation occurs when someone with a grievance voices it to the person or entity believed to be responsible and asks for some remedy. We call this communication *claiming*. A claim is transformed into a dispute when it is rejected in whole or in part. Rejection need not be expressed by words. Delay that the claimant construes as resistance is just as much a rejection as is a compromise offer (partial rejection) or an outright refusal.

The sociology of law should pay more attention to the early stages of disputes and to the factors that determine whether naming, blaming, and claiming will occur. Learning more about the existence, absence, or reversal of these basic transformations will increase our understanding of the disputing process and our ability to evaluate dispute processing institutions. We know that only a small fraction of injurious experiences ever mature into disputes. Furthermore, we know that most of the attrition occurs at the early stages: experiences are not perceived as injurious; perceptions do not ripen into grievances; grievances are voiced to intimates but not to the person deemed responsible. A theory of disputing that looked only at institutions mobilized by disputants and the strategies pursued within them would be seriously deficient. It would be like constructing a theory of politics entirely on the basis of voting patterns when we know that most people do not vote in most elections.

NOTES AND QUESTIONS

1. As highlighted in the extract from Felstiner, disputes are social constructs, their boundaries flexible, changing over time in response to the social context in which the conduct is situated. Marc Galanter, in an article entitled, "Reading the Landscape of Disputes: What We Know and Don't Know (and Think We Know) About Our Allegedly Contentious Society" (1983), 31 *UCLA Law Review* 4, describes the process of dispute formation as follows:

> Disputes are drawn from a vast sea of events, encounters, collisions, rivalries, disappointments, discomforts and injuries. The span and composition of that sea depend on the broad contours of social life. For example, the introduction of machinery brings increases in non-intentional injuries; higher population densities and cash crops bring raised expectations and rivalry for scarce land; advances in knowledge enlarge possibilities of control and expectations of care.

2. What are the factors that will influence whether one names, blames, and/or claims? In what ways might the organization and distribution of legal services play a role? Consider, for example, that most legal services are provided on a fee-for-service basis, such that, by and large, only persons with considerable economic resources can access legal information and advice. Do we believe that a person with a recognized claim should make the claim? Or do we think it is better not to encourage people to "stir up trouble"? If we think that someone should make a recognized claim, do we think that doing so is a right? Do we think it is a duty? If it is a right, what responsibility do we have to facilitate that right? If it is a duty, what means should we use to encourage them? Finally, do we think that aggrieved persons should promote the recognition of new claims? Should they do so through the civil litigation process? If so, how should the process operate to encourage this?

B. The Forms of Dispute Resolution

In the following excerpt, Marc Galanter explains the key differences between civil litigation and other major forms of dispute resolution.

> **Marc Galanter, "Adjudication, Litigation, and Related Phenomena"**
> in Leon Lipson and Stanton Wheeler, eds., *Law and Social Sciences* (New York: Russell Sage Foundation, 1986) 152, at 152-60 (footnotes omitted)

[The accompanying table] distinguishes several prominent varieties of third-party dispute processing.

... [A]*djudication* [is] a kind of third-party processing of disputes, in which disputants or their representatives present proofs and arguments to an impartial authoritative decision-maker who gives a binding decision, conferring a remedy or award on the basis of a preexisting general rule.

... [A]*rbitration* refers to a family of processes that share such features as an impartial decision-maker, who enters a binding final award on the basis of proofs and arguments presented by the disputants (or their representatives). It commonly departs from adjudication in that the forum is selected by the parties (either ad hoc, by contractual undertaking, or by adhesion to a standing procedure) and that the forum is nongovernmental. There is also variation as to whether the arbitrator is constrained to decide in accordance with a prefixed body of norms and whether the norms applied are public ones or indigenous to a particular setting. Arbitration may be present in an attenuated form of *fact-finding* in which the parties accept the decisional implications of a finding on the facts and delegate the latter to an agreed upon third party—such as the lumber grader or the patent office. (Fact-finding may have important effects on negotiating positions even where parties have *not* agreed to accept its decisional implications.)

Many kinds and styles of arbitration can exist within a single society. Among the common varieties in the United States are labor arbitration, in which the "law of the shop" is applied; commercial arbitration in the standing bodies of self-contained trade associations applying norms of the trade; commercial arbitration by ad hoc arbitrators applying some version of governmental law; and the arbitration of tort cases or small claims under the auspices of a court that urges or requires that such cases be diverted to arbitration.

Mediation refers to a contrasting cluster of dispute processes in which the forum, rather than imposing a binding solution on the parties, arranges a settlement that is agreeable to them. Mediators range from the mere go-between carrying messages, to one who actively devises a solution and persuades the parties to accept it. The mediator may be a specialized standing body or a notable mobilized ad hoc for the purpose. Mediators may be reactive, or they may be proactive like the mediators in pre-Communist China and Communist China. Judges or arbitrators often seek to mediate a dispute, holding in reserve their power of binding decision. Although this mixed form ("med-arb") has been attacked as compromising the integrity of each process, it is strikingly prevalent in American dispute processing in settings as varied as labor arbitration, arrangement of consent orders by administrative agencies, plea bargaining in criminal cases, and judicial arrangement of settlements in civil suits.

Table 1.1   A Taxonomy of Modes of Dispute Processing

Three Parties	Adjudication
	Arbitration
	Fact-Finding
	Mediation
	Therapy
	Administrative Decision-Making
	Political Decision-Making
Immediate Forms	Champion (e.g., ombudsman)
	Parental Dyad (i.e., one party decides)
Two Parties	Bargaining / Negotiation
	Under threat of resort to third party
	In present of group norms
	Under threat of exit, or other unilateral action
One Party	Exit
	Avoidance
	Self-help
	Resignation ("lumping it")
No Parties	Failure to Apprehend Remedy
	Claim
	Violation

NOTE: Arranged by the number of principal persons / roles involved in the process of seeking a remedy or resolution. This classification omits various support roles (informer, adviser, advocate, ally, and surrogate) described by Black and Baumgartner 1983.

Mediation shades off into *therapy*—that is, modes of dispute processing that aim not to secure agreement from parties as they are, but to change the parties by giving them insight into their situation or themselves. Therapy, too, may be mixed with other forms, as in counseling under court auspices.

Like mediation and therapy, *administrative decision-making* is prospective. But the administrator (for example, the school principal or welfare official) exercises control over the subject matter or parties that extends beyond the immediate dispute; he is responsible for fulfilling the goals of his organization; his aims are not confined to the universe of claims posed by the parties. His inquiry is not restricted by limiting rules of relevance and admissibility; his decision need not apply preexisting general standards. Of course, agencies with administrative responsibilities may commit themselves to abide by adjudicatory forms.

With *political decision-making* we move away from the impartial and independent decision-maker to one who can be recruited as an ally. The permissible devices of persuasion are enlarged to include exchanges with the decision-maker (support, fealty) as well as proofs and arguments. We move away from the bi-polar case to the polycentric dispute and away from the obligation to decide by reference to a closed stock of preexisting rules to forthright fashioning of new rules—or away from general rules to individual ad hoc decisions. The same subject matters (divorce, incorporation, franchise, territorial dispute) may be handled by political, administrative, or adjudicative decision. Political decision-makers will often act as if they are subject to the constraints of an adjudicator and will engage in mock-adjudicative forms and justifications.

Although the most prestigious and visible third-party processes are governmental in location, sponsorship, personnel, norms, and sanctions, modern societies are honey-combed with third-party processes that are nongovernmental. These range from forums that are relatively independent in all of these respects (for example, religious courts) to those that are closely appended to governmental processes, dependent on them for norms and sanctions. These appended processes include private forums established to forestall governmental intervention in a trade as well as systems of negotiation or mediation that flourish in the anterooms and hallways of official adjudicatory or administrative decision-makers.

Dispute forums may be separate institutions (a court, the American Arbitration Association, or the like) or embedded within the social setting (workplace, school, church, and so forth) where a dispute occurs. Embedded forums range from those barely distinguishable from the everyday decision-making within the institution to those such as grievance hearings specifically constituted to handle disputes that cannot be resolved by everyday processes.

These three-party processes stand in contrast to *bargaining* or *negotiation* between two disputing parties. Negotiation ranges from that which is indistinguishable from the everyday adjustments that constitute the relationship between the parties to that which is "bracketed" as an emergency or a disruption of that relationship. Negotiations among businessmen, between injury victims and insurers, among parties to an uncontested divorce, or in (some styles of) plea bargaining of criminal charges are alike in that no third party is present; but the course of the negotiations is importantly affected by the kind, feasibility, and cost of potential third-party intervention. The ability to invoke a third party of a particular sort may be a crucial element in the bargaining, but such a threat may be insignificant compared with (usually tacit) threats to withdraw from beneficial relations or to cause reputational damage by circulating information to other interested parties. The bargaining parties may themselves have internalized the normative idiom of the third party.

The contrast between two- and three-party modes is further blurred by the presence of intermediate forms. The *champion*—neither an arbiter with authority to render a binding decision or a mere representative of one party—combines advocacy on behalf of one disputant with an element of investigative judging. The champion is familiar to us in his recent incarnation as the (government) ombudsman; and in the media ombudsman such as "action line" columns, the complaint bureau, the Better Business Bureau, and the elected official who intervenes on behalf of constituents.

The champion is a third party who is something less than a decision-maker. In another intermediate form which I call the *parental dyad* one of the two parties serves as decision-maker as well as disputant. Thus, insurance companies decide the complaints of aggrieved policy holders; automobile manufacturers decide the warranty claims of car buyers; architects serve as both arbitrators and owners' representatives in disputes between owners and building contractors. Such decision-makers may be obligated to observe some or many of the requirements ordinarily incumbent on an adjudicator—such as hearing arguments or deciding according to preexisting rules. When we recall administrators disposing of subordinates' complaints and parents deciding (their) disputes with their children, it is evident that the parental dyad is one of the most frequent dispute configurations.

So far I have been discussing modes of disputing that are discursive. But there are also unilateral—hence, nondiscursive—modes of processing disputes. These include *exit*— that is, withdrawal from a situation or relationship by moving, resigning, or severing relations, as well as various lesser forms that might better be termed *avoidance*.

Exit and avoidance may be the goal, as well as the sanction, in the dispute process. A disputant may threaten resort to a court in order to effectuate a desired exit. On the other hand, the presence of exit as a credible sanction may be important to the working of other remedies; that is, the threat of resort to exit may create a "bargaining endowment" just as does the threat of resort to adjudication. A remedy for one party may be a sanction to the other, and the threat of sanction may induce remedial action. Exit options are not inherently incompatible with the pursuit of other remedies. The rights-assertion dimension may be usefully distinguished from the exit-versus-remain dimension: an aggrieved party can remain and acquiesce (lump it) or remain and assert his claim; similarly, he may simply leave or he may leave and assert his claim as well.

Exit and avoidance do not exhaust the possibilities of unilateral dispute processing. *Self-help* includes various forms of direct action—taking or retaining possession of property as well as physical retaliation, overt or covert. Direct physical violence may be the most prominent element in a system of disputing or it may play an interstitial role.

Disputants may decline to pursue any of these options and may resign themselves to an unfavorable situation: gains of the available dispute options may appear too low or the cost too high (including opportunity costs, the psychic costs, and physical risks of disputing). Such *resignation* ("lumping it") behavior may be a matter of allowing a single incursion to pass without protest or it may involve acquiescence in continuing predation.

Resignation—"lumping it"—shades off into *failure to apprehend* a violation or grievance (or underestimation of its seriousness) or the possibility of remedy. Vast numbers of warranty violations, exposures to dangerous substances and conditions, acts of malpractice, and so forth remain undetected. With these cognitive barriers we eliminate the last of the parties and with it the dispute. ...

· · ·

Adjudication refers to one of the core phenomena of the legal process. Though not one of the most frequent, it is important not only when it does occur, but also

1. as a potential recourse—a threat or escape;
2. hence, as a source of counters that can be used for bargaining or regulation in other settings;
3. as a model for other processes;
4. as a symbol exemplifying shared or dominant values and hence as a source of legitimacy for norms, offices, acts and so forth. (This aspect is compounded in common-law systems, where adjudication is the primary focus of legal scholarship and holds sway over legal thought vastly disproportionate to its prominence as a source of rules.)

Much of the meaning of other activities in the legal process is expressed in terms of this adjudication core. The making of claims, the arrangement of settlements, the assessment of official action—all these frequently involve reference to adjudication—to actual adjudication or to some imaginary adjudication that could take place.

. . .

Forum Governance

Once initiated, the case proceeds under the control of the forum, according to procedures prescribed by the forum. The forum cannot be dismissed by the parties—as can an arbitrator—nor can they amend its procedures. ...

Narrow Scope of Relevance

The case is defined by claims that specific events, transactions, or relations should be measured by application of some delimited conceptual categories. The forum will hear only matters that are relevant to application of those categories. Frequently its willingness to admit proof and arguments is limited further by other policies—such as those crystallized in rules of evidence, and *res judicata*. Here the forum contrasts with other remedy agents like mediators and counselors who are open to a wide range of matters underlying and connected to the immediate dispute. ...

Formal Rationality

The discourse that goes on in connection with adjudication is not open and unbounded. There is a repertoire of legal concepts that is less inclusive than the whole universe of moral discourse or the whole array of sanctioned social norms. The claims of parties are assessed in the light of some bounded body of preexisting authoritative normative learning, to which the forum is committed in advance. Typically, the forum renders a decision by judging the conformance of the parties' claims to established general categories or classificatory concepts. Application of these general standards precludes response to the unique particularity of the situation or to the external consequences of the decision and proceeds without a fresh assessment of the wider consequences of the general norm that is being applied. Thus, adjudication approximates to "logically formal rationality" as postulated by Weber.

[In fact, courts depart from this model of austere formalism in various ways. Appellate judges frame general rules in the hope of producing optimum results. Judges at all levels are imbued with a sense that it is their mission to facilitate governmental policies of minimizing drunk driving, prostitution, or pollution. Or—in the style that Weber called "khadi justice"—judges feel impelled to respond to the particular circumstances rather than subsuming cases under general rules.

The inherent ambivalence of general standards requires that judges choose among alternative specifications of norms. In complex legal systems, choice is amplified by the inevitable conflicts and overlaps within a body of norms and among competing bodies—as, for example, in situations of "legal pluralism," where more than one system of legal concepts may be present and available to the disputants and the forum.]

At least some adjudication involves parts of the law that are "open-textured," and judges have to choose among variant readings of the existing body of normative learning. Such open-ended rule-making authority may be acknowledged and cultivated or covert and confined. There may be more or less emphasis on the obligation to apply concepts consistently with earlier applications. One dramatic sort of unacknowledged change is the presence of legal fictions, in which fictitious recitals are employed to trigger a desired result without departing from the constraints of authoritative conceptual categories.]

Decision and Remedy

Rendering of some authoritative disposition is mandatory: the adjudicator, with her agenda assembled by the parties, is obliged to hear all those cases properly before her. She cannot (as can, for example, the legislature or executive) decline to render a decision. The judge renders her decision on the merits (ascertained in terms of the authoritative learning) rather than arranging an agreement acceptable to the parties. The forum renders an award or remedy to one party rather than engaging in therapeutic reintegration of the parties. The decision is all or none: the forum grants or denies the claim of one party. Indeed, there may be norms against compromise. The decision is binding rather than advisory. The decision is final. Although there are procedures for trying to reopen it, there are also norms that render readjudication difficult. Typically, the forum cuts its links with the dispute and closes the case rather than undertaking a course of continuing supervision or readjustment of its decree. ...

Differentiation

Adjudication is differentiated from other activities. Typically, adjudication involves special locations, persons, roles, language, postures, costumes, and furniture. Often it involves moving to unfamiliar places and settings, movement that may represent substantial cost or an insurmountable barrier. Many reform schemes aim to dispel this remoteness and lower this cost.

Adjudication is, typically, conducted by professional specialists who have recourse to special forms of knowledge, discontinuous with everyday understandings, and not expressed in everyday language. This specialized learning may be generated in the adjudicative institutions themselves—as in common-law systems where the higher strata of judges produce the doctrinal literature—or there may be, as in contemporary Europe (continuing the Roman tradition), a division between the judge who decides the cases and the legal expert who cultivates and transmits doctrine.

Participation is, typically, indirect and through specialist intermediaries who are attached to the forum or have a monopoly on such intermediation. Enforcement, too, is entrusted to specialized functionaries (bailiffs, jailers) rather than carried out by the parties, their allies, or the community through ostracism or direct physical imposition.

The whole process is insulated from general knowledge about persons and their histories and statutes. Justice is blind; the decision-maker excludes the perceptions and

commitments of everyday life to render a decision based solely on those aspects identified as salient by applicable legal categories. ...

Impartiality and Independence

The forum is impartial. It is not predisposed toward any party. The decision-maker is not
an ally of either (set of) disputant(s), but is poised evenly between (or above) them. Unlike the manager or administrator, the adjudicator has nothing of her own at stake in the
controversy. Nor is the judge an agent of any entity outside the forum, with responsibility
to forward policies other than those crystallized in the applicable legal learning. Impartiality and independence are institutionalized in restrictions on contact with disputants
and such devices as tenure and fixed pay to protect the judges against "command influence" and retaliation. ...

[Eagerness to preserve a visibly independent judiciary may induce regimes to remove
from regular courts classes of cases thought to require politically responsive judging.]

Connection to Organized Power

The prototypical adjudicative institution is an organ of government: it is located in a
public building, it is staffed by state officers who apply public norms, and its sanctions
are imposed by the compulsory powers of the state.

[Historically, the notion that adjudication is a state monopoly is a relatively recent one.
In practice, there is an immense amount of adjudication in the private sector—in tribunals embedded in various institutions (churches, universities, labour unions, exchanges,
trade associations, and so forth) as well as specialized institutions for arbitration. The
line between public and private is not a sharp one. Public norms may be applied in private tribunals and enforced by private sanctions; conversely, public tribunals, officials,
and sanctions may be used to enforce private norms.]

Courts are coercive rather than voluntary. They impose outcomes regardless of the
assent of the parties. But, in fact, their decrees are often unenforced. The coercive powers
of courts are important even when they are not utilized, for the threat of their use in-
duces settlements between the parties—often, capitulation by one party. The degree of
compliance with settlements is higher than with verdicts.

NOTES AND QUESTIONS

1. Could the prototypical model described by Galanter accommodate a "collective"
complaint brought by all of the individuals affected? In general, what would the procedures
look like? How would issues particular to individuals be addressed?

2. The prototypical model of adjudication presented by Galanter suggests that our courts
are primarily designed to resolve disputes concerning the private grievances of individual
citizens. Are the courts able to respond to the "public interest" nature of some claims?

CHAPTER TWO

The Economic and Professional Context

I. ACCESS TO JUSTICE

A. Introduction

No matter how well-organized or progressive, societies cannot avoid generating a large number of disputes. While efforts must be made to ensure that the extent and character of such disputes are kept within reasonable limits, every society must ensure that there are readily available forums and devices through which disputes can be effectively and fairly resolved. Traditionally, the legal system has been at the heart of this dispute resolution process. In societies devoted to the virtues of the rule of law, judges and lawyers have been entrusted with the task of fulfilling this responsibility in a manner that works for the general benefit at large. However, in recent years, widespread dissatisfaction with the performance of the legal process has developed. In blunt terms, it is contended that existing arrangements are too expensive (the costs of obtaining justice too often outweigh the benefits of the justice obtained), too delayed (the inordinate time it takes to obtain justice amounts to a denial of any justice), too distant (people are not actively involved in the pursuit of justice, but function only as the statistical objects of a bureaucratic processing), and too individualistic (the legal system is oriented around the resolution of individual disputes and is unable to deal with or comprehend disputes of a more collective or structural nature).

In addition to these concerns, we need to consider whether access to the legal system necessarily means access to justice—that is, the existence of barriers that impede access to the legal system may constitute an injustice, but it does not necessarily follow that the removal of these barriers will result in access to justice.

As you read the following extract ask yourself whether denying access to the legal system or failing to render truly just access is destructive of the whole basis of the legal system. Should access be available on an equal basis? After all, there are many goods and services that are not equally available in our society and we tolerate (perhaps even approve of) such disparities. What exactly is wrong with allowing people to have as much or as little law as they are willing to pay for and can afford? If access to the legal system is not synonymous with access to justice then should it be a matter of concern that access to legal services is not equally available to all?

Rod Macdonald, "Access to Justice and Law Reform"
(1990), 10 *Windsor Yearbook of Access to Justice* 287 (footnotes omitted)

In order to work oneself back to an integrated, social construction of complex justice which is both more encompassing than, and prior to, our current conception of justice according to law, it is helpful to examine the premises of the access debate, at least as it now stands. As I read it, mainstream access to justice literature is largely instrumental; it is a literature about access to law, rather than access to justice. In this perspective, whatever else justice might be for philosophers, it is, for access to justice proselytizers, fundamentally a product marketed by the state through its dispute processing agencies to which all citizens should have access. Justice is neither an aspiration, nor an ideal which demands engagement by those who pursue it. Rather, like data-banks stored by computer systems, justice is a commodity which can be made more accessible by removing interface obstacles. Access to justice is, therefore, really about access to the systemic equivalent of hardware—to the processes and institutions of formalized law.

Given this model of justice and its accessibility, it is hardly surprising that the law reform agenda consists of a series of issues relating to operation of various state agencies. The *problematique* is simply: "What measures can be implemented in order to facilitate the recognition and exercise by citizens of those rights and entitlements which existing law puts at their disposal?" It is on this ground, and not on the ground of re-examining the existing distribution of rights and entitlements, or of questioning the centrality of the concept of rights to the achievement of justice that most lawyers and politicians who are interested in "access to justice" take their stand. The identification and removal of obstacles to the deployment of the legal instruments with which they are familiar and over which they exercise some control exhausts the law reform agenda.

Yet it is not evident that the lay population of the country has willingly accepted its preordained non-role in the officially-organized justice system. For example, many citizens reject the idea that the definition of those procedures and institutions to which access must be enhanced should be entirely captured by groups who have a personal interest in maintaining a monopoly over a limited set of such dispute-processing institutions. Non-state agencies of affect and disaffect, and especially those from which lawyers are routinely excluded, still play important roles in assisting people to discern the entailments of justice. The scepticism of ordinary citizens goes even much deeper: for they understand that it is the acquisition of *knowledge* and not just the availability of "expertise" which is a precondition to achieving justice. Thus, most citizens can still draw a distinction between access to legal services (and to official institutions such as courts) and access to legal knowledge. As in health care, the maxim "an ounce of prevention" applies; and knowledge is believed to be a prerequisite to prevention. Nevertheless, as in health care, instrumental maxims about the virtue of prevention present only a small part of the picture of legal knowledge. If the object of knowledge is seen only in these instrumental terms, it can easily be captured by special interests. That is, if the concept of legal information is restricted to data about rights or about the powers of the police, or more generally to data about those claims arguable in official institutions, capture is complete.

I would claim that enhancing access to legal knowledge is a valuable goal not just because it can serve to further the agenda of preventive law. Law is powerfully symbolic. Legal knowledge is about control over law's symbolism as well as over its instruments. Unfortunately, even as uninstitutional a theme as access to legal knowledge typically has been co-opted into a reinforcing mechanism of the existing legal order. Rather than knowledge about law being used to situate formal legal institutions and processes in a wider, more democratic and less professional normative context, the dissemination of legal information is often consciously advanced in professional circles as a means to expand the reach of law.

The same is true of attempts to make legal jargon more comprehensible—in legislation, contracts, court documents, and so on. To the extent that the arcane vocabulary of official law remains largely inaccessible and incomprehensible, subtle legal ordering outside the domain of this official law retains a healthy presence in people's lives. Legal text, like scripture or religious canon, is the preserve of the priesthood. And fortunately, just as not all spiritual needs require the ministry of clergy, neither do all social needs require the attornment of lawyers. Once the processes of formal law are democratized, however, and especially once its texts are rendered "vulgar," the penetration of formal law into everyday life is enhanced. In the present state of Canadian political life, dejargonizing the law does not empower the citizen by disseminating broadly the previously private knowledge of legal professionals; quite the contrary, by legalizing the vocabulary of routine human interaction it makes the services of professional advisers and decoders even more indispensible to everyday life. And so, even though access to justice could mean access to legal knowledge for the symbolic reasons suggested, to all intents and purposes it means access to legal information for the instrumental purpose of reinforcing the centrality of those formal institutions and procedures which comprise the real field on which the contemporary access to justice agenda is played out.

Not surprisingly, therefore, in both the public and professional sectors access to justice is strongly focused on the delivery of traditional legal services. Access to information is only a beginning. For true believers, the principle of equality before the law (now conveniently entered in the most hallowed ground—section 15 of the *Charter of Rights and Freedoms*) can only be made operational if all citizens have equal access, as a very first step, to those state institutions charged with applying the law and allocating its sanctions. Hence, the conditions for ensuring equal access to courts and administrative tribunals assume a primary place in policy recommendations. The lawyer's trite saying that "a right which one cannot vindicate in court is no right at all" is the touchstone of this conception of access.

But little attention is devoted by those who are concerned with access to justice to ensuring access to other state institutions for the production of law which are closely associated with these adjudicative and quasi-adjudicative bodies. I have in mind here the executive, and to a lesser extent the legislature. Among executive agencies one could identify the police, licensing bodies, inspectorates, and various officials in the public service. It is at this level of administration of the law that the principle of equal access (even in the limited sense here used) is most often put to its severest test. For it is often at the level of street contact with the police that the various injustices of law are most manifest to ordinary citizens.

In an even larger perspective of formal law one must also consider access to legislative institutions. Should not the notion of equal access also comprise equal access to the legislative body which most often announces the state normative order defining the rights and entitlements thought to ensure justice? Conceived in this fashion, equal access would demand the allocation of equal resources to all citizens in order to influence policy by way of lobbying, pressure groups or the submission of briefs to working groups, consultative committees and legislative hearings. Those who dismiss these concerns as hyperbolic by pointing to the equality of access which is reflected in the exercise of the electoral franchise make two mistakes. First, they conflate politics with law, and second they conflate the state in its various managerial roles with the state as legislator.

These last forms of equal access lead to a conception of access to justice which is congruent with the major concern of most commissioned studies of the phenomenon—equal access to legal services, whether provided by lawyers or licensed paralegals. The recognition that access to institutions in a purely formal sense is an inadequate conceptualization (after all, every criminal accused has equal formal access to the criminal courts) leads to concern for equal access to the means to make use of that institution. Nevertheless, given the professionalization of modern social reflexes, just as equal access to health is immediately translated into medicare—equal access to doctors—so too the primary thrust of the movement to equal access to justice is translated into some variant of judicare—equal access to lawyers. Only on the margins of the system, and only under strict control of the primary profession, does this notion of judicare suggest the need for equal access to paralegals, legal technicians and so on.

This preoccupation with the delivery of legal services is a reflection of a conception of justice which discounts true preventive law as an object of concern. The curative focus of investigations into access to justice not only makes a mockery of the idea that equal access to law-making and law administering institutions is important, but also minimizes the idea of equal access to public legal education. Hence, in addition to a neglect of paralegals or their telescoping into the professional hierarchy, one finds that access to formal legal education, community clinics, information provided via the mass media, and even indirect behaviour modifying inducements designed to forestall legal difficulty are not privileged as access to justice themes.

As a final observation about the professional model of access to justice, it is worth noting that, consistent with its etymology, access is conceived largely in individualized and instrumental terms. The notion of access is individualized because late-20th century notions of rights are localized in individuals, and justice is seen almost exclusively in Aristotelian "commutative justice" terms. Social justice, or the idea of just distributions even in existing legal arrangements is discounted because of its aggregative orientation. Thus, concepts such as class actions, broadened standing for non-hohfeldian plaintiffs, and the possibility of impleading unspecified "industry defendants" get marginalized as policy initiatives. Moreover, institutional considerations like the representativity of the police, the bar, the judiciary, faculties of law, are not viewed as important aspects of the access agenda. Here the individual orientation merges with [the] instrumental. Law, being neutral, is not in need of aggregated representativity in order to maintain its symbolic efficacy. Put bluntly, access to justice is the access of a disembodied individual to the institutions of formal law, when the latter are seen only as instruments for enforcing pre-established "just" rights and claims.

NOTES AND QUESTIONS

1. What does Macdonald mean by "access to justice"? Do you agree with this understanding?

2. Even if we accept that access to legal services may not be synonymous with access to justice, might we nonetheless want to take the position that access to the legal system should be equally available to all? Although we have taken some public goods—such as education and health—out of the market, we still feel that it is appropriate to distribute legal services largely on the basis of people's ability to pay. What does this say about our conception of justice? Is there a realistic alternative?

3. Does Macdonald engage in an analysis that is theoretically illuminating, but practically of little use? What can individual lawyers and law reform agencies do to respond to Macdonald's critiques?

4. There is considerable literature that emphasizes that how and why disputes come to be recognized and identified is of great significance; it is not the simple or value-free process that many assume. Disputes are social constructs, their boundaries flexible, changing over time in response to the social context in which the conduct is situated. Marc Galanter, in "Reading the Landscape of Disputes: What We Know and Don't Know (and Think We Know) About Our Allegedly Contentious Society" (1983), 31 *UCLA Law Review* 4, describes the process of dispute formation as follows:

> Disputes are drawn from a vast sea of events, encounters, collisions, rivalries, disappointments, discomforts and injuries. The span and composition of that sea depend on the broad contours of social life. For example, the introduction of machinery brings increases in non-intentional injuries; higher population densities and cash crops bring raised expectations and rivalry for scarce land; advances in knowledge enlarge possibilities of control and expectations of care.

What are the factors that will influence whether one names, blames, and/or claims? In what ways might the organization and distribution of legal services play a role? Consider, for example, that most legal services are provided on a fee-for-service basis, such that, by and large, only persons with considerable economic resources can access legal information and advice. A study of civil disputes in Ontario found that a tendency to complain about a

perceived problem (even without necessarily initiating formal legal process) is heavily dependent on the type of problem. See Bogart and Vidmar, "Personal Experience with the
Ontario Civil Justice System: An Empirical Assessment," in A. Hutchinson, ed., *Access to
Justice* (Toronto: Carswell, 1990). For example, people with perceived problems arising out
of auto accidents are much more likely to complain than those with problems concerning
discrimination. What does this tell us? Do people complain about auto accidents because
they see them as a legal problem, as opposed to discrimination? Or do they perceive that an
automobile accident is worth complaining about but that discrimination is not?

4. In attempting to define the phrase "access to justice," various commentators have
identified two discreet, yet related, issues—equal access to the system and access to a system
that generates results that are individually and socially just. In other words, as Macdonald
insisted, one cannot simply equate, without inquiry, access to the legal system with access
to justice. Indeed, many individuals and groups lack confidence that access to the legal system will ensure access to justice and for this reason choose not to enter the legal arena. How
might the question of who the judge is, for example, make a difference about whether a particular litigant's claim is, and is perceived to be, treated fairly or justly?

B. A Constitutional Right to Legal Services

Recently, courts have struggled with the question of how to understand access to justice in
the context of litigation surrounding a possible constitutional right to legal services. As you
are reading the following Supreme Court of Canada case, consider what conception of access to justice drives the Court's reasoning. Do you agree with the Court's analysis?

British Columbia (Attorney General) v. Christie
[2007] 1 SCR 873

THE COURT: In 1993, British Columbia enacted the *Social Service Tax Amendment Act
(No. 2), 1993, SBC 1993*, c. 24, imposing a 7 percent tax on the purchase price of legal
services. The purpose of the tax was said to be to fund legal aid in the province. However,
the tax collected is put into general revenue, and it is difficult to ascertain how much (if
any) of the tax collected is put towards legal aid, or other initiatives aimed at increasing
access to justice. The legal profession is the only profession in British Columbia whose
services are taxed in this way.

This case is the latest in a series of challenges to the tax and its predecessor, the *Social
Service Tax Amendment Act, 1992*, SBC 1992, c. 22. It was brought by Mr. Dugald Christie, a litigation lawyer who worked with poor and low income people in Vancouver. Mr.
Christie was consumed by a passion to provide legal services to those at the margins of
society. It was a passion that ultimately took his life; last year, on a cross-Canada bicycle
trip to raise funds for the cause, he was struck and killed on a stretch of highway near
Sault Ste. Marie, Ontario.

Mr. Christie's action to have the legal services tax declared unconstitutional was rooted in his experience of the effects of the tax on his practice. Mr. Christie charged low fees.

His net income in the years 1991 to 1999 did not exceed $30,000 per year. Often his clients were not able to pay the bills he rendered for legal services, either on time or at all. Yet the Act required him to submit the tax to government even though the fees on which it had been levied had not been paid. Mr. Christie's small income made this difficult. On March 10, 1997, the government sent Mr. Christie a demand notice. A few days later, without ascertaining the reason for non-payment or attempting to work out a payment schedule, the province seized $972.11 from Mr. Christie's bank account. It seized a further $5,349.64 in December 1997. Mr. Christie stopped practising law and did not resume the practice until July 2000. ...

Mr. Christie claimed that the net effect of the tax was to make it impossible for some of his clients to retain him to pursue their claims. ...

II. Analysis

The respondent's claim is for effective access to the courts which, he states, necessitates legal services. This is asserted not on a case-by-case basis, but as a general right. What is sought is the constitutionalization of a particular type of access to justice—access aided by a lawyer where rights and obligations are at stake before a court or tribunal (Court of Appeal, at para. 30). In order to succeed, the respondent must show that the Canadian Constitution mandates this particular form or quality of access. The question is whether he has done so. In our view, he has not.

We take as our starting point the definition of the alleged constitutional principle offered by the majority of the Court of Appeal (para. 30)—the right to be represented by a lawyer in court or tribunal proceedings where a person's legal rights and obligations are at stake, in order to have effective access to the courts or tribunal proceedings.

We will first discuss what the proposed right entails. We will then ask whether the right, thus described, is prescribed by the Constitution.

This general right to be represented by a lawyer in a court or tribunal proceedings where legal rights or obligations are at stake is a broad right. It would cover almost all—if not all—cases that come before courts or tribunals where individuals are involved. Arguably, corporate rights and obligations would be included since corporations function as vehicles for individual interests. Moreover, it would cover not only actual court proceedings, but also related legal advice, services and disbursements. Although the respondent attempted to argue otherwise, the logical result would be a constitutionally mandated legal aid scheme for virtually all legal proceedings, except where the state could show this is not necessary for effective access to justice.

This Court is not in a position to assess the cost to the public that the right would entail. No evidence was led as to how many people might require state-funded legal services, or what the cost of those services would be. However, we do know that many people presently represent themselves in court proceedings. We also may assume that guaranteed legal services would lead people to bring claims before courts and tribunals who would not otherwise do so. Many would applaud these results. However, the fiscal implications of the right sought cannot be denied. What is being sought is not a small, incremental change in the delivery of legal services. It is a huge change that would alter the legal landscape and impose a not inconsiderable burden on taxpayers.

The next question is whether the Constitution supports the right contended for. In support of this contention, two arguments are made.

First, it is argued that access to justice is a fundamental constitutional right that embraces the right to have a lawyer in relation to court and tribunal proceedings. This argument is based on *BCGEU v. British Columbia (Attorney General)*, [1988] 2 SCR 214, where this Court affirmed a constitutional right to access the courts, which was breached by pickets impeding access. It is argued that a tax on legal services, like pickets, prevents people from accessing the courts. It follows, the argument concludes, that a tax on legal services also violates the right to access the courts and justice.

The right affirmed in *BCGEU* is not absolute. The legislature has the power to pass laws in relation to the administration of justice in the province under s. 92(14) of the *Constitution Act, 1867*. This implies the power of the province to impose at least some conditions on how and when people have a right to access the courts. Therefore *BCGEU* cannot stand for the proposition that every limit on access to the courts is automatically unconstitutional.

A second argument is that the right to have a lawyer in cases before courts and tribunals dealing with rights and obligations is constitutionally protected, either as an aspect of the rule of law, or a precondition to it.

The rule of law is a foundational principle. This Court has described it as "a fundamental postulate of our constitutional structure" (*Roncarelli v. Duplessis*, [1959] SCR 121, at p. 142) that "lie[s] at the root of our system of government" (*Reference re Secession of Quebec*, [1998] 2 SCR 217, at para. 70). It is explicitly recognized in the preamble to the *Constitution Act, 1982*, and implicitly recognized in s. 1 of the Charter, which provides that the rights and freedoms set out in the Charter are "subject only to such reasonable limits prescribed by law as can be demonstrably justified in a free and democratic society." And, as this Court recognized in *Reference re Manitoba Language Rights*, [1985] 1 SCR 721, at p. 750, it is implicit in the very concept of a constitution.

The rule of law embraces at least three principles. The first principle is that the "law is supreme over officials of the government as well as private individuals, and thereby preclusive of the influence of arbitrary power": *Reference re Manitoba Language Rights*, at p. 748. The second principle "requires the creation and maintenance of an actual order of positive laws which preserves and embodies the more general principle of normative order": ibid., at p. 749. The third principle requires that "the relationship between the state and the individual ... be regulated by law": *Reference re Secession of Quebec*, at para. 71. (See also *British Columbia v. Imperial Tobacco Canada Ltd.*, [2005] 2 SCR 473, 2005 SCC 49, at para. 58; *Charkaoui v. Canada (Citizenship and Immigration)*, [2007] 1 SCR 350, 2007 SCC 9, at para. 134.)

It is clear from a review of these principles that general access to legal services is not a currently recognized aspect of the rule of law. However, in *Imperial Tobacco*, this Court left open the possibility that the rule of law may include additional principles. It is therefore necessary to determine whether general access to legal services in relation to court and tribunal proceedings dealing with rights and obligations is a fundamental aspect of the rule of law.

Before examining this question, it is important to note that this Court has repeatedly emphasized the important role that lawyers play in ensuring access to justice and upholding the rule of law: *Andrews v. Law Society of British Columbia*, [1989] 1 SCR 143, at p. 187; *MacDonald Estate v. Martin*, [1990] 3 SCR 1235, at p. 1265; *Fortin v. Chrétien*, [2001] 2 SCR 500, 2001 SCC 45, at para. 49; *Law Society of British Columbia v. Mangat*, [2001] 3 SCR 113, 2001 SCC 67, at para. 43; *Lavallee, Rackel & Heintz v. Canada (Attorney General)*, [2002] 3 SCR 209, 2002 SCC 61, at paras. 64-68, per LeBel J (dissenting in part but not on this point). This is only fitting. Lawyers are a vital conduit through which citizens access the courts, and the law. They help maintain the rule of law by working to ensure that unlawful private and unlawful state action in particular do not go unaddressed. The role that lawyers play in this regard is so important that the right to counsel in some situations has been given constitutional status.

The issue, however, is whether general access to legal services in relation to court and tribunal proceedings dealing with rights and obligations is a fundamental aspect of the rule of law. In our view, it is not. Access to legal services is fundamentally important in any free and democratic society. In some cases, it has been found essential to due process and a fair trial. But a review of the constitutional text, the jurisprudence and the history of the concept does not support the respondent's contention that there is a broad general right to legal counsel as an aspect of, or precondition to, the rule of law.

The text of the Charter negates the postulate of the general constitutional right to legal assistance contended for here. It provides for a right to legal services in one specific situation. Section 10(b) of the Charter provides that everyone has the right to retain and instruct counsel, and to be informed of that right "on arrest or detention." If the reference to the rule of law implied the right to counsel in relation to all proceedings where rights and obligations are at stake, s. 10(b) would be redundant.

Section 10(b) does not exclude a finding of a constitutional right to legal assistance in other situations. Section 7 of the Charter, for example, has been held to imply a right to counsel as an aspect of procedural fairness where life, liberty and security of the person are affected: see *Dehghani v. Canada (Minister of Employment and Immigration)*, [1993] 1 SCR 1053, at p. 1077; *New Brunswick (Minister of Health and Community Services) v. G. (J.)*, [1999] 3 SCR 46. But this does not support a general right to legal assistance whenever a matter of rights and obligations is before a court or tribunal. Thus in *New Brunswick*, the Court was at pains to state that the right to counsel outside of the s. 10(b) context is a case-specific multi-factored enquiry (see para. 86).

Nor has the rule of law historically been understood to encompass a general right to have a lawyer in court or tribunal proceedings affecting rights and obligations. The right to counsel was historically understood to be a limited right that extended only, if at all, to representation in the criminal context: M. Finkelstein, *The Right to Counsel* (1988), at pp. 1-4 to 1-6; W.S. Tarnopolsky, "The Lacuna in North American Civil Liberties—The Right to Counsel in Canada" (1967), 17 *Buff. L Rev.* 145; Comment, "An Historical Argument for the Right to Counsel During Police Interrogation" (1964), 73 *Yale LJ* 1000, at p. 1018.

We conclude that the text of the Constitution, the jurisprudence and the historical understanding of the rule of law do not foreclose the possibility that a right to counsel may be recognized in specific and varied situations. But at the same time, they do not support the conclusion that there is a general constitutional right to counsel in proceedings before courts and tribunals dealing with rights and obligations.

This conclusion makes it unnecessary to inquire into the sufficiency of the evidentiary basis on which the plaintiff bases his claim. However, a comment on the adequacy of the record may not be amiss, in view of the magnitude of what is being sought—the striking out of an otherwise constitutional provincial tax. Counsel for Mr. Christie argued before us that the state cannot constitutionally add a cost to the expense of acquiring counsel to obtain access to justice when that cost serves no purpose in furthering justice. This assumes that there is a direct and inevitable causal link between any increase in the cost of legal services and retaining a lawyer and obtaining access to justice. However, as the Attorney General of British Columbia points out, the economics of legal services may be affected by a complex array of factors, suggesting the need for expert economic evidence to establish that the tax will in fact adversely affect access to justice. Without getting into the adequacy of the record in this case, we note that this Court has cautioned against deciding constitutional cases without an adequate evidentiary record: *R v. Edwards Books and Art Ltd.*, [1986] 2 SCR 713, at pp. 762 and 767-68, per Dickson CJ; *MacKay v. Manitoba*, [1989] 2 SCR 357, at p. 361; *Danson v. Ontario (Attorney General)*, [1990] 2 SCR 1086, at p. 1099.

III. Conclusion

Notwithstanding our sympathy for Mr. Christie's cause, we are compelled to the conclusion that the material presented does not establish the major premise on which the case depends—proof of a constitutional entitlement to legal services in relation to proceedings in courts and tribunals dealing with rights and obligations.

We would allow the appeal and dismiss the cross-appeal, without costs.

NOTES AND QUESTIONS

1. In this decision, the court holds that there is no general constitutional right of access to legal services. However, the court also noted that there are types of litigation that do attract a specific constitutional right to legal services. Outside the criminal law context, the court suggests that this includes cases involving a person's constitutional right not to be deprived of life, liberty, and security of the person, except in accordance with the principles of fundamental justice. In your view, are there other types of litigation that attract (or that ought to attract) a specific constitutional right to legal services?

2. What implications do you think this decision might have with respect to constitutional challenges brought by individuals who are excluded from eligibility for provincial legal aid programs?

C. Cross-Cultural Considerations

One factor that compounds the difficulty in articulating how to best understand access to justice is that an understanding that is generally accepted in one community may be deeply contested in another of the many communities that make up contemporary multicultural societies such as Canada. This point becomes particularly pressing where courts are asked to adjudicate conflicts that involve multiple communities with different conceptions of access to justice. However, it also poses challenges when communities, responding to the perceived failure of civil courts to provide adequate access to justice, create alternative adjudicative institutions for members of those communities. These are the issues taken up in the next two excerpts.

Consider, first, aboriginal communities in Canada. According to some members of these communities, the existing civil courts cannot, by their very nature, take seriously the culture of the First Nations peoples. For many, tinkering at the edges of what is, at its core, a white man's justice system, will never lead to access to justice for aboriginal communities. See the *Royal Commission on Aboriginal Peoples* (Ottawa: Supply and Services, 1996). In response to such concerns about access to justice for aboriginal peoples in Canadian civil courts, Sam Stevens makes a number of recommendations, which are reproduced in the following extract. As you are reading the extract, consider what criteria should be employed in evaluating these proposals and who should have the final word in undertaking this evaluation.

Sam Stevens, "Access to Civil Justice for Aboriginal Peoples"
in A. Hutchinson, ed., *Access to Civil Justice* (Toronto: Carswell, 1990), at 203

[I]t may be useful to summarize the reasons why aboriginal people do not feel they can gain access to the civil justice system.

1. Aboriginal people have been conditioned to distrust the Canadian judicial system, part of which includes the civil court process. They will therefore not usually use the civil justice system.
2. The Canadian justice system does not recognize aboriginal customary laws, laws that have been used by aboriginal peoples, in some cases, for thousands of years. As a result, aboriginal people feel their disputes cannot be resolved by the present justice system in a meaningful way.
3. The adversarial system used by the Canadian judicial system is antithetical to the traditional aboriginal dispute resolution system.
4. The aboriginal people in Canada are unfamiliar with the courts and their right as Canadians; they therefore do not generally assert their rights as recognized under federal or provincial laws.
5. Until recently, there has been an obvious lack of representation in the Canadian judicial system by aboriginal lawyers and judges.
6. A majority of aboriginal people have incomes substantially less than those of average Canadians, and, as a result, many of the problems that aboriginal people experience are "poor people problems." Lawyers generally do not want to deal with these "poor people problems."
7. The time it takes to solve their legal problem is something that aboriginal people cannot accept.
8. The cost of having a civil suit adjudicated by the court is prohibitive.
9. The socio-economic position of aboriginal peoples makes the court more inaccessible for aboriginal peoples than for non-aboriginal peoples.
10. The civil court system is an inappropriate forum for the resolution of issues dealing with claims and aboriginal rights.

To begin to solve these problems, I have proposed solutions based on three broad approaches. First, there are disputes of a private, individual nature, involving an aboriginal
person and a non-aboriginal person or one of the governments. These disputes should
continue to be settled by the present civil courts. So, what can be done to ensure that the
civil courts are more accessible to aboriginal people or other people in circumstances
similar to those of aboriginal peoples? Second, there are disputes that are of a civil, private law nature but that are between two aboriginal people from the same community or
from another aboriginal community. Aboriginal people have proposed, and it seems
reasonable and indeed feasible, to have these disputes resolved by the aboriginal community and according to their laws and standards. Third, there are disputes that are of a
public law nature and that involve aboriginal community rights on the one hand, and
either the Canadian or provincial community or private law rights on the other hand.
The civil courts are being asked to resolve increasingly more disputes of this nature. It is
questionable whether the present civil courts are necessarily the best forums to settle
these kinds of disputes. If we continue to use the present civil court system to resolve
some of these disputes, what can we do to ensure aboriginal people get a just resolution
of their disputes, and are there other alternative dispute resolution forums that can be
implemented to resolve these types of disputes?

Although aboriginal communities are in a unique position in Canada because of historical
and constitutional considerations, there are many other communities that have similarly
critiqued the ability of Canadian civil courts to provide access to justice for members of
their community. Some such communities have attempted to move litigation involving
members of their community to other adjudicative forums. One recent example of this
phenomenon has proven especially controversial: Sharia family law arbitration tribunals in
Toronto.

Marion Boyd, *Dispute Resolution in Family Law:*
Protecting Choice, Promoting Inclusion
(Toronto: Attorney General's Office, 2004)

This Review began as a result of developments that came to public attention in the fall of
2003. After more than twenty years of effort, Syed Mumtaz Ali, a retired Ontario lawyer
determined to ensure that Islamic principles of family and inheritance law could be used
to resolve disputes within the Muslim community in Canada, announced that a new organization, the Islamic Institute of Civil Justice (IICJ), had been established. The Institute
would be conducting arbitrations according to Islamic personal law. According to Mumtaz Ali these services would be offered to the Muslim community of Ontario in the form
of a "Sharia Court" authorized by the *Arbitration Act, 1991*.

    In initial comments to the media in late 2003 Syed Mumtaz Ali, president of the IICJ,
stated, "[n]ow, once an arbitrator decides cases, it is final and binding. The parties can go
to the local secular Canadian court asking that it be enforced. The court has no discretion in the matter. The … impracticality [of not being allowed to use Sharia] has been removed. In settling disputes, there is no choice but to have an arbitration board." His

statement went on to suggest that, once the "Sharia Court" was available to Muslims, they would be required, as part of their faith position, to settle disputes only in that forum, if they were to be regarded as "good Muslims." The Institute proposed that it would offer memberships to Muslims, who would then be bound to settle personal disputes only in this forum, without recourse to the courts of Canada and Ontario. However, the statement also emphasized that the "Sharia Court" would be bound by the laws of Canada and Ontario, as it is a requirement for Muslims living in non-Islamic countries to obey the laws of their country of residence.

These announcements, and the subsequent media interviews which discussed the issue of arbitration in the context of family and inheritance law, raised acute alarm throughout Ontario and Canada. In particular, there was intense fear that the kind of abuses, particularly against women, which have been exposed in other countries where "Sharia Law" prevails, such as Afghanistan, Pakistan, Iran, and Nigeria, could happen in Canada. A related fear, expressed by many groups throughout the Review was that the many years of hard work, which have entrenched equality rights in Canada, could be undone through the use of private arbitration, to the detriment of women, children and other vulnerable people. ...

Summary of Consultations ...

The use of arbitration based on religious law is most familiar in Ontario in the context of the Jewish faith. In Ontario, the Jewish Court in Toronto is called the Beis Din of the Vaad Harabonim, made up of ordained Rabbis who have a higher ordination as Rabbinic Judges. It has been operating for many years. According to the information given to the Review by representatives of the Beis Din, Orthodox Jews are forbidden to bring a lawsuit before secular judges. There is a strong emphasis on helping the disputants to reach an agreed settlement of issues and only if a matter cannot be settled through agreement, will arbitration prevail. Enforcement of arbitration decisions is through the court, pursuant to the *Arbitration Act*. ... [I]n the vast majority of family law cases, in the Orthodox, Conservative and Reform traditions of Judaism, parties approach the Beis Din only for a get, the religious divorce necessary to satisfy the requirements of Jewish law. However, in about thirty cases a year the Beis Din may deal with all issues, such as support, property division, custody and access, according to the oral presentation of Rabbi Reuven Tradburks, Secretary of the Beis Din. ...

Every submission we received from those advocating for the continued use of religiously based arbitration stressed the importance for people of faith to have the opportunity to live in the world according to their beliefs, even if those choices affect their material well being. A couple of those eloquent arguments are worth repeating here:

> By choosing to utilize a system of religious arbitration the parties are doing two things: adhering to their faith; and resolving the dispute on the basis of their religious law, rather than the secular civil law. So long as the choice to do so is a free, informed and voluntary one, and there is no contravention of the Charter of Rights, not only should they be permitted to do so, they have a right to do so as part of the expression of their freedom of religion.

> Simply stated, a secular court or tribunal bases its decision on all of the applicable state law. The religious-based system treats the tenets of the faith as paramount in reaching its

decision. The conscious and voluntary decision to participate in the faith-based systems includes a knowledge that in doing so, rights that exist in the secular system may be given
up. …

     … one can easily understand that the reason why a Muslim chooses to go to a Muslim
Court of Arbitration instead of a secular Canadian court, is that he or she must bring in a
spiritual dimension and let this spiritual consideration play a determining role. A Muslim,
consequently, makes their decision in this respect not because they are likely to get the same
or better rights or material benefits from a Canadian Court or the Muslim Court. …a Muslim must take their dispute for settlement so as to be a good Muslim. …

Many of the Muslims who responded to the Review, talked about how severely
stressed their community has been since the terrorism attacks of 9/11 and the subsequent incidents that have arisen from security measures taken by the Canadian government. Some spoke of increased fear of discrimination against their community in the
court system. Many are very aware of the criticisms raised in the Cole/Gittens Report on
Systemic Racism in the Criminal Justice System and made the point that similar issues
of discrimination have been experienced in the civil justice system, particularly in family
courts. This fear of discrimination in the mainstream society may make private arbitrations under Muslim law seem more attractive and safer, especially to younger people
seeking to establish their identity as a minority within a larger community that is seen as
hostile. …

Access to Justice Issues …

Financial considerations can be a serious constraint to access to justice. Litigation of
family disputes in courts is often a very expensive and lengthy process. As a result, the financial burden of litigation can be a substantial detriment to access to justice for women.
In many cases, women who enter into litigation pay legal costs over several years, and
end up depleting a substantial portion of any assets awarded at the end of the process.
Women who cannot afford the cost of litigation often apply for legal aid, and then must
repay the fees when they reach a financial settlement, often finding they paid more in
legal fees than they received at the end of the day. Many women who work outside the
home are not eligible for legal aid at all and must finance their legal costs privately; some
are forced to seek out loans on which they may have to pay interest over a lengthy period
of time.

     Alternative dispute resolution mechanisms, such as mediation and arbitration, are
flagged as low-cost, faster alternatives to the court system. While some respondents suggested that arbitrators, particularly those who operate their services as businesses, rather
than non-profit enterprises, charge excessive fees, parties who have used the system have
indicated that it is certainly a less expensive alternative to litigation through the courts
"100% of the time."

     In the realm of religiously-based mediation and arbitration services, the majority of
those appearing before the Review offered their services at very low cost, partly as a community service and partly to encourage the members of their communities to choose this
dispute resolution route.

It is important to note, however, that "cheaper" does not necessarily make the system affordable or accessible to all people, and parties who chose this route of dispute resolution may still require some financial assistance in accessing justice. Based on current criteria, it does not seem that Legal Aid or any other public funding would be available for arbitration cases, either to pay for the arbitrator, to finance independent legal advice or to pay any costs for accountants, expert witnesses, child assessments, and so on. Without resources, it is often hard to put forward a convincing case. Although arbitrators are able to assign costs at the end of the process, the most frequent decision is for the parties to share costs equally.

Most respondents stressed the importance of access to independent legal advice in family matters. Parties who choose arbitration may not have any legal advice on their rights or options under the law. However, it was pointed out that the Supreme Court of Canada has noted that independent legal advice at the time of negotiation (in family disputes) is an important means of ensuring an informed decision to enter an agreement.

If independent legal advice is required for all parties in arbitration as a means to ensure complete understanding of legal rights and options as well as free consent, the question of who will pay for the advice remains. While some respondents looked hopefully at the possibility of pro bono services or duty counsel, most advocated for an expansion of Legal Aid funding to ensure that those using mediation and arbitration get the independent legal advice they require. Some respondents pointed out that widespread use of arbitration would free up the courts and save many dollars now spent on litigation which could then be transferred to finance better access to legal advice. Many opponents of arbitration were cynical, stating that the only reason the government is permitting arbitration of family matters is to save court costs; they urged the government to put access to justice ahead of cost considerations.

Critics of arbitration argue that the public court system, in spite of its problems, at least offers some safeguards and support services such as Legal Aid, language interpretation, information services, duty counsel, a public legal forum, and other resources for vulnerable people. This is particularly significant for women who have little or no knowledge of their options and rights under the law. While even many well-educated and informed women lack an understanding of their legal rights, this problem is compounded when considering immigrant women or women who are isolated in their communities.

Under the arbitration system, there are currently no provisions that require arbitrators, or any other third party, to inform parties involved in the process of their rights and options under the law. In fact, women's organizations believe that in religiously-based arbitration, arbitrators may strongly encourage parties into opting for religious-based dispute resolution as the only religiously acceptable choice. In the absence of clear information about options and the consequences of choosing religious arbitration, women are not making informed choices and may choose a form of law that will deprive them of rights they don't even know they have in Canada.

Immigrant women who may come from countries where the laws on gender equality and family matters are very different from Canada may accept, or be coerced into accepting, arbitration as their only option by their community, religious leader, family or spouse. As well, for some, linguistic and economic barriers may have a negative impact on their ability to educate themselves on their options and make them dependent only on the information provided by their community, religious leader, family or spouse.

Parties to a family dispute are not required to use litigation to decide their matter. Under the law, it is not illegal for either party in a family dispute to opt out of his or her rights in making a separation agreement, with or without mediation. It is argued that in many cases it is the female partner who decides to contract out of property and support settlement rights in order to facilitate the separation process and ensure her safety as well as custody of or access to her children.

While this can happen both in the court system and in alternative dispute resolution processes, under Ontario's family law regime "agreements on property division and spousal support require full disclosure of finances from each party and a clear understanding of the consequences of the agreement." A clear understanding of the nature and consequences of the agreement typically includes the ability to read legal documents and to access to independent legal advice. If these criteria are not met, a court can set the agreement aside if one party applies to the court for relief. Further, "where as a result of a marriage breakdown one party would require social assistance, the government would rather have that party's former spouse pay spousal support as required than burden the state with this matter."

Arbitration, on the other hand, allows parties to agree to have their civil dispute settled by a third party in a private setting, using any rules of law that may exclude safeguards set under the *Family Law Act*. Critics of this process are concerned that the private, unregulated and informal nature of arbitration and the possible power imbalance in partners is more likely to result in unfair settlements where "women may cede hard won rights behind closed doors," and that may result in their being dependent on social welfare, thus putting further pressure on the system. As the arbitration process is private, the court would have no knowledge of such unfair or unequal decisions unless the arbitration decision is contested on the grounds currently available for appeal.

Although the court system offers interpretation services to accommodate the needs of Ontario's diverse community, it is widely accepted that many concerns with respect to its cultural sensitivities remain. Many of those working with immigrant and refugee people, particularly those who may be perceived as hostile to Canada by virtue only of their race or national origin, identified incidents of discrimination and racism that impede access to justice. In the court system, parties have no control over which judge will preside over their case. In some instances, presiding judges have indicated discomfort in dealing with cultural and religiously based issues, such as Mahr. Some contributors have pointed out that there is "an 'apparent cultural anxiety' in Ontario associated with entering the 'religious thicket,' a place that the courts cannot safely and should not go."

Ultimately, parties looking for a more personalized and thus a more acceptable form of dispute resolution may find it in the arbitration process. For many people, this means choosing a dispute resolution mechanism that recognizes their cultural background and personal value system, beliefs and faith, which is simultaneously a voluntary process, and affords them some control over the situation. The arbitration may be conducted in the parties' own language, thus ensuring them better understanding of the process and the evidence. For many, the privacy of the process is consistent with their priority for "modesty" and "discretion." Some respondents pointed out the lack of success in the court system of ensuring compliance with support or restraining orders, and argued that the decision of faith-based arbitrators may be more respected and obeyed if recalcitrant parties feel obliged by their faith to follow the orders made.

In spite of strides made in achieving gender equality in Canada, many mainstream and new immigrant communities are largely patriarchal in nature. A woman may be told that it is her religious or community duty to accept whichever adjudicative route is chosen for her. Her fear of isolation from her community, the possible negative impact on her children, and concerns of being considered an apostate in her faith may force her into submitting to one form of dispute resolution over another. The problem may be compounded by the intersectionalities of vulnerabilities that include perceived immigration sponsorship debt, disabilities, issues of class and race, violence and abuse.

While coercion and pressure can influence any settlement, even in the court system, "the Family Law regime in Ontario (including the *Family Law Act, Divorce Act, Children's Law Reform Act*, other statutes and common law) represents years of important reform in the area of women's rights and women's equality. This work has been aimed at dismantling the legal perpetuation of the patriarchal model of family relations, through reforms such as support requirements for dependent spouses, equalization of net family property, and common law constructive trust principles." Some feel that using arbitration, particularly in faith-based settings, may mean these protections will not be honoured by more patriarchal cultures and women may not be treated with justice according to those hard-won rights. Others believe that religiously based mediation and arbitration is a forum in which the values of equality, fairness and justice can be insisted upon because those values are being espoused by the religious and cultural leaders the parties respect.

Women's organizations and other critics of the arbitration system assert that there are currently very limited grounds for appealing a decision made under the *Arbitration Act* and that women's rights are better safeguarded under the traditional justice system employing Ontario's family law regime. In its present state, the *Arbitration Act* does not provide for appeals if a party did not understand the nature or consequences of the domestic contract, or on grounds of incomplete financial disclosure, or duress, misrepresentation or inequality in bargaining power. The ability to appeal a decision on the above mentioned grounds are considered of utmost importance to women. It is argued that women with vulnerabilities that include lack of information, linguistic barriers, risk of coercion etc. would benefit from a wider range of grounds for appeal under arbitration. Only one group, FACT, urged that there be fewer grounds for appeal.

It is clear, then, that the access to justice considerations look quite different from the perspective of the opponents and proponents of arbitration. The challenge for the Review is to take account of all sides of the issue in an attempt to provide recommendations that may resolve these disparate concerns.

NOTES AND QUESTIONS

1. In your view, how should the balance be struck between the competing perspectives evident in the excerpt from the Boyd Report? Does family law arbitration—based on secular or religious norms—enhance or detract from access to justice?

2. The Boyd Report recommends that Ontario continue to allow family law arbitration, whether based on religious norms or otherwise. However, to address concerns expressed regarding gender equality, the report also recommends a number of procedural protections, including requiring that parties to family law arbitration obtain independent legal advice, mechanisms for court oversight, and explicit authorization for courts to overturn family law arbitral awards that are not in the best interests of any children. In 2006, the Ontario legislature rejected the recommendations in the Boyd Report. Instead, the legislature amended the *Arbitration Act, 1991*, SO 1991, c. 17, s. 1, such that family law arbitral awards that meet certain conditions can be enforced, but only where the arbitration "is conducted exclusively in accordance with the law of Ontario or of another Canadian jurisdiction." Some Canadian provinces have taken other approaches to the subject. In Quebec, for example, family law arbitral awards are unenforceable, irrespective of the substantive law applied. *Civil Code of Quebec*, SQ 1991, c. 64, art. 2639. Which of these approaches do you prefer?

II. THE ECONOMICS OF LITIGATION

A. Paying for Canadian Legal Work

There are two dynamics at work that influence the economics of Canadian litigation. The first is the actual cost to the client in paying his or her own lawyer—the bill the client receives at the end of the matter for services the lawyer rendered on behalf of the client. The second is the costs that may be payable by one party to another in the litigation as a result of Canada's fee-shifting regime. The loser in the litigation pays a proportion of the successful litigant's legal fees for the matter. Each of these dynamics will be explained in turn. For further details concerning the law of costs, see M. Orkin, *The Law of Costs*, 3rd ed. (Aurora, ON: Canada Law Book, looseleaf).

1. The Lawyer and the Client

The financial relationship between lawyer and client is governed through a contractual relationship. The client is ultimately responsible for the lawyer's bill, even though some of that bill may be paid by the opposing litigant due to fee shifting. The client chooses the lawyer and strikes an agreement with him or her. There is little mandatory control over the form and type of agreement. Most Canadian jurisdictions, however, have rules of professional conduct that highlight the nature of the economic relationship between lawyer and client. See, for example, Ontario *Rules of Professional Conduct*, rules 2 and 3 (rules respecting reasonableness of fees). For a high proportion of litigation in Canada, there is no specific agreement regarding what precisely a client will pay his or her lawyer for legal services. It is therefore implied that, because the client requested services from the lawyer, the lawyer will provide such services and the client will pay. There is rarely an up-front written estimate as to fees for services, though a lawyer may provide the client with an oral "ball-park" figure, based on how far the lawyer expects the litigation to go and with what degree of complexity.

In all cases, as a matter of law a Canadian lawyer's fees are to be "fair and reasonable" (*Boucher v. Public Accountants Council (Ontario)*, [2004] OJ No. 2634 (Ont. CA)). Yet what is "fair and reasonable" can often be an ambiguous and unpredictable range. Non-repeat clients are at an obvious disadvantage to judge what is fair and reasonable in a lawyer's fee. Provincial rules of professional conduct often enumerate what factors make up a "fair and reasonable" fee, such as those found in the commentary to Ontario's *Rules of Professional Conduct*, rule 2.08:

> (a) the time and effort required and spent,
> (b) the difficulty and importance of the matter,
> (c) whether special skill or service has been required and provided,
> (d) the amount involved or the value of the subject-matter,
> (e) the results obtained,
> (f) fees authorized by statute or regulation,
> (g) special circumstances, such as the loss of other retainers, postponement of payment, uncertainty of reward, or urgency.

If a client or lawyer has a dispute regarding payment of the fee, the courts can supervise the arrangement through a process called assessment (or "taxation" in some Canadian jurisdictions). A court assessment officer examines the lawyer's account and determines whether the fee is "fair and reasonable." If so, the assessment officer's findings are enforceable as a judgment of the court, and the lawyer and client can rely on it as such. Typical criteria for assessing a lawyer's bill, like those found in Ontario's *Rules of Civil Procedure*, rule 58.06(1), include the following factors, which closely parallel those found in the professional conduct rules:

> (a) the amount involved in the proceeding;
> (b) the complexity of the proceeding;
> (c) the importance of the issues;
> (d) the duration of the hearing;
> (e) the conduct of any party that tended to shorten or to lengthen unnecessarily the duration of the proceeding;
> (f) whether any step in the proceeding was,
>   (i) improper, vexatious or unnecessary, or
>   (ii) taken through negligence, mistake or excessive caution;
> (g) a party's denial of or refusal to admit anything that should have been admitted; and
> (h) any other matter relevant to the assessment of costs.

A lawyer will often get written instructions from the client confirming that the lawyer has been hired. In essence, this "retainer agreement" is a contract where the lawyer undertakes to fulfill certain obligations in return for the client's offer to pay the lawyer. The retainer agreement describes the ambit of the legal services to be provided by the lawyer. Most retainer agreements in litigation are very broadly drafted, leaving the lawyer wide discretion as to what tasks to do and whose services to engage, all on behalf of the client. For example, a retainer might provide as follows:

I, Amir Smith, of the City of Toronto, hereby retain and employ Harriet Johns, of the City of Hamilton as my lawyer and hereby authorize her to commence and prosecute an action in the Ontario Superior Court of Justice against XYZ Ltd. of the City of Windsor for damages I suffered due to my consumption of certain goods manufactured and sold by XYZ Ltd. I authorize my lawyer to take such actions and conduct such proceedings as she may consider necessary or proper for conducting this action on my behalf.

A lawyer is the client's agent. Since the client is the principal, the lawyer is obliged to take instructions from the client. Thus, a lawyer who acts outside the authority granted by the client may end up in serious difficulties.

The retainer agreement may also cover the subject of lawyer remuneration. Lawyers in Canada are generally paid by one of two methods: on an hourly basis or on a contingency fee basis. The retainer agreement will set out the method of calculating the lawyers' fee (i.e., either hourly basis or on contingency) and the time for collection of the fee (either periodically or at the conclusion of the matter). The agreement will also explain whether or not the client is responsible to pay disbursements throughout the litigation, or at the end of the matter. Disbursements are the out-of-pocket expenses the lawyer pays on the client's behalf, such as fees for experts, photocopying, postage, and court fees. The retainer agreement may also demand from the client an up-front sum of money, also confusingly referred to as a "retainer" sum. The lawyer holds this money in trust, and uses it to fund the initial disbursements required to get the litigation going.

a. Hourly Basis

Most Canadian legal work such as corporate and commercial litigation, as well as most defence litigation for institutional defendants like insurance companies or banks is billed to the client on an hourly basis. In other words, clients pay for increments of a lawyer's time. Clients are billed periodically (e.g., monthly) for the lawyers' time plus any disbursements expended on the client's behalf. The amount the client pays the lawyer is not dependent on whether or not the lawyer is successful in the litigation. A lawyer's hourly fee ranges greatly, depending on the lawyer's experience and geographic market. For example, a lawyer's hourly fee in a smaller, rural setting could be $125 an hour. In a larger urban setting, an experienced lawyer at a large firm could charge $900 or more an hour.

The largest exception to the lawyer being compensated by the client on an hourly basis is the wide array of lawyers who are in salaried positions and who either work in that position for one single client—in-house counsel for a corporation—or who are government staff lawyers whose client is the particular government department or legal aid clinic for whom they work.

b. Contingency Fee Basis

A smaller proportion of Canadian lawyers are paid on a contingency fee basis, usually for plaintiff personal injury litigation. A contingency fee arrangement is an agreement between the lawyer and client whereby the lawyer's fee is tied to the success of the client's matter. If the client is successful in the litigation, the lawyer takes a certain percentage of the proceeds of the litigation as a fee. If the client is unsuccessful, the lawyer does not charge the client. A contingency fee arrangement is typically for between 20 and 35 percent of the client's end-result proceeds of the litigation. Factors that may affect the agreed-upon fee proportion include the expense and risk that will be undertaken by the lawyer, the complexity and type of matter, the likelihood of success, and the amount the client and lawyer expect to recover. Clients generally do not shop around among lawyers for preferable contingent fee rates. Some type of contingency fee arrangements are permitted in all Canadian jurisdictions by statute, rule, case law, or as a matter of practice. See, for example, Ontario's *Rules of Professional Conduct*, rule 2.08 and Ontario's *Solicitors Act*, RSO 1990, c. S.15, as amended by SO 2002, c. 24, Sch. A.

Contingency fees have been heralded as providing greater access to justice for clients who are unable, or unwilling, to pay for a lawyer on an hourly basis. See, for example, *McIntyre Estate v. Ontario (Attorney General)* (2002), 61 OR (3d) 257 (CA). In theory, the lawyer's and client's interests are entirely aligned if the lawyer takes the case on a contingency basis. The lawyer only gets paid if the matter is completed and, the higher the amount the client receives at the conclusion of the matter, the more the lawyer is paid. This also incentivizes the lawyer to seek a timely conclusion to the client's matter. The plaintiff personal injury bar in Canada regularly uses contingency fees because the vast proportion of injured litigants do not have the personal funds to launch or sustain a lawsuit over time.

Class action litigation also uses a contingency fee and multiplier arrangement. Fees in class actions are strictly controlled by the judiciary. All class action legal fees must be approved by the court, in the best interests of the class members. See chapter 11 on class action fees.

c. Pro Bono Legal Services

In addition to "for fee" legal services for paying clients, there is a strong tradition among Canadian litigation lawyers for *pro bono*, or "no fee," litigation work. Depending on the case, many lawyers and law firms regularly take cases for indigent clients or clients whose matter has a strong social justice component. These clients will pay no fee for the lawyer's work. This *pro bono* work is seen as part of the professional duty of a lawyer to promote access to justice. It is up to the individual lawyer whether or not to take a case on a *pro bono* basis. See Lorne Sossin, "The Public Interest, Professionalism, and *Pro Bono Publico*" (2008), 46 *Osgoode LJ* 131.

d. Publicly Funded Litigation

Beyond providing the courthouse backdrop for civil litigation, the Canadian government funds a very small proportion of civil litigation in the country. The federal and provincial governments in Canada fund the state administrative machine behind Canada's civil litigation. The federal and provincial governments pay for the courthouses and for the salaries of the judges and court administrative staff. Federal and provincial governments also have their own in-house, salaried litigation lawyers who regularly argue cases where the government is a party to the litigation.

The provinces in Canada each have publicly funded legal assistance for those who cannot afford a lawyer. This "legal aid" has strict requirements as to who can qualify. The legal aid framework in Canada will be discussed further in section E. below.

Most provinces have also set up some legal aid clinics, which are specialized government-funded law centres where those with modest means can go for legal assistance. The centres are staffed by salaried lawyers. The focus of these centres is often on poverty law issues, immigration, landlord and tenant issues, family matters, and issues affecting certain vulnerable populations of Canadian society.

Although there exists a method in case law for interim funding of public interest cases from government funding sources, as will be shown in section II.D. below, the legal test a litigant must meet to access such funding is exceedingly high. A litigant must fit within the narrow category of a "public interest" case. The courts, therefore, keep tight reins on accessing public interim funding for disputes.

NOTES AND QUESTIONS

1. Many have criticized the lawyers' hourly billing practice as inefficient and unfair because it incentivizes a work rate tied not to results but to the time the lawyer spends on the case. Are contingency fees the answer? See, for example, Alice Woolley, "Time for Change: Unethical Hourly Billing in the Canadian Profession and What Should Be Done About It" (2004), 83 *Can. Bar Rev.* 859.

2. Most liability insurance policies in Canada provide for the funding of the cost of a defence in the event the insured is sued. Insurers generally negotiate preferential rates with particular law firms because of the high volume of defence-side legal work created in the liability insurance industry. There is no meaningful "litigation insurance" market in Canada for insurance geared toward bringing a lawsuit. However, most private law tort and insurance lawsuits are brought in the names only of the insureds in the policy, but are actually litigated solely by insurers, to protect the insurers' subrogated interests. The insurance policies provide that the insurance company has the right to sue the wrongdoer in the insured's name. The insureds themselves are paid directly by their insurer, which then chases the alleged wrongdoer to recoup its losses from the one at fault.

3. A relatively small proportion of litigation work (though large by volume in terms of individual matters) is contracted on a negotiated bulk rate, mostly for work done by large law firms on behalf of large institutional clients who are often defendants (e.g., railways and banks). In this fashion, institutional clients who can expect to have regular litigation work benefit from being repeat players with a particular law firm. These institutional clients negotiate preferential or block rates of the law firm's hourly time in exchange for exclusive guaranteed legal work from the institution.

4. There is only some evidence in Canada of third parties financing civil litigation in exchange for a proportion of the proceeds because of the concerns about maintenance and champerty—both illegal actions in Canada. However, see Poonam Puri, "Financing Litigation by Third Party Investors: A Share of Justice" (1998), 36 *Osgoode Hall LJ* 515 (arguing that, in the interests of access to justice, the Canadian legal market should allow greater participation of third-party investor financing in litigation).

B. Fee Shifting in Canada

In Canada, the losing party in civil litigation pays a proportion of the successful party's legal fees. This is called "fee shifting." In an environment of escalating legal costs, where so much is at stake in litigation in legal costs alone, the present fee-shifting regime has created an entire body of substantive law regarding costs in additional to the procedural and statutory framework for operating fee shifting. Legal costs are often not a mere collateral concern in most Canadian litigation. Instead, costs often play an important role in driving the very result in litigation, sometimes more so than the substantive matter that is the very subject of the litigation.

Canada adopted a modified fee shifting-regime, modelled on the English fee-shifting system. Unlike the American fee model, where each litigant is typically only responsible to pay his or her own lawyer, the Canadian fee-shifting regime allows the successful litigant to recoup a proportion of his or her legal costs from the unsuccessful litigant. The original reasoning behind fee shifting was to compensate a successful party in civil litigation for some of the cost to which he or she was put in exercising a legal right. Had the defendant not resisted the civil action and instead paid the plaintiff's claim, the plaintiff would not have incurred the cost of initiating the lawsuit. Similarly, if the defendant is successful in resisting the plaintiff's claim, the defendant is put to legal costs he or she otherwise would not have, but for the actions of the unsuccessful plaintiff. Costs, then, are a type of damage award consistent with the notion that it is the losing party's fault that the successful party was put to the cost of hiring a lawyer and to prosecute or defend the claim. The losing party should, therefore, reimburse the plaintiff for these legal costs if the plaintiff is successful in the claim.

However, that reimbursement is mediated by what the unsuccessful party would reasonably expect to pay for costs to the successful party. Courts are expected to police cost awards such that they bear some rational relationship with expected reasonable market rates for such a proceeding, thus theoretically aiding predictability of an award so a litigant can better make an informed decision about the risk of costs in a matter. To further aid in this predictability, courts are to consider whether the costs to be paid by the unsuccessful litigant are rationally proportional to the matter litigated. The amount of the claim, the amount of the judgment at the end of the matter, the complexity, and the importance of the dispute are all considerations in assessing proportionality of the costs award. For example, if a successful party's actual costs to litigate the matter were $80,000 and the amount at stake was $100,000, those costs are likely not proportional in relation to the amount at stake. The problem with the current economics of legal services is that, more and more, actual legal costs are getting close to eclipsing the amount at stake in small to medium-sized lawsuits.

1. The Court's Discretion

Canadian courts enjoy enormous discretion with respect to awarding costs throughout the life of a lawsuit. The basis for a court's discretionary power as to costs is statutory. For example, s. 131(1) of Ontario's *Courts of Justice Act*, RSO 1990, c. C.43 provides:

> Subject to the provisions of an Act or rules of court, the costs of and incidental to a proceeding or a step in a proceeding are in the discretion of the court, and the court may determine by whom and to what extent the costs shall be paid.

Most jurisdictions in Canada have established some rules to assist judges in exercising this discretion with respect to costs. For example, see British Columbia's *Supreme Court Rules*, rule 57 and Nova Scotia's rule 77. In Ontario, rule 57.01(1) of the *Rules of Civil Procedure* sets out the following factors for judicial consideration of cost awards:

> 57.01(1) In exercising its discretion under section 131 of the *Courts of Justice Act* to award costs, the court may consider, in addition to the result in the proceeding and any offer to settle or to contribute made in writing,
>
>> (0.a) the principle of indemnity, including, where applicable, the experience of the lawyer for the party entitled to the costs as well as the rates charged and the hours spent by that lawyer;
>>
>> (0.b) the amount of costs that an unsuccessful party could reasonably expect to pay in relation to the step in the proceeding for which costs are being fixed;
>>
>> (a) the amount claimed and the amount recovered in the proceeding;
>>
>> (b) the apportionment of liability;
>>
>> (c) the complexity of the proceeding;
>>
>> (d) the importance of the issues;
>>
>> (e) the conduct of any party that tended to shorten or to lengthen unnecessarily the duration of the proceeding;
>>
>> (f) whether any step in the proceeding was,
>>
>>> (i) improper, vexatious or unnecessary, or
>>>
>>> (ii) taken through negligence, mistake or excessive caution;
>>
>> (g) a party's denial of or refusal to admit anything that should have been admitted;
>>
>> (h) whether it is appropriate to award any costs or more than one set of costs where a party,
>>
>>> (i) commenced separate proceedings for claims that should have been made in one proceeding, or
>>>
>>> (ii) in defending a proceeding separated unnecessarily from another party in the same interest or defended by a different lawyer; and
>>
>> (i) any other matter relevant to the question of costs.

The multiple factors a court uses to consider an appropriate costs award under fee shifting serve two broad-spectrum purposes: a fault-based compensatory purpose, and a larger civil justice regulatory purpose. In all cases, a court is to assess an unsuccessful party's cost awards based on what is "fair and reasonable" for that party to pay. See, for example, *Boucher v. Public Accountants Council (Ontario)*, [2004] OJ No. 2634 (Ont. CA).

2. Scales of Costs

a. The Norm: Partial Indemnity Costs

Under Canadian fee shifting, there are theoretically three scales of costs on which a court may order an unsuccessful party to pay a successful party: party-and-party costs (called "partial indemnity costs" in Ontario and "ordinary costs" in British Columbia), solicitor-and-client costs (called "substantial indemnity costs" in Ontario and "special costs" in British Columbia), and full indemnity. The standard order for costs a court awards is costs payable on a partial indemnity scale. This scale of costs is not full, dollar-for-dollar indemnity but is only a proportion of the successful party's legal costs. Surprisingly, what that proportion is has never been defined with any precision. Partial indemnity costs are designed to provide some contribution toward the successful party's legal costs without putting the award out of reach of the unsuccessful defendant to pay. Traditionally, partial indemnity costs range from 40 to 75 percent of the actual, reasonable legal bill the successful party will have to pay, with 60 percent being a frequent representative proportion. Because cost awards are to be "fair and reasonable" and depend on so many factors in a case—from the experience and market of the lawyers involved to the length and complexity of the lawsuit to the behaviour of the parties—it is impossible to pin down any predictable range for partial indemnity costs in Canadian case law beyond 40 to 75 percent. When the actual legal costs to prosecute a small to medium-size case could run in the $50,000 to $150,000 range, the costs award in the fee-shifting regime could range from $20,000 to $112,500.

b. The Exception: Substantial and Full Indemnity Costs

The second and third scales for costs are substantial indemnity and full indemnity costs. These are exceptional costs awards, reserved only for unique circumstances where either sanctionable behaviour or the failure to reasonably settle a case dictate such an award. A substantial indemnity costs award is closer to full, dollar-for-dollar indemnity, yet is still mediated as always by fairness and reasonableness. Substantial indemnity awards typically are 90 percent of a successful litigant's actual legal costs. In Ontario, substantial indemnity costs are 1.5 times partial indemnity costs. Full indemnity is, of course, dollar-for-dollar indemnity for legal services. The ceiling for Canadian costs awards is the actual, dollar-for-dollar amount a client will pay his or her lawyer. Successful parties cannot profit from cost awards.

An unsuccessful party will have to pay a substantial indemnity cost awards in two instances: (1) egregious behaviour in the litigation, which attracts the punitive sanction of costs, or (2) a failure to accept a reasonable settlement offer.

i. Costs as Behaviour Sanction

If a party conducts the litigation in a manner that unnecessarily increases time and expense, the court may order that party to pay substantial indemnity costs as punishment for such behaviour. For example, adverse cost awards can be used to discourage frivolous or vexatious behaviour or to punish failure to respond to requests to admit information and thereby unnecessarily lengthen proceedings. See, for example, *Lanty v. Ontario (Ministry of Natural Resources)* (2007), 61 RPR (4th) 161 (Ont. CA), where the plaintiff's unreasonable and uncooperative behaviour warranted a higher costs award. Certain other instances also attract sanctions of substantial indemnity costs. If a party brings a motion for summary judgment, advocating there is no genuine issue for trial, and loses such a motion, the losing party is subject to substantial indemnity costs. There are similar sanctions for bringing a claim which attacks integrity, such as fraud or punitive damages, and failing to prove such a claim.

ii. Costs and Settlement Incentives

Canadian provincial jurisdictions have statutory procedural mechanisms designed to use fee-shifted costs to prompt early settlement of lawsuits. The settlement-costs dynamic is a fundamental aspect of Canada's fee-shifting costs regime, and provides a powerful incentive to settle a case early. If a party fails to accept a reasonable settlement offer before trial, that party is sanctioned with an adverse costs award. See chapter 7 on settlement.

For example, in Ontario, under rule 49, parties are incentivized to settle the case before trial or risk being punished with costs, even if that party is ultimately successful at trial. If a plaintiff offers to settle the case at least seven days before trial, and that offer is not accepted by the defendant, and the plaintiff obtains a judgment at trial that is at least as favourable as the terms of the plaintiff's offer, then the plaintiff is to receive her partial indemnity costs up to the date of the offer, and her substantial indemnity costs from the date of the offer onward. If a defendant makes an offer to settle the case, and the plaintiff obtains a judgment at trial no more favourable than the terms of the defendant's offer, then the plaintiff gets her partial indemnity costs up to the date of the defendant's offer and the defendant gets his partial indemnity costs from the date of the offer onward.

3. Calculating Costs

It is difficult to predict a costs award in Canadian civil litigation. Guided by the principle that costs borne by an unsuccessful litigant in Canada's fee-shifting regime are to be "fair and reasonable," courts fix cost awards on a contextual, case-by-case method. Courts must account not only for the market rates the successful party would pay but also for the behaviour of the parties throughout the litigation, the proportionality of the costs award to the amount at stake in the matter, and whether or not there were any offers to settle that attract costs consequences. The end result: a multifactoral, fact-specific analysis that varies from case to case.

At the end of a matter before the court, or at the end of an interlocutory step in a matter before the court, the parties make submissions to the court with respect to costs. If possible, the parties may agree on costs. If the parties do not agree, each submits a costs outline that details the years of experience of each lawyer involved, the partial indemnity and the actual hourly rate of each lawyer, a detailed description of the time spent on the matter, and all disbursements spent on the client's behalf. The court hears submissions and then determines the costs. If it is a trial, the trial judge will determine the total cost award for the entire life of the matter, including any interlocutory motions, discovery, and other steps in the litigation. Costs follow the matter in Canada, such that the losing party pays the cost of prosecuting the entire claim. If the matter is an interlocutory motion, the numerical value of the costs for that step in the proceeding will be set by the judge who heard the motion but those costs will only be borne by the eventual losing party, barring exceptions where the motions judge wishes to sanction a party's behaviour on the motion with costs. Ironically, a party can include as part of her costs submissions the time her lawyer spent in preparing for, and arguing for, the costs themselves. In many instances, a separate hearing on costs is required post-trial. There is thus often significant procedure wrangling—and cost—to a litigant in dealing with the costs stage of litigation.

The court's process in arriving at the end-result costs award is not strictly mathematical, where the judge takes the hours spent and multiplies that figure by the lawyer's hourly rate. In addition to the economic reality of the actual cost of the litigation, a court must make certain that the cost award to the unsuccessful party is not putting litigation out of reach, in a general sense. The amount must be what the losing party would reasonably expect to pay. In arriving at such an amount, some Canadian jurisdictions provide some guidance as to reasonable lawyers' hourly rates.

While unsuccessful litigants would not be forced to pay costs of a "Cadillac variety," courts also do not expect that successful litigants would have shopped around for a less expensive alternative to their counsel of choice. (See, for example, *Liu v. Sung* (1995), 37 CPC (3d) 44 (BCSC).) Courts also expect that the lawyers take responsibility for keeping costs proportional to the matter at stake.

Awards for costs, left to the discretion of the judge hearing the matter, are nuanced and contextual, depending on the nature of the litigation, the behaviour of the parties involved, and the cost of the litigation itself in the market. The dynamic is even more complicated when a court must also balance the cost awards inherent in the settlement regime, which incentivizes early reasonable offers to settle and uses adverse cost consequences for failing to accept a reasonable settlement offer. The following two cases explore many of the typical factors and legal considerations that courts must balance in awarding costs that are "fair and reasonable."

Maracle v. Brant
2008 CarswellOnt 5232 (Ont. SCJ)

L. RATUSHNY J:

Costs Endorsement

Further to Reasons for Judgment released March 27, 2008 in this matter (the "Decision") and the awarding of costs to the plaintiffs as the successful party, each party has forwarded written submissions on their quantum.

The plaintiffs request substantial indemnity costs throughout based on the nature of the defendants' allegations and their conduct, in the amount of $274,579.00 exclusive of disbursements and GST.

The defendants submit partial indemnity costs are appropriate throughout, in the amount of $106,982.19 all inclusive.

A number of issues have been raised by the costs submissions and I deal with them in the same order.

Whether Certain of the Plaintiffs' Time and Disbursements
Form Part of the Proper Costs of the Action

In response to the defendants' costs submissions, the plaintiffs concede that the correct fee amount for work performed before their offer to settle (the "Offer") is reduced by $6,023.00, resulting in a total pre-Offer fee amount of $148,633.00.

However, the defendants submit there should be further exclusions for three other matters that occurred prior to the trial of this action, involving fees in the total amount of $35,549.26.

The first of these three other matters was a motion for an interlocutory injunction brought by the plaintiffs against the defendants that was ultimately dismissed with costs of the motion awarded against the plaintiffs. The second was a motion for summary judgment brought by the plaintiffs that was later abandoned with costs ultimately awarded against the plaintiffs.

The plaintiffs claim these costs because of the usefulness in the action of the material prepared and filed and the cross-examinations conducted for each of these motions.

However, to award costs in respect of these previous motions where costs have already been dealt with would, in my view, amount to the trial judge varying previous costs orders without having been given any power to do so and inappropriately interfering with the discretion already exercised by the motions judges in respect of costs: Mark Orkin, *The Law of Costs*, 2nd ed. 1987 (Aurora: Canada Law Book Inc., 1999) at pp. 4-11.

The third of these other matters was an action commenced against the plaintiffs, the defendant Maracle and others by the County of Hastings in relation to a gasoline spill in a ditch in proximity to the plaintiffs' Lands as defined in the Decision. This action was ultimately settled between the plaintiffs' insurers, the defendant Maracle and the other defendants in that action.

While the plaintiffs' claim in the present action resulting in the Decision was not amended to make claims in respect of issues relating to the fuel spill, the plaintiffs include the costs of that action because it had as its basis the same claim as in the present action, namely, the defendants' illegal occupation of the plaintiffs' Lands.

However, I decline to include the plaintiffs' fees incurred in respect of the fuel spill action. It was open for the plaintiffs to have sought to have the fuel spill issues included in the present action. They chose not to do so for their own reasons. Even if I were disposed to include those fees because they were incurred as a result of the defendants' illegal occupation of the Lands, I would have no facts before me regarding that other action on which to weigh the appropriate scale and quantum of costs and to form the basis for the exercise of my discretion.

I agree with the defendants, therefore, that the plaintiffs' fees for these three other matters should be excluded.

The plaintiffs' pre-Offer fee amount is revised to be the sum of $113,084.24. I accept the plaintiffs' submission that their disbursements for this revised fee amount are in the total sum of $10,834.52.

Whether the Plaintiffs Should Be Awarded Substantial Indemnity Costs Throughout Based On the Conduct of the Defendants

The plaintiffs seek substantial indemnity costs throughout, as stated before, based on the pre-litigation conduct of the defendants and based also on unproven allegations made by them during their testimony at trial regarding the plaintiffs' fraud or misconduct in public office.

The defendants' counsel submits that he told the Court in his opening and closing arguments that his clients were not alleging fraud or deliberate misconduct by anyone.

The Decision finds otherwise, however, and particularly so, at paragraph 55. The defendants' pre-litigation conduct included their theory of fraud or misconduct in public office and at trial they continued to make these allegations notwithstanding their counsel's statement that this was not part of their legal claim.

The Decision awarded punitive damages of $50,000.00. At paragraphs 132-136, the Decision reviewed the basis for these punitive damages, including not only the defendants' pre-litigation misconduct but also the theory presented at trial of fraud or misconduct particularly in relation to the allotment resolution.

To award extra costs for the same conduct that has been the subject of punitive damages would amount to additional punishment or compensation when the appropriate level of compensation has already been determined. It would amount to an inappropriate topping up, in effect, of the punitive damages award: *Panapers Inc. v. 1260539 Ontario Ltd.*, [2007] OJ No. 204 (Ont. CA), at para. 5 and following *Gerula v. Flores* (1995), 83 OAC 128 (Ont. CA), at para. 74.

I decline, therefore, to award substantial indemnity costs throughout based on the conduct of the defendants.

Whether the Plaintiffs Should Be Awarded Substantial Indemnity Costs from the Date of Their Offer

The defendants submit that while the Offer falls within r. 49.10 of the *Rules of Civil Procedure*, RRO 1990, Reg. 194 (the "*Rules*"), it was an invitation to surrender and not a genuine offer of compromise such that I should exercise my discretion and decline to award substantial indemnity costs from the date of the Offer.

The policy of encouraging settlements is inherent in r. 49, so that an offer to settle should reflect some element of compromise and if it does not, the court can exercise its discretion in the interests of fairness to order "otherwise" under r. 49.10: *Celanese Canada Inc. v. Canadian National Railway*, [2005] OJ No. 1122 (Ont. CA), at paras. 33-36.

I accept the plaintiffs' submissions that the Offer, at least in its monetary portion, was an offer to accept less than they could have claimed at trial and of course, did not include substantial trial costs about to be incurred. In this way and provided the defendants recognized the plaintiffs' assertions that they had never given up control of the Lands, the Offer did reflect an element of compromise regarding the level of compensation to be paid to the plaintiffs.

The plaintiffs obtained about twice the amount of the Offer at trial. I agree with the plaintiffs that rule 49.10 is fairly applicable and I award them substantial indemnity costs from the date of the Offer.

Whether the Costs Claimed by the Plaintiffs Are Excessive

The plaintiffs acknowledge that the costs incurred are substantial. They make the point that they faced "hard to refute" allegations made over events that covered a 16-year time period.

The defendants' counsel submits that compared to his total fees of $122,315.00 billed to his clients, the plaintiffs are claiming costs for fees of $113,084.24 for the pre-Offer period and fees of $153,677.00 for the post-Offer period, for a total fee amount of $266,761.24. The plaintiffs' fees are, therefore, more than double the defendants' fees.

I accept, as referred to in the Decision, that there were important issues in this action for the plaintiffs, particularly regarding the issues of control of the Lands, the reinforcement of the rule of law on the Territory and the defendants' allegations of fraud or misconduct in public office. In addition, these issues had percolated for 16 years before the trial commenced. In my view, these factors justify extra time and costs by the plaintiffs' counsel.

I also recognize that there is a further valid justification for extra time and costs by the plaintiffs. They first retained their trial counsel, Mr. Roger Horst, in April 2002. By that time, 10 years of events and numerous court orders relevant to the action had occurred. All of these had to be assembled, organized and analyzed, as they were for trial, in chronological order for the 16 years in question. In contrast to the situation for the plaintiffs' counsel, the evidence at trial was that the defendants' counsel, Mr. Robert Reynolds, had acted for the Brants from time to time during those first ten years. It is reasonable to assume that he was already quite familiar with the events and court orders by the time the plaintiffs' counsel was retained so that in addition to not having to start an action, it is likely that he had to spend substantially less time in becoming knowledgeable about those events.

I accept that the work done by the clerks and articling students in preparation for the plaintiffs' case and for senior trial counsel, Mr. Roger Horst, resulted in a high quality of organization regarding the exhibit books at trial. The trial was well organized and efficiently run, by both counsel, and a planned 10-day trial was able to be reduced to 5 days.

Mr. Reynolds submits that after allowing for a comparative amount of time spent by his clerk on the action, there are approximately 485 hours of clerk or student time at an approximate average rate of $155 per hour, being about $75,000.00 of the total fee amount, being claimed by the plaintiffs. There is no doubt some duplication of effort in this time and fee amount incurred by the plaintiffs but it is difficult to conclude from this kind of numerical analysis that this amount of time is manifestly excessive: *Hague v. Liberty Mutual Insurance Co.*, [2005] OJ No. 1660 (Nordheimer J), at paras. 12, 13 and 15.

The overall objective is to award costs that are "fair and reasonable," taking into account r. 57.01 factors and including, if this is able to be discerned, the reasonable expectation of the parties as to costs: *Hague*, at paras. 12 and 15, referring to *Boucher v. Public Accountants Council (Ontario)*, [2004] OJ No. 2634 (Ont. CA), at paras. 24-26, 37-38.

The parties have each revealed their own legal fees in connection with the action. I accept that the fees billed to the plaintiffs for the action are roughly double those billed to the defendants.

On a partial indemnity basis for the plaintiffs' pre-Offer revised fees of $113,084.24, 60% of that sum is an amount of $67,850.54 in costs.

On a substantial indemnity basis for the plaintiffs' post-Offer fees of $153,677.00, 90% of that sum is an amount of $138,309.30 in costs.

These sums result in a total costs amount of $206,159.84 exclusive of disbursements and GST.

This amount does not appear to me to be an unfair or unreasonable amount in all the circumstances. Nor should the defendants have reasonably expected that the plaintiffs' costs would not almost double their own legal fees in all of the circumstances and particularly given the issues at play as referred to above.

I do, however, allow for some inevitable duplication of effort in the plaintiffs' time dockets between the numerous law clerks and students-at-law on the file. By way of rough measure and keeping the overall picture in mind as reviewed above, a "backing out" of 50 hours at a billing rate of $155.00 per hour is reasonable in my view, resulting in a reduction in fees in the sum of $7,750.00. If this amount is divided equally to reduce the fees both pre and post Offer, the new total costs amount on the basis of the partial and substantial indemnity split is approximately $200,350.00 exclusive of disbursements and GST.

The plaintiffs' disbursements both pre and post Offer are in a total amount of $20,127.17 ($10,834.52 + $9292.65).

Mr. Horst asks for an additional sum of $2,500.00 for the extra work necessary regarding costs. This is a reasonable request.

With all of these factors in mind, I fix the costs to be paid by the defendants, namely the Brants and Miracle, in the amount of $223,000, inclusive of all fees and disbursements but exclusive of GST.

Barlow v. Citadel General Assurance Co.
2008 CarswellOnt 2199 (Ont. SCJ)

P.F. LALONDE J:

Amended Decision on Costs

This matter arose out of a claim for long-term disability benefits. The defendant insurance company paid benefits from June 1, 2004 to September 19, 2005 at which time the defendant ceased making payments. The defendant had decided that the plaintiff was no longer disabled. Following a seven-day jury trial, the jury found that the plaintiff was entitled to her disability payments of $4,000.00 per month from October 1, 2005 to the date of trial in November 2007, together with a return of the premiums she had paid during that period of time.

The plaintiff's request to add a claim for aggravated and punitive damages was denied prior to the opening of the trial, as was a motion to strike out the defendant's jury notice.

I was asked by both parties to fix costs in this matter. As I have received their written submissions, ruled on their pre-trial motions and directed the jury in this trial, I am in a position to assess costs in this matter.

The Plaintiff's Position

Counsel for the plaintiff seeks a $50,000.00 premium on the basis that he took on the plaintiff's case on the basis that he would not recover any fees or disbursement unless the plaintiff was successful in a settlement or at trial. He states that his client had no financial ability to retain his services.

The plaintiff also claims that the award made by the jury was as good or better than was made by the plaintiff's offer to settle. The plaintiff made two offers to settle and she claims costs on a substantial indemnity basis from the date of her first offer.

Counsel for the plaintiff further claims that this mater was a complex matter, vigorously defended by the insurance company and of great importance for his client.

The Defendant's Position

I agree with the following submissions made by the defendant.

Premiums are no longer payable in cases where a lawyer takes on a claim for a plaintiff on a contingency fee basis since *Walker v. Ritchie*, [2006] SCJ No. 45 (SCC) was decided by the Supreme Court of Canada.

Many offers were put forward by the plaintiff. The plaintiff cannot claim costs consequences on previous offers as a subsequent offer implies the cancellation of a previous offer.

Decision

It is not my role in fixing costs to engage in another piece of litigation. I find that the argumentative supplementary costs submissions of plaintiff's counsel were not helpful. Counsel can find any number of costs decisions that, if improperly applied, can support outlandish positions.

The plaintiff claimed a premium of $50,000.00 basically because she did not have the financial means to retain counsel (paragraph 3 of the plaintiff's submissions on costs). The Supreme Court of Canada in *Walker v. Ritchie, supra*, stated that Rule 57.01(1) does not make the risk of non-payment a relevant factor in determining costs. That decision was followed by the Ontario Court of Appeal in *Ward v. Manufacturers Life Insurance Co.*, [2007] OJ No. 4882 (Ont. CA). In that case, *Manufacturers Life* froze Mr. Ward's vested commission account. Weiler JA referring to the Supreme Court of Canada decision in *Walker* found that recent amendments passed in 2005 did not change the new Rule 57.01. ...

Weiler JA cancelled the $50,000.00 premium award. For the same reasons, I dismiss the plaintiff's claim for a $50,000.00 costs premium in this case.

With regards to motions or costs for steps in the proceeding prior to trial, the recent Court of Appeal decision in *Islam v. Rahman*, 2007 CarswellOnt 5718 (Ont. CA) settled the issue and I accept that while a trial judge has the right to order full recovery of costs for the entire case, there should be excluded from that award, all costs related to steps in the case where either the order was no costs or the order was silent as to costs. I will therefore only consider the motions brought before me at the commencement of trial before the jury was brought in to hear the case. I need not and will not consider any claim for costs that arose due to motions made during the months that preceded the trial. I reproduce the history of these motions taken from the defendant's submissions, as I agree with them without reservation.

In the bill of costs submitted by the plaintiff, there is an amount in excess of $30,000.00 claimed for motions.

Motions were heard on September 29, 2006, December 21, 2006, May 10, 2007, August 27, 2007 and November 14, 2007.

. . .

Therefore, the plaintiff was not successful on any of the motions for which she is seeking costs, with the exception of the motion of August 27, 2007 for which she already agreed to $2,000.00 in costs.

Considering the fact that the plaintiff was generally unsuccessful in all of the motions and that costs have already been considered by the judges who heard the motions, the plaintiff should not receive any costs for these motions. If the plaintiff wanted to receive costs for these motions then she should have appealed the orders of the judges who heard the motion.

In connection with mediation on August 21, 2007, the plaintiff claims 33.50 hours spent by her counsel and 2.20 hours spent for a law clerk for a mediation that lasted three hours. I agree with the defendant's submissions that this is an example of gross overbilling and I will only compensate the plaintiff for eight hours.

The $58,000.00 claimed for trial by the plaintiff is excessive also. The plaintiff's counsel prepared a statement of law and case brief that included more than 75 cases. I agree that the majority of these cases were with respect to the claims for aggravated, punitive and exemplary damages that were struck by me. On November 14, 2007 following my decision on plaintiff counsel's many motions, I admonished counsel in the absence of his client for citing no less than eight cases to support a simple proposition. His factum was rife with such examples.

On the matters of disbursements, the plaintiff has included expenses for a Dr. Cooke in the amount of $2,142.14. Dr. Cooke was never called as a witness at trial and that expense is refused.

The plaintiff has included $635.00 for motion records. For reasons mentioned earlier, the claim for such disbursements is rejected.

The plaintiff has also included a flat amount of $5,000.00 for printing expense that is not supported by any documents and $2,025.40 for photocopies that again is not supported by any documents. Those claims are also rejected as of the many cases cited most were not useful to this particular case.

As noted earlier, costs are awarded pursuant to Rule 57.01(1) of the *Rules of Civil Procedure*. ...

I agree with counsel for the defendant as to how the above principles should be applied and reproduce his submissions.

Rates Charged

I take no issue with the rates charged by counsel for the plaintiff. However, as the defendant takes the position that there is no reason to award substantial indemnity costs, I will review the scale of costs to be awarded.

Amount Claimed and the Amount Recovered in the Proceeding

The plaintiff claimed for: (a) damages for breach of contract in the sum of $1,000,000.00; (b) damages for negligent adjusting in the amount of $1,000,000.00; (c) aggravated, exemplary and punitive damages in the amount of $1,000,000.00, plus interest and costs.

The plaintiff received $100,000.00 for breach of contract. The claim for negligent adjusting was determined to have no basis in law and was struck prior to trial. The claims for aggravated, exemplary and punitive damages were also struck prior to trial. The plaintiff was awarded nothing for mental distress.

Therefore the plaintiff recovered $100,000.00 out of a claim of $3,000,000.00. The defendant submits that costs should be proportional to the recovery. The modest recovery for damages should be coupled with a modest recovery for costs.

In *Boucher v. Public Accountants Council (Ontario)*, [2004] OJ No. 2634 (Ont. CA), the Ontario Court of Appeal states that an award of costs is not simply a mechanical exercise. Instead, the overall objective is to fix an amount that is fair and reasonable for the unsuccessful party to pay in the particular circumstances of the case rather than an amount fixed by the actual costs incurred by the successful party.

In *Zesta Engineering Ltd. v. Cloutier*, [2002] OJ No. 4495 (Ont. CA), another Ontario Court of Appeal decision, the Court states that the costs award should reflect more what the court views as a fair and reasonable amount that should be paid by the unsuccessful party rather than an exact measure of the actual costs of the successful litigant.

The principle of proportionality is essentially a principle of common sense and is fundamental to any decision on what constitutes a fair and just order of costs. This principle was considered in the case of *Buchanan v. Geotel Communications Corp.*, [2002] OJ No. 3063 (Ont. SCJ) where Ferguson J at paras. 10-11 states:

> ¶ 10 Having said all that, the bottom line is that the proposed costs are excessive. They are excessive from two perspectives: costs of this magnitude will make litigation inaccessible as a method of dispute resolution; costs of this magnitude are also disproportionate to the value of the legal work reasonably necessary to represent a client in this dispute.
>
> ¶ 11 If counsel do not use more restraint in deciding how much to invest in litigation they will put both the bar and the courts out of business which will profoundly harm the public whom we both serve.

Further, with regard to escalating costs and proportionality, Mr. Justice Killeen in *Pagnotta v. Brown*, [2002] OJ No. 3033 (Ont. SCJ) at paras. 24-25 states:

> ¶ 24 From my perspective, if lawyers wish to expend such grossly inordinate amounts of billable hours on relatively routine cases, they may feel free to do so, subject to their client's approval, but they cannot expect judges to encourage such inefficient expenditures of time when their costs are to be fixed following upon a trial.
>
> ¶ 25 Judges and assessment officers have a duty to fix or assess costs at reasonable amounts and, in this process, they have a duty to make sure that the hours spent can be reasonably justified. The losing party is not to be treated as a money tree to be plucked, willy nilly, by the winner of the contest.

I agree that it would be extremely excessive to award approximately two and a half times more in costs than the plaintiff recovered at trial. When I gave my directions to the jury, I told them to treat an insurance company as they would treat an individual. Obvi-

ously counsel for the plaintiff was not listening as he would not have made this outlandish claim for costs.

Conduct of the Plaintiff That Unnecessarily Lengthened the Proceeding

This action was unnecessarily complicated by the plaintiff. This was a relatively straightforward action for breach of contract. The plaintiff engaged in the following conduct that
lengthened the proceedings:

- unnecessary motions with no basis in law;
- pursuing claims for "negligent adjusting," exemplary, aggravated and punitive damages that were not supported by any evidence.

I agree with J. MacDonald J's decision on limited success and small recovery in *Stewart v. Canadian Broadcasting Corp.*, [1997] OJ No. 4077 (Ont. Gen. Div.). She states as
follows:

> In fixing an award of costs that reflected the plaintiff's limited success and small recovery,
> the court holds that the plaintiff failed in numerous aspects of his claims against the defend-
> ant. Further, the legal requirement that determine costs on the merits of the lawsuit must
> take into account both the lack of merit in the plaintiff's failed allegations against the de-
> fendant and the low assessed value of the plaintiff's successful allegations.

The plaintiff seems to rely on the fact that the defendant will continue to pay benefits
on the policy in the future. This argument does not warrant granting additional costs.
The fact that payments will continue flows directly from the jury's decision of reinstating
the plaintiff's rights under the contract. In *Family Law*, increased costs are not granted
because a wife obtains lifetime support from her husband that could amount to millions
of dollars in the future.

I agree with the defendant that the decision in *Mills v. Raymond*, [1997] OJ No. 4083
(Ont. Div. Ct.) stands for the proposition that where a party makes a subsequent offer, it
implies the cancellation or withdrawal of a previous offer. As a result, I rule that only the
plaintiff's October 12, 2007 offer and not her August 11, 2006 offer need be considered
here.

Further, I rule that the plaintiff's November 12, 2007 offer can be considered and can
attract Rule 49 consequences. *Lindsay Paper Box Co. v. Schubert International Manufacturing Inc.*, [1992] OJ No. 798 (Ont. Gen. Div.) was such a case where the court found
that an offer to settle does not have to be in the form prescribed by Rule 49. Rule 49.13
also states that a judge "may take into account any offer to settle made in writing, the date
the offer was made and the terms of the offer."

I rule that the plaintiff's offer made on November 12, 2007 to settle for $480,000.00
plus costs to have the defendant buy out the plaintiff's contract entitles the plaintiff to a
$10,000.00 increase on my award of costs to her. I further rule that if substantial indem-
nity costs are considered, it would be for services rendered after the plaintiff's October
12, 2007 offer. However since this litigation was not complex and taking into consideration what the defendant ought to have expected to pay, I award the plaintiff $90,000.00
inclusive of fees, disbursements and GST.

The plaintiff is asking for the following award on costs:

Total Fee	$124,830.00
Total Law Clerk Fee	$ 6,602.00
Counsel Fee	$ 14,000.00
Premium	$ 50,000.00
Disbursements	$ 37,500.98
GST	$ 13,975.98
Grand Total	**$246,908.96**

I am using my discretion to award $90,000.00 in costs and I reject the following claims for the reasons mentioned earlier:

(a) I refuse the claim for premium—$50,000.00
(b) Motion's work (rejected)—$30,000.00
(c) Disbursements:
   Claim for Dr. Cooke (rejected)—$2,142.14
   Claim for printing (rejected)—$5,000.00
   Claim for photocopies (rejected)—$2,025.40
(d) The plaintiff's bill of costs claims $58,000.00 or $34,112.32 more for trial. I rule that it is excessive and reduce it by $23,887.68

I further rule that because the plaintiff made an offer on the eve of trial, to settle all matters for $480,000.00, I grant the plaintiff $10,000.00 that is included in the $90,000.00 awarded. While the jury awarded the plaintiff less money, her entitlement is nevertheless ongoing until such time in the future when her disability benefits might cease for a number of reasons that I need not go into.

Order accordingly.

NOTES AND QUESTIONS

1. Do the amounts awarded for costs in *Maracle* and *Barlow* seem "fair and reasonable"? Why or why not?

2. Are the cost awards in *Maracle* and *Barlow* proportional to the specific matter pursued by the litigants? If not, why not? For example, in *Barlow*, the plaintiff asked for costs in an amount equal to two and a half times the value of the monetary damages awarded in the case.

3. How do the cost awards parallel the market price paid for legal services in each case? Should cost awards be a more exact measure of what are the actual costs to the litigant?

4. Are there any problems with the contextual, case-by-case approach to costs? How predictable are the results? Can litigants predict their costs with enough accuracy to make cost awards an appropriate incentive or disincentive to litigate?

The following case from the Supreme Court of Canada exposes the two dominant tensions within the law of costs: economics versus access to justice. The case also provides an important glimpse into the realities of the high cost of litigation today.

Kerr v. Danier Leather Inc.
[2007] 3 SCR 331

BINNIE J:

I. Introduction

This appeal raises questions about the continuous disclosure obligations of an issuer seeking to sell its shares to the public by a prospectus governed by the Ontario *Securities Act*, RSO 1990, c. S.5. Purchasers under a prospectus are given a statutory right of action if the prospectus or any amendment contains a misrepresentation against the issuer and officers of the issuer who signed the prospectus. ...

II. Overview

The warm days of spring are not a blessing for everyone, it seems. As temperatures rise, the sales of leather clothing can lag even in otherwise prospering leather goods retail stores. The downturn in sales may simply reflect the weather and indicate nothing negative about the strength of the underlying business, as turned out to be the case here. Nevertheless, about two weeks *after* closing, the respondents did issue a revised forecast indicating that Danier would fall short of the sales and net income figures in the original forecast. Danier's share price dropped by about 22 percent. It took until August 2000 for the shares to get back to their issue price. By then, Danier's business had grown substantially.

A number of purchasers had sold their new shares soon after the announcement and lost money. The appellants then initiated a class action against the respondents for failure to disclose material information, i.e., the disappointing intra-quarterly results. They argued that the prospectus contained a misrepresentation on the closing date (May 20), because even though the year-end sales forecast was reasonable on the filing date (May 6), lagging sales thereafter rendered it misleading to management's knowledge at the date of closing. The respondents, they argued, "omi[tted] to state a material fact [i.e., lagging sales] that is ... necessary to make a statement [i.e., the sales forecast in the prospectus] not misleading in the light of the circumstances in which it was made," and this constituted an actionable misrepresentation within the meaning of ss. 1 and 130 of the Act.

The respondents reply, in essence, that they fully complied with their regulatory obligations. The legislature cannot have intended to punish under s. 130(1) what it has permitted under s. 57(1). Moreover, they say a sales forecast is not a "fact" but reflects the opinions of management, and such opinions when held in good faith (as here) are protected by the Business Judgment Rule. The issues were thus joined.

. . .

VII. Costs

The appellant Durst argued that the Court of Appeal erred as a matter of law in awarding costs against him as the representative plaintiff because of its misinterpretation of s. 31(1) of the *Class Proceedings Act, 1992*. Quite apart from s. 31(1), he says, general concerns about access to justice justified a departure from the usual rule that costs follow the event. The Court of Appeal, in effect, held that there was no more reason in this case for the successful defendants to carry the full costs of the defence than in any other commercial litigation.

The costs of the proceedings in the courts below were very much in the discretion of the Court of Appeal: *Courts of Justice Act*, RSO 1990, c. C.43, s. 131. I would not interfere with its disposition.

There is no doubt that the representative plaintiff, Mr. Durst, was outraged by what he regarded as the devious conduct of the respondents, and considered that it was in the public interest to call them to account. Nevertheless, he also has a major personal financial interest in the outcome. He purchased 222,600 shares in Danier's IPO and made a profit of approximately $1.5 million when he sold these shares. If the trial judgment had not been reversed on appeal, he would also have recovered an additional $518,410 by way of damages. He acknowledged that he was a person of substance, with an investment portfolio in the range of $11-22 million. (Although put forward as potential representative plaintiffs, the certification judge considered the appellants Douglas Kerr and S. Grace Kerr unacceptable in that role because Ms. Kerr was a partner in the law firm seeking to be class counsel (para. 68) and that "[a]s a general principle, it is best that there is no appearance of impropriety. In this situation, there is the perception of a potential for abuse by class counsel through acting in their own self-interest rather than in the interests of the class" (para. 72). Accordingly, "the Kerrs are not approved as representative plaintiffs. Mr. Durst is approved as the sole representative plaintiff" (para. 73).)

There is nothing to be criticized in any of this. The trial judge noted that the costs incurred by Mr. Durst in this litigation outweighed any personal financial benefit. However, protracted litigation has become the sport of kings in the sense that only kings or equivalent can afford it. Those who inflict it on others in the hope of significant personal gain and fail can generally expect adverse cost consequences.

The appellants are correct to point out that there is a strong public interest in setting the rules of adequate disclosure by issuers prior to closing, that indeed proper disclosure is the heart and soul of the securities regulations across Canada. However, regard must also be had to the situation of the respondents/defendants who have incurred the costs of a 44-day trial and 5 days in the Court of Appeal and one day here to defend themselves against serious allegations, and who in this instance have prevailed.

Section 31(1) of the *Class Proceedings Act, 1992*, provides:

> 31(1) In exercising its discretion with respect to costs under subsection 131(1) of the *Courts of Justice Act*, the court may consider whether the class proceeding was a test case, raised a novel point of law or involved a matter of public interest.

It has not been established that this is a "test case" in the conventional sense of a case selected to resolve a legal issue applicable to other pending or anticipated litigation. Nor have the appellants raised a "novel point of law." As we have seen, the heart of the case is simply a shareholder dispute over a lot of money requiring the application of well settled principles of statutory interpretation to particular legislative provisions. This is the usual fodder of commercial litigation (see generally *Gariepy v. Shell Oil Co.* (2002), 23 CPC (5th) 393 (Ont. SCJ), aff'd. [2004] OJ No. 5309 (Ont. SCJ), at para. 8; *Moyes v. Fortune Financial Corp.* (2002), 61 OR (3d) 770 (Ont. SCJ), at paras. 4-5).

While counsel for the appellants have put before the Court exhaustive research into the US jurisprudence on different variants of statutory language, and have said what could be said on their clients' behalf, the proper interpretation of s. 130(1) of the Ontario Act has from the outset been the time bomb ticking under their case. The respondents attempted to have this issue determined in their favour on a motion for summary judgment heard in December 2000 but were unsuccessful. The result was a very expensive piece of shareholder litigation, but there is no magic in the form of a class action proceeding that should in this case deprive the respondents of their costs. The language of s. 31(1) is permissive.

The *Class Proceedings Act, 1992* uses the expression "matter of public interest" in s. 31(1) in the sense of a matter that involves "either issues of broad public importance or persons who are historically disadvantaged in society" (footnotes omitted) (M.M. Orkin, *The Law of Costs* (2nd ed., loose-leaf ed.), vol. 1, at § 208.2.1). The appellants contend that the present case raises a matter of public interest, indeed they say that this may well be "the first Canadian case to consider statutory prospectus misrepresentation" (Supp. AF, at para. 1). However, this is a dispute where private commercial interests predominated.

We are certainly not dealing with people on either side who are historically disadvantaged. Nor, as the Court of Appeal noted, "is it a contest characterized by significant power imbalance" ([2006] OJ No. 3770 (Ont. CA), at para. 6). Though many Canadians are investors and the resolution of the present dispute will affect future actions for prospectus misrepresentation, the Court of Appeal rightly concluded that this is, in essence, "a commercial dispute between sophisticated commercial actors who are well resourced" (*ibid.*). If anything, converting an ordinary piece of commercial litigation into a class proceeding may be seen by some observers simply as an *in terrorem* strategy to try to force a settlement. Be that as it may, Mr. Durst was well aware that as a representative plaintiff he ran the risk of being held solely responsible for the defendants' costs if the action failed. He gambled on his interpretation of s. 130(1) and lost.

Nor do general concerns about access to justice warrant a departure from the usual cost consequences in this case. While I agree with counsel for the appellants that "[a]n award of costs that exceeds or outweighs the potential benefits of litigation raises access to justice issues" (Supp. AF, at para. 39), it should not be assumed that class proceedings invariably engage access to justice concerns to an extent sufficient to justify withholding costs from the successful party. I agree with the observation of Nordheimer J in *Gariepy* that caution must be exercised not to stereotype class proceedings. "[T]he David against Goliath scenario" he writes, "does not necessarily represent an accurate portrayal of the real conflict" (para. 6). Class actions have become a staple of shareholder litigation. The Court of Appeal took the view that this case is a piece of Bay Street litigation that was well run and well financed on both sides. Success would have reaped substantial rewards for the representative plaintiff and his counsel. He put the representative respondents to enormous expense and I see no error in principle that would justify our intervention in the discretionary costs order made against him by the Court of Appeal.

By the time it reached this Court, the case had narrowed to a half-day argument about statutory interpretation. The legal issue is important, as is required for leave to be granted under s. 40 of the *Supreme Court Act*, RSC 1985, c. S-26, but the circumstances already discussed do not justify our Court in departing from the usual rule that costs follow the result.

In the Court of Appeal, the costs were awarded only against the then respondent Durst. In this Court, the respondents claim costs only against the appellant Durst. It appears from the material before us that the appellants Douglas Kerr and S. Grace Kerr took no active role in the appeal to this Court. Yet, the appellants' supplementary factum speaks of costs for or against "the appellants" (plural) (para. 8). On this record, costs should be awarded against the respondent Durst only, with leave to Durst, if he contends that the costs order should go against the Kerrs as well, to apply in writing to the Court for a variation of the costs order to include the Kerrs within 30 days from the date of this judgment. ...

NOTES AND QUESTIONS

1. Does the Supreme Court strike the right balance with respect to basic principles for awarding costs? Is this just a "piece of Bay Street litigation" or is there a public interest to this case?

2. Has litigation become too expensive—the "sport of kings?" What are the possible solutions for escalating costs of litigation? How can access to justice be achieved with such spiralling costs?

The dynamic between the economics of litigation and access to justice is markedly prevalent in cases where a lawyer takes the case on a contingency fee basis. Often, the lawyer must risk his or her time plus all the outstanding disbursements for months or years before any payment is made to the lawyer (assuming the client is successful in the case). If the client loses the case, the lawyer is not compensated and must cover the cost of disbursements himself or herself. In addition, the lawyer also has a lost opportunity cost—the lawyer could have worked on another matter that had a greater certainty of payment. Contingency fees are designed to provide access to legal services to those who could not afford to pay a lawyer's hourly rate up-front. Lawyers, therefore, often take cases on a contingency basis for indigent plaintiffs, particularly in personal injury litigation. The concept of a risk premium was introduced in order to incentivize lawyers to risk their time and money on behalf of indigent clients by taking on meritorious cases which have a high risk element (See, for example, *Desmoulin v. Blair* (1994), 21 OR (3d) 217 (Ont. CA).) The following case from the Supreme Court of Canada explored not only the notion of a risk premium on costs but the underpinnings of both contingency fees and fee shifting in the Canadian legal landscape.

Walker v. Ritchie
[2006] 2 SCR 428

ROTHSTEIN J:

I. Introduction

This appeal involves the appropriateness of an increase to a costs award, payable by the unsuccessful defendants to the plaintiffs, on the basis that counsel for the impecunious plaintiffs carried the risk of non-payment through the course of the litigation. This Court is asked to determine whether this risk was a relevant consideration within the costs scheme in place in Ontario at the time costs were fixed in this case. I conclude that it was not.

II. Facts

Stephanie Walker suffered serious personal injuries as a result of a motor vehicle accident. Ms. Walker and her family (the "plaintiffs") initiated litigation against Donald Ritchie, a truck driver, and his employer, Harold Marcus Limited (the "defendants"). The defendants denied liability throughout the course of the litigation and did not admit facts. The matter took four years to proceed to trial and involved issues the trial judge described as complex. During the litigation, the plaintiffs issued an offer to settle pursuant to Rule 49 of the Ontario *Rules of Civil Procedure*, RRO 1990, Reg. 194. The defendants rejected this offer.

At trial, the defendants were found 100 percent liable for the accident. Brockenshire J awarded the plaintiffs $5,168,317 in damages, inclusive of pre-judgment interest. As the plaintiffs' award exceeded their Rule 49 offer, the plaintiffs were entitled under Rule 49 to partial indemnity costs for the litigation up to the date of service of the offer and substantial indemnity costs from that point onward.

III. Decisions Below

A. Ontario Superior Court (2004), 2 CPC (6th) 163

Brockenshire J awarded $577,879.69 to the plaintiffs for fees and disbursements, inclusive of GST. He did so after reviewing the bill of costs submitted by the plaintiffs, which included claims for disbursements and fees for each step in the litigation.

Brockenshire J noted that a "huge amount of time went into this file" (para. 13). Nevertheless, he found that most of the hours claimed by the plaintiffs' counsel in the bill of costs were reasonable. This determination was based primarily upon the complexity of the proceedings and the fact that the plaintiffs were put to their proof on every issue because of the defendants' refusal to admit facts. Moreover, Brockenshire J held that it was appropriate for the hourly rate for the plaintiffs' primary counsel to be set at the highest level on both the partial indemnity and the substantial indemnity scales under the Tariff. As Brockenshire J stated: "the top rate is for the most experienced lawyer in the most complex and important cases" (para. 18).

In addition, Brockenshire J also ordered the defendants to pay a premium of $192,600, inclusive of GST. He found that counsel for the plaintiffs had carried the litigation for four years without remuneration because the plaintiffs could not afford it. Liability was not admitted, and as such, plaintiffs' counsel faced the risk of non-payment. On the basis of this risk and the result achieved, Brockenshire J held it was appropriate to award the premium.

B. *Ontario Court of Appeal (2005), 12 CPC (6th) 51*

Gillese and Lang JJA, for a unanimous panel, upheld the risk premium of $192,600 awarded by Brockenshire JA premium payable by defendants had been upheld by the Ontario Court of Appeal previously, where the defendant was required to pay substantial indemnity costs: *Lurtz v. Duchesne* (2005), 194 OAC 119 (Ont. CA). Gillese and Lang JJA held that a risk premium can be awarded against a defendant where the plaintiff is entitled to substantial indemnity costs under Rule 49, but rejected the argument that premiums are available when the plaintiff is only entitled to partial indemnity costs.

Gillese and Lang JJA emphasized that risk premiums should rarely be awarded. The imposition of such a premium can only be justified where there is both risk of non-payment and an "outstanding result."

They defined risk as having the following features: (1) the plaintiff lacked the financial resources to fund lengthy and complex litigation; (2) plaintiff's counsel financed the litigation; (3) the defendant contested liability; and (4) plaintiff's counsel assumed the risk not only of delayed but possible non-payment of fees.

IV. Analysis

A. *Development of Risk Premiums as Between Plaintiff and Plaintiff's Counsel*

While this case does not concern fee arrangements between solicitor and client, it is first necessary to provide some background about these arrangements before turning to the question of whether a risk premium should be payable by an unsuccessful defendant.

As between solicitor and client, fees for litigation may be payable without regard to the outcome of the case or may be contingent on the result obtained. A contingency fee arrangement is typically used by plaintiff's counsel where there is the prospect of receiving a damages award. If the plaintiff's case is lost, the lawyer receives no payment. If the plaintiff's case is won, the lawyer receives a pre-determined percentage of the damages award or a fixed fee. Thus, where counsel expends time and incurs disbursements on behalf of a client, that lawyer assumes the risk of non-payment for those services and disbursements should the litigation prove unsuccessful. To compensate for this risk, a contingency fee will typically be higher than that which would have been payable had counsel billed the client irrespective of the outcome.

Prior to 2002, and at the time applicable to this case, contingency fee arrangements were barred in Ontario. Contingency fee arrangements had been seen as violating the rule against champerty, as it was considered undesirable for lawyers to have a pecuniary interest in the outcome of their clients' litigation. As a means of promoting access to justice, contingency fee arrangements are now permitted in Ontario, but are regulated by the *Solicitors Act*, RSO 1990, c. S.15 (as amended by SO 2002, c. 24, Sched. A). See also *McIntyre Estate v. Ontario (Attorney General)* (2002), 61 OR (3d) 257 (Ont. CA).

Even before the introduction of contingency fee arrangements, lawyers still represented impecunious plaintiffs. Given the plaintiff's impecuniosity, efforts to enforce a debt for fees and disbursements against the plaintiff might prove fruitless. However, where the plaintiff successfully received a damage award, he/she would now have the means to pay counsel. In *Stribbell v. Bhalla* (1990), 73 OR (2d) 748 (Ont. HC), Osborne J (as he then was) held it was not champertous for an impecunious plaintiff to pay his counsel fees out of his damage award. In his view, such a payment by the plaintiff was necessary to ensure access to justice and to ensure that deserving actions be prosecuted by competent counsel.

In *Desmoulin v. Blair* (1994), 21 OR (3d) 217 (Ont. CA), Austin JA upheld a risk premium payable by a plaintiff to his counsel out of his award of damages. The plaintiff was impecunious. Counsel pursued the lengthy personal injury litigation without being paid and obtained a large judgment in favour of the plaintiff. After the successful conclusion of the trial, plaintiff's counsel rendered a bill to the client, a portion of which represented an amount over and above counsel's hourly rate. This premium was added by counsel to take into account the risk of non-payment borne by counsel. Austin JA held that the premium was justified as the taking on of litigation on behalf of impecunious plaintiffs should be encouraged in appropriate ways. The plaintiff did not qualify for legal aid but could not otherwise fund the litigation, as contingency fee agreements were not permitted in Ontario at the time. Austin J.A. emphasized that premiums should only be assessed where there "was a very real risk of an adverse finding on the issue of liability": *Desmoulin*, at p. 223.

As indicated, when counsel took on the plaintiffs' claims in this case, contingency arrangements were not permitted. The trial judge found plaintiffs' counsel carried the litigation, in the face of the defendants' denial of liability, through its four-year duration with no remuneration due to the impecuniosity of the plaintiffs. According to *Desmoulin* it appears plaintiffs' counsel may have been entitled to charge the plaintiffs a risk premium.

The propriety of a risk premium between lawyer and client is not challenged in this appeal. At issue is whether the plaintiffs' costs award, payable by the unsuccessful defendants, should be increased to take into account the risk of non-payment to the plaintiffs' counsel.

B. Ontario Costs Scheme at the Relevant Time

Costs awards made by trial judges should be accorded a high degree of deference: *British Columbia (Minister of Forests) v. Okanagan Indian Band*, [2003] 3 SCR 371, 2003 SCC 71 (SCC), at paras. 42-43; *Hamilton v. Open Window Bakery Ltd.* (2003), [2004] 1 SCR 303, 2004 SCC 9 (SCC), at para. 27. However, as LeBel J stated in *Okanagan Indian Band*, at para. 43: "An appellate court may and should intervene where it finds that the trial judge has misdirected himself as to the applicable law." In this case, the Court must look to the law governing costs in Ontario.

Ontario courts have discretion over costs; however, that discretion is not unlimited. [The Court cited to s. 131(1) of the *Courts of Justice Act*, RSO 1990, c. C.43.]

Thus, the determination of whether risk of non-payment to plaintiff's counsel was an appropriate consideration requires an examination of the relevant Ontario legislative scheme governing the fixation of costs, which is contained in the *Rules of Civil Procedure*.

Rule 57.01(1) sets out the factors a court is to consider when exercising its discretion over costs. [At the time costs were fixed in this case, Rule 57.01(1) did not have subsections (0.a) and (0.b).] ...

Rule 57.01(1) guides a court's determination of the quantum of a costs award. While indemnification is and always has been one of the cornerstones of a costs award, the scheme in place at the time costs were fixed in this case was not one of full indemnity. An entitled party did not simply send its lawyer's bill to the other side. Rather, the quantum a party would receive as an indemnity was governed by the factors set out in Rule 57.01(1) and the Tariff. Rule 57.01(3) provided: "When the court awards costs, it shall fix them in accordance with subrule (1) and the Tariffs."

At the time costs were fixed in this case, the fee portion of the Tariff consisted of a costs grid with two scales: "partial indemnity" and "substantial indemnity." Each scale set hourly or daily maximums for various steps in the litigation process taking into consideration the experience and expertise of counsel.

Where a plaintiff makes an offer under Rule 49 and the plaintiff obtains a judgment as favourable or more favourable than that offer, the plaintiff is entitled to costs on the partial indemnity scale up to the point of offer and on the substantial indemnity scale from the point of offer onward unless the court orders otherwise. In this way, Rule 49 acts as a settlement incentive for a defendant to accept a reasonable offer. This settlement incentive under Rule 49, however, works both ways. If a defendant makes an offer to settle and the plaintiff obtains a judgment as favourable or less favourable than the offer, the plaintiff is entitled to costs on the partial indemnity scale up to the date of the service of the offer, but the unsuccessful defendant is entitled to costs on the partial indemnity scale from the point of offer onward unless the court orders otherwise. ...

C. Does Risk of Non-Payment to Plaintiffs' Counsel Fall Within Rule 57.01(1)(i)?

Risk of non-payment to plaintiffs' counsel is not an enumerated factor under Rule 57.01(1). Can it be said that such risk falls within para. (i) as "any other matter relevant to the question of costs"? While these words are broad, from the scheme of Rule 57.01(1) I infer they are not unlimited. If the court's discretion to consider costs was unlimited, there would have been no need for paras. (a) to (h). On the contrary, I think the enumerated considerations in paras. (a) to (h) provide guidance as to matters that might be considered relevant in para. (i).

Indeed, the Latin maxim *esjudem generis*, or the limited class rule, is helpful in determining legislative intent when a court is faced with a list of items followed by a general term. As R. Sullivan explains in *Sullivan and Driedger on the Construction of Statutes* (4th ed. 2002), at pp. 175-77, the scope of the general term may be limited to any genus or class to which the specific items all belong. An examination of the factors that were expressly included at the time the costs award was fixed in this case reveals some common features among them.

First, the factors in place at the relevant time could be described as neutral. They applied to either a plaintiff or a defendant and typically either increased or decreased a costs award against one of those parties. Risk of non-payment to plaintiff's counsel lacks such neutrality. Taking risk into consideration would result in an increase in the costs awarded only against the defendant.

Second, the enumerated factors in place at the relevant time fell within one of two categories. They dealt either with the nature of the case or the conduct of the parties in the litigation. Parties to litigation have knowledge about the nature of the case and can control their own conduct in the litigation. Therefore, the parties are capable of predicting, generally, how such factors would affect a costs award against them, and may thereby be guided as to whether or not to settle or to proceed. By contrast, a risk premium is a financial arrangement between the plaintiffs and their counsel. It is not a matter about which the defendant would normally have knowledge, nor is it a matter about which the defendant is entitled to know. The risk premium does not fall within either of the categories of knowledge or control. It is a function of either the plaintiff's financial circumstances or simply the fee agreement between the plaintiff and counsel.

Application of the *esjudem generis* rule would suggest that it was not the intention of its framers that para. (i) would include the risk of non-payment to plaintiffs' counsel as a relevant factor to consider in an award of costs against an unsuccessful defendant. Unsuccessful defendants should expect to pay similar amounts by way of costs across similar pieces of litigation involving similar conduct and counsel, regardless of what arrangements the particular plaintiff may have concluded with counsel.

In the Ontario Court of Appeal, Gillese and Lang JJA concluded that the specific arrangement between plaintiff and counsel was not to be considered when an award of partial indemnity costs was ordered. Thus, a risk premium could not be assessed against a different unsuccessful defendant in this case. (At trial, an award of damages and partial indemnity costs including a risk premium was made against the Wawanesa Mutual Insurance Company. The Court of Appeal reversed on the issue of risk premium and that aspect of the decision was not appealed to this Court.) At para. 113 of their reasons, Gillese and Lang JJA stated:

> A defendant has no knowledge of the private arrangements between the plaintiff and his or her counsel and thus has no means of measuring the risk of engaging in litigation. Defendants would be unable to gauge their exposure to costs when deciding whether and how to defend as exposure would be dependent, at least in part, on the financial means of the plaintiff. This difficulty would be compounded by the fact that many plaintiffs would happily agree to any amount of premium if the premium were to be paid by the losing party. In situations where a party realistically understands that his or her exposure for costs is limited to an award on a partial indemnity basis, counsel ought not to be concerned that the normal elements of costs will be inflated by a private arrangement made between the other side and his or her counsel.

I agree with that reasoning. However, I see no reason why it would not be applicable when the court, under Rule 49, makes an award of costs on the substantial indemnity scale as opposed to the partial indemnity scale. Substantial indemnity costs were defined simply as costs payable on a higher scale than partial indemnity costs. As their name suggests, they were not intended to fully indemnify a party for any amount it may have undertaken to pay its counsel. I therefore see no basis for a difference in approach to the issue of a risk premium as between an award of partial or substantial indemnity costs.

In *Finlayson v. Roberts* (2000), 136 OAC 271 (Ont. CA), Carthy JA found that a risk premium was not assessable against the unsuccessful defendant when costs were awarded pursuant to Rule 49. At para. 25 he stated:

> A premium fee does not fit with rule 49 concerns and is unfair to a defendant. On the date of an offer to settle, the risk of refusal is of future costs which can be measured against general experience. A defendant has no knowledge of private arrangements between the plaintiff and her counsel, and thus has no means of measuring the risk of refusing the plaintiff's offer. ... To inflict [a risk premium] upon the defendant under rule 49 turns the rule from one that induces and encourages settlements, to a rule that penalizes a defendant for not accepting an offer by imposing what may be a totally unexpected obligation in an unknown amount. It also introduces the added difficulty presented by typical plaintiffs who would happily agree to any amount of premium that an insurer pays to counsel.

Finlayson was distinguished in *Lurtz* on the basis that in *Finlayson* liability was admitted and the risk premium was pursuant to an agreement and not necessarily because the plaintiff was impecunious. However, I see nothing in Carthy JA's reasons that purports to limit his view to cases where liability is admitted or to cases in which the risk premium agreement is not as a result of the impecuniosity of the plaintiff. As I read *Finlayson*, its reasoning can and should be applied to any assessment of costs flowing from a Rule 49 offer to settle. Carthy JA concludes at para. 28 of *Finlayson*:

> I therefore conclude that what is commonly known as a "risk premium" should not be included in a solicitor and client assessment under rule 49.

Carthy JA's approach, with which I am in substantial agreement, provides strong reasoning as to why a risk premium is not to be included in an award of substantial indemnity costs under Rule 49.

The assessment of risk premiums against unsuccessful defendants has been rejected in the United States. While there are different considerations as between the United States and Ontario cost schemes, the risk analysis by the United States Supreme Court is instructive. As pointed out by Scalia J for the majority of the Court in *City of Burlington v. Dague*, 505 US 557 (USSC 1992), where payment to plaintiff's counsel is dependent upon the plaintiff achieving a favourable result, counsel's risk of non-payment is directly related to the plaintiff's risk of losing his/her case. Scalia J determined that a plaintiff's risk of loss is a product of two factors: (1) the factual or legal merits of the plaintiff's case; and (2) the difficulty in establishing those merits. He explained that assessing costs against the defendant for the first component of risk leads to undesirable consequences while the second component of risk is already subsumed in the costs award without the need for a premium.

In my view the same reasoning applies to the Ontario costs scheme. As to the legal and factual merits of the plaintiff's claim, the more risky a case is to the plaintiff, the more defensible it is to the defendant. The threat of a risk premium would incline defendants with meritorious defences to settle. This increased tendency to settle brings with it an undesirable corollary effect—it would encourage plaintiffs to pursue the least meritorious claims. Encouraging plaintiffs to pursue the least meritorious claims is not an objective which the costs scheme should promote.

As to the difficulty of establishing the legal and factual merits of the plaintiff's claim, the complexity of the legal and factual issues in a particular case and the unwillingness of a defendant to admit liability or facts make it more difficult for the plaintiff to prove his/her case. This necessarily increases the risk of the plaintiff achieving an unfavourable result, and in turn, increases the risk to a lawyer whose payment is contingent upon that result. Moreover, these factors often lead to protracted litigation requiring additional time on behalf of plaintiff's counsel thereby increasing counsel's investment in the matter. Complexity may also require a more experienced or expert counsel to achieve a favourable result, whose investment of time is more valuable.

These factors, however, should already be taken into account by a court when it fixes costs. Complexity, length, result, and a failure to admit are enumerated factors under Rule 57.01(1) and experience and expertise of counsel were taken into consideration according to the express terms of the Tariff. Indeed, in this case the trial judge noted that while the costs award was "substantial" it was fair and reasonable. A full reading of his reasons indicates that he considered all of the above factors in arriving at that award. Compensating for these factors again through the addition of a risk premium arguably constitutes a double count in the costs award against the unsuccessful defendant.

D. Do Access to Justice Considerations Make Risk of Non-Payment a Relevant Factor Under Rule 57.01(1)(i)?

The plaintiffs argued that risk premiums payable by defendants encourage counsel to take on the cases of impecunious plaintiffs and therefore promote access to justice. They rely on *Okanagan Indian Band* in arguing that access to justice makes risk of non-payment to plaintiffs' counsel a relevant consideration under the Ontario scheme.

Okanagan Indian Band involved an interim award of costs payable by the government to enable the Indian Band to engage in the litigation. LeBel J emphasized that a defendant should only be required to carry the burden of ensuring an opponent's access to justice in the most exceptional of circumstances. One of the requirements of the test is that the plaintiff "no other realistic option exists for bringing the issues to trial": *Okanagan Indian Band*, at para. 40.

Personal injury cases involve the prospect of receiving a favourable judgment out of which an impecunious plaintiff can pay a lawyer's fee. Thus, if successful, counsel will receive payment for the disbursements made and services rendered, i.e. what counsel would have received on an ongoing basis had the client been financially capable of paying. In addition to the delay in payment, however, such counsel bears the risk of non-payment if success is not achieved. This requires a further incentive for counsel to be willing to take on such cases. In other words, counsel will look to be compensated for providing the additional service of financing the litigation at his/her own risk.

This is the concern that the Ontario courts first responded to by permitting counsel to charge plaintiffs a risk premium. In addition, it is now met through legislation permitting counsel to charge contingency fees: see the *Solicitors Act* and the *Class Proceedings Act, 1992*, SO 1992, c. 6. The opportunity for counsel to charge his or her own client a risk premium, or now a contingency fee, encourages competent counsel to take on the cases of impecunious plaintiffs. Such a charge is not dependent upon the amount the plaintiff recovers from the opposing party in a costs award. The appropriate source of encourage-ment lies with the client not with his or her opponent. Requiring unsuccessful defend-ants to pay a premium to the plaintiffs in personal injury cases is not compelled on the theory of promoting access to justice.

The plaintiffs have also argued that risk premiums payable by unsuccessful defendants are required to provide access to justice to impecunious plaintiffs who, even if successful, will receive no or minimal damages given the nature of their case, such as a challenge under the *Canadian Charter of Rights and Freedoms*. In the absence of the prospect of a significant damage award out of which fees may be charged, there is little incentive for competent counsel to take on such cases. Nonetheless, I have difficulty placing serious weight on this argument. There are a number of other alternatives that bring these cases to trial. For example, plaintiffs in such cases may qualify for some form of legal aid, re-ceive funds to pursue the litigation from a private source, find counsel to take on the case on a *pro bono* basis, or, in rare cases, be entitled to an interim costs award. While there may be a plaintiff who is unable to secure one of these alternatives, the costs scheme does not aim at perfection. Risk premiums cannot be justified on this basis.

V. *Conclusion*

I conclude that risk of non-payment to the plaintiffs' lawyer was not a relevant factor under the costs scheme in Rule 57.01(1) at the time costs were fixed in this case. The ap-peal is allowed with costs and the premium in the amount of $192,600 is set aside.

These reasons apply to the costs scheme in place in Ontario at the time costs were fixed in this case. Since that time the costs scheme has been modified in a number of ways. Whether or not the reasoning in this judgment applies to the costs scheme cur-rently in place will be an issue for the courts as the occasion arises.

NOTES AND QUESTIONS

1. In July 2005, prior to the Supreme Court of Canada's reasons in *Walker v. Ritchie*, On-tario's Civil Rules Committee revised rule 57.01 to include two additional factors:

(0.a) the principle of indemnity, including, where applicable, the experience of the lawyer for the party entitled to the costs as well as the rates charged and the hours spent by that lawyer;

(0.b) the amount of costs that an unsuccessful party could reasonably expect to pay in rela-tion to the step in the proceeding for which costs are being fixed;

The specific inclusion of "indemnity" is noteworthy. The "costs grid" was also abolished.

2. The *Walker* case appeared to end the practice of courts granting additional risk pre-miums to successful plaintiffs. Courts reversed such awards post-*Walker*. In *Ward v. Manu-facturers Life Insurance Co.*, 2007 ONCA 881, the Court of Appeal for Ontario reversed a

risk premium and interpreted the newly worded rule 57.01 within the context of "indemnity" at para. 69:

> The concerns underlying the decision in *Walker* apply equally to the new language of Rule 57.01. First, the new factors, like the old ones, are neutral in character and can apply equally to plaintiffs or defendants. Second, although the new factors do not specifically relate to the nature of the case or the conduct of the parties, they serve to uphold the principles of transparency and predictability that should govern costs awards. The two new factors merely make explicit the fact that, in the absence of a costs grid, there should be fairness and consistency in the amount that can be charged for lawyers' time across similar pieces of litigation involving similar conduct and counsel.
>
> I would note that the phrase "the principle of indemnity" in the new legislation is qualified. The listed considerations are the experience of the lawyer, the rates charged, and the hours spent. While the clause is phrased inclusively, a risk premium is not of like kind to these considerations.
>
> Clause (0.b) confirms this interpretation by insisting that costs be what the unsuccessful party could "reasonably expect to pay." This engages the other concern about risk premiums explicit in *Walker*: that the defendant is not aware of his potential cost exposure because the premium is a private agreement between the plaintiff and his counsel. As noted in *Walker*, this is particularly important where, as here, a Rule 49 offer to settle has been made, and the defendant must be aware of the risk of refusing the plaintiff's offer.

3. However, despite *Walker* and cases such as *Ward*, some courts continue to award a kind of risk premium to lawyers who take on meritorious, risky cases. They do so by reference to the enumerated factors in rule 57.01. For example, in *Sandhu v. Wellington Place Apartments*, 2008 ONCA 215, the Court of Appeal for Ontario reversed a $350,000 risk premium awarded at trial because it was awarded for reasons of risk. Instead, the Court increased the costs award by $50,000 and used the enumerated factors in rule 57.01 to justify the increase—namely, that the case was complex and lengthy, the issues were important, and the result achieved was outstanding. In *Berendsen v. Ontario*, 2008 CarswellOnt 4142 (SCJ), while acknowledging that *Walker* and *Ward* eliminated risk premiums, the trial judge nevertheless awarded a $50,000 "cost premium" to the plaintiff's counsel because the case was complex and important.

4. Why are courts compelled to award such premiums? Are cost premiums a good idea? Fair to defendants? Do they incentivize lawyers to take on meritorious, risky cases? Do they provide greater access to justice?

5. The dynamic of fee shifting is complicated when multiple parties participate in a litigation matter. To who are the fees shifted? What if there is divided success among various parties? Courts have used two types of costs orders when determining costs in multiparty litigation: Bullock and Sanderson orders. A Bullock order directs an unsuccessful defendant to reimburse a plaintiff for the fee-shifted costs that the plaintiff had to pay to a successful defendant. A Sanderson order directs that the unsuccessful defendant pay the successful defendant's costs directly. For the specific legal doctrine behind each of these costs orders in multiparty litigation, see *Rooney v. Graham* (2001), 53 OR (3d) 685 (CA) and *Moore v. Weinecke*, 2008 ONCA 162 (CA). Strategically, when should courts use a Sanderson order instead of a Bullock order, or vice versa (hint: think of the inability of a party to collect from another party)?

C. Disciplinary Use of Costs

The normal practice of ordering costs to follow the event is itself a rule for regulating the conduct of litigation because it is designed to discourage unmeritorious litigation. A court can use the device of costs to discourage abuse of the procedural system; to regulate the conduct of parties and their lawyers; and, in some small way, to deal more equitably with distributing the cost of litigation.

The court's use of costs as a disciplinary tool has as its starting point the generally expected outcome that the successful party will receive an award of costs on a party-and-party or partial indemnity scale. If the court wants to discipline a successful party, all or part of that expected award of costs may be disallowed. If the court wanted to discipline an unsuccessful party, the court may increase the ordinary award of costs on a party-and-party scale to an award of costs on a solicitor-and-client or substantial indemnity scale. The latter scale is intended to be a more complete indemnity for the actual costs and fees incurred in the litigation.

The Rules provide some guidance as to when a lawyer may be subject to discipline through the costs system. For example, Ontario's rule 57.07 states:

> 57.07(1) Where a lawyer for a party has caused costs to be incurred without reasonable cause or to be wasted by undue delay, negligence or other default, the court may make an order,
>
> > (a) disallowing costs between the lawyer and client or directing the lawyer to repay to the client money paid on account of costs;
> >
> > (b) directing the lawyer to reimburse the client for any costs that the client has been ordered to pay to any other party; and
> >
> > (c) requiring the lawyer personally to pay the costs of any party.

See also British Columbia (rule 57(30)) and Nova Scotia (rule 63.15(2)). There is some ambiguity in the case law as to when a court will intervene to award solicitor-and-client or substantial indemnity costs for disciplinary reasons. The criteria expressed in the rules are not intended to be exhaustive; there are a multitude of judicial decisions considering the factual circumstances for an award of costs on an enhanced scale and the results often seem to be contradictory.

Apart from proven or unproven allegations of fraud or dishonest conduct, the assessment of the basis for solicitor-and-client or substantial indemnity costs is fact-specific and guided by prior examples and the court's own assessment of what is "exceptional." In *Hamilton v. Open Window Bakery Ltd.*, [2004] 1 SCR 303, 2004 SCC 9, the Supreme Court of Canada stated:

> In *Young v. Young*, [1993] 4 SCR 3, at p. 134, McLachlin J (as she then was) for a majority of this Court held that solicitor-and-client costs "are generally awarded only where there has been reprehensible, scandalous or outrageous conduct on the part of one of the parties." An unsuccessful attempt to prove fraud or dishonesty on a balance of probabilities does not lead inexorably to the conclusion that the unsuccessful party should be held liable for solicitor-and-client costs, since not all such attempts will be correctly considered to amount to "reprehensible, scandalous or outrageous conduct." However, allegations of fraud and dishonesty are serious and potentially very damaging to those accused of deception. When, as here, a party makes

such allegations unsuccessfully at trial and with access to information sufficient to conclude that the other party was merely negligent and neither dishonest nor fraudulent (as Wilkins J found), costs on a solicitor-and-client scale are appropriate: see, generally, M.M. Orkin, *The Law of Costs* (2nd ed. (loose-leaf)), at para. 219.

One of the issues raised by disciplinary costs orders is whether they are the most effective means of disciplining a party's conduct in litigation. Disciplinary costs orders also raise the question of the allocation of responsibility for wrongful acts in litigation between a party and his or her lawyer or in relation to non-parties. These issues are featured in the following case.

Standard Life Assurance Co. v. Elliott
(2007), 86 OR (3d) 221 (SCJ)

MOLLOY J:

Introduction

The plaintiff ("Standard Life") commenced this action against Bonnie Elliott in December, 2004 seeking to recover an overpayment of long-term disability benefits it alleged it paid to Ms Elliott mistakenly. Ms Elliott defended and counterclaimed. Ms Elliott also issued a Third Party Claim against KPMG and KPMG Management Services (Ms Elliott's employer at the time of her disability benefit claim) and against every individual past and present employee of Standard Life who had ever handled her file. She sought contribution and indemnity from those individual employees for any amount she might be found liable to repay to Standard Life. In its defence, Standard Life acknowledged that it is vicariously liable for all the acts of its employees.

On July 21, 2006, I heard a motion brought by the plaintiff and by those third parties who are current employees of the plaintiff seeking an order dismissing the third party claim in its entirety as against all the individual third parties. Counsel for the plaintiff also represented the position of the former employees who had been added as third parties, although not formally retained by them and although none of those individuals had as yet been served with the pleadings.

There is no additional recovery possible against the individuals that is not recoverable from Standard Life, given its admission of vicarious liability for all employees. I found that the third party claim failed to disclose a cause of action against the individuals and was an abuse of process as it had been brought solely for "procedural advantage." I struck out the third party claim as against those individuals and ruled that the successful parties were entitled to their costs. The successful parties sought those costs against the solicitor for the defendant in his personal capacity. Accordingly, the matter was adjourned for the filing of appropriate material and to permit both Ms Elliott and Mr. Masters (Ms Elliott's counsel in the action and on the motion) to obtain independent legal advice.

In the motion now before me, Standard Life (which funded the defence costs of the motion to dismiss the third party claim) seeks the costs of that earlier motion on a substantial indemnity basis, payable by Mr. Masters personally, or, alternatively, payable by Ms Elliott.

Material Filed on the Costs Motion

The moving parties filed a 10½ page solicitor's affidavit setting out the history of the action and referring to some conduct by Mr. Masters which is alleged to have unreasonably run up costs, specifically: threatening a class action if Standard Life did not abandon its defence; alleging deliberate withholding of evidence and production by Standard Life; refusing to meet to discuss settlement because of the alleged failure to make full production; persisting with the third party claim although warned that it was abusive and that a motion would be brought to strike it; and sending numerous repetitive and verbose letters. The moving parties also filed a 15-page factum and a case book containing the applicable Rules and six relevant cases.

Mr. Masters retained counsel to represent him on the motion. In response to the costs motion, he filed a two-volume affidavit, including 99 exhibits. The affidavit itself covers 89 pages of text and contains 375 paragraphs. Much of this material is completely irrelevant to anything I have to decide. A considerable amount of the material deals with the merits of Ms Elliott's defence to the action itself. Mr. Masters also filed a 28-page factum and a brief containing 17 cases.

In response to Mr. Masters' affidavit, the moving parties filed a supplementary affidavit addressing some of what they alleged were inaccuracies and a brief supplementary factum.

Ms Elliott retained independent counsel to represent her on the motion. She filed a brief affidavit in which she said she agreed with the accuracy of Mr. Masters' affidavit and stated that she was aware of all steps taken by Mr. Masters on her behalf in the litigation, had been kept fully informed of those steps as they were being taken, and that all steps he had taken were on her express instructions. It is clear from the material that Ms Elliott is an independent, well-educated and intelligent woman. She holds a Masters in Business Administration and has considerable experience in finance and accounting. She had almost completed her training to be a Chartered Accountant at the time she went on disability benefits.

The Scale of Costs

Costs on a partial indemnity basis are the norm and are awarded on that scale in the vast majority of cases. The situations in which costs on a substantial indemnity basis are appropriate are rare. However, one of the situations in which such an award is appropriate is where one party to the litigation has behaved in an abusive manner, brought proceedings wholly devoid of merit, and unnecessarily run up the costs of the litigation: *Shier v. Fiume* (1991), 6 OR (3d) 759 (Ont. Gen. Div.); *Benquesus v. Proskauer, Rose, LLP*, [2005] OJ No. 2418 (Ont. SCJ); *Donmor Industries Ltd. v. Kremlin Canada Inc.* (1992), 6 OR (3d) 506 (Ont. Gen. Div.); *Aspiotis v. Coffee Time Donuts Inc.*, [1995] OJ No. 419 (Ont. Gen. Div.); *Apotex Inc. v. Egis Pharmaceuticals* (1991), 4 OR (3d) 321 (Ont. SCJ).

In exercising discretion as to an appropriate costs award, it is relevant to take into account "the conduct of any party that tended to shorten or lengthen unnecessarily the duration of the proceeding" and "whether any step in the proceeding was improper, vexatious or unnecessary": *Rules of Civil Procedure*, Rule 57.01(1)(e) and (f).

It is apparent from Mr. Masters' affidavit, and from the exchange of correspondence between counsel prior to the commencement of the third party claim, that Mr. Masters added the individual employees as third parties as a tactic to put further pressure on Standard Life to settle on terms advantageous to his client and to obtain the procedural advantage of multiple examinations for discovery of all employees of Standard Life. I had concluded this was the case at the time of the original motion before me, and this is now confirmed by the material filed. Standard Life's counsel had been attempting to persuade Mr. Masters to meet so they could discuss outstanding issues. Mr. Masters repeatedly responded by insisting that Standard Life had failed to produce all of the relevant documents and was trying to pressure his client into a settlement without allowing her the opportunity to be fully informed. There are, of course, remedies in the Rules for obtaining production of documents from a party who has failed to make full disclosure. Mr. Masters made no attempt to do that. Instead, he proceeded to add as parties every single employee of Standard Life who had ever had anything to do with Ms Elliott's file. In my view, this was a vexatious and unnecessary step in the proceeding and one which had the effect of unnecessarily lengthening the proceeding and driving up costs. As such, it falls squarely within the kind of conduct contemplated under the Rules as warranting an increased level of costs to the other party.

In addition to having brought the third party proceeding in the first place, there was also considerable repetitive and lengthy correspondence from Mr. Masters that increased the legal costs of the other side. Also, he twice amended the third party claim, again necessitating further time and expense for the plaintiff.

Counsel for Standard Life gave Mr. Masters several opportunities to drop the third party claim against the employees without the necessity of a motion, but he refused.

Standard Life's original claim against Ms Elliott for overpayment of benefits is in the approximate amount of $30,000.00. Ms Elliott has defended and counterclaimed for a total of $900,000.00, which includes a claim of $100,000 for aggravated damages and $500,000 for punitive damages.

As a result of the third party proceeding alone, Standard Life will have incurred nearly $40,000.00 in legal fees. This kind of tactical litigation is not conducive to the legitimate settlement of disputes in our judicial system. On the contrary, it is exactly the kind of conduct that makes litigation so prohibitively expensive that legitimate disputes cannot be litigated. It is appropriate in this kind of situation to discourage such conduct by imposing stiff costs consequences. As was stated by my colleague, Stach J in *Benquesus v. Proskauer, Rose, LLP* (at para. 17):

> One of the legitimate functions of the costs system is to discourage frivolous and unnecessary litigation. Doing so in the proper case enhances access to the justice system for other litigants.

In view of all of the circumstances, I consider an order for costs at the substantial indemnity level to be appropriate.

Liability for Costs

Ms Elliott has filed an affidavit stating that all steps in the litigation, including the bringing of the third party proceeding and resisting the motion to strike it, were taken with her knowledge and on her informed instructions. Before swearing that affidavit she had the benefit of independent legal advice. On the evidence before me, there is no basis to excuse her from the responsibility to pay those costs.

The moving parties also seek to have those costs jointly payable by the solicitor personally.

Mr. Masters argues that the claim for costs against him personally has the "intended effect of intimidating the plaintiff personal injury bar with objectionable threats of costs which are contrary to the interests of justice and meant to inhibit the fulfillment of a lawyer's duty to their [sic] clients": factum, para. 2. Paragraph 38 of his factum alleges, without any reference to evidence, that:

> Mr. Masters is not being pursued to recover costs from Standard Life. Rather, Standard Life has targeted Mr. Masters so that he may be made an example of what happens to aggressive plaintiff lawyers who take on insurance companies. Standard Life is sending a signal to the plaintiff personal injury bar to not aggressively and forcefully advocate for their clients against insurance companies.

There is no evidence whatsoever to support that accusation. There is, in my view, considerable merit to Standard Life's request that Mr. Masters be personally liable for the costs. Although Ms Elliott is an intelligent, well-educated person, she is not a lawyer, has no legal training and cannot have been the inspiration behind the third party proceeding. That litigation strategy must have been developed and recommended by her lawyer. In my decision on the original motion, I held that the third party claim against the employees was an abuse of process. I further stated, "Procedural advantage is not a proper basis to add a host of individual third parties, and that is the most innocuous characterization of the tactic, in my view." While costs would certainly also have been recoverable from Ms Elliott, she has been on disability benefits for over a decade. The legal costs in this proceeding have been escalating out of control and now vastly exceeds the value of the claim itself. Given my findings, and the realistic prospect that as a practical matter costs might never be recovered from Ms Elliott, it was no means unreasonable for Standard Life to proceed against Mr. Masters.

Furthermore, from what I have seen of Mr. Masters' conduct in the material before me, I believe it goes well beyond a lawyer "forcefully and aggressively" advocating for his client. In all of the circumstances, adding all of these individual third parties was a completely unnecessary step that was grossly out of proportion to the actual amount in dispute between the parties. I see the position taken by Standard Life on the motion before me as a legitimate step to try to curb these excesses by counsel and to attempt to focus the litigation on the real matters in dispute. I reject the suggestion that this motion was brought improperly to intimidate the entire plaintiffs' bar.

Mr. Masters submits that before a lawyer can be found personally responsible for costs, there must be a finding he acted in bad faith or has been derelict in his duty to his client or the court, relying on the historic roots of the power to make such an order as articulated in cases such as *Myers v. Elman*, [1939] 4 All ER 484 (UK HL); *R. & T. Thew Ltd. v. Reeves (No. 2)*, [1982] 3 All ER 1086 (Eng. CA). While those cases still apply to a residual discretion in the court at common law to award costs against a solicitor, I do not believe that is the applicable test now in Ontario.

In Ontario, the test is now set out in Rule 57.07(1)(c), which states:

> 57.07(1) Where a solicitor for a party has caused costs to be incurred without reasonable cause or to be wasted by undue delay, negligence or other default, the court may make an order,
>
> > (c) requiring the solicitor personally to pay the costs of any party.

There is no reason not to apply the plain meaning of those words. There is no requirement of bad faith or dereliction of duty before the power under Rule 57.07(7) to award costs against a solicitor personally is triggered. Indeed, the Rule specifically refers to negligence as a ground for recovery of such costs.

However, just because the actions of a solicitor may fall within the defined circumstances in which costs may be awarded against him personally, does not mean that the court's discretion ought to be exercised in that manner. On the contrary, the discretion ought to be exercised sparingly and only in exceptional circumstances. In this regard, I agree with the observations of Granger J in *Marchand (Litigation Guardian of) v. Public General Hospital Society of Chatham*, [1998] OJ No. 527 (Ont. Gen. Div.) at para. 115, as follows:

> … As I am satisfied that Rule 57.07 is not a codification of the common law, the ordinary meaning of the words contained therein can be applied to determine if an order for costs should e made against the solicitor personally. Applying the ordinary meaning to the words found in Rule 57.07, costs incurred without reasonable cause, or by reason of undue delay, negligence or other default can be charged back to the solicitor who is responsible for such costs being incurred. Pursuant to Rule 57.07 mere negligence can attract cost consequences. In addition, actions or omissions which fall short of negligence may also attract cost consequences. Causing undue delay in a trial could be the result of bad judgment as opposed to negligence. The reference to "negligence or some other default" indicates that the categories for making an award under rule 57.07 are within the discretion of the court. Although "bad faith" is not a requirement to invoking the costs sanctions of Rule 57.07 against a solicitor, such an order should only be made in rare circumstance and such orders should not discourage lawyers from pursuing unpopular or difficult cases. It is only when a lawyer pursues a goal which is clearly unattainable or is clearly derelict in his or her duties as an officer of the court that resort should be had to R. 57.07.

In *Young v. Young* (1993), 108 DLR (4th) 193 (SCC), the Supreme Court of Canada held that costs ought not to have been awarded personally against the solicitor for the father in protracted child custody proceedings dealing with the extent to which the father could involve the children in his Jehovah's Witness religious activities during periods of access. The Supreme Court recognized that the proceedings had been lengthy and acrimonious. However, the Court held, at p. 284 that costs are compensatory and are not awarded for the purpose of punishing a barrister. McLachlin J (writing for the majority on this point), stated p. 284:

> … Any member of the legal profession might be subject to a compensatory order for costs if it is shown that repetitive and irrelevant material, and excessive motions and applications, characterized the proceedings in which they were involved, and that the lawyer acted in bad

faith in encouraging that abuse and delay. It is as clear that the courts possess that jurisdiction to make such an award, often under statute and, in any event, as part of their inherent jurisdiction to control abuse of process and contempt of court. ... Moreover, courts must be extremely cautious in awarding costs personally against a lawyer, given the duties upon a lawyer to guard confidentiality of instructions and to bring forward with courage even unpopular causes. A lawyer should not be placed in a situation where his or her fear of an adverse order of costs may conflict with these fundamental duties of his or her calling.

The Supreme Court in *Young* did not purport to interpret every statutory provision dealing with costs payable by a solicitor personally and to read into each such statute a requirement that the solicitor must have acted in bad faith before such an award could be made. The decision in *Young*, does not, therefore, restrict the application of Rule 57.07(1)(c) to cases of bad faith, or otherwise limit the broader language of the Rule. However, the cautionary advice of the Court is applicable to any situation in which a trial judge is called upon to exercise the costs jurisdiction. Before ordering costs against any solicitor in his personal capacity, it is important to bear in mind the nature of the solicitor and client relationship, the importance of fostering the confidentiality underlying that relationship and the necessity of giving leeway to solicitors who find themselves acting for clients with unpopular or difficult causes. As was stated by Doherty JA in *Carmichael v. Stathshore Industrial Park Ltd.*, [1999] OJ No. 2182 (Ont. CA) at para. 15:

> Bearing in mind the extreme caution which should be exercised before awarding costs personally against a solicitor, I am not satisfied that the respondent has made out a case for ordering costs personally against Mr. Wysocky: *Young v. Young*, [1992] 4 SCR 3. In my view, the caution expressed in *Young v. Young*, *supra*, applies to applications for costs made under Rule 57.07, just as it does to applications under the inherent jurisdiction of the court.

One of the difficulties faced by the Court in *Carmichael* was that the principle basis advanced for ordering costs personally against the solicitor for the appellant was that the appeal had been brought frivolously. Since the appeal had been dismissed on consent, there was no determination of the merits of the appeal, and the Court could not know if it was indeed frivolous. However, Doherty JA did note, at para. 9, "I would not order costs against a solicitor personally solely on the basis that the solicitor took an appeal which I regarded as frivolous." In my view, it follows that a mere finding that a step in a proceeding is an abuse of process does not automatically trigger an award of costs against a solicitor personally.

Applying those principles to the case before me, I conclude that it is not necessary for me to find that Mr. Masters acted in bad faith before he can be held personally liable for the payment of costs. However, neither does my finding that issuing the third party claim against the individual employees was an abuse of process necessarily mean that Mr. Masters should pay the costs personally.

I would not go so far as to say that Mr. Masters did act in bad faith. He cited some case authority for the position he took on behalf of his client. I did not elect to follow that authority, but the position taken was not totally devoid of merit. Further, I accept that Mr. Masters himself believed he had an arguable case on the point. That said, in my view, his conduct went well beyond what was necessary to protect the interests of his client. He waged a war of attrition against the insurer company, intending to make it so expensive for the insurer to litigate his client's claim that they would simply give up. The fact that he felt there was some case law to support his position, does not mean that the position was legitimately taken, as opposed to being taken for an ulterior purpose. Based on my review of the material filed, I am satisfied that Mr. Masters was using the Rules as a weapon in his war against the insurer, rather than as a mechanism for obtaining a fair and just result for his client. He deliberately caused excessive costs to be incurred without reasonable cause in order to put pressure on the insurance company. Even though his client approved what he did, I do not see her as the instigator. She was following her counsel's advice.

Costs are meant to be compensatory. The likelihood of recovering the costs thrown away as against the defendant are remote. The only way to truly compensate the plaintiff insurer for its costs would be to make them payable by the solicitor. Given my finding that Mr. Masters was the instigator of the action taken and that he took the steps he did for an improper purpose, as well as the fact that his general conduct of the litigation excessively drove up costs, it is in my view appropriate that he pay the costs personally.

That is not the end of the matter, however, in so far as the allocation of the ultimate responsibility for those costs between Mr. Masters and Ms Elliott is concerned. It is difficult while the action is still ongoing and the solicitor and client relationship still in existence to determine the extent to which Ms Elliott approved the steps taken with full knowledge of the purpose of those steps and the potential for adverse costs consequences. If Ms Elliott instructed Mr. Masters to take those steps based on his advice that it was appropriate to do so and without any appropriate warning as to costs consequences, justice might well require the costs to be fully borne by Mr. Masters, or at least reflected in the bill Ms Elliott is ultimately required to pay. On the other hand, if this strategy was discussed between them and Ms Elliott approved it as a way of driving up the insurer's costs in order to pressure the insurer into settling more advantageously for her than might otherwise be the case, then this may well be a factor to be taken into account in placing the liability for those costs, at least in part, on Ms Elliott. Likewise, if the merits of proceeding in this manner were fairly discussed with her and the costs consequences reviewed and she nevertheless insisted that her solicitor proceed, notwithstanding his advice to the contrary, then she might well be required to reimburse him for the costs he has had to pay in following her instructions.

That allocation of responsibility as between the solicitor and client are not the concern of the plaintiff, however, and should await the conclusion of the proceeding, or at least the termination of the solicitor/client relationship. For purposes of this application, the order shall simply be that the costs are payable to the plaintiff by Ms Elliott and Mr. Masters, jointly and severally, on a substantial indemnity basis. ...

D. Costs for Public Interest Work

Litigation is expensive. This makes it extraordinarily difficult for public interest litigants to access the Canadian justice system. Lawyers can assist by providing their services for free, *pro bono*. But how does such assistance operate in an environment where there is fee shifting? Can a successful litigant obtain costs from the unsuccessful party when he or she is actually not paying for the lawyer's services? Would such a system incentivize lawyers to take on more public interest work? Does such a system provide greater access to justice for these particular types of cases? The following case explores this issue.

1465778 Ontario Inc. v. 1122077 Ontario Ltd.
(2006), 82 OR (3d) 757 (CA)

K. FELDMAN JA: At a hearing before this panel on December 1, 2005, the appellants were successful in setting aside three orders that (1) did not allow the appellant Cavalieri, as the sole shareholder of the plaintiff numbered company, to represent the company in the litigation; (2) ordered security for costs against Cavalieri; and (3) dismissed the application. When the court read its endorsement, counsel for the appellants asked for costs of the appeal. Counsel for the respondent objected on the basis that counsel for the appellant was acting *pro bono*, through the auspices of the Advocates' Society *pro bono* program.

The costs issue raised is whether, in a private action that does not involve public law, the *Charter* or similar issues of general public importance, the court can or should make costs orders in favour of a party represented by counsel acting *pro bono*. Because of the significance of the issue to the legal profession and the public, the court adjourned the costs issue and invited representatives of the profession to act as *amici curiae*. These *amici* submitted briefs and made oral submissions advising the court on the policy considerations that inform the issue, as well as the positions taken by the profession.

. . .

Positions of the Parties

Mr. Rosenstein of Pape Barristers acted *pro bono* on the appeal on behalf of the appellants, and was successful in setting aside the default judgment and order for security for costs, the breach of which led to the dismissal of the application. He also obtained an order allowing Mr. Cavalieri, the sole shareholder of the numbered company, to represent his company in the litigation. He asked for costs of the appeal fixed in the amount of $4,500. Based on his bill of costs, that amount represents a substantial reduction from a partial indemnity award. His position is that there is no reason why *pro bono* counsel should be denied their costs, and that recent case law and the principles in s. 131 of the *Courts of Justice Act*, RSO 1990, c. C.43 and Rule 57 of the *Rules of Civil Procedure*, RRO 1990, Reg. 194 support this submission.

Mr. Dallal on behalf of the respondents opposed the request for costs. He provided detailed written submissions following the original hearing for the purpose of allowing the court to consider all sides of the issue. He also presented a practical compromise submission if costs were to be awarded in this case.

His first position is that where lawyers agree to act *pro bono*, they have no expectation of payment. They are making a contribution to the administration of justice as part of their professional obligation as lawyers, again in the best tradition of the bar. Therefore, the potential for a costs award is contrary to the concept of acting *pro bono*. I add at this point the question whether, if costs are available, counsel considering a *pro bono* retainer may factor into their decision the potential for the recovery of costs.

Mr. Dallal also submits that in the "loser pay" costs regime, a party represented by *pro bono* counsel needs no indemnification from the losing party for legal fees incurred because that party is not paying counsel. This case, an ordinary commercial dispute, can be distinguished from recent case law that has allowed costs in favour of *pro bono* counsel acting in *Charter* cases, where there is a significant public interest component to the subject of the litigation.

Although there are other purposes to an award of costs besides indemnification, specifically to encourage settlement, prevent frivolous or vexatious litigation and to discourage unnecessary steps, in cases such as this one, the playing field is not level. The impecunious party has an effective immunity from paying costs ordered in interlocutory matters and at the conclusion of the case.

A further argument is that if costs are to be awarded, then the financial terms of the retainer of the *pro bono* lawyer should be disclosed, including whether there is indemnity from another source or any contingency fee arrangement. An anomalous situation is created if the only parties with an interest in litigating the issue of costs are the *pro bono* lawyer and the losing party.

Finally, Mr. Dallal submits in the alternative, that the court should make all costs of interlocutory proceedings payable only at the end of the litigation rather than forthwith, because only the non-*pro bono* party would be able to pay forthwith. He suggests that this resolution will have two advantages. First, it will discourage interlocutory motions and create a more level playing field for the balance of the litigation. Second, it will prevent the problematic situation in which costs are awarded forthwith against a *pro bono* litigant who is unable to pay, entitling the opposing party to seek security for costs and ultimately, when such security cannot be paid, dismissal of the application.

On the alternative submission, Mr. Rosenstein responded in his written reply submission that the proper way to deal with a party unable to satisfy interlocutory costs orders is under rule 56.01(1)(c), security for costs.

Amicus curiae briefs were filed and oral representations made on behalf of three legal organizations with a special interest in advocacy issues: the Ontario Trial Lawyers Association, *Pro Bono* Law Ontario and The Advocates' Society. In response to the issues raised, all three refer to the noble tradition of the bar to take on cases without remuneration when the need of a potential litigant comes to its attention. This tradition was discussed by Major J in a speech titled "Lawyers' Obligation to Provide Legal Services" delivered to the National Conference on the Legal Profession and Professional Ethics at the University of Calgary in 1994 (33 *Alta. L Rev.* 719) where he said:

> It has long been part of the duty and tradition of the legal profession to provide services gratuitously for those who require them but cannot afford them. The profession, recognizing its commitment to the larger principle of justice, has traditionally not let such cases go unanswered merely because the individual is impecunious. Instead, the profession has collectively accepted the burden of such cases, thereby championing the cause of justice while at the same time, sharing the cost that such cases entail. This is a tradition which dates to the very inception of the profession in medieval Europe in the thirteenth century.

All *amici* submit, however, that it is not inappropriate for counsel who volunteer to act *pro bono* to be able to be reimbursed for their services to some extent by costs awards. They also agree that the potential for such awards would encourage more lawyers to take on *pro bono* cases and thereby increase access to justice for many people in Ontario.

The Ontario Trial Lawyers Association also adopts the view that the purposes of costs awards in litigation other than indemnity apply equally to cases where a party is represented by *pro bono* counsel. It is therefore inappropriate to remove from the process the potential sanction of a costs order to promote settlement, to prevent litigants from causing needless delays and to allow the court to control its process.

Pro Bono Law Ontario ("PBLO") takes a somewhat more radical position. Established in 2002, its mission statement is:

> To improve access to justice by providing strategic guidance, training and tailored technical assistance to law firms, law associations, legal departments and other groups that are dedicated to addressing the legal needs of low income and disadvantaged individuals as well as the communities and charitable organizations that serve them.

PBLO works to promote a *pro bono* culture within the legal profession by developing and enhancing the *pro bono* capacity of the bar. Lawyers have an obligation to ensure that everyone who needs it has access to justice, and acting *"pro bono publico,"* in the public good, helps to fulfill that objective. *Pro bono* legal services are offered without the expectation of payment to people who cannot afford a lawyer, in order to increase access to justice. The underlying charitable motivation distinguishes *pro bono* work from contingency fee or class action arrangements. However, because some lawyers are not in a position to absorb the financial obligations attached to *pro bono* work easily, the court's recognition of the potential for costs awards may allow or encourage more lawyers to offer their services.

The position of PBLO is that there should be no special rule either for or against costs where parties are represented by *pro bono* counsel. In some cases, *pro bono* counsel may choose not to seek costs or may elect to donate any costs received to charity. However, because costs serve several normative functions within the litigation process, it is important that the court retain its discretion to make costs orders to control its own process and ensure that the system works fairly. To that end, the court should recognize access to justice as a fifth purpose underlying an award of costs that will be particularly relevant in *pro bono* cases. In that context, other costs remedies such as security for costs orders should be equally available to defendants with *pro bono* counsel who are sued, for example, by an impecunious plaintiff.

Further, where a party represented by *pro bono* counsel is unsuccessful, PBLO suggests that access to justice considerations may weigh against making a costs award against that party. The fear of such an adverse costs award may deter parties with limited means from litigating issues that are legitimately important to them. On the other hand, PBLO recognizes that other considerations in the specific litigation may lead the court to conclude that an adverse costs award is appropriate.

Although the issue before the court involves private litigation, PBLO also refers to cases such as *Charter* litigation, which seek to advance the public interest. In public interest cases, there is more reason for a court to avoid penalizing the *pro bono* litigant. It may even be appropriate for the court to grant costs, or at least disbursements, to an unsuccessful *pro bono* party. In England, for example, there is a limited practice of granting "pre-emptive costs orders" or "protective costs orders" ("PCO"s) in public interest cases where the applicant has no private interest in the case. In *R (on the application of Corner House Research) v. Secretary of State for Trade & Industry*, [2005] 4 All ER 1 (Eng. CA), the English Court of Appeal explained these orders as follows at para. 6:

> The general purpose of a PCO is to allow a claimant of limited means access to the court in order to advance his case without the fear of an order for substantial costs being made against him, a fear which would inhibit him from continuing with the case at all.

PBLO concludes its submissions by suggesting that the court should develop criteria for awarding or denying costs in *pro bono* cases on a case-by-case basis that will serve the traditional purposes of costs awards, but also reflect an overriding concern for access to justice.

As I mentioned earlier, The Advocates' Society's position is that it is not inconsistent with the charitable objective of taking on *pro bono* work that counsel be able to request and accept an award of costs, if successful. The Society points out that it would be a windfall in the context of our "loser pay" system, for an unsuccessful party to avoid paying costs just because the opposite party is represented by *pro bono* counsel. Or, looking at the issue another way, in some cases, it will be appropriate for the unsuccessful party to bear a portion of the costs of the litigation instead of the whole burden falling on volunteer *pro bono* counsel.

On the other hand, there could be cases where a costs order ought not to be made. One such case may be where the *pro bono* party would not have been able to pay costs if unsuccessful, and would not have expected to do so. The Society's view is that this may be a relevant consideration for the court. In other words, the Society agrees with the respondent in this case that it may be problematic to have an uneven playing field, where one party is impecunious and represented by *pro bono* counsel, while the other has retained counsel in the ordinary way.

The Society accepts that the law in this area should develop on a case-by-case basis, but within the framework of allowing the court to apply ordinary costs principles, while also reacting to specific issues raised in the *pro bono* context. Such an approach will have a salutary effect on facilitating access to justice and will improve the efficiency of the administration of justice.

Legislative and Case Law Background

By s. 131 of the *Courts of Justice Act*, costs of a proceeding are in the discretion of the court but that discretion, although very broad, is to be exercised in accordance with the provisions of an Act or the *Rules of Civil Procedure*. Section 131(1) provides:

> 131(1) Subject to the provisions of an Act or rules of court, the costs of and incidental to a proceeding or a step in a proceeding are in the discretion of the court, and the court may determine by whom and to what extent the costs shall be paid.

Traditionally the purpose of an award of costs within our "loser pay" system was to partially or, in some limited circumstances, wholly indemnify the winning party for the legal costs it incurred. However, costs have more recently come to be recognized as an important tool in the hands of the court to influence the way the parties conduct themselves and to prevent abuse of the court's process. Specifically, the three other recognized purposes of costs awards are to encourage settlement, to deter frivolous actions and defences, and to discourage unnecessary steps that unduly prolong the litigation. See *Fellowes, McNeil v. Kansa General International Insurance Co.* (1997), 37 OR (3d) 464 (Ont. Gen. Div.), at 467 and 472.

In *British Columbia (Minister of Forests) v. Okanagan Indian Band*, [2003] 3 SCR 371 (SCC) at paras. 25 and 26, LeBel J discussed the natural evolution of the law in recognizing these policy objectives:

> As the *Fellowes* [*supra*] and *Skidmore* [*infra*] cases illustrate, modern costs rules accomplish various purposes in addition to the traditional objective of indemnification. An order as to costs may be designed to penalize a party who has refused a reasonable settlement offer[.] … Costs can also be used to sanction behaviour that increases the duration and expense of litigation, or is otherwise unreasonable or vexatious. In short, it has become a routine matter for courts to employ the power to order costs as a tool in the furtherance of the efficient and orderly administration of justice.
>
> Indeed, the traditional approach to costs can also be viewed as being animated by the broad concern to ensure that the justice system works fairly and efficiently. Because costs awards transfer some of the winner's litigation expenses to the loser rather than leaving each party's expenses where they fall (as is done in jurisdictions without costs rules), they act as a disincentive to those who might be tempted to harass others with meritless claims. And because they offset to some extent the outlays incurred by the winner, they make the legal system more accessible to litigants who seek to vindicate a legally sound position. These effects of the traditional rules can be connected to the court's concern with overseeing its own process and ensuring that litigation is conducted in an efficient and just manner. In this sense it is a natural evolution in the law to recognize the related policy objectives that are served by the modern approach to costs.

As part of the recognition that costs serve a purpose beyond indemnification, the courts began to award costs in favour of litigants who were traditionally viewed as disentitled to costs. For example, costs have been awarded in cases where the litigant was self-represented (*Skidmore v. Blackmore* (1995), 2 BCLR (3d) 201 (BC CA) and *Fong v. Chan* (1999), 46 OR (3d) 330 (Ont. CA)); where the winning party was a law firm represented by one of its partners who was not charging fees (*Fellowes, McNeil, supra*); where counsel was salaried (*Solicitors Act*, RS 1990, c. S.15, s. 36); and, where the responsibility for a party's legal fees was undertaken by a third party (*Lavigne v. OPSEU* (1987), 60 OR (2d) 486 (Ont. HC)).

Costs have also been awarded to counsel acting *pro bono* in *Charter* or public interest cases such as *Rogers v. Greater Sudbury (City) Administrator of Ontario Works* (2001), 57 OR (3d) 467 (Ont. SCJ). In that case, Epstein J awarded costs payable forthwith on an injunction application. She stated at para. 21:

Through granting, when appropriate, cost awards payable forthwith during the course of what is frequently protracted litigation, the financial burden assumed by the lawyers doing *pro bono* work is reduced. Orders of this nature would allow more lawyers to accept this kind of retainer thereby increasing the opportunity for people, such as Ms. Rogers, to have access to justice. As well, applicants who may suffer irreparable harm as a result of the application of a law that is the subject of a legitimate *Charter* challenge have increased opportunity to seek interlocutory relief since counsel acting for them have a chance of being paid promptly for the often very expensive process of preparing for and arguing a motion for an interlocutory injunction.

There have also been some recent instances, both in Ontario and in British Columbia, where costs orders have been made in favour of *pro bono* counsel in non-public interest cases. See for example, *Mackay Homes v. North Bay (City)*, [2005] OJ No. 3263 (Ont. SCJ), *Spatone v. Banks*, [2002] OJ No. 4647 (Ont. SCJ), and *Jacks v. Victoria Amateur Swimming Club*, [2005] BCJ No. 2086 (BC SC [In Chambers]). In *Ontario (Human Rights Commission) v. Brockie* (2004), 185 OAC 366 (Ont. CA), this court reversed a decision of the Divisional Court that denied costs to *pro bono* counsel, holding that "[s]uch a policy would act as a severe penalty to lawyers acting in the public interest by making it possible for litigants of modest means to access the courts."

[The court then set out the factors in rule 57.01 of Ontario's *Rules of Civil Procedure* that a court may consider when deciding on a costs award.]

All the *amici* agree that these factors, which reflect the four principles referred to in *Fellowes* and in *Fong v. Chan* of indemnity, encouragement of settlements, discouragement of frivolous actions and defences, and discouragement of unnecessary steps in the litigation, can be applied in *pro bono* cases. PBLO submits that access to justice should be added as a fifth purpose.

In its brief, the Advocates' Society submits that costs should be available to *pro bono* parties based on the factors set out in rule 57.01(1) as well as on the principles of access to justice and the efficient administration of the courts. However, it argues that while the court should encourage access to justice through *pro bono* litigation, it should be mindful of considerations that may uniquely arise in such cases. It is important that there always be the potential for costs consequences to ensure that both parties adopt appropriate litigation strategies. However, an award of costs in favour of a successful *pro bono* party will not always be appropriate. For example, an award might not be made in a case where there was never an expectation that the *pro bono* party would be able to pay costs if unsuccessful.

Analysis

Issue 1: Can Pro Bono Counsel Seek Costs?

It is clear from the submissions of the *amici* representing the views of the profession, as well as from the developing case law in this area, and I agree, that in the current costs regime, there should be no prohibition on an award of costs in favour of *pro bono* counsel in appropriate cases. Although the original concept of acting on a *pro bono* basis meant

that the lawyer was volunteering his or her time with no expectation of any reimbursement, the law now recognizes that costs awards may serve purposes other than indemnity. To be clear, it is neither inappropriate, nor does it derogate from the charitable
purpose of volunteerism, for counsel who have agreed to act *pro bono* to receive some
reimbursement for their services from the losing party in the litigation.

To the contrary, allowing *pro bono* parties to be subject to the ordinary costs consequences that apply to other parties has two positive consequences: (1) it ensures that
both the non-*pro bono* party and the *pro bono* party know that they are not free to abuse
the system without fear of the sanction of an award of costs; and (2) it promotes access
to justice by enabling and encouraging more lawyers to volunteer to work *pro bono* in
deserving cases. Because the potential merit of the case will already factor into whether
a lawyer agrees to act *pro bono*, there is no anticipation that the potential for costs awards
will cause lawyers to agree to act only in cases where they anticipate a costs award.

Issue 2: Does the Costs Award Belong to Pro Bono Counsel or to the Litigant?

Where costs are awarded in favour of a party, the costs belong to that party. See Mark M.
Orkin, Q.C., *The Law of Costs*, looseleaf (Aurora: Canada Law Book, 2005) at §204 and
Rules of Civil Procedure, rule 59.03(6). However, *pro bono* counsel may make fee arrangements with their clients that allow the costs to be paid to the lawyer. This ensures that
there will be no windfall to the client who is not paying for legal services.

Issue 3: Is It Fair To Award Costs in Favour of a Pro Bono Party if That Party Would Be Unable To Pay Costs Ordered Against It?

The case law makes it clear—and the submissions of the *amici* support the proposition—
that although it is open to a judge to award costs to a successful *pro bono* party, such an
award is not mandatory and will depend on the rule 57.01 factors, considerations of access to justice, and the need to maintain a level playing field between the parties.

This is particularly true with respect to interlocutory costs awards that are ordered to
be paid forthwith. If a *pro bono* party has unsatisfied costs orders outstanding, there may
well be potential unfairness in obliging a non-*pro bono* party who is unsuccessful on an
interlocutory motion to pay costs of a motion forthwith without offset.

The effectiveness of the system relies on the fact that all parties are at risk to pay costs
if they are unwilling to consider a reasonable settlement, or if they unnecessarily bring
or oppose motions. In its recently released decision in *Walker v. Ritchie*, 2006 SCC 45
(SCC), denying a risk premium to plaintiff's counsel as part of the losing defendant's
costs obligation, the Supreme Court of Canada affirmed the concept that all defendants
must face the same risk of costs:

> Unsuccessful defendants should expect to pay similar amounts by way of costs across simi-
> lar pieces of litigation involving similar conduct and counsel, regardless of what arrange-
> ments the particular plaintiff may have concluded with counsel. (para. 28)

The same proposition applies to unsuccessful plaintiffs. However, if the *pro bono* party
is effectively immune from any real obligation to pay interlocutory costs because of impecuniosity, then the purpose of the costs rule is undermined.

The issue of the costs obligations of impecunious parties represented by *pro bono* counsel presents a delicate problem from the point of view of the profession, as its members not only have a collective obligation to provide services *pro bono* in appropriate cases, but they also, of course, act for clients who may be litigating against a *pro bono* party. In that context, the *amici* have been careful to encourage the court to maintain flexibility and to develop the principles on a case-by-case basis. I agree with that approach. As Mr. Dallal, counsel for the respondent, points out, the situation may become somewhat anomalous if the *pro bono* party has nothing at stake regarding the costs, and the real adversaries on that issue are the non-*pro bono* party and the *pro bono* lawyer.

The concern for levelling the playing field for *pro bono* and non-*pro bono* litigants does not require, however, that the parties be placed in equal positions in every case. As the approaches adopted in some foreign jurisdictions illustrate, the policy objective of facilitating access to justice may be of sufficient importance to warrant placing the *pro bono* litigant in a more favourable position in some cases. …

There are provisions in the rules that can be used to level the playing field when costs are awarded to a *pro bono* party. For example, rule 57.03(2) allows the court to dismiss a party's proceeding, strike the party's defence or "make such other order as is just" where that party fails to pay the costs of a motion as ordered. Rule 57.01(4)(b) allows the court to award only a percentage of assessed costs. These two rules can be used by the court to reduce an award of costs to a *pro bono* party who wins an interlocutory motion, where that party has failed to pay costs previously ordered against it.

The correct approach, then, is for the judge in each case to be apprised of the status of outstanding costs orders, and then weigh the access to justice issues together with the particular circumstances of the interlocutory matter, including the conduct of the parties and the relative importance of the motion within the context of the litigation. The judge will have the discretion to make the order that fits the circumstances, including ordering costs payable to the *pro bono* party, reducing the quantum of those costs or limiting the order to disbursements, making the costs payable only at the end of the case, or making no order.

Issue 4: Should the Court Develop a Set of Rules Governing the Availability of Costs Awards in Favour of Pro Bono Parties?

I agree with the submission of PBLO that the list of the purposes of costs awards should now include access to justice as a fifth consideration. It is clear that the profession sees the availability of costs orders in favour of *pro bono* counsel as a tool to potentially reduce the necessary financial sacrifice associated with taking on *pro bono* work and to thereby increase the number of counsel who may be willing and able to accept *pro bono* cases. This will facilitate access to justice.

Because of the discretion accorded to judges to award and fix the quantum of costs (subject to s. 131 of the *Courts of Justice Act*, the *Rules of Civil Procedure* and the Supreme Court's decision in *Walker*), they have the necessary scope to respond to any potential unfairness that may arise as a result of the parties' unequal abilities to pay costs, and the fact that the *pro bono* party is not paying a lawyer. They also have the flexibility to craft a costs order that addresses the potential unfairness where the circumstances, including all the other relevant factors, call for it.

Where a case is brought to assert a *Charter* claim or other matter of general public importance, different considerations may apply when deciding whether to award costs in favour of the *pro bono* party. In those cases, for example, it may be appropriate for the court to consider potentially insulating the *pro bono* party from exposure to costs, or limiting the party's exposure, in order to facilitate the resolution of an important public interest issue by the court. The principles that will be applied in this type of litigation will also develop as the cases arise.

The legal profession in Ontario has a history of commitment to ensuring access to justice and providing *pro bono* services through its members. That history is reflected in today's litigation environment where it is both appropriate and necessary that costs awards be available to successful *pro bono* litigants in ordinary private law cases both at the end of the case and on interlocutory motions. The principles that will guide the exercise of the court's discretion in deciding when such costs will be awarded should be developed over time on a case-by-case basis.

The Award in This Case

This matter came before the Court of Appeal primarily as an appeal from an order dismissing the appellants' application without a determination on the merits. Because the appellant was successful in having that order set aside, the issue of the availability of an arbitration clause in a franchise agreement may now be able to be heard on the merits. In the ordinary course, costs would follow the event of a successful appeal and would be ordered payable by the respondents on the partial indemnity scale. The appellants were represented by *pro bono* counsel on the appeal only. Is there any reason in this case why the ordinary order should not be made?

The respondents point to the fact that the appellants are impecunious and that it was because they were unable to pay a costs order that the case was dismissed. However, that costs order has also been set aside. In my view, there is no reason why the losing party should not be ordered to pay costs of this appeal forthwith. If an issue with respect to future costs orders arises as the litigation progresses, either with *pro bono* counsel or with an in-person litigant, it can be addressed by the judge who hears the issue. I do not find it appropriate at this stage not to make the costs order payable forthwith.

Pro bono counsel has asked for $4,500 on the partial indemnity scale. The respondent suggests $2,000. Costs of $1,500 were fixed on a motion to extend the time for bringing this appeal to be payable in accordance with the order of the panel. In the circumstances, I would order total costs to the appellants in the amount of $4,500, inclusive of disbursements and GST.

There will be no costs of the appeal relating to the general issue of costs in *pro bono* cases. Again, I thank all counsel for advising the court of the position of the profession and for all of their very helpful assistance on this important issue.

Cases in litigation can take years to complete. Public interest litigants therefore may have difficulty in continuously funding their matters. In addition to *pro bono* legal services provided by lawyers, a court may, in rare instances, order interim cost awards funded by the public purse. The following case further develops the test for public funding of public interest litigation, which was first explored in *British Columbia (Minister of Forests) v. Okanagan Indian Band*, [2003] 3 SCR 371, 2003 SCC 71. The compelling question is: which cases are worthy of public financing?

Little Sisters Book and Art Emporium v. Canada
(Commissioner of Customs and Revenue)
[2007] 1 SCR 38

BASTARACHE AND LeBEL JJ:

1. Introduction

The appellant, Little Sisters Book and Art Emporium, is a corporation that operates a bookstore serving the gay and lesbian community in Vancouver. The issue in this appeal is whether it is proper for the appellant to have the costs of its court battle against the respondents (collectively referred to as "Customs") funded by the public purse by means of the exceptional advance (or interim) costs order contemplated in *British Columbia (Minister of Forests) v. Okanagan Indian Band*, [2003] 3 SCR 371, 2003 SCC 71 (SCC). In our view, the appellant cannot succeed.

The situation in *Okanagan* was clearly out of the ordinary. The bands had been thrust into complex litigation against the government that they could not pay for, and the case raised issues vital both to their survival and to the government's approach to aboriginal rights. The issue before the Court in that case was whether the bands' inability to pay should have the effect of leaving constitutional rights unenforceable and public interest issues unresolved. Mindful of the serious consequences to the bands and of the contours of the anticipated litigation, this Court decided that a real injustice would result if the courts refused to exercise their equitable jurisdiction in respect of costs and if, as a consequence, the bands' impecuniosity prevented the trial from proceeding.

The situation in the present case differs from that in *Okanagan*. A small business corporation is in particular engaging in litigation to gain the release of merchandise that was stopped at the border. On its face, this dispute is no different from any other one that could be initiated by the many Canadians whose shipments may be detained and scrutinized by Customs before they are allowed to receive them. But the history of this case reveals more. Understandably frustrated after years of court battles with Customs over similar issues, this corporation has chosen to enlarge the scope of the litigation and to pursue a broad inquiry into Customs' practices. The appellant wants its present interests, as well as its (and other importers') future interests, settled for good, and it wants to stop Customs from prohibiting any more imports until its complaints are resolved.

The question in this appeal is not whether the appellant has a good cause of action, but whether the cost of the corporation's attempt to get Customs to release its merchandise, or the costs of its broad inquiry into Customs' practices, should be borne by the Canadian taxpayer. An exceptional order such as this can be made only in special circumstances, like those in *Okanagan*, subject to stringent conditions and to the appropriate procedural controls. In our opinion, the appellant's application meets none of the requirements developed by the Court in that decision.

The fact that the appellant's claim would not be summarily dismissed does not suffice to establish that interim costs should be granted to allow it to proceed. That is not the proper test. Quite unfortunately, financial constraints put potentially meritorious claims at risk every day. Faced with this dilemma, legislatures have offered some responses, although these may not address every situation. Legal aid programs remain underfunded and overwhelmed. Self-representation in courts is a growing phenomenon. *Okanagan* was not intended to resolve all these difficulties. The Court did not seek to create a parallel system of legal aid or a court-managed comprehensive program to supplement any of the other programs designed to assist various groups in taking legal action, and its decision should not be used to do so. The decision did not introduce a new financing method for self-appointed representatives of the public interest. This Court's *ratio* in *Okanagan* applies only to those few situations where a court would be participating in an injustice—against the litigant personally and against the public generally—if it did not order advance costs to allow the litigant to proceed.

· · ·

4. Analysis

4.1 Rule in Okanagan

Okanagan concerned logging rights of four Indian bands on Crown land in British Columbia. These bands had begun logging in order to raise funds for housing and desperately needed social services. Contending that they had no right to do so, the Minister of Forests served them with stop-work orders and then commenced proceedings to enforce the orders. The bands tried to prevent the matter from going to trial, seeking to have it determined summarily by arguing that it would be impossible for them to finance a full trial.

An exceptional convergence of factors occurred in *Okanagan*. At the individual level, the case was of the utmost importance to the bands. They were caught in a grave predicament: the costs of the litigation were more than they could afford, especially given pressing needs like housing; yet a failure to assert their logging rights would seriously compromise those same needs. On a broader level, the case raised aboriginal rights issues of great public importance. There was evidence that the land claim advanced by the bands had *prima facie* merit, but the courts had yet to decide on the precise mechanism for advancing such claims—the fundamental issue of general importance had not been resolved by the courts in other litigation. However the case was ultimately decided, it was in the public interest to have the matter resolved. For both the bands themselves and the public at large, the litigation could not, therefore, simply be abandoned. In these exceptional circumstances, this Court held that the public's interest in the litigation justified a structured advance costs order insofar as it was necessary to have the case move forward.

In essence, *Okanagan* was an evolutionary step, but not a revolution, in the exercise of the courts' discretion regarding costs. As was explained in that case, the idea that costs awards can be used as a powerful tool for ensuring that the justice system functions fairly and efficiently was not a novel one. Policy goals, like discouraging—and thus sanctioning—misconduct by a litigant, are often reflected in costs awards: see M.M. Orkin, *The*

Law of Costs (2nd ed. (loose-leaf)), vol. 1, at § 205.2(2). Nevertheless, the general rule based on principles of indemnity, i.e., that costs follow the cause, has not been displaced. This suggests that policy and indemnity rationales can co-exist as principles underlying appropriate costs awards, even if "[t]he principle that a successful party is entitled to his or her costs is of long standing, and should not be departed from except for very good reasons": Orkin, at p. 2-39. This framework has been adopted in the law of British Columbia by establishing the "costs follow the cause" rule as a default proposition, while leaving judges room to exercise their discretion by ordering otherwise: see r. 57(9) of the Supreme Court of British Columbia *Rules of Court*, BC Reg. 221/90.

Okanagan did not establish the access to justice rationale as the paramount consideration in awarding costs. Concerns about access to justice must be considered with and weighed against other important factors. Bringing an issue of public importance to the courts will not automatically entitle a litigant to preferential treatment with respect to costs: ... By the same token, however, a losing party that raises a serious legal issue of public importance will not necessarily bear the other party's costs: ... Each case must be considered on its merits, and the consequences of an award for each party must be weighed seriously: ... .

Okanagan was a step forward in the jurisprudence on advance costs—restricted until then to family, corporate and trust matters—as it made it possible, in a public law case, to secure an advance costs order in special circumstances related to the public importance of the issues of the case (*Okanagan*, at para. 38). In other words, though now permissible, public interest advance costs orders are to remain special and, as a result, exceptional. These orders must be granted with caution, as a last resort, in circumstances where the need for them is clearly established. The foregoing principles could not yield any other result. If litigants raising public interest issues will not always avoid adverse costs awards at the conclusion of their trials, it can only be rarer still that they could benefit from advance costs awards. An application for advance costs may be entertained only if a litigant establishes that it is impossible to proceed with the trial and await its conclusion, and if the court is in a position to allocate the financial burden of the litigation fairly between the parties.

The nature of the *Okanagan* approach should be apparent from the analysis it prescribes for advance costs in public interest cases. A litigant must convince the court that three absolute requirements are met (at para. 40):

1. The party seeking interim costs genuinely cannot afford to pay for the litigation, and no other realistic option exists for bringing the issues to trial—in short, the litigation would be unable to proceed if the order were not made.
2. The claim to be adjudicated is *prima facie* meritorious; that is, the claim is at least of sufficient merit that it is contrary to the interests of justice for the opportunity to pursue the case to be forfeited just because the litigant lacks financial means.
3. The issues raised transcend the individual interests of the particular litigant, are of public importance, and have not been resolved in previous cases.

In analysing these requirements, the court must decide, with a view to all the circumstances, whether the case is sufficiently special that it would be contrary to the interests of justice to deny the advance costs application, or whether it should consider other methods to facilitate the hearing of the case. The discretion enjoyed by the court affords it an opportunity to consider all relevant factors that arise on the facts.

It is only a "rare and exceptional" case that is special enough to warrant an advance costs award: *Okanagan*, at para. 1. The standard was indeed intended to be a high one, and although no rigid test can be applied systematically to determine whether a case is "special enough," some observations can be made. As Thackray JA pointed out, it was in failing to verify whether the circumstances of this case were "exceptional" enough that the trial judge committed an error in law.

First, the injustice that would arise if the application is not granted must relate both to the individual applicant and to the public at large. This means that a litigant whose case, however compelling it may be, is of interest only to the litigant will be denied an advance costs award. It does not mean, however, that every case of interest to the public will satisfy the test. The justice system must not become a proxy for the public inquiry process, swamped with actions launched by test plaintiffs and public interest groups. As compelling as access to justice concerns may be, they cannot justify this Court unilaterally authorizing a revolution in how litigation is conceived and conducted.

Second, the advance costs award must be an exceptional measure; it must be in the interests of justice that it be awarded. Therefore, the applicant must explore all other possible funding options. These include, but are not limited to, public funding options like legal aid and other programs designed to assist various groups in taking legal action. An advance costs award is neither a substitute for, nor a supplement to, these programs. An applicant must also be able to demonstrate that an attempt, albeit unsuccessful, has been made to obtain private funding through fundraising campaigns, loan applications, contingency fee agreements and any other available options. If the applicant cannot afford all costs of the litigation, but is not impecunious, the applicant must commit to making a contribution to the litigation. Finally, different kinds of costs mechanisms, like adverse costs immunity, should also be considered. In doing so, courts must be careful not to assume that a creative costs award is merited in every case; such an award is an exceptional one, to be granted in special circumstances. Courts should remain mindful of all options when they are called upon to craft appropriate orders in such circumstances. Also, they should not assume that the litigants who qualify for these awards must benefit from them absolutely. In the United Kingdom, where costs immunity (or "protective orders") can be ordered in specified circumstances, the order may be given with the caveat that the successful applicant cannot collect anything more than modest costs from the other party at the end of the trial: see *R (on the application of Corner House Research) v. Secretary of State for Trade & Industry*, [2005] 1 WLR 2600, [2005] EWCA Civ 192 (Eng. CA), at para. 76. We agree with this nuanced approach.

Third, no injustice can arise if the matter at issue could be settled, or the public interest could be satisfied, without an advance costs award. Again, we must stress that advance costs orders are appropriate only as a last resort. In *Okanagan*, the bands tried, before seeking an advance costs order, to resolve their disputes by avoiding a trial altogether. Likewise, courts should consider whether other litigation is pending and may be conducted for the same purpose, without requiring an interim order of costs. Courts should also be mindful to avoid using these orders in such a way that they encourage purely artificial litigation contrary to the public interest.

Finally, the granting of an advance costs order does not mean that the litigant has free rein. On the contrary, when the public purse—or another private party—takes on the burden of an advance costs award, the litigant must relinquish some manner of control over how the litigation proceeds. The litigant cannot spend the opposing party's money without scrutiny. The benefit of such funding does not imply that a party can, at will, multiply hours of preparation, add expert witnesses, engage in every available proceeding, or lodge every conceivable argument. A definite structure must be imposed or approved by the court itself, as it alone bears the responsibility for ensuring that the award is workable.

For example, the court should set limits on the chargeable rates and hours of legal work, closely monitor the parties' adherence to its dictates, and cap the advance costs award at an appropriate global amount. It should also be sensitive to the reality that work often expands to fit the available resources and that the "maximum" amounts contemplated by a court will almost certainly be reached. As well, the possibility of setting the advance costs award off against damages actually collected at the end of the trial should be contemplated. In determining the quantum of the award, the court should remain aware that the purpose of these orders is to restore some balance between litigants, not to create perfect equality between the parties. Legislated schemes like legal aid and other programs designed to assist various groups in taking legal action do not purport to create equality among litigants, and there is no justification for advance costs awards placing successful applicants in a more favourable position. An advance costs award is meant to provide a basic level of assistance necessary for the case to proceed.

A court awarding advance costs must be guided by the condition of necessity. For parties with unequal financial resources to face each other in court is a regular occurrence. People with limited means all too often find themselves discouraged from pursuing litigation because of the cost involved. Problems like this are troubling, but they do not normally trigger advance costs awards. We do not mean to minimize their unfairness. On the contrary, we believe they are sufficiently serious that this Court cannot purport to solve them all through the mechanism of advance costs awards. Courts should not seek on their own to bring an alternative and extensive legal aid system into being. That would amount to imprudent and inappropriate judicial overreach.

4.2 Applying the Rule in Okanagan to the Facts of This Appeal

The appellant has asked this Court to award it advance costs with respect to two separate issues it raises in its litigation against Customs. The Four Books Appeal concerns Customs' prohibition of four books imported by the appellant for sale in its store. The Systemic Review, on the other hand, involves a broad investigation of Customs' practices relating to obscenity prohibitions.

We will first consider the merit of these claims, and will then discuss their public importance. We want to emphasize that the impecuniosity requirement, though listed first in *Okanagan*, cannot be used to give impecunious litigants a *prima facie* right to advance costs, as some interveners before this Court have suggested. Accordingly, we will consider it last. The question of impecuniosity will not even arise where a case is not otherwise special enough to merit this exceptional award.

4.2.1 Standard of Review

A trial judge enjoys considerable discretion in fashioning a costs award. This discretion
has two corollaries.

First, a plethora of options are available to a judge when rendering a decision on costs.
While the general rule is that costs follow the cause, as we have seen, this need not always
be the case.

Second, a judge's decision on costs will generally be insulated from appellate review.
In the past, this Court has established that costs awards should not be interfered with
lightly: see *Odhavji Estate*, at para. 77. But this does not mean that no decision on costs
should ever be interfered with. For instance, in *Okanagan*, advance costs were granted
on appeal after having been denied by the trial judge. A costs award can be set aside if it
is based on an error in principle or is plainly wrong: *Hamilton v. Open Window Bakery
Ltd.* (2003), [2004] 1 SCR 303, 2004 SCC 9 (SCC), at para. 27. In exercising their discretion regarding costs, trial judges must, especially in making an order as exceptional as
one awarding advance costs, be careful to stay within recognized boundaries.

Despite the deference owed to the exercise of a discretion by a trial judge, we conclude
that, in the present case, Bennett J went beyond the boundaries this Court set in
Okanagan.

4.2.2 Prima Facie Merit and Public Importance

As was explained in *Okanagan*, the merit requirement involves the following
consideration:

> 2. The claim to be adjudicated [must be] *prima facie* meritorious; that is, the claim is at
> least of *sufficient merit that it is contrary to the interests of justice for the opportunity to pursue
> the case to be forfeited* just because the litigant lacks financial means. [Emphasis added;
> para. 40.]

The explicit reference in this passage to the interests of justice suggests that the test
requires something more than mere proof that one's case has sufficient merit not to be
dismissed summarily. Rather, an applicant must prove that the interests of justice would
not be served if a lack of resources made it necessary to abort the litigation. The very
wording of the requirement confirms that the interests of justice will not be jeopardized
every time a litigant is forced to withdraw from litigation for financial reasons. The reason for this is that the context in which merit is considered is conditioned by the need to
show that the case is exceptional. This does not mean that the case must be shown to
have exceptional merit; rather, it must be shown to have sufficient merit to satisfy the
court that proceeding with it is in the interests of justice. In the case at bar, as found by
Bennett J, there is obviously a serious issue justifying a decision to have the matter proceed to trial. The question is whether a claim such as the one made by the appellant is
sufficient to support a finding that the requirement of special circumstances is met. It is
difficult to dissociate one from the other. We think there is no need to do so and will
proceed accordingly.

. . .

The nature of the injustice at stake in the case at bar can be contrasted with the one that was at stake in *Okanagan*. In that case, the bands, having been thrust into a situation requiring litigation, could not afford to pay for the litigation themselves, but could not afford the costs of forfeiting it either. The appellant in the instant case, on the other hand, has taken the Systemic Review upon itself even though it characterizes the fight as one that "makes no business sense."

The requirement that the issues raised transcend the litigant's individual interests and that it be profoundly important that they be resolved in the interests of justice (*Okanagan*, at para. 46) can be disposed of with little difficulty where the Four Books Appeal is concerned. Because the appellant has chosen to investigate Customs' general operations under the Systemic Review, it is clear that the Four Books Appeal concerns no interest beyond that of the appellant itself and, as a consequence, is not special enough to justify an award of advance costs. This is especially so given that all the legal issues the appellant has canvassed in that appeal were already considered, and ruled upon, by this Court in *Little Sisters No. 1*. As the appellant itself observes at para. 10 of its factum, Binnie J left the door open to further actions by the appellant with the words, "[t]hese findings should provide the appellants with a solid platform from which to launch any further action in the Supreme Court of British Columbia should they consider that further action is necessary" (*Little Sisters No. 1*, at para. 158). At most, the Four Books Appeal deals with the application of *Little Sisters No. 1* to a specific set of facts.

· · ·

… Where only one of the possible results on the merits could render the case publicly important, the court should not conclude that the public importance requirement is met. It is in general only, when the public importance of a case can be established regardless of the ultimate holding on the merits, that a court should consider this requirement from *Okanagan* satisfied.

4.2.3 Impecuniosity

In a case like the present one, it is not even necessary for a court to consider the applicant's impecuniosity. The access to justice purpose of advance costs cannot be triggered absent the kind of exceptional circumstances that the Court discussed in *Okanagan*.

We agree that corporations are not barred from receiving advance costs awards. However, the judge should ask in every case whether the applicant has made the effort that is required to satisfy a court that all other funding options have been exhausted. In *Okanagan*, this requirement was described as follows:

> 1. The party seeking interim costs genuinely cannot afford to pay for the litigation, and no other realistic option exists for bringing the issues to trial—in short, the litigation would be unable to proceed if the order were not made. [para. 40]

In evaluating whether the impecuniosity requirement is met, a court should also consider the potential cost of the litigation. In the present appeal, the cost estimate for the trial is well over $1 million. The Four Books Appeal alone is somewhat more affordable according to the appellant's estimate: approximately $300,000. Such cost estimates form an integral part of the evidence; the court should subject them to scrutiny, and then use them to consider whether the litigant is impecunious to the extent that an advance costs order is the only viable option.

A court should generally consider whether the applicant has tried to obtain a loan. In the criminal law context, financing litigation through credit is something that courts will look for before deciding that an accused's failure to obtain counsel merits a constitutional remedy: *R v. K. (K.K.)* (1997), 159 NSR (2d) 357 (NS CA). An application for advance costs should demand no less.

The impecuniosity requirement from *Okanagan* means that it must be proven to be impossible to proceed otherwise before advance costs will be ordered. Advance costs should not be used as a smart litigation strategy; they are the last resort before an injustice results for a litigant, and for the public at large.

5. Conclusion

Once the three-part test from *Okanagan* has been met, the court must exercise its discretion to decide whether advance costs ought to be awarded or whether another type of order is justified. In exercising its discretion, the court must remain sensitive to any concerns that did not arise in its analysis of the test. Although the appellant in the case at bar has failed to meet the *Okanagan* test, we believe that this case also raises issues that should in any event have prompted Bennett J to exercise her discretion against an advance costs award in respect of the Systemic Review even if the *Okanagan* test had satisfied.

As we have stressed, the *Okanagan* test requires that an advance costs award be used only as a last resort in order to protect the public interest. The test prevents an applicant from succeeding in an advance costs application where legal action is unnecessary (the merit requirement) or where private funding has not been diligently sought (the impecuniosity requirement). But there will sometimes be other options that are not contemplated by the *Okanagan* analysis.

· · ·

To proceed in this way is consistent with the principle stated above that an applicant must be willing to relinquish some control over the litigation to benefit from an advance costs award. Since a litigant who has been awarded advance costs is proceeding with the aid of funds received from another party, the litigant must accept certain limitations. These may be strictly financial—e.g., caps on spending—but they may also go more directly to the litigant's litigation strategy. For instance, spending limits will mean that litigants proceeding with the aid of advance costs awards may be limited in their choice and in the number of counsel and experts. Also, the court awarding advance costs must consider whether the litigant's chosen method of proceeding at trial is compatible with the notion of advance costs being a last resort and may thus need to establish a framework for the conduct of the planned litigation. In the present appeal, while the appellant understandably wants to resolve the issues in the Systemic Review as quickly as possible, it may be preferable to proceed first with the Four Books Appeal before deciding the issues arising out of the Systemic Review. In response to an argument of this sort, an applicant must be able to prove either that modifying its litigation strategy would not be more efficient and would not lead to demonstrable savings, or that retaining its original litigation strategy is necessary to ensure that justice is done.

The rule in *Okanagan* arose on a very specific and compelling set of facts that created a situation that should hardly ever reoccur. As this Court held in *Okanagan*, an advance costs award should remain a last resort. The costs award in the instant case did not meet the required standards.

[McLachlin CJC also agreed to dismiss the appeal, but for different reasons. She held that the third criteria to award advanced costs must comprise an acknowledgment of "special circumstances" warranting public funding beyond just the "public interest" of the case. Binnie J dissented. He would have granted public funding because of the "pressing public interest" of this particular case.]

NOTES AND QUESTIONS

1. With reference to the theory behind Canada's costs system, how can you explain such divergence from the judges with respect to how to apply the *Okanagan* test? Do you think it explains the result because Binnie J was the judge in a case involving the Little Sisters bookstore before? Does one's perspective of access to justice affect the result? Or is it something else?

2. There has been a remarkable amount of scholarship exploring public interest cases, Canada's costs regime and how to foster access to justice within that regime. See, for example, Chris Tollefson, "When the 'Public Interest' Loses: The Liability of Public Interest Litigants for Adverse Costs Awards" (1995), 29 *UBC L Rev.* 303; Lara Friedlander, "Costs and the Public Interest Litigant" (1995), 40 *McGill LJ* 55; Chris Tollefson, Darlene Gilliland, and Jerry DeMarco, "Towards a Costs Jurisprudence in Public Interest Litigation" (2004), 83 *Can. Bar Rev.* 473; Brian McLaughlin, Cheryl Tobias, and Craig Cameron, "Interim Costs: The Impact of *Okanagan Indian Band*" (2005), 54 *UNBLJ* 126; and Chris Tollefson, "Costs and the Public Interest Litigant: *Okanagan Indian Band* and Beyond" (2006), 29 *Can. J Admin. L and Prac.* 39.

3. Why is interim public funding for litigation restricted only to "public interest" cases? Are there not more people hurt in private law personal injury cases, where the law often also needs developing? Do more citizens have a constitutional question to resolve?

E. Public Funding of Litigation

1. Institutional Support

Although litigation is largely funded by the litigants, there is a sizable public contribution to the maintenance of the litigation process. The state assumes responsibility for the provision of buildings, judges, and support staff. A small charge is made for the issuing of various documents, but the major portion of these other expenses is assumed by the state. There is a division of responsibility between the federal and provincial governments. In accordance with the Constitution, the federal government funds the federal court system, the Supreme Court of Canada, and the salaries of the provincial superior district and county courts. The provincial governments assume financial responsibility for the administration and costs of all courts in the province and for the salaries of lower court judges.

2. Legal Aid

The primary means of public support of certain parties in litigation is legal aid. How should society decide who gets legal aid and for what purposes? What does the "access" in access to justice mean? If there is a basic entitlement to justice, how does society ensure that this is obtainable? Also, how realistic is it to imagine that there will be a significant appetite to adequately fund legal aid programs?

The three extracts that follow seek to place present legal arrangements in a broad context. The first extract looks to the public policy justifications for providing legal aid and asks whether it is possible to provide a rank ordering of legal aid needs and expenditures. The second extract introduces the basic structure of legal aid delivery schemes and assesses future challenges. The third extract is an analysis of the economic and human resources feasibility of the current model and its need to change.

A Blueprint for Publicly Funded Legal Services
Report of the Ontario Legal Aid Review (Toronto: Queen's Printer, 1997), 67-74
(footnotes omitted)

In order to identify the underlying moral or political justification for the state's obligation to provide legal aid, if indeed it has one, some basic issues of political or democratic theory must be considered. Our purpose in doing so is to inform our understanding of how priority-setting, as a matter of principle, might best be conducted in the legal aid context. It might be assumed that the most fruitful analytical path for achieving this purpose is to identify the normative justifications for the state's obligation to provide legal aid in particular contexts, such as criminal law and family law, and evaluate those justifications with a view to placing them in an order that would suggest, at the level of general principle, that preference should be given to the funding of criminal law or family law legal aid or vice versa.

We have come to the conclusion that such an approach is not fruitful. In coming to this conclusion, we have been much influenced by a thoughtful background paper prepared for the Review by Professor David Dyzenhaus. Indeed, in his view, this approach, which he terms the "box approach," is misguided. In what follows we suggest that the underlying normative foundation for the state's obligation to provide some form of legal aid is to be found in Canadians' shared commitment to the Rule of Law as an essential feature of the Canadian political system. Further, we attempt to demonstrate why the "box approach" to priority-setting is not satisfactory and, more particularly, why a preoccupation with the value of avoiding incarceration, or "negative liberty," will distort priority-setting for legal aid. Finally, we identify the implications of these conclusions for legal aid priority-setting.

· · ·

As a matter of principle, then, the underlying rationale for the state's obligation to facilitate access to the law is not restricted to any particular kind of law or type of legal situation. The normative foundations for legal aid do not assist us in making an argument for giving priority to one domain of law over another in terms of access to legal aid resources.

One further implication of some importance can be drawn from the relationship of the Rule of Law, through the publicity condition, to the state's obligation to facilitate access to the law. To the extent that the law is needlessly complex or in some other respect designed in a manner that indirectly or, indeed, directly requires legal advice and assistance, it may be that the legal regime in question has unnecessarily imposed burdens on the state to facilitate access to the law. If, for example, the defective design of a particular statutory scheme makes it necessary that individualized legal problems be handled on a case-by-case basis, the defect in question will have imposed on the parties, and upon the state, a very expensive burden. In some instances, then, the state's obligation to facilitate access might be much better served by removing the defect from the statutory scheme. This is, in our view, an important point, and one which we discuss at some length in chapter 6 of this report.

(b) Beyond "Negative Liberty"

Having set out our conclusion that an examination of the normative foundations of legal aid does not provide a principled basis for giving priority access to legal aid resources to one legal domain over another, we must consider at some length a serious argument to the contrary. Some would suggest that it is easiest to justify imposition of an obligation on the state to fund legal aid in the criminal law context. Two reasons for this suggestion are typically offered.

First, it is suggested that it is in the domain of criminal law that the accused individual is at risk of losing his or her physical liberty, and this factor engages the important value we place on not losing one's freedom, or the "negative liberty" interest. Second, in the context of criminal law, the accused is pitted against the massive resources of the state, and it may be argued that simple obligations of fairness require the state to provide assistance to an accused person facing such an unequal contest. For reasons such as these, it is arguable that the allocation of public resources to legal aid in the criminal law context can be defended on grounds that are unrelated to the publicity condition and the Rule of Law.

· · ·

Similarly, the "negative liberty" test is not particularly helpful in drawing clear distinctions for priority-setting purposes between criminal law and other legal domains. In the first place, it can be and has been argued that "negative liberty" interests are often at stake in other legal domains. In refugee determinations, for example, the unsuccessful claimants may well face a period of incarceration, or worse, if returned to their jurisdiction of origin. The involuntary civil commitment of a psychiatric patient, although clearly not a criminal law matter, unquestionably engages the "negative liberty" interest. In the family law context, some observers have argued, in effect, that "negative liberty" issues are often at stake. Thus, for example, where an administrative agency threatens to remove a child from the family home because of an allegedly unsafe environment, the situation might be characterized as involving "negative liberty" (at least for the child) and, indeed, as one which places the family in a contest with a powerful agency of the state. Cases of domestic violence where the victim is in need of legal assistance simply to get out of the home or to establish any freedom of movement in the community may also be considered to engage the "negative liberty" interest. In short, the boundaries between the domains based on the "negative liberty" test begin to crumble on closer examination.

More important, perhaps, the kinds of cases in these other domains which would fail a "negative liberty" test are not necessarily less deserving than many criminal law "negative liberty" cases. ...

. . .

For all of these reasons, then, we have come to the conclusion that the "negative liberty" interest does not provide a satisfactory basis for a rank-ordering of claims to legal aid resources from one legal domain to the next or, indeed, within particular legal domains. Although the "negative liberty" interest is, indeed, one of the important normative justifications for providing legal aid, it is only one of several such interests. Focusing on the "negative liberty" interest for priority-setting purposes at the expense of others will lead, we suggest, to a distorted analysis of the relative weight to be given to any particular claim for legal aid.

(c) Conclusion

Our conclusion, then, is that an examination of the normative foundations for legal aid supports the notion that the state has an obligation, varying with the circumstances at issue, to facilitate access to law. This obligation flows from the condition of publicity, which is an inherent requirement in the use of law in a society such as ours, which accepts the fundamental importance of the Rule of Law. Where the law deployed by the state is complex, and affects important interests of those with limited means, the publicity condition will require the state to facilitate access to the law. Legal aid is one, but not the only, device that might be used to meet that obligation. Another, for example, might be to render the law less complex. An examination of the normative justifications for legal aid does not, however, appear to provide a basis for a rank-ordering of claims that might be made by various legal domains, nor, within such domains, a basis for rank-ordering the claims of particular case types. More specifically, the interest in "negative liberty" does not appear to facilitate such an exercise. Indeed, we adopt the view that undue reliance on the "negative liberty" interest causes a number of distortions in the analysis of the relative weight of particular claims for access to legal aid resources.

The interests that support claims to legal aid resources are various, both within criminal law and in other fields. Analysis at the level of general principle, then, suggests that priority-setting in legal aid should be premised on the assumption that a rank-ordering of this kind cannot be sustained. Further, our difficulty in identifying general principles which will facilitate a rank-ordering of entitlements to legal aid suggests that priority-setting in the legal aid context needs to be based on the circumstances of particular cases and the parties to them, should retain an element of flexibility, and should be subject to revision in the light of experience.

Fred Zemans and Patrick Monahan, *From Crisis to Reform:*
A New Legal Aid Plan for Ontario
(Toronto: Osgoode Hall Law School, 1996) (Revised and updated)

A. Introduction

There is no single standard method of administering and/or delivering legal aid services. Within Canada, each province has developed its own unique plan. Legal aid plans in England and Wales, Australia, and the United States are different again.

Seven legal aid plans in Canada are administered by independent statutory organizations. Only two are administered by provincial legal aid societies: New Brunswick and Alberta. Legal aid services in Prince Edward Island are administered directly by the provincial government.

Some plans deliver services through a "judicare" model, whereby services are provided by private practitioners who are paid by the plan on a fee-for-services basis according to a predetermined tariff. Other plans deliver services through a "staff lawyer" model, whereby the plan provides services through salaried staff lawyers who work directly for the plan (when a staff lawyer model provides criminal services, it is generally referred to as a "public defender" model). Other models are also used, such as the "neighbourhood law office" model or "contract" model. Several plans, including Ontario, use a "mixed" system, employing several different models to deliver services to clients. No two "mixed" plans are alike, however, as each utilizes a different selection and proportion of models to deliver services.

Two issues cross almost all jurisdictional boundaries. First, almost all of these jurisdictions have had to take steps to reduce costs in the face of rapidly escalating costs and the resulting pressure from governments—who provide the vast majority of legal aid funding—to reduce or limit those costs. Many of these plans have had to make major structural reforms live within newly imposed fiscal limits. Second, most plans have had to address the changing nature of the demand for legal aid services. For example, in almost all jurisdictions, family law cases have a much greater prominence than they did ten or fifteen years ago. Plans have had to adapt to providing these services, often within the context of reduced revenues.

This section will briefly review the administration and delivery of legal aid services in Canadian jurisdictions and in England and Wales. Legal aid in the United States is sufficiently unique that a detailed review of American models would not be productive.

This section illustrates that there are many different ways of delivering legal aid services and many different ways of coping with change.

· · ·

C. Legal Aid in Canada

1. Newfoundland

The *Legal Aid Act* governs the legal aid system in Newfoundland. The Act establishes an independent seven-member commission as the body responsible for administering legal aid services in the province. The provincial government names five members of the commission. The Deputy Minister of Justice and the Provincial Director serve as *ex officio* members.

Services are delivered through a mixed system of both private and staff lawyers. Approved applicants obtain a certificate that can be presented to a staff lawyer or a private lawyer who belongs to a legal aid panel. From 2000-2001, staff lawyers took on approximately 94 percent of the total caseloads.

The plan's substantive coverage closely follows the terms of the federal–provincial cost-sharing agreement on criminal and young offenders. The plan covers most family cases. Coverage for other civil legal aid is discretionary, subject to an evaluation of both the likely success of the matter and its cost relative to the anticipated recovery.

2. Prince Edward Island

Prince Edward Island has no legislative legal aid program. Rather, the Provincial Attorney General directly administers the plan.

Services are provided through a salaried public defender office. In 2004, there were four full-time staff lawyers. Private counsel are retained if a staff lawyer has a scheduling conflict, conflict of interest in a particular case, or in a "mandatory choice of counsel" case, as defined by the federal–provincial cost-sharing agreement. Mandatory-choice cases exist where the charge carries a mandatory sentence to life imprisonment upon conviction.

Criminal law legal aid is available to financially eligible individuals charged with those offences described in the federal–provincial cost-sharing agreement. With regards to family law matters, the plan offers full coverage where there is a present or ongoing threat of domestic violence, and limited coverage for all other family cases involving child custody, access, and support. The plan also covers matters under the *Mental Health Act* dealing with child protection, adult protection, and involuntary hospitalization. Other civil matters are not covered.

3. Nova Scotia

The *Legal Aid Act* governs legal aid in Nova Scotia. The Act establishes the Legal Aid Commission, a seventeen-member independent commission. Two of the directors are non-voting members selected from the public service. The Provincial Governor-in-Council appoints all other directors; 8 are nominated by the Minister of Justice (Attorney General) and 7 are nominated by the Council of Nova Scotia Barristers' Society.

The Commission delivers most of its services via a network of 13 community-based law offices as well as 2 sub-offices known as Nova Scotia Legal Aid. The offices are staffed by salaried lawyers and, in certain situations, supplemented by lawyers in private practice on a fee-for service basis.

No type of case is expressly excluded from coverage. Cases are, however, prioritized. Criminal law cases have the highest priority, followed by family law cases. Cases in which the applicant is likely to lose his or her home or livelihood, or cannot retain counsel without suffering undue financial hardship, are third priority.

4. New Brunswick

Legal aid in New Brunswick is governed by the terms of the *Legal Aid Act*. The Act allows the Law Society of New Brunswick to administer the legal aid plan via regional legal aid offices. The Law Society has established a Legal Aid Committee which oversees the administration of the plan. The Committee is composed of at least three persons appointed by the Law Society, at least one of who must be a member of the Law Society. The provincial government also appoints an Advisory Committee to review legal aid issues. The Committee reports to the Minister of Justice and consists of provincial judges, the Deputy Minister of Justice, the Deputy Minister of Family and Community Services, and two lawyers in private practice.

Legal aid in New Brunswick is delivered exclusively through a judicare model. There is no staff delivery of services. Legal aid certificates are generally provided for accused charged with serious criminal or young offender offences. Duty Counsel are also available daily in Provincial Court for accused who wish to speak to a lawyer. Civil legal aid is available for a wide range of matters—such as bankruptcy, divorce, and appeals.

5. Quebec

The *Legal Aid Act* governs legal aid in Quebec. This Act establishes the Commission des services juridiques, a twelve-member independent commission with responsibility for administering legal aid in Quebec. The Government chooses the Commission's members from groups who, because of their activities, are likely to contribute to the study and solution of the legal problems of the underprivileged.

The Commission creates and supervises the work of several regional and local legal aid centres. These regional and local centres operate the plan within specified administrative areas. A board of directors appointed by the Commission oversees each centre. The membership of these boards is generally divided equally between the legal profession and residents of the area.

Quebec operates a mixed model of service delivery. Within their specific areas, regional and local centres provide services through a staff model. The Act specifies, however, that services may be provided to approved applicants by a private lawyer if the applicant specifically requests it, or in the event of a conflict of interest, or the need for specific legal expertise. If no request is made, the case will usually be assigned to a staff lawyer. The legal aid program covers almost all areas of law.

6. Ontario

The terms of the *Legal Aid Services Act* govern legal aid in Ontario. The Act establishes Legal Aid Ontario (LAO), an independent statutory corporation responsible for legal aid in the province. The eleven members of LAO's Board of Directors are appointed by the provincial government: the chairperson is selected by the Attorney General from a list recommended by a government committee, five others are selected from a list recommended by the Law Society, and five others are recommended by the Attorney General.

Services are delivered through a mixed model. Approved applicants obtain a certificate that can be presented to a staff lawyer, duty counsel, or a private lawyer who belongs to a legal aid panel. From 2002-2003, private lawyers took on approximately 72 percent of the total caseloads. LAO also provides funding for clinics, student legal aid services societies, and alternative dispute resolution services. Finally, assistance is offered to individuals representing themselves through the provision of summary advice, assistance in preparing documents, and information packages or self-help kits.

Services are provided in the areas of criminal, family, clinic and mental health law. Comprehensive civil legal aid is also offered, subject to a few exceptions such as defamation and realtor proceedings.

7. Manitoba

Legal aid in Manitoba is governed by the terms of the *Legal Aid Services Society of Manitoba Act*. The Act establishes the Legal Aid Services Society, an independent, statutory corporation. The provincial government appoints the Society's twelve-member Board. Four of the Board members must be non-lawyers, three must be chosen from a list submitted by the Law Society of Manitoba, and one must be a staff lawyer.

Legal Aid Manitoba (LAM) uses a mixed-delivery model, employing both private lawyers and nine staff-lawyer offices around the province. The plan also operates two specialty clinics. Approved applicants have the right to choose between private lawyers and staff lawyers. Historically, about 70 percent of applicants have chosen private lawyers.

LAM has been described as "the best example to date of a fully elaborated mixed model of service delivery." LAM projects include the development of a Public Interest Law Centre, the Northern Paralegal Project, the Expanded Eligibility Program, the Portage Legal Services Initiative, other block contracting projects, and the Full Service Duty Counsel Project.

8. Saskatchewan

Legal aid in Saskatchewan is governed by the *Legal Aid Act, 1983*. The Act establishes a ten-member independent statutory commission responsible for the delivery of legal aid services throughout the province.

Legal aid services are provided through a staff delivery system. Legal advice and representation are provided by lawyers and non-lawyers employed by the Commission. Cases are only referred to the private bar in mandatory-choice-of-counsel cases or, occasionally, in cases of a staff lawyer conflict. In conflict cases, the applicant has the option of choosing another staff lawyer or a private lawyer from a panel of lawyers.

Criminal law coverage is provided for all indictable offences. Summary conviction offences and provincial offences are only covered when there is a likelihood of imprisonment or loss of livelihood. All young offender charges are covered. Civil law coverage is restricted to family law matters. Coverage also extends to groups, organizations, or societies, if the majority of their members are eligible applicants and if the matter is within the range of services offered by legal aid.

9. Alberta

Alberta does not have specific legal aid legislation. Rather, the legal aid program is governed by an agreement between the provincial government and the Law Society of Alberta giving the Law Society statutory authority to establish, maintain, and operate a provincial legal aid plan. The eleven members of the Board of Directors are appointed by the Law Society from a list of candidates recommended by a Nominating Committee. The Board appoints an executive director who is responsible for the administration of the plan.

Services are delivered almost entirely through a judicare model. Clients can choose their own counsel or have one appointed from a roster of participating lawyers if they have not stated a preference.

Criminal law legal aid extends to all matters covered by the federal–provincial agreement. Unlimited coverage is extended to all applicants who are young offenders. Civil coverage is extended when plan officials determine that the case has merit and that the cost of the probable action is reasonable in relation to the remedy sought. The case must also be one in which a reasonable person of modest means would pay for a lawyer. The majority of civil law cases are divorce and related domestic matters.

10. British Columbia

Legal aid in British Columbia is governed by the terms of the *Legal Services Society Act*. This act establishes the Legal Services Society (LSS), an independent statutory body responsible for the administration of legal aid in the province. The Board of directors is comprised of nine directors: five directors are to be appointed by the provincial government and four directors are to be appointed by the Law Society of British Columbia after consultation with the executive of the British Columbia branch of the Canadian Bar Association.

Legal aid in British Columbia is delivered through a mixed model. Approved applicants obtain a certificate that can be presented to a staff lawyer, duty counsel, or a private lawyer who belongs to a legal aid panel. Legal aid and legal information services are provided through 7 regional centres and 21 local agents across British Columbia. From 2002-2003, private lawyers took on approximately 74 percent of the total caseloads. The LSS also provides funding for alternative dispute resolution services. Finally, assistance is offered to individuals representing themselves through the provision of summary advice, assistance in preparing documents, and information packages or self-help kits.

Criminal legal aid covers all indictable offences and summary conviction offences in which imprisonment or loss of livelihood is likely upon conviction. Civil law coverage is provided for serious family and immigration law matters.

Michael Trebilcock, *Report of the Legal Aid Review*
(Toronto: Ontario Ministry of Attorney General, 2008)

In the course of my consultations with stakeholder groups, no issue engaged more attention and provoked more criticism than the management of the legal aid tariff, and more
specifically, the hourly rates payable under the tariff and, to a lesser extent, the maximum
time allocation for particular proceedings and maximum allocations for disbursements
and travel time. The anger within the private bar at what they regard as grossly inadequate hourly rates for services provided by members of the private bar under certificates
issued by LAO was palpable, and the sense of alienation from the legal aid system ubi-
quitous. They are not only outspoken in exercising voice, but more to the point are voting
with their feet in exiting the system in increasing numbers. On the criteria of exit, voice
and loyalty, the certificate system is in tenuous condition. The diminishing commitment
by the private bar to the provision of legal aid services poses a fundamental challenge to
the sustainability of the legal aid system as we have known it. This issue is one that requires urgent and immediate attention. My terms of reference require me to examine
"alternatives to the current tariff process, including methods of ensuring regular reviews
to set and adjust the hourly rate paid to lawyers doing legal aid work."

The legal aid tariff has a long history in Ontario that was reviewed at some length in
the Holden-Kaufman Task Force Report for LAO in 2000 and is briefly summarized and
updated in an appendix to this section of my report (along with a brief review of comparative experience). In brief, the legal aid tariff was created by the *Legal Aid Act* of 1967
to provide for the payment of fees out of public revenues to lawyers providing legal services under the certificate system with a view to approximating the modest fees that
would be charged to a client who could pay, but for whom the payment of a larger fee
might involve some hardship (the so-called "client of modest means" test). At that time
the certificate (or judicare) system was the only delivery mechanism for legal aid services, prior to the emergence of the clinic system beginning in the late 1970s.

The tariff and the maximum hour allocations and the maximum allocations for various related matters such as disbursements and travel time are set out in a complex regulation promulgated by the Lieutenant Governor in Council. While the tariff and its
structure have been revised from time to time, often long periods of time have elapsed
without significant revision. For example, hourly rates for legal aid work were not
changed between 1987 and 2001, although in the last several years the tariff has been increased by about 16 per cent as a result of several modest changes to it. As of 2006-07 the
tariff rates for legal aid services provided under certificates are as follows:

- Tier I (0-4 years) $ 77.56
- Tier II (4-10 years) $ 87.26
- Tier III (10 years +) $ 96.95

In submissions that I received and in consultations which I held with various stakeholder groups, most of the attention was focused on the inadequacy of these hourly rates,
but given the increasing complexity of many kinds of legal proceedings covered by legal
aid certificates, a number of concerns were also addressed to the permitted maximum

hourly allocations for various legal proceedings under the regulations prescribing the tariffs (a matter which I do not feel equipped to deal with in detail in this review).

LAO's submission to me reported the effect of low tariffs on lawyer participation rates. The number of private lawyers providing legal aid services dropped steadily between 1999 and 2007, notwithstanding an increase in both the tariff and the number of certificates issued during this period.

- Between 1999-00 and 2006-07, the total number of lawyers paid by LAO has fallen by 16 per cent (4,932 to 4,119)
- Between 1999-00 and 2006-07, the total number of *criminal* lawyers paid by LAO has fallen by 14 per cent (2,875 to 2,460)
- Between 1999-00 and 2006-07, the total number of *family* lawyers paid by LAO has fallen by 29 per cent (2,964 to 2,109)

LAO data also show that there is a significant "drop off" in the number of lawyers providing legal aid services once they become more experienced. Again, this trend is most notable in the area of family law. For example, in 1999-00 there were 855 "basic level" lawyers (0-4 years' experience) providing family certificates compared to 722 lawyers at the next tier (4-10 years' experience). By 2006-07, there were only 392 lawyers at the 4 to 10 years' experience level providing family certificate services, a decline of 46 per cent.

The seniority profile, when combined with an analysis of the "participation mix" (amount of legal aid work undertaken by different categories of legal aid lawyers), illustrates the risks to sustainability of the certificate program, particularly in family law. LAO data show that LAO relies upon a small number of experienced family lawyers to deliver a significant proportion of its family law services. In 2006-07, only 11 per cent of family lawyers paid by LAO can be said to have a significant legal aid practice by accepting more than 60 certificates for the entire year (an average of more than five certificates per month). By way of contrast, 60 per cent of family lawyers paid by LAO accepted fewer than 12 certificates for the entire year (an average of less than one certificate per month).

On the criminal side, the data show that LAO relies on upon a comparatively larger number of experienced criminal lawyers to deliver a significant proportion of its criminal law services. In 2006-07, 22 per cent of criminal lawyers paid by LAO had a significant legal aid practice (accepted more than 60 certificates for the entire year). Fifty per cent of criminal lawyers paid by LAO accepted fewer than 12 certificates for the entire year.

In both cases, LAO relies on a small proportion of senior lawyers to provide the bulk of legal aid services. In family law, more than half (52 per cent) of lawyers with a significant legal aid practice have more than 10 years' experience. In criminal law, the proportion is even higher, at 61 per cent.

Relying on a small number of significant, experienced providers to supply the bulk of legal aid certificate services, while realizing the benefits of experience and specialization, is also quite risky. It means that even a minor reduction in the number of providers could have important consequences for client services. Those consequences will be serious if LAO loses significant providers in small or rural communities.

Equally important, the data suggest that the legal aid system may not be generating enough new lawyers to replace the more experienced lawyers who now make up the bulk of LAO's service providers. The situation in family law is particularly acute. In 2006-07 there were 58 Tier I and 56 Tier II (i.e. less than 10 years' experience) family lawyers across Ontario who had what could be described as a significant legal aid practice. In other words, there were slightly more than 100 relatively young family lawyers in Ontario who maintained a significant legal aid caseload. This is a small number of practitioners given the size and diversity of Ontario. On the other hand, there are more young and relatively young criminal lawyers with significant legal aid practices. In 2006-07 there were 214 criminal lawyers in this category (105 Tier I and 109 Tier II).

· · ·

In considering issues relating to the tariff, I accept as a premise the fairness and efficiency rationales for an appropriate tariff set out by the Holden-Kaufman Task Force in its report in 2000:

> In thinking about the appropriate level of the hourly rate of the legal aid tariff as opposed to its structure (such as maximum hours per service, the use of block or lump sum tariffs, counsel fees, or per diems), one could adopt a fairness perspective, an efficiency perspective, or both. We are influenced by both perspectives.

From a fairness perspective, one might argue that it is unfair for current and prospective providers of legal aid services to receive an hourly rate for their services that has declined through time while the compensation levels for lawyers in private practice, federally and provincially appointed judges, crown attorneys and other government lawyers, and physicians has increased. Thus, lawyers that are committed to allocating a significant portion of their practices to some of the least advantaged members of society are being asked to make financial sacrifices, on account of their commitment, that most lawyers in private practice and most lawyers or judges in the public sector are not required to make.

From an efficiency perspective, concerns about the level of the tariff must focus not on the fairness of comparisons between lawyers providing legal aid services and other professional groups, but rather the short and long-run incentive effects of undercompensation of lawyers providing legal aid services relative to lawyers pursuing other kinds of practices or non-private practice careers. These incentive effects are likely to affect both lawyers currently providing legal aid services and existing or future lawyers who might prospectively provide such services. With respect to the existing cohort of lawyers providing legal aid services, any deterioration of the legal aid tariff through time may induce an increasing percentage of lawyers to substitute fee-paying clients for legal aid clients. One would predict that young lawyers entering the profession committed to areas of private practice covered by the legal aid plan (e.g., criminal law, family law, and immigration law), with excess capacity and relatively fewer fee-paying clients, in the early years of their practice may be prepared to take on legal aid cases at very low rates, because the opportunity costs of doing so are so low. However, as they become established, develop reputations in their fields, and acquire a significant fee-paying client base that reduces or eliminates any excess capacity, they will increasingly withdraw from the legal aid services segment of the market as their opportunity costs of undertaking legal aid cases rise.

However, older lawyers who have acquired over time highly specialized expertise in particular areas of practice covered by the legal aid plan, such as criminal law and refugee law where private fee-paying clients constitute a smaller percentage of total users of legal services in these areas, may well continue to provide legal aid services despite declining real legal aid rates through time. For them, writing off their investments in specialized expertise and incurring the cost of developing new expertise, along with their commitment to particular areas of law and particular client needs, may induce them to remain participants in the legal aid plan. In some cases, older lawyers with excess capacity and relatively fewer fee-paying clients may be prepared to provide legal aid services at low rates (because of low opportunity costs in so doing), but there may be serious questions about the quality of service that they provide. On the other hand, with respect to established lawyers providing competent legal aid services in areas of practice dominated by legal aid clients, the legal aid plan and the governments which finance it may be primary purchasers of legal services (Legal Aid Ontario is the monopoly purchaser of legal aid services) and hence may be able to depress legal aid rates through time without inducing major substitution or exit effects.

However, in our view, to endorse this approach is ultimately myopic because many students embarking upon programs of formal legal education and then contemplating various choices among areas of specialised legal practice following admission to the profession, may be influenced in their choice of areas of legal specialisation by comparisons of the legal aid rate with prevailing rates of compensation in other areas of private practice or in legal careers in the public sector. That is to say, long-term career choices may be influenced by the opportunity costs of specialising in areas of law dominated by legal aid clients in terms of foregone alternative career options.

Thus, in the long-run, maintaining legal aid tariff levels substantially below prevailing compensation levels in private legal practice and in legal careers in the public sector is likely to reduce both the number and quality of legal practitioners providing legal aid services to the most disadvantaged members of our community.

NOTES AND QUESTIONS

1. What is the rationale for legal aid—effective or formal equality? Is it to put a poor person in the same position as the more comfortable or is it to provide a set of services more sensitive to the different needs of the poor? Does legal aid merely ensure minimal access, but to a system that is tilted against the needs of the poor?

2. The extracts draw a distinction between judicare, where the client brings a legal-aid certificate to a lawyer of his or her choice, and clinics staffed by employed lawyers. What are the arguments for each type of service? Are the clinics an improvement? Is it argued that they are because they offer services not available under traditional legal-aid schemes, such as representation before tribunals and general welfare issues? But are they a real solution to the problem of the poor or are they anything more than a band-aid for deeper wounds?

3. The hourly rates paid by legal aid may be substantially lower than those which lawyers earn in private practice. Lower fees lead to a situation where only relatively junior lawyers are prepared to act on a certificate. An additional access concern regarding the low fees of legal aid is that lawyers may refuse to act in matters that are particularly complicated. Note

that the *Rules of Professional Conduct* state that "[i]t is in keeping with the best traditions of the legal profession to reduce or waive a fee in a situation where there is a hardship or poverty, or the client or prospective client would otherwise effectively be deprived of legal advice or representation" (see rule 9, commentary 2). Do you think that this rule goes far enough? Should lawyers be obliged to provide free services, or services at reduced fees? Why or why not? Some law schools have instituted a requirement that all students perform a predetermined number of hours of public-interest legal services as a prerequisite to graduation. At least part of the rationale is to try to instill in soon-to-be lawyers the "best traditions" of the legal profession referred to in rule 9.

4. Canada has presently experienced a rise of formal institutions devoted to *pro bono* work, including provincial *pro bono* groups like Pro Bono Law Ontario (and similar groups in British Columbia, Saskatchewan, Alberta, and Quebec), as well as Pro Bono Students Canada, now active in every law school in Canada. For more on this legal trend and what it means for the Canadian legal landscape, see Lorne Sossin, "The Public Interest, Professionalism, and *Pro Bono Publico*" (2008), 46 *Osgoode Hall LJ* 131.

III. THE ETHICS OF LAWYERING

A. Introduction

Before embarking on a discussion of the ethical norms governing lawyers within the traditional model of litigation, it is useful to review some of the basic features of the legal profession. The regulation of the practice of law is a matter within provincial jurisdiction and, as is the case for many professions, the provinces have delegated to the legal profession the power to determine and enforce standards for admission to the practice of law and standards of practice for the profession. These governance functions are carried out by the "benchers" of the provincial law society, who are elected by the members of the profession.

As such, we might think of the legal profession as having two central features—self-regulation (through its admission of members and enforcement of standards of conduct) and (near) monopoly (the legal profession is based on a licensure regime in which only those granted a licence, having satisfied the criteria established by the profession, are entitled to practise law). In most circumstances it is a provincial offence for a person to engage in the unauthorized practice of law—that is, to practise as a barrister or solicitor without a licence.

Each provincial and territorial law society has developed its own code of conduct for practising lawyers. Most of these codes have been closely modelled after the *Code of Professional Conduct* prepared by the Canadian Bar Association (CBA). There are, however, many important differences between the codes of various jurisdictions, particularly in their treatment of the issue of confidentiality and its limitations. The preface to the CBA code notes that

> [t]he pertinent laws in Canada use various terms to describe conduct that subjects the lawyer to discipline, for example "professional misconduct," "conduct unbecoming," and "acts derogatory to the honour or dignity of the bar."

Codes do not attempt to define these terms; rather, they serve only as guides. As a former chair of the discipline committee of the Law Society of Upper Canada noted, not every breach of a rule contained in the applicable code will constitute professional misconduct, and, similarly, following each rule will not ensure that one has not engaged in professional misconduct: see Marc Somerville, "Applying Ethical Standards to Lawyers" (1993), 6:1 *Westminster Affairs* 11. Examine any code closely and you will find inconsistencies, ambiguities, conflicts, and gaps; the rules do not always speak clearly and unequivocally. If a lawyer is found guilty of misconduct and is subject to discipline, that discipline may range from a reprimand to disbarment.

Much of the literature addressing the ethical norms that ought to govern a lawyer's conduct, and much in the model code, presupposes that lawyers are acting within a traditional adversarial paradigm when, in reality, a significant portion of the profession does not do so. For example, corporate lawyers frequently complain that the CBA code and the applicable codes of many jurisdictions fail to address the practice of corporate law; hence, on many issues, they provide little useful guidance. Moreover, the traditional model of litigation has increasingly come under challenge and, in response to these challenges, has been modified in many ways. These modifications also invite questions about whether the role of lawyers has changed or ought to change and, accompanying that change of role, whether the ethical norms that ought to guide lawyers' conduct should similarly change.

B. Models and Critiques of Professional Ethics

Until recently, a dominant model of lawyering has understood the exclusive professional interest of lawyers to be the interests of their clients. Important to this model is the notion that clients, and not lawyers, are responsible for the practical and moral consequences of the clients' actions. Under this model, lawyers have been referred to as "zealous advocates," "amoral technicians," "hired guns," and "neutral partisans." More recently, lawyers (and others) have become increasingly dissatisfied with this dominant, role-differentiated vision of lawyers. One of the major dissatisfactions is the private and public consequences of continuing to pursue this model, particularly in the context of increasingly pluralistic communities. As such, alternative models are being actively considered and pursued, some of which have been referred to as "moral lawyering," lawyering with "critical morality," "sustainable professionalism," and the like.

The following extracts explore some of these models and issues in the context of debates over the appropriate role of lawyers and the professional and ethical duties placed on them.

**Rob Atkinson, "How the Butler Was Made To Do It: The Perverted
Professionalism of the Remains of the Day"**
(1995), 105 *Yale LJ* 177, at 181-94 (footnotes omitted)

The larger story is about an English butler looking back over his career in one of the great English country houses. The butler's name is Stevens, and he has been in service for most of his professional life to the fictitious but typical Lord Darlington. His retrospective is set in 1956, when the great era of the country house is over, and with it the age of the classic English butler. The Labor Government's wealth transfer taxes have begun to break up the ancestral estates of people like Lord Darlington. Members of the aristocracy are now opening their houses to throngs of tourists or, worse still, conveying them to the National Trust or, worst of all, selling them to foreign, even American, millionaires. This last indignity has befallen Lord Darlington's house.

Even for those with the money, like Darlington Hall's new owner, things are not what they were. In Stevens's words, "finding [staff] recruits of a satisfactory standard is no easy task nowadays." Even in the old days, as Stevens frequently laments, the less ambitious often opted out of domestic service to marry and raise families of their own. Stevens himself, however, has no children; he has never been married. For that matter, he has never taken a vacation.

When Stevens's new American employer learns of this, he insists that Stevens take the estate's Ford out for a week's holiday in the late summer when he is himself away in the United States. Stevens eventually assents, but only when he is able to convince himself that the trip has a professional purpose. He has just received the first letter in a long while from a former head housekeeper at the Hall, Miss Kenton, and he interprets this to mean that she may be ready, after twenty years of married life, to leave her husband and return to domestic service. He recalls "her great affection for this house, ... her exemplary professionalism." His taking a trip to her home in the West Country, he persuades himself, may convince her to return in her former professional capacity. But we begin to suspect that he has been interested in more than her exemplary professionalism, and that her affection was not always limited to the house.

In the course of his trip, Stevens reflects that social life in the country house is not all that has suffered since the war; the personal reputation of the recently deceased Lord Darlington is at a low ebb as well. In the mid-thirties, he had hosted several "unofficial" meetings between the British Foreign Secretary and German Ambassador von Ribbentrop, in an effort, as we would now say, to reanchor Germany in the West. In recognition of his good offices, he had been rather graciously received in the reconstituted Reich. Stevens is at pains to point out that many entirely loyal English aristocrats were initially inclined to trust the new German leadership, and that Lord Darlington was not the last to realize the true nature of Nazism. More ominously, Stevens admits, Darlington had flirted, intellectually and otherwise, with a female member of the British Union of Fascists and had entertained that organization's leader, Sir Oswald Mosley, at the Hall. But Stevens tries to minimize Darlington's association with the Black Shirts, reducing it to a very few incidents over a very brief time. It is on one of those incidents that I want to focus.

B. *What the Butler Did*

One summer afternoon Lord Darlington calls Stevens into the study, and, after the usual pleasantries, asks whether there are any Jews on the house staff. When informed that there are two Jewish housemaids, Lord Darlington tells Stevens, "Of course, you'll have to let them go." Apparently prompted by Stevens's barely perceptible surprise, Lord Darlington explains: "It's regrettable, Stevens, but we have no choice. There's the safety and well-being of my guests to consider. Let me assure you, I've looked into this matter and thought it through thoroughly. It's in all our best interests."

Because the two maids are under Miss Kenton's direct supervision as housekeeper, Stevens thinks it appropriate to inform her of their dismissal. He brings the matter up that very night at their routine meeting for cocoa in her parlor. Stevens offers Miss Kenton the opportunity to speak with the maids herself before sending them along to his pantry for their dismissal the next morning. Miss Kenton expresses outrage and warns Stevens that if the maids are dismissed, she will leave as well. But Stevens carries out the order, and Miss Kenton does not leave.

Before examining the incident in more detail, I want briefly to reassure the skittish, those who are beginning to wonder how this tale can possibly relate to the practice of law other than perhaps to imply a deprecating comparison between lawyers and domestic servants. Thus, for those of you who think the assertedly parallel lines are diverging, let me offer a brief aside. Suppose Lord Darlington, punctilious in all his affairs, had called his London solicitors to confirm that his firing of the maids was legally proper. He might have asked for a written opinion on the subject and for carefully drafted dismissal papers to effect their discharge. Predictably, Lord Darlington would have rung up a senior member of the firm, and that member might well have assigned the research and drafting to a junior associate. The subordinate would have discovered that, under traditional common law notions of employment, the Jewish maids could be dismissed for even immoral reasons. I suspect, however, that both he and his senior would have been troubled by the prospect of playing a part in that morally sordid but perfectly legal action. It thus takes no great stretch of the imagination to see the dilemma of the butler and the maid played out in perfectly parallel fashion in a law firm of their day—or of ours.

As the next part shows, the responses of Stevens and Kenton are typical of two competing approaches open to contemporary American lawyers in such a situation. Either answer, standing alone, is inadequate, and the story itself presents a more satisfactory, but by no means perfect, response. The medium in which Stevens and Kenton give their answers—a story—reveals not only the relative merits of the alternative answer, but also why Stevens and Kenton failed to choose that alternative, and at what cost. The factors influencing their choices operate on us as well, and we are at risk of incurring similar costs. To shift from the terminology of economics to the language of literature, we are in danger of suffering the same fate.

II. Perverted Professionalism

Whenever someone serves another, that service poses a question: Should the service be limited by anything other than the principal's will? Modern society imposes one obvious set of constraints: the outer bounds of the state's positive law. But are there other limits? That is a fundamental question of professional ethics: Should a professional always do all that the law allows, or should the professional recognize other constraints, particularly concerns for the welfare of third parties? This question divides scholars of legal ethics and thoughtful practitioners into two schools: those who recognize constraints other than law's outer limit, and those who do not. Mr. Stevens and Miss Kenton, in their treatment of the maids and in their professional lives generally, fall on opposite sides of this divide. The course of their lives suggests not so much that one answer is wrong and the other right, but that each poses distinct dangers to moral integrity and that each is the beginning, rather than the end, of moral analysis.

A. Mr. Stevens's Neutral Partisanship

Stevens's position closely parallels what students of the legal profession call "neutral partisanship." The second of these two correlated principles, partisanship, entails advancing client ends through all legal means, and with a maximum of personal determination, as long as the ends are within the letter of the law. The first principle, neutrality, lets the professional claim personal disinterest in, or even antipathy toward, client ends and moral nonaccountability for helping to advance them. So it was with Stevens's firing of the Jewish maids. Looking back on the incident, he sees it this way:

> [M]y every instinct opposed the idea of their dismissal. Nevertheless, my duty in this instance was quite clear, and as I saw it, there was nothing to be gained at all in irresponsibly displaying such personal doubts. It was a difficult task, but as such, one that demanded to be carried out with dignity.

When Miss Kenton expresses her outrage, he reminds her that "our professional duty is not to our own foibles and sentiments, but to the wishes of our employer."

For Stevens and the neutral partisans, the ultimate decision, in matters of morality and public policy, is the client's to make. Furthermore, this has an important corollary: The professional's job is essentially technical. In the words of a prominent academic proponent of neutral partisanship, the client is like an "individual facing and needing to use a very large and very complicated machine (with lots of whirring gears and spinning data tapes) that he can't get to work." In Stevens's words, "Let us establish this quite clearly: a butler's duty is to provide good service. It is not to meddle in the great affairs of the nation." Neutral partisanship tends to reduce the human dimensions of one's professional life, to deal with its unpleasantries in abstract and impersonal terms. Thus, for example, Stevens speaks of the "particular contracts to be discontinued," and refers to the maids as "the two employees concerned." And as neutral partisanship reduces professional service to technical assistance, so it tends to reduce moral concerns to matters of individual taste, if not idiosyncrasy. We have already heard Stevens dismiss his moral qualms as "foibles and sentiments."

This is not to say, however, that Stevens's position is totally divorced from morality, any more than is the contemporary justification of neutral partisanship as practiced by lawyers. Rather, Stevens firmly grounds his position in morality, in very much the same way today's neutral partisan lawyers do. Stevens insists that the moral dimension of one's professional role as a butler derives from the moral standing of one's employer:

> [T]he question was not simply one of how well one practised one's skills, but *to what end* one did so; each of us harboured the desire to make our own small contribution to the creation of a better world, and saw that, as professionals, the surest means of doing so would be to serve the great gentlemen of our times in whose hands civilization had been entrusted. …
>
> A "great" butler can only be, surely, one who can point to his years of service and say that he has applied his talents to serving a great gentleman—and through the latter, to serving humanity.

· · ·

Defenders of neutral partisan lawyering are also at pains to show how the professional role they prescribe serves the public good. In contrast to Stevens, they do not focus on the humanitarian impulses, or even on the moral status, of the client. Rather, the reverse is true: They are at pains to show that whenever the lawyer helps a client exercise legal rights, even in an immoral way, the lawyer has acted well as a professional. Yet this professional probity, like Stevens's, is grounded in an ethical good. In the case of neutral partisan lawyers, that ethical good is the client's exercise of moral autonomy as authorized by the law. Society recognizes individual autonomy as a good of the highest order, so the argument runs, and carves out a sphere in which individuals can exercise that autonomy without interference. By helping lay folk operate within that envelope—sometimes even by pressing its edge—the lawyer is accomplishing a moral and social, not just professional, good. When, accordingly, proponents of neutral partisanship describe their model as amoral, they are not referring to its ultimate grounding, which is emphatically moral. They are referring, rather, to the lawyer's immunity from the task of scrutinizing the morality of particular client acts. Theirs is morality at the wholesale but not the retail level; a morality of the long run, not the particular case; a morality of fidelity to role obligations, not attention to particular acts. ...

The skepticism at the root of neutral partisanship in lawyering generally takes a less personal, and more radical, form. It has been traced to the Hobbesian, positivist notion that "[e]nds are natural, individual, subjective, and arbitrary." On that view, the only ends individuals share are the desire to be free to pursue their private ends and the corollary desire for security in that pursuit. The legitimate function of law is to define limits within which individuals can exercise autonomy without impinging upon each other. The lawyer's job is to advise the client, faced with a bafflingly complex legal order, about where the outer edge of this sphere of autonomy lies. Not to assist the client in exercising autonomy up to the very margin allowed by law would be to usurp the role not just of judge and jury, but of the legislature as well. Ultimately, it would undermine the legitimacy of government itself. Thus, though the moral skepticism of neutral partisan lawyers is more global and less self-effacing than that of Stevens, it produces the same result: deferring to clients on moral judgments within the letter of the law. Thus, moral skepticism, somewhat paradoxically, is the foundation of Stevens's and the neutral partisan lawyers' faith in the rightness of fidelity to clients' ends.

B. Miss Kenton's Moral Activism

Miss Kenton's reaction to the firing of the maids offers a striking contrast to Mr. Stevens's response, and it implies a vision of professionalism quite different from neutral partisanship. She recoils from the technocratic, antiseptic attitude of Stevens, his treatment of the dismissals "as though [he] were discussing orders for the larder." In contrast to his references to "contracts" and "employees," she persistently refers to the maids by their first names, Ruth and Sarah, and invokes her long, personal relationship with them. And she does not dismiss deeply held personal aversions as "foibles and sentiments." She says she's outraged, and she puts her position in unmistakably moral terms: "Does it not occur to you, Mr Stevens, that to dismiss Ruth and Sarah on these grounds would be simply— *wrong*? I will not stand for such things." A bit later, she refers to the dismissals as "a sin as any sin ever was one." Most significantly, she takes direct moral responsibility for the immediate consequences of her actions, rather than insulating herself within her role. She will not be a partisan for what she believes to be a moral wrong, because she cannot be neutral professionally toward what she opposes personally.

In all of these respects, and most fundamentally in the last, Miss Kenton implicitly anticipates the growing ranks of scholarly critics of neutral partisanship in the legal profession. Although they differ on details, these critics all agree that, with narrow exceptions like criminal defense work and other David-versus-Goliath analogues, lawyers cannot claim moral absolution for unquestioningly assisting their clients in unjust acts, however legally proper. In their view, lawyers should not merely decline to assist in such acts; they should also act affirmatively to promote justice in their representation of private clients. Accordingly, following one of its chief proponents, I will call this position "moral activism."

Defenders of moral activism in the legal profession look to several sources outside the letter of the law for additional limits on what lawyers may properly do for clients, and these sources support Miss Kenton's position. Some moral activists factor ordinary morality, the shared moral norms of society—in particular, our common obligation not to harm the innocent—directly into the professional's ethical calculus. On that view, because the function of the professional role itself is to advance ordinary moral values, such as the discovery of truth and the protection of individual rights, any departure that the professional role requires from ordinary morality must be strongly justified in terms of ordinary morality itself. Ordinary morality is the most obvious source of Miss Kenton's resistance, sounded in her objection that "to dismiss Ruth and Sarah on these grounds would be simply—*wrong*." And moral objections can be grounded in religious as well as secular ethics; lawyers, like Miss Kenton, can conclude that complying with their employers' wishes would be "a sin as any sin ever was one."

Other moral activists, anticipating Stevens's dismissal of moral limits as subjective or idiosyncratic, find limits to the law's letter in its spirit. At the most basic level, they point out, lawyers justify their role in service to the law as "officers of the court," and the purpose of the law itself is to promote justice. Thus, when lawyers invoke particular laws on behalf of clients in ways that threaten to subvert justice, they undercut the very basis of their professional status. ...

Finally, some moral activists, skeptical of finding general agreement on either ordinary moral norms or professional values, look for the limits of professional conduct in the fundamental beliefs of smaller communities united in a common faith. Such faiths need not be conventionally religious and need not rest on anything beyond their adherents' personal commitments. Miss Kenton, echoing the prototypical Protestant, sounds this theme as well, albeit in a minor key: "I will not stand for such things."

C. Stevens and Kenton's Common Ground: Moral Isolationism

Stevens's vision of professionalism, like that of the neutral partisan lawyer, leaves the ultimate moral judgment to the client; Kenton, like neutral partisanship's critics, reserves that judgment for herself. It is important to note at this point, however, that it is the *ultimate* decision on which neutral partisans and their critics divide. More subtle proponents of neutral partisanship agree with their detractors on one critical point: the appropriateness of raising moral concerns with a client in an effort to discourage the client from committing what the professional believes to be a moral wrong.

On this point, both schools of lawyering would fault Stevens *and* Kenton—Stevens, for going along without remonstrating; Kenton, for believing that she should resign without remonstrating. Moreover, the official codes of legal ethics stand squarely behind the united front of neutral partisans and their critics on the point of giving moral advice to clients. The codes and virtually all commentators agree that, having determined that a client is about to do something legal but morally reprehensible, lawyers have an option before they reach the decision that divides neutral partisans from moral activists. Before deciding to assist in the wrong or terminate the representation, the lawyer may—in some views, should—try to persuade the client to do the morally right thing. Curiously, both Miss Kenton and Mr. Stevens skipped this step; in fact, this step does not seem to have occurred to either of them as a live option.

There was, in addition, another element of moral isolationism in Stevens and Kenton's story. They failed not only to talk with Lord Darlington, but also to talk in any meaningful way with each other. The importance of this second dialogue, a dialogue among professionals themselves or between professionals and their personal friends, is not well reflected either in codes of legal ethics or in academic treatments of lawyer professionalism.

D. Kennedy, "The Responsibility of Lawyers for the Justice of Their Causes"
(1987), 18 *Texas Technical L Rev.* 1157, at 1157-63

Begin with a vacuous piety: Try your best, oh graduating students of the Washington College of Law, to avoid doing harm with your lawyer skills.

If I asked each of you to swear an oath to try to avoid doing harm with your lawyer skills, I bet most of you would say, "Why object? All right, boss, you're the graduation speaker, sounds harmless, even obvious, to me, I hereby pledge myself to avoid doing harm with my lawyer skills."

But I think this vacuous piety has some controversial bite. It would get many lawyers into trouble. To make the pledge controversial, let me put aside two of its easy meanings. When you represent a client, you should do your best for her, or him. That means: *avoid malpractice*, and who can quarrel with that. Then there's another, slightly more touchy point. I think we would all agree that a lawyer doesn't in most situations have to take on a client. If you think the client is trying to do something terrible, and wants to use your lawyer skills to do harm, you don't have to take the case, unless a court appoints you to take it.

Your right-to-turn-down-a-case goes beyond just not having to do something to help a person with evil intentions. You might not take the case because you didn't want to contribute or even be associated in any way with a client you thought was bad. Your cases are yours to choose on any basis you want.

I know this is a *little* controversial because of the reaction from the establishment bar and editorial writers when students around the country began a boycott of hiring interviews with firms that represent the South African government. A lot of lawyers thought it was outrageous for students to try to influence law firms, or to interfere with the ability of the South African government to get counsel, by threatening not to go to work for those firms.

I want to go a step further than those students. While it's true no one should blame you for refusing to represent a client whose activity your disapprove of, that's not enough. You should feel guilty, and we should disapprove of you, if you go ahead and argue a cause you think will do more harm than good. You shouldn't take the case if you think it would be better for society, or more moral, for the client to lose. You shouldn't take the case if you think the client shouldn't be in court in the first place, for example, because the client should morally have made recompense even though he has a technically good legal defense. You shouldn't take the case if your client is enforcing his legal rights, but is *using* his legal rights in a bad cause.

This is the tough meaning of the vacuous piety that you should avoid doing harm with your lawyer skills. Most lawyers don't agree with it at all. They believe that you are not tarred morally by your clients' underlying intentions, or character, or by the outcome, as long as you don't participate in law breaking yourself. Maybe they make an exception and condemn Mafia lawyers, even when they aren't involved directly in criminal activity. But that's about it. I think you are tarred with bad actions of clients that you facilitate in your work as a lawyer.

To the extent this is right, it is wrong to represent an abortion clinic that's trying to lease a new building to expand its operations, if you are pro-life. And it's wrong to represent a landlord who has been intimidated into trying to evict an abortion clinic if you are pro-choice. It's wrong to work against unionization if you believe everyone should have a labor union; and wrong to work for union rights to picket a shopping center if you think unions are generally evil. It's wrong to lobby for the postponement of environmental controls if you think they should be imposed right now; and wrong to do antitrust work against a corporate merger, if you believe mergers are good for the economy.

My position is extreme, and it will certainly apply to you at some point in your lives as lawyers. I suppose that's what graduation speeches are at least sometimes for. I'm saying you should turn down the client even though she isn't trying to get you to do anything illegal, and even though she isn't doing anything illegal herself. She just wants you to argue that the abortion clinic has violated its lease, which you don't believe is the case, or that the merger violates the anti-trust laws. I'm saying that if you think the outcome of winning-for-your-client would be on balance a bad thing, socially unfortunate, you should decline to participate, in spite of the fact that the client will pay, and that you wouldn't be doing anything that came close to violating the canons of professional ethics. You'd be in the clear as far as "unethical conduct" is concerned, as it's defined by your profession. But I'm suggesting that you'd be morally in the wrong anyway.

There are lots and lots of objections to what I've just said. I'm going to try to shoot down about twenty of them in rapid succession. First, what about the Porsche? I don't mean mine (I don't have one); I mean the one you might imagine in your future. The short answer is that there's plenty of money to be made out there, for most lawyers most of the time, without becoming a hired gun—that's what we're talking about, the lawyer as a gun for hire regardless of the morals of the client. At least at present, there are tons of morally innocuous, or positively beneficial, or neutral, lawyer work. *Most* lawyer work falls into that category for most people. If sticking to that type of work involves some loss of income, so be it. Maybe you'll win a Porsche in the lottery.

Second, if I don't do it, someone else will. But that doesn't make it right for you to do it. You should avoid doing harm with your lawyer skills even if there is someone else waiting to take your place.

Third, what can be wrong, indeed why isn't it a good thing, to help people enforce their rights? Lawyers should be devoted to legality, but I am proposing that they refuse clients on non-legal grounds—on the grounds that, though within their rights, the clients in question are doing more harm than good.

The simple answer is that law is not coterminous with morality: there is a vast range of behavior that harms people without legal remedy, and when lawyers help people do that harm, they can't escape responsibility for it if it is immoral. Legality is important. It's a good starting point for the discussion. But that your client had a legal right to injure and get away with it doesn't mean that you can have a clear conscience, even if your role was just routinely technical, and it wasn't you who chose the course of action, if the course of action was immoral.

Further, lawyers are often—maybe usually—more than just legal technicians. They shape deals and they make law. They invent new forms of social life, they fill gaps, resolve conflicts and ambiguities. They mold the law, through the process of legal argument, in court, in briefs, in negotiations. It won't do to say, look, I molded the law this way, and this way, and this way. I've made a lot of law. But don't hold me responsible for the actual content of the law I made. That was determined by who happened to be my client at the time. I chose my clients according to their ability to pay. What concern is it of mine if the law they paid me to make goes against my own moral beliefs? I'm just an advocate and I leave the final decision to others.

The trouble with this is that your activity is not neutral, and the better your legal skills, the less neutral you become. Lawyers think up new rules, ideas, arrangements and arguments. Which ones win, which ones judges and juries and legislatures adopt, is a function of who has the legal talent on their side, as well as a function of the justice of the position. If you put your legal talent on the side of outcomes you disapprove of, you make it at least a little more likely that bad outcomes, bad new inventions of your own, will prevail. You bear responsibility when *your* unique way of molding the law, your work product, wins out to the detriment of the community, even if it was not you, but a judge or administrator who "pulled the trigger," so to speak, by actually deciding the case, and even if someone else would have done it if you didn't.

But what would happen to the right to counsel if lawyers were always second-guessing the justice of their clients' causes? And what about Our Adversary System? Isn't it based on the lawyers going all out for their clients, and letting truth emerge through conflict? It's up to the jury or the judge to decide on the justice of the case; it's up to the *lawyer* to present the best possible case for her side, whichever it may be.

These are serious objections, and I'm willing to make some concessions to recognize some counterprinciples to the one I'm arguing for. After all, even on this day of days there are no absolutes.

First, I am not saying that you should represent bad clients half-heartedly or incompetently. I'm talking about the choice of clients. Once you sign on, it seems to me you *are* somewhat stuck with being an adversary within the adversary system, unless something unexpected happens that means you have to withdraw. This can pose a lot of delicate problems, if you are really trying not to use your lawyer skills in ways that harm people. But that's not my issue.

Second, people, including your potential clients, have a *right* to counsel, in the sense that the state will provide one if they can't afford one, only in a few situations—in some aspects of the criminal justice system, and in some, though by no means all, family law situations. The only other sense in which they have a right to counsel is that the state will not forbid them to have a lawyer *if* they can find one they can afford. The right to counsel does not mean that clients whose causes hurt the body politic have a right to your counsel just because they have the money to pay for it.

I think it's morally fine to be a public defender or a legal services lawyer, in spite of the fact that you will sometimes find yourself representing guilty or immoral people. In those cases, there has been a *social* decision that people should have lawyers even if they can't afford them. I'd go further, and say that if a prospective client can't get a lawyer unless *you* represent them, and if they are likely to be treated unfairly by the system if they don't have a lawyer, then you ought to take the case to prevent the injustice of their being unrepresented.

But what I'm talking about is this: ought you, or ought you *not* to do the paperwork for a real estate developer who is acting legally and completely within his rights in buying up 100 low income apartments housing 400 poor people and converting them to 40 condominiums housing 80 yuppies, when the poor people will have to move into smaller apartments for higher rents and increase the starch content of their children's diets? I say you ought not to do it, and the right to counsel is irrelevant, Let some other lawyer do it, or let the developer do it himself, in the unlikely event that no one else can be bought.

I think the real objection to my proposal is that it contradicts our sense that it's okay to distribute legal services among people according to how much money they can pay. Lawyers want to feel that because society has left the decision about who gets a lawyer, and what lawyer (an incompetent or the best money can buy) to the market, then it's all right for them to forget about it, while selling their own services for what they will command, regardless of the morality of the legal activity.

If you—if most lawyers—took the choice of clients seriously according to the vacuous piety that you should avoid doing harm with your lawyer skills, it seems likely that some clients would have to pay more for less legal service, and other people would get more service for less money. Your moral intuitions would influence the distribution of legal talent, through the market, along with the buying power of clients. Would that be better or worse than the current situation?

I think it would be better. At present, the distribution of legal services is a disgrace: rich people get vastly more than they need or deserve; middle income people can't afford a lawyer in numerous situations in which they are ripped off for relatively small amounts of money, or discriminated against on sexual or racial grounds, or seriously injured. Poor people have virtually no access to legal services, given the abysmal underfunding of the Legal Services Corporation. If lawyers felt morally responsible for their individual contribution to this allocation of legal services, it seems likely to me that they would improve it, though perhaps only marginally. This would hurt, probably, some current excess consumers of lawyer time.

If you applied your moral judgment to the choice of clients not just occasionally but in every case, you might often choose in ways that I disagreed with. Though I think the overall pattern of choices would probably be better than that which emerges from a market where human suffering counts for nothing and dollars for everything, I am in favor of taking client morality into account for its own sake. My proposal is left-wing only in the very general sense of being for liberation and responsibility, even if the consequences may sometimes be conservative.

A.C. Hutchinson, "Legal Ethics for a Fragmented Society: Between Professional and Personal"
(1997), 5 *International Journal of the Legal Profession* 175 (footnotes omitted)

Traditional views and understandings about what it means to be an ethical lawyer are based upon narrow and unrealistic assumptions about what ethical decisions address and involve, who lawyers are and what they do, what constitutes law, and the professional contexts in which these arise. To be a legal professional is to enter into a community that has developed a shared set of normative practices and expectations that it is authorised or prepared to enforce in the face of recalcitrant behaviour. While several devices are used to curb and monitor lawyers' behaviour, codes of professional conduct lie at the heart of the profession's focus on legal ethics and responsibility. The reasons for having codes of professional conduct are fairly obvious—to educate lawyers on communal expectations; to affect behaviour; and to offer a basis for discipline. ...

To read any of the provincial codes of professional conduct is to encounter a series of pronouncements that are long on righteous aspiration and vague generalities, but short on serious instruction and concrete guidance. It is a case of not seeing the ethical forest for the law-like trees. Although lawyers are weighed down with discrete and detailed directives on this or that matter, there is little to counsel the floundering or jaded lawyer in establishing an overall and professional *modus vivendi*. Like the formalist lawyering that many claim to embody and extol, ethics is reduced to a technical compliance with a set of simple do's and don'ts—more of a shopping list than a genuine effort to inculcate a style and substance of legal practice that addresses the whole lawyer, not merely the occasional legal transaction. It is as much about conformity as it is about conscience. Lawyers approach ethics in the same way that they approach law—as a set of rules to be mastered and manipulated to serve the purpose in hand. Indeed, under the sway of a legalistic mentality, the teaching of legal ethics and responsibility is more like a course on office management; it is as much about techniques in filing and organisation as it is about thinking through dilemmas and difficulties. ...

[A]n exclusive concentration on the rules is misplaced. There is little to be gained by providing an elaborate and exhaustive annotation of the rules of professional conduct because, not only has this been adequately done, but it ignores the very real fact that the influence on lawyers' daily routines and rituals is small: the constant attention to and redrafting of the rules is of decreasing marginal utility. Nevertheless, this does not mean that the codes have no place in any appreciation of legal ethics and their actual improvement; they are an important resource in discussion and decision-making, but they are not a decisive or determinate play-book that relieves lawyers of the personal responsibility to develop an ethical style and substance of legal practice. The codes are a site at which ethical debate can be joined and developed. As with many catalogues of rights and responsibilities, there will be competing and occasionally contradictory imperatives; duties to one's clients might suggest a different course of action to those recommended by the lawyers' responsibilities as an officer of the court. In some instances, the rules demand that lawyers "must" make certain choices and give priority to certain actions. However, the rules more often offer no definite resolution and simply provide a rudimentary framework within which lawyers can debate and develop an ethical practice of law. It is important therefore to remember that the rules do not and cannot relieve lawyers of the continuing responsibility to exercise their own professional and moral judgement about the appropriate course to follow.

In many ways, therefore, the interpretation of the professional codes and rules resembles other modes of legal interpretation. In the same way that the meaning of constitutional or statutory law is not fixed or exhausted by their textual renderings, so the requirements of professional responsibility and legal ethics are not reducible to the four textual corners of the codes: both require reference to a wide range of interpretive aids and sources, including conventions, customs, tradition, cultural expectations, institutional norms, and social values. As with teaching legal doctrine generally, little is achieved by simply asking students to learn rote-like the rules of professional conduct without also providing them with some critical framework within which to understand how those particular rules came into being, what they are intended to do, etc. It is the same with legal ethics. If students are taught only the rules of professional conduct, they will be ill-prepared to adapt those sweeping injunctions to changing circumstances or to respond to uncertainty in the rules' meaning or application. As so much contemporary jurisprudence insists, it is never possible simply to "follow the rules," as the question of what "the rules" mean and what it means to "follow" them are never beyond dispute. Legal interpretation is an ungrounded practice in that it cannot be engaged in without taking a stand on values or choices that are themselves always open to challenge; the distinction between "following the rules" and "following one's conscience" is neither as clear nor as uncontroversial as traditionalists suggest. Accordingly, the suggestion that a viable and satisfying legal ethics can be maintained by adopting the professional role of a rule-ordered mentality is sorely mistaken. ...

Although it is often forgotten by most lawyers, the study of legal ethics is a branch of ethics generally; it is not a subject unto itself. At its broadest, ethics involves a meditation on what is wrong and right and, most importantly, how such standards are arrived at and validated. Traditionally, the task was to elaborate and justify a set of ethical norms that provide an authoritative code that people could consult and follow in resolving difficult dilemmas. However, faith in the possibility of sketching such a body of enduring and universally-valid rules has been waning. There is now the less absolutist and more sceptical acceptance that ethics is a much more situational practice that cannot claim objective or neutral justification. As with general ethics, the prevailing standards of right and wrong do not exhaust ethical inquiry into legal professionals' behaviour; those standards must themselves be subject to scrutiny and challenge. The different ethical theories seek to examine critically conventional moral judgments and practices; they offer methods and devices through which to justify or condemn particular moral answers to controversies or dilemmas. There are almost as many ethical theories as there are ethical philosophers. In many instances, all ethical theories will converge on a similar set of generally accepted norms and standards of moral conduct. However, many moral theorists contend that a moral approach to life consists of more than a hell-or-high-water allegiance to one overarching code of moral rules and principles; there will be a pragmatic willingness to resist hard-and-fast solutions that are supposed to work in all situations.

None of this should be taken to mean that ethical behaviour and decision-making is condemned to be irrational or arbitrary, only that what counts and operates as reason is never outside of its informing context. In this way, legal ethics can be viewed less as a fixed and independent code of professional conduct and more as continuing practice within which lawyers construct acceptable norms of behaviour as they struggle to comply with them. To be an ethical lawyer involves more than learning and applying a set of rules; it also demands the cultivation of a critical reflection upon the professional role and responsibilities of lawyers. In short, a fully ethical practice requires an independent sense of moral virtue that involves the life-long development of personal moral character. Because there is no one answer to ethical dilemmas, it does not mean that reasoning can be abandoned or that "anything goes."

In ethical debate, a wide range of arguments can be supported by sophisticated chains of reasoning: moral reasoning is not, therefore, something that stands outside or in judgment on moral decision-making; it is made and re-made in the situational process of moral engagement and debate. As such, what counts as a good moral reason is a matter of justification and persuasion, not proof and authority. Accordingly, I do not offer a recommendation that is relativistic (or nihilistic) in which each person's conception of right and wrong is as good as or as valid as any one else's. While values are constructed within particular social and historical contexts, standards do develop about what is and is not acceptable behaviour, even though those standards are never themselves outside of debate and transformation. My approach does have the merit of demanding that, if ethical issues are to be taken seriously, there must be an acceptance that debate and reflection on moral issues is a useful and worthwhile pursuit and that the upshot of such engagement might have an effect upon or make a difference to a person's decisions and actions. Most importantly, it suggests that acting ethically is not about adherence to a code that is resorted to in occasional moments of indecision, but is about the development of a moral way of living and lawyering that encompasses an organic set of attitudes, dispositions, and values and that can be incorporated into each lawyer's daily routines and regimen. It is to such a recommendation and its practical implications that I now turn. …

Legal ethics is a life-long challenge in which lawyers must be encouraged to go beyond simply learning the rules and how to apply them; they should constantly interrogate themselves and their colleagues about the moral status of their work and practices. Accordingly, lawyers must be helped to hone and question a sense of moral judgment about themselves and their work. While many lawyers lead ethical lives and carry much of that over into their professional lives, there is still a depressing indifference to issues of legal ethics and a lamentable ignorance about how to identify and deal with situations that raise ethical queries and challenges. The first task, therefore, is for people to enhance and interrogate their own sense of moral judgement and responsibility; this is too often assumed to be in place. Mindful that ethical training is primarily concerned with learning about oneself, students need to confront ethical dilemmas in concrete circumstances in order to begin to discover (or construct), question and articulate their own moral views before they struggle with the complex demands of a professional ethic. There is an urgent need to stimulate the moral imagination and cultivate each person's sense of moral responsibility, such that they are able to develop a moral facility that is capable of recognising ethical dilemmas, analysing them, and responding to them in a responsible and realistic way. A pervasive difficulty in achieving this is that legal ethics is more about responsibilities than rights and, therefore, does not sit easily or well with much of the legal education that lawyers receive.

Insofar as the practice of legal ethics is in disarray, the law societies and the law schools must shoulder a considerable share of the blame for failing to provide an institutional setting for establishing a sophisticated understanding of professional responsibility and its demands. Few law schools take very seriously the need to offer training of a mandatory or optional kind to its graduates. Certainly, the extent and sophistication of courses in legal ethics comes nowhere close to mirroring those of the substantive courses. Furthermore, the courses that do exist tend to treat the teaching of legal ethics as if it were simply one more course, with the same intellectual ambitions and pedagogical techniques as business association or torts. In an important sense, although law schools have not taken the teaching of legal ethics seriously, they have still instilled within students and lawyers a certain sense of professional ethics. Indeed, law schools cannot avoid teaching legal ethics as "the very act of teaching ... creates images of law and lawyering when we teach doctrine through cases and hypotheticals." Unfortunately, reinforced by the general rule-centred attitude to the study of legal doctrine, law students settle neatly into thinking of legal ethics as involving a similar process of role-detachment and legalistic application. ...

As well as altering their attitudes and approach to the teaching of legal ethics, law societies must encourage their members to adopt a much more expansive understanding of their ethical responsibilities. It can do this in a number of ways. At an institutional level, lawyers can be constantly reminded that they must not neglect or overlook the opportunity to converse with other lawyers. This can be done by proliferating the forums—in law schools, in professional gatherings, in law firms, etc.—within which dialogue and engagement can be nurtured and thrive. In this way, lawyers might explore their own moral intuitions in the testing context of others' views without risking public criticism or risk. Also, it can be made clear to lawyers that their moral obligations as professionals extend beyond concern with their own individual actions and should encompass a responsibility to monitor the actions of other lawyers. In this way, professional responsibility is as much a collective as well as personal undertaking in which each lawyer should contribute to the moral health of the profession as a whole. ...

Although traditional versions of legal ethics are still defended in the name of public service, there are few lawyers who conduct their daily professional lives in such a spirit. It is unrealistic to imagine or expect that every lawyer will, like Socrates, only be guided by the need to do right rather than wrong: most lawyers are reasonably concerned about their jobs, paying their mortgages, providing for their kids, etc. Indeed, there is ample evidence to demonstrate that lawyers will hold to ethical principles when it is in their interests to do so or, more accurately, when their financial considerations coincide with their ethical ones. However, it is neither unreasonable nor unrealistic to expect that they can be persuaded, collectively and individually, to accept the noble challenge of redeeming the legal profession's moral standing and of fashioning a fresh image of legal ethics and professional responsibility that serves a fragmented society.

At the heart of any efforts to re-affirm the profession in its own and the public's moral esteem must be the commitment to emphasise that lawyers need not and should not spend the bulk of their professional lives doing what they would shy away from in their personal lives—can it really be appropriate that lawyers should act in wilful disregard of moral considerations that would weigh heavily on them and others in their personal lives? In short, lawyers must stop asking whether a good lawyer can be a bad person and begin providing answers to how good persons and good lawyers can co-exist in the same person. This is a task that all lawyers should relish. Moreover, legal ethics should not be thought of as something that arises in discrete and exceptional circumstances. Everything that lawyers do, from the selection of clients to their involvement in civic affairs, implicates and reflects a lawyer's approach and understanding of what it means to be an ethical lawyer. A lawyer who appreciates the full import of what it demands to be an ethical lawyer understands that ethical considerations are at the heart of lawyering, not a peripheral concern. To be a good person and a good lawyer need not be the oxymoron that Plato and more modern pessimists seem to believe it to be.

Justice Rosalie Abella, "Professionalism Revisited"
Speech to the Benchers of the Law Society of Ontario (October 14, 1999)
http://www.ontariocourts.on.ca/coa/en/ps/speeches/professionalism.htm

My thesis is that there are three basic values which merge in a good lawyer: a commitment to competence, which is about skills; a commitment to ethics, which is about decency; and a commitment to professionalism, which transfuses the public interest into the two other values. My sense is that while there is a crisis neither of competence nor of ethics, most lawyers having both in laudable abundance, the same cannot be said of the spirit of professionalism. …

When I graduated from law school, no one taught ethics or professionalism. In the Bar Admission course, the then Chief Justice of the province gave a one-hour lecture on how lawyers should behave. He told the over 500 students never to wear brown suits and white socks, a largely irrelevant observation for the 10 women in the room who nonetheless shared the Chief Justice's view of brown suits.

Yet despite the fact that the only lecture on being a lawyer in four and a half years of my legal education was about what a lawyer should look like, there was a tacit consensus about what it meant to be a lawyer. It meant being a professional, which meant all of those romantic notions about decency, civility, trustworthiness, and fairness, to name a few. The lawyers who had good reputations were the lawyers who practised law with these adjectives as conduct guides. Some of them made a lot of money, which no one be-grudged them or presumed. And quite a few of them were very smart. But they were also overwhelmingly white, male, able-bodied, and socially advantaged. Diversity was a word we used to describe the variety of cases we handled, not our consumer or collegial environments.

We have come a long way. When I was appointed to the bench in 1976 there were fewer than a dozen women judges in Canada. I was the first pregnant woman to be made a judge. That pregnancy offered me my first close-up of stereotyping. I was home on ma-ternity leave 2 months after my appointment with our 3-year-old son, Jacob, having given birth to his brother, Zachary, two months earlier. I was reading to him what he obviously found to be a tantalizing book called "If I Were a Bus Driver." When I finished the book he said, "When I grow up, I want to be a bus driver." "Don't you want to be a judge?" I gently pressured. He looked up at me, confused, and replied assertively, "Only girls are judges."

That 3 year old is now articling, and his baby brother has just started law school, but they are graduating into a very different professional environment from mine three de-cades ago. It is bursting with diversity, far better educated about ethics, far better paid, and far more stressful. But it is also a professional environment where the consensus about what it means to be a professional has broken down, as has the consensus about what the criteria should be for awarding good reputations.

What worries me about this is not so much the absence of a consensus, although this is undoubtedly an unsettling reality, it is the threat I fear to the very legitimacy of the profession, and to the professionals and institutions in it. Although I quickly concede that this is not a new issue, it has a feel of urgency to me in this ideologically polarized, intellectually sclerotic, and frenetically fluid era.

There is undoubtedly a crisis of professionalism generally, and that crisis in turn is having a supply-side impact on everyone, including lawyers. It should surprise no one that lawyers are affected by the spirit of the times, but neither should it surprise lawyers that the public expects them to rise above it.

The fact that the public is so nervous should at least give us pause. It is certainly true that we cannot expect to be popular with the public all the time. The independence of the Bench and Bar means we have to be prepared to be unpopular with the public from time to time, and even on occasion controversial; but our independence does not absolve us from the responsibility of listening and being open to the possibility that the public's suggestions and criticisms are relevant. We cannot, of course, accede to every request for a response just because it comes from the public, but neither should we decry every criti-cism as irrelevant just because it had never occurred to us before, or came from an un-familiar source, or met with no support from our colleagues. ...

The public is our audience, the people for whom we perform the justice play. They do not direct us, but they are very interested in what is going on. If they stop clapping, we are in deep trouble. We have to figure out if it is because of the script, the props, the cast, or all of them. We know we will always have an audience, because the play is called the Rule of Law, and the public's attendance is mandatory. Since we give the public no choice about whether or not they are subject to the rule of law, we have to care about whether they like the performance. They may not always be right, but they always have a right to be heard.

This is how, in large part, we discharge our accountability to the public without compromising our independence: through an empathetic hearing of its concerns, being open to the possibility that its concerns may be valid, and responding as effectively and quickly as possible when they are.

To me, the Law Society got it right when it said in its 1994 Role Statement that the legal profession exists in the public interest to advance the cause of justice and the rule of law. So did the American Bar Association's 1996 Professionalism Report on Teaching and Learning Professionalism, when it said that professionalism was about "dedication to justice and the public good."

High-sounding and high-minded ideals, but they are for me not mere rhetorical flourishes—they are bedrock aspirations. They are how we should be seeing ourselves, how we should be seen by others, and how we should continually strive to be seen. Professionalism is more than about being a lawyer—it is about why we are lawyers.

But in my view, two headwinds are polluting, or at least threatening to pollute, the ideal professional environment, and therefore the centrality of our relationship with the public: economic pressures and a misplaced preoccupation with process. These Zeitgeist forces create a kind of turbulence in our pursuit to narrow the gap between our professional ideals and the competing realities.

1. Economic Pressures

Lawyers, like everyone else, relished the boon economy of the 80's, and raised their financial aspirations and expectations accordingly. Many people got rich in the 80's, including many lawyers, and, understandably, no one was eager to give any of it up. When it looked as if they might have to, fear of loss took over. It was, I think, this intense fear of losing the economic benefits so intensely accumulated in the 80's that largely sedated people's impulse for generosity.

The fear of economic loss played out in different ways for different groups, but among lawyers it played out in rigid billing requirements, increased competition, and a restricted willingness to acknowledge requests for lifestyles that included living a life.

But to me, the most worrying repercussion of the economic Darwinism at work in the legal profession was the extent to which its impact was a perception by the public that the profession had adopted many of the practices not of a profession, but of a trade. When the public starts thinking of the practice of law as a trade like any other trade, it may well start asking itself why the practice of law should not be treated like a trade. Why, for instance, if lawyers are going to behave like a trade, should they be self-governing? Or why is a lawyer needed at all if lawyering is simply a matter of skill and not professionalism.

The economic amenities lawyers pursue must be seen as the earned rewards of the primary pursuit of serving the public. If they are, no one will begrudge their fair, and even generous, accumulation. If, on the other hand, they are seen as the object of the exercise, we risk ultimately being judged unworthy of the presumption of professional independence.

On the other hand, sometimes the economic pressures lawyers face, especially lawyers in small or sole practitioner firms, arise from not being able to keep up with the extraordinary costs—technological and otherwise—of doing business today. Pressure from clients to do more faster and for less, competition from non-lawyers, the relentless pace and face of change, reduced legal aid work at staggeringly stagnant tariffs—all these and more impose enormous tensions which should be acknowledged.

But in my view economic pressures, while generating inevitable stress for lawyers which may require responsive policy measures from a governing body, cannot be seen as a legitimate excuse to avoid practising in a professional way. Nothing justifies the absence of professionalism for a lawyer, at either end of the economic continuum.

2. Process Preoccupation

We have moved from being a society governed by the rule of law to being a society governed by the law of rules. We have become so completely seduced by the notion, borrowed from criminal law, that process ensures justice, that we have come to believe that process is justice. Yet to members of the public who find themselves mired for years in the civil justice system's process, process may be the obstacle to justice. It may be time—again—to rethink how civil disputes are resolved.

For a start, we need to sever the philosophies of dispute resolution in the civil and criminal justice systems. The dispute in criminal law is between an individual and the state. Process protects that individual's presumption of innocence from the overwhelming power of the state, and necessarily so. But civil justice is usually a dispute between two private parties. Can we honestly say that the fair resolution of such a dispute requires several years and resort to hundreds of rules? It would be worth asking a client who has just lost a lengthy trial how good he or she feels about having had the benefit of an elaborate procedural journey. Would it really surprise anyone if we learned from such a client that the result was of more interest than the process, and that all he or she wanted was a fair chance to be heard? People want their day in court, not their years. ... The public does not believe it should take years to decide where their children should live, whether their employer should have fired them, or whether their accident was compensable. Maybe for a constitutional case, but decidedly not for the resolution of a dispute between two private parties.

We cannot talk seriously about access to justice without getting serious about how inaccessible the result, not the system, is for most people. The public knows we are the only group who can change the process. They are very interested in, but less understanding of, our explanations as to why we resist streamlining the system from the inside. When we say, "It can't be done," and the public asks, "Why not," they want a better reason than "Because we've always done it this way."

Our monopoly puts us in a fiduciary relationship with the public. We are the gatekeepers and groundskeepers of the fields of the law. As such, we should be on the front line for reform, taking on outmoded systems, and being seen to be putting the public before our pockets or our prestige. Process is the map, lawyers are the drivers, law is the highway, and justice is the destination. Lawyers are supposed to be experienced about the best, safest, and fastest way to get there. If, much of the time, they are unable to get there because the maps are too complicated, then, as Gertrude Stein said, "There's no there, there." And if there's no "there, there," there's no point in having a whole system to get to where almost no one can afford to go.

I know this has been a difficult time for the legal profession. Through it all, most law-yers carry on with pride and professionalism, and with more than a touch of frustration at their seeming inability to synchronize their professional reputations with fluctuating public expectations.

There remains, however, one public expectation that does not fluctuate. It is the expec-tation that the profession will always, no matter the times or their permutations, behave professionally. It is an expectation to which the profession has always expressed a deep commitment, and it is an expectation to which most lawyers remain deeply committed.

The legal system represents the ideals of the public, and because as lawyers we are the interpreters and translators of those ideals, it is therefore a system that deserves our ide-alism, courageously and optimistically.

Having set the cluttered stage, what can be done to reinstate a commitment to profes-sionalism as the lawyer's—and the public's perception of the lawyer's—transcendent vi-sion? And, more particularly, what can be done by the Law Society? ... [H]ere are some thoughts:

1. The Law Society cannot solve all the problems lawyers face in the practice of law. Not every market force is surmountable and not every contingency is prevent-able. It may be time to stop the hand-wringing over how many lawyers should be allowed to practise on the head of a pin, and more on how many are doing it as professionally as possible. Establish your priorities in a way that facilitates as many ethical options for as many lawyers as possible, but don't try to be all things to all lawyers.

2. On the other hand, a lot of lawyers are hurting. It is worth knowing why, and which are the most vulnerable. What services could they use from the Law Soci-ety, besides a Code of Conduct, to help them navigate the breathless rates of change in law, information, and technology. In other words, how much more of the Law Society's energy and resources could or should be spent on facilitating access to what small firms, sole practitioners, and non-Toronto lawyers need to practise law as effectively and professionally as possible.

3. Having welcomed women into the profession in droves, we wallowed in smug-ness at our generosity, then forgot to pay attention to the droves who were leav-ing. To what extent are we acknowledging that life in a law firm may be no life? I appreciate that the environment is hotly competitive and that fear inspires des-perate measures, like 2000 hours of billings a year. But not only are we ignoring the reality that the gender that historically made and cared for babies still wants to, we are also forgetting that we spent the 60's and 70's telling the other gender that they too are important to children. So not only will female lawyers be either depressed, torn or childless, so will the males. Life matters—movies, books, friends, and family keep us humane, and if we are not humane we cannot deliver a humane justice system to the public. We should take as much pride in how di-verse and accommodating our law firms are—for both men and women—as in how big their billings are.

   How many minorities and women run major law firms. How many are part-ners, or Bar leaders? It's no good talking about the merit system any more because the curtain's been pulled and, like Dorothy, we know that the Wizards who make promotions and appointments are just real people. The "merit system" always operated idiosyncratically, and words like "qualified" tended to mean "who'll fit in best." So we should stop pretending about why the profession is still so top heavy with able-bodied members of only one of this country's official genders and colours and get on aggressively with making it possible for the public to see itself reflected at all layers in the lawyers who serve it.

4. ... [W]hy do we have articling and Bar Admission courses? Whose interests does this pedagogical gauntlet really serve? It has for too long survived the establishment of the university law schools whose absence was the original rationale for its existence. Is there really an evidentiary foundation for concluding that this is the most reasonable way for the Law Society to ensure that people entering the profession have the requisite educational arsenal of knowledge and skill? Has anyone taken a survey to gauge the utility of, or consumer satisfaction with the humiliating beauty pageant that is the gatekeeper to articling, or with the Bar Ad's income-delaying months which either repeat the job the law schools were doing, or teach the courses few graduates will ever need. How positively can a newly emerging lawyer be expected to feel about a Law Society which imposes either the frenzy of the match programme or the irrelevance of an accounting exam. Are the gains really worthy of the financial burdens these educational enhancements impose on students?

5. ... A sense of professionalism may well start before law school, but there is no doubt that it can take full flight in those three formative years. A good legal education teaches not just technical proficiency with laws and rules, but an ability to exercise judgment empathetically and wisely by blending that proficiency with the particular client or conflict. This is a lifelong career requirement that starts in law school and continues until retirement.

    But that good education will atrophy if the professional culture in which it is applied shrinks the idealism most students graduate from law school with. This professional culture is in the Law Society's jurisdiction, and it could do worse than spending time thinking about how to keep that idealistic sense of professionalism vibrant. Cultures are generated by shared values and expectations. It's time to concentrate on how to make those of professionalism culturally transcendent. ...

6. Which brings me to Leadership. We learn by watching and we teach by example. Who are the profession's designated role models and what are they saying? Are they talking about how many people find the legal system too cumbersome, costly and inaccessible, or are they talking about the opportunities globalization offers? Are they Generals in the war against disadvantage, or are they on the front lines of the battle to protect the honour of the status quo? Do they promote taking risks on behalf of social justice or do they promote complacency on behalf of a collegial life? Who we venerate today determines who we are served by tomorrow. Is the Law Society prepared to take a leadership role, or will it hide behind the impossibility of a consensus from its almost 30,000 members before it confronts the public's cynicism? Will it continue to jerk from agitating crisis to critical agitation, or will it undertake to prevent the legal system's ambush at Credibility Gap by a public who got tired of waiting for us to understand that their confi-

dence was a sacred trust? Will its misconduct preoccupations remain fixated on the sanctity of the trust fund or will it rebuke professional incivility and discourtesy? The gratuitously insulting crankiness which has now replaced critical analysis with depressing frequency, is a hole in our profession's ozone layer and requires the Law Society's protective public response, not only to remind the public and the profession that professional discourse is different from schoolyard discourse, but to maintain a professional culture lawyers should be proud to be a part of and clients should be proud to be served by.

It is not just a question of what the Law Society stands for, it is also a question of what the Law Society stands up for.

7. And finally, how will we define success in this profession? By money? By partnership? By hard work? Of course. But also by integrity, by decency, by compassion, by wisdom, by courage, by vision, by innovation, and by idealism.

If we venerate these qualities and reward those who have them with our respect, we send signals to the profession that our shared values and expectations exceed the tangible economic consequences of the expertise we enjoy. Lawyers have many contributions to make in many different ways. And they should feel pride, despite the reality of their fears and tensions and challenges, in what they do, who they do it for, and how they do it.

And this the Law Society can do best—promote that sense of pride, repair it when it suffers injury, and satisfy the public that we have earned the right to have them share in that sense of pride.

Let me end with a story that explains one lawyer's passionate belief in the justice system. Seventy years ago, a young Jewish man from a small town in Europe won a scholarship to the Jagiellonian University in Krakow to study law. There was a quota on the number of Jews, and he was one of only 4 admitted to the law school in a class of over 100. The Jewish students were assigned special seats in the lecture rooms. Rather than sit in them, he stood through most of his first year at University. World War II broke out one year after his graduation as a lawyer and on the day of his marriage. He and his wife spent 4 years in a concentration camp. Their 2½ year old son and the man's parents and three brothers died at Treblinka.

After the war, the man and his wife went to Germany. They had two more children. He learned English and German, and was appointed by the Americans to develop the system of legal services for displaced persons in Southwest Germany and to act as their senior legal advisor. He developed a deep respect for the American legal system, which he passed on to his children. He applied for, but was denied entry into Canada because his legal training was not a skill then considered necessary to Canada.

He eventually was permitted entry after teaching himself and passing licensing tests. He was admitted as a men's underwear cutter and as a shepherd, and arrived in Canada in 1950 with his wife and two children. In Canada, he was not permitted to become a member of the bar because he was not a Canadian citizen. This would have taken five years so he became an insurance agent instead to support his family.

He did very well as an insurance agent, and for the rest of his life felt deeply grateful for the opportunity to come to a new country and raise his two daughters in freedom. One of his daughters became the lawyer he couldn't be, but he died two months before her graduation. That daughter stands before you today, believing as did her father, that democracies and their laws represent the possibility of justice, and that lawyers are the people who have the duty to make that justice happen. I am very proud to be a lawyer, but I will never forget why I became one.

Constance Backhouse, "Gender and Race in the Construction of 'Legal Professionalism': Historical Perspectives"
Paper presented to the 1st Colloquium of Chief Justice of Ontario series, Law Society of Upper Canada (October 20, 2003)
www.lsuc.on.ca/news/pdf/constance_backhouse_gender_and_race.pdf

This is a paper solicited to contribute to a colloquia canvassing issues of "legal professionalism." When first asked to participate, I was advised that the colloquia had been designed by the Chief Justice of Ontario's Advisory Committee on Professionalism to "promote professionalism, civility, and a spirit of community and collegiality in the legal profession." The concept of "professionalism" is one that has always caused me a certain degree of hesitation. I think back to the Osgoode Hall classroom in which I sat as a third year law student, decades ago in the mid 1970s, listening to Dean Harry Arthurs lecture on "The Legal Profession." Try as I might, I could never quite get over my bewilderment that the hallmarks of "professions" apparently included self-regulating codes of conduct, and an ethic of public service. I remember leaning back in my chair, surprise twinned with skepticism, and wondering, as I have more than once in subsequent years, "just whom do they think they are kidding?"

So it was with some sense of unease that I asked myself whether I was actually the right person to agree to contribute to the colloquium. While mulling this over, I was out walking with a professor of history who teaches at Carleton University. I told her about the professionalism colloquium and mentioned my hesitation. She retorted, "Professionalism? Professionalism is all about power and exclusion." I returned home slowly from that walk, pondering the connections between professionalism, power and exclusion. My expertise is within the field of history. And what I have learned about the history of the Canadian legal profession resonates far more with words such as power, exclusion, and dominance than it does with concepts such as civility, or the extension of community and collegiality.

In the end, I resolved to prepare a paper for the professionalism colloquium, but a paper that attempts to chronicle what we know about how lawyers have resorted to ideas of "professionalism" to exercise power and exclusion based on gender, race, class and religion. It describes some of the barriers that were placed before the working class, Black, Jewish, Aboriginal and female individuals who sought admission to the legal profession.

[After offering an extensive history of exclusionary practices in the name of professionalism among lawyers, law societies and judges in Canada, Backhouse goes on to inquire why this history matters for contemporary understandings of legal professionalism.]

Why does it matter that the norms of the legal profession have historically been framed around deeply entrenched notions of masculinity, white supremacy, and class privilege? Obviously, the costs to those who have been excluded from the profession because of their gender, race, and class, have been enormous in terms of career opportunities, economic benefits, and social status. But the consequences run much, much deeper. The homogeneous nature of the profession and its resistance to diversification in the name of preserving professionalism have serious implications for the services that lawyers offer to the public, the arguments that lawyers make in courtrooms, and the decisions that are rendered by judges.

Our understandings of the most beneficent theories of professionalism suggest that legal services should be available to all, and that lawyers should provide well-honed advocacy skills that properly represent the interests of their clients' causes. Yet communities that have gone underrepresented in the profession have substantially less access to information about legal rights, and to the lawyers who could represent them. If and when they do identify the legal aspects of their problems and retain legal services, the lawyers are often unable to represent them properly.

No where is this more evident than with Aboriginal communities. The historical record is replete with examples of completely inept lawyering on cases of critical importance to Aboriginal clients. When Euro-Canadian legal authorities first attempted to assert jurisdiction over Aboriginal communities—in terms of criminal, civil and property law—there were a host of arguments that should have been made contesting the validity of this assertion. There had been no conquest, no surrender of sovereignty on the part of Aboriginal nations, and where there were treaties, these were woefully vague on issues of legal jurisdiction. Yet Euro-Canadians blithely arrested Aboriginal individuals, imposed their own understandings of substantive law, and scheduled trials that operated under Euro-Canadian procedural rules, presided over by Euro-Canadian judges. Aboriginal peoples frequently contested the right of European newcomers to assert such jurisdiction, but their voices were ignored. When Aboriginal clients were represented by white lawyers, almost every effort to put the jurisdictional question on the record was misconstrued by counsel, unheard or mangled. White lawyers seem to have been simply incapable of comprehending the complex Aboriginal political and justice systems that had been operating for centuries before contact, or of imagining that the Euro-Canadian system was not the only option. The basic questions of sovereignty, then, were never truly considered or adjudicated. Not only did this result in the failure to accord Aboriginal communities basic legal rights, but it also left these questions outstanding, continuing to plague Aboriginal–Canadian relations into the present and the future.

Historical court archives are also filled with examples of white male lawyers making blatantly racist and sexist arguments. Hamilton barrister, C.W. Reid Bowlby, was representing a group of Ku Klux Klansmen from south-western Ontario, after they had used mob intimidation in 1930 to prevent a marriage in Oakville between a white woman and an African-Canadian man. During the criminal trial, Bowlby proclaimed that his clients had done "a humane, decent thing in taking her away from that man." He begged the court for a dismissal of all charges, adding "I am sure that there are hundreds of parents throughout the Dominion of Canada who would be eternally thankful that such a step had been taken." Regina lawyer Douglas J. Thom K.C. appeared before Regina City Coun-

cil in 1924, to argue that Chinese-Canadian restaurateur Yee Clun ought not to be granted a licence that would enable him to hire white female employees. In an unabashedly
racist argument, Thom asserted that "Chinatowns have an unsavory moral reputation,"
and that "white girls lose caste when they are employed by Chinese." Nineteenth- and
early twentieth-century sexual assault and seduction trials are filled with misogynistic
arguments. Generally without any evidentiary basis whatsoever, male lawyers asserted
that victims of sexual abuse lied, and were sexually promiscuous, rabble-rousing, foul-
tongued, ill-mannered and intemperate in drinking habits. They accused women and
children of fabricating sexual complaints out of delusional fantasies, desires for revenge,
and conspiracies to blackmail. These character assassinations, pursued in zealous efforts
to protect accused men, frequently convinced all-male juries to acquit in trials where the
evidence of the crime was strong and convincing.

The fact that so many lawyers were drawn from the ranks of privileged white males
also affected their understandings of the world when they later became judges. ... To
provide only a few examples, George T. Denison, a white judge who became Toronto's
most famous magistrate from 1877 to 1921, openly referred to Jews as "neurotic," southern Europeans as "hot-blooded," the Chinese as "degenerate," Aboriginal peoples as
"primitive," and Blacks as "child-like savages." William Renwick Riddell, a white Court of
Appeal judge in early twentieth-century Ontario, described the Inuit and First Nations'
people of western and northern Canada as people with "savage appetites," who "seldom
considered themselves to be bound by anything but their own desires," in contrast to
whites, whom he designated as a "higher race." Riddell publicly portrayed Blacks as incompetent and uncivilized. The historical record reveals countless statements made by
male Canadian judges exhibiting explicit suspicion of, and hostility towards, women.
William Campbell, who served as Ontario Chief Justice in the early nineteenth century,
heard a family law dispute in which a husband had brandished a whip over his wife in
front of multiple witnesses, after beating his wife repeatedly for a long period of time. Mr.
Justice Campbell declared that "a man had a right to chastise his wife moderately," and
ruled that the wife had had no justification in leaving the marital home. This legitimation
of wife-battering stood for years as the prevailing Canadian judicial edict on husband's
rights. More recently, R.M. Bourassa, a white male Territorial Court judge from the
Northwest Territories, made a remarkable series of statements that attracted widespread
criticism as being both racist and sexist. The judicial inquiry into his conduct found no
reasonable apprehension of bias. The shocking revelation of the wrongful criminal conviction of Donald Marshall Jr., an Aboriginal man from Nova Scotia, resulted in an inquiry into the behaviour of the five white appellate judges who upheld his conviction.
The white judges of the Judicial Council of Canada concluded that there was nothing to
impugn the impartiality of the court.

The Future of the Concept of Legal Professionalism

The examples I have produced in this short paper cannot capture the fullness of the historical record, in part because this research is so new, and in part because the recipients
of such behavior did not commit thorough accounts to writing in forms that have survived in archival collections. Yet what is here allows us to get some sense of the climate

that fostered a deep and longstanding intolerance of lawyers and judges who were not male, white, economically privileged Gentiles. The history of the legal profession illustrates that concepts such as professionalism, civility, community, and collegiality have been imbued with discriminatory intent and practice. These are, indeed, ideas that have been pressed into service to allow the most privileged of lawyers and judges to exercise power and promulgate exclusion based on gender, race, class and religion.

What does this mean for the future? Are such concepts so tainted by their historical foundations that they are impossible to rehabilitate? Are efforts to promote an ethic of professionalism doomed to failure? Certainly, I would argue that some of these concepts are irretrievably misconceived. "Collegiality" is a word that has long been used within the academy to justify the need to hire and retain faculty members who "fit the mold," who blend well into existing structures and ways of doing things. It almost never represents a desire to extend camaraderie or support to individuals and groups who have long been outside the fold. When previously excluded groups articulate the problems they perceive, they are accused of "lack of collegiality," of "lack of civility," of failing to behave "professionally." The concepts are turned on their heads, and those who have been exercising power for the purpose of exclusion claim that it is they who are aggrieved.

Perhaps we are better to turn away from words that are so laden with historical baggage. I think we might move forward from our history of exclusion more quickly if we were to focus upon different ideals, such as anti-racism, gender equality, respect for Aboriginality, religious tolerance, reduction in wealth disparity, and social justice. The legacy left by our profession's historical practices continues to impact upon the present. Major structural changes are required to set things right. These, far more than "professionalism" and "civility" are the principles that require the utmost of urgent attention if we are to achieve a profession worthy of the name.

Trevor C.W. Farrow, "Sustainable Professionalism"
(2008), 46 *Osgoode Hall LJ* 51, at 53-55, 57, 83-87, and 96-100
(footnotes omitted)

The traditional narrative of the legal profession has run its course. Lawyers are looking for ethically sensitive ways to practice law that "assume greater responsibility for the welfare of parties other than clients" and that increasingly amount "to a plus for this society and for the world of our children." Lawyers are also seeking ways to practice law that allow them to get home at night and on weekends, see their families, work full or part-time, practice in diverse and "alternative" settings, and generally pursue a meaningful *career* in the law rather than necessarily a total *life* in the law. Similarly, law students are hoping not to be asked to make a "pact with the Devil" as the cost of becoming a lawyer, and are instead looking to find areas in the law that fit with their personal, political, and economic preferences. An increasing number of legal academics are teaching, researching, and writing about progressive changes to the way we view the role and purpose of lawyering. Law faculties are actively reforming their programs and creating centres and initiatives designed to make space for innovative ethics offerings and public interest programs. Law societies and other regulatory bodies are slowly chipping away at some of the time-honoured shields of ethically suspect client behaviour, while at the same time facing demands for increased accountability. The bench and the bar are taking an active interest in addressing a perceived growing lack of professionalism within the practice. The public is increasingly skeptical of the distinction that continues to be drawn between legal ethics and "ordinary standards of moral conduct." Finally, clients are not only expecting lawyers to actively canvass methods of alternative dispute resolution—the alternative to the adversarial and costly litigation process—but they are also demanding evidence of general sustainable professional practices from their legal counsel.

These current, contextual, and contested realities have become badges of modern progressive lives in the practice of law, as well as its visions. Taken together, they are forming a new discourse for lawyers and the legal profession that is seeking to become personally, politically, ethically, economically, and professionally sustainable. It is a discourse that makes meaningful space for a lawyer's own principles, interests, and life preferences by balancing them with other important interests—including, but not dominated by, those of the client—in the context of the overall calculus of what counts as the "right" course of conduct both in a given retainer as well as, more generally, in a given career. It is a discourse that seeks to make good on what has largely only amounted to aspirational promises of equality, access to justice, and the protection of the public interest. And it is a discourse that seeks both to benefit from and take seriously its obligations to address the culturally complicated makeup of the bar and our general pluralistic and globalized civil societies. This modern discourse of an ethically sustainable profession challenges the "time-honoured" centrality of client autonomy and a lawyer's unqualified loyalty to the client's interests. Specifically, it rejects stories of lawyers, collectively, as members of a relatively homogenized profession and who, individually, are single-tasked "hired guns" focused on only one interest "in all the world." According to this new model, those stories are no longer—if they ever were—sustainable. ...

The resulting paradox created by the dominant narrative is that, although the stories that continue to be told are becoming less attractive to more people, the stories continue to be told. To my mind, given the complex realities of the current professional trajectory, lawyers need another story—a sustainable story—that captures those complex realities and provides for a meaningful prospect of broad-based buy-in. ...

[After offering competing principle, policy and practice-based articulations of the dominant and alternative models of lawyering, Farrow proceeds to set out his vision of professionalism, which makes use of aspects of both the dominant and alternative models, and that is anchored in notions of general sustainability.]

A key aspect of the problem is that the two stories, on their face, disagree about how to evaluate what counts as the "right" course of action in a given circumstance. Their positions on [Atkinson's] ... fundamental question compete. If we continue to assert these competing positions without uncovering the interests that underlie their positions—unless we find some common ground or more specifically, a persuasive lens through which to see this potential common ground—we will maintain this gridlock. By uncovering the underlying interests at stake in each of the two versions, we will start to see who and what we need to address and to protect in order to develop a story of professionalism that addresses all (or at least as many as possible) of those underlying interests. We will find common ground on which to build a theory of professionalism that is (as far as possible) acceptable to, or sustainable for, both sides. ...

So what are those underlying interests? For the dominant model, the client maintains the ultimate interest. More specifically, this model preferences the client's ability to maximize his or her autonomy and rights within the broad parameters of what counts as legal, and free from the moralizing of the advising lawyer. For the alternative visions, some version of "justice" or the "public interest" is the primary interest at stake. Again, this model specifically cares about the interests of a number of stakeholders—the client, the lawyer, the judge, the other side, and the public (present and future)—who, taken together, describe the interests of justice or what is thought of as the public interest. Under this model, discovering and balancing these interests actively engages the lawyer's own moral opinions and preferences in the dialogue.

The primary points of disagreement between these approaches are the number of relevant stakeholders (client versus client and others) and the relevance of a lawyer's own moral opinions (vis-à-vis the client's chosen course of legal conduct). Otherwise, both sides seem to agree on the basic justice-seeking premise of the lawyering exercise. We can recast this discussion, taking account of both the shared and competing interests, through a lens of sustainability. ...

As a general matter, sustainability has come to be primarily identified with three particular approaches: "sustainability as optimal living resource exploitation"; "sustainability as respect for ecological limits"; and "sustainability as sustainable development." While all three approaches characterize the *typical* use of the concept in modern legal parlance, they do not preclude other, more general uses of the idea. ...

To my mind, the legal profession provides a new terrain for "continuing debate" about the utility of sustainability, broadly defined. ...

From before, we saw that the primary conflicting agendas involved those solely of the client as compared to those of a broader range of voices. Further, the theories of professionalism disagree as to the relevance or prominence of a lawyer's individual moral opinions vis-à-vis a client's legal course of action. Therefore, a useful lens of sustainability must take into account a broad range of these competing interests, which I have organized into four main groups: client interests, lawyer interests, ethical and professional interests (of lawyers and the profession), and the public interest. ...

[After looking at how these four main groups of underlying interests are accommodated by a general notion of sustainability, Farrow proceeds to articulate his theory of sustainable professionalism.]

So where does this leave us? From a review of the competing principle, policy, and practice-based arguments that animate the dominant and alternative models of professionalism, and trying to make sense of these various complex, contextual, and sometimes competing interests. ... what remains is a challenge that neither the dominant nor the alternative model has fully overcome. As I argued earlier, both sides must learn to think and speak in terms that are sustainable to a wide range of voices and interests. The dominant model, through its narrow focus primarily on one interest "in all the world," misses a variety of other relevant people and interests. The alternative model, on the other hand—through its typical focus on the "good lawyer"—has been seen to be unrealistic in practice. …

This theory of sustainable professionalism addresses the gridlock created by these competing notions of professionalism. It purports to do so by harnessing both the energy and optimism of the alternative models as well as the tenacity of the dominant model. Even more importantly, it self-consciously identifies the myriad interests that are at stake in the context—those of the client, lawyer, profession, and public—and draws them into a theory of professionalism that is sustainable.

By moving beyond the centrality of the client's interest as championed by the dominant model, instantly we open ourselves up to competing and potentially irreconcilable interests. This theory of sustainable professionalism takes seriously the complex and pluralistic landscapes of lawyers, clients, and the public. But in order to have a chance of buy-in from those broad-based stakeholders, we need to live in the world of those complexities, not in a world of fictional simplicity. As Backhouse reminds us, doing otherwise simply perpetuates exclusion. Such exclusion, in turn, fails to develop a professionalism that is sustainable on any calculus. We also need to live in a world that is not afraid of those complexities. At times conflict will be unavoidable. And when it does occur, a sustainable theory of professionalism will seek to balance and respect as many interests as possible. For example, allowing for client autonomy and meaningful space for moral deliberation by a lawyer is not necessarily a mutually exclusive exercise. In fact, as Hutchinson argues, it is an exercise that can in fact be mutually beneficial: "To provide sound professional judgment, it is necessary to resort to a well-honed and mature sense of moral acuity." Further, failing to develop "bridges" between the "professional role" and the "dictates of a personal morality" will "impoverish both professional and personal pursuits."

At times, however, the conflict will be irreconcilable. The legal demands of a client retainer may collide head-on with the dictates of a lawyer's own personal moral code. For example [as Kennedy essentially contemplates in the excerpt above], what if a rich, speculative, private land developer wishes to negotiate a deal with a slum landlord over the purchase of a fully functioning, low-income rental facility that currently houses eighty subsistence-income-level families, in favour of its demolition and replacement with a high-end, multi-use condo facility that would house eight high-income families? Would you take the retainer? How would you advise the developer? Would it make a difference if you knew that alternative housing arrangements, given the current rental market, were not immediately available to those other families? Alternatively, what if the CEO of a large privately-held downsizing transnational security firm came to you and asked you to negotiate a deal in private that would result in the termination of all employees of the Muslim faith, based on your client's unfounded occupational requirement theory that these employees, while good people, simply pose too much of a reputational and security risk (in terms of attacks against security officers in the field) and are therefore too costly to the firm? What course of action would avoid an "injustice," would avoid "dishonourable" or "morally reprehensible" conduct, and would promote a generally accepted notion of "social justice"?

The dominant model and alternative models have not been able to find common ground on these sorts of questions. The dominant model provides that if the lawyer decides to accept the retainer (which is itself, although not required, an act that is encour-aged by the dominant model), he or she must background his or her own moral views and proceed to effect the client's legally permitted instructions. Based on anecdotal ex-perience, that is not a personally satisfying, acceptable, and therefore sustainable ap-proach for many students and lawyers.

The alternative models, by typically asking the question "what does justice require?" in a given situation, immediately open the door to contextual analysis. By so doing, com-peting interests can be balanced and, in the end, be prioritized on a calculus of what a lawyer thinks is a "good" course of conduct. ... As they currently stand, however, the al-ternative models—by perceiving themselves as taking the moral (justice-seeking) high ground and by casting the lawyering exercise into a normative hierarchy—have alienated both members of the dominant model and closet members of the alternative models who fail to see room for a theory of professionalism that makes space for the institutional practicalities and realities of the practice of law.

By seeking to normalize these competing interests and discourses, through an exercise of interest identification and rationalization, the theory of sustainable professionalism re-casts these interests into a broad collective of inputs. These inputs are the landscape of what amounts to the "real world" of the modern lawyering project. Seeing competing interests in this light normalizes them. It also forces any theory of professionalism to take them into account in order to be sustainable in the eyes of its various interested stakeholders.

If a lawyer chooses to represent the "rich, speculative, private land developer," then—pursuant to a theory of sustainable professionalism—he or she is doing so because, based on an interest-based calculus that includes a broad range of voices (including the client, the lawyer, and the public), the lawyer thinks it is a "good" thing to do, not because of the feeling that he or she "has to do it." The lawyer may choose to do so because he or she agrees with the client's motivations. Alternatively, the lawyer may be persuaded by the principle of client autonomy that underlies the dominant model of professionalism. In the further alternative, the lawyer may choose to take on the client but then try hard to persuade the client to pursue a different course of action. The lawyer's motivations may be that he or she disagrees with the goals of the retainer and seeks to change the client's mind. The lawyer may simply think that it is not the kind of work that he or she wants to do. Or the lawyer may think that it is not in the public interest, or that it is not "honour-able," "moral," or in the pursuit of "social justice." Regardless, the goal is to foster deliber-ation both for the lawyer and between the client and the lawyer, in the spirit of enabling a sustained and engaged discussion that takes seriously a variety of potentially compet-ing interests. This is not simply an exercise in client autonomy or an exercise in moral superiority. It is an exercise in real world, sustainable lawyering.

NOTES AND QUESTIONS

1. Each of the above authors adopts a distinct approach to understanding the role of lawyers and "legal professionalism." Is there one (or more) of these approaches that you find particularly persuasive or particularly problematic?

2. How might one or more of these visions of lawyers and/or the profession help with the first topic discussed in this chapter—namely, access to justice (broadly or narrowly

defined)? What is the connection, if any, between lawyers, the legal profession, and access to justice?

3. How would you respond to the following scenarios?

(a) A well-dressed couple come to your office seeking your services. They tell you that they made an arrangement with an elderly couple to take care of a property they own while they were out of the country for a year. Now that they have returned, they no longer want to pay the couple the $3,000 that they had informally promised to pay, even though the elderly couple had done the work in an exemplary fashion and now need the money. Do you agree to help them get out of the deal? Would it make a difference to you if, for example, these people were already clients of yours in other matters; they were willing to pay you handsomely; they had discovered that the elderly couple were cheating Revenue Canada; or you were short of clients?

(b) A client wants you to advise her about her overall tax liability. You tell her that your rate is $200 an hour. You are able to devise a simple solution after a couple of hours work that will save her almost $30,000 annually in tax. Rather than bill her for $600 (which represents the time you spent on her file), you send her a bill for $2,000 on the basis that this amount is reasonable in the light of the money you have saved her. Should you do this? What could you have done differently? Should your client's ability to pay be a factor in your approach?

(c) You have a few years experience under your belt in a family law practice. You negotiate for your client in a divorce where the other spouse is represented by a brash, know-it-all young lawyer with little family law experience. In the final negotiations, you agree on a deal that is, because of tax consideration, beneficial to your client and onerous to the other spouse. You are certain that the other lawyer is not aware of the disadvantageous tax consequences of the deal. What can or should you do?

(d) You represent a plaintiff in a personal injury action. There have been active settlement discussions with the defendant's lawyer. You have obtained a written medical report from your client's doctor stating that it is unlikely that your client can return to her former employment. The report has been furnished to the defendant's lawyer. You subsequently learn from your client that another physician has prescribed a new medication that has been completely effective but your client doesn't want to return to work until after the case is settled or tried. You receive a call from the defendant's lawyer who wants to engage in further settlement discussions. What is your duty in the circumstances?

(e) You are representing your client in negotiations with a businessperson, represented by counsel, who wants to buy your client's business. Financial statements prepared one month ago have been supplied to the other side. As the deal is being finalized, but before it has been concluded, your client tells you that there has been a dramatic decline in sales during the last month. What is your obligation with respect to this information?

(f) You are authorized by your clients to settle the case for $20,000, but they want you to get more if you can. Is it proper for you to say to defendant's counsel, "My client will take $25,000 and not one penny less"?

CHAPTER THREE

Commencing Civil Proceedings

I. COURTS AND TRIBUNALS

This part of the chapter places civil litigation in the context of the various kinds of tribunals in which disputes are resolved. It begins with a brief overview of the history of court organization and civil procedure in Canada; next, it describes the organization of Canada's courts of civil jurisdiction; and finally, it considers the differences between courts and administrative and arbitral tribunals.

A. The History of the Courts and Civil Procedure in Canada

Though courts existed in Canada before 1791, the evolution of Canada's court system effectively began with the passage of the *Constitution Act, 1791*, which created Upper Canada and Lower Canada, the precursors of the provinces of Ontario and Quebec, respectively. At this time, or shortly thereafter, there were several trial-level courts in Upper Canada, including the Court of King's Bench, District Courts, and the Court of Requests. The *Court of King's Bench* was a court of original and essentially unlimited jurisdiction in law. In the

Court of King's Bench all issues of fact were determined by a jury, not by a judge. As in England, this court went on circuit to try cases in the various district towns. (Interestingly, in 1849, the Court of Common Pleas with the same jurisdiction, practice, and course of proceedings as the Ontario's Court of Queen's Bench was established, leaving claimants to choose between identical court systems.) *District Courts* existed in each district for the "cognizance of small causes." These courts had jurisdiction in actions of contract for sums above 40 shillings and not exceeding £15. Each district was divided into divisions, and each division had a Court of Requests, the ancestor of the modern day small claims courts. In the *Court of Requests*, judges sitting alone (i.e., without a jury) had full power to give judgment in cases of claims not exceeding 40 shillings. At this time, no general appellate court existed within Upper Canada. Appeals from the Court of King's Bench, if the matter in controversy exceeded £100, were taken to the governor and the Executive Council. Where the matter in controversy exceeded £500, a further appeal lay to the Privy Council in England. A general appellate court was not established in Upper Canada until 1849.

One matter that should be quite obvious, and rather surprising, from the foregoing description, is that there was no court that exercised equitable jurisdiction—that is, there was no Court of Chancery. However, from time to time, after 1795, there was agitation for the creation of a court that could exercise jurisdiction based on equitable rather than legal principles. Eventually, the judges of Upper Canada advised the British Parliament that all of the judges of the King's Bench should be given equitable jurisdiction "with competent authority to one or more of them to hold a Court of Equity ... at certain periods distinct from the existing law Terms."

One pamphlet by John Godfrey Spragge, later a Chancellor of Upper Canada, argued for the need for a court of equity as follows:

> The common law was never meant, nor is it calculated, by itself to form the jurisprudence of a country. Without being tempered by equity law, it would often work injustice, and in its actual operation the application of its rules did work injustice, until a language began to be used in our Court of King's Bench which would have sounded strangely in the ear of a common lawyer in England. What was called the equitable jurisdiction of the court was not unfrequently appealed to as absolutely necessary, in the absence of a Court of Equity, to correct the rigour of the common law; a more dangerous doctrine could scarcely be broached, or one more calculated to subvert the common law itself. There are judges whose bent of mind would incline them to strain the common law rather than that a flagrant injustice should be committed, by applying its rules in their integrity to the case before them—"to do a great good, do a little wrong." The temptation to do so flowing from a love of justice and a hatred of wrong, thus, by degrees the common law would cease to be what it is and ought to be—a system of law built upon precedent and authority—so that a man may, with reasonable certainty, know what the law is, and govern himself accordingly; but it would degenerate into an uncertain hybrid system, neither common law nor equity, but an incongruous compound of both, so that no man could tell what his rights were, inasmuch as they would, in so great a measure, depend on the half-legal half-equitable view which the judge or judges might take of them.
>
> The law would soon deserve a reproach such as Selden applied to the Court of Chancery in his time: "In law we have a measure, and know what to trust to. Equity is according to the conscience of him that is Chancellor; and as that is larger or narrower so is equity. 'Tis all one, as if

they should take the standard for the measure, the Chancellor's foot. What an uncertain measure this would be! One Chancellor has a long foot, another a short foot, a third an indifferent foot. It is the same thing with the Chancellor's conscience." For the word equity, substitute law, and for the word Chancellor, substitute judges, and you have a quaint but forcible and true description of what our law would become.

This proposal met with serious opposition on the ground that equity could never be administered in a court of law. The outcome was the establishment, in 1837, of a separate Court of Chancery. Almost from the outset, however, jealousy and discord existed between the Courts of Queen's Bench and Chancery in what seemed to be a repetition of the historic conflict seen in England more than two centuries before. At various times, proposals were made for the creation of a single court to administer both law and equity, but such a radical departure from tradition was viewed with alarm and it drew strong opposition. Accordingly, common law courts and courts of equity were not merged until the latter half of the 1800s.

The remaining major developments in the structure and procedure of Ontario courts in the 19th century parallel the English reforms of that period. In the mid to late 1800s, statutory reforms were enacted to unify the court system and to codify court procedure, setting the stage for many of the modern rules of civil procedure. For example:

- The requirement that every issue of fact be decided by a jury was revised so that most issues could be decided by a judge alone, unless either party served a notice requiring a jury. In certain classes of cases a jury trial was *prima facie* mandatory, but even in such cases the parties might at trial dispense with the jury on consent. This is essentially the system that prevails today.
- Judges were authorized to make rules for enabling a clerk of the Court of Queen's Bench to exercise the jurisdiction of a judge in chambers. This was a significant change and it is the origin of the jurisdiction today exercised by masters.
- The shrouds of secrecy that had previously surrounded the pretrial stages of an action were swept away by granting to any party the right to obtain an order for oral examination of his or her opponent touching the matters in question in the action. By this provision the basis was laid for our modern system of discovery.
- Civil claims could not be defeated on the basis of a formal objection alone. This laid the foundation for the liberal power of amendment to cure errors in procedure that plays such a major and pervasive role in procedure today.

In summary, until the passage of 19th-century statutory reforms, the Canadian court system suffered under a system of multiple courts, a division in the administration of law and equity, and different procedures at law and in chancery. Statutory reforms such as Ontario's *Judicature Act, 1881* unified the administration of law and equity in one court and the statutory rules reforms of the late 1800s finally brought about the replacement of common law and chancery procedure with a written code of rules.

The history of procedure in England, Canada, and the United States can be divided into analogous periods. All three jurisdictions experienced a period in which law and equity were administered by separate courts and procedure was largely governed by non-statutory rules developed by the judges on a case-by-case basis, the period of "common law pleading and procedure." In essence, this was the pre-*Judicature Act* period in Ontario and England, and the pre-*Field Code* period in the United States.

Following the reforms of the middle or late 19th century, all three jurisdictions entered a period of "code-pleading and procedure"—a period in which the rules of procedure were set out in a statutory or written form. The common aim and achievement in each country was to codify rules for the conduct of litigation that were considerably less technical and formal than the common law rules. In basic philosophy and approach, though not in details, the procedural codes in the three jurisdictions were similar.

In 1938, US procedure was radically altered. By contrast, major procedural reform did not take place in England and the Canadian common law provinces until the onset of a reform movement spanning the period 1965 to 1985, and which stopped short of embracing the most radical changes in procedural philosophy that occurred in the United States. However, it is not to be assumed that English and Canadian procedure were identical; the differences have become more pronounced with the recent Wolfe reforms. In particular, they differ with regard to the important matter of the availability of pre-trial discovery. The English rules make no provision for the oral examination for discovery of parties, whereas this procedure is universal in Canada (although recent reform initiatives in many jurisdictions seek to impose certain limits on these processes). Instead, discovery in England is limited to discovery of documents and, with leave of the court, the administration of interrogatories. These are written questions to be answered on oath in writing by the opposing party. These procedures are changing with the introduction of witnesses' statements to be made available before trial.

The basic principles of procedure are similar throughout the common law provinces of Canada; in the period following 1965, the provinces and the Federal Court of Canada revised their rules on more than one occasion. These revisions drew on each other, on the English rules of 1965, and, to a certain extent, on the US *Federal Rules of Civil Procedure*.

With the passage of the US *Federal Rules of Civil Procedure* in 1938, procedure in the United States moved into a third period—one into which the courts in Canada and England, generally, did not enter. The *Federal Rules* represented a radical revision of the former US code procedure; they were so well received in the United States that they were adopted by, or influenced subsequent revisions in, most of the states of the Union. The chief reform occasioned by the *Federal Rules* of 1938 was to de-emphasize and simplify pleadings and to place a much greater emphasis on pre-trial discovery and the pre-trial conference as devices for defining the issues in an action. A major feature of the *Federal Rules* is that the scope of pre-trial discovery is broad and extends not only to the examination of the parties, but also to non-party witnesses.

While the US *Federal Rules* had a substantial impact on recent Canadian procedural reforms, those reforms stopped short of adopting the most radical aspects of US procedure. Typically, in Canada, only parties may be examined for discovery orally as a right and, typically, non-parties can be examined only with leave of the court. Also, Canadian procedure still places more emphasis on the pleadings than does US procedure; the liberal class action rules available in the United States have only recently been adopted in Canada. However, several features of the US *Federal Rules*—for example, broad summary judgments procedure and pre-trial conferences—have generally been adopted in Canada.

NOTES AND QUESTIONS

1. More detailed historical accounts appear in Williston and Rolls, *The Law of Civil Procedure*, vol. 1 (1970), at 4159 (on which the above description is based); in Riddell, *The Bar and Courts of the Province of Upper Canada* (1928); and in McRuer, *Royal Commission Inquiry Into Civil Rights*, Report No. 1 (1968), at 865-91. Falconbridge, "Law and Equity in Upper Canada" (1914), 63 *University of Pennsylvania L Rev.* 1, provides an account of the "equityless" period and of the establishment of the Court of Chancery.

2. What are the differences between equity and common law? Can one exist without the other? Note that Ontario and some US states had an "equityless" period, but also note Spragge's criticisms of what this did to the common law. Some now believe that we have gone too far and that contemporary procedure is all based on the exercise of equitable discretion. These critics claim that there are no rules—for example, any party or claim can be joined in an action; there are no limits to discovery; and judges face no constraints in the exercise of their remedial discretion.

3. Is it fair to say that equity and common law are truly merged? Note that many equitable subjects such as trusts, specific performance, and injunctions are still taught separately.

B. Courts of Civil Jurisdiction in Canada

Any discussion of the organization of the courts in Canada must begin with an examination of the *Constitution Act, 1867*, which created the Dominion of Canada. This statute divides legislative power in Canada between the Parliament of Canada, on the one hand, and the provincial legislatures, on the other. Sections 92(14) and 96 to 101 of the *Constitution Act, 1867* authorize Parliament and the provincial legislatures to create and administer Canadian courts. Section 92(14) gives the provincial legislatures exclusive jurisdiction over "the administration of justice in the Province, including the constitution, maintenance and organization of provincial courts both of civil and criminal jurisdiction and including procedure in civil matters in these courts." Sections 96 to 100 impose some requirements on the federal government with regard to the superior, district, and county courts in each province. In particular, section 96 requires that the judges of these courts be federally appointed and section 100 provides that the salaries of these judges are to be set by Parliament. Both of these requirements were designed to promote judicial independence by distancing the appointment and compensation of superior court judges from local politics. Finally, s. 101 empowers the Parliament of Canada to establish a "General Court of Appeal for Canada, and ... any additional Courts for the better Administration of the Laws of Canada."

The Parliament of Canada has used its s. 101 power to create the Supreme Court of Canada and the federal courts. Each of the provinces has used its s. 92(14) authority to create two levels of trial courts (superior and inferior) and provincial courts of appeal. The Yukon Territory and the Northwest Territory have created similar court structures using legislative authority delegated by the federal government. The Nunavut Territory is unique in using its federally delegated authority to create a single, unified trial level court and an appellate court.

Generally the court structure in Canada can be represented diagrammatically as shown in figure 3.1. A more thorough description of each court level follows.

Figure 3.1

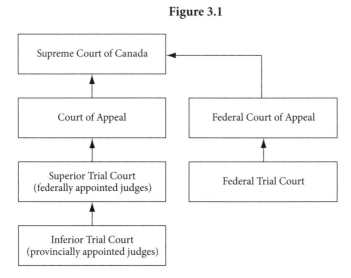

1. The Supreme Court of Canada

The Supreme Court of Canada was established by federal statute in 1875. The Supreme Court of Canada is a general court of appeal that hears matters relating to legislation applicable to the whole country (e.g., criminal law) or to provincial legislation that raises questions of national interest. Note, however, that on appeals from provincial courts of civil or criminal jurisdiction, the court sits as a court of appeal for that province and not as a federal court. This is crucial, for example, in appeals from the courts of Quebec. In these appeals, the civil as opposed to the common law governs. Before 1933 in the case of criminal appeals and before 1949 in the case of civil appeals, a further appeal could be taken from an order of the Supreme Court of Canada to the Judicial Committee of the Privy Council in England. However, since these dates, the Supreme Court of Canada has acted as the final court of appeal for Canada.

The Supreme Court hears appeals from the courts of appeal of the provinces and from the Appeal Division of the Federal Court of Canada. The jurisdiction and procedure of the court are regulated by the *Supreme Court Act*, RSC 1985, c. S-26, as amended, and regulations made thereunder. The court is composed of the (chief) justice of Canada and eight puisne judges. The *Supreme Court Act* requires that three of the judges should be appointed from Quebec; by convention the court includes three appointees from Ontario, one from the Atlantic provinces, and two from Western Canada. Sittings of the court are held in Ottawa from October to June.

Except in certain criminal cases, an appeal does not lie as of right from the court of appeal of a province to the Supreme Court of Canada. In all civil cases leave to appeal is necessary. Leave may be obtained from the provincial court of appeal or from the Supreme Court of Canada itself.

The Supreme Court of Canada may grant leave to appeal where the court is of the opinion that the question involved is, by reason of its public importance or the importance of any issue of law or any issue of mixed law and fact involved in such question, one that ought to be decided by the Supreme Court or is, for any other reason, of such a nature of significance as to warrant decision by it. This has been the situation since the *Supreme Court Act* was amended in 1974. Before then, an appeal in civil cases lay as of right if the amount or value of the matter in controversy exceeded $10,000. Leave had to be obtained if the amount or value in question was less than that sum. Practice before this court is governed by a separate body of rules, promulgated by the judges of the court pursuant to the *Supreme Court Act*.

2. *The Federal Courts*

Generally, the federal Parliament has been content to leave the provincial courts with jurisdiction to determine federal as well as provincial issues. Until 1875, there were no federal courts at all. In 1875, the federal Parliament established the Exchequer Court of Canada, which had a limited jurisdiction over cases involving the revenue and the Crown in Right of Canada. Over time, this jurisdiction was gradually increased to cover intellectual property, admiralty, tax, citizenship, and a few other matters regulated by federal laws. When the Exchequer Court was replaced by the Federal Court of Canada in 1971, the new court inherited the jurisdiction of its predecessor, but was also given additional jurisdiction, including the power to review the decisions of federal agencies and officials. Following changes in 2003, two divisions of the Federal Court of Canada were divided into two separate courts: the Federal Court of Appeal (formerly the Appeal Division), and the Federal Court (formerly the Trial Division). The seat of the court is in Ottawa, but each division of the court can sit at any place in Canada "to suit, as nearly as may be, the convenience of the parties." The procedure of the court is regulated by the *Federal Court Rules, 1998*.

The jurisdiction of the Federal Court is of two kinds—exclusive jurisdiction and concurrent jurisdiction—that is, concurrent with the provincial superior courts. Speaking broadly (until recently) the court had *exclusive* jurisdiction with respect to actions *against* the Crown, administrative appeals, and judicial review of the decisions of federal agencies and officials. The court has *concurrent* jurisdiction with respect to action *by* the Crown, intellectual property claims (copyright, trademarks, and patents), and admiralty claims. (An appeal lies to the Supreme Court of Canada from a final judgment or determination of the Federal Court of Appeal, with the leave of the Supreme Court.)

The establishment of the Federal Court, with its broader jurisdiction and more elaborate structure—that is, a trial division and an appeal division—represents a step in the direction of the dual court system in the United States, a system that leads to multiple litigation and complex jurisdictional disputes. See, generally, P. Hogg, *Constitutional Law of Canada*, 4th ed. (Toronto: Carswell, 2002). For a time, the jurisdiction of the Federal Court was surrounded in controversy that was compounded by a series of court decisions. The federal Parliament's power to establish courts is limited by the terms of s. 101 of the *Constitution Act, 1867*, which does not authorize the establishment of courts of general jurisdiction akin to provincial courts. It authorizes only courts "for the better administration of the laws of Canada," which means that the Federal Court can be given jurisdiction over only subject matters governed by "the laws of Canada." In a series of restrictive decisions, the Supreme Court of Canada has given the phrase "the laws of Canada," and hence the jurisdiction of the Federal Court, an extremely narrow interpretation. Beginning in 1976, the court rejected the view that a federal court could be given jurisdiction over any matter in relation to which the federal Parliament had legislative competence, even if that matter was not in fact regulated by federal statute law. On this view, the "laws of Canada" could include a rule of provincial statute law or a rule of the common law if its subject matter was such that the law could have been enacted or adopted by the federal Parliament. The Supreme Court of Canada held that the federal court could not constitutionally assume jurisdiction over a case unless the case was governed by "applicable and existing federal law."

This doctrine adopted by the Supreme Court created difficult questions surrounding the federal court's jurisdiction. Moreover, the situation was complicated by the court's refusal to adopt techniques developed in the United States to prevent the fragmentation of jurisdiction between two court systems and to avoid a multiplicity of litigation by allowing a federal court to settle matters of "state" law presented in one functional dispute. Eventually, the controversy was resolved in favour of concurrent jurisdiction with the superior courts of the provinces.

3. *Superior Courts of the Provinces*

Each province, as well as the Yukon Territory and the Northwest Territory, has created a superior court system consisting of a trial court and an appellate court. Although the titles and the subdivisions of the superior trial courts vary between some provinces, these courts are courts of inherent and general jurisdiction, like the superior courts in existence in the provinces at the time of confederation. This means that the superior courts are able to hear all matters that are not otherwise exclusively designated by statute to another court or tribunal. Currently, the superior trial court is called the "Supreme Court" in British Columbia, Nova Scotia, Prince Edward Island, Newfoundland, the Yukon Territory, and the Northwest Territory; the "Court of Queen's Bench" in Alberta, Saskatchewan, Manitoba, and New Brunswick; the "Superior Court of Justice" in Ontario; and the "Superior Court" in Quebec. As noted above, the Nunavut Territory is unique in having a single unified superior trial court (instead of superior and inferior trial courts). In Ontario, the Superior Court of Justice branches into the Divisional Court, which has a limited appellate jurisdiction. Generally, however, appeals from the superior trial courts are heard by each province or territory's superior appellate court. Because the superior courts of the provinces are captured by sections 96 to 100 of the *Constitution Act, 1867*, the judges of the superior trial and appeal courts are federally appointed and paid, although the courts are otherwise administered by the provinces.

4. *Provincial Courts*

Each province and territory (except Nunavut) has an inferior trial court. Generally, these courts are known as "provincial courts" or "territorial courts" and the judges of these courts are appointed by the relevant province or territory. The jurisdiction of these courts is limited and defined by statute. In a number of provinces, these courts are subdivided into criminal, family, and other specialized areas of law. Their jurisdiction over civil claims is usually limited to small claims (see below).

5. *Small Claims Courts*

Each province and territory has also used its s. 92(14) power to create a small claims court to hear civil claims for limited damages. In all jurisdictions except Manitoba and Ontario (where the small claims courts are adjuncts of the superior trial court) and Nunavut (where the small claims court is an adjunct of the Nunavut Court of Justice), the small claims courts are subdivisions of the provincial court. Currently, British Columbia, Alberta, and Nova Scotia have the highest small claims court limits of $25,000, with the limit in Ontario being raised to that amount in January 2010. Small claims court procedure is defined by statute in each jurisdiction. While the procedures resemble the rules applicable to the superior courts, they are intended to provide for a less formal hearing, which often does not involve legal counsel.

Marvin A. Zuker, *Small Claims Court Practice*
(Toronto: Carswell, 1998), 2-3, 6, 20-21

Small Claims Courts originated in response to a perception that the complex and technical regular civil procedure made it virtually impossible for wage earners and small [businesses] to use the court system to collect wages or accounts which they were owed. The basic problem was perceived to be caused by cumbersome formal civil court procedures that resulted in unreasonable delay and expense, since a lawyer was a virtual necessity to enable litigants to find their way through the complex procedural requirements. The primary aim was to reduce delay by simplifying the court process by reducing the need for litigants to be represented by a lawyer.

While the adversary process was retained, in the sense that each side to a dispute was responsible for presenting the arguments and facts in its favour, it was envisioned that the judge in a small claims proceeding would play an active role at trial—assisting litigants in bringing out relevant facts and clarifying the legal issues involved. Trial procedures and rules of evidence were to be "informal" and were left largely to the discretion of the trial judge. Generally, a small claims judgment was still required to accord to the rules of substantive law, although in some jurisdictions the small claims judge was directed, in addition, to do "substantial justice" between the parties.

The crux of the small claims procedure is informality and simplicity, in the sense that little paperwork is required beyond a brief initial claim commencing the action. Formal rules of trial procedure and rules of evidence are often waived. In some jurisdictions, no formal answer is required of the defendant beyond appearing in court on the trial date to explain his or her side of the case. ...

Over the years, a number of goals have been identified for the small claims process. Early reformers emphasized providing accessibility to the machinery of law for all classes—specifically, working and tradespeople. Since the primary problem with existing civil procedure was seen to be its complexity with resulting delay and expense, early goals were simplicity, speed and low cost. By simplifying the process of adjudication, early reformers also hoped to maximize self-representation by litigants. Small claims decisions were intended to be "fair," in that judges were required to arrive at even-handed decisions by applying the regular substantive law to the facts of a case.

Generally, all Small Claims Courts share the basic characteristics of informal adjudication … [in that] most procedural steps and paperwork are eliminated, and informal rules of procedure and informal rules of evidence are often used at trial. Small claims jurisdiction is almost always limited to a specified monetary range of civil claims that can be satisfied in money damages. Beyond these common features, however, several other procedural features have evolved as different paths of moving closer to the goals of the small claims process. …

An important development in the small claims process is using Small Claims Court clerks to assist litigants in filing (such as filling out a claim form) and to provide information on what types of proof will be needed at trial, or when supporting witnesses may be required and how to subpoena them. Some courts presently permit court clerks to give quasi-legal advice to litigants, such as how to determine the correct defendant, how to sue business defendants, and so on.

Small Claims Courts are organized administratively around the small claims clerk's office. …

The most common types of claims are actions for debt recovery or damages. A debt is a sum of money due by certain and expressed agreement where the amount is fixed and specified and does not depend on any subsequent valuation by the court to settle it. Examples of debt actions include those for services rendered, goods sold and delivered, promissory notes or dishonoured cheques. Damage claims are those for loss, injury or deterioration caused by the negligence, design or accident of one person to another, the amount claimed being a sum which must be evaluated by the court. …

In order to simplify and speed up the process of getting to trial, the focusing and clarification of issues is often left to the trial. This requires a more judicially active role at trial. Even in courts which permit lawyers, in a significant number of cases the judge will still have to assist the parties without a lawyer to explain their side of the controversy and to identify the relevant facts in a case.

The inquisitorial trial procedure used in a small claims court is much more efficient than rigid formal trial procedure in getting quickly to the heart of a dispute, since the judge has more control over the trial and can question litigants and witnesses to draw out relevant facts and clarify conflicting testimony.

Typically, small claims trials are conducted as follows. The judge summarizes the small claims complaint in his or her case file, identifying the plaintiff and defendant and describing the alleged cause of action and the amount claimed as damages. The plaintiff is then asked if this is correct in order to verify the claim. The plaintiff is then sworn in and told to tell his story in his own words. Testifying parties are directed to sit in a witness chair in front of the judge's bench or to stand in front of the bench. Generally, judges do not permit any interruptions or questions by the other side or by a solicitor while a litigant is testifying; also, judges assist the testifying party in laying out the facts and examining receipts or other documents which the plaintiff has brought to court. If the plaintiff has brought any witnesses, these witnesses are then sworn in and testify after the plaintiff. Finally, the defendant tells his story and presents witnesses, if any. Judges then permit the plaintiff and defendant to cross-examine each other, or their witnesses.

The degree of judicial activism observed in small claims trials is usually reflected in the extent to which judges "control" the trial process. More active judges, many "inquisitorial" or "investigatory," move from a brief review of the case to questioning the plaintiff to establish the necessary cause of action and proof of damages. They then shift to questioning the defendant to clarify his side of the case to bring out any defences or any facts by the plaintiff. After an opportunity for questions by the litigants, the judge announces a decision, explaining how he arrived at the dollar amount of the award. Judges who use this inquisitorial approach justify it on the grounds that it speeds up trials, enabling the judge to skip over or to cut short rambling or extraneous testimony and take the burden off inexperienced litigants.

NOTES AND QUESTIONS

1. For a review of the literature on and issues facing small claims court, see I. Ramsay, "Small Claims Courts: A Review," in Ontario Law Reform Commission, *Rethinking Civil Justice Research Studies for the Civil Justice Review* (Toronto: Ministry of the Attorney General, 1996).

2. Should lawyers be banned from small claims courts? One study suggests that fewer than 25 percent of small claims court litigants use lawyers and that they do not fare better than other litigants. See K. Hildebrandt, B. McNeely, and P. Mercer, "The Windsor Small Claims Court: An Empirical Study of Plaintiffs and Their Attitudes" (1982), *Windsor Yearbook of Access to Justice* 86.

3. Another alternative is to make better use of mediation in the small claims context. Traditionally, small claims courts have made extensive use of pre-trial conferences where the parties meet together with a court officer in an attempt to settle the case or narrow the issues for trial. During these meetings the court officer often acts as a facilitator of the discussions between the parties. At times, court officers apply considerable pressures on the parties to settle. Further, at the date scheduled for trial, it is not uncommon for the judge to summon the parties into his or her chambers and attempt to settle the case there. Increasingly, provinces are requiring or providing the option of mediation services prior to a small claims court hearing. (Alberta, for example, has a civil mediation program as part of its small claims court procedures; British Columbia has a pilot mediation project underway for small claims; and other jurisdictions, such as Ontario and Quebec, offer mediation options for small claims proceedings). What are the advantages and disadvantages of such procedures?

4. In May 2009, the government of New Brunswick introduced legislation to abolish the province's small claims court as a cost-cutting measure. (See Bill 66, *An Act To Repeal the Small Claims Act*.) If this legislation passes, the civil cases which would have been heard in small claims court will come under the jurisdiction of the province's superior trial court. This proposal has raised considerable controversy, because opponents fear that the elimination of the small claims court will make civil justice more expensive, time consuming, and generally less accessible to the public. See, for example, the response issued by the Canadian Bar Association at http://www.cba.org/NB/pdf/New%20Release%20March%202009.pdf.

C. Courts and Other Tribunals

The courts of civil jurisdiction in Canada are not the only state-regulated fora in which disputes are resolved through third-party binding decision making. Arbitration is increasingly being used in commercial disputes where parties wish to have the advantages of a customized process for resolving their disputes. Typically, the process is founded on an arbitration clause in a commercial agreement in which the parties undertake to submit their disputes to an arbitral tribunal rather than to the courts. However, the agreement to arbitrate is sometimes entered into after a dispute has arisen, and, occasionally, it is pursued after trial in lieu of an appeal in the regular courts. Because arbitration is a private form of dispute resolution, it affords the parties the benefits of confidentiality and the flexibility to tailor the process to suit their needs. It is often more efficient, but not necessarily less expensive. Although it is a private form of dispute resolution, it is supported and supervised by the courts through the various legislative schemes passed for this purpose.

In addition, administrative tribunals play an important role in dispute resolution in Canada. The following excerpt considers the role of administrative tribunals and their relationship to the courts.

W. Bogart, *Courts and Country*
(Toronto: Oxford University Press, 1994), 107-24 (footnotes omitted)

[T]he relationship between courts and the huge administrative state that has developed in Canada ... may be summarized as follows. First, courts over the last century blocked many progressive attempts to deal with widely applicable issues such as compensation for injury in the workplace, unionization, and human rights, with the result that the administrative state frequently displaced courts in dealing with such issues. Competition law provides a more complex example where the courts' failure to enforce laws regarding economic competition echoed vacillation in the political process that continues today. Second, courts continue to exert at least ideological influence through a review process (that is mostly constructed by themselves) of administrative actors' decisions. Such a process has the capacity to prune administrative programs in the name of the highly contentious concept of "jurisdiction." Finally, the foregoing suggests little basis for concluding that courts are capable of or willing to intervene systematically and to devise effective solutions to social problems in the face of powerful economic forces. ...

In administrative issues our judges have mostly been the keepers of pure liberal ideology: the state assigned minimalist policing functions, and the market was the best distributor of goods and services. Whether it was in such matters as occupational health and safety, the development of human rights, or the advent of unions and collective bargaining, the courts' activities wove a pattern of indifference, even hostility towards state activities. With a few notable exceptions, judges have raised the sanctity of the common law, which brought market principles to bear on the resolution of such issues: that everyone should be free to contract and negotiate the terms on an individual basis, and that only establishing fault should determine the basis for compensation of injury. Yet, under the guise of principles that seemed to treat everyone equally, the health and safety of workers were ignored with abandon, poisons were dumped into the environment, and the most insidious acts of prejudice were taken as a hallmark of self-regarding behaviour.

Change to curb the most dire consequences of such rules came from the legislatures, but was resisted by the courts. This opposition had two clear consequences. First, it led to the removal of several important areas of law from the courts. Second, when the areas were taken from the courts and a new regime was established and carried out by an administrative board, the courts insisted on overseeing their activities through a process of judicial review, which provoked much controversy among legal commentators.

The Establishment of Tribunals as Alternatives to Courts

While many instances exist (for example, regarding the environment or in terms of public interest groups participating in the process itself) three prominent illustrations spanning the better part of the twentieth century will be discussed regarding the courts' resistance to change aimed at altering the minimalist state. As a result of such resistance, the legislatures not only had to alter judge-made law but also took the task of implementing the new regime away from the courts. We will look at a fourth example—competition policy and law—which illustrates a more complex set of attitudes on the part of the courts and legislatures and a more ambiguous solution.

Workers' Compensation, Labour Relations, and Human Rights

The first illustration of resistance by courts and intervention by the administrative state concerns compensation of workers who were injured as a result of industrial accident. By the mid-nineteenth century, it was clear that only the most hardened could be indifferent to the toll industrialization had taken on human lives. Mishaps in the workplace injured and killed workers with alarming frequency, but the courts' response to this demonstrated a distressing rigidity. They insisted that fault must be established as a basis for recovery. In such a regime, individual workers fighting over a specific claim were almost always no match for employers, who were better organized and more financially able to resist. Courts placed workers at an even greater disadvantage with such holdings as that negligence of fellow workers would bar injured ones from recovering on the theory that they must have agreed to the joint enterprise that resulted in the damage. This "fellow servant" rule and other doctrines propounded by the courts were compatible with broader ideas about the role of the common law. Its purpose was to augment autonomy by creating spheres where individuals were free from state or any other interference. Accompanying such independence was a person's responsibility for his own fate. Such responsibility depended upon free will, with fault both a moral failing and a condition of liability.

Studies done of court cases just before substantial change was effected by legislation suggest that despite impediments, those workers who turned to litigation may have been successful more often than the rules would suggest, but these few cases may illustrate how pathetic some work conditions actually were. These results conveyed a possibility for compensation while leaving untampered a severe regime weighted against the injured labourer:

> Recovery by a few workers could satisfy the impulse of sympathy without challenging the settled doctrine and without making a shift in the balance of power between employers and labour or a threat to the established economic order. It may also be seen as giving the subtle control that can come from being merciful.

After much debate, the legislatures in many industrialized countries, including Canada, established a regime to compensate workers injured on the job. The details varied markedly, but the schemes had two characteristics. First, recovery was to be based on "no fault"; that is, the injured worker had to prove that she was injured as a result of an accident in the workplace, regardless of whose responsibility it was. Second, the regime of compensation was taken from the courts and handed to an administrative agency. Injuries were compensated by a system that provided for filing and adjudication of claims (where necessary) and for a system of appeals, all housed within an administrative structure established by the statutory regime.

A similar pattern developed with workers' rights to organize and bargain collectively, providing the second example of resistance by courts and intervention by the administrative state. During the nineteenth century, employees began to consolidate to demand some minimum benefits that came with the Industrial Revolution. Concerns for safety, exploitation of women and children, limits to hours worked, and the desire for increased wages all drove the union movement on. When it was not attacked by brute force, it was assaulted in the courts, where judges were mostly the allies of management. The cudgel was the concept of restraint of trade. Liberal values, at least in this context, espoused free markets where goods and services could flow unimpeded. Any clog was to be removed, hence any agreements or activities that restrained trade were to be suppressed. Courts used this concept to pummel any formal organizing by workers and attempts to bargain collectively.

Again, it was for the legislatures to reformulate the structure between employees and management by recognizing the workers' rights to form unions and requiring employers to bargain with them collectively and, of course, freeing them from the threat of criminal conspiracy for asserting their own interests: "the statutory freeing of unions from criminal responsibility for conspiracy or combination in restraint of trade is the cornerstone on which the trade movement rests. From it flows also collective bargaining and the later legislation dealing with labour relations."

Further, the implementation of such a regime was ultimately handed to administrative tribunals. A number of attempts to leave the issues with the courts foundered. Their focus on one-time disposition based on winners and losers, their adherence to a passive model where all aspects of an issue were to be brought and shaped by the parties, and their abiding hostility to the notion that workers should be able to bind together to improve their lot doomed the courts' role to failure. Ultimately, all legislatures in Canada ousted them from a direct role in collective bargaining issues. Yet the courts did not ease silently away but reasserted themselves in another role, a matter discussed below.

The last example of resistance by courts and intervention by the administrative state comes from the law's treatment of discrimination. One of the most cherished ideals of justice is the law's equal treatment of everyone. But like so many ideals, it is utterly compelling as an abstraction and extraordinarily difficult as a reality. Does everyone have at least a basic claim to society's economic resources for minimum food, shelter, medical care, education, and access to the justice system? Does equality always mean equal treatment or is it sometimes necessary to treat individuals differently so as to achieve equal results?

Whatever equality should convey, it has come to mean at least a claim to treatment freed from discrimination based on religion, race, and sex. A man's chances for being hired for a job should be based on his competence as compared with that of other applicants. His ethnic background should be irrelevant. A black woman's desire to rent an apartment should depend on her ability to pay and her willingness to use the premises reasonably. The fact that she is a woman and black should be beside the point. Even this negative sense of equality can be problematic. Should it allow for affirmative action programs to rectify past injustices? Should a criminal record be taken into account when hiring or should it be regarded as irrelevant like religion, at least for some positions? Is it appropriate to allow certain institutions that overtly espouse a particular religion or set of beliefs to hire only those who adhere to those beliefs in order to foster the institution itself?

These issues illustrate the complexity of the concepts of equality and discrimination regardless of which government agency grapples with them. What is clear from the historical record is the courts' antagonism to even minimum notions of equality of freedom from discrimination. For decades the courts were given a number of opportunities to nurture or at least tolerate the concepts, but, with few exceptions, they were hostile and unyielding.

The market was once again the frequent watchword. The free and uninterrupted flow of goods and services needed to be enhanced, while individual proprietors of those goods and services decided to contract with whomever they wished. If an owner refused to serve blacks, that was his right, subject to discipline by the market, because he would be deprived of that group's commerce. That a group as weak and diffuse as blacks in this country at that time could actually discipline bigotry through market forces was a fantasy that escaped the courts' notice.

This fidelity to freedom of contract was not subtle in any way. In one of the most notorious cases in Quebec before the Second World War, a black was refused service by a tavern owner. In upholding his right to do so, the Supreme Court of Canada made these comments:

> [T]he general principle of the law of Quebec was that of complete freedom of commerce. ... Any merchant is free to deal as he may choose with any individual member of the public. It is not a question of motives or reasons for deciding to deal or not to deal; he is free to do either. The only restriction to this general principle would be the existence of a specific law, or, in the carrying out of the principle, the adoption of a rule contrary to good morals or public order ... [and it cannot] be argued that the rule adopted by the respondent in the conduct of its establishment was contrary to good morals or public order.

Over time, there were a number of cases dealing with similar issues that venerated contract and dishonoured human dignity.

A similar atmosphere surrounded the "Persons" case, which raised the question of whether women could be appointed to the Senate as "qualified persons," ... . In denying the entitlement to women, the Supreme Court of Canada engaged in tortuous reasoning based on the historical intent when the provision was created in 1876. That is how things would have stood had an English appellate court, the Judicial Committee of the Privy Council (at that time Canada's highest court of appeal), not disagreed, ruling that women were qualified. This case is but one example of how the courts treated women ... .

To be sure, the legislatures perpetuated their own discriminatory horrors. But again, challenges to these wrongs, particularly against the Chinese, were continually rebuffed

by the courts. Often the legislation restricted the rights of the Chinese to gain a livelihood or employ certain people, particularly "white women." On these occasions freedom
of contract was subordinated to the higher cause of "morals" and "bodily health." This is
typical judicial reaction:

> It would require some evidence of it to convince me that the right and opportunity to em-
> ploy white women is, in any business sense, a necessary condition for the effective carrying
> on by Orientals of restaurants and laundries and like establishments. … Neither is there any
> ground for supposing that this legislation is designed to deprive Orientals of the opportun-
> ity to gain a livelihood.

Hesitantly and piece by piece, the legislatures eradicated discrimination after the Second World War. Though fragmentary and incomplete, the idea behind the statutes was
basic: equal treatment for all individuals without regard to particular characteristics that
are irrelevant to the decision being made. It is well to remember that the process is still
unfolding and is almost always controversial. …

Yet the process continues and these issues have been removed from the courts' jurisdiction. Human rights commissions have been established to implement the legislation,
fight discrimination with education, conciliation and, if necessary, through adjudication
that brands particular actions as wrong and awards compensation to victims when the
allegations are proven. Reviewing the courts' performance and legislative reaction, a
leading text on discrimination concludes, "[I]t is no wonder, then, that the legislatures,
with no aid from the judiciary, had to move into the field and start to enact antidiscrimination legislation, the administration and application of which have largely been
taken out of the courts."

The examples drawn from these three areas are merely illustrative of a pattern: initially, the courts' propounding of rules that mostly honoured strict liberal notions of individual responsibility, autonomy, and freedom centred on economic entitlement; then a
reaction by legislatures that adopted a more communitarian perspective, inquired into
the actual results, and recognized other values (such as need for compensation, legitimacy of collective action, and claims to equal treatment), frequently combined with the
creation of an administrative body. Finally, the removal of these issues, in large part,
from the courts, at least in terms of initial decision-making and the creation of some administrative agency to decide such questions. Other contemporary examples include pay
equity, redress for environmental harm, and compensation for injuries from motor
vehicle accidents. …

This is not to say that the legislative response has been flawless. Workers' compensation boards, grappling with rising costs, have come to be seen as unresponsive to very
serious issues that affect health in the workplace, such as occupational disease, though
most standard claims are handled promptly and to the satisfaction of the injured. Human
rights tribunals are criticized for being slow and backlogged. Indeed, such problems have
grown to crisis proportions in Ontario and have been the subject of a very critical report.
There are many examples of discrepancy between the high ideals espoused by these tribunals and related initiatives and the underlying reality. For example, despite strict laws
prohibiting discrimination against the disabled, Canada's record for employing people
with disabilities appears to be among the worst.

Yet in terms of responding with solutions other than those centred on economic individualism when it comes to issues that affect ordinary men and women, there has been a consistent division in this century between the courts and the legislatures and their agencies. Reviewing the historical record on this question, Arthurs has flatly asserted, "the courts utterly failed to deal with the most significant legal repercussions of the Industrial Revolution in the nineteenth century and with the revolution of rising expectations in the twentieth." In suggesting that judges by and large should not deal with human rights cases, a former justice of the Ontario courts has observed recently that:

> Judges as a group have been traditionally drawn from social classes unsympathetic to social change. This has been perceived as clouding their judgment by inclining them to decide against the change the legislation seeks to achieve. Judges have been perceived as unsympathetic to the problems of the "common-man."
>
> . . .

Judicial Review of Administrative Action

The clash between the judiciary and the administrative state—illustrated by our discussion of workers' compensation, labour relations, and human rights—developed on another front. Even before the advent of industrialization and capitalism, the courts had claimed the right to review the workings of government, though actual review was unsystematic. The growth of government was accompanied by the courts' increasing propensity to intervene and set aside orders made illegally.

But how was illegality to be determined? The courts vowed that this review was focused not on the correctness of the ultimate decision but on whether the decision-maker was empowered by the authorizing legislation to make the decision and the procedures the decision-maker was required to use. But even if this was the ambit of review, deciding what legislation empowered and what procedures could be used left plenty of scope for review. It was easy to see how a view that suggested the courts should not have such power of scrutiny would arise. Such an opinion was grounded in the belief that each administrative actor was as well situated or even better situated because of expertise to determine how his decisions ought to be made. Any review or appeal should come from that structure. The courts should keep out, as history indicates this was not a task for them, either as initial decision-makers or as reviewers of administrative actors' decisions, unless there was some appeal made to them that was authorized by statute.

Those who subscribed to this view were outraged that legislatures often inserted in relevant statutes sections declaring that the tribunal's decision was final and not to be reviewed in any way, specifically by a court. Yet these admonitions—known as "privative clauses"—were frequently defied by courts. To do this, they declared that all administrative tribunals had limited jurisdiction assigned to them by the legislatures. Therefore, whenever the tribunal made decisions that exceeded the limits of the jurisdiction assigned to them, they stepped outside the ambit of protection afforded by these clauses and the courts as protectors of the rule of law could—and indeed were obliged to—step in and corral them.

As logic, this manoeuvre was fine; as policy, it was highly dubious. It was true that administrative tribunals were assigned limited functions. Labour relation boards were to deal with issues arising between properly certified unions and management but were not to set milk production quotas. But the flaw was that issues submitted to the court as jurisdictional ones were far less clear than that. They almost always dealt with questions critical to the task the administrative actor was performing. The courts were frequently ignorant and even hostile to the thrust of the underlying legislative policy. When they brought to the interpretive exercise notions about the rule of law that idealized courts and the common law as its embodiment, there were bound to be clashes.

Perhaps at this point an example would be helpful. Any number could be provided, but let us take a classic one from the wranglings between courts and human rights tribunals, since we have already looked at the courts' response to issues of discrimination in the previous section. In 1968 McKay, a black, phoned about renting an apartment in the home of Bell. When he arrived to look at it, Bell informed him that the flat was rented. McKay, who was suspicious of the circumstances, had an acquaintance of his phone Bell soon after and she was told it was still available. Faced with this revelation, McKay went to the Ontario Human Rights Commission and filed a complaint. Bell explained that he lied because he did not rent to young men who could be students, and lying was a means to avoid argument and confrontation. However, at the board of inquiry—the hearing to adjudicate whether a discriminatory act had taken place—Bell raised a more formidable point that, if accepted, would prevent the board from proceeding at all.

Preventing discrimination has been given a high value in our society through the statutory prohibitions against it, but compromises have been made. Rightly or wrongly— at the time of this case—the legislation only prohibited discrimination in rental accommodation for "self-contained dwelling units." The idea behind the qualification was that the physical setup is likely to engender even more hostility between bigot and victim if the bigot is forced to accept the victim into what is basically her own home.

However, the matter for debate was what qualified as a "self-contained dwelling unit" since this term was not defined in the code. Bell went to court to have the judges stop the board of inquiry on the grounds that the flat was not a self-contained dwelling unit and, therefore, the board had no "jurisdiction" to decide whether acts of discrimination had occurred. Despite dissents, Bell won in the Supreme Court of Canada, the majority characterizing the issue as a "perfectly simple, short and neat question of law."

What irks defendants of administrative tribunals is the attitude typified by this quote. In fact the issue is complex and heavily dependent on a sense of the entire antidiscrimination structure and where and how to draw boundary lines in terms of, on the one hand, resisting discrimination and, on the other, realizing that insistence on enforcing the Human Rights Code will result in even more rancour. Such a decision should not be reached in the abstract, but only after carefully examining the facts in the particular case and relating them to appropriate circumstances where boundary lines have had to be drawn to enforce human rights legislation and mindful of the fact that premises such as the one in the *Bell* case are likely to be rented by individuals most in need of protection from discrimination.

Instead the Court based the meaning it attributed to "self-contained dwelling unit" on a mechanical and selective application of the previous formulation of the legislation. Initially the code forbade discrimination in "any apartment in any building that contains more than six self-contained dwelling units." An amendment in 1965 included buildings with more than three such units. Finally, in 1967 the legislation was altered again to prevent discrimination because of race to "any self-contained dwelling unit." Responding to these evolving formulations, the Court asserted that: "[T]he premises leased by the appellant, located in his upstairs floors, may well be 'dwelling units' but they were not 'self-contained' dwelling units."

It is small wonder then, with the *Bell* case as an example, that courts' review of administrative action has been characterized as subjective, inconsistent, hostile to the purpose of the agency and the legislation being scrutinized, and just plain muddled. Adams, a leading author in labour law (and himself now a judge) explains that since substantive rules of law applicable to judicial control of administrative action are so general in nature, they may actually invite intervention based on "subjective judicial opinion." Statutes like those dealing with labour relations issues were enacted to reflect particular economic and social policy, but any number of judges' personal views may be quite contradictory and lead to any number of conflicting decisions. ...

[In recent years, the Supreme Court has attempted to subsume the question of judicial intervention in administrative decision-making within a more coherent analytical framework. To determine what degree of deference a court should show a tribunal—in other words, what standard the administrative decision should be reviewed upon—a pragmatic and functional approach will be followed. This involves the reviewing court looking to the presence or absence of a privative clause, the nature of the administrative bodies' expertise, the purpose of the statute empowering the administrative body and the nature of the problem being challenged (e.g., was it a question of law, or fact or discretion?). Based on these criteria, a court will decide on one of three standards of review: correctness, reasonableness or patent unreasonableness. Correctness implies the least deference and implies a court will overturn an administrative decision that it believes is in error. Patent unreasonableness suggests the most deference, and where this standard applies, a court should not intervene unless a decision is clearly irrational on its face. The middle standard of reasonableness will justify intervention where a somewhat probing examination reveals a flaw in the reasoning of the administrative body. *Ryan v. Law Society of New Brunswick*, 2003 SCC 28.]

... [C]ourts have also sought to fulfill a second function with their review. In this second role, they recognize the importance of reviewing an administrative decision to ensure that one who has been affected by a decision has been accorded minimal procedural decencies. At first glance, this too may seem intrusive since the courts' power to intervene is so embracing. Still, most of the criticism of courts' interference with tribunals, much of it justified, has been directed towards their mangling of the agencies' substantive programs by second-guessing how their legislative mandate is to be carried out. Critics have been much less bothered by the courts' role in assuring that decisions accord with appropriate procedural safeguards free of bad faith and bias, and giving those who are affected adequate opportunities to participate in the process. That these two processes supervising the scope of administrative agencies' power and scrutinizing the procedures used to arrive at their decisions can be very different is obvious if one realizes that former Chief Justice Dickson, the primary architect of deference to boards working out their regulatory scheme, was also one of the judges who favoured the most intervention to ensure that individuals affected by administrative actors' decisions have an adequate opportunity to present their arguments and evidence.

Deference to an agency's decisions in determining its mandate will alleviate problems of courts crippling tribunals' substantive programs. On the other hand, respect for persons—not just in terms of economic rights but in all aspects of individual integrity—should inform any kind of decision made by anyone empowered to decide. Even the staunchest defenders of administrative law are willing to admit that agencies' records at times have not been good in this regard. While indicating their willingness to intervene on this basis, the courts have simultaneously indicated that they will not use a fixed and immutable standard for evaluating the decencies of the procedures used unless required to do so by some statutory directive. The person affected must be given an adequate opportunity to participate and be treated fairly, but what is adequate and fair will vary from the most perfunctory right of oral reply to written submissions to a more formal hearing.

II. JURISDICTION

A. The Inherent Authority of the Superior Courts

In a civil dispute, "jurisdiction" refers to the authority of the court to decide the case. The jurisdiction of the court was once a purely procedural matter. As Professor Glenn explained in the excerpt in Chapter 1, "the writs were all there was. If the harm suffered could not be pleaded in accordance with the forms of action, no remedy was available." The claim was simply not cognizable at law. Perhaps nowhere has this approach to civil justice changed more than in the superior courts in Canada where the authority of the courts to fashion a remedy for a wrong is regarded as plenary and inherent. Where the civil justice system once operated on the theory that where there was no remedy there had been no wrong, it now seems to aspire to a situation in which "where there is a wrong, there must be a remedy."

The inherent authority of the courts to provide a remedy is affirmed in many of the statutes governing the superior courts of justice. For example, the Ontario Superior Court of Justice, the *Courts of Justice Act*, RSO 1990, c. C.43 states in s. 11(2) that "[t]he General Division has all the jurisdiction, power and authority historically exercised by courts of common law and equity in England and Ontario." In view of the limited authority once available under the writs, there is a certain irony in describing the breadth of the authority of the Ontario Superior Court of Justice by reference to the English courts of law. However, that reference includes both the courts of law and equity. And, in any event, the inherent jurisdiction of the superior courts of justice in Canada has been interpreted in the broadest possible manner.

Despite the breadth of the courts' authority, some limits remain, and these give rise to questions of the courts' jurisdiction. As in many federations, one limit on that jurisdiction is created by the division of authority between the federal courts and the superior courts of the provinces. In the United States, this limit is usually described in terms of *subject matter* jurisdiction. In Canada, conflicts between the jurisdiction of the federal courts and the superior courts of the provinces have largely been resolved in favour of the superior courts of the provinces as is explained in the following excerpt.

J. Walker, *The Constitution of Canada and the Conflict of Laws*
(Oxford: Oxford University DPhil Thesis, 2001), at 85-87
(footnotes omitted or incorporated)

[The] Ontario Court of Appeal described the jurisdiction of the Canadian superior courts (in *80 Wellesley St. East Ltd. v. Fundy Bay Builders Ltd.*, [1972] 2 OR 280 (CA)) as follows:

> ... As a superior Court of general jurisdiction, the Supreme Court of Ontario has all of the powers that are necessary to do justice between the parties. Except where provided specifically to the contrary, the Court's jurisdiction is unlimited and unrestricted in substantive law in civil matters. ... Starke J ... said:
>
> > It appears clear that the Supreme Court of Ontario has broad universal jurisdiction over all matters of substantive law unless the Legislature divests from this universal jurisdiction by legislation in unequivocal terms. The rule of law relating to the jurisdiction of superior Courts was laid down at least as early as 1667 in the case of *Peacock v. Bell and Kendall* (1667), 1 Wms. Saund. 73 at p. 74, 85 ER 84:
> >
> > > ... And the rule for jurisdiction is, that nothing shall be intended to be out of the jurisdiction of a Superior Court, but that which specifically appears to be so; and, on the contrary, nothing shall be intended to be within the jurisdiction of an Inferior Court but that which is so expressly alleged.

In contrast, the federal courts in Canada, though not inferior courts, have a limited jurisdiction that has been analogized to the jurisdiction of inferior courts by the Supreme Court of Canada as follows:

> It is well settled, and the defendants do not dispute, that as a general rule provincial superior courts have plenary and inherent jurisdiction to hear and decide all cases that come before them, regardless of whether the law applicable to a particular case is provincial, federal or constitutional. ...

As a statutory court, the Federal Court of Canada has no jurisdiction except that assigned to it by statute. In light of the inherent general jurisdiction of the provincial superior courts, Parliament must use express statutory language where it intends to assign jurisdiction to the Federal Court. In particular, it is well established that the complete ouster of jurisdiction from the provincial superior courts in favour of vesting exclusive jurisdiction in a statutory court (rather than simply concurrent jurisdiction with the superior courts) requires clear and explicit statutory wording to this effect. This latter principle finds early expression in the judgment in *Peacock v. Bell* (1677), 1 Wms. Saund. 73, 85 ER 84, at pp. 87-88:

> And the rule for jurisdiction is, that nothing shall be intended to be out of the jurisdiction of a Superior Court, but that which specially appears to be so; and, on the contrary, nothing shall be intended to be within the jurisdiction of an Inferior Court but that which is so expressly alleged.

The source of the jurisdiction of the federal courts is found in section 101, which is the last of the Judicature sections in Part VII of the Constitution. This section provides in part "The Parliament of Canada may, notwithstanding anything in this Act, from Time to Time provide for ... the Establishment of any additional Courts for the better Administration of the Laws of Canada." A plain reading of the grant of authority to the Parliament of Canada to establish federal courts suggests that it is merely permissive because it is qualified by the phrase providing that it be exercised "for the *better* Administration of the Laws of Canada" and therefore, that for federal courts was not obvious to the founders of Canadian Confederation. The authority to create federal courts was exercised only in 1875, and it has never been fully exercised in respect of the "Laws of Canada." Where the federal legislation in question does not stipulate a forum for adjudicating disputes, the provincial superior courts have jurisdiction. Where the federal legislation in question *does* stipulate a forum, as it does in the Criminal Code and the Divorce Act, it frequently stipulates that the provincial superior courts have jurisdiction.

When the federal Parliament did exercise its authority under section 101 to establish the Exchequer Court of Canada in 1875, the court was empowered to determine only matters of the revenue and the Crown in right of Canada. Gradually, the court's jurisdiction was enlarged to include matters of intellectual property, maritime law, tax and citizenship. In 1971 it was replaced by the Federal Court of Canada, which continues to have exclusive jurisdiction in certain specialized areas such as maritime law, and patent and copyright. The court consisted of 14 judges until 1983, when its numbers were increased to 21, and in 1985, to 25. The court is based in Ottawa but it sits in various places throughout the country. In addition to the Federal Court of Canada, the Tax Court of Canada was created in 1983 to replace the Tax Review Board in adjudicating income tax appeals.

Although the mandate to establish the Federal Court of Canada might have a superficial resemblance to the mandate in the United States Constitution to establish the United States Federal Courts, there are important differences between the adjudicative functions of these courts and the roles that they are expected to play in the maintenance and development of the federation. The most obvious differences have emerged in the interpretation of the mandate of the Federal Court of Canada by the Supreme Court of Canada, which serves as a court of appeal from the Federal Court of Appeal. The Federal Court serves an important function in adjudicating disputes that fall within its subject matter jurisdiction, but the Supreme Court of Canada's concern for the jurisdictional complexities that might arise from the operation of parallel court systems has fostered a restrictive interpretation of the Federal Court's jurisdiction.

In a series of cases, the Supreme Court determined that the Federal Court's mandate was limited to the adjudication of disputes involving matters that fall within the classes of subjects on which the federal Parliament is authorized to legislate and on which the federal Parliament has legislated (*Quebec North Shore Paper Co. v. Canadian Pacific*, [1977] 2 SCR 1054 (1976) 71 DLR (3d) 111; *McNamara Construction v. The Queen*, [1977] 2 SCR 654, 75 DLR (3d) 273). Further, the Supreme Court has determined that the Federal Court has neither pendent jurisdiction (*Roberts v. Canada*, [1989] 1 SCR 322, 57 DLR (4th) 197; *Quebec Ready Mix v. Rocois Construction*, [1989] 1 SCR 695, 60 DLR

(4th) 124; but see *ITO International Terminal Operators v. Miida Electronics*, [1986] 1 SCR 752, 28 DLR (4th) 641), nor ancillary jurisdiction. (*R v. Thomas Fuller Construction*, [1980] 1 SCR 695, (1979) 106 DLR (3d) 193). Pendent jurisdiction and ancillary jurisdiction are important features of the jurisdiction of the United States Federal Court and they account for a substantial portion of its caseload. Pendent jurisdiction would allow the Federal Court of Canada to decide issues or claims that did not otherwise fall within its mandate provided that they arose in a case that did fall within its mandate. In other words, pendent jurisdiction would permit joinder of claims the subject matter of which would otherwise place them beyond the Court's jurisdiction. Ancillary jurisdiction would permit joinder of claims that would otherwise be beyond the Court's jurisdiction by reason of the parties involved.

At one time, the lack of ancillary jurisdiction threatened to force cases to be split between the Federal Court and the provincial superior courts because the Federal Crown had exclusive jurisdiction over claims against the Federal Crown. A claim against the Federal Crown had to be brought in the Federal Court, even if it was a counterclaim to a claim by the Federal Crown that related to laws other than "the laws of Canada" that, as a result, had to be brought in one of the provincial superior courts. Recognizing ancillary jurisdiction was one possible response because it would have allowed the whole claim to be brought in the Federal Court. However, the Supreme Court of Canada chose not to read such a jurisdiction into the grant in section 101 of the Constitution. Instead, the difficulty was addressed by amendments to the Federal Court Act that made its jurisdiction over the proceedings against the federal Crown concurrent with the provincial superior courts rather than exclusive of them as previously had been the case. The result was that a case that once would have been split between the two courts could be brought in one proceeding, but the proceeding would have to be brought in the provincial superior court and not in the Federal Court.

NOTES AND QUESTIONS

1. In *80 Wellesley St. East Ltd. v. Fundy Bay Builders Ltd.*, [1972] 2 OR 280 (CA) mentioned in the excerpt above, the plaintiff agreed to sell a piece of property to one of the defendants. Before the date for closing, that defendant assigned the agreement to another defendant, who registered the assignment of the agreement against the title to the property. The transaction did not close and a dispute arose over whether the deposit should be refunded and whether the registration of the assignment on title should be discharged. The plaintiff took the position that the deal was at an end, that the registration of the assignment (which blocked any further sale) should be discharged, and that the plaintiff should be able to keep the deposit. The defendants argued that the deposit should not be forfeited. In the course of the litigation, the plaintiff wished to sell the property to another person and brought an application to discharge the assignment to allow the new sale to proceed. The plaintiff offered to post security in respect of the defendant's claim to a refund of the deposit. The application was dismissed because although the judge believed that the security that was proposed was adequate, he found that he had no jurisdiction to require the defendants to look to such security for satisfaction of their claim in lieu of the assignment. The Court of Appeal held that this was wrong because as a superior court of general jurisdiction, the

Supreme Court of Ontario (as it was then called) has all of the powers that are necessary to do justice between the parties.

The Court of Appeal in *Wellesley* discussed the jurisdiction of the Supreme Court, the predecessor to the Ontario Superior Court of Justice, from two points of view:

1. the power of the court to grant an appropriate remedy; and
2. the power of the court to control its own process.

Brooke JA expressed a view of judicial jurisdiction that was extremely broad. He said that "the Court's jurisdiction is unlimited and unrestricted in substantive law in civil matters." This seems to be a far broader view of judicial jurisdiction than that with which lawyers and jurists in the United States and Australia would be comfortable. Can you explain this?

2. As a result of the approach taken to the potential for overlap between the jurisdiction of the federal courts and that of the superior courts of the provinces, the question of *subject matter* jurisdiction rarely arises.

3. In the following decision, the Court of Appeal for Ontario considers another limit on the jurisdiction of the courts, that of justiciability, which operates in addition to the question of the relationship between the jurisdiction of the federal courts and that of the superior courts of the provinces. The question of justiciability will be considered in more detail in chapter 5 in the section on Standing. Note, however, that although the court dismisses the appeal in this case because the question is not justiciable, the court nevertheless goes on to dismiss the cross-appeal as well, in order to clarify that had the matter been justiciable, it would have fallen within the jurisdiction of the Superior Court of Justice of Ontario, and not that of the Federal Court.

Black v. Canada (Prime Minister)
(2001), 54 OR (3d) 215 (CA)

LASKIN JA: ... The appellant Conrad Black wants to be appointed a peer in the United Kingdom, which would allow him to sit in the House of Lords. He alleges that Prime Minister Jean Chrétien intervened with the Queen to oppose his appointment and that, but for the Prime Minister's intervention, he would have received the honour and title of peer. Mr. Black has sued the Prime Minister for abuse of power, misfeasance in public office and negligence. He has sued the Government of Canada, represented by the Attorney General of Canada, for negligent misrepresentation. He seeks declaratory relief and damages of $25,000.

The respondents Prime Minister Chrétien and the Attorney General of Canada brought a motion to dismiss all of Mr. Black's claims (except the claim for negligent misrepresentation against the Government) on two grounds: first, that the claims are not justiciable and therefore disclose no reasonable cause of action; and second, that the Superior Court has no jurisdiction to grant declaratory relief against the respondents because that jurisdiction lies exclusively with the Federal Court.

In a decision reported as *Black v. Canada (Prime Minister)* (2000), 47 OR (3d) 532 (Sup. Ct.), LeSage CJSC held that the Superior Court had jurisdiction to entertain Mr. Black's claims. However, the motions judge dismissed these claims, concluding at p. 544

that "[i]t is [the Prime Minister's] prerogative, non-reviewable in court, to give advice and express opinions on honours and foreign affairs ... His actions and his reasons for giving that advice or expressing those opinions are not justiciable."

Black appeals on the issue of justiciability and the respondents cross-appeal on the jurisdiction of the Superior Court to grant declaratory relief. Together, the appeal and the cross-appeal raise the following three issues:

1. Is it plain and obvious that, in advising the Queen about the conferral of an honour on a Canadian citizen, the Prime Minister was exercising a prerogative power of the Crown?;

2. If so, is it plain and obvious that this exercise of the prerogative is not reviewable by the courts?; and

3. If the Prime Minister's exercise of the prerogative is reviewable, does the Superior Court have jurisdiction to grant declaratory relief?

For the reasons that follow, I would answer yes to all three questions. Because of my answers to the first two questions, I would dismiss Mr. Black's appeal. In my view, in advising the Queen about the conferral of an honour on a Canadian citizen, the Prime Minister was exercising his honours prerogative, a prerogative power that is beyond the review of the courts.

First Issue: Was the Prime Minister Exercising a Prerogative Power?

. . .

... whether one characterizes the Prime Minister's actions as communicating Canada's policy on honours to the Queen, giving her advice on Mr. Black's peerage, or opposing Mr. Black's appointment, he was exercising the prerogative power of the Crown relating to honours.

. . .

... Because I am satisfied that the Prime Minister was exercising prerogative power relating to the granting of honours, it is unnecessary to consider the alternative basis for the motions judge's decision, the foreign affairs prerogative, or Mr. Black's submissions on it.

Second Issue: Is the Prerogative Power Exercised by the Prime Minister Reviewable in the Courts?

This is the main question on this appeal. The motions judge concluded at p. 541 that Mr. Black's complaint about the Prime Minister was not justiciable. He wrote: "It is not within the power of the court to decide whether or not the advice of the PM about the prerogative honour to be conferred or denied upon Black was right or wrong. It is not for the court to give its opinion on the advice tendered by the PM to another country. These are non-justiciable decisions for which the PM is politically accountable to Parliament and the electorate, not the courts."

. . .

At the core of the subject matter test is the notion of justiciability. The notion of justiciability is concerned with the appropriateness of courts deciding a particular issue, or instead deferring to other decision-making institutions like Parliament. ... Only those exercises of the prerogative that are justiciable are reviewable. The court must decide "whether the question is purely political in nature and should, therefore, be determined in another forum or whether it has a sufficient legal component to warrant the intervention of the judicial branch." ...

Under the test set out by the House of Lords, the exercise of the prerogative will be justiciable, or amenable to the judicial process, if its subject matter affects the rights or legitimate expectations of an individual. Where the rights or legitimate expectations of an individual are affected, the court is both competent and qualified to judicially review the exercise of the prerogative.

Thus, the basic question in this case is whether the Prime Minister's exercise of the honours prerogative affected a right or legitimate expectation enjoyed by Mr. Black and is therefore judicially reviewable. To put this question in context, I will briefly discuss prerogative powers that lie at the opposite ends of the spectrum of judicial reviewability. At one end of the spectrum lie executive decisions to sign a treaty or to declare war. These are matters of "high policy." ... Where matters of high policy are concerned, public policy and public interest considerations far outweigh the rights of individuals or their legitimate expectations. In my view, apart from Charter claims, these decisions are not judicially reviewable.

At the other end of the spectrum lie decisions like the refusal of a passport or the exercise of mercy. The power to grant or withhold a passport continues to be a prerogative power. A passport is the property of the Government of Canada, and no person, strictly speaking, has a legal right to one. However, common sense dictates that a refusal to issue a passport for improper reasons or without affording the applicant procedural fairness should be judicially reviewable. ...

· · ·

The refusal to grant an honour is far removed from the refusal to grant a passport or a pardon, where important individual interests are at stake. Unlike the refusal of a peerage, the refusal of a passport or a pardon has real adverse consequences for the person affected. Here, no important individual interests are at stake. Mr. Black's rights were not affected, however broadly "rights" are construed. No Canadian citizen has a right to an honour.

And no Canadian citizen can have a legitimate expectation of receiving an honour. In Canada the doctrine of legitimate expectations informs the duty of procedural fairness; it gives no substantive rights. ... Here Mr. Black does not assert that he was denied procedural fairness. Indeed, he had no procedural rights.

But even if the doctrine of legitimate expectations could give substantive rights, neither Mr. Black nor any other Canadian citizen can claim a legitimate expectation of receiving an honour. The receipt of an honour lies entirely within the discretion of the conferring body. The conferral of the honour at issue in this case, a British peerage, is a discretionary favour bestowed by the Queen. It engages no liberty, no property, no economic interests. It enjoys no procedural protection. It does not have a sufficient legal component to warrant the court's intervention. Instead, it involves "moral and political considerations which it is not within the province of the courts to assess." See *Operation Dismantle, supra,* per Dickson J at p. 465.

In other words, the discretion to confer or refuse to confer an honour is the kind of discretion that is not reviewable by the court. In this case, the court has even less reason to intervene because the decision whether to confer a British peerage on Mr. Black rests not with Prime Minister Chrétien, but with the Queen. At its highest, all the Prime Minister could do was give the Queen advice not to confer a peerage on Mr. Black.

For these reasons, I agree with the motions judge that Prime Minister Chrétien's exercise of the honours prerogative by giving advice to the Queen about granting Mr. Black's peerage is not justiciable and therefore not judicially reviewable.

Once Prime Minister Chrétien's exercise of the honours prerogative is found to be beyond review by the courts, how the Prime Minister exercised the prerogative is also beyond review. Even if the advice was wrong or careless or negligent, even if his motives were questionable, they cannot be challenged by judicial review. To paraphrase Dickson J in *Thorne's Hardware, supra*, at p. 112: "It is neither our duty nor our right" to investigate the Prime Minister's motives or his reasons for his advice. Therefore, the declaratory relief and the tort claims asserted by Mr. Black cannot succeed. For these reasons, I would dismiss his appeal.

Third Issue: Does the Superior Court Have Jurisdiction To Grant Declaratory Relief Against the Prime Minister and the Government of Canada?

Although raised only on the cross-appeal, the Superior Court's jurisdiction over Mr. Black's claim is a threshold issue. For that reason, and because it was fully argued, I will consider it in these reasons.

Under the recent amendments to the *Federal Court Act* and the *Crown Liability and Proceedings Act*, the general rule is that the Federal Court and the courts of the provinces have concurrent jurisdiction to entertain claims for relief against the Crown. In their cross-appeal, however, the Prime Minister and the Government of Canada submit that even if Mr. Black's claims are justiciable, the Superior Court does not have jurisdiction to grant the declaratory relief he seeks because that jurisdiction rests exclusively with the Federal Court (Trial Division). The respondents ask us to dismiss Mr. Black's claims for declaratory relief under Rule 21.01(1)(3)(a) of the *Rules of Civil Procedure*. This Rule permits a court to dismiss an action on the ground that "the court has no jurisdiction over the subject matter of the action." The motions judge concluded that the Superior Court had jurisdiction to entertain the claim against the Prime Minister. He also held that the Superior Court could deal with the claim against the Government of Canada because for the purpose of jurisdiction it was in the same position as the Prime Minister.

The respondents rely on s. 18(1) of the *Federal Court Act*, which gives the Trial Division of the Federal Court exclusive original jurisdiction to grant declaratory relief against any "federal board, commission or other tribunal":

> 18(1) Subject to s. 28, the Trial Division has exclusive original jurisdiction to issue an injunction, writ of *certiorari*, writ of prohibition, writ of *mandamus* or writ of *quo warranto*, or grant declaratory relief, against any federal board, commission or other tribunal; and to hear and determine any application or other proceeding for relief in the nature of relief contemplated by paragraph (a), including any proceeding brought against the Attorney

General of Canada, to obtain relief against a federal board, commission or other tribunal. ...

(3) The remedies provided for in subsections (1) and (2) may be obtained only on an application for judicial review made under s. 18(1).

Thus, the narrow question on this cross-appeal is whether the Prime Minister or the Government of Canada was acting as a federal board, commission or other tribunal.

When the *Federal Court Act* was first enacted, the phrase "federal board, commission or other tribunal" was defined in s. 2 to mean a body exercising jurisdiction or powers conferred by or under an Act of Parliament:

... any body or persons having, exercising or purporting to exercise jurisdiction or powers conferred by or under an Act of Parliament, other than any such body constituted or established by or under a law or a province or any such person or persons appointed under or in accordance with a law of a province or under section 96 of the *Constitution Act, 1867*.

However, in 1990, this definition was amended to include the exercise of power conferred by or under an order made pursuant to a prerogative of the Crown. Section 2 was replaced by a new definition in s. 2(1), which reads:

"federal board, commission or other tribunal" ... means any body or persons having, exercising or purporting to exercise jurisdiction or powers conferred by or under an Act of Parliament or *by or under an order made pursuant to a prerogative of the Crown*, other than any such body constituted or established by or under a law or a province or any such person or persons appointed under or in accordance with a law of a province or under section 96 of the Constitution Act, 1867. [Emphasis added.]

The respondents acknowledge that the actions complained of by Mr. Black were not performed "by or under an Act of Parliament." Even if Prime Minister Chrétien acted under the 1919 Nickle Resolution or the 1968 Regulation or the 1988 Policy, none of these policy statements gives powers conferred by or under a federal statute. Therefore, the Federal Court has exclusive jurisdiction only if Prime Minister Chrétien exercised powers conferred "by or under an order made pursuant to a prerogative of the Crown." LeSage CJSC concluded, and the respondents accept, that Prime Minister Chrétien did not make any order. What he did, according to the amended statement of claim, was intervene with the Queen to block Mr. Black's peerage or advise the Queen not to appoint Mr. Black. There was no "order."

However, the phrase "by or under an order made pursuant to a prerogative of the Crown" admits of two possible interpretations. Under the first interpretation, advanced by Mr. Black and accepted by the motions judge, "an order" modifies both "by" and "under." Under this interpretation, the Federal Court (Trial Division) would have exclusive jurisdiction if the Prime Minister exercised powers conferred by an order made pursuant to a prerogative of the Crown or exercised powers conferred under an order made pursuant to a prerogative of the Crown. As Prime Minister Chrétien did neither, under this interpretation the Superior Court has jurisdiction to entertain Mr. Black's claim for declaratory relief.

Under the second interpretation, advanced by the respondents, "an order" modifies "under" but not "by." Under this interpretation, the Federal Court would have exclusive jurisdiction if the respondents exercised powers conferred by a prerogative of the Crown or exercised powers conferred under an order made pursuant to a prerogative of the Crown. As the Prime Minister exercised a prerogative power, under this interpretation only the Federal Court (Trial Division) would have jurisdiction to grant declaratory relief, at least against him.

The respondents submit that their interpretation is more plausible. They argue that the motions judge's interpretation of the Act is contrary to Parliament's intention to make the Federal Court the only forum for review of federal administrative action. They point out that under the motions judge's interpretation, if the prerogative were exercised pursuant to an order, it could only be reviewed by the Federal Court; but if the prerogative were exercised directly, that is, without an order, it could be reviewed by the Superior Court. The respondents contend that such a result is anomalous. And they point out that judicial review of administrative action does not depend on the existence of an order.

One possible answer to the respondents' argument is that by defining "federal board, commission or other tribunal" in the way it did, Parliament intended that the exercise of the prerogative be immune from judicial review. However, accepting—as I have—that some prerogative powers are reviewable, the respondents' argument must yield to the wording and structure of s. 2(1) of the statute. A fair reading of s. 2(1) suggests that "an order made pursuant to" modifies both "by" and "under." This interpretation is supported by the parallel structure of s. 2(1)—"by or under an Act of Parliament" and "by or under an order made pursuant to a prerogative of the Crown." The former phrase must mean by an Act of Parliament or under an Act of Parliament; similarly, the latter phrase must mean by an order made pursuant to a prerogative of the Crown or under an order made pursuant to a prerogative of the Crown.

Even if the respondents' interpretation is plausible, it collides with the principle that clear and explicit statutory language is required to oust the jurisdiction of provincial superior courts, which, unlike the Federal Court, are courts of inherent general jurisdiction. The Supreme Court of Canada articulated this principle in *Ordon Estate v. Grail*, ... Section 18(1) of the Federal Court Act does not clearly and explicitly oust the jurisdiction of the Superior Court to grant declaratory relief in respect of the Prime Minister's exercise of the honours prerogative.

Put differently, if Parliament has left a "gap" in its grant of statutory jurisdiction to the Federal Court, the institutional and constitutional position of provincial superior courts warrants granting them this residual jurisdiction over federal matters. ... I therefore conclude that absent an order, the exercise of a prerogative power may be reviewable in the Superior Court. Thus, I agree with the motions judge and would dismiss the cross-appeal.

NOTES AND QUESTIONS

1. Despite dismissing the appeal on the basis that the matter was not justiciable, the Court of Appeal for Ontario found that "clear and explicit statutory language is required to oust the jurisdiction of provincial superior courts, which, unlike the Federal Court, are

courts of inherent general jurisdiction" and that any gap in the statutory grant of jurisdiction to the Federal Court is to be filled by jurisdiction in the Superior Court of the Province. Note that this determination is being made by a Provincial Appellate Court. Would this ruling bind the Federal Court?

2. One might expect that a court's authority could ultimately be traced to the Constitution. Because descriptions of the inherent authority of the provincial superior courts may be found in provincial legislation such as the Ontario *Courts of Justice Act*, above, it has been suggested that the court's authority is subject to the limitations of provincial statutes, including the limitations on their extraterritorial reach, that are prescribed by the *Constitution Act, 1867*. The *Constitution Act, 1867*, s. 92 includes the following in a list of matters over which the provinces have exclusive legislative power:

> 13. Property and Civil Rights in the Province. [In this context, the term "property and civil rights" encompasses most areas of private law.]
> 14. The Administration of Justice in the Province, including the Constitution, Maintenance, and Organization of Provincial Courts, both of Civil and of Criminal Jurisdiction, and including Procedure in Civil Matters in those Courts.

As is discussed more fully in J. Walker, *The Constitution of Canada and the Conflict of Laws* (Oxford: Oxford University D. Phil. thesis, 2001), at 35-44, it is not obvious that judicial authority is subsumed under provincial legislative authority simply because the superior courts are administered by the provinces. As we know, the superior court judges are appointed and compensated by the federal government in Canada, and the courts are thereby established and maintained cooperatively by the federal and provincial governments. Indeed, a review of the *Constitution Act, 1867*, suggests that judicial authority is not derivative of provincial *legislative* authority at all. The Canadian Constitution is different from that of the United States and Australia, in which each of the three branches of government—the legislature, the executive, and the judiciary—have a section in the Constitution that provides for their authority (for example, article III of the *United States Constitution*, which establishes the authority of the US federal courts). Here is a summary of the parts of our Constitution:

Part I:	Preliminary
Part II:	Union
Part III:	Executive Power
Part IV:	Legislative Power
Part V:	Provincial Constitutions
Part VI:	Distribution of Legislative Powers
Part VII:	Judicature
Part VIII:	Revenues; Debts; Assets; Taxation
Part IX:	Miscellaneous Provisions
Part XI:	Admission of Other Colonies

The "judicature" part of the *Constitution Act, 1867* contains provisions such as those for appointing and remunerating judges, but it does not provide in any general way for "judicial power" or court authority. The preamble to the *Constitution Act, 1867* suggests that this was not an oversight. It specifies that the Constitution provides for "Legislative Authority" and for "the Nature of Executive Government"—there is no mention of the need to provide for judicial authority:

> Whereas the Provinces of Canada, Nova Scotia and New Brunswick have expressed their Desire to be federally united into One Dominion under the Crown of the United Kingdom of Great Britain and Ireland, with a Constitution similar in Principle to that of the United Kingdom:
>
> • • •
>
> And whereas on the Establishment of the Union by Authority of Parliament it is expedient, not only that the Constitution of the Legislative Authority in the Dominion be provided for, but also that the Nature of the Executive Government therein be declared.

The intention to provide only for legislative and executive authority and not for judicial authority seems to be confirmed by s. 129, which provides:

> 129. Except as otherwise provided by the Act ... all Courts of Civil ... Jurisdiction ... existing ... at the Union, shall continue ... as if the Union had not been made; subject nevertheless [to applicable legislation].

Accordingly, it may be suggested that the *Constitution Act, 1867* does not create, but merely continues the authority of the superior courts, which is described in the *Courts of Justice Acts* of the various provinces.

B. Territorial Considerations Affecting the Courts' Authority

The early common law rule: Service in the jurisdiction or consent. In the early days of the common law, the jurisdiction of the courts was limited to the territory governed by the state. Thus, the courts could take jurisdiction over a civil matter only where the defendant had been served with the originating process within the territory in which the court sat. For example, if such a rule were applied in Canada, an Ontario court would have jurisdiction only where the defendant had been served in Ontario, or an Alberta court would have jurisdiction only where the defendant had been served in Alberta. This was sometimes called jurisdiction "as of right." The courts would also have authority over the matter if the defendant consented. If the defendant appeared and defended the claim on its merits, the court would generally be regarded as having authority to decide the matter.

Under this traditional common law rule, if the defendant could not be served in the jurisdiction and did not submit to the court's authority, the plaintiff had no alternative but to go to a court in a place in which one of these requirements could be met (for example, where the defendant resided) and commence proceedings there.

Expanded rules for service outside the jurisdiction. The rules based on service and consent have long since been modified by rules that authorize service "*ex juris*"—that is, the service of process on a defendant outside the territory of the issuing court. This makes good sense when the forum is the most suitable for the resolution of the dispute even though it is not the defendant's home court and the defendant has not consented to it. For example, if the events giving rise to the matter occurred in the forum, access to evidence and witnesses might be facilitated by trial there. Similarly, in situations involving consumers, workers, and other plaintiffs who might unlikely be able to travel to sue defendants in distant fora, it can seem unfair to require them to do so.

This was illustrated in *Moran v. Pyle National (Canada) Ltd.*, [1975] 1 SCR 393. In that case, the Supreme Court of Canada considered a situation in which the widow of a man, who had been electrocuted in Saskatchewan when removing a spent light bulb that had been manufactured in Ontario by the defendant, commenced an action in Saskatchewan based on the rules that applied then for service outside Saskatchewan. The Supreme Court was asked to decide where the tort occurred in order to determine whether the Saskatchewan court had jurisdiction to hear the matter. Dickson J held that, in determining where a tort has occurred for the purposes of establishing jurisdiction, "it is unnecessary, and unwise, to have resort to any arbitrary set of rules." Further, borrowing from the US tradition of emphasizing fairness to the defendant, he reasoned that

> where a foreign defendant carelessly manufactures a product in a foreign jurisdiction which enters into the normal channels of trade and he knows or ought to know both that as a result of his carelessness a consumer may well be injured and it is reasonably foreseeable that the product would be used or consumed where the plaintiff used or consumed it, then the forum in which the plaintiff suffered damage is entitled to exercise judicial jurisdiction over that foreign defendant.

The rules for "service out" (or "long arm" statutes as they are called in the United States) permit defendants to be served outside the jurisdiction in which the proceeding has been commenced. These rules vary from province to province. Initially, they were relatively narrow, but they were gradually extended in Canada in the 1970s and 1980s to give plaintiffs access to more courts in more types of cases. Today, in some provinces, some of the rules permit service *ex juris* in cases that have little connection to the forum province. For example, under Ontario rules 17.02(h) and (o), defendants can be served without leave in cases in which the damage was suffered in Ontario, regardless where the wrong occurred, or in which the defendant is merely a necessary party to a proceeding against another defendant served in Ontario; under NS rule 10.07, a defendant can be served without leave anywhere in Canada or the United States, apparently in any type of case. Further, in regimes like that established by the Ontario rules, there is generally provision for plaintiffs to seek the leave of the court to serve out if their case does not fit into one of the categories of cases for service out without leave. See Ontario rule 17.03.

Despite its increasing prevalence, jurisdiction based on service out has been exercised with some degree of caution and the courts in some Canadian provinces still require plaintiffs to obtain leave to serve out by persuading the court that it is an appropriate forum for the resolution of the dispute. Even in places such as Ontario, where the rules have been amended to permit service out without leave in certain established categories of cases, it has been held that this does not signal a change in the care that should be exercised by courts in assuming jurisdiction over cases against foreigners. (See *Frymer v. Brettschneider* (1994), 19 OR (3d) 60 (CA).)

One important practical problem in using service out rules to sue a foreign party is how to effect service in a foreign country. Rules about service differ substantially from country to country. For example, while anyone can serve an originating process under the Ontario rules, in some jurisdictions service must be effected by a state official. Whose rules as to the method of service apply? For many countries, this is answered by *The Hague Convention on the Service Abroad of Judicial and Extrajudicial Documents in Civil or Commercial Matters,* which establishes the regime for how service abroad is to be effected. In Ontario, rule 17.05 provides for the application of the convention in serving parties in countries that have acceded to the convention, and it sets out how service is to be effected in countries who have not acceded to the convention.

Service out and the enforcement of judgments. One reason for exercising caution is that even if jurisdiction is assumed over a foreign defendant the resulting judgment might not be enforceable in the places where the foreign defendant's assets are located. A judgment granted by a court, say, in Ontario is, of course, enforceable in Ontario, but if the defendant has no assets in Ontario, the plaintiff (now a judgment creditor) must take the Ontario judgment to a jurisdiction where the defendant's assets are located and bring an action on the judgment there. Generally speaking, it will be enforced only if that court recognizes the jurisdiction of the Ontario court over the defendant.

Until 1990, the rules in Canada about when a court would recognize and enforce the judgments of other courts were narrower than the jurisdiction asserted by the recognizing court itself under its own service out rules. Courts would generally recognize and enforce the judgments of courts only in cases in which the court issuing the judgment had exercised jurisdiction on the basis of the traditional rules—that is, the defendant had been served in the territory of the court or had submitted to the court's jurisdiction. There was no obligation, or requirement of "comity," to respect the jurisdiction of a court when it had been assumed over a defendant outside the court's territory (by service out) without the defendants' consent. These narrow enforcement rules helped to make the expanded service *ex juris* rules tolerable because defendants who were served under the expanded rules and who had no assets in the jurisdiction could ignore the proceeding and the default judgment would not be enforceable in the place where their assets were located. This gave plaintiffs the opportunity to suggest a forum for the proceeding other than the defendants' home forum or one which the defendants had previously approved, but it gave defendants a veto over the plaintiffs' choice.

The Morguard revolution. This asymmetry in the rules for jurisdiction and for judgments continues to prevail between the majority of *independent sovereign states*. Courts will assume jurisdiction over foreigners in certain situations in which there are connections between the forum and the action but they are not prepared to recognize the jurisdiction of other courts that do so when asked to enforce the other courts' judgments. In 1990, the Supreme Court of Canada decided that this was not an appropriate model for jurisdictional relations or comity between the courts of the provinces *within the Canadian federation*. The court looked to the United States and the European Union as models. The founders of the American and Australian Federations and of the European Union thought it was not suitable for their internal arrangements to have the courts of constituent jurisdictions treat one another like different countries; they therefore created special rules for the assumption of jurisdiction and the enforcement of judgments by the courts of the constituent parts of their unions. Article IV of the US Constitution requires the courts of the states to give "full faith and credit" to the judgments of the courts of other states, as does the Australian Constitution. Article 220 of the *Treaty of Rome*, which was the basis for the *Brussels I Regulation*, provides for similarly generous rules for the recognition of judgments. In 1990, the Supreme Court of Canada held that it was time to change the rules under which the superior courts of the Canadian provinces had treated one another as if they were the courts of different countries for the purposes of jurisdictional relations.

The decision in *Morguard Investments Ltd. v. De Savoye*, [1990] 3 SCR 1077 marked a new approach to jurisdiction and the recognition and enforcement of judgments in Canada. In that case, the court unanimously upheld the enforceability of an Alberta judgment for the shortfall from a mortgage of Alberta land on which a BC resident had defaulted, despite the fact that the BC defendant had not been served in Alberta (the judgment was based on service out, in British Columbia) and had not consented to adjudication of the matter in Alberta. Speaking for the court, La Forest J acknowledged that the facts of *Morguard* would not satisfy the common law rule of recognition because the defendant was outside the jurisdiction of the Alberta court at the time of the action and had never submitted to the jurisdiction. However, La Forest J said, at 1098, that Canadian courts had in the past "made a serious error in transposing the rules developed for the enforcement of foreign judgments to the enforcement of judgments from sister-provinces" and he noted that the old rules for jurisdiction and judgments "seem ... to fly in the face of the obvious intention of the Constitution to create a single country." For the purpose of recognizing each other's judgments, the provinces should not be regarded as "foreign" jurisdictions—they were part of one nation; "various constitutional and sub-constitutional arrangements and practices make unnecessary a 'full faith and credit' clause. ... [T]he application of the underlying principles of comity and private international law must be adapted to the situations where they are applied, and ... in a federation this implies a fuller and more generous acceptance of the judgments of the courts of other constituent units of the federation."

Despite the emphasis on the constitutional basis for expanding the bases for enforcing judgments from other provinces, Canadian courts were quick to extend this generous approach to the enforcement of truly foreign judgments. In doing so, they relied on the extensive discussion in *Morguard* of the importance to international trade of liberal rules for the recognition and enforcement of judgments. Observations of La Forest J, like "modern states ... cannot live in splendid isolation" and "accommodating the flow of wealth, skills and people across state lines has now become imperative," supported the view that this new approach should be applied to all judgments, whether issued in other provinces or other countries. This approach has since been affirmed by the Supreme Court of Canada in *Beals v. Saldanha*, [2003] 3 SCR 416.

The implications of the Morguard principles for jurisdiction. This expansive approach to the recognition of judgments is fair to defendants only if the courts exercise restraint in the assumption of jurisdiction over persons in other provinces and confine themselves to cases in which there is a "real and substantial connection" between the matter and the province in which the action is to be tried. Accordingly, Canadian courts still retain the power to refuse to deny enforcement of a judgment where there is no real and substantial connection between the matter and the forum in which the judgment was issued. The British Columbia courts demonstrated this when they refused to enforce a judgment issued by a Texas court that had assumed jurisdiction solely on the basis that a passive website hosted in British Columbia might have been viewed by persons in Texas: *Braintech v. Kostiuk* (1999), 171 DLR (4th) 46 (BCCA); leave to appeal to SCC refused, SCC Bulletin 2000, at 453.

Although *Morguard* was neither argued nor decided in constitutional terms, the subsequent decision of the Supreme Court of Canada in *Hunt v. T&N plc*, [1993] 4 SCR 289 held that the jurisdictional principles it enunciated were founded on the Constitution and that Canadian courts must exercise jurisdiction in accordance with "the principles of order and fairness." Accordingly, the "real and substantial connection" test for the jurisdiction of the superior provincial courts supersedes the rules for service outside the province as the basis for judicial jurisdiction. While the categories of cases set out in the rules for service outside the province provide a rough guide to the kinds of cases in which persons outside the province will be regarded as subject to the jurisdiction of the courts, they are not determinative of the existence of a "real and substantial connection" for establishing jurisdiction. Accordingly, such categories are incorporated into the scheme proposed by the Uniform Law Commission of Canada in the *Uniform Jurisdiction and Proceedings Transfer Act* as presumptively real and substantial connections. The Supreme Court of Canada has held that the bases of jurisdiction over out-of-province defendants contained in book X of the *Quebec Civil Code* also comply with the principles of order and fairness: *Spar Aerospace Ltd. v. American Mobile Satellite Corp.*, 2002 SCC 78.

Thus, if a court takes jurisdiction over a case that meets the requirements of the rules for service out, but, on closer inspection, has no real and substantial connection to the forum, the assumption of jurisdiction could be challenged on constitutional grounds. This was done in a series of five cases decided by the Court of Appeal for Ontario in 2002 in which a constitutional challenge was brought against the exercise of jurisdiction based on rule 17.02(h). These appeals involved the exercise of jurisdiction by Ontario courts over defendants served outside Ontario in cases in which the only connection to Ontario was the fact that the plaintiff had continued to suffer in Ontario from injuries that occurred elsewhere. As the court explained:

> An Ontario resident suffers serious personal injury in another province or in another country. The injured party returns home to Ontario, endures pain and suffering, receives medical treatment, and suffers loss of income and amenities of life, all as a result of the injury sustained outside the province. The question is whether the courts of Ontario should entertain the injured party's suit against the out-of-province defendants who are alleged to be liable in tort for damages.

The Court of Appeal enunciated a flexible and fact-specific test based on eight factors, including:

1. the connection between the forum and the plaintiff's claim;
2. the connection between the forum and the defendant;
3. unfairness to the defendant in assuming jurisdiction;
4. unfairness to the plaintiff in not assuming jurisdiction;
5. the involvement of other parties to the suit;
6. the court's willingness to recognize and enforce an extra-provincial judgment rendered on the same jurisdictional basis;
7. whether the case is interprovincial or international in nature; and
8. comity and the standards of jurisdiction, recognition, and enforcement prevailing elsewhere.

See *Muscutt v. Courcelles* (2002), 60 OR (3d) 20 (CA).

In *Muscutt*, the court found that the Ontario courts could exercise jurisdiction in the matter because the defendant's insurer was part of a federal auto insurance regime that had undertaken to defend in the provinces of the claimant's residence. However, the court held that jurisdiction could not be exercised in the other four cases because they were matters in which the foreign defendants had not engaged in conduct in which they would reasonably have foreseen the obligation to defend against a claim in Canada. Despite the relatively detailed analytic structure established by the court, the results in the cases seem explicable in terms of the concern for access to justice that underlies the particular ground for service outside the province relied on in these cases. In two of the cases, which involved claims against local tour operators in the Caribbean, the plaintiffs' claims against other members of the travel industry were unaffected. In a third case, the individual defendants, who were drivers of cars involved in collisions in New York state, might themselves have had difficulty travelling to defend against the claims brought in Ontario; and in the last case, the plaintiffs' alternative forum for a claim relating to a slip-and-fall injury appeared to be the American town two hours' drive from the plaintiffs' residence in Ontario.

In another ruling by the Court of Appeal for Ontario concerning rule 17.02(o), the court similarly rejected a simplistic, territorial approach to determining the scope of the court's jurisdiction based on service outside the province. In *McNichol Estate v. Woldnik* (2001), 13 CPC (5th) 61, the Court of Appeal decided that a court could assume jurisdiction over all the defendants, including the foreign defendant, even though the claim might not have met the test for jurisdiction if it were constituted as a separate action. As the court explained:

> I do not agree that where an action has some claims with an extra-territorial dimension, and others which have none, the former must be separated and tested in isolation. To do so would, in my opinion, be contrary to the direction set by *Morguard* and *Hunt*. It would be a step backwards, towards a focus on territoriality and away from the recognition of the increasingly complex and interdependent nature of the modern world community which lies at the heart of La Forest J's reasoning. Moreover, it would introduce a rigidity to a test clearly designed to be flexible. Finally, it would mute the influence of the underlying requirements of order and fairness by preventing an assessment of the entire action against these requirements to determine whether they made it proper to take jurisdiction over the action as framed by the plaintiffs, including the extraterritorial claim.
>
> Rather, I think that the approach prescribed by *Morguard* and *Hunt* requires the court to evaluate the connection with Ontario of the subject matter of the litigation framed as it is to include both the claim against the foreign defendant and the claims against the domestic defendants. In doing so, the courts must be guided by these requirements of order and fairness. If it serves these requirements to try the foreign claim together with the claims that are clearly rooted in Ontario, then the foreign claim meets the real and substantial connection test. This is so even if that claim would fail the test if it were constituted as a separate action. This approach goes beyond showing that the foreign defendant is a proper party to the litigation. It rests on those values, namely order and fairness, that properly inform the real and substantial connection test and allows the court the flexibility to balance the globalization of litigation against the problems for a defendant who is sued in a foreign jurisdiction.

As the *McNichol* decision suggests, just as the concern to secure access to justice for plaintiffs incapable of travelling to sue could provide support for service on the basis of rule 17.02(h), so too could the concern to prevent a multiplicity of actions and inconsistent results provide support for service on the basis of rule 17.02(o). Nevertheless, these two bases of jurisdiction remain controversial and they are not necessarily endorsed in all the Canadian provinces.

Forum non conveniens—stays and injunctions. The rules for basic jurisdiction sometimes permit the exercise of jurisdiction over matters that are better decided elsewhere. Where this occurs, Canadian courts may stay proceedings pursuant to the doctrine of *forum non conveniens*. As the Supreme Court of Canada suggested in the passage below from *Hunt v. T&N plc*, [1993] 4 SCR 289, at 326, the two jurisdictional analyses work hand-in-hand to meet the constitutional requirements of the principles of order and fairness.

> I need not, for the purposes of this case, consider the relative merits of adopting a broad or narrow basis for assuming jurisdiction and the consequences of this decision for the use of the doctrine of *forum non conveniens* … . Whatever approach is used, the assumption of and the discretion not to exercise jurisdiction must ultimately be guided by the requirements of order and fairness.

Thus, the broad authority to assume jurisdiction described above would be overreaching if it were not for the fact that Canadian courts (including Quebec courts), like other common law courts, may exercise discretion to decline to hear a matter where there is a clearly more appropriate forum elsewhere. The law governing discretionary relief from jurisdiction is derived from the Scottish doctrine of *forum non conveniens* and it forms a potent remedy for defendants who wish to resist trial in the forum chosen by the plaintiff where that forum is unsuitable. In fact, the doctrine of *forum non conveniens* fulfills such a fundamental role in discouraging plaintiffs from commencing proceedings in inappropriate fora that it is an integral feature of the law of jurisdiction in common law countries. As Lord Goff explained in *Airbus Industrie GIE v. Patel*, [1998] 2 All ER 257:

> In the common law world … [t]here is, so to speak, a jungle of separate, broadly based, juris-dictions all over the world … . But the potential excesses of common law jurisdictions are generally curtailed by the adoption of the principle of *forum non conveniens*—a self-denying ordinance under which the court will stay (or dismiss) proceedings in favour of another clearly more appropriate forum … . The principle is directed against cases being brought in inappro-priate jurisdictions and so tends to ensure that, as between common law jurisdictions, cases will only be brought in a jurisdiction which is appropriate for their resolution … . It is however de-pendent on the voluntary adoption of the principle by the state in question; and … if one state does not adopt the principle, the delicate balance which the universal adoption of the principle could achieve will to that extent break down.

Relying on this doctrine, defendants have two remedies. First, they may bring a motion in the proceeding commenced by the plaintiff to ask that court to stay its proceedings; or, second, they may apply to another court (one that has jurisdiction over the plaintiff and that is an appropriate forum for the action) for an order restraining the plaintiff from continuing the proceeding. Although an "anti-suit injunction" is binding only on the plaintiff in the foreign action, it has the potential to pre-empt the decision of a foreign court regarding its own jurisdiction. This raises sensitive issues of comity, so injunctions are treated with con-siderable caution. To maintain the "delicate balance" described by Lord Goff, the leading common law courts, including the Supreme Court of Canada in its judgment in *Amchem v. British Columbia Worker's Compensation Board*, [1993] 1 SCR 897, have demonstrated an interest in aligning their principles with those guiding judicial discretion in other countries.

The following excerpt from the decision in *Muscutt v. Courcelles* considers many of these issues in the light of implications of the constitutional foundations of the law of jurisdiction.

Muscutt v. Courcelles
(2002), 213 DLR (4th) 577 (Ont. CA)

SHARPE JA: This appeal, argued together with four other appeals, involves the important issue whether the Ontario courts should assume jurisdiction over out-of-province defendants in claims for damage sustained in Ontario as a result of a tort committed elsewhere.

. . .

This appeal raises three issues:

(1) Is Rule 17.02(h) *ultra vires* the province?
(2) Did the motions court judge err in finding that the Ontario Superior Court could assume jurisdiction against the out-of-province defendants? ...

. . .

It is important to place the issues raised by this appeal in their proper legal context.

The jurisdictional issues that arise on this appeal emerge from a rapidly evolving area of law. Until the early 1990s, this area was governed by a set of rigid common law rules developed in England in the nineteenth century. These rules, discussed below, were shaped by the sovereignty concerns of a dominant nineteenth century world power anxious to safeguard its territorial sovereignty and jealous of any attempt by foreign states to intrude.

Towards the end of the twentieth century, it became increasingly apparent that these rules were out of keeping with the reality of modern interprovincial and international commerce and the frequent and rapid movement of people, goods and services across borders. The rules were especially ill-suited for resolving issues of jurisdiction, enforcement and choice of law between the interdependent sister provinces of Canada.

In four seminal decisions between 1990 and 1994, the Supreme Court of Canada radically changed the entire area of law. The decisions recognized that a new approach was necessary for a modern federal state with integrated national markets and a justice system that featured closely-shared values, a common appointment process for judges and a single final court of appeal for all courts.

Morguard and *Hunt* rewrote the law of jurisdiction and enforcement. For the first time, jurisdiction and enforcement were recognized as being governed by common values. The Supreme Court held that the principles of "order and fairness" require limits on the reach of provincial jurisdiction against out-of-province defendants and that jurisdiction can only be asserted against an out-of-province defendant on the basis of a "real and substantial connection." However, the Court also held that the courts of a province must give "full faith and credit" to the judgments of the courts of a sister province where the real and substantial connection test is satisfied.

(a) The Development of Assumed Jurisdiction

There are three ways in which jurisdiction may be asserted against an out-of-province defendant: (1) presence-based jurisdiction; (2) consent-based jurisdiction; and (3) assumed jurisdiction. Presence-based jurisdiction permits jurisdiction over an extra-provincial defendant who is physically present within the territory of the court. Consent-based jurisdiction permits jurisdiction over an extra-provincial defendant who consents, whether by voluntary submission, attornment by appearance and defence, or prior agreement to submit disputes to the jurisdiction of the domestic court. Both bases of jurisdiction also provide bases for the recognition and enforcement of extra-provincial judgments.

This appeal raises the issue of assumed jurisdiction. Assumed jurisdiction is initiated by service of the court's process out of the jurisdiction pursuant to Rule 17.02. Unlike presence-based jurisdiction and consent-based jurisdiction, prior to *Morguard* and *Hunt*, assumed jurisdiction did not provide a basis for recognition and enforcement.

. . .

Rule 17.02(h) was enacted in 1975. As mentioned above, this Rule allows for service out of the jurisdiction in respect of a claim for damage sustained in Ontario arising from a tort committed elsewhere. This "damage sustained" rule represented a legislative response to the type of problem confronted by the Supreme Court of Canada in *Moran v. Pyle*.

Courts have given the "damage sustained" rule a generous and liberal interpretation. The rule has been applied to a plaintiff who undergoes medical treatment and endures pain and suffering in Ontario as a result of a tort committed elsewhere. In *Vile v. Von Wendt* (1979), 26 OR (2d) 513 at 517 (Div. Ct.), the court held that the rule was intended "to enable the people of Ontario to use their own Courts more easily" and to overcome decisions under the old rule, which had required Ontario residents to pursue foreign tortfeasors elsewhere. In *Poirier v. Williston* (1980), 31 OR (2d) 320 (CA), this court affirmed the Divisional Court's decision ((1980), 29 OR (2d) 303 at 304), that, subject to *forum non conveniens*, "it was quite right, proper, and just" for the injured party to bring the action in Ontario.

As will be explained below, the "damage sustained" rule is now subject to the principles articulated in *Morguard* regarding the need for a real and substantial connection and the need for order, fairness and jurisdictional restraint.

(c) The Relationship Between Assumed Jurisdiction and Recognition and Enforcement

Although *Morguard* dealt with the proper exercise of jurisdiction from the perspective of recognition and enforcement, La Forest J made it clear that precisely the same real and substantial connection test applies to the assumption of jurisdiction against an out-of-province defendant. As La Forest J held at p. 1103, "the taking of jurisdiction by a court in one province and its recognition in another must be viewed as correlatives." Likewise, La Forest J made it clear that the need for order, fairness and jurisdictional restraint also applies to assumed jurisdiction. At pp. 1103-1104, La Forest J wrote:

[I]t hardly accords with principles of order and fairness to permit a person to sue another in any jurisdiction, without regard to the contacts that jurisdiction may have to the defendant or the subject-matter of the suit … . Thus, fairness to the defendant requires that the judgment be issued by a court acting through fair process and with properly restrained jurisdiction. …

· · ·

… [I]f the courts of one province are to be expected to give effect to judgments given in another province, there must be some limits to the exercise of jurisdiction against persons outside the province.

In *Tolofson*, the Supreme Court reaffirmed that the same test and the same need for restraint apply to both assumed jurisdiction and jurisdiction for recognition and enforcement purposes. Further, at p. 1049, La Forest J held that it is the real and substantial connection test that prevents jurisdictional overreaching: "This test has the effect of preventing a court from unduly entering into matters in which the jurisdiction in which it is located has little interest."

Having provided the background necessary to consider the issues in this appeal, it is now possible to turn to those issues.

Issue 1: Is Rule 17.02(h) Ultra Vires the Province?

The appellants submit that Rule 17.02(h) should be struck down as *ultra vires* the province of Ontario. They submit that Rule 17.02(h) asserts jurisdiction against extra-provincial defendants on a basis that exceeds the limits of the principles of order and fairness and the real and substantial connection test articulated in *Morguard* and *Hunt*.

The motions court judge dismissed the constitutional challenge on the basis that Rule 17.02(h) is purely procedural and does not confer jurisdiction on the court. By contrast, in *Duncan (Litigation guardian of) v. Neptunia Corp.* (2001), 53 OR (3d) 754 (SCJ), the court held that Rule 17.02(h) does confer jurisdiction on the court.

For the reasons that follow, I agree with the motions court judge that Rule 17.02(h) is procedural in nature and does not by itself confer jurisdiction. I would therefore dismiss this ground of appeal and hold that Rule 17.02(h) is not *ultra vires* the province.

It is clear that *Morguard* and *Hunt* together impose constitutional limits on the assumption of jurisdiction against extra-provincial defendants. As P.W. Hogg states in *Constitutional Law in Canada*, looseleaf (Toronto: Carswell, 2000) at 13-15, "the constitutional rule of extraterritoriality requires that the only causes of action in respect of which service *ex juris* is available are those in which there is a substantial connection between the defendant and the forum province." It follows that provincial rules of court allowing for service out of the jurisdiction, including Rule 17.02(h), must now be read in the light of the constitutional principles of "order and fairness" and "real and substantial connection."

In fact, it has long been accepted that service in accordance with the rules of court does not determine the issue of jurisdiction: see *Singh v. Howden Petroleum, supra.* Service merely ensures that the parties to an action receive timely notice of the proceeding so that they have an opportunity to participate. Moreover, the constitutional validity of Rule 17.02(h) cannot be determined by reading the Rule in isolation. Rule 17.02(h) is part of a procedural scheme that operates within the limits of the real and substantial connection test.

In G.D. Watson & L. Jeffrey, *Holmested and Watson: Ontario Civil Procedure* (Carswell: Toronto, 2001) at p. 17-9, the authors explain that the grounds outlined in Rule 17.02 "provide a rough guide to the kinds of cases in which persons outside Ontario will be regarded as subject to the jurisdiction of the Ontario courts." However, these grounds do not determine the issue of jurisdiction.

Several subsections of Rule 17.02 indicate that the Rule was not intended as a complete description of the requirements for assumed jurisdiction. For example, Rules 17.02(j), (k), and (l) provide for service outside Ontario for support claims, claims for custody of or access to a minor, and claims to declare the invalidity of a marriage. Each of these claims has well-established legal standards governing jurisdiction that must be satisfied notwithstanding the fact that the defendant has been served in accordance with the Rule. In my view, the same conclusion follows for Rule 17.02(h), which must now be read as being subject to the real and substantial connection requirement.

A party who is served in accordance with Rule 17.02(h) has several means of challenging the jurisdiction of the court on the basis that the real and substantial connection test has not been met. First, Rule 17.06(1) allows a party who has been served outside Ontario to move for an order setting aside the service or staying the proceeding. Second, s. 106 of the *Courts of Justice Act* provides for a stay of proceedings, and it is well established that a defendant may move for a stay on the ground that the court lacks jurisdiction. Third, Rule 21.01(3)(a) allows a defendant to move to have the action stayed or dismissed on the ground that "the court has no jurisdiction over the subject matter of the action." Together, this procedural scheme adequately allows for jurisdictional challenges to ensure that the interpretation and application of Rule 17.02(h) will comply with the constitutional standards prescribed by *Morguard* and *Hunt*.

Issue 2: Did the Motions Court Judge Err in Finding that the Ontario Superior Court Could Assume Jurisdiction Against the Out-of-Province Defendants?

The appellants urge us to adopt an interpretation of the real and substantial connection test that focuses on the nature and extent of the defendant's contacts with the jurisdiction. The appellants submit that a court can only assume jurisdiction against an extraprovincial defendant where it is reasonable to infer that the defendant has voluntarily submitted to Ontario's jurisdiction or where it was reasonably within the defendant's contemplation that his or her conduct could cause an injury in Ontario and give rise to a claim in Ontario courts.

The respondents contend that an approach that focuses solely upon the nature and extent of the defendant's contacts with the jurisdiction would be unduly restrictive and would fail to pay adequate heed to the interests of the injured plaintiff. They submit that the connection between the forum and the subject matter of the action and the connection between the forum and the damages suffered by the plaintiff are equally relevant in determining whether there is a real and substantial connection.

The Supreme Court of Canada has insisted that the real and substantial connection test must be flexible. The Court has not attempted to define the precise nature of the connection to the jurisdiction that is required, and the Court's language is ambiguous. While certain passages in *Morguard* suggest that the connection must be with the defendant, others suggest that the connection must be with the subject matter of the action or with the damages suffered by the plaintiff.

In his comment on *Morguard*, (1991) 70 *Can. Bar Rev.* 733 at 741, Professor Joost Blom observes that the Court's language lends itself to two possible approaches: the "personal subjection" approach, and the "administration of justice" approach. Under the personal subjection approach, jurisdiction is legitimate if the defendant regularly lived or carried on business in the province, or if the defendant voluntarily did something that related to the province so as to make it reasonable to contemplate that he or she might be sued in the province. By contrast, under the administration of justice approach, the basis for assuming jurisdiction is broader than personal subjection. The forum need only meet a minimum standard of suitability, under which it must be fair for the case to be heard in the province because the province is a "reasonable place for the action to take place."

These two approaches provide a useful way of analyzing the case law. In the discussion that follows, I outline the cases that have emphasized personal subjection as a basis for assumed jurisdiction as well as the cases that have followed a broader approach. I then explain why I consider the broader approach to be supportable and outline several factors relevant to assumed jurisdiction under this broader approach.

(a) The Personal Subjection Approach

The personal subjection approach has been followed in the United States and in several Canadian decisions at the trial level.

Under American law, state courts are obliged under Article IV of the Constitution to give "full faith and credit" to the judgments of sister states. However, when exercising jurisdiction against an out-of-state defendant, a court must observe the due process guarantee, which stems from the Fifth and Fourteenth Amendments to the Constitution. The United States Supreme Court has held that the due process guarantee means that a state can only exercise jurisdiction over a defendant from another state where the defendant has "minimum contacts" with the state purporting to exercise jurisdiction. In *International Shoe Co. v. State of Washington*, 326 US 310 at 316 (1945), the Court held:

> ... [D]ue process requires only that in order to subject a defendant to a judgment in personam, if he be not present within the territory of the forum, he have certain minimum contacts with it such that the maintenance of the suit does not offend "traditional notions of fair play and substantial justice."

In *World-Wide Volkswagen Corp. v. Woodson*, 444 US 286 (1980), the Court held at pp. 291-92:

> The concept of minimum contacts ... can be seen to perform two related, but distinguishable, functions. It protects the defendant against the burdens of litigating in a distant or inconvenient forum. And it acts to ensure that the States, through their courts, do not reach out beyond the limits imposed on them by their status as coequal sovereigns in a federal system.

The Court rejected the argument that jurisdiction could be assumed on the basis that it was foreseeable that a product would arrive and cause injury in the forum. At p. 297, the Court held that under due process analysis, "the mere likelihood that a product will find its way into the forum State" does not suffice. Rather, "it is that the defendant's conduct and connection with the forum State are such that he should reasonably anticipate being haled into court there."

Although Canadian decisions do not use the term "minimum contacts," several trial level decisions have adopted a similar personal subjection approach, under which a significant degree of contact between the defendant and the forum is a pre-requisite for the assumption of jurisdiction. ...

An Approach Broader than Personal Subjection

The weight of post-*Morguard* appellate authority holds that a real and substantial connection may be found on a broader basis than personal subjection. One of the leading authorities is the Nova Scotia Court of Appeal's decision in *Oakley v. Barry* (1998), 158 DLR (4th) 679. The plaintiff, at the time a resident of New Brunswick, received treatment from the defendant physicians and hospital in New Brunswick. The defendant physicians performed a liver biopsy and told the plaintiff that she suffered from infectious hepatitis "B." The plaintiff then moved to Nova Scotia, where physicians advised her that she did not suffer from that illness. The plaintiff was in poor health, lacked financial resources and was unable to travel. She brought her action against the New Brunswick defendants in Nova Scotia.

Pugsley JA dismissed the defendants' appeal from an order refusing to stay the action. Acknowledging the ambiguity in *Morguard's* articulation of the real and substantial connection test, Pugsley JA held at p. 691 that there was "a real and substantial connection between the *subject matter of the action* and the Province of Nova Scotia, as well as a real and substantial connection between the *damages* caused by the alleged negligence of the appellant physicians, and the defendant hospital, and the Province of Nova Scotia." [Emphasis added]. In support of this finding, he noted that the plaintiff's cause of action did not accrue until she was advised in Nova Scotia of the problems with the diagnosis she had been given in New Brunswick and that, since the plaintiff was being treated in Nova Scotia, that province had a significant financial interest in her well-being.

Pugsley JA pointed out at p. 692 that the "[i]nterprovincial mobility of Canadian citizens was specifically noted by Justice La Forest in both *Morguard* and *Hunt* as one of the factors supporting a more cooperative spirit in recognizing and enforcing judgments in a sister province." He added at pp. 695-96 that:

> Whether the decision in *Morguard* which involved a fact situation that was entirely Canadian, and depended to a significant extent on the "essentially unitary structure of our judicial system with the Supreme Court of Canada at its apex" ... should be applied to cases in the international sphere is an interesting question that does not require our consideration.

Pugsley JA also held that the requirements of fairness emphasized in *Morguard* and *Hunt* concerned not only the interests of the defendant but also the interests of the plaintiff.

Since the plaintiff was unable to travel and financially incapable of proceeding with litigation outside Nova Scotia, fairness to the plaintiff favoured jurisdiction.

Oakley v. Barry was followed in *O'Brien v. Canada (Attorney General)*, [2002] NSJ No. 57, which also involved a medical malpractice claim against out-of-province doctors following further treatment in Nova Scotia. At para. 20, Hallett JA held:

> The concept of order and fairness is integral to the question of determining whether there is a real and substantial connection between the cause of action and the forum province. This Court has held in *Oakley* that it is not inappropriate for a court to consider, as a component of the test, the fairness to the parties in determining if there is a real and substantial connection between the cause of action and the forum province that warrants a finding that the court has jurisdiction simpliciter.

This court's decision in *McNichol Estate v. Woldnik* (2001), 13 CPC (5th) 61 also supports the argument that the real and substantial connection test may be satisfied despite a lack of contact or connection that amounts to personal subjection by the defendant.

The British Columbia Court of Appeal's approach is also not limited to considering personal subjection by the defendant. In claims for damages arising from motor vehicle accidents in another province, the Court has held that jurisdiction cannot be assumed against an out-of-province defendant where the plaintiff's residence is the only link to the forum. See *Ell v. Con-Pro Industries Ltd.* (1992), 11 BCAC 174 and *Jordan v. Schatz* (2000), 77 BCLR (3d) 134 (CA). However, in *Pacific International Securities Inc. v. Drake Capital Securities Inc.* (2000), 194 DLR (4th) 716 at 722, the Court held that it was appropriate to consider damage sustained in the jurisdiction and that prior decisions did not preclude "the British Columbia Courts from taking *jurisdiction simpliciter* where the damages, either in contract or tort, are sustained in British Columbia." Further, in *Cook v. Parcel, Mauro, Hultin & Spaanstra, PC* (1997), 143 DLR (4th) 213 at 219, the Court accepted that a real and substantial connection could be based on a connection either with the defendant or with the subject matter of the litigation:

> It is common ground that the test to be applied in determining whether the BC Supreme Court has jurisdiction over these proceedings is whether there is a real and substantial connection between the court and either the defendant … or the subject-matter of the litigation (occasionally referred to in the authorities as the "transaction" or the "cause of action").

Similarly, in *Duncan v. Neptunia, supra*, at p. 768, the court held that the real and substantial connection test should be interpreted in a flexible manner and that "it is clear that a real and substantial connection *between the forum province and the subject matter of the litigation, not necessarily the defendant*, is sufficient to meet the test." [Emphasis added]

Finally, I note that in *Spar Aerospace Ltd. c. American Mobile Satellite Corp.*, [2000] JQ No. 1717 (CA), leave to appeal granted [2000] SCCA No. 397, the Quebec Court of Appeal implicitly rejected a personal subjection approach. Although the case appears to have been argued primarily in terms of *forum non conveniens*, the Court upheld the trial judge's order finding a real and substantial connection and dismissing a challenge to the jurisdiction of the Quebec Superior Court.

The Relevant Factors Under the Broader Approach

It is apparent from *Morguard*, *Hunt* and subsequent case law that it is not possible to reduce the real and substantial connection test to a fixed formula. A considerable measure
of judgment is required in assessing whether the real and substantial connection test has
been met on the facts of a given case. Flexibility is therefore important.

But clarity and certainty are also important. As such, it is useful to identify the factors
emerging from the case law that are relevant in assessing whether a court should assume
jurisdiction against an out-of-province defendant on the basis of damage sustained in
Ontario as a result of a tort committed elsewhere. No factor is determinative. Rather, all
relevant factors should be considered and weighed together. In my view, a weighing of
the factors in the present case favours the assumption of jurisdiction against the out-of-
province defendants in this case.

1) The Connection Between the Forum and the Plaintiff's Claim

The forum has an interest in protecting the legal rights of its residents and affording injured plaintiffs generous access for litigating claims against tortfeasors. In *Moran v. Pyle*
at p. 409, Dickson J spoke of "the important interest a state has in injuries suffered by
persons within its territory." The *Moran* decision and the introduction of the "damage
sustained" rule in 1975 were both motivated by the perception that the interests of justice
required a more generous approach to assumed jurisdiction. The connection between
the forum and the plaintiff's claim is therefore relevant.

This factor was important in *Oakley*, where the Nova Scotia Court of Appeal took into
account the significant connection that arose from the extensive medical attention the
plaintiff had received in Nova Scotia.

On the other hand, if the plaintiff lacks a significant connection with the forum, the
case for assuming jurisdiction on the basis of damage sustained within the jurisdiction
is weaker. If the connection is tenuous, courts should be wary of assuming jurisdiction.
Mere residence in the jurisdiction does not constitute a sufficient basis for assuming
jurisdiction. See V. Black, "Territorial Jurisdiction Based on the Plaintiff's Residence:
Dennis v. Salvation Army Grace General Hospital" (1998), 14 CPC (4th) 222 at 232, where
the author writes:

> Permitting a plaintiff to assume a new residence and sue a defendant there in respect of
> events that occurred elsewhere seems to be harsh to defendants, and this is particularly so
> when those events comprise a completed tort.
>
> Even if the connection is significant, however, the case for assuming jurisdiction is pro-
> portional to the degree of damage sustained within the jurisdiction. It is difficult to justify
> assuming jurisdiction against an out-of-province defendant unless the plaintiff has suffered
> significant damage within the jurisdiction.

As with all of the following factors, the nature of the connection between the forum
and the plaintiff is only one factor to consider. As La Forest J explained in *Hunt* at p. 327,
while "a province undoubtedly has an interest in protecting the property of its residents
within the province ... it cannot do so by unconstitutional means." Similarly, in *Tolofson*,
at p. 1055, La Forest J stated that "the mere fact that another state (or province) has an

interest in a wrong committed in a foreign state (or province) is not enough to warrant its exercising jurisdiction over that activity in the foreign state for a wrong in one state will often have an impact in another."

In the present case, the plaintiff has required extensive medical attention in Ontario. His claim is, *inter alia*, for pain and suffering in Ontario. These damages represent a significant connection with Ontario.

2) The Connection Between the Forum and the Defendant

If the defendant has done anything within the jurisdiction that bears upon the claim advanced by the plaintiff, the case for assuming jurisdiction is strengthened.

Moran v. Pyle holds that conduct outside the territory may render the defendant subject to the jurisdiction of the forum where it was reasonably foreseeable that the defendant's conduct would result in harm within the jurisdiction. This forseeability should be distinguished from a situation in which the wrongful act and injury occur outside the jurisdiction and the plaintiff returns and suffers consequential damage. It seems to me that in the latter situation, the fact that it was foreseeable that the plaintiff would return home does not bring the case within the *Moran* principle.

In this case, the defendants did not have any connection with Ontario that would justify the assumption of jurisdiction. Although the defendants were engaged in an activity that carried with it an inherent risk of an accident with an out-of-province party, their conduct fell well short of what might constitute personal subjection or submission to the jurisdiction of the Ontario courts.

While conduct of the defendant amounting to personal subjection provides a strong basis for assumed jurisdiction, such conduct is not necessary in all cases. Even if there is no act or conduct by the defendant that amounts to personal subjection or makes litigation in the forum a foreseeable risk, it is still necessary to consider other factors to determine whether or not the real and substantial connection test has been met.

3) Unfairness to the Defendant in Assuming Jurisdiction

The consideration of the defendant's position should not end with an inquiry as to acts or conduct that would render the defendant subject to the jurisdiction. The principles of order and fairness require further consideration, because acts or conduct that are insufficient to render the defendant subject to the jurisdiction may still have a bearing on the fairness of assumed jurisdiction. Some activities, by their very nature, involve a sufficient risk of harm to extra-provincial parties that any unfairness in assuming jurisdiction is mitigated or eliminated.

In my view, in the present case, the assumption of jurisdiction would not result in any significant unfairness to the defendants. The defendants were engaged in an activity that involves an inherent risk of harm to extra-provincial parties. Mandatory motor vehicle insurance requirements across Canada reflect the reciprocal risk of harm caused and faced by all motorists. There was evidence that the defendants are insured and that the terms of their insurance clearly contemplate and provide coverage for suits in other Canadian provinces, which would include a suit involving an accident with an out-of-province defendant. The standard form Power of Attorney and Undertaking requires motor vehicle insurers to appear and defend claims brought in any Canadian province or territory. These insurance arrangements reflect the reasonable expectations of the motoring public. The burden of defending the suit will fall on the defendants' insurer and not on the defendants themselves. I would give no weight to the argument that the assumption of jurisdiction would be unfair to the defendants.

4) Unfairness to the Plaintiff in Not Assuming Jurisdiction

The principles of order and fairness should be considered in relation to the plaintiff as well as the defendant. In *Morguard*, La Forest J recognized the need to consider the plaintiff's interest in access to the courts of his or her home jurisdiction. At p. 1108, he stated that "permitting suit where there is a real and substantial connection with the action provides a reasonable balance between the rights of the parties."

Morguard and *Moran* both hold that given the realities of modern commerce and the free flow of goods and people across borders, plaintiffs should not be saddled with the anachronistic "power theory" that focuses exclusively on subjection and territorial sovereignty. Although *Tolofson* dealt with choice of law, at pp. 1071-72, the court also speaks of the need to balance the interests of the plaintiff and defendant. Further, in *Oakley v. Barry*, Pugsley JA held at p. 699 that "[t]he concept of fairness in determining jurisdiction should be considered from the point of view of both the respondent [plaintiff], as well as the appellants [defendants]." I agree that it is important to consider fairness to the plaintiff and to balance this against fairness to the defendant.

In this case, if jurisdiction were refused, the plaintiff would be compelled to litigate in Alberta. This would undoubtedly be inconvenient to the plaintiff, especially given the injuries he has sustained. Further, unlike the defendant, the plaintiff does not have the benefit of an insurer to cover the cost of litigation. While the unfairness to the plaintiff of having to litigate in Alberta may not be as strong as it was in *Oakely v. Barry*, on balance, a consideration of unfairness favours the plaintiff.

5) The Involvement of Other Parties to the Suit

The decision in *McNichol*, *supra* indicates that the involvement of other parties bears upon the real and substantial connection test. The twin goals of avoiding a multiplicity of proceedings and avoiding the risk of inconsistent results are relevant considerations. Where the core of the action involves domestic defendants, as in *McNichol*, the case for assuming jurisdiction against a defendant who might not otherwise be subject to the jurisdiction of Ontario courts is strong. By contrast, where the core of the action involves other foreign defendants, courts should be more wary of assuming jurisdiction simply because there is a claim against a domestic defendant.

In this case, the involvement of other parties to the suit is not a significant factor.

6) The Court's Willingness To Recognize and Enforce an Extra-Provincial Judgment Rendered on the Same Jurisdictional Basis

In considering whether to assume jurisdiction against an extra-provincial defendant, the court must consider whether it would recognize and enforce an extra-provincial judgment against a domestic defendant rendered on the same jurisdictional basis, whether pursuant to common law principles or any applicable legislation. Every time a court assumes jurisdiction in favour of a domestic plaintiff, the court establishes a standard that will be used to force domestic defendants who are sued elsewhere to attorn to the jurisdiction of the foreign court or face enforcement of a default judgment against them. This principle is fundamental to the approach in *Morguard* and *Hunt* and may be seen as a self-imposed constraint inherent in the real and substantial connection test. It follows that where a court would not be willing to recognize and enforce an extra-provincial judgment rendered on the same jurisdictional basis, the court cannot assume jurisdiction, because the real and substantial connection test has not been met.

In my view, it is appropriate for Ontario courts to recognize and enforce judgments from the courts of sister provinces rendered on the same jurisdictional basis as in the case at bar. *Morguard* and *Hunt* recognize the modern reality of rapid and frequent movement by Canadian citizens across provincial borders. Further, the risk of accidents with and injury to the residents of another province is inherent in motor vehicle travel, and insurance arrangements reflecting this risk are common across Canada. The spirit of *Morguard* and *Hunt* favours recognition and enforcement of the judgments of the courts of sister provinces where jurisdiction has been assumed on the basis that serious damages have been suffered within the province as a result of a motor vehicle accident in another province.

7) Whether the Case Is Interprovincial or International in Nature

The decisions in *Morguard*, *Tolofson* and *Hunt* suggest that the assumption of jurisdiction is more easily justified in interprovincial cases than in international cases. The jurisdictional standards developed in *Morguard* and *Hunt* were strongly influenced by the need to adapt the rules of private international law to the demands of the Canadian federation.

In *Morguard* at pp. 1098 and 1101, La Forest J held that the "considerations underlying the rules of comity apply with much greater force between the units of a federal state," that a federation "implies a fuller and more generous acceptance of the judgments of the courts of other constituent units of the federation," and that "the rules of comity or private international law as they apply between the provinces must be shaped to conform to the federal structure of the Constitution." At pp. 1099-1100, La Forest J mentioned several features that foster consistency and uniformity between provinces and thereby minimize the risk of unfairness within Canada:

> The Canadian judicial structure is so arranged that any concerns about differential quality of justice among the provinces can have no real foundation. All superior court judges—who also have superintending control over other provincial courts and tribunals—are appointed and paid by the federal authorities. And all are subject to final review by the Supreme Court of Canada, which can determine when the courts of one province have appropriately exercised jurisdiction in an action and the circumstances under which the courts of another province should recognize such judgments. Any danger resulting from unfair procedure is further avoided by sub-constitutional factors, such as for example the fact that Canadian lawyers adhere to the same code of ethics throughout Canada.

· · ·

8) Comity and the Standards of Jurisdiction, Recognition, and Enforcement Prevailing Elsewhere

In *Morguard* at p. 1096, La Forest J adopted the following formulation of comity expressed in *Hilton v. Guyot*, 159 US 113 at 163-64 (1895):

> [T]he recognition which one nation allows within its territory to the legislative, executive or judicial acts of another nation, having due regard both to international duty and convenience, and to the rights of its own citizens or of other persons who are under the protection of its laws. ...

One aspect of comity is that in fashioning jurisdictional rules, courts should consider the standards of jurisdiction, recognition and enforcement that prevail elsewhere. In interprovincial cases, this consideration is unnecessary, since the same standard necessarily applies to assumed jurisdiction, recognition and enforcement within Canada. However, in international cases, it may be helpful to consider international standards, particularly the rules governing assumed jurisdiction and the recognition and enforcement of judgments in the location in which the defendant is situated.

. . .

(e) Conclusion

In my view, a fair weighing of the factors I have outlined clearly favours assumed jurisdiction in the present case. Accordingly, I would affirm the finding of the motions court judge that the real and substantial connection test has been met.

NOTES AND QUESTIONS

1. Following the release of the *Muscutt* decision, a number of courts across Canada adopted its eight-factored test for judicial jurisdiction. However, the test has not been universally endorsed, see *André Gauthier v. Coutu* (2006) 296 NBR (2d) 34; and it has received some academic criticism, see Tanya Monestier, "A Real and Substantial Mess: The Law of Jurisdiction in Canada" (2007), 33 *Queen's LJ* 179.

2. Since 2006, several provinces have adopted the Uniform Law Conference of Canada's *Court Jurisdiction and Proceedings Transfer Act*, which was developed in 1993. The central provisions of this legislation are discussed in the following article by Elizabeth Edinger.

Elizabeth Edinger, "New British Columbia Legislation: The Court Jurisdiction and Proceedings Transfer Act: The Enforcement of Canadian Judgments and Decrees Act"
(2006), 39 *UBC L Rev.* 407-421

The *Court Jurisdiction and Proceedings Transfer Act* ... provides that "the territorial competence of a court is to be determined solely by reference to this Part." Sections 3 to 6, therefore, now represent an exhaustive statement of the circumstances in which a British Columbia court will have jurisdiction *simpliciter*. The statutory rules thus replace both the common law rule that presence in the province at the time of commencement of the proceedings gives the court jurisdiction *simpliciter* as of right and the rules for service *ex juris* formerly found in R. 13(1) of the Rules of Court. However, except for ss. (d), s. 3 tracks the current common law rules as modified, of course, by *Morguard*. The defendant may consent to the court's jurisdiction in one of three ways: by commencing an action in the province "to which the proceeding in question is a counterclaim"; by submitting during the proceeding; or by having entered into an agreement with the other party. Presence at the time the action is commenced has been replaced by "ordinary residence at the time of commencement of the proceedings." The last basis for territorial competence, derived directly from *Morguard*, is the existence of "a real and substantial connection between British Columbia and the facts on which the proceeding against that person is brought." What degree of nexus constitutes a real and substantial connection for purposes of jurisdiction *simpliciter* is still not settled but s. 10 of the *Act* is helpful in this respect. It sets out a variety of circumstances "presumed" to constitute a real and substantial connection. What evidence it will take to rebut the presumption and how often that will be accomplished is speculative. What is needed in this area is a bit more of the pre-*Morguard* certainty about jurisdiction *simpliciter* so it is to be hoped that the presumption will prove to be rarely, if ever, rebuttable.

Sections 4 and 5 deal respectively with unnamed defendants (there must be a real and substantial connection between the facts and the province) and actions *in rem* against vessels, for which presence is still sufficient.

Section 6 may be fragile from a constitutional point of view but it is undoubtedly very practical and very desirable from a litigation point of view. The section provides that a British Columbia court may assume jurisdiction if there is no other court available or if commencement of an action elsewhere "cannot reasonably be required" ... even though the court lacks territorial competence. The possible fragility arises from the fact that territorial competence has been defined so as to satisfy constitutional principles. How can a British Columbia court validly assume jurisdiction when the constitutional principle has not been satisfied? And when jurisdiction is assumed pursuant to s. 6, will British Columbia judgments be recognized by other Canadian courts which are not subject to the *Enforcement of Canadian Judgments and Decrees Act* and which, therefore, still require there to have been a real and substantial connection?

Because ordinary residence is now a basis for territorial jurisdiction, sections 7, 8, and 9 provide definitions of ordinary residence for corporations, partnerships and unincorporated associations respectively. These definitions govern for purposes of determining territorial jurisdiction under the *Act* but are essentially codifications of the common law. Ordinary residence for natural persons is governed by unadulterated common law, no statutory definition having been attempted.

Section 10 of the *Act* sets out a variety of circumstances in which a real and substantial connection will be presumed to exist. The new R. 13(1) authorizes service of process outside British Columbia without leave in any of the circumstances listed in s. 10 of the *Act*. But s. 10 is not an exhaustive statement of the circumstances in which process may be served outside the province. R. 13(3) still authorizes a plaintiff to seek leave to serve process outside the province if some other circumstance can be said to constitute a real and substantial connection. The case law interpreting the pre-*Court Jurisdiction and*

Proceedings Transfer Act R. 13(3) should all still be relevant and applicable to such applications for leave.

It is beyond the scope of this article to discuss each of the circumstances set out in s. 10 in detail but a few comments are warranted.

Property is now referred to throughout as movable and immovable instead of as real and personal. That change reflects the terminology in common law choice of law rules and should pose no difficulty. The common law rule that characterization of property as movable or immovable is governed by the law of the *situs* will, one assumes, still apply. On the other hand, terminology in the Rules of Court which used to couple territorial jurisdiction with the connecting factor in the choice of law rules for succession to movable property and questions of status has been abandoned. A British Columbia court will be presumed to have territorial jurisdiction to deal with movable property or make a declaration as to status or capacity of a person who was at the time of death or now is (respectively) ordinarily resident in British Columbia. The connecting factor for the relevant choice of law rules is still domicile. Ordinary residence makes practical and legal sense as a basis for territorial jurisdiction, however, because it is never technical, is likely to be easier to establish than domicile and, of course, may often actually coincide with domicile.

The circumstances connecting both trust and contract actions to the province have been significantly expanded. A connecting circumstance has been added for restitutionary actions. Another circumstance, new to the *Act* and thus to British Columbia, consists of an action (any juridical category) which "concerns a business carried on in British Columbia." This is probably redundant if the defendant is a corporation because a corporate defendant carrying on business in the province is likely ordinarily resident here and, by s. 3(d), ordinary residence gives the court territorial jurisdiction under the *Act* but there may be some cases which require the extended definition of a real and substantial connection in s. 10.

Oddly, a real and substantial connection is presumed to exist for all actions to enforce judgments and arbitral awards *per se*. Neither the ordinary residence of the judgment debtor or the location of the judgment debtor's assets is made a relevant additional factor. Like s. 6, this is, arguably, a fragile provision constitutionally speaking. Either assets in the province against which the converted judgment could be enforced or the ordinary residence of the judgment debtor must surely be required for a real and substantial connection. The fact that most judgment creditors are practical and will be unlikely to commence an action to enforce a judgment unless there are exigible assets locally cannot cure the constitutional invalidity of a provision which fails to describe a real and substantial connection. A statute which describes connections, each of which constitutes a real and substantial connection *per se*, would reintroduce certainty to jurisdictional decisions and permit litigants to focus on the *forum non conveniens* issue without repeating their arguments and so blurring the issues.

Finally, there is a potentially significant omission from the old R. 13(1) list of connections considered sufficient to authorize service of process without leave. Necessary and proper parties have been excluded. The ULCC commentary explains that "such a rule would be out of place in provisions that are based, not on service, but on substantive connections between the proceeding and the enacting jurisdiction." Addition of necessary and proper parties is still possible but it will require an application for leave under R. 13(3).

The *Act* preserves judicial discretion to stay local proceedings on the grounds that British Columbia is *forum non conveniens*. Unless a defendant over whom a British Columbia court has territorial jurisdiction under s. 3 has attorned, that defendant may object to the exercise of jurisdiction by the court pursuant to s. 11 of the *Act* and R. 14 of the Rules of Court. Section 11(2) sets out a non-exhaustive list of circumstances which must be considered by the court. Most are on the lists of factors found in judgments from courts in all provinces and are uncontroversial. Only one, s. 11(2)(e), could prove problematical.

Section 11(2)(e) directs the court to consider "the enforcement of an eventual judgment." The difficulty is that there are two levels on which this factor may play out, one pragmatic and one legal, and the *Act* does not indicate which level it intends the court to consider. On a pragmatic level, the location of the defendant's assets is often considered by the courts already, and makes practical sense. However, if the "eventual enforcement" is considered at the legal level, there could be an inconclusive war of affidavits from experts hypothesizing about a judgment which does not yet exist and so cannot be evaluated properly.

If the court decides that it is not *forum conveniens*, and if it is a superior court, it now has options. Until the *Act* was proclaimed, the only options were to stay the local action, temporarily or indefinitely, or to stay it subject to conditions. Part 3 of the *Act* provides another option new to Canada. It sets out mechanisms for the *in media res* transfer of actions or parts of actions to courts outside the province and for the reception of actions from such courts. The order to transfer an action may be made at the instance of a party but, like letters rogatory, it is a court to court request.

Whether sending an action or refusing to receive an action, the court must give reasons for its decision.

"For all purposes of the law of British Columbia" transfers from British Columbia take effect when the order accepting the transfer is filed in the receiving court and thereafter there is no jurisdiction remaining in the British Columbia court except in the very limited circumstances set out in s. 16(2) and (3). Section 19 makes mirror image provisions for the reception of actions in British Columbia.

Any orders made in the proceedings, except the transfer order itself, are appealable in British Columbia. Ordinarily, the British Columbia court will implement any terms imposed by the transferring court but s. 22 authorizes departure from those terms "if it is just and reasonable to do so." Section 23 requires the British Columbia courts to respect any limitation periods which would have been applied by the transferring court. In light of the fact that *Tolofson* requires courts to apply the limitation period of the *lex causae* and that most provinces apply the same common law choice of law rules to select the *lex causae*, there should not often be disagreements within Canada about the appropriate limitation period but non-Canadian jurisdictions may still characterize limitation periods as procedural or have different choice of law rules.

Part 3 constitutes legislative facilitation of increased judicial comity to achieve both fairness and efficiency. However, until more jurisdictions set themselves up to transfer and receive, Part 3 will be admired in principle but not in practice.

NOTES AND QUESTIONS

1. In 2009, a Consultation Paper was published by the Law Commission of Ontario to promote discussion of the various standards of jurisdiction operating in Canada and the question whether there was a need for uniformity. The paper further sought to promote discussion whether this warranted the adoption in Ontario of the *Court Jurisdiction and Proceedings Transfer Act* or, alternatively, some other codification of the law of judicial jurisdiction. In the autumn of 2009, the Court of Appeal for Ontario decided to hear two pending appeals concerning the *Muscutt* test together before a panel of five judges to consider whether the framework of analysis should be changed.

2. *Applicable law.* A plaintiff may resort to the rules for service out of the jurisdiction, or may go and sue in a jurisdiction where the defendant can be served locally. Thus, the plaintiff is often presented with a choice of fora in which to sue. This may give rise to "forum shopping"—that is, seeking out a forum that will apply substantive law favourable to the plaintiff. When this is done in an opportunistic way as a means of manipulating the outcome of the dispute, it is frowned upon by Canadian courts.

3. However, this is not always possible. Although courts assume jurisdiction over matters involving foreign defendants and claims arising in foreign countries, this does not necessarily mean that they will apply their own law to resolve the dispute. For example, a BC court might hear an action for breach of contract that occurred in Saskatchewan but apply Saskatchewan law to decide the case. If one of the parties argues that the connections between the case and a foreign country (or another province) warrant the application of the law of that country to the dispute, the court will engage in what is known in the conflict of laws as "choice of law" analysis to decide which law will govern the dispute.

4. The *Morguard* decision marked the beginning of a revolution, not only in the approach taken in Canadian law to the relations between the courts of different provinces in the rules for assuming jurisdiction and enforcing judgments, but also in the rules for choice of law. In *Tolofson v. Jensen*, [1994] 3 SCR 1022, the Supreme Court held that the flexibility afforded through the application of the new rules for jurisdiction and for judgments created a "structural problem." This problem needed to be addressed by the establishment of uniform forum-neutral choice-of-law rules. Such rules would diminish the incentives to select a forum on the basis of attempting to manipulate the outcome of the dispute because the same law would be applied regardless of which court decided the matter. In the case of tort claims, the court held that the law of the place where the wrong occurred should apply, and exceptions to this rule should be carefully defined.

5. In *Tolofson*, the plaintiff in an automobile accident case sued in British Columbia, the province in which he resided, rather than in Saskatchewan, the province in which he was injured, because he hoped to avoid the application of the shorter limitation period in Saskatchewan. Even if the court decided to apply the law of Saskatchewan, he hoped that the court would apply the BC limitation period. This litigation strategy relied both on the well-established rule that courts always apply their own procedural rules, even where a foreign law governs the substance of the rights and obligations of the parties, and on an old common law rule that statutes of limitation were classified as procedural and not substantive in nature. Accordingly, even if a BC court determined that it should apply the law of Saskatchewan, it was likely to apply the BC limitation period. The routine application of local limita-

tion periods, coupled with choice-of-law rules that could lead courts to apply their own tort law rather than the law of the place where the accident occurred, led to a great deal of "forum shopping" in personal injury cases in Canada.

6. When *Tolofson* reached the Supreme Court of Canada, La Forest J held that these rules were out of place in the modern context and that courts had to apply the law of the place where the tort occurred, including its limitation period—that is, limitation periods were no longer to be characterized as procedural for choice-of-law purposes, but as substantive law. La Forest J reasoned that "to permit the court of the forum to impose its views over those of the legislature endowed with power to determine the consequences of wrongs that take place within its jurisdiction would invite the forum shopping that is to be avoided if we are to attain the consistency of result an effective system of conflict of laws should seek to foster." Accordingly, most Canadian courts continue to apply the local rules of procedure that are essential to the efficient adjudication of the matter but limitation periods are no longer regarded as fitting in that category. Some provinces, however, have passed legislation requiring the application of local limitations statutes to all matters that come before the courts.

III. LIMITATION OF ACTIONS

A. The Purpose and Operation of Limitation Periods

Limitation periods define the time limits within which a potential litigant must commence a civil action. If a lawsuit is not commenced within a certain proscribed period of time, in most circumstances the right to bring the legal claim will extinguish, regardless of the merits of the underlying claim. Limitation periods are therefore vital considerations for lawyers and clients alike. Someone has to keep an eye on the limitation timeline to avoid losing the client's right to sue. Lawyers therefore often have reminder systems in place to keep track of running limitation periods, in order to protect the rights of their clients to bring a claim.

Limitation periods attempt to strike a fair balance between the rights of litigating plaintiffs and defendants. These temporal limitations act as a procedural backstop to provide some degree of closure and finality to defendants targeted in potential lawsuits. The right of potential plaintiffs to bring legal claims against defendants is not completely unfettered in that such a right does not normally exist forever. Through limitations legislation, provincial legislatures have defined specific timeframes in which plaintiffs must commence a civil proceeding. Limitation periods are created to balance a plaintiff's right to sue with a defendant's right to arrange its affairs with some predictability. Statutes of limitation benefit defendants by incentivizing plaintiffs to exercise their rights to sue in a reasonable timeframe. These benefits are realized because limitation periods define a temporal period when potential defendants may no longer need to worry about prior obligations and potential liabilities. Limitation periods also make certain evidence is not lost due to the passage of time, because plaintiffs must get on with the lawsuit. For more background about the historical, procedural, and cultural purposes behind limitation periods, see Graeme Mew, *The Law of Limitations*, 2nd ed. (2004).

Provincial limitations regimes are generally outlined in specific provincial limitations statutes, such as British Columbia's *Limitation Act*, RSBC 1996, c. 266, Alberta's *Limitations*

Act, RSA 2000, c. L-12, and Ontario's *Limitations Act, 2002*, SO 2002, c. 24, Sched. B. While these statutes often contain the general default limitation periods for most standard legal claims, a lawyer must always be aware of other applicable limitation periods in subject-specific statutes that may provide for longer or shorter limitation periods for certain specific types of claims.

The time frame for commencing an action can vary depending on the precise nature of the claim. Most provincial limitations regimes specify a period of two years for the most common types of actions, such as actions for damages in property, injury, and contract cases. One must also be mindful of the event that starts the limitation clock running, because the triggering event may differ from claim to claim. In some instances in some provinces, the limitation clock begins to run on the date that the right to bring a claim arises (often called the date on which the cause of action "accrues" or "arises"). In Alberta and Ontario, however, the limitation clock begins to run when the plaintiff discovers or ought to have discovered the right to claim against the defendant (Alberta s. 3, Ontario s. 4). Some specific claims in some provinces are not subject to any limitation period. These often include claims based on fraud or claims of sexual assault.

In many provinces, the force of the general limitations legislation is undercut by a significant number of special limitations provisions contained in other statutes. They have the effect of overriding the otherwise applicable period under the general limitations legislation, and almost always shorten that period. For example, the insurance legislation of some provinces provide for a limitation period of one year for an action on an insurance policy against an insurer, with various definitions as to when time commences running. See, for example, Nova Scotia *Insurance Act*, RSNS 1989, c. 231, ss. 145, 209(1); Ontario *Insurance Act*, RSO 1990, c. I.8, s. 259.1. The result can be somewhat of a labyrinth for lawyers and clients alike to navigate. One must therefore be mindful of the type of claim and any exceptions to the limitation regime in the particular province's various topical legislation.

Because limitation periods are primarily designed to benefit defendants and streamline the civil justice system with reasonable time frames in which litigants must act, it is up to defendants to plead limitation periods as a defence in a lawsuit. If a limitation defence is raised in a pleading, this issue is often dealt with by way of a motion before the trial on the merits is commenced, as a successful limitation defence by a defendant eclipses the plaintiff's very right to bring the claim.

B. Discoverability

In order to optimally and fairly balance the competing rights of plaintiffs and defendants in any limitations regime, it is sometimes necessary to consider the particular individual circumstances of the litigants to ensure that limitation periods are not unfairly eclipsing the rights of plaintiffs to pursue their claims. The concepts of discoverability and capacity act to mediate this often challenging balance.

Discoverability was a common law creation that grew out of the recognition that it is manifestly unfair to allow a limitation period to expire in certain circumstances when certain plaintiffs are unaware they even have a legally cognizable claim. Discoverability delays the start of a limitation period until a time when a reasonable plaintiff in the plaintiff's position knew or ought to have known that the right to sue existed. In most instances, plaintiffs (and their lawyers) are deemed to know the law and that includes the myriad applicable limitation periods for legal claims. There is generally no legal recourse for a missed limitation period. The applicability of the discoverability doctrine is usually the only legal remedy a plaintiff can use to cure a missed limitation period. Discoverability is only applicable in certain circumstances and its applicability is assessed on a case-by-case basis. Conceptually, courts have held that it is unfair to have a limitation clock expire on a plaintiff if that plaintiff reasonably could not have known the connection between an injury suffered and the fault of the potential defendant for that injury. A plaintiff must therefore know, first, that he or she has suffered a legally cognizable injury and, second, that that injury was potentially caused by the fault of a defendant. Without those two pieces of information, limitation periods work an injustice toward unaware plaintiffs. The following two cases demonstrate how the discoverability doctrine rests on the paramount importance of a plaintiff's knowledge of a defendant's fault (*M. (K.)*) and the connection of that fault to a legally cognizable injury (*Peixeiro*).

M. (K.) v. M. (H.)
[1992] 3 SCR 6

LA FOREST J (Gonthier, Cory, and Iacobucci JJ concurring): This case concerns the procedural obstacles facing victims of childhood incestuous abuse who attempt to vindicate their rights in a civil action for damages against the perpetrator of the incest. While the problem of incest is not new, it has only recently gained recognition as one of the more serious depredations plaguing Canadian families. Its incidence is alarming and profoundly disturbing. The damages wrought by incest are peculiarly complex and devastating, often manifesting themselves slowly and imperceptibly, so that the victim may only come to realize the harms she (and at times he) has suffered, and their cause, long after the statute of limitations has ostensibly proscribed a civil remedy. It has been said that the statute of limitations remains the primary stumbling block for adult survivors of incest, and this has proved to be the case thus far for the appellant in the present action. The appellant commenced this action for damages occasioned as a result of recurrent sexual assaults between the ages of eight and sixteen when she was twenty-eight. A jury found that the respondent committed sexual assault upon the appellant and assessed damages at $50,000, but her action was dismissed on the basis of a statute of limitations.

. . .

In 1985 the appellant sued her father for damages arising from the incest, or in the alternative for the infliction of mental distress. Further damages were claimed for breach of a parent's fiduciary duty to care for and minister to his child. The claims of mental distress and breach of fiduciary duty were also made against the appellant's mother. Before the trial began, counsel for the respondent moved for dismissal of the action on the ground that it was barred by the passage of time pursuant to s. 45 of the *Limitations Act*, RSO 1980, c. 240. It reads:

45(1) The following actions shall be commenced within and not after the times respectively hereinafter mentioned, ...

(j) an action for assault, battery, wounding or imprisonment, within four years after the cause of action arose;

However, s. 47 of the Act postpones the limitation period if the plaintiff is under a legal disability—i.e., is a minor, mental defective, mental incompetent or of unsound mind, and the appellant had pleaded that she had been of unsound mind until she underwent therapy. It reads:

47. Where a person entitled to bring an action mentioned in section 45 or 46 is at the time the cause of action accrues a minor, mental defective, mental incompetent or of unsound mind, the period within which the action may be brought shall be reckoned from the date when such person became of full age or of sound mind.

The trial judge postponed the limitations motion until the end of the trial, so that it could be decided in light of all the evidence.

The jury found that the respondent had sexually assaulted his daughter, and awarded $50,000 in damages. However, Maloney J allowed the respondent's limitations application, and found that action statute barred. He ruled that the appellant had been of sound mind from the age of majority, in that she had been capable of retaining and instructing counsel. Moreover, assuming that her cause of action only accrued when it was reasonably discoverable, Maloney J found that from the age of sixteen the appellant was aware that she had been wronged and had suffered adverse effects. Accordingly, her cause of action was reasonably discoverable at that time, and the subsequent lapse of time before commencing the action contravened the *Limitations Act*.

• • •

For the reasons that follow, I am of the view that this appeal should be allowed. Incest is both a tortious assault and a breach of fiduciary duty. The tort claim, although subject to limitations legislation, does not accrue until the plaintiff is reasonably capable of discovering the wrongful nature of the defendant's acts and the nexus between those acts and her injuries. In this case, that discovery took place only when the appellant entered therapy, and the lawsuit was commenced promptly thereafter. The time for bringing a claim for breach of a fiduciary duty is not limited by statute in Ontario, and therefore stands along with the tort claim as a basis for recovery by the appellant. ... Fraudulent concealment was not considered by the courts below, and the respondent argued that additional evidence might have been adduced had the issue been raised in those courts. As such, I make no finding on that issue, but I would not foreclose considering its availability for postponing limitation periods in other cases.

• • •

The Limitations Act and Reasonable Discoverability

The appellant argues that her cause of action did not accrue until she went through a form of therapy, because her psychological injuries were largely imperceptible until later in her adult life and thus not reasonably discoverable until she was able to confront her past with the assistance of therapy. During the hearing, counsel for the respondent conceded that the doctrine of reasonable discoverability had application to an action grounded in assault and battery for incest. He submitted, however, that the appellant was aware of her cause of action no later than when she reached the age of majority. In order to determine the time of accrual of the cause of action in a manner consistent with the purposes of the *Limitations Act*, I believe it is helpful to first examine its underlying rationales. There are three, and they may be described as the certainty, evidentiary, and diligence rationales; see Rosenfeld, "The Statute of Limitations Barrier in Childhood Sexual Abuse Cases: The Equitable Estoppel Remedy" (1989), 12 *Harv. Women's LJ* 206, at p. 211.

Statutes of limitations have long been said to be statutes of repose. ... The reasoning is straightforward enough. There comes a time, it is said, when a potential defendant should be secure in his reasonable expectation that he will not be held to account for ancient obligations. In my view this is a singularly unpersuasive ground for a strict application of the statute of limitations in this context. While there are instances where the public interest is served by granting repose to certain classes of defendants, for example the cost of professional services if practitioners are exposed to unlimited liability, there is absolutely no corresponding public benefit in protecting individuals who perpetrate incest from the consequences of their wrongful actions. The patent inequity of allowing these individuals to go on with their life without liability, while the victim continues to suffer the consequences, clearly militates against any guarantee of repose.

The second rationale is evidentiary and concerns the desire to foreclose claims based on stale evidence. Once the limitation period has lapsed, the potential defendant should no longer be concerned about the preservation of evidence relevant to the claim. ... However, it should be borne in mind that in childhood incest cases the relevant evidence will often be "stale" under the most expedient trial process. It may be ten or more years before the plaintiff is no longer under a legal disability by virtue of age, and is thus entitled to sue in her own name. ... In any event, I am not convinced that in this type of case evidence is automatically made stale merely by the passage of time. Moreover, the loss of corroborative evidence over time will not normally be a concern in incest cases, since the typical case will involve direct evidence solely from the parties themselves.

Finally, plaintiffs are expected to act diligently and not "sleep on their rights"; statutes of limitation are an incentive for plaintiffs to bring suit in a timely fashion. ...

There are, however, several reasons why this rationale for a rigorous application of the statute of limitations is particularly inapposite for incest actions.

As I mentioned earlier, many, if not most, of the damages flowing from incestuous abuse remain latent until the victim is well into adulthood. Secondly, and I shall elaborate on this further, when the damages begin to become apparent, the causal connection between the incestuous activity and present psychological injuries is often unknown to the victim. Needless to say, a statute of limitations provides little incentive for victims of incest to prosecute their actions in a timely fashion if they have been rendered psychologically incapable of recognizing that a cause of action exists.

Further, one cannot ignore the larger social context that has prevented the problem of incest from coming to the fore. Until recently, powerful taboos surrounding sexual abuse have conspired with the perpetrators of incest to silence victims and maintain a veil of secrecy around the activity. The cogency of these social forces would inevitably discourage victims from coming forward and seeking compensation from their abusers. …

The foregoing discussion has examined the policy reasons for limitations from the perspective of fairness to the potential defendant. However this court has also said that fairness to the plaintiff must also animate a principled approach to determining the accrual of a cause of action. In *Nielsen v. Kamloops (City)*, [1984] 2 SCR 2, one of the issues that arose was whether the plaintiff's action was statute-barred by the British Columbia *Municipal Act*, RSBC 1960, c. 255, where the plaintiff first became aware of the damage after the one year prescription. Wilson J, writing for the majority, observed that the injustice which statute-bars a claim before the plaintiff is aware of its existence takes precedence over any difficulty encountered in the investigation of facts many years after the occurrence of the allegedly tortious conduct.

This principle was later adopted in *Central & Eastern Trust Co. v. Rafuse*, [1986] 2 SCR 147, where the court held that the reasonable discoverability rule was as applicable to cases involving professional negligence as it was to actions involving injury to property. Le Dain J thus articulated the general rule, at p. 224:

> … a cause of action arises for purposes of a limitation period when the material facts on which it is based have been discovered or ought to have been discovered by the plaintiff by the exercise of reasonable diligence …

That essentially mirrors the delayed discovery doctrine developed in the United States, where the rationale most often cited is the plaintiff who is "blamelessly ignorant" of his injury; see *Urie v. Thompson*, 337 US 163 (1949).

• • •

Application of the Discoverability Rule to Incest

In my view the only sensible application of the discoverability rule in a case such as this is one that establishes a prerequisite that the plaintiff have a substantial awareness of the harm and its likely cause before the limitations period begins to toll. It is at the moment when the incest victim discovers the connection between the harm she has suffered and her childhood history that her cause of action crystallizes. I am in complete agreement with Professor Des Rosiers that the causal link between fault and damage is an important fact, essential to the formulation of the right of action, that is so often missing in cases of incest; see "Les recours des victimes d'inceste et d'agression sexuelle" to be published in Legrand, ed., *Common law d'un siècle à l'autre* (1992). What is more, I am satisfied that the weight of scientific evidence establishes that in most cases the victim of incest only comes to an awareness of the connection between fault and damage when she realizes who is truly responsible for her childhood abuse. Presumptively, that awareness will materialize when she receives some form of therapeutic assistance, either professionally or in the general community. I have come to this conclusion after studying the expert evidence in this case and the American jurisprudence which has wrestled with this problem over the past decade. The presumption will, of course, be displaced when the evidence establishes that the victim discovered the harm and its likely cause at some other time.

• • •

In my view the approach taken by the court in *Evans v. Eckelman* cuts to the heart of the matter: when does the plaintiff become aware of the wrongful nature of the defendant's acts? Battery consists of wrongful touching, and it is the wrongfulness of the contact and its consequential effects that are the material facts the plaintiff must discover before her cause of action accrues. Much of the expert evidence given at trial in the present case was directed to the question of when the plaintiff, after reaching the age of majority, remembered or became aware of her childhood abuse. There was conflicting evidence as to whether the plaintiff could have an intellectual, but not an emotional awareness of the abuse. To my mind, no useful purpose is served by engaging in this metaphysical debate on the epistemology of discovery. In the end I am satisfied that the issue properly turns on the question of when the victim becomes fully cognizant of who bears the responsibility for her childhood abuse, for it is then that she realizes the nature of the wrong done to her.

I would note that a similar approach has recently been taken by a Canadian court. In *Gray v. Reeves* (1992), 64 BCLR (2d) 275 (SC), Hall J concluded that the victim's recognition of the nexus between her injuries and the earlier incest is the point when time should begin to run against the victim. In that case the plaintiff was sexually assaulted by her uncle on approximately fifteen occasions between the ages of four and twelve. She commenced action at the age of thirty, after receiving therapy which identified the true cause of certain psychological problems suffered by the plaintiff during her adult life. This is clearly a "Type 1" case, as the plaintiff always remembered the assaults, had revealed the incestuous abuse to her family, and indeed had fought continuously to have her uncle excluded from family gatherings during her adult life. Nevertheless, the trial judge found as follows, at p. 306:

> Here, the plaintiff Ms. Gray knew from a very early age that the assaultive behaviour of her uncle, the defendant, was disgusting to her. She knew at least from the time when she was a teenager that these acts were wrong and she sought to protect younger children from any assaults by the defendant. I am of the view that the evidence in the case discloses that, although the plaintiff was repelled by the assaults, she had no reason to believe and did not believe that she had suffered any material harm, mental or physical, from the assaults. While she had these feelings of revulsion or repugnance to the activities of the defendant concerning herself or others, I am quite unable to find that she was able, until a point in time after the commencement of her therapy with Dr. Way in 1988, to perceive any link between the earlier wrongful conduct of the plaintiff and her depression and inability to establish a satisfactory relationship with a member of the opposite sex.

British Columbia's limitations legislation is very different from the statute before us in the instant case. It creates a form of statutory reasonable discoverability test, and I note with interest that this legislation emphasizes the importance of professional treatment and advice by stating the test (s. 6(3)) as the knowledge of a reasonable person "having taken the appropriate advice." [The meaning of this provision has most recently been considered by British Columbia's Court of Appeal in *Levitt v. Carr* (1992), 66 BCLR (2d) 58.] Despite the differences in legislation, the conclusions of Hall J in *Gray v. Reeves*, at p. 309, are worthy of note:

… it seems to me that the hypothetical reasonable person in the shoes of the plaintiff here would not have been acting sensibly in commencing an action until such a person came to appreciate that a wrong or wrongs that had occasioned significant harm to her wellbeing could be established.

This is essentially the test I propose in the instant case.

· · ·

The close connection between therapy and the shifting of responsibility is typical in incest cases. In my view, this observed phenomenon is sufficient to create a presumption that certain incest victims only discover the necessary connection between their injuries and the wrong done to them (thus discovering their cause of action) during some form of psychotherapy. I base this proposition on the scientific evidence presented at trial and to this court which confirms a post-incest syndrome amongst incest survivors. If the evidence in a particular case is consistent with the typical features of this syndrome, then the presumption will arise. Of course, it will be open to the defendant to refute the presumption by leading evidence showing that the plaintiff appreciated the causal link between the harm and its origin without the benefit of therapy.

Application to the Present Case

After hearing the evidence, the trial judge concluded that from the age of sixteen the appellant was aware that she had been wronged and had suffered adverse effects. I will not expound on the role of an appellate court when reviewing findings of fact. Here, in my view, the trial judge did not address himself to the critical issue—i.e., when did the appellant discover her cause of action in the sense of having a substantial awareness of the harm and its likely cause? With respect, the trial judge made no finding that the appellant had made the necessary connection at any time before entering therapy.

In my view, this is a case in which it can be presumed that the nexus between the appellant's injuries and incest was discovered only when the appellant received therapy. The evidence presented at trial shows the appellant to be a typical incest survivor. Her experiences as a child and later in life correspond closely to the symptoms of post-incest syndrome. As a child, she was subjected to the threats and bribes that enforce secrecy on the assaults. Her mental defence mechanism was dissociation, typical in incest cases. Later in life, her attempts at disclosure were met with skepticism, denial and evasion, again a typical feature of post-incest syndrome. As an adult she suffers from depression and difficulty with intimate relationships, which are classic symptoms of the syndrome.

Aside from the presumption available to the appellant, the evidence overwhelmingly indicates that she did not make the causative link between her injuries and childhood history until she received therapeutic assistance, and the evidence proffered to the contrary was entirely speculative. In any event there was no direct evidence to overcome the presumption that the appellant's therapy was the triggering event for discovering her cause of action. As such, the statute of limitations did not begin to run against her until that time, and this action was commenced within all relevant statutory limitation periods. On this basis, together with the reasons which follow, I would allow the appeal and restore the jury's verdict both as to liability and damages.

I cannot leave this topic without adding my voice to the chorus calling for reform in this area of limitations law. I note that a recent consultation draft prepared by the Attorney General of Ontario has proposed the abolition of limitation periods in cases of incestuous sexual assault: A Consultation Draft of the General Limitations Act, s. 18(h), in "Recommendations for a New Limitations Act," report of the Limitations Act Consultation Group (Toronto: Ministry of the Attorney General, March 1991). As well, British Columbia has recently amended its *Limitation Act* to permit survivors of childhood sexual abuse to pursue legal action at any time; see *Limitation Amendment Act, 1992*, SBC 1992, c. 44. In light of the existing evidence on the nature and extent of the problems faced by incest survivors, these are welcome developments.

. . .

There remains the issues of determining the meaning of fraudulent concealment, and its application to cases of incest. In my view, incest cases will often be amenable to the application of fraudulent concealment as an answer to a limitations defence. Incest takes place in a climate of secrecy, and the victim's silence is attained through various insidious measures. As we have seen, these actions by the perpetrator of the incest condition the victim to conceal the wrong from herself. The fact that the abuser is a trusted family authority figure in and of itself masks the wrongfulness of the conduct in the child's eyes, thus fraudulently concealing her cause of action. On this basis, I am satisfied that fraudulent concealment can be applied in incest cases.

. . .

… In cases of incest there is, of course, a grievous abuse of a position of confidence. I will have more to say later about the fiduciary nature of the parent-child relationship, but for now it is enough to say that incest is clearly an abuse of a confidential position. As the authorities make clear, incest is really a double wrong—the act of incest itself is followed by an abuse of the child's innocence to prevent recognition or revelation of the abuse; see *Evans v. Eckelman*, supra. I should add that given the nature of the concealment in abuse cases, namely, that the abuser compels the complicity of the victim in denying the harm done to her, it may be that the doctrine can operate in a tort as well as fiduciary context to toll the limitation period because of the deliberate attempts at concealment on the part of the abuser.

Peixeiro v. Haberman
[1997] 3 SCR 549

MAJOR J:

I. Introduction

This appeal arises from a motion brought by the respondents Peixeiro to determine whether their action against the appellant Haberman was statute-barred. The appeal was heard and dismissed on March 13, 1997.

The question raised was whether the discoverability principle applied to postpone the commencement of the two-year limitation period contained in s. 206(1) of the *Highway*

Traffic Act, RSO 1990, c. H.8 ("HTA"). It stipulates that actions for "damages occasioned by a motor vehicle" must be commenced within two years of the time when the "damages were sustained." The respondents commenced their action against the appellant three years and nine months after the motor vehicle accident. In that action they claimed that Mr. Peixeiro's injuries met the requirement of the exception to the general liability immunity afforded to persons involved in a motor vehicle accident by s. 266(1) of the *Insurance Act*, RSO 1990, c. I.8. This liability immunity is a key feature of the statutory no-fault automobile accident compensation scheme. It operates to effectively bar causes of action in tort in all but a few cases. [In order to maintain the right to sue in tort for compensation, motor vehicle accident victims in Ontario must experience injuries that pass a statutory "threshold"—i.e., they must sustain serious, permanent impairment to an important bodily function.] The resolution of the issue in this appeal requires a consideration of the liability immunity and the no-fault scheme before consideration of the applicability of the discoverability principle.

II. Statement of Facts

The application before the motions judge proceeded on agreed facts. A two-car accident occurred on October 11, 1990 at the intersection of Ossington Avenue and Harbord Street in the City of Toronto. The appellant Haberman and the respondent Mauricio Peixeiro were the drivers. Liability in the accident is disputed but it is agreed that Mr. Peixeiro knew he was injured.

Mr. Peixeiro consulted his family doctor and was told that he had suffered soft tissue injuries in the form of a severe contusion to the right side of his back. He was also referred to a specialist who recommended a course of physiotherapy. X-rays were taken at that time but disclosed nothing unusual. He was unable to work as a general contractor, from the date of the accident to November 1991, a period of over 13 months.

On January 7, 1992, Mr. Peixeiro was involved in a second two-car accident. Mr. Jose Silva was the other driver in this second accident. Mr. Peixeiro's resultant injuries were again diagnosed as being soft tissue in nature. Mr. Peixeiro was unable to work from the date of the second accident until May 1992. He ceased employment again in August 1992 and has not returned to work.

On January 15, 1993, Mr. Peixeiro consulted his family physician. As a result, a CT scan was performed in June 1993. The scan revealed a disc protrusion in the respondent's spine at L5-S1. At that time, Mr. Peixeiro was not a good candidate for surgery. However, on December 8 when he developed paresis on his right leg, he was admitted to emergency. He underwent a hemilaminectomy and a discectomy to remove the herniated disc on December 22, 1993.

On December 17, 1993, the respondents commenced an action against Mr. Silva. The respondents initially attempted to add the appellant as a defendant to the Silva action. By agreement, a separate action was commenced on July 27, 1994 against the appellant and a motion on a question of law was brought to determine whether the claim against him for the injuries of October 11, 1990 was statute-barred by s. 206(1) *HTA*.

On November 1, 1994, the chambers judge Paisley J held that the respondents' action against Haberman was statute-barred.

The Court of Appeal for Ontario allowed the respondents' appeal on September 5, 1995. ...

The parties agreed that the respondents first learned about a herniated disc in Mr. Peixeiro's back in June 1993.

. . .

It was conceded by the respondents that Mr. Peixeiro suffered a back injury and was aware of it immediately after the first accident. It was of sufficient severity that he remained off work for a period of 13 months. After the second accident of January 1992, he only worked three months between May 1992 and August 1992 and has not worked since.

While the respondents knew of some injury, they did not know within the limitation period that the damage Mr. Peixeiro sustained as a result of the first accident was a herniated disc. They did not know that it met the threshold for an action under s. 266(1) of the *Insurance Act*. He did not sue because he thought that his injuries were not serious enough to qualify for compensation in tort.

It was conceded that at common law ignorance of or mistake as to the extent of damages does not delay time under a limitation period. The authorities are clear that the exact extent of the loss of the plaintiff need not be known for the cause of action to accrue. Once the plaintiff knows that some damage has occurred and has identified the tortfeasor (see *Cartledge v. E. Jopling & Sons*, [1963] AC 758 (UK HL), at p. 772 *per* Lord Reid, and *July v. Neal* (1986), 57 OR (2d) 129 (Ont. CA)), the cause of action has accrued. Neither the extent of damage nor the type of damage need be known. To hold otherwise would inject too much uncertainty into cases where the full scope of the damages may not be ascertained for an extended time beyond the general limitation period.

However, it was submitted that because of Ontario's no-fault insurance scheme at the time of the accident, the starting point of the running of time is when the damages are known to comprise "permanent serious impairment" within the meaning of s. 266 of the *Insurance Act*. The argument was that the intervention of the liability immunity, one of the mandatory features of Ontario's no-fault system, alters the time of accrual of the cause of action until the material fact of sufficient injury is reasonably discoverable.

. . .

In my view, the right of action contemplated in s. 206(1) *HTA* must refer to an action that is not excluded by s. 266 of the *Insurance Act*. It cannot be otherwise. Ontario's system of mandatory automobile insurance is not a pure no-fault system; it cannot be said that the legislature intended to preclude all causes of action arising from motor vehicle accidents.

In this case, had the respondents started an action prior to June 1993, they would not have had evidence of a sufficient serious physical injury. ... It is unreasonable to suggest that the respondents, given the existing knowledge of the injury, should have proceeded. It would have been futile.

B. *Does the Discoverability Rule Apply?*

The cause of action under s. 206(1) does not arise unless the injury meets the statutory exceptions set out in the *Insurance Act*. The question which remains is whether the discoverability principle applies to postpone the running of time until the material facts underlying the cause of action, including extent of the injury, are known.

Short limitation periods indicate that the legislature put a premium on their function as a statute of repose. This is one of the three rationales which serve society and the courts' continued interest in maintaining the respect of these statutes. Whatever interest a defendant may have in the universal application of a limitation period must be balanced against the concerns of fairness to the plaintiff who was unaware that his injuries met the conditions precedent to commencing an action. ...

M. (K.) v. M. (H.) applied the three rationales to the fact situation there and found that neither the guarantee of repose, the evidentiary concerns nor the expectation of diligence on the part of the plaintiff precluded the application of the discoverability principle.

Since this Court's decisions in *Nielsen v. Kamloops (City)*, [1984] 2 SCR 2 (SCC), and *Central & Eastern Trust Co. v. Rafuse*, [1986] 2 SCR 147 (SCC), at p. 224, discoverability is a general rule applied to avoid the injustice of precluding an action before the person is able to raise it. ... See also *M. (K.) v. M. (H.)*, *supra*, at p. 32 and *Murphy v. Welsh*, *supra*, at pp. 1079-81.

In this regard, I adopt Twaddle JA's statement in *Fehr v. Jacob* (1993), 14 CCLT (2d) 200 (Man. CA), at p. 206, that the discoverability rule is an interpretive tool for the construing of limitations statutes which ought to be considered each time a limitations provision is in issue:

> In my opinion, the judge-made discoverability rule is nothing more than a rule of construction. Whenever a statute requires an action to be commenced within a specified time from the happening of a specific event, the statutory language must be construed. When time runs from "the accrual of the cause of action" or from some other event which can be construed as occurring only when the injured party has knowledge of the injury sustained, the judge-made discoverability rule applies. But, when time runs from an event which clearly occurs without regard to the injured party's knowledge, the judge-made discoverability rule may not extend the period the legislature has prescribed.

The appellant submitted here that the general rule of discoverability was ousted because the legislature used the words "damages were sustained," rather than the date "when the cause of action arose." It is unlikely that by using the words "damages were sustained," the legislature intended that the determination of the starting point of the limitation period should take place without regard to the injured party's knowledge. It would require clearer language to displace the general rule of discoverability. The use of the phrase "damages were sustained" rather than "cause of action arose," in the context of the *HTA*, is a distinction without a difference. The discoverability rule has been applied by this Court even to statutes of limitation in which plain construction of the language used would appear to exclude the operation of the rule. *Kamloops*, *supra*, dealt in part with s. 739 of the *Municipal Act*, RSBC 1960, c. 255, which required that notice should be given within two months "from and after the date on which [the] damage was sustained." However, this Court applied the discoverability rule even with respect to this section; see *Kamloops*, *supra*, at pp. 35-40.

I agree with the Court of Appeal that to hold that the discoverability principle does not apply to s. 206 *HTA* would unfairly preclude actions by plaintiffs unaware of the existence of their cause of action. In balancing the defendant's legitimate interest in respecting limitations periods and the interest of the plaintiffs, the fundamental unfairness of requiring a plaintiff to bring a cause of action before he could reasonably have discovered that he had a cause of action is a compelling consideration. The diligence rationale would not be undermined by the application of the discoverability principle as it still requires reasonable diligence by the plaintiff.

The appellant submitted that as a matter of law, the discoverability principle was inapplicable to personal injury actions. Notwithstanding *Cartledge v. E. Jopling & Sons, supra*, there is no principled reason for distinguishing between an action for personal injury and an action for property damage (see *Kamloops, Sparham-Souter* and *M. (K.) v. M. (H.))*.

. . .

C. Application of the Discoverability Principle to the Facts

The respondent Mr. Peixeiro was injured in October 1990 and first discovered that his injury was physical in nature, within the meaning of *Meyers*, in June 1993. He commenced his action against the appellant in July 1994. Given the medical advice that Mr. Peixeiro had, and in spite of reasonable diligence by him, his injury was reasonably discoverable for the first time in June 1993.

As a matter of law, I do not think that the existence of a cause of action was reasonably discoverable until the respondents learned that Mr. Peixeiro had a herniated disc. Therefore, the respondents' action is not statute-barred, as it was started within two years of the time when they first learned that they had a cause of action.

VII. Conclusion

Under s. 206(1) *HTA*, there is no cause of action until the injury meets the statutory exceptions to liability immunity in s. 266(1) of the *Insurance Act*. The discoverability principle applies to avoid the injustice of precluding an action before the person is able to sue. Time under s. 206(1) does not begin to run until it is reasonably discoverable that the injury meets the threshold of s. 266(1). It was agreed that the respondents first learned of the herniated disc in June 1993. The respondents were reasonably diligent in this respect. It cannot be said that they ought to have discovered the serious nature of the damage earlier. As the action was commenced in July a year later within the limitation period, it cannot be statute-barred.

In the continual quest to balance a defendant's desire for peace with the sometimes draconian effect limitation periods have on unsuspecting plaintiffs who seek to assert their rights after a limitation period has expired, courts have developed a more individually specific and contextual consideration of discoverability. The Supreme Court of Canada established in the above two cases that the limitation clock does not begin to run until the plaintiff can make the factual connection between the defendant's fault and the injury suffered by the plaintiff. In the case that follows, the Supreme Court subsequently adopted a more nuanced subjective-objective approach to how the plaintiff must prove precisely when that connection was made or ought to have been made.

Novak v. Bond
[1999] 1 SCR 808

McLACHLIN J (L'Heureux-Dubé, Gonthier, and Cory JJ concurring):

. . .

II. Facts

The appellant, Dr. Bond, was the respondent Mrs. Novak's physician. Between October 18, 1989 and October 1, 1990, Mrs. Novak saw him about a lump and soreness in her left breast on at least six occasions. Each time, Dr. Bond told her that she had "mammary dysplasia" and "'lumpy' breasts," reassuring her that "cancer is not like this" and that she had nothing to worry about. He told her to exercise more, drink less coffee, and take Vitamin E, Diazide and Advil.

On October 1, 1990, Mrs. Novak was referred to a specialist, and on October 3, 1990, was examined by a surgeon, Dr. T.E. Abraham. On October 4, 1990, Dr. Abraham performed a biopsy which established that Mrs. Novak had cancer of the left breast. On October 9, 1990, she had a partial radical mastectomy and it was discovered that the cancer had spread to at least twelve of her thirteen lymph nodes. From October 1990 until April 1991, Mrs. Novak underwent chemotherapy and radiation therapy. Later in October 1990, she began seeing a new physician as she no longer had confidence in Dr. Bond.

From the time of her diagnosis in October 1990, Mrs. Novak believed that Dr. Bond should have taken action earlier than he did. She believed that she would have required less extensive medical treatment had an earlier diagnosis been made, although she still would have had to undergo the mastectomy. Although she did not know the specific extent of her lymph node involvement in October 1990, she was aware by at least December 1990, that it was heavy or extensive.

In the late summer or early fall of 1991, Mrs. Novak considered whether she should sue Dr. Bond. She did not consult a lawyer, but discussed the issue with her parish priest. She decided not to pursue litigation. At her Examination for Discovery, she explained the reasons for her decision:

> That would have taken place probably after my—after my chemo. I remember distinctly thinking, I'm not going to worry about litigation until I get my treatment. It was very profound, I was extremely ill for about a year, and I started to get back on my feet and—so it was after my chemo, probably the summer of '90, and then my father died and I was dealing with my dad's death. So it would have been the late summer maybe early fall of '91, somewhere around there, and I tossed it about and tossed it about and thought, well do I have the strength to really go through this at this stage of the game? And I talked to my parish priest about it and thought, well I'm well, I have to believe that I'm well, I have to believe that I've been cured, if I go for litigation it brings back all the horrible memories and I won't at this point, we'll wait to see for a few years what's going to happen down the road.

Mrs. Novak had no symptoms of cancer from April 1991 to May 1995, a time during which her health was closely monitored. In May 1995, she was diagnosed with cancer of the spine, liver and lung and became aware of the actual extent of the lymph node involvement that had been found in 1990. The cancer was a recurrence of the breast cancer originally diagnosed and treated in October 1990.

When her cancer recurred, Mrs. Novak and her husband decided to initiate legal action against Dr. Bond, and commenced these proceedings on April 9, 1996. They made no claim with respect to the initial cancer, nor for its treatment. They claimed only damages relating to the recurrence of cancer in May 1995 on the basis that those damages arose from Mrs. Novak's increased susceptibility to recurrence caused or contributed to by the late diagnosis of her breast cancer.

Dr. Bond successfully moved to have the action dismissed as statute-barred. The Court of Appeal allowed Mrs. Novak's appeal and reinstated her action. Dr. Bond now appeals that decision to this Court.

In order for Mrs. Novak's action to be within the time limit set by s. 3(2)(a) of the Act, she must establish that the running of time was postponed by s. 6(4) until at least *April 9, 1994*.

III. Statutory Provisions

Limitation Act, RSBC 1996, c. 266

Section 3(2)(a) provides that an action claiming damages for personal injury must be brought within two years of the date the right to bring the action arose.

> 3. ...
> (2) After the expiration of 2 years after the date on which the right to do so arose a person may not bring any of the following actions:
>> (a) subject to subsection (4)(k), for damages in respect of injury to person or property, including economic loss arising from the injury, whether based on contract, tort or statutory duty. ...

In certain circumstances, s. 6 allows the running of time to be postponed.

> 6. ...
> (3) The running of time with respect to the limitation periods set by this Act for any of the following actions is postponed as provided in subsection (4):
>> (a) for personal injury;
>> • • •
>> (c) for professional negligence. ...
> (4) Time does not begin to run against a plaintiff with respect to an action referred to in subsection (3) until the identity of the defendant is known to the plaintiff and those facts within the plaintiff's means of knowledge are such that a reasonable person, knowing those facts and having taken the appropriate advice a reasonable person would seek on those facts, would regard those facts as showing that
>> (a) an action on the cause of action would, apart from the effect of the expiration of a limitation period, have a reasonable prospect of success, and
>> (b) the person whose means of knowledge is in question ought, in the person's own interests and taking the person's circumstances into account, to be able to bring an action.

(5) For the purpose of subsection (4),

(a) "appropriate advice," in relation to facts, means the advice of competent persons, qualified in their respective fields, to advise on the medical, legal and other aspects of the facts, as the case may require,

(b) "facts" include

(i) the existence of a duty owed to the plaintiff by the defendant, and

(ii) that a breach of a duty caused injury, damage or loss to the plaintiff. ...

Section 7 allows the running of time to be postponed if the plaintiff is under a legal disability.

7(1) For the purposes of this section,

(a) a person is under a disability while the person

(i) is a minor, or

(ii) is in fact incapable of or substantially impeded in managing his or her affairs, and

(b) "guardian" means a parent or guardian who has actual care and control of a minor or a committee appointed under the *Patients Property Act*.

(2) If, at the time the right to bring an action arises, a person is under a disability, the running of time with respect to a limitation period set by this Act is postponed so long as that person is under a disability.

(3) If the running of time against a person with respect to a cause of action has been postponed by subsection (2) and that person ceases to be under a disability, the limitation period governing that cause of action is the longer of the following:

(a) the period that the person would have had to bring the action had that person not been under a disability, running from the time the cause of action arose;

(b) the period running from the time the disability ceased, but in no case does that period extend more than 6 years beyond the cessation of disability.

(4) If, after time has begun to run with respect to a limitation period set by this Act, but before the expiration of the limitation period, a person who has a cause of action comes under a disability, the running of time against that person is suspended so long as that person is under a disability.

(5) If the running of time against a person with respect to a cause of action has been suspended by subsection (4) and that person ceases to be under a disability, the limitation period governing that cause of action is the longer of the following:

(a) the length of time remaining to bring an action at the time the person came under the disability;

(b) one year from the time that the disability ceased.

Section 8 provides an ultimate limitation period of six years for proceedings against medical practitioners.

8(1) Subject to section 3(4) and subsection (2) of this section, but despite a confirmation made under section 5, a postponement or suspension of the running of time under section 6 or 11(2) or a postponement or suspension of the running of time under section 7 in respect of a person who is not a minor, no action to which this Act applies may be brought

· · ·

    (b) against a medical practitioner, based on professional negligence or malpractice,
    after the expiration of 6 years from the date on which the right to do so arose. ...

What is the proper approach to be taken when interpreting s. 6(4)(b) of the *Limitation Act*, RSBC 1996, c. 266?

VI. *Analysis*

A. *Approaches Suggested by the British Columbia Court of Appeal*

The British Columbia Court of Appeal has been engaged in an ongoing struggle to define the content of s. 6(4)(b) of the Act. At least four different approaches to s. 6(4)(b) have emerged in the decisions of the Court of Appeal. To a greater or lesser extent, they are reflected in the positions taken by the appellant and the respondent.

(1) *Broad Subjective/Objective Approach: Whether Reasonable Plaintiff "Should" Bring Action*

This approach suggests that s. 6(4)(b) postpones the running of time until a reasonable person would hold that the plaintiff, taking his or her own circumstances and interests into account, should bring an action, i.e., until it is in the plaintiff's best interests to do so. Such an interpretation was advocated in *Evans v. Vancouver Port Corp.* (1989), 42 BCLR (2d) 174 (CA), per Wood JA, additional reasons at (1990), 46 BCLR (2d) 334 (CA), *per* Macdonald JA, and in *Karsanjii Estate v. Roque*, [1990] 3 WWR 612 (BCCA), *per* Taylor JA. On this interpretation, great deference is given to the course of action that is best for the plaintiff.

(2) *Restrictive Subjective/Objective Approach: Whether Reasonable Plaintiff "Could" Bring Action, Taking into Account Plaintiff's "Important and Substantial Interests"*

Later cases have restricted the broad approach taken by Wood JA in *Evans*, supra, and by Taylor JA in *Karsanjii*, supra. These cases attempt to give effect to the inclusion of the words "to be able" in s. 6(4)(b) and strive to identify the point at which a reasonable person, taking into account the plaintiff's "important and substantial interests," would conclude that the plaintiff *could*—not necessarily *should*—sue the defendant.

    The leading case adopting this interpretation is *Frosch Construction Ltd. v. Volrich* (1995), 7 BCLR (3d) 72 (CA). Lambert JA, writing for the court, compared s. 6(4)(b) to the New South Wales legislation on which it was based, and expressed the opinion, at p. 78, that the addition to the British Columbia Act of the words "to be able" made "a significant difference to the meaning of the provision." At p. 79, he set out his understanding of how s. 6(4)(b) should be interpreted, emphasizing that postponement cannot be justified by tactical considerations:

> In short, the effect of the addition of the words "to be able" is, in my opinion, to take out of
> consideration matters of tactics to do with the lawsuit itself and to do with any other matters
> that affect only questions of tactical timing, and to leave for consideration only those mat-
> ters where important and substantial interests of the plaintiff in his or her own circum-

stances should be open for consideration by a reasonable person in deciding whether a person in the plaintiff's position ought to be able to bring an action. "Ought to bring an action" involves a wider range of factors for consideration than "ought to be able to bring an action." By the addition of the words "to be able" the meaning is changed from whether a reasonable person would consider that someone in the plaintiff's position *should*, acting reasonably, bring an action at that time, to whether a reasonable person would consider that someone in the plaintiff's position *could*, acting reasonably, bring an action at that time. [Emphasis in original.]

Lambert JA proposed a similar interpretation of s. 6(4)(b) in *Vance v. Peglar* (1996), 22 BCLR (3d) 251 (CA), leave to appeal refused, [1997] 1 SCR x.

(3) Restrictive Objective Approach: Plaintiff Generally "Ought To Be Able To Bring Action" if Legally Capable of Bringing Action

A third interpretation of s. 6(4)(b) was proposed by McEachern CJ in *Karsanjii, supra*. There, he suggested that s. 6(4)(b) essentially referred only to the plaintiff's legal capacity to bring an action. Once the plaintiff is legally entitled to bring an action, he or she "ought to be able" to do so. At pp. 616-17, McEachern CJ expressed his views with respect to what is now s. 6(4)(b) as follows:

> ... I must respectfully reject the suggestion that personal, economic or embarrassing reasons are sufficient to postpone the commencement of a limitation period. It must be remembered that the plaintiff has two years to bring an action after the means of knowledge test is satisfied.
>
> Therefore, without knowing precisely what this section means, it is my view that any plaintiff who ought, in his own interests and taking his circumstances into account, to bring an action should do so if he is able, that is, if he has legal capacity to be able to do so.
>
> • • •
>
> In my view, any person who is able to bring an action is also a person who ought to be able to bring an action.

(4) Discretionary Approach: Court Has Discretion To Assess Action and Decide Whether Plaintiff "Ought To Be Able To Bring" It

In *Vance, supra*, McEachern CJ offered a fourth interpretation of s. 6(4)(b). The main question posed by this approach is whether the plaintiff (who would otherwise be out of time) has established a cause of action with a reasonable chance of success under s. 6(4)(a). If so, s. 6(4)(b) is then considered to determine whether there are any factors which negative the plaintiff's right to bring the action, i.e., which show that the plaintiff ought *not* to be able to bring the action. McEachern CJ elaborated at pp. 263-64:

> It may be, for example, that a plaintiff has already been compensated adequately for the lost cause of action, or that the cause of action is trivial, frivolous, vexatious or not *bona fide*. No doubt there are other examples of cases where the court, having regard to all relevant considerations, would properly conclude that the plaintiff ought not to be able to bring an action even though his or her cause of action has a reasonable prospect of success.

B. How Should Section 6(4)(b) Be Interpreted?

(1) Statutory Interpretation

Although the judicial debate about the proper interpretation of s. 6(4)(b) has assumed an independent life in British Columbia legal circles, it remains a question of statutory interpretation. The cardinal principle of statutory interpretation is that a legislative provision should be construed in a way that best furthers its objects: see *Rizzo & Rizzo Shoes Ltd. (Re)*, [1998] 1 SCR 27, at paras. 21-22, *per* Iacobucci J, and *Interpretation Act*, RSBC 1996, c. 238, s. 8. Subsidiary rules of statutory interpretation provide that each part of an enactment must be given meaning, and that statutes must be construed in such a way that absurdities are avoided: see *Rizzo Shoes, supra*, at para. 27, *per* Iacobucci J. The task faced by the Court on this appeal is therefore to first identify the scheme and purpose of the *Limitation Act* and then identify the interpretation of s. 6(4)(b) that best furthers its goals.

(2) Scheme and Purpose of the Limitation Act

In *Peixeiro v. Haberman*, [1997] 3 SCR 549, this Court affirmed its earlier identification of the traditional rationales of limitations statutes in *M. (K.) v. M. (H.)*, [1992] 3 SCR 6, at pp. 29-30. Limitations statutes were held, at p. 29, to rest on "certainty, evidentiary, and diligence rationales." In *M. (K.), supra*, this Court noted at pp. 29-30:

> Statutes of limitations have long been said to be statutes of repose. ... The reasoning is straightforward enough. There comes a time, it is said, when a potential defendant should be secure in his reasonable expectation that he will not be held to account for ancient obligations. ...
>
> The second rationale is evidentiary and concerns the desire to foreclose claims based on stale evidence. Once the limitation period has lapsed, the potential defendant should no longer be concerned about the preservation of evidence relevant to the claim. ...
>
> Finally, plaintiffs are expected to act diligently and not "sleep on their rights"; statutes of limitation are an incentive for plaintiffs to bring suit in a timely fashion.
>
> It is apparent that these rationales generally reflect the interests of the potential defendant: *Murphy v. Welsh*, [1993] 2 SCR 1069, at pp. 1079-80, *per* Major J. They rest on the view that a potential defendant should not have to defend a stale claim brought by a plaintiff who has chosen not to assert his or her rights diligently. Indeed, although there have traditionally been doctrines or statutory provisions that recognized the plaintiff's interests, such as the exceptions applicable to persons under a disability or victims of concealed frauds, limitations statutes have generally been oriented towards the interests of the potential defendant.

Over the last several decades, however, many legislatures have moved to modernize their limitations statutes, most of which were formerly based on diverse collections of centuries-old English statutes: see Law Reform Commission of British Columbia, *Report on Limitations, Part 2: General* (1974), at pp. 9-16; Alberta Law Reform Institute, Report No. 55, *Limitations* (1989), at pp. 15-16 and Appendix A. As part of this process, renewed attention has been given to ensuring that the limitations statutes are framed in a manner that addresses more consistently the plaintiff's interests, not just those of the defendant. This trend has also been reflected in the more balanced way that courts have sought to interpret these statutes. Arbitrary limitation dates have been discouraged in favour of a more contextual view of the parties' actual circumstances. To take just one example, it has been well-recognized that it is unfair for the limitation period to begin running until the plaintiff could reasonably have discovered that he or she had a cause of action: see *Kamloops (City of) v. Nielsen*, [1984] 2 SCR 2; *Central Trust Co. v. Rafuse*, [1986] 2 SCR 147; *M. (K.)*, *supra*; *Peixeiro*, *supra*. Even on this new approach, however, limitation periods are not postponed on the plaintiff's whim. There is a burden on the plaintiff to act reasonably.

Contemporary limitations statutes thus seek to balance conventional rationales oriented towards the protection of the defendant—certainty, evidentiary, and diligence—with the need to treat plaintiffs fairly, having regard to their specific circumstances. As Major J put it in *Murphy*, *supra*, "[a] limitations scheme must attempt to balance the interests of both sides" (p. 1080). See also *Peixeiro*, *supra*, at para. 39, *per* Major J.

The result of this legislative and interpretive evolution is that most limitations statutes may now be said to possess four characteristics. They are intended to: (1) define a time at which potential defendants may be free of ancient obligations, (2) prevent the bringing of claims where the evidence may have been lost to the passage of time, (3) provide an incentive for plaintiffs to bring suits in a timely fashion, and (4) account for the plaintiff's own circumstances, as assessed through a subjective/objective lens, when assessing whether a claim should be barred by the passage of time. To the extent they are reflected in the particular words and structure of the statute in question, the best interpretation of a limitations statute seeks to give effect to each of these characteristics.

The general scheme of the British Columbia *Limitation Act* reflects this evolution. Section 3 provides concrete limitation periods for most actions. Depending on the cause of action, an action must be commenced within two, six, or ten years after the date on which the right to bring it arose, i.e., the date on which all the elements of the cause of action came into existence: see s. 3(2), (3), (5) and (6); *Bera v. Marr* (1986), 1 BCLR (2d) 1 (CA).

At the same time, the Act contains provisions aimed at treating plaintiffs fairly. For example, s. 6(3) to (5) reflect the common law view that it is unfair to the plaintiff if the running of time commences before the existence of the cause of action is reasonably discoverable. To determine when the running of time should commence for the enumerated actions, the court is generally directed to consider the actions of a reasonable person in the particular plaintiff's circumstances. Except where certain claims are made against a trustee, the plaintiff bears the burden of proving that, on the basis of these tests, the running of time has been postponed in a particular case: see s. 6(2), (6), and *Zeidan v. British Columbia*, [1989] BCJ No. 598 (QL) (SC). Section 7 of the Act allows the running of time to be postponed if the plaintiff is under a legal disability, a provision that is also directed to ensuring fairness to plaintiffs.

Certainty and diligence, however, remain important goals. The running of time cannot be postponed indefinitely. Therefore, s. 8 of the Act sets forth a series of *ultimate* limitation periods, the length of which depends on the particular type of action in issue. Generally, regardless of whether the running of time has been postponed or the cause of action confirmed by the defendant, no action can be brought after the expiration of—depending on the classification of the action—six or thirty years after the date on which the right to bring the action arose. Where the plaintiff is a minor, the running of time for the purposes of the ultimate limitation period is postponed until he or she reaches the age of majority: see s. 8(2). Only upon the expiration of the relevant ultimate limitation period can the potential defendant truly be assured that no plaintiff may bring an action against him or her. At that time, any cause of action that was once available to the plaintiff is extinguished: see s. 9(1). See generally Law Reform Commission of British Columbia, *Report on the Ultimate Limitation Period: Limitation Act, Section 8* (1990), especially at pp. 21-23. With respect to the case on appeal, the appellant is protected by a six-year ultimate limitation period: see s. 8(1)(b).

Viewed in this context, s. 6(4)(b) may be seen as operating to adjust the position of the limited window of time within which a plaintiff may bring an action. This section is constrained at one end by the specific date on which the cause of action actually arose in fact and, at the other end, by the ultimate limitation period of six or thirty years. Within that longer time period, and regardless of when it is considered to begin running, time may generally only be permitted to run for two, six, or ten years. The debate in this case is over the type of circumstances in which, *within that larger period of time*, the commencement of the limitation period for the initiation of an action that has a reasonable prospect of success should be postponed. The answer to this question must be resolved in a manner that maintains the traditional defendant-oriented rationales of limitations statutes, while also reflecting the modern need to balance those rationales against the plaintiff's circumstances and his or her interest in bringing an action to redress a wrong.

(3) Meaning of the Troublesome Phrase in Section 6(4)(b)

After stipulating that the identity of the defendant must be known to the plaintiff, s. 6(4) sets out the parameters of knowledge and advice that determine whether the commencement of the running of time will be postponed beyond the date on which the right to bring the action arose in fact. The question is whether a reasonable person, knowing the facts within the plaintiff's means of knowledge and having taken the appropriate advice a reasonable person would take on those facts, would regard those facts as showing *both* that the action would have a reasonable prospect of success (s. 6(4)(a)), and that the plaintiff "ought … to be able to bring an action," given the person's "own interests" and "circumstances" (s. 6(4)(b)). Time does not begin to run until both s. 6(4)(a) and s. 6(4)(b) are satisfied. The question before this Court is the meaning to be ascribed to the opaque phrase, "ought, in the person's own interests and taking the person's circumstances into account, to be able to bring an action." The word "ought" suggests an objective "reasonable person" standard. On the other hand, the reference to the plaintiff's "own interests" and "circumstances" introduces subjective considerations. How are the two to be reconciled?

The interpretation given to s. 6(4)(b) must give proper weight to: (1) the Legislature's inclusion of a subjective/objective standard in s. 6(4)(b); (2) the broad wording it has used in that provision; (3) the contemporary view that when construing a limitations statute the plaintiff's concerns must be considered together with the defendant's need to be protected from stale claims brought by dilatory plaintiffs; and (4) the interpretive presumption that s. 6(4)(b) adds something to s. 6(4)(a) and, to the rest of the Act. Many of the proposed interpretations fail to meet one or more of these requisites.

One suggestion is that the phrase "ought ... to be able to bring an action" in s. 6(4)(b) is concerned with legal capacity. A minor or a mentally incompetent person might argue that, owing to a disability, he or she was not able to bring the action at the time the right to do so arose. The first problem with this suggestion is that the Legislature has addressed questions of the plaintiff's legal capacity to bring an action in s. 7 of the Act, not s. 6(4)(b). This interpretation would therefore render s. 6(4)(b) superfluous. The second problem with this suggestion is that it fails to reflect fully the broad wording of s. 6(4)(b). Section 6(4)(b) expressly directs the court to consider the plaintiff's "own interests" and "circumstances." These expansive words go far beyond bare legal capacity and effect must be given to the Legislature's decision to include them in s. 6(4)(b).

Another suggestion is that s. 6(4)(b) is primarily designed to address the situation of the plaintiff who considers that, while an action would have a reasonable prospect of success, the amount likely to be recovered would be so little, or the remedy so unimportant, that practical considerations weigh against bringing it. Again, this suggestion fails to acknowledge the broad ambit of the phrase, "in the person's own interests and taking the person's circumstances into account." To be sure, there may be cases where the plaintiff's "own interests" and "circumstances" make the significance of the remedy an important consideration under s. 6(4)(b). But to confine the ambit of s. 6(4)(b) to these situations seems to me to run against the broad language the Legislature chose to employ.

A third suggestion is that the Legislature intended that s. 6(4)(b) should prevent the postponement of the limitation period where the action—which the plaintiff only lately discovered has a reasonable prospect of success—is trivial, frivolous, vexatious, or not bona fide. This suggestion seems to assume that s. 6(4)(b) "revives" an extinguished cause of action and confers upon the court the discretion to decide which causes of action should be "revived" and which should not. Frivolous, vexatious, trivial, or non-bona fide actions are examples, the argument runs, of proceedings that should not be revived.

With respect, this interpretation overlooks the wording and function of s. 6(4). First s. 6(4) provides that time does not *begin* to run until the identity of the defendant is known and the provisions of *both* s. 6(4)(a) and s. 6(4)(b) are satisfied. Thus, the question of whether s. 6(4)(b) should be used to "revive" the plaintiff's particular action is inapposite: the action has not yet been extinguished at the time s. 6(4)(b) is considered. It is accordingly incorrect to posit that s. 6(4)(b) allows the limitation period to be postponed only if the action appears meritorious.

This interpretation also threatens to render s. 6(4)(b) superfluous. To the extent that the merits of the particular action are relevant to the s. 6(4) analysis, they more naturally fall for consideration under s. 6(4)(a). An action that is trivial, frivolous, vexatious, or not *bona fide* is, by definition, an action that does not have a "reasonable prospect of success." If this be so, this interpretation deprives s. 6(4)(b) of any purpose. Alternatively, on the assumption that the character of the action may also figure in the plaintiff's "own interests" and "circumstances," s. 6(4)(b)'s broad wording belies the view that the character of the action is the only thing to be considered, to the exclusion of the rest of the plaintiff's interests and circumstances. In fact, if the character of the action were the exclusive focus of s. 6(4)(b), it would be indistinguishable from s. 6(4)(a).

Having considered and found wanting the narrower interpretations proposed, I turn to the broader interpretations of s. 6(4)(b). Two possibilities emerge: a broad subjective/objective approach akin to that suggested by Wood JA and Taylor JA in *Evans, supra*, and *Karsanjii, supra*, and a more restrictive subjective/objective approach similar to that offered by Lambert JA in *Frosch Construction, supra*, and *Vance, supra*.

The broad subjective/objective approach interprets the phrase "ought … to be able to bring an action" as meaning "should bring an action, in light of the plaintiff's interests and circumstances." This gives effect to the subjective component of s. 6(4)(b). However, it begs the question of why the Legislature did not simply use "should" if that is what it intended. Why did it choose the phrase "ought … to be able" with its connotation of capacity? Moreover, this interpretation is open to the practical objection that it might allow the running of time to be postponed for mere tactical reasons, a result that does not accord with the need to balance the four characteristics of limitations statutes discussed earlier.

The other option, a more restrictive subjective/objective test similar to that adopted by Lambert JA in *Frosch Construction, supra*, and *Vance, supra*, gives full effect to the language of s. 6(4)(b) while avoiding both the distortion of the phrase "ought … to be able to bring an action" and the misuse of the provision for tactical purposes. On this approach, s. 6(4)(b) may be read as denoting a time at which a reasonable person would consider that someone in the plaintiff's position, acting reasonably in light of his or her own circumstances and interests, *could*—not necessarily *should*—bring an action. This approach is neither purely subjective nor purely objective. The question becomes: "in light of his or her own circumstances and interests, at what point could the plaintiff reasonably have brought an action?" The reasonable person would only consider that the plaintiff could not have brought an action at the time the right to do so first arose if the plaintiff's own interests and circumstances were serious, significant, and compelling. Purely tactical considerations have no place in this analysis. In my view, this approach best accords with the purposes of modern limitations statutes, gives a sensible meaning to the terms of s. 6(4)(b), and is most likely to result in clear and fair results in the majority of cases.

This approach addresses the heart of the problem posed by this difficult provision: how to reconcile the words "ought … to be able to bring an action," with their connotation of capacity or ability, and the section's insistence that full account also be taken of the plaintiff's "own interests" and "circumstances." As suggested above, the two directions may seem contradictory on one level. The phrase "ought … to be able" suggests objective ability or capacity. The reference to the plaintiff's personal circumstances and interests, on the other hand, is the language of choice, of a situation where the plaintiff has the ability to do two or more things, and chooses one.

The proposed interpretation resolves this apparent conundrum by relying on the fact that there are different kinds of "ability." "[O]ught … to be able to bring an action" can certainly be interpreted narrowly in the sense of legal capacity. But it also may be interpreted more broadly, in the sense of a practical ability to choose a particular course in light of the factual circumstances in which a person finds himself or herself. We speak of not being "able" to do something not only when we lack the legal or physical capacity to do it, but also when our circumstances are such that we cannot reasonably contemplate doing the thing.

Interpreting "ought ... to be able to bring an action" in the second sense permits full weight to be given to all the words of s. 6(4)(b). The running of the limitation period is therefore postponed when the plaintiff shows that practical considerations arising from his or her "circumstances" and "own interests" render him or her unable, as a reasonable person, to bring an action at the earlier prescribed date. "[O]ught ... to be able to bring an action," interpreted thus, is very different from the normative "should bring an action." "Should" connotes subjective choice; "could" connotes practical ability. On the interpretation I have proposed, the court's central task is to identify the point at which the reasonable person who animates s. 6(4) would consider that the plaintiff, in light of his or her own interests and circumstances, could reasonably have brought an action. Section 6(4)(b) therefore refers to a time at which, in light of the plaintiff's particular situation, the bringing of a suit is reasonably *possible*, not when it would be *ideal* from the plaintiff's perspective to do so.

What "interests and circumstances" should be considered at this stage? In *Frosch Construction, supra*, at p. 79, Lambert JA held that only "important and substantial interests of the plaintiff in his or her own circumstances" should be considered. Practically speaking, the reasonable person would only consider that the plaintiff could not have brought an action at the time the right to do so first arose if the plaintiff's own interests and circumstances were serious, significant, and compelling. For example, a plaintiff may not reasonably be able to bring an action when, viewed objectively but with regard to the plaintiff's own situation, the costs and strain of litigation would be overwhelming to him or her, the possible damages recoverable would be minimal or speculative at best, or other personal circumstances combine to make it unfeasible to initiate an action. Litigation is never a process to be embarked upon casually and sometimes a plaintiff's individual circumstances and interests may mean that he or she cannot reasonably bring an action at the time it first materializes. This approach makes good policy sense. To force a plaintiff to sue without having regard to his or her own circumstances may be unfair to the plaintiff and may also disserve the defendant by forcing him or her to meet an action pressed into court prematurely: see generally B. Legate, "Limitation Periods in Medical Negligence Actions Post-*Peixeiro*" (1998), 20 *Advocates' Q* 326, at p. 334.

Whether a particular circumstance or interest has the practical effect of preventing the plaintiff from being able to commence the action must be assessed in each individual case. Section 6(4)(b) requires that the circumstances and interests of the *individual plaintiff* be taken into account. What is a serious, substantial, and compelling interest in one case may not be so in another case. Purely tactical concerns play no role in this analysis because they do not relate to the practical *ability* of the plaintiff to bring an action, as assessed by a reasonable person who takes into account all his or her circumstances and interests. See *Trueman v. Ripley*, [1998] BCJ No. 2060 (QL) (SC).

• • •

I conclude that delay beyond the prescribed limitation period is only justifiable if the individual plaintiff's interests and circumstances are so pressing that a reasonable person would conclude that, in light of them, the plaintiff could not reasonably bring an action at the time his or her bare legal rights crystallized. The task in every case is to determine the point at which the plaintiff reasonably could bring an action, taking into account his or her own interests and circumstances.

C. Application to the Case on Appeal

The motions judge did not engage in a detailed consideration of the requirements of s. 6(4)(b) and whether they were met in this case. The justices of the Court of Appeal considered the test in greater detail, noting that it appeared not to have been fully argued and considered at first instance. In separate reasons, the three Justices each found that Mrs. Novak's conduct in delaying the commencement of her action was reasonable having regard to her own interests and circumstances. These findings must be approached with caution, however, since the test applied, particularly by Southin and Newbury JJA, differed in some respects from the test adopted in these reasons. The test I have proposed places greater emphasis than did these judges on the importance of evaluating the plaintiff's decision not to sue from the objective standpoint of a reasonable person, of insisting that the circumstances must be such that a person in Mrs. Novak's position could not reasonably have brought an action at the time the right to do so first arose, and of requiring that the factors inducing the decision to delay suing must be serious, significant and compelling. We must therefore consider anew the facts of the case on appeal, in light of the test here proposed.

One starts with the motions judge's holding that the primary limitation period began to run in October 1990. Therefore, without a postponement, the two-year limitation period prescribed by s. 3(2)(a) would have expired in October 1992. The motions judge also held that, before that time, Mrs. Novak had sufficient knowledge of the facts that, had she obtained the appropriate advice a reasonable person would have taken on those facts, she would have been advised that she had the right to bring an action and that such an action would have had a reasonable prospect of success. The provisions of s. 6(4)(a) were therefore met prior to the expiry of the primary limitation period.

However, s. 6(4) postpones the running of time until *both* s. 6(4)(a) and s. 6(4)(b) are satisfied. Section 6(4)(b) requires an analysis of Mrs. Novak's interests and circumstances at the time she considered and decided against bringing an action prior to the expiration of the primary limitation period. Having identified these interests and circumstances, one then asks whether those interests and circumstances were so serious, significant and compelling that she could not reasonably bring an action within the limitation period. If those circumstances and interests were not so pressing—if they were tactical, trivial or unreasonable, for example—they cannot serve as a basis for postponing the running of the limitation period under s. 6(4)(b).

Mrs. Novak's personal interests and circumstances prior to the expiry of the primary limitation period were these. Between 1990 and the summer of 1991 she was extremely ill. She had undergone a partial radical mastectomy and was receiving debilitating radiation treatment and chemotherapy for her breast cancer. She was just starting "to get back on [her] feet" in the summer of 1991 when her father died, presenting her with new difficulties. She actively considered starting an action in the late summer or fall of 1991. She described her decision not to sue in these terms:

... I tossed it about and tossed it about and thought, well do I have the strength to really go
through this at this stage of the game? And I talked to my parish priest about it and thought,
well I'm well, I have to believe that I'm well, I have to believe that I've been cured, if I go for
litigation it brings back all the horrible memories and I won't at this point, we'll wait to see
for a few years what's going to happen down the road.

In fact, Mrs. Novak had reason to believe herself cured at this point. She had no symptoms of cancer from April 1991 to May 1995.

Hall JA summarized Mrs. Novak's situation (at p. 113) as follows:

... the plaintiff ... , after her initial surgery, was determined to devote all her energies to attempting to recover from her illness and took the not unreasonable view that expending
time and energy on a lawsuit that would largely concentrate on what she hoped were minimal future contingencies would be harmful to her.

Having concluded that these were Mrs. Novak's "interests" and "circumstances" under
s. 6(4)(b), he held, at p. 113, that:

People ought to be encouraged to take reasonable steps short of litigation to cope with their
problems. I consider that what this plaintiff did accorded not only with good public policy
but was clearly in her own best interests. It was far better for her to maintain a positive attitude and concentrate on the hopes of a continuing healthy life as opposed to dwelling on the
possibility of a recurrence of illness.

Although I disagree that the test is what is in Mrs. Novak's "best interests," I nonetheless agree with Hall JA's assessment of her situation. More importantly in light of the test
here proposed, I am also satisfied that her concerns were so serious, substantial and
compelling that, taking into account all of her circumstances and interests, she could not
reasonably have commenced a suit at the time the cause of action first arose. She certainly did not approach the matter lightly, going so far as to consult her parish priest. Nor is
there any evidence that her decision was taken for tactical reasons. She was concerned
with nothing less than how to maintain her threatened hold on life, a serious and compelling concern by any measure. She hoped that her health would improve and that her
cancer would not recur. In light of these interests and circumstances, Mrs. Novak decided against bringing an action against Dr. Bond, a proceeding that would have required
her to prove the likely recurrence of the very cancer she was trying so desperately to
eradicate. I am satisfied that, in light of her own particular interests and circumstances
at the time, Mrs. Novak could not reasonably have sued Dr. Bond in the spring of 1991.

Mrs. Novak's determination to get better continued after 1991 and, for a time, it
seemed that the cancer no longer posed a threat. However, her interests and circumstances changed dramatically in May 1995. It was then that she learned that her cancer
had returned, this time to her spine, liver, and lung. She no doubt understood that she
was in great jeopardy and that her previous attempts to regain her health and avoid any
harm that may have been caused by Dr. Bond's alleged negligence had been to no avail.
The circumstances that precluded a decision to sue earlier—the need to maintain a positive outlook and believe herself cured—were no longer operative. Absent these considerations, her need to redress the serious wrong allegedly done to her and her consequent

willingness to undergo the stresses and strains of litigation outweighed her intensely felt desire to concentrate on regaining her health. Litigation became a realistic option.

After May 1995, it is my view that a reasonable person would consider that, taking into account her own unique interests and circumstances, Mrs. Novak "ought to be able" to bring an action, i.e., that she reasonably could bring an action. Section 6(4)(b) of the *Limitation Act* therefore postponed the running of time to at least that date. Because this action was brought by Mrs. Novak and her husband within two years of May 1995, it follows that it is not barred by s. 3(2)(a) of the Act. Neither is it barred by the ultimate limitation period of six years prescribed by s. 8(1) of the Act, running from the time the right to bring the action arose in October 1990.

VII. Conclusion

I would dismiss the appeal and confirm the Court of Appeal's order that the order of the motions judge be set aside and the action permitted to proceed. The respondent shall have her costs in this Court and in the courts below.

[Lamer CJ and Iacobucci and Major JJ dissented, agreeing on the test propounded by the majority, but arguing that the test was not the test applied in reaching the majority decision.]

A number of provinces have enacted specific discoverability provisions in their limitations statutes. For example, Ontario's *Limitations Act, 2002* provides that:

> 5(1) A claim is discovered on the earlier of,
>> (a) the day on which the person with the claim first knew,
>>> (i) that the injury, loss or damage had occurred,
>>> (ii) that the injury, loss or damage was caused by or contributed to by an act or omission,
>>> (iii) that the act or omission was that of the person against whom the claim is made, and
>>> (iv) that, having regard to the nature of the injury, loss or damage, a proceeding would be an appropriate means to seek to remedy it; and
>> (b) the day on which a reasonable person with the abilities and in the circumstances of the person with the claim first ought to have known of the matters referred to in clause (a).
> (2) A person with a claim shall be presumed to have known of the matters referred to in clause (1)(a) on the day the act or omission on which the claim is based took place, unless the contrary is proved.

The common law doctrine of discoverability does not apply to extend the limitation period in claims where the timing of an event upon which a limitation period is based is unrelated to the plaintiff's knowledge. See, for example, *Ryan v. Moore*, [2005] 2 SCR 53, where the trigger of the limitation period was the death of a party, not the knowledge of injury or death by a party.

C. Capacity

Courts and legislatures have also held that it is unfair to have a plaintiff's claim expire due to lapse of a limitation period when that plaintiff suffers from some incapacity that prevents him or her from taking the necessary steps toward starting a lawsuit to exercise his or her legal rights. Incapacity may be a result of age or of some psychological incapacity. If a plaintiff is incapacitated or under some legal disability (such as a minor), the limitation period is stalled, or tolled. Ontario's *Limitations Act, 2002*, for example, provides for such tolling in s. 6 for minors and s. 7 for those suffering from mental incapacity.

The steps involved in initiating a legal claim are not simple steps. A potential plaintiff must not only have the capacity necessary to pass the discoverability test (i.e., be able to establish the connection between the injury suffered and the defendant's fault). A plaintiff must also be able to contact a lawyer or direct someone to do so on the plaintiff's behalf. That plaintiff must be able to balance the risks of starting litigation, be able to understand legal advice given, and be able to direct someone about whether or not to take procedural steps necessary to preserve the right to sue. These are not simplistic considerations and require some level of cognitive capacity. For example, in *Bannon v. City of Thunder Bay*, [2002] 1 SCR 716, the Supreme Court of Canada tolled the 7-day notice period for the plaintiff in that case who was in the hospital and on pain medication. While she was able to perform some simple functions of living, such as eating and speaking, she was incapable of directing her mind to the more intricate steps of determining whether or not to sue for her injuries. Perhaps capacity to commence a lawsuit may best be measured by a "business transactions" threshold, where a court asks whether or not a reasonable plaintiff in the plaintiff's position has the capacity to undertake a business transaction of similar seriousness and complexity as the commencement of a lawsuit. Such was suggested in Erik S. Knutsen, "Limitation Periods and the Symbiosis of Capacity and Discoverability," in T. Archibald and M. Cochrane, eds., *Annual Review of Civil Litigation 2002* (Toronto: Carswell, 2003), at 237-53.

D. Ultimate Limitation Periods

In order to further the tenuous balance between plaintiffs' and defendants' rights, and partly in answer to the development and proliferation of the discoverability doctrine, some provinces have enacted ultimate limitation periods, which are absolute upper-limit limitation periods that cannot be tolled by the discoverability doctrine. The time clock for ultimate limitation periods begins on the date the act or omission on which the claim is based took place, not on the date the claim is discovered by the plaintiff. For example, in Ontario, the ultimate limitation period is 15 years. No claim can be pursued after 15 years have passed since the events giving rise to the claim took place. In British Columbia, the ultimate limitation period is 30 years, except for claims against a hospital or medical practitioner for negligence, in which case the ultimate limitation period is 6 years. In Alberta, the ultimate limitation period is 10 years. Ultimate limitation periods do not exist for causes of action for which there is no limitation period at all.

NOTES AND QUESTIONS

1. Why is there such a wide range among different provinces in Canada for each province's ultimate limitation period for most legal claims, from 10 years to 30 years (the one claim-specific exception being British Columbia's 6-year ultimate limitation period for claims against physicians and hospitals)?

2. Why do physicians and hospitals enjoy such a short ultimate limitation period—6 years—in British Columbia?

3. If limitation periods in general favour defendants, and if discoverability is an attempt to redress the imbalance created by strict adherence to limitation periods in some individual instances, why is it necessary to have an "ultimate" limitation period at all? Does not discoverability achieve the same results? Is the price of a defendant's peace really equivalent to the eclipsing of a plaintiff's claim?

4. How might insurance concerns influence and drive the enactment of ultimate limitation periods? Are these concerns real or illusory? For a critical evaluation of ultimate limitation periods, see Erik S. Knutsen, "The Ultimate Limitation Period: Updating the Limitation Act" (2003), 39 *Can. Business LJ* 148.

5. Limitation issues are litigated with remarkable frequency. The greatest proportion of cases about limitation periods involve those who have suffered personal injuries. England and Wales have made a policy choice to not have an ultimate limitation period for victims of personal injury. Might such a policy in Canada achieve desirable cost savings in litigation and streamlining of legal issues to focus on the merits, instead of the procedure, of claims?

6. Limitation periods are creatures of statute and, as such, are subject to the same tenets of statutory interpretation as other statutes. However, because limitation statutes have such a dramatic effect on a person's right to sue—the potential extinguishing of such a right—they are subject to a highly contextual reading. For example, in *York Condominium Corp. v. Jay-M Holdings Ltd.* (2007), 84 OR (3d) 414 (CA), a case about Ontario's ultimate limitation period, the court held that limitation statues are to be read in their ordinary grammatical sense in context, and with the purpose and intent of the legislature in mind. In addition, the court stressed that the statute should be liberally construed in favour of the person seeking to pursue his or her claim. Is this the correct balance to strike when interpreting what are, at heart, defence-sensitive statutes?

7. In order to argue a missed limitation period as a defence, defendants often have to prove that there would be no prejudice to them if the claim were allowed to proceed (i.e., if discoverability were invoked by the plaintiff). Prejudice can be established if a defendant can prove that some evidence has disappeared which would unduly prejudice the defence of the claim. For example, witnesses may have died or moved away, evidence may have been destroyed, or the passage of time might make the evidence too stale in the memories of witnesses. In *Coutanche v. Napoleon Delicatessen* (2004), 72 OR (3d) 122 (CA), the Court of Appeal for Ontario rejected a college defendant's argument that it would be prejudiced if the plaintiff's three-year and three-month-old claim went ahead, despite the passing of the limitation period. The plaintiff sued in negligence both a college alleged to have served alcohol to the deceased student as well as the drivers who struck and killed the student. The plaintiff in that case had been awaiting a report from the Alcohol and Gaming Commission that would have assisted her with establishing liability against that college defendant. The court

held that the report, for her, may have been necessary to provide some missing facts. However, the plaintiff's lawsuit against the defendant drivers was held to be statute-barred as it was commenced past the two-year limitation period. The plaintiff knew the identity and fault of those defendant drivers and there was no excuse for not starting the claim, even though the plaintiff had some communication difficulties with her lawyer. How often do you think a defendant can successfully establish prejudice if the claim is allowed to go ahead when a plaintiff invokes the discoverability doctrine? Also, is it fair to punish a plaintiff by extinguishing her claim when, in fact, it was the fault of her lawyer that a limitation period was missed? How difficult might it be to pursue a claim for negligence against the lawyer?

E. Notice Periods

Notice periods parallel limitation periods in general operation and effect. Certain specific legislation may require a potential plaintiff to provide written notice to a potential defendant within a prescribed time period as a condition precedent to bringing an eventual lawsuit. The plaintiff's claim is barred if the plaintiff fails to provide such notice on time. Many government entities require notice to be given before a legal claim is launched. For example, s. 7(1) of Ontario's *Proceedings Against the Crown Act* requires that, 60 days before launching a lawsuit against the Crown, potential plaintiffs serve a notice of claim with sufficient particulars to identify the claim. Section 44(1) of Ontario's *Municipal Act, 2001* requires that plaintiffs contemplating suing a municipality for injury on a highway or bridge provide written notice to the city within 10 days of the accident. See also s. 286 of British Columbia's *Local Government Act* for similar requirements.

Notice periods are designed to alert the defendant to a pending lawsuit. This prompts a potential defendant to not only preserve evidence but, in some instances, even rectify an unsafe or undesirable situation. Some notice periods are remarkably short—a matter of days. This tends to indicate that the legislature put a premium on time for reasons of evidence preservation and maintenance of safety.

NOTES AND QUESTIONS

1. Is a notice period of a matter of days too short, considering the complex decision analysis required when a plaintiff is considering launching a lawsuit? See, for example, *Bannon v. City of Thunder Bay*, [2002] 1 SCR 716, which involved a plaintiff who was unable to comply with a seven-day notice period that was a required preliminary step at that time before suing municipalities for injuries resulting from a slip and fall on ice and snow.

2. Why is it that legislatures see the need to protect government entities with not only limitation periods but notice periods as well? Are these "double" limitation periods necessary? Are they unfair to potential plaintiffs who have two time-frames about which to worry?

IV. SERVICE OF ORIGINATING PROCESS

A. Personal Service and Alternatives

The rules of court in every province and territory require commencement documents to be personally served on the party or parties against whom a claim is being made (i.e., the defendant(s)). Generally, personal service means leaving a copy of the commencement document with the party being sued; however, the rules also provide specific methods of achieving personal service, depending on the capacity of the party being served. For example, the rules typically provide for different methods of personally serving an individual, a corporation, an unincorporated association, an infant, and a mental incompetent. After service of the commencement document, subsequent documents are usually served on each party's solicitor of record. The rules generally provide for various methods of achieving such non-personal service, including service by mail, by facsimile, by courier, and by e-mail.

The requirement for personal service of commencement documents is designed to ensure that a party being sued receives adequate notice of the commencement of proceedings and to permit the court to take jurisdiction over the party being sued. While these are important objectives, the requirement for personal service can also be used as a technical defence by a recalcitrant defendant. The following case illustrates the court's attempt to reconcile the need for adequate notice with the need to discourage a defendant from relying upon a technical deficiency in service to avoid a civil claim.

Rupertsland Mortgage Investment Ltd. v. Winnipeg
(1981), 23 CPC 208 (Man. Co. Ct.)

JEWERS CO. CT. J: This case raises the question of whether documents have been personally served when the process server has not himself delivered them to, but they have nevertheless reached, the intended recipient.

Rupertsland Mortgage Investment is appealing against four orders issued by the City of Winnipeg Health Department pursuant to the *Public Health Act* of Manitoba, CCSM 1970, c. P.210 requiring Rupertsland to effect certain repairs and do certain things at 530 Croydon Avenue in the City, being residential premises owned by Rupertsland.

One of the grounds of appeal is that the orders were not properly served upon Rupertsland. If that is a valid ground of appeal, consideration of other grounds of appeal raised by Rupertsland would not be necessary.

A sheriff's officer delivered two copies of the orders to Esther Matz at 187 Montrose Street in the City of Winnipeg on December 30, 1980. That address is the head office and business address of Rupertsland. Mrs. Matz is neither a director nor officer, nor employee, of Rupertsland, but she is the company's solicitor. As well, she is the wife of the sole director of Rupertsland, Mr. Waldemar H. Matz. Mrs. Matz is not authorized to accept service of process on Rupertsland. Nevertheless, she accepted delivery of the orders and, in turn, delivered them to her husband who received them not later than December 31, 1980. The question is whether, in these circumstances, the documents can be said to have been personally served upon Rupertsland.

The City of Winnipeg was proceeding pursuant to revised regulation P210-R3, being a regulation respecting sanitation under the *Public Health Act*. Section 6(1) of that regulation provides that, where the medical officer of health or an inspector becomes aware of the existence of any insanitary condition, he shall serve on the person responsible, a written order to abate the condition. The Act does not expressly authorize substituted service and, unless authorized by statute, there is no substitute for personal service. See *Smith v. Smith* (1952), 7 WWR (NS) 163, affirmed 9 WWR (NS) 144, 61 Man. R 105, [1953] 3 DLR 682 (CA). There is no doubt that Rupertsland is the person responsible for any alleged insanitary condition, and so the service of the orders must be effected personally on Rupertsland.

There is no definition in the Act or the Regulations of "personal service." A good discussion of what is meant by the term "personal service" may be found in the case of *Orazio v. Ciulla* (1966), 57 WWR 641, 59 DLR (2d) 208 (BCSC) a decision of Kirke Smith LJSC. That learned Judge adopted, as I do, the following statement of Lord Cransworth LC in *Hope v. Hope* (1854), 4 De GM & G 328, 43 ER 534 [at 664 WWR]:

> The object of all service is of course only to give notice to the party on whom it is made, so that he may be made aware of and may be able to resist that which is sought against him; and when that has been substantially done, so that the Court may feel perfectly confident that service has reached him, everything has been done that is required.

In the instant case, the object referred to by Lord Cranworth has been attained. Mr. Matz, a responsible officer of Rupertsland, actually received the orders not later than December 31st, 1980, and was fully apprised of their contents. The material makes it clear that he read the orders and knew precisely what was required of Rupertsland. Does it legally make any difference that the orders were not given to him directly by the process server but rather through the intermediary, Mrs. Matz?

The case of *Re Consiglio*, [1971] 3 OR 798 (MC), a decision of Senior Master Rodger, is instructive. In the headnote of that case, which dealt with an application to set aside a writ on the ground that it had not been personally served, it is stated that, "If the writ comes to the knowledge, or into the possession, of the person to be served, either directly or indirectly from a third party, then it may be found that there has been personal service."

In that case, the process server attempted to serve the writ upon the defendant's brother-in-law, outside of certain residential premises, in the mistaken belief that the brother-in-law was the proper party to be served. The brother-in-law refused to accept the document and went into the premises, whereupon the process server followed, and, as the brother-in-law closed the door of the premises, the server threw the papers between the screen and the door. The Senior Master held that, if it could be established that the papers had actually come into the possession of the defendant, it could be considered that there has been personal service upon him. He therefore ordered the brother-in-law to attend and be cross-examined on an affidavit which he had filed in the proceedings, so that he could answer questions bearing upon that point.

In the course of his reasons, the Senior Master referred to the following cases:

(a) *O'Neil v. O'Neil* (1913), 4 WWR 478, 11 DLR 440, a Saskatchewan decision in which there was obiter to the effect that, if the plaintiff could show that a copy of

the writ ultimately came to the knowledge or possession of the defendant, the
Court would have been disposed to allow the service of the writ to stand;

(b) *Rhodes v. Innes* (1831), 7 Bing. 329, 131 ER 127, where a copy of the writ enclosed
in a letter was left with the defendant's son at the defendant's residence; the son
was asked to give the letter to his father, which he promised to do, and such service was held to be equivalent to personal service;

(c) *Vidito v. Veinot* (1912), 3 DLR 179, 10 ELR 292, where the writ of summons was
given to the defendant's wife and there was evidence that she had given it to her
husband on the same day when he returned from his work (that, of course, is essentially the case at Bar);

(d) *Phillips v. Ensell* (1834), 1 CM & R 374, 149 ER 1124, where the writ was given to
the defendant's brother living in the same house and where, because it was not
sworn that the writ did not come to the knowledge or possession of the defendant, the application to set aside the writ was refused.

It is clear, then, that there is precedent for the proposition that, for "personal service"
to be effected, the process need not be delivered directly by the process server to the intended recipient, just as long as the party to be served actually does receive the process
into his possession. I am content to adopt and follow these precedents, which recognize,
and apply, the essential principle: that the whole purpose of service is to apprise, and give
a party notice of, proceedings intended to be taken against him, and if that object has
been satisfied, and the process has actually reached the party, the precise manner in
which that has occurred should not be of concern.

I hold, therefore, that, in this case, the orders were personally served upon the appellant, Rupertsland, on December 31st, 1980.

NOTES AND QUESTIONS

1. Consider the rule for service in your province. What would constitute valid service of
an originating process on Rupertsland if it were in your province? Would the facts in that
case constitute valid or potentially valid service in your province? What specific rules would
you rely on?

2. In *Bhatnager v. Canada (Minister of Employment and Secretary of State for External Affairs)* (1990), 71 DLR (4th) 84, the issue before the Supreme Court of Canada was whether
two ministers could be held in contempt for disobeying a court order to produce immigration files when the order was served on government lawyers but not on the ministers personally. The Supreme Court held unanimously that personal service was necessary, overturning
a decision of the Federal Court of Appeal that the federal rules authorized service on the solicitor. Sopinka J stated:

On the cases, there can be no doubt that the common law has always required personal service
or actual personal knowledge of a court order as a precondition to liability in contempt. Almost
two centuries ago, in *Kimpton v. Eve* (1813), 2 V & B 349, 35 ER 352, Lord Chancellor Eldon
held that a party could not be held liable in contempt in the face of uncontradicted evidence
that he or she had no knowledge of the order. In *Ex parte Langley* (1879), 13 Ch. D 110 (CA),
Thesiger LJ stated the principle as follows, at p. 119:

… the question in each case, and depending upon the particular circumstances of the case, must be, was there or was there not such a notice given to the person who is charged with contempt of Court that you can infer from the facts that he had notice in fact of the order which had been made? And, in a matter of this kind, bearing in mind that the liberty of the subject is to be affected, I think that those who assert that there was such a notice ought to prove it beyond reasonable doubt.

More recently, this Court adverted to the knowledge requirement in contempt in *Baxter Travenol Laboratories of Canada Ltd. v. Cutter (Canada), Ltd.*, [1983] 2 SCR 388, per Dickson J (as he then was), at pp. 396-97.

This lengthy history of a strict requirement at common law that the party alleging contempt must prove actual knowledge on the part of the alleged contemnor is inconsistent with the submission that a rebuttable presumption arises in every case upon service of the order on the solicitor. In my opinion, a finding of knowledge on the part of the client may in some circumstances be inferred from the fact that the solicitor was informed. Indeed, in the ordinary case in which a party is involved in isolated pieces of litigation, the inference may readily be drawn. In the case of Ministers of the Crown who administer large departments and are involved in a multiplicity of proceedings, it would be extraordinary if orders were brought, routinely, to their attention. In order to infer knowledge in such a case, there must be circumstances which reveal a special reason for bringing the order to the attention of the Minister. Knowledge is in most cases (including criminal cases) proved circumstantially, and in contempt cases the inference of knowledge will always be available where facts capable of supporting the inference are proved: see *Avery v. Andrews* (1882), 51 LJ Ch. 414.

This does not mean that Ministers will be able to hide behind their lawyers so as to flout orders of the court. Any instructions to the effect that the Minister is to be kept ignorant may attract liability on the basis of the doctrine of wilful blindness. Furthermore, the fact that a Minister cannot be confident in any given case that the inference will not be drawn will serve as a sufficient incentive to see to it that officials are impressed with the importance of complying with court orders.

Applying the foregoing to this case, it is plain that Strayer J did not infer knowledge on the part of the Ministers in the circumstances; nor did the Court of Appeal. Indeed, for reasons which I shall address shortly, Urie J imputed the requisite knowledge to the appellants in such a way that even conclusive proof of an absence of knowledge on their part would not have availed. There is, therefore, no finding of fact on the record that the appellants had knowledge of the order of August 15. Neither is one warranted. Accordingly, at common law they cannot be held liable in contempt.

· · ·

The respondent, supporting Urie J's judgment, claims that these rules provide a comprehensive code for effecting notice of court orders. Urie J held that the service of the order on the appellants' counsel created a "presumption of proper notice" that could be rebutted only if the appellants led evidence to show that their counsel acted without authority in accepting service. The appellants reject this interpretation of the Rules and, taking the matter one step further, argue that if the Rules were interpreted to have this effect they would be *ultra vires* the rule-making power granted to the judges of the Federal Court by s. 46 of the *Federal Court Act*.

With respect to Urie J, I cannot interpret the *Federal Court Rules* as having the effect he ascribed to them, apart altogether from any Charter considerations that might have come into play if I had held otherwise. While it is true that there are provisions in the Rules for personal service (e.g., Rule 355(4)), it does not follow that the permission in Rule 308 to effect service other than personally is determinative of the issue of knowledge in a contempt of court proceeding. The relevant Rules define what is effective service for the purposes of the expeditious conduct of litigation in the Federal Court, but they do not purport to detract from the elements necessary to establish contempt. It seems to me that a crucial requirement for the proof of a serious offence such as contempt of court could not be implicitly abrogated by a provision in subordinate legislation; such an alteration of the general law would require explicit language. As Hogg JA stated in *Re Gordon MacKay & Co. and Dominion Rubber Co.*, [1946] 3 DLR 422 (Ont. CA), at p. 425:

> The common law rights of the subject are not to be taken away or affected except only to such extent as may be necessary to give effect to the intention of Parliament when clearly expressed or when such result must follow by necessary implication, and if the rights of persons are encroached upon, this intention must be made manifest by the language of the statute, if not by express words then by clear implication and beyond reasonable doubt.

It cannot be doubted that the knowledge of a solicitor is the knowledge of the client for some purposes, particularly in civil cases in which an individual's knowledge of the status of a commercial transaction is at issue: see *Bank of British North America v. St. John & Quebec R. Co.* (1920), 52 DLR 557 (NBCA); aff'd. (1921), 62 SCR 346; *Re Botiuk and Collision* (1979), 26 OR (2d) 580 (CA), per Wilson JA (as she then was), at p. 589; and *Re National Trust Co. and Bouckhuyt* (1987), 61 OR (2d) 640 (CA), per Cory JA (as he then was), at pp. 643-44. While this principle of imputation of knowledge is a necessary feature of our adversary system of civil litigation, in which representation by counsel is the rule rather than the exception, it ought not to apply in the criminal or quasi-criminal context of a contempt prosecution in the absence of express legislative language to the contrary. As the *Federal Court Rules* do not contain such language, it is unnecessary to deal with the argument that the Rules are *ultra vires*.

The Supreme Court saw personal service of the order as an important element of due process before the two ministers were exposed to possible incarceration as a result of a finding of contempt for disobeying the order. Do the same type of considerations apply in the civil context?

3. Why is there the insistence that the originating process must be served on the defendant personally? Can we design more convenient and less expensive methods of service that will ensure that the defendant receives actual notice of the proceeding?

One alternative to personal service has long been recognized. Personal service of the originating process is not necessary where the solicitor for the defendant accepts service on behalf of the defendant. This is a useful procedure for a plaintiff because it avoids the necessity of finding and serving the defendant. Obviously, though, it can be used only if the plaintiff knows the defendant is represented in the matter and the solicitor is prepared to accept service. It may only occur, however, where the solicitor is authorized by the client to accept service.

Some jurisdictions have gone much further in relaxing the requirement of personal service by providing that adequate service can be achieved by mail and by leaving a copy of the document at the residence of the person to be served with a person who appears to be an adult member of the household. Are such relaxations of the requirements of personal service appropriate?

B. Substitutional Service

Although the rules typically require personal service of a commencement document on a defendant, in some cases this may be impossible to achieve. For example, the defendant may be actively trying to avoid service or the location of the defendant may be unknown. To overcome this problem, and to prevent the plaintiff from being stopped in his or her tracks by the inability to serve the defendant personally, every jurisdiction has rules permitting the courts to authorize a substitutional form of service or to dispense with service when personal service cannot practically be achieved. To successfully obtain an order for substitutional service, a plaintiff is usually required to demonstrate that personal service is impractical or impossible and that the proposed alternative service method has a reasonable possibility of bringing the claim to the defendant's attention. For an order dispensing with service, a plaintiff typically must prove that all reasonable attempts have been made to serve the defendant and that it is in the interests of justice to permit the action to proceed despite the lack of service. As illustrated by the following excerpt, in considering alternatives to personal service, a court's primary consideration is complying as near as possible with the principle of natural justice which affords every person adequate notice of proceedings commenced against him or her.

Gallacher v. Hashim
[1989] OJ No. 1642 (HC)

DANDIE LJSC: The petitioner wife asks for an order dispensing with the service of the petition of divorce on the grounds that the petitioner has no knowledge of the whereabouts of the respondent and on the further ground that the respondent suffers from schizophrenia and has threatened the petitioner's life in the past and that the petitioner is fearful that the respondent may become violent and attack her upon receipt of the petition. Rule 16.04(1) reads as follows:

> 16.04(1) Where it appears to the court that it is impractical for any reason to effect prompt service of an originating process or any other document required to be served personally or by an alternative to personal service under these rules, the court may make an order for substituted service or, where necessary in the interest of justice, may dispense with service.

Service of a process is so fundamental to our system of justice that it would appear, at first blush, that the present application should be denied. It is clear to me that there are two branches to Rule 16.04(1), namely where it appears to the Court that it is impractical to serve the document and where it is necessary in the interests of justice, the Court may dispense with service. It may be that when a petitioner has reasonable cause to fear for his or her life in the event a petition is served on the respondent, that service of the petition may be dispensed with. Although such relief may be available, the issue must be established by more than an affidavit of the petitioner. The least degree of proof required is an opinion by the attending psychiatrist, Dr. Ahmed, that service needs to be dispensed with. It is apparent from the material that such a letter will not be forthcoming and I am not prepared to dispense with service in these circumstances on the untested affidavit of the petitioner. As the relief asked is for an order dispensing with service, the motion is denied. I would think that if the petitioner were to make an application asking for substitutional service upon Dr. Ahmed and provided there are sufficient facts to determine that the petition will come to the respondent's attention then I might be persuaded to order substitutional service upon Dr. Ahmed.

NOTES AND QUESTIONS

1. Do you agree with this decision? Why would it matter in this case whether the respondent husband was served or not? Would it be wise to order substituted service on Dr. Ahmed? What will he do with the commencement document?

2. An order for substitutional service is obtained by applying to the court "ex parte" (that is, without notice). What facts do you think the plaintiff will have to set forth in his supporting affidavit to obtain this order?

3. Common modes of substitutional service include: by mail addressed to the defendant at his or her last known address; by delivery to a person who is shown to be in communication with the defendant or likely to be in communication—for example, the spouse or other relative of the defendant or a solicitor known to have represented the defendant in other matters; by delivery to the defendant's last known address; or by advertisement in a newspaper circulating in the area where the defendant is believed to be living. More recently, taking advantage of Internet technology, courts in Canada and in Australia have permitted substitutional service by posting notice on the defendant's Facebook page.

4. The relevant considerations in deciding whether service should be dispensed with are the same whether service is attempted pursuant to provincial rules of court or pursuant to international agreements (such as the Hague convention). See *Zhang v. Jiang* (2006), 82 OR (3d) 306 (SCJ).

5. In motor vehicle litigation, because of liability insurance, the named defendant is often not the "real" defendant that the plaintiff seeks to bring into the action. The plaintiff is seeking to involve the defendant's motor vehicle liability insurer. The defendant's insurer is entitled and required by the policy to take charge of defending the action and to pay any judgment issued against the defendant. Further, provincial legislation provides the insurer with an independent right to involve itself in the claim against the defendant insured. In cases where the named defendant cannot be found, and an application for substituted service is made, the court must, in effect, decide whether the injured plaintiff or the insurer should bear the risk of the defendant's disappearance. If the insurer has notice of the claim, why should the court require that the named defendant be served? Is it fair to force the insurer to defend without the assistance of the defendant? Would the defendant be prejudiced in any way? Consider the solution adopted by Cory J in *Meius v. Pippy* (1980), 20 CPC 215 (Ont. HC), excerpted below, a decision followed and approved in *Kalser et al. v. Brine* (1981), 126 DLR (3d) 190; aff'd. 133 DLR (3d) 512 (Ont. Div. Ct.):

In this case the plaintiff has taken every reasonable step to locate the defendant, Pippy. When the sheriff was unable to effect service at the last noted addresses of Patricia Pippy, a special investigator was retained. The special investigator, by his report, indicated that Patricia Pippy was no longer within the jurisdiction and could not be located. An application was then made for the substitutional service upon the insurer.

On behalf of the insurer it has been argued firstly, that there is no indication that the insurer was able to conduct its investigation at least to the extent of conferring with its insured, the defendant Pippy. Secondly, it was pointed out that in light of the difficulty the insurer would have in producing Pippy for discovery that substitutional service ought not to be permitted.

The material indicates that the insurer was sufficiently satisfied with its investigations to confirm in writing on two occasions that its "investigations" had reached such a stage that it was able to deny liability on behalf of its insured Pippy.

In light of the correspondence from the insurer, there is no prejudice at least at this stage in permitting the substitutional service. Further, I am satisfied that the plaintiff has taken all requisite steps and proceeded with all due diligence both with regard to the action itself and with regard to the attempts to locate the defendant Pippy. Substitutional service therefore should be permitted upon the defendant. I would ordinarily have been more concerned with the problems that would arise and beset the insurer in attempting to produce the missing Patricia Pippy for discovery. However, that problem has been resolved by the undertaking of counsel which is confirmed by this order that the plaintiff will not move to strike out the defence of the defendant Pippy if the insurer is unable to produce Patricia Pippy for discovery.

The application will therefore be granted. Costs in the cause.

Note that the courts have taken a different approach to liability insurance coverage that does not provide the insurer with the same rights and obligations as provided under statutorily mandated motor vehicle liability insurance. For example, in *Chambers v. Muslim*, [2007] OJ No. 3855, the Ontario Superior Court of Justice held that substitutional service on a professional liability insurer was not appropriate where the insurer did not know the whereabouts of the insured. The court held that an order dispensing with service on the insured was preferable in such a case.

C. Time for Service and Extensions

The *Rules of Civil Procedure* provide a fixed period of time for serving a commencement document on the defendant once the commencement document has been issued (filed with the court). This time period for service is distinct from, but related to, the statutory limitation period for commencing litigation. A limitation period is satisfied by the act of issuing the commencement document—an act that is not designed to come to the attention of the defendant. However, the ultimate purpose of a limitation period is timely notice to the defendant that he or she is being sued; this is not met by the mere issuing of the commencement document, but by service of this document on the defendant. Hence, in a real sense, the time limit for service by the rules forms part and parcel of the overall scheme of limitation periods.

The court has no general power to relieve against limitation periods. So, if the plaintiff fails to commence the action within the limitation period, the court cannot protect the plaintiff from the bar of the limitation period. Under the rules of civil procedure, however, the courts usually are authorized to extend the time for serving the commencement document, either through application of the general power of the court to extend time limits under the rules or pursuant to a specific power to "renew" the commencement document. What happens, however, if the plaintiff fails to serve the originating process within the time limit set by the rules and the relevant limitation period expires during that period of time? Consider the approach taken to this issue in the following case.

Buleychuk v. Danson
(1992), 8 OR (3d) 762 (Gen. Div.)

O'LEARY J: The issue on this appeal is the test to be applied where a solicitor asks the court to extend time for service of a statement of claim that he has failed to serve within the six-month period provided for in rule 14.08(1) of the *Rules of Civil Procedure*, O. Reg. 560/84.

The master, who refused to extend the time for service and from whose decision this appeal is taken, seems to have reasoned as follows.

(1) Not only had the six-month period for service of the statement of claim expired, but the statutory two-year limitation period for commencing an action under the *Highway Traffic Act*, RSO 1990, c. H.8, had also long expired by the time the solicitor asked the court to extend time for service.

(2) The statutory limitation period having expired, the principles laid down by the Court of Appeal in *Deaville v. Boegeman* (1984), 48 OR (2d) 725, 14 DLR (4th) 81, and *Aliferis v. Parfenuik* (1985), 1 CPC (2d) 41, 9 OAC 215, come into play, those principles being:

   (a) The expiry of a limitation period created by statute for the commencement of an action creates a presumption the defendant has been prejudiced through not having been served with the document that commenced the action.

   (b) The plaintiff must rebut (and here he has failed to rebut) this presumption of prejudice to the defendant before the court will extend time for service of the statement of claim and, presumably but not so expressed by the master, "special circumstances" or "exceptional circumstances" must exist before it can be said such prejudice has been rebutted.

(3) In any event, an order extending time for service of the statement of claim should be refused because to adopt the words of Lacourcière JA in *Laurin v. Foldesi* (1979), 23 OR (2d) 321, 96 DLR (3d) 503 (CA), this was "an unpardonable and inexcusable laxity" on the part of the plaintiffs' solicitor.

I agree with the learned master that *Deaville* and *Aliferis* appear to enunciate the principles he has outlined. I suggest, however, that based on their facts those two cases have little in common. In *Deaville* the Court of Appeal was dealing with the question as to when, following the expiry of a statutory limitation period, it is permissible to add a new plaintiff to an action that was commenced within the statutory limitation period. In

Aliferis the Court of Appeal was dealing with the question as to when it is proper to re-new a writ of summons issued within the statutory limitation period but not served within one year from the date it was issued as was required by the former Rules of Practice, RRO 1980, Reg. 540.

The court has no power (except to correct administrative error or avoid a fraud or like impropriety) to permit the commencement of an action that is barred by statute. It is not surprising then that the court allows a new plaintiff to be added beyond the statutory limitation period in only "special circumstances." That is the basis for the reasoning be-hind *Deaville*.

But once an action has been commenced within the period allowed by statute, as was the case in *Aliferis*, it is only a rule that requires service on the defendant within a speci-fied period. As was stated by MacKay JA in *Brown v. Humble*, [1959] OR 586, 21 DLR (2d) 38 (CA), at p. 594 OR, p. 55 DLR:

> I am in agreement with the statement of McRuer CJHC in the Robinson case [*Robinson v. Cornwall*, [1951] OR 587, [1951] 4 DLR 161] … . At p. 597 he said
>
> > With the greatest respect, I do not think there is a strict analogy between a case where a writ has been issued within the time allowed by a statute of limitations but not served until after the time has expired and one where no action is brought against a party until after the period has run.

The words of Laskin JA in *Clairmonte v. Canadian Imperial Bank of Commerce*, [1970] 3 OR 97, 12 DLR (3d) 425 (CA), at p. 113 OR, p. 441 DLR, are to the like effect but more enlightening:

> I say, with respect, that where an action has been commenced within the proper limitation period, there can be no pretence that any right of a defendant to rely on a limitation period is prejudiced, because the course of the action is protracted … . Indeed, to speak of preju-dice to the defendant on the basis of the expiry of a limitation period which would protect him only if the application to dismiss the action for want of prosecution succeeded, is to beg the very question that has to be decided; it is to use the results of success on the application as a ground for granting it.

It is evident then that the question before the court in *Aliferis* was quite different from that facing the court in *Deaville*. While Cory JA, speaking for the court in *Aliferis*, did say, "The disposition of this appeal is in accord with the most recent decision of this Court pertaining to extension of limitation periods: see *Deaville v. Boegeman* (1984), 48 OR (2d) 725," I suggest it is obvious that the ratio of the decision in *Aliferis* is that it is proper to renew a writ that has not been served when such renewal will not prejudice the defendant. Indeed Cory JA said as much at p. 43 CPC, pp. 216-17 OAC:

> With all due respect to the Judge hearing the motion, we are of the opinion that he erred in concluding that the plaintiff had failed to satisfy the onus resting upon him to demonstrate that the defendant would not be prejudiced by an order renewing the writ. Here the facts are quite exceptional and make it clear that the defendant will not, in fact, be prejudiced by an extension of time.

So even if this application had been dealt with under the former Rules of Practice, time for service should have been extended, for counsel for the defendant admitted before me that, save for the loss of the six-month time limit for service fixed by rule 14.08(1), the defendant will not be prejudiced by late service of the statement of claim.

I respectfully disagree with the learned master that Lacourcière JA in *Laurin v. Foldesi*, supra, purported to enunciate an inflexible rule that a plaintiff will be denied an extension of time for service where his solicitor has been guilty of unpardonable and inexcusable laxity. Rather, Lacourcière JA said in *Laurin*, at p. 323 OR, p. 505 DLR:

> The basic consideration in these matters is whether the renewal post diem will advance the just resolution of the dispute, without prejudice or unfairness to the parties.

That then was the test for renewal or extension of time for service under the former *Rules of Practice* and, in my view, remains the test under the *Rules of Civil Procedure*, which came into force in 1985. That such is the test can be established by the mere recitation of rules 1.04(1), 2.01(1) and 3.02(1) and (2):

> 1.04(1) These rules shall be liberally construed to secure the just, most expeditious and least expensive determination of every civil proceeding on its merits.
>
> 2.01(1) A failure to comply with these rules is an irregularity and does not render a proceeding or a step, document or order in a proceeding a nullity, and the court,
>
> (a) may grant all necessary amendments or other relief, on such terms as are just, to secure the just determination of the real matters in dispute; or ...
>
> 3.02(1) Subject to subrule (3), the court may by order extend or abridge any time prescribed by these rules or an order, on such terms as are just.
>
> (2) A motion for an order extending time may be made before or after the expiration of the time prescribed.

The court must then examine the facts in each case to determine whether time for service of the statement of claim can be extended and the terms on which such time can be extended in an effort to secure a just determination of the real matters in dispute.

The task of the court is easy and time for service should be extended where the defendant frankly admits, or it is in any event obvious, that extending time for service will cause the defendant no prejudice. Such is the case here.

This action arises out of a motor vehicle accident that occurred on January 30, 1987. The police accident report indicates that the defendant, who had been travelling westbound on Highway 26, lost control of his vehicle, crossed the centre line and came into collision with the plaintiffs' motor vehicle which had been travelling eastbound. It appears the defendant was completely responsible for the accident.

The plaintiffs retained a solicitor on February 6, 1987. On February 9, 1987 that solicitor sent a letter to the defendant, which reads as follows:

Re: *Buleychuk & Danson*—Auto Accident

We have been retained on behalf of Mr. & Mrs. Walter Buleychuk in connection with injuries and damages sustained by them in a motor vehicle accident which occurred on or about the 30th day of January, 1987.

> Please accept this correspondence as notice of an intention on the part of Mr. & Mrs. Buleychuk to claim prejudgment interest in connection with damages arising out of this accident.
>
> We understand that the adjuster will be in touch with us in due course.

The solicitor sent a copy of this letter to the Advocate Insurance Company, the defendant's insurer. On February 2, 1987, Advocate Insurance appointed A.W. Masterton to be its adjuster in the matter and he became aware on that date of the particulars surrounding the accident. Mr. Masterton had a telephone conversation with the plaintiff, Walter Buleychuk, on February 17, 1987. In October 1987 Masterton had a further telephone conversation with Walter Buleychuk at which time he obtained from Walter Buleychuk the name of his solicitor. Masterton could also have obtained that information from Advocate Insurance.

On January 29, 1988 Masterton telephoned the office of the plaintiffs' solicitor and left a message for him to contact Masterton with respect to the plaintiffs' claims. On February 11, 1988 the plaintiffs' solicitor's secretary telephoned Masterton's secretary and advised that medical reports on the plaintiffs' injuries would be forthcoming.

On April 12, 1988 Masterton wrote to the plaintiffs' solicitor as follows:

Re: Your Client: Buleychuk Our Insureds: Isobel & Barnett Danson Date of Loss: January 30, 1987

In February 1988 we contacted your office in an effort to learn the status of your client's claim. We were told you were awaiting medical reports.

Have you now received any medical reports on Mr. Buleychuk's condition? If so, we would be pleased to pay for the acquisition costs of those reports. If none have been obtained then perhaps now would be the appropriate time to have examinations done. Again, our principals would be willing to reimburse those costs.

It is my understanding that Mr. Buleychuk is back at work but we have no idea at this time as to the extent of the special damage claim and I would be grateful for an opportunity to discuss that portion of his claim so our principals can have an opportunity to reserve their funds accordingly.

In spite of further letters and telephone calls made during the following months to the office of the plaintiffs' solicitor, Masterton received no information about the plaintiffs' injuries. Finally, in January 1989, Masterton spoke to the plaintiffs' solicitor who advised him that he would send him medical reports with respect to the claims of both plaintiffs. The solicitor advised Masterton at that time that a statement of claim had been issued. On April 17, 1989 Masterton wrote to the solicitor again asking for medicals, details of the special damages and a copy of the statement of claim. Those were not sent to him. Not having heard from the solicitor, Masterton closed his file on this claim on December 11, 1989.

As indicated, the accident occurred January 30, 1987. If the plaintiffs had waited two years before issuing their statement of claim and then had waited a further six months before serving it, the defendant and his insurer might not have learned until approximately the end of July 1989 that he was being sued as a result of the accident. In fact the defendant, and perhaps more importantly his insurer, knew within a few days of the accident that the plaintiffs were claiming damages for their injuries.

The neglect and incompetence of the solicitor for the plaintiff is obvious and little is to be gained by dwelling on it. The fact is, however, it did not prejudice the defendant, that is to say, the evidence does not suggest that the defendant is less able because of it to defend in regard to liability or damages.

The statement of claim was issued December 20, 1988 and so should have been served by June 20, 1989. The solicitor's affidavit in support of his motion to extend the time for service of the statement of claim was sworn on May 10, 1990, although the evidence before me does not disclose just when the notice of motion was served. The fact that Advocate General Insurance Company, the defendant's insurer, went into receivership at some point has tended to delay this matter and the parties are in agreement that any delay since June 15, 1990, when the motion was first returnable, is not to be held against the plaintiffs.

Since the solicitor for the defendant admits that in fact the defendant has suffered no prejudice by the delay in serving the statement of claim and since the evidence in any event makes that obvious, the defendant should not have resisted the motion to extend time for service, unless he wanted some conditions attached to any order extending time for service. No such conditions have been asked for.

I, therefore, allow the appeal and extend time for service of the statement of claim for one month from this date. Costs both before me and before the master to the plaintiff in any event of the cause.

Appeal allowed.

NOTES AND QUESTIONS

1. Would the result have been different if the lawyer in *Danson* had failed to issue a statement of claim? Why?

2. What would have happened if the time for service had not been extended? Would the client have a good cause of action in negligence against the lawyer? To what extent do you think that factor played a role in the decision of the judge to extend service?

3. The issue of whether an extension for service should be allowed when the limitation period has expired is more likely to arise in jurisdictions where the court's power to extend the time for service is part of a general rule authorizing the court to extend time periods otherwise provided by the rules. The question is less likely to arise in jurisdictions where the court's power to extend the time for service is provided by a rule that specifically defines the circumstances in which a court can (and cannot) extend the service time.

The Scope of the Matter

I. INTRODUCTION

The doctrine of joinder, and that of *res judicata* is designed to prevent address the dilemma of duplicative litigation. While it generally becomes an issue only in subsequent litigation, from the outset it operates as a key consideration in framing the initial litigation. Duplicative litigation is a dilemma because more than one piece of litigation seeking to resolve a single dispute risks inconsistent decisions, extra burdens of time and expense on the parties, and a drain on public resources in the administration of justice.

If a plaintiff has a number of factually and legally related claims, and pursues each in a separate action, the rules permitting joinder will permit the court to exercise a broad discretion to merge or "join" these various claims together.

By virtue of this the doctrine, of *res judicata*, if one party sues another and the matter is resolved, the losing party cannot sue again either for the same cause of action or for a different cause of action that turns on the same issue. The goal is to provide closure and fairness to the winning parties in litigation and to ensure that scarce judicial resources are distributed efficiently. Binnie J, writing for a unanimous court in *Danyluk v. Ainsworth Technologies Inc.*, [2001] 2 SCR 460, discussed below, describes the doctrine this way (at para. 18):

> The law rightly seeks a finality to litigation. To advance that objective, it requires litigants to put their best foot forward to establish the truth of their allegations when first called upon to do so. A litigant, to use the vernacular, is only entitled to one bite at the cherry.

In the classic scenario of the same parties seeking to relitigate the same matter, the rationale and operation of *res judicata* is clear. However, where some of the parties to the relitigation of a matter are the same and some are not, the rationale is less clear. For the new parties, this relitigation represents their first "bite at the cherry." Is it fair to prevent their day in court? Also, in the classic scenario, both the litigation and the relitigation take place in court. How does the operation of *res judicata* change when the first or second proceeding takes place not in a court but before an administrative decision-maker such as a board, tribunal, or arbitrator? Does this amount to comparing cherries with raspberries? When deciding whether to prevent relitigation, does it matter whether the procedural protections and fairness of the first proceeding were adequate? Does *res judicata* amount to an automatic bar to relitigation or does it merely provide the judge with the discretion to prevent duplicative litigation? These questions are addressed below.

II. JOINDER OF CLAIMS

A. Introduction

Having considered a number of issues that must be addressed in the course of commencing litigation, we now turn to the rules governing which claims and parties may be included or joined together in a single proceeding. This subject is known as "joinder."

The starting point in any discussion of joinder is the proposition that the interests of both society and litigants are better served by one lawsuit than by several. It is usually more economical for the litigants and for the court system to litigate matters in one action than in numerous separate actions. In most cases, the trial in a single action of all the matters in dispute between the parties will take less time, trouble, and money than several actions. Thus, the gain to be derived from broad joinder is the convenience and utility of settling all differences between parties at one time. A further factor often favours a single action rather than a multiplicity of actions. If a plaintiff has a number of claims that are factually or legally related to each other, and pursues each in a separate action, there is a risk of different or inconsistent findings—and no recovery at all—on matters common to each claim. The law views the possibility of inconsistent verdicts as something to be avoided.

This general policy in favour of a single action rather than a multiplicity of actions is sometimes enshrined in statute—see, for example, s. 138 of the Ontario *Courts of Justice Act* ("[a]s far as possible, multiplicity of legal proceedings shall be avoided"); it is often referred to in cases interpreting and applying rules relating to joinder—see, for example *McNaughton v. Baker* (1988), 28 CPC (2d) 49 (BCCA). This policy is implemented, *inter alia*, by (1) rules making generous provision for the joinder of multiple claims and parties; (2) rules that prohibit the splitting of a cause of action and the relitigation of issues (the doctrine of *res judicata*); and (3) the practice of allowing either party to obtain consolidation or the trial of actions together. However, the policy in favour of joinder of claims and parties is not an absolute one. An unlimited right of joinder could lead to confusion and complexity, a situation that would result if too many diverse issues were attempted to be litigated in one action. Consequently, the court has a broad discretion to refuse to permit claims or parties to be joined in the same action. This is a discretion that will be exercised when it is demonstrated that fairness and trial convenience favour separate actions rather than a single action.

With some exceptions, the modern joinder rules allow parties and actions to be joined in almost any circumstances, leaving the court with a residual discretion to forbid joinder if it would lead to inconvenience or injustice. In the following sections, the emphasis is on explaining the situations in which the different mechanisms for joinder might be used and on identifying the limits that ought to be respected if the litigation is not to become so unwieldy and complex as to defeat the general objectives of efficiency and justice that led to liberal joinder rules in the first place.

In this section, we look at the scope of the plaintiff's entitlement through "permissive joinder" to increase the size of litigation beyond the simple situation of one plaintiff asserting one claim against one defendant. The plaintiff may do this by uniting (1) multiple claims against one defendant in one action (joinder of claims); (2) multiple plaintiffs, multiple defendants, or *both* in an action (joinder of parties); or (3) both multiple claims and multiple parties. Thus, in its most elaborate form, joinder may result in multiple plaintiffs suing multiple defendants on multiple claims.

The major issue is how far plaintiffs may go in joining multiple claims and parties in one action when they believe such joinder is desirable. In other words, what is the maximum size of the litigation using permissive joinder? We will see that the rules of procedure and the courts tend to be liberal in allowing permissive joinder. Why is this? When courts do confine joinder, is a consistent guideline applied?

A less obvious issue concerns the *minimum* size of the litigation. As we will see, rules exist that may compel a plaintiff in a narrow range of circumstances to join multiple parties and to assert multiple claims. The situation in which a plaintiff is required to join either parties or claims or both is referred to as compulsory joinder. How can requiring a plaintiff to add certain parties or claims be reconciled with party control of litigation, one of the hallmarks of the adversary system?

At common law, restrictive rules prevailed regarding the joinder of multiple claims and multiple parties. For an account of these rules, see Hazard, Fleming, and Leubsdorf, *Civil Procedure*, 5th ed. (2001), chapter 9. In the following pages, we concern ourselves only with the modern rules on the subject.

1. Permissive Joinder

Permissive joinder relates to circumstances where a plaintiff is permitted to join several claims in a single proceeding. See Ontario rules 5.01 and 5.05. Other examples are BC rule 5(1), Man. rule 5.01, NB rule 5.01, NS rule 5.01, and Sask. rule 35.

Stevens v. Sun Life Assurance Co. of Canada
2004 BCSC 468

ALLAN J:

Background

The plaintiff, Lorne Stevens, received Long Term Disability ("LTD") benefits from the defendant, Sun Life Assurance Company of Canada ("Sun Life"), until September 30, 2002, at which time Sun Life terminated those benefits. Mr. Stevens sued Sun Life, claiming that the insurer has breached its contractual obligation to pay LTD benefits to him (the contract claim) and has acted in bad faith (the bad faith claim). It is common ground that a bad faith claim continues throughout the litigation if the insurer continues to improperly deny LTD benefits to its insured.

In its statement of defence, Sun Life denies that Mr. Stevens was totally disabled after September 30, 2002, alleges that he suffered from a pre-existing disability, alleges that the plaintiff's disability is due to abuse of drugs or alcohol, and counterclaims for reimbursement of alleged over-payments. ...

Sun Life applies for an order pursuant to Rules 5(6) and 39(29) severing those portions of the statement of claim that deal with the bad faith claim and directing that the plaintiff's contract claim be determined before the bad faith claim. ...

Sun Life submits that severance is appropriate in the circumstances of this case. It says that when a plaintiff advances a contractual claim for insurance moneys in combination with a claim for extra-contractual punitive and aggravated damages for bad faith, a conflict is bound to arise between the insurer's right to solicitor–client privilege and the plaintiff's right to discovery in relation to the bad faith claims.

Sun Life also submits that it is "just and convenient" to sever the claims and try the contract claim first in order to prevent undue complexity, inconvenience and expense. The tort claim and the contract claim are two "distinct and separate causes of action."

Mr. Craig has deposed that the defendant has sought legal advice from its present counsel regarding Mr. Stevens' claims. Mr. Samuel, counsel for the defendant, submits that Sun Life should not be put in the position of having to defend the contract claim and, at the same time, disclose legal opinions relating to the subject matter of the contract claim because they are relevant to the bad faith claim.

The plaintiff contends that the contract and bad faith claims should not be severed for the following reasons:

- The court should exercise its discretion to sever only for "extraordinary, exceptional or compelling reasons" and not merely where it would be "just and convenient" to order severance.
- The plaintiff seeks to have the case heard by a jury and the balance of convenience and prejudice to Mr. Stevens favors the matter be heard at one trial to avoid different findings by two juries.
- The issues are interwoven and require the same witnesses and facts.
- Mr. Stevens is entitled to a single trial "as of right" and a single trial will not prejudice Sun Life.
- Severance would lead to increased time and costs. Having both claims heard at the same time would not unduly lengthen the trial.

· · ·

The Relevant Law

Rules 5(1) and 5(6) of the *Rules of Court* provide:

> 5(1) Subject to subrule (6) a person, whether claiming in the same or different capacities, may join several claims in the same proceeding.
>
> 5(6) Where a joinder of several claims or parties in a proceeding may unduly complicate or delay the trial or hearing of the proceeding or is otherwise inconvenient, the court may order separate trials or hearings or make any other order it thinks just.

[The defendant] relies on a number of recent cases of this Court that have severed contract and bad faith claims. ...

In *Wonderful Ventures, supra*, Madam Justice Garson allowed the insurer's application to sever the insured's claim for money owed under the insurance contract from its claim for punitive damages for bad faith. The insured had argued that the insurer bore a heavy burden of showing that there were exceptional or compelling reasons to grant the extraordinary remedy of severance. The insured further submitted that it would be prejudiced, *inter alia*, by the delay, the extra expense, the duplication of evidence and the potential for inconsistent findings of fact. The insurer argued that if both claims were to be held at the same time, it might have to disclose what would otherwise be privileged communications in the trial of the contract claim, in order to defend the bad faith claim. Garson J concluded that the prejudice to the insurer of having both claims tried together overrode any inconvenience, cost or expense that might be suffered by the insured as a result of severing the claims. She ordered that discovery on the severed paragraphs relating to the bad faith claim be delayed until the conclusion of the contract claim. ...

Wonderful Ventures, supra, was also followed by Mr. Justice Goepel in *Read*, [[2002] BCJ No. 2617], and by Mr. Justice Hutchison in *Sanders*, [[2003] BCJ No. 596].

In the latter case Hutchison J noted at [para.] 7:

> The surge of claims for bad faith and punitive damages arises out of the recent Supreme Court of Canada decision in *Whiten v. Pilot Insurance Co.*, [2002] SCJ No. 19, 209 DLR (4th) 257. At page 302, Binnie J for the court in upholding a jury award of $1 million in punitive damages (a sufficient sum to activate the saliva glands of trial lawyers) at paragraph 122, says the following:
>
>> [122]   Where a trial judge is concerned that the claim for punitive damages may affect the fairness of the liability trial, bifurcated proceedings may be appropriate. ...

[The plaintiff] seeks to distinguish *Wonderful Ventures, supra*, and the cases which have followed it on the basis that, in those cases, severance was granted primarily on the basis that privileged information would have to be disclosed. He asserts, incorrectly in my opinion, that privileged information is not a significant issue in this case.

[The plaintiff] refers to the cases of *Evans v. Crown Life Insurance Co.* (1996), 25 BCLR (3d) 234, 37 CCLI (2d) 61 (SC) and *D.E. v. Unum Life Insurance Co. of America* (1998), 52 BCLR (3d) 69, 4 CCLI (3d) 223 (SC), where the plaintiff succeeded in recovering aggravated damages for mental distress caused by the insurer's conduct, and *McIsaac v. Sun Life Assurance Co. of Canada* (1997), 48 CCLI (2d) 299, [1997] BCJ No. 2164, aff'd. 1999 BCCA 299, 65 BCLR (3d) 60, application for leave to appeal to SCC dismissed without reasons, [1999] SCCA No. 320, in which contractual and bad faith claims were heard together. In those cases, the issue of severance was not raised.

The plaintiff also relies on one case of this Court, *Randall v. ICBC* (1999), 13 CCLI (3d) 318, [1999] BCJ No. 2330 (SC), and two cases decided in Ontario and Newfoundland, *Sempecos v. State Farm Fire and Casualty Co.* (2001), 17 CPC (5th) 371, [2001] OJ No. 4887 (SCJ), and *Lundrigan v. Non-Marine Underwriters, Lloyd's, London* (2002), 36

CCLI (3d) 263, [2002] NJ No. 30 (SCTD), in which the Courts declined to sever similar contract and tort claims. ...

The test applied in Ontario and Newfoundland is different from that in BC. There, severance is granted only in "exceptional circumstances."

In *Lundrigan, supra,* the relevant Rule provides that "[w]here a joinder of causes of actions or parties in a proceeding may embarrass or delay the trial or hearing of the proceeding or is otherwise inconvenient, the Court may order separate trials or hearings, or make such other order as is just." The Court followed other Newfoundland cases that have held that a separate trial should be ordered "only in exceptional cases" and where the issues are not interwoven.

The relevant Ontario Rule is permissive:

> Rule 5.05 Where it appears that the joinder of multiple claims or parties in the same proceeding may unduly complicate or delay the hearing or cause undue prejudice to a party, the court may
>
> (a) order separate hearings ...

However, the case authorities in Ontario make it clear that a split trial should only be ordered "in the clearest of cases." Moreover, s. 148 of the *Courts of Justice Act,* 1984 (Ont.), c. 11, provides, "As far as possible, multiplicity of legal proceedings shall be avoided."

In *Sempecos, supra,* the Court considered but declined to follow *Wonderful Ventures, supra.* Mr. Justice Killeen followed earlier Ontario authority, including the judicial admonition of Meredith CJCP in *Waller v. Independent Order of Foresters* (1905), 5 OWR 421 at 422: "Experience has shown that seldom, if ever, is any advantage gained by trying some of the issues before the trial of the others is entered upon." Waller followed an earlier English decision, *Emma Silver Mining Co. v. Grant* (1878), 11 Ch. D 918 at 928. Historically, the questions of severance arose most commonly in the context of severing liability and quantum in a personal injury action. It is perhaps trite to observe that the landscape of litigation has changed dramatically in the past 100 years.

In this case, I am bound by the decision of Garson J in *Wonderful Ventures, supra,* which I also respectfully consider to have been correctly decided. Here, there is also a live issue of solicitor–client privilege that should be protected until Mr. Stevens has proven his entitlement to LTD benefits. ...

Conclusion

The claims will be severed and the contract claim will be determined first.

NOTES AND QUESTIONS

1. The law respecting the privilege (that is, the right of non-disclosure) that may attach to communications between a lawyer and client and to documents prepared for the purpose of pending or anticipated litigation is dealt with in chapter 8. Why would lawyer–client communications be potentially relevant to a bad-faith claim against an insurer? How could they be prejudicial to the contract claim?

2. What practical effects will the result in *Stevens* have on the plaintiff's ability to pursue the action? Do you agree with the court's balancing of the interests of the plaintiff and defendant? What approach did the court use in dealing with conflicting lines of cases?

3. In the Ontario case cited in *Stevens*, *Sempecos v. State Farm Fire and Casualty Co.* (2001), 17 CPC (5th) 371 (SCJ), the decision of Killeen J was subsequently upheld by the Ontario Divisional Court: 29 CPC (5th) 99. The Court of Appeal for Ontario dismissed a subsequent appeal with the following cryptic endorsement (2003 ONCA 10419):

> The issue on this appeal is whether the appellant insurance company is entitled to have the court order that the trial of the plaintiff's action on the insurance contract and for bad faith punitive damages be bifurcated in order to protect the insurance company from disclosing privileged communications in the bad faith claim, which could also be used to its prejudice in the contract claim.
>
> The Divisional Court noted that on the evidence in the record, the appellant has not provided evidence that it in fact intends, or will be obliged, to waive privilege in respect of solicitor–client communications in order to defend the bad faith claim. Counsel has explained that when the motion was initiated, several of the important cases in this area were not yet decided, including the Supreme Court's decision in *Whiten v. Pilot Insurance Co.*, [2002] SCJ No. 19 (SCC) and this court's decision in *Khazzaka v. Commercial Union Assurance Co. of Canada*, [2002] OJ No. 3110 (Ont. CA).
>
> We accept that the law in this area has changed since the appellant's material was prepared. However, on the record before this court, we agree with the Divisional Court that there is no evidence that the appellant will actually suffer the prejudice alleged from disclosing privileged communications. We would therefore dismiss the appeal but without prejudice to the appellant's right, if so advised, to bring a further motion on the appropriate evidence. The respondents of course will be able to respond as advised.

Has the Ontario court signalled a possible shift in the law, and a more accommodating approach to severance in bad-faith claims? Is this a good thing?

4. *Joining claims that may cause prejudice.* In relatively rare circumstances, a defendant can make a credible argument that joining claim B with claim A will prejudice the defendant in his defence of claim B—see, for example, *Heider v. Levine*, [1955] OWN 936 (the court held improper the joinder of a claim for indecent assault with one for breach of contract, although a causal connection between the two was alleged); *Sporn v. Hudson Transit Lines*, 265 App. Div. 360, 38 NYS 2d 512 (NY 1942) (the plaintiffs, the driver of a car and his passengers, joined claims that each of them had against the defendant bus company for personal injuries sustained in a collision between the car and the bus, allegedly due to the negligent operation of the bus, with a claim by the driver for malicious prosecution; the basis of the second claim was that, following the accident, the defendant had maliciously caused the arrest of the driver for reckless driving; joinder was held to be improper). Are the decisions in *Sporn* and *Heider* justifiable? Contrast the following statement by Friedenthal, "Joinder of Claims, Counterclaims and Cross-Complaints: Suggested Revision of the California Provisions" (1970), 23 *Stanford Law Review* 1, at 5-6:

> Any undesirable effects resulting from unlimited joinder of causes can be remedied by a severance of causes for trial. Joinder of causes, in and of itself, is never harmful. A joint trial of causes

may be unjustified, however, either because the trial may become too complex for rational decision, or because evidence introduced on one cause may so tend to prejudice the trier of fact that
it will be unlikely to render a fair decision on another cause.

5. *Joinder and relief against joinder.* The rules regarding the joinder of multiple claims
by a plaintiff are extremely broad. Under the rules, the plaintiff may join any number of
claims against the same defendant, subject to the power of the court to exclude or to direct
separate trials in respect of causes of action that cannot be conveniently disposed of together. Essentially, the question is determined on the basis of fairness and convenience and
it involves a balancing of interests. On the one hand, the court seeks to avoid prejudice to
the defendant by joinder of multiple causes of action. On the other hand, it seeks to avoid
putting the plaintiff to unwarranted expense by forcing separate proceedings where the
claims could more conveniently and less expensively be tried together.

When the court exercises its power, it usually does so by ordering separate trials of the
plaintiff's claim rather than by excluding claims from the plaintiff's action (but note the decisions in *Sporn* and *Heider*). If the court orders claims that were initially joined to be excluded, then the plaintiff is forced to abandon these claims altogether or to assert them in a
separate action. However, where separate trials are ordered, all the claims remain in the action and the separation takes place only at the trial stage. Instead of one trial in which all the
claims are tried and determined, separate trials on the different claims are held. Usually the
issue of whether there should be separate trials is left to the trial judge to decide.

6. In Alberta, part 5 of the Alberta Rules governs joinder of parties and causes of action.
The procedures set out in this part of the Rules provide for a generous ability to join parties
and causes of action in the spirit of making litigation more efficient and cost-effective. To
the extent that parties seek to add parties after the expiration of the limitation period—in
the context of Alberta's *Limitations Act*, RSA 2000, c. L-12—see the court's discussion in
Stout Estate v. Golinowsky Estate (2002), 100 Alta. LR (5), at para. 83 *et seq.* (CA); *Alberta v.
Canadian National Railway Co.* (2003), 12 Alta. LR (4th) 4 (CA).

2. Compulsory Joinder

Generally, the plaintiff is free to assert any or all claims against a defendant but there is no
obligation to do so. The court will not, in a particular action, force a plaintiff to assert any
particular claim. However, as you will see below, the law relating to *res judicata* has the
practical effect of requiring a plaintiff to join, in one action, all potential claims arising out
of a single factual scenario. While failure to join a claim in an action does not prevent the
plaintiff from proceeding with that action, *res judicata* may operate to bar other related
claims from being asserted in any other proceedings. Therefore, it places the onus on the
plaintiff either to ensure that all relevant aspects of a claim or claims are argued in the one
proceeding or to lose the opportunity to argue them in the future.

III. RES JUDICATA

A. Introduction

In general terms, the doctrine of *res judicata* prevents the relitigation of matters already decided. So, for example, it will prevent a losing plaintiff from suing the defendant again on the same cause of action. The operation of the doctrine is summarized in G. Spencer Bower and A.K. Turner, *The Doctrine of Res Judicata*, 2nd ed. (London: Butterworths, 1969), at 9:

> The rule of estoppel by *res judicata* ... is a rule of evidence [and] may thus be stated:
>
> > [W]here a final judicial decision has been pronounced by ... [a] judicial tribunal of competent jurisdiction over the parties to, and the subject of, the litigation, any party or privy to such litigation, as against any other party or privy thereto ... is estopped in any subsequent litigation from disputing or questioning such decision on the merits, whether it be used as the foundation of an action, or relied upon as a bar to any claim, indictment or complaint, or to any affirmative defence, case or allegation.

Although united in the same doctrine, there are two quite distinct limbs to the general principle of *res judicata*: claim preclusion or cause of action estoppel (sometimes referred to as "claim preclusion"; and issue estoppel (sometimes referred to as "issue preclusion" or as "collateral estoppel").

1. Cause of Action Estoppel

The first limb arises when a court has adjudicated a claim between two or more parties and a second action is brought between the same parties that is in some way related to the first. The decision in the first action may bind the parties. If the same cause of action is involved in both actions, the second action is precluded and must fail. If the plaintiff wins the first action, his or her cause of action is said to *merge* in the judgment and it cannot be reasserted. If the plaintiff was unsuccessful in the first action, the cause of action is said to be *barred* by the judgment for the defendant. This is called merger and bar or, more commonly, "cause of action estoppel." The term used in the United States—"claim preclusion"—is the most descriptive: the rule precludes a party from relitigating a claim.

2. Issue Estoppel

The second limb of the doctrine arises when the second action does not involve the same cause of action or claim. In certain circumstances, the courts are prepared to treat any issues decided in the first case that also arise in the second case as settled and, therefore, not open to relitigation. This is known as issue estoppel or issue preclusion: the rule estops or precludes a party from relitigating an issue.

It is important to distinguish the operation of *res judicata* from the doctrine of *stare decisis*. A rule of law decided in an earlier case can determine or control the result in a later case but, under *stare decisis*, the parties to the second case are free to argue that the principle does not apply to their particular set of facts. Nonetheless, the courts give considerable weight to earlier precedents, and past decisions therefore exert a gravitational pull on later decisions.

The difference between *stare decisis* and *res judicata*, and how the latter binds more strictly than the former, is dramatically illustrated by the *Re Waring* decisions. In *Re Waring (No. 1)*, [1942] Ch. 426, trustees under a will applied to the court for the determination of the question whether two annuities granted under the will were subject to taxation. The Court of Appeal interpreted the relevant statute as making the annuities taxable. Subsequently, in *Berkeley v. Berkeley*, [1946] AC 555, the House of Lords overruled the Court of Appeal's decision in *Re Waring (No. 1)* and its interpretation of the taxing statute. The trustees of the Waring estate then made another application, *Re Waring (No. 2)*, [1948] 1 Ch. 221, to determine the liability of the annuities to taxation. There were two annuities payable under the will; one of the annuitants was a party in *Re Waring (No. 1)*, and one was not. Surprisingly, it was held that the action by the annuitant who was a party to the first action was *res judicata*, but the action by the annuitant who was not a party to the original proceeding could take advantage of the *Berkeley* decision and take the annuity tax-free. The English courts have since granted relief against such a rigorous application of issue estoppel in "special circumstances." In *Arnold v. Westminster Bank plc*, [1991] 3 All ER 41 (HL), a continuing contractual obligation by way of long lease was held to be sufficient to permit the courts to reopen the issue already decided between the same parties where, since the original decision, the law had been judicially changed.

3. Hypothetical

In reading the following materials, consider this situation. An accident occurs between two cars at an intersection. The driver of one car, Allan, is charged with proceeding from a stop sign before it was safe to do so. He was acquitted. He then brought an action against the other driver, Nancy, in the Small Claims Court to recover $1,000 for damage to his car. What should be the effect, if any, of his earlier acquittal on the outcome of this action? Would it make any difference if he had been convicted? Assume that Allan succeeds in his action against Nancy. He now brings an action against Nancy to recover $50,000 in damages for personal injuries. Allan's daughter, Sarah, was also injured in the action and she joins her father's action as another plaintiff; her claim is also for $50,000. Also, Nancy counterclaims for $1,000 for property damage and $50,000 for personal injuries. Can Allan claim that Nancy is estopped from defending his action and from proceeding with her counterclaim? Or can Nancy claim that Allan is estopped from proceeding with his claim? Can she claim a similar estoppel against Sarah's action? Or can Sarah plead that Nancy is estopped from defending Sarah's action?

B. Cause of Action Estoppel

Britannia Airways Ltd. v. Royal Bank of Canada
(2005), 5 CPC (6th) 262 (Ont. SCJ)

LAX J: This is a motion by Royal Bank of Canada to strike, stay or dismiss the action on the grounds of *res judicata* or abuse of process.

[This dispute concerned Britannia Airways Limited, a charter airline that flies from the United Kingdom around the world, including Egypt. Nile Valley Aviation ("Nile Valley") was Britannia's ground-handling agent in Egypt. In the 1990s, Britannia became a customer of the Jet Card System, which was a credit card for the aviation industry, and allowed customers to use the card to pay for aviation goods and services. In 1997, Britannia started using the Jet Card System to pay for goods and services purchased in Egypt. Sometime thereafter, Britannia alleged that Nile Valley Aviation overcharged the company by more than US$9 million. In 1999, Britannia commenced a lawsuit against the companies that offered the Jet Card System—launching a claim against Air Routing in Texas and a claim against the Royal Bank of Canada in Ontario ("RBC").]

Pleadings were exchanged in the Ontario action, but Britannia's action against Royal Bank otherwise remained dormant. It proceeded with its lawsuit in Texas and in March 2002, this went to trial by judge and jury. Through a combination of summary judgment orders, directed verdicts, and jury findings, Britannia lost the Texas lawsuit in its entirety.

Two years later, Britannia revived the Ontario action by bringing a motion to amend the Statement of Claim to add Air Routing and a number of related parties as defendants, in addition to the original defendant, RBC. RBC brought a cross-motion for summary judgment and to strike, stay or dismiss the Ontario action. The summary judgment portion of RBC's cross-motion was deferred pending the outcome of the other motions. Britannia and Air Routing later settled the motion to amend on the basis of a consent dismissal. These reasons address RBC's cross-motion to strike, stay or dismiss Britannia's action against it on the grounds of *res judicata* and abuse of process.

Issues

The motion turned on three main questions. First, what was claimed or could have been claimed in the Texas action? Second, what is the nature of the allegations that Britannia is making against RBC in Ontario, and on what basis does Britannia seek to hold RBC liable? Third, was RBC privy in interest to the matters and issues in the Texas lawsuit? ...

The nutshell position of RBC is that, having lost the Texas litigation, Britannia is now seeking to relitigate the same underlying "Air Routing" factual allegations in Ontario, although dressed up in a different way. It submits that all of the causes of action against RBC, in one way or another, deal with Nile Valley Aviation's fraud and the failure of Air Routing to detect this, which were determined against Britannia in Texas. It submits that if Britannia had won against Air Routing in Texas, RBC could not have challenged Air Routing's liability to Britannia, but would have been limited in this action to the question of its own vicarious liability for what happened. Britannia, it argues, must be equally bound by Air Routing's exoneration in the Texas action and may only assert claims in Ontario for RBC's actions that were not or could not have been brought in the Texas action.

The nutshell position of Britannia is that the claims in Texas and Ontario are different. It submits that the heart of the Texas claim was a claim in fraudulent or negligent misrepresentation on the part of the representative of Nile Valley, as an agent of Air Routing, who had falsely represented to Britannia that Air Routing would validate and verify invoices from suppliers such as Nile Valley before the charges were forwarded to Britannia for payment. In contrast, it says that the heart of the Ontario claim is based on breach of contract and negligence of Royal Bank in the design and operation of the Jet Card System, which Britannia asserts was flawed and prone to fraud.

Legal Principles

By and large, the parties agree on the legal doctrines relevant to this motion. They disagree on the application of these doctrines to this action. I begin by setting out the law that applies.

Res Judicata

The doctrine of *res judicata* prevents relitigation of matters that have already been determined by a court of competent jurisdiction. There are two branches of the doctrine: cause of action estoppel and issue estoppel. Both branches are founded on the twin principles that the same party shall not be harassed twice for the same complaint and that there is societal value in the finality and conclusiveness of judicial decisions: *Angle v. MNR*, [1975] 2 SCR 248 at 267.

Cause of Action Estoppel

Cause of action estoppel prevents not only the same cause of action from being litigated again, but also bars claims which properly belonged to the subject matter of previous litigation: *Maynard v. Maynard*, [1951] SCR 346. Put another way, "an adjudication of a particular set of facts does not raise an estoppel with respect to every cause of action which is subsequently based on the same facts, but only those claims which properly belonged to the first proceeding": Sopinka, Lederman, Bryant, *The Law of Evidence in Canada*, 2nd ed. (Markham: Butterworths, 1999) at 1079.

A cause of action is the group of operative facts giving rise to one or more bases for suing, or the factual situation that entitles one person to obtain a remedy from another. Accordingly, cause of action estoppel operates to prevent a party from attempting to relitigate a case by advancing a new legal theory in support of a claim based on essentially the same facts or combination of facts. *Las Vegas Strip Ltd. v. Toronto (City)* (1996), 30 OR (3d) 286 (Gen. Div.), aff'd. (1997), 32 OR (3d) 651 (CA).

This principle has been applied to bar a second proceeding in Ontario where the same underlying facts were relied on in an action in New York: *Peterson v. New York Life Insurance Co.*, [1992] OJ No. 2503 (Gen. Div.).

It has also been applied to bar a second proceeding based on breach of fiduciary duty where the first action in contract involved a claim for the same sum of money, arising out of the same relationship and for the same services: *Morgan Power Apparatus Ltd. v. Flanders Installations Ltd.* (1972), 27 DLR (3d) 249 (BCCA) at 251; see also *Hoque v. Montreal Trust Co. of Canada*, [1997] NSJ No. 430 (CA) where the court discusses the relationship between cause of action estoppel and underlying factual allegations. *Hoque* was followed in *Freedman v. Reemark Sterling I Ltd.* (2003), 62 OR (3d) 743 (CA).

Britannia relies on *Doering v. Grandview (Town)*, [1976] 2 SCR 621 and the decision in *Abramson v. Oshawa (City)*, [1998] OJ No. 2205; aff'd. [1999] OJ No. 339 (CA) as authority for the proposition that the key consideration is whether the second action sets up a separate and distinct cause of action, regardless of common facts. *Grandview* was a case where the second action was barred because the plaintiff failed to bring forward all of the facts in the first action and failed to demonstrate why those facts could not have been ascertained with reasonable diligence. The majority held that the plaintiff was suing for the same cause of action in nuisance as before. In *Abramson*, the second action truly was a separate and distinct cause of action.

In my view, these decisions do not detract from the principle articulated in *Las Vegas Strip Club*, *supra*, that cause of action estoppel is not limited to an examination of the claims that were brought or properly belonged to the first action. It is not the legal label, but the underlying factual basis for the claim that counts. A party cannot recast the claim arising out of the same facts using a different legal description without bumping up against the doctrine of cause of action estoppel and, if the parties or privies requirement is met, it will operate to bar the second action.

Issue Estoppel

Issue estoppel applies to prevent relitigation of issues that have previously been determined. The constituent elements are: (1) the same question has been decided; (2) the prior judicial decision was final; (3) the parties to both proceedings are the same, or their privies: *Toronto (City) v. Canadian Union of Public Employees (CUPE), Local 79*, [2003] 3 SCR 77, referencing, *Danyluk v. Ainsworth Technologies Inc.*, [2001] 2 SCR 460 at 476-7.

[Lax J reviewed the factual allegations in both actions and determined that the lawsuits rested on the same factual allegations, and the Texas decision was final.]

Privity

Cause of action estoppel operates to bar claims against RBC in Ontario if RBC is privy in interest to the matters and issues that were raised or could have been raised in the Texas proceeding between Britannia and Air Routing relating to the same subject matter as the Ontario action.

Privity of interest rests on the concept of mutuality. There must be a sufficient degree of connection or identification between the two parties, thus making it fair to permit a party to rely on the earlier determination involving the other party. The determination of privity is made on a case-by-case basis because, "[i]t is impossible to be categorical about the degree of interest which will create privity: *Machin v. Tomlinson* (2000), 51 OR (3d) 566 at paras. 20, 22-4 (CA).

There are few guideposts to assist with the determination of whether parties are privy in interest, but a helpful consideration is whether the party seeking to take advantage of the judgment would have been bound had the judgment gone the other way: Sopinka, Lederman, Bryant, *The Law of Evidence in Canada, supra*, at 1090.

I agree with the submission of Royal Bank that if Britannia had been successful against Air Routing in Texas, RBC could not have challenged Air Routing's liability to Britannia. It would have been limited in this action to the question of its own vicarious liability for Air Routing's conduct and required to answer allegations of direct and independent liability for its own conduct that do not depend on Air Routing's actions or omissions.

The matter may also be tested by examining what would have happened if Britannia had asserted claims against both Air Routing and RBC in the same lawsuit. It seems clear that Britannia's claims against RBC would have fallen away. For example, after Britannia decided it was not claiming negligence *per se* against Air Routing, there would have been no basis for a finding that RBC was liable for Air Routing's allegedly negligent acts. The trial judge in Texas dismissed Britannia's claim against Air Routing for negligent misrepresentation, by way of a directed verdict. Although he gave no reasons, he must have found that Britannia did not provide evidence to support the claim. RBC could not have been found liable for a non-existent negligent misrepresentation or for a non-existent fraudulent misrepresentation even if the jury had decided that Air Routing was RBC's agent.

. . .

For these reasons, I conclude that RBC is privy in interest to the matters that were or could have been raised in Texas, relating to the same subject matter as this action.

Conclusion on Res Judicata

In the Texas lawsuit, Britannia litigated a set of facts which it alleged constituted fraud, negligent misrepresentation, civil conspiracy and theft. RBC has established that, although different legal labels have been applied, the underlying factual allegations are the same in Ontario as in Texas and the privity requirement is met. The doctrine of *res judicata* operates to bar the claim for fraud and the claim for an alleged breach of an implied term of the Jet Card Service Agreement on the basis that Air Routing would validate and verify billing information. Both branches of the doctrine apply to these claims. The claim for negligence is barred by operation of the doctrine of cause of action estoppel as this is a claim that properly belonged to the subject matter of the Texas lawsuit.

NOTES AND QUESTIONS

1. In *Britannia*, after her conclusion that the fraud, negligent misrepresentation, civil conspiracy, and theft actions were barred in Ontario due to cause of action estoppel, Lax J went on to find that another aspect of Britannia's claim, dealing with breach of contract between it and RBC, was not subject to cause of action estoppel because it was not determined by the Texas court, and could proceed. Does this finding defeat the purpose of the doctrine of *res judicata*? Explain.

2. According to Cromwell JA (as he then was), writing in *Hoque v. Montreal Trust Co. of Canada* (1997), 162 NSR (2d) 321 (CA), one of the cases Lax J relied on in Britannia, Canadian courts have not embraced the broad principle that everything that should have been raised in the first action cannot then be raised in a subsequent action. This principle prevents litigants from suing first on one theory of liability and, if unsuccessful, suing again on a different theory. *Hoque* suggests that the modern day approach of courts to frustrate the relitigation of matters that could have been but were not raised in earlier proceedings is not a bright-line test but an inquiry into the context of the first proceeding and the issues raised there. The outcome of such an analysis is not always predictable as the following examples illustrate:

   a. *Freedman v. Reemark Sterling Ltd.* (2003), 62 OR (3d) 743 (CA), where a defendant's cross-claim against a co-defendant was held not to be barred by cause of action estoppel even though the liability of the co-defendant to the plaintiff had already been established in a prior proceeding. The Ontario Court of Appeal, applying the framework from *Hoque*, held that the cross-claim related to a "distinct cause of action" and permitted it to proceed.

   b. *Las Vegas Strip Ltd. v. Toronto (City)* (1996), 30 OR (3d) 286 (Gen. Div.), relied on by Lax J in *Britannia*, above, where the plaintiff, having previously failed in an application to show that its activities were consistent with the bylaw, sought to invalidate a municipal bylaw restricting its commercial activities. The court held the second application to be barred. It also held that it was open to the plaintiff to have raised the validity of the bylaw in the first application, but, because it had freely chosen not to, it was now bound by the decision.

   c. *Gallant v. Bembridge* (1993), 140 NBR (2d) 119 (QB), where a plaintiff's first action for defamation had been dismissed for failure to comply with notice provisions. The court refused to dismiss a second action against the same defendants for tortious conspiracy for conspiring to injure him by disseminating certain information. The second action was neither grounded on defamation nor on conspiracy to commit libel and, therefore, a *res judicata* argument was without merit.

   d. *Batchelor v. Morden* (1985), 50 CPC 39 (Ont. Dist. Ct.), where the court refused to dismiss an action by a tenant against a landlord claiming a rent rebate and damages for invasion of privacy. The tenant had brought an earlier action for breach of a covenant of quiet enjoyment in which the claims might have been included. Although the claims could have been set up in the first action, they had no relevancy to that action and the tenant was not precluded from now advancing them.

   e. *Decorby v. Decorby* (1985), 34 Man. R (2d) 124 (QB), aff'd. 37 Man. R (2d) 271 (CA), where a son who had previously, unsuccessfully, challenged the interpretation of his father's will was not barred from bringing a subsequent action claiming entitlement to all his father's land pursuant to an agreement or, alternatively, claiming unjust enrichment or *quantum meruit*.

3. *Defining "cause of action" or "claim."* The different approaches to defining "cause of action" or "claim" are canvassed in American Law Institute, *Restatement of the Law (Second), Judgments* (1982), 196-97:

> "Claim" in the context of *res judicata*, has never been broader than the transaction to which it related. But in the days when civil procedure still bore the imprint of the forms of action and the division between law and equity, the courts were prone to associate claim with a single theory of recovery, so that, with respect to one transaction, a plaintiff might have as many claims as there were theories of the substantive law upon which he could seek relief against the defendant. Thus, defeated in an action based on one theory, the plaintiff might be able to maintain another action based on a different theory, even though both actions were grounded upon the defendant's identical act or connected acts forming a single life-situation. In those earlier days there was also some adherence to a view that associated claim with the assertion of a single primary right as accorded by the substantive law, so that, if it appeared that the defendant had invaded a number of primary rights conceived to be held by the plaintiff, the plaintiff had the same number of claims, even though they all sprang from a unitary occurrence. There was difficulty in knowing which rights were primary and what was their extent, but a primary right and the corresponding claim might turn out to be narrow. Thus it was held by some courts that a judgment for or against the plaintiff in an action for personal injuries did not preclude an action by him for property damage occasioned by the same negligent conduct on the part of the defendant—this deriving from the idea that the right to be free of bodily injury was distinct from the property right. Still another view of [cause of action] looked to sameness of evidence; a second action was precluded where the evidence to support it was the same as that needed to support the first. Sometimes this was made the sole test of identity of claim; sometimes it figured as a second action might be precluded although the evidence material to it varied from that in the first action. Even so, claim was not coterminous with the transaction itself.
>
> The present trend is to see claim in factual terms and to make it coterminous with the transaction regardless of the number of substantive theories, or variant forms of relief flowing from those theories, that may be available to the plaintiff; regardless of the number of primary rights that may have been invaded; and regardless of the variations in the evidence needed to support the theories or rights. The transaction is the basis of the litigative unit or entity which may not be split.

In Canadian law, this trend is illustrated by contrasting *Brunsden v. Humphrey* (1884), 14 QBD 141 and *Cahoon v. Franks*, [1967] SCR 455. In *Brunsden v. Humphrey*, the Court of Appeal concluded that the second action was not barred by the first, holding that different rights were infringed in the two actions—that a tort causing both injury to the person and injury to the property gave rise to two distinct causes of action. In *Cahoon v. Franks*, the plaintiff commenced an action for property damage suffered in an automobile accident. After the expiry of the relevant limitation period, the plaintiff sought leave to amend to add a claim for $150,000 for personal injuries. The defendant opposed leave on the ground that the plaintiff was attempting to add a new cause of action (citing *Brunsden*) after the expiry of the limitation period (discussed in chapter 4, Pleadings). The Supreme Court of Canada held that the

tort of negligence involves a breach by the defendant of the duty owed to the plaintiff resulting in damage to the plaintiff and that there is only one cause of action, notwithstanding that
the plaintiff suffers both personal injury and property damage. In so holding, the court concluded that *Brunsden* is not good law in Canada and ought not to be followed.

4. *Splitting the cause of action in negligence.* In *Cox v. Robert Simpson Co. Ltd.* (1973), 1
OR (2d) 333, the plaintiff sued in Small Claims Court for damage to his automobile. The
defendant paid the amount claimed into court and the plaintiff took the money out in satisfaction of his claim. Subsequently, the plaintiff commenced a County Court action in respect of the same accident claiming damages for personal injury. The defendant moved for
an order dismissing the action by reason of what occurred in the Small Claims Court proceedings. Section 84 of the *Small Claims Court Act*, RSO 1980, c. 476 provided that "the sum
so paid shall be paid to the plaintiff, and he shall be deemed to have accepted it in full satisfaction of his claim, and all proceedings in the action shall be stayed." The Ontario Court of
Appeal, following *Cahoon*, held that the negligence of the defendant gave the plaintiff but
one cause of action, which could not be split, and the plaintiff's second action was barred.
(The court indicated that this may be a harsh result as far as the plaintiff is concerned, particularly having regard to the fact that he conducted the first action himself.)

Should it make any difference if A had collision insurance on his automobile and the insurance company had paid A the amount of the damages to the vehicle; then, in accordance
with a provision in his insurance policy, A assigned to the insurer his claim for such damage; subsequently, the insurer instituted the first action in A's name and A subsequently
instituted his own action for his personal injuries? Some courts in the United States have
created an exception to the rule against splitting a cause of action that permits a separate
suit for property damage to be brought by the insurer without jeopardizing the insured's
own claim for personal injuries. See the cases referred to in *Weekes v. Atlantic National Insurance Company*, 370 F2d 264 (9th Cir. 1966).

In *Vaughan v. Scott* (1980), 15 CPC 219 (Ont. Co. Ct.), the plaintiff suffered both property damage and personal injuries in a motor vehicle accident with the defendant in June
1976. The plaintiff's insurer paid the property damage claim and, in November 1976, commenced an action in the plaintiff's name pursuant to its subrogation rights. Default judgment was obtained against the defendant and damages were assessed in June 1977. In May
1978, the plaintiff personally commenced an action for personal injuries and the defendant
applied to dismiss the action as being an abuse of process—that is, *res judicata*—and the application was dismissed. *Cox v. Robert Simpson* was distinguished as a case turning on the
interpretation of s. 8 of the *Small Claims Court Act*. While plaintiffs may not split their cause
of action, the reality here was that it was the insurance contract and the *Insurance Act* (not
the plaintiff) that split the cause of action. The insurer was given the subrogation right when
it paid the property claim, whereas the plaintiff personally retained the right to sue for personal injuries. For a similar result see *Malcolm v. Carr* (1996), 40 Alta. LR (3d) 29 (QB).

5. *How should the question of attempts to relitigate claims be approached?* It will be clear
that it is often not easy to determine what is a cause of action. Louisell and Hazard have
suggested that it would facilitate "analysis of the problem of bar and merger to eliminate
'cause of action' as an intermediate terminological repository and to put the [real issue] directly: Is there any satisfactory explanation why this claim was not presented in the prior

action?" Their basic position is that "a plaintiff should be compelled to join all those claims arising from the same out-of-court transaction that he could have joined" on penalty of being barred from bringing any subsequent action for such claims: Louisell and Hazard, *Cases and Material on Pleading and Procedure*, 2nd ed. (Mineola, NY: Foundation Press, 1968), at 590. Do you agree with them? Are their views consistent with the decision in *Hoque*?

Edward Cleary, in "Res Judicata Re-Examined" (1948), 57 *Yale Law Journal* 339, takes a very different view. First, he would like to see the bar and merger doctrine given a quite narrow scope. He argues that broad tests, like that proposed by Louisell and Hazard, requiring extensive joinder of claims "usually effect no saving except paper and filing fees and [result] as a practical matter in breaking the case back down into some sort of units for the purposes of trial." Second, he believes that the present penalty for "splitting" a cause of action—dismissal of the latter action—is too severe. Instead, he would impose, in the US context, the sanction of requiring the plaintiff to pay the defendant's costs, including attorney's fees, of litigating the second action. Do you agree? Adapting his suggestions to the Canadian context, would a preferable solution in *Hoque* have been to allow the plaintiff to proceed, but on condition that it pay the defendant's costs, on a substantial indemnity scale, in any event? (It should be noted that Cleary would retain the present rules relating to issue estoppel to prevent relitigation of matters actually decided in the first action.)

In respect of Cleary's second proposal, Louisell and Hazard, above, at 591, ask, does the proposed sanction "take adequate account of the human and social costs of litigation? What about compensation for defendant's mental anguish? Doesn't final disposition of the controversy, even on terms less than fully just have a value in and of itself?"

In "Res Judicata Redux" (1986), 24 *Osgoode Hall Law Journal* 713, at 735, Tim Pinos suggests a similar policy-based solution:

> The first temptation is to try to supplant the concept of a *cause of action* with another concept that directs the court's attention more broadly. In other contexts, and other jurisdictions, the concepts *matter*, or *transaction* have been construed fairly broadly, and may provide possible candidates for a *test*. An alternate approach would be to say that when litigation arises between two parties, both are under an obligation to raise all claims, counterclaims, and defences arising out of or connected to the original subject-matter of the lawsuit, and whether raised or not, they may not be raised in a subsequent proceeding.
>
> Regardless of the choice, it is suggested that the following criteria are relevant to the scope of the judge's power under either formulation of the rule:
>
> 1. Would a reasonably diligent party, acting with reasonably diligent legal advice, have been aware of the opportunity to advance the claim or defence?
>
> 2. Was the claim or defence connected in any way with the subject-matter of the earlier litigation?
>
> 3. Was the claim or defence available at the time of the earlier proceeding, in the sense of having accrued?
>
> 4. Did the court in the prior proceeding have jurisdiction over the claim or defence asserted in the subsequent proceeding?

If the answer to these questions is yes, then *prima facie*, the attempt to litigate the claim or defence in a subsequent proceeding should fail.

6. *What types of former adjudications attract cause of action estoppel?* The application of cause of action estoppel applies not only to judgments rendered by domestic courts after a contested hearing, but also extends to *default judgments*—see, for example, *Miscouche Sales & Service Ltd. v. Massey Ferguson Industries Ltd.* (1992), 12 CPC (3d) 63 (PEITD) (where a first action resulted in a default judgment; a subsequent action relating to the same transaction was dismissed on the grounds of *res judicata*; the claim now sought to be asserted by the plaintiff should have been raised in the earlier action instead of permitting default judgment to be taken); to *consent judgments*—see, for example, *Patterson v. Antonucci*, [1988] WDFL 1744 (Ont. CA) (a family law case in which a woman was not permitted to claim damages for assault when she could have made such a claim in earlier proceedings between the parties that had been settled); and to *foreign judgments* entitled to recognition under conflicts of laws principles—see, for example, *Pervez (Litigation Guardian of) v. Carpenter Technology (Canada) Ltd.* (1992) (Ont. Gen. Div.), aff'd. (1995) (Ont. CA) (where, in an Ontario action that was virtually identical to one in the United States that had been dismissed, the court held that the matter was *res judicata* and to allow it to continue against the defendants would be an abuse of process). The question whether decisions of administrative decision makers or tribunals can give rise to *res judicata* is discussed separately below.

7. *Application of cause of action estoppel to counterclaims.* Cause of action estoppel clearly applies to a defendant in requiring him or her to put forward any and all defences to the plaintiff's claim in the first action. (See, for example, *Four Embarcadero Centre Venture v. Kalen* (1988), 65 OR (2d) 551 (HC) (a default judgment results in the merits becoming *res judicata*; a foreign money judgment that is final and enforceable settles the issues between the parties just as an Ontario judgment would do; when sued on the foreign judgment, the defendant may not attack it on the ground that the foreign court never considered the merits of the claim). But what if the claim the defendant now seeks to assert could have been asserted by him or her as a counterclaim in an earlier action by the plaintiff? In the United States, the *Federal Rules of Civil Procedure*, rule 13(a) specifically makes "compulsory" any counterclaim that the defendant may have *that arises out of the same transaction or occurrence* on which the plaintiff sues. Canadian authority on the issue is sparse, but compare *Ranch des Prairies Ltée (Prairie Ranch Ltd.) v. Bank of Montreal* (1988), 69 CBR (NS) 180 (Man. CA) (shareholders of a bankrupt company were precluded from suing a bank, the company's receiver/manager, and their solicitors for damages because the shareholder's claims should have been raised in earlier proceedings—that is, when the receiver was appointed by the court, when the sale of the company's assets was approved by the court, or when default judgment was signed against the shareholders) with *Roque v. Brown* (1977), 2 CPC 243 (Ont. HC) (the present plaintiff, P, had been unsuccessfully sued by the defendant, D, in earlier proceedings for malicious prosecution where there was a finding that D had assaulted P, who then commenced this action; commencement of action that might have been raised as a counterclaim in prior proceedings between the same parties may amount in certain circumstances to an abuse of process, but in normal circumstances (as here) there is a right to wait and bring a separate and subsequent action, although the plaintiff may in consequence be deprived of costs in the second action).

8. *Requirements for the application of res judicata (both claim and issue estoppel).* There are several requirements for the application of both streams of *res judicata*.

a. *Generally, the two actions must involve the same parties or their privies*

As a matter of due process or fundamental justice, a person's legal rights should not be determined without an opportunity to litigate them. This principle is so important that any exceptions to it are carefully and narrowly defined in the law of *res judicata*. There are only two exceptions to the general rule in which a judgment may have preclusive effects with respect to a non-party. One exception is that for privies—a person may be bound by the decision in a former litigation to which he or she was not a party because he or she was "in privity" with a person who was a party to the earlier litigation. The other is non-mutual issue estoppel, discussed below under the heading "Issue Estoppel." (The debate concerning the abandonment of the requirement of "same parties" (mutuality) in the context of issue estoppel has no application to claim preclusion; the only exception to the "same parties" requirement re claim preclusion is privity.)

b. *Claim now sought to be asserted must have been within the prior court's jurisdiction*

The reason for this requirement is straightforward and obvious; for the defence of *res judicata* to succeed, a plaintiff must have had the opportunity to recover in the first action and, but for his own fault, might have recovered then what he seeks to recover in the second: *Horsman Bros. Holdings Ltd. v. Dolphin Electrical Contractors Ltd.* (1987), 10 BCLR (2d) 213 (CA).

c. *Prior adjudication must have been on the merits*

This requirement denies preclusive effect to adjudications that result in the first action being dismissed for procedural reasons not going to the merits of the claim asserted—for example, dismissal for want of prosecution or for lack of jurisdiction: Ontario rule 24.05; *Sharma v. Ouellette* (1991), 2 CPC (3d) 289 (Ont. Gen. Div.) (for *res judicata* to apply, the judgment in the first action must have been on its merits; where the previous action against an insurer was dismissed solely on the basis of a finding that the plaintiff did not commence the action within the limitation period, that action was not determined on its merits; the limitation period did not apply to the claim made in the second action for declaratory relief). The rationale is that if the prior court did not get to the merits of the plaintiff's claim, but dismissed the proceeding on some preliminary or procedural point, it would be too harsh to foreclose the plaintiff; an adjudication on the merits of the plaintiff's claim is a prerequisite to this. However, note that there are limits to this reasoning and to the principle. Where it is held that the claim now sought to be asserted is barred because, though it was not asserted in the prior proceeding it should have been (as in *Hoque*), the claim will be barred even though there was no adjudication on the merits of that claim. Also, for the purposes of this principle, a default judgment is an adjudication of the merits; in rendering a default judgment, a court intends to finally adjudicate on the merits of the plaintiff's claim, albeit without considering the merits.

d. *The prior decision must have been a final judgment*

As to this requirement—that of finality of the prior decision—F. James and G.C. Hazard, *Civil Procedure*, 3d ed. (Boston: Little, Brown, 1985), 591 state:

> Both branches of the rules of res judicata, that is claim preclusion and issue preclusion, depend on there having been a final determination of the claim or issue with respect to which rules are applied. The reason is virtually definitional: The rules preclude relitigation of a matter previously determined, and a matter has not been "determined" until a judgment has been rendered concerning it. It follows that the rules of res judicata do not come into operation before a final judgment.

For examples of the principle that the prior decision must have been a final judgment, see *Westcoast Energy Inc. v. Husky Oil Operations Ltd.* (March 13, 1995), doc. Calgary Appeal 13415 (Alta. CA) (where the court held that because of the broad powers granted to the provincial Public Utilities Board by its enabling legislation, there was no finality to its earlier decision refusing to make an award of interest that would invoke the doctrine of *res judicata*) and *Barwell Food Sales Inc. v. Snyder & Fils Inc.* (1988), 38 CPC (2d) 192 (Ont. HC) (where the plaintiff commenced separate actions in Quebec and Ontario for the same relief; the failure to obtain an interlocutory injunction in Quebec did not render the interlocutory injunction motion in Ontario *res judicata*; the refusal to grant injunctive relief did not constitute a final order and hence *res judicata* was not applicable). See also, to similar effect, *Global Petroleum Corp. v. Point Tupper Terminals Co.* (1998), 170 NSR (2d) 367 (CA).

James and Hazard point out that a troubling point is whether preclusive effect should be given to a judgment that is under appeal; the US decisions are divided on the issue, reflecting the dilemma posed. On the one hand, it makes little sense to give preclusive effect to a determination that may be reversed on appeal; on the other hand, it may be a waste of effort to retry an issue just because an appeal is pending in the earlier case (and hence there is no "final judgment").

9. *Exceptions to the application of res judicata (both claim and issue estoppel).* The law recognizes certain exceptional circumstances where some overriding question of fairness requires a rehearing of a matter that is otherwise *res judicata*. The two most important exceptions are (1) fraud or other misconduct in the earlier proceedings; or (2) the discovery of fresh evidence that "entirely changes the aspect of the case" that could not, by the exercise of reasonable diligence, have been adduced in the earlier proceeding. Both exceptions are discussed by Lord Denning in *McIlkenny*, below; both are narrowly construed and rarely, if ever, applied.

10. *Review exercise.* Consider the hypothetical case, above, that precedes *Brittania*. How many of the questions posed can you now answer? What are your answers?

C. Issue Estoppel

The legal doctrine of issue estoppel is in a state of considerable flux in Canadian law. Pulled between the traditional rigidity of English law and the modern flexibility of US law, Canadian courts have developed this area of the law cautiously, borrowing elements from both the United States and the United Kingdom and developing a distinctively Canadian approach to issue estoppel.

1. *The Basic Requirements of Issue Estoppel and an Introduction to Non-Mutuality*

As Garry Watson has observed, "Issue estoppel is an extension of the same rule of public policy, but it focuses not on claims or causes of actions, but on *issues*. It precludes relitigation of issues that a court has decided in a prior suit. If the cause of action involved in a subsequent proceeding is a separate and distinct one, cause of action estoppel will not apply. However, within a given cause of action there may be several issues that have to be adjudicated. If an issue has been determined in prior litigation, issue estoppel—even if the new litigation involves a different cause of action—will prevent relitigation of the issue already decided." (Garry D. Watson, "Duplicative Litigation: Issue Estoppel, Abuse of Process and the Death of Mutuality" (1990), 69 *Can. Bar Rev.* 623).

For issue estoppel to apply, three elements must be present: (1) the parties to both proceedings must be the same (or those in privity with the original parties); (2) the same issue must be involved in the first and subsequent litigation; (3) the issue must have been actually litigated and determined in a final fashion.

The mutuality requirement has proven the most contentious of these elements. In the United States, the requirement of mutuality has been abandoned. In *Blonder-Tongue Laboratories Inc. v. University of Illinois Foundation*, 402 US 313 (1971), the United States Supreme Court confirmed that mutuality would not be a requirement where issue estoppel (referred to as "collateral estoppel in the US context) was sought to be used defensively. Defensive issue estoppel arises where a subsequent defendant seeks to preclude an issue from being litigated which the plaintiff argued unsuccessfully against the original defendant. *Blonder-Tongue* approved the *defensive* use of non-mutual issue estoppel. In *Parklane Hosiery Co. v. Shore*, 439 US 322 (1979) the US Supreme Court approved *the offensive* application of non-mutual issue estoppel, though allowed lower courts a discretion in applying this doctrine to prevent unfairness to the parties.

Watson provides three arguments in favour of Canada abandoning mutuality in relation to issue estoppel:

> The purpose of issue estoppel is to "relieve parties of the cost and vexation of multiple lawsuits, conserve judicial resources, and, by preventing inconsistent decisions, encourage reliance on adjudication." The basic arguments in favour of nonmutual preclusion are that it reduces the risk of inconsistent adjudication, spares one party the cost of ever litigating the issue, and protects the court system and other litigants against the delay and burdens entailed by relitigation. These are substantial values, which go far to support the argument that one full and fair opportunity to litigate an issue is enough.

But the abandonment of mutuality, and the use of offensive non-mutual collateral estoppel in particular, has its opponents and there are policy arguments to the contrary. The first is that the case for non-mutual preclusion is weaker than that which supports preclusion between the same parties. The need to foster repose and reliance on judgments that support the general doctrine of preclusion is greatly diluted in the context of non-mutual issue preclusion. Moreover, the argument that a party should not be "twice-vexed"—burdened with relitigating the same issues—is inapplicable to offensive non-mutual preclusion. The defendant in the second action usually resists the application of issue estoppel and is quite happy to be "twice-vexed," if this means that he or she will have a second chance at a better result. In the final analysis it is the justice system, and other litigants within the system with unrelated disputes, that benefit from non-mutual preclusion's avoidance of duplicative litigation.

A second argument against non-mutual preclusion points to the fact that the first determination of an issue is not always correct, and refers to special dangers peculiar to non-mutual preclusion. Experienced litigators know that any decision may be strongly affected by the identity of the parties. For example, a badly disfigured survivor of an accident may have a much better chance of recovery than the estate of someone killed in the accident. Moreover, chance may not determine the identity of the plaintiff in the first action, since plaintiffs' lawyers may see to it that the most sympathetic claim is tried first. This argument rejects the notion that "fact finders compartmentalize their decision making and ignore 'irrelevant' information that one case is as good as another for establishing the liability facts for future cases. ... The damages proof often spills over into liability issues so that a case weak on liability is saved if the damages are strong and vice-versa." That the first court may be ignorant of the potential impact of its findings is seen as aggravating these difficulties. "No one involved in the first case can be sure whether its outcome will have collateral estoppel effects." The court "may yield to the temptation to make a sympathetic award, even if the liability proof does not quite justify it, if it appears that the defendant can easily afford to pay."

A third argument questions the contribution of non-mutual preclusion in preventing the legal system from embarrassing itself through inconsistent determinations. Although it "somewhat reduces the potential for inconsistent decisions," it in no way ensures this because (a) it is unavailable where its application would be unfair to the defendant, and (b) it does nothing to prevent relitigation of the same question if the plaintiff loses the first case.

Even accepting the merit of these arguments, offensive non-mutual preclusion remains justified because of (a) "its contribution to judicial efficiency" (sparing one party the cost of ever litigating the issue and protecting the court system and other litigants against the delay and burdens entailed by relitigation) and (b) its ability to bring about at least a partial reduction of inconsistent decisions. And surely these are sufficient justifications. To be acceptable, however, the doctrine must ensure fairness to the defendant by a careful determination that, in the first action, the defendant had a full and fair opportunity to litigate and that, therefore, to apply preclusion would be fair. Moreover, the doctrine must be administered in such a way as to disarm the "option effect" (the "free-riderism") that it offers to "wait and see" plaintiffs.

2. The Emergence of Non-Mutual Issue Estoppel (and Abuse of Process)

Confronted with a similar concern about mutuality in the application of issue estoppel, Lord Denning, writing for English Court of Appeal, unsuccessfully attempted to bring English law in line with the approach adopted by the US Supreme Court.

McIlkenny v. Chief Constable of the West Midlands
[1980] QB 283 (CA)

[The plaintiffs, who were alleged to be members of the IRA, had been previously convicted of the horrible bombing of a hotel that caused the death of numerous people. Subsequently, they brought a damage action against the police for allegedly beating them during their interrogation. During the course of the earlier criminal trial the accused had specifically raised this issue by alleging that their confessions had been beaten out of them, and both the judge (on the *voir dire*) and the jury had rejected this contention and held the confessions to be voluntary. In the subsequent civil action, the police argued that there was an issue estoppel arising from earlier criminal proceedings. In the Court of Appeal, Lord Denning based the dismissal of the action on the ground of non-mutual issue estoppel, holding that, for issue estoppel to apply, it should no longer be necessary, as required by traditional doctrine, that there be the same parties in both the former and the present action. What was essential, he held, is that the person against whom the estoppel was now sought to be pleaded (that is, the present plaintiffs) have been a party to the earlier proceeding. In so doing, Lord Denning referred to, and specifically embraced, the doctrine of non-mutual issue estoppel as developed in the United States. On the question of abandoning mutuality, Goff LJ dissented, insisting that mutuality and privity must remain, but holding that the action should be dismissed on the grounds of "abuse of process" arising from the fact that the very issue that the plaintiffs sought to raise had already been decided against them in the prior proceeding on the criminal standard of proof beyond a reasonable doubt. In his reasons, Lord Denning anticipated Goff LJ's invocation of abuse of process and stated that "the real reason why the claim was struck out was because the self-same issue had previously been determined *against* the party by a court of competent jurisdiction. What is that but issue estoppel?"]

DENNING MR: In seeking to strike out these actions, the police rely first on the law as to issue estoppel. They say that the six men are estopped from raising again an issue which was decided by Bridge J. Secondly, if that be wrong, the police say that these actions are an abuse of the process of the court. Now of these two propositions, I feel that priority should be given to issue estoppel. For this reason: It is admitted that the six men, if they are to be believed, have a reasonable cause of action for damages against the police officers: just as they have against the prison officers. On the ground that they, the six men, say that they were subjected to serious assaults—violence and threats—whilst in custody. The action itself is not therefore an abuse of the process. If it is to be called an abuse, it is because of the previous decision against them in the "trial within a trial." If they are to be stopped, it must be by way of an estoppel of some kind or other.

From that simple origin there has been built up over the centuries in our law a big house with many rooms. It is the house called Estoppel. In Coke's time it was a small house with only three rooms, namely, estoppel by matter of record, by matter in writing, and by matter in pais. But by our time we have so many rooms that we are apt to get confused between them. Estoppel per rem judicatam, issue estoppel, estoppel by deed, estoppel by representation, estoppel by conduct, estoppel by acquiescence, estoppel by election or waiver, estoppel by negligence, promissory estoppel, proprietary estoppel, and goodness knows what else. These several rooms have this much in common: They are all under one roof. Someone is stopped from saying something or other, or doing something or other, or contesting something or other. But each room is used differently from the others. If you go into one room, you will find a notice saying, "Estoppel is only a rule of evidence." If you go into another room you will find a different notice, "Estoppel can give rise to a cause of action." Each room has its own separate notices. It is a mistake to suppose that what you find in one room, you will also find in the others.

Privity and Mutuality

Today we go into a room described as estoppel *per rem judicatam*: in which there is an alcove which has sometimes passed unnoticed. It is called issue estoppel. In this room there are several chairs to sit on. One is called the doctrine of privity. The other is the doctrine of mutuality. The two look all right but they are both a bit rickety.

The doctrine of *privity* says that the only persons who can take advantage of the estoppel or be bound by it are the two parties to the previous proceedings themselves or their privies. No third person can take advantage of it or be bound by it; because he was no party to the previous proceedings. Those proceedings, so far as the third person is concerned, were *res inter alios acta*.

The doctrine of *mutuality* says that, in order that there should be an estoppel, it must be such that both of the two parties and their privies must be bound by the estoppel, whichever way it goes. Win or lose, each party must be bound. It is said that, in any contest, that is the only fair thing.

Now although those two chairs look all right to start with, you will soon find that they are quite unsafe. Jeremy Bentham as long ago as 1827 told people not to rely on them. In his "Rationale of Judicial Evidence," *Jeremy Bentham's Works* (Bowring ed., 1843), vol. VII, Book VI, p. 171, he said that: "This rule of *mutuality* is destitute of even that semblance of reason, which there is for the rule concerning *res inter alios acta*." And 10 years later in 1837 John William Smith in the 1st edition of his *Smith's Leading Cases* gave a warning more politely: "Yet this rule that an *estoppel must be mutual, otherwise neither party is bound*, must be taken with some limitation." Then in 1856 Martin B. in *Petrie v. Nuttall* (1856), 11 Exch. 569, 576-577, castigated the consequences of it as "absurd" and said it should be reconsidered by the court of error.

Our friends in the United States have been just as scathing as Jeremy Bentham. They have rejected the doctrine of mutuality altogether:, and they have limited the doctrine of privity. They take a distinction between a decision *in favour* of man and a decision *against* him. If a decision has been given *against* a man on the identical issue arising in previous proceedings—and he had full and fair opportunity of defending himself in it—

then he is estopped from contesting it again in subsequent proceedings. Not only is he estopped but so are those in privity with him. But there is no corresponding estoppel on the person in whose favour it operates.

This is no new departure. It was foreseen as long ago as 1776 when the judges of England advised the House of Lords in the *Duchess of Kingston's Case* (1776), 2 Smith LC (13th ed., 1929), pp. 644, 647-648:

> But in all these cases, the parties to the suits, or at least the parties against whom the evidence was received, were parties to the sentence, or had acquiesced under it; or claimed under those who were parties and had acquiesced. ...

Exceptions

It has long been recognised that estoppel per *rem judicatam* or issue estoppel is not an absolute bar to the matter in dispute being tried again. The party concerned can avoid the effect of the previous decision if he can prove the same to have been obtained by fraud or collusion. That was the unanimous opinion of the judges in the *Duchess of Kingston's Case*, 2 Smith LC (13th ed.), pp. 644, 652. To which we can add now that the party concerned can avoid the effect of the previous decision if he can show that a new fact has come to light (which he could not have ascertained before by reasonable diligence) which entirely changes the aspect of the case: see *Phosphate Sewage Co. Ltd. v. Molleson* (1879), 4 App. Cas. 801, 814, *per* Earl Cairns LC. This is a much stricter test than we require when we admit fresh evidence on an appeal. On an appeal (which is a re-hearing) we have said that the fresh evidence must be such that, if given, it would probably have an important influence on the result of the case, though it need not be decisive: see *Ladd v. Marshall*, [1954] 1 WLR 1489, 1491, and *Skone v. Skone*, [1971] 1 WLR 812, 815. But in order to avoid the effect of an estoppel (when there is no re-hearing) the fresh evidence must, I think, be decisive. It must be such as to show that the previous decision was wrong. Oath against oath will not do. An "important influence on the result" will not do. ...

[I]it seems to me that a previous decision in a civil case against a man operates as an estoppel preventing him from challenging it in subsequent proceedings unless he can show that it was obtained by fraud or collusion: or he can adduce fresh evidence (which he could not have obtained by reasonable diligence before) to show conclusively that the previous decision was wrong. ...

To illustrate my view of the present law, I would take this example. Suppose there is a road accident in which a lorry driver runs down a group of people on the pavement waiting for a bus. One of the injured persons sues the lorry driver for negligence and succeeds. Suppose now that another of the injured persons sues the lorry driver for damages also. Has he to prove the negligence all over again? Can the lorry driver (*against* whom the previous decision went) dispute his liability to the other injured person? It seems to me that if the lorry driver (with the backing of his employer) has had a full and fair opportunity of contesting the issue of negligence in the first action, he should be estopped from disputing it in the second action. He was a party to the first action and should be bound by the result of it. Not only the lorry driver, but also his employer should be estopped from disputing the issue of negligence in a second action: on the ground that the employer was in privity with the lorry driver.

Thus in all cases, both criminal and civil, our law is now brought into line with that of the United States. This should give an English lawyer satisfaction just as it did Lord Atkin in *Donoghue v. Stevenson*, [1932] AC 562, 598. As he paid tribute to the judgment of Cardozo J so I would pay tribute to the illuminating judgment of my friend Traynor J in *Bernhard v. Bank of America* (1942), 122 P2d 892 and equally of my friend White J in the Supreme Court in *Blonder-Tongue Laboratories v. University of Illinois* (1971), 402 US 313. ...

Abuse of the Process of the Court

In some cases in the past when the self-same issue has been decided *against* a party in previous proceedings, the courts have said that they will not allow him to raise it again in a subsequent proceeding. These decisions have been put on the ground that it is an abuse of the process of the court. ...

The truth is that at the date of those cases the doctrine of issue estoppel had not emerged as a separate doctrine. So the courts found it necessary to put it on "abuse of the process of the court." Now that issue estoppel is fully recognised, it is better to reach the decision on that ground: rather than on the vague phrase "abuse of the process of the court." Each doctrine is based on the same considerations and produces the same result.

Conclusion

This case shows what a civilised country we are. Here are six men who have been proved guilty of the most wicked murder of 21 innocent people. They have no money. Yet the state lavished large sums on their defence. They were convicted of murder and sentenced to imprisonment for life. In their evidence they were guilty of gross perjury. Yet the state continued to lavish large sums on them—in their actions against the police. It is high time that it stopped. It is really an attempt to set aside the convictions by a sidewind. It is a scandal that it should be allowed to continue. The issue was fully tried out and decided by Bridge J at the "trial within a trial." His finding on that issue is decisive unless there are circumstances which make it fair or just to reopen it. I see no such circumstances. I would allow the appeal and strike out these actions on the ground of issue estoppel.

NOTES AND QUESTIONS

1. On appeal to the House of Lords, in *McIlkenny* (*sub nom. Hunter v. Chief Constable of the West Midlands*, [1982] AC 529 (HL)), the court rejected Denning MR's attempt to reform the mutuality requirement of issue estoppel stating that it preferred the reasoning of Goff LJ. The following is an excerpt from the speech of Lord Diplock:

> My Lords, this is a case about abuse of the process of the High Court. It concerns the inherent power which any court of justice must possess to prevent misuse of its procedure in a way which, although not inconsistent with the literal application of its procedural rules, would nevertheless be manifestly unfair to a party to litigation before it, or would otherwise bring the administration of justice into disrepute among right-thinking people. The circumstances in

which abuse of process can arise are very varied; those which give rise to the instant appeal must surely be unique. It would, in my view, be most unwise if this House were to use this occasion to say anything that might be taken as limiting to fixed categories the kinds of circumstances in which the court has a duty (I disavow the word discretion) to exercise this salutary power. …

Lord Denning MR and Sir George Baker were also in favour of extending the description "issue estoppel" to cover the particular example of abuse of process of the court presented by the instant case—a question to which much of the judgment of Lord Denning is addressed. Goff LJ, on the other hand, expressed his own view, which had been shared by Cantley J, that such extension would involve a misuse of that expression. But if what Hunter is seeking to do in initiating this civil action is an abuse of the process of the court, as I understand all your Lordships are satisfied that it is, the question whether it also qualifies to bear the label "issue estoppel" is a matter not of substance but of semantics. Counsel for the appellant was therefore invited to address this House first upon the broader question of abuse of process and to deal in particular with the reasoning contained in the judgment of Goff LJ who dealt with the matter more closely than the other members of the court and bases his decision solely on that ground. In the result, counsel for the appellant, Hunter, who argued the case with their accustomed ability and diligence, were quite unable to persuade any of us that there was any error in the reasoning of Goff LJ in what proved to be the last judgment that he prepared before his much lamented and untimely death. In the result it became unnecessary to call on counsel for the police. So the debate upon semantics did not take place. It could not possibly affect the outcome of the appeal or justify the public expense that would have been involved in prolonging the hearing any further.

Nevertheless it is my own view, which I understand is shared by all your Lordships, that it would be best, in order to avoid confusion, if the use of the description "issue estoppel" *in English law, at any rate* (it does not appear to have been adopted in the United States), were restricted to that species of estoppel per rem judicatam that may arise in civil actions between the same parties or their privies, of which the characteristics are stated in a judgment of my own in *Mills v. Cooper*, [1967] 2 QB 459, 468-469 that was adopted and approved by this House in *Reg. v. Humphrys*, [1977] AC 1, the case in which it was also held that "issue estoppel" had no place in English criminal law.

The abuse of process which the instant case exemplifies is the initiation of proceedings in a court of justice for the purpose of mounting a collateral attack upon a final decision against the intending plaintiff which has been made by another court of competent jurisdiction in previous proceedings in which the intending plaintiff had a full opportunity of contesting the decision in the court by which it was made.

The proper method of attacking the decision by Bridge J in the murder trial that Hunter was not assaulted by the police before his oral confession was obtained would have been to make the contention that the judge's ruling that the confession was admissible had been erroneous a ground of his appeal against his conviction to the Criminal Division of the Court of Appeal. This Hunter did not do. Had he or any of his fellow murderers done so, application could have been made on that appeal to tender to the court as "fresh evidence" all material upon which Hunter would now seek to rely in his civil action against the police for damages for assault, if it were allowed to continue.

2. Does it matter whether we eliminate the mutuality requirement for issue estoppel or rely on abuse of process? What is at stake in this distinction between issue estoppel and abuse of process? Is it important that one is a rule and the other a involves the exercise of discretion? Is it a debate of technical significance or does it have practical significance?

Whether or not the distinction affects the outcome in any particular case, the rejection of Denning MR's position by the House of Lords in *Hunter* (coupled with the adoption of the reasoning of *Hunter* by the Ontario Court of Appeal in *Demeter*, see below) has introduced considerable confusion into Anglo-Canadian law on the continuing requirement of mutuality. Current case law suggests that English and Canadian judges no longer "buy" mutuality as a requirement of issue estoppel—that is, they agree with Denning and the US authorities—but they feel they must resort to abuse of process when faced with a case in which this requirement is not met. (Could it be that they do this just to confuse law students?)

In an article in (1986), 64 *Can. Bar Rev.* 437, at 453, Michael Herman and Gerald Hayden argue that *McIlkenny* collapsed the two questions into one:

> It does seem that this attempt to collaterally attack the finding of the trial judge in the criminal proceedings is an abuse of process, and it may well be that this is another, independent ground on which the civil action for assault could have been dismissed or stayed. However, to preserve clear thinking, it is important to realize that the application of the doctrine of abuse of process for their purpose is quite different and distinct from the narrower and more specific doctrine of issue estoppel, which seems to deal with the more salient complaint in the case; namely that the defendants ought not to be able to relitigate a matter which has already been found against them in the prior criminal adjudication. In the instant case, the application of the doctrine of issue estoppel was sufficient to dispose of the case, whether or not the plaintiffs' conduct in the subsequent civil proceeding was abusive as an improper collateral attack on the criminal trial judge's findings. By simply relying on the generalized and multi-purpose principle of abuse of process, the House of Lords has muddied the waters, and has failed to distinguish between two distinct, albeit complementary, bases on which the civil cause of action was properly dismissed.

Do you agree?

3. How should the legal system deal with wrongful convictions? Subsequent to their civil action, the case was investigated by a different police force whose findings were considered by the Court of Appeal in January 1987, at which time the court upheld the convictions. In March 1990, the home secretary ordered that the police inquiry into the case be reopened to examine new evidence that might provide grounds for further reference to the Court of Appeal. The new evidence included revelations that several members of the now disbanded West Midlands Serious Crime Squad (which had investigated the Bombers) extracted confessions from men, allegedly by brutality. Subsequently, the home secretary again referred the case to the Court of Appeal on the ground that new evidence "might be thought to cast doubt on the safety of the convictions," notwithstanding that the pending police inquiry was not expected to be completed for several months. In March 1991, the six were acquitted and released.

It eventually came to light that the police had withheld exculpatory evidence, fabricated inculpatory evidence, and, indeed, extracted confessions through the use of force and intimidation. As Gerry Hunter, one of the six men, stated, the only thing he was guilty of was being Irish and leaving on a train from Birmingham to Belfast to attend an IRA funeral.

These events may seem to make it ironic to use their civil case as a major basis for an argument for issue preclusion, particularly in the light of the ultimate acquittal of the "Guildford Four" (whose bombing convictions were referred to and quashed by the Court of Appeal after they had spent 15 years in prison) and the release of the "Maguire Seven" (whose convictions for operating a bomb factory were declared by the director of public prosecutions to be unsafe after the accused had spent 10 years in jail). In cases like these, to avoid the chaos of relitigation of all criminal convictions, should we leave reconsideration of unsound verdicts to the type of rehearings used in those cases (satisfactory or unsatisfactory as they may be), rather than to private attempts at collateral attack?

In Canada, the wrongful convictions of Donald Marshall, David Milgaard, and Guy Paul Morin have heightened public concern about wrongful convictions generally. The Royal Commission on the Donald Marshall Jr. Prosecution recommended the establishment of an independent review body to investigate cases of alleged wrongful conviction. As a public inquiry, this body would have coercive powers to compel witnesses to testify and provide evidence.

Some still contend that to blame the application of a *res judicata* principle for wrongful convictions is to miss the point and purpose of the principle. Those who blame a rigorous use of estoppel argue that it is important that every opportunity must be given to ensure that truth is arrived at in the judicial process: systemic efficiency ought not to trump substantive justice. Others disagree. While the appeal process is primarily directed to ensuring adequate safeguards against erroneous decisions, the doctrine of *res judicata* is more concerned with matters of judicial efficiency and procedural fairness—it wishes to allocate scarce institutional resources sensibly and to ensure that everyone has a full and fair opportunity to present their case, but only once. Does the ultimate outcome affect your confidence in a rigorous application of estoppel? Could there have been a more appropriate result?

4. In the opposite vein, many were puzzled that the families of Nicole Brown and Ronald Goldman were able to obtain determinations of liability against O.J. Simpson in civil actions for wrongful death after Simpson had been acquitted of criminal charges based on the same events. Why was the civil action not a collateral attack on the result of the criminal trial?

5. *The power of offensive non-mutual estoppel and its problems.* A plane crashes, killing all 250 passengers. Wrongful death actions are commenced by the next of kin of the deceased against the airline. Of these actions, 24 are consolidated for trial and result in a verdict for the plaintiffs based on a finding of negligence on the part of the airline. Subsequently, in 10 further actions, the plaintiffs move for summary judgment on the issue of liability on the ground that in view of the earlier decision the issue is *res judicata*. What will the decision be? Compare *United States v. United Airlines, Inc.*, 216 F Supp. 701, aff'd. *sub nom. United Airlines v. Wiener*, 335 F2d 379 (9th Cir. 1964) and *Zdanok v. Glidden Co.*, 327 F2d 944 (2d Cir. 1964) with *Berner v. British Commonwealth Pacific Airlines, Ltd.*, 346 F2d 532 (2d Cir. 1965).

What if instead the 24 plaintiffs had sued the airline in successive actions and lost and a 25th plaintiff sues and wins. May the 26th plaintiff (and all other persons suing in respect of the death of the passengers) rely on the judgment in the 25th case?

P1 sues D for demolishing his new car in an auto accident; D is found negligent and ordered to pay $20,000. D is then sued by P1's passenger, P2, for $500,000 for personal injuries. May P2 rely on issue estoppel? What if D had won the first action on a finding that he had not been negligent. Can D rely on this finding as issue estoppel in P2's action?

In *Parklane Hosiery Co. v. Shore*, 439 US 322 (1979), mentioned above, the US Supreme Court concluded that the preferable approach is not to preclude the use of "offensive collateral estoppel" (that is, preventing a plaintiff who has been successful in a claim against one defendant from bringing a similar claim against another defendant and seeking to prevent the subsequent defendant from relitigating the issues decided in the first claim) but to grant trial courts broad discretion to determine when it should be applied. The general rule should be that in cases where a plaintiff could easily have joined in the earlier action or where the application of offensive estoppel would be unfair to a defendant, a trial judge should not allow the use of offensive collateral estoppel.

6. In *Bomac Construction Ltd. v. Stevenson* (1986), 48 Sask. R 62, two people were injured in a plane accident. The first plaintiff succeeded in a negligence action and damages against the plane owners and the pilot. A second plaintiff brought a similar action. The plaintiff moved to have the defendants' defence struck out. In allowing the application, the Saskatchewan Court of Appeal stated that

> [i]t is usual to consider that the concept of abuse of process is applicable only to a plaintiff's claim to prevent the commencement of certain types of actions, but there is no apparent reason for its restriction to such circumstances when it is considered that the purpose is to prevent the raising of an issue which has already been squarely before the courts once before and decision rendered. There seems little justification for concluding that such an issue cannot be raised by a plaintiff but may be raised in defence by a defendant. If the concern is a valid one, it should not matter by what process the concern is raised.
>
> In any event, there would be great difficulty in thinking that courts would permit a rule to evolve which in negligence cases involving a claim and counterclaim the defendant could be permitted to challenge the previous trial finding out of the same occurrence but as plaintiff by counterclaim he would be precluded from doing so on the basis of abuse of process.
>
> What is involved here is that the plaintiff wishes to deny the defence the opportunity to have a second chance to avoid liability, whereas the defence contend that by not joining in the first action the plaintiff has sought to assure its opportunity for two chances to succeed. If the first action was successful she would seek to rely on it, whereas if the first action was not successful she would have a second chance to succeed by proceeding with this case. One cannot conclude that the ends of justice are best served by permitting such a situation to prevail. If the plaintiffs in separate actions wish to stand on their right to a separate trial where the facts and issues and defendants are identical with another claim, they must take the chance of having their claim follow the result of the first action. Similarly, the defendant liability must be taken as having been established in the first action. To rule otherwise would be to permit an abuse of process through the prospect of a multiplicity of actions, inconsistent results and no fitting end to the litigation process.
>
> Courts are always reluctant to prevent an issue from proceeding to trial. This reluctance has been expressed time and time again, particularly in relation to applications to set aside statements of claim as disclosing no cause of action. The same reluctance arises here but it is tem-

pered somewhat by the knowledge that the basic issues raised by the plaintiff and the third party claim have been fully canvassed, and if any injustice arises from an inability to litigate the said issues again it is less than the potential injustice perpetuated both on the parties and the judicial system by having the same basic issues dealt with in two or perhaps three separate trials.

7. *Offensive non-mutual estoppel in Canadian courts.* In his survey of Anglo-Canadian doctrine, "Duplicative Litigation: Issue Estoppel, Abuse of Process, and the Death of Mutuality" (1990), 69 *Can. Bar Rev.* 623, Garry Watson argues that, while Canada lacks a landmark decision of an appellate court clearly abandoning the mutuality requirement in favour of non-mutual issue estoppel, the *Bomac* decision (above), and concludes that the rise of abuse of process cases has achieved the "the death of mutuality" in Canada without ever formally abandoning the requirement of mutuality in the context of issue estoppel.

8. *Application of issue estoppel to interlocutory orders and to decisions made within one proceeding.* Here there are two distinct situations and questions. The first is what preclusive effect will be given in action number 2 to a decision made in action number 1 where the decision is one that did not dispose of action number 1—that is, it was not embodied in the final judgment but was merely embodied in an order giving some form of interim relief or deciding some interlocutory procedural point—for example, whether a claim for privilege was valid? Generally, the answer in this situation is that because the decision was not a final one (said to be a prerequisite to the application of any form of *res judicata*), issue estoppel is inapplicable and there is no preclusion: see, for example, *Barwell Food Sales Inc. v. Snyder & Fils Inc.* (1988), 38 CPC (2d) 192 (Ont. HC) (where the plaintiff commenced separate actions in Quebec and Ontario for the same relief; the failure to obtain an interlocutory injunction in Quebec did not render the interlocutory injunction application in Ontario *res judicata*; the refusal to grant injunctive relief did not constitute a final order and hence *res judicata* was not applicable).

The second situation is what preclusive effect will be given to issues decided within a given proceeding—that is, if an issue is raised and decided at one stage in the proceeding, may the parties relitigate it at a later stage—for example, on a subsequent interlocutory motion or at trial? The answer is that, in terms of statements of general principle, the case law is in hopeless confusion. Compare the following rulings. *Res judicata* applies to interlocutory orders in the absence of an appeal, a material change in circumstances, or new evidence that had been previously suppressed or unavailable: *Newmarch Mechanical Constructors Ltd. v. Hyundai Auto Canada Inc.* (1994), 26 CPC (3d) 289 (Ont. Gen. Div.). For issue estoppel to apply, the subject order must finally determine an issue; because the interlocutory injunction in question was not final but interlocutory in nature, the court was prepared to review the issue afresh: *Trilea Centres Inc. v. Cumming Cockburn Ltd.* (1991), 5 OR (3d) 598 (Gen. Div.). Where an issue is raised and determined in the context of an interlocutory motion, as a general rule, issue estoppel applies and neither party will be permitted to relitigate the issue in the same or a subsequent proceeding: *Ward v. Dana D. Colson Management Ltd.* (1994), 24 CPC (3d) 211 (Ont. Gen. Div.), aff'd. [1994] OJ No. 2792 (CA). In *Ward*, Macdonald J observed (at para. 12):

I am satisfied the issue estoppel is not eliminated as an issue because O'Brien J's order was made in the context of an interlocutory application. A decision in an interlocutory application is binding on the parties, at least with respect to other proceedings in the same action. I agree with the submission that the general principle is that it is not open for the court, in a case of the same question arising between the same parties, to review a previous decision not open to appeal. If the decision was wrong, it ought to have been appealed within the appropriate time-frames. This principle is not affected by the fact that the first decision was pronounced in the course of the same action.

This passage has been applied several times since. For an example, see *Roseau River Anishinabe First Nation v. Atkinson* (2001), 107 ACWS (3d) 2 (FCTD).

Where the plaintiff had been refused an order for disclosure of documents in the defendant's possession on the ground that they were protected by public interest immunity, the court held that a further application by the plaintiff would be considered; a ruling on an interlocutory application that does not adjudicate on issues of fact or law raised by the pleadings is not *res judicata* if the same interlocutory issue is raised again: *Pocklington Foods Inc. v. Alberta (Provincial Treasurer)* (1993), 25 CPC (3d) 292 (Alta. QB), varied (1995), 28 Alta. LR (3d) 96 (CA).

In part, these conflicting statements reflect uncertainty about the role and application of the "final order" requirement to issues decided within a given proceeding. In the United States, much of the confusion found in the Canadian case law in our attempts to apply the *res judicata* principles to issues decided within a given proceeding, has been avoided by removing such cases from the operation of *res judicata* and subjecting them to a separate (but clearly related) doctrine called "the law of the case." James and Hazard, *Civil Procedure*, 593 explain this doctrine as follows:

> The rules of *res judicata* are to be distinguished from a related but distinct rule, that of the "law of the case." The law-of-the-case rule has application to a determination of a question of law at an earlier stage of a proceeding. The rule is that a determination once made will be treated as correct through all subsequent stages of the proceeding except when the question comes before a higher court. Thus, a trial court will treat its own earlier rulings as conclusive in subsequent trial proceedings. Similarly, when there has been an interlocutory appeal in which a legal question was decided, that decision will be treated as conclusive by the same appellate court if the case later comes before it on an appeal from the final judgment. The law of the case rule thus applies within one action regarding issues of law previously determined that action, while the rules of *res judicata* apply between successive actions.

9. Issue estoppel has created challenges for Canadian courts in criminal as well as civil settings. In *R v. Mahalingan* 2008 SCC 68, the Supreme Court was divided on whether issue estoppel applies in the context of criminal law:

> I have read the reasons of my colleague Justice Charron and agree with them, with the exception of their treatment of issue estoppel. Issue estoppel, as applied in Canada since *Grdic v. The Queen*, [1985] 1 SCR 810, has created perplexing difficulties and fostered calls for reform. That reform is required is beyond doubt. The only question is whether that reform should take the form of excising issue estoppel entirely from the criminal law, as my colleague contends, or whether the principle should be retained in a narrower, less problematic form.
>
> I favour the latter approach. In my view, the difficulties associated with the application of issue estoppel in criminal law arise from the fact that it has been extended to circumstances

where justice does not support its application. Properly confined, in accordance with a proper reading of the majority reasons in *Grdic*, issue estoppel plays an indispensable role in ensuring fairness to the accused, avoiding inconsistent verdicts and maintaining the principle of finality. Other concepts, such as abuse of process, character evidence rules, and the rules governing the admissibility of similar fact evidence, do not completely or effectively guarantee these goals. Though it shares many features with its civil law equivalent, criminal law issue estoppel is a stand-alone doctrine responsive to the unique characteristics of criminal trials. I would therefore decline to throw out issue estoppel in its entirety. Rather, I would modify the current Canadian approach to issue estoppel in criminal law, confining it to the focused compass of precluding the Crown from leading evidence which is inconsistent with findings made in the accused's favour in a previous proceeding.

Applying this principle to the facts in this case, I conclude that issue estoppel does not operate against the Crown. The accused argues that issue estoppel means that evidence admitted on his first trial, the verdict under appeal, must now be deemed to have been improperly admitted on the ground that he was acquitted on a second charge where the subject matter of the second charge was the same as the impugned evidence led at the first trial. In my view, this argument invokes the doctrine of issue estoppel in a manner that is overbroad. I agree with Blair JA, dissenting in the Court of Appeal, that properly understood, issue estoppel does not operate retrospectively to require the ordering of a new trial. However, as a new trial is required on other grounds, I would dismiss the appeal.

A specific problem for Canadian courts has been how to deal with the attempt to relitigate a criminal matter in civil courts. Since mutuality will not be present in such cases, the courts have turned to the doctrine of abuse of process to preserve the finality of judgments in criminal proceedings.

3. *The Impact of Criminal Convictions on Civil Proceedings*

Demeter v. British Pacific Life Insurance Co.
(1983), 150 DLR (3d) 249 (Ont. SC)

OSLER J: These three actions, which are, with the exception of minor details, identical, are brought by the plaintiff against the three defendant insurance companies upon policies of insurance whereby the defendants, respectively, agreed to pay to the survivor of the plaintiff and Christine Demeter, his wife, specific sums of money upon the death of the other. The statements of claim allege that on July 18, 1973, the plaintiff's wife, Christine Demeter, died; that proof of her death was duly filed; that each of the policies was in full force and effect at the material time; and that payment has been refused by each of the defendants. In their amended statements of defence each of the defendants plead that Christine Demeter came to her death by reason of the criminal conduct of the plaintiff and that the purported policy was thereby rendered void and unenforceable, that public policy precludes any person benefiting from his own criminal act, and the death of the life insured resulted from a criminal act of the plaintiff. They add certain technical defences.

[The defendants moved for an order to determine as a question of law the effect of the criminal conviction on the civil claims and for an order dismissing the claims as an abuse of process. Counsel for the plaintiff relied heavily on the decision of the English Court of Appeal in *Hollington v. F. Hewthorn & Co. Ltd.*, [1943] 1 KB 587, holding that in a motor vehicle action, evidence of the defendant's conviction for driving without due care and attention was inadmissible. Osler J reviewed the authorities dealing with *Hollington* and concluded that it had not been followed in Canada, had been overruled by the House of Lords in *McIlkenny*, *supra*, and that proof of the conviction of the plaintiff for the murder of his wife may be adduced in evidence and, if this is done, should be regarded as *prima facie* proof of that issue, subject to rebuttal by the plaintiff on the merits.]

That, however, does not end the matter. [The defendants contend that] the claim of the plaintiff in the statements of claim constitutes an abuse of the process of the court in light of the conviction of the plaintiff for the murder of his wife.

In *McIlkenny*, Lord Diplock was careful to emphasize that the inherent jurisdiction of the court to dismiss or stay an action as an abuse of its own process was one to be sparingly exercised but one that undoubtedly existed and should be exercised if the circumstances should warrant. In *McIlkenny's* case, what was said to be an abuse of the process of the court was the collateral attack inherent in the civil action upon not simply and plainly the prior criminal conviction but really upon a subordinate finding that it must have been assumed the jury made, as well as the trial judge, in the light of the verdict it reached. ...

The gravamen of the abuse is the attempt to relitigate an issue already tried. True, Lord Diplock did refer to what he concluded was an improper motive for proceeding with the action, namely, the desire to influence the Home Secretary to pardon the offenders rather than the purported aim of the action to secure damages. He reached this conclusion because one of the defendants, the Home Secretary on behalf of prison guards, had caused a payment to be made into court or an offer to be tendered which the plaintiffs disregarded. It is, therefore, perhaps not entirely out of place to refer to what was placed before me as an excerpt from the *de bene esse* examination of Csaba Szilagyi on April 17, 1978, when the plaintiff, conducting the examination on his own behalf, stated in part:

> ... I am not here for the money, I am here to reopen my case. The only reason I decided to—planning this on the record—the reason I am going to publish in the first volume only until the night of my wife's death, July 18th, '73, which is mostly about us, mostly about Mr. Szilagyi and my wife. To put him into the position to have to go to court and refute it, because only through these reactions and an action he has to start, can I reopen my case, can I bring my new witnesses and prove my total innocence and vindicate myself.

Those words do not suggest a man who is single-mindedly pursuing a series of actions for purely financial reasons.

In fairness, however, it must be said that Ms Belman put it forcefully that such an interpretation does not accord with reason and common sense. The plaintiff Demeter has now served almost ten years of a life sentence for non-capital murder. He is now on day parole and stands an excellent chance of being placed on full parole in the very near future. An attempt to prove his innocence, Ms Belman says, might well result in a new trial being ordered, a trial which would of necessity be for first degree murder and which would carry with it the risk of conviction and a sentence of not less than 25 years, with no credit for the time already served.

The motive of the plaintiff, then, may be dubious. Nevertheless, the circumstances of this case, the fact of conviction for the non-capital murder of his wife, the dismissal of his appeals up to and including the Supreme Court of Canada, and the refusal of the Minister of Justice to reopen the case, persuade me beyond peradventure that to permit these actions to go forward would result in a travesty of justice and would bring the administration of justice into disrepute. It would be, in the most fitting phrase of Schroeder JA, in *Kennedy v. Tomlinson et al.* (1959), 20 DLR (2d) 273, 126 CCC 175, "an unedifying spectacle." ...

Nothing is put forward, therefore, by the plaintiff to justify me in concluding that, if the prior conviction were admitted in the present actions as *prima facie* evidence of the fact that the plaintiff killed his wife, any evidence is available to the plaintiff that would cast doubt upon that proposition. In view of the solemn verdict of the jury, properly charged with respect to the burden of proof, the fact that proof must be beyond a reasonable doubt, and the identity of the issue before the jury with the issue in the present actions, it would be an affront to one's sense of justice and would be regarded as an outrage by the reasonable layman to let these actions go forward. In the exercise of the court's inherent jurisdiction they will each be dismissed with costs.

Actions dismissed.

[Demeter's appeal to the Ontario Court of Appeal was dismissed: (1984), 13 DLR (4th) 318, per MacKinnon ACJO:]

We agree with Mr. Justice Osler's careful and thoughtful analysis of the authorities and his conclusions that *Hollington v. F. Hewthorn & Co., Ltd. et al.*, [1943] 1 KB 587, which held that the fact that the defendant driver in that case had been convicted of careless driving at the time and place of the accident did not amount to even *prima facie* evidence of his negligent driving at the time and place, is not the law in Ontario. We are equally of the view that the use of a civil action to initiate a collateral attack on a final decision of a criminal court of competent jurisdiction in an attempt to relitigate an issue already tried is an abuse of the process of the court. The alleged fresh evidence or evidence of fraud or collusion falls far short of supporting an argument that an exception should be made to the general rule of public policy.

On the facts of this case it would be, as the learned motions court judge pointed out, an affront to one's sense of justice to let these actions go forward and, for the reasons given by him, the appeals are dismissed with costs as of one appeal.

Appeal dismissed.

NOTES AND QUESTIONS

1. The BC *Evidence Act*, RSBC 1996, c. 124, s. 71 provides that evidence of a prior conviction may be admitted in a subsequent civil action, and that the weight to be given to the
conviction is a matter for the trier of fact. In other provinces, the matter is governed by the
common law. For instance, in Ontario, there is authority that a criminal conviction is admissible as *prima facie* evidence only and the reasons for conviction or findings of fact in
support of the conviction are not admissible in evidence in civil proceedings; see *Re Del
Core and Ontario College of Pharmacists* (1985), 51 OR (2d) 1 (CA) (discipline hearing following a criminal conviction) and *Taylor v. Baribeau* (1985), 51 OR (2d) 541 (Div. Ct.)
(personal injury action following a conviction for dangerous driving).

2. Was *Q. v. Minto Management Ltd. and Halliday* (1984), 15 DLR (4th) 581 (Ont. HC)
correctly decided? The plaintiff sued for damages resulting from an assault committed by
the defendant Halliday, an employee of the corporate defendant, Minto. The plaintiff resided
in a building owned by Minto, and alleged that Minto was negligent in permitting Halliday
to have access to her apartment. Prior to the civil action, Halliday had been convicted of
sexual assault and sentenced to seven years' imprisonment. Steele J held that proof of the
conviction was admissible against *both* defendants, but that *both* should be permitted to
challenge the correctness of the conviction on the ground that it could not be said they were
guilty of abuse of process, since they had not initiated the proceedings but were merely defending themselves.

3. *How should criminal convictions be used in subsequent civil actions?* Should a distinction be drawn between criminal convictions for serious criminal offences and convictions
for less serious matters, such as careless driving and other traffic offences? In the United
States, many jurisdictions prevent a party from relitigating issues determined by conviction
where the offence was a serious one (such as in *Demeter* or *Q. v. Minto Management Ltd. et
al.*), but provide that in less serious matters (such as traffic offences) the conviction should
be evidence only. The distinction is explained in H. Karlson, "Criminal Judgments as Proof
of Civil Liability" (1982), 31 *Defense Law Journal* 173:

> In order for a criminal conviction to preclude a party from relitigating issues determined in the
> criminal proceeding, the defendant must have had an adequate opportunity and incentive to
> obtain a full and fair adjudication in the criminal action. When a criminal trial concerns a seri-
> ous offense, the accused clearly has motivation to defend himself fully, and the procedural re-
> quirements of our criminal justice system ensure a fair day in court. These characteristics,
> however, are not always present in proceedings arising out of minor traffic offenses. Unless a
> defendant is aware that the outcome of the traffic court proceeding will create a substantial risk
> of civil liability, he usually has little incentive to contest the issue of guilt. Minor fines imposed
> by traffic courts create no desire on the part of a defendant to expend the funds necessary to
> obtain an attorney and litigate the issues. A driver may plead guilty to a minor traffic offense
> because the cost of defending outweighs the burden of having such a conviction on his
> record.
>
> Even where a driver has the incentive to contest his guilt, traffic courts are neither designed
> nor equipped to become the crucial forums in deciding issues for civil actions. The incredible
> volume of convictions generated by traffic courts must be routinely handled in as expeditious
> a manner as possible. If the effect of a minor traffic conviction is to preclude relitigation of

important issues in a civil action, drivers involved in traffic accidents will have a strong incentive to contest traffic citations. This would increase, not decrease, litigation. Therefore, one of the main justifications for the doctrine of collateral estoppel, the reduction of litigation, will not result from permitting traffic convictions to be used in subsequent civil actions. The overwhelming majority of jurisdictions that have considered the questions have, by either statute or court decision, refused to permit a minor traffic conviction to preclude relitigation of issues in a civil action.

In his "Duplicative Litigation" article, above, Garry Watson notes that generally the Canadian case law envisages prior judgments being used in subsequent proceedings in two different ways: as truly preclusive issue estoppel (which prevents relitigation), and as *prima facie* evidence subject to rebuttal (which permits relitigation, but with the prior judgment being admitted in evidence in the second litigation). The first approach has been taken with regard to the use of prior civil determinations, while the second approach has been taken with the use of prior criminal convictions.

He then poses some questions. If mutuality is openly abandoned, and non-mutual preclusion is adopted subject to appropriate qualifications, why should criminal convictions be treated any differently from civil determinations? He also raises the question whether there is any role at all for prior determinations as merely "*prima facie*" evidence subject to rebuttal?

He argues that reason dictates that where the conditions for non-mutual preclusion are met, this "stronger" doctrine should apply, leaving no room for the *prima facie* evidence approach. If the dual components of the doctrine—fairness and efficiency—are met, then issue estoppel should apply and the former judgment should preclude relitigation: preclusive effect should be given to the prior judgment, rather than merely making it a matter of evidence.

But accepting this general proposition still leaves circumstances where it will be appropriate to use the evidentiary approach. This can be seen by examining the *Hollington v. Hewthorn* type of scenario, that is, a prior traffic conviction followed by a subsequent civil motor vehicle action. Here, if we apply the tests necessary to determine whether nonmutual preclusion should be available it will often lead to the conclusion that it is inapplicable. First, frequently in such cases the "full and fair opportunity to defend" test will not be met because given the nature of most traffic court proceedings the now convicted person will often have lacked the incentive to litigate fully the issue in the traffic court. Second, if we accept the notion that the driving force behind non-mutual preclusion is judicial efficiency and that it should not apply where efficiencies are minimal or non-existent, then there may be a further reason for not applying preclusion in the subsequent civil negligence action. Often in such cases, issues other than the liability of the convicted person are present (for example, the plaintiff's contributory negligence and the comparative negligence of other defendants) so that all the evidence relating to the accident has to be adduced (including the evidence relating to the convicted person's negligence). The end result is that there may be no efficiency gains and, moreover, giving preclusive effect to the conviction may actually complicate the second adjudication. (A further argument for not giving preclusive effect to traffic convictions, involving both fairness and efficiency, is that often the real party in interest in the subsequent civil action will be an insurance company, which will not have participated in the criminal defence of the insured. From an efficiency point of view, the last thing we want to do is to have insurance companies defending every traffic prosecution against their insured on the off chance that there may subsequently be a civil negligence claim.)

If, however, in any given circumstances it is inappropriate to give preclusive effect to a prior judgment, resort may still be had to admitting the prior judgment as *prima facie* evidence subject to rebuttal, since the fairness rights of all persons affected are protected by their ability to call evidence to rebut the *prima facie* evidence arising from the earlier judgment. But in some cases involving the use of prior criminal convictions in subsequent civil actions, non-mutual preclusion will be quite appropriate, for example, after a fully contested rape trial where the accused was vigorously represented and faced a substantial period of imprisonment, and was convicted. If the convicted person is subsequently sued for damages for assault, a court should normally conclude that such an accused had a full and fair opportunity to defend. [Footnote: This will also be true of some traffic convictions, for example, for impaired driving, where there was a vigorous defence. I am not suggesting a separate rule for traffic convictions and other convictions (but see, *supra*, as to the role of insurance). In all cases a functional analysis is required.] The conditions for non-mutual preclusion will have been met and issue estoppel should apply to the exclusion of giving the previous conviction effect as *prima facie* evidence subject to rebuttal.

Toronto (City) v. CUPE, Local 79
2003 SCC 63

[O worked as a recreation instructor for the respondent City. He was charged with sexually assaulting a boy under his supervision. He pleaded not guilty. At trial before a judge alone, he testified and was cross-examined. The trial judge found that the complainant was credible and that O was not. He entered a conviction, which was affirmed on appeal. The City fired O a few days after his conviction. O grieved the dismissal. At the arbitration hearing, the City submitted the complainant's testimony from the criminal trial and the notes of O's supervisor, who had spoken to the complainant at the time. The complainant was not called to testify. O testified, claiming that he had never sexually assaulted the boy. The arbitrator ruled that the criminal conviction was admissible evidence, but that it was not conclusive as to whether O had sexually assaulted the boy. No fresh evidence was introduced. The arbitrator held that the presumption raised by the criminal conviction had been rebutted, and that O had been dismissed without just cause. The Divisional Court quashed the arbitrator's ruling. The Court of Appeal upheld that decision.]

ARBOUR J:

V. Analysis

[A discussion of standard of review and s. 22.1 of the Ontario *Evidence Act* has been omitted.]

. . .

C. The Common Law Doctrines

Much consideration was given in the decisions below to the three related common law doctrines of issue estoppel, abuse of process and collateral attack. Each of these doctrines was considered as a possible means of preventing the union from relitigating the criminal conviction of the grievor before the arbitrator. Although both the Divisional Court and the Court of Appeal concluded that the union could not relitigate the guilt of the grievor as reflected in his criminal conviction, they took different views of the applicability of the different doctrines advanced in support of that conclusion. While the Divisional Court concluded that relitigation was barred by the collateral attack rule, issue estoppel and abuse of process, the Court of Appeal was of the view that none of these doctrines as they presently stand applied to bar the rebuttal. Rather, it relied on a self-standing "finality principle." I think it is useful to disentangle these various rules and doctrines before turning to the applicable one here. I stress at the outset that these common law doctrines are interrelated and in many cases more than one doctrine may support a particular outcome. Even though both issue estoppel and collateral attacks may properly be viewed as particular applications of a broader doctrine of abuse of process, the three are not always entirely interchangeable.

(1) Issue Estoppel

Issue estoppel is a branch of *res judicata* (the other branch being *cause of action* estoppel), which precludes the relitigation of issues previously decided in court in another proceeding. For issue estoppel to be successfully invoked, three preconditions must be met: (1) the issue must be the same as the one decided in the prior decision; (2) the prior judicial decision must have been final; and (3) the parties to both proceedings must be the same, or their privies (*Danyluk v. Ainsworth Technologies Inc.*, [2001] 2 SCR 460, 2001 SCC 44, at para. 25, *per* Binnie J). The final requirement, known as "mutuality," has been largely abandoned in the United States and has been the subject of much academic and judicial debate there as well as in the United Kingdom and, to some extent, in this country. (See G.D. Watson, "Duplicative Litigation: Issue Estoppel, Abuse of Process and the Death of Mutuality" (1990), 69 *Can. Bar Rev.* 623, at pp. 648-51.) In light of the different conclusions reached by the courts below on the applicability of issue estoppel, I think it is useful to examine that debate more closely.

The first two requirements of issue estoppel are met in this case. The final requirement of mutuality of parties has not been met. In the original criminal case, the *lis* was between Her Majesty the Queen in right of Canada and Glenn Oliver. In the arbitration, the parties were CUPE and the City of Toronto, Oliver's employer. It is unnecessary to decide whether Oliver and CUPE should reasonably be viewed as privies for the purpose of the application of the mutuality requirement since it is clear that the Crown, acting as prosecutor in the criminal case, is not privy with the City of Toronto, nor would it be with a provincial, rather than a municipal, employer (as in the *Ontario v. OPSEU* case, released concurrently).

There has been much academic criticism of the mutuality requirement of the doctrine of issue estoppel. In his article, Prof. Watson, *supra*, argues that explicitly abolishing the mutuality requirement, as has been done in the United States, would both reduce confusion in the law and remove the possibility that a strict application of issue estoppel may work an injustice. The arguments made by him and others (see also D.J. Lange, *The Doctrine of Res Judicata in Canada* (2000)), urging Canadian courts to abandon the mutuality requirement have been helpful in articulating a principled approach to the bar against relitigation. In my view, however, appropriate guidance is available in our law without the modification to the mutuality requirement that this case would necessitate.

In his very useful review of the abandonment of the mutuality requirement in the United States, Prof. Watson, at p. 631, points out that mutuality was first relaxed when issue estoppel was used defensively:

> The defensive use of non-mutual issue estoppel is straight forward. If P, having litigated an issue with D1 and lost, subsequently sues D2 raising the same issue, D2 can rely defensively on the issue estoppel arising from the former action, unless the first action did not provide a full and fair opportunity to litigate or other factors make it unfair or unwise to permit preclusion. The rationale is that P should not be allowed to relitigate an issue already lost by simply changing defendants. ...

Prof. Watson then exposes the additional difficulties that arise if the mutuality requirement is removed when issue estoppel is raised offensively, as was done by the United States Supreme Court in *Parklane Hosiery Co. v. Shore*, 439 US 322 (1979). He describes the offensive use of non mutual issue estoppel as follows (at 631):

> The power of this offensive non-mutual issue estoppel doctrine is illustrated by single event disaster cases, such as an airline crash. Assume P1 sues Airline for negligence in the operation of the aircraft and in that action Airline is found to have been negligent. Offensive non-mutual issue estoppel permits P2 through P20, *etc.*, now to sue Airline and successfully plead issue estoppel on the question of the airline's negligence. The rationale is that if Airline fully and fairly litigated the issue of its negligence in action #1 it has had its day in court; it has had due process and it should not be permitted to re-litigate the negligence issue. However, the court in *Parklane* realized that in order to ensure fairness in the operation of offensive non-mutual issue estoppel the doctrine has to be subject to qualifications.

Properly understood, our case could be viewed as falling under this second category—what would be described in US law as "non-mutual offensive preclusion." Although technically speaking the City of Toronto is not the "plaintiff" in the arbitration proceedings, the City wishes to take advantage of the conviction obtained by the Crown against Oliver in a different, prior proceeding to which the City was not a party. It wishes to preclude Oliver from relitigating an issue that he fought and lost in the criminal forum. US law acknowledges the peculiar difficulties with offensive use of non-mutual estoppel. Prof. Watson explains, at pp. 632-33:

> First, the court acknowledged that the effects of non-mutuality differ depending on whether issue estoppel is used offensively or defensively. While defensive preclusion helps to reduce litigation, offensive preclusion, by contrast, encourages potential plaintiffs not to join in the first action. "Since a plaintiff will be able to rely on a previous judgment against a defendant but will not be bound by that judgment if the defendant wins, the plaintiff has every incentive to adopt a 'wait and see' attitude, in the hope that the first action by another plaintiff will

result in a favorable judgment." Thus, without some limit, non-mutual offensive preclusion would increase rather than decrease the total amount of litigation. To meet this problem the *Parklane* court held that preclusion should be denied in action #2 "where a plaintiff could easily have joined in the earlier action."

Second, the court recognized that in some circumstances to permit non-mutual preclusion "would be unfair to the defendant" and the court referred to specific situations of unfairness: (a) the defendant may have had little incentive to defend vigorously the first action, that is, if she was sued for small or nominal damages, particularly if future suits were not foreseeable; (b) offensive preclusion may be unfair if the judgment relied upon as a basis for estoppel is itself inconsistent with one or more previous judgments in favour of the defendant; or (c) the second action affords to the defendant procedural opportunities unavailable in the first action that could readily result in a different outcome, that is, where the defendant in the first action was forced to defend in an inconvenient forum and was unable to call witnesses, or where in the first action much more limited discovery was available to the defendant than in the second action.

In the final analysis the court declared that the general rule should be that in cases where a plaintiff could easily have joined in the earlier action or where, either for the reasons discussed or for other reasons, the application of offensive estoppel would be unfair to the defendant, a trial judge should not allow the use of offensive collateral estoppel.

It is clear from the above that American non-mutual issue estoppel is not a mechanical, self-applying rule as evidenced by the discretionary elements which may militate against granting the estoppel. What emerges from the American experience with the abandonment of mutuality is a twofold concern: (1) the application of the estoppel must be sufficiently principled and predictable to promote efficiency; and (2) it must contain sufficient flexibility to prevent unfairness. In my view, this is what the doctrine of abuse of process offers, particularly, as here, where the issue involves a conviction in a criminal court for a serious crime. In a case such as this one, the true concerns are not primarily related to mutuality. The true concerns, well reflected in the reasons of the Court of Appeal, are with the integrity and the coherence of the administration of justice. This will often be the case when the estoppel originates from a finding made in a criminal case where many of the traditional concerns related to mutuality lose their significance.

For example, there is little relevance to the concern about the "wait and see" plaintiff, the "free rider" who will deliberately avoid the risk of joining the original litigation, but will later come forward to reap the benefits of the victory obtained by the party who should have been his co-plaintiff. No such concern can ever arise when the original action is in a criminal prosecution. Victims cannot, even if they wanted to, "join in" the prosecution so as to have their civil claim against the accused disposed of in a single trial. Nor can employers "join in" the criminal prosecution to have their employee dismissed for cause.

On the other hand, even though no one can join the prosecution, the prosecutor as a party represents the public interest. He or she represents a collective interest in the just and correct outcome of the case. The prosecutor is said to be a minister of justice who has nothing to win or lose from the outcome of the case but who must ensure that a just and true verdict is rendered. (See Commentary Rule 4.01(3) of the *Rules of Professional*

Conduct, Law Society of Upper Canada (2002), at pp. 58 and 61; *R v. Regan*, [2002] 1 SCR 297, 2002 SCC 12; *Lemay v. The King*, [1952] 1 SCR 232, at pp. 256-57, *per* Cartwright J; and *R v. Banks*, [1916] 2 KB 621 (CCA), at p. 623.) The mutuality requirement of the doctrine of issue estoppel, which insists that only the Crown and its privies be precluded from relitigating the guilt of the accused, is hardly reflective of the true role of the prosecutor.

As the present case illustrates, the primary concerns here are about the integrity of the criminal process and the increased authority of a criminal verdict, rather than some of the more traditional issue estoppel concerns that focus on the interests of the parties, such as costs and multiple "vexation." For these reasons, I see no need to reverse or relax the long-standing application of the mutuality requirement in this case and I would conclude that issue estoppel has no application. I now turn to the question of whether the decision of the arbitrator amounted to a collateral attack on the verdict of the criminal court.

(2) Collateral Attack

The rule against collateral attack bars actions to overturn convictions when those actions take place in the wrong forum. As stated in *Wilson v. The Queen*, [1983] 2 SCR 594, at p. 599, the rule against collateral attack

> has long been a fundamental rule that a court order, made by a court having jurisdiction to make it, stands and is binding and conclusive unless it is set aside on appeal or lawfully quashed. It is also well settled in the authorities that such an order may not be attacked collaterally—and a collateral attack may be described as an attack made in proceedings other than those whose specific object is the reversal, variation, or nullification of the order or judgment.

Thus, in *Wilson, supra*, the Court held that an inferior court judge was without jurisdiction to pass on the validity of a wiretap authorized by a superior court. Other cases that form the basis for this rule similarly involve attempts to overturn decisions in other fora, and not simply to relitigate their facts. In *R v. Sarson*, [1996] 2 SCR 223, at para. 35, this Court held that a prisoner's *habeas corpus* attack on a conviction under a law later declared unconstitutional must fail under the rule against collateral attack because the prisoner was no longer "in the system" and because he was "in custody pursuant to the judgment of a court of competent jurisdiction." Similarly, in *R v. Consolidated Maybrun Mines Ltd.*, [1998] 1 SCR 706, this Court held that a mine owner who had chosen to ignore an administrative appeals process for a pollution fine was barred from contesting the validity of that fine in court because the legislation directed appeals to an appellate administrative body, not to the courts. Binnie J described the rule against collateral attack in *Danyluk, supra*, at para. 20, as follows: "that a judicial order pronounced by a court of competent jurisdiction should not be brought into question in subsequent proceedings except those provided by law for the express purpose of attacking it" (emphasis added).

Each of these cases concerns the appropriate forum for collateral attacks upon the judgment itself. However, in the case at bar, the union does not seek to overturn the sexual abuse conviction itself, but simply contest, for the purposes of a different claim with different legal consequences, whether the conviction was correct. It is an implicit attack on the correctness of the factual basis of the decision, not a contest about whether that decision has legal force, as clearly it does. Prohibited "collateral attacks" are abuses of the court's process. However, in light of the focus of the collateral attack rule on attacking the order itself and its legal effect, I believe that the better approach here is to go directly to the doctrine of abuse of process.

(3) Abuse of Process

Judges have an inherent and residual discretion to prevent an abuse of the court's process. This concept of abuse of process was described at common law as proceedings "unfair to the point that they are contrary to the interest of justice" (*R v. Power*, [1994] 1 SCR 601, at p. 616), and as "oppressive treatment" (*R v. Conway*, [1989] 1 SCR 1659, at p. 1667). McLachlin J (as she then was) expressed it this way in *R v. Scott*, [1990] 3 SCR 979, at p. 1007:

> ... abuse of process may be established where: (1) the proceedings are oppressive or vexatious; and, (2) violate the fundamental principles of justice underlying the community's sense of fair play and decency. The concepts of oppressiveness and vexatiousness underline the interest of the accused in a fair trial. But the doctrine evokes as well the public interest in a fair and just trial process and the proper administration of justice.

The doctrine of abuse of process is used in a variety of legal contexts. The unfair or oppressive treatment of an accused may disentitle the Crown to carry on with the prosecution of a charge: *Conway, supra*, at p. 1667. In *Blencoe v. British Columbia (Human Rights Commission)*, [2000] 2 SCR 307, 2000 SCC 44, this Court held that unreasonable delay causing serious prejudice could amount to an abuse of process. When the *Canadian Charter of Rights and Freedoms* applies, the common law doctrine of abuse of process is subsumed into the principles of the *Charter* such that there is often overlap between abuse of process and constitutional remedies (*R v. O'Connor*, [1995] 4 SCR 411). The doctrine nonetheless continues to have application as a non-*Charter* remedy: *United States of America v. Shulman*, [2001] 1 SCR 616, 2001 SCC 21, at para. 33.

In the context that interests us here, the doctrine of abuse of process engages "the inherent power of the court to prevent the misuse of its procedure, in a way that would ... bring the administration of justice into disrepute" (*Canam Enterprises Inc. v. Coles* (2000), 51 OR (3d) 481 (CA), at para. 55, *per* Goudge JA, dissenting (approved [2002] 3 SCR 307, 2002 SCC 63)). Goudge JA expanded on that concept in the following terms at paras. 55-56:

> The doctrine of abuse of process engages the inherent power of the court to prevent the misuse of its procedure, in a way that would be manifestly unfair to a party to the litigation before it or would in some other way bring the administration of justice into disrepute. *It is a flexible doctrine unencumbered by the specific requirements of concepts such as issue estoppel.* See *House of Spring Gardens Ltd. v. Waite*, [1990] 3 WLR 347 at p. 358, [1990] 2 All ER 990 (CA).

> One circumstance in which abuse of process has been applied is where the litigation before the court is found to be in essence an attempt to relitigate a claim which the court has already determined. [Emphasis added.]

As Goudge JA's comments indicate, Canadian courts have applied the doctrine of abuse of process to preclude relitigation in circumstances where the strict requirements of issue estoppel (typically the privity/mutuality requirements) are not met, but where allowing the litigation to proceed would nonetheless violate such principles as judicial economy, consistency, finality and the integrity of the administration of justice. (See for example, *Franco v. White* (2001), 53 OR (3d) 391 (CA), *Bomac Construction Ltd. v. Stevenson*, [1986] 5 WWR 21 (Sask. CA), and *Bjarnarson v. Government of Manitoba* (1987), 38 DLR (4th) 32 (Man. QB), aff'd. (1987), 21 CPC (2d) 302 (Man. CA)). This has resulted in some criticism, on the ground that the doctrine of abuse of process by relitigation is in effect non-mutual issue estoppel by another name without the important qualifications recognized by the American courts as part and parcel of the general doctrine of non-mutual issue estoppel (Watson, *supra*, at pp. 624-25).

It is true that the doctrine of abuse of process has been extended beyond the strict parameters of *res judicata* while borrowing much of its rationales and some of its constraints. It is said to be more of an adjunct doctrine, defined in reaction to the settled rules of issue estoppel and cause of action estoppel, than an independent one (Lange, *supra*, at p. 344). The policy grounds supporting abuse of process by relitigation are the same as the essential policy grounds supporting issue estoppel (Lange, *supra*, at pp. 347-48):

> The two policy grounds, namely, that there be an end to litigation and that no one should be twice vexed by the same cause, have been cited as policies in the application of abuse of process by relitigation. Other policy grounds have also been cited, namely, to preserve the courts' and the litigants' resources, to uphold the integrity of the legal system in order to avoid inconsistent results, and to protect the principle of finality so crucial to the proper administration of justice.

The *locus classicus* for the modern doctrine of abuse of process and its relationship to *res judicata* is *Hunter* [*v. Chief Constable of the West Midlands Police et al.*, [1982] AC 529], aff'g. *McIlkenny v. Chief Constable of the West Midlands*, [1980] QB 283 (CA). The case involved an action for damages for personal injuries brought by the six men convicted of bombing two pubs in Birmingham. They claimed that they had been beaten by the police during their interrogation. The plaintiffs had raised the same issue at their criminal trial, where it was found by both the judge and jury that the confessions were voluntary and that the police had not used violence. At the Court of Appeal, Lord Denning MR endorsed non-mutual issue estoppel and held that the question of whether any beatings had taken place was estopped by the earlier determination, although it was raised here against a different opponent. He noted that in analogous cases, courts had sometimes refused to allow a party to raise an issue for a second time because it was an "abuse of the process of the court," but held that the proper characterization of the matter was through non-mutual issue estoppel.

On appeal to the House of Lords, Lord Denning's attempt to reform the law of issue estoppel was overruled, but the higher court reached the same result via the doctrine of abuse of process. Lord Diplock stated, at p. 541:

The abuse of process which the instant case exemplifies is the initiation of proceedings in a court of justice for the purpose of mounting a collateral attack upon a final decision against the intending plaintiff which has been made by another court of competent jurisdiction in previous proceedings in which the intending plaintiff had a full opportunity of contesting the decision in the court by which it was made.

It is important to note that a public inquiry after the civil action of the six accused in *Hunter, supra*, resulted in the finding that the confessions of the Birmingham six had been extracted through police brutality (see *R v. McIlKenny* (1991), 93 Cr. App. R 287 (CA), at pp. 304 *et seq.* In my view, this does not support a relaxation of the existing procedural mechanisms designed to ensure finality in criminal proceedings. The danger of wrongful convictions has been acknowledged by this Court and other courts (see *United States v. Burns*, [2001] 1 SCR 283, 2001 SCC 7, at para. 1; and *R v. Bromley* (2001), 151 CCC (3d) 480 (Nfld. CA), at pp. 517-18). Although safeguards must be put in place for the protection of the innocent, and, more generally, to ensure the trustworthiness of court findings, continuous re-litigation is not a guarantee of factual accuracy.

The attraction of the doctrine of abuse of process is that it is unencumbered by the specific requirements of *res judicata* while offering the discretion to prevent relitigation, essentially for the purpose of preserving the integrity of the court's process. ...

Critics of that approach have argued that when abuse of process is used as a proxy for issue estoppel, it obscures the true question while adding nothing but a vague sense of discretion. I disagree. At least in the context before us, namely, an attempt to relitigate a criminal conviction, I believe that abuse of process is a doctrine much more responsive to the real concerns at play. In all of its applications, the primary focus of the doctrine of abuse of process is the integrity of the adjudicative functions of courts. Whether it serves to disentitle the Crown from proceeding because of undue delays (see *Blencoe, supra*), or whether it prevents a civil party from using the courts for an improper purpose (see *Hunter, supra* and *Demeter, supra*) the focus is less on the interest of parties and more on the integrity of judicial decision making as a branch of the administration of justice. In a case such as the present one, it is that concern that compels a bar against relitigation, more than any sense of unfairness to a party being called twice to put its case forward, for example. When that is understood, the parameters of the doctrine become easier to define, and the exercise of discretion is better anchored in principle.

The adjudicative process, and the importance of preserving its integrity, were well described by Doherty JA. He said, at para. 74:

The adjudicative process in its various manifestations strives to do justice. By the adjudicative process, I mean the various courts and tribunals to which individuals must resort to settle legal disputes. Where the same issues arise in various forums, the quality of justice delivered by the adjudicative process is measured not by reference to the isolated result in each forum, but by the end result produced by the various processes that address the issue. By justice, I refer to procedural fairness, the achieving of the correct result in individual cases and the broader perception that the process as a whole achieves results which are consistent, fair and accurate.

When asked to decide whether a criminal conviction ... ought to be ... taken as conclusive, courts will turn to the doctrine of abuse of process to ascertain whether relitigation would be detrimental to the adjudicative process as defined above. When the focus is thus properly on the integrity of the adjudicative process, the motive of the party who seeks to relitigate, or whether he or she wishes to do so as a defendant rather than as a plaintiff, cannot be decisive factors in the application of the bar against relitigation.

Thus, in the case at bar, it matters little whether Oliver's motive for relitigation was primarily to secure re-employment, rather than to challenge his criminal conviction in an attempt to undermine its validity. Reliance on *Hunter, supra*, and on *Demeter* (HC), *supra*, for the purpose of enhancing the importance of motive is misplaced. It is true that in both cases the parties wishing to relitigate had made it clear that they were seeking to impeach their earlier convictions. But this is of little significance in the application of the doctrine of abuse of process. A desire to attack a judicial finding is not in itself an improper purpose. The law permits that objective to be pursued through various reviewing mechanisms such as appeals or judicial review. Indeed reviewability is an important aspect of finality. A decision is final and binding on the parties only when all available reviews have been exhausted or abandoned. What is improper is to attempt to impeach a judicial finding by the impermissible route of relitigation in a different forum. Therefore, motive is of little or no import.

There is also no reason to constrain the doctrine of abuse of process only to those cases where the plaintiff has initiated the relitigation. The designation of the parties to the second litigation may mask the reality of the situation. In the present case, for instance, aside from the technical mechanism of the grievance procedures, who should be viewed as the initiator of the employment litigation between the grievor, Oliver, and his union on the one hand, and the City of Toronto on the other? Technically, the union is the "plaintiff" in the arbitration procedure. But the City of Toronto used Oliver's criminal conviction as a basis for his dismissal. I cannot see what difference it makes, again from the point of view of the integrity of the adjudicative process, whether Oliver is labelled a plaintiff or a defendant when it comes to relitigating his criminal conviction.

· · ·

Rather than focus on the motive or status of the parties, the doctrine of abuse of process concentrates on the integrity of the adjudicative process. Three preliminary observations are useful in that respect. First, there can be no assumption that relitigation will yield a more accurate result than the original proceeding. Second, if the same result is reached in the subsequent proceeding, the relitigation will prove to have been a waste of judicial resources as well as an unnecessary expense for the parties and possibly an additional hardship for some witnesses. Finally, if the result in the subsequent proceeding is different from the conclusion reached in the first on the very same issue, the inconsistency, in and of itself, will undermine the credibility of the entire judicial process, thereby diminishing its authority, its credibility and its aim of finality.

In contrast, proper review by way of appeal increases confidence in the ultimate result and affirms both the authority of the process as well as the finality of the result. It is therefore apparent that from the system's point of view, relitigation carries serious detrimental effects and should be avoided unless the circumstances dictate that relitigation is in fact necessary to enhance the credibility and the effectiveness of the adjudicative process as a whole. There may be instances where relitigation will enhance, rather than impeach, the integrity of the judicial system, for example: (1) when the first proceeding is tainted by fraud or dishonesty; (2) when fresh, new evidence, previously unavailable, conclusively impeaches the original results; or (3) when fairness dictates that the original result should not be binding in the new context. This was stated unequivocally by this Court in *Danyluk*, *supra*, at para. 80.

The discretionary factors that apply to prevent the doctrine of issue estoppel from operating in an unjust or unfair way are equally available to prevent the doctrine of abuse of process from achieving a similar undesirable result. There are many circumstances in which the bar against relitigation, either through the doctrine of *res judicata* or that of abuse of process, would create unfairness. If, for instance, the stakes in the original proceeding were too minor to generate a full and robust response, while the subsequent stakes were considerable, fairness would dictate that the administration of justice would be better served by permitting the second proceeding to go forward than by insisting that finality should prevail. An inadequate incentive to defend, the discovery of new evidence in appropriate circumstances, or a tainted original process may all overcome the interest in maintaining the finality of the original decision (*Danyluk*, *supra*, at para. 51; *Franco*, *supra*, at para. 55).

These considerations are particularly apposite when the attempt is to relitigate a criminal conviction. Casting doubt over the validity of a criminal conviction is a very serious matter. Inevitably in a case such as this one, the conclusion of the arbitrator has precisely that effect, whether this was intended or not. The administration of justice must equip itself with all legitimate means to prevent wrongful convictions and to address any real possibility of such an occurrence after the fact. Collateral attacks and relitigation however, are not in my view appropriate methods of redress since they inordinately tax the adjudicative process while doing nothing to ensure a more trustworthy result.

In light of the above, it is apparent that the common law doctrines of issue estoppel, collateral attack and abuse of process adequately capture the concerns that arise when finality in litigation must be balanced against fairness to a particular litigant. There is therefore no need to endorse, as the Court of Appeal did, a self-standing and independent "finality principle" either as a separate doctrine or as an independent test to preclude relitigation.

D. Application of Abuse of Process to Facts of the Appeal

I am of the view that the facts in this appeal point to the blatant abuse of process that results when relitigation of this sort is permitted. The grievor was convicted in a criminal court and he exhausted all his avenues of appeal. In law, his conviction must stand, with all its consequent legal effects. Yet as pointed out by Doherty JA (at para. 84):

> Despite the arbitrator's insistence that he was not passing on the correctness of the decision made by Ferguson J, that is exactly what he did. One cannot read the arbitrator's reasons without coming to the conclusion that he was convinced that the criminal proceedings were badly flawed and that Oliver was wrongly convicted. This conclusion, reached in proceedings to which the prosecution was not even a party, could only undermine the integrity of the criminal justice system. The reasonable observer would wonder how Oliver could be found guilty beyond a reasonable doubt in one proceeding and after the Court of Appeal had affirmed that finding, be found in a separate proceeding not to have committed the very

same assault. That reasonable observer would also not understand how Oliver could be found to be properly convicted of sexually assaulting the complainant and deserving of 15 months in jail and yet also be found in a separate proceeding not to have committed that sexual assault and to be deserving of reinstatement in a job which would place young persons like the complainant under his charge.

As a result of the conflicting decisions, the City of Toronto would find itself in the inevitable position of having a convicted sex offender reinstated to an employment position where he would work with the very vulnerable young people he was convicted of assaulting. An educated and reasonable public would presumably have to assess the likely correctness of one or the other of the adjudicative findings regarding the guilt of the convicted grievor. The authority and finality of judicial decisions are designed precisely to eliminate the need for such an exercise.

In addition, the arbitrator is considerably less well equipped than a judge presiding over a criminal court—or the jury—guided by rules of evidence that are sensitive to a fair search for the truth, an exacting standard of proof and expertise with the very questions in issue, to come to a correct disposition of the matter. Yet the arbitrator's conclusions, if challenged, may give rise to a less searching standard of review than that of the criminal court judge. In short, there is nothing in a case like the present one that militates against the application of the doctrine of abuse of process to bar the relitigation of the grievor's criminal conviction. The arbitrator was required as a matter of law to give full effect to the conviction. As a result of that error of law, the arbitrator reached a patently unreasonable conclusion. Properly understood in the light of correct legal principles, the evidence before the arbitrator could only lead him to conclude that the City of Toronto had established just cause for Oliver's dismissal.

VI. *Disposition*

For these reasons, I would dismiss the appeal with costs.

[Concurring reasons of LeBel J are omitted.]

NOTES AND QUESTIONS

1. The court notes in *City of Toronto* that the use of the "abuse of process" doctrine in Canada has resulted in some criticism, on the ground that it is tantamount to non-mutual issue estoppel by another name without the important qualifications recognized by the American courts as part and parcel of the general doctrine of non-mutual issue estoppel. Is the abuse-of-process doctrine simply a grant of open-ended discretion to courts? What constraints are imposed, implicitly or explicitly, on this discretion by virtue of the discussion of the policy goals that the doctrine is intended to advance?

2. The Supreme Court emphasized in *City of Toronto* that "[c]asting doubt over the validity of a criminal conviction is a very serious matter. Inevitably in a case such as this one, the conclusion of the arbitrator has precisely that effect, whether this was intended or not. The administration of justice must equip itself with all legitimate means to prevent wrongful convictions and to address any real possibility of such an occurrence after the fact. Collateral

attacks and relitigation, however, are not in my view appropriate methods of redress since they inordinately tax the adjudicative process while doing nothing to ensure a more trustworthy result." Based on *City of Toronto*, are there any circumstances when it could be appropriate to relitigate a criminal matter in a civil or administrative forum.? What about if the sexual assault conviction had been obtained as a result of a plea bargain without the benefit of a trial or the presentation of any evidence—would it be open to the union to claim before the arbitrator that the truth of the allegations had not been "litigated" in the criminal process?

In *Fischer v. Halyk*, [2003] Sask. DJ 16124 (CA), the Saskatchewan Court of Appeal considered the case of a registered nurse convicted of theft over $1,000, who subsequently brought a civil suit in negligence against her criminal defence lawyer. A civil jury found that the defence lawyer's conduct had fallen below the standard of care but his actions did not cause her to be convicted. Both parties appealed. The Court of Appeal held that it constituted a *prima facie* abuse of process to initiate a collateral civil challenge to a criminal conviction and that where the case constituted a direct attack on the conviction and the administration of justice that resulted in that conviction it would ordinarily be struck as being an abuse of process. Jackson JA, writing for the court, observed that the evidence in the case did not indicate any damage suffered that was not linked to the criminal conviction so that the only way the nurse could succeed in the civil action would be to attack the decision of the criminal trial. In the court's view, there could not be the possibility of a civil judgment that was inconsistent with a criminal conviction. The claim was struck as an abuse of process. Jackson JA suggests the value of finality in a criminal matter is, as a matter of principle and policy, greater than the value of finality in other legal settings (at paras. 77-82):

> In deciding whether to permit relitigation, a court or tribunal must decide whether finality concerns should outweigh an individual litigant's claim that the justice of the specific case warrants relitigation. That determination is fact-specific and requires that the court or tribunal weigh these competing considerations in the context of the facts of the particular case. Not all relitigation compromises finality concerns to the same extent and finality is not as important in some facets of the law as in others. Similarly, a claim that the justice of the individual case requires relitigation is much stronger in some situations than in others.
>
> • • •
>
> Finality is essential to the maintenance of a fair and effective adjudicative process. The values it serves are fundamental to that process and to the community. Firstly, relitigation raises the spectre of inconsistent results. Such results create a myriad of problems for those involved in the proceedings, including, but not limited to those arising from attempts to enforce conflicting orders. Inconsistent results are also capable of bringing the administration of justice into disrepute in the eyes of reasonable and well informed members of the community. In this case, the conflicting results arrived at in the criminal proceedings and in the arbitration would, in my view, cause reasonable persons to wonder about the rationality of the adjudicative process.
>
> Secondly, relitigation diminishes the overall authority of the adjudicative process. What value is a result if that result can be challenged and relitigated in another forum at any time? Thirdly, relitigation breeds uncertainty. How can those drawn into the adjudicative process determine when they have reached the end of that process, get on with the rest of their lives and arrange their affairs in reliance on the decisions reached in that process? Finally, relitigation

drains individual and institutional resources. Neither individuals, nor the community as a whole, have the resources or the lifespan required to permit the continual relitigation of decided issues.

In emphasizing the importance of finality, I do not pretend that the decision made in the first proceeding is always correct. It must, of course, be observed that relitigation is not a guarantee of a more accurate result. The simple truth is that finality is so essential that it is routinely given priority over the possibility that relitigation would achieve a more accurate result. The importance of finality is best seen in those cases where finality has trumped individual constitutional rights: *Reference re Manitoba Language Rights*, [1985] 1 S SCR 721, 19 DLR (4th) 1; *R v. Thomas*, [1990] 1 SCR 713, 75 CR (3d) 352; and *R v. Sarson*, [1996] 2 SCR 223, 107 CCC (3d) 21. In those cases, even though the decision is wrong in the most important sense in that it denies someone a fundamental right, the courts have held that finality precludes relitigation. A desire to avoid the harm caused by permitting relitigation is given paramountcy over the rights of the individual and the accuracy of the result in the particular case.

As indicated above, finality concerns are given more prominence in some areas of the law than others. For example, finality carries less weight in cases involving child support and custody orders than in cases involving the ownership of real property. Finality is very important in criminal cases. A criminal verdict is not simply a determination of an issue as between two private litigants. The prosecution is taken on behalf of the community and the verdict is the verdict of the community. The community has a real stake in that verdict. To permit relitigation of issues decided in criminal cases in subsequent private litigation is to seriously diminish the force of the criminal law in the community.

What does this say about the possibility of using civil actions to expose wrongful criminal convictions?

3. What would happen if a court were asked to relitigate a matter that had been the subject of a prior criminal proceeding which resulted in an acquittal? This was the issue in *Peel Police Service v. Watson*, [2005] OJ 3525 (Div. Ct.). In that case, the Ontario Divisional Court considered whether a disciplinary hearing against a police officer should be stayed on abuse of process grounds where the officer had been charged with a criminal offence based on the same circumstances (involving an allegation of shoplifting) and had been acquitted. The Divisional Court found that it was not an abuse of process to hold a disciplinary hearing in these circumstances as whether or not the police officer committed a crime, the issue of whether he had brought discredit to the police force in a fashion sufficient to lead to a disciplinary sanction was a separate and distinct issue.

4. In *Britannia Airways Ltd. v. Royal Bank of Canada* (2005), 5 CPC (6th) 262 (Ont. SCJ), discussed above in relation to cause of action estoppel, Justice Lax also considered whether abuse of process would preclude Britannia from reviving their claim in Ontario after its claim was dismissed in Texas. Lax J held:

> In view of the conclusion I have reached, it is probably unnecessary to deal with the remaining issue of abuse of process, but in the event I have erred in my understanding of the privity doctrine, I will do so briefly.
>
> The decision of the Supreme Court of Canada in *Toronto (City) v. CUPE, supra*, is the most recent, comprehensive and authoritative analysis of the doctrine of abuse of process. There, it expressed the underlying policy reasons for the doctrine at paras. 51-52:

First, there can be no assumption that relitigation will yield a more accurate result than the original proceeding. Second, if the same result is reached in the subsequent proceeding, the relitigation will prove to have been a waste of judicial resources as well as an unnecessary expense for the parties and possibly an additional hardship for some witnesses. Finally, if the result in the subsequent proceeding is different from the conclusion reached in the first on the very same issue, the inconsistency, in and of itself, will undermine the credibility of the entire judicial process, thereby diminishing its authority, its credibility and its aim of finality.

... [F]rom the system's point of view, relitigation carries serious detrimental effects and should be avoided unless the circumstances dictate that relitigation is in fact necessary to enhance the credibility and the effectiveness of the adjudicative process as a whole.

In this case, there are compelling reasons to avoid relitigation. The Texas proceeding afforded a comprehensive and fair examination of the issues. There is no suggestion that it was tainted by fraud or dishonesty. There are neither new facts, nor fresh evidence. A second proceeding years later on the same issues would unquestionably violate the principles referred to in *Toronto v. CUPE*, including judicial economy, consistency, finality and the integrity of the administration of justice (at para. 37).

Moreover, it would be manifestly unfair to RBC to require it to reproduce the evidence and arguments on Air Routing's liability, which were determined in Texas. The Jet Card System no longer operates. Some of the Air Routing entities are no longer in operation. Many of the individuals involved with Air Routing have left or retired. As the Court of Appeal stated in *Vos v. Hospital for Sick Children*, [1998] OJ No. 4369 at para. 36, "it would be an affront to one's sense of justice" and would cause "an outrage by a reasonable person"; see also, *Jaremko v. Metropolitan Toronto Condominium Corp. No. 875* (1998), 20 CPC (4th) 85 (Ont. CA).

Britannia submits that the doctrine of abuse of process has no application to a claim or issue that has not previously been litigated. It relies on the dissenting judgment of Goudge JA in *Canam Enterprises v. Coles* (2000), 51 OR (3d) 481 (CA) rev'd. [2002] 3 SCR 307. In that case, the majority of the Court of Appeal found abuse of process. Justice Goudge dissented on the basis that there was no abuse of process because the claims had never been litigated. He agreed with the majority that issue estoppel did not apply because the same issue requirement of issue estoppel was not met (at para. 49). The Supreme Court of Canada agreed with Goudge JA that the case there did not represent an abuse of process for the reasons he gave.

Here, the Air Routing case has been litigated in Texas. It would be an abuse of process to litigate these claims again in Ontario.

5. Part of the court's logic in *City of Toronto* is that a judge presiding over a criminal trial is better equipped to reach the truth than an arbitrator presiding over an administrative process. What if the circumstances were reversed? According to this same logic, when an issue is decided through an administrative process, should relitigation be possible before a civil court? This issue is discussed in the next section.

4. The Impact of the Decisions of Administrative Tribunals on Civil Proceedings

Earlier in this section we noted that preclusion may arise from decisions rendered by administrative tribunals of competent jurisdiction. In an earlier chapter we observed that the procedures followed by some administrative tribunals may be very simple—summary and quite uncourt-like. The combination of these two factors produces its own problems as the following case and notes demonstrate.

The first significant appellate case to explore whether a decision by an administrative tribunal could give rise to issue estoppel if relitigated in a civil proceeding was *Rasanen v. Rosemount Instruments Ltd.* (1994), 17 OR (3d) 267 (CA). *Rasanen* involved a plaintiff employed by the defendant as manager of nuclear/aerospace, marketing, and sales, based in Toronto, and reporting directly to the defendant's Canadian president. In 1984, as a result of a corporate restructuring, the plaintiff's position became redundant. He was offered two alternative positions, both at the same salary level as his old position, one in Calgary, reporting to the president, and one in Toronto, reporting to the president through the sales manager. The plaintiff, through his lawyer, stated that he viewed both alternatives as representing a unilateral and fundamental change in his employment position amounting to a constructive dismissal. The defendant's response was to terminate the plaintiff's employment because of his refusal to accept either offer. The plaintiff made a claim under s. 40 of the *Employment Standards Act* ("the ESA") for eight weeks' termination pay and commenced an action for damages for wrongful dismissal. After a hearing during which Rasanen and his employer gave evidence, the referee, appointed pursuant to s. 50(1) (now s. 68(1)) of the *Employment Standards Act*, concluded that no money for termination pay was owing to Rasanen. Rasanen then brought a civil claim for wrongful dismissal based on the same allegations. The trial judge concluded that the issue before him was the same as that before the Employment Standards referee and dismissed the action on the basis of issue estoppel. The Ontario Court of Appeal upheld that decision. In applying the three-pronged test for issue estoppel, Abella JA (as she then was) found that the same issue clearly arose in both proceedings. With respect to the second prong, she affirmed that an administrative finding could qualify as a "final, judicial decision":

> The second requirement is that there be a prior, final, judicial decision. The appellant argued that the procedure before the referee was not sufficiently "judicial," and that the absence of discovery, costs, production of documents and a judge rendered it so dissimilar a process to that of the courts that no decision resulting from it should be binding.
>
> This is an argument, in my opinion, which seriously misperceives the role and function of administrative tribunals. They were expressly created as independent bodies for the purpose of being an alternative to the judicial process, including its procedural panoplies. Designed to be less cumbersome, less expensive, less formal and less delayed, these impartial decision-making bodies were to resolve disputes in their area of specialization more expeditiously and more accessibly, but no less effectively or credibly. ...
>
> As long as the hearing process in the tribunal provides parties with an opportunity to know and meet the case against them, and so long as the decision is within the tribunal's jurisdiction, then regardless of how closely the process mirrors a trial or its procedural antecedents, I can see no principled basis for exempting issues adjudicated by tribunals from the operation of issue estoppel in a subsequent action. If the purpose of issue estoppel is to prevent the retrial of "[a]ny right, question, or fact distinctly put in issue and directly determined by a court of competent jurisdiction" (*McIntosh v. Parent, supra*), then it is difficult to see why the decisions of an administrative tribunal having jurisdiction to decide the issue, would not qualify as decisions

of a court of competent jurisdiction so as to preclude the redetermination of the same issues. ...
On the contrary, the policy objectives underlying issue estoppel, such as avoiding duplicative
litigation, inconsistent results, undue costs, and inconclusive proceedings, are enhanced in appropriate circumstances by acknowledging as binding the integrity of tribunal decisions. ...

There is no basis for restricting the application of issue estoppel to decisions made by judges
in the ordinary course of litigation. By analogy, the hearing by the referee, if not technically
"judicial," is designed to be an independent, fair, impartial and binding adjudicative process,
and therefore satisfies the spirit of the requirement. It was a decision made in a hearing in
which the appellant knew the case he had to meet, had a chance to meet it, and lost. Had he
won, the decision would have been no less binding.

Turning to the third prong, that of mutuality, Abella JA (as she then was) found that
while it was the Ministry of Labour rather than the employee who initiated the first administrative proceeding against the employer, the employee was nonetheless a privy to the
Ministry, and shared a "community of interest."

Carthy JA disagreed with the application of issue estoppel in these circumstances,
explaining:

It would be unfair to an employee who sought out immediate and limited relief of $4,000, for-
saking discovery and representation in doing so, to then say that he is bound to the result as it
affects a claim for ten times that amount. Neither representation nor discovery is affordable for
a $4,000 claim and that is undoubtedly why the Act provides for representation on behalf of the
employee by a representative of the ministry. I would adopt the language of Lord Upjohn in
Carl-Zeiss-Stiftung, supra, at p. 947:

All estoppels are not odious but must be applied so as to work justice and not injustice,
and I think that the principle of issue estoppel must be applied to the circumstances of
the subsequent case with this overriding consideration in mind.

It is my conclusion that, in this case, it would be unfair to the appellant to consider him as
so closely associated with the proceeding under the ESA as to invoke issue estoppel against his
common law claim for wrongful dismissal damages.

Carthy JA nonetheless concurred in the result on the basis that the wrongful dismissal claim
should have been dismissed in any event on its merits.

The decision of the Ontario Court of Appeal in *Rasanen* raised an important question:
what degree of procedural fairness in tribunal hearings should be required before persons
who go before them are held to be estopped in litigating their claim in court? Recall that in
Parklane Hosiery the court said that it might be unfair to apply issue estoppel where the second action affords the party against whom the estoppel is sought procedural advantages that
were unavailable in the first proceeding. The American Law Institute, *Restatement of the
Law (Second), Judgments* (1982) provides as one of the exceptions to the general rule of issue
preclusion estoppel in § 28(3) that "[a] new determination of the issue is warranted by differences in the quality or extensiveness of the procedures followed in the two courts." Although not referring to these authorities, was Carthy JA in *Rasanen* essentially saying the
same thing? On the issue estoppel point, whose decision is preferable—that of Abella JA or
that of Carthy JA?

In a further concurring decision in *Rasanen*, Morden ACJO left open the possibility that deficiencies in the procedure relating to the first decision could be taken into account in determining whether to apply issue estoppel. He stated:

> I do not exclude the possibility that deficiencies in the procedure relating to the first decision could properly be a factor in deciding whether or not to apply issue estoppel. However, in this case, whatever the procedure was that governed the statutory proceeding, the appellant frankly admitted that it placed him at no disadvantage in the presentation of his case and so I do not think that the procedural aspect is relevant in this case.

This issue arose in *Minott v. O'Shanter Development Co.*, a subsequent decision before the Ontario Court of Appeal five years later.

Minott v. O'Shanter Development Co.
1999 ONCA 44

[*Minott* involved an appeal by the defendant employer from the trial judge's decision to award the plaintiff employee, Minott, a wrongful dismissal award of $40,537.47. Minott worked in O'Shanter's maintenance department for 11 years. He was a loyal worker with a good work record. However, after a dispute with a supervisor, he took two days off without permission and received a two-day suspension. He was then fired when he did not come to work on the day after his suspension. He was 43 years old and had little formal education and few skills. There was a job slump in construction. He applied for unemployment insurance (UI) benefits. The UI Board of Referees found that Minott was disqualified from receiving benefits for three weeks because he had lost his job by reason of his own conduct. Minott then sued O'Shanter for damages for wrongful dismissal. At trial, O'Shanter moved to dismiss the action on the ground of issue estoppel based on the board's finding that Minott was fired for cause. The trial judge dismissed the motion, allowed the action, and awarded damages. O'Shanter's appeal was dismissed by the Court of Appeal.

Following is part of the court's judgment written by Laskin JA (with numerous footnotes omitted). Earlier in the judgment, Laskin JA held that the board's finding did not give rise to issue estoppel because the issues were not the same in the two proceedings. The board's finding did not answer the same question that had to be answered in the wrongful dismissal action. Misconduct under the *Unemployment Insurance Act* and just cause for dismissal at common law did not necessarily raise the same question.]

(iii) Were the Parties the Same?

To apply issue estoppel, the parties to the first proceeding must be the same as the parties to the second proceeding. Deciding whether this requirement has been met causes difficulty when one of the parties to the second proceeding is entitled to participate actively in the first proceeding and to exercise fully the rights of a party in that proceeding, but chooses not to do so. That is the case here. Although O'Shanter could have taken part in the oral hearing before the Board of Referees, it declined to do so. In such cases, whether a person is a party for the purpose of issue estoppel depends on its degree of participation. Because O'Shanter did not actively participate in the hearing before the Board of Referees, I conclude that it was not a party for the purpose of issue estoppel.

The provisions of the *Employment Insurance Act* and the regulations passed under it, the *Employment Insurance Regulations* ... give the employer the right to participate at the various stages of the proceedings before the Commission, the Board of Referees and the Umpire. The employer is entitled to notice, has the right to make representations at the hearings, is notified of the outcome and has a right to appeal a decision of the Commission or of the Board of Referees. ... For example, s. 83(1) of the Regulations, which contemplates that an employer is a party, states: "A board of referees shall give each of the parties interested in an appeal a reasonable opportunity to make representations concerning any matter before the board."

O'Shanter took no part in the proceedings before the Board of Referees, although it received notice of Minott's appeal. O'Shanter did not appear before the Board; it did not seek to introduce any evidence; and it made no written representations. It did, however, file with a Commission a written statement in response to Minott's application for benefits. This statement, to which I referred earlier, was given at the invitation of the Commission under s. 42 of the *Unemployment Insurance Act*, which provided:

> 42. Where, in considering a claim for benefit, the Commission finds an indication from the documents relating to the claim that the loss of employment resulted from the claimant's own misconduct or that the claimant voluntarily left employment, the Commission shall
>
> > (a) provide an opportunity to the claimant and the employer to provide information as to the reasons for the loss of employment; and
> >
> > (b) where any such information is provided, take it into account in determining the claim. ...

This statement, which said that Minott had received written warnings and had been offered a job he could reach by public transportation, was in the Board's file on appeal and was apparently relied on by the Board in reaching its decision. The giving of this statement, however, was the only way that O'Shanter participated in the proceedings before the Commission and the Board. In my view, that limited participation was not sufficient to make O'Shanter a party for the purpose of issue estoppel.

Recent case law in this province suggests that a person must actively participate in administrative proceedings to meet the "same parties" requirement of issue estoppel. In both *Schweneke v. Ontario* (1996), 1 CPC (4th) 35 (Ont. Gen. Div.) and *Randhawa v. Everest & Jennings Canadian Ltd.* (1996), 22 CCEL (2d) 19 (Ont. Gen. Div.), also cases concerning proceedings under the *Unemployment Insurance Act*, the employer actively participated in the hearing before the Umpire or the Board of Referees and was therefore held to be a party. Similarly, in *Rasanen*, Abella JA held that the appellant, the employee, if not a party to the proceedings under the *Employment Standards Act*, was at least a privy. She wrote:

> The appellant clearly called the witnesses he wanted, introduced the relevant evidence he needed, and had the chance to respond to the evidence and arguments against him. ... He had a meaningful voice, through his own evidence and through the assistance of the minis-

try, in a proceeding which decided the very issue he sought to raise in his subsequent action. ...

In contrast, in the recent case of *Wood v. Nor-Sham (Markham) Hotels Inc.* (1998), 35 CCEL (2d) 206 (Ont. Gen. Div.) Sharpe J held that an employer who chose not to contest an employee's appeal before a Board of Referees under the Act was not bound by the Board's decision in the subsequent wrongful dismissal action. As in the case before us, in *Wood* the employer had provided information about the employee's dismissal to the unemployment insurance officer adjudicating the claim for benefits. The employer, however, did not attend the hearing before the Board of Referees and instead wrote the Chairman of the Board saying it would not attend. Sharpe J held that "the letter, together with the other conduct of the employer taken as a whole, do not constitute participation in the process sufficient to render the employer bound by the Board of Referees' decision."

In their article, "Ties that Bind at Common Law: Issue Estoppel, Employment Standards and Unemployment Insurance Adjudication" (1997), 24 CCEL (2d) 291, at 310, Jeffrey Goodman and Jeff Murray accurately summarize the caselaw:

> The case law to date suggests that employers can avoid creating an estoppel either by not appealing a decision favourable to an employee or not attending an employee's appeal. The cases have held that by appealing or attending at an employee's appeal, the employer becomes a party to that appeal.

The recent Australian High Court case, *Australian Securities Commission v. Marlborough Gold Mines Limited* (1993), 177 CLR 485 (Aust. HC), also lends support to the need for active participation to become a party for the purpose of issue estoppel. A company had applied to the trial court for an order to summons a meeting of its members to consider a scheme to convert the company from one of limited liability to one of no liability. The Australian Securities Commission appeared and told the court that it neither consented to nor opposed the application. The order was made and a meeting was held to approve the scheme. The Commission then learned of a recent judgment suggesting that the scheme was illegal. The trial court approved the scheme and the Commission filed a notice to intervene, opposing the approval and then appealing against the approval. The Australian High Court had to consider whether issue estoppel arose in this context, estopping the Commission from its opposition. The High Court held that the Commission's appearance before the court on the application for leave to summons a meeting was not sufficient to make it a party for the purpose of issue estoppel. The High Court wrote: ...

> The fact that the Law requires that notice be given to the Commission does not make the Commission a party. Nor, in our view, does the fact that the Commission appeared to announce its attitude make it a party. That, if anything, was something done by way of making information available to the Court.

A person can be a party for one purpose and not for another. In the present case, O'Shanter provided information to the Commission. By doing so it did not become a party for the purpose of issue estoppel. In addition to the case law, I think that policy considerations justify focusing on the degree of participation to determine whether an employer in O'Shanter's position is a party for the purpose of issue estoppel. Holding that an employer who merely provides information to an insurance officer becomes a party and thus bound by the Commission's or the Board's findings could turn a right to participate into a practical obligation to do so. Ordinarily, employers do not appear on applications for unemployment insurance benefits or even on appeals because the stakes are small and they do not have a direct financial interest in the outcome, although they may be liable under s. 46(1) of the Act to repay any benefits received by an employee who subsequently succeeds in a wrongful dismissal action. Thus, to give employers in O'Shanter's position party status for the purpose of issue estoppel would provide a perverse incentive for employers to participate actively in hearings before the Board of Referees or before an Umpire.

Implicit in this discussion is my rejection of any notion of non-mutual issue estoppel. The doctrine of non-mutual issue estoppel, which was not argued before us, has roots in American jurisprudence. … It permits a judgment to operate in favour of a non-party. Applied here, it might permit an employer to refrain from participating in a hearing before a Board of Referees yet rely on a favourable Board decision in a subsequent wrongful dismissal action. By adopting a "wait and see" approach to the Board's decision, an employer could rely on issue estoppel if the employee lost, but be no worse off if the employee won, because issue estoppel could not be applied against an employer who had not had its day in court. Applying non-mutual issue estoppel would allow the employer to "have it both ways." In my view, in these cases issue estoppel should be mutual … . An employer should only be able to invoke issue estoppel for a favourable decision if issue estoppel could also be invoked against it for an unfavourable decision. I do not consider O'Shanter bound by the Board's decision any more than I consider it would have been bound in the wrongful dismissal action had Minott succeeded in his appeal before the Board of Referees. O'Shanter was not a party for the purpose of issue estoppel and the third requirement is therefore not satisfied.

I have concluded that the Board's finding of misconduct under the Act does not satisfy the first and third requirements of issue estoppel. Therefore the Board's finding did not prevent Minott from maintaining his action for wrongful dismissal. Even had the three requirements been met, however, in my view the court has always retained discretion to refuse to apply issue estoppel when to do so would cause unfairness or work an injustice. As Lord Upjohn observed in *Carl Zeiss Stiftung v. Rayner Keeler Ltd.*, [1967] 1 AC 853, at 947, "[a]ll estoppels are not odious but must be applied so as to work justice and not injustice, and I think the principle of issue estoppel must be applied to the circumstances of the subsequent case with this overriding consideration in mind."

Issue estoppel is a rule of public policy and, as a rule of public policy, it seeks to balance the public interest in the finality of litigation with the private interest in achieving justice between litigants. Sometimes these two interests will be in conflict, or at least there will be tension between them. Judicial discretion is required to achieve practical justice without undermining the principles on which issue estoppel is founded. Issue estoppel should be applied flexibly where an unyielding application of it would be unfair to a party who is precluded from relitigating an issue.

That the courts have always exercised this discretion is apparent from the authorities. For example, courts have refused to apply issue estoppel in "special circumstances," which include a change in the law or the availability of further relevant material. If the decision of a court on a point of law in an earlier proceeding is shown to be wrong by a later judicial decision, issue estoppel will not prevent relitigating that issue in subsequent proceedings. It would be unfair to do otherwise. In *Arnold v. National Westminster Bank plc*, [1991] 3 All ER 41, at 50 (HL), Lord Keith wrote:

> … there may be an exception to issue estoppel in the special circumstance that there has become available to a party further material relevant to the correct determination of a point involved in the earlier proceedings, whether or not that point was specifically raised and decided, being material which could not by reasonable diligence have been adduced in those proceedings. One of the purposes of estoppel being to work justice between the parties, it is open to courts to recognize that in special circumstances inflexible application of it may have the opposite result. …

Applying issue estoppel to the findings of an administrative tribunal to foreclose a subsequent civil proceeding may also be unfair or work an injustice. Its application to findings made in proceedings under the Employment Insurance Act is a good example. Looking at legislative intent, nothing either in the scheme of the Act or in its individual provisions suggests, for example, that the finding of misconduct by a Board of Referees or by an Umpire is binding in a civil action for wrongful dismissal. Issue estoppel is a common law rule and therefore the courts must consider the appropriateness of applying it to the findings of a tribunal under the Act to prevent those finding findings from being relitigated in a subsequent action for wrongful dismissal.

In my opinion, invoking issue estoppel for the findings of a Board of Referees or of an Umpire raises several concerns. Some of these concerns are alleviated by holding that the "same parties" requirement turns on the employer's degree of participation. But issue estoppel affects employees as well as employers and thus other concerns remain, which I will discuss briefly.

First, the scheme of the Act contemplates that claims for unemployment insurance benefits be adjudicated quickly, inexpensively and summarily. To inject issue estoppel into these claims adjudications would undermine the aim of the legislative scheme. [See also N. Grosman, "No Estoppel" (April 1997), 7 EMP Bul. 2.] Employers and employees may overlitigate these adjudications, hire lawyers unnecessarily or pursue appeals they might not otherwise take out of fear of the consequences in later civil litigation. As Molloy J [the trial judge in *Minott*] sensibly observed:

> If the decisions of Boards of Referees as to misconduct are held to always be determinative of whether there has been cause for dismissal at common law, it will be necessary for employees to retain counsel and litigate before the Board in the same manner as before a court in a wrongful dismissal action. This would not be a desirable result for any of the parties involved, including the administrative board itself which would soon find its expeditious summary process clogged with parties litigating their civil causes of action.

Second, employees apply for benefits when they are most vulnerable, immediately after losing their job. The urgency with which they must invariably seek relief compromises their ability to adequately put forward their case for benefits or to respond to the case against them. [See *Restatement of the Law (Second), Judgments*, 2d (1982), s. 83(2)(e).] Applying issue estoppel may therefore cause real injustice to an aggrieved employee. As Langdon J noted in *Hough v. Brunswick Centres*, "[t]o become unemployed is a fairly universal experience in modern days. It is an almost automatic reaction for anyone who is terminated or laid off to file for benefits. One does not do so with the thought in mind that if one loses one's claim, one is at risk of having all legal remedies foreclosed.". . .

Third, the financial stakes in an application for unemployment insurance benefits are typically insignificant compared to the financial stakes in an action for wrongful dismissal. [*Restatement*, at 279.] Here, before the Board of Referees, only a few weeks of benefits were at stake, but in the wrongful dismissal action $40,000 was at stake. As Sharpe J observed in *Randhawa* [above], "there may well be situations where one would hesitate to apply the doctrine of issue estoppel where a party participated in an administrative hearing having insignificant consequences and the result of that hearing was then raised later in a suit which had enormous consequences." To apply issue estoppel in such a case may be as unfair to the employer as to the employee.

Fourth, the procedural differences between a hearing under the Act and a civil action for wrongful dismissal may cause a court to exercise its discretion against applying issue estoppel. The Restatement (Second) of Judgments sets out several exceptions to the application of issue estoppel. [See *Restatement*, para. 28, "Exceptions to the General Rule of Issue Preclusion."] One exception recognizes that procedural differences in the two proceedings may be a sufficient reason not to apply issue estoppel. Section 28(3) of the Restatement states that "a new determination of the issue is warranted by differences in the quality or extensiveness of the procedures followed in the two courts ... ." Morden ACJO expressed a similar view in his concurring judgment in *Rasanen* when he said "I do not exclude the possibility that deficiencies in the procedure relating to the first decision could properly be a factor in deciding whether or not to apply issue estoppel." In *Rasanen* itself, Morden ACJO held that the tribunal procedures were sufficient to apply issue estoppel. Carthy JA, dissenting on this point, held that they were insufficient.

Procedural differences should be looked at in practical terms. In the present case, Minott did not have a prehearing discovery. Although he had limited formal education, he appeared before the Board of Referees unrepresented, led no evidence, called no witnesses and had no opportunity to build his case through cross-examination. His claim failed because the Board had in its file, and apparently acted on, information from O'Shanter later proved incorrect in the wrongful dismissal action. I do not say that the procedures before the Board of Referees were deficient. They may have been appropriate for the purpose of the Act and for the summary determination of the disqualification period to be made by the Board, but entirely inappropriate for the determination in the wrongful dismissal action of Minott's claim for damages and of O'Shanter's defence of just cause.

Finally, the expertise of the Board of Referees is quite different from the expertise needed to decide a wrongful dismissal action. The Board of Referees must consider misconduct in the context of a claim for unemployment insurance not in the context of a dispute between an employer and an employee over just cause. [See *Re Toronto Police Services Board and Toronto Police Association* (1998), 71 LAC (4th) 289, at 306-7.]

Because I take the view that O'Shanter has not met all of the three basic requirements of issue estoppel, I need not invoke discretion to hold that the Board's finding of misconduct does not prevent Minott from maintaining his action for wrongful dismissal. Had I concluded otherwise, however, I would have been prompted by the concerns that I have listed to exercise my discretion to refuse to apply issue estoppel to the finding of misconduct made by the Board of Referees. I do not intend by anything I have said to undermine the role of the tribunals under the Employment Insurance Act. They play a vital role because they decide entitlement to benefits that are of great importance to many workers. But because of the very different characteristics of decision making under the Act, the findings of these tribunals should not automatically be imported into a subsequent civil action. I would not give effect to this ground of appeal.

NOTES AND QUESTIONS

1. Consider the treatment of the Court of Appeal's earlier decision in *Rasanen*—was the court in *Minott* effectively overruling *Rasanen*? On what basis can the two cases be distinguished?

2. In *Minott*, Laskin JA based his decision to permit the relitigation of an issue decided by an administrative tribunal on the possibility that the administrative tribunal's proceeding lacked the fairness guarantees of a court proceeding. Strangely, he made no reference to *Danyluk v. Ainsworth Technologies Inc.* (1998), 42 OR (3d) 235 (CA), in which another Ontario Court of Appeal panel precluded a civil suit on the ground of issue estoppel where the same issue—namely, whether an employee of a technology company who was involved in a dispute over unpaid commissions with her employer had been improperly dismissed—already had been decided by an employment standards officer. The Court of Appeal held that issue estoppel applied, even though it also concluded that the earlier administrative proceeding had been procedurally unfair. Rosenberg JA, writing for the court, based his conclusion on the fact that the plaintiff in *Danyluk* could have appealed the administrative decision (and likely succeeded) but instead chose to abandon the administrative appeal process and pursue a wrongful dismissal action in civil court. Because this constituted an "adequate alternative remedy" the court held that to allow the civil action to continue would condone a "collateral attack" on the administrative decision. Of course, by the time the court held her civil action estopped, the time within which she would have had to file an appeal to the administrative decision had long since expired. This left Danyluk in the position of never having had a fair hearing on her claim. The Court of Appeal was mindful of this result but concluded that Danyluk had been the author of her own misfortune. Danyluk appealed to the Supreme Court of Canada. By the time the court decided *Danyluk*, the Ontario Court of Appeal's decision in *Minott*, as well as related decisions in *Heynen v. Frito Lay Canada Ltd.* (1999), 179 DLR (4th) 317 (Ont. CA); *Schweneke v. Ontario* (2000), 47 OR (3d) 97 (CA); and *Machin v. Tomlinson* (2000), 194 DLR (4th) 326 (Ont. CA) had all been released.

Danyluk v. Ainsworth Technologies Inc.
[2001] 2 SCR 460, 2001 SCC 44

[The appellant was involved in a dispute with her employer over alleged unpaid commissions of $300,000. In October 1993, she filed a complaint under the *Employment Standards Act*, RSO 1990, c. E.14 (ESA). The employment standards officer assigned to investigate the matter interviewed the appellant over the phone for an hour. In March 1994, the appellant commenced a court action for wrongful dismissal. In June 1994, the respondent employer answered the appellant's ESA complaint, but the appellant was neither provided with any of this information nor given an opportunity to respond. On September 23, 1994, the appellant was informed that the employment standards officer had rejected her claim of $300,000 in unpaid commissions. She did not pursue an appeal of this decision to the director of Employment Standards. In response to her action for wrongful dismissal, the respondent moved to strike the paragraphs regarding unpaid wages and commissions on the basis of issue estoppel. The Ontario Court (General Division) granted this motion, and it was upheld by the Ontario Court of Appeal.]

BINNIE J:

IV. Analysis

The law rightly seeks a finality to litigation. To advance that objective, it requires litigants to put their best foot forward to establish the truth of their allegations when first called upon to do so. A litigant, to use the vernacular, is only entitled to one bite at the cherry. The appellant chose the ESA as her forum. She lost. An issue, once decided, should not generally be re-litigated to the benefit of the losing party and the harassment of the winner. A person should only be vexed once in the same cause. Duplicative litigation, potential inconsistent results, undue costs, and inconclusive proceedings are to be avoided.

Finality is thus a compelling consideration and judicial decisions should generally be conclusive of the issues decided unless and until reversed on appeal. However, estoppel is a doctrine of public policy that is designed to advance the interests of justice. Where, as here, its application bars the courthouse door against the appellant's $300,000 claim because of an administrative decision taken in a manner which was manifestly improper and unfair (as found by the Court of Appeal itself), a re-examination of some basic principles is warranted.

The law has developed a number of techniques to prevent abuse of the decision-making process. One of the oldest is the doctrine estoppel *per rem judicatem* with its roots in Roman law, the idea that a dispute once judged with finality is not subject to re-litigation: *Farwell v. The Queen* (1893), 22 SCR 553, at p. 558, *Angle v. Minister of National Revenue*, [1975] 2 SCR 248, at pp. 267-68. The bar extends both to the cause of action thus adjudicated (variously referred to as claim or cause of action or action estoppel), as well as precluding relitigation of the constituent issues or material facts necessarily embraced therein (usually called issue estoppel): G.S. Holmested and G.D. Watson, *Ontario Civil Procedure* (loose-leaf), vol. 3 Supp. at 21§17 *et seq.* Another aspect of the judicial policy favouring finality is the rule against collateral attack, i.e., that a judicial order pronounced by a court of competent jurisdiction should not be brought into question in subsequent proceedings except those provided by law for the express purpose of attacking it: *Wilson v. The Queen*, [1983] 2 SCR 594; *R v. Litchfield*, [1993] 4 SCR 333; *R v. Sarson*, [1996] 2 SCR 223.

These rules were initially developed in the context of prior court proceedings. They have since been extended, with some necessary modifications, to decisions classified as being of a judicial or quasi-judicial nature pronounced by administrative officers and tribunals. In that context the more specific objective is to balance fairness to the parties with the protection of the administrative decision-making process, whose integrity would be undermined by too readily permitting collateral attack or relitigation of issues once decided.

The extension of the doctrine of issue estoppel in Canada to administrative agencies is traced back to cases in the mid-1800s by D.J. Lange in *The Doctrine of Res Judicata in Canada* (2000), at p. 94 *et seq.*, including *Robinson v. McQuaid* (1854), 1 PEIR 103 (SC), at pp. 104-5, and *Bell v. Miller* (1862), 9 Gr. Ch. 385 (UC Ch.), at p. 386. The modern cases at the appellate level include *Raison v. Fenwick* (1982), 120 DLR (3d) 622 (BCCA); *Rasanen, supra*; *Wong v. Shell Canada Ltd.* (1995), 15 CCEL (2d) 182 (Alta. CA); *Machin v. Tomlinson* (2000), 194 DLR (4th) 326 (Ont. CA); and *Hamelin v. Davis* (1996), 18 BCLR (3d) 86 (CA). See also *Thrasyvoulou v. Environment Secretary*, [1990] 2 AC 273 (HL). Modifications were necessary because of the "major differences that can exist between [administrative orders and court orders] in relation, *inter alia*, to their legal nature and the position within the state structure of the institutions that issue them": *R v. Consolidated Maybrun Mines Ltd.*, [1998] 1 SCR 706, at para. 4. There is generally no dispute that court orders are judicial orders; the same cannot be said of the myriad of orders that are issued across the range of administrative tribunals.

In this appeal the parties have not argued "cause of action" estoppel, apparently taking the view that the statutory framework of the ESA claim sufficiently distinguishes it from the common law framework of the court case. I therefore say no more about it. They have, however, joined issue on the application of issue estoppel and the relevance of the rule against collateral attack.

Issue estoppel was more particularly defined by Middleton JA of the Ontario Court of Appeal in *McIntosh v. Parent*, [1924] 4 DLR 420 (Ont. CA), at p. 422:

> When a question is litigated, the judgment of the Court is a final determination as between the parties and their privies. Any right, question, or fact *distinctly put in issue and directly determined* by a Court of competent jurisdiction as a ground of recovery, or as an answer to a claim set up, cannot be re-tried in a subsequent suit between the same parties or their privies, though for a different cause of action. The right, question, or fact, *once determined*, must, as between them, be taken to be conclusively established so long as the judgment remains. [Emphasis added.]

This statement was adopted by Laskin J (later CJ), dissenting in *Angle, supra*, at pp. 267-68. This description of the issues subject to estoppel ("[a]ny right, question or fact distinctly put in issue and directly determined") is more stringent than the formulation in some of the older cases for cause of action estoppel (e.g., "all matters which were, or might properly have been, brought into litigation," *Farwell, supra*, at p. 558). Dickson J (later CJ), speaking for the majority of *Angle, supra*, at p. 255, subscribed to the more stringent definition for purpose of issue estoppel. "It will not suffice" he said, "if the question arose collaterally or incidentally in the earlier proceedings or is one which must be inferred by argument from the judgment." The question out of which the estoppel is said to arise must have been "fundamental to the decision arrived at" in the earlier proceeding. In other words, as discussed below, the estoppel extends to the material facts and the conclusions of law or of mixed fact and law ("the questions") that were necessarily (even if not explicitly) determined in the earlier proceedings.

The preconditions to the operation of issue estoppel were set out by Dickson J in *Angle, supra*, at p. 254:

(1) that the same question has been decided;

(2) that the judicial decision which is said to create the estoppel was final; and,

(3) that the parties to the judicial decision or their privies were the same persons as the parties to the proceedings in which the estoppel is raised or their privies.

The appellant's argument is that even though the ESA officer was required to make a decision in a judicial manner, she failed to do so. Although she had jurisdiction under the ESA to deal with the claim, the ESA officer lost jurisdiction when she failed to disclose to the appellant the case the appellant had to meet and to give the appellant the opportunity to be heard in answer to the case put against her. The ESA officer therefore never made a "judicial decision" as required. The appellant also says that her own failure to exercise her right to seek internal administrative review of the decision should not be given the conclusive effect adopted by the Ontario Court of Appeal. Even if the conditions precedent to issue estoppel were present, she says, the court had a discretion to relieve against the harsh effects of estoppel *per rem judicatem* in the circumstances of this case, and erred in failing to do so.

[A discussion of the statutory scheme and review process for decisions by *Employment Standards Act* officials is omitted.]

B. The Applicability of Issue Estoppel

1. Issue Estoppel: A Two-Step Analysis

The rules governing issue estoppel should not be mechanically applied. The underlying purpose is to balance the public interest in the finality of litigation with the public interest in ensuring that justice is done on the facts of a particular case. (There are corresponding private interests.) The first step is to determine whether the moving party (in this case the respondent) has established the preconditions to the operation of issue estoppel set out by Dickson J in *Angle, supra*. If successful, the court must still determine whether, as a matter of discretion, issue estoppel ought to be applied: *British Columbia (Minister of Forests) v. Bugbusters Pest Management Inc.* (1998), 50 BCLR (3d) 1 (CA), at para. 32; *Schweneke v. Ontario* (2000), 47 OR (3d) 97 (CA), at paras. 38-39; *Braithwaite v. Nova Scotia Public Service Long Term Disability Plan Trust Fund* (1999), 176 NSR (2d) 173 (CA), at para. 56.

The appellant was quite entitled, in the first instance, to invoke the jurisdiction of the Ontario superior court to deal with her various monetary claims. The respondent was not entitled as of right to the imposition of an estoppel. It was up to the court to decide whether, in the exercise of its discretion, it would decline to hear aspects of the claims that were previously the subject of ESA administrative proceedings.

[Binnie J next considers whether the *Employment Standards Act* can be considered a "judicial" decision for purposes of setting up the possibility of issue estoppel. He found that while the employment standards officer failed to provide a fair hearing, the decision remained a "judicial decision."]

3. Issue Estoppel: Applying the Tests

(a) That the Same Question Has Been Decided

A cause of action has traditionally been defined as comprising every fact which it would be necessary for the plaintiff to prove, if disputed, in order to support his or her right to the judgment of the court: *Poucher v. Wilkins* (1915), 33 OLR 125 (CA). Establishing each such fact (sometimes referred to as material facts) constitutes a precondition to success. It is apparent that different causes of action may have one or more material facts in common. In this case, for example, the existence of an employment contract is a material fact common to both the ESA proceeding and to the appellant's wrongful dismissal claim in court. Issue estoppel simply means that once a material fact such as a valid employment contract is found to exist (or not to exist) by a court or tribunal of competent jurisdiction, whether on the basis of evidence or admissions, the same issue cannot be relitigated in subsequent proceedings between the same parties. The estoppel, in other words, extends to the issues of fact, law, and mixed fact and law that are necessarily bound up with the determination of that "issue" in the prior proceeding.

The parties are agreed here that the "same issue" requirement is satisfied. In the appellant's wrongful dismissal action she is claiming $300,000 in unpaid commissions. This puts in issue the same entitlement as was refused her in the ESA proceeding. One or more of the factual or legal issues essential to this entitlement were necessarily determined against her in the earlier ESA proceeding. If issue estoppel applies, it prevents her from asserting that these adverse findings ought now to be found in her favour.

(b) That the Judicial Decision Which Is Said To Create the Estoppel Was Final

As already discussed, the requirement that the prior decision be "judicial" (as opposed to administrative or legislative) is satisfied in this case.

Further, I agree with the Ontario Court of Appeal that the employee not having taken advantage of the internal review procedure, the decision of the ESA officer was final for the purposes of the Act and therefore capable in the normal course of events of giving rise to an estoppel.

I have already noted that in this case, unlike *Harelkin, supra*, the appellant had no right of appeal. She could merely make a request to the ESA Director for a review by an ESA adjudicator. While this may be a factor in the exercise of the discretion to deny issue estoppel, it does not affect the finality of the ESA decision. The appellant could fairly argue on a judicial review application that unlike Harelkin she had no "adequate alternative remedy" available to her as of right. The ESA decision must nevertheless be treated as final for present purposes.

(c) The Parties to the Judicial Decision or Their Privies Were the Same Persons as the Parties to the Proceedings in Which the Estoppel Is Raised or Their Privies

This requirement assures mutuality. If the limitation did not exist, a stranger to the earlier proceeding could insist that a party thereto be bound in subsequent litigation by the findings in the earlier litigation even though the stranger, who became a party only to the subsequent litigation, would not be: *Machin, supra, Minott v. O'Shanter Development Co.* (1999), 42 OR (3d) 321 (CA), *per* Laskin JA, at pp. 339-40. The mutuality requirement was subject to some critical comment by McEachern CJBC when sitting as a trial judge in *Saskatoon Credit Union Ltd. v. Central Park Ent. Ltd.* (1988), 22 BCLR (2d) 89 (SC), at p. 96, and has been substantially modified in many jurisdictions in the United States: see Holmested and Watson, at 21§24, and G.D. Watson, "Duplicative Litigation: Issue Estoppel, Abuse of Process and the Death of Mutuality" (1990), 69 *Can. Bar Rev.* 623.

The concept of "privity" of course is somewhat elastic. The learned editors of J. Sopinka, S.N. Lederman, A.W. Bryant in *The Law of Evidence in Canada* (2nd ed. 1999), at p. 1088 say, somewhat pessimistically, that "[i]t is impossible to be categorical about the degree of interest which will create privity" and that determinations must be made on a case-by-case basis. In this case, the parties are identical and the outer limits of "mutuality" and of the "same parties" requirement need not be further addressed.

I conclude that the preconditions to issue estoppel are met in this case.

4. The Exercise of the Discretion

The appellant submitted that the Court should nevertheless refuse to apply estoppel as a matter of discretion. There is no doubt that such a discretion exists. In *General Motors of Canada Ltd. v. Naken*, [1983] 1 SCR 72, Estey J noted, at p. 101, that in the context of court proceedings "such a discretion must be very limited in application." In my view the discretion is necessarily broader in relation to the prior decisions of administrative tribunals because of the enormous range and diversity of the structures, mandates and procedures of administrative decision makers.

In *Bugbusters, supra*, Finch JA (now CJBC) observed at para. 32:

> It must always be remembered that although the three requirements for issue estoppel must be satisfied before it can apply, the fact that they may be satisfied does not automatically give rise to its application. Issue estoppel is an equitable doctrine, and as can be seen from the cases, is closely related to abuse of process. The doctrine of issue estoppel is designed as an implement of justice, and a protection against injustice. It inevitably calls upon the exercise of a judicial discretion to achieve fairness according to the circumstances of each case.
>
> Apart from noting parenthetically that estoppel *per rem judicatem* is generally considered a common law doctrine (unlike promissory estoppel which is clearly equitable in origin), I think this is a correct statement of the law. Finch JA's dictum was adopted and applied by the Ontario Court of Appeal in *Schweneke, supra*, at paras. 38 and 43:

> The discretion to refuse to give effect to issue estoppel becomes relevant only where the three prerequisites to the operation of the doctrine exist. ... The exercise of the discretion is necessarily case specific and depends on the entirety of the circumstances. In exercising the discretion the court must ask—is there something in the circumstances of this case such that the usual operation of the doctrine of issue estoppel would work an injustice? ...
>
> ... The discretion must respond to the realities of each case and not to abstract concerns that arise in virtually every case where the finding relied on to support the doctrine was made by a tribunal and not a court.

See also *Braithwaite, supra*, at para. 56.

Courts elsewhere in the Commonwealth apply similar principles. In *Arnold v. National Westminster Bank plc.*, [1991] 3 All ER 41, the House of Lords exercised its discretion against the application of issue estoppel arising out of an earlier arbitration, *per* Lord Keith of Kinkel, at p. 50:

> One of the purposes of estoppel being to work justice between the parties, it is open to courts to recognise that in special circumstances inflexible application of it may have the opposite result. ...

In the present case Rosenberg JA noted in passing at pp. 248-49 the possible existence of a potential discretion but, with respect, he gave it short shrift. There was no discussion or analysis of the merits of its exercise. He simply concluded, at p. 256:

> In summary, Ms. Burke did not accord this appellant natural justice. The appellant's recourse was to seek review of Ms. Burke's decision. She failed to do so. That decision is binding upon her and her employer.

In my view it was an error of principle not to address the factors for and against the exercise of the discretion which the court clearly possessed. This is not a situation where this Court is being asked by an appellant to substitute its opinion for that of the motions judge or the Court of Appeal. The appellant is entitled at some stage to appropriate consideration of the discretionary factors and to date this has not happened.

The list of factors is open. They include many of the same factors listed in *Maybrun* in connection with the rule against collateral attack. A similarly helpful list was proposed by Laskin JA in *Minott, supra*. The objective is to ensure that the operation of issue estoppel promotes the orderly administration of justice but not at the cost of real injustice in the particular case. Seven factors, discussed below, are relevant in this case.

(a) The Wording of the Statute from Which the Power To Issue the Administrative Order Derives

In this case the ESA includes s. 6(1) which provides that:

> No civil remedy of an employee against his or her employer is suspended *or affected* by this Act. [Emphasis added.]

This provision suggests that at the time the Ontario legislature did not intend ESA proceedings to become an exclusive forum. (Recent amendments to the Act now require an employee to elect either the ESA procedure or the court. Even prior to the new amendments, however, a court could properly conclude that relitigation of an issue would be an abuse: *Rasanen, supra*, per Morden ACJO, at p. 293, Carthy JA, at p. 288.)

While it is generally reasonable for defendants to expect to be able to move on with their lives once one set of proceedings—including any available appeals—has ended in a rejection of liability, here, the appellant commenced her civil action against the respondents before the ESA officer reached a decision (as was clearly authorized by the statute at that time). Thus, the respondents were well aware, in law and in fact, that they were expected to respond to parallel and to some extent overlapping proceedings.

(b) The Purpose of the Legislation

The focus of an earlier administrative proceeding might be entirely different from that of the subsequent litigation, even though one or more of the same issues might be implicated. In *Bugbusters, supra*, a forestry company was compulsorily recruited to help fight a forest fire in British Columbia. It subsequently sought reimbursement for its expenses under the *BC Forest Act*, RSBC 1979, c. 140. The expense claim was allowed *despite* an allegation that the fire had been started by a Bugbusters employee who carelessly discarded his cigarette. (This, if proved, would have disentitled Bugbusters to reimbursement.) The Crown later started a $5 million negligence claim against Bugbusters, for losses occasioned by the forest fire. Bugbusters invoked issue estoppel. The court, in the exercise of its discretion, denied relief. One reason, *per* Finch JA, at p. 11, was that

> a final decision on the Crown's right to recover its losses was not within the reasonable expectation of either party at the time of those [reimbursements] proceedings [under the *Forest Act*].

A similar point was made in *Rasanen, supra*, by Carthy JA, at p. 290:

> It would be unfair to an employee who sought out immediate and limited relief of $4,000, forsaking discovery and representation in doing so, to then say that he is bound to the result as it affects a claim for ten times that amount.

A similar qualification is made in the American *Restatement of the Law, Second: Judgments 2d* (1982), vol. 2 § § 83(2)(e) which refers to

> procedural elements as may be necessary to constitute the proceeding a sufficient means of conclusively determining the matter in question, having regard for the magnitude and complexity of the matter in question, the urgency with which the matter must be resolved, and the opportunity of the parties to obtain evidence and formulate legal contentions.

I am mindful, of course, that here the appellant chose the ESA forum. Counsel for the respondent justly observed, with some exasperation:

> As the record makes clear, Danyluk was represented by legal counsel prior to, at the time of, and subsequent to the cessation of her employment. Danyluk and her counsel were well aware of the fact that Danyluk had an initial choice of forums with respect to her claim for unpaid commissions and wages. ...

Nevertheless, the purpose of the ESA is to provide a relatively quick and cheap means of resolving employment disputes. Putting excessive weight on the ESA decision in terms of issue estoppel would likely compel the parties in such cases to mount a full-scale trial-type offence and defence, thus tending to defeat the expeditious operation of the ESA scheme as a whole. This would undermine fulfilment of the purpose of the legislation.

(c) The Availability of an Appeal

This factor corresponds to the "adequate alternative remedy" issue in judicial review: *Harelkin, supra,* at p. 592. Here the employee had no *right* of appeal, but the existence of a potential administrative review and her failure to take advantage of it must be counted against her: *Susan Shoe Industries Ltd. v. Ricciardi* (1994), 18 OR (3d) 660 (CA), at p. 662.

(d) The Safeguards Available to the Parties in the Administrative Procedure

As already mentioned, quick and expeditious procedures suitable to accomplish the objectives of the ESA scheme may simply be inadequate to deal with complex issues of fact or law. Administrative bodies, being masters of their own procedures, may exclude evidence the court thinks probative, or act on evidence the court considers less than reliable. If it has done so, this may be a factor in the exercise of the court's discretion. Here the breach of natural justice is a key factor in the appellant's favour.

Morden ACJO pointed out in his concurring judgment in *Rasanen, supra,* at p. 295: "I do not exclude the possibility that deficiencies in the procedure relating to the first decision could properly be a factor in deciding whether or not to apply issue estoppel." Laskin JA made a similar point in *Minott, supra,* at pp. 341-42.

(e) The Expertise of the Administrative Decision Maker

In this case the ESA officer was a non-legally trained individual asked to decide a potentially complex issue of contract law. The rough-and-ready approach suitable to getting things done in the vast majority of ESA claims is not the expertise required here. A similar factor operates with respect to the rule against collateral attack (*Maybrun, supra,* at para. 50):

> … where an attack on an order is based on considerations which are foreign to an administrative appeal tribunal's expertise or *raison d'être,* this suggests, although it is not conclusive in itself, that the legislature did not intend to reserve the exclusive authority to rule on the validity of the order to that tribunal.

(f) The Circumstances Giving Rise to the Prior Administrative Proceedings

In the appellant's favour it may be said that she invoked the ESA procedure at a time of personal vulnerability with her dismissal looming. It is unlikely the legislature intended a summary procedure for smallish claims to become a barrier to closer consideration of more substantial claims. (The legislature's subsequent reduction of the monetary limit of an ESA claim to $10,000 is consistent with this view.) As Laskin JA pointed out in *Minott, supra,* at pp. 341-42:

... employees apply for benefits when they are most vulnerable, immediately after losing their job. The urgency with which they must invariably seek relief compromises their ability to adequately put forward their case for benefits or to respond to the case against them. ...

On the other hand, in this particular case it must be said that the appellant with or without legal advice, included in her ESA claim the $300,000 commissions, and she must shoulder at least part of the responsibility for her resulting difficulties.

(g) The Potential Injustice

As a final and most important factor, the Court should stand back and, taking into account the entirety of the circumstances, consider whether application of issue estoppel in the particular case would work an injustice. Rosenberg JA concluded that the appellant had received neither notice of the respondent's allegation nor an opportunity to respond. He was thus confronted with the problem identified by Jackson JA, dissenting, in *Iron v. Saskatchewan (Minister of the Environment & Public Safety*, [1993] 6 WWR 1 (Sask. CA), at p. 21:

> The doctrine of res judicata, being a means of doing justice between the parties in the context of the adversarial system, carries within its tenets the seeds of injustice, particularly in relation to issues of allowing parties to be heard.

Whatever the appellant's various procedural mistakes in this case, the stubborn fact remains that her claim to commissions worth $300,000 has simply never been properly considered and adjudicated.

On considering the cumulative effect of the foregoing factors it is my view that the Court in its discretion should refuse to apply issue estoppel in this case.

NOTES AND QUESTIONS

1. To many administrative law scholars, the most puzzling aspect of issue estoppel in the context of administrative tribunal decisions is the relevance of whether the administrative decision maker was acting "judicially." Before *Nicholson v. Regional Board of Commissioners of Police*, [1979] 1 SCR 311, the question whether a decision was "judicial," "quasi-judicial," or "administrative" was of central importance to Canadian administrative law. The rules of natural justice were held not to apply to administrative decisions. In *Nicholson*, Laskin CJ held that categorizing administrative action in this fashion was both inherently difficult and potentially unjust. He endorsed, in its stead, the concept of a spectrum of administrative action, with differing degrees of fairness applicable to different points along the spectrum. In *Danyluk*, the Supreme Court accepted, without comment, that only administrative decisions that may be characterized as "judicial" can give rise to issue estoppel. The court's source for this requirement is the pre-*Nicholson* decision of the court in *Angle v. Minister of National Revenue*, [1975] 2 SCR 248. In commenting on the Ontario Court of Appeal's judgment in *Danyluk*, which had also held that issue estoppel could only arise where the administrative ruling was both final and "judicial," David Mullan observed that "[t]he effect of this is, of course, to re-insinuate into the law one of the most problematic distinctions ever encountered in Canadian judicial review law" (D. Mullan, *Administrative Law* (Toronto: Irwin, 2001), 474).

2. Binnie J appears to leave open the possibility that a procedurally unfair administrative decision might nonetheless give rise to issue estoppel. Is this consistent with Laskin JA's position in *Minott*? Can you think of circumstances when this might occur?

3. How does the discretion to be exercised by the court in cases such as *Danyluk* (whether to apply issue estoppel) differ, if at all, from the discretion to be exercised by the court in cases such as *City of Toronto* (whether to apply abuse of process)? Is there any aspect of *res judicata* that should not be left, ultimately, within the discretion of the judge?

CHAPTER FIVE

Parties and Participants

I. STANDING

What interest does a person seeking to litigate have to demonstrate in order to be permitted to sue and how does he or she demonstrate such an interest? With the advent of the *Canadian Charter of Rights and Freedoms*, the question of standing has arisen in the context of public interest litigation when the plaintiff is trying to vindicate rights not possessed by him or her personally, but rather by the public. But the question of which claims ought to be recognized and allowed to be litigated can be viewed more fundamentally. Take an obvious case: Why do we let someone who has been run down by a car and has had an arm broken sue? The answer, of course, is because he or she has suffered physical damages for which he or she seeks compensation based on harm done by the negligence of the driver. However, we do not permit someone who has observed the incident and is horrified by the mayhem caused by negligent driving to sue. Why not? Is it because such an individual has no interest in what has transpired or is it because the interest is one that the law is not, in any event as yet, willing to protect? Is the difference that, in the former case, the plaintiff can show harm that can be compensated in damage or some other form of relief and that will benefit that person directly, or is it something more fundamental? We do not, after all, protect all claims for relief that allege injury, even if the injury is a traditional one. In the classic case of *Donoghue v. Stevenson*, the plaintiff had to go to the House of Lords and, even there, only a majority of that court decided that the interest she was asserting ought to be protected. If the decision to recognize a claim does depend on something more fundamental, what is it?

Let's return to the question of standing when someone wishes to litigate and cannot claim an invasion of any interest to himself or herself directly, at least as traditionally conceived, and, therefore, seeks to litigate in the "public interest" or to vindicate "public rights." What does "public interest" or "public rights" mean? Does it mean only where a court decides to allow the litigation for other reasons it is in the "public interest," but, if the plaintiff is refused standing, the litigation is not in the "public interest"?

The following is a description of how courts have traditionally treated standing to litigate "public rights." Why do you think the attorney general was accorded such deference? How did the attorney general know where the public interest lay in any question?

W.A. Bogart, "Developments in the Canadian Law of Standing"
(1984), *Civil Justice Quarterly* 340-42 (footnotes omitted)

The traditional common law position in Canada is based on standing rules formulated by the English courts, which in turn, had their origins in the law of public nuisance. Gradually, the rules formulated in that context spread to other areas, namely "public rights," where individuals were attempting to seek redress for wrongs which affected many people but no one of them in particular.

The basic rule which developed is that suits to redress infringement of public rights are a matter for the Attorney-General to enforce. The Attorney-General may enforce the rights in two ways: either he initiates and prosecutes the action himself or he permits some private individual or public authority to bring a relator action which is an action in the name of the Attorney-General "on the relation of" that private individual or public authority. The Attorney-General is exclusively empowered to refuse or permit an individual to commence a relator action and his decision is not reviewable by a court.

However, the need to vindicate public rights through the Attorney-General by having him initiate the litigation himself or through a relator action can be circumvented if the individual can demonstrate that either his private right will be infringed or that he will suffer "special damages." What constitutes "special damages" has spawned all sorts of litigation. A favourite question is whether the damage to the individual seeking to litigate has to be of a different kind and not just different in degree from that suffered by the rest of the public.

Canadian courts have recognised some exceptions to the "special damages" rule. The first allowed municipal ratepayers standing where a municipality made an expenditure alleged to be ultra vires, that is, outside the scope of its authority. Even in these cases some deference was paid to the notion of special damages, for the courts said that they presumed that the ratepayer suffered special damages in the form of increased taxes over and above other residents in the municipality and the public in general. Moreover, the municipal ratepayers exception has been, at least by some courts, only tolerated and has often been interpreted narrowly.

The second kind of exception to the "special damages" rule was that found in statutes which widened standing in order to permit a body, a class, or specific individuals to maintain suits, without the need to demonstrate special damages arising out of the subject of the litigation, or without the need to obtain the Attorney-General's consent. These statutory standing provisions break down into three categories. In the first category are statutes which allow the governing body of a profession to seek court orders when the governing statute is being infringed. Canadian courts have held that in the absence of such statutory provisions, a professional body cannot seek an injunction to restrain persons from acting in breach of the statute unless the Attorney-General is joined as a plaintiff. Secondly, under certain provincial acts, municipalities are given the right to obtain an injunction to restrain a breach of the municipality's by-laws. In addition, sometimes an elector or "person interested in a by-law" is granted standing to apply to have a by-law quashed. Thirdly, certain acts, particularly those designed to protect consumers' interests, grant broad standing to individuals to apply to court when the act in question is being contravened.

The third type of exception focusses on the remedies sought. While it is not entirely clear, it seems that the courts are more disposed to give an individual standing when review by the court of administrative action is sought. The reasons for the courts' more liberal view have never been fully articulated though the courts' general desire to check administrative action may be significant. There is evidence that courts treat the question of standing as a matter of discretion when review of administrative action is in issue though, again, it is uncertain how this discretion is to be exercised.

NOTES AND QUESTIONS

Standing is but one aspect of the "gatekeeping" discretion exercised by courts. It concerns "who" is eligible to seek remedies from the court. A related concern is justiciability, which concerns "what" matters may be brought to court. There are a range of factors that might render a matter non-justiciable. Disputes that raise purely hypothetical, abstract, or academic questions will usually be held non-justiciable. With respect to disputes that have become moot or that are not yet ripe, courts exercise a discretion as to whether the matter should nonetheless be adjudicated: see *Borowski v. Canada*, [1989] 1 SCR 342.

It also may be that a dispute was intended to be resolved by non-judicial means. For example, in *Canada (Minister of Energy, Mines and Resources) v. Canada (Auditor General)*, [1989] 2 SCR 49, Dickson CJ held that a dispute between the auditor general and a minister was intended to be resolved by Parliament, not the courts. He stated (at 90-91), "An inquiry into justiciability is, first and foremost, a normative inquiry into the appropriateness as a matter of constitutional judicial policy of the courts deciding a given issue."

Tom Cromwell (now Mr. Justice Cromwell of the Supreme Court of Canada) summarized this approach to justiciability in the following terms:

> The justiciability of a matter refers to its being suitable for determination by a court. Justiciability involves the subject matter of the question, the manner of its presentation and the appropriateness of judicial adjudication in light of these factors. This appropriateness may be determined according to both institutional and constitutional standards. It includes both the

question of the adequacy of judicial machinery for the task as well as the legitimacy of using it. [T. Cromwell, *Locus Standi: A Commentary on the Law of Standing in Canada* (Toronto: Carswell, 1986), 192.]

As the following excerpt suggests, there is a close relationship between justiciability and standing.

L. Sossin, *Boundaries of Judicial Review: The Law of Justiciability in Canada*
(Toronto: Carswell, 1999), 202-6 (some footnotes omitted)

Standing addresses the question of who is entitled to bring proceedings to a court. Those parties directly affected by an impugned action or law are generally entitled to standing. Canadian courts have also expanded the availability of discretionary public interest standing. Part of the test which public interest litigants must satisfy is that the claim they seek to advance is a justiciable one. [Note: See *Thorson v. Attorney General of Canada*, [1975] 1 SCR 138; *Nova Scotia Board of Censors v. McNeil*, [1976] 2 SCR 265; *Canada (Minister of Justice) v. Borowski*, [1981] 2 SCR 575; and *Canada (Minister of Finance) v. Finlay*, [1986] 2 SCR 607.] Thus, once a party is granted public interest standing, the subject matter of its claim must also have been held to be justiciable. [Note: However, standing may be granted on the basis, in part, of a justiciable claim, but later removed when the dispute becomes non-justiciable. This occurred in the case of *Borowski v. Canada (Attorney General)*, [1989] 1 SCR 342 at 367-368. Borowski was granted public interest standing to challenge s. 251 of the *Criminal Code* permitting therapeutic abortions and thereby infringing the rights of foetuses. However, when his appeal on the merits reached the Supreme Court, the impugned law already had been struck down on separate grounds in *Morgentaler*. As a result, the Court dismissed Borowski's appeal as moot and added that the basis on which he had been granted standing had disappeared.]

Because justiciability so often is raised in public interest standing challenges, much of the case-law relating to justiciability has emerged from the case-law on standing. Furthermore, these analyses are related as both the doctrines of standing and justiciability call upon a court to consider, as Le Dain J observed in *Finlay v. Canada*, "the proper role of the courts and their constitutional relationship to the other branches of government" [at 631]. In this sense, both the law of standing and justiciability may be said to define the legal limits of judicial review.

It is well established that the granting of public interest standing is a discretionary matter. Further, it is trite law that a court must exercise its discretion judicially and in accordance with established principles. The Supreme Court of Canada, in a preCharter trilogy of decisions, *Thorson v. Attorney General of Canada*, *Nova Scotia Board of Censors v. McNeil*, and *Minister of Justice of Canada v. Borowski*, set out the requirements for a discretionary grant of public interest standing to challenge the validity of legislation.

The standing trilogy established that, before a court will exercise its discretion in favour of an applicant seeking public interest standing, three criteria must be met:

(a) there must be a justiciable and serious issue as to the validity of the Act;

(b) the applicant must be directly affected by the Act or have a genuine interest in its validity; and

(c) there must be no other reasonable and effective way to bring the Act's validity before the court.

Courts have confirmed in a number of post*Charter* cases that this criteria should not be considered as "mere technical requirements," nor should they be applied in a "mechanistic fashion." [Note: See, for example, *Corp. of Canadian Civil Liberties Assn. v. Canada (Attorney General)* (1998), 161 DLR (4th) 225 (CA).] In *Finlay v. Canada*, the Supreme Court extended the scope of the trilogy to non-constitutional challenges of administrative action. Le Dain J, in writing for the court, emphasized the role an analysis of justiciability plays in the determination of standing:

> The traditional judicial concerns about the expansion of public interest standing may be summarized as follows: the concern about the allocation of scarce judicial resources and the need to screen out the mere busybody; the concern that in the determination of issues the courts should have the benefit of the contending points of view of those most directly affected by them; and the concern about the proper role of the courts and their constitutional relationship to the other branches of government. ...
>
> *The concern about the proper role of the courts and their constitutional relationship to the other branches of government is addressed by the requirement of justiciability,* which Laskin J held in *Thorson* to be central to the exercise of the judicial discretion whether or not to recognize public interest standing [at 631]. [Emphasis added]

In a dissenting opinion in *Hy and Zel's* [*Inc. v. Ontario (Attorney General)*, [1993] 3 SCR 675], L'Heureux-Dubé J elaborates on the place of justiciability in the principles and policy rationales underlying standing:

> Three major concerns are typically identified: the proper allocation of judicial resources; the prevention of vexatious suits brought at the behest of mere "busybodies"; and the particular requirements of the adversary system. The first category includes such concerns as fears about a multiplicity of suits, otherwise known as the "floodgates" argument. Within the second category, courts have employed standing restrictions to ensure that issues are fully canvassed by promoting the use of the judicial process to decide live disputes between parties as opposed to hypothetical ones. Under the latter category are subsumed such matters as the "justiciability" of the issue before the courts, whether the full dimensions of the issue can be expected to be aired before the court and limits on the exercise of judicial power [at 702-3].

While Le Dain J appears in *Finlay* to identify justiciability as a separate requirement, justiciability is often subsumed as simply a part of the consideration of the "serious issue" criterion. This approach is at first glance sensible, as only a justiciable issue could qualify as a serious one, but it conflates the question of whether a matter is appropriate for adjudication, with the question of whether a matter is sufficiently important for adjudication. The test for discretionary public interest standing, therefore, is more accurately applied in four distinct phases: (1) is the matter justiciable? (2) is the matter serious? (3) is the person directly affected or genuinely interested in the litigation? and (4) is there an alternative means of challenging the validity of the Act or action at issue?

While standing is a frequent procedural juncture at which justiciability ... is considered, there is no [different or altered threshold] of justiciability applied in standing cases than elsewhere.

However, as decision-making trends move from more liberal to conservative approaches on public interest standing (or in the reverse direction), the analysis of justiciability may be influenced as well. For example, the Supreme Court's decision in *Hy and Zel's* to many signalled a retreat from the high-water mark of flexibility and access reflected in the *Finlay* decision. [Note: See P. Bowal and M. Cranwell, "Case Comment: Persona Non Grata: The Supreme Court of Canada Further Constrains Public Interest Standing" (1994), 33 *Alta. L Rev.* (No. 1) 192.]

[While *Hy and Zel's* was decided on the basis that private litigants could have brought the litigation at issue forward to a court, this decision also addressed the hypothetical nature of the claim and the lack of any evidence put before the court. While the majority decision written by Major J does not expressly deal with the relationship between standing and sufficiency of evidence], this case may also suggest that justiciability issues could be relevant to the other aspects of the standing test [beyond the "serious issue" component, especially the third prong of that test relating to alternative means of the matter coming before the court]. In *Canadian Civil Liberties Association v. Canada*, Charron JA, writing for the majority, interpreted *Hy and Zel's* as standing for the proposition that sufficiency of evidence was relevant to the analysis of standing:

> If one considers the rationales for imposing restrictions on standing which were identified by L'HeureuxDubé J, it would seem to me quite clear that the lack of a proper evidentiary basis could have a bearing on considerations such as "the proper allocation of judicial resources," "ensuring that issues are fully canvassed," "promoting the use of the judicial process to decide live disputes between parties as opposed to hypothetical ones" and determining "whether the full dimensions of the issue can be expected to be aired before the court" [at 239].

In *CCLA*, the Canadian Civil Liberties Association ("CCLA") sought to have certain provisions of the *Canadian Security Intelligence Service Act* declared unconstitutional. The federal government challenged the standing of the CCLA to bring this challenge. The motions judge granted standing and dismissed the challenge. On appeal, however, the majority of the Ontario Court of Appeal found the CCLA lacked standing to challenge the legislation. Charron JA found that the CCLA did not meet the first prong of the standing test due to the insufficiency of the evidence on which they based their allegations of unconstitutionality. She would also, if necessary, have concluded that there were alternative means by which the challenge could be advanced by a private litigant.

Therefore, the analysis of justiciability and standing are properly viewed as related but distinct inquiries into the efficacy of devoting judicial resources to a particular dispute or issue. Usually, justiciability concerns will be raised in the first part of the test for standing in the determination of whether there is a serious issue before the court. Concerns over ripeness, mootness and the political nature of the issue all may constitute grounds for denying standing.

NOTES AND QUESTIONS

1. *The expansion of standing in public interest litigation.* In the last three decades the Supreme Court of Canada has decided a number of cases dealing with challenges to the plaintiff's standing to raise constitutional and other issues and each time has confirmed the plaintiff's entitlement to sue. The first three of these, *Thorson v. Attorney General of Canada*, [1975] 1 SCR 138, *Nova Scotia Board of Censors v. McNeil*, [1976] 2 SCR 265, and *Minister of Justice of Canada v. Borowski*, [1981] 2 SCR 575 greatly liberalized the test for granting standing in public interest litigation.

Thorson, a constitutional challenge to the *Official Languages Act*, was framed as being brought by a taxpayer on behalf of all taxpayers. This basis for standing was rejected because "the claim to legal standing could not be founded solely on the damage resulting from an illegal expenditure of public funds." However, it was recognized that "the Act was not a regulatory type of statute, but was declaratory and directory in respect of the use of English and French by and in federal authorities and agencies and did not, itself, create offences or impose penalties. There was thus no person or class of persons particularly aggrieved who might raise the issue of its constitutional validity." Accordingly, standing was granted to prevent such legislation from being immune from judicial review.

Thorson was soon followed by a challenge to the constitutional validity of censorship provisions of the Nova Scotia *Theatres and Amusements Act* in *McNeil*. Standing was granted by the court in a decision by Laskin J, who said:

> [M]embers of the Nova Scotia public are directly affected in what they may view in a Nova Scotia theatre, albeit there is a more direct effect on the business enterprises which are regulated by the legislation. The challenged legislation does not appear to me to be legislation directed only to the regulation of operators and film distributors. It strikes at the members of the public in one of its central aspects.
>
> In my view, this is enough, in the light of the fact that there appears to be no other way, practically speaking, to subject the challenged Act to judicial review to support the claim of the respondent to have the discretion of the Court exercised in his favour to give him standing.

In the third decision of the trilogy, *Borowski*, the issue of standing arose in a challenge by an anti-abortionist pursuant to the *Canadian Bill of Rights* to certain exculpatory provisions to the *Criminal Code* permitting doctors to perform abortions when authorized to do so by a hospital committee. The court granted standing (Laskin J dissenting) based on the following reasoning:

> The legislation under attack here is not declaratory or directory as in the case of the *Official Languages Act* nor is it regulatory as in the case of the *Theatres and Amusements Act*. It is exculpatory in nature. It provides that in certain specified circumstances conduct which otherwise would be criminal is permissible. It does not impose duties, but instead provides exemption from criminal liability. That being so, it is difficult to find any class of person directly affected or exceptionally prejudiced by it who have cause to attack the legislation.
>
> Doctors who perform therapeutic abortions are protected by the legislation and would have no reason to attack it. Doctors who do not perform therapeutic abortions have no direct interest to protect by attacking it, and, consequently, an attack by a doctor in that category would be no different from that made by any other concerned citizen. The same thing applies to hospitals.

A hospital which appoints a therapeutic abortion committee has no reason to attack the legislation. A hospital which does not appoint such a committee has no direct reason to attack the legislation.

There is no reason why a pregnant woman desirous of obtaining an abortion should challenge the legislation which is for her benefit. The husband of a pregnant wife who desires to prevent an abortion which she desires may be said to be directly affected by the legislation in issue in the sense that by reason of that legislation she might obtain a certificate permitting the abortion if her continued pregnancy would be likely to endanger her life or health and thus prevent the abortion from constituting a crime. However, the possibility of the husband bringing proceedings to attack the legislation is illusory. The progress of the pregnancy would not await the inevitable lengthy lapse of time involved in court proceedings leading to a final judgment. The abortion would have occurred, or a child would have been born long before the case had been finally terminated, perhaps in this Court.

The legislation proposed to be attacked has a direct impact upon the unborn human foetuses whose existence may be terminated by legalized abortions. They obviously cannot be parties to proceedings in court and yet the issue as to the scope of the Canadian Bill of Rights in the protection of the human right to life is a matter of considerable importance. There is no reasonable way in which that issue can be brought into court unless proceedings are launched by some interested citizen.

In the light of the *Thorson* and *McNeil* cases, it is my opinion that the respondent should be recognized as having legal standing to continue with his action. In the *Thorson* case, the plaintiff, as an interested citizen, challenged the constitutional validity of the *Official Languages Act*. The legislation did not directly affect him, save in his position as a taxpayer. He had sought, without avail, to have the constitutional issue raised by other means. He was recognized to have status. The position is the same in the present case. The respondent is a concerned citizen and a taxpayer. He has sought unsuccessfully to have the issue determined by other means.

In the *McNeil* case, the plaintiff was concerned about censorship of films in Nova Scotia. He had sought by other means to have the validity of the *Theatres and Amusements Act* tested, but without success. In that case there were other classes of persons directly affected by the legislation who might have challenged it. Nonetheless, he was recognized as having legal standing because it also affected the rights of the public. The position of the respondent in this case is at least as strong. There are in this case no persons directly affected who could effectively challenge the legislation.

I interpret these cases as deciding that to establish status as a plaintiff in a suit seeking a declaration that legislation is invalid, if there is a serious issue as to its invalidity, a person need only to show that he is affected by it directly or that he has a genuine interest as a citizen in the validity of the legislation and that there is no other reasonable and effective manner in which the issue may be brought before the Court. In my opinion, the respondent has met this test and should be permitted to proceed with his action.

2. *Extension of public interest standing to challenges to administrative action.* In 1986, Finlay, a Manitoba resident who relied on social assistance, sought declaratory and injunctive relief from the Federal Court to the effect that the transfer payments made by the federal government to Manitoba under the *Canada Assistance Plan*, RSC 1970, c. C-1 were illegal

(*Finlay v. Canada (Minister of Finance)*, [1986] 2 SCR 608). The basis for this claim was that the relevant Manitoba social welfare legislation did not comply with the Plan's requirements for transfer payments to the provinces. Compliance allegedly would have produced a higher level of assistance for Finlay whose assistance payments were clawed back when a previous overpayment was discovered. His claim was struck out at the trial level but restored on appeal. On appeal by the Crown to the Supreme Court of Canada, standing was upheld. The court found that although Finlay had a direct, personal interest in provincial non-compliance with the Plan, the relationship between the prejudice suffered and the illegality of the transfer payments was too remote for standing under traditional rules. However, the court reviewed the *Thorson, McNeil,* and *Borowski* trilogy and held that public interest standing could be applied as a matter of judicial discretion to cases such as *Finlay* in which the challenge was not made to the constitutionality of legislation but to administrative action.

Canadian Council of Churches v. The Queen
[1992] 1 SCR 236

CORY J: … At issue on this appeal is whether the Canadian Council of Churches should be granted status to proceed with an action challenging, almost in its entirety, the validity of the amended *Immigration Act, 1976*, which came into effect January 1, 1989.

Factual Background

The Canadian Council of Churches ("the council"), a federal corporation, represents the interests of a broad group of member churches. Through an inter-church committee for refugees it coordinates the work of the churches aimed at the protection and resettlement of refugees. The council, together with other interested organizations, has created an organization known as the Concerned Delegation of Church, Legal, Medical and Humanitarian Organizations. Through this body the council has commented on the development of refugee policy and procedures both in this country and in others.

In 1988 the Parliament of Canada passed amendments to the *Immigration Act, 1976*, SC 1976-77, c. 52, by SC 1988, c. 35 and c. 36. The amended Act came into force on January 1, 1989. It completely changed the procedures for determining whether applicants come within the definition of a Convention refugee. While the amendments were still under consideration the council expressed its concerns about the proposed new refugee determination process to members of the government and to the parliamentary committees which considered the legislation. On the first business day after the amended Act came into force, the council commenced this action, seeking a declaration that many if not most of the amended provisions violated the *Canadian Charter of Rights and Freedoms* and the *Canadian Bill of Rights*, RSC 1985, App. III. The Attorney General of Canada brought a motion to strike out the claim on the basis that the council did not have standing to bring the action and had not demonstrated a cause of action.

The Question of Standing in Canada

Courts in Canada, like those in other common law jurisdictions, traditionally dealt with individuals. For example, courts determine whether an individual is guilty of a crime; they determine rights as between individuals; they determine the rights of individuals in their relationships with the state in all its various manifestations. One great advantage of operating in the traditional mode is that the courts can reach their decisions based on facts that have been clearly established. It was by acting in this manner that the courts established the rule of law and provided a peaceful means of resolving disputes. Operating primarily, if not almost exclusively, in the traditional manner, courts in most regions operate to capacity. Courts play an important role in our society. If they are to continue to do so care must be taken to ensure that judicial resources are not overextended. This is a factor that will always have to be placed in the balance when consideration is given to extending standing.

On the other hand there can be no doubt that the complexity of society has spawned ever more complex issues for resolution by the courts. Modern society requires regulation to survive. Transportation by motor vehicle and aircraft requires greater regulation for public safety than did travel by covered wagon. Light and power provided by nuclear energy require greater control than did the kerosene lamp.

The State has been required to intervene in an ever more extensive manner in the affairs of its citizens. The increase of State activism has led to the growth of the concept of public rights. The validity of government intervention must be reviewed by courts. Even before the passage of the Charter this court had considered and weighed the merits of broadening access to the courts against the need to conserve scarce judicial resources. It expanded the rules of standing in a trilogy of cases; *Thorson v. Canada (Attorney General)*, supra, *McNeil v. Nova Scotia (Board of Censors)* (1975), [1976] 2 SCR 265, 12 NSR (2d) 85, 32 CRNS 376, 5 NR 43, 55 DLR (3d) 632, and *Borowski v. Canada (Minister of Justice)*, [1981] 2 SCR 575, [1982] 1 WWR 97, 24 CPC 62, 24 CR (3d) 352, 12 Sask. R 420, 64 CCC (2d) 97, 130 DLR (3d) 588, 39 NR 331. Writing for the majority in *Borowski*, Martland J set forth the conditions which a plaintiff must satisfy in order to be granted standing, at p. 598 [SCR]:

> [T]o establish status as a plaintiff in a suit seeking a declaration that legislation is invalid, if there is a serious issue as to its invalidity, a person need only to show that he is affected by it directly or that he has a genuine interest as a citizen in the validity of the legislation and that there is no other reasonable and effective manner in which the issue may be brought before the Court.

Those then were the conditions which had to be met in 1981.

In 1982, with the passage of the Charter, there was for the first time a restraint placed on the sovereignty of Parliament to pass legislation that fell within its jurisdiction. The Charter enshrines the rights and freedoms of Canadians. It is the courts which have the jurisdiction to preserve and to enforce those Charter rights. This is achieved, in part, by ensuring that legislation does not infringe the provisions of the Charter. By its terms the Charter indicates that a generous and liberal approach should be taken to the issue of standing. If that were not done, Charter rights might be unenforced and Charter freedoms shackled. The *Constitution Act, 1982* does not of course affect the discretion courts possess to grant standing to public litigants. What it does is entrench the fundamental right of the public to government in accordance with the law.

The rule of law is recognized in the preamble of the Charter, which reads:

> Whereas Canada is founded upon principles that recognize the supremacy of God and the rule of law:

The rule of law is thus recognized as a cornerstone of our democratic form of government. It is the rule of law which guarantees the rights of citizens to protection against arbitrary and unconstitutional government action. The same right is affirmed in s. 52(1), which states:

> 52(1) The Constitution of Canada is the supreme law of Canada, and any law that is inconsistent with the provisions of the Constitution is, to the extent of the inconsistency, of no force or effect.

Parliament and the legislatures are thus required to act within the bounds of the Constitution and in accordance with the *Canadian Charter of Rights and Freedoms*. Courts are the final arbiters as to when that duty has been breached. As a result, courts will undoubtedly seek to ensure that their discretion is exercised so that standing is granted in those situations where it is necessary to ensure that legislation conforms to the Constitution and *Canadian Charter of Rights and Freedoms*.

The question of standing was first reviewed in the post-Charter era in *Finlay v. Canada (Minister of Finance)*, [1986] 2 SCR 607, 23 Admin. LR 197, [1987] 1 WWR 603, 17 CPC (2d) 289, 71 NR 338, 33 DLR (4th) 321, 8 CHRR D/3789. In that case Le Dain J, speaking for the court, extended the scope of the trilogy and held that courts have a discretion to award public interest standing to challenge an exercise of administrative authority as well as legislation. He based this conclusion on the underlying principle of discretionary standing which he defined as a recognition of the public interest in maintaining respect for "the limits of statutory authority."

The standard set by this court for public interest plaintiffs to receive standing also addresses the concern for the proper allocation of judicial resources. This is achieved by limiting the granting of status to situations in which no directly affected individual might be expected to initiate litigation. In Finlay, it was specifically recognized that the traditional concerns about widening access to the courts are addressed by the conditions imposed for the exercise of judicial discretion to grant public interest standing set out in the trilogy. Le Dain J put it in this way, at p. 631 [SCR]:

> [T]he concern about the allocation of scarce judicial resources and the need to screen out the mere busybody; the concern that in the determination of issues the courts should have the benefit of the contending points of view of those most directly affected by them; and the concern about the proper role of the courts and their constitutional relationship to the other branches of government. These concerns are addressed by the criteria for the exercise of the judicial discretion to recognize public interest standing to bring an action for a declaration that were laid down in *Thorson, McNeil* and *Borowski*.

Should the Current Test for Public Interest Standing Be Extended?

The increasing recognition of the importance of public rights in our society confirms the need to extend the right to standing from the private law tradition which limited party status to those who possessed a private interest. In addition, some extension of standing beyond the traditional parties accords with the provisions of the *Constitution Act, 1982*. However, I would stress that the recognition of the need to grant public interest standing in some circumstances does not amount to a blanket approval to grant standing to all who wish to litigate an issue. It is essential that a balance be struck between ensuring access to the courts and preserving judicial resources. It would be disastrous if the courts were allowed to become hopelessly overburdened as a result of the unnecessary proliferation of marginal or redundant suits brought by well-meaning organizations pursuing their own particular cases certain in the knowledge that their cause is all-important. It would be detrimental, if not devastating, to our system of justice and unfair to private litigants.

The whole purpose of granting status is to prevent the immunization of legislation or public acts from any challenge. The granting of public interest standing is not required when, on a balance of probabilities, it can be shown that the measure will be subject to attack by a private litigant. The principles for granting public standing set forth by this court need not and should not be expanded. The decision whether to grant status is a discretionary one with all which that designation implies. Thus, undeserving applications may be refused. Nonetheless, when exercising the discretion the applicable principles should be interpreted in a liberal and generous manner.

The Application of the Principles for Public Interest Standing to This Case

It has been seen that when public interest standing is sought, consideration must be given to three aspects. First, is there a serious issue raised as to the invalidity of legislation in question? Second, has it been established that the plaintiff is directly affected by the legislation or if not does the plaintiff have a genuine interest in its validity? Third, is there another reasonable and effective way to bring the issue before the court?

(1) Serious Issue of Invalidity

It was noted in *Finlay, supra,* that the issues of standing and of whether there is a reasonable cause of action are closely related and indeed tend to merge. In the case at bar the Federal Court of Appeal in its careful reasons turned its attention to the question of whether the amended statement of claim raised a reasonable cause of action. The claim makes a wide-sweeping and somewhat disjointed attack upon most of the multitudinous amendments to the *Immigration Act, 1976*. Some of the allegations are so hypothetical in nature that it would be impossible for any court to make a determination with regard to them. In many ways the statement of claim more closely resembles submissions that might be made to a parliamentary committee considering the legislation than it does an attack on the validity of the provisions of the legislation. No doubt the similarity can be explained by the fact that the action was brought on the first working day following the passage of the legislation. It is perhaps unfortunate that this court is asked to fulfill the function of a motions court judge reviewing the provisions of a statement of claim. However, I am prepared to accept that some aspects of the statement of claim could be said to raise a serious issue as to the validity of the legislation.

(2) Has the Plaintiff Demonstrated a Genuine Interest?

There can be no doubt that the applicant has satisfied this part of the test. The council enjoys the highest possible reputation and has demonstrated a real and continuing interest in the problems of the refugees and immigrants.

(3) Whether There Is Another Reasonable and Effective Way To Bring the Issue Before the Court

It is this third issue that gives rise to the real difficulty in this case. The challenged legislation is regulatory in nature and directly affects all refugee claimants in this country. Each one of them has standing to initiate a constitutional challenge to secure his or her own rights under the Charter. The applicant council recognizes the possibility that such actions could be brought but argues that the disadvantages which refugees face as a group preclude their effective use of access to the court. I cannot accept that submission. Since the institution of this action by the council, a great many refugee claimants have, pursuant to the provisions of the statute, appealed administrative decisions which affected them. The respondents have advised that nearly 33,000 claims for refugee status were submitted in the first 15 months following the enactment of the legislation. In 1990, some 3,000 individuals initiated claims every month. The Federal Court of Appeal has a wide experience in this field. MacGuigan JA, writing for the court, took judicial notice of the fact that refugee claimants were bringing forward claims akin to those brought by the council on a daily basis. I accept without hesitation this observation. It is clear therefore that many refugee claimants can and have appealed administrative decisions under the statute. These actions have frequently been before the courts. Each case presented a clear, concrete factual background upon which the decision of the court could be based.

The appellant also argued that the possibility of the imposition of a 72-hour removal order against refugee claimants undermines their ability to challenge the legislative scheme. I cannot accept that contention. It is clear that the Federal Court has jurisdiction to grant injunctive relief against a removal order: see *Toth v. Canada (Minister of Employment & Immigration)* (1988), 6 Imm. LR (2d) 123, (sub nom. *Toth v. Minister of Employment & Immigration*) 86 NR 302 (Fed. CA). Further, from the information submitted by the respondents it is evident that persons submitting claims to refugee status in Canada are in no danger of early or speedy removal. As of March 31, 1990, it required an average of five months for a claim to be considered at the initial "credible basis" hearing. It is therefore clear that in the ordinary case there is more than adequate time for a claimant to prepare to litigate the possible rejection of the claim. However, even where the claims have not been accepted "the majority of removal orders affecting refugee claimants have not been carried out." (See *Report of the Auditor General of Canada to the House of Commons, Fiscal Year Ended 31 March 1990*, at pp. 352-353, para. 14.43.) Even though the Federal Court has been prepared in appropriate cases to exercise its jurisdiction to prevent removal of refugee claimants there is apparently very little need for it to do so. The means exist to ensure that the issues which are sought to be litigated on behalf of individual

applicants may readily be brought before the court without any fear that a 72-hour removal order will deprive them of their rights.

From the material presented, it is clear that individual claimants for refugee status,
who have every right to challenge the legislation, have in fact done so. There are, therefore, other reasonable methods of bringing the matter before the court. On this ground
the applicant council must fail. I would hasten to add that this should not be interpreted
as a mechanistic application of a technical requirement. Rather it must be remembered
that the basic purpose for allowing public interest standing is to ensure that legislation is
not immunized from challenge. Here there is no such immunization as plaintiff refugee
claimants are challenging the legislation. Thus the very rationale for the public interest
litigation party disappears. The council must, therefore, be denied standing on each of
the counts of the statement of claims. This is sufficient to dispose of the appeal. The respondents must also succeed on their cross-appeal to strike out what remained of the
claim as the plaintiff council does not satisfy the test for standing on any part of the statement of claim. I would simply mention two other matters.

Intervenor Status

It has been seen that a public interest litigant is more likely to be granted standing in
Canada than in other common law jurisdictions. Indeed, if the basis for granting status
were significantly broadened, these public interest litigants would displace the private
litigant. Yet the views of the public litigant who cannot obtain standing need not be lost.
Public interest organizations are, as they should be, frequently granted intervenor status.
The views and submissions of intervenors on issues of public importance frequently
provide great assistance to the courts. Yet that assistance is given against a background of
established facts and in a time-frame and context that is controlled by the courts. A
proper balance between providing for the submissions of public interest groups and preserving judicial resources is maintained.

Disposition of the Result

In the result I would dismiss the appeal and allow the cross-appeal on the basis that the
plaintiff does not satisfy the test for public interest standing. Both the dismissal of the
appeal and the allowance of the cross-appeal are to be without costs.

Appeal dismissed; cross-appeal allowed.

NOTES AND QUESTIONS

1. What is the relationship between "cause of action" and "standing"? Is "standing" simply about the ability to be heard or is it the "public" part to the "private" "cause of action"—
that is, a recognition of entitlement so long as the underlying factual basis is established? In
his book *Locus Standi* (Toronto: Carswell, 1986), at 208, T.A. Cromwell suggests that standing should essentially be confined to the ability to be heard: "[I]f the definition of standing
includes such issues [relating to cause of action], it fails to isolate a set of legal issues concerned solely with access to adjudication that may be usefully analyzed as a unit."

2. In contrast, consider the position of the Ontario Law Reform Commission in its *Report on the Law of Standing* (1989), at 87-91:

> Any new test to be proposed by the Commission must guide courts to make decisions that are consistent with the legitimate rationalia of standing rules. Moreover, the test must be animated by a recognition of what courts really do when they make standing decisions. The Commission believes that, in deciding questions of standing in any type of civil proceeding, courts essentially determine whether a particular claim or interest, advocated by a particular plaintiff, should be recognized as worthy of protection by, and therefore deserving of advancement in, the courts.
>
> In our view, it is critical for the law of standing to recognize a broadened array of interests. In order to do so, courts must necessarily become sensitive to the existence and implications of various values in our society—values that have dramatically altered from the time when the public nuisance rule first developed. Focusing on normative values will permit courts to utilize decision-making tools that further a serious consideration of potentially novel kinds of interest and a sensitivity to the place of such interests in various contexts. Courts need to abandon tools to the extent that they promote the notion that standing decisions are made according to rigid rules, and in a sort of normative vacuum.
>
> Reflecting on the circumstances and situations where standing issues have arisen or will likely arise suggests that there is no single factor, no one element, that should invariably lead to the grant or denial of standing in any particular case. Instead, as we shall see below, it is sensitivity to the existence of a variety of factors, and a sophisticated evaluation and balancing of them, that we believe should lie at the heart of the court's decision-making process.
>
> This is not easy or uncontroversial. Deciding which interests to recognize and for what purposes is a complex and sensitive task, one in which courts are always actively engaged, whether explicitly recognized or not. By granting standing, a court indicates that it is prepared to place a certain value on an interest and to protect it by allowing it to be the subject of litigation, and that the individual or group seeking to litigate is not disputing something of, for example, merely idiosyncratic interest. One commentator has described the process in this way: "What we need to attend to is separating out interests sincerely held, but which nevertheless are too embryonic or too idiosyncratic, from those which represent a common interest of sufficient importance to merit the law's protection."
>
> This process, in our view, links the notion of standing and the notion of cause of action at the theoretical, and certainly at the practical, level. Both concepts essentially involve asking the same questions. Accordingly, whether or not courts explicitly acknowledge the link—and whether they use the term "standing" or "cause of action"—the process of decision-making in respect of both "private" and "public" litigation does not, in fact, "keep the recognition of rights and standing as separate exercises." Courts do focus, in effect, on the normative values underlying any determination of standing (and therefore, cause of action) and do not in practice make decisions that reflect a rigid dichotomy between who should be permitted to proceed and what claims, whether traditional or otherwise, should be recognized. We believe this is the correct approach for all types of civil litigation—a rational and principled approach to the issue of entitlement to seek relief in the courts under the rubric of standing or cause of action. One commentator has put the matter in this way:

Toward the end of his judgment in *Finlay* Le Dain J, in responding to an argument of the defendant that even if Finlay had standing the proceedings should nonetheless be struck out because the plaintiff still had no cause of action, made a brief but critical observation:

> I question whether there is a true issue of reasonable cause of action distinguish-able, as an alternative issue from that of standing. ... Clearly, if a plaintiff has the requisite standing an action will lie for a declaration that an administrative au-thority has acted without statutory authority.

This is important because it indicates that recognizing someone's standing and founding a cause of action are closely related processes, that there is no clear line of division be-tween different kinds of interest and that the recognition of any interest is grounded in a common process—the law's pronouncement about which values it will enhance and protect.

The regime that we propose in this report is intended to, and will, deal fully and adequately with what courts and commentators have hitherto called either "cause of action" or "standing" (although, as indicated in the General Introduction, for convenience we use only the latter term throughout this report). In the end then, we believe that cause of action and standing are suffi-ciently intertwined and co-extensive, if not identical, to warrant their continued assimilation in practice by the courts.

The assimilation of these two concepts—which, as we have said, is a feature of existing practice in all civil proceedings—is reflected in the manner in which a plaintiff's entitlement to commence and maintain a proceeding is challenged. In Ontario, there is no discrete rule per-mitting a challenge on the basis of "standing." However, rule 21.01(1)(b) of the Rules of Civil Procedure provides for motions "to strike out a pleading on the ground that it discloses no rea-sonable cause of action. ... Notwithstanding this terminology, it is clear that where a defendant wishes to challenge the plaintiff's standing," he may wish to proceed under this rule.

It is, we believe, critically important to understand the essential nature of the defendant's at-tack on the plaintiff's right to commence and maintain an action, and to emphasize that no change in principle or practice is intended to be made by the proposals set forth in this report. Whether this view of the practical effect of our recommendations requires the amendment of any rule, or of any other provision, is a matter we leave to the appropriate authority.

Which view do you prefer? Why? In answering, is there a particular model of litigation you are drawing upon?

While the trend to more restrictive approaches to standing alluded to above has been apparent in constitutional cases, courts appear to have extended the more liberal approach to non-constitutional challenges. Consider the following example of how the law of public interest standing was applied to a class action by a group of taxpayers seeking a declaration from the court that preferential treatment was unlawfully given to a family trust. Revenue Canada (now the Canada Revenue Agency) permits taxpayers to request advance income tax rulings where they want to know how specific provisions of the *Income Tax Act* will be applied to proposed transactions. In 1985 and 1991, Revenue Canada made nonpublic rul-ings with the implicit assumption that Canadian residents could hold taxable Canadian property and that a deemed disposition and corresponding tax liability would not occur when such taxable Canadian property was transferred out of Canada. The effect of this ruling was alleged to be that millions of dollars of tax liability owed by the unnamed family trust would be deferred. The advance judgment issued by Revenue Canada appeared to contradict a public opinion released in 1985. In response to the 1991 ruling, the auditor general issued a strongly worded report criticizing the ruling itself, the seeming covertness and the lack of documentation associated with the way in which it was made. Following the auditor general's report, Harris, a taxpayer and member of a group called CHO!CES, issued a statement of claim, alleging that Revenue Canada acted illegally or for ulterior motives by providing preferential treatment to a taxpayer in issuing an advance tax ruling in 1991. Revenue Canada moved to strike out the statement of claim on the basis that it disclosed no cause of action because no one is permitted to challenge another's income tax treatment and because the respondent lacked public-interest standing. Two issues were raised on appeal: (1) whether the statement of claim described a reasonable cause of action arising out of the respondent's allegations, and (2) whether the respondent had public interest standing to seek declaratory relief in alleging maladministration of the *Income Tax Act* by Revenue Canada.

Harris v. Canada
[2000] 4 FC 37, 2000 CanLII 15738

SEXTON JA:

Introduction

Mr. Harris issued a statement of claim, alleging that the Ministry of National Revenue acted illegally or improperly or for ulterior motives by providing preferential treatment to a taxpayer when the Ministry of National Revenue issued an advance tax ruling in 1991. The Ministry of National Revenue moved to strike the statement of claim on the basis that it disclosed no cause of action because one person is not permitted to challenge another's income tax treatment, and because Mr. Harris lacked public interest standing.

The following issues are raised by this appeal:

Issues

. . .

[A discussion of why the Attorney General cannot succeed on its motion to strike the claim for failing to disclose a reasonable cause of action is omitted.]

2. Does Mr. Harris have public interest standing to seek declaratory relief relating to the alleged maladministration of the Income Tax Act by the Minister of National Revenue?

The Attorney General submits that public interest standing may be granted to permit a citizen to litigate a non-constitutional issue only where the issue raised concerns the limits of statutory authority for administrative action. The Attorney General relies heavily on Le Dain JA's (as he then was) decision in *Rothmans v. Pall Mall Canada Ltd. v. MNR et al. (No. 1)* [[1976] 2 FC 500 (CA)].

. . .

In the *Thorson, McNeil* and *Borowski* cases, the Supreme Court established the conditions under which a public interest plaintiff could challenge legislation on constitutional grounds.

. . .

In *Finlay v. Canada (Minister of Finance)*, Le Dain J considered whether the principles of public interest standing that applied to litigants who seek to challenge legislation on constitutional grounds ought to be extended to a "non-constitutional challenge ... for a declaration to the statutory authority for public expenditure or other administrative action." [*Finlay*, supra, at 630.] Le Dain J confirmed that public interest standing should be so extended to ensure "the maintenance of respect for the limits of administrative authority."

By contrast, in *Rothmans*, Le Dain JA [as he then was] declined to grant Rothmans standing to challenge the Minister's calculations. He held:

> The decisions of the Supreme Court of Canada in *Thorson v. Attorney General of Canada* [1975] 1 SCR 138, and *McNeil v. Nova Scotia Board of Censors* (1975) 5 NR 43, were urged upon us as indicating a relaxation of the requirement of *locus standi*. A careful reading of these decisions shows, in my respectful opinion, that the principal consideration governing them is the importance in a federal state of opportunity to challenge the constitutional validity of statutes. No such consideration is applicable here. It was suggested that there is a comparable consideration of public policy in broad access to challenge the validity of administrative action, and this view finds some support in the recognition of a judicial discretion to permit a stranger to bring *certiorari* or prohibition in certain cases. *The present case is not one that raises any question of the limits of statutory authority. The most that is raised is a question of administrative interpretation that the authorities are obliged to make in their application of the governing statute.* [Ibid., at 510 (emphasis added).]

The essential difference between *Rothmans* and the instant appeal is that in *Rothmans*, the Court concluded that the issues raised did not involve a question of the respect of the limits of administrative authority. By contrast, Mr. Harris' statement of claim does. He complains that certain taxpayers have been afforded tax advantages by Revenue Canada that were not afforded to other taxpayers. In other words, he alleges that Revenue Canada has afforded preferential treatment to certain taxpayers, something that raises a question of the limits of statutory authority.

This Court has recognized that where strong public interest issues arise, a Court may exercise its discretion to recognize public interest standing. In *Distribution Canada Inc. v. MNR* [[1993] 2 FC 26 (CA)], a case in which a plaintiff sought to require the Minister to comply with certain provisions of the *Customs Tariff* [RSC 1985 (3d Supp.), c. 41], Desjardins JA held that public interest standing may exist where "the matter raised ... is one of strong public interest and there may be no other way such an issue could be brought to the attention of the Court, were it not for the efforts of the [public interest litigant]. [Ibid., at 39.]

Similarly, in *National Federation of Self-Employed*, despite holding that "as a matter of general principle I would hold that one taxpayer has no sufficient interest in asking the court to investigate the tax affairs of another taxpayer or to complain that the latter has been underassessed or overassessed" [*Federation of Self-Employed*, supra, at 99], Lord Wilberforce held:

> That a case can never arise in which the acts or abstentions of the Revenue can be brought before the court I am certainly not prepared to assert, nor that, in a case of sufficient gravity, the court might not be able to hold that another taxpayer or other taxpayers could challenge them. Whether this situation has been reached or not must depend on an examination, on evidence, of what breach of duty or illegality is alleged. On this, and relating it to the position of the complainant, the court has to make its decision [ibid.].

In the same vein, Lord Diplock held:

> I do not doubt, however, and I do not understand any of your Lordships to doubt, that if it were established that the Board were proposing to exercise or to refrain from exercising their powers not for reasons of "good management" but for some extraneous or ulterior reason that inaction or inaction of the Board would be *ultra vires* and would be a proper matter for judicial review if it were brought to the attention of the court by an applicant with "a sufficient interest" in having the Board compelled to observe the law [ibid., at 101].

Lord Diplock added that it would "be a grave lacuna in our system of public law if a pressure group, like the federation, or even a single public spirited taxpayer, were prevented by outdated technical rules of locus standi from bringing the matter to the attention of the court to vindicate the rule of law and get the unlawful conduct stopped" [ibid., at 107].

Again, as I have explained earlier in these reasons, Revenue Canada would not have the power to conclude the compromise agreement that was at issue in *National Federation of Self-Employed*. Accordingly, I do not think that the reason for which the House of Lords denied public interest standing to the Federation of Self-Employed constitutes good law in Canada. Therefore, I do not think that the House of Lords' decision demonstrates that Mr. Harris is precluded from obtaining public interest standing to challenge the tax treatment afforded to other taxpayers by Revenue Canada. Indeed, I think that the *obiter* statements of Lord Wilberforce, Lord Diplock and Lord Scarman reproduced above demonstrate the opposite: namely, that if Revenue Canada concludes compromise agreements or covert deals or provides preferential treatment to certain taxpayers without statutory authority, public interest standing may be granted to challenge the tax treatment that Revenue Canada affords to taxpayers who benefit from those actions.

I now turn to the four criteria established in *Finlay* to determine whether this Court should exercise its discretion to recognize Mr. Harris' public interest standing. In *Finlay*, Le Dain J held that courts should be concerned about their proper role and their constitutional relationship to other branches of governments. He held that where an issue may be appropriately decided by a court, a court "should not decline to determine it on the ground that because of its policy context or implications it is better left for review and determination by the legislative or executive branches of government." [*Finlay*, supra, at 632.]

In my view, Mr. Harris' statement of claim raises a justiciable issue. His claim that the Minister of National Revenue acted illegally or improperly or for ulterior motives, namely favouritism and preferential treatment by way of a covert deal when he interpreted the provisions of the Act in favour of a specific trust, raises a question of a potential violation of the Act that a court may assess by reference to the Minister's duty to follow the Act "absolutely," as this Court held in *Ludmer* [supra, at 5317].

The second criterion established by Le Dain J in *Finlay* was that a public interest litigant must raise a serious issue. As Le Dain J concluded in *Finlay*, the issues raised by Mr. Harris are "far from frivolous." [*Finlay*, supra, at 633.] Mr. Harris does not merely bring an action to obtain a declaration for an interpretation of particular sections of the Act. Rather, as stated above, he alleges that the Minister of National Revenue acted for ulterior motives with a view to favouring particular taxpayers, in circumstances where there was a "lack of documentation and analysis of key decisions made by Crown officials in this regard." [Statement of Claim, para. 13.] The issues are serious.

The third criterion is that the public interest litigant must have a genuine interest in the issue. On appeal, the Attorney General did not seriously contest that Mr. Harris did have a genuine interest in the issues he raises. Mr. Harris is a taxpayer. He is a member of an organization that seeks to ensure the fair administration of the taxation system. Accordingly, I conclude that Mr. Harris has a genuine interest in the issues he raises.

Finally, in exercising its discretion to recognize public interest standing, a court must be satisfied that there is no other reasonable and effective manner in which the issue may be brought before a court. Here too, the Attorney General did not seriously contend that there was another reasonable or effective manner in which the issue could be brought before a court. Mr. Harris requested the Attorney General to do so twice, but to this date, the Attorney General has not yet complied. It cannot be seriously contended that the taxpayers who were provided with the 1991 ruling favourable to them would raise the issues brought by Mr. Harris. Therefore, I conclude that there is no other reasonable and effective manner in which the issue could be brought before a court.

Conclusion on Standing

Public interest standing has been granted in analogous cases. For example, in *Greater Victoria Concerned Citizens Association v. Provincial Capital Commission* [[1990] 46 Admin. LR 74 (BCSC)], a citizens group successfully obtained standing to seek to obtain a declaration that an agreement to lease certain heritage property as a tourist attraction was beyond the Provincial Capital Commission's jurisdiction. In *Union of Northern Workers v. Jewell* [[1991] NWTJ No. 40 (SC)], a union was granted public interest standing to seek to compel a government minister to hold occupational health and safety board meetings. In *Sierra Club of Canada v. Canada (Minister of Finance)* [[1999] 2 FC 211 (TD)], an organization promoting protection of the environment was granted standing to seek to compel several government ministers to subject the sale of nuclear reactors to a full environmental assessment under the *Canadian Environmental Assessment Act* [SC 1992, c. 37], the absence of which was said to be unlawful.

I do not think that there is a principled basis for concluding that the Minister of National Revenue is somehow protected from a similar action by a public interest litigant to compel the Minister to perform his or her statutory duties. Accordingly, I conclude that Muldoon J properly ruled that Mr. Harris could be granted public interest standing and therefore correctly set aside the Prothonotary's granting of the Crown's motion to strike.

I wish to emphasize the narrow cause of action for which public interest standing has been granted. Mr. Harris does not merely seek to obtain the interpretation of a particular provision of the Act, akin to requesting a court to provide a legal opinion. A mere *bona fide* change of position on interpretation of a statute, without more, would be insufficient to constitute a cause of action and would have been insufficient to persuade this Court to exercise its discretion to recognize public interest standing. Nevertheless, in considering Mr. Harris' cause of action for which public interest standing has been granted, the trial judge may incidentally find it necessary to consider whether, on a proper construction of the Act, "taxable Canadian property" may be held by a resident of Canada.

• • •

I would therefore dismiss the appeal, with costs.

NOTES AND QUESTIONS

1. The Supreme Court of Canada refused leave to appeal the decision of the Federal Court of Appeal in *Harris*. After confirming the public interest standing of taxpayers to bring an action against the minister of national revenue, the class action proceeded to trial in 2001. Harris lost a motion to obtain disclosure of the identity of the family trust at the centre of the allegations and lost a further motion for disclosure of ministry documents relating to the advance judgment provided on the family trust rollover. After a trial lasting three weeks, the claim was dismissed by the Federal Court, Trial Division, [2001] FC No. 1876 (TD). Having dismissed the claim, Dawson J considered the issue of costs where public interest standing has been granted. She ruled as follows (at paras. 221-25):

> The question of costs is of considerable significance when rationally deciding whether to bring an action. Where a plaintiff lacks a personal, proprietary or pecuniary interest in an action the plaintiff is effectively deterred from bringing the action, notwithstanding he or she may have, as a matter of law, public interest standing.
>
> In its Report on Standing (Toronto: Minister of the Attorney General, 1989) the Ontario Law Reform Commission proposed criteria to determine the circumstances where costs should not be awarded against a person who commences public interest litigation. Those criteria were:
>
> a) The proceeding involves issues the importance of which extends beyond the immediate interests of the parties involved.
>
> b) The person has no personal, proprietary or pecuniary interest in the outcome of the proceeding, or, if he or she has an interest, it clearly does not justify the proceeding economically.
>
> c) The issues have not been previously determined by a court in a proceeding against the same defendant.
>
> d) The defendant has a clearly superior capacity to bear the costs of the proceeding.
>
> e) The plaintiff has not engaged in vexatious, frivolous or abusive conduct.

In my view, those criteria also provide a principled foundation for considering a claim to costs in the context of public interest litigation. As I conclude that the facts of the present case fall within those criteria, I find, in the exercise of my discretion, that Mr. Harris is entitled to some award of costs. This recognizes that absent an award of costs public interest status may be of theoretical but not practical effect.

Mr. Harris should not however receive costs on a solicitor and client basis. Such awards are exceptional and are generally awarded only where there has been reprehensible conduct on the part of one of the parties. There has been no such conduct and no circumstances in my view [that] otherwise warrant an award of costs on this basis. The appropriate scale of costs is in accordance with column III of the Table to Tariff B of the *Federal Court Rules, 1998*.

Given my conclusion that any award of costs should be on a party and party basis, another important principle is that such costs are to be a partial indemnity, not a windfall, or a bonus. This is reflected in the Court's Tariff B which represents a compromise between compensating the payee while not unduly burdening the payor. I am therefore concerned at the absence of information before the Court as to the funds already given to Mr. Harris, likely by other Canadian taxpayers, to finance this action.

Therefore if Mr. Harris continues to seek costs, and they can not be agreed between the parties, as a condition for such award and pursuant to my discretion as set out in Rule 400(1), I find it appropriate that Mr. Harris provide a full accounting to the Court and the defendants in satisfactory form as to the amount of the funds received by him and expended or owing in respect of the costs of this litigation. This accounting is for the purpose of ensuring that any award of costs paid by the Canadian government goes toward indemnity, not profit.

2. Compare this reasoning with the treatment of costs in the context of intervention, where intervenors typically may be liable for costs but cannot be entitled to them. Are costs intended to provide an incentive for worthy litigants to bring lawsuits, to implicitly deter litigants, or to be a "neutral" factor in the decision to launch an action? What principles underlie Dawson J's concern over the possibility that Harris has received funds from other sources? Does this concern relate exclusively to public interest litigants or should the court inquire into the financing of all civil actions? Would the award of costs in *Harris* have been any different if Harris had won the action? Should there be a difference in costs between winning and losing in public interest litigation? Note that in the Federal Court of Appeal judgment on standing, which went in Harris's favour, costs were awarded against the Crown. What different principles applied, if any, in that decision?

Canadian Bar Assn. v. British Columbia
2006 BCSC 1342

BRENNER CJSC:

Introduction

The plaintiff The Canadian Bar Association ("CBA") seeks a series of declarations and orders regarding the provision of civil legal aid in British Columbia. The Attorney General of Canada ("Canada") applies to dismiss this action on the grounds that the plaintiff has no standing to bring the claim and that therefore this court has no jurisdiction to hear it. Alternatively, Canada applies under Rule 19(24) of the Rules of Court to strike the statement of claim on the basis that it discloses no reasonable claim.

The defendant Her Majesty the Queen in Right of the Province of British Columbia ("BC") also applies to strike the statement of claim under R. 19(24) and to have the action dismissed for lack of standing. The defendant Legal Services Society ("LSS"), the organization that administers and delivers legal aid in British Columbia, did not take any position on these applications.

For the reasons that follow, I am of the view that the plaintiff has no standing to bring this action and that it must therefore be dismissed. Alternatively, the action must be struck out under Rule 19(24).

The CBA claims public interest standing to bring this action:

> ... on behalf of people living on low incomes as defined by Statistics Canada Low Income Cut-offs ("LICOS") and who lack sufficient means to obtain proper advice and redress, including legal representation if necessary, in matters where their Fundamental Interests are threatened. ("Poor People"). (statement of claim at para. 8).

The CBA alleges that Canada and BC are jointly responsible for the provision of civil legal aid, and that the LSS administers civil legal aid on their behalf.

In substance, the CBA claims that the provision of civil legal aid in British Columbia ("BC Civil Legal Aid") is inadequate and that these inadequacies amount to breaches of the *Canadian Charter of Rights and Freedoms*, written and unwritten provisions of the Constitution, and international human rights instruments. The CBA contends that BC Civil Legal Aid is inadequate because matters that engage fundamental interests are excluded from coverage, financial eligibility guidelines exclude many poor people and, where legal aid coverage is provided, the services provided are too restrictive.

In its statement of claim the CBA does not attack the constitutionality of any statute or regulation. However it does allege that the current *Legal Services Society Act*, SBC 2002, c. 30, "radically altered and reduced the provision of BC Civil Legal Aid" in comparison to its predecessor statute, RSBC 1996, c. 256. The statement of claim also states that reduced federal and provincial funding has resulted in less access to civil legal aid since 1995.

The plaintiff claims that the unwritten constitutional principle of the rule of law requires that every person have equal and meaningful access to justice and that inadequate civil legal aid denies such access. Similarly, inadequate civil legal aid undermines the unwritten constitutional principle of judicial independence by drawing judges and tribunals into the fray to assist unrepresented persons, thus compromising the adversarial system.

The plaintiff further claims that inadequate civil legal aid contravenes sections 7, 15(1), and 28 of the Charter, s. 36(1) of the *Constitution Act, 1982*; and various international human rights instruments.

The plaintiff claims remedies under s. 24(1) of the Charter, s. 52(1) of the *Constitution Act, 1982*, and the inherent jurisdiction of the court.

· · ·

In summary, the plaintiff CBA seeks a declaration that unwritten and express constitutional provisions require Canada and BC to "establish and maintain a civil legal aid regime that ensures meaningful and effective access to justice by Poor People where their Fundamental Interests are at stake"; a further declaration that such a legal aid system is subject to eligibility, coverage, and quality of service requirements; and finally, an order directing Canada and BC to maintain a legal aid system compliant with the declarations and with the Constitution. The plaintiff also requests that this court retain ongoing supervisory jurisdiction to ensure compliance with the declarations and order.

· · ·

In the case at bar, the plaintiff CBA is not a litigant seeking civil legal aid funding in the context of a particular case. Rather, the plaintiff is a national bar organization that has long advocated for adequate legal aid funding across Canada. In pursuit of that objective it brings the within action to obtain the declarations and orders to which I have earlier referred. Since the CBA has no direct interest in this action, it must meet the criteria for public interest standing in order for the case to proceed in its current form.

Prior to the Charter, the test for public interest standing was set out in three cases: *Thorson v. Canada (Attorney General)*, [1975] 1 SCR 138; *Nova Scotia Board of Censors v. McNeil*, [1976] 2 SCR 265; *Canada (Minister of Justice) v. Borowski*, [1981] 2 SCR 575; these authorities were joined post-Charter by *Finlay v. Canada (Minister of Finance)*, [1986] 2 SCR 607. The parties agree that this quartet sets out the current test the court must apply in order to determine public interest standing. However, they agree neither on precisely how that test is articulated, nor how it applies to the present action.

The quartet displaced, or at least qualified, the general rule that only the Attorney General had the legal standing necessary to maintain an action to assert a purely public right or interest. Prior to these cases, an individual citizen or taxpayer was unable to challenge the validity of legislation unless they were either directly affected by it or threatened by sanctions for an alleged violation of it.

Laskin J (as he then was) for the majority in *Thorson* expressed doubt as to whether the traditional rule "can have any application in a federal system where the Attorney General is the legal officer of a Government obliged to enforce legislation enacted by Parliament" (at 146). This is not surprising since in such a system, simultaneously enforcing and challenging legislation is practically perverse, if not legally untenable. As Laskin J pointed out, the situation in Canada "is markedly different from that of unitary Great Britain where there is no unconstitutional legislation and the Attorney General, where he proceeds as guardian of the public interest, does so against subordinate delegated authorities" (at 146).

In *Thorson*, the majority held that the constitutionality of legislation is always justiciable; and that maintenance of the traditional rule would immunize legislation from review in circumstances where an Attorney General was unwilling to institute proceedings, or where a government was unwilling to direct a reference, and where there was no person or class of persons particularly aggrieved by the law. Holding that a grant of standing in such circumstances by a court was discretionary and borrowing from the language of private law, Laskin J characterized such a discretionary grant of standing as arising from "the right of the citizenry to constitutional behaviour by Parliament" (at 163).

Laskin J clearly viewed this displacement of discretion from the legislative and executive branches to the judicial branch as consistent with principle, jurisprudence and public policy. He also saw the ready availability of the declaratory remedy as ensuring that these considerations would not be trumped in the end by a remedial void:

> The expansion of the declaratory action, now well-established, would to me be at odds with a consequent denial of its effectiveness if the law will recognize no one with standing to sue in relation to an issue which is justiciable and which strikes directly at constitutional authority (at 162).

However, while *Thorson* did modify the traditional common law rule, it did so in a cautious and limited manner. It emphasized that the decision to grant standing was purely discretionary.

Martland J for the majority in *Borowski* summarized the three part test emerging from *Thorson* and *McNeil* as follows (at 598):

> I interpret these cases as deciding that to establish status as a plaintiff in a suit seeking a declaration that legislation is invalid, if there is a serious issue as to its validity, a person need only show that he is affected by it directly or that he has a genuine interest as a citizen in the validity of the legislation and that there is no other reasonable and effective manner in which the issue may be brought before the Court.

Therefore, in order to obtain public interest standing to challenge legislation, a party must establish:

(1) there is a serious issue as to the invalidity of the legislation;
(2) the plaintiff is affected directly by or has a genuine interest in the validity of the legislation; and
(3) there is no other reasonable and effective manner in which the issue may be brought before the Court.

[A discussion of whether standing should be decided as a preliminary matter is omitted.]

The Three Part Test:

1. "No serious issue"

The plaintiff CBA asserts that a party seeking public interest standing must satisfy, on a balance of probabilities, the following three requirements:

(a) Is there a serious issue?
(b) Does the plaintiff have a direct interest or a genuine interest in the matter?
(c) Is there another reasonable and effective way to bring the matter to court?

However, more accurately the first test requires that: "there be a serious issue as to the validity of the Act." The second requires that "the applicant be directly affected or have a genuine interest in the Act's validity"; and the third requires that there be "no other reasonable and effective way to bring the Act's validity before the court."

The plaintiff's recasting of the test, while understandable, does highlight the difficulties with this action. The CBA does not challenge any legislation, nor indeed, any government action. It does not challenge the existing legal aid legislation in British Columbia (the *Legal Services Society Act*). Nor does it challenge the expenditures being made for legal aid. Rather, it seeks a sweeping review of an entire program for compliance with not only written constitutional provisions, but also with unwritten constitutional principles. This raises the question as to whether the scope of public interest standing is broad enough to accommodate the CBA's claim.

The "serious issue" requirement reflects a concern over justiciability which Laskin J held in *Thorson* to be "central to the exercise of judicial discretion whether or not to recognize public interest standing" (*Finlay* at 632). As discussed above, a challenge to the constitutionality of legislation is always justiciable. However, as the passage from *Borowski* quoted above at para. 26 demonstrates, the Supreme Court intended the modification of the traditional common law rule for public interest standing to apply only in circumstances where the party is "seeking a declaration that legislation is invalid." Further, the first requirement set out in that paragraph is that there must be "a serious issue as to its [the legislation's] invalidity."

Where the Supreme Court has decided to expand public interest standing beyond strict challenges to legislation, it has done so only incrementally. In *Finlay*, where the court did choose to expand the scope of public interest standing established by the pre-*Charter* cases of *Thorson*, *McNeil*, and *Borowski*, it did so with considerable caution.

In *Finlay* there was a challenge, not to the validity of legislation, but rather to the legality of certain payments out of the Consolidated Revenue Fund. Le Dain J for the court in *Finlay* introduced the case (at 610):

> This appeal raises the question whether a private individual has standing to sue for a declaration that certain payments out of the Consolidated Revenue Fund of Canada are illegal *on the ground that they are not made in accordance with the applicable statutory authority*. [Emphasis added.]

The "new" question posed in *Finlay* was "whether the approach to public interest standing reflected in those cases, in which there was a challenge to the constitutionality or operative effect of legislation, applies to a non-constitutional challenge to the statutory authority for administrative action" (at 614).

In my view … there can be little doubt that the limitation of public interest standing to legislative challenges is both express and intentional.

· · ·

This was re-affirmed in *Canadian Council of Churches v. Canada (Minister of Employment and Immigration)*, [1992] 1 SCR 236 at para. 252, where Cory J for the court observed that "the whole purpose of granting status is to prevent the immunization of legislation or public acts from any challenge." While "public acts" was not defined, the quotation from Finlay makes it clear that the Supreme Court intended to extend public interest standing only in those circumstances where a challenge to administrative action was analogous to a challenge to legislation. In other words, public expenditure or other administrative action could be challenged but only on the basis that it was without or in excess of statutory authority.

There are other examples of the Supreme Court extending public interest standing in circumstances that do not involve challenges to specific legislation. In *Finlay* itself, the court concluded that a challenge to public spending on the ground that it was not made in accordance with the applicable statutory authority was justiciable. In *Operation Dismantle v. The Queen*, [1985] 1 SCR 441, a constitutional challenge to a specific decision of the executive was also considered justiciable.

But of significance is that these cases addressed the public interest in the maintenance of respect for the limits of administrative and executive authority, respectively. It is for that reason that they were therefore considered analogous to *Thorson, McNeil*, and *Borowski*, all of which addressed the limits of legislative authority (see *Finlay* at 631).

However, in the case at bar, there is no challenge to legislation or to administrative action said to be *ultra vires*. Instead, there is a challenge attacking a failure to legislate or a failure to have a scheme in place that meets appropriate constitutional criteria as contended by the CBA. This is a significant distinction. Instead of considering a specific statute or a specific administrative act or expenditure for constitutional compliance, this case would ultimately require the court to define a constitutionally valid civil legal aid scheme and order its provision by the defendants.

The plaintiff correctly submits that the principles governing public interest standing must be applied in a "liberal and generous manner." In *Canadian Council of Churches*, Cory J stated that "the post-*Charter* era calls for a liberal and purposive approach to standing." However, he also emphasized that the approach must remain balanced (at 250). In my view, the balanced approach will not be served by removing the requirement that the "serious issue" must relate to invalidity of legislation, or to a public act undertaken without or in excess of statutory authority.

In the case at bar, there is no challenge to a specific governmental decision, act, or statute. The case cannot be characterized as raising an issue with respect to the limits of statutory, administrative, or executive authority. The challenge is to the funding, content, administration, operation, and effect of an entire public program that invokes various federal and provincial statutes, ministries, agencies, and non-governmental entities and actors.

There is no question that the provision of legal aid for non-criminal matters is a serious public issue, but that does not render it a serious issue warranting the grant of public interest standing. I am reluctant to extend the concept of public interest standing so far beyond what has been clearly set out by the Supreme Court of Canada.

What the plaintiff effectively seeks in the case at bar is to have the court conduct an inquiry on the subject of civil legal aid, define a constitutionally compliant civil legal aid scheme, order the defendants to implement such a scheme, and oversee the process to ensure compliance.

This issue highlights the difficulty with the form of this action. Here the plaintiff claims declaratory remedies and an order under s. 24(1) of the *Charter*, s. 52(1) of the *Constitution Act, 1982*, and the court's inherent jurisdiction. BC denies that these remedies are available under either the constitutional provisions or the court's inherent jurisdiction. It also says that the unavailability of a remedy vitiates a reasonable cause of action under R. 19(24), or standing, or both. Canada says that there is no cause of action under the *Charter* because no individual claims have been advanced. If this is correct, how does the non-availability of a remedy impinge upon the issue of standing?

Standing is not merely the right to assert a legal claim, but the "right to seek particular relief" (*Finlay* at 635). The right to seek particular relief is not the same as the entitlement to such relief, which is a matter for a trial court to decide after a consideration of the merits of the case. Where a party is precluded from seeking particular relief, the party has no standing.

The precondition of an individual remedy in the *Charter* context was considered in *Borowski v. Canada (Attorney General)*, [1989] 1 SCR 342 [*Borowski (No. 2)*]. *Borowski (No. 2)* was decided after the Supreme Court of Canada had struck down the abortion provisions of the *Criminal Code* in their entirety (*R v. Morgentaler (No. 2)*, [1988] 1 SCR 30). This rendered the *Borowski (No. 2)* appeal moot since the legislative provisions under attack in that case were those that had been struck down.

However, of significance for the case at bar are the court's findings with respect to standing. The court found that Mr. Borowski had lost his standing under both s. 24(1) and s. 52(1). Sopinka J for the court stated (at 367):

> In my opinion s. 24(1) cannot be relied upon here as a basis for standing. Section 24(1) clearly requires an infringement or denial of a *Charter*-based right. The appellant's claim does not meet this requirement as he alleges that the rights of a foetus, not his own rights, have been violated.
>
> Nor can s. 52(1) of the *Constitution Act, 1982* be invoked to extend standing to Mr. Borowski.
>
> Nevertheless, in the same manner that the "standing trilogy" referred to above was based on a challenge to specific legislation, so too a challenge based on s. 52(1) of the *Constitution Act, 1982* is restricted to litigants who challenge a law or governmental action pursuant to power granted by law. The appellant in this appeal challenges neither "a law" nor any governmental action so as to engage the provisions of the *Charter*. What the appellant now seeks is a naked interpretation of two provisions of the *Charter*. This would require the Court to answer a purely abstract question which would in effect sanction a private reference. In my opinion, the original basis for the appellant's standing is gone and the appellant lacks standing to pursue this appeal.

Sopinka J's concerns are apposite here. The court is being asked to "answer a purely abstract question which would in effect sanction a private reference" (*Borowski (No. 2)* at 367). In order for the intended beneficiaries of this action to obtain a meaningful remedy, the CBA asks the court to identify the parameters of a constitutionally valid scheme of civil legal aid. Just as Mr. Borowski was unable to advance a s. 24(1) claim on behalf of a third party, the CBA here has no standing to assert a claim on behalf of an amorphous group of individuals whose *Charter* rights may have been, or in the future may be, breached by the operation (or more accurately the non-operation) of a public program.

In saying this I am mindful of the plaintiff's submission that the court should be "flexible, responsive and purposive" and further, that "if there is a right there is a remedy." The plaintiff says that the court should be guided by the Supreme Court's decision in *Operation Dismantle* However, in that case no issue was raised as to standing. There were also twenty other activist groups along with the nominate plaintiff. The statement of claim alleged potential violation of the plaintiffs' s. 7 rights. In that case, no issue appears to have been taken with the fact that there were no individual plaintiffs.

Also of note is that the individual members of all of the groups in *Operation Dismantle* alleged that their s. 7 rights were at issue; in the case at bar the CBA does not contend that any of its *Charter* rights or its members' *Charter* rights are at issue. As attempted in *Borowski (No. 2)*, it is advancing a claim, including a *Charter* claim, on behalf of third parties with whom it stands at arm's length.

I conclude therefore that the plaintiff has failed to meet the first requirement for public interest standing.

[A discussion of the "genuine interest" prong of the test is omitted.]

In my view, the third requirement for standing and its underlying concern that the courts have the benefit of the contending points of view of those most directly affected by them, is entirely consonant with the common law method. The voices of organizations such as the CBA in this type of litigation are capable of being heard. Our judicial system accommodates professional expertise through generous intervenor provisions and by permitting expert evidence.

The defendants say that as individual cases are decided, the parameters of constitutional civil legal aid will continue to emerge. The numbers of individual challenges to legal aid denial suggests that the availability of individual plaintiffs is fatal to the plaintiff's argument for public interest standing. In *Federation of Newfoundland Indians v. Canada*, 2003 FCT 383, that court stated at para. 14:

> The jurisprudence on public interest standing suggests that requests by aboriginal groups are routinely denied when individual aboriginals are already listed as plaintiffs: see *Landry v. Canada (Indian and Northern Affairs)*, [1994] FCJ No. 2004 (QL); *Nolan v. Canada (Attorney General*, [1997] OJ No. 3361 (QL). The major hurdle for aboriginal "umbrella" groups is the third branch of the public interest standing test. In the instant case, since individual aboriginal plaintiffs are already named as plaintiffs, it cannot be said there is no other way to bring the litigation. Therefore, I find that the plaintiffs have not satisfied the third branch of the test set out by the Supreme Court of Canada in *Canadian Council of Churches*, supra, and consequently the FNI will not be accorded public interest standing.

In *Canadian Council of Churches*, the plaintiff challenged amendments to the *Immigration Act*. The Supreme Court refused standing to the Council on the basis that all refugee claimants were directly affected and that many had filed refugee claims. The court also noted that the imposition of a 72 hour removal order against refugee claimants did not undermine their ability to challenge the legislative scheme.

This was described by the court as the "real difficulty in this case" (at 254) and it was the basis on which the court denied public interest standing to the Council. Given the history of individuals challenging the availability of civil legal aid, it is difficult to distinguish the *Canadian Council of Churches* decision from the case at bar.

In the subsequent case of *Hy and Zel's Inc. v. Ontario (Attorney General)*, [1993] 3 SCR 675, public interest standing was again denied, by a majority decision, on the basis that other reasonable and effective ways to bring the issue before the court existed.

These authorities were applied by the Ontario Court of Appeal in *Corp. of the Canadian Civil Liberties Assn. v. Canada (Attorney General)* (1998), 40 OR (3d) 489. In that case, an application by the plaintiff for public interest standing to challenge certain provisions of the *Canadian Security Intelligence Act* was dismissed.

In my view, these authorities make it clear that in the case at bar the plaintiff CBA does not meet the third test for public interest standing since it fails to meet the "no other reasonable and effective manner" requirement for a discretionary grant of public interest standing.

In addition to the authorities, the extensive affidavit material filed by the CBA in support of its claim tends to undermine its submissions on this branch of the test. The CBA has long practiced direct advocacy and intervention on appeal cases as one method of addressing its concerns about legal aid. In its most recent *Legal Aid Advocacy Resource Kit*, the CBA states:

> Until our lobbying efforts are successful at improving access to justice for the less advantaged in our society across the country, we will need to turn to the courts to decide on the right to publicly-funded representation on a case-by-case basis. (Affidavit of Gayle Schellenberg, Exhibit Q at 772.)

The CBA material strongly suggests that bringing this "systemic claim," rather than any of the more traditional forms of test case, representative action, class action or individual challenge, was a strategic choice. I conclude that there are other reasonable and effective methods for bringing the issues before the court.

I conclude that the CBA has failed to establish that there is a serious issue as to the invalidity of legislation or as to the invalidity of particular public acts. Further, the CBA has failed to establish that there is no other reasonable or effective manner by which the issue may be brought before the court. I therefore decline to exercise my discretion to grant standing to the CBA in this matter.

[A discussion of Brenner CJSC's conclusion that the statement of claim fails to disclose a reasonable claim pursuant to any of the Charter or constitutional provisions pleaded is omitted.]

NOTES AND QUESTIONS

1. In "The Justice of Access: Who Should have Standing to Challenge the Constitutional Adequacy of Legal Aid?" (2007), 40 *UBC L Rev.* 727-44, Lorne Sossin argues that Brenner CJSC misconstrued the test for public interest standing and failed to appreciate the role of *Charter* principles, including the principle of access to justice, in applying this test. The Court has created an artificial dichotomy between "individual" and "systemic" Charter litigation, the result of which will be to further erode access to justice in Charter cases involving social rights.

2. The BC Court of Appeal dismissed an appeal from the Canadian Bar Association to the decision of Brenner CJSC (2008 BCCA 92). The Court of Appeal held that the issue of whether the claim discloses a reasonable cause of action (as required by rule 19(24) of the BC *Rules of Court*), had to be decided prior to an analysis of standing. In other words, unless

the claim as pleaded discloses a reasonable cause of action, the issue of standing does not arise. In this case, the BC Court of Appeal concluded that Brenner CJSC was correct to conclude that the claim disclosed no reasonable cause of action.

The BC Court of Appeal held that the pleadings did not give rise to a reasonable cause of action under the Constitutional grounds raised, and that such facts, even if proven, could not justify the relief sought. The BC Court of Appeal expressed no view on the conclusions of Brenner CJSC regarding standing.

What do you think of the logic of determining whether there is a reasonable cause of action prior to the determination of standing?

3. The BC Court of Appeal relied on the Supreme Court decision in *British Columbia (Attorney General) v. Christie*, [2007] 1 SCR 873, which was released the year after the decision of Brenner CJSC. The Court of Appeal observed:

> However, the invocation of unwritten constitutional principles in this case is in the context of a dispute over the funding of legal aid. In this, the statement of the Supreme Court of Canada in *British Columbia (Attorney General) v. Christie*, [2007] 1 SCR 873, 2007 SCC 21 ["Christie (SCC)"] rules out, in my view, a broad-based systemic claim to greater legal services based on unwritten principles:
>
> > The issue, however, is whether general access to legal services in relation to court and tribunal proceedings dealing with rights and obligations is a fundamental aspect of the rule of law. In our view, it is not. Access to legal services is fundamentally important in any free and democratic society. In some cases, it has been found essential to due process and a fair trial. But a review of the constitutional text, the jurisprudence and the history of the concept does not support the respondent's contention that there is a broad general right to legal counsel as an aspect of, or precondition to, the rule of law.
> >
> > Nor has the rule of law historically been understood to encompass a general right to have a lawyer in court or tribunal proceedings affecting rights and obligations. The right to counsel was historically understood to be a limited right that extended only, if at all, to representation in the criminal context: M. Finkelstein, *The Right to Counsel* (1988), at pp. 1-4 to 1-6; W.S. Tarnopolsky, "The Lacuna in North American Civil Liberties—The Right to Counsel in Canada" (1967), 17 *Buff. L Rev.* 145; Comment, "An Historical Argument for the Right to Counsel During Police Interrogation" (1964), 73 *Yale LJ* 1000, at p. 1018.
> >
> > We conclude that the text of the Constitution, the jurisprudence and the historical understanding of the rule of law do not foreclose the possibility that a right to counsel may be recognized in specific and varied situations. But at the same time, they do not support the conclusion that there is a general constitutional right to counsel in proceedings before courts and tribunals dealing with rights and obligations.
>
> Whether there are unwritten principles that may be invoked in an individual case, I leave to another day. This statement of claim does not purport to advance individual cases that may resonate more loudly on the issues mentioned.
>
> In my view, the broadly-directed pleadings of a systemic problem violating unwritten constitutional principles do not raise a reasonable claim, and I see no basis upon which to interfere with the Chief Justice's conclusion on this question."

II. JOINDER OF MULTIPLE PARTIES

Which parties may be included or joined together in a single proceeding? The desire to prevent duplicative litigation has given rise to liberal joinder rules. These rules are balanced by the countervailing concern that the litigation not become unduly complex and burdensome.

A lawsuit in its simplest form involves a single plaintiff asserting a single claim against a single defendant. However, most cases are more complex. This section of the chapter examines the rules governing the extent to which a lawsuit can be expanded or confined within particular limits. A plaintiff can (or, sometimes, must) add multiple parties. A defendant can expand the size of the litigation by claiming relief against the plaintiff (counterclaims), other defendants (cross-claims), or an entirely new party (third-party claims). Separate actions can be united in a single proceeding (consolidation). There are rules that have developed to allow those who have not been joined by the plaintiff or defendant to be involved in litigation (known as "intervention"). Class proceedings, cases in which one person can bring an action on behalf of a large number of others, are discussed separately in the final chapter.

The starting point in any discussion of joinder is the proposition that the interests of both society and litigants are better served by one lawsuit than by several. It is usually more economical for the litigants and for the court system to litigate matters in one action than in numerous separate actions. In most cases, the trial in a single action of all the matters in dispute between the parties will take less time, trouble, and money than several actions. Thus, the gain to be derived from broad joinder is the convenience and utility of settling all differences between parties at one time. A further factor often favours a single action rather than a multiplicity of actions. If a plaintiff has a number of claims that are factually or legally related to each other, and pursues each in a separate action, there is a risk of different or inconsistent findings—and no recovery at all—on matters common to each claim. The law views the possibility of inconsistent verdicts as something to be avoided.

This general policy in favour of a single action rather than a multiplicity of actions is sometimes enshrined in statute—see, for example, s. 138 of the Ontario *Courts of Justice Act* ("[a]s far as possible, multiplicity of legal proceedings shall be avoided"); it is often referred to in cases interpreting and applying rules relating to joinder—see, for example *McNaughton v. Baker* (1988), 28 CPC (2d) 49 (BCCA). This policy is implemented by (1) rules making generous provision for the joinder of multiple claims and parties; (2) rules that prohibit the splitting of a cause of action and the relitigation of issues (the doctrine of *res judicata*, discussed in chapter 4); and (3) the practice of allowing either party to obtain consolidation or the trial of actions together. However, the policy in favour of joinder of claims and parties is not an absolute one. An unlimited right of joinder could lead to confusion and complexity, a situation that would result if too many diverse issues were attempted to be litigated in one action. Consequently, the court has broad discretion to refuse joining claims or parties in the same action. This is a discretion that will be exercised when it is demonstrated that fairness and convenience favour separate actions rather than a single action.

With some exceptions, the modern joinder rules allow parties and actions to be joined in almost any circumstances, leaving the court with a residual discretion to forbid joinder if it would lead to inconvenience or injustice. The following sections emphasize the situations in which the different mechanisms for joinder might be used. The sections also explore the limits that ought to be respected if the litigation is not to become so unwieldy and complex as to defeat the general objectives of efficiency and justice that led to liberal joinder rules in the first place.

A. Permissive Joinder

In terms of parties, how large may the plaintiff make the litigation through joinder of multiple plaintiffs or defendants? This issue arises regularly because it is common for plaintiffs to wish to join together in bringing an action, or for them to seek to sue multiple defendants. The rules relating to the joinder of multiple plaintiffs and defendants in one action are broad and permissive. But such joinder is not unlimited. Multiple joinder of either plaintiffs or defendants is only proper if the conditions set out in the applicable rules of practice, as interpreted by the courts, are met. Even if the joinder attempted in a particular case satisfies the requirements of the appropriate rule, the court has broad discretion to order separate trials where fairness and convenience so require.

1. Multiple Plaintiffs

Cases in which joinder of multiple plaintiffs would be proper occur where the defendant owes an obligation jointly to numerous plaintiffs—for example, where the plaintiffs are partners who have entered into a contract. Other cases in which joinder of multiple plaintiffs would be proper occur where a number of persons are injured as a result of an automobile accident—for example, where three persons travelling in a car are all injured in a collision. In what way does the automobile accident case just described satisfy the conditions of the rules concerning joinder? What policy objectives justify joinder of the claims of several plaintiffs injured in an automobile accident in one action? Most provinces have specific rules about joinder. See Ontario rules 5.02(1) and 5.05; Alberta rule 36; British Columbia rule 5.02; Manitoba rule 5.02; New Brunswick rule 5.03(1); Nova Scotia rule 5.02; and Prince Edward Island rule 5.02(1).

Iovate Health Sciences Inc. v. NxCare Inc.
2007 CarswellOnt 7459 (SCJ)

B. ALLEN J: ... Iovate brings a motion under Rule 5.04(2) for an order to add new parties to the action underlying this motion and seeks leave to amend the style of cause by changing the name of the Defendant NxCare Inc. to WellNx Life Sciences Inc.

Background

Iovate and WellNx are competitors in the business of manufacturing and marketing weight loss and nutritional products. The Former Employees were at one time employees of Iovate who subsequently began employment with WellNx. In early 2004, Iovate began research into the development of a weight loss product for women that its research showed would be a profitable venture. The Defendant, Scott Welch, in the position of Senior Marketing Manager for Iovate, had knowledge of the product, its trade name

"LeanBalance," and details of the marketing research, plans and targets, and of Iovate's anticipated February 2005 launch date. Iovate alleges Welch shared that confidential information with Bradley Woodgate, Vice President of WellNx, and Derek Woodgate, President and Secretary of WellNx.

Iovate alleges WellNx rushed its product through development and brought it to market in December 2004, before Iovate's anticipated launch date. WellNx's product, "SlimQuick," being the first to market, was more successful than LeanBalance. Iovate alleges WellNx misappropriated Iovate's confidential information and as a result profited at Iovate's expense by gaining an advantage in the market that would have been captured by LeanBalance.

Iovate further alleges WellNx, the Woodgates, Welch and Stevenson entered into a conspiracy to gain access to Iovate's confidential information and to induce Iovate employees to leave Iovate and to go to work for WellNx. Eighteen employees voluntarily left or were terminated as employees of Iovate and went to work for WellNx. The Former Employees were employed with Iovate in such positions as product development, accounts, graphic design, marketing, sales and sales management, research, writing, media, data coordination, call centre representative, and in the athletics area. Iovate alleges the Former Employees provided extensive privileged and confidential information to WellNx.

In Paragraphs 34-42, Iovate alleges confidential information taken and misused by the Former Employees includes, but is not limited to: advanced copies of advertisements; media and marketing plans; advertising rates; the identities of key suppliers and manufacturers and the prices paid to them; details of the quality control systems; information about direct customer and distributor networks; information relating to the development of new Iovate products; information related to contracts with athletes who endorsed Iovate products; and privileged email communications between Iovate and its legal counsel.

Iovate claims $100,000,000 in compensatory damages for lost profits; in the alternative, it seeks an accounting of WellNx's sales of SlimQuick; punitive damages of $10,000; injunctive relief; and the return to Iovate of any of its confidential information.

In its motion to add parties, Iovate seeks to add five new plaintiffs that are related to the originally named Plaintiff and form part of the Iovate group of companies. The additional parties are: Iovate Health Sciences Research Inc., Iovate Health Sciences International Inc., Iovate Health Sciences U.S.A. Inc., Iovate Health Sciences Fulfilment Inc., and Smartburn Formulations Inc. ("the new Plaintiffs").

· · ·

B. *Iovate's Motion to Add New Parties*

1. *The Parties' Positions*

Iovate asks the Court to exercise its discretion under Rule 5.04(2) to add the five new Plaintiffs to the action. Iovate argues, in accordance with the requirements of the Rule, the addition of those parties would not result in prejudice to the Defendants that could not be compensated for by costs or an adjournment.

Iovate further submits adding the new Plaintiffs satisfy the criteria set down by the court in a recent decision. The pleadings as they relate to the new parties are legally tenable and comply with the rules of pleading. The new Plaintiffs will plead the necessary elements of conspiracy and breach of confidence and misappropriation of confidential information. [*D.W. Lorentz Construction Inc. v. Andaman Construction Ltd.*, [2007] OJ No. 1534 (Ont. SCJ), at para. 14]. Iovate submits it is not a breach of the rules of pleading to allege that the Defendants have collective responsibility for wrongs against all the Plaintiffs. Adding the parties also meets the requirements of Rule 5.02(1) in that the claims by the original Plaintiff Iovate and the new Plaintiffs raise common questions of law and arise from a common occurrence. Delay will not result from adding parties since no statement of defence has yet been served. Iovate submits it seeks to add the new parties to assist the court by ensuring all proper parties are before the court and not for the purpose of abusing the judicial process. In Iovate's view, the Defendants have failed to establish that irremediable prejudice will result from adding the new parties.

The Defendants argue Iovate should not be permitted to add the new parties because it seeks to do so outside the two-year limitation period after the alleged wrongs occurred. According to the Defendants, the alleged misappropriation and misuse of the confidential information took place from October 2004 to December 2004, but the motion to add the new parties was not served until March 2007, more than two years after the alleged wrongs occurred. The Defendants acknowledge the evidence shows Iovate's in-house counsel began instructing outside counsel on the alleged misuse of confidential information in February 2005 so, based on this, it could be argued the limitation period expired either in December 2006 or February 2007. The Defendants also point to a letter, dated April 1, 2005 by Iovate's then outside counsel directed to certain of the Defendants, raising allegations of theft of confidential information, which indicates, in the Defendants' view that Iovate's senior people knew of the wrongs before April 2005.

Iovate relies on the evidence of its Chief Operating Officer, Terrence Begley, to establish the limitation period for adding new parties had not expired. Iovate says it did not learn of the alleged breach of confidence until after March 2005, nor did it have knowledge of the alleged conspiracy until the second half of 2005. Iovate submits Mr. Begley was unaware of the April 1, 2005 letter, and moreover, no copy of that letter could be found in Iovate's records.

Iovate advances the further argument that a cause of action does not arise until after harm is suffered which is an essential element of a cause of action. Iovate says the evidence shows it was not known to Iovate that an alleged conspiracy was afoot until the second half of 2005 when Iovate became aware the departure of the employees from Iovate was the result of a conspiracy rather than natural employee turn-over. Iovate was not aware of the damage suffered in the form of lost sales and lost market advantage—a necessary element of the claims of conspiracy and breach of confidence—until well after March 5, 2005. [*Air Canada v. WestJet Airlines Ltd.*, [2005] OJ No. 5512 (Ont. SCJ), at para. 18; *Lysko v. Braley*, [2006] OJ No. 1137 (Ont. CA), at paras. 19 and 20]. Iovate submits since the causes of action plead did not arise until the second half of 2005, the limitation period had not expired when it brought the motion to add parties.

Iovate argues, in the alternative, that if the limitation period did expire, there are special circumstances the Court should consider to allow the addition of the parties. The Ontario Court of Appeal has allowed proper parties to be added after the expiry of the limitation period when the failure to name the party from the outset was the result of error or inadvertence. [*Mazzuca v. Silvercreek Pharmacy Ltd.*, [2001] OJ No. 4567 (Ont. CA) at para. 56]. Iovate points to Mr. Begley's evidence that failure to add the parties at the outset was the result of an oversight. Iovate argues the additional parties should be allowed because, similar to the circumstances in *Mazzuca*, no additional causes of action are raised, nor are further remedies being sought in adding the new parties.

The Defendants argue Iovate has failed to meet the limitation period for adding parties and has been unsuccessful in establishing special circumstances. They point out Iovate has a complex corporate structure about which it likely did not advise the counsel who commenced the action on its behalf. The fault for that rests with Iovate and, in the Defendants' view, is not the type of circumstance the court in *Mazzuca* had in mind as a basis to set aside the effect of the limitation period.

2. Analysis

I accept Iovate's position on this issue and grant the motion to add the five new Plaintiffs.

I find Iovate has satisfied the requirements of Rule 5.04(2) as expanded upon by the criteria discussed in *D.W. Lorentz*.

I can find no prejudice that would result to the Defendants by the addition of the new Plaintiffs that could not be compensated for by costs. A statement of defence has not yet been served so the Defendants would not be disadvantaged by having to amend its defence as a result of the joinder. The addition of the new parties will not result in increased complexity in the proceedings from the point that the new parties neither raise new claims nor request additional remedies beyond those of the original Plaintiff. The addition of the parties does not appear to be motivated by an improper purpose. The intention of the motion seems clearly to be to ascertain that all proper parties will be before the court in the action.

On the question of whether Iovate exceeded the limitation period in bringing the motion to add parties, I accept Iovate's position. I accept it can be concluded on the evidence that Iovate could reasonably have been unaware by December 2004 that it might have had causes of action against the Defendants for alleged conspiracy or breach of confidence. It is not clear that the Iovate representatives had sufficient knowledge of the breach of confidential information and conspiracy at the time of and before the April 1, 2005 letter. Even accepting the Defendants' point that Iovate knew of the April 1, 2005 letter and the matters raised in it, I do not find that shows the necessary elements to establish the causes of action existed at the time or were known to Iovate.

I accept Iovate's argument that the essential element of damage or harm would have to have been suffered in relation to both breach of confidence and conspiracy before those causes of action can be properly raised. On balance, I accept Mr. Begley's evidence that Iovate did not learn of the breaches of confidence until after March 2005 and was not aware of the alleged conspiracy involving the Former Employees leaving Iovate until the second half of 2005. I accept Mr. Begley's evidence that Iovate did not suffer damages resulting from lost sales until after March 2005. I find, as a result, Iovate did not bring the Motion to add parties outside the two-year limitation period. I find there is no need to consider whether special circumstances apply. I therefore grant Iovate's motion to add the five new Plaintiffs pursuant to Rule 5.04(2).

Tactical consequences. There are some tactical considerations to be borne in mind by a plaintiff contemplating bringing suit with other co-plaintiffs. These include liability for costs, possible conflict of interest or division of opinion, the possible delay and expense that might result from the defendant's counterclaiming against a co-plaintiff or bringing in a third party with reference to the co-plaintiff's claim, and the possible prejudice resulting from discovery of a co-plaintiff. To these may be added the consideration that all the plaintiffs have to be represented by the same counsel (see, for example, Ontario rule 5.02(1)).

2. Multiple Defendants

A plaintiff may also join multiple defendants in a single lawsuit. See Ontario rules 5.02(2) and 5.05, Alberta rules 36 and 39, Manitoba rule 50.2(2), New Brunswick rule 5.03(2), Nova Scotia rule 5.02, PEI rule 5.02, and Saskatchewan rule 37(2). The following excerpt explains the purpose and strategy behind joining multiple defendants in a single lawsuit. The case that follows is an example of the strategic use of joinder of defendants.

Garry D. Watson, "Joinder of Defendants Sued in the Alternative: Solicitors as Co-Defendants"
(1981), 2 *Advocates' Quarterly* 365

Joinder of multiple defendants is permitted for two basic policy reasons; reasons which underlie many civil procedural rules: economy and justice. Typically, in most cases where joinder is sought both policies will be operative. However, as we will see, this will not always be so.

Economy. A plaintiff is permitted to join multiple defendants to achieve a saving of time and costs, both to himself and to the court, through the avoidance of a multiplicity of actions where there are questions of law or fact common to the claims asserted. This is *one* of the policies which justifies, for example, the most common instance of multiple joinder of defendants—that of several defendants sued in respect of the plaintiff's injuries incurred in an automobile accident. To require the plaintiff to sue each defendant separately would involve the plaintiff in additional costs and would require the court to go over much of the same area twice.

Justice and the risk of inconsistent determination. Economy (or convenience) is not the only policy underlying multiple joinder. There is a second and, it is submitted, a more important one: to assure that justice is done by avoiding the risk of inconsistent determinations. This risk arises because, under the traditional rules of *res judicata*, only the parties to the litigation (and privies) are bound thereby. Hence, if P sues D1 and is unsuccessful because the court concludes that the injuries were a result not of the negligence of D, but rather of the negligence of D2 (who is not a party), and P then turns around and sues D2, D2 is in no way bound by the "decision" in the first action that his negligence caused the plaintiff's injuries. He is completely free to relitigate the question and, moreover, to blame the accident on D1's negligence. A major reason for allowing the joinder of multiple defendants is to spare the plaintiff this risk of inconsistent determinations: to force both defendants where the plaintiff is in doubt as to the persons from whom he is entitled to relief to defend in one action. A primary purpose of multiple joinder of defendants is to get D2 bound by the decision as against D1, and *vice-versa*. It stops D1 from blaming D2 in D2's absence, and then D2 blaming D1 in Dl's absence (or, put more generally, it stops the second defendant from questioning the underlying basis of the decision in favour of the first defendant) which may leave the plaintiff unjustly uncompensated.

The second policy is arguably the more important of the two because it involves a more significant value. It is concerned not merely with convenience and economy, but with justice in terms of the ultimate outcome. It assures that a fair and proper result is achieved and that if the plaintiff is to lose he does so on the merits, rather than as a result of procedural manoeuvering. However, the existence and importance of the second policy is often overlooked, for several reasons. In most cases the two policies favouring joinder will be operative where multiple joinder is sought. This is because the existence of a common question of law or fact normally invokes both policies: it will usually make it convenient to try the claims together and it will present the plaintiff with the risk of inconsistent determinations if joinder is disallowed. Moreover, the economy-convenience policy is the more obvious of the two and the one most often referred to. Recognition of the second policy has been somewhat obscured by the judge-made rule which has emerged in Ontario as the test for the propriety of multiple joinder of defendants: "it depends upon convenience and the existence of a common question of law or fact." This formulation, while it makes overt reference to convenience (economy), makes no explicit reference to the second policy.

Brown v. Mendis

2003 CarswellOnt 3581 (SCJ)

MORIN J: The plaintiffs instituted action against the defendant Dr. T. Mendis by statement of claim issued on September 4, 2002.

In their statement of claim the plaintiffs allege that in 1989 the plaintiff Brian Brown was referred by his family physician to the defendant neurologist Dr. Mendis for an assessment of a dysfunction of his shoulder girdle and that Dr. Mendis eventually gave a diagnosis that Mr. Brown was suffering from amyotrophic lateral sclerosis (ALS—commonly referred to as Lou Gehrig's Disease). It is further alleged that after the diagnosis, Dr. Mendis continued to treat Mr. Brown for Lou Gehrig's Disease until 2001 when it was determined that, in fact, Mr. Brown's condition was caused by what is known as an Arnold-Chiari Malformation and Syringomyelia. It is alleged that as a result of Dr. Mendis' negligent misdiagnosis and mistreatment, Mr. Brown is now condemned to a life of complete physical dysfunction which has totally immobilized him except for the most rudimentary functions.

In his statement of defence dated January 6, 2003, Dr. Mendis pleaded that in 1989 he had referred Mr. Brown to a consultant specializing in neuro-muscular disorders and that the consultant had diagnosed Mr. Brown with Lou Gehrig's Disease, a non-treatable and progressive neuro-degenerative disease.

Plaintiffs' counsel served a demand for particulars dated January 17, 2003 requesting, *inter alia*, that the consultant be identified. At his examination for discovery held April 15, 2003, Dr. Mendis confirmed that the consultant to whom he had initially referred Mr. Brown was neurologist Dr. David Preston. As well, on his examination for discovery, Dr. Mendis made it very clear that the diagnosis of Lou Gehrig's Disease made in the original instance, was that of Dr. Preston and not his. Dr. Mendis, on discovery, took the position that he had sent Mr. Brown to Dr. Preston "for a diagnosis" and that he was "depending on Dr. Preston for diagnosis" (see questions 188 and 189 of Dr. Mendis' discovery).

Following examination for discovery the plaintiff brought on this motion for an order granting leave to add Dr. David Preston as a party defendant in the within action and for leave to deliver an appropriately amended statement of claim. In the ordinary course it would be appropriate for such an order to issue. See Rules 5.02, 5.03, 5.04 and 26.01. Here, however, counsel for Dr. Preston, who is also counsel for Dr. Mendis, takes the position that the applicable limitation period for bringing action against Dr. Preston has expired and that the test for adding a defendant after expiry of the limitation period, has not been met by the plaintiffs.

Section 89 of the *Health Professions Procedural Code* provides:

> No person who is or was a member is liable to any action arising out of negligence or malpractice in respect of professional services requested of or rendered by the person unless the action is commenced within one year after the date when the person commencing the action knew or ought to have known the fact or facts upon which the negligence or malpractice is alleged.

On the materials before the court, there is a very live issue as to whether the limitation period has run with respect to any action against Dr. Preston. (While Section 89 was not pleaded by Dr. Mendis in his original statement of defence, that statement of defence has now been amended to include the plea.)

On the materials before me, I am satisfied that the issue of the application of Section 89 of the *Health Professions Procedural Code* and more particularly the issue as to when the plaintiffs knew or ought to have known the fact or facts upon which their allegations of negligence are based, are issues of fact best left to the trial judge and should not be finally disposed of on this motion. See *Aguonie v. Galion Solid Waste Material Inc.* (1998), 38 OR (3d) 161 (Ont. CA).

It is clear that where there are special circumstances and a lack of prejudice, the court has a general discretion to add defendants to an existing action even after the expiry of the limitation period. See *Swain Estate v. Lake of the Woods District Hospital* (1992), 9 OR (3d) 74 (Ont. CA) and *Mazzuca v. Silvercreek Pharmacy Ltd.* (2001), 56 OR (3d) 768 (Ont. CA). Indeed, in *Mazzuca*, Laskin JA in his concurring judgment questioned whether "special circumstances" are required to add a party after the expiry of a limitation period. At page 789 he said the following:

> Cronk JA concludes that when a plaintiff wants to add a party or substitute one party for another after the expiry of a limitation period, showing an absence of non-compensable prejudice is not enough. The plaintiff must also show that special circumstances are present to justify the amendment. I take a different view. I accept that unlike Rule 26.01 which governs

motions to amend proceedings, Rule 5.04(2) gives the court discretion to refuse to add or substitute a party even absent non-compensable prejudice. But I see no reason to burden that discretion with a "special circumstances" component. Requiring "special circumstances" is unnecessary, contrary to the underlying philosophy of the Rules and in some cases may impose a heavier burden on the moving party than called for by Rule 5.04(2). In my view, courts ought to be guided by the principle that ordinarily an amendment should be granted "where the opposite party has not been misled or substantially injured by the error," or in other words, has not suffered prejudice that cannot be compensated for by costs or an adjournment.

On the issue of prejudice it seems clear that where a defendant is sought to be added after the expiry of a limitation period, prejudice is presumed and the burden is on the moving party to rebut this presumption. See *Deaville v. Boegeman* (1984), 48 OR (2d) 725 (Ont. CA).

In his affidavit filed in opposition to this motion, Dr. Preston deposes that he has no recollection of his treatment of Mr. Brown, that he retired from practice in the Summer of 1998 at which time he destroyed all of his clinical notes and records including those relating to Mr. Brown and at which time he gave away all of the text books or journals that he would have consulted when making a diagnosis of Lou Gehrig's Disease. He claims, therefore, that he will be prejudiced if he is now added as a party defendant in this action. However, in his cross-examination, Dr. Preston conceded that his typewritten reports to Dr. Mendis, which have been preserved, were intended to and likely did reflect the significant observations that Dr. Preston made with respect to Mr. Brown and which he recorded in his handwritten notes. It appears as well that upon his retirement Dr. Preston's library was donated to the Ottawa Civic Hospital and to the extent that any of the books might be relevant in this litigation there has been no real effort made to track them down.

Certainly, nothing has transpired between the issuance of the statement of claim and the bringing of this motion which has caused Dr. Preston any prejudice. Mr. Brown was advised by a specialist on June 27, 2001 that he did not in fact have Lou Gehrig's Disease. The earliest that the limitation period could possibly expire would have been on June 27, 2002. The action was started on September 2, 2002 and the loss of Dr. Preston's handwritten notes and library occurred in 1998.

In all of the circumstances, and assuming that the limitation period has in fact run, to the extent that there is a presumption that Dr. Preston will be prejudiced by being added as a party defendant in this action, that presumption has, in my view, been rebutted.

To the extent that special circumstances are required to be shown before the plaintiff is given leave to add Dr. Preston as a party defendant, I am satisfied that those circumstances exist. There is no indication of any bad faith on the part of the Brown family or their counsel. Dr. Mendis advised on examination for discovery on April 15, 2003 that the diagnosis of Lou Gehrig's Disease was not his but rather that of Dr. Preston and a motion was then brought without delay to add Dr. Preston as a party defendant. Mr. Brown has suffered gross damages as a result of not being treated for his actual condition. While Mr. Brown was certainly aware throughout of Dr. Preston's involvement in his diagnosis and treatment, the first time that it was clearly indicated that the diagnosis of Lou Gehrig's Disease was made by Dr. Preston as opposed to Dr. Mendis was during the course of the examination for discovery of Dr. Mendis held April 15, 2003.

Accordingly, the plaintiffs will be granted leave to add Dr. Preston as a party defendant in the within action and to deliver an amended statement of claim.

Motion granted.

NOTES AND QUESTIONS

1. Adding defendants after the expiring of a limitation period is always challenging and, in many cases, cannot be done (see the section on "Limitation of Actions" in chapter 3). Various jurisdictions deal with the problem in their Rules. See, for example, British Columbia's rule 15(5), which grants a court wide discretion to add parties, in the interest of justice. Note that the considerations to add a party after the expiry of a limitation period are far more nuanced and complex than the considerations to merely add the party before a limitation period's expiry.

2. *Persons injured in successive accidents.* Is joinder of multiple defendants permissible in the case of the plaintiff who is allegedly injured by two different defendants acting independently and at different times. For example, (1) plaintiff's injuries were purportedly sustained by the negligence of A and were aggravated by the subsequent negligence of B, an ambulance driver, while taking the plaintiff to the hospital; (2) plaintiff was a passenger in a car that was struck from the rear twice in one day—once when en route to work in the morning and again when returning home in the afternoon; or (3) in an accident caused by the first defendant the plaintiff loses a leg and suffers a whiplash, while in the accident caused one year later by the second defendant the plaintiff suffers brain damage and a further whiplash. Is joinder of both defendants proper in each case?

3. *Costs in actions against two or more defendants.* While it may seem a good idea on the part of plaintiffs to sue "everyone in sight," this may prove to be an imprudent tactic. It must be remembered that the general rule with regard to costs is that a winning party is usually entitled to costs against the loser. Consequently, a plaintiff who sues two defendants and recovers against only one of them faces the prospect of being ordered to pay costs to the successful defendant. Chapter 2 deals with the purpose and strategy behind Bullock and Sanderson orders, two orders a court can make in multiparty litigation for direction of payment of costs.

4. *Joinder and examination for discovery.* Generally, in Canada, only parties may be orally examined for discovery, although there are exceptions (see chapter 7 on discovery). This general limitation on who may be examined for discovery may lead a plaintiff to name a person as a defendant partly to ensure the right to examine that person for discovery. A typical example is where a plaintiff sues an employer, alleging that the employer is vicariously liable for a tort committed by an employee against the plaintiff. In such a case, the plaintiff would normally join the employee as a co-defendant. One reason for so doing would be to ensure the right to examine the employee for discovery.

This tactic of joining a party "for the purposes of discovery" is subject to one obvious limitation—a plaintiff may not name a person as a defendant solely for the purpose of obtaining discovery. The plaintiff may join a person as a defendant only if there is a claim for relief against that person in the action.

B. Compulsory Joinder

Compulsory joinder addresses problems with the minimum size of the litigation—how few parties may a plaintiff join in the litigation and still have the court adjudicate a claim? Unlike issues of the permissive joinder of parties—that is, how large an action may become through joinder of parties—problems of compulsory joinder are relatively rare.

Ordinarily, it is up to the plaintiff to decide which persons will be involved in the litigation. Whether the plaintiff chooses to sue B alone and not B and A is ordinarily of no concern either to B or A or to the court. So, too, is whether the plaintiff sues with or without A as co-plaintiff. While this is the general rule, the plaintiff's choice as to the minimum number of parties to the lawsuit will not always be conclusive. Occasionally, there are persons whose presence before the court is "necessary" in the sense that, on the application of the defendant, the court will order them to be joined as a precondition to the court deciding the case. To this extent the question of who are to be the parties to the litigation is not always in the sole discretion of the original plaintiff. See Reed, "Compulsory Joinder of Parties in Court Actions" (1957), 55 *Michigan L Rev.* 327.

Hazard, Fleming, and Leubsdorf, *Civil Procedure*, 5th ed. (2001), in c. 9, explain the rationale for the necessary parties/compulsory joinder rule, and its narrow scope of operation, as follows:

> The absence of C as a party to an action may work prejudice to D, who is a party, in at least two ways. In the first place it may expose D to multiplicity of suits, which is itself something of an evil. But beyond that is the exposure to possible injustice, particularly double liability, if inconsistent results are reached in two or more lawsuits where the nonparty is not bound by the first judgment.
>
> An example of simple multiplicity is found in the case of partial assignment or subrogation: when debtors have incurred a single obligation they ought not to be subjected to multiple suits for its breach. Partial assignees are therefore regarded as necessary parties.
>
> Multiplicity of suits is a burden not only on [the] defendant, but also on society because of the expense to the taxpayers and the burden of crowded dockets on the administration of justice. Curiously, this interest has been given little recognition when it comes to joinder of plaintiffs. As expressed in Federal Rule 20 [see Ont. rule 5.02(1)], plaintiffs who have claims arising out of the same transaction may join in one action but are not obliged to do so. This reflects the old common law's preference for simple lawsuits, but it does not make sense in [the] modern context, especially in two frequently recurring situations. One is where several members of a family are hurt in the same accident, for example in an automobile accident. Since their interests are compatible, and often overlap so far as damages are concerned, and since they are usually represented by the same counsel, it would seem that they should be compelled to sue in one action. But the rules do not so require, except that in a few jurisdictions a spouse's claim for loss of consortium by reason of injury to the other spouse can be asserted only if joined in the latter's own action for his or her injury. The reason why plaintiffs bring separate actions in such situations sometimes is to avoid the possibility that the jury may be inclined to put a "cap" on defendant's total liability, or to get "two bites" at the issue of defendant's liability—since one family member is not bound by a judgment against another family member.
>
> The other situation is where a large number of persons are injured in one transaction—for example, a plane crash. As we shall see, defendants in such situations are usually bound in sub-

sequent litigation if they lose, but unjoined plaintiffs are free to sue even if some of their number have lost. Yet the rules do not require joinder, with [the] result that the same issue of liability can be thoroughly litigated more than once, at resultant public expense.

In insisting on compulsory joinder, the court is usually pursuing one or both of the policies offered by Hazard, Fleming, and Leubsdorf. Consider the applicable rules regarding compulsory joinder of parties—for example, Ont. rule 5.03(1), NB rule 5.02(2), Man. rule 5.03(1). Is it difficult to deduce when a party will be considered a "necessary" party? Does it depend on the party to be joined being "jointly entitled"? If so, how do courts conceive of joint entitlement? In the following case, assess the defendant's arguments against the narrow scope of compulsory joinder described above.

Swearengen v. Bowater Canadian Forest Products Inc.
(2007), 54 CPC (6th) 131 (Ont. SCJ)

S.J. KERSHMAN J:

Overview

This motion is brought by the Defendants Bowater Canadian Forest Products Inc., Bowater Pulp and Paper Canada Inc., Bowater Canadian Limited, Bowater Belledune Sawmill Inc., (hereinafter referred to as "Bowater") for an order adding the Ministry of Natural Resources (hereinafter referred to as "MNR") as a party defendant to the action, on the grounds that the MNR is a necessary party in order to enable the court to adjudicate effectively and completely on the issues raised by the Plaintiffs in the proceeding.

Issue

The issue to be decided in this case is whether the MNR should be brought in, or, more correctly, brought back in as a party defendant in this matter, pursuant to Rule 5.03 of the *Rules of Civil Procedure*.

Decision

The motion must fail.

Factual Background

This matter was started by a Notice of Action issued by the Plaintiffs on June 7, 2006. At that time, the Notice of Action included the current Defendants, the MNR, the Attorney General of Canada and the Government of Canada.

The Statement of Claim was issued on July 7, 2006.

A Notice of Discontinuance dated October 25, 2006 was filed whereby the Plaintiffs discontinued their claims against the Attorney General of Canada and the Government of Canada.

On November 6, 2006, Bowater served a Notice of Intent to Defend. An agreement was reached with the Plaintiffs whereby Bowater was not required to deliver a Statement of Defence as the Plaintiffs were considering certain amendments to the Statement of Claim.

By Notice of Discontinuance dated February 2, 2007, the Plaintiffs discontinued the claim against the MNR.

An Amended Statement of Claim initially dated February 5, 2007 and thereafter formally amended, was served on July 16, 2007. The Plaintiffs' claim relates to the harvesting of trees in Northern Ontario.

A Jury Notice was delivered by the Plaintiffs on July 16, 2007.

Analysis

Bowater contends that the MNR is a necessary Defendant to this action in order to enable the Court to adjudicate effectively and capably on all the issues raised by the Plaintiffs in the proceeding.

The Plaintiffs and the MNR argue against the adding of the MNR as a party Defendant to the action and claim that there are other ways that the MNR can be involved in the action.

The MNR says that there is no requirement that there be a compulsory joinder of it as a party Defendant to the action. It argues that the case law has established that a compulsory joinder is the least desirable way to join a non-party to an action. It further argues that joinder is an inappropriate mechanism by which to gather evidence and establish a complete and factual record so that the issues between Bowater and the Plaintiffs can be properly adjudicated.

The MNR cites the case of *Peigan Indian Band v. Alberta*, [1998] AJ No. 1108 (Alta. QB) at para. 29.

> Alberta states that Canada is a necessary party because it has documents that Alberta needs. I am satisfied that most, if not all, of the documents relating to this action are in public archives or otherwise available to Alberta. Moreover, the Band states that all documents relating to the natural resources transfer legislation are available to Alberta from Canada. For example, s. 23 of the Schedule to the Alberta Natural Resources Act, 1930, SC 20-21 Geo. V, c. 3 provides that Canada will deliver to Alberta, or allow Alberta access to, all relevant documents. Alberta gave no satisfactory response to this contention. Alberta is a sophisticated and represented party, with extensive resources. It has the knowledge, ability and finances to locate the documents on its own, through searching the archives or requesting the documents. Even if Canada does have some documents that are not otherwise available to Alberta, the simple fact is that Canada can be required to produce such documents without having to be a party.

The MNR argues that the Plaintiffs can use various of the *Rules of Civil Procedure* to obtain what is required from the MNR. The MNR argues that the *Rules of Civil Procedure* provide documentary discovery to obtain a full factual record through Rule 30.10 which is the rule for an order for inspection of documents. In addition, Rule 31.10 provides for discovery of non-parties with leave of the Court.

Lastly, Bowater has the option under the *Rules of Civil Procedure* of commencing a third party claim against the MNR, pursuant to Rule 29.

For unknown reasons, Bowater has not chosen to take any of these courses of action, but rather seeks to add the MNR by Rule 5.03.

Rule 5.03 of the Rules of Civil Procedure

Joinder of Necessary Parties

General Rule

5.03(1) Every person whose presence is necessary to enable the court to adjudicate effectively and completely on the issues in a proceeding shall be joined as a party to the proceeding. RRO 1990, Reg. 194, r. 5.03(1).

Claim by Person Jointly Entitled

(2) A plaintiff or applicant who claims relief to which any other person is jointly entitled with the plaintiff or applicant shall join, as a party to the proceeding, each person so entitled. RRO 1990, Reg. 194, r. 5.03(2).

Claim by Assignee of Chose in Action

(3) In a proceeding by the assignee of a debt or other chose in action, the assignor shall be joined as a party unless,

(a) the assignment is absolute and not by way of charge only; and

(b) notice in writing has been given to the person liable in respect of the debt or chose in action that it has been assigned to the assignee. RRO 1990, Reg. 194, r. 5.03(3).

Power of Court to Add Parties

(4) The court may order that any person who ought to have been joined as a party or whose presence as a party is necessary to enable the court to adjudicate effectively and completely on the issues in the proceeding shall be added as a party. RRO 1990, Reg. 194, r. 5.03(4).

Party Added as Defendant or Respondent

(5) A person who is required to be joined as a party under subrule (1), (2) or (3) and who does not consent to be joined as a plaintiff or applicant shall be made a defendant or respondent. RRO 1990, Reg. 194, r. 5.03(5).

Relief Against Joinder of Party

(6) The court may by order relieve against the requirement of joinder under this rule. RRO 1990, Reg. 194, r. 5.03(6).

Bowater's position is that the presence of the MNR is required to enable the Court to adjudicate effectively and completely on the issues in this claim.

Bowater argues that if the Court agrees with this position, then Rule 5.03 provides that the MNR *shall* (my emphasis) be added as a party defendant to the proceedings.

Bowater claims that the allegations against it are interwoven with the role of the MNR in the regulating and supervising the rights and obligations of both Bowater and the Plaintiffs in respect of the licensing and cutting of timber. According to Bowater, the MNR is a necessary party to the resolution of the issues in the claim.

Bowater relies upon the case of *School of Dance (Ottawa) Pre-Professional Programme Inc. v. Crichton Cultural Community Centre*, [2006] OJ No. 5224 (Ont. SCJ). There, the City of Ottawa voluntarily sought to be added as a party defendant to the proceedings in accordance with various other *Rules of Civil Procedure*, including Rule 5.03.

Justice Hackland, at paragraph 9, states:

> The question of whether the City is a necessary party to this proceeding is significantly dependent on whether they are likely to be affected or prejudiced by a Court order that will dispose of the rights of the parties to this proceeding. This consideration must be weighed against the jurisprudence relied on by the defendants which establishes that the application of the necessary parties/compulsory joinder principle is very narrow in recognition of the fact that the *plaintiff is normally accorded the right to decide who it will sue* (emphasis added). A very helpful statement of the rationale for the "necessary parties rule" is found at page 5-25 of *Holmstead and Watson*, Ontario Court Procedure, 2003:
>
> > (b) Rationale for the necessary parties rule
> >
> > But, while "plaintiff's choice" is the general rule, the plaintiff's choice as to the minimum number of parties to the lawsuit will not always be conclusive. Occasionally, there are persons whose presence before the court is "necessary" in the sense that on the application of the defendant the court will order them to be joined as a precondition to the court deciding the case. To this extent the question of who are to be the parties to the litigation is not always in the sole discretion of the original plaintiff. See Reed, "Compulsory Joinder of Parties in Court Actions" (1957), 55 Mich. L Rev. 327. Professors Louisell and Hazard, *Cases and Materials on Pleading and Procedure* (4th ed. 1979), p. 571 summarize the reasons for the compulsory joinder of necessary parties succinctly as follows:
> >
> > > [T]he objectives of the rule were, and still are, simple enough: from the viewpoint of the court, to do a complete job on the controversy in one sitting; from the view-point of those already parties, to protect them against the consequences of subsequent litigation reaching inconsistent results; from the view-point of those not made parties but by the rule required to be brought in, to assure that their practical out-of-court situation would not be adversely affected by changes in the *status quo* wrought in consequence of the judgment.
>
> As already indicated, the compulsory joinder principle is a narrow exception to the general rule that a plaintiff is free to decide whom to sue.

Professors Louisell and Hazard in the 4th edition of *Cases in Material on Pleadings and Procedure* say that the objective of the rule for compulsory joinder of necessary parties is to "do a complete job on the controversy in one sitting;"

If the MNR is added as a party defendant, one hearing will not resolve the controversy in this case. The filing of the Jury Notice will require a 2-step trial process—in effect 2 trials, as follows:

(1) a jury trial between the Plaintiffs and Bowater; and

(2) a second trial between the Plaintiffs and the MNR as a non-jury trial since jury trials are not permitted where Crown entities are involved (Section 26 of the *Crown Liability and Proceedings Act*, RSC 1985, c. C-50).

In this case, the Plaintiffs do not want to sue the MNR. By adding them as party defendants, the MNR will be negatively affected and prejudiced. Inclusion of the MNR as a party defendant would cause it to incur significant time and expense in dealing with the issue. In addition, the Plaintiffs will incur significant time and expense if the MNR is added as a party defendant. Lastly, there is the issue as to costs. If the MNR is added as a party defendant, costs could potentially be awarded against the MNR in the action.

Conclusion

Bowater has other methods of including the MNR in this matter, involving through Rule 30.10 for an order to inspect documents, Rule 31.10 which provides for discovery of non-parties and through Rule 29 by commencing a third party claim against the MNR. Given the negative consequences set out in the previous paragraph, the Bowater motion is dismissed on a without prejudice basis to the defendants to commence a third party proceeding against the MNR, provided that the third party rules apply to grant a right to commence third party proceedings.

NOTES AND QUESTIONS

1. *Should the absence of a "necessary party" be the plaintiff's or the defendant's problem?* Third-party rules like Ontario rule 29.01 provide a means by which defendants can solve the absent party problem themselves:

> A defendant may commence a third party claim against any person who is not a party to the action and who, ...
>
> (c) should be bound by the determination of an issue arising between the plaintiff and the defendant.

Instead of bringing a motion to force the plaintiff to join a necessary party, the defendant could simply join the party as a third party under the above provision. But can the plaintiff argue that this is the proper approach and that it is the obligation of the defendant to join a necessary party? Perhaps not, if only because (1) the necessary parties law is old and well established, and (2) the question of who may become liable to pay the necessary party's costs is possibly different depending on who joins that party.

2. As already indicated, the compulsory joinder principle is a narrow exception to the general rule that a plaintiff is free (within the limits of the permissive joinder rules) to decide who to sue. This is well illustrated by the attitude of the courts to joinder in most tort cases. If injured in a multiple-car collision, the plaintiff is free to select one of several tortfeasors as a sole defendant. In view of the policy against a multiplicity of actions, this seems odd because there is nothing (except limitation periods and rules forbidding double recovery) to stop the plaintiff from subsequently suing the other tortfeasors. The explanation is to be found in several factors.

The first is the basic commitment of our law to the adversary system with its principle of party presentation and formulation of the case as opposed to presentation and formulation by the court. The court will force a party on the plaintiff only where the absent party or the defendant will be prejudiced by the absence, even though by so doing the court may also avoid a multiplicity of actions. The principle of party formulation of the case, coupled with the risks involved in non-joinder, will usually result in the plaintiff suing all persons reasonably thought to be liable. Thus, defining the minimum size of the litigation can generally be safely left to the plaintiff and this relieves the court of having to concern itself with the problem. On balance the legal system is probably better served by leaving the choice of parties to the plaintiff, since enforced joinder enlarges a lawsuit to avoid a subsequent lawsuit that might never be brought. Second, compulsory joinder could cause expense for, and even produce injustice to, the plaintiff, since the additional party must then be served and fought in the litigation. Finally, the problem of a multiplicity of proceedings of a kind that compulsory joinder might avoid is perhaps more theoretical than real. The subsequent litigation usually does not materialize, either because the plaintiff chooses not to sue or because the running of limitation periods prevents it.

III. ADDITION OF CLAIMS AND PARTIES BY THE DEFENDANT

A. Introduction

Litigation may be expanded by the defendant in three ways. First, defendants can assert claims against plaintiffs through *counterclaims*. Second, defendants can assert claims against other co-defendants through *cross-claims*. Third, defendants can assert claims against persons who are not yet formal parties to the litigation through *third-party proceedings*. Are there common concerns regarding these three devices in terms of their capacity for expanding lawsuits and for setting proper limits on them?

B. Counterclaims

If the defendant has a claim against the plaintiff, is it necessary for a separate action to be brought, or can the claim be asserted and relief recovered from the plaintiff in the original action? Considerations of economy and convenience favour a determination of the claims of each party against the other by the same tribunal at the same time in a single action. See, for example, Ontario rule 27. To require the defendant to bring a separate action against the plaintiff might cause financial hardship. If the plaintiff is successful on the initial claim, the defendant will become immediately liable to satisfy such a judgment, notwithstanding that the defendant might have a claim against the plaintiff, possibly for an amount equal to or greater than the judgment debt.

At one time, a defendant could assert a claim in the plaintiff's action in only a restricted number of situations. Today, a defendant can assert any claim against the plaintiff by counterclaim, subject only to the power of the court to exclude the defendant's claim where it cannot conveniently be dealt with in the plaintiff's action.

Lid Brokerage & Realty Co. (1977) v. Budd
[1992] 2 WWR 453 (Sask. QB)

BAYNTON J: The plaintiffs allege that the defendants through breach of trust, breach of employment contracts, and by means of a conspiracy, have caused financial damage to the produce brokerage business operated by the plaintiffs.

. . .

One of the existing defendants, Star Produce Ltd., applies for leave under R. 165 to counterclaim against the plaintiffs and against seven proposed defendants by counterclaim who are not now parties to the lawsuit. Star Processing Ltd. (one of the four proposed defendants I have permitted the plaintiffs to add as parties), also desires to join in the counterclaim as one of the plaintiffs by counterclaim. Although the application is made under R. 165 which requires leave to amend pleadings, the applicant points out that there is no rule which requires leave to counterclaim. Rule 105B(1), however, requires a counterclaim to be served on the plaintiff within the time limited for the delivery of the statement of defence. In this action that time limit has expired.

The applicants point to the provisions of R. 105(1) and 105(2) which respectively authorize a defendant to assert any claim he may have against the plaintiff by way of counterclaim, and to join any third party who is a necessary party as a defendant by counterclaim. ...

The gist of the proposed counterclaim is that the proposed defendants by counterclaim have conspired to injure the business operated by the proposed plaintiffs by counterclaim. It is alleged that the two corporate entities proposed to be added as parties and as defendants to the counterclaim carry on the business of produce brokers. It is also alleged that the individuals proposed to be added as parties and as defendants to the counterclaim are the senior management and directing minds of these two corporations and of the two corporate plaintiffs in this lawsuit. These two corporate plaintiffs are the only existing parties who are proposed to be added as defendants to the counterclaim. Particulars of the alleged conspiracy are that the proposed defendants to the counterclaim have attempted to persuade suppliers and customers not to deal with the proposed plaintiffs by counterclaim, have established a pricing policy designed to injure contrary to the *Competition Act*, RSC 1985, c. C-34, and have wrongfully used confidential information obtained contrary to an undertaking given to the court.

The grounds upon which the applicant relies to obtain leave to counterclaim, are that the counterclaim will avoid a multiplicity of proceedings and that the claim and counterclaim arise out of the same series of transactions. ...

One ground of opposition put forward by the plaintiffs is that the defendants' alleged claim is unrelated to this lawsuit, and as it involves seven individuals and corporate entities who are not parties to this action, the defendants should be required to proceed with their alleged claim by way of a separate action. Reliance is placed on *Co-op Trust Co. of Canada v. Target 21 Industries Ltd.*, [1982] 6 WWR 465, 20 Sask. R 200 (QB), for the proposition that the counterclaim must be related to the claim in the main action. The facts in *Target 21 Industries* are quite different than those in this case. It does, however, deal with an application to strike out a counterclaim or in the alternative with an application for separate trials of the main issue and the counterclaim. The plaintiffs contend that the case is authority for the proposition that a counterclaim must be connected with the claim in the main action where a third person is made a defendant. This proposition is found on p. 206 of the decision and is contained within a quotation taken from a 1920 British Columbia decision [Sask. R]:

> It [a counterclaim] need not be connected with the original matter of the plaintiff's action except where a third person is made defendant to the counterclaim along with the plaintiff in which case it must be so connected. If the subject-matter of the counterclaim is not outside of, and independent of, the subject-matter of the claim, it is then, as here, in the nature of a defence.

It is significant that Grotsky J, in quoting the BC case, did so with the stated purpose of explaining the difference between a set-off and a counterclaim. His conclusions were not based upon this principle. It is noteworthy that he determined not to strike out the counterclaim nor to order a separate trial of the counterclaim. As well, although this principle seems to have foundation in s. 44(3) of the *Queen's Bench Act*, it appears to be inconsistent with the tenor of R. 105. I need not in this case decide whether this principle is a limiting requirement of counterclaims brought in Saskatchewan. Although the plaintiffs allege a different conspiracy than that alleged by the defendants, there is a common subject matter to the main action and the counterclaim. It is the previous employment relationship of the primary parties and the alleged injury to the respective competing produce brokerage businesses in which all the parties are involved, directly or indirectly. The counterclaim is accordingly connected to the matter in the main action.

· · ·

Another ground of opposition to the proposed counterclaim is that it is a stalling tactic of the defendants and will complicate and delay the main action. The plaintiffs point to the difficulties they have had to date in obtaining adequate disclosure and production of documents, the fact that the examinations for discovery of the defendants involving some 18 days has now been completed, and the detrimental effect further delays will have on their claim for injunctive relief. They contend that there is no valid reason the counterclaim could not have been made at the time the statement of defence was filed. They rely on R. 105E(2) which enables the court to strike out a counterclaim, even if properly brought within time (without prejudice to the right of the defendant to assert the claim in a separate action) where it appears that the counterclaim may unduly complicate or delay the trial of the main action. They submit that this principle should apply all the more to this case in that the defendants are out of time and require leave to amend their pleadings.

I have considerable sympathy with this last submission. I have no doubt that if leave is granted, the counterclaim will delay and complicate the main action and result in prejudice to the plaintiffs. The issue, however, should not be determined solely from the perspective of the main action. Consideration must also be given to the likely result to the plaintiffs if leave is denied. There will be little overall net benefit to the plaintiffs or to any of the parties if leave is refused, a separate action is commenced, and the action is later consolidated with the main action. The same result will ensue if any judgment obtained in the main action is stayed until the separate action is determined. It must also be borne in mind that Star City Processing Ltd. (one of the proposed defendants now added to the main action by leave, and one of the proposed plaintiffs by counterclaim) would have the right without leave, to file a statement of defence and counterclaim. Accordingly, refusing leave would not in any event necessarily result in the counterclaim issue being conducted or determined completely apart from the main action.

I am persuaded, by the thrust of recent decisions, by the provisions referred to earlier in the *Queen's Bench Act*, and by the provisions of Pt. Six I and II of the Rules dealing with parties and joinder of actions, that the Rules must be interpreted to facilitate and expedite the effective and final resolution of all the issues in contention between the parties. The claim in the counterclaim is to some degree related to or connected with the claim in the main action, the parties are substantially the same, counsel representing the parties are the same, and a good portion of the documentation will be the same. As well, a finding of fact on the evidence to be presented and the determination of legal issues raised in the main action will have a significant impact on a finding of fact and determination of legal issues raised by the proposed counterclaim. There are accordingly obvious advantages to the litigants, including the plaintiffs, in having these matters considered at one pre-trial conference, and if not resolved at that stage, in having them determined by one judge in one trial. As counsel for the defendants put it, the paramount test is one of convenience. Geatros J in *Neufeld v. UFCW, Local 1400 (No. 2)* (1984), 32 Sask. R 245 (QB), refusing to strike out a counterclaim pursuant to R. 173 or 105E(2), at pp. 248-50 states:

> So it is that the claim and counterclaim "for convenience of procedure, are combined in one action" even if the counterclaim "is in respect of a wholly independent transaction." All the more so where, as in the present case, the counterclaim has a relationship with the main action.
>
> I think it is a fair proposition that wherever possible a multiplicity of proceedings should be avoided.
>
> . . .
>
> I am of the view that the trial of the main action would not be unduly delayed within the meaning of the Rule if an order for separate trials is not made.
>
> . . .
>
> At all events, any increase in time must be considered in tandem with the overriding factor that a multiplicity of litigation will have been prevented.

I am also persuaded, as evidenced by recent judicial decisions, by a review of the *Queen's Bench Act*, and by the provisions of R. 165, that the objective of promoting the expeditious and final resolution of legal actions between parties is not to be achieved at the expense of a party who has been prejudiced by the delay of another party. In such a case, the granting of discretionary relief to a party from the strict application of the Rules should be conditional. The conditions (whether they are in the form of an order for costs or an order setting out a time schedule for the completion of certain steps in the action) should as far as reasonably possible mitigate the prejudice that would otherwise be suffered.

It seems to me that the potential delay and prejudice to the plaintiffs that will arise in the circumstances of this case if leave is granted can be addressed in this fashion. As well, if the counterclaim is a stalling tactic and without foundation as alleged by the plaintiffs, then the trial judge can take this into account in the award of costs. The immediate impact on costs is the delay and additional expense which will be incurred by the plaintiffs in rescheduling examinations for discovery of those defendants already examined this fall. The material filed by the defendants indicates that many of the incidents relied on in the counterclaim occurred before or during this past spring. Had the counterclaim been proceeded with at that time, substantial costs and delays would have been avoided. The defendants allege that they advised the plaintiffs during the examinations for discovery that they would be counterclaiming, but a substantial delay was involved even at that date. Another indication of procrastination on the part of the defendants are the strong comments of Matheson J in his July 5, 1991 fiat. He states that it appears the defendants not only were initially "stonewalling," but were subsequently deliberately defying court orders. As previously indicated, he awarded costs to the plaintiffs, in any event of the cause.

In summary on this issue, I find that discretion to grant leave to amend pleadings under R. 165 to permit a counterclaim should be based on the following principles:

1. Leave should be granted to the applicant (the paramount consideration being convenience and the avoidance of multiple proceedings) unless the party opposing the proposed counterclaim establishes that:
   a. the counterclaim, even if delivered on time, could have been struck under R. 173 (e.g., on the basis it discloses no cause of action); or
   b. there are extenuating circumstances which would render it inequitable to grant leave (such as an intervening limitation period barring the defendant from bringing a separate action); or
   c. the proposed counterclaim will so unduly complicate or delay the trial of the main action that the benefits of avoiding multiple legal actions are outweighed by prejudice to the plaintiff that cannot reasonably or adequately be compensated by conditions attached to such leave.
2. Leave should be granted on conditions where the plaintiff will otherwise suffer prejudice due to the delay on the part of the defendant in bringing the counterclaim in time. Such conditions should, as far as reasonably possible, adequately compensate the plaintiff for such unnecessary prejudice.
3. If the counterclaim will add new parties to the action, consideration should be given as to whether the subject matter of the counterclaim is related to or connected with the subject matter of the main action.

NOTES AND QUESTIONS

1. To what extent is the potential for a counterclaim to serve as a "stalling tactic" relevant to whether a defendant should be permitted to bring a counterclaim? Are the sanction and the remedies for such conduct identified by Baynton J in the *Lid Brokerage* case sufficient to discourage such conduct?

2. *Joining other persons as defendants to the counterclaim.* As is illustrated in *Lid Brokerage*, the rules permit a defendant asserting a counterclaim to expand the size of the litigation by joining other persons as defendants to the counterclaim. Until recently, the defendant's

right to add additional parties as defendants to a counterclaim was limited. The defendant could bring in new parties by counterclaim only where the relief claimed related to or was connected with the original subject of the plaintiff's claim. Modern rules (for example, Ontario rule 27.01(2)) typically impose no such limitation. The only requirement now is that the person to be added as a defendant to the counterclaim must be "a necessary or proper party to the counterclaim." Hence, the counterclaim may be unrelated to the plaintiff's claim and it may involve bringing in a new party as defendant to the counterclaim. Of course, the court has power "where it appears that a counterclaim may unduly complicate or delay the trial of the main action, or cause undue prejudice to a party," to order separate trials or to order the counterclaim to proceed as a separate action: Ontario rule 27.08(2).

3. *Setting off judgments on the claim and counterclaim.* Suppose the plaintiff succeeds on a claim and is awarded $25,000 and the defendant is successful on a counterclaim and is awarded $19,000. In most such situations, it will be convenient and just to order that, for the purposes of execution, the two judgments be set off against one another and that the defendant pay the plaintiff the balance of $6,000. This is indeed the general practice followed by the court. However, there are sometimes dynamics in particular cases where setting off judgments is not appropriate, such as occurs when an insurer, for example, has a subrogated interest to pursue. See, for example, *Colonial Furniture Co. (Ottawa) Ltd. v. Saul Tanner Realty Ltd.* (2001), 52 OR (3d) 539 (CA) where the Court of Appeal for Ontario affirmed that equitable set-off is not available in such a situation because of a lack of mutuality.

4. *Counterclaims for the tort of abuse of process.* Some defendants have asserted, by way of counterclaim, that the very bringing of the main action by the plaintiff constitutes the tort of abuse of process. The following case illustrates "the problem" and how the courts are handling it.

Lee v. Globe and Mail
(2002), 17 CPC (5th) 342 (Ont. SCJ)

[This is a motion by the plaintiff for an order striking out a counterclaim.]

GREER J: The Plaintiff, Lee Kuan Yew ("Lee") is the former Prime Minister of the Republic of Singapore and is now Senior Minister of Singapore. He took offence at the content of an article entitled "Singapore Sage," which appeared on March 29, 1999, in the *Globe & Mail.* The article was written by Marcus Gee about Singapore, the government of Lee and included an interview with the Defendant, Devan Nair ("Nair"), a former President of Singapore from October 1981 to March of 1985. Nair is now a resident of Hamilton, Ontario. Nair had once been the head of Singapore's most powerful trade union association, and he believes that he had been perceived by Lee as being a potential political threat. By Statement of Claim dated June 19, 1999, Lee sued the above-named Defendants, saying that he has suffered damage and "been brought into hatred, ridicule and contempt," by reason of the libel he says is contained in the article.

Nair, in his Statement of Defence and Counterclaim dated July 6, 2001, by way of Counterclaim, claims damages for the tort of abuse of process. The abuse is said to include, but is not limited to loss of income, out-of-pocket expenses, unrecoverable costs, and mental anguish, distress and anxiety associated with defending the litigation financed on Lee's behalf with the essentially unlimited resources of the Government of the Republic of Singapore. Nair says this could prove to be financially ruinous to him.

Lee moves for an Order striking out the Counterclaim in its entirety on the grounds that the Counterclaim for the tort of abuse of process, on its face, fails to plead the necessary elements of the tort. He says that the Counterclaim discloses no reasonable cause of action and that it is scandalous, vexatious or an abuse of process of the Court. Finally he says that it constitutes, includes or directs an inflammatory attack on the integrity of the Government of Singapore, which is not a party to this action.

Some of the Background

The article notes that Nair left Singapore in approximately 1988, and did not return, after "publicly quarrelling with Mr. Lee over the arrest of a well-known government critic. Then he dropped from sight." It sets out the earlier history between the two men, when they both fought together to prevent an attempted takeover of Singapore by the Communists and helped build their country to an "economic dynamo bristling with skyscrapers." It also sets out some of the problems Nair experienced when he and Lee began disagreeing about how Lee was governing Singapore and how Nair found himself the centre of a "rumour-mongering campaign that labelled him a drinker and a womanizer." Nair says that he was neither. The article says that Nair suspects that Lee had government doctors slip him hallucinatory drugs to make him appear befuddled in order to "begin a total demolishment of his character. He's very good at that." The article then says that "Singapore doesn't lock up its critics any more; it sues them, instead," noting that a critic of the government, Mr. Jeyarethnam has faced countless libel suits from Mr. Lee and other members of his government.

Nair's Factum sets out, in some detail, more of what Nair says Lee did to remove him as a political threat. This includes a white paper tabled in the parliament of Singapore before Nair left, because of Nair's public statements in opposition to what the government was doing to oppress a leading dissident in Singapore. Further, it is Nair's position that this action was commenced by Lee for the collateral and improper purpose of silencing his critics, including but not limited to Nair. In Singapore, this is done, says Nair by fostering a climate of fear and intimidation among residents.

It is Nair's position in paragraph 16 of his Factum that:

> Mr. Lee is indifferent to his reputation among the readership of the *Globe & Mail*, but has an established and well publicized record within the Republic of Singapore for suing his critics for defamation, and using other measures which are contrary to established international rights in respect of freedom of expression, with a view to silencing his critics.

It is within the framework of this background that the action was brought on, and that the Counterclaim of Nair is structured. Lee asks the Court to strike the whole Counterclaim.

The Issues

Lee says that the issue to be determined by the Court is whether it is plain and obvious that the Counterclaim cannot succeed because the pleading does not disclose a reasonable cause of action in that Nair has failed to plead the necessary elements of the tort of abuse of process.

Nair says that the issues are what is the test on a motion to strike a Counterclaim as not disclosing a cause of action; and does the Counterclaim set out the two constituent elements of the tort of abuse of process namely, that in prosecuting the action, Mr. Lee is using the process of this court for a collateral and improper purpose; and, that Mr. Lee has made an overt and definite act or threat, separate and distinct from the proceedings themselves in furtherance of this improper purpose.

Test on the Motion

Lee moves under rule 21.01(1)(b) of the *Rules of Civil Procedure* to strike out the Counterclaim on the grounds that it discloses no reasonable cause of action or defence. He says that the libel is a precise, narrow libel, and claims that Nair has invented false allegations in his Statement of Defence and Counterclaim.

The court may also, under rule 25.11, strike out or expunge all or part of a pleading on the ground that the pleading is scandalous, frivolous or vexatious, or that it is an abuse of the process of the court.

The test for determining whether a pleading should be struck is set out by the Supreme Court of Canada in *Hunt v. T & N plc*, [1990] 2 SCR 959, 74 DLR (4th) 321 (SCC). Assuming that the facts as stated in the Counterclaim can be proven, the Court said in *Hunt*, supra, one must look to see if it is "plain and obvious" that the Counterclaim discloses no reasonable cause of action. The Court also notes that if there is a chance that the plaintiff might succeed, then the plaintiff should not be "driven from the judgment seat." In *Falloncrest Financial Corp. v. Ontario* (1995), 27 OR (3d) 1 (Ont. CA), the Court of Appeal, at p. 6 says:

> On a motion to strike out a pleading, the court must accept the facts alleged in the statement of claim as proven unless they are patently ridiculous or incapable of proof, and must read the statement of claim generously with allowance for inadequacies due to drafting deficiencies.

Nor, should the Court dispose of matters of law that are not fully settled.

The Court of Appeal in *Prete v. Ontario* (1993), 16 OR (3d) 161, [1993] OJ No. 2794 (Ont. CA), Action No. C9963 at p. 9 of the Quicklaw version, examines both the tests under rule 21.01(1) and rule 25.11. In that case, the Court was split on the issue of whether the Court can look beyond the pleadings and determine if the action has a chance of success. The majority found that it could not because if you consider the statement of claim to be an abuse of the process of the court, it can only be because it discloses no reasonable cause of action. Weiler JA, in dissent, found that the Court could look beyond the pleading. Even if one cannot look beyond the pleading, the pleading must be examined to see if it is scandalous, frivolous or vexatious, or otherwise constituting an abuse of the court's process.

The Tort of Abuse of Process

The two elements of the tort of abuse of process, both of which must be pleaded, are whether the plaintiff, in bringing the action, is using the court process for a collateral and improper purpose; and whether he or she has made an overt and definite act or threat, separate and distinct from the proceedings themselves, in furtherance of the improper purpose. See: *Tsiopoulos v. Commercial Union Assurance Co.* (1986), 57 OR (2d) 117 (Ont. HC) at pp. 119 and 120, where the Court notes that the process is very narrow in scope. Further, the Court has noted that the alleged collateral and improper purpose cannot be related to a direct or indirect purpose or to an intended or unintended purpose such as intimidation or the fact that it would impoverish the defendant. See also: *Dooley v. C.N. Weber Ltd.* (1994), 19 OR (3d) 779 (Ont. Gen. Div.).

The Courts have consistently held that the intention to silence through a defamation action is not a collateral or improper purpose, as this is a result, which naturally flows from the litigation itself and is a legitimate purpose. See: *Pizza Pizza Ltd. v. Toronto Star Newspapers Ltd.* ((July 24, 1996)), Doc. 93-CQ-33824 (Ont. Gen. Div.); aff'd., [1997] OJ No. 3891 (Ont. CA).

The second element of the tort, that is an act or threat in furtherance of the improper purpose, must be separate and distinct from the proceedings themselves. If it is not, there cannot be an abuse of process. This has been set out by Eberle J in *Teledata Communications Inc. v. Westburne Industrial Enterprises Ltd.* (1990), 65 DLR (4th) 636 (Ont. HC). The Court has also said that there must be a nexus between any threat and the improper pleading complained of. See: *Dooley*, supra at p. 791. It is Lee's position that Nair's pleading in his Counterclaim, has not met the two elements of the test.

Nair says that he has met the two-part test. He says that Lee commenced the libel action for the collateral and improper purpose of silencing all of Mr. Lee's critics, including Nair, but not limited to him. It must be remembered, in examining what is in the article itself, not only can the writer be considered a critic, and Nair considered a critic, but others in Singapore and elsewhere, who attempt to criticize Lee and his government's methods of trying to silence critics and opposition, are open to silencing because of what Nair says is a pattern of using the libel process to succeed in generally using whatever measures Lee considers necessary to thwart the "established international rights in respect of freedom of expression." Whether or not this can be supported at Trial is not for me to decide. It is, however, not scandalous, frivolous or vexatious. Lee's action is being brought in a country which prides itself in allowing freedom of political expression. Nair says that this is not the case in Singapore, where there is a climate of fear and intimidation among the residents.

Nair says that his situation can be distinguished from that in *Pizza Pizza*, supra, where Cameron J struck the counterclaim as having a purpose concurrent with the legitimate purpose of the plaintiff in bringing its libel action. Nair claims that there is no legitimate purpose which could save Lee's libel action since Lee is indifferent to his reputation among the readership of the *Globe & Mail*. Nair says that Lee's action ... "is a mere stalking horse intended to further foster and continue a climate of fear and intimidation." I agree with Nair's position that the issue is whether the "predominate" (as opposed to exclusive) purpose is ulterior. Given the political and international aspect of the tenor of the article, and given that Lee has seemingly no residence/domicile or other connection to Canada, it is within the scope of the test for Nair to argue that the predominate purpose is ulterior. See: *Hilltop Group Ltd. v. Katana*, [2000] OJ No. 2576 (Ont. SCJ), Court File No. 96-CU-106768, where Campbell, Colin J examines what Sharpe J, as he then was, set out in *Scintilore Explorations Ltd. v. Larche* (1999), 48 BLR (2d) 248 (Ont. SCJ). There Sharpe J noted at p. 317 that the predominate purpose must "be outside the ambit of the legal claim on which the Court is asked to adjudicate." I am satisfied that the first element of the tort, as pleaded, has been met.

Nair says that he has also met the second part of the test, in that Lee has taken an overt act or step in furtherance of his improper purpose in invoking the legal process. Nair says that he was forced to resign as President of the Republic of Singapore in March of 1985 and was falsely labeled as an alcoholic. Several years later when Nair says he first spoke out politically for the first time since resigning, Lee tabled a white paper in the Singapore's parliament, which included extracts of a confidential nature from Nair's personal medical records and correspondence. Nair says this was done to silence his political views and Nair says that Lee further threatened to and ultimately did arrange to have Nair's pension withheld. Nair then left Singapore and did not speak out politically from 1988 until he granted the interview for the *Globe and Mail* article in question. Given these actions and steps taken by Lee in Singapore to create a climate of fear and intimidation of critics, Nair says that this new action is intended to be and is a threat which is on-going and pervasive. Nair says these overt acts and threats in the past by Lee against Nair only went below the surface, but remained always there even though Nair left Singapore and remained silent for over a decade. These threats have resurfaced and re-emerged in this new libel action in the country in which Nair sought freedom from political threats and overt legal actions against him. To Nair, the threat is on-going and pervasive, and in my view, it meets the second part of the test.

I am therefore satisfied, in these unusual circumstances, that Nair has met the two-part test. Lee's Motion is therefore dismissed. If the parties cannot otherwise agree on Costs, I will receive brief written submissions by them.

Motion dismissed.

Garry Watson and Tim Pinos, "A Note on Counterclaims and Set-Off"
(2004)

History of counterclaims and set-off. Originally at common law, with one very minor exception, the defendant could not assert in the same action a claim against the plaintiff. A complaint by the defendant about a different cause of action necessitated a separate action. The inconvenience caused by these restrictions produced some legislative reform in England early in the 18th century. The legislation consisted of two enactments, known as the statutes of set-off. For example, in Ontario, see s. 111 of the *Courts of Justice Act* (in Manitoba, see *Queen's Bench Act*, ss. 78-79):

> (1) In an action for payment of a debt, the defendant may, by way of defence, claim the right to set off against the plaintiff's claim a debt owed by the plaintiff to the defendant. ...

(3) Where, on a defence of set off, a larger sum is found to be due from the plaintiff to the defendant than is found to be due from the defendant to the plaintiff, the defendant is entitled to judgment for the balance.

Some provinces still rely on the original English statutes, whereas other have enacted legislation similar to that in Ontario: see K. Palmer, *The Law of Set-Off in Canada* (Toronto: Canada Law Book, 1993), 8.

The statutes of set-off (now generally referred to as *legal set-off*) allowed only *mutual debts* to be set off. However, the defendant could not set off a debt that was incurred by the plaintiff after the issue of the writ in the action; if the amount of the defendant's debt was less than that due by the plaintiff, the excess was not recoverable. Moreover, because the statutes allowed only *mutual debts* to be set off, the defendant could not set off *a claim that sounded in damages*, nor could a debt be set off in answer to a claim by the plaintiff for damages. It is important to note that legal set-off was (and is) considered to be a *defence*, rather than cross-actions by the defendant. This was so because the common law would not accept the notion of the defendant pursuing its own claim in the plaintiff's action. The main consequence of this view was that the excess of the defendant's claim over that of the plaintiff's claim was never recoverable. A separate action would have to be commenced to recover this excess. This was changed in 1830 when the original English predecessor to s. 111(3) of the *Courts of Justice Act* was first enacted.

The counterclaim is a creature of the late 19th century *Judicature Act* reforms. It was devised to overcome the restrictions that applied to legal set-off. A defendant may now assert any counterclaim against a plaintiff, whatever the nature of the claim and the date of its accrual, and whether it arises out of the same transaction as that relied on by the plaintiff or not. In short, provided that it is substantively adequate, the defendant may assert any claim against the plaintiff as a counterclaim. The defendant is also permitted to counterclaim against both the plaintiff and a person who is not already a party to the action, but who is a proper party defendant to the counterclaim. This right is subject only to the discretionary power in the court to sever the claims where the trial of claim and counterclaim together might cause inconvenience or unfairness.

It might have been expected that the statutory provisions relating to legal set-off would be repealed with the creation of the more liberal device of the counterclaim. However, this did not occur and legal set-off continues to co-exist with the counterclaim. Set-off is still largely subject to the same restrictions that applied before the counterclaim was devised.

The subject has been further complicated by the development and expansion of a common law doctrine known as equitable set-off. Under this doctrine, equitable set-off is available whether or not the cross-obligations are mutual debts, or even debts at all, provided that the relationship between the cross-obligations is such that it would be inequitable to permit one to proceed without taking the other into account. It is enough that the opposing claims flow from the same transaction or relationship between the parties, or are otherwise closely connected. Equitable set-off as a distinct principle can be traced to the early 19th century, and has been the subject of many judicial decisions in Canada. See, generally, K. Palmer, *The Law of Set-Off in Canada* (Toronto: Canada Law Book, 1993) and S.R. Derham, *Set-Off*, 2d ed. (Oxford: Oxford University, 1996).

Modern consequences of the distinction between set-off and counterclaim. As already indicated, because set-off has survived the creation of the counterclaim, in certain situations the defendant can plead a claim against the plaintiff either as a counterclaim or by way of set-off, or both. Today there are still some significant procedural differences between counterclaim and set-off.

Suppose that A claims $1,000 from B for the price of goods sold and delivered and, at the date of commencement of A's action, A owes a sum to B for money lent. B's liability for the price of the goods can be set off against the unpaid loan. Because set-off is a defence proper to the plaintiff's claim, where it is pleaded there will be only one judgment in the action. If the amount of the set-off equals the amount of the plaintiff's claim, there will be judgment for the defendant simply dismissing the plaintiff's action. If it is for less, the plaintiff will be given judgment for the balance. Because the set-off is a defence, a shield for the defendant, the defendant originally could not recover any excess from the plaintiff. This is now altered by statute for legal set-off, but not equitable set-off. See *Courts of Justice Act*, s. 111(3).

Where a counterclaim is asserted, it is for the purposes of judgment treated as a separate action and there will be not one judgment but two—one on the plaintiff's claim and the other on the defendant's. This means that if the defendant counterclaims and both parties are successful, there will be judgment for the plaintiff against the defendant with costs on the claim, and judgment for the defendant against the plaintiff with costs on the counterclaim. For the purposes of enforcement, however, one judgment will usually be offset against the other.

As already noted, legal and equitable set-off are much narrower in scope than the counterclaim. In almost every case where a defendant has a claim against the plaintiff, the claim can be asserted by way of counterclaim. However, the defendant can plead by way of set-off only in situations of mutual debts or where the requirements of equitable set-off can be satisfied. But apart from the different forms of judgment that are pronounced according to whether the defendant has pleaded a set-off or delivered a counterclaim, does the distinction today produce any important practical consequences?

The continued distinction between set-off and counterclaim has two important practical consequences—the awarding of costs and the operation of limitation periods.

Costs. Because set-off is a defence, if it is successful for the full amount of the plaintiff's claim, the action will be dismissed and the defendant will be entitled to the costs of the action. By contrast, in the case of a counterclaim, when a plaintiff succeeds on a claim and the defendant on a counterclaim, each party, subject to judicial discretion, is entitled to the costs incurred to recover the claim and counterclaim respectively. For the purposes of costs, a claim that could be pleaded by way of set-off does not lose its real character by being asserted as a counterclaim. Of course, it should be noted that a set-off, because it is a defence, can simply be pleaded in the defendant's statement of defence or can be asserted as a counterclaim. However, claims that can only be the subject of a counterclaim cannot be asserted as a defence, but must be asserted in a separate portion of the defendant's pleading entitled a "counterclaim" (see Ontario rule 27.02).

Is any useful purpose served by retaining the dichotomy between set-off and counterclaim? Does it make any sense to have the issue of costs depend on whether the defendant's claim is a set-off or a counterclaim? If so, why?

The decision in *Reid (E.D.) Produce Ltd. v. Bayside Transport Ltd.* (1986), 64 Nfld. & PEIR 55 (PEI TD) illustrates the costs consequences of proceeding by counterclaim rather than set-off. The plaintiff was a buyer of empty beer bottles and whenever it had assembled enough to make up a trailer load, it would contact the defendant, a licensed carrier, which had an arrangement with a Saint John brewery for delivery. The defendant would purchase the load of bottles from the plaintiff, for which it would either pay cash immediately upon loading, or, as sometimes happened, the first business day following, if the pick-up was made on a weekend. The loading of the trailer would normally be at the cost of the plaintiff. The plaintiff obtained judgment against the defendant for $3,500.50 for a dishonoured cheque and other shortages in payment. Of the defendant's counterclaim of $8,840 made up of six different and distinct accounts, two items were allowed in part for a total amount of $2,800. Since the defendant was successful, at least in part, on two of six counts, but unsuccessful on the remaining four, it was entitled to recover one-third of its taxed costs against the plaintiff.

Limitation periods. The application of limitations periods to counterclaims and set-off is varied. With respect to counterclaims, and as a general rule only, a party cannot raise a claim in a counterclaim that is barred by a limitation period when the counterclaim is first asserted. Some statutes, to the contrary, permit counterclaims to proceed where the main action was commenced in time, and notwithstanding the intervening expiry of a limitation period applicable to the counterclaim. See G. Mew, *The Law of Limitations*, 2d ed. (Toronto: Butterworths, 2004), 95-96. The situation with regard to set-off is even more confusing. Some provinces explicitly make limitations legislation applicable to set-off generally, in the same manner as counterclaims. In those cases where the statutes are silent, the situation may be different with respect to each of legal and equitable set-off. Caselaw with respect to legal set-off has held that a statute-barred debt owed to a defendant cannot form the basis for set-off on the basis of mutual debts owing. Some courts have found differently in the case of equitable set-off, holding that a statute barring the assertion of a right in an action does not extinguish the underlying legal right and, accordingly, it may be raised as a defence to reduce or eliminate the claim. The reason for the apparently different treatment of legal and equitable set-off in this respect is obscure and difficult to rationalize. See Palmer, supra, at 29-30 and Derham, supra, at 27-28 and 64-65.

C. Third-Party Claims

Suppose a defendant in an action believes that he or she has a claim against someone who is not a party and that claim is related to issues that have arisen or could arise between the plaintiff and the defendant. If such a claim is against the plaintiff, the defendant may assert it by counterclaim. If it is against another defendant, it may be asserted by cross-claim (as discussed below). However, if the claim is against someone else, the defendant will have to bring that person into the action by way of third-party proceedings. The defendant may assert such a claim because he or she believes that there is a right of contribution or indemnity against the third party—that is, if the defendant is liable to the plaintiff, that defendant has a right to demand compensation from the third party, in whole or in part, for the relief the defendant will be ordered to pay the plaintiff. Historically, third-party procedures were limited to this situation, which still arises frequently. However, under many modern rules, a defendant may also initiate a third-party proceeding for a claim against the third party regardless of whether the plaintiff prevails against the defendant.

An example will illustrate how a defendant might have a claim against a person not a party to the action in respect of the relief claimed against that defendant by the plaintiff. Suppose that Chen has entered into a contract with Air Canada to have a quantity of goods shipped from Toronto to Vancouver. Air Canada, in turn, enters into a contract with Mary to have the goods picked up and taken to the Toronto airport. On the way to the airport, the goods, while in the custody of Mary, disappear. Chen now sues Air Canada, claiming damages for breach of the contract to deliver the goods from Toronto to Vancouver. Air Canada is likely to be primarily liable to Chen, but because the goods were lost while in the possession of Mary, Air Canada feels that Mary should have to pay Air Canada the amount that Air Canada must pay Chen. Air Canada could wait until Chen has obtained judgment against it and then bring a separate action against Mary, claiming the amount of damages that Air Canada had to pay to Chen. However, to bring a second action in such a situation is not only cumbersome, expensive, and a violation of the principle that a multiplicity of proceedings should be avoided, but it also exposes Air Canada to the risk of inconsistent decisions in the two actions—that is, Air Canada might lose to Chen and then lose against Mary. It was for this reason that the third-party procedure was developed. Thus, Air Canada, rather than bringing a separate action against Mary, in which it would have to prove the matters already determined in the action brought by Chen, may join Mary as a third party via a process known as a third-party claim or a third-party proceeding. What results is really two linked actions under the umbrella of a single title (and, usually, court file number) in which the title of proceedings would read:

Between:	
Chen	Plaintiff
	and
Air Canada	Defendant
	and
Mary	Third Party

If, in addition, Air Canada wished to assert a claim against Mary for return of money paid under the contract because of non-performance by Mary, such an assertion would illustrate the use of third-party procedures to assert a claim by the defendant regardless of the plaintiff's claim. Should Air Canada be able to assert an unrelated claim by means of third-party proceedings?

Although the special words "contribution or indemnity" may no longer be in many rules (although they are clearly encompassed by the language that appears in Ontario rule 27.01(a)), they represent situations in which third-party proceedings will be frequently employed. The term *indemnity* applies to the situation where the defendant claims against the third party that, in the event of the defendant being found liable to the plaintiff, the third party must provide full compensation to the defendant including any costs awarded the plaintiff and the defendant's personal costs. When *contribution* is sought, the defendant claims that the third party is liable to pay *part* of any amount for which the defendant is adjudged liable to the plaintiff. The extent of the contribution and the way it is determined will depend on the nature of the relationship between the defendant and the third party out of which the liability to contribute arises.

The following are examples of relationships between two persons that give one the right to be indemnified by the other: an agent by a principal for liabilities incurred in the course of the agency; a guarantor by the principal debtor in respect of liability to the creditor under the guarantee to satisfy the debt; and any contract by which one party agrees to indemnify the other—for example, an insurance contract.

The right of contribution is implied by law in relationships such as that existing between partners, trustees, guarantors, and joint debtors. Further, there is a statutory right of contribution between concurrent tortfeasors.

However, third-party proceedings in many jurisdictions are not limited to situations involving claims for contribution or indemnity. For example, Ontario rule 29 contemplates assertion of claims by the defendant independent of the claims of the plaintiff. One of the most significant features of third-party procedure is that the decision reached by the court on the issues between the plaintiff and the defendant binds the third party. This follows because the rules permit the third party not only to defend against the defendant's claim, but also to participate in the main action and to defend the claim of the plaintiff against the defendant. Of course, it is in the interest of the third party to defend the plaintiff's claim against the defendant if the situation is one in which, should that claim fail, the third-party claim will also fail. The third party has substantial leeway in defending the main action and can raise any defence open to the defendant, including defences not raised by the defendant or defences that contradict those presented by the defendant: see *Van Patter v. Tillsonburg District Memorial Hospital* (1999), 45 OR (3d) 223 (CA).

Negligence Act. Ontario's *Negligence Act*, RSO 1990, c. N.1, and its provincial corollaries, has a major impact on joinder generally, and on third-party claims in particular. This legislation, and similar legislation in most Commonwealth jurisdictions, does two things. First, it does away with contributory negligence as a complete defence, which was the prior situation at common law—that is, if the plaintiff caused or contributed to her own injuries through her own fault, or negligence to any degree, that was a complete defence to any claim by the plaintiff. Instead, under the legislation, the absolute defence is abolished in favour of a regime in which the plaintiff's contributory negligence merely goes to reduce *pro rata* the plaintiff's recovery, according to the relative degrees of fault. So even a plaintiff whose own injuries are adjudged 90 percent her own fault can still recover 10 percent of her assessed damages from a defendant. However, it is the second aspect of the legislation that is most important regarding joinder. The legislation makes all concurrent tortfeasors jointly and severally liable for the plaintiff's injuries—that is, if D1 and D2 contribute equally to the plaintiff's injuries through their fault or negligence, the plaintiff will normally be given a judgment against both of them for the full amount of the damages. While the plaintiff is entitled to satisfaction of the amount of the judgment only once, the plaintiff can execute for the whole of the amount of the judgment against any one of the defendants. So as between a solvent and insolvent defendant, the plaintiff can choose to execute her judgment against the solvent defendant who has assets to satisfy the judgment. The legislation further provides a right of contribution between tortfeasors who are held jointly and severally liable.

Accordingly, if one tortfeasor is called to pay the plaintiff more than her *pro rata* share of the damages then she can recover that amount from the other tortfeasor (a right that will be worth nothing if the other tortfeasor defendant is insolvent). The overall effect of this regime is to place the risk of insolvency of one of the defendants on the defendants, rather than the plaintiff. This contributory negligence regime is in contrast to the "comparative negligence" regime in place in some US states under which a defendant is only ever liable for his or her *pro rata* share. The contributory negligence regime can be characterized as an "in for a penny, in for a pound" regime because it can lead to situations where a defendant who is only adjudged slightly at fault for the plaintiff's injuries having to pay for all of the plaintiff's damages. This regime can prompt a search to include "deep pocket" defendants in a lawsuit who made only a small contribution to the plaintiff's damages.

The contributory negligence regime of the *Negligence Act* impacts on joinder decisions in various other ways. A plaintiff may join both D1 and D2 as defendants, not merely because she is in doubt about from whom she is entitled to relief, but to guard against the risk that one of them will not be able to satisfy the whole judgment. While the legislation gives joint tortfeasors a right of contribution, this right (like any right) is one for which a claim has to be asserted and a judgment obtained. Consequently, in an action where contributory negligence is alleged against multiple defendants, those defendants should, and normally will, "claim over" against each other for contribution by means of a cross-claim. What if the plaintiff sues D1 alone and D1 believes that D2 contributed to the plaintiff's injuries? Here D1 can join D2 as a third party, assert the latter's negligence and claim contribution from D2. This, in turn, will likely lead the plaintiff to amend his or her claim to add D2 as a defendant because, if D2 is merely a third party and is found to be 100 percent at fault for the damages, the plaintiff will fail in the action. In order to recover damages, he or she must establish that *a defendant* was at fault for his or her injuries; the plaintiff can never obtain a judgment directly against a third party.

Daniel Industries Inc. v. Alberta Energy Co.
(1989), 37 CPC (2d) 118 (Alta. CA)

[Appeal from order staying third-party notice pending trial of main action.]

PER CURIAM (memorandum of judgment): … At issue here is a stay of a third party proceeding.

The plaintiff contracted with the defendant (or its distributor) to supply 16 valves manufactured by the defendant for an oil pipeline. The plaintiff also contracted with the third party to design how to install them, and to supervise installation. After operation for some time, one of the valves blew up. Another valve was removed for inspection. On advice of the third party, all the valves from the defendant were removed and replaced by valves from another manufacturer.

The plaintiff sued only the defendant manufacturer (and its distributor). It did not sue the third party. The defendant issued a third party notice against the third party. The plaintiff moved to strike out the third party notice, or in the alternative to stay it until after trial. The chambers judge stayed it, and the defendant appeals.

The learned judge's reasons are not recorded. The plaintiff first argues that the third party notice contravenes a rule of law. The appellant agrees that the rule of law exists, so the question is its application. The rule forbids a third party notice which is based solely on facts which, if proved, would give a complete defence to the main action. In such a case the very facts which would make the third party liable to the defendant would make the defendant not liable to the plaintiff. So the main action would be dismissed, and there would be no need for contribution or indemnity.

Some cases have applied that rule in situations where the plaintiff and the third party are identified with and responsible for each other's fault, by statute, for example, a passenger and his driver; or the government guaranteeing a student loan, and the lending bank. The defendant here offered to abandon its appeal and its third party notice if the plaintiff would agree to be identified with any fault or liability of the third party. But the plaintiff did not volunteer such liability. No one argued that the plaintiff and the third party are in law identified or vicariously liable for each other here, so the identification doctrine does not apply.

Here the third party notice denies liability to the plaintiff. But should there be such liability, it claims indemnity "in whole or in part." It alleges that the third party (a) inspected and approved the valves, (b) had fabrications built incorporating those valves, (c) undertook to inspect and ensure proper construction, (d) did all those things "negligently" and failed to do them properly (with extensive particulars), (e) caused the one explosion by those defaults, and (f) improperly advised the plaintiff after one valve exploded that all the rest should be replaced, and did not tell the plaintiff that the cause was its own previous defaults.

The plaintiff suggests that the facts alleged in the third party notice will either be found or not be found at trial. It says if they are found, they will give a complete defence to the action, and so render the third party notice unnecessary. That may be so at common law, but the defendant points out that s. 3 of Alberta's *Tort-Feasors Act* and s. 2 of its *Contributory Negligence Act* change that. They allow for partial defences and percentages of liability. If the defendant is partly to blame, the plaintiff will recover a judgment for all its loss against the defendant. The defendant may then claim contribution against the other tortfeasor for the portion which was the latter's fault. The courts have often held that such a claim over for contribution may be made by third party notice.

Therefore, the trial or the third party notice need not produce an all-or-nothing situation. The trial judge might find that the first valve exploded because of the combined effects of the defendant's poor design or manufacture, and of the third party's poor inspection or installation method or supervision. He might also find that the other valves were removed and replaced because of the combined effects of some of those things plus poor advice by the third party. In any such event, the third party claim would be well-founded. The third party claim is necessary, since the plaintiff chose not to sue one of the alleged original tortfeasors.

Counsel for the plaintiff admitted in argument that such trial results were possible, but contended that they were very unlikely, especially respecting the one valve which exploded. Counsel for the defendant contended that such results were not improbable. There have been fairly extensive examinations for discovery to date, which are detailed by an affidavit of the plaintiff's officer for discovery. That affidavit is the only evidence. It says nothing about the merits of the main lawsuit, or the merits of the third party claim. We are unwilling to assume that it is very unlikely that there could be a mixed result in this three-cornered suit. Such mixed results are not uncommon in construction litigation. We cannot see that finding bad manufacture of the valves would render bad installation improbable. Negligence by the manufacturer and the installer could co-exist and compound each other.

Therefore, in our view, the third party notice cannot be struck out, and must be taken to be a proper third party notice.

The chambers judge granted the alternative relief of a stay, and counsel gave us brief argument on that topic. A few days have been reserved for further examination for discovery by both parties. The plaintiff's counsel believes that the main action will then be ready to set down for trial, but the defendant's counsel believes that it will not. How long the third party proceedings would delay trial (if not stayed) is not clear. But the evidence before us is that a great deal of the third party's information and documents have already been produced to the defendant in the main action. In argument, the plaintiff suggests that little, if any, has not. Therefore, the only evidence suggests that additional discovery from the third party would not take long, and so would not long postpone trial. The benefits of having the identical fact issue tried once by one judge and not twice by two judges are always great, and must be doubled in such a technical suit. Inconsistent findings by the two judges would be a disaster, and the cost of trying the same issues twice would be no kindness to anyone.

The plaintiff suggests that the third party notice may have been issued only to get discovery and not in good faith because the third party is out of business. The defendant's counsel assures us that is not so, and there is no evidence that the third party lacks assets or lacks insurance. We would not find bad faith or oblique motives without evidence.

The plaintiff briefly suggested delay by the defendant, but the only affidavit does not address that point. The motion to strike out the third party notice was filed over two years after the third party notice was issued. It is alleged that the defendant had issued formal notices against the third party for discovery of documents and examination for discovery many months before the notice of motion. There is no basis in evidence for finding delay, let alone undue delay.

That covers all the grounds argued to support the order for a stay. We allow the appeal, discharge the order of the learned chambers judge, and dismiss the motion to strike out or stay the third party proceedings. As each party sought costs of the appeal, the defendant will have costs of the appeal. As the reasons of the chambers judge and the arguments before him are not known, costs of the Queen's Bench motion to strike out or stay the third party notice will be awarded by the trial judge.

Appeal allowed.

Freudmann-Cohen v. Tran
(2004), 70 OR (3d) 667 (CA)

BLAIR JA: The court is called upon to resolve the interaction between two well-established principles on this appeal. The first of these is the tenet of insurance subrogation law that an insurer may sue only in the name of the insured in relation to a subrogated claim. The second relates to the policy underlying the third party provisions of the *Rules of Civil Procedure* (rule 29.01), which seeks to promote efficiency, cost effectiveness, and the avoidance of multiplicity of proceedings in civil actions. The tension arises because the respondent, Zurich Insurance Company, seeks to pursue, in its own name, what is in reality a subrogated claim on behalf of the plaintiff, by way of a third party claim against the appellants. The appeal also entails an examination of the nature of the subrogation right in the context of a limitation period defence.

Introduction

The defendants Tran and Vu (the "Tran defendants") were respectively the operator and owner of a motor vehicle that struck another motor vehicle being operated by the plaintiff, Ms. Freudmann-Cohen. She was injured in the accident.

Zurich is Ms. Freudmann-Cohen's insurer. It is a defendant in the action because the Tran defendants are underinsured and the plaintiffs have asserted a claim under their underinsured motorist coverage pursuant to Zurich's Family Protection Endorsement OEF 44.

Zurich subsequently learned that Mr. Tran had been delivering pizza for Pizza Nova franchise #81 at the time of the accident and that the franchisee had insurance coverage. Zurich then issued a third party claim against Pizza Nova Restaurants and Pizza Nova #81 (together "Pizza Nova") pursuant to rule 29.01 of the *Rules of Civil Procedure*.

Pizza Nova moved for an order striking out the third party claim as failing to disclose a reasonable cause of action, or, in the alternative, for summary judgment dismissing the claim. Justice Dambrot dismissed the motion, and in so doing concluded that Zurich could bring the third party claim in its own name. Pizza Nova appeals from that decision.

I would dismiss the appeal, for the reasons that follow.

Facts

The accident occurred on October 15, 1993 and the action was commenced against the Tran defendants on October 10, 1995. On June 18, 1996 Zurich was added as a defendant, after the plaintiffs' solicitors formed the opinion that the Tran defendants were underinsured.

For reasons that are not explained, Mr. Tran was not examined for discovery until April 30, 2001. At that time Zurich became aware that he had been delivering pizza for Pizza Nova at the time of the accident. After further research, it discovered in February 2002 that Pizza Nova had Non-Owned Automobile Insurance Coverage. In May 2002, the plaintiffs consented to the issuance of Zurich's third party claim, and on June 12, 2002, the third party claim was issued against Pizza Nova.

The Family Protection Endorsement—OEF 44 is a prescribed form under the *Insurance Act* RSO 1990, c. I.8, as amended, for insertion into policies of automobile insurance where a premium is paid in consideration of which the insurer agrees to indemnify the insured for the amount that he or she is entitled to recover from an inadequately insured motorist. The insurer is then subrogated to the claimant's rights in accordance with section 20 of OEF 44, which states:

> Where a claim is made under this endorsement, the insurer is subrogated to the rights of the eligible claimant by whom a claim is made, and may maintain an action in the name of that person against the inadequately insured motorist and the persons referred to in section 7.

As Dambrot J noted, it is common ground that Pizza Nova falls within section 7.

It appears to be common ground as well that the nature of the claim being asserted by Zurich is a subrogation claim. Although the claim is framed in terms of contribution and indemnity, contributory negligence and vicarious liability, it is in substance the claim that the plaintiffs could have made against Pizza Nova as Mr. Tran's employer, alleging that the appellants are jointly liable with Mr. Tran for the plaintiffs' claims. No explanation has been provided for why the plaintiffs have not themselves sought to add Pizza Nova as a party defendant, but they have not done so.

Analysis

Pizza Nova's argument is two-fold. First, it submits that Zurich's only claim against it is a subrogated claim. As such, the claim must therefore be brought in the name of the insured (Freudmann-Cohen), by virtue both of the language of OEF 44 and at common law; it cannot be brought as an independent third party claim in the name of the insurer, as Zurich has purported to do. Secondly, Pizza Nova argues that a subrogated action is a derivative action and Zurich accordingly has no greater right than the plaintiffs. Since the limitation period for a claim by the plaintiffs against Pizza Nova has expired, Zurich's claim is precluded as well. I shall refer to these arguments as "the third party/subrogation argument" and "the limitation period argument."

The Third Party/Subrogation Argument

An insurer's right to bring a subrogated claim to enforce the rights of an insured, and to do so in the name of the insured, is now provided by s. 278(1) of the *Insurance Act* RSO 1990, c. I.

The doctrine of subrogation is not confined to insurance law, but it has a strong foothold in that domain. The fundamental principle of insurance is indemnity, and subrogation law is closely aligned with that principle. …

The appellants' argument is based upon the common law notion whereby an insurer with a subrogated claim is said to be required to pursue that claim in the name of the insured; it cannot sue in its own name. … Section 278(1) of the *Insurance Act* and OEF 44 reflect this principle, providing, as they do, that the subrogated insurer "may maintain an action in the name of the insured [or the eligible claimant]." Accordingly, the appellants submit, the third party proceeding cannot be brought in the insurer's name.

An analysis of this position requires an examination of the third party rule (rule 29.01) and its underpinnings, on the one hand, and the rationale underlying the subrogation principle requiring the insurer to sue in the name of the insured alone, on the other hand.

The motions judge recognized the conflict between these two principles. At para. 13 of his reasons he said:

> The position taken by E. Macdonald J in *Morey v. Knipple* that the right of the insurer to subrogate should not be defeated by the technical impediment that it cannot, in the particular circumstances, bring the third party claim in the name of the insured, but only in its own name, is a fair and just position. It is consistent with the policy objective underlying the amendment to Rule 29 of having the rights of all the parties involved in the same factual situation determined without a multiplicity of proceedings. It does appear, however, to fly in the face of the words of OEF 44, and the common law, which both appear to permit the insurer to maintain an action of this sort only in the name of the insured.

The motions judge had reservations about the reasoning in *Morey v. Knipple*, [1994] OJ No. 2181 (Ont. Gen. Div.), which followed an earlier decision, *Carswell v. Traders General Insurance Co.* (1987), 19 CPC (2d) 126 (Ont. Dist. Ct.), affirmed (1987), 20 CPC (2d) 117 (Ont. HC). However, he felt obliged to follow the prevailing view as laid down in those authorities, particularly since the Divisional Court had approved the same approach in *Nuvo Electronics Inc. v. London Assurance*, [2000] OJ No. 808 (Ont. Div. Ct.). Although there is some basis for the reservations of the motions judge, I am satisfied after considering the provisions of rule 29.01, and the policy underlying it, in the context of the nature of the subrogation rule in question, that his decision was correct.

Rule 29.01 provides:

> A defendant may commence a third party claim against any person who is not a party to the action and who,
>
> > (a) is or may be liable to the defendant for all or part of the plaintiff's claim;
> >
> > (b) is or may be liable to the defendant for an independent claim for damages or other relief arising out of,
> >
> > > (i) a transaction or occurrence or series of transactions or occurrences involved in the main action, or
> > >
> > > (ii) a related transaction or occurrence or series of transactions or occurrences;
> >
> > or
> >
> > (c) should be bound by the determination of an issue arising between the plaintiff and the defendant.

This language is quite different from the provisions of the third party rule, as it existed prior to 1985. Zurich submits that the changes are pivotal to the disposition of this matter and that they support Zurich's right to assert its third party claim. In effect, Zurich argues that rule 29.01 constitutes a procedural scheme, with the force of regulation, which overrides the normal subrogation principle requiring an insurer claiming a subrogated right to sue in the name of the insured in circumstances such as these. I agree.

As several authorities have noted, the amendments effected by rule 29.01 were intended to make substantial changes in the law; claims which could not previously have been asserted under the former Rule 167 may well be allowed under rule 29.01: see *Nuvo Electronics Inc.*, *Morey v. Knipple*, and *Carswell v. Traders General Insurance Co.*, *supra*. In a notation to rule 29.01, the authors of Holmested and Watson, *Ontario Civil Procedure, 2003*—Volume 1, state, at 604:

> The significance of this change should not be underestimated. It changes the very nature of a third party claim. No longer is it limited to situations designed to obtain "a flow through of recovery" to D from the third party because of the judgment that the plaintiff may obtain against the defendant. Instead, it is now a general joinder device by which a defendant may engraft on to the main action any "related claim" he or she may have against non-parties, subject to the severance power given to the court by rule 29.09.

The purpose of the new rule was to simplify third party procedure and to avoid multiplicity of proceedings: *Carswell v. Traders General Insurance Co.*, at p. 129. This promotes efficiency and expedition in litigation, lowers costs, and enhances accessibility to the system. As E. Macdonald J noted, in *Morey* at para. 26, one of "the policies underlying the amendment to the rules, as reflected in Rule 29 is the objective of having the rights of all parties involved in the same factual situation determined without a multiplicity of proceedings." See also *Sanga v. Bettridge* (1994), 17 OR (3d) 773 (Ont. CA) at p. 777.

It is significant, in my view, that under Rule 29.01(c)—the provision relied on by Zurich in this case—it is not necessary for the person against whom the third party claim is asserted to be a person who "is or may be liable to the defendant." Rather, it is sufficient that the party sought to be added "should be bound by the determination of an issue arising between the plaintiff and the defendant." The fact that Zurich seeks to add Pizza Nova on the basis of a claim by which Pizza Nova is or may be liable to *the plaintiff* is not fatal to the operation of the third party procedure; in fact, it is exactly what that procedure is now designed to do (assuming the other criteria for its operation are also met).

Pizza Nova argues that the requirement for an insurer, as subrogee, to sue in the name of the insured is not merely a "technical impediment," as the motions judge suggested, but rather a matter of substantive law. Therefore it must be adhered to. I agree it is doubtful whether a procedural rule—desirable as its objectives may be—can override a substantive common law principle. But is the insurance law requirement that Zurich put forward its claim in the name of the plaintiffs a matter of procedural or substantive law?

There are cases that have allowed the third party procedural rule to supersede the common law requirement; however, they had done so without analysis of the rationale underlying the subrogation principle: see *Morey*, *Carswell*, and *Nuvo Electronics Inc.*, *supra*. There are other authorities that have declined to do so: see *Harris v. Floyd* (1991), 7 OR (3d) 512 (Ont. Master); *Metz v. Breland* (1990), 47 CCLI 107 (Alta. CA).

In my view, the provisions of rule 29.01 do permit a subrogated insurer to issue a third party claim in circumstances such as this. I have reached this conclusion because the subrogation principle obliging the insurer to sue in the name of the insured—as well embedded in insurance law as it is—is nonetheless a procedural requirement itself, as opposed to a substantive obligation. While subrogation is a matter of substance rather than form (see *Somersall v. Friedman*, 2002 SCC 59 (SCC), per Binnie J at para. 97), this aspect of subrogation is a matter of the procedure to be followed in the exercise of the substantive right of subrogation.

To understand this conclusion it is important to understand the rationale underlying the principle that a subrogated insurer must sue in the name of the insured. That rationale has its roots in the need to provide a process by which the insurer would be able to exercise its subrogated rights. The principle of "indemnity-but-no-more-than-indemnity" required that the insured take—or, on being indemnified as to costs, permit to be taken—all steps within the insured's power to reduce the amount of loss for which indemnity had been received. This included exercising the insured's remedies against third parties. Since those remedies were remedies personal to the insured, however, they could only be exercised in the name of the insured as a matter of procedural law. ...

The requirement to sue in the name of the insurance claimant is therefore procedural in origin, not substantive. A reference to assignment law is helpful by way of analogy, too. Although subrogation is not the equivalent of assignment, it has assignment-like aspects to it ... . Whether an assignee can or cannot sue in his or her own name is another facet of the law that is shrouded in mystery and history; but it is also based upon the personal nature of the claim being asserted. It is clear that this same type of requirement in assignment law is a procedural one. See rule 5.03(3); *DiGuilo v. Boland*, [1958] OR 384 (Ont. CA).

If the common law requirement that a subrogee must sue in the name of the insured claimant is procedural in nature, the provisions of OEF 44 that incorporate it are procedural as well, as are the provisions of s. 278(1) of the *Insurance Act*. I note in passing that neither of these provisions specify that the insurer *must* sue in the name of the insured, but merely that it *may* do so. This suggests they are designed to facilitate the insurer's subrogation right, not to circumscribe it. I am satisfied, therefore, that what is at issue here is a competition between two *procedural* principles—the one founded in the law of subrogation; the other embodied in the provisions of rule 29.01—rather than between a *procedural* and a *substantive* right. In that competition the objectives expressed in the rule, namely, more effective and less costly litigation, and the avoidance of multiplicity of proceedings, should carry the day.

The fact that Zurich has resorted to the third party procedure to put its subrogated claim on behalf of the plaintiffs in play in the action does not mean that Zurich is asserting the plaintiffs' claim against Pizza Nova in Zurich's own name. As I have earlier pointed out, rule 29.01 merely provides a mechanism whereby the defendant Zurich may ensure that an issue regarding which the third party should be bound is determined in the action; it is not necessary that that issue arise out of a claim whereby the defendant says the third party is or may be liable to the defendant. In my view, Zurich is entitled to resort to the third party rule in its own name in these circumstances. ...

That an insurer may not recover on a subrogated claim of the insured against a third party is, I agree, substantive law. As a matter of principle, it does not seem to me that it necessarily follows that, as a matter of procedure, the insurer should therefore not be entitled to employ third party procedure unless it has first indemnified the insured, at least in the circumstances of this case.

If as important a principle as the requirement that an insurer pay the claim before suing to recover on its subrogated rights can yield to the desired goal of promoting the disposition of all relevant issues between all relevant parties in one action, thus avoiding the multiplicity of proceedings, I see no reason in principle why the same result should not flow when the provisions of rule 29.01 collide with the procedural principle in subrogation law requiring the insurer to sue in the name of the insured.

Mr. Strung concedes on behalf of the appellants that, leaving aside the third party/ subrogation issue and the limitation period defence, Pizza Nova is a person who is not a party to the action but who "should be bound by the determination of an issue arising between the plaintiff and the defendant" pursuant to rule 29.01(c). The appellants fit into this category because of the limits of Zurich's coverage under s. 4 of OEF 44, which provides:

> The insurer's maximum liability under this endorsement … is the amount by which the limit of family protection coverage exceeds the total of all limits of motor vehicle liability insurance … of the inadequately insured motorist *and of any person jointly liable with that motorist* [emphasis added].

Thus, the issues that must be sorted out between the plaintiffs and Zurich in the main action include not only the amount, if any, by which the liability of the Tran defendants exceeds the limits of their own insurance coverage, but also the amount for which Pizza Nova (and therefore its insurer) may be liable. The question of Zurich's liability cannot be settled until the latter issue has been determined. Pizza Nova should be bound by that determination so that it cannot take a different position at a later time. …

I would not give effect, therefore, to the appellants' arguments on the third party/ subrogation issue. A subrogated insurer is entitled to resort to rule 29.01 in its own name for purposes of instituting third party proceedings, provided the circumstances are such that the criteria set out in that Rule are otherwise met. …

Hannah v. Canadian General Insurance Co.
(1989), 90 NSR (2d) 83 (SC)

HALLETT J: This is a motion made by the defendant at the pretrial conference that the action be adjourned and an order made requiring the plaintiff to add a blasting contractor as a defendant. The plaintiff's action is against the insurer of his home for damages caused to his home from blasting carried out on an adjacent lot. The insurance contract provides for coverage caused by "explosion."

Civil Procedure Rule 5.04(2)(b) provides:

> 5.04(2) At any stage of a proceeding the court may, on such terms as it thinks just and either of its own motion or on application, …
>
>   (b) order any person, who ought to have been joined as a party or whose participation in the proceeding is necessary to ensure that all matters in the proceeding may be effectually adjudicated upon, be added as a party.

This motion comes very late in the proceedings, just four days prior to trial, the action having been commenced in November of 1987, and the trial dates set many months ago. The defendant raises the point that if the trial goes ahead and the plaintiff succeeds and the defendant then exercises his right of subrogation and sues the blasting contractor, there is a danger of inconsistent findings as to what damage was caused by the blasting as a result of two proceedings dealing with this issue and, secondly, by not joining the blasting contractor as a defendant, there will be a duplicity of proceedings and the attendant increased costs; he suggests this is not in the interest of justice. ...

In *Canada Permanent Trust Co. v. Rao et al.* (1981), 46 NSR (2d) 336; 89 APR 236, at p. 343, Cowan CJTD, quoted from *The Law of Civil Procedure*, Williston and Rolls, vol. 1, p. 426, that the objects of third party proceedings are:

> (1) to avoid a multiplicity of actions. The procedure provides a substitute for another action, and disposes of all issues arising out of a transaction as between the plaintiff and the defendant, and between the defendant and a third party;
>
> (2) to avoid the possibility that there might otherwise be contradictory or inconsistent findings in two different actions on the same facts;
>
> (3) to allow the third party to defend the plaintiff's claim against the defendant;
>
> (4) to save costs; and
>
> (5) to enable the defendant to have the issue against the third party decided as soon as possible, in order that the plaintiff can not enforce a judgment against him before the third party issue is determined.

In *Burry v. Centennial Properties Ltd.* (1979), 38 NSR (2d) 450; 69 APR 450, the court, in considering the scope of rule 17.02, stated at paragraph 32:

> The only real limitation on the use of third party proceedings is contained in the *Judicature Act* where the second cause of action must be "relating to or connected with the original subject of the proceeding," but once that connection is established then procedurally all common issues should be tried and disposed of at the one time.

In my view, the defendant's counsel puts too narrow an interpretation on rule 17.02 as the blasting contractor should, in the interest of the efficient administration of justice, be bound by a determination of the issue of causation and damages that arises between the plaintiff and the defendant in these proceedings. The defendant could have applied to join the blasting contractor as a third party as provided for by rule 17.02(1)(c); it chose not to do so. The plaintiff is entitled to choose his remedy and has chosen to sue his insurer under the insurance contract which provides for extended coverage, including damage from explosion. The plaintiff opposes the granting of the order. This motion, on the eve of the trial, comes too late. While it would be desirable to have the blasting contractor before the court, it would be unfair and not in the best interests of the administration of justice to adjourn this case four days before trial when trial dates were set so many months ago and the defendant could have applied months ago to join the blasting contractor. I am dismissing the motion.

NOTES AND QUESTIONS

1. Rule 29.01(b) in Ontario *expressly* authorizes that an independent claim the defendant may have against a third party may be asserted via a third-party claim. This can occur as

long as the claim arises out of the transaction or occurrence involved in the main action or a related series of transactions or occurrences.

2. Issues with counterclaims, setoffs, and third-party claims as presented in this chapter relate primarily to joinder of additional parties. However, issues may also be raised with respect to the scope of the matter, such as those issues dealt with in chapter 4.

3. Where a third party has a claim to assert, fourth-party proceedings are available, and claims by fourth and subsequent parties may also be asserted: see, for example, Ontario rule 29.11.

4. *The mechanics of third-party proceedings.* See Ontario rule 29. For other examples, see Alberta rules 66-79; British Columbia rule 22; New Brunswick rule 30; Nova Scotia rule 17; and Saskatchewan rules 1070 and 1071.

The defendant is required to serve the third-party notice within a stipulated time after the defendant has delivered the statement of defence or the time limited for its delivery has expired. The defendant must also serve the third party with a copy of the pleadings previously delivered. (Where a defendant counterclaims, any defendant to the counterclaim may take third-party proceedings—for example, see Ontario rule 29.13.)

In reality, third-party proceedings are just another action (defendant v. third party) engrafted onto the main action. However, the *plaintiff's* procedural rights may be adversely affected by the addition of third-party claims. For this reason, under Ontario rule 29, only the plaintiff in the main action, and not the third party, is given the express right to challenge the propriety of a third-party claim: rule 29.09. It is, however, open to the third party to move under the general relief against joinder (rule 5.05) in an appropriate case.

If the motion is unsuccessful, or if no motion is brought, the third party is required to file a statement of defence and the defendant may then deliver a reply. As previously indicated, the third party may also deliver a statement of defence to the plaintiff's statement of claim. The third party and the defendant (and the third party and the plaintiff, where the main action is being defended by the third party) may have production and discovery from each other in the same manner as between a plaintiff and a defendant. The third-party issue is set down for trial at the same sitting of the court for which the action between the plaintiff and defendant is set down. However, rule 29.09 provides that "a plaintiff is not to be prejudiced or unnecessarily delayed by reason of a third-party claim."

4. *Conduct of the trial where third-party proceedings are taken.* The third-party action is placed on the list for trial following the main action: see, for example, Ontario rule 29.08(1). The rule also provides: (1) that the third-party action shall be tried at or after the trial of the main action, as the trial judge may direct; (2) that the third party shall be at liberty to appear at the trial of the action and to take part in the trial in such manner and to such extent as the trial judge may direct; and (3) that the third party shall be bound by any judgment or decision in the action. The extent to which there will be a separate trial in the third-party action depends on the nature of the main action and the claims asserted in the third-party proceeding.

In a typical motor vehicle accident case where the defendant joins a third party alleging that the third party caused or contributed to the accident, and is thus potentially liable to contribute under the *Negligence Act*, all the issues between the defendant and the third party will, typically, simply be litigated in the trial of the main action and there will be no separate trial in the third-party proceeding. The reason for this is that usually, in such a case, the only issue between the defendant and the third party is fault-based responsibility for the plaintiff's injuries and, if both defendant and third party are found at fault, what their respective degrees of responsibility are. In this kind of action, it is convenient for the court and the parties, when considering the issues between the plaintiff and the defendant, to consider also those issues between the defendant and the third party. However, in other types of actions, there may be issues between the defendant and third party—for example, where the defendant is asserting an independent claim—that are unrelated to the issues between the plaintiff and the defendant. In such a case, the main action will be disposed of and then the third-party proceedings will be heard.

D. Cross-Claims

Cross-claims permit claims between co-defendants and are provided for in some jurisdictions. See, for example, Ontario rule 28; New Brunswick rule 29; Nova Scotia rule 17A; and Saskatchewan rule 106. Such a situation can easily arise. Take for example the situation where P, a passenger in a car, suffers injuries in a collision and sues D1 (the owner-driver of the vehicle in which P was a passenger) and D2 (the driver of the other vehicle). Assume that, after the action is commenced, D1 wishes to claim against D2 for personal injuries and property damage. Note that D1 cannot simply assert this claim by serving a counterclaim on D2, because a counterclaim is available for use only by a defendant against a plaintiff either alone or with another person. Defendants who, under provincial comparative negligence statutes like Ontario's *Negligence Act*, claim contribution and indemnity from other potential tortfeasor co-defendants do so by way of cross-claim. For example, in *Veffer v. Feldman* (2007), 85 OR (3d) 772 (Div. Ct.), a plaintiff was injured in two motor vehicle accidents and sued two separate defendants. The action was dismissed against the first defendant but the cross-claim against that defendant was allowed to continue because the first defendant might be required to contribute to damages awarded against the second defendant. Maintaining the cross-claims among the two co-defendants allows for such contribution.

IV. CONSOLIDATION AND ORDERS FOR THE TRIAL OF ACTIONS TOGETHER

The rules give the court power to relieve against the consequences of joinder where it threatens to give rise to inconvenience or injustice. See, for example, Ontario rule 5.05 and the specific provisions under the rules relating to counterclaims (rule 27.08(2)), cross-claims (rule 28.10), and third-party claims (rule 28.09).

What can a party do if, despite the availability of joinder, cross-claims, counterclaims, or third-party procedures, the party capable of using such procedures does not do so but, instead, commences a separate action? For example: a car driven by A and in which B is a passenger is involved in a collision with a car owned and operated by C. A institutes an action for personal injuries against C, claiming that the latter's negligence caused the injuries. B institutes a separate action against C, making similar allegations. Can C force A and B to join their claims together or must C face the prospect of two trials?

The answer is to be found in provisions, such as rule 6 in each of Ontario, Manitoba, New Brunswick, and Prince Edward Island; Nova Scotia rule 39.02; Alberta rule 229; and British Columbia rule 5(8), giving the court power to order *consolidation* of actions or the trial of actions together. Generally speaking, the court will order consolidation of actions whenever joinder would have been proper. There are, however, certain exceptions—for example, the court will not order the plaintiffs to consolidate their actions if they are represented by different solicitors. Also, as a general rule, an order for consolidation will be refused if a trial of the claims together would not be convenient.

However, in those situations in which the court will refuse to consolidate actions, it nevertheless has a broad discretion to invoke a closely analogous device—that of directing that the actions be tried together. The difference between an order for consolidation and an order that the actions be tried together is as follows: if actions are consolidated, the two actions are completely melded into one and they proceed in all respects as if there had been initial joinder of the claims. There is but one set of pleadings, one set of discoveries, one judgment, and one costs order. If an order is made that actions be tried together, the actions maintain their separate identity and there are separate pleadings, discoveries, judgments, and costs orders. But the actions are set down on the court's trial list one after the other to be "tried in such manner as the court directs." Usually, the trial judge will order that the evidence in one action is to be taken as evidence in the other action or actions. In this way, both or all of the actions are tried together by the same judge or jury. The purpose of directing the trial of actions together is the same as consolidation—to save time and to avoid inconsistent determinations.

It is important to note that applying for an order for trial of actions together may be an appropriate step for a plaintiff to take when an initial joinder of claims and parties has been successfully challenged by the defendant. Denial of the plaintiff's right to join multiple claims and parties may be less significant where the plaintiff is able to obtain an order for trial of the actions together.

Mernick v. Mernick
(2006), 34 CPC (6th) 326 (Ont. SCJ)

MASTER R. DASH:

Joinder of Actions and Separation of Counterclaim

The defendant moves under rule 6.01 for common trial of actions 05-CV-294375PD2 (the "Settlement Action") and 06-CV-311208PD3 (the "Possession Action"). The plaintiff resists this motion and further moves under rule 27.08(2) to sever the counterclaim to the Possession Action and have it proceed as a separate action or by separate trial.

Background

Farley Mernick is the plaintiff and Stephen Mernick is the defendant in both actions. They are brothers and named co-executors of the estate of Belle Mernick (their mother). They are also residual beneficiaries of the estate together with two other brothers, Neil and Earl. The portion in favour of Earl was to be held in trust subject to a monthly income. Neil subsequently died intestate without spouse or children resulting in three residual beneficiaries. There were other certain specific bequests. When the plaintiff and defendant could not agree on any issues with respect to management or distribution of the estate they agreed to submit the dispute to a rabbinical tribunal—a Beis Din ("BD")—pursuant to an Arbitration Agreement dated May 6, 1998 to determine what joint submissions should be made to the court respecting the estate, disposition of assets and related issues. The parties agreed to be bound by the BD's award.

After a lengthy hearing the BD denied the specific claims to estate assets of both parties and ordered that they resign as executors and arrange for an institutional executor to replace them. ... Neither party resigned as executor. The parties however continued to negotiate. The plaintiff pleads that an agreement was reached to confirm the BD award other than the provision with respect to the resignation of the executors and to divide estate assets into two lots, one for each of the plaintiff and the defendant with the plaintiff paying an amount to equalize the division and each would pay Earl a monthly payment for his support (referred to in these reasons as the "Subsequent Agreement"). The defendant denies that any binding Subsequent Agreement was reached, that the BD award remains valid in its entirety and that the plaintiff must resign as executor.

The plaintiff has effectively been managing the day-to-day affairs of the estate since his mother's death in 1997 and the BD had made an interim order that the status quo continue until a new executor was appointed. In 2002 the defendant moved into the home at 128 Clanton Park Rd. owned by his mother (the "Property") despite the plaintiff's opposition thereto and has allegedly let the Property deteriorate and prevented the plaintiff from effecting repairs. The BD had denied Stephen any rights to the Property. In the alleged Subsequent Agreement the Property was part of the lot to be distributed to Stephen.

The Pleadings

The Settlement Action is between Farley as plaintiff personally and Stephen as defendant personally. In that action the plaintiff seeks a declaration that the BD award is valid, enforceable and final for purposes of constituting part of the joint submission except for provisions of the award relating to the resignation of executors, a declaration that Belle Mernick's will is valid and enforceable and a declaration that the plaintiff and defendant reached a binding agreement for distribution of assets that constitute the remainder of the joint submissions. In his statement of defence, the defendant pleads that no binding Subsequent Agreement was ever reached and that the entirety of the BD award is valid, enforceable and final for purposes of the joint submission including the provisions ordering the resignation of the executors. Therefore the only issues in the Settlement Action are whether there was a Subsequent Agreement as to division of assets and whether that part of the BD order that requires the executors to resign is to be severed from the BD award for purposes of the joint submissions. There is no dispute that the reminder of the BD award is final and binding and no issue that Belle Mernick's will is valid and enforceable. A consequence of the determination of that action will be whether the plaintiff is entitled to apply to be an executor of his mother's estate. ...

The Possession Action was commenced a few days later, on May 1, 2006, and is between Farley as plaintiff personally and as estate trustee and Stephen as defendant personally and as estate trustee. The plaintiff seeks an order that Stephen deliver up to Farley "as executor" vacant possession of the Property and a writ of possession. The plaintiff pleads that he has sole responsibility to administer the estate, that the Property is an estate asset, that the BD denied Stephen's claims to the property and that Stephen is a trespasser. Stephen delivered a statement of defence and counterclaim. In his statement of defence, Stephen pleads that the entire award of the BD became effective 30 days after its decision when no MS were filed, that the award required Farley to resign as executor and that an institutional executor be appointed, that Hoilett J confirmed that the award was valid for all purposes, that Farley continues to administer the estate and ignore the order to resign and as a result "the plaintiff has no standing to bring this action or deal with the distribution of the Estate assets as he was ordered to be removed on May 26, 2003 and has continued to disregard the arbitration decision." He pleads that the Settlement Action was commenced to delay the appointment of an institutional executor. He also pleads that there was an agreement to allow him to remain on the Property, which I refer to herein as the "Clanton Agreement." (There are other alleged provisions to the Clanton Agreement that are discussed later in this endorsement.) Although the action is framed as an action for possession of one of the estate assets, the defendant asserts the plaintiff has no standing to bring the action. On September 8, 2006 I denied the plaintiff's motion for summary judgment for possession on the basis that there was a genuine issue to be tried whether the plaintiff has standing as executor (or as beneficiary) to bring the action and seek recovery of estate property. The issues to be tried in the Possession Action, aside from the counterclaim, are whether the defendant has the right to remain in possession of the Property and whether the plaintiff has standing to bring the action.

Trial Together of Main Actions

Rule 6.01 provides:

> 6.01(1) Where two or more proceedings are pending in the court and it appears to the court that,
>
> (a) they have a question of law or fact in common;
>
> (b) the relief claimed in them arises out of the same transaction or occurrence or series of transactions or occurrences; or
>
> (c) for any other reason an order ought to be made under this rule, the court may order that,
>
> (d) the proceedings be consolidated, or heard at the same time or one immediately after the other; or
>
> (e) any of the proceedings be,
>
> > (i) stayed until after the determination of any other of them, or
> >
> > (ii) asserted by way of counterclaim in any other of them.

Both actions arise out of the same series of transactions, namely the Arbitration Agreement, the BD award, the subsequent negotiations and the failure of Farley to resign as executor. Both actions require the court to determine whether Farley has a right to act as executor of the estate of Belle Mernick. To that end both actions depend on the determination by the trial judge whether there was a binding Subsequent Agreement to vary the BD award by severing the provisions requiring the parties to resign as executors and appoint an institutional executor. This is a common issue of fact that is central to both actions. If the court upholds the Subsequent Agreement respecting distribution of assets and varying the resignation provisions of the BD award to allow Farley to remain as executor, the declarations Farley seeks in the Settlement Action will follow as will his standing to bring the Possession Action. The only remaining issue (as currently pleaded) would be whether Stephen has a right to remain on the Property as a result of the Clanton Agreement. However, if the Subsequent Agreement is upheld, that determination would be moot since the Subsequent Agreement included the distribution of the Property to Stephen as part of his share. If the Subsequent Agreement is not upheld the declarations sought by the plaintiff in the Settlement Action that the resignation provisions of the BD award be severed would not be granted and it is unlikely he would have standing to bring the Possession Action, subject to consideration of his right to bring the action as beneficiary (although this would require an amendment to the statement of claim). To allow the two main actions to proceed separately could result in inconsistent verdicts and contravene section 138 of the *Courts of Justice Act* that provides that the court should as far as possible avoid a multiplicity of proceedings. Neither action is complex or document intensive and much of the discoveries will involve the same issue. Neither action will be unduly delayed by common discoveries or by common or consecutive trials. ...

Conclusion

I am therefore of the view that only those portions of the counterclaim dealing with removal of the executor based on the BD award and the penalty resulting from Farley's contesting the BD award should be tried with the main actions. ... In all other respects actions 05-CV-294375PD2 and 06-CV-311208PD3 shall be tried together or one after the other as the trial judge may direct and shall have common discoveries and a common mediation. The defendant shall deliver a fresh as amended statement of defence and counterclaim in action 06-CV-311208PD3 deleting references to the severed issues, and further to the particulars required and discussed further in these reasons. If the plaintiff commences a fresh action on a timely basis for the relief severed from action 06-CV-311208PD3 it shall be deemed to have been commenced on the date that the statement of defence and counterclaim in the Possession Action was delivered. I am prepared to conduct a case conference at the request of either party to set a timetable for the remaining litigation events in the main actions and the severed action. ...

Rae-Dawn Construction Ltd. v. Edmonton (City)
(1992), 10 CPC (3d) 356 (Alta. CA)

COTÉ JA (for the court): In 1986 and 1987, a number of construction suits were begun, two of them being builders' lien suits. They all involve the same construction failure, and unpaid construction bills. In 1987, by agreement those parties all sued the common construction insurers. In 1987, there was a motion to have all the suits tried together, but after discussion that was dropped. Instead, a master was simply asked to order that the construction suits be tried together, and he so ordered.

Since then, a large number of discoveries have been held in the construction suits, and they are close to being ready for trial, and have been so ready for about a year. Counsel for the insurers has taken no part in them. Much less has been done about discoveries in the insurance suit. If its discoveries are to plow any of the same ground, they will take a long time to complete. But little has been done with the insurers' counsel to discuss or agree on whether the construction suit discoveries can be used in the insurance suit. One of the parties to one construction suit accepted the money paid into court respecting his part of the insurance suit, and so he and his claim are now gone from the insurance suit. The insurers never were parties to any construction suit.

After those things occurred, one party common to both suits secured an order from a justice in chambers. The order directs that the construction suits cannot be tried until after judgment is given in the insurance suit. It also directs that the same trial judge is to try all the suits, and that the evidence from the insurance suit is to apply in the construction suits. Many of the other parties opposed that order, and now appeal.

It is desirable to try to do something to avoid duplication of proceedings or inconsistent verdicts. But in our view that cannot always be done, and should not be done where it unfairly retards litigation.

The construction suits are as much as six years old. It is entirely possible that at least one of the plaintiffs is free of blame for the construction failure. Many seem to have large prima facie debts owing to them, and the defence is essentially a set-off for the loss from the construction failure. Two of the suits are builders' lien actions, and the *Builders' Lien Act*, RSA 1980, c. B-12, contains a number of provisions suggesting that such suits should move speedily. One such plaintiff is no longer a party to the insurance suit, and so has no responsibility to keep it moving, and no interest whatever in it. While some issues overlap between the construction suits and the insurance suit, not all do. Even the issue of responsibility for the construction failure may not be legally identical in the two suits.

What is more, all parties agree that even under the order appealed some evidence would be led in the construction trial which would not be led in the earlier insurance trial. And as counsel differ somewhat, different arguments might well be heard at the two trials, even on supposedly identical issues. Therefore, even if the same trial judge heard both, inconsistent verdicts in the two trials would be possible.

The order appealed directs that the construction trial not start until after judgment has been rendered in the insurance suit. As there must be some waiting time between setting down and trial, and as one cannot tell how long judgment would be reserved in the insurance suit, that could easily add another year or two of delay. What is more, if the trial judgment in the insurance suit were appealed by any party (as seems fairly likely), that could add yet another two years' delay. Therefore, it might be years before the trial of the construction suits could begin.

Therefore, it seems to us that far too high a price has been paid in an uncertain attempt to achieve consistency and economy.

The construction suits should not have to wait for the insurance suit. The construction suits should be set down for trial as soon as they are ready, even though the insurance suit may well not be ready then. If they are tried before the insurance suit, or even by different judge, so be it.

Of course we do not forbid trial of the construction suits and the insurance suits at different times, but before the same judge. When the suit which is ready for trial later comes to be set down, if the judge who heard the other suits happens to be available, or can be made available, doubtless all concerned would prefer that she or he hear the later trial.

The respondents argued that the insurance suit can be got ready for trial as quickly as can the construction suits. As noted, we doubt that that is possible, and will not hold up the construction suits to see if that is so. But if it should happen that in fact the insurance suit is made ready as quickly, our decision does not preclude an application putting down both trials consecutively on the same trial list before the same trial judge.

However, it seems to us that trial together is not now possible. The parties differ in the construction and insurance suits, and many issues and pleadings are radically different. For example, in the insurance suit only the insurers are defendants. All the other players (except the one who has settled) are co-plaintiffs with no issues framed between them. When parties and issues differ significantly and there is no consent, we cannot imagine how simultaneous trials could be made to work. Nor is trial together what was directed by the order now appealed, nor is it the real thrust of any party's factum.

A large feature of trial together would presumably [be] the use of common evidence, rather than its segregation. In any event, that was ordered here. The evidence in the insurance suit is automatically to apply in the construction suits. How that would work is not entirely clear.

And we see some grave objections to that. First, the subcontractor who settled with the insurer (long before the motions in question were launched) would not take any part in the insurance suit. It could not object to the admissibility of evidence, nor cross-examine. That violates natural justice. Nor would it make sense to make that subcontractor again a party for that purpose, for its quarrel is with its former co-plaintiffs, not with the insurers who are the only defendants. Those insurers strenuously and correctly object to having to fight afresh in any respect with someone whom they have paid to go away and drop his claim.

Second, it is most unusual to tell a trial judge in advance what evidence he can and cannot admit. What evidence is proper often depends on the course of trial, and what evidence has preceded. No one can foresee all the twists and turns of a long trial. Ever since the Judicature Acts, civil trials have been before one trial judge who decides all the issues, factual, procedural and legal, and decides those issues in whatever order to him seems most fit.

Therefore, the order that the evidence in one trial apply maybe years later in a different trial with somewhat different players, appears to us to be unjust and unworkable.

The appeal is allowed and the order appealed is set aside.

V. INTERVENTION

The question whether, and if so in what circumstances, persons who are not parties should be permitted to intervene in litigation raises issues of safeguarding the public interest, party autonomy, and control over litigation, as well as issues of administrative and judicial efficiencies. Courts have historically favoured a very narrow approach to allowing non-parties to participate in litigation in an effort to preserve private party autonomy and control over litigation. However, where actions framed between private parties raise important issues of public policy, there may be room to ensure that the public interest (which may or may not correspond with the interests of the private parties) is represented and addressed. This issue has been most squarely raised in constitutional litigation, in which the very public nature of the matters in dispute has attracted attention from public interest groups wishing to assist the court in understanding the broader social, ethical, and political dimensions of the legal matters at stake.

A non-party can serve one of two roles as intervenor in a case. A party can be granted intervenor status to intervene as another interested party in the litigation, with all the rights and liabilities of the other parties. Alternatively, a party can be granted intervenor status to act as a friend of the court (amicus curiae). An amicus curiae informs the court about a particular position or interest not represented by the parties. An amicus curiae does not have the same full participatory rights in the litigation as do other parties (that is, usually no rights to file pleadings and evidence or examine witnesses). It is there for informational purposes only.

The legal process for intervention differs somewhat among the provinces. Manitoba, New Brunswick, Ontario, and Prince Edward Island have similarly worded statutory mechanisms that guide a court in determining whether or not to grant intervenor status to a particular party in a particular case. (See Manitoba rule 13.01, New Brunswick rule 15.02, Ontario rule 13.01, and PEI rules 13.01 and 13.02). The following case is an example of the process for deciding intervenor status in those provinces.

Canadian Blood Services v. Freeman
2004 CarswellOnt 4514 (SCJ)

MASTER BEAUDOIN:

Nature of the Motion

[1] The Canadian Aids Society ("CAS") moves for an order granting it leave to intervene as an added party in the within action, including the counterclaim, with the full rights of a party pursuant to Rule 13.01(1) of the *Rules of Civil Procedure*. In the alternative, CAS seeks an order granting leave to intervene as a friend of the Court pursuant to Rule 13.02 of the Rules.

Background

[2] Canadian Blood Services ("CBS") is responsible for collecting, processing and distributing blood products in Canada with the exception of Quebec. As part of its

screening process in the collection of blood products, a CBS representative will ask each donor to answer standard questions prior to donating blood. The questions are designed to identify donors whose blood might pose a risk to recipients. Question 18 addresses only intended male donors. That question asks whether the intended donor has had sex with a man, even once, since 1977.

[3] Kyle Freeman is a former blood donor. CBS launched this action for damages after Mr. Freeman allegedly falsely and negligently responded to the questionnaire that he had not had sex with a man, not even once, since 1977. According to the claim issued in this action, Mr. Freeman later contacted CBS anonymously to advise that he had lied when he had answered that question. CBS seeks damages in the amount of $100,000.00 for Mr. Freeman's alleged negligent misrepresentation.

. . .

The Intervenor

[8] In his affidavit, Paul Lapierre, the Executive Director of CAS, states that CAS was formed in 1985 as the national umbrella group for local AIDS service organizations across Canada, including the AIDS Committee of Toronto ("ACT") and AIDS Vancouver ("AV"). Many of CAS's member groups have existed since the emergence of AIDS in Canada in 1982. Some of CAS's member groups emerged from local gay and lesbian organizations which turned their attention to AIDS when it first appeared. CAS currently comprises over 120 local, regional and national AIDS service organizations.

[9] CAS's mandate includes public education on HIV and AIDS to prevent transmission of HIV and to advocate for those people who are HIV positive. CAS has a long history of participation in consultations, both formal and informal, with the Plaintiff, the Canadian Red Cross Society (former national blood transfusion service administrator) and representatives of Health Canada regarding the safety of the blood supply in Canada.

[10] CAS has intervened in the Supreme Court of Canada in cases which involved gay and lesbian equality rights, specifically section 15(1) of the *Canadian Charter of Rights and Freedoms*. These cases included *Vriend v. Alberta* [1998 CarswellAlta 210 (SCC)] and *Little Sisters Book & Art Emporium v. Canada (Minister of Justice)* [2000 CarswellBC 2442 (SCC)].

[11] CAS has also intervened at the Supreme Court of Canada in *R. v. Latimer* [2001 CarswellSask 4 (SCC)] because assisted suicide was an issue of some importance to people in the last stages of AIDS and one in which CAS had developed a position paper. CAS also sought and was granted intervenor status in *Hodge v. Canada (Minister of Human Resources Development)* [2004 CarswellNat 3695 (SCC)] which raised issues of entitlement to a survivor pension for common law spouses under the Canada Pension Plan. This issue was of importance to people with HIV and AIDS who need the additional financial assistance provided by a survivor pension.

[12] CAS has intervened in other courts and tribunals on behalf of the gay and lesbian community and persons with HIV/AIDS. ...

[13] In 1993, CAS was granted standing at the Commission of Inquiry of the blood system in Canada (the "Krever Inquiry") ... .

[14] In 1994, CAS was an applicant before the Ontario Court (General Division), against the province of Ontario and the CRCS. In that proceeding CAS was seeking to prevent the identities of donors of frozen blood samples from being released to public health authorities and tested for HIV without the consent of donors. In the *Vriend v. Alberta, Little Sisters v. Canada* and *R v. Latimer*, CAS was allowed to file a factum and present oral submissions in all the appeals. In *Hodge*, CAS's intervention was limited to filing a factum. It appears that CAS was granted the right to file a factum and make oral submissions in the *Hodder* and *Boulais* cases however those cases settled before the appeals were heard. From the record, the only cases where CAS was directly involved in developing the record before the Court were the 1994 matter, wherein CAS was the applicant, and the Krever Inquiry. With respect to the latter, the Attorney General of Canada notes that the test for standing at a public inquiry is different from Rule 13 of the *Rules of Civil Procedure*. Although CBS submits that the Lapierre affidavit fails to define CAS's legal status, its membership or its precise mandate, I take notice that other courts have recognized CAS as an organization entitled to seek standing. ...

• • •

Intervention

[21] Rule 13 allows a non-party to intervene in a proceeding and it provides for two distinct forms of intervention; leave to intervene as an added party; and leave to intervene as a friend of the Court. In this case, CAS seeks firstly to intervene as an added party and, alternatively, to intervene as a friend of the Court. The Attorney General of Canada submits that CAS might intervene only as a friend of the Court. CBS argues that CAS does not meet the test for intervention in either case.

[22] Rule 13.01 provides:

(1) A person who is not a party to a proceeding may move for leave to intervene as an added party if the persons claims,

(a) an interest in the subject matter of the proceeding;

(b) that the person may be adversely affected by a judgment in the proceeding; or

(c) that there exists between the person and one or more of the parties to

(2) On the motion, the court shall consider whether the intervention will unduly delay or prejudice the determination of the rights of the parties to the proceeding and the court may add the person as a party to the proceeding and may make such order as is just.

[23] Rule 13.02 states:

Any person may, with leave of a judge or at the invitation of the presiding judge or master, and without becoming a party to the proceeding, intervene as a friend of the court for the purpose of rendering assistance to the court by way of argument.

[24] In determining whether or not a moving party should be granted leave to intervene as an added party, it must be noted that the moving party need only meet any one of the criteria set out in 13.01(1)(a), (b) or (c). Once that is done, the Court must consider "whether the intervention will unduly delay or prejudice the determination of the rights of the parties." If the Court is then satisfied by the moving party that there will be

no such undue delay or prejudice, the Court can exercise its discretion in determining if the moving party should be added as a party and if so, on what terms it considers just.

[25] As Molloy J in *Trempe v. Reybroek* (2002), 57 OR (3d) 786 (Ont. SCJ) stated at page 796:

> Rule 13.01 contains a built-in safeguard in the form of judicial discretion. The right to inter-
> vene is not automatic upon meeting one of the three tests set out in the sub-clauses of the
> rule. Rather, there is an overriding discretion set out in rule 13.01(2) based on whether the
> intervention would "delay or prejudice the determination of the rights of the parties to the
> proceeding." Further, the intervention may be granted on such terms as the court considers
> just. That might extend to granting full rights to participate on the same basis as any party,
> but might also be more restrictive. For example, the intervening party might be restricted
> to argument only with no right to file evidence. The broad judicial discretion afforded by
> this sub-rule prevents the addition of a party if this would cause an injustice to the existing
> parties.

[26] There are two significant principles to consider in deciding this issue. The first is that greater latitude is to be given in intervenor motions in cases involving *Charter* chal-
lenges since such challenges generally involve a greater public interest. (See *Peel (Regional Municipality) v. Great Atlantic & Pacific Co. of Canada* (1990), 74 OR (2d) 164 (Ont. CA) at p. 167, (1990), 2 CRR (2d) 327 (Ont. CA), and *Halpern v. Toronto (City)* (2000), 51 OR (3d) 742 (Ont. Div. Ct.) at para. 16.) The second is the distinction between intervenor status at an appellate level and intervenor status before a Court of first instance. At this level, and in this particular proceeding, the proposed intervenor is asking for input into the formation of the record. As noted by Lang J in *Halpern*, "the potential scope for intervention is far greater where the intervenor wishes to participate fully in setting the rec-
ord. Such an intervention would potentially result in dramatic increase in delay and expense for all parties."

[27] The *Halpern* decision is of considerable guidance since Justice Lang thoroughly canvassed the relevant case law. At paragraph 21, Justice Lang refers to the criteria in Rule 13.01 and sets out the following test:

(1) Does the proposed intervenor have sufficient, direct "interest" in this *Charter* challenge judicial review?

(2) What useful contribution could the proposed intervenor make to the proceeding?

(3) If such interest and useful contribution are established, would the intervenor's involvement either prejudice or delay the determination of the rights of the parties to the proceeding?

(4) Is any such prejudice or delay counterbalanced by the useful contribution of the proposed intervenor?

(5) What terms or conditions might be imposed on the intervention to ensure that the goals are met of useful contribution without undue delay or prejudice?

[28] On the facts of that case, Justice Lang found that there was a sufficient interest on the part of EGALE to be granted intervenor status as an added party on that applica-

tion for judicial review. For that reason she did not have to consider sub-paragraphs (b) and (c) of Rule 13.01(1).

Does CAS Have an Interest?

[29] In determining whether or not a proposed intervenor has a sufficient "interest" in the subject matter of the proceeding, it is helpful to review the case law and the following statements are of assistance:

- The intervenors' interest must be a public interest but also one that is over and above that of the general public.
- The proposed intervenor must do more than state that it is an organization that is representative of certain groups across the country that agrees with one of the parties.
- Experience as an interest group is insufficient to meet the test.
- Witness experience is not helpful.
- Ability to give expert evidence on particular matters is non-determinative since that activity can be more appropriately undertaken by providing the expert testimony on behalf of one of the parties.
- Past role as an advocate and as an intervenor may not be enough.
- Experience as a lobbyist is insufficient to meet the test; and some cases add that lobbyists should not be given access to the courts.

[30] Rule 13.01(1)(a) only requires that "an interest" be demonstrated by the proposed intervenor and the case law requires that interest to be "direct." In *Halpern*, Justice Lang reviewed EGALE'S experience as an interest group and concluded that its interest extended beyond its involvement as a lobbyist or as a witness. She noted that EGALE had developed institutional knowledge and "represented a broad based spectrum of gays and lesbians across Canada" and that its "members would be directly affected by the outcome of this proceeding in one manner or another. It has also shown appreciation for diverse perspectives of gays and lesbian on equality issues." The impact on its members was sufficient to meet the test of an "interest in the subject matter."

[31] Notwithstanding its other deficiencies, the affidavit of Paul Lapierre discloses that CAS is an umbrella group for approximately 120 local, regional and national AIDS service organizations. CAS represents a broad spectrum of blood consumers and suppliers, same-sex oriented or otherwise. It also represents people with HIV. Because they are immune suppressed, they are more susceptible to infections. CAS's mandate includes public education on HIV and AIDS to prevent the transmission of HIV. Because HIV and AIDS have had a disproportionate impact on the gay community, Mr. Lapierre deposes that CAS has always had an interest in sexual orientation equality issues. CAS and its member groups have been involved in messages to promote the safety of Canada's blood supply.

[32] Mr. Freeman is a gay male who does not have AIDS. No other party to this proceeding represents the interests of the groups that CAS represents. The screening criteria used by CBS will impact CAS's members who are consumers of blood products and its public education mandate. I am satisfied that CAS and its members will be directly

affected by the outcome of this proceeding and that CAS has met the first branch of the test set out in Rule 13.01.

Useful Contribution

[33] Following *Halpern*, I must now consider what useful contribution that CAS can provide to the proceeding. Once again, the case law provides some direction and I note the following:

- The proposed intervenor cannot simply repeat another party's evidence or argument or give a slightly different emphasis on arguments presented by the parties. The fact that intervenors might be prepared to make a more sweeping constitutional argument does not mean that they will be added as a party to the dispute.
- The fact that one party to the proceeding may lack resources is insufficient to advance an intervenor application. In this case, Mr. Freeman's counsel points to his client's lack of resources and expertise. In *Halpern*, Justice Lang determined that intervention is not granted simply to provide help to a party. As she said at paragraph 30:

> If a party has difficulty with resources, such a difficulty must be addressed in other ways. Of course, nothing in these reasons would preclude EGALE's counsel or other likeminded counsel from rendering assistance to counsel for the applicants if they so choose.

- It's insufficient for a proposed intervenor to promise not to overlap or duplicate any of the arguments from materials of the original parties. The onus is on them to persuade the Court of the significance of what they will be contributing rather than the significance of what they will not be doing.

[34] The comments of Justice Epstein in the *M. v. H.* decision (supra) are helpful. She states at pp. 79-80:

> Typically, when intervention is sought, the nature of the interest and potential contribution of the proposed intervenors is put forward to enable the court to have some idea how they would fit into the case. ... The moving parties have presented the court with no information as to what contribution they can make to the legal arguments in this proceeding, over and above that which will be made by the parties.

Finally she concludes:

> The intervention of third parties into a private dispute, in particular such a personal one, should not be lightly entertained. An intervention adds to the costs and complexity of the litigation, regardless of agreements to restrict submissions. It always constitutes an inconvenience that ought not to be imposed on the parties except under compelling circumstances, which do not exist in this case.

[35] These comments are echoed in the *Halpern* decision where Justice Lang noted the distinction that needs to be made when a proposed intervenor is seeking to have input into the formation of the record. In the end, the proposed intervenor has to dem-

onstrate that the Court's ability to determine the constitutional question in issue will be enhanced by their intervention as a party.

[36] I have closely examined the evidence that has been placed by CAS in support of the relief that it seeks. CAS seeks to be added as a party with all of the attendant rights and responsibilities including, but not limited to, the rights to adduce evidence and to make written and oral submissions on the legal issues in dispute. It seeks to participate as a party on discoveries although it promises not to duplicate questions. It asks for leave to file expert reports and call expert witnesses at trial.

[37] At paragraph 21 of his affidavit, Mr. Lapierre states that CAS will be able to provide this the Court with "legal argument on the issues relevant to the case." He repeats this at paragraph 35 where he says that CAS's submissions will focus on the legal arguments and any policy considerations that CAS believes to be of assistance to the Court. He adds that CAS may decide not to participate in the examinations for discovery except to the extent that they deal with the overall equality of rights and policy arguments. Ms. LeFebour, in her affidavit, states she recognized many of the documents listed in the affidavits of documents filed in these proceedings and that CAS has extensive knowledge of these documents. She adds at paragraph 30 that "the extensive institutional knowledge CAS could provide regarding these documents would not otherwise be provided by the parties to these proceedings."

[38] Nowhere in its affidavit material does CAS identify any experts that it proposes to call at trial. No additional documents have been identified by Ms. LeFebour. While Mr. Lapierre states that CAS may or may not participate in discovery, its questions would be limited to issues involving discrimination and policy issues. These are the very issues raised by Mr. Freeman in his statement of defence. Mr. Freeman supports CAS's application as intervenor because he recognizes and acknowledges that CAS has resources and expertise that he and his counsel do not possess. As noted in *Halpern* (supra), that is insufficient to grant an intervenor full party status. In that case, Lang J limited EGALE to filing an affidavit on 2 issues that were not being addressed by any of the parties.

Conclusion

[39] Although CAS has demonstrated that it has a direct interest in this action, I cannot conclude that CAS can make a useful contribution to the development of the record in this proceeding by adding them as a party to the action. If it has additional expertise and resources, CAS can make this available to Mr. Freeman and his counsel or provide expert testimony at trial. Accordingly, I order that CAS be allowed to intervene as a friend of the Court pursuant to Rule 13.02 subject to the following terms:

1) that CAS take the record as it is and not be permitted to file further material without consent of the other parties or without leave of the trial judge;
2) that it not seek or be subject to an award of costs;
3) that its written arguments not duplicate the arguments of any other parties to the proceedings. They not exceed 20 pages in length unless otherwise ordered by the trial judge;
4) that it adhere to any case management timetables set by this Court;

5) that the time allocated for oral submissions be limited to 30 minutes or less otherwise permitted by the trial judge.

[40] If I do not hear from the parties in writing on or before November 30th, 2004, I
would direct that there should be no costs.

Order accordingly.

Contrast *Canadian Blood Services* with the decision below. How does the nature and context
of the case affect a court's granting of intervenor status?

Hollinger Inc. v. Ravelston Corp.
(2008), 89 OR (3d) 721 (Ont. CA)

JURIANSZ JA: [1] The plaintiffs in this action obtained a Mareva injunction against
Conrad Black and Barbara Amiel-Black. The motion judge made a protective order sealing the motion material making it unavailable to the public. Bell Globemedia Publishing
Inc. ("the Globe") moved to intervene to set aside the protective order. The motion judge
dismissed the Globe's motion. The Globe appeals. ...

· · ·

Facts

[4] The motion judge was case managing the action of the plaintiffs (referred to collectively as "Hollinger") against the Blacks and others. At the time, Mr. Black was facing
a number of highly publicized criminal charges in the US, and his trial was scheduled to
begin in March, 2007.

[5] On August 18, 2006, the motion judge made two orders on motions brought by
Hollinger without notice to the Blacks. In the first order, the motion judge granted a Mareva injunction against the Blacks freezing their assets worldwide. Hollinger was required
to give notice to the Blacks and then apply to have the order confirmed within ten days.
The order contained a term that "the Motion Record, the Affidavits filed and this Order
shall remain sealed until the return of this motion [after service of the order on the
Blacks]." The parties refer to this term as the "sealing order." In the second order, the motion judge ordered "that the Motion material is hereby subject to a protective Order,
subject to further Order of this court." The parties refer to this as the "protective order."

[6] When the Blacks received notice of the Mareva order, they brought a motion to
set it aside. Their motion and Hollinger's motion to continue the Mareva order were both
scheduled to be heard on September 29, 2006. The motion judge made an interim order
on August 29, 2006 continuing both the Mareva order and the protective order to September 29, 2006.

[7] On August 30, 2006 the Globe learned about the August 18, 2006 orders. It filed
a motion seeking:

1) intervenor status for the purpose of challenging the sealing and protective orders;
2) permission to have its counsel and Deputy Editor, upon giving appropriate confidentiality undertakings to the court, review the sealed material in order to provide and receive instructions and to permit counsel to make informed submissions on its motion;
3) to set aside the sealing and protective orders, and in the alternative, to vary the sealing orders so that they limited public access to the motion material to the minimal extent possible. ...

. . .

Denial of Intervenor Status

[36] While the decision to recognize an intervenor is largely discretionary, in my view the motion judge erred in principle in refusing to grant the Globe intervenor status. He failed to give sufficient weight to the Globe's constitutionally guaranteed freedom of the press and to the fact the Globe sought standing to assert a position coincident with the public's interest that would not be raised otherwise.

[37] Public access to the court system promotes confidence in the judicial system and enables oversight of the functioning of the courts. In this case, the parties to the action asked the motion judge for an order that the protective order continue. The public had an interest in whether it was continued or set aside, but that interest was not represented. Except for the Globe, there was no one, first to raise the issue whether the protective order should be set aside and then to advocate the position that it unnecessarily violated the open court principle.

[38] In *Dagenais*, Lamer CJC set out general guidelines for the Crown, the accused, the media, and the courts in criminal cases where a party has applied for a publication ban pending the completion of trial. He addressed the role of the court at 872:

> Upon a motion for a ban under the common law rule, the court should give standing to the media who seek standing (according to the rules of criminal procedure and the established common law principles) and follow the general guidelines for practice set out in ... these reasons.

[39] This edict rests comfortably with the *Rules of Civil Procedure*. Rule 13 allows a person who is not a party to move for leave to intervene where he or she "may be adversely affected" by a judgment. The appellant brought its motion relying on the guarantee of freedom of expression including freedom of the press in s. 2(b) of the *Charter*. I have no doubt the Globe's constitutional rights were "adversely affected" by the protective order.

[40] Given these factors and their importance, the motion judge erred by refusing the Globe intervenor status for the purpose of dealing with the question whether the protective order should be continued or set aside.

[41] It may be suggested that the error was one of form rather than substance since the motion judge did allow the Globe to make submissions. I do not accept the suggestion. In my view, the motion judge's perception that the Globe lacked sufficient connection to

challenge the sealing order would have undermined the force of the Globe's position. The procedure he adopted and the conclusions he reached might have been different had he appreciated the Globe's status. It might have been less likely that he would have lost sight of the fact the onus was on the respondents. The Globe, as an intervenor, would have had a stronger claim to review the material for the limited purpose of making informed argument. If the rights of an intervening party were at stake, the judge might have been persuaded to undertake a review of the material. If the judge had undertaken a review, he may have concluded that some or all of it could be released.

[42] I would conclude that the motion judge's refusal to accord intervenor status to the Globe was not merely an error of form, and must be set aside. ...

NOTES AND QUESTIONS

1. How might rulings with respect to costs and imposing limits on the role of intervenors affect the willingness and ability of interest groups to meaningfully participate in litigation, as well as the willingness of the courts to permit intervention?

2. For a useful overview of the law of intervention in Manitoba, see *Sawatzky v. Riverview Health Centre*, [1998] MJ No. 574 (QB), a Charter case about the rights of health care facilities to make "do not resuscitate" orders without patient consent. Rule 8.01(1)(c) of Nova Scotia's *Civil Procedure Rules* and rule 7.05(1)(c) of Newfoundland and Labrador's *Rules of the Supreme Court* are nearly identical and allow intervenors if "that person has a right to intervene under a statute or rule."

3. Alberta and British Columbia have not yet adopted stand-alone rules for intervention but instead rely on the breadth of discretion built into the general rules, as well as a common law approach, to measure a court's discretion to add intervenors to a case. Compare whether or not the approach in these two provinces differs in the following two cases from the statutory approach in the previous two cases.

Athabasca Tribal Council v. Alberta (Minister of Environmental Protection)
[1998] 67 Alta. L Rep. (3d) 232 (QB)

MEDHURST J:

Background

[1] This is an application on behalf of the Canadian Association of Petroleum Producers, ("CAPP") for leave to intervene in the proceedings between The Athabasca Tribal Council ("ATC") and The Province of Alberta. The original action concerns exploration approvals granted to Rio Alto Exploration Ltd. ("Rio Alto") pursuant to the *Mines and Minerals Act*, RSA 1980, c. M-15 and the accompanying regulations. The exploration approvals were granted in respect of lands within the registered trapping areas of the ATC. The ATC has challenged the land use decisions made by the Province based on their treaty rights and s. 35(1) of the *Constitution*. ...

CAPP's Position

[2] CAPP bases its application for intervenor status on the fact that it is an organization which represents 170 producer members who produce 95% of the oil and gas produced in Canada. CAPP claims that its members will be substantially affected if the relief sought by the ATC is granted and that any such relief will have far reaching impact on the industry. Furthermore, CAPP claims that as the representative of the oil and gas industry as a whole, it can provide the Court with submissions which will be of assistance in weighing the competing values and interests before the Court. According to CAPP, neither the Public Respondents nor Rio Alto can sufficiently represent the views and concerns of the industry as a whole with respect to the issues raised by this litigation. Finally, CAPP claims that the justification required in a s. 35(1) analysis is analogous to a s. 1 analysis under the *Charter* and, therefore, the Court should be more willing to grant the application for intervenor status.

ATC's Position

[3] The ATC opposes CAPP's application. The ATC claims that CAPP has nothing to add to the action by virtue of its position in the industry. The ATC has characterized the issue before the Court as a very narrow one, affecting only the rights of the one named oil and gas exploration company, Rio Alto. The ATC further argues that any evidence regarding the oil and gas exploration regime in Alberta could effectively be put before the Court by Rio Alto, an experienced and sophisticated industry member. Simply put, the ATC maintains that the inclusion of CAPP as an intervenor in the action will complicate matters unnecessarily and serve no useful purpose. The ATC strongly disagrees with CAPP's assertion that the justification analysis required by s. 35(1) is analogous to a s. 1 consideration in *Charter* cases. The ATC argues that Treaty and Aboriginal rights are unique in nature and they are outside of the rights recognized by the *Charter*. Consequently, the same standards and issues should not be applied in this case as would be applied in a *Charter* case.

Analysis

[4] Whether or not a party can intervene in an action is a matter that is to be decided at the discretion of the judge hearing the application. While many Canadian jurisdictions have rules which specify conditions in which intervenor status will be granted, Alberta has no such rules and reference must be had to the common law. The test developed in the common law is essentially that a party should only be granted intervenor status if the party will be directly affected by the ultimate decision of the case and/or where the presence of the party is necessary for the Court to properly decide the matter.

[5] The ATC submits that the judicial review at issue will not directly affect the legal interests of CAPP and therefore CAPP should not be granted intervenor status. The ATC argues that the relief they claim is limited to relief against Rio Alto and the effects of the judicial review will go no further. CAPP asserts that if the relief sought in the judicial review is granted, it will affect the ability of individual CAPP members to obtain approvals to conduct seismic activities on the lands covered by Treaty 8. Their position is that while

the relief sought is as against only Rio Alto, the precedential effect of the granting of that relief will have wide reaching impact on all of the industry members that CAPP represents.

[6] In making a determination on this issue, a two step approach is appropriate: "The first step is to characterize the subject-matter or the nature of the proceeding. The second step is to determine what interest the proposed intervenor has in it." (P. Muldoon *Law of Intervention Status and Practice* (Ontario: Canada Law Books Inc. 1989) at 40.) The subject matter of this proceeding is a series of exploration approvals granted by the Minister of Environmental Protection to Rio Alto. The ATC is seeking an order which would require the Minister to consult with the ATC with respect to the scope, nature and extent of the impact of exploration activities within the lands covered by Treaty 8. The ATC is essentially asking that no exploration approvals be granted by the Minister until they are consulted.

[7] The ATC claims that CAPP has no interest in the subject matter because it only affects one exploration company, namely, Rio Alto. CAPP contends that the interests of all of its members could be affected by the outcome of the judicial review requested by the ATC if the ATC is successful.

[8] If the ATC is successful against Rio Alto then, given the application of the *Stare Decisis* doctrine in our judicial system, it is likely that the decision would be determinative in future cases. For all intents and purposes, the decision in this case will determine what procedures exploration companies will have to follow in the future in order to get Ministerial approval for exploration activities on Treaty lands. If the ATC is successful and the orders they are requesting are granted, it is difficult to see how a different exploration company could then get Ministerial approval for exploration on Treaty land without going through the same consultations that were required of Rio Alto. Every exploration company that has interests in the expansive areas covered by Treaty 8 would likely be affected by a decision in favour of the ATC. CAPP therefore has an interest in the litigation by virtue of the fact that it is the organization responsible for advancing the interests of its constituent members.

[9] It is true that the decision regarding the matter as between the ATC and Rio Alto will not have a direct affect on the legal rights of the corporate entity known as CAPP. CAPP does not itself engage in oil and gas exploration in Northern Alberta. It is a organization that is designed to protect and advance the interests of its members who are oil and gas exploration companies and, regardless of any orders granted in the matter between the ATC and Rio Alto, CAPP will continue to exist and operate just as before. Its constituent members however, may not be able to continue to operate as they did before. They may be adversely affected. Given that the members of CAPP have an interest in the litigation, and given that CAPP is a body designed to protect and advance the interests of its members, it appears logical to find that CAPP has an interest sufficient to grant it intervenor status. Comments made in the decision of the Ontario Court of Appeal in *Schofield v. Ontario (Minister of Consumer & Commercial Relations)* (1980), 112 DLR (3d) 132 (Ont. CA) at 141 apply to this point:

> As an example of one such situation, one can envisage an applicant with no interest in the
> outcome of an appeal in any such direct sense but with an interest, because of the particular

concerns which the applicant has or represents, such that the applicant is in an especially advantageous and perhaps even unique position to illuminate some aspect or facet of the appeal which ought to be considered by the Court in reaching its decision but which, but for the applicant's intervention, might not receive any attention or prominence, given the quite different interests of the immediate parties to the appeal.

[10] In the present case, Rio Alto is going to be most concerned about its immediate predicament respecting the oil and gas exploration approvals that it had been granted and are now under scrutiny. It may not be in the best position to inform the Court of the impact of any potential orders on the industry as a whole over an extended period of time. CAPP is in such a position and it is an important issue that represents the other side of the position advanced by the ATC. Based on the nature of this case and the fact that CAPP is the organization that represents affected industry members, it is reasonable that CAPP be granted intervenor status on the grounds that it has (or represents those who have) a direct interest in the outcome of the hearing.

[11] CAPP advances the position that a s. 35 justification is analogous to the process in a s. 1 analysis under the *Charter*. Consequently, they argue, the Court should be more willing to grant intervenor status. The authorities are consistent in the application of the law with respect to intervenors in *Charter* matters. For example, in *Alberta Sports & Recreation Assn. for the Blind v. Edmonton (City)* (1993), 20 CPC (3d) 101 (Alta. QB) at 103, Ritter J said:

> The courts have consistently stated that the application of s. 1 of the *Charter* requires evidence. If that evidence is either within the abilities of a proposed intervenor or its adduction can be assisted by the proposed intervenor, then it is not unreasonable to presume that the difficulties with application of s. 1 of the *Charter* can more readily be avoided.

Similarly in *CLC v. Bhindi* (1985), 17 DLR (4th) 193 (BC CA) at 201, Anderson JA stated:

> In my view, it is imperative in dealing with important constitutional issues and, in particular, Charter issues requiring the production of an evidentiary record, that the trial court be empowered to grant" intervenor" status.

Further, at 204, he said:

> I would add on this point, that it is important in dealing with Charter issues raised for the first time, that the courts have the assistance of argument from all segments of the community. The courts should not resist but should welcome such assistance.

Finally at 205, he said:

> While no doubt the intervention of the appellant will add to the length and complexity of the trial, the additional expense is, on balance, justified. Issues relating to s. 1 of the Charter cannot and should not be addressed in a vacuum.

[12] The ATC argues that principles which apply to *Charter* inquiries do not apply in the case of a s. 35 analysis. The ATC relies on authority which characterizes Treaty and

Aboriginal rights as unique and they argue that this uniqueness prevents the application of any authority that deals expressly with the *Charter* and s. 1. ...

[13] ... Clearly, many of the same considerations come into play in determining whether there is a justification for an infringement on Aboriginal rights as in determining whether there is justification for an infringement on an individual's *Charter* rights. Consequently, the Courts should be more willing to permit intervenors where it would assist the Court in adducing evidence as to the justification or lack thereof.

[14] Neither party would dispute the statement that these are important matters which have the potential for long term effects on the Aboriginals and the oil and gas industry. CAPP brings to the litigation a unique perspective, that of the industry as a whole. They are likely in the best position to inform the Court of the impact of any decision on the industry as a whole. That is important evidence for the Court to have in order to make a proper determination of the issue before it. Given that CAPP has an interest in the outcome of the litigation, and given the importance of the question to be determined, CAPP should be granted intervenor status in the present matter. The Order as requested is therefore granted.

Application granted.

Mullins v. Levy
2002 CarswellBC 2222 (SC)

HOLMES J: [1] The British Columbia Schizophrenic Society ("BCSS") is a non-profit society serving the interests of persons seeking to alleviate the suffering caused by schizophrenia through support to families, public education, research and advocacy.

[2] The BCSS is an organization knowledgeable regarding the difficulties and issues faced by persons suffering schizophrenia or serious mental illnesses.

[3] The BCSS applies for an order pursuant to the Court's inherent jurisdiction to grant it leave to intervene in this action in respect of the Notice of Constitutional Question Particulars dated April 9, 2002.

[4] The BCSS seeks only to participate in the proceeding in respect of the issues raised by the plaintiff seeking to have certain of the provisions of the *Mental Health Act*, RSBC 1996, c. 288, declared invalid or alternatively "read down." Certain specific sections challenged by the plaintiff allow for the involuntary taking in custody and detaining for admission and treatment of patients suffering from a mental disorder.

[5] The established guidelines for consideration canvassed in relevant authorities include:

(a) whether the intervenor can bring a different perspective to the issues;

(b) whether the intervenor has a special interest in the outcome;

(c) whether the intervenor could make a contribution to the resolution of the issues;

(d) whether the intervenor will impose no additional burden on the litigation.

. . .

[6] The application is supported by the affidavit evidence of it's executive director Gary Glacken and by a psychologist John Grey who is also a director. The plaintiff filed an affidavit in opposition.

[7] None of the defendant's oppose the application.

[8] The plaintiff opposes the application on the basis the BCSS is not an appropriate interest group; the health concerns of the BCSS do not arise in this action; all constitutional issues will be adequately dealt with by the Attorney General; intervention by the BCSS will delay or prolong the trial without useful purpose.

[9] The BCSS has a membership of 1600 persons comprised of those suffering from schizophrenia and their relatives. They are concerned with the plight of persons in the community suffering serious mental illnesses.

[10] The BCSS has no direct interest in the plaintiff's primary cause of action against the defendants for damages. It certainly has an interest in the plaintiff's application to strike down the impugned provisions of the *Mental Health Act* concerning the involuntary apprehension, detention and treatment of schizophrenics and other serious mentally ill persons.

[11] The concern of the BCSS is simple and direct. If the impugned sections of the *Mental Health Act* are restricted or declared invalid many persons who suffer serious mental illnesses will be denied essential medical treatment and care.

[12] The perspective the BCSS can bring to the consideration of the constitutionality of the impugned provisions of the *Act* is that of a significant disadvantaged group within society whose well being requires medical treatment at times and in circumstances when the nature of their mental illness requiring treatment impairs or distorts their ability for rational consent.

[13] The issue of the constitutionality of the impugned sections of the *Mental Health Act* are secondary to the plaintiff's main cause of action. The constitutional issues the plaintiff has raised go beyond the *lis* between the parties to the action and are of primary interest to BCSS as a public law issue.

[14] Intervenor status ought to be more liberally granted to an interest group in these circumstances.

Special Interest in the Outcome

[15] I am satisfied the BCSS has a special interest in the outcome of the constitutional issue. Should the impugned sections be struck the lack of provision for involuntary admission and treatment will certainly impact upon their membership and the wider constituency of mentally ill persons who derive benefit and protection from the existing legislation.

Contribution to the Resolution of Issues

[16] The BCSS has knowledge of the practical application of the Mental Health Act and the needs of the mentally ill to access treatment. The BCSS has a history of research and advocacy which may benefit the court in addressing the wider public law issue raised by the plaintiff's constitutional challenge to the *Mental Health Act*.

Additional Burden of the Litigation

[17] The BCSS does not seek to raise any new issue in this action. It restricts it's application to an issue raised by the plaintiff. The parties apparently agreed that the time necessary to address the constitutional issues is one week.

[18] The BCSS will apparently seek to call evidence that in direct is unlikely to be lengthy. Counsel for the plaintiff anticipates it may be necessary to cross examine extensively. I have difficulty as to why an unduly lengthy cross examination would be necessary given counsel's reputation for concise and relevant questioning.

[19] I am of the view that the defendants will co-ordinate their evidence and submissions on the constitutional issues so that the trial will not be unduly lengthened, nor will leave to the BCSS to intervene impose a burden on the litigation.

[20] I would assume that absent the BCSS as an intervenor it is likely the defendants or the Attorney General might well call evidence similar to that contemplated in any event. I have every confidence the parties are prepared to avoid duplication in this matter and the court will have the overall benefit of focused submissions.

Conclusion

[21] The BCSS is granted leave to intervene in the trial of the issues raised by the particulars of Constitutional Question. The intervenor will be permitted to adduce evidence, cross examine witnesses and make submissions in respect of those issues.

[22] I make no finding as to the admissibility of any expert evidence, or the expertise of any witness presented, on behalf of the intervenor. Expert evidence will be advanced and challenged in the usual manner.

Application granted.

NOTES AND QUESTIONS

1. Philip Bryden articulates three arguments against taking a liberal approach to intervenors in "Public Interest Intervention in the Courts" (1987), 66 *Can. Bar Rev.* 490, at 513:

The first are what might be described as arguments of principle. What is considered objectionable about public interest intervention is that it is believed to be incompatible with the proper functioning of the judicial system, or that it is unfair to the parties, who may be deprived of control over the litigation. The second type of objection can be termed arguments of practicality. Public interest intervention is not considered undesirable in and of itself, but only to the extent that it represents an unproductive use of the court's time and energy. The third type of argument is one of balance. The concern here is not that intervention is wrong or impractical but that it will not work well enough, so that the courts will be presented with an unequal or unrepresentative sample of the views of members of the public. I do not think that these objections can be dismissed out of hand, but I do believe that they must be weighed carefully in light of the positive contribution that public interest intervention can make to the process of judicial law-making.

Do you find these arguments persuasive? Are Bryden's arguments being put into practice in all provinces in the same fashion, and to the same effect?

VI. EXPERT WITNESSES

A. Introduction

In this section we consider the evidence of expert opinion in civil cases. The general rule is that opinion evidence is excluded: witnesses testify as to their observations and the trier of fact decides what to make of all the evidence in deciding the case. Often, however, relevant evidence cannot be understood or properly evaluated without the assistance of an expert. For example, motor vehicle accident cases may require a witness who can explain the way in which a particular vehicle will operate under specific road conditions. In tort cases involving medical injuries, medical experts are called by both parties to prove or disprove the cause of action and damages. Most civil trials involve expert evidence. Rules of civil procedure anticipate this and require disclosure of the names, qualification, and substance of an expert opinion in advance of trial so that parties can prepare for trial in a more effective and informed manner (see, for example: Nova Scotia rule 55; Ontario rule 53.03; and British Columbia rule 40A). In many, the outcome—whether by way of negotiated settlement or judicial ruling—will be significantly determined by expert reports and testimony. The testimony of experts is subject to detailed and complex rules of evidence law; our coverage is introductory. The legal "test" for admission of expert evidence is simple to articulate but quite demanding to apply. Moreover, the legal system has come under attack for both allowing and for rejecting expert evidence. This is a topic of enormous philosophical, political, and legal controversy. The leading cases in Canada are criminal, and in both civil and criminal contexts trial judges must assess the value of opinion evidence against the disadvantages of admission in a particular case. Our modest goal here is to highlight the following: the Supreme Court of Canada cases; key areas of contention and dispute; and reform to various jurisdictions' rules of civil procedure as a means of responding to the increased use and abuse of expert opinion evidence in civil cases.

B. Supreme Court of Canada Jurisprudence

R v. Mohan is the leading case on expert evidence in Canada for both civil and criminal cases. In it the court conceives of the trial judge as the protective "gatekeeper." The key issue for the trial judge is the assessment of the threshold reliability of the opinion evidence. Ultimate reliability is up to the trier of fact. The four broad criteria that must be considered by the trial judge in determining whether to admit expert opinion evidence are: relevance, necessity, the absence of any exclusionary rule, and whether the proposed witness is a properly qualified expert (see *R v. Mohan*, [1994] 2 SCR 9). The prejudicial effect may outweigh the probative value if the evidence would take more time than is justified or the impact of hearing it is out of proportion to its reliability. While expert evidence must be related to a fact in issue, and be necessary for a correct disposition of the case, it must also pass a cost–benefit analysis: it has to be worth it.

R v. Mohan
[1994] 2 SCR 9

. . .

(1) Expert Opinion Evidence

Admission of expert evidence depends on the application of the following criteria:

(a) relevance;
(b) necessity in assisting the trier of fact;
(c) the absence of any exclusionary rule;
(d) a properly qualified expert.

(a) Relevance

Relevance is a threshold requirement for the admission of expert evidence as with all other evidence. Relevance is a matter to be decided by a judge as question of law. Although *prima facie* admissible if so related to a fact in issue that it tends to establish it, that does not end the inquiry. This merely determines the logical relevance of the evidence. Other considerations enter into the decision as to admissibility. This further inquiry may be described as a cost benefit analysis, that is "whether its value is worth what it costs." See *McCormick on Evidence* (3rd ed. 1984), at p. 544. Cost in this context is not used in its traditional economic sense but rather in terms of its impact on the trial process. Evidence that is otherwise logically relevant may be excluded on this basis, if its probative value is overborne by its prejudicial effect, if it involves an inordinate amount of time which is not commensurate with its value or if it is misleading in the sense that its effect on the trier of fact, particularly a jury, is out of proportion to its reliability. While frequently considered as an aspect of legal relevance, the exclusion of logically relevant evidence on these grounds is more properly regarded as a general exclusionary rule (see *Morris v. The Queen*, 1983 CanLII 28 (SCC), [1983] 2 SCR 190). Whether it is treated as an aspect of relevance or an exclusionary rule, the effect is the same. The reliability versus effect factor has special significance in assessing the admissibility of expert evidence.

There is a danger that expert evidence will be misused and will distort the fact-finding process. Dressed up in scientific language which the jury does not easily understand and submitted through a witness of impressive antecedents, this evidence is apt to be accepted by the jury as being virtually infallible and as having more weight than it deserves. As La Forest J stated in *R v. Béland*, 1987 CanLII 27 (SCC), [1987] 2 SCR 398, at p. 434, with respect to the evidence of the results of a polygraph tendered by the accused, such evidence should not be admitted by reason of "human fallibility in assessing the proper weight to be given to evidence cloaked under the mystique of science." The application of this principle can be seen in cases such as *R v. Melaragni* (1992), 73 CCC (3d) 348, in which Moldaver J applied a threshold test of reliability to what he described, at p. 353, as "a new scientific technique or body of scientific knowledge." Moldaver J also mentioned two other factors, *inter alia*, which should be considered in such circumstances (at p. 353):

(1) Is the evidence likely to assist the jury in its fact-finding mission, or is it likely to confuse and confound the jury?

(2) Is the jury likely to be overwhelmed by the "mystic infallibility" of the evidence, or will the jury be able to keep an open mind and objectively assess the worth of the evidence?

A similar approach was adopted in *R v. Bourguignon*, [1991] OJ No. 2670 (QL), where, in ruling upon a *voir dire* concerning the admissibility of DNA evidence, Flanigan J admitted most of the evidence but excluded statistical evidence about the probability of a match between the DNA contained in samples taken from the accused and those taken from the scene of a crime. The learned judge explained:

> This Court does not think that the criminal jurisdiction of Canada is yet ready to put such an additional pressure on a jury, by making them overcome such fantastic odds and asking them to weigh it as just one piece of evidence to be considered in the overall picture of all the evidence presented. There is a real danger that the jury will use the evidence as a measure of the probability of the accused's guilt or innocence and thereby undermine the presumption of innocence and erode the value served by the reasonable doubt standard. As said in the Schwartz case: "dehumanize our justice system."
>
> I would therefore, rule admissible the D.N.A. testing evidence but not the statistic probabilities. This restriction can be easily overcome by evidence that "such matches are rare" or "extremely rare" or words to the same effect, which will put the jury in a better position to assess such evidence and protect the right of the accused to a fair trial.

It should be noted that, subsequently, other courts have rejected the distinction drawn by Flanigan J and have admitted both DNA evidence and the evidence regarding statistical probabilities of a match. (See, *e.g.*, *R v. Lafferty*, [1993] NWTJ No. 17 (QL)). I rely on *R v. Bourguignon*, *supra*, simply to illustrate the mode of approach adopted there and leave the specific issue decided by Flanigan J to be considered when it arises.

(b) Necessity in Assisting the Trier of Fact

In *R v. Abbey*, *supra*, Dickson J, as he then was, stated, at p. 42:

> With respect to matters calling for special knowledge, an expert in the field may draw inferences and state his opinion. An expert's function is precisely this: to provide the judge and jury with a ready-made inference which the judge and jury, due to the technical nature of the facts, are unable to formulate. "An expert's opinion is admissible to furnish the Court with scientific information which is likely to be outside the experience and knowledge of a judge or jury. If on the proven facts a judge or jury can form their own conclusions without help, then the opinion of the expert is unnecessary" (*Turner* (1974), 60 Crim. App. R 80, at p. 83, *per* Lawton LJ)

This pre-condition is often expressed in terms as to whether the evidence would be helpful to the trier of fact. The word "helpful" is not quite appropriate and sets too low a standard. However, I would not judge necessity by too strict a standard. What is required is that the opinion be necessary in the sense that it provide information "which is likely to be outside the experience and knowledge of a judge or jury": as quoted by Dickson J in *R v. Abbey, supra*. As stated by Dickson J, the evidence must be necessary to enable the trier of fact to appreciate the matters in issue due to their technical nature. In *Kelliher (Village of) v. Smith*, 1931 CanLII 1 (SCC), [1931] SCR 672, at p. 684, this Court, quoting from *Beven on Negligence* (4th ed. 1928), at p. 141, stated that in order for expert evidence to be admissible, "[t]he subject-matter of the inquiry must be such that ordinary people are unlikely to form a correct judgment about it, if unassisted by persons with special knowledge." More recently, in *R v. Lavallee, supra*, the above passages from *Kelliher* and *Abbey* were applied to admit expert evidence as to the state of mind of a "battered" woman. The judgment stressed that this was an area that is not understood by the average person.

As in the case of relevance, discussed above, the need for the evidence is assessed in light of its potential to distort the fact-finding process. As stated by Lawton LJ in *R v. Turner*, [1975] QB 834, at p. 841, and approved by Lord Wilberforce in *Director of Public Prosecutions v. Jordan*, [1977] AC 699, at p. 718:

> An expert's opinion is admissible to furnish the court with scientific information which is likely to be outside the experience and knowledge of a judge or jury. If on the proven facts a judge or jury can form their own conclusions without help, then the opinion of an expert is unnecessary. In such a case if it is given dressed up in scientific jargon it may make judgment more difficult. The fact that an expert witness has impressive scientific qualifications does not by that fact alone make his opinion on matters of human nature and behaviour within the limits of normality any more helpful than that of the jurors themselves; but there is a danger that they may think it does.

The possibility that evidence will overwhelm the jury and distract them from their task can often be offset by proper instructions.

There is also a concern inherent in the application of this criterion that experts not be permitted to usurp the functions of the trier of fact. Too liberal an approach could result in a trial's becoming nothing more than a contest of experts with the trier of fact acting as referee in deciding which expert to accept.

These concerns were the basis of the rule which excluded expert evidence in respect of the ultimate issue. Although the rule is no longer of general application, the concerns underlying it remain. In light of these concerns, the criteria of relevance and necessity are applied strictly, on occasion, to exclude expert evidence as to an ultimate issue. Expert evidence as to credibility or oath-helping has been excluded on this basis. See *R v. Marquard*, 1993 CanLII 37 (SCC), [1993] 4 SCR 223, *per* McLachlin J.

(c) The Absence of any Exclusionary Rule

Compliance with criteria (a), (b) and (d) will not ensure the admissibility of expert evidence if it falls afoul of an exclusionary rule of evidence separate and apart from the opinion rule itself. For example, in *R v. Morin*, 1988 CanLII 8 (SCC), [1988] 2 SCR 345, evidence elicited by the Crown in cross-examination of the psychiatrist called by the accused was inadmissible because it was not shown to be relevant other than as to the disposition to commit the crime charged. Notwithstanding, therefore, that the evidence otherwise complied with the criteria for the admission of expert evidence it was excluded by reason of the rule that prevents the Crown from adducing evidence of the accused's disposition unless the latter has placed his or her character in issue. The extent of the restriction when such evidence is tendered by the accused lies at the heart of this case and will be discussed hereunder.

(d) A Properly Qualified Expert

Finally the evidence must be given by a witness who is shown to have acquired special or peculiar knowledge through study or experience in respect of the matters on which he or she undertakes to testify.

In summary, therefore, it appears from the foregoing that expert evidence which advances a novel scientific theory or technique is subjected to special scrutiny to determine whether it meets a basic threshold of reliability and whether it is essential in the sense that the trier of fact will be unable to come to a satisfactory conclusion without the assistance of the expert. The closer the evidence approaches an opinion on an ultimate issue, the stricter the application of this principle.

NOTES AND QUESTIONS

1. *Recent Supreme Court of Canada cases.* The Court in *Mohan* noted special scrutiny of the scientific theory or technique is required where it is "novel." In the United States, expert evidence was initially only admissible when there was scientific consensus as to its reliability (*Frye v. United States*, 293 F 1013, at 1014 (DC Cir. 1923)), but this was criticized as imposing too high of a standard. In *Daubert* the US Supreme Court took a new approach and held the issue is whether the evidence has scientific validity, not general acceptance (*Daubert v. Merrell Dow Pharmaceuticals*, 509 US 579 at n. 9 (1993)). Note that one commentator has warned against the ready import into Canada of the approaches in the United States, where the developments are largely driven by large-scale product liability litigation. (See David M. Paciocco, "Context Culture and the Law of Expert Evidence" (2001), 24 *Advocates Quarterly* 42). In *R v. J.-L.J.*, [2000] 2 SCR 600 the Supreme Court of Canada adopted as useful the factors in *Daubert* in considering scientific validity: testing (can others duplicate the results?), peer review and publication (have others offered critiques?), standards for evaluation and rates of errors (what are the criteria for understanding the results of tests?), and acceptability within the scientific community (are others in agreement? How big is this community?). In *J.-L.J.*, the court affirmed the trial judge's decision not to permit defence-led expert testimony in which a penile plethysmograph (used in therapeutic treatment of sex offenders) was relied on as a forensic tool to exclude the accused from the group of likely offenders. This was a novel use of the technique. The court found two problems. First, the so-called distinctive group of likely offenders was vague. Second, the test results showed high rates of error. In short, the evidence failed to meet threshold reliability. The more recent decision on expert evidence, *R v. Trochym*, 2007 SCC 6, split the court. The majority held that previously admissible post-hypnosis testimony is now unreliable and presumptively inadmissible. The majority noted that, "the Court's framework for assessing novel science ensures that only scientific opinions based on a reliable foundation are put to the trier of fact ... , and the same principle applies to scientific techniques" (*Trochym*, at para. 24).

Not all cases require this scrutiny—it varies depending on the state of the underlying science, which itself can change, making the old newly unreliable (e.g., in-dock identification), and vice versa (e.g., DNA evidence) (*Trochym*, at para. 32).

2. *Criticism.* A particular concern with experts relates to their role. They are called, and paid for by, a specific litigating party. Obviously experts would not be put forward as witnesses unless they were useful to a party's cause. But experts are not retained as *advocates* of any party's cause and their evidence is not admissible on that basis. Rather, their role is to assist the *court*—not a particular party—and the basis for the admissibility of their evidence is their *objective* expertise. This inherent tension between the theory of expert opinion and the realities of an adversarial system is not easily resolved, and generates demand for reform. Many divergent views have been expressed on reform of the rules for common law courts: see Guy Pratte, Nadia Effendi, and Jennifer Brusse, "Experts in Civil Litigation: A Retrospective on Their Role and Independence with a View to Possible Reforms" in *Annual Review of Civil Litigation 2008*, eds. Todd L. Archibald and Randall Scott Echlin (Toronto: Carswell, 2008), at 169; William G. Horton and Michael Mercer, "The Use of Expert Witness Evidence in Civil Cases" (2004), 29 *Advocates Quarterly* 153; Paul Michell and Renu Mandhane, "The Uncertain Duty of the Expert Witness" (2005), 42 *Alta. L Rev.* 635; and also Canadian Judicial Council's model instructions to jurors on expert evidence online at http://www.cjc-ccm.gc.ca/english/lawyers_en.asp?selMenu=lawyers_pmf_types_en.asp. Lawyers have been urged to do more to ensure expert evidence does not undermine the legitimacy of the legal system. In this regard, see Tania M. Bubela, "Expert Evidence: The Ethical Responsibility of the Legal Profession" (2004), 41 *Alta. L Rev.* 853, who argues ethical obligations do generate this responsibility on lawyers.

3. *Goudge Inquiry.* We noted in the introduction that the rules of evidence for experts are the same in civil and criminal cases. But the legal context of a ruling matters; errors in fact-finding in criminal cases can lead to incorrect outcomes regarding guilt and innocence, and improperly admitted expert evidence is a major cause of wrongful convictions. The most recent treatment of the issue in Canada is by the Honourable Justice Stephen Goudge, Commissioner for the *Inquiry into Pediatric Pathology in Ontario* (Toronto: Ontario Ministry of the Attorney General, 2008). In chapter 18, The Role of the Court, in volume 3 of his report, Justice Goudge forcefully argues that the emphasis on a careful evaluation of threshold reliability first advanced in *Mohan*, elaborated in *J.-L.J.*, and applied in *Trochym*, should extend to all scientific evidence: "Reliability must ... be a constant concern of judges in their gate-keeping role, whether the science is classified as novel or not and even though reliability does not have its own separate label when *Mohan* is reduced to a four-part test for the admissibility of expert evidence" (at 477-78). This point is equally applicable to civil cases.

After a thorough canvass of a variety of checklists for assessing threshold reliability, all of which are considerably more detailed than anything offered by the Supreme Court of Canada to date, the Goudge Report recommended the following for use by trial judges in assessing threshold reliability under *Mohan* factors, and by triers of fact if the evidence is admitted (at 495):

1. the reliability of the witness, including whether the witness is testifying outside of his or her expertise;

2. the reliability of the scientific theory or technique on which the opinion draws, including whether it is generally accepted and whether there are meaningful peer review, professional standards, and quality assurance policies;

3. whether the expert can relate his or her opinion in the case to a theory or technique that has been or can be tested, including substitutes for testing that are tailored to the particular discipline;

4. whether there is serious dispute or uncertainty about the science and, if so, whether the trier of fact will be reliably informed about the existence of that dispute or uncertainty;

5. whether the expert has adequately considered alternative explanations or interpretations of the data and whether the underlying evidence is available for others to challenge the expert's interpretation;

6. whether the language that the expert proposes to use to express his or her conclusions is appropriate, given the degree of controversy or certainty in the underlying science; and

7. whether the expert can express the opinion in a manner such that the trier of fact will be able to reach an independent opinion as to the reliability of the expert's opinion.

4. *Limitations on Experts.* Provincial and Federal evidence statutes may have an impact of the form of civil trials. In Ontario, s. 12 of the *Evidence Act* limits the number of expert witnesses that can be called without leave of the court: "Where it is intended by a party to examine as witnesses persons entitled, according to the law or practice, to give opinion evidence, not more than three of such witnesses may be called upon either side without the leave of the judge or other person presiding." RSO 1990, c. E.23, s. 12. Similar provisions exist in other jurisdictions, for example in Saskatchewan and in courts applying the federal evidence law, the number of expert witnesses is limited to five (*Saskatchewan Evidence Act*, SS 2006, c. E-11, s. 43; *Canada Evidence Act*, RSC 1985, c. C-5, s. 7). In some jurisdictions, the statutory limit is not a serious problem because it has been interpreted so to apply to each separate disputed issue in a case, but in Ontario the governing law holds that the limit applies to the case as a whole, see: *Bank of America Canada v. Mutual Trust* (1998), 39 OR (3d) 134, at 137-38.

5. *Expert evidence and sustainable justice.* While in civil cases there is no liberty interest at stake, similar concerns with respect to expert evidence have arisen and reforms demanded. Issues of cost and efficiency are rightly seen as important in the overall sustainability of the civil justice system. Expert evidence increases accuracy but at significant expense. We live in a hyperspecialized age. In any one trial, several experts may be required to address contested facts. While knowledge may be increasingly complex and differentiated, we have yet to provide judges—much less lay fact finders—with the training that may be essential for meaningful assessment of expert evidence, despite urgent calls to do so. Views on how the adversarial system could be adapted are the subject of extrajudicial comment by the Honourable Justice W. Ian C. Binnie in his article, "Science in the Courtroom: The Mouse that Roared" (Autumn 2008), 27 *Advocates' Soc. J* No. 2, 11-23, at paras. 40-46, and provide the basis for proposed rule changes (see: Coulter A. Osborne in *Civil Justice Reform Project: Summary of Findings & Recommendations* (Toronto: Ministry of the Attorney General,

2007, at 82.). Changes are needed because expert evidence that cannot be properly assessed will either be ignored or deferred to by the trier of fact, and both of these responses impair accuracy and the long-term sustainability of the justice system. Significant and widespread reform to the civil procedure rules governing expert evidence is taking place currently. It is beyond the scope of this text to detail all of the proposed changes but a few may be briefly noted. Rule 53.03 of the Ontario *Rules of Civil Procedure* currently states that parties intending to call an expert witness at trial must serve an expert report to all other parties in the action at least 90 days before the commencement of the *trial*. The report must be "signed by the expert, setting out his or her name, address and qualifications and the substance of his or her proposed testimony." However, this Rule will be changed on January 1, 2010, so that the report must be served 90 days before the *pre-trial conference* that will be mandated by rule 50 under the new rules. Furthermore, the required content of the report will also be made more extensive by the amendments, under rule 53.03(2.1). Further extensive reform will also occur in Ontario as of January 1, 2010, when the Ontario *Rules of Civil Procedure* will be amended to include rule 4.1 "Duty of Expert":

> 4.1.01(1) It is the duty of every expert engaged by or on behalf of a party to provide evidence in relation to a proceeding under these rules,
>> (a) to provide opinion evidence that is fair, objective and non-partisan;
>> (b) to provide opinion evidence that is related only to matters that are within the expert's area of expertise; and
>> (c) to provide such additional assistance as the court may reasonably require to determine a matter in issue. O. Reg. 438/08, s. 8.
> (2) The duty in subrule (1) prevails over any obligation owed by the expert to the party by whom or on whose behalf he or she is engaged. O. Reg. 438/08, s. 8.

Major reforms regarding expert evidence have also been recommended and are currently under review for the Federal Court: (Rules Committee of the Federal Court of Appeal and of the Federal Court, "Expert Evidence in the Federal Courts Update" (Federal Court of Appeal, March 16, 2009), online at: http://www.fca-caf.gc.ca/bulletins/notices/Update_2009-03-16.pdf). If adopted, these would: require experts to testify when the court considers it necessary; to sign a code of conduct as a precondition to admissibility of a report; allow for discretionary expert conferencing in advance of trial (on a without prejudice basis) to be agreed to or ordered by the court; allow parties to nominate a single joint expert; allow for "hot-tubbing" in which panels of experts, who are addressing the same issue, are sworn in together; and to be questioned by counsel or the court but not by each other (without leave of the court). With respect to the number of witnesses, as noted, s. 7 of the *Canada Evidence Act* limits the number of expert witnesses that may be called by a party to five, unless leave is granted. The proposed reform is to make explicit reference to factors to be considered in exercising that discretion: (a) the nature of the litigation, its public significance, and the need to clarify the law; (b) the number and complexity or technical nature of the issues in dispute; and (c) the likely expense involved in relation to the amount in dispute.

In Nova Scotia, reforms to the *Civil Procedure Rules* have now been implemented. Rule 55.02 precludes experts from testifying unless they have submitted a report, and that report must follow a standardized format that is designed to make the opinion transparent and accessible by including in it "qualifications, acknowledgement of an overriding duty to the Court, assumptions made, tests carried out, and reasons for opinions" (rule 55.04). After submission, opposing parties have up to 30 days to request clarification of a report through written questions but there is no discovery of experts as of right (rule 55.11). Standardized reports have also been proposed for Alberta (Alberta Law Reform Institute, *Alberta Rules of Court Project: Proposed Rules of Court* (Edmonton: ALRI, 2008), at *Proposed Rules* 5.34).

Pleadings

I. INTRODUCTION

Chapter 3 on commencing proceedings looked at the preliminary issue of choice of procedures and, specifically, the difference between actions and applications. This chapter looks at
pleadings, which are the primary documents by which actions are commenced and
defended.

The exchange of allegations between parties in the form of pleadings serves several purposes, including: (1) defining the questions to be determined as between the parties; (2) notifying the opposing party of the case to be met; (3) framing the issues to be determined by
the court; (4) providing a clear record of the issues involved in the action to prevent relitigation of the same issues at a later date; and (5) advocating to the opposing party and to
the court the justice of the pleader's case. While the importance of the advocacy function of
pleadings in creating a favourable first impression of a client's case cannot be overstated, that
is more properly the subject of an advocacy text than one on civil procedure.

This chapter focuses on pleadings as a vehicle for the exchange of information and the
provision of fair notice to other parties of the case to be met. All Canadian jurisdictions require material fact pleading and provide for significant pre-trial disclosure in an effort to
limit unfair surprise at trial and to ensure, as far as possible, that litigation proceeds as fairly
and as efficiently as possible. Despite broad pre-trial disclosure obligations, material fact
pleading remains an important mechanism for addressing the risk of unfair surprise. The
role of material fact pleading is taking on renewed significance as mechanisms for the efficient and fair administration of justice continue to evolve. For example, case management
regimes requiring parties to evaluate their cases relatively early in the proceeding in order
to participate in mandatory mediation or other pre-trial dispute resolution processes, and

rules establishing simplified procedures eliminating examinations for discovery in some circumstances, enhance the importance of detailed pleading to ensure proper notice and issue framing.

Following this introductory section, section II of this chapter begins with an overview of the nature and function of pleadings, followed by a brief outline of the mechanics of pleading and an examination of the rules relating to the form and content of pleadings. The form and content section focuses on the degree to which the type of allegation made or relief claimed affects the specificity required in pleading material facts.

Section III deals with issues related to the substantive content of pleadings. This section addresses the threshold requirement for a pleading to be substantively adequate and discusses the implications that the substantive content of a pleading has on the issues that may be raised at trial. The section concludes with a review of the basic principles that apply to the amendment of pleadings.

Further reference to limitation periods, striking a pleading, and summary judgment are found in chapters 3 and 9.

II. NATURE AND FUNCTION OF PLEADINGS

A. Overview of the Pleading Process

The present rules of pleading in Canada are based on the exchange of "alternate allegations" between parties. This reflects an English tradition stemming at least from the time of the reign of Henry II (see *Odgers' Principles of Pleading and Practice in Civil Actions in the High Court of Justice*, 22nd ed. (London: Stevens & Son, 1981), at 88-89). The issues that must ultimately be tried are identified through the exchange of allegations between the parties. Other procedural tools, such as pre-trial disclosure obligations and requests to admit, also assist in distinguishing the facts and issues agreed on from those requiring judicial resolution.

The exchange of allegations typically begins with the issuance and service of the statement of claim, in which the plaintiff sets out the relief claimed, as well as the facts that are said to give rise to a legal entitlement to relief. For example, the plaintiff might claim damages on the ground that the defendant has refused to pay for goods supplied under a contract.

Should the defendant wish to defend the action, the defendant must respond to the statement of claim, unless the defendant wishes to make a preliminary attack on the statement of claim—for example, by moving to strike all or a portion of it (see further chapter 9). Barring delivery of a response or initiation of a preliminary attack, the defendant risks summary disposition of the claim in favour of the plaintiff through default proceedings. The defendant, in a statement of defence, must respond to the allegations in the statement of claim. Four general types of responses are typically possible:

1. *Admissions.* The defendant is required to admit those allegations in the statement of claim that are true, knowing that admission of certain allegations may entitle the plaintiff to judgment. As a result, in practice, defendants are frequently slow to admit allegations contained in the statement of claim, typically admitting only those

that are obviously true. Even if the admissions made by the defendant do not entitle the plaintiff to judgment, admitted allegations are deemed to be facts and they need not be proven at trial.

2. *Denials.* Where a defendant denies the truth of an allegation or is not prepared to declare the truth or falsity of an allegation in the statement of claim due to uncertainty, the defendant will deny the allegation. For example, in an action for payment for goods supplied, the defendant may admit that there was a contract for the supply of goods, but deny that the goods ordered were actually delivered. Allegations denied must be proven at trial, unless an admission is subsequently obtained.

3. *No knowledge.* Where the defendant has no knowledge of a fact alleged in the statement of claim, the defendant may plead lack of knowledge. Without a formal admission at a later stage, the plaintiff will be required to prove that fact at trial. Typically, a defendant responds in this manner to the plaintiff's allegations about its own circumstances or behaviour. For example, when a plaintiff corporation claims that it was incorporated on a certain date, the defendant might respond that it has no knowledge of such a fact.

4. *Affirmative defences.* The defendant may admit a fact alleged in the statement of claim, but provide further facts in the statement of defence that, if true, would allow the defendant to avoid the result claimed by the plaintiff (known as "confession and avoidance"). In our supply-of-goods example, the defendant may admit or "confess" that the plaintiff delivered the goods, but plead that a later agreement with the plaintiff absolved the defendant of any obligation to pay, thereby allowing the defendant to "avoid" the legal result claimed by the plaintiff. Typically, an affirmative defence through "confession and avoidance" will be pleaded in a statement of defence in the alternative to a denial. For example, a defendant might deny entering into the contract alleged in the statement of claim, but plead "in the alternative" that if there was such a contract, a subsequent agreement brought it to an end. At trial, the plaintiff will be required to prove entry into the first contract and the defendant, if necessary, will have to prove the subsequent agreement.

Statements of defence are likely to include a mixture of admissions, denials, assertions of lack of knowledge, and affirmative defences, as defendants respond to the allegations framed in the statement of claim.

The exchange of alternate allegations may not end with delivery of the statement of defence. If the defendant has pleaded an affirmative defence—raising new allegations—the plaintiff may be required to file a reply. Generally, a reply will not be necessary if the plaintiff simply denies the allegations in the statement of defence. For example, if no reply is filed in response to the affirmative defence of a subsequent agreement, the plaintiff will be deemed to deny that allegation and the defendant will be required to prove it at trial. In some situations, a plaintiff *may* file a reply to expressly deny the allegation. However, the plaintiff *must* file a reply if he or she wishes to assert an affirmative defence, rather than a mere denial. For example, the plaintiff may wish to admit (or "confess") to a subsequent agreement with the defendant, but to "avoid" the legal result of that agreement by asserting that it was attained by fraud. Further pleadings beyond the reply are possible only with leave or on consent, but they are rarely used.

Other types of pleadings may be required in addition to the statement of claim, statement of defence, and reply. For example, a defendant can respond not simply with a statement of defence, but with a statement of defence and counterclaim, in which the defendant, in addition to defending the plaintiff's claim, asserts a claim back against the plaintiff (and, potentially, against strangers to the litigation). Further, the defendant may bring in new parties by issuing third- and subsequent-party claims, and co-defendants may issue crossclaims against one another. Counterclaims, third-party and subsequent claims, and crossclaims are discussed further in Chapter 5 on parties and participants in the litigation. While each type of claim requires its own type of pleading, these will not be specifically addressed here; rather, their mechanics can be understood by comparison to statements of claim and statements of defence.

The process of exchanging alternate allegations carries with it the advantage of notifying the opposing party of the case to be met as well as defining the issues and clarifying which issues are agreed on and which must be tried. As discussed further in chapter 4 on the scope of litigation, issue definition in pleadings may play a crucial role in ensuring that issues resolved in one action cannot be retried in subsequent actions between the same or related parties.

Pleadings and the rules of pleading are strategically important for other reasons. In most jurisdictions, the scope of the parties' discovery obligations will be determined by reference to the matters raised in the pleadings (see further chapter 7 on discovery). Further, the content of pleadings may also influence substantive legal matters within and outside the scope of the dispute between the immediate parties.

As we will see, the rules of pleading require parties to cast their "story" into a legal narrative that articulates the "material facts" relied on to support the claim for legal relief (the cause of action) that is being made. The materiality requirement mandates the inclusion of facts necessary to establish the legal result claimed *and* the exclusion of facts that are extraneous to that claim.

B. Mechanics of Pleading

The rules of procedure in each jurisdiction specify the time within which each of the various pleadings must be served and filed. While these rules should be followed, courts generally have broad discretion to extend the time for delivery of pleadings in appropriate circumstances. Often the parties to a proceeding will also agree to reasonable extensions. In considering requests for extensions of time, plaintiff's counsel in case-managed or simplified procedure actions should take into account the fact of automatic administrative dismissal mechanisms if statements of defence are not delivered within fixed periods of time following issuance of the statement of claim. Absent an extension of time, by court order or by agreement, a party that fails to meet prescribed time limits risks being noted in default by the opposing party. Finally, rules of professional responsibility often contemplate cooperation between counsel in the context of reasonable requests to extend filing deadlines.

C. Form and Content of Pleadings

As discussed previously, pleadings perform multiple functions in litigation, including providing notice to the other side as well as defining the issues among the parties. Generally, in Canada, parties are required to plead the "material facts" relied on in support of the claim or defence. Material fact pleading may be contrasted to the "notice pleading" approach more traditionally followed in the United States. Under the material fact approach, the pleadings arguably continue to serve both notice and issue definition functions. Under the notice approach, much of the issue-definition function is left to later stages in the action when documentary production and oral examinations take place. The Canadian approach to material fact pleading more closely resembles the approach taken in England, although pre-trial discovery in Canada is generally much broader than that permitted in England.

Procedural considerations with respect to pleadings may directly affect the substantive rights of the parties. As will be discussed in chapter 9 on pre-trial relief and disposition without trial, failure to plead the material facts with a sufficient degree of specificity may result in a summary disposition of the case without trial. Further, the degree of specificity required will depend, in part, on the nature of the allegations asserted. In many cases, the court will insist on more detailed material facts where allegations of moral wrongdoing are made. This "sliding scale" of material facts serves both the notice and issue definition functions: seeking to ensure detailed notice to the party accused of wrongdoing and to require the accuser to be specific about the exact issues raised.

The following two cases discuss the concept of "material facts": one in the case of alleged wrongdoing by an employee who is suing for wrongful dismissal; the other in the case of a claim for punitive damages. In both cases, the courts indicate that the requisite level of material fact disclosure in a pleading is directly related to the nature of the allegations being made. In the first case, the court's decision is rendered in response to a motion for particulars by the plaintiff employee. By way of background, a party served with a pleading may request additional particulars in relation to the allegations made in that pleading. Requests for particulars are designed to assist the requesting party in responding to the allegations made against him or her. If particulars are not provided, the requesting party can then move for a court order compelling their production. As Master Sandler indicates in the *Copland* decision below, "particulars" might best be understood in relation to "material facts" as providing greater detail of the material facts alleged. As a result, consideration of what level of material fact is necessary to ground an adequate pleading will often occur in the context of a motion for particulars.

Copland v. Commodore Business Machines Ltd.
(1985), 52 OR (2d) 586, 3 CPC (2d) 77 (Sup. Ct.); leave to appeal to Ont. HCJ
denied (1985), 52 OR (2d) 586n., 3 CPC (2d) 77n., Henry J

MASTER SANDLER: This motion raises the question of how much information must be set forth in a statement of defence, in a wrongful dismissal action, when the defendant employer seeks to plead dismissal for cause. This issue has practical significance because of the frequency with which this type of action and this type of defence comes before this Court.

The statement of claim reveals that the plaintiff started his employment in May of 1982 as a national sales manager. This employment was terminated on July 5, 1984, without any prior warning. There follows the usual claims for relief.

The key paragraph in the statement of defence is para. 9, containing the pleas of "cause," and I now set out each of the subparagraphs of para. 9, together with the relief that the moving party-plaintiff seeks in relation to each subparagraph.

9(a) The plaintiff attempted to mislead representatives of the defendant as to the amount of his salary and as to his obligation to repay advances provided to him by the defendant;

The plaintiff seeks "particulars" of the "times" at which and the "nature of the attempts" which the plaintiff is alleged to have made, to "mislead" the defendant as alleged; and also particulars of the "circumstances in which such attempts are alleged to have been made."

9(b) The plaintiff knowingly or incompetently permitted excessive costs of sales;

The plaintiff seeks particulars of the "instances of and the manner in which the plaintiff permitted excessive costs of sales."

9(c) The plaintiff entered into imprudent personal transactions which brought his personal interests into conflict with his duties to the defendant;

The plaintiff seeks particulars of the "imprudent personal transactions" … as pleaded in para. 9(c).

9(d) The Plaintiff treated other employees of the Defendant in an abusive and improper manner;

The plaintiff seeks particulars of this allegation, being the times and nature of such treatment and the names of the employees in question.

9(e) The plaintiff abused limousine and entertainment privileges provided to him at the defendant's expense;

The plaintiff seeks "particulars of the instances and circumstances" in which he is alleged to have abused these privileges.

9(f) The plaintiff was insubordinate at and systematically attempted to undermine the position and authority of the defendant's president by misrepresentations made with respect to the latter's conduct and abilities;

The plaintiff seeks "particulars of the occasions and circumstances in which the plaintiff is alleged to have been insubordinate" and how he attempted to "undermine the position and authority of the defendant's president," and particulars of the "misrepresentation" referred to in para. 9(f).

9(g) On the final day of his employment the plaintiff openly confronted the defendant's president in the presence of another employee, in a manner which was abusive, improper, and incompatible with the continuance of the plaintiff's employment relationship with the defendant.

The plaintiff seeks particulars of this "confrontation" which would include a general description of exactly what the defendant did on this particular occasion.

The plaintiff's counsel argued that these particulars are not within the plaintiff's knowledge and that they are necessary in order to enable the plaintiff to plead to the statement of defence. There is no affidavit filed by the plaintiff (or by anyone else) to this effect.

Under r. 25.06(1):

> Every pleading shall contain a concise statement of the material facts on which the party relies ... , but not the evidence by which those facts are to be proved.

... Material facts must be pleaded; evidence must not be pleaded. In between the concept of "material facts" and the concept of "evidence" is the concept of "particulars." These are additional bits of information, or data, or detail, that flush out the "material facts," but they are not so detailed as to amount to "evidence." These additional bits of information, known as "particulars," can be obtained by a party under ... r. 25.10, if the party swears an affidavit showing that the particulars are necessary to enable him *to plead* to the attacked pleading, and that the "particulars" are not within the knowledge of the party asking for them. An affidavit is not necessary only where the pleading is so bald that the need for particulars is patently obvious from the pleading itself. ...

Rule 25.06(1) mandates a minimum level of material fact disclosure and if this level is not reached, the remedy is not a motion for "particulars," but, rather, a motion to strike out the pleading as irregular. It is only where the minimum level of material fact disclosure has been reached that the pleading becomes regular. Thereafter, the discretionary remedy of "particulars" under r. 25.10 becomes available, if the party seeking particulars can qualify for the relief under the provisions of that rule.

Thus it becomes necessary, in any specific type of action, to determine the minimum level of material fact disclosure required for any particular pleading, in order to determine if the pleading is or is not regular. This is not an easy task by any means, and much common sense must be brought to bear in this endeavour. As well, the purpose and function of pleadings in modern litigation must be kept constantly in mind. It is often difficult to differentiate between, and articulate the difference between material facts, particulars, and evidence.

Some assistance is obtained, as to statements of defence, from ... r. 25.07(4). ... Under this ... rule, a party must plead "... any matter on which the party intends to rely to defeat the claim of the opposite party ... ," and the "material facts" in relation to such matters must be set forth as required by r. 25.06(1).

Further assistance is obtained from Bullen and Leake and Jacob's Precedents of Pleadings (12th ed., 1975) at pp. 1207 to 1208, where the precedent sets forth a plea of misconduct of an employee, in wilfully disobeying the reasonable orders of his employer, or by habitually neglecting his duties, or by dishonestly converting to his own use money which he had received to the use of the employer. The precedent then indicates that the pleading is to "state the particulars of the misconduct which justified the dismissal according to the fact." Further on, the notes say "The ground of dismissal must be specifically pleaded (*Tomlinson v. London Midland & Scottish Ry.*, [1944] 1 All ER 537 at 541 (CA))." And further, "The defendant must in his defence give particulars of the misconduct to show clearly in what it consisted, so as to enable the plaintiff to meet the charge, and if this is not done, further particulars will be ordered: see *Saunders v. Jones* (1877), 7 Ch. D 435 (CA)." ...

In my view, the minimum level of material fact disclosure for a statement of defence in a wrongful dismissal action, where the defendant employer relies on cause for the dismissal, is very high, and the pleading must contain sufficient detail so that the employee and the Court can ascertain the exact nature of the questions to be tried, and so that the employee can meet the charge and respond in his reply accordingly.

As one studies the allegations in paras. 9(a) through 9(g) of this statement of defence, it becomes apparent that material facts relating to each of these allegations are missing and have not been pleaded. For example, the material facts of the "imprudent personal transactions" referred in 9(c) are missing. The material facts concerning which employees were abusively and improperly treated and of what the plaintiff's conduct consisted are missing from 9(d). The material facts concerning how the plaintiff abused his limousine and entertainment privileges, as pleaded in para. 9(e), are missing.

I am satisfied that each of paras. 9(a) through 9(g) fails to meet the minimum level of material fact disclosure required by rule 25.06(1) in the particular context of this particular action, and I thus strike out para. 9 in its entirety, with leave to the defendant to amend as it may be advised. (I suggest that the amended para. 9 be divided into additional paras. 9A, 9B, etc. containing all the necessary material facts, so that the numbering of the remaining paras. 10-18 of the statement of defence is not changed, which will make any subsequent review of the amended pleading much easier.)

Costs of this motion to the plaintiff in the cause.

Order striking out paragraphs of statement of defence granted.

NOTES AND QUESTIONS

1. The *Copland* decision demonstrates the risk to substantive legal rights posed by inadequate pleadings. Failure to meet the minimum material fact requirement will lead the court to strike paragraphs containing deficient allegations from the pleading (with or without leave to amend). Further, Master Sandler concludes that the threshold for material facts alleging cause in a wrongful dismissal action is "very high." What purposes might a very high level of material fact disclosure serve in a case such as this? Is it necessary to serve the notice function of pleadings, given that the parties are generally entitled to broad rights of pre-trial discovery? As discussed below and in chapter 7, the pleadings play a role in determining the scope of these pre-trial discovery obligations. As such, requiring a high level of specificity in pleading may confine the issues as well as narrowing the scope of pre-trial discovery.

2. The decision also assists in elucidating the difference between "material facts" and "evidence"—a distinction made relevant by procedural rules that require parties to plead material facts but not evidence. Master Sandler suggests that material facts, particulars, and evidence fall along a spectrum from least to most detailed. Material facts are the minimum required to meet the basic threshold for sufficiency. Particulars may be required to ensure that the responding party has sufficient information to respond. Neither material facts nor particulars should be equated with "evidence." While the distinction between the levels of

particularity on the spectrum is often difficult to discern, a general rule may assist in identifying the difference between material facts and evidence. Facts that simply tend to prove allegations already made tend to fall into the category of evidence and, therefore, should not typically be pleaded. For example, in a car accident case, the allegation that car A struck car B may constitute a material fact; however, it is not generally necessary to plead that witness X will testify that car A struck car B, because the information relating to witness X merely describes how the pleading party intends to prove the allegation that car A struck car B. With this discussion in mind, look at the pleading paragraphs in *Copland* again and articulate some further examples of particulars. Then see if you can articulate some examples of evidence that might be used to prove those particulars at trial.

3. At play in *Copland* is the general rule that material facts must be pleaded. The corollary of this rule is that "immaterial" or irrelevant facts should not be pleaded. The rules of civil procedure in all Canadian jurisdictions address this issue. Frequently, the rules provide a mechanism for "scandalous," "embarrassing," "frivolous," and/or "vexatious" pleadings to be struck out by a court. See, for example, *Sherman v. Giles* (1994), 130 NSR (2d) 52 (CA), which summarizes the principles governing whether an action is frivolous, vexatious, or an abuse of process.

"Scandalous" refers to indecent or offensive allegations made for the purpose of abusing or prejudicing the other party. However, no relevant allegation will be considered scandalous. Take, for example, a defamation case. If the defendant is alleged to have defamed the plaintiff by stating that the plaintiff is a criminal, it is not "scandalous" (in the legal sense) for the defendant to plead that the plaintiff committed a notorious crime in support of a defence of justification; the allegation of the commission of a crime would be material to the legal determination of the defendant's liability. Similarly, so long as a fact alleged is relevant to the legal result in the case, it will not be considered "embarrassing."

4. Generally, the allegations in a statement of claim must be taken as true for the purpose of pleading. Even where an allegation is clearly disputable, a court will be hesitant to grant a motion to strike on the grounds that the pleading is scandalous, frivolous, vexatious, or an abuse of process. For example, in *Sherman v. Giles*, above, the Nova Scotia Court of Appeal disallowed the use of affidavit evidence to prove that a statement of claim was frivolous and vexatious. It also dismissed the application to strike out the statement of claim, holding that however improbable it was that the claim would succeed, it could not be said that the claim was unsustainable beyond a doubt. The court emphasized that the power to strike out a pleading should be used only in the narrowest of circumstances where a statement of claim is "obviously unsustainable" or "devoid of all merit." For a further discussion of striking a pleading, see chapter 9.

5. For a recent discussion of the *Copland* case, see Trevor C.W. Farrow, "Five Pleadings Cases Everyone Should Read" (2009), 35 *Advocates' Quarterly* 466.

While the *Copland* decision illustrates the impact that the nature of the allegations will have on the degree of specificity required in pleadings, the Supreme Court of Canada's decision in *Whiten* demonstrates that the nature of the relief claimed may also have an impact on the degree of specificity required.

Whiten v. Pilot Insurance Co.
[2002] 1 SCR 595, 2002 SCC 18

BINNIE J (for the majority): This case raises once again the spectre of uncontrolled and uncontrollable awards of punitive damages in civil actions. The jury was clearly outraged by the high-handed tactics employed by the respondent, Pilot Insurance Company, following its unjustified refusal to pay the appellant's claim under a fire insurance policy (ultimately quantified at approximately $345,000). Pilot forced an eight-week trial on an allegation of arson that the jury obviously considered trumped up. It forced her to put at risk her only remaining asset (the insurance claim) plus approximately $320,000 in legal costs that she did not have. The denial of the claim was designed to force her to make an unfair settlement for less than she was entitled to. The conduct was planned and deliberate and continued for over two years, while the financial situation of the appellant grew increasingly desperate. Evidently concluding that the arson defence from the outset was unsustainable and made in bad faith, the jury added an award of punitive damages of $1 million, in effect providing the appellant with a "windfall" that added something less than treble damages to her actual out-of-pocket loss. The respondent argues that the award of punitive damages is itself outrageous.

The appellant, Daphne Whiten, bought her home in Haliburton County, Ontario, in 1985. Just after midnight on January 18, 1994, when she and her husband Keith were getting ready to go to bed, they discovered a fire in the addition to their house. They and their daughter, who had also been upstairs, fled the house wearing only their night clothes. It was minus 18 degrees Celsius. Mr. Whiten gave his slippers to his daughter to go for help and suffered serious frostbite to his feet for which he was hospitalized. He was thereafter confined to a wheelchair for a period of time. The fire totally destroyed the Whitens' home and its contents, including their few valuable antiques and many items of sentimental value and their three cats.

The appellant was able to rent a small winterized cottage nearby for $650 per month. Pilot made a single $5000 payment for living expenses and covered the rent for a couple of months or so, then cut off the rent without telling the family, and thereafter pursued a hostile and confrontational policy which the jury must have concluded was calculated to force the appellant (whose family was in very poor financial shape) to settle her claim at substantially less than its fair value. The allegation that the family had torched its own home was contradicted by the local fire chief, the respondent's own expert investigator, and its initial expert, all of whom said there was no evidence whatsoever of arson. The respondent's position, based on wishful thinking, was wholly discredited at trial. Pilot's appellate counsel conceded here and in the Ontario Court of Appeal that there was no air of reality to the allegation of arson.

A majority of the Ontario Court of Appeal allowed the appeal in part and reduced the punitive damage award to $100,000. In my view, on the exceptional facts of this case, there was no basis on which to interfere with the jury award. The award, though very high, was rational in the specific circumstances disclosed in the evidence and within the limits that a jury is allowed to operate. The appellant was faced with harsh and unreasoning opposition from an insurer whose policy she had purchased for peace of mind and protection in just such an emergency. The jury obviously concluded that people who sell peace of mind should not try to exploit a family in crisis. Pilot, as stated, required the appellant to spend $320,000 in legal costs to collect the $345,000 that was owed to her. The combined total of $665,000 at risk puts the punitive damage awards in perspective. An award of $1 million in punitive damages is certainly at the upper end of a sustainable award on these facts but not beyond it. I would allow the appeal and restore the jury award of $1 million in punitive damages.

(2) Was the Claim for Punitive Damages Properly Pleaded?

The respondent says that even if a separate claim arising under the insurance contract could provide the basis for punitive damages, none was pleaded in this case.

In other words, while "punitive and exemplary damages" are explicitly requested in para. 13 of the statement of claim, the material facts necessary for the grant of such an award are not spelled out in the body of the pleading. Further, the respondent in its cross-appeal says that even if the plaintiff has established an "independent actionable wrong," she failed to prove any separate and distinct damage flowing from it. The appellant thus failed, Pilot says, to meet the *Vorvis* requirements and her claim for punitive damages ought to have been dismissed.

There is some case law that says a claim for punitive damages need not be specifically pleaded as it is included conceptually in a claim for general damages. ... In my view, the suggestion that no pleading is necessary overlooks the basic proposition in our justice system that before someone is punished they ought to have advance notice of the charge sufficient to allow them to consider the scope of their jeopardy as well as the opportunity to respond to it. This can only be assured if the claim for punitive damages, as opposed to compensatory damages, is not buried in a general reference to general damages. This principle, which is really no more than a rule of fairness, is made explicit in the civil rules of some of our trial courts. For example, in Saskatchewan the Queen's Bench Rules require that claims for punitive damages be expressly pleaded and specify the misconduct which is claimed to give rise to such damages (*Rieger v. Burgess*, [1988] 4 WWR 577 (Sask. CA); *Lauscher v. Berryere* (1999), 172 DLR (4th) 439 (Sask. CA)). Rule 25.06(9) of the Ontario *Rules of Civil Procedure* also has the effect of requiring that punitive damages claims be expressly pleaded. It is quite usual, of course, for the complexion of a case to evolve over time, but a pleading can always be amended on terms during the proceedings, depending on the existence and extent of prejudice not compensable in costs, and the justice of the case.

One of the purposes of a statement of claim is to alert the defendant to the case it has to meet, and if at the end of the day the defendant is surprised by an award against it that is a multiple of what it thought was the amount in issue, there is an obvious unfairness. Moreover, the facts said to justify punitive damages should be pleaded with some particularity. The time-honoured adjectives describing conduct as "harsh, vindictive, reprehensible and malicious" (*per* McIntyre J in *Vorvis*, ... [[1989] 1 SCR 1085], p. 1108) or their pejorative equivalent, however apt to capture the essence of the remedy, are conclusory rather than explanatory.

Whether or not a defendant has in fact been taken by surprise by a weak or defective pleading will have to be decided in the circumstances of a particular case.

In this case, the plaintiff specifically asked for punitive damages in her statement of claim and if the respondent was in any doubt about the facts giving rise to the claim, it ought to have applied for particulars and, in my opinion, it would have been entitled to them.

However, the respondent did not apply for particulars, and I think there is sufficient detail in the statement of claim to show that its failure to do so was not a self-inflicted injustice. There was no surprise except perhaps as to the quantum, which resulted in an amendment of the statement of claim at trial. Quite apart from the advance notice that she was seeking punitive damages (para. 1(e)), the appellant specifically pleaded the basis for the independent "actionable wrong" in para. 10:

> 10. The Plaintiff pleads an implied term of the insurance contract was a covenant of good faith and fair dealings which required the Defendant, Pilot Insurance Company to deal fairly and in good faith in handling the claim of the Plaintiff.

The appellant also pleaded that Pilot's manner of dealing with her claim had created "hardship" of which "the Defendants, through their agents and employees always had direct and ongoing knowledge" (para. 8). In para. 14 she pleaded that "as a result of the actions of the Defendants, the Plaintiff has suffered and continues to suffer great emotional stress" (although there was no claim for aggravated damages). The respondent specifically denied acting in bad faith (Statement of defence and Counterclaim of the Defendant, at para. 6). The statement of claim was somewhat deficient in failing to relate the plea for punitive damages to the precise facts said to give rise to the outrage, but Pilot was content to go to trial on this pleading and I do not think it should be heard to complain about it at this late date.

As to the respondent's objection that the pleading does not allege separate and distinct damages flowing from the independent actionable wrong, the respondent's argument overlooks the fact that punitive damages are directed to the quality of the defendant's conduct, not the quantity (if any) of the plaintiff's loss. As Cory J observed in *Hill*, ... [[1995] 2 SCR 1130], at para. 196, "[p]unitive damages bear no relation to what the plaintiff should receive by way of compensation. Their aim is not to compensate the plaintiff, but rather to punish the defendant. It is the means by which the jury or judge expresses its outrage at the egregious conduct of the defendant." In any event, there is a good deal of evidence of emotional stress and financial cost over and above the loss that would have been incurred had the claim been settled in good faith within a reasonable time.

IV. Conclusion

I would allow the appeal and restore the jury award of $1 million in punitive damages, with costs in this Court on a party-and-party basis.

The respondent's cross-appeal against the award of any punitive damages is dismissed with costs to the appellant, also on a party-and-party basis.

NOTES AND QUESTIONS

1. The majority's decision in *Whiten* makes it clear that pleadings for punitive damages ought to be "more rigorous" in future to avoid unfairness to the defendant. However, the majority also notes an onus on defendants to seek particulars of punitive damages. Failure to do so in a timely way may undermine later arguments by defendants that punitive damages should not be awarded, or should be confined to a limited amount.

2. *Whiten* affirms the need for specificity in pleadings for punitive damages, but could also enlarge the permissible scope of material facts. At paragraph 130 of the judgment, Binnie J suggests that evidence of an overall corporate strategy to deny claims might strengthen the claim for punitive damages. This statement has been duly noted by plaintiffs' counsel, and relied on as a basis for the propriety of pleading that a defendant insurer engaged in an overall strategy of denying claims. For example, in *National Steel Car Ltd. v. Factory Mutual Insurance Co.*, [2002] OJ No. 4536 (SCJ), Master Kelly accepted that an allegation of an overall corporate strategy to deny claims might be material to a claim for punitive damages, but noted the significant impact of such an allegation on the breadth of the issues and discovery obligations of the defending insurer. The resulting order preserved the possibility of such a broad claim being asserted in future, should evidence of a corporate strategy to deny the particular plaintiff's claim be demonstrated on discovery.

3. The imposition of a higher level of specificity in pleading material facts in wrongful dismissal cases where cause is asserted and in claims for punitive damages has also been followed in cases pleading battery. For example, in *Allen v. Mt. Sinai Hospital* (1981), 33 OR (2d) 603, the Court of Appeal held that a plaintiff who had failed to plead battery specifically in a medical malpractice claim was not permitted to advance the theory of battery, but allowed the plaintiff to amend her claim in order to do so.

4. In some situations, it will be difficult for the plaintiff to know the material facts supporting his or her claim in advance of pre-trial discovery. Is it useful to require plaintiffs to "guess" at plausible fact patterns supporting their claims, for example, when asserting negligence against a municipality in a "slip and fall" case? Mere assertions of negligence in these situations have been held to fall short of the material facts required by the rules of pleading (see, e.g., *Thompson v. TTC*, [1947] OWN 920 (Master)).

5. *Whiten* also raises the issue of the nature of statements made in pleadings. It is understood that statements made in pleadings are simply assertions of facts, which the party hopes to prove. However, the court in *Whiten* made clear that defendants who continue to assert allegations throughout trial, in the face of overwhelming evidence to the contrary, may expose themselves to higher punitive damage awards.

In a similar vein, in *Lammie v. Belair*, [2002] OJ No. 4732, [2002] OTC 958 (SCJ), the court exercised its discretion to award costs on a substantial indemnity scale against a plaintiff who had made serious, broad-ranging allegations of misconduct against her insurer. Although the court noted that the plaintiff was obliged to plead with specificity in order to support her claim for punitive damages, it held as follows:

> To commence an action with pleadings that are unsubstantiated is not a rare phenomenon. Presumably, counsel hope that something will "fall out of the tree," something will come out of the discoveries. This bold start is not necessarily unreasonable. However, to maintain a pleading knowing that there is no evidentiary basis beyond a point, especially on the eve of trial, is

unreasonable. In other words, there is a point when counsel must jettison scandalous and embarrassing pleadings in order to minimize cost consequences.

Given what the courts have said about costs and their disciplinary use (discussed in chapter 2), to what extent is it fair to impose increased costs on a client for what the court in *Lammie* described as "mirror[ing] the beliefs of [her former counsel], the self-styled advocate for insurance consumers, as to the shortcomings of the insurance industry"? Note that the court in *Lammie* invited submissions from the plaintiff's then-current and former counsel as to whether and to what extent they should contribute to those costs.

6. Concerns about maintaining "untruths" in pleadings have been addressed in the United States by requiring lawyers (or unrepresented parties) to verify their pleadings. Rule 11 of the US *Federal Rules of Civil Procedure* requires certification, about a pleading, that:

> ... to the best of the person's knowledge, information, and belief, formed after an inquiry reasonable under the circumstances: (1) it is not being presented for any improper purpose, such as to harass, cause unnecessary delay, or needlessly increase the cost of litigation; (2) the claims, defenses, and other legal contentions are warranted by existing law or by a nonfrivolous argument for extending, modifying, or reversing existing law or for establishing new law; (3) the factual contentions have evidentiary support or, if specifically so identified, will likely have evidentiary support after a reasonable opportunity for further investigation or discovery; and (4) the denials of factual contentions are warranted on the evidence or, if specifically so identified, are reasonably based on belief or a lack of information.

To the extent that verification is a response to concerns about a proliferation of baseless lawsuits, it may be that Canadian courts' discretion with respect to awarding costs, as exemplified in *Lammie*, provides a more effective response. However, for a proposed certification requirement in Canada, see, for example, the proposed reforms to the rules of civil procedure in British Columbia (mentioned below). Which approach do you prefer? Why?

7. Further, and in any event, codes of professional conduct prohibit the knowing prosecution by counsel of "unmeritorious steps in the litigation process." Trevor C.W. Farrow, "Ethics in Advocacy" in Alice Woolley et al., eds., *Lawyers' Ethics and Professional Regulation* (Markham, ON: LexisNexis, 2008) c. 5, at 206. Given these professional obligations, are certification requirements or costs sanctions necessary? Why or why not?

8. As discussed further in chapter 10, there are a number of current reform projects ongoing in Canada, the outcomes of which will impact the form and content of pleadings rules. See, for example, BC Justice Review Task Force, Civil Justice Reform Working Group, online at: http://www.bcjusticereview.org/working_groups/civil_justice/civil_justice.asp; Alberta Law Reform Institute (ALRI), Rules of Court Project, "Final Report No. 95" (October 2008), at Appendix H ("Proposed Rules of Court"), online at: http://www.law.ualberta .ca/alri/Rules-of-Court.php; Ontario Civil Justice Reform Project, "Findings and Recommendations" (Hon. Coulter A. Osborne, QC) (November 2007), online at: http://www .attorneygeneral.jus.gov.on.ca/english/about/pubs/cjrp/. For a further useful source of rules and reform initiatives, see Canadian Forum on Civil Justice (CFCJ), "Inventory of Reforms," online at: http://cfcj-fcjc.org/inventory/.

III. SUBSTANTIVE CONTENT

This section addresses three fundamental issues regarding the substantive content of pleadings. Part A addresses the threshold requirement of substantive adequacy. It focuses on the drafting of pleadings in order to prevent or survive a preliminary motion to strike the pleading. (Preliminary motions to strike are discussed in chapter 9, Pre-Trial Relief and Disposition Without Trial.) Part B discusses the impact that pleadings have on limiting or defining the matters to be proven at trial. This discussion references the problem of variance—that is, where the facts alleged in the pleading differ from the facts that are proven, or sought to be proven at trial. Finally, Part C deals with strategies for amending or rectifying the content of pleadings in order to meet the threshold requirements of substantive adequacy or to re-define the issues for trial.

A. Substantive Adequacy

The most basic requirement of a pleading is that it must disclose or defend a cause of action. In order to be considered "substantively adequate," a statement of claim must articulate a set of facts which, if true, would entitle the plaintiff to the legal relief claimed. If a statement of claim fails to fulfill this requirement, the defendant may attack the pleading through a motion to strike. Similarly, a statement of defence must articulate a set of facts that, if true, would provide the defendant with a valid defence to the plaintiff's claim. If the statement of defence fails in this respect, the plaintiff may bring a preliminary application to strike out the defence pleading. All Canadian jurisdictions require substantive adequacy in pleadings and they all provide mechanisms for a preliminary determination of this issue.

The substantive adequacy of a pleading is typically assessed by the courts in the context of a preliminary application to strike out a pleading. (These motions are dealt with further in chapter 9.) When drafting a pleading, it is therefore important to keep in mind what a court will be looking for if the pleading is ever challenged on the grounds of substantive inadequacy. The test for substantive adequacy is whether, on the face of its pleadings, a party (1) has advanced a valid cause of action or defence, and (2) has plead all the material facts needed to support that cause of action or defence. It is important to note that the substantive adequacy test focuses solely on the allegations raised in the pleadings and does not involve a consideration of whether sufficient evidence may be raised at trial to prove these allegations. This point is clearly articulated in the following excerpts from *Dawson v. Rexcraft* and *Wyman and Moscrop Realty Ltd. v. Vancouver Real Estate Board*. (See also *Jane Doe v. Board of Commissioners of Police for the Municipality of Metropolitan Toronto* (1990), 74 OR (2d) 225 (Div. Ct.), which is discussed further in chapter 9.)

Dawson v. Rexcraft Storage and Warehouse Inc.
(1998), 164 DLR (4th) 257, [1998] 111 OAC 201 (CA)

BORINS JA: ... a defendant may move to strike out a plaintiff's statement of claim on the ground that it does not disclose a reasonable cause of action. The essence of the defendant's motion is that the "wrong," described in the statement of claim, is not recognized as a violation of the plaintiff's legal rights, with the result that the court would be unable to grant a remedy, even if the plaintiff proved all the facts alleged. Thus, to permit the plaintiff to litigate the claim through discovery and trial would be a waste of both the parties' and the court's time.

Because the purpose of a rule 21.01(1)(b) motion is to test whether the plaintiff's allegations (assuming they can be proved) state a claim for which a court may grant relief, the only question posed by the motion is whether the statement of claim states a legally sufficient claim, i.e., whether it is substantively adequate. Consequently, the motions judge, as mandated by rule 21.01(2)(b), does not consider any evidence in deciding the motion. The motions judge addresses a purely legal question: whether, assuming the plaintiff can prove the allegations pleaded in the statement of claim, he or she will have established a cause of action entitling him or her to some form of relief from the defendant. Because dismissal of an action for failure to state a reasonable cause of action is a drastic measure, the court is required to give a generous reading to the statement of claim, construe it in the light most favourable to the plaintiff, and be satisfied that it is plain and obvious that the plaintiff cannot succeed. See *Hunt v. Carey Canada Inc.*, [1990] 2 SCR 959.

In some cases, a statement of claim will be vulnerable to dismissal under rule 21.01(1)(b) because the plaintiff has sought relief for acts that are not proscribed under the law. The typical textbook example is a statement of claim that alleges that the defendant made a face at the plaintiff, or that the defendant drove a car of an offensive colour. In other cases, however, the statement of claim may be defective because it has failed to allege the necessary elements of a claim that, if properly pleaded, would constitute a reasonable cause of action.

To illustrate the second situation, suppose, for example, that P sues D for damages for malicious prosecution. To recover for malicious prosecution, a plaintiff must establish these elements: institution of criminal proceedings by the defendant without reasonable and probable cause; an improper purpose in instituting the proceedings such as malice, or a primary purpose other than that of carrying the law into effect; termination of the criminal proceedings in favour of the plaintiff; and damages: J. Fleming, *The Law of Torts* (8th ed., 1992, The Law Book Co. Ltd.) at 610. If P fails to plead favourable termination of the criminal proceedings, D may move to strike out the statement of claim on the ground that P failed to allege a necessary element of the tort. P's failure to plead favourable termination may simply be an oversight. If so, the court should allow P to amend the statement of claim to add this allegation, and the lawsuit will proceed. See *AGF Canadian Equity Fund v. Transamerica Commercial Finance Corp. Canada* (1993), 14 OR (3d) 161 at 172-74 (Gen. Div.).

Although I have analyzed rule 21.01(1)(b) from the perspective of a defendant's motion to strike out a statement of claim on the ground that it is substantively inadequate, a similar analysis applies to a plaintiff's motion to strike out a statement of defence on the ground that it does not state a reasonable defence.

Thus, while a rule 21.01(1)(b) motion focuses on the substantive adequacy of a claim, or a defence, it offers no assistance in weeding out cases where a substantively adequate claim, or defence, has been pleaded, but cannot be proved. This is the function of a motion for summary judgment. This can be illustrated by reference to the hypothetical action for malicious prosecution. Suppose that P has pleaded the essential elements of the tort, and D knows that the case was stayed by the court, rather than dismissed. If this disposition does not constitute "favourable termination," P cannot win his malicious prosecution action. Under Rule 20, D may challenge P's ability to prove favourable termination by moving for summary judgment, supported by evidence that provides proof that the case was stayed without a finding, and legal argument that a stay is insufficient to meet the "favourable termination" element of a malicious prosecution action.

Wyman and Moscrop Realty Ltd. v. Vancouver Real Estate Board
[1957] BCJ No. 135 (CA)

COADY JA: This is an appeal from the order of Whittaker J dismissing the defendant's application to strike out the statement of claim herein on the ground that it discloses no reasonable cause of action in that the plaintiffs had not pleaded that they or either of them are members of the defendant's society.

The endorsement on the writ is as follows:

The plaintiffs' claim is for: (a) Damages for wrongful expulsion from the Vancouver Real Estate Board; (b) damages for loss of reputation, business and profits arising out of such wrongful expulsion; (c) an order directed to the defendant to restore the plaintiffs to membership in good standing in the defendant, and to restore to the plaintiffs all rights and privileges incidental to such membership, and (d) costs.

It has not been suggested that this was not a sufficient endorsement. What is complained of is that the plaintiffs in their statement of claim do not specifically plead that they or either of them are members of the defendant's organization.

Paragraph 4 of the statement of claim sets out in some detail the investigation made by the defendant, on notice to the plaintiff, of a complaint made to the defendant with respect to a salesman employed by the plaintiff company. Paragraph 5 alleges that following this investigation the plaintiff company was expelled from membership in the defendant organization. Paragraph 6 alleges that the appeal taken by the plaintiffs to the directors of the defendant organization from such expulsion was disallowed. Paragraph 7 states that the further appeal of the plaintiffs to the full membership of the defendant was also disallowed. In para. 8 of the statement of claim the plaintiffs allege that all the aforesaid proceedings, including the expulsion, were wrongful as contrary to law, contrary to natural justice and contrary to the constitution and by-laws of the defendant.

The defendant has denied para. 4 but has not specifically pleaded to the factual allegations in paras. 5, 6 and 7 of the statement of claim, but in reply to para. 8 thereof denies that the pleadings referred to in paras. 5, 6 and 7 of the statement of claim were contrary to law, or contrary to natural justice, or contrary to the constitution and by-laws of the defendant, as alleged by the plaintiffs, and further denies that the expulsion of the plaintiff was contrary to law, contrary to natural justice and contrary to the constitution and by-laws of the defendant. The defendant further pleads that the statement of claim alleges no cause of action against the defendant.

Counsel for the plaintiffs admits, as I understand it, that proof of membership is essential if the plaintiff is to succeed in this action. He admits too, as I understand, that a plea of membership is essential, but maintains that the statement of claim, as it stands, including the prayer for relief, while not expressly alleging membership, does so by clear inference and there can therefore be no misunderstanding or confusion arising from the absence of any express plea.

It would therefore appear to be common ground that a plea of membership is essential and proof of membership is likewise essential to the plaintiffs' case.

The first and only substantial point for decision in this case is whether or not the plaintiffs in the statement of claim have with sufficient clarity pleaded membership in the defendant organization. It is unnecessary in the circumstances to discuss cases dealing with whether the plea is essential or not. The only point is whether it has been sufficiently pleaded.

Order 19, r. 4, provides that: "Every pleading shall contain, and contain only, a statement in a summary form of the material facts on which the party pleading relies for his claim or defence, as the case may be."

The cases make it clear that a party must plead all the material facts on which he intends to rely at the trial, otherwise he is not entitled to give evidence of them at the trial. It is clear too, I think, that no averment must be omitted which is essential to success.

In *Cooke v. Gill* (1873), LR 8 CP 107 at p. 116, Brett J defines "cause of action" as "every fact which is material to be proved to entitle the plaintiff to succeed—every fact which the defendant would have a right to traverse." See also *Read v. Brown* (1888), 22 QBD 128. As said by Hunter CJ in *Centre Star Mining Co. v. Rossland Miners Union* (1903), 9 BCR 531 at p. 534: "Pleadings should be concise and positive with no ambiguity."

In the present case there is no express plea of a necessary averment, namely, membership. At best the plea can only be described as an attempt in an indirect and oblique way to express a claim to membership. Such necessary averment ought not to be left to mere inference or mere implication to be deduced from the form in which the pleading is framed. The defendant is entitled to know definitely the case he is called upon to meet. It is necessary for the plaintiffs to establish by evidence that the plaintiffs, or either of them, are legally members of the defendant. The pleading as it stands, if it can be interpreted inferentially as a plea of membership, may mean nothing more than a claim to *de facto* membership which would be insufficient to constitute the basis for the relief claimed. Legal membership has to be established. Counsel for the defendant has moreover pointed out that in the absence of any express plea of membership, he has not pleaded a further defence that will be open to him and will be relied upon if an express plea of membership is made. That defence he says is to the effect that the constitution and by-laws of the defendant provide that the decision of the domestic tribunal shall be final and that no recourse shall be had to the Courts by a member with respect to any decision of this domestic tribunal.

There is a second point raised by counsel for the plaintiffs, namely, that the failure of the defendant to specifically deny the factual allegations in paras. 5, 6 and 7 of the statement of claim, constitutes an admission of these paragraphs and consequently an admission of the membership of the plaintiffs in the defendant organization, and the defendant is now on the pleadings estopped from denying that membership, and this appeal for that reason should therefore be dismissed. I cannot agree that the failure to deny the factual allegations in the said paragraphs involves any admission by the defendant of membership. But if it were held that it did, the defendant, in the circumstances, faced as he was with an uncertain and indefinite pleading would be granted leave to amend. No advantage therefore can be obtained by counsel for the plaintiffs based on any such suggested admission. We cannot escape the burden of proving membership and I find it difficult to understand why the reluctance to pleading it expressly. The present pleading, insofar as it is intended to be a plea of membership, is at best too vague, indefinite and misleading.

The learned Judge below concluded that the matter should be left to the trial Judge. The cases relied upon are, I think, distinguishable. The only matter for consideration at present is, assuming all the allegations in the statement of claim are true, whether there is a cause of action disclosed: *Anderson v. Midland R. Co.*, [1902] 1 Ch. 369. It is not a case of hearing evidence and then deciding. The matter should be decided now, it seems to me, and not left in the present uncertain and indefinite state. The parties should not be compelled to go down to trial before having the position clarified.

The appeal should be allowed and the respondents given 15 days to amend as they may he advised; otherwise the statement of claim to be struck out. This is in effect the order made in *Roberts v. Pollock*, [1926] 4 DLR 1145, 21 SLR 141, except that the time for amendment was there extended for 30 days. The appellant is entitled to the costs of the appeal and the costs below as costs to the appellant in any event.

NOTES AND QUESTIONS

1. The test for substantive adequacy requires not only that the pleading be premised on a legally recognized cause of action (or, at least, one not plainly and obviously destined to fail), but also that the pleading must articulate sufficient material facts to demonstrate a factual foundation for each element of that cause of action. The facts alleged are deemed to be proved in determining the existence of a cause of action for the purposes of determining the substantive adequacy of a pleading. Actually proving the alleged facts is a matter for trial.

2. One important concern raised with respect to substantive adequacy at the pleading stage is whether the requirement to show a legally recognized claim at the outset will discourage the advancement of novel claims and causes of action. Canadian courts have grappled with this issue and have generally concluded, as per the Supreme Court of Canada's ruling in *Holland v. Saskatchewan*, below, that, although a cause of action is novel, a pleading should not be struck unless it is clear that the cause of action could not succeed at trial. See also *Jane Doe v. Board of Commissioners of Police for the Municipality of Metropolitan Toronto* (1990), 74 OR (2d) 225 (Div. Ct.), included in chapter 9.

Holland v. Saskatchewan
[2008] SCJ No. 43

McLACHLIN CJ: The issue in this case is whether the Court of Appeal erred in striking out the plaintiff's cause of action in negligence. The result of this order was to prevent the claim in negligence from proceeding to trial.

The appellant, Roger Holland, represents a group of approximately 200 game farmers who refused to register in a federal program aimed at preventing chronic wasting disease ("CWD") in domestic cervids, because they objected to a broadly worded indemnification and release clause in the registration form. As a result of their refusal to sign the form, the game farmers lost the CWD-free herd certification level which they had acquired by conforming to provincial CWD prevention rules, before the merging of the provincial and federal programs. The down-grading of the farmers' certification status both reduced the market price of their product and diminished their ability to sell it. This resulted in a financial loss to the farmers.

The game farmers successfully established on judicial review that the indemnification and release clauses had been invalidly included in the registration form. These clauses required that game farm operators would not only assume "sole responsibility for any death losses ... which may occur when animals are being handled for purposes of inspection, sampling or testing," but would also indemnify the federal and provincial governments "from and against all claims and demands ... arising out of or attributable or with respect to the Program, or any aspect of the Program or its implementation." Gerein CJQB found that the Minister had no legislative authority to make acceptance of these clauses, which he characterized as "broad in the extreme," a condition to participate in the CWD program ((2004), 258 Sask. R 243, 2004 SKQB 478, at para. 38). The program's reliance upon game farm operators might justify limited indemnification and release clauses restricted to the operator's actions, but it could not validly extend to the actions of government employees (para. 37). While Gerein CJQB found that the applicants' herd status was wrongly reduced to the lowest level of "surveillance," he declined to reinstate the prior herd status in the absence of any evidence on the current circumstances of the game farm operations. He specified, however, that if the applicants met the certification program conditions, the court's declarations would "serve to remove the earlier impediments" (para. 50). The government did not appeal this decision.

Despite the court's declaration that the government's reduction of the herd status was invalid, the government did not take the necessary steps to consider reinstating the farmers' certification or take any steps to compensate the farmers for the revenue they lost through the wrongful cancellation of their prior certification level.

Seeking a remedy for the financial loss they suffered as a result of the government's wrongful reduction of certification status, the game farmers turned to the law of tort. They commenced a class action, in the name of the appellant, claiming damages on three alleged grounds: (1) the tort of misfeasance in public office; (2) the tort of intimidation; and (3) the tort of negligence.

The government brought a motion to strike out the farmers' claims. The motions judge, Laing CJ, struck the intimidation claim for lack of evidence of any threat (2006), 277 Sask. R 131, 2006 SKQB 99, at (para. 36), granted leave to amend the statement of claim with regard to the misfeasance claim (para. 33), and denied the motion on the negligence claim (para. 34). The Court of Appeal of Saskatchewan allowed the government's appeal from the ruling on negligence, holding that no action lies against public authorities for negligently acting outside their lawful mandates (2007), 299 Sask. R 109, 2007 SKCA 18, at para. 40). The question before this Court is whether the Court of Appeal erred in striking out the appellant's negligence claim in its entirety.

The Court of Appeal read the appellant's negligence claim as a claim for negligently acting outside the law (paras. 18-21). With one exception, discussed more fully later, I agree with this characterization of the negligence claim. For purposes of these reasons, I would characterize the imputed fault as breach of statutory duty. The statement of claim, read generously as required in an application to strike, focused mainly on two alleged acts of negligence: requiring the game farmers to enter into the broad indemnification agreement, and down-grading the status of those who refused to do so. In both cases, the alleged fault may be described as failing to act in accordance with the authorizing acts and regulations. As the statement of claim puts it at para. 58, the government and its employees "were under a duty of care to the Class [game farmers] to ensure those Acts and Regulations were administered in accordance with law and not to operate in breach of them."

I agree with the Court of Appeal that the claim, thus characterized, discloses no cause of action recognized by law and must be struck. The Court of Appeal correctly concluded that the viability of the action in negligence falls to be determined by application of *Anns v. Merton London Borough Council*, [1978] AC 728 (HL), adopted and refined by this Court in *Cooper v. Hobart*, [2001] 3 SCR 537, 2001 SCC 79. The Court of Appeal concluded that to date the law has not recognized an action against a government authority for negligent breach of statutory duty by acting outside or contrary to the law. This being the case, the question was whether a new instance of negligence should be permitted. This question is resolved by asking whether a new kind of duty of care arises under the two-step *Anns* inquiry. The Court of Appeal did not find it necessary to consider the first branch of *Anns*, holding that even if the requirement of proximity were established, residual policy considerations at the second step militate against recognizing such a cause of action.

In my view, the Court of Appeal was correct in these conclusions. The law to date has not recognized an action for negligent breach of statutory duty. It is well established that mere breach of a statutory duty does not constitute negligence: *The Queen in Right of Canada v. Saskatchewan Wheat Pool*, [1983] 1 SCR 205. The proper remedy for breach of statutory duty by a public authority, traditionally viewed, is judicial review for invalidity. The appellant pursued this remedy before Gerein CJQB and obtained a declaration that the government's action of reducing the herd certification status was unlawful and invalid. No parallel action lies in tort.

The next question was whether a hitherto unrecognized relationship of potential liability in negligence should be recognized under the *Anns* test. Assuming, without deciding, that the legislative and regulatory matrix established proximity between the Class and the government at the first step, policy considerations would negate recognition of liability, as the Court of Appeal detailed. These include the chilling effect and specter of indeterminate liability. As Richards JA stated at para. 43 of the Court of Appeal's decision:

> … the respondent's theory of liability would fundamentally shift the way in which the public and private spheres historically have carried the consequences or burden of governmental action which is shown to be *ultra vires*. I see no policy reason which would warrant such a dramatic revision in the shape of the law and, as indicated above, see much which cuts tellingly against shaping the law in the manner sought by the respondent.

I therefore agree with the Court of Appeal that the appellant's claim for negligently acting outside the law, or breach of statutory duty, cannot succeed and that the paragraphs of the statement of claim asserting this cause of action were rightly struck.

One allegation of negligence, however, appears to fall into a different category. Clause 61.1(f) of the appellant's statement of claim alleges that the Minister was negligent because "[n]otwithstanding the declarations of Mr. Justice Gerein that the indemnification and release clauses were invalid and [of] no effect, and that the herd status of 'surveillance' was wrongfully assigned, [he] refused to restore the CWD herd status ... to the level ... enjoyed before or to pay compensation ... for ... loss."

The claim is essentially one of negligent failure to implement an adjudicative decree.

The Court of Appeal treated this claim as separate and different from the claim for breach of statutory duty, dealing with it under the heading "The Other Alleged Duties of Care." However, it did not address the central assertion in this claim that the Minister was under a duty to implement the judicial decree of Gerein CJQB. Gerein CJQB's order arguably placed the Minister under a duty to remedy the wrongful reduction of the applicants' herd status. The Court of Appeal never discussed this question. Instead, it held that the pleadings' reference to restoration of herd status must be struck, not because it disclosed no cause of action, but because the appellant "has not pleaded any facts to the effect his herd or any other farmer's herd had been maintained so as to warrant any particular CWD status, including the status it enjoyed before being reduced to 'surveillance'" (para. 49). "[T]he failure to plead such facts in the statement of claim," it concluded, "means this aspect of the negligence action must fail."

With respect, it is not clear to me that the reasons given by the Court of Appeal provide a sound basis for striking para. 61.1(f) at the outset of the proceedings. The real issue, not addressed by the Court of Appeal, is whether a claim for negligent failure to implement a judicial decree clearly cannot succeed in law and hence must be struck at the outset. Such a claim is not a claim for negligent breach of statute. It stands on a different footing. In *Welbridge Holdings Ltd. v. Greater Winnipeg*, [1971] SCR 957, at p. 970, this Court noted the difference in terms that appear to recognize the possibility of an action for failure to implement a judicial decree:

> ... the risk of loss from the exercise of legislative or adjudicative authority is a general public risk and not one for which compensation can be supported on the basis of a private duty of care. *The situation is different where a claim for damages for negligence is based on acts done in pursuance or in implementation of legislation or of adjudicative decrees.* [Emphasis added.]

More recent authorities describe the distinction in terms of "policy" versus "operational" decisions. Policy decisions about what acts to perform under a statute do not give rise to liability in negligence. On the other hand, once a decision to act has been made, the government may be liable in negligence for the manner in which it implements that decision: *Kamloops (City of) v. Nielsen*, [1984] 2 SCR 2; *Just v. British Columbia*, [1989] 2 SCR 1228; *Laurentide Motels Ltd. v. Beauport (City)*, [1989] 1 SCR 705; *Lewis (Guardian ad litem of) v. British Columbia*, [1997] 3 SCR 1145. Public authorities are expected to implement a judicial decision. Consequently, implementation of a judicial decision is an "operational" act. It is therefore not clear that an action in negligence cannot succeed on the breach of a duty to implement a judicial decree.

The remaining question is whether para. 61.1(f) must be struck because it fails to plead sufficient facts. In my view, it should not. The government's refusal "to restore CWD herd status" is pleaded as a fact. It is also pleaded, elsewhere, that loss of herd status led to losses to the members of the Class. These facts, in my view, were sufficient to support the claim for negligent failure to implement a judicial decree. It might be argued that facts relating to the conditions for restoration should have been pleaded. However, I am satisfied that the pleading was sufficient to put the government on the notice of the essence of the appellant's claim. Taking a generous view, it should not have been struck.

I do not comment on whether the evidence and the applicable law will in fact establish a claim for negligence on this head at the time of trial. However, applying the rule that, on an application to strike, pleadings must be read broadly and that it must be clear that the claim cannot succeed if it goes to trial, I am of the view that para. 61.1(f) should not be struck.

I would therefore confirm the order of the Court of Appeal that paras. 58 to 63.1 of the statement of claim should be struck out, with the exception of para. 61.1(f). I add that this order should not be read as precluding further applications by the appellant to amend the statement of claim, nor to prevent reliance on facts mentioned in the portions of the claim struck out, insofar as such facts relate to the actions properly raised in the statement of claim.

In the result, I would allow the appeal in part, with costs in the cause.

B. Setting the Boundaries of Litigation and Trial

Pleadings define and set the outer limits of the issues to be addressed in an action. Since pleadings are intended to provide notice to the opposing party of the case that he or she has to meet, fairness ordinarily dictates that a party will not be permitted to raise new issues at trial or to call evidence not relevant to the issues as pleaded. Even where the requirement of substantive adequacy is met, failure to plead one's case fully may raise a problem of variance: a difference between that which is pleaded and that which one wishes to argue or prove at trial. As illustrated by the following excerpts from *Rodaro v. Royal Bank of Canada* and *MacDonald Construction Company v. Ross*, respectively, Canadian courts have consistently held that lawsuits should be tried and resolved within the parameters defined by the pleadings.

Rodaro v. Royal Bank of Canada
[2002] OJ No. 1365 (CA)

[This case involved, in part, an appeal of the trial judge's finding that the defendant was liable on the grounds of lost opportunity, a cause of action that was not pleaded by the plaintiff. The following excerpt is the Court of Appeal's ruling on this point.]

DOHERTY JA: ... The lost opportunity analysis adopted by Spence J was theoretically sound. I am satisfied, however, that it could not be applied in this case. First, it was never pleaded or otherwise raised by Mr. Rodaro at any stage of the lengthy proceedings. Second, there was no evidence that the disclosure of the confidential information by RBC to Barbican caused Mr. Rodaro to lose the opportunity described by Spence J. To the contrary, to the extent that the evidence speaks to the loss of the opportunity at all, it demonstrates that Mr. Rodaro "lost" the opportunity to negotiate with Barbican for reasons that had nothing to do with the disclosure of the information to Barbican.

Mr. Rodaro did not plead that RBC's improper disclosure to Barbican deprived him of the opportunity to negotiate a "package deal" involving the sale of the debt and his equity in the project. At no time during the months of trial or the course of lengthy argument did Mr. Rodaro suggest that the improper disclosure had caused him to lose the opportunity described by Spence J. That theory appeared for the first time in the reasons of Spence J.

It is fundamental to the litigation process that lawsuits be decided within the boundaries of the pleadings. As Labrosse JA said in *460635 Ontario Limited v. 1002953 Ontario Inc.*, [1999] OJ No. 4071 at para. 9 (CA) (QL):

> ... The parties to a legal suit are entitled to have a resolution of their differences on the basis of the issues joined in the pleadings. A finding of liability and resulting damages against the defendant on a basis that was not pleaded in the statement of claim cannot stand. It deprives the defendant of the opportunity to address that issue in the evidence at trial. ...

By stepping outside of the pleadings and the case as developed by the parties to find liability, Spence J denied RBC and Barbican the right to know the case they had to meet and the right to a fair opportunity to meet that case. The injection of a novel theory of liability into the case via the reasons for judgment was fundamentally unfair to RBC and Barbican.

In addition to fairness concerns which standing alone would warrant appellate intervention, the introduction of a new theory of liability in the reasons for judgment also raises concerns about the reliability of that theory. We rely on the adversarial process to get at the truth. That process assumes that the truth best emerges after a full and vigorous competition amongst the various opposing parties. A theory of liability that emerges for the first time in the reasons for judgment is never tested in the crucible of the adversarial process. We simply do not know how Spence J's lost opportunity theory would have held up had it been subject to the rigours of the adversarial process. We do know, however, that all arguments that were in fact advanced by Mr. Rodaro and were therefore subject to the adversarial process were found wanting by Spence J.

Spence J erred in finding liability on a theory never pleaded and with respect to which battle was never joined at trial. This error alone requires reversal. However, I am also satisfied that the lost opportunity analysis could not succeed on this evidence.

Given that Mr. Rodaro did not plead or argue the lost opportunity approach adopted by Spence J, it is not surprising that he led no evidence in support of that approach. Counsel for Mr. Rodaro does not suggest that there was any direct evidence to support the lost opportunity analysis. He submits, however, that Spence J was entitled to draw inferences from the evidence as to what likely would have happened had there not been improper disclosure of the confidential information: *Cadbury Schweppes*, supra, at p. 186.

I accept that Spence J was entitled to draw inferences from the evidence. I also accept that in doing so, he could consider what a reasonable person in the position of Mr.

Rodaro would have done but for the improper disclosure of the confidential information. However, where, as here, the lost opportunity identified by Spence J was never identified by Mr. Rodaro at any stage in the proceedings, and was not touched on at all in the evidence, I think Spence J's findings that the opportunity existed and was lost as a result of the improper disclosure of confidential information amount to speculation and not inference.

MacDonald Construction Company v. Ross
(1980), 17 CPC 142 (PEISC)

McQUAID J: This is an action for damages which the plaintiff is alleged to have suffered by reason of the negligence of the defendant.

Briefly, the plaintiff is a building contractor and the defendant was, at all material times, solicitor to the plaintiff. One of the plaintiff's properties was destroyed by fire, and the plaintiff instructed the defendant, as its solicitor, to take the necessary steps to realize upon a fire insurance policy earlier placed on the property. The main action arises out of the defendant's alleged negligence in not so doing until after the limitation period of one year had expired, thus rendering any such claim barred by statute.

Upon the completion of the taking of evidence, counsel for the defendant proceeded to make his argument. During the course of his presentation he advanced the proposition that even if the defendant were negligent, which he did not admit, and even if he had pursued the claim for insurance with due diligence, he would not have been successful in any event, since the property in question was vacant on the date of the loss, contrary to the terms of the policy. Since the plaintiff's claim against the defendant was for loss allegedly incurred in the defendant's failure to pursue the insurance claim to recovery, his alleged loss being the amount which he claims he should have recovered, the defendant's argument was that no loss would have been recovered in any event, the policy being voided by vacancy, and hence the plaintiff had no recoverable claim against the defendant.

Counsel for the plaintiff objected to the defendant being permitted to advance this line of argument, since it had never been pleaded, that had such been pleaded as a defence, his examination of witnesses would have taken a different course, and that he was taken by surprise and therefore prejudiced. Counsel for the defendant argued that this defence was implicit in his pleadings, or in the alternative, that he be permitted to amend his pleadings, and moved accordingly.

The issues presently before the Court are twofold, first whether he is to be permitted to pursue this argument without amendment, or is he precluded from so doing by his pleadings; second, whether he be permitted to amend, and, if so, the implications of any such amendment.

In his defence, the defendant pleaded:

> 2. The Defendant denies that the Plaintiff retained the defendant as its solicitor as alleged or at all.

3. If the Plaintiff retained the Defendant as its solicitor (which is denied) the Defendant denies that he was instructed to take any action against The Casualty Company of Canada within the limitation period, or at all.

4. The Defendant does not admit that the Plaintiff suffered the damages alleged or at all.

The proposed amendment would be in the following words:

5. In the alternative, the Defendant denies liability to the Plaintiff for his failure to take action against The Casualty Company of Canada as alleged in paragraph 6 of the Plaintiff's Statement of Claim, because such an action, had it been taken within the limitation period, would have been unsuccessful by reason that the Plaintiff's building referred to in the Statement of Claim at the time of the fire had been vacant for more than thirty (30) consecutive days and, therefore, was a loss excluded under the Plaintiff's fire insurance policy with The Casualty Company of Canada.

Paragraphs 2 and 3 of the defence are, I think, immaterial to the issue at hand. The first question to be determined here is whether para. 4 is sufficiently broad to encompass the particular line of argument on defence.

The purpose of pleadings is to enunciate to the opposing party, and to the Court, precisely and with some degree of definition the issues in dispute as between the parties, to enable each to know, in advance of trial the issues to be met, the evidence which will be required, and the shape which the trial is likely to take.

Rule 14.04 provides:

Every pleading shall contain a statement in summary form of the material facts on which the party pleaded relies on for his claim or defence. … and the statement shall be as brief as the nature of the case admits.

And Rule 14.14:

Subject to Rules 14.15 to 14.18 [not relevant here], a party in his defence or in any subsequent pleading shall,

(c) specifically plead any matter, for example, performance, release, payment, or any relevant statute of limitation, statute of frauds, fraud, or any fact showing illegality that,

(i) might make any claim or defence of the opposing party not maintainable;

(ii) if not specifically pleaded, might take the opposing party by surprise;

(iii) raises issues of fact not arising out of the preceding pleadings.

The requirement is, therefore, that pleadings are required to be so framed that they contain all material facts and matters in a manner sufficiently clear and concise to present the nature of the claim, or defence, so that the opposing party will not reasonably be taken by surprise, or which, in themselves will not raise collateral or subsidiary issues not otherwise pleaded. (*Cherry v. Petch*, [1946] OWN 383; *Saliarius v. Saunders; Saunders v. Saliarius*, [1948] 2 WWR 706). The commentary on the corresponding English Rule, 18/8, as it appears at p. 271 of the *1976 Annual Practice* indicates that the defendant must make it quite clear what line of defence he is adopting.

Referring back to the defence as filed, "The Defendant does not admit that the Plaintiff suffered the damages alleged or at all," this does not, in my opinion, meet the requirements of the Rule. It is a simple traverse which, in effect, does little other than to put the plaintiff to the proof of his allegations. It does not, as I suggest it should, alert the plaintiff to the line of defence which the defendant intends to advance, that is to say, that the plaintiff was in breach of his insurance contract, and by reason of such breach could not have recovered in any event.

I would therefore be of the opinion, and so hold, that, on the basis of the pleadings as they stood at the time of trial, the defendant is precluded from pursuing this line of argument.

Rule 15 provides that a party may amend his pleadings at any time with leave of the Court. The granting or withholding of such leave is discretionary in the Court, and although the evidence, but not the argument, had been completed, the application for amendment was made "at trial," and hence not out of time. The wording of the proposed amendment is appropriate in that it clearly defines the issue and line of argument on which the defendant presumably will rest his defence.

The first question is: should I exercise that discretion, and permit such an amendment? I am grateful to counsel for providing me with their many authorities, all of which I have reviewed, but out of which I will refer only to those which appear to me to be the most applicable.

In *Re Robinson's Settlement; Gant v. Hobbs*, [1912] 1 Ch. 717 (CA) Fletcher Moulton LJ states at p. 726:

> With regard to the other question, I would point out that these rules are meant to assist the administration of the judicial functions of the Court, and they are not meant to introduce rigid technicalities which would militate against full justice being done by the Court. They are there to protect litigants, and in cases where there is no wrong done, and nobody is taken by surprise or put at a disadvantage thereby, it is perfectly open to the Court either to grant an amendment or to decline to enforce strict obedience to these rules, more especially in the case of rules to the breach of which no penalty is affixed.

In the same case at p. 728, Buckley LJ said:

> The effect of the rule is, I think, for reasons of practice and justice and convenience to require the party to tell his opponent what he is coming to the Court to prove. If he does not do that the Court will deal with him in one of two ways. It may say that it is not open to him, that he has not raised it and will not be allowed to rely on it; or it may give him leave to amend by raising it, and protect the other party if necessary by letting the case stand over. The rule is not one that excludes from the consideration of the Court the relevant subject-matter for decision simply on the ground that it is not pleaded. It leaves the party in mercy and the Court will deal with him as is just.

This case was cited as an authoritative statement of the law in *Pirie v. Richardson*, [1927] 1 KB 448, Lord Hanworth MR at p. 453. Two Canadian cases on point are *Toronto v. Hutton*, [1951] OWN 639, and *Simrod v. Cooper*, [1952] OWN 720.

Thus, the principle is established that the Rules of Court, at least insofar as they apply to pleadings, are intended to constitute the criteria required to be met in case disclosure, for the information of the litigants, and, insofar as the Court is concerned, to enable it to adjudicate with equal fairness to those litigants on all matters in issue as between them. Where, however, either party may not have complied with those criteria, the Rules should not be strictly and rigidly construed to preclude amendment, and thus defeat justice being done. This is not to say that in all cases will such amendment be allowed, or if allowed, without terms and conditions. ...

Having reviewed these authorities, it now becomes necessary to attempt to relate them to the present matter. Reference has already been made to the defendant's pleadings with respect to which I have held that they are, in themselves, insufficient to permit the defendant to develop the line of defence upon which he launched in his argument.

Next, I think the evidence must be looked at to determine whether the question of vacancy was raised. I have examined the evidence of Earl Beaton, the representative of the insuring company and can find no reference therein to the possibility that the property was vacant, or even that he was aware or suspected it might have been. The matter was not in any way broached.

The cross-examination of Dewar MacDonald, president of the plaintiff company contains the following exchange beginning at the foot of p. 34 of the transcript:

Q. Did anybody live in it after the first week of September?
A. No.
Q. So, the property was vacant until September 1 until the fire, is that correct?
A. Oh, six weeks, a month, somewheres around there.
Q. I see. When you obtained your insurance, did you advise Mr. Beaton that the property was vacant?
A. It wasn't vacant at the time I put insurance on it.
Q. I see, but it was vacant from somewhere around September the 1st, on?
A. Approximately there.
Q. And this fire occurred when?
A. October the 31st, '75.
Q. That's normally Hallowe'en night?
A. That's right.
Q. And you knew on Hallowe'en night that this property was vacant?
A. That's right.
Q. And this property was not a summer or seasonal dwelling, this was a property you had for purposes of rental the full year around, is that correct?
A. That's right.

Apart from a casual reference to vacancy on Halloween night on p. 78(a), there appears to be no other mention of the fact of vacancy.

It is on the basis of this brief passage of evidence that the defendant would introduce his proposed line of argument. It could be said, that, in a subtle way, a groundwork had been laid. However, there was nothing in the defendant's pleadings which would alert the plaintiff, which, of course, is the purpose of pleadings. The evidence of MacDonald, above quoted, was subsequent to that of the insurer, Beaton. I am quite sure, knowing the examining capabilities of both counsel, had there been any prior intimation that the vacancy element would be a factor, the examination of Beaton might well have taken a different course. Indeed one can speculate that the entire thrust of the plaintiff's case, pleadings, discovery and evidence, might well have been different. I think it would be extremely difficult for any counsel, upon reading para. 4 of the defence, to anticipate this line of defence.

I do not believe that, as the pleadings now stand, the defendant should be permitted to pursue it.

However, as Fletcher Moulton LJ pointed out in *Re Robinson's Settlement*, supra, the function of rules is to present the respective position of the litigants in such a manner as will enable the Court to administer justice between them, and where they appear to militate against this end, they should either be interpreted flexibly, or where this is not possible, amendment on terms should be permitted in the discretion of the Court.

It is possible that had the defendant's suggested defence been properly pleaded, rather than approached obliquely, it might conceivably constitute a good defence to the action, and he should not be denied his defence by a rigid application of the rule. On the other hand, had the defendant so pleaded, it is equally conceivable that the plaintiff might well have countered it either by way of a pleading in reply, or by evidence led.

I would be of the opinion that the proposed amendment should be allowed in order to bring all proper issues before the Court, for that is the purpose of the trial process. To allow the amendment may change substantially the entire thrust of the proceeding, and this should not be done to the prejudice of the plaintiff.

The amendment will be allowed on the following terms. The pleadings will be deemed to be re-opened with the plaintiff being allowed to reply, if he considers it appropriate to do so; the plaintiff may discover, or rediscover any witness; when trial resumes either party should have the right to recall and re-examine any witness on matters touching or arising out of the substance of the amendment.

In addition the plaintiff shall have its costs as taxed in any event from the time of the close of the initial pleadings to the date of resumption of trial. In addition, if it should be that the end result of the trial shall be in favor of the plaintiff, the plaintiff will be entitled to interest, at present bank rates, from the date on which the application to amend was made to the date on which the taking of any further evidence which either counsel may elect to adduce, as a result of such amendment, shall be concluded.

Application allowed.

NOTES AND QUESTIONS

1. The relationship between a novel cause of action and a pleaded cause of action was recently considered by the Supreme Court of Canada in *British Columbia v. Canadian Forest Products Ltd.*, [2004] SCJ No. 33. In this case, the court refused to consider the Crown's claim for environmental damage as a matter of public trust or *parens patriae* for the environment because this claim was not made out by the pleadings. While acknowledging that this novel cause of action may merit judicial consideration, the court nonetheless referred to the Crown's pleadings to restrict the plaintiff's entitlement in this case to compensation to the Crown's role as landowner. The court stated, at para. 145, that while "the courts should not strangle legitimate claims that are properly pleaded because of overly technical objections

to novel methods of assessment," the Crown could not succeed "in an unpleaded claim for 'ecological' or 'environmental' damage simply because the Crown on this issue occupies the moral high ground."

2. While variance between pleading and proof in relation to material facts may present an obstacle to success in many cases, in defamation claims the courts will not necessarily require an exact match between the words pleaded and the words ultimately proven to have been spoken (*Grant v. Cormier* (2001), 56 OR (3d) 215 (CA)). Why would this exception be made in the context of defamation?

3. *Special rules re statements of defence.* The general requirement to plead material facts applies to statements of defence as well. This means that, depending on the nature of the defence being advanced, a defendant may be required to do more than merely plead denials of the plaintiff's claim. Further, in most (but not all) Canadian jurisdictions, silence in a defence pleading is deemed to be an admission of the plaintiff's allegations.

4. *Impact of the scope of pleadings.* Pleadings affect matters both within and outside of the dispute between the parties to litigation. For example:

a. Within the litigation itself, they will assist in determining the scope of the parties' obligations in documentary and oral discovery. For this reason, it is important for counsel to recognize that broad allegations in pleadings may well increase the resources required to comply with production obligations at a later stage in the proceeding. Note, however, that while the pleadings remain a touchstone for determining production obligations in jurisdictions across Canada, the breadth of the obligations vis-à-vis the pleadings may vary. For example, in Ontario, parties are obliged to disclose any material having a "semblance of relevance to the matters in issue as delineated by the pleadings" (*Axa Pacific Insurance Co. v. R.J. Nicol Construction (1975) Ltd.*, [2001] OJ No. 4020 (Master)). In contrast, in Alberta, disclosure obligations flow from showing that material will "significantly help determine one or more issues raised in the pleadings" or "ascertain evidence that could reasonably be expected to significantly help determine one or more" of those issues (*750869 Alberta Ltd. v. Cambridge Shopping Centres Ltd.* (2001), 283 AR 391 (QB)). Proposed amendments to the Ontario rules, discussed further in chapter 7, will likely narrow the scope of discovery in Ontario.

b. In class proceedings (discussed in chapter 11), strategic framing of pleadings may well play a role in determining whether a proceeding will be certified. For example, structuring statements of claim to target only a small group of defendants can assist in limiting the common issues raised in the proceeding and may improve chances for certification (see *Collette v. Great Pacific Management Co.* (2001), 86 BCLR (3d) 92, [2001] BCTC 237 (SC)).

c. With respect to matters outside the immediate dispute between the parties to the litigation, pleadings can play an integral role in determining whether an insurer has a duty to defend and/or indemnify a defending policyholder. In these situations, courts will examine the pleadings against the policyholder to determine whether they allege behaviour falling within the scope of the relevant insurance policy. One strategy for plaintiffs suing impecunious defendants, therefore, might have been to allege negligent conduct, rather than intentional acts by the policyholder, as the latter frequently do not fall within the scope of insurance policies. To the extent that the behaviour was covered by the policy, plaintiffs might expect to be in a better position to recover damages. However, the Supreme Court of Canada has made it clear that "what really matters is not the labels used by the plaintiff, but the true nature of the claim" (*Non-Marine Underwriters, Lloyds of London v. Scalera*, [2000] 1 SCR 551). As a result, courts asked to determine an insurer's duty to defend or indemnify a policyholder will look not only at the words pleaded, but the substance of the claim. In so doing, they may also review documents explicitly referred to in the pleading (*Monenco Ltd. v. Commonwealth Insurance Co.*, [2001] 2 SCR 699).

C. Amendment

In all Canadian jurisdictions, courts have broad powers to permit amendments to pleadings. Amendments can be used to rectify problems of substantive adequacy or to redefine or expand the issues for trial. As illustrated in *MacDonald Construction Company v. Ross*, above, amendments can be granted at a late stage of the litigation. However, a central consideration of a court in permitting an amendment is whether the amendment would result in prejudice to the opposing side that cannot be compensated for in costs and/or by an adjournment. This test may be more difficult to meet in the late stages of litigation. Where late amendments are permitted, courts may address prejudice through the order of costs and/or through an adjournment to allow the opposing party time to respond and obtain additional disclosure.

Nevertheless, "late in the day" amendments are not a forgone conclusion. In *Severin v. Vroom* (1977), 3 CPC 183, the Ontario Court of Appeal denied the defendant's motion on appeal to amend the statement of defence to assert an affirmative defence based on the *Statute of Frauds*. The court found the failure to seek an amendment at trial constituted a waiver of the defence (and also found evidence of past performance that rendered the agreement enforceable against the defendant notwithstanding the *Statute of Frauds*). In the result, parties ought to move as quickly as possible on recognizing that an amendment is necessary to close a gap between pleading and proof. The later the request for the amendment, the greater the likelihood of the responding party establishing incompensable prejudice (such as the death of a key witness or destruction of a document made material by the amendment) in the interim between the original pleading and the amendment.

In some circumstances, a court may conclude that an amendment requested late in the day is nevertheless proper if the issue was not specifically pleaded, but was canvassed on examinations for discovery (see *Sullivan v. Hoffman Bros. Ltd.*, [1968] 2 OR 201 (HC)). In any event, however, as illustrated by the following case, the prevailing consideration for the court in assessing an application to amend is fairness. Where prejudice can be compensated for in costs, an amendment should not be refused as a method of punishing the party seeking the amendment.

Miguna v. Ontario (Attorney General)
[2005] OJ No. 5346 (CA)

R.A. BLAIR JA:

Background

Miguna Miguna is a barrister and solicitor, practising in the areas of human rights law and immigration and refugee law, amongst others. He was born in Kenya, subsequently immigrated to Canada and became a Canadian citizen. He was called to the Ontario Bar in 1995.

On November 4, 2002, he was arrested at his law offices and charged with sexual assault following a complaint from one of his immigration clients. On July 14, 2003, when he appeared in court for the commencement of his trial on that charge, he was arrested again and charged with three further counts of sexual assault arising out of the complaints of another immigration client. Both arrests took place in front of colleagues and the public. He alleges that he was arrested, searched, handcuffed and detained in full public view at the court house on July 14 notwithstanding that he had, four days earlier, attended voluntarily at the police station, with his lawyer, in response to a police query to his staff about his whereabouts during an absence from his office while he was in Kenya.

On June 23, 2004, he was acquitted of all charges by Justice Moore of the Ontario Court of Justice. The trial judge accepted his evidence, found that there were contradictions in the testimony of the two complainants and was suspicious that they had a common motive to implicate Mr. Miguna and concluded that the police investigation of the case was wanting in some respects.

Mr. Miguna commenced these two proceedings against the Crown Attorney defendants, the Police defendants, Her Majesty the Queen, and the Attorney General for Ontario and Legal Aid Ontario, alleging malicious prosecution (including a serious allegation of racial profiling), breach of his Charter rights, negligent investigation and assault on the part of the police, and a galaxy of other "causes of action," some of which exist in law and some of which do not. On motion of the Crown and police defendants, Justice Paisley struck the statements of claim and refused leave to amend. He awarded substantial indemnity costs against Mr. Miguna in the total amount of $89,243.00.

Mr. Miguna appeals these orders and seeks to have the two actions reinstated except as against the defendants the Attorney General for Ontario and Legal Aid Ontario.

For the reasons that follow, I would allow the appeal, set aside the order striking the statement of claim in the action against the Crown and police defendants (except with respect to the Attorney General for Ontario and Legal Aid Ontario), and grant the plaintiff leave to amend. The appeal from the order striking the claim in the second action against Her Majesty the Queen is dismissed. The cost order falls with the granting of the first appeal.

The Action Against Her Majesty the Queen

The action against Her Majesty the Queen is a nullity because it was not commenced in compliance with s. 7(1) of the Proceedings Against the Crown Act, RSO 1990, c. P.27.

That section provides that no action may be commenced against the Crown without sixty days prior notice having been given. Here, the Crown was provided with notice of intention to sue on September 1, 2004. The statement of claim was issued on September 13, 2004.

As a result of the failure to comply with these requirements the action is a nullity and was properly struck. The appeal in this respect must therefore be dismissed.

The Action Against the Crown Attorneys and Police Defendants

On a motion to strike a pleading pursuant to Rule 21 of the Rules of Civil Procedure the facts as pleaded in the statement of claim must be taken to be true, although allegations of assumptions and speculation need not be accepted as such: see *Operation Dismantle v. The Queen*, [1985] 1 SCR 441 at 455. Where malice is alleged, full particulars must be provided: Rule 25.06(8). For a claim to be struck, it must be "plain and obvious" that no cause of action is disclosed: *Hunt v. Carey*, [1990] 2 SCR 959.

In *Nelles v. Ontario*, [1989] 2 SCR 170, and later in *Proulx v. Quebec (Attorney General)*, [2001] 3 SCR 9, the Supreme Court of Canada emphasized that the threshold for Crown liability for prosecutorial misconduct is very high. This is—as Binnie and Iacobucci JJ said in *Proulx* at para. 4—"so as to deter all but the most serious claims against the prosecuting authorities, and to ensure that Crown liability is engaged in only the most exceptional circumstances." At para. 8 they added, "[a] failed prosecution does not without more—much more—give rise to a viable claim for prosecutorial wrongdoing." In *Nelles*, Lamer J expressed the view that the availability of the Rule 21 motion to strike a claim as disclosing no cause of action would serve as a healthy brake on such actions (p. 197). At p. 199 he said:

> There is no doubt that the policy considerations in favour of absolute immunity have some merit. But in my view those considerations must give way to the right of a private citizen to seek a remedy when the prosecutor acts maliciously in fraud of his duties with the result that he causes damage to the victim. In my view the inherent difficulty in proving a case of malicious prosecution combined with the mechanisms available within the system of civil procedure to weed out the meritless claims is sufficient to ensure that the Attorney General and Crown Attorneys will not be hindered in the proper execution of their important public duties.

Thus there exists a narrow exception to the Crown's immunity from suit for prosecutorial misconduct in cases where "the prosecutor acts maliciously in fraud of his duties with the result that he causes damage to the victim." Whether that narrow exception is confined to the tort known as "malicious prosecution" is not clear from the authorities. But one thing is clear: however the claim is framed, the Crown's conduct must rise to the level of malice. Malice is defined for these purposes as "a deliberate and improper use of the office of the Attorney-General or Crown Attorney, a use inconsistent with the status of 'minister of justice'" and one in which the defendant "perpetrated a fraud on the process of criminal justice and in doing so has perverted or abused his office and the process of criminal justice": *Nelles*, at 193-194. No action lies against a Crown Attorney for prosecutorial misconduct that sounds in negligence.

There is a claim in law against the police for negligent investigation, however: see *Beck-stead v. Ottawa (City) Chief of Police* (1997), 37 OR (3d) 62 (Ont. CA); *Hill v. Hamilton-Wentworth Regional Police Services Board*, [2005] OJ No. 4045. As well, police may be liable for independent torts committed during the course of their duties, such as false arrest, false imprisonment, and assault and battery.

The issue here is whether Mr. Miguna's statement of claim discloses permissible causes of action against the Crown Attorney defendants and/or the Police defendants, or whether, if leave to amend is granted, the statement of claim could do so. We must be satisfied that the motion judge erred in the exercise of his discretion not to permit leave to amend, before we can interfere.

By any standards, Mr. Miguna's statement of claim is not well pleaded. He is claiming $17.5 million in damages and alleging the gravest of allegations against the Crown Attorney and Police defendants. Yet, instead of focusing his claim and the factual assertions supporting it on the few bases that may be open to him, he has taken the scattergun approach and raises—according to the respondents' count—somewhere between sixteen and twenty-five causes of action. These include: malicious prosecution, breach of Charter rights, prosecutorial misfeasance (abuse of process, abuse of power), negligent investigation, conspiracy, fraudulent misrepresentation, unlawful arrest and detention, assault and battery, defamation, incompetence, recklessness, wilful blindness, racial profiling, interference with bodily security, cruel unusual and oppressive treatment, and breach of trust.

In addition, Mr. Miguna's statement of claim confuses the need to plead the material facts relied upon—and in the case of malicious prosecution, the need to do so with full particularity—with the view that superimposing pejorative adverbs or adjectives one upon the other is a suitable substitute for pleading facts. For example, each of the Crown Attorney defendants is repeatedly alleged to have "negligently, incompetently, unethically, recklessly, and unprofessionally" (and, occasionally, "arrogantly") engaged in various types of impugned activities. But the pleading is very sparse when it comes to setting out material facts in support of the sweeping allegations made.

Having said that, however, the statement of claim does contain some basis for alleging the core causes of action that are asserted, and in my view, Mr. Miguna should be given an opportunity to amend to make out his case properly on a pleading basis. For instance, he alleges that:

a) he was arrested without reasonable cause and without the police having conducted a proper investigation on both November 4, 2002 (at his law office) and July 14, 2003 (at the courthouse);

b) both arrests were made publicly with a view to embarrassing and humiliating him in front of staff, professional colleagues, the judiciary, members of courts administration and the public;

c) the July 14 arrest was carried out in full public view, and on the instructions of the Crown, notwithstanding that Mr. Miguna and his lawyer had only four days previously attended at the police station in response to an indication that the police had been looking for him;

d) Crown Attorney Shallow directed the police officers to have Mr. Miguna arrested;

e) the trial judge acquitted him because, amongst other things, (i) the police failed to conduct a full investigation and to interview important witnesses, (ii) he was suspicious the complainants had a common motive to implicate Mr. Miguna, and (iii) he found Mr. Miguna to be a credible witness; in addition, the trial judge also alluded to the fact that Mr. Miguna was arrested on July 14, 2003, "despite offers by Mr. Miguna and his counsel to present himself to the police prior to that date";

f) Crown Attorney Shallow, alone or with the other defendants, sent fake clients to Mr. Miguna with the aim of entrapping him;

g) Crown Attorney Shallow continued to prosecute him when he (Shallow) knew or ought to have known that the complainants had falsely accused Mr. Miguna, misrepresented facts and evidence to the Ontario Court of Justice, interfered with witnesses, concealed evidence from the defence and the Court and counselled witnesses to commit perjury;

h) Crown Attorney Braley engaged in activities similar to those outlined in (g) above;

i) both Shallow and Braley participated in causing the venue of Mr. Miguna's trial to be changed from the Ontario Court of Justice at 1000 Finch Ave. to the Court located at College Park in downtown Toronto with the intention of further injuring his professional reputation;

j) all individual defendants participated in racial profiling against him;

k) the Police defendants failed to investigate the complainants' allegations against him prudently and to follow up where required, continued with the prosecution when they knew or ought to have known there was no reasonable basis for it, participated in the presentation of false evidence, failed to make full disclosure, and withheld evidence; and

l) he was assaulted by the police and subject to an illegal strip search during his detentions.

These are very serious allegations, and are, of course, only allegations at this stage of the proceedings. Mr. Miguna fails to establish them at his peril in terms of costs and, possibly, his reputation. For the most part, the allegations are pleaded in an unacceptably bald fashion. However, if appropriately supported by material facts, and proven, they—and other facts pleaded—could support claims for malicious prosecution, breach of the Charter and misfeasance in public office as against the Crown Attorney and Police defendants, and as against the Police defendants alone claims for negligent investigation, unlawful arrest, false imprisonment, and assault and battery. In my view, the plaintiff should be entitled to one more chance to attempt to plead these claims properly.

At the same time, it is appropriate to reiterate at this point the observation of Dickson J in *Operation Dismantle*, supra, at p. 455 that "allegations based on assumptions and speculation" need not be taken as true, because it would be improper to do so, as they are incapable of proof. Mr. Miguna must have knowledge of the facts supporting his claims and not merely plead allegations that he believes may or may not be true. Rosenberg J put it this way, in *Region Plaza Inc. v. Hamilton-Wentworth (Regional Municipality)* (1990), 12 OR (3d) 750 (HCJ) at 757:

... If the plaintiff does not at the outset have knowledge of the facts that give rise to the con-clusions of malice, breach of duty, conspiracy to intentionally injure, etc., then it is inappro-priate to make these allegations in the statement of claim. It may be that in the future the plaintiff will determine facts as a result of discovery or in some other way that will support some or all of the allegations ... [B]ut until the plaintiff has knowledge of some facts on which to base the conclusions alleged in the statement of claim, it is improper to allow these conclusions to be pleaded baldly and without any supporting facts.

The motion judge accepted the respondents' arguments that the statement of claim in its entirety was deficient, as several torts alleged were unknown to law, Her Majesty, the Attorney General and the Crown Attorneys were immune from suit with respect to others that were raised, and sufficient facts were not pleaded to support the claims that could be asserted in law. In spite of these factors, it seems that the motion judge, himself, was of the view that the deficiencies might be cured by amendment with respect to the permissible causes of action. He concluded, however, that he should exercise his discre-tion not to grant leave to amend. His exercise of discretion was based upon the following considerations:

a)   the appellant had been made aware of the deficiencies in the pleading and had had ample opportunity to amend, but had not done so (and the proposed amend-ed statement of claim presented at the hearing was deemed to be similarly deficient);

b)   the appellant had committed a grievous error in misrepresenting the reasons of the trial judge at the criminal trial on the charges of sexual assault; and,

c)   the appellant had made bald allegations of racial profiling, which amounted to a serious abuse.

Respectfully, the motion judge erred in principle in refusing to grant Mr. Miguna leave to amend his statement of claim for the foregoing reasons, in the circumstances of this case. He placed too much emphasis on what he perceived as the appellant's failure to move quickly to deliver a proper amended statement of claim, in the face of the respond-ents' criticisms of his pleading, and he appears to have reacted so as to punish Mr. Migu-na for his erroneous characterization of the reasons of the trial judge at his criminal trial and for his allegations of racial profiling. These are factors that might well attract cost consequences as a sanction, but they do not justify a refusal to grant leave to amend in the circumstances.

The plaintiff's pleading is bald and wanting in supporting material facts. The factual assertions gleaned from the statement of claim and outlined above, however—together with certain others not mentioned—if proved, could give rise to the essentials of the causes of action also summarized above. Those claims, at least, are not claims that Mr. Miguna is forbidden by law from asserting.

Of the three principal grounds relied upon by the motion judge for declining to grant leave to amend, the fact that the allegations are bald is not, in itself, a basis for refusing leave. It is only where it is clear that the plaintiff cannot allege further material facts that he knows to be true to support the allegations that leave to amend will be refused. While it may turn out that such is the case here, I am not satisfied at this stage that that is necessarily so.

There was much debate at the hearing about the motion judges' first basis for declining leave, namely the notion that Mr. Miguna had had ample opportunity to attempt to correct the deficiencies in his statement of claim but had refused or failed to do so. The motion judge was very impressed with the factums of the Crown defendants and the Police defendants that were filed before him—he relied upon them very heavily—and was of the view that anyone reading their detailed critique of the statement of claim would have been aware of the weaknesses in it and would have taken steps to correct them. While the motion judge was entitled to be impressed with the factums filed before him, as they were excellent factums and undoubtedly very helpful to him, it does not follow that they were necessarily instructive to the opposing pleader as to how to redraft the pleading. In any event, the time delay was nowhere near, for example, the nine months that was involved in *Wilson v. Toronto (Metropolitan Police Service)*, [2001] OJ No. 2434 (SCJ) on which the motion judge relied. Here, the delay was only approximately two and a half months. I note as well that this was the first time his pleading had been considered by the court.

Finally, I do not think it was permissible for the motion judge to overreact—as he seems to have done—to the misstatements admittedly made by Mr. Miguna in his statement of claim respecting the trial judge's reasons for acquittal and to the allegation of racial profiling. Both are ominous allegations, and it is true, as the motion judge observed, that the trial judge did not state the defendants had acted maliciously or were actuated by malice, or find that a conspiracy existed, or find that anyone had lied—all of which the pleading suggests. However, the test for granting leave to amend a pleading is not whether the pleader should be punished for previous misstatements or for making serious but bald allegations; rather, the test is whether the amendment can properly be made without prejudice to the other side. Here, there is no prejudice to the respondents in permitting Mr. Miguna an opportunity to rescue his statement of claim by properly pleading the facts within his knowledge relevant to the causes of action available to him that do exist in law.

Disposition

For the foregoing reasons, then,

a) the appeal with respect to the dismissal of the action against Her Majesty the Queen (action No. 04-CV-275438CM1) is dismissed;

b) the order of Paisley J dismissing the action against the Crown Attorney defendants and the Police defendants (action No. 04-CV-272928CM1) is set aside, except with respect to the defendants Attorney General of Ontario and Legal Aid Ontario; and,

c) the plaintiff is granted leave to deliver a fresh statement of claim, within 30 days of the date of this order.

d) The order of Paisley J fixing costs is set aside.

Even if Paisley J had made the order I would now make, striking the statement of claim with leave to amend, the respondents would have been entitled to partial indemnity costs of the motion before him. I would award the respondents costs of the motion before Paisley J, on the basis of a motion to strike with leave to amend, payable on a partial indemnity basis and in the cause.

In view of the indulgence being granted Mr. Miguna, I would not award any costs of the appeal.

NOTES AND QUESTIONS

Amending after expiry of a limitation period. The broad power to grant amendments at any stage in a proceeding may be limited in situations where the plaintiff waits until after the expiration of a limitation period to request the amendment. The first consideration is the extent to which amendments after expiry of the limitation period are permitted or restricted by the limitations legislation in the jurisdiction in question. More generally, however, the court must determine whether an amendment in the circumstances would incompensably prejudice the defendant by depriving him or her of the relevant limitations defence, as illustrated in *Basarsky v. Quinlan*, below.

Basarsky v. Quinlan
(1971), 24 DLR (3d) 720 (SCC)

HALL J: This is an appeal from the Appellate Division of the Supreme Court of Alberta in which an application by the appellant to amend the statement of claim in the action was dismissed.

Gordon Stewart Onishenko was killed in an automobile accident on September 9, 1967, near Lacombe in the Province of Alberta. The appellant Basarsky was appointed administrator of the estate of the deceased Onishenko under letters of administration granted to him on January 17, 1968. On October 18, 1968, the appellant commenced an action against the respondents.

The defendants entered a statement of defence in the action and para. I of that defence reads:

> THAT the Defendants admit the accident referred to in the Statement of Claim and further admit that the said accident occurred as a result of the negligence of the Defendant, JOE QUINLAN.

The action proceeded limited to the quantum of damages recoverable as liability had been admitted.

On August 26, 1970, the appellant applied to the presiding Judge in Chambers at Edmonton for leave to amend the statement of claim in certain particulars which were not objected to by the respondents and for which leave was given, and in the same application the appellant asked leave to amend the statement of claim by adding two new paragraphs, 7(a) and (b), as follows:

7(a) The said Gordon Stewart Onishenko before the time of his death was 43 years of age, employed as a sheet metal shop foreman and his wife and children aforesaid were entirely dependent upon his earnings as such, for their support and education, and in consequence of the death of the said Gordon Stewart Onishenko they have been deprived of that means of support and education.

7(b) The plaintiff, as Administrator aforesaid, incurred expense for the burial of the said Gordon Stewart Onishenko and therefore claims the sum of $500.00.

and by changing the prayer for relief to read:

(c) Under the provisions of the Fatal Accidents Act and on behalf of the widow and children of Gordon Stewart Onishenko, deceased, damages in the sum of $150,000.00.

The application was dismissed without written reasons by Primrose J and on an appeal to the Appellate Division the appeal from Primrose J was dismissed, again with no written reasons.

The issue here is as to whether the proposed amendments could be made, having regard to the fact that the two-year period under which an action could be brought under the *Fatal Accidents Act*, RSA 1955, c. 111 [now RSA 2000, c. F-8] had expired before the application to amend was made.

The respondents in their factum rely principally on what is known as the rule in *Weldon v. Neal* (1887), 56 LJQB 621, and the jurisprudence emanating therefrom and quote from Lord Esher MR in that case as follows:

It has been urged that if the Court were to allow an amendment by adding a cause of action which, if the writ were issued at the time when such amendment is allowed, would be barred, this would be giving the plaintiff an advantage and taking away from the defendant a right which he would have had—the effect of such an amendment being to allow the plaintiff to take advantage of the original writ of summons for the purpose of defeating the Statute of Limitations.

and:

The effect of allowing these amendments would be to deprive the defendant of his right to plead the Statute of Limitations. …

It must be pointed out that there was omitted from the remarks attributed to Lord Esher MR in the Law Journal Queen's Bench Report between the two quotations as given above the following:

The Court, inasmuch as they have power to allow amendment, would, under very peculiar circumstances, allow it to be made; but, as a general rule, such an amendment will not be allowed. There are no peculiar circumstances here. The plaintiff originally brought an action for slander alone; and if the matters now sought to be put into the statement of claim had been included in the writ of summons, they would not have been barred; whereas if a new writ were to be issued in respect of these matters they would be barred. (Emphasis added.)

It is of some significance to point out that Lord Esher MR's judgment in *Weldon v. Neal* is also reported in the Law Reports, 19 QBD 394, and the complete text of his judgment in the latter report of the case is as follows:

We must act on the settled rule of practice, which is that amendments are not admissible when they prejudice the rights of the opposite party as existing at the date of such amendments. If an amendment were allowed setting up a cause of action, which, if the writ were issued in respect thereof at the date of the amendment, would be barred by the Statute of Limitations, it would be allowing the plaintiff to take advantage of her former writ to defeat the statute and taking away an existing right from the defendant, a proceeding which, as a general rule, would be, in my opinion, improper and unjust. Under very peculiar circumstances the Court might perhaps have power to allow such an amendment, but certainly as a general rule it will not do so.

This case comes within that rule of practice, and there are no peculiar circumstances of any sort to constitute it an exception to such rule. For these reasons I think the order of the Divisional Court was right and should be affirmed.

In the light of the special circumstances existing in this case, I would allow the appeal and order that the statement of claim be amended as asked for. The appellant will have his costs in this Court and in the Appellate Division. The respondents are entitled to their costs of the application before Primrose J.

NOTES AND QUESTIONS

1. Adding parties or claims after expiry of a limitation period arises with some frequency. The courts and academic commentators, however, do not necessarily agree on the appropriate approach to the issue. Which of the following two approaches do you consider to be more compelling? Why?

a. *Deaville v. Boegeman* (1984), 48 OR (2d) 725, at 729-30, *per* Mackinnon ACJO:

A number of courts have made rather heavy weather out of the meaning of "special circumstances" and have sought to establish conditions or detailed guide-lines for the granting of relief after the expiry of the limitation period. This is a discretionary matter where the facts of the individual case are the most important consideration in the exercise of that discretion. While it is true that the discretion is not one that is to be exercised at the will or caprice of the court, it is possible to outline only general guidelines to cover the myriad of factual situations that may arise.

When limitation periods were under consideration by the common law courts in the 18th and the 19th centuries, the judges described these limitation statutes as "statutes of repose" or "statutes of peace": *Tolson v. Kaye* (1822), 3 Brod. & B 217, 129 ER 1267; *A'Court v. Cross* (1825), 3 Bing. 329 at p. 332, 130 ER 540; *Hunter v. Gibbons* (1856), 26 LJ Ex. 1 at p. 5; *Scales v. Jacob* (1826), 3 Bing. 638 at p. 645, 130 ER 660. The emphasis then was as it is today, on the necessity of giving security to members of society. Citizens would not expect to be disturbed once the limitation period had expired. Today when a limitation period has expired it is considered that, generally speaking, a defendant need no longer be concerned about the location or preservation of evidence relevant to the particular claim or relevant to a claim which has not been made. Further, the defendant is, presumably, at the stage free to act and plan his life without concern for stale claims or claims of which he has no knowledge which have arisen out of the original incident. When considering the purpose of limitation periods, the maxim, although used frequently in other connections, *expedit reipublicae ut sit finis litium* is appropriate; it is indeed in the public interest that there should be an end to litigation: *Smith v. Clay* (1767), 3 Bro. CC 646, 29 ER 743.

Some courts have suggested that in applications of the nature of the one in the instant case, limitation periods can be ignored. Limitation periods, however, were not enacted to be ignored. It has also been suggested that the mere bringing of such an application as in the instant case immediately shifts the burden of establishing prejudice to the defendant. I do not agree. In my view, the expiry of the limitation period creates a presumption, however slight in some cases, of prejudice to the defendant. It may be that the mere recitation of the facts and history of the case makes it clear there is no prejudice to the defendant and it can be inferred that he knew, within the limitation period, of the case and the nature of the claims now being made against him. Alternatively the defendant may file material which establishes prejudice. If matters are left in balance, the usual rules apply and the applicant upon whom the burden lies has not discharged that burden. The facts of the case and the claims and the history of the dealings with the defendant are within the knowledge of the plaintiff and there is no unfairness in placing upon the plaintiff the burden of establishing those facts.

b. Watson, "Amendment of Proceedings After Limitation Periods" (1975), 53 *Can. Bar Rev.* 237, at 276-78:

> In exercising the amendment power the goal must be to strike a balance between the plaintiff's interest in fully developing the action he has diligently commenced and the interests of the defendant which the limitation period seeks to protect. As we have already seen, the policies underlying statutes of limitations seek to protect two interests of the defendant through the device of timely notice of the plaintiff's claim. The first is that the defendant need no longer preserve or seek out evidence to use in defence of the claim. The second is that he need no longer fear the insecurity that his business and social activities will be disrupted by the reactivation of claims which he reasonably believes are dead. To the extent consistent with the protection of these interests the plaintiff should be entitled to freely amend his action.
>
> Hence, where a plaintiff seeks leave to amend after the expiration of the limitation period, then (irrespective of whether analytically it may involve the addition of a new cause of action, a change of parties or the curing of a nullity) the amendment should be allowed whenever the defendant has received such timely notice that he will not be prejudiced by an actual infringement of either of the interests sought to be protected by the limitations statute. As to the "evidentiary interest" the amendment should only be refused when the defendant can show that through lack of notice the change sought will require the use of evidence now unavailable to him but which would have been available had the action been constituted in this manner at the outset. With regard to his "interest in security" the amendment should be permitted unless the defendant can show that through lack of notice of the claim now sought to be asserted he actually changed his position, to his detriment, in reasonable reliance on the fact that the claim now sought to be asserted was dead.
>
> It will be observed that, while giving a plaintiff broad scope for amendment, two requirements are contained in this suggested approach. The first is timely notice to the defendant. Notice is the device by which the interests sought to be protected by the statute of limitations are protected in the ordinary course and this is retained. But here the concept of notice should not be restricted merely to formal notice of the kind given by the writ or the statement of claim. As

many courts have already done in the context of amendments after the limitation period, and analogous situations, all sources of notice formal and informal (for instance, correspondence or discovery) should be taken into account.

The second requirement is that an amendment will not be permitted if it can be shown that actual prejudice to the defendant will result from his lack of timely notice. This requirement assures that the legitimate interests of the defendant sought to be protected by the statute of limitations remain inviolate but beyond this, amendments should be freely allowed. It is also explicit in the above formulation that the burden of proving the existence of actual prejudice should be placed on the defendant. This seems reasonable and is in accord with the general principle that where the facts necessary to establish a proposition are peculiarly within the knowledge of one of the parties, that party should bear the burden of proof. If the amendment will cause actual prejudice to the defendant, he is in the better position to prove it. Generally, the plaintiff will not know whether the defendant is prejudiced or not, and if the burden were placed on him he will be faced with the difficulty of establishing a negative proposition.

2. The Ontario Court of Appeal grappled with the burden of proof for permitting amendments following the expiry of limitation periods in *Mazzuca v. Silvercreek Pharmacy Ltd.* (2001), 56 OR (3d) 768. The majority concluded that the party seeking the amendment must show *both* that there was no incompensable prejudice to the responding party *and* that there were "special circumstances." The dissent held that the only applicable test was whether the amendment, if allowed, would incompensably prejudice the responding party.

3. See chapter 3 for further discussion of limitation periods and the commencement of civil proceedings.

Discovery

I. INTRODUCTION

In chapter 6, Pleadings, we saw that the pleadings in an action serve to define the issues that the court will determine at trial, and to give notice to each party of the case to be met. The processes of issue-defining and notice-giving are far from exhausted with the exchange of pleadings; they continue with the discovery stage of the proceedings.

Issue-defining. Pleading rules only require the party to provide a bare outline of the case that he or she will actually attempt to prove at trial. When the action reaches trial, the party may have modified or abandoned some aspect of the claim or defence initially set up by the pleadings. Particulars—which are often overinclusive—provide a good illustration. It by no means follows that a party plans to establish all particulars at trial that are contained in the pleading. Similarly, although a party should admit facts that he or she knows to be true, there are many occasions in which a pleading will contain a denial of facts not genuinely in dispute. Thus, although they may be formally correct, the pleadings do not typically give a full picture of the claims or defences that will actually be presented at trial, and they hardly provide sufficient information to allow for adequate trial preparation. With the increased use in some jurisdictions in Canada of pre-trial, court-annexed ADR processes (see chapter 10), issue-defining at the pleading stage—and potentially further at the discovery stage—continues to be important.

Notice-giving. Another important function of discovery is to facilitate an exchange of information and evidence between the parties. Discovery allows the parties to a lawsuit to obtain access to documents in the other party's possession that are relevant to their claim or defence and to require at least one representative of the other party—and possibly more depending on the case and the jurisdiction—to attend an oral examination for discovery. This exchange of information stands in tension with the adversary system's emphasis on party presentation and prosecution of claims in civil litigation and it presents potential ethical problems. Nevertheless, as we will see in chapter 8, full exchange of information is limited by rules of privilege, which allow parties to shield from discovery, among other things, matters that involve attempts to obtain legal advice (the solicitor-and-client privilege), documents prepared for litigation (litigation privilege), and matters that involve attempts to settle a dispute (settlement privilege).

Despite the potential cost and the limits posed by privilege, it is important not to lose sight of the fact that discovery can often be crucial in many types of cases. Imagine, for example, a products liability case. The plaintiff will usually only know that he or she has been injured. It is only in the discovery process that the plaintiff can learn about the manufacturing process and the risks that the defendant contemplated or ought to have contemplated.

This section will provide a general introduction to the different types of discovery and their purpose and to the reform initiatives designed to reduce costs and inefficiencies that interfere with access to justice, as well as to address the impact of technology on litigation.

A. Overview

1. Discovery of Documents

While oral discovery is often considered to be the most significant pre-trial information-gathering device, rules of court provide for other important methods of discovery, most notably the compulsory disclosure and production of documents relevant to the case. Documentary discovery is particularly important in complex litigation where reconstruction of the events giving rise to the dispute can only be accomplished through detailed and laborious documentary research. In such cases, documents disclosed on discovery will often be decisive.

After the completion of pleadings, each party is required to prepare a statement listing all documents relevant to the proceedings that the party has or formerly had in his or her possession or control. (See, for example, Ontario rule 30, Nova Scotia rule 15, and BC rule 26.) In Alberta, the rules were amended in 1999—by Alta. reg. 172/99—requiring the production of "records," which includes the "physical representation or record of any information, data or other thing that is or is capable of being represented or reproduced visually or by sound, or both." See Alberta rule 186. The statement listing a party's records or documents is called, variously in different provinces, an "affidavit of documents," an "affidavit of records," or a "list of documents." The opposite party is entitled to inspect and take copies of all documents listed to which the party making discovery takes no objection to producing. As we shall see in chapter 8, rules of privilege protect from production certain types of documents. Such documents must also be listed, and the grounds given for refusal to disclose them. Should there be any dispute as to the validity of the privilege claimed, the matter will be raised on a motion to a master or judge to determine the validity of the claim to privilege.

Typically, discovery of documents should be conducted before the oral examination so that counsel conducting the oral discovery is fully prepared to ask the right relevant questions. Often, on oral discovery, the process of document production will continue and questions relating to the documents and the facts disclosed from the documents will be explored in greater depth.

Each party is *unilaterally obligated* to disclose all documents that are relevant and (if requested) to produce all such documents that are not privileged. This imposes important obligations—including ethical obligations—on the party making disclosure (and that party's counsel) to ensure that all relevant documents are produced.

2. *Examination for Discovery*

It is through the process of oral examination for discovery that each party can require his or her opponent to provide a much fuller and more complete statement of the basis of the claim or defence. Allegations or denials in a pleading are not made on oath. Pleadings represent initial statements of position, not sworn testimony. On discovery, a party is examined under oath and is sworn to tell the truth. He or she can be asked to provide sworn answers as to the position he or she takes on all points in issue in the litigation. By defining the issues more sharply, discovery enables the parties to concentrate their energies on the matters that are really in dispute. In this way, discovery also often assists in fostering settlement.

Oral discovery takes place after the close of pleadings. Rules of court typically provide that a party may initiate oral discovery by serving an appointment or notice, requiring the person to be examined to attend at a specified place and date. In practice, arrangements for discovery are usually made by agreement between the lawyers representing the parties. The examination itself will not take place in a courtroom but rather in the office of a lawyer or court reporter. The witness is sworn to tell the truth and responds to questions put by counsel for the party on whose behalf the examination is being conducted. The questions and answers are recorded by a court reporter who later prepares a certified transcript of the examination that will be used by the lawyers in preparation for the trial. (As we will see later, this transcript is often referred to at the trial.) Ordinarily, only the witness, other parties, all counsel, and the court reporter will be present. Questions may be asked to which exception is taken as being improper by opposing counsel, who will likely instruct the witness not to answer. After the transcript has been prepared, the party who asked the question to which objection was taken will have to consider whether the information sought is sufficiently important to warrant a formal motion to the court. If it is, a motion will be brought to the appropriate judicial officer who will consider the arguments of the parties with respect to the propriety of the question or the objection. Should it be determined that the question should have been answered, the usual order will be for the party subject to examination to re-attend so that the question and any questions logically flowing from it may be asked and the answers recorded. In practice, these answers are often provided in writing.

Use of examination for discovery at trial. Examination for discovery would be extremely useful if it did no more than provide each party with an insight into or a preview of the other side's case. While this is probably the most important aspect of the procedure, it does much more. Discovery is also an important evidence-gathering tool because the transcript of the examination for discovery may be used at trial in two ways. Evidence can be gathered by means of *obtaining admissions* that can be used at trial to prove facts that are in dispute. An admission is a statement made by a party before a trial that is adverse to his or her case. It can be received at trial as proof of the truth of its contents. Admissions may be obtained otherwise than through oral discovery, but oral discovery remains the most important opportunity to obtain an admission as it will ordinarily be the only pre-trial opportunity whereby one party can require the other to answer questions about sensitive issues in the case.

Another evidentiary device arising from discovery is the use of a *prior inconsistent statement* to impeach the credibility of a witness at trial. The use of a prior inconsistent statement is a familiar technique in cross-examination whereby the credibility of a witness is attacked by demonstrating that the witness has said something different on an earlier occasion from what he or she is now saying at the trial. As the discovery will have canvassed the important issues in the case, it operates to commit a witness to the version he or she has given at discovery. If the witness varies from that version at trial, he or she will risk having the inconsistency brought to light in cross-examination. The trier of fact may not believe the version given at trial in light of the prior inconsistent version given on discovery.

The rules of most provinces—to varying degrees—provide for discovery of non-party witnesses and thereby significantly expand the information-gathering possibilities offered by oral discovery. By examining potential witnesses under oath, a party can obtain a much more detailed account of the evidence that he or she will be faced with at trial, and may also be able to collect from non-parties information in support of his or her own case.

So far, we have been discussing oral examination for discovery. However, another method of examination for discovery is available in most Canadian jurisdictions: *examination by written questions (interrogatories)*. Typically, the two forms of examination—oral or written—are alternatives; that is, a party must choose one method or the other and may not use both, except with leave (see, for example, Ontario rule 35, BC rule 29, and Nova Scotia rule 19). An examination by written questions is conducted by delivering a list of written questions that must be answered in writing under oath or affirmation. It is a device that might be useful where the witness is to be examined on some very specific point or where the cost of conducting an oral examination is unwarranted. While it may be considerably cheaper, it is generally considered to be inferior to an oral examination for discovery; the answers received are typically answers that have been drafted by a lawyer (and so do not include the actual words of the witness), and it is more difficult to ask spontaneous follow-up questions in response to the answers received. Further, there is no opportunity to assess the strengths and weaknesses of the witness himself or herself. Its use in Canada is infrequent.

As we will see, however, the costs associated with extensive documentary discovery and examination for discovery have led to a push to insure proportionality between the scope of disclosure obligations and the significance of what is at stake in the litigation.

3. Physical Discovery

While examination for discovery (fact discovery) and documentary discovery are by far the most important forms of discovery (and are used on a regular basis), the rules in virtually every common law jurisdiction also provide for two forms of "physical discovery." The more rarely used is *inspection of property* (see, for example, Ontario rule 32, BC rule 30, and Nova Scotia rule 17). This may be useful in certain cases to inspect physical premises, articles, or other things, the condition of which is relevant to the action. For example, a plaintiff injured when struck by a car driven by the defendant in which the brakes were faulty may wish to inspect the brakes to determine whether the allegation that the brakes were defective can be substantiated.

A much more commonly used form of physical discovery is a *medical examination*, which is especially important in personal injury litigation. This procedure permits the defendant in such actions to require that the plaintiff be medically examined on the defendant's behalf (see, for example, Ontario rule 33, Alberta rule 217, BC rule 30, and Nova Scotia rule 21). This provides independent information about the plaintiff's medical condition that would otherwise be unavailable to the defendant. (This procedure is further examined below.)

4. Continuing Discovery Obligations

Examinations for discovery and documentary discovery may take place relatively early in the life of a lawsuit; in any event, they typically occur well before trial. What happens if a party subsequently acquires information that was unknown to him or her at the time of discovery, and therefore was not disclosed to the other side? As we will see below, the law imposes obligations of "continuing discovery" that usually require the party to inform his or her opponent of subsequently acquired information.

5. Request To Admit

One further procedural device should be noted, although it is not strictly a discovery device. Modern rules typically provide for a *request to admit* procedure (see, for example, Ontario rule 51.02 *et seq.*, Alberta rule 230, BC rule 231, and Nova Scotia rule 20.03-05. This procedure permits a party at any time to serve on any other party a request to admit the truth of a fact or the authenticity of a document. Typically, this procedure is used on the eve of trial for the purpose of narrowing the issues or dispensing with the proof of documents. However, it can be used at any time.

B. Philosophy and Developing Approaches to Discovery

Canadian discovery practice has been inspired by American sources, although important differences do exist. In England, discovery—governed by the amended *Civil Procedure Rules*—is comparatively limited, particularly with respect to oral discovery. Modern Canadian oral discovery rules are, in a sense, an expansion of a practice that originated in the English Court of Chancery. (See Garry D. Watson and Craig Perkins, eds., Holmested and

Watson, *Ontario Civil Procedure* (Toronto: Carswell, 1984).) While the general philosophy underlying discovery has tended to presume that the search for truth is best aided by extensive disclosure, concerns about the rising costs of litigation have led to reform initiatives designed to streamline discovery processes. Reform initiatives have been particularly pronounced in relation to electronic discovery in light of both the explosion of digital records that are potentially producible and the data management systems available to facilitate the exchange of information and documents in digital form.

The philosophy of modern discovery is discussed further in the following American excerpt, which largely reflects Canadian attitudes toward discovery. The analysis of Louisell and Wally is primarily focused on oral examination for discovery.

David W. Louisell and Barry M. Wally, *Modern California Discovery*
2nd ed. (San Francisco: Bancroft-Whitney, 1972), 1-6 (footnotes omitted)

Uncovering Evidence. The primary purpose of modern discovery procedures is to enable the litigants to obtain a more informed picture of the facts of the case more quickly and at less expense than they could by relying on their own unaided initiative. The basic premise of modern discovery, then, is that fuller disclosure, which may ultimately entail enforced disclosure, will permit each party to present the most complete and favorable case that can be made on his behalf at trial, and will minimize the possibility that ignorance of relevant facts, or the adversary's sudden presentation of unanticipated evidence, will obscure the true state of affairs out of which the controversy arose. ...

[T]he underlying goal of the federal discovery rules and the growing number of modern state discovery schemes is the same: To cause disclosure of relevant information before trial in order to render the judicial process more accurate and fair.

As Justice Peters stated in the landmark case of *Greyhound Corp. v. Superior Court*:

> Certainly, it can be said, that the Legislature intended to take the "game" element out of trial preparation while yet retaining the adversary nature of the trial itself. One of the principal purposes of discovery was to do away "with the sporting theory of litigation," namely, surprise at the trial. (... (D)iscovery tends to "make a trial less a game of blindman's bluff" and more a fair contest with the basic issues and facts disclosed to the fullest practical extent.)

This theme, that a lawsuit should be an intensive search for truth and not a game to be won by bluff or surprise, has today become commonplace. The widespread acceptance by the bar of the modern federal and state discovery rules attests to the vitality of this philosophy. Furthermore, there is nothing to suggest that the new discovery devices constitute a retreat from the common law's firm conception of litigation as a *competitive adversary* proceeding. The historic notice that a contest between vitally interested partisans is the best mechanism for exposing the truth is consistent with discovery principles.

The rules simply develop discovery, which has its antecedents in English chancery practice, into an efficient technique for fact ascertainment, to take its place in the common law's arsenal along with the advocate's other efficient weapons such as testimony in open court, cross-examination, impeachment, forensic skill, and mastery of legal principles.

In the United States Supreme Court decision in *Hickman v. Taylor* this theme was again emphasized:

> [Counsel for plaintiff] bases his claim to [the conversations of defendants' counsel with witnesses] on the view that the Rules were to do away with the old situation where a law suit developed into a "battle of wits between counsel." But a common law trial is and always should be an adversary proceeding. Discovery was hardly intended to enable a learned profession to perform its functions either without wits or on wits borrowed from the adversary.

Encouraging Settlement. In addition to the primary role that comprehensive discovery devices play in facilitating disclosure of information relevant to the litigation, they also serve other functions. Chief among these is the promotion of settlement. Settlement is typically reached when the parties' respective assessments of the value of the case are in substantial agreement. These appraisals are calculations of the maximum worth of the case in the event of recovery, discounted by the likelihood of defeat and of intermediate possibilities. The accuracy of these estimates obviously depends on the factual data available for analysis. Thus, to some extent at least, discovery aids the settlement process by increasing the quantum of information available to the parties. In addition, discovery costs and expenses increase the parties' investment in the case and may make the prospect of total defeat all the more disastrous. This, too, may induce settlement.

Emphasizing Issues. Another function of modern discovery is to isolate issues and facts over which there is no material controversy. In some cases this may lead to a motion for summary judgment. More often, discovery operates like the pretrial conference and obviates the need for costly litigation to establish facts which are not controverted in the lawsuit. Conversely, discovery tends to highlight those claims and defenses for which there is some basis in fact, thus pointing the way for further investigation. ...

Pinning the Witness Down. Discovery presents the opportunity for skilful counsel to compel a witness to commit himself to one version of the facts. In one context this may involve a simple, but nevertheless crucial, admission of lack of knowledge on a given subject. In other situations, the witness may espouse a particular description of an important event or transaction. Of course, the witness may subsequently change his testimony even up to the time of trial. But careful documentation of his testimony at the time of discovery can make subsequent alteration more difficult and embarrassing.

Sizing Up Witnesses and Counsel. Discovery presents the opportunity for observation of the demeanor, attitudes, and responses of a witness and opposing counsel. The former information will dictate how the witness should be handled at trial if he appears. The latter is less important, but may be useful in negotiating a settlement and planning other work connected with the case.

Undesirable Uses of Discovery. It has occasionally been suggested that discovery facilitates perjury by a litigant who "reconstructs" evidence during the discovery proceedings. While this possibility is indeed a fact of life, the very nature of discovery itself tends to minimize such danger. By permitting the broadest and most complete acquisition of information, discovery tends to make perjury difficult to conceal. Further, discovery occurs early in the litigation and is more likely to produce statements that are recorded when they are fresh and unrehearsed or concocted.

NOTE

Notwithstanding the theoretical benefits of the discovery process in the search for truth, civil justice reform initiatives for at least two decades have focused on developing procedural rules to assist in actualizing the benefits theorized, without unduly increasing the associated costs. Some of the more recent reforms are discussed below in relation to the scope of documentary and oral discovery.

In 1995 the Canadian Bar Association created the Systems of Civil Justice Task Force (the "CBA Task Force") to identify weaknesses in the civil justice system and propose reforms designed to make it "more efficient, accessible, accountable, fair and able to deliver timely results in a cost-efficient manner" (Canadian Bar Association, "Systems of Civil Justice Task Force Report" (CBA, 1996), online at: http://www.cba.org/cba/pubs/pdf/systemscivil_tfreport.pdf ("CBA Report"). In light of common complaints concerning the impact of delay and prohibitive costs in accessing justice, the CBA Task Force recommended, among other things, that every jurisdiction "amend its rules of procedure to limit the scope and number of oral examinations for discovery" and develop a means to "assist parties in scheduling discoveries and in resolving discovery disputes in an efficient manner" (CBA Report, p. VI). The push toward imposing limits on discovery processes also included recommendations for establishing the simplified processes that are discussed in detail in chapter 10. In explaining the recommendation, the CBA Report stated at p. 43:

> The objectives of discovery are to learn the case to be met, to obtain admissions (thereby reducing trial time); and, to avoid ambush. There are different rules governing discovery across Canada, but there is nearly universal dissatisfaction with most of them. The discovery process, and particularly oral examinations for discovery, lengthen the litigation process and add considerably to costs. …
>
> Oral discovery is the target of much dissatisfaction under the current litigation process. It is seen as an expensive and sometimes wasteful exercise. Reforms, therefore, should enhance the efficient and timely use of discovery. This means a significant contraction of the scope of discovery. All jurisdictions need to explore ways to limit discovery.

The CBA Task Force also noted the increasing costs of production of documents, particularly in complex cases, as well as the role of document imaging and management in that process. However, it made no specific recommendations with respect to document production.

Subsequently, in 2001, the Attorney General of Ontario appointed a Discovery Task Force (the "Ontario Discovery Task Force"), whose findings were reported in 2003 (*Report of the Task Force on the Discovery Process in Ontario* (Ontario Courts, 2003), online at: http://www.ontariocourts.on.ca/scj/en/reports/discoveryreview/) and in a supplementary report released in 2005 (*Supplemental Discovery Task Force Report* (Ontario Bar Association, 2005), online at: http://www.oba.org./en/pdf_newsletter/DTFFinalReport.pdf). Reiterating many of the themes identified by the CBA Task Force, the Ontario Discovery Task Force recommended that the Ontario Rules be amended to narrow the scope of discovery and to impose time limits on the duration of examinations for discovery; that parties be given easier access to case management in order to resolve disputes relating to discovery; that all parties to the litigation develop a discovery plan; and that best practices be developed relating to the production of electronic documents. These themes and concerns were again addressed in the 2007 recommendations of the task force headed by Coulter Osborne (*Civil Justice Reform Project: Summary of Findings and Recommendations* (Ontario Ministry of the Attorney General, 2007), online at: http://www.attorneygeneral.jus.gov.on.ca/english /about/pubs/cjrp/CJRP-Report_EN.pdf).

Studies undertaken in other Canadian jurisdictions, including Alberta, British Columbia, and Nova Scotia revealed similar concerns regarding the cost and delay endemic in discovery processes. See, for example, Alberta Law Reform Institute, *Alberta Rules of Court Public Consultation Report* (Edmonton: ALRI, September 19, 2002), online at: http://www. law.ualberta.ca/alri/docs/Banister2Finalrptl.pdf; BC Civil Justice Reform Working Group, *Effective and Affordable Civil Justice* (BC: November, 2006); Nova Scotia Discovery and Disclosure Working Group, *Final Report: Civil Procedure Rules Revision Project* (Nova Scotia: 2005), online at http://www.courts.ns.ca/rules_revision/reports/discovery.pdf. As will be discussed below, many of these recommendations have been or will shortly be implemented through rule reform.

II. DOCUMENTARY DISCOVERY

A. Affidavit of Documents

Each party is typically entitled to discovery of documents from every other party in the action as of right (see, for example, Ontario rule 30, Alberta rule 186, and Nova Scotia rule 20.1).

Discovery of documents from parties is a two-step procedure. The first step—disclosure— is the preparation and service of an "affidavit of documents" (see, for example, Ontario rule 30.03), or an "affidavit of records" (see, for example, Alberta rule 187). (In some jurisdictions—for example, British Columbia—a party is required in the first instance only to provide an unsworn list of documents. If the other party so wishes, it can apply to have this list of documents sworn.) The scope of the production obligation is not uniform across Canada and is undergoing revision in some jurisdictions. For example, in Ontario, prior to January 1, 2010, a party in its affidavit of documents is required to list and describe, in separate schedules, all documents relating to any matter at issue in the action: (1) that are in the party's possession, control, or power and that the party does not object to producing; (2) that are or were in the party's possession, control, or power and for which the party claims privilege, together with the grounds for the claim; and (3) that were formerly in the party's possession, control, or power, together with a statement of when and how the party lost possession and the documents' present location (rule 30.03). The affidavit must also state that the party has never had in his or her possession, control, or power any other documents relating to any matter at issue in the action other than those listed in the affidavit. As of January 1, 2010, the Ontario standard will change, narrowing the production obligation from materials "relating" to any matter in issue to those materials that are "relevant" to any matter in issue (see O. Reg. 438/08). This will bring the scope of the production obligation in Ontario into line with that provided for in other jurisdictions, like Alberta (see rule 186.1. Moreover, at least in some jurisdictions (for example, see Ontario rule 30.03(4)), the party's solicitor must certify that he or she has explained to the deponent the necessity of making full disclosure of all documents relating to any matter in issue in the action.

The second step is the production of documents for inspection. Each party is entitled to inspect the documents listed by another party, *other than those documents for which privilege is claimed* (for example, see Ontario rules 30.02 and 30.04, Alberta rule 188, BC rule 26(7), and Nova Scotia rule 14.10). In short, a party has to disclose relevant documents—including privileged documents—but only non-privileged documents have to be produced for inspection. Typically, the obligation under the rules is merely to make the documents available for inspection at the office of the lawyer acting for the party making production. In practice, the parties often exchange copies of the documents.

Grossman v. Toronto General Hospital
(1983), 146 DLR (3d) 280 (Ont. HC)

REID J: The action arises out of the death of Howard Grossman who is claimed to have been lost while a patient in the Toronto General Hospital ("the Hospital"). It is alleged that his body was discovered after 12 days in an air-duct shaft in the hospital.

The defence entered by the Hospital for itself and its staff amounts to a general traverse. Not even the death was directly admitted.

That document gave a hint of what was in store for plaintiffs. The Hospital's affidavit on production (the affidavit) revealed only one thing the Hospital had no objection to producing: the deceased's hospital record. That was the only entry made in the first part of the first schedule of the form (Form 23) required by the Rules of Practice.

Defendants' position is essentially this: plaintiffs have failed to establish that any documents exist that should be produced other than the deceased's medical record and those now described in paras. 1(a) and (b) of the master's order [requiring production of exhibits filed at a Coroner's Inquest and our investigation report]. When I expressed surprise that a 12-day search for a missing patient in a hospital would not have produced one scrap of paper relevant to the issues in this lawsuit Mrs. Farrer replied that any such piece of paper would be privileged, the Hospital having retained solicitors at a very early point.

That may be so. It may be a proper basis for a claim of privilege for any and all documents other than the one thing produced voluntarily and the others forced out of defendants' hands by reason of the motion before the master (in paras. 1(a) and (b) of Master Sandler's order). However, no one could have told from reading defendants' original affidavit whether or not that claim was justified. The answer made in the second part of the first schedule is a mere boiler-plate calculated to conceal all and any documents from inspection. The result was to deprive opposing counsel of any basis for challenging the privilege claimed. Equally, if a challenge had been made, no court could have decided it, without resorting to ordering production to the court of all the documents referred to in the second part of the first schedule. Since no one could have known from reading the schedule what documents are referred to, that would have been an order made in the dark.

The Rules of Practice are designed to facilitate production, not frustrate it.

Honest differences of opinion might arise over the question whether a given document should or must be produced. If that occurs, the court has power to decide the issue.

It becomes quickly clear to anyone setting out to practice in the courts that "production" is open to serious abuse. The integrity of the system depends upon the willingness of lawyers to require full and fair discovery of their clients. The system is, in a sense, in the hands of the lawyers. The opportunity for stonewalling and improper concealment is there. Some solicitors grasp it. They will make only such production as can be forced from them. That is bad practice. It can work real injustice. It causes delay and expense while the other side struggles to see that which they had a right to see from the first. In such a contest the advantage is to the long purse. The worst consequence is that the strategy is sometimes successful, giving its perpetrators a disreputable advantage. The practice must be condemned. If it were widespread it would undermine the trial system.

Master Sandler has written of the susceptibility of the system to abuse. In *Bow Helicopters v. Textron Canada Ltd. et al.; Rocky Mountain Helicopters Inc. et al., Third Parties* (1981), 23 CPC 212, he said at p. 215:

> I also observe that under our present system of documentary discovery, the choice as to what documents that are in a party's possession are relevant is, in the first instance, left up to the party itself, and my experience and observations have taught me that nowhere is the abuse of our rules of procedure greater than in this area of documentary production and in the failure of each party to fairly and reasonably disclose and produce to the opposite party all relevant documents, and to disclose the existence of all relevant but privileged documents. (This abuse has been recognized and has attempted to be remedied by the Civil Procedure Revision Committee, chaired by the late Walter B. Williston, QC, in draft Rules 31.03(4), 31.06(a), and 31.08 and 31.09 of their Report of June, 1980.)

The duty upon a solicitor is now, and always has been, to make full, fair and prompt discovery. Williston and Rolls, in *The Law of Civil Procedure* (1970), vol. 2, put it this way, at pp. 892-4:

> A party giving discovery is under a duty to make a careful search for all relevant documents in his possession and to make diligent inquiries about other material documents which may be in the possession of others for him. A solicitor has a duty of careful investigation and supervision and of advising his client as to what documents should be included in the affidavit, because a client cannot be expected to know the whole scope of his obligation without legal assistance. In *Myers v. Elman* [[1940] AC 282] a solicitor was ordered to pay the costs of the proceedings because his managing clerk was guilty of misconduct in the preparation and filing of an incorrect and inadequate affidavit. …
>
> It has equally always been the case that sufficient information must be given of documents for which privilege is claimed to enable a party opposed in interest to be able to identify them. It is not, however, necessary to go so far as to give an indirect discovery. …

The sufficiency of the description given to documents must be governed by the circumstances. The rule must be that enough must be given to enable a court to make a *prima facie* decision as to whether the claim for privilege has been established from what appears *on the face of the affidavit*. …

The rule is, therefore, that a party must candidly describe in an affidavit on production not only documents for which no privilege is claimed but also those for which a privilege is claimed. It is not enough to do the one but not the other.

Litigation is, after all, a search for truth. Its processes are, we all know, imperfect. To permit advantage to be taken of its weaknesses to the point of injustice and unfairness would be wrong. Defendants' strategy in this case must not be tolerated. The appeal must be dismissed.

Plaintiffs ask for costs on a solicitor and his own client scale. That is a punitive award. Yet it was the disposition made by Master Sandler in both orders under appeal. It reveals his view of defendants' course of action.

That course of action may reflect merely excessive concern for the protection of his clients' rights or it may reveal simple stonewalling. My concern that it may be the latter is deepened by the decision of my brother Carruthers in *Fiege v. Cornwall General Hospital et al.* (1980), 30 OR (2d) 691, 117 DLR (3d) 152. I am informed by counsel that the solicitor responsible for the defence in that case up to the point of trial is the solicitor responsible for the conduct of the defence herein. (That is not, I must add, Mrs. Farrer, whose lot it was to seek to justify someone else's conduct, and who did so with much skill and fortitude.) The failure in *Fiege* to produce an important document was strongly condemned by Carruthers J. He awarded costs on a solicitor and his own client scale against the defendant in that case because of the waste of time and money that resulted. The same may be said of this case. Time has been wasted and money thrown away. There is no merit in defendants' position.

The seriousness of a failure to make proper production is recognized in the rules. Rule 352 states:

> 352(1) If a party fails to comply with any notice or order for production or inspection of documents, he is liable to attachment and is also liable, if a plaintiff, to have his action dismissed, and, if a defendant, to have his defence, if any, struck out.

Attachment of a party is a severe sanction. Defendants' conduct in this case amounts to a deliberate refusal to comply with the notice to produce and is subject to that sanction. But in the absence of any indication that defendants' conduct was other than as advised by their solicitor, the responsibility for it must fall on the solicitor.

The consequences for a solicitor can be severe. In *Myers v. Elman*, [1940] AC 282, [1939] 4 All ER 484 (HL), the solicitor was ordered to pay the costs. If the course of action followed in this case were shown to be widespread, an order to that effect would be appropriate as a general deterrent.

It could be argued that, because this case is a repetition of conduct that has already been deplored, that order should be made here. Although I have some doubt, I am satisfied to treat this case as an example of excessive zeal and to adopt Master Sandler's order. His order shall stand. The costs of the appeal shall be to plaintiffs in any event of the cause as between a solicitor and his own client. However, because this is a repetition of the same error found in *Fiege*, *supra*, the costs may be taxed forthwith and shall be payable forthwith thereafter.

The further affidavit, or affidavits, shall be delivered forthwith subject to any extension allowed by Master Sandler.

Appeal dismissed.

NOTES AND QUESTIONS

1. As a preliminary matter, Reid J's judgment makes it clear that documentary production "is open to serious abuse ... . The system is, in a sense, in the hands of the lawyers." As such, documentary discovery is an area where the rules of court, the rules of professional conduct, and codes of civility meet head on. It is critical, when learning the obligations required by the discovery rules, to keep in mind parallel obligations under the various provincial codes of conduct and civility initiatives. For further reform initiatives, see below.

2. Was the court's costs order appropriate in this case or should the lawyer have been held personally liable? Who has the power in this relationship? Who of the lawyer and the client is likely to have a more precise sense of what documents need to be disclosed and what should be contained in the affidavit of documents? If a client refuses to follow the lawyer's advice regarding the production of documents, what is the lawyer's responsibility? If a lawyer knows that a client is actually destroying relevant documents, what is his or her responsibility? In *Myers v. Elman*, [1940] AC 282, a leading case at common law about awarding costs against a lawyer personally, the House of Lords held that a solicitor may not assist a client who, to his or her knowledge, has sworn a false affidavit. If a solicitor discovers that his or her client has sworn a false affidavit, the solicitor must decline to act further in the matter. In *Myers*, the solicitor, who knew the client had sworn a false affidavit and did not withdraw, was ordered to pay part of the opposing party's costs.

3. In *Waxman v. Waxman* (1990), 42 CPC (2d) 296 (Ont. Master), the court had to work out the implications of *Grossman*. (You will be in a better position to understand the *Waxman* decision after you have considered the materials on privilege, chapter 8.) The defendants claimed privilege in their affidavit of documents for:

> Letters, statements and memoranda passing between the corporations' solicitors and third parties in connection with the litigation herein and in preparation therefor, the earliest of which is dated November 9, 1988.

The plaintiffs moved for an order to require the defendants to produce a further and better affidavit of documents, setting out a detailed list of documents referred to in the paragraph including, with respect to each such document, the name and identity of the "third parties," the dates of communication, and whether any of the communications were expert reports.

Master Sandler granted the motion in part. He held that the rules require that the documents for which privilege is claimed should be described, with the description including the function, role, and status of sender and receiver, and their relationship to the party to the action. However, he held that a party was not required to give particulars that would destroy the benefit of any privilege that might properly have attached to the documents. Under Ontario rule 31.06(3), the names and addresses of experts who are retained solely for the purpose of litigation, and whom the party undertakes not to call at trial, need not be disclosed. Moreover, under Ontario rule 31.06(2), even the names and addresses of potential witnesses can be kept from disclosure if the court so orders. Consequently, to require the disclosure of the name of every person whose reports or interviews were the subject of a claim for privilege in an affidavit of documents before a ruling on the validity, if such a claim were made, would destroy, in part, the benefit of the privilege that might properly have attached to the document. Accordingly, the defendants were not required to set forth the names or identities of the creators of the documents; the witnesses who gave the statements that formed the substance of the documents; or the names of the experts, investigators, or adjusters who authored any report to whom the solicitors wrote. Master Sandler further held that in certain circumstances, the use of categories for the listing of certain types of documents might be appropriate, so long as such use was not a strategy to avoid revealing documents that ought to be revealed.

4. While both the *Grossman* and *Waxman* decisions condemn the use of general, "boilerplate" claims for privilege, such claims are often used in practice. Why? Are lawyers simply flouting the requirements of discovery? One answer is that compliance with the two decisions is expensive. It takes time and money to go through the productions and identify each document for which a claim for privilege is made and describe it individually. Many lawyers avoid this expense for their clients by making a general privilege claim, knowing that if called on to do so by their opponents they will have to describe the documents individually. In cases where both parties are interested in avoiding this expense, and have little interest in the details of the privilege claim, it is still not uncommon to see them making "boilerplate" privilege claims. Of course, in cases where the parties are interested in such details, they will insist on compliance with the *Grossman* and *Waxman* principles. Moreover, parties who know at the time of preparing their affidavits that they will be insisting on compliance by their opponents will themselves comply from the outset.

5. *Solid Waste Reclamation Inc. v. Philip Enterprises Inc.* (1991), 2 OR (3d) 481 (Gen. Div.) involved voluminous documentary discovery. In such cases, counsel are increasingly employing electronic storage and retrieval systems for productions. In *Solid Waste*, the defendants complained that Schedule A of the plaintiff's affidavit was inadequate because it described and numbered many of the documents in bundles rather than individually. Mr. Justice Lane observed:

> A modern rule as to identifying documents cannot ignore the computer and its need for a unique identifier for every item to be retrieved. ... [P]roper identification demands numbering each document with a unique number. Such a number is far more valuable than a long-winded description of each document including its sender, addressee, date, etc. ... . My experience in matters involving thousands of documents is that the initial cost of proper identification of each document with a unique identifier is surprisingly small and is repaid many times over by savings in time during discovery, preparation of witnesses and trial. Whatever the [numbering] system, it must, as a minimum:
>
> (1) enable swift and sure retrieval at trial or discovery;
>
> (2) enable counsel examining the documents of another party to relate each document to its reference on Schedule A and to satisfy himself that all documents listed are actually in the collection he is examining;
>
> (3) enable counsel at trial to ascertain swiftly that a document which is tendered to become an exhibit is in fact a document produced in Schedule A;
>
> (4) be compatible with computer retrieval systems;
>
> (5) be implemented before copies of the documents are made, so that the copies in the hands of all parties bear the identifier.

To what extent do you think these standards for document identification are realistic and cost efficient? The Alberta Court of Appeal, in *Dorchak v. Krupka; Roy v. Krilow* (1997), 196 AR 81, relied on the Ontario court's approach in *Solid Waste* in the following statement by Côté JA:

> An affidavit of documents must show unambiguously what documents' existence it does or does not disclose. It must remove any uncertainty on the following vital question. If a piece of paper turns up later, or is tendered on a motion or at trial, has it been disclosed by the previous affidavit of documents? That question can arise in a motion for a further and better affidavit of documents, under R. 194(1). It also arises when there is an objection to putting a document into evidence at trial, for failure to disclose it, under R. 195. It is important that the affidavit remove any doubt on the topic.

6. Note again the distinction between the process of oral examination and documentary discovery. The procedure for oral examination is adversarial in the sense that while a party is entitled to have its proper questions answered, the opposing party's obligation is simply to answer the questions asked. It is not permissible for the examining party to ask the party examined, "Tell me everything you know that is relevant to the issues in this action." By contrast, the process of documentary discovery imposes a unilateral obligation upon each party to identify and disclose every relevant document or record that is or was in their possession and control and to disclose it to the opposing party and then (if requested) to produce to the other side for inspection every such document or record, other than those for which privilege is claimed.

Can this distinct approach to documentary discovery be reconciled with the basic adversarial nature of our litigation process? Why? The approach typically taken by US courts is quite different: there is no general obligation of documentary disclosure, and a party's only obligation is to disclose classes of documents demanded by their opponent. Is the Anglo-Canadian approach, in essence, grounded on efficiency; that is, is it simply more efficient to require the parties to make disclosure of all documents relevant to the issues in the action rather than have the parties make up lists of classes of documents they wish to have produced? If efficiency is the explanation, should we adopt the same approach with regard to fact discovery? For a further discussion of various reform proposals, see below.

7. Most Canadian jurisdictions specifically define the parties' productions obligations to include digital matter. (See Alberta rule 186, Manitoba rules 30.01 and 31.01, New Brunswick rule 31.01, NWT rule 218, Ontario rules 30.01 and 31.01, PEI rules 30.01 and 31.01, Saskatchewan rule 211, and federal rules 222 and 225.) However, they do not uniformly approach production of digital matter as a matter of *documentary* production *per se*. In Ontario, rule 30.01(1) defines "document" to include "a sound recording, videotape, film, photograph, chart, graph, map, plan, survey, book of account and data and information in electronic form." In contrast, Nova Scotia's discovery rules distinguish between "documents" (rule 15.01) and "electronic information" (rule 16.01) and articulate different processes and expectations for production in each category. With the explosion of digital record creation, retention and retrievability has come a whole new wave of issues often referred to under the heading electronic discovery or e-discovery. These are discussed in detail below in part C.

B. Scope of Documentary Discovery

The general scope of documentary discovery has tended to be extremely broad. The various provincial rules—compare, for example, Ontario rule 30.02 and Alberta rule 186.1—specify the scope. As the following case illustrates, the rules as to the scope of discovery have typically been given an expansive interpretation by the courts. However, as will be seen below, different jurisdictions may impose different limits on the scope of discovery and some that have traditionally imposed extensive production obligations (e.g., Ontario, British Columbia, and Nova Scotia) appear to be moving toward narrowing the obligation to ensure production costs are generally proportional to what is at stake in the litigation.

Peter Kiewit Sons Co. of Canada Ltd. v. British Columbia Hydro and Power Authority
(1982), 134 DLR (3d) 154 (BCSC)

McEACHERN CJSC: The plaintiffs entered into a contract with the defendant British Columbia Hydro & Power Authority (BC Hydro) for the construction of Segment 5 of a transmission line comprising 189 steel towers between Kingsvale and the Giant Mascot Mine. This project was part of the Mica Creek transmission line.

At the same time BC Hydro had let contracts for other segments of the same transmission line, and for portions of the Kootenay Canal transmission line.

It was a term of the plaintiffs' contract that BC Hydro would furnish the required structural steel for this project on a timely basis at its Kidd Steelyard in Richmond, BC. The plaintiffs contracted with the defendant Columbia Hydro Constructors Ltd. that the latter would furnish all labour required by the plaintiffs for the performance of their contract. The contractors on the other projects mentioned above had similar contractual arrangements for the timely supply of steel and labour for their projects.

The plaintiffs and the contractors on the other projects employed a common trucking contractor, Pe Ben Industries Company Limited (Pe Ben), to take delivery, at the Kidd Steelyard, of any steel the contractors required for transportation to various locations.

The plaintiffs' job did not go well, and one of the principal allegations against BC Hydro is that it did not properly manage the supply of steel. Amongst other things, the plaintiffs say steel was not available as required; that steel intended for one contract was diverted to other jobs with the squeaky contractor getting the steel; and other shortcomings on the part of BC Hydro. The defendant Columbia Hydro Constructors Ltd. is not directly involved in this application.

The foregoing is a brief but sufficient description of the scope of one part of this case.

It is clear that these were major projects requiring much planning and organization. The plaintiffs claim substantial damages on a number of grounds for the failure of the defendants properly to supply steel, designs and labour; and there are also claims in deceit and negligent misstatement. On this application I am concerned only with the question of steel.

In my view, it is appropriate to describe this case as major litigation of a type which is not uncommon in our Courts. I do not suggest that this case is necessarily comparable to *Morrison-Knudsen Co., Inc. et al. v. British Columbia & Power Authority* (1978), 85 DLR (3d) 186, [1978] 4 WWR 193 (CA) (which lasted over 400 days at trial), but the conduct of this case is a very substantial undertaking. It is estimated by counsel to require 20 days for trial.

BC Hydro has furnished about 30,000 documents for inspection by the plaintiffs and, just before the hearing of this motion, BC Hydro tendered a further 12-page inventory of documents it is prepared to make available for inspection.

The plaintiffs now seek an order:

> (1) pursuant to Rule 27(10) of the Rules of Court that the Defendant, British Columbia Hydro and Power Authority, produce the documents referred to in the Schedule to this Notice of Motion for inspection and copying by the Plaintiff at such time, place and manner as the Court thinks just.

> (2) pursuant to Rule 27(4) of the Rules of Court that the Defendant, British Columbia Hydro and Power Authority, deliver an Affidavit stating whether the documents or class of documents specified or described in the Schedule to this Notice of Motion is or has been in the possession or control of that Defendant and, if not then in the possession or control of the Defendant, when that Defendant parted with it and what has become of it.

Attached to these reasons is the schedule to the notice of motion which sets out what the plaintiffs seek on both branches of its application.

One of the matters in issue between these parties is the extent to which the plaintiffs may require production and inspection of documents relating to this and other contracts which were underway at the same time as the contract in question. The plaintiffs say documents relating to these contracts may contain statements (described, hopefully, by counsel for the plaintiff as "confessions") which may assist the plaintiffs to prove their case or, possibly, impeach the case of the defendants.

BC Hydro says it has now produced all documents relating to the operation of the Kidd Steelyard in connection with this and the other contracts, including Pe Ben's "pullsheets" which record all steel ordered for the project and removed from the Kidd Steelyard. BC Hydro declines to produce all its other "mountains of documents" which relate to various phases of this and other contracts.

BC Hydro says it has complied with the requirements of paras. IV, VI, and VII of the schedule, and will produce bar graphs of progress on all its transmission line contracts, but it objects to a search of everything it has relating to the Mica Creek and Kootenay Canal transmission lines in order to see if anything which may possibly be relevant is resting there. This, I am sure, would be a very extensive undertaking, and no likelihood has been established that anything worthwhile will be found.

The plaintiffs rely on *Compagnie Financiere et Commerciale du Pacifique v. Peruvian Guano Co.* (1882), 11 QBD 55 (CA), which has been followed and applied in numerous cases in this Court for many years. The Rule the Court was there considering required discovery of "a document relating to any matter in question in the action." Our present Rule 26(1) is in practically the same terms.

The *Peruvian Guano* case (as it is usually called) indicates (at pp. 56-7) that the plaintiffs made an affidavit of documents in the usual form, in which they disclosed, *inter alia*, their minute-book. The defendant brought an application for a further affidavit of the following documents, which were described in the minute-book:

> ... first, drafts of arrangement between the Peruvian Guano Company, and the plaintiff company, referred to in the board minutes of the plaintiff company, dated the 28th of September, 1881; secondly, the letter and two telegrams received by the plaintiffs from Mr. Adam, referred to in the board minutes of the plaintiff company, dated the 2d of November, 1881; thirdly, two further drafts relating to the form of communication to be made, and the letter from M. de Germiny to M. Homeberg, respectively referred to in the board minutes, dated the 3d of November, 1881; fourthly, a letter addressed to Mr. Adam, referred to in the board minutes, dated the 8th of November, 1881; and, fifthly, several letters written from London by Mr. Adam to the plaintiff company, or directors thereof, and the several letters and telegrams sent by the plaintiff company, or directors thereof, to Mr. Adam, as referred to in the board minutes, dated the 16th of November, 1881.

The Master declined to order a further affidavit. Pearson J, sitting in Chambers, made an order as to the first class of documents only. An appeal to the Queen's Bench Division was dismissed, and a further appeal was taken to the Court of Appeal.

Baggailay LJ at pp. 59-60 said:

> I assent to the suggestion made by Brett LJ in the course of the argument, that a document, which, it is not unreasonable to suppose, may tend either to advance the case of the party seeking discovery, or to damage the case of his adversary, should be regarded as a document relating to a matter in question in the action. I proceed to apply these tests to the documents in respect of which this appeal is brought. As regards No. 3, the objection taken by the plaintiffs, that it does not appear from the affidavit already sworn that is in the possession or power of the plaintiffs, must I think prevail; but as regards Nos. 2, 4, and 5, I am of opinion that it appears from the minutes that they are in the possession or power of the plaintiffs, and that it is not unreasonable to suppose that they may contain information, directly or indirectly, enabling the defendants to advance their own case or to damage the case of their adversaries.
>
> > Brett LJ in the *locus classicus* on this question said at p. 63:
> >
> > > It seems to me that every document relates to the matters in question in the action, which not only would be evidence upon any issue, but also which, it is reasonable to suppose, contains information which *may*—not which *must*—either directly or indirectly enable the party requiring the affidavit either to advance his own case or to damage the case of his adversary. I have put in the words "either directly or indirectly," because, as it seems to me, a document can properly be said to contain information which may enable the party requiring the affidavit either to advance his own case or to damage the case of his adversary, if it is a document which may fairly lead him to a train of inquiry, which may have either of these two consequences ...

It appears from the foregoing that the documents in question in the *Peruvian Guano* case were probably not as extensive as the record of pleadings in this case.

It also appears that a literal reading of Rule 26(1) and the application of the *Peruvian Guano* case leads inexorably to the conclusion that the plaintiffs should succeed on this application.

I hesitate to disturb an authority as ancient and well-established as the *Peruvian Guano* case which has stood unchallenged in Britain and in this Province for 100 years. But Lord Diplock said that all judicial reasoning must be considered "*secundum subjectam materiam*": *Mutual Life & Citizens' Ass'ce Co. Ltd. et al. v. Evatt*, [1971] 1 All ER 150 at p. 161. The Rules of Court are our servants, not our masters.

I respectfully decline to follow the *Peruvian Guano* case, *supra*, or slavishly to apply Rule 26(1) in a case such as this, where thousands or possibly hundreds of thousands of documents of only possible relevance are in question. I do not intend to suggest, however, that the *Peruvian Guano* case does not correctly state the law in most cases. That question does not arise for consideration here.

It does not follow that this motion should be dismissed because, notwithstanding the foregoing, every reasonable effort must be made to enable the plaintiffs to locate any documents which may assist the parties to ascertain the truth. What is not permissible, or reasonable, in my view, is to require a party, in a case as this, to incur enormous expense in what may be a futile search for something which may not exist.

One solution would be to permit the most extensive possible search and inquiry to be made at the plaintiffs' non-recoverable expense; or, alternatively, to require the plaintiffs to post security for the cost of the search, with the cost thereof being assessed ultimately by the Court when the results of both the search and the action are known.

Another suggestion might be to try an issue, if one could be defined, which might resolve this question without the kind of search which the plaintiffs' motion requires. Rule 26(15) provides for such an order. In this connection the plaintiffs' claim is that they did not directly, or by their agent Pe Ben, obtain steel in the manner required by the contract. If that question could be resolved objectively, it might not be necessary to go any further. I suspect, however, that the plaintiffs would wish to have the information they seek on the trial of even a limited issue.

I would give consideration to any reasonable proposal the parties may make regarding the foregoing. If they cannot agree, then, in order to make an effective order, I would direct only that the plaintiffs may apply again for an affidavit, and subsequent inspection, of documents which may be uncovered by a search of greatly reduced scope. To put it differently, the plaintiffs must choose a smaller target within BC Hydro. As is well known, BC Hydro is the largest enterprise in the Province, and the plaintiffs must define a more manageable area for inquiry. In addition, the plaintiffs must establish a *prima facie* case that something relevant will be uncovered before a further affidavit and further inspection will be ordered.

Upon any such further application I would expect a senior responsible officer of BC Hydro to verify on oath the extent of its production to date, the magnitude and estimated expense of the search required to satisfy the further production which is being sought, and such further circumstances as may be necessary to enable the Court to decide whether a further search will be fruitful. In addition, I would expect such deponent to verify, upon grounds which are stated, what his belief is regarding the likelihood of further relevant documents being uncovered.

I hesitate to make pronouncements such as this which carry the risk of being mis-understood. I therefore wish it to be known that what I say in these reasons applies par-ticularly to discovery of documents in cases of this kind. The production of documents made by BC Hydro up to this stage is entirely appropriate, and, notwithstanding any-thing I have said, I would have ordered production at least of all the defendant's documents relating to the operation of the Kidd Steelyard—for all contractors. I do not, however, foreclose the right of any party to major litigation to apply at any stage for dir-ections regarding discovery of documents. The time has arrived, in my view, for the Court to become concerned about the cost of litigation subject, of course, to the right of any party to the Court's assistance in the reasonable preparation of his claim or defence.

Order accordingly.

NOTES AND QUESTIONS

1. The court suggested a number of solutions to the thorny problem of voluminous docu-ment production. Was one more appropriate than the other? Why? One of the suggested options "might be to try an issue, if one could be defined, which might resolve this question without the kind of search which the plaintiffs' motion requires." A number of jurisdictions permit divided discovery of documents and have similar rules regarding oral discovery; for example, see Ontario rule 30.04(8) and New Brunswick rule 31.04(6). Courts have been re-luctant to order such procedure, but instances certainly exist. See, for example, *Diamond v. Kaufman* (1985), 1 CPC (2d) 1 (Ont. Master). There, the court ordered divided production and discovery in an action seeking an accounting of the business receipts and disburse-ments of a computer software business operated by the defendants. Only if the plaintiff had succeeded on the liability issue would the accounting have been necessary, since disclosure of the information could have seriously prejudiced the defendants.

2. The court in *Peter Kiewit Sons* further referred to the cost of litigation—and in the context of that case, discovery—as a consideration for the scope of permissible discovery. Should cost be a factor when interpreting a procedural rule? Should the application of rules differ depending on the size, scope, type, and potential complexity of litigation?

3. In Great Britain, Lord Woolf—in his seminal report: *Access to Justice* (London: HMSO, 1996)—made ambitious recommendations for civil justice reform. He found that, as in Canada and the United States, there was a general consensus that documentary discov-ery in more complex litigation can present real problems because of the sheer volume of documents and resulting high costs. Interestingly, he also expressed concern that the breadth of documentary discovery in England (which is certainly no broader than other common law jurisdictions) was having an adverse impact on the ability of English courts to continue to attract important international litigation. Lord Woolf found the answer to his concerns in judicial management and discretion:

> As part of the case management process, the judiciary will have both the means and the respon-sibility to ensure that discovery is limited to what is really necessary (Interim Report, at 168, para. 20).

Lord Woolf recommended that the court retain jurisdiction to order full discovery of the kind now available, but he anticipated that this will be rare and, generally, discovery will be more limited. Lord Woolf's proposals depend on distinctions that he draws among what are today considered relevant and, hence, producible documents. Documents are divided into four categories: (1) documents that a party relies on to support its case; (2) documents that, to a material extent, adversely affect a party's case or support the other party's case; (3) documents that are relevant to the issues in the proceeding but do not fall into the preceding categories; and (4) documents that are not relevant in and of themselves but might lead to a "train of inquiry" leading to relevant documents. Documents in categories (1) and (2) are to be available as "standard discovery," while the documents in categories (3) and (4) are to be available only as "extra discovery." Normally, in fast-track cases, the parties will be required to give only "standard discovery." In other cases (multitrack cases), discovery will be tailored to the circumstances of the particular case and the procedural judge will decide whether and when "extra discovery" will be available.

In making his recommendation, Lord Woolf observed:

> The core of the problem is that conscientious lawyers and their clients might feel obliged to troll through all category (3) documents in order to eliminate the possibility of overlooking category (2) documents. To do so would be to defeat the aims of controlled discovery.

He resolved this matter by stating that "initial disclosure should apply to documents of which a party is aware at the time when the obligation to disclose arises." The court and the parties, he said, will have to work out in practice the appropriate balance between what should properly be disclosed under that test and what can legitimately be left for the opponent to canvas on an application for further discovery.

When thinking about discovery reform in Canada (see below), what is your reaction to Lord Woolf's findings and recommendations? Is it worrying to hear him say that a party is not required to "troll through" all of the documents in its possession to find out if category (2) documents exist, because this may open the door to the non-production of damaging documents? Is relieving a party of the obligation to "troll through" all of its documents an open invitation to parties to never "turn up" the smoking gun that favours the opponent's case? For a useful summary of the reforms in England resulting from Lord Woolf's report, see Task Force on the Discovery Process in Ontario, *Report of the Task Force on the Discovery Process in Ontario* (November 2003), part III, at 46-48, available online at: http://www .ontariocourts.on.ca/scj/en/reports/discoveryreview/toc.pdf.

4. As mentioned above, studies undertaken in many Canadian jurisdictions, including Alberta, British Columbia, and Nova Scotia revealed similar concerns regarding the cost and delay endemic in discovery processes. See, for example, Alberta Law Reform Institute, *Alberta Rules of Court Public Consultation Report* (Edmonton: ALRI, September 19, 2002), online at: http://www.law.ualberta.ca/alri/docs/Banister2Finalrptl.pdf; BC Civil Justice Reform Working Group, *Effective and Affordable Civil Justice* (BC: November 2006); Nova Scotia Discovery and Disclosure Working Group, *Final Report: Civil Procedure Rules Revision Project* (Nova Scotia: 2005), online at: http://www.courts.ns.ca/rules_revision/reports/ discovery.pdf.

Many study recommendations have been incorporated into amendments to the discovery related rules of civil procedure in Ontario, Alberta, British Columbia, and Nova Scotia.

For example, "[t]he 1999 amendments to [Alberta] Rules 186.1, 187.1(2), and 200(1.2) narrowed the scope of relevance for written and oral discovery, excluding tertiary relevance" (*Hirtz v. Alberta (Public Trustee)* (2002), 303 AR 25. See also: Glen Poelman et al. "Civil Procedure and Practice: Recent Developments" (2003), 41 *Alta L Rev.* 449.) Amendments to the Nova Scotia rules, effective January 1, 2009, also narrow the scope of discovery and disclosure (see rule 14.01(1)) and provide specific rules for production of documents (rule 15) and production of electronic information (rule 16). Rule amendments to take effect in Ontario and in British Columbia in 2010 will impose time limits on examinations for discovery, as well as narrowing the scope of discovery and disclosure (see O. Reg. 438/08, rules 26, 27, and 31.05(1) and Supreme Court civil rules 7-1 and 7-2 online at: http://www .ag.gov.bc.ca/justice-reform-initiatives/publications/pdf/CivilRules07-07-09.pdf. In addition, the revised Ontario rules will impose an obligation on parties to develop a discovery plan (O. Reg. 438/08, rule 29.1) and will specifically require courts to take into account the principle of proportionality in deciding whether to order further production of documents or to order that additional questions be answered (O. Reg. 438/08, rule 29.2).

Taken together, these developments seem to suggest that future case law relating to discovery obligations in these jurisdictions is likely to focus more explicitly on balancing the right to production against the expense and delay associated with responding to any particular production request. On the other hand, cases such as *Peter Kiewit Sons*, above, demonstrate that even where discovery rules have not previously explicitly provided for it, at least some judges and masters have already been taking these concerns into account in their production rulings.

Rule reforms relating to discovery have also focused on e-discovery, an area in which principles such as proportionality have been gaining credence in Canadian case law.

C. Electronic Discovery

1. Overview

Concerns regarding the impact of electronic information on discovery obligations and production practices (including such things as digital imaging and management techniques) were being raised in Canada as early as 1995 in the CBA Report. Subsequently, the Ontario Discovery Task Force, recommended that best practices be established relating to the production of electronic documents, as part of a sweeping set of reform recommendations intended to address the rising costs of discovery. (See: *Report of the Task Force on the Discovery Process in Ontario* (Ontario Courts 2003), online at: http://www.ontariocourts.on.ca/ scj/en/reports/discoveryreview/ and, in a supplementary report released in 2005, *Supplemental Discovery Task Force Report* (Ontario Bar Association: 2005), online at: http://www .oba.org./en/pdf_newsletter/DTFFinalReport.pdf.) The BC Supreme Court's Practice Direction Re: Electronic Evidence took effect on July 1, 2006, addressing both practical considerations in terms of producing and filing electronic documents, as well as recommending best practices for counsel in developing preservation and production plans. (See: BC Supreme Court *Practice Direction Re: Electronic Evidence* (July 1, 2006), online at: http://www .commonwealthlegal.com/pdf/ElectronicEvidenceJuly2006.pdf.)

It was quickly recognized that e-discovery issues warranted attention on a national scale and the Sedona Canada Working Group was formed. Working in part with models previously developed in the United States, the Canadian working group developed the Sedona Canada Principles designed to assist parties from across Canada in working through e-discovery issues in accordance with the discovery rules in their particular jurisdictions. The Sedona Canada Principles define "e-discovery" as (Public Comment Draft 2007, p. 1, online at: http://www.thesedonaconference.org/dltForm?did=2_07WG7pubcomment.pdf):

> refer[ring] to the discovery of electronically stored information, including email, web pages, word processing files, computer databases and virtually any information that is stored on a computer or other electronic device. Technically, electronically stored information is electronic if it exists in a medium that can be read through the use of computers or other digital devices. Such media include cache memory, magnetic disks (such as computer hard drives or floppy disks), optical disks (such as DVDs and CDs), and magnetic tapes. Electronic discovery can be distinguished from "paper discovery," which refers to the discovery of writings on paper that can be read without the aid of electronic devices.

E-discovery presents unique challenges in the litigation process. Among others, the Sedona Canada Working Group noted the greater rate at which electronic documents are produced and the ease of their duplicability, the relatively greater difficulty of disposing of electronic information, the availability of "metadata" that can be used to reveal considerable information about the creation and modification of documents, and the tendency toward greater levels of dispersion and searchability of electronic information (Sedona Canada Principles, pp. 2-5). In light of these kinds of material distinctions between electronic information and traditional paper documents, the Working Group developed 12 principles addressing electronic document production, some of which have also been adopted in relation to documentary discovery more generally in light of their potential to reduce litigation costs:

1. Electronically stored information is discoverable.

2. In any proceeding, the parties should ensure that steps taken in the discovery process are proportionate, taking into account (i) the nature and scope of the litigation, including the importance and complexity of the issues, interest and amounts at stake; (ii) the relevance of the available electronically stored information; (iii) its importance to the court's adjudication in a given case; and (iv) the costs, burden and delay that may be imposed on the parties to deal with electronically stored information.

3. Counsel and parties should meet and confer as soon as practicable and on an ongoing basis, regarding the identification, preservation, collection, review and production of electronically stored information.

4. As soon as litigation is reasonably anticipated, parties must consider their obligation to take reasonable and good faith steps to preserve potentially relevant electronically stored information.

5. The parties should be prepared to disclose all relevant electronically stored information that is reasonably accessible in terms of cost and burden.

6. A party should not be required, absent agreement or a court order based on demonstrated need and relevance, to search for or collect deleted or residual electronically stored information.

7. A party may satisfy its obligation to identify electronically stored information in good faith by using electronic tools and processes such as data sampling, searching and/or the use of selection criteria to collect potentially relevant electronically stored information.

8. Parties should agree as early as possible in the litigation process on the format in which electronically stored information will be produced. Parties should also agree on the format, content and organization of information to be exchanged in any required list of documents as part of the discovery process.

9. During the discovery process parties should agree to, or if necessary, seek judicial direction on, measures to protect privileges, privacy, trade secrets and other confidential information relating to the production of electronic documents and data.

10. During the discovery process, parties should anticipate and respect the rules of the forum in which the litigation takes place, while appreciating the impact any decisions may have in related actions in other forums.

11. Sanctions should be considered by the court where a party will be materially prejudiced by another party's failure to meet any obligation to preserve, collect, review or produce electronically stored information. The party in default may avoid sanctions if it demonstrates the failure was not intentional or reckless.

12. The reasonable costs of preserving, collecting and reviewing electronically stored information will be borne by the party producing it. In limited circumstances, it may be appropriate for the parties to arrive at a different allocation of costs on an interim basis, by either agreement or court order. (Sedona Canada Principles, p. vi.)

The Ontario Bar Association has developed a series of model e-discovery precedents to assist parties in planning and reaching agreement on electronic document production. See: Ontario Bar Association, "Model E-Discovery Precedents" (OBA: 2007), online at: http://www.oba.org/en/publicaffairs_en/E-discovery/model_precendents.aspx.

A significant body of case law on these issues has been building over the last several years. The Ontario Bar Association maintains a very useful e-discovery case law digest online at http://www.oba.org/En/publicaffairs_en/E-Discovery/digest.aspx. In considering requests for further production of electronic documents, courts in a number of Canadian jurisdictions referred to guidelines developed by the Ontario Task Force (which have now been superseded by the Sedona Canada Principles), particularly in relation to the importance of cost/benefit analysis in determining whether to order further production.

2. Scope of E-Discovery

Spar Aerospace Limited v. Aerowerks Engineering Inc.
2007 ABQB 543

[On an application before Veit J, the plaintiff Spar argued that the defendants had failed to meet their production obligations under the Alberta Rules. Included among the alleged deficiencies were emails from and to individuals involved in the transaction at issue, documents that had been deleted from the defendants' hard drives, but were retrievable, relevant metadata relating to those documents, and "properly processed electronic documents for the records listed in the Affidavit of Records, with complete database information; and, passwords, operating systems, and system-related files necessary to view all producible records" (para. 2). Veit J allowed the plaintiff's application and, in light of the particular parties and allegations before her, issued an order for broad-ranging production of electronic documents and information.]

· · ·

[7] In addition to the failure to provide the documents relating to the Cascade consortium, the defendants have also failed to provide all relevant e-mails, and, in the circumstances here, all relevant and retrievable documents that have been deleted from the drives, all relevant meta-data, all passwords, operating systems and system-related files necessary to view all producible documents and to properly process electronic documents for the records listed in the affidavit of records, with complete database information. In reviewing each of these situations, the court observes that production of electronic records should be produced electronically; hence, the party to whom the records are produced is entitled to all passwords, operating systems and system-related files to allow real access the produced material. In each of these situations, the court is satisfied that Spar has proven that the records requested do or did exist and are relevant and material; some e-mails refer to other e-mails and some e-mails explicitly refer to the deletion of materials.

[8] The unusually high level of disclosure imposed in this case is justified by: the underlying fact that the defendants were employees of the plaintiff when they began working in competition with the plaintiff, the judicial determination that this was an appropriate case in which to issue an Anton Piller order, the size of the claim, which exceeds $50 million, and the great IT expertise of the parties which presupposes that at least some of the work required to provide the required level of disclosure can be done in-house.

· · ·

4. What Are the Limits of Electronic Disclosure?

[56] Although recent developments in the law have clarified the law relating to disclosure of electronic records, some work remains to be done in this area. Alberta has not yet adopted an electronic document production Rule, although it is on the verge of doing so. It is a given, in this context, that electronically stored information is discoverable.

[57] It appears to be accepted in Canadian practice that the obligation of discovery is tempered by the application of proportionality or cost/benefit ratio: in Alberta, this means that records must be only be disclosed if they are not only relevant, but also material. Although this is a principle of general proportionality that is articulated in the Rules of Court, I accept that there is an implicit requirement that limits production to those records which are reasonably accessible. However, in this case, Spar claims damages of $50 million, or an accounting of profits, and punitive damages in the amount of $1 million. Moreover, all the parties are extremely IT competent. In those circumstances, proportionality is not a major feature of the discovery process.

[58] Here, the onus was on the defendants to satisfy the court that they should be relieved of production that would notionally have been required because of the cost or burden of providing that discovery. Given the circumstances outlined above, the defendants have failed to meet that test

[59] Indeed, the last two facts mentioned—the large size of the claim and the IT competence of the parties, along with two more important facts, on the one hand that, while the defendants were employees of Spar, they began to compete with Spar and, on the other, that this court has already determined that it was appropriate to issue an exceptional Anton Piller order, combine to justify a high level of disclosure, a level which may not be required in standard litigation.

[60] Here, the former case manager, Binder J, wisely encouraged the parties to meet and to attempt a collaborative effort on disclosure; indeed, the case manager directed such a meeting in his June 15, 2006 order. Although such a meeting was held, and a later meeting did eventually produce a consent confidentiality order as discussed above, those meetings unfortunately did not resolve all the discovery disputes between the parties.

[61] An element of the background that must be considered in this case is the fact that this court concluded, in December 2004, that the circumstances known at that time warranted the issuance of an exceptional Anton Piller order. Clearly, therefore, at that time the court was satisfied that this extraordinary measure was necessary in order to ensure that no vital evidence relating to the issues between the parties would be destroyed.

[62] The various specific issues that have arisen in this lawsuit relative to electronic production of documents is discussed below.

a) Must E-mails Be Produced?

[63] Here, the court is satisfied that the defendants have not produced all relevant and material e-mails.

[64] The defendants have provided over 300 e-mails from Kevin Morris to Steven Gentles and Tyler Pahl, but only one e-mail from either of those recipients to Kevin Morris. Moreover, it is clear from the Morris e-mails that he did receive e-mails from Gentles and Pahl.

b) Must Deleted or Destroyed Records Be Produced?

[65] Here, the court is satisfied that the defendants can, and should, list on their affidavit of documents all of the material and relevant records that have been deleted if no electronic or paper copy exists.

[66] As demonstrated in the document reproduced in para. 65 above, the defendants or some of them deleted relevant and material records. In the exceptional circumstances here, as described above, the defendants were required to list all deleted and destroyed records, and were required, moreover, to make reasonable efforts to produce those deleted records.

c) Must Required Passwords, Systems, and Software Be Provided?

[67] The defendants are required to provide to Spar all passwords, systems and software necessary to access the records produced.

[68] Here, the defendants have provided approximately 1.2 gigabytes of information, much of which is password protected and therefore inaccessible to Spar.

[69] It was always the case that production included an obligation to provide all technical information necessary to allow the receiving party to access the production: *Canadian Engineering and Surveys (Yukon) Limited.*

[70] That general principle carries over to electronic disclosure. Moreover, it is obvious that the defendants should produce their electronic records electronically: not only is hard copy production considerably more expensive, but it is also less searchable and is inferior because it does not retain potentially critical meta-data such as when and by whom a record was created or amended: *Cholakis.* In order to access the electronic disclosure, it is obvious that a receiving party requires from the producing party whatever passwords and other systems necessary in order to constitute real disclosure.

d) Must Unprocessed Records Be Produced?

[71] The defendants must produce their electronic records in a meaningful way. Here the electronic records provided have not been processed for export into an electronic document database program.

[72] The principles of meaningful disclosure are the same, whether disclosure is made by electronic or paper means: *Wilson, Prism Hospital Software Inc., Nicolardi.*

e) Must Metadata Be Produced?

[73] In the circumstances here, the defendants must produce their metadata.

[74] Metadata is a record: *Desgagne.*

[75] While metadata presumably need not be produced in most situations, because it is irrelevant to know, for example, when a document was printed, the production of such records is material and relevant here where the pleadings disclose that the identity of the author of electronic records, the timing of the treatment of those records— including if and when they were modified, the dates and tracking routes of e-mail, are all potentially at the very core of the issues that are raised in the litigation.

· · ·

5. Must the Hard Drives Be Produced?

[80] Spar has proven its entitlement to access to the defendants' hard drives and is entitled to immediate access to them.

[81] It goes without saying, that access to the opponent's hard drives will not always be granted by a court: *Baldwin Janzen, Ireland*. The then case managing judge presumably took all of those situations into account in determining that failure to provide adequate, timely, disclosure would result in the release of the hard drives to Spar. His order was not appealed.

[82] However, where, as in this case, a party satisfies the court that required disclosure has not been made and the missing disclosure is likely stored on a computer's hard drive, a court would normally grant access to the hard drive itself: *Nicolardi*. Such an approach was presumably the basis for the then case manager's order of June 15, 2006.

[83] If the failure to provide the required affidavit of records had been inconsequential, this court presumably would have had the equitable jurisdiction to relieve the defendants from the full force of the June 15, 2006 order.

[84] In the circumstances here, however, where the deficiencies in the affidavit of records are many and material, there is no basis for this court to interfere with the order granted on June 15, 2006.

NOTES AND QUESTIONS

1. Broad-ranging production orders, particularly of parties' hard drives carry with them the threat of undue privacy intrusions and the related risk of disclosure of irrelevant information. In *Innovative Health Group Inc. v. Calgary Health Region*, 2008 ABCA 219, Madam Justice Conrad noted that Veit J's broad-ranging order in *Spar* was merited on the unique facts of the case, but emphasized the important role that the proportionality principle outlined in the Sedona Canada Principles will play in most cases. Further, she cautioned at para. 41 that where "the court deems it appropriate to order production of a hard drive, measures should be taken to protect disclosure of irrelevant and immaterial information that the producing party objects to produce. Although litigation confidentiality exists, many times that will not be sufficient to protect personal, confidential and private material. A judge should always hear representations as to how information that is neither material nor relevant can be protected from exposure, and frame any production order in the least intrusive manner."

2. In Ontario, electronic copies of documents already produced in paper form have been ordered produced, in part in reliance on Principle 11 the OBA's Guidelines for Discovery of Electronic Documents (OBA, "Ediscovery Guidelines, 2004), online at: http://www.oba.org/En/pdf_newsletter/E-DiscoveryGuidelines.pdf at p. 15), which suggests that the parties should agree early on in what form the documents will be produced and that "documents may be producible in electronic form" in certain kinds of circumstances, including allowing more complete access to relevant information, to preserve data security and integrity and to minimize the costs of production. See, for example, *Hummingbird v. Mustafa*, 2007 CanLII 39610 (Ont. SCJ) and *Ritchie v. 830234 Ontario Inc.*, 2008 CanLII 4787 (Ont. SCJ). As noted above, the OBA Guidelines have since been superseded by the Sedona Canada Principles.

3. Must a party to litigation produce for discovery information they have posted about themselves on their Facebook site? See: *Leduc v. Roman*, [2009] OJ No. 681 (SCJ). Is a website operator compelled to disclose information that could lead to revelation of the identities of subscribers to its site? See: *Warman v. Wilkins-Fournier*, 2009 CanLII 14054 (Ont. SCJ).

D. Documentary Discovery from Non-Parties

In most jurisdictions, some level of documentary discovery is available from non-parties (see, for example, Ontario rule 30.10, Alberta rule 209, and Nova Scotia rule 18.05). However, non-parties are not required to produce an affidavit of documents—that is, to make general disclosure of the documents within their possession (however, note Ontario rule 30.02(4) with regard to documents in the possession of a corporation related to a corporate party)—but they can, if the court so orders, be required to produce specific documents. As with examination for discovery of non-parties, the rules may specifically place limits on this power to obtain production from non-parties; for example, see Ontario rule 30.10(1). The following case was decided under an earlier version of the Ontario rule.

Ontario (Attorney General) v. Stavro
(1995), 26 OR (3d) 39 (CA)

[The plaintiffs sought declarations pursuant to the Ontario *Charitable Gifts Act* that the executors of the estate of Harold Ballard had acted in breach of their fiduciary duties to the estate as a result of actions leading to the sale of the estate's interest in Maple Leaf Gardens Ltd. (MLG) to MLG Ventures ("Ventures"), a company controlled by Stavro (one of the estate's executors). The plaintiffs also sought an order that the sale was null and void; a declaration that all dividends received by Ventures on the shares of MLG Ltd. were received in trust for the estate, and an order enjoining the defendants from taking steps to amalgamate MLG Ltd. and Ventures, from conducting a shareholders' meeting, or from taking steps to cancel the estate's interest in MLG Ltd. Pursuant to the oppression remedies under the Ontario *Business Corporations Act*, the plaintiffs further sought a declaration that the affairs of MLG Ltd. had been carried on in a manner that was oppressive to, unfairly prejudicial to, and unfairly disregarded the interests of, security holders of MLG Ltd., including the estate and beneficiaries of the estate, and an order setting aside the acquisition of the shares of MLG Ltd. by Ventures.

After obtaining an interim injunction, the plaintiffs brought two motions pursuant to rule 30.10(1) of the Ontario *Rules of Civil Procedure* for production of documents in the possession, control or power of four non-party financial institutions. Two of these non-parties, the Toronto-Dominion Bank and TD Capital Group Limited, opposed production. The motions judge found that the documents were relevant to material issues in the litigation, but he concluded that the plaintiffs had not established that it would be unfair to require them to proceed to trial without the documents or that the documents were vital or crucial to preparation for trial. Consequently the motions were dismissed. The plaintiffs appealed.]

BY THE COURT: The appellants (plaintiffs) appeal from the order of the motion judge dismissing two motions brought pursuant to rule 30.10(1) of the *Rules of Civil Procedure* seeking production of documents in the possession, control or power of four non-parties to this action. Two of the non-parties did not oppose the motions.

Briefly stated, the action is with respect to issues dealing with the fiduciary duties of the executors in dealing with assets of the estate of Harold E. Ballard, deceased.

The rule provides as follows:

> 30.10 (1) The court may, on motion by a party, order production for inspection of a document that is in the possession, control or power of a person not a party and is not privileged where the court is satisfied that,
>
> (a) the document is relevant to a material issue in the action; and
>
> (b) it would be unfair to require the moving party to proceed to trial without having discovery of the document.

The motion judge found that the documents were relevant to material issues in the litigation. He then proceeded to consider whether it would be unfair to require the appellants to proceed to trial without having discovery of those documents. After alluding to a number of factors relevant to that determination, the motion judge turned to the importance of the documents in the litigation. He referred to this consideration as the "most important factor" in the fairness assessment. After reviewing the authorities he said [at 44 ante]:

> [T]he evidence sought must be vital or crucial and such that the moving party cannot adequately prepare its case for trial without access to such documents.

The appellants submit that in holding that the documents must be "vital" or "crucial" to their preparation for trial, the motion judge departed from the test set out in rule 30.10(1).

We agree. The fairness assessment required by rule 30.10(1)(b) is made only after the documents are found to be relevant to a material issue. By requiring that the documents be "vital" or "crucial" before it could be said that it would be unfair to refuse their production, the motion judge combined the separate considerations identified in rule 30.10(1)(a) and (b) into a single test which imposed a higher standard of materiality than that contemplated by the rule. The rule envisions cases where it will be unfair to require a party to proceed to trial without the production of relevant documents even though those documents are not crucial or vital to that party's preparation for trial. By limiting the production of documents to those found to be vital or crucial, the trial judge elevated the materiality standard in rule 30.10(1)(a) and effectively neutered the fairness assessment demanded by rule 30.10(1)(b).

The motion judge did refer to various factors which could be relevant to the inquiry required by rule 30.10(1)(b). He then proceeded, however, to consider the significance of the documents in the litigation to the virtual exclusion of all other factors in determining whether it would be unfair to require the appellants to proceed to trial without production of the documents. In doing so, he erred.

In holding that the motion judge erred, we do not suggest that the importance of the documents in the litigation is not relevant to the fairness assessment required by rule 30.10(1)(b). In *Metropolitan Life Insurance Co. v. Frenette*, [1992] 1 SCR 647, 89 DLR (4th) 653, the defendant sought production of medical records referable to the plaintiff's mental condition before his death. In considering a provision of the *Quebec Code of Civil Procedure*, RSQ, c. C-25, which was said to be analogous to rule 30.10 (p. 690), L'Heureux-Dubé J said at p. 685:

Otherwise, judges must exercise their discretion under art. 402 CCP *according to the degree of relevance and importance of the information sought relative to the issue between the parties.* In exercising that discretion, a court must weigh the diverse interests in conflict. (Emphasis added)

Clearly, if a moving party can show that the documents requested are crucial to its preparation for trial, that party has gone a long way to demonstrating that it would be unfair to require the party to proceed to trial without production of those documents. It does not, however, follow that absent a demonstration that the documents are crucial to the litigation, the moving party cannot demonstrate that it would be unfair to require that party to proceed to trial without production of the documents. The importance of the documents requested is a factor, but only one factor to be considered in making the determination required by rule 30.10(1)(b).

The appellants submitted that if we concluded that the motion judge applied the wrong test in denying production that we should vacate that order and require production.

We do not agree. An order requiring production should be made only after a full consideration of all of the relevant factors. The motion judge, who is case managing this complex litigation, is in a much better position than this court to determine whether fairness requires production of all, some or none of the demanded documents at this stage of the litigation. In our view, the policy underlying the case management system is best served by remitting the matter to the motion judge for a determination of the merits.

In making the fairness assessment required by rule 30.10(1)(b), the motion judge must be guided by the policy underlying the discovery regime presently operating in Ontario. That regime provides for full discovery of, and production from parties to the litigation. It also imposes ongoing disclosure obligations on those parties. Save in the circumstances specifically addressed by the rules, non-parties are immune from the potentially intrusive, costly and time-consuming process of discovery and production. By its terms, rule 30.10 assumes that requiring a party to go to trial without the forced production of relevant documents in the hands of non-parties is not *per se* unfair.

The discovery process must also be kept within reasonable bounds. Lengthy, some might say interminable, discoveries are far from rare in the present litigation environment. We are told that discovery of these defendants has already occupied some 18 days and is not yet complete. Unless production from and discovery of non-parties is subject to firm controls and recognized as the exception rather than the rule, the discovery process, like Topsy, will just grow and grow. The effective and efficient resolution of civil lawsuits is not served if the discovery process takes on dimensions more akin to a public inquiry than a specific lawsuit.

The motion judge was properly concerned about the ramifications of a production order in this case. Many litigants, especially those involved in complex commercial cases, find themselves in the position where non-party financial institutions are in possession of documents which are relevant to material issues in the litigation, and which those institutions cannot, or will not, voluntarily produce prior to trial. If this situation alone is enough to compel production during the discovery stage of the process, then production from and discovery of non-parties would become a routine part of the discovery process in complex commercial cases. It may be that it should be part of that process, but that is not the policy reflected in the rules as presently drafted.

In deciding whether to order production in the circumstances of this case, the factors to be considered by the motion judge should include:

- the importance of the documents in the litigation;
- whether production at the discovery stage of the process as opposed to production at trial is necessary to avoid unfairness to the appellant;
- whether the discovery of the defendants with respect to the issues to which the documents are relevant is adequate and if not, whether responsibility for that inadequacy rests with the defendants;
- the position of the non-parties with respect to production;
- the availability of the documents or their informational equivalent from some other source which is accessible to the moving parties;
- the relationship of the non-parties from whom production is sought, to the litigation and the parties to the litigation. Non-parties who have an interest in the subject-matter of the litigation and whose interests are allied with the party opposing production should be more susceptible to a production order than a true "stranger" to the litigation.

In addressing these and any other relevant factors (some of which were identified by the motion judge in his reasons), the motion judge will bear in mind that the appellants bear the burden of showing that it would be unfair to make them proceed to trial without production of the documents.

In our opinion, a consideration of some of these factors will require an examination of the documents as contemplated by rule 30.10(3). That rule provides in part:

> 30.10(3) … where the court is uncertain of the relevance of or necessity for discovery of the document, the court may inspect the document to determine the issue.

For example, in considering whether it would be unfair to require the appellants to wait until trial to obtain the documents, the number, content and authorship of the documents may be very important. Those facts could be ascertained only from an examination of the documents or perhaps from an examination of an appropriate summary prepared by those in possession of the documents. Similarly, the importance or unimportance of the documents in the litigation may best be determined by an examination of them.

We recognize that this process will be time consuming and will place an additional burden on the motion judge. We are satisfied, however, that in the circumstances of this case and considering the material filed on the motions, that an informed decision requires an examination of the documents. A decision made without reference to the documents runs the very real risk of being either over- or under-inclusive. No doubt, as the case management judge, the motion judge will have a familiarity with the case which will facilitate his review of the documents.

In the result, the appeal is allowed, the order made by the motion judge is set aside, and the matter is remitted to the motion judge for further consideration in accordance with the principles outlined above. The costs of this appeal and of the motion below are left to the motion judge.

Appeal allowed.

NOTES AND QUESTIONS

1. Is the potential complexity of the analysis and the time and expense involved in moving for production from an unwilling non-party likely in most cases to serve to limit such motions to cases in which the evidence is "vital" or "crucial" to preparation for trial? If so, should the rules change?

2. What should be the position of non-party financial institutions? Do they have a responsibility to the public to facilitate the discovery process regarding legitimate claims? Or should courts be concerned about the potential expense to such institutions of producing documents in litigation in which they have no interest?

3. When assessing the relevance of potential non-party documents, the court in *Miller (Ed) Sales and Rentals Ltd. v. Caterpillar Tractor Co. et al.* (1988), 94 AR 17, at 18 (para. 8) (QB)—relying on the British Columbia Court of Appeal in *Rhoades v. Occidental Life Insurance of California*, [1973] 3 WWR 625—identified four "caveats" when considering a document's probable relevance:

> 1. The rule should not be used as a fishing expedition to discover whether or not a person is in possession of a document.
>
> 2. The documents need not necessarily be admissible in evidence at trial.
>
> 3. The documents of which production is sought must be adequately described, but not necessarily so specifically that they can be picked out from any number of other documents.
>
> 4. The third party's objections to production must be considered, but are not determinative.
> [Emphasis omitted.]

Further, the Alberta court added an "additional condition" that "the Rule cannot be used as a method of obtaining discovery of a person not a party to the action." Through these various jurisdictional approaches, have the courts correctly balanced the rights of non-parties with those of litigants?

4. *Internet.* In *Irwin Toy Ltd. v. Doe* (2000), 12 CPC (5th) 103 (Ont. SCJ), the moving party plaintiff brought a motion for an order pursuant to Ontario rules 30.10 and 31.10 in the context of an "action against a phantom 'nom de guerre' John Doe," seeking damages for "defamation in respect of an individual plaintiff and breach of confidence and conversion with respect to the corporate plaintiff and punitive damages in respect of both plaintiffs." The court, taking the claim on its face, found that the action arose as against the unidentified defendant "by reason of a publication sent by electronic mail message to approximately 75 persons utilizing the services of the internet." In deciding the issue, Wilkins J reasoned as follows:

It is alleged that the message sent was defamatory with respect to the individual plaintiff and it is further alleged that, attached to the electronic message, were two private and confidential electronic files which had been wrongfully removed from the corporate plaintiffs' computer system.

At the time of the issuance of the Statement of Claim, neither plaintiff was in a position to be able to identify the person who had published the electronic mail message and the two allegedly confidential files. Utilizing the services of CDC Inc., a communications and internet consulting firm, the plaintiffs were able to identify the internet alias of the sender to be george .jodie@spinfinder.com.

Further investigation identified that this particular internet alias was tracked to an internet protocol address of 216.200.145.35. This particular address was further traced and ascertained to refer to a subscriber of iPrimus Canada, an internet service provider.

The plaintiffs, through their counsel, contacted the technical administrator of iPrimus Canada who confirmed that the electronic records would be preserved and identified that the numerical protocol address was a subscriber with iPrimus internet service provider. The representative of iPrimus, however, declined to identify the subscriber although, ultimately, through their counsel they informed the plaintiffs' counsel that they would not oppose an application to the court for an order obliging iPrimus Canada to disclose the identity of the internet protocol address 216.200.145.35.

In the case at bar, the internet service provider has been given notice of this motion. The internet service provider has closed the account of the customer in question, and there is no evidence before me that it had any knowledge of the alleged conduct of its customer.

Although the internet service provider does not oppose this application, it is my view that it is important to comment on this form of motion as it is anticipated that the courts will be seeing motions of this nature on a more frequent basis, as members of the public become curious to determine the true identity of the originator of messages, and/or information passed through the internet, or posted on "notice boards" or disclosed in "chat rooms" therein.

The development of information and disclosure and exchange by electronic means through the auspices of the internet is an informational disclosure process in common use to any member of the public, the mechanics of which are simple, straightforward and inexpensive. As a consequence of the evolution of this process, the volume of electronic disclosure of information has been expanding explosively on an exponential basis.

Implicit in the passage of information through the internet by utilization of an alias or pseudonym is the mutual understanding that, to some degree, the identity of the source will be concealed. Some internet service providers inform the users of their services that they will safeguard their privacy and/or conceal their identity and, apparently, they even go so far as to have their privacy policies reviewed and audited for compliance. Generally speaking, it is understood that a person's internet protocol address will not be disclosed. Apparently, some internet service providers require their customers to agree that they will not transmit messages that are defamatory or libelous in exchange for the internet service to take reasonable measures to protect the privacy of the originator of the information.

In keeping with the protocol or etiquette developed in the usage of the internet, some degree of privacy or confidentiality with respect to the identity of the internet protocol address of the originator of a message has significant safety value and is in keeping with what should be perceived as being good public policy. As far as I am aware, there is no duty or obligation upon the internet service provider to voluntarily disclose the identity of an internet protocol address, or to provide that information upon request.

In the case at bar, the moving party has demonstrated on a *prima facie* basis that the originator of the message in question has released, by electronical mailing, words which are capable of being construed by a properly charged jury as being defamatory. Similarly, a *prima facie* case has been demonstrated that the unidentified originator of the message had access to two private and confidential electronic files wrongfully removed from the corporate plaintiffs' computer system, and converted by the originator of the message to their own use.

The moving parties seek to obtain the identity of "Joe Doe" in order that they might properly bring action against the proper defendant against whom they make the allegations in the Statement of Claim. Rules 30.10 and 31.10 provide for production for inspection of documents in the possession, control or power of persons not a party to the action, and leave to examine for discovery any person who there is reason to believe has information relevant to a material issue in the action subject to certain tests provided for in rule 31.10.

On the facts of the case at bar the moving parties, in my view, meet all of the tests necessary to obtain the information in the possession of iPrimus Canada identifying the subscriber with the internet protocol address 216.200.145.35. To date, the moving parties have been unable to obtain information as to the identity of "Joe Doe" which is clearly information to which they would be entitled on any examination on discovery from "Joe Doe," who will be the very person they wish to examine. In addition, it would be unfair to require the moving party to attempt to proceed without having the opportunity of identifying the true defendant.

In my view there would be no unfairness to iPrimus Canada to oblige them to disclose the identity of the specific internet protocol address subscriber by way of answering a written interrogatory containing the name, address or other identification information that would be available in their electronic records.

Ordinarily, under Rule 31.10, the moving party must satisfy the court that they have been unable to obtain the information from other persons whom the moving party is entitled to examine for discovery. In something so fundamental as the proper identification of the true defendant in circumstances such as the case at bar, one has difficulty imagining how the moving parties could ever make that identification by any other means than disclosure from the internet service provider.

Rule 31.10 contemplates that the moving party will demonstrate that there is reason to believe that the person sought to be examined has information relevant to a material issue in the action. Presumably, the true identity and appropriate address for service for a defendant could arguably always be something of such importance as to require its disclosure. Such disclosure, however, in my view, should not be automatic upon the issuance of the Statement of Claim. If such were to be the case, the fact of the anonymity of the internet could be shattered for the price of the issuance of a spurious Statement of Claim and the benefits obtained by the anonymity lost in inappropriate circumstances.

In the circumstances of the case at bar, the moving party has demonstrated on the affidavit material filed before me that it has a *prima facie* case as against Joe Doe in respect to the allegations of claim made in the Statement of Claim. In my view, that is the appropriate test for the court to apply in determining whether or not to order a non-party internet service provider to disclose the identity of an internet protocol address.

The law in Ontario respecting the liability of an internet service provider for the actions of its customer is not clear. It would be unjust and expensive to require a plaintiff to commence a potentially losing law suit just to obtain the identity of the real tortfeasor from the service provider.

The moving party shall therefore be entitled to their order as requested and the internet service provider, iPrimus Canada, is directed to provide that information to the plaintiffs.

As agreed between the parties, there are to be no costs as against iPrimus Canada. The costs of this motion however, with respect to Joe Doe in the ultimate result of the litigation are reserved to the trial judge.

Did the court properly balance the various competing interests at stake in *Irwin Toy*? Could a higher expectation of privacy on the part of "Joe Doe" be justified? For further considerations in relation to disclosure of subscriber identity or information tending to reveal subscriber identity see: *BMG Canada Inc. v. Doe*, 2005 FCA 193 (CanLII); Jane Bailey, "The Substance of Procedure: Non-Party Disclosure in the Canadian and U.S. Online Music Sharing Litigation" (2006), 43 ALR 615.

III. PHYSICAL DISCOVERY

A. Medical Examinations

As already indicated, the rules of the various jurisdictions invariably provide that where the physical and mental condition of a party to a proceeding is in question, the court may order a party to undergo a physical or mental examination: see, for example, Ontario rule 33, Alberta rule 217, BC rule 30, and Nova Scotia rule 21. What is the policy behind allowing the courts to order parties to undergo such intrusive examinations even against their will?

Manuel v. Head

(1988), 72 Nfld. & PEIR (2d) 211 (Nfld. TD)

BARRY J: This is an application by the defendant under rule 34 of the Rules of the Supreme Court contained in Schedule D of the Judicature Act (Statutes of Newfoundland 1986) for an order that the first plaintiff be examined by two medical practitioners for the purpose of enabling them to make an assessment of injuries sustained by him in a motor vehicle accident which occurred on June 30, 1984, and of the result of the medical treatment subsequently received. ...

The first plaintiff has alleged in his statement of claim that he sustained serious personal injuries in the automobile accident, above referred to, for which he now claims damages from the defendant. The first plaintiff has already supplied the defendant with medical reports prepared by his own physicians but the defendant alleges that it is necessary to make his own assessment of those injuries to enable him to prepare a proper defence to this action.

Rule 34.01(1) provides for issuance of an order by this court for an examination of a party to an action by a qualified medical practitioner upon application of another party in the same action in the following terms:

> 34.01(1) Where the physical or mental condition of a party is in issue, the court may, at any time on the application of an opposing party or on its own motion, order the party to submit to a physical or mental examination by a qualified medical practitioner.

… The plaintiff alleges that rule 34.01 is unconstitutional because it offends sections 7, 8, and 9 of the Charter by providing means whereby a litigant may be compelled to submit to a medical examination or face the prospect of having his case stayed or dismissed. These provisions are as follows:

> 7. Everyone has the right to life, liberty and security of the person and the right not to be deprived thereof except in accordance with the principles of fundamental justice.
>
> 8. Everyone has the right to be secure against unreasonable search or seizure.
>
> 9. Everyone has the right not to be arbitrarily detained or imprisoned.

In my view, there cannot be a deprivation of liberty within the meaning of s. 7 unless there is a compulsory restriction of movement of one person by another through the exercise by the latter of some measure of authority or control by threat or force. In this case, the order of the court if granted would require the plaintiff to submit his person for a medical examination by two medical practitioners selected by the defendant. While at first sight this measure appears to be an infringement upon the liberty or security of the first plaintiff, yet when put into proper context, it appears in a different light.

The proper context is that of a civil action taken by the first plaintiff against the defendant claiming damages for injuries allegedly caused by the defendant's negligence. The application herein has been made to enable the defendant to defend himself against the first plaintiff's claim. What is involved is a balancing of the first plaintiff's right to sue the defendant for damages and the right of the defendant to inform himself prior to trial by inspection of the damages which the first plaintiff claims from him. There was no obligation upon the first plaintiff to institute action against the defendant seeking damages for the injuries he sustained. However, by doing so, he voluntarily accepted the procedure provided in the Rules of the Supreme Court for the processing of his claim. The question arising upon the application is whether the first plaintiff can invoke the Charter to assist him in avoiding a procedural step which provides that upon application of the defendant the court may order that he be examined by qualified medical practitioners for an assessment of his injuries. The Charter was not designed to take away rights of others in order to convenience persons who themselves are seeking to establish rights before the law. Accordingly, I hold that an order of the court directing the first plaintiff to submit himself to a medical examination would not offend s. 7 of the Charter because it is a necessary step in a proceeding which he himself initiated.

The same reasoning applies to the first plaintiff's allegation that the order requires that he submit to an unreasonable search of his person in violation of his right to the protection from such searches afforded him by s. 8 of the Charter. The search to which he refers is the proposed medical examination which an order under rule 34.01 would direct him to undergo. If the examination can be properly termed a search within the meaning of s. 8 of the Charter, it cannot be held to be unreasonable in view of the fact that it is a necessary part of the procedure involved in the course of his own suit against the defendant. Nor does the proposed order constitute detention within the meaning of s. 9 of the Charter. That section relates to a situation where a person in authority forcefully holds or takes another into custody without his consent. It appears that its scope overlaps that of s. 7 of the Charter to some degree, and for the reasons above set out with reference to that section it is not applicable to a case such as this where the detainment apprehended is merely an order of the court directing the first plaintiff to comply with a necessary procedural requirement in the legal proceeding commenced by the first plaintiff.

If I am wrong in so holding, and the infringements of the Charter alleged or any of them are truly violations of its provisions, I am satisfied that any such infringement is a reasonable limit upon guaranteed freedoms and for the reasons given above, can be demonstrably justified in a free and democratic society in accordance with the provisions of s. 1 of the Charter, which I now quote:

> 1. The Canadian Charter of Rights and Freedoms guarantees the rights and freedoms set out in it subject only to such reasonable limits prescribed by law as can be demonstrably justified in a free and democratic society.

… The purpose of pretrial procedures such as the medical examination of a party is to enable parties to be informed of each other's claims and contentions and of the evidence to be presented at trial in order that they will be prepared to meet the issues involved in particular actions. Such procedures result in narrowing issues, obviating unnecessary evidence and obtaining agreement upon undisputed relevant evidence at trial. These procedures when utilized by parties often lead to settlement of many issues before trial, as well as out-of-court settlements of the claims themselves. The many benefits and advantages which result from pretrial procedures are well-known and generally operate to the benefit of parties to civil actions. In this case the pretrial medical examination sought by the defendant is intended to give him an opportunity to conduct an independent examination of the first plaintiff in order to satisfy himself as to the nature and extent of the injuries complained of.

To recover, the plaintiff must prove his claim not only in respect of the tort involved but also in respect of the damages sustained. Proof of damages involves presentation to the court of creditable evidence to substantiate the nature and extent of the injuries sustained by the first plaintiff as a result of the wrongdoing of the defendant. It is, inter alia, a condition of acceptance of such evidence by the court that upon application the defendant be permitted, where applicable, to examine the objects damaged and to cross-examine the plaintiff's witnesses as to the accuracy of their observations and conclusions respecting such damage.

Rule 30.01 provides for the oral examination of a person intended by a party to be called as a witness in an action at any time before trial, whether such person resides within or without the jurisdiction of the court. Similar provision has been made in rule 32 for the discovery and inspection of documents before trial and in rule 36 for the inspection of real and personal property. While an examination of injuries sustained by a person cannot be equated to an oral examination of a person under rule 30 or the inspection of a damaged motor vehicle under rule 36, nevertheless, a defendant in an action for personal damages has the right to make his own assessment of injuries sustained by the plaintiff to test the accuracy and veracity of allegations of damages made by the plaintiffs. It is alleged that the first plaintiff cannot be ordered to submit to a medical examination because such an order involves a form of restriction upon rights granted him by the Charter, and therefore, the subject of his claim, i.e. his own injuries, should be allowed to escape scrutiny by the defendant. However, the Rules of Court are intended to introduce a procedure which will bring a maximum degree of fairness to parties who are involved in actions before this court. Of the essence of this procedure is the principle that facts in issue be made known by parties relying upon them to other parties and the court. This means that a plaintiff, upon application by the defendant, must make available the subject matter of the damage claimed so that the defendant can inspect the objects about which the issues revolve. To deprive a defendant of an opportunity to make such an examination is to prevent him from exercising his right to inspect the principal object of the plaintiff's claim.

The importance of according such a right to a defendant to a medical examination of the plaintiff to be conducted by a qualified medical practitioner becomes obvious where, as here, he alleges to have sustained very severe injuries for which he claims substantial monetary damages. If an inspection is not allowed, the defendant and the court must accept, without means of testing or verification, the testimony which the plaintiffs will adduce on the nature and the extent of the injuries and the disabilities which ensue therefrom. While the plaintiff is entitled to claim against the defendant the damages he suffered arising out of the alleged wrongful conduct of the defendant, those damages must be proved and assessed in accordance with the Rules of Court. The plaintiff can succeed in his action, only by following the rules of procedure enacted under the authority of the Judicature Act including the rule that he make available for medical inspection the person who sustained the injuries for which damages are claimed, i.e., himself, even though it may be repugnant to him.

In issuing an order for the medical examination of a party under rule 34 the court does not direct that such party be forced or compelled to undergo the examination. The order really means that the defendant is entitled to have the plaintiff's injuries examined by a medical practitioner and that if the plaintiff does not submit to such an examination, he will not be permitted to prove his damages solely upon the evidence of the medical practitioners whom he may choose to call as witnesses. Rule 34.06 states:

> 34.06(1) When a party fails to submit to an examination or deliver a medical report as required by rule 34, the party shall not be liable to contempt but shall, if a plaintiff, be liable to have his or her proceedings dismissed, or, if a defendant, to have his or her defence struck out.

I interpret this as meaning that the court, upon the plaintiff's refusal or failure to comply with an order under s. 36.01, may, not "must," dismiss the plaintiff's action. It appears to me that it is implicit in this rule (34.06) that the plaintiff will not be allowed to adduce the evidence of damages which he alleges to have suffered, where he has refused to undergo a medical examination which has been ordered by the court upon the application of the defendant.

I have referred above to the defendant's application for a medical examination of the plaintiff, but it should be noted that rule 34.01 also permits the court of its own motion to order a medical examination of the plaintiff. The reason for this rule in both instances is to provide a means whereby another assessment of the plaintiff's injuries may be placed before the court so that it will be in a better position to make its own appraisal of the plaintiff's injuries. ...

If all of the above objections were decided in favour of the defendant, I would still have to reject this application because the proposed site of the examination, i.e., Halifax in the Province of Nova Scotia, is clearly very inconvenient to the first plaintiff. There are extensive hospital facilities in this province and many qualified medical practitioners. No evidence has been adduced or offered to show that the site proposed for the examination is the nearest one where the required facilities or the qualified professional personnel are available. In the absence of such evidence, there is no justification for issuance of an order requiring the first plaintiff to go to another province for the requested medical examination. ...

Application dismissed.

NOTES AND QUESTIONS

1. In *Schlagenhauf v. Holder*, 379 US 104 (1964), the court similarly held on fairness grounds that provisions in the US federal rules authorizing medical examinations did not violate a litigant's rights to privacy under the *Bill of Rights*, but stressed that the mental or physical condition of the party to be examined must be "in controversy" and the party asking for the examination show "good cause."

2. How should the court deal with an argument based on s. 7 of the Charter where the order for a medical examination (authorized by, for example, the Ontario *Courts of Justice Act*, ss. 105(2) and (3)) is sought against a party who did not put its own physical or mental condition in issue and is not making any claim in respect thereof—for example, where a husband brings a divorce proceeding, contests his wife's claim for custody on the ground that she is mentally unfit, and seeks a court-ordered medical examination of the wife with a view to establishing her mental instability?

3. When determining whether to order a medical examination of the plaintiff, the court may take into account the existence and number of previous examinations, the usefulness of the purported further examination, and the examination's potential intrusiveness as balanced against its purported benefits: *Soodhar v. Bagley*, [2003] AJ No. 766 (QB).

B. Inspection of Property

As noted above, a medical examination is not the only form of physical discovery (though it is the most common). The rules also provide for the inspection of property: for example, see Ontario rule 32, BC rule 30(4), and Nova Scotia rule 17.05.

Callis v. Stop 48 Ltd.
(1990), 50 CPC (2d) 304 (Ont. Ct. Gen. Div.)

POTTS J: The defendants appeal from the June 27, 1990 order of Judge Crossland that gave permission to the plaintiffs to inspect the go-cart involved in an accident. The appeal was heard on September 5, 1990, and at that time I dismissed the appeal, reserving costs to be determined by the trial judge. The following are my reasons. ...

The plaintiffs Tommy Callis and his mother Koula Callis were at a go-cart track at Kirkfield, Ontario, on June 4, 1988. The track was operated by the defendant Stop 48 Ltd., who leased the track from the defendants Giampiero and Daphne Baldini. Tommy paid an admission fee, rode a go-cart and was in an accident. Subsequently, the plaintiffs Tommy and his mother sued the defendants for damages. ...

Rule 32.01(1) of the Ontario *Rules of Civil Procedure* states:

> 32.01(1) The court may make an order for the inspection of real or personal property where it appears to be necessary for the proper determination of an issue in a proceeding.

The defendants submit that the words "necessary for the proper determination of an issue in a proceeding" dominate R. 32: *Nichols v. Toronto Transportation Commission* (1928), 62 OLR 124, 33 OWN 412, 34 CRC 252, [1928] 2 DLR 364 (CA), at 127 [OLR]. By this the defendants seem to suggest that an inspection of the go-cart is not necessary for the determination of an issue in the trial. The plaintiffs respond, however, that the inspection is necessary for a proper determination of one of the principal issues in the action, namely, liability for the accident: *PPG Industries Canada Ltd. v. Tioxide Canada Inc.* (1986), 12 CPC (2d) 158 (Ont. Master), at p. 162. The plaintiffs argue that an inspection should be granted where there is sufficient relevancy between the inspection of the property and a material issue in the action: *Bank of Nova Scotia v. Wu* (1986), 15 CPC (2d) 283 (Ont. Dist. Ct.), at p. 286. The plaintiffs argue R. 32 should be construed liberally to permit inspections: *Farhi v. Wright* (1987), 26 CPC (2d) 88 (Ont. HC), at p. 91.

The defendants submit that even though the plaintiffs' statement of claim states that the defendants did not properly inspect the brakes on the go-cart or maintain the go-cart in a proper condition, there is no issue with respect to these points. The defendants submit that the examinations for discovery disclose that the go-cart was inspected on the day of the accident and its brakes were working and that the plaintiff did not attempt to use the brakes until he had already lost control of the cart. The defendants submit that the plaintiffs' assertions in the statement of claim are mere bald assertions and are not sufficient grounds to order an inspection: *Lacosse v. Nygard* (1989), 16 WDCP 234 (Ont. HC) [reported 20 MVR (2d) 179]. The plaintiffs, however, respond that they do not agree that the go-cart was inspected on the day of the accident or that its brakes were working. Furthermore, the plaintiffs respond that they wish to look at the go-cart not only to inspect the brakes, but also to look at the overall condition of the go-cart and see how it operates generally. The plaintiffs also argue that *Lacosse* states that the plaintiff is entitled to full disclosure, including inspection, on an issue that is crucial to the action.

The defendants submit that to allow an inspection now, more than two years after the accident, would be extremely prejudicial to the defendants since the defendants have continued to use the go-cart at the track since the accident. Any conclusions drawn from an inspection now will not accurately reflect the condition of the go-cart at the time of the accident. The plaintiffs respond that this sort of prejudice is not a factor to be considered. The plaintiffs state that if there are concerns about the validity of the evidence, this is a factor to be considered at trial when the weight of the evidence is assessed.

I believe the inspection of the go-cart should be allowed to proceed. I agree with the plaintiffs that the inspection is relevant to and necessary for the determination of the issue of liability. *Nichols* and *Lacosse* do not assist the defendants, since these cases concerned the different question of whether the court should permit a re-enactment of the accident. In the case at bar, we are concerned only with the question of whether the plaintiffs should be allowed an inspection. I share some of the defendants' concern that any evidence about the state of repair of the go-cart at the time of the inspection may have little to do with the state of repair of the go-cart at the time of the accident, but this concern can be addressed at trial when the evidence is assigned its probative weight. However, the most important reason for allowing the plaintiffs to inspect the go-cart is that the trial court should be informed of the general operating characteristics of the go-cart. Does the cart have rear-wheel drive and front-wheel steering? Does it have a manual clutch and shift? How are the brakes designed? How are the brakes operated? These and other questions may be crucial to the proper determination of the issue of liability. These questions are independent of the question of the state of repair of the go-cart. A delayed inspection on these general features of the go-cart is not likely to affect the validity of this evidence, thus the defendants will not be prejudiced by the late inspection on these issues. ...

Appeal dismissed.

NOTES AND QUESTIONS

1. In addition to allowing for inspections, courts may also permit the inspecting party to take photographs to supplement the oral testimony given at trial. Finding that the right to take photographs need not be limited to situations in which the "physical make-up of the premises itself was in issue," Griffiths J dismissed an appeal from the decision of a master allowing for the inspecting party to take moving and still photographs of the manufacturing processes of the defendant: *Lagerquist v. Labatts Ltd.* (1978), 19 OR (2d) 586 (HCJ).

2. Do these decisions adequately balance the competing burdens placed on the parties? Do inspection orders unnecessarily raise the cost of discovery? Are there any privacy issues that ought to be considered?

IV. EXAMINATION FOR DISCOVERY

A. Purposes of Examination for Discovery

Garry D. Watson and Craig Perkins, eds., Holmested and Watson,
Ontario Civil Procedure
Rule 31 §7: Purposes of Examination for Discovery
(Toronto: Carswell, 1984) (looseleaf)

Of all the discovery devices provided by the rules, the most important and powerful is examination for discovery. A key element of examination for discovery is that it permits the proceeding to descend from the mere paper allegation of lawyers to sworn statements by the parties themselves.

The purposes of examination for discovery were conveniently summarized by Trainor J in *Ontario Bean Producers Marketing Bd. v. W.G. Thompson & Sons* (1981), 32 OR (2d) 69, affirmed 35 OR (2d) 711 (Div. Ct.):

 (a) to enable the examining party to know the case he has to meet;

 (b) to procure admissions to enable one to dispense with formal proof;

 (c) to procure admissions which may destroy an opponent's case;

 (d) to facilitate settlement, pre-trial procedure and trials;

 (e) to eliminate or narrow issues;

 (f) to avoid surprise at trial.

Montgomery J in *Malofy v. Andrew Merrilees Ltd.* (1982), 28 CPC 284 (Div. Ct.), after quoting the above, stated "I add to this, to enable payment into Court" (see now rule 49, Offer to Settle). Montgomery J went on to quote Brooke JA in *Perini Ltd. v. Parking Authority of Toronto* (1975), 6 OR (2d) 363 (CA): "These Rules form a scheme to provide procedures through which knowledge of all relevant facts is available to both sides so that each will know his opponent's case and be better able to evaluate his own and so to assist in the early resolution of litigation either by settlement or shorter trials."

Since the answers given by a person on his or her examination for discovery can be used at trial to impeach the witness should the witness give different testimony at trial (see rule 31.11(2)), examination for discovery enables the examining party to pin down the witness by his or her answers on discovery. Examination for discovery also provides an opportunity for counsel to assess the effectiveness and believability of both his or her own client and the opposing party, and to assess the effectiveness of opposing counsel. ...

While intuitively discovery appears to aid the settlement process, such empirical evidence as exists on the relationship between discovery and settlement does not suggest a straight cause and effect relationship. See Glaser, *Pretrial Discovery and the Adversary System* (1968), 91-100; Note, "Discovery: Boon or Burden?" 36 Minn. L Rev. 364 (1952).

Glaser, reporting on a major empirical study of discovery in the United States, found that while 96 per cent of all lawyers surveyed in the study felt that discovery promoted settlement, empirical support for such a conclusion was lacking. Cases employing discovery were more likely to reach trial. Discovery did not produce any large statistical increment beyond what lawyers had originally expected would be the settlement prospect for their cases, nor were the settlement rates higher than for cases where no discovery was employed. Not only did the use of discovery correlate inversely with settlement, but so did the intensity of discovery—the greater the time spent in discovery the more likely it was that the case would reach trial. Glaser observed that "the common belief that discovery increases settlement may be due to the fact that a large majority of cases with discovery settle, but this is true simply because most cases settle." It is also interesting to note that in England, where broad-ranging discovery, and particularly examination for discovery, does not exist, a lower percentage of cases proceed to trial than in Canada. (The English figures are in the 2-3 per cent range, whereas the Canadian figures are in the 3-5 per cent range.) It may be that in Canada settlement is often postponed until after discovery, rather than being caused by discovery. If so, presumably discovery does make settlement better informed.

For further discussion on the purposes of discovery, see W.A. Stevenson and J.E. Côté, *Civil Procedure Encyclopedia*, chapter 28, at 28-3.

B. Use of Examination for Discovery at Trial

The dynamics of examination for discovery will be easier to understand if we first recall the uses that can be made of the examination at trial. The use that counsel can make of an examination for discovery at trial conditions what they try to achieve in conducting the examination.

There are two basic ways in which an examination for discovery may be used at trial. First, a party may *read into evidence* any part of the examination for discovery of an adverse party (if otherwise admissible)—for example, see Ontario rule 31.11(1), Alberta rules 200.1(1) and 214, BC rules 40(27)-(29), and Nova Scotia rules 18.20 and 18.21 (for a discussion of the Nova Scotia rule, see *Burton v. Howlett* (2001), 191 NSR (2d) 147 (CA)). Second, the evidence given on an examination may be used for the *purpose of impeaching* the deponent in the same manner as any previous inconsistent statement. For example, see Ontario rule 31.11(2) and Nova Scotia rule 18.20). To ensure fairness, where only part of the examination is used in evidence, the trial judge may direct the introduction of any other part that qualifies the part used. See, for example, *Smith v. British Columbia Television Broadcasting Ltd. (BCCA)* (1988), 32 BCLR (2d) 18 (CA). See also, for example, Alberta rule 214(4). While these uses of examination for discovery are in rules of practice, they in fact flow from well-established rules of the law of evidence. Answers given on an examination for discovery are hearsay (because they are not the evidence of a witness present and testifying at trial and are being tendered for the truth of their content). However, there is a basic exception to the hearsay rule for "admissions made by an opposing party." This is the basis for the "reading in" use of discovery answers. The law of evidence also permits any witness who has given evidence at trial to be impeached by use of a prior inconsistent statement. This can come from any source. For example, a conversation at a cocktail party, a statement made in an affidavit, or a statement made in prior correspondence. It is this principle that permits the "impeachment use" of discovery answers. For an analysis of these principles, see, for example, *Edmonton (City) v. Lovat Tunnel Equipment Inc.* (2000), 260 AR 245 (QB). See also *Mikisew Cree First Nation v. Canada* (2002), 2 Alta. LR (4th) 1 (CA), supplementary memorandum of judgment (2002), 2 Alta. LR (4th) 24.

The examination of a non-party "witness," where available, may not be read into evidence as an admission, but may be used to impeach the non-party should he or she testify. For example, see Ontario rules 31.11(1) and (2) and 31.10(5).

The two uses of examination for discovery described above condition the conduct of the examination in the following ways. First, counsel will be looking for answers that can be *used as admissions* and hence read in at trial. A simple example may illustrate the importance of admissions. Assume a motor vehicle accident in which the plaintiff alleges that the defendant was negligent in driving at an excessive speed. The plaintiff may have no direct evidence of the speed at which the defendant was travelling. However, on discovery, the plaintiff can require the defendant to state the speed the car was travelling. If the defendant admits to driving too fast, that answer can be used in evidence by the plaintiff (in a way we will explore in greater detail below) to establish that crucial fact. Second, and this may often be difficult to distinguish from the first objective, counsel will be seeking to exhaust the recollection of the witness and tie the witness down to a story so that, if the witness changes his or her story at trial, the discovery transcript can be used to *impeach the witness.* Of course, at discovery, counsel will also be pursuing objectives that are not so directly related to "trial usage"—for example, trying to understand the opponent's case and evidence to back it up and searching for evidence that can be used to support counsel's own case.

Discovery is a pre-trial process; it is not available to a party following trial, but pending appeal. For further discussion see: *Atchison v. Manufacturers Life Insurance Co.* (2003), 330 AR 123 (CA).

C. Who May Be Examined for Discovery

1. *Parties Generally*

On this subject, Ontario rule 31.03 is typical in providing that a party may examine for discovery any other party "adverse in interest." See also Alberta rules 200 and 200.1, BC rule 27(1), and Nova Scotia rule 18.03. The various provincial rules generally also make special provisions for corporations (which we will discuss in some detail below) and for other types of parties, such as partnerships, persons under disability, or assignees. The following case explores the meaning of the central phrase "parties adverse in interest."

Aviaco International Leasing Inc. v. Boeing Canada Inc.
(2000), 2 CPC (5th) 48 (Ont. SCJ)

NORDHEIMER J: [1] The plaintiffs move for directions regarding the examinations for discovery that are to take place in this action . ...

[2] Central to [this determination] is the issue of whether the defendants are adverse in interest to each other such that the defendants should have the right to examine their co-defendants for discovery ... .

[3] ... The action involves a claim by the plaintiffs arising out of an alleged payment of bribes by some of the defendants to other of the defendants through yet other of the defendants regarding the purchase of five Dash-8 commuter aircraft. The plaintiffs allege that this scheme of payments led to the termination of contracts relating to these aircraft to which they were parties which in turn led to the destruction of their businesses. They claim, as a consequence, damages in excess of $400,000,000 and punitive damages of $50,000,000. The causes of action alleged include conspiracy, inducing breach of contract, intentional interference with economic relations, fraud and deceit.

[4] The defendants, other than Bethel, Williams, Murray and Famona, have defended the plaintiffs' claims. There are not currently, however, any crossclaims among the defendants. Rather, the defendants have each essentially asserted that the plaintiffs' allegations are not substantiated by the facts in that any monies that were paid among certain of the defendants were legitimate payments and not bribes in any sense and that the ultimate transaction which the plaintiffs attempt to impugn was, in fact, entirely proper.

The Examinations for Discovery

[5] The plaintiffs contend that the defendants cannot in such circumstances establish a sufficient adversity in interest among themselves in order to be entitled to examine each other for discovery purposes. Rule 31.03(1) of the *Rules of Civil Procedure* states:

> A party to an action may examine for discovery any other party adverse in interest, once, and may examine that party more than once only with leave of the court, but a party may examine more than one person as permitted by subrules (3) to (8).

[6] A classic statement of the meaning of the expression "adverse in interest" is contained in *Menzies v. McLeod* (1915), 34 OLR 572 in which Chancellor Boyd said, at p. 575:

> An actual issue in tangible form spread upon the record is not essential, so long as there is manifest adverse interest in one defendant as against another defendant. "Adverse interest" is a flexible term, meaning pecuniary interest, or any other substantial interest in the subject-matter of litigation.

[7] It is apparent from the above quotation that the issue of adversity in interest is not to be determined from the state of the pleadings alone but upon the state of the record as a whole. Inherent in that observation, in my view, is that an adversity of interest may arise at any point in the proceeding as the record and evidence develop. Of particular

importance in this regard, is the practical reality that any of the witnesses to be examined for discovery may well give evidence that is inconsistent with their pleading. Therefore, while the defendants might not appear to be adverse in interest on the face of their pleadings, it does not follow that an adversity of interest will not become apparent as the discoveries take place. Further, in a case such as this one which is based primarily on an alleged conspiracy among the defendants, and on the existence and characterization of payments that may have flowed among some or all of the defendants, it seems to me there is every possibility that some element of adversity of interest may well appear among the defendants as the discovery process proceeds.

[8] In any event, there are already harbingers to the possibility of the defendants becoming adverse in interest on the face of the pleadings as they currently exist. By way of one example only, and there are others, paragraph 24 of the fresh statement of claim states, in part:

> Moreover, Rapier (and Sovereign), to the knowledge of Boeing and Boeing U.S., never performed any meaningful sales or promotional activity for Boeing aside from acting as a funnel through which the Boeing Payments could be channelled to the Bahamian Officials.

[9] If the plaintiff, in examining the defendant Rapier for discovery, were to obtain evidence in support of this allegation (which are denied by the Boeing defendants in their statement of defence), then it would seem self-evident that Rapier and the Boeing defendants would then become adverse in interest. In such an eventuality, Boeing's counsel ought to have the right, at that point, to examine the defendant Rapier for discovery in relation to such evidence. In *Frobisher Ltd. v. Canadian Pipelines & Petroleums Ltd.* (1957), 10 DLR (2d) 338 (Sask. CA); aff'd. [1960] SCR 126, McNiven JA said at p. 403:

> However, the weight of authority supports the right of counsel for a defendant to cross-examine a witness called by a codefendant, particularly where the witness gives evidence adverse to the party desiring to cross-examine.

I consider this observation to be equally applicable in the context of an examination for discovery.

[The court went on to find a similar example in relation to the Boeing defendants.]

· · ·

[12] Central to the plaintiffs' concern about the co-defendants being permitted to examine among themselves is that the examinations will be conducted as so-called "sweetheart" examinations and will be used to undermine any admissions which the plaintiffs might obtain from the defendants. I consider the plaintiffs' concern in this regard to be an entirely legitimate one. However, there is a protection against the use of such "sweetheart" examinations built into the *Rules of Civil Procedure*. Rule 31.11(1) states:

> At the trial of an action, a party may read into evidence as part of the party's own case against an adverse party any part of the evidence given on the examination for discovery of,
>
> > (a) the adverse party; or

(b) a person examined for discovery on behalf or in place of, or in addition to the adverse party, unless the trial judge orders otherwise,

if the evidence is otherwise admissible, whether the party or person has already given evidence or not." ...

[13] It seems to me that in order for the evidence from an examination for discovery to be admissible, it has to have been properly obtained under the *Rules of Civil Procedure* and in accordance with the normal rules of evidence. If no adversity in interest in fact appears among the defendants, or any subset of them, any examination for discovery undertaken by any defendant of a co-defendant may well be ruled by the trial judge not to have been proper and the evidence obtained thereby would, consequently, be inadmissible. On the same analysis, a trial judge could refuse to allow any such examination to be used to qualify or explain earlier answers under rule 31.11(3). I will make it clear now, and will repeat it at the conclusion of these reasons, that I do consider it appropriate, nor do I intend, for anything that I decide on these motions to be in any way binding on the trial judge in terms of his or her right to decide what adversity of interest, if any, in fact exists among the defendants. In my view, the trial judge ought to have the unfettered discretion to decide whether there is any adversity of interest between any of the defendants particularly since the trial judge will have a much fuller and more complete record on which to make that determination than is currently before me.

[14] As a further measure of protection, and while this is not something that it appears I could order, I will also mention that the defendants have offered to permit counsel for the plaintiffs to ask further questions of the representatives being examined for discovery after any of the co-defendants have asked questions. In a sense, this gives counsel for the plaintiffs a right of re-examination to rehabilitate any earlier evidence that might have been impacted by the examination undertaken by any co-defendant.

[15] Further, if I were to now rule that there is no adversity of interest between the defendants, and therefore that they are not entitled to any examination for discovery among themselves, one of two possibilities may result. First, after the examinations for discovery if evidence is given which clearly gives rise to an adversity of interest among the defendants, or any of them, a motion may be brought for permission to then have examinations among the defendants, and, if that motion were granted, there would be additional delay and expense incurred by everyone in trying to have all of these many parties and their counsel come together again for further examinations. Alternatively, the matter might not arise until the trial. If, at that time, the trial judge was of the view that there was an adversity of interest among the defendants, either the defendants would then be put into the position of having to cross-examine other defendants without the benefit of the disclosures which the discovery process is supposed to achieve, or an adjournment of the trial might be necessary to allow the discoveries to take place. The advent of either of those eventualities is clearly to be avoided—see a similar observation made by Sheppard J in *800715 Ontario Inc. v. Mitchell*, [1994] OJ No. 2127 (Gen. Div.) at para. 5.

[16] I am satisfied that there is currently both a measure of adversity of interest shown on the pleadings, and the very real possibility that a more apparent adversity of interest may appear during the course of the discoveries, that I would be in error to make

what is essentially a declaration at this stage that the defendants are not adverse in interest. If no real adversity in interest appears during the examinations for discovery and the defendants choose to conduct examinations among themselves, then they do so at their peril. That seems to me, however, in these circumstances to be a matter that is best left to counsel to decide, at least in the first instance.

NOTES AND QUESTIONS

1. *Federal Crown.* For a discussion of the circumstances in which discovery is available against the federal Crown, see *Logan v. Harper*, [2003] OJ No. 4098 (Master). For a discussion of documents purportedly subject to Cabinet confidentiality, see *Babcock v. Canada (Attorney General)*, [2002] 3 SCR 3.

2. *Class actions.* In class actions (see further chapter 11), discovery is typically available against the class representatives only. According to the Supreme Court of Canada:

> One of the benefits of a class action is that discovery of the class representatives will usually suffice and make unnecessary discovery of each individual class member. Cases where individual discovery is required of all class members are the exception rather than the rule. Indeed, the necessity of individual discovery may be a factor weighing against allowing the action to proceed in representative form ... examination of other class members should be available only by order of the court, upon the defendants showing reasonable necessity.

(*Western Canadian Shopping Centres Inc. v. Dutton*, [2001] 2 SCR 534, at paras. 59-60.) See further *Gerber v. Johnston* (2002), 8 BCLR (4th) 46 (CA); review application dismissed, [2003] BCJ No. 810 (CA).

3. *Who may attend?* As Burrows J stated in *Austec Electronic Systems Ltd. v. Mark IV Industries Ltd.* (2001), 284 AR 386, at para. 13 (QB), the "normal rule" regarding who can attend at discovery is that, in addition to the court reporter, "only the parties, counsel and persons present by consent can attend at examinations for discovery." Deviation from this rule, however, remains in the court's discretion. See, for example, *Wilson v. Servier Canada Inc.*, [2001] OJ No. 4636 (SCJ); leave to appeal to Ont. Div. Ct. dismissed, [2002] OJ No. 60. The principle that only parties and their counsel may attend is consistent with the general principle that, "[i]n return for this freedom to investigate [on discovery], an implied obligation of confidentiality has emerged in the case law" at the discovery stage: *Lac d'Amiante du Québec Ltée v. 2858-0702 Québec Inc.*, [2001] 2 SCR 743, at para. 60 (LeBel J).

4. *Discovery by video conference.* Being present in the same room as a discovery witness typically facilitates the assessment of that witness's credibility and effectiveness as a witness. However, various provincial rules contemplate potential examinations by video conference. See, for example, Ontario rule 34.19 and Nova Scotia rules 18.15 and 82.06. The court in *De Carvalho v. Watson* (2000), 83 Alta. LR (3d) 354, at paras. 15-16 (QB)—involving a request to continue the examination for discovery of a witness, commenced in person, by video conference—highlighted some of the factors to be considered when determining the availability of examination by video conference:

> Another factor ... is ... that technology continues to evolve apace. Video conferencing is now accepted as being a reliable and improving method of communication between persons. It has

even improved to the point that in given circumstances, arrangements can be made so that a person being examined or cross-examined by video conference can even be presented with documents which can be dealt with appropriately. It would require one to have "one's head in the sand," as it were, to not recognize that there are circumstances where the use of such technology can properly be made use of.

It is not the suggestion of this Court that because video conferencing is an available form of technology suitable for examination and cross-examination of witnesses or potential witnesses that such use of technology should be used generally as a substitute for personal appearances on either trials, examinations on affidavits or examinations for discovery. But it seems to me that where there are circumstances such as the present where an individual is a long way away from the jurisdiction in which the examination would normally take place, where the costs for the personal attendance of that individual would be extremely substantial, where the examination can be carried out with a minimum of difficulty by the use of such video conferencing technology, and where there has already been a[n] opportunity for counsel to engage in personal cross-examination of an extensive nature of the particular witness or potential witness, with the witness having been present for that examination or cross-examination, that this is an appropriate type of case for a Court to look positively upon a request made on behalf of such witness that the witness be allowed in a civil action such as this to provide continued evidence on examination for discovery by way of video conference. This would be inappropriate only where there is some other circumstance which would cause a meaningful risk of causing prejudice to the party seeking to require the witness to appear in person.

2. Examining a Corporation

Because a corporation is not a natural person, and hence cannot be orally examined for discovery, the rules must regulate who may be examined on behalf of the corporation. As discussed further below, this is an area where the rules of various Canadian jurisdictions differ. Ontario rules 31.03(2) and (3) provide that the examining party may "examine any officer, director or employee on behalf of the corporation, but the court on motion of the corporation before the examination may order the examining party to examine another officer, director or employee"; "the examining party may examine more than one officer, director or employee only with the consent of the parties or the leave of the court"; and, where such person has been examined, no other such person may be examined without leave of the court. In British Columbia, see rules 27(4)-(6). In Nova Scotia, see rule 18.01. In Alberta, the corporation chooses its representative (see Alberta rule 200.1). Further, the Alberta rules provide that "if the other adverse party is a corporation," the examining party may examine "one or more officers of the corporation" (Alberta rule 200(1)(b)). For amendments that were proposed as at the date for publication of this edition, see Proposed Alberta Rules of Court rule 5.17(1)(b)(i), online at: http://www.law.ualberta.ca/alri/docs/1.%20Appendix%20H%20-%20Proposed%20Rules%20of%20Court.pdf.) The following case examines how the Ontario rule has been interpreted.

Clarkson Mews Properties Inc. v. Angel Creek Estates Ltd.
(1989), 37 CPC (2d) 104 (Ont. HC)

MASTER DONKIN: The plaintiff brings a motion for two items of relief, one of which has been dealt with. The remaining part of the motion is to substitute Mr. Hrycyna, an officer of the plaintiff, to be examined for discovery in place of Mr. Forgione.

The plaintiff's action is to recover a deposit made in connection with a proposed purchase of real estate. The purchase agreement was entered into by Forgione Investments & Developments Inc., and that company paid a deposit of $200,000 to the defendant Gitalis, who is the real estate agent. The agreement provided that the purchaser had the right to assign to a limited company or individuals. The agreement was in fact assigned to the plaintiff on June 29, 1988. The transaction was to close on July 5, 1988. It failed to close and the contest in the action appears to involve the incidents from about June 30, 1988 to July 5 or 6, 1988. During that time it is alleged that there were requisitions on title and there is a contest as to whether these were proper. A repudiation of the agreement in that period is alleged and contested, and there is a contest as to whether the vendor actually had title in such a way that it could transfer the property on the scheduled date for closing.

Mr. Hrycyna has filed an affidavit in which he says that the plaintiff is a corporation that was set up in order to purchase this property; and when Mr. Forgione had signed the agreement of purchase and sale, he approached Mr. Hrycyna and several other people with respect to participating with him in the purchase. At that point, Mr. Hrycyna swears that he took over as the principal person dealing with this matter and that Mr. Forgione's involvement, other than his monetary involvement, ceased. Mr. Hrycyna looked after the arrangements to set up the corporation and for the purchase. Although he is not able to provide first-hand information on all the issues, he kept himself informed throughout the transaction, and he was the person who provided instructions to the plaintiff's solicitors.

Parts of the affidavit are set out below in full:

> 5. Gus Forgione does not have sufficient knowledge to deal with the examination properly. In fact, his attendance may be embarrassing to the plaintiff.

> 12. Mr. Forgione was not involved during this time and has absolutely no knowledge of any of the issues in the action. His only involvement was in the negotiation of the agreement of purchase and sale, which is not an issue in this action.

> 13. I have discussed with Mr. Forgione the possibility of his being examined for discovery. Based on my discussions with him, I verily believe [that] he will not properly prepare himself for the examination for discovery and that he will not inform himself of all of these issues in the lawsuit. I verily believe that he, in fact, may damage the plaintiff's case because of his lack of knowledge and because of his refusal to participate fully in this lawsuit.

In *Protter Management Ltd. v. Ont. Housing Corp.* (1975), 8 OR (2d) 445, at 447 (Ont. HC), Pennell J states that:

> I am of opinion that applications must be dealt with upon the circumstances in particular cases rather than by a "fixed standard of measurement."

In most of the cases to which counsel have referred me where the court permitted substitution of a different officer, there was some form of conflict of interest between the officer selected and the corporation, or at least a divergence of interest. In *Protter Management v. Ont. Housing Corp.*, *supra*, the corporation had suspended the officer who was selected because certain charges had been laid against him in connection with his employment. In *Kowk v. Kitchener Waterloo Record Ltd.* (1985), 2 CPC (2d) 250 (Ont. Dist. Ct.), there was not only the factor that the person sought to be examined was not a particularly senior employee but also he had been disciplined by the defendant corporation for writing a letter about the plaintiff. In *Exhibition Assn. of Saint John (City & County) v. Cdn. Imperial Bank of Commerce* (1987), 21 CPC (2d) 88, 82 NBR (2d) 337, 208 APR 337, decided by Jones J of the New Brunswick Court of Queen's Bench, the Court accepts that the officer selected to be examined was in a position of conflict of interest with the corporation on whose behalf it was sought to examine them.

There are other cases in which the ground for substitution has been that the person selected is not a responsible officer and does not have knowledge of the matter. That is not the case in this matter. It is true that Forgione apparently does not have sufficient knowledge. It is not alleged that he cannot get that knowledge. It is not alleged that he is not an officer or responsible person. He does have some connection with the transaction, inasmuch as he entered into the original agreement of purchase and sale on behalf of his own company and paid the deposit. The real problem as set out in the affidavit is that the deponent believes that Forgione will not properly prepare himself for examination for discovery and will not inform himself of all the issues in the lawsuit.

It is trite law that initially the examining party can select the officer or person whom the plaintiff wishes to examine on behalf of the defendant. It seems to me that it does not lie in the mouth of the person selected who is a responsible person to simply say that he refuses to be involved. If that were permitted, examining parties would be frustrated extremely easily. It is perhaps worth noting that in *Cineplex Odeon Corp. v. Toronto Star Newspapers Ltd.* (1986), 11 CPC (2d) 291 (Ont. Master), the officer of the defendant being examined refused to answer questions on the basis that they could better be answered by one of the individual defendants, and the corporation undertook to be bound by his answers to those questions. Master Peppiatt decided that that was not a proper course and that the officer who was being examined was bound to obtain the answers from the defendant who knew the answers and to give those answers on discovery on behalf of the corporation. In effect, that case was similar because the officer selected was refusing to obtain the information necessary to allow him to answer properly.

In my view, this part of the motion should be dismissed.

The better part of the argument on this motion was directed to this issue, and, in my view, costs should be to the defendant Angel Creek in the cause. If counsel wish to submit argument on a different disposition of costs, they may request an appointment.

Motion dismissed.

NOTES AND QUESTIONS

1. *Who is an "officer, director, or employee"?* The courts have generally taken a flexible and functional approach to interpreting these terms. For example, in *Bell v. Klein (No. 3)*, [1955] 1 DLR 37 (BCCA), in an action in which a corporation was being sued for fraud, it was held that the company's auditors (an independent firm of accountants) were "officers" and could be examined by the plaintiff:

> As one of the chief functions of auditors is to present to shareholders a true account of a company's financial position, I see no reason why auditors should not be examined on discovery in an action which rightly or wrongly challenges the good faith of directors in the management of company affairs. ... The test to which these decisions point seems to be whether the person sought to be examined can be regarded as an officer or servant in any permissible sense if he is the one person connected with the company best informed of matters which may define or narrow the issues between the parties at the trial.

In *Atherton v. Boycott* (1989), 36 CPC (2d) 250 (Ont. HC), it was held that for the purpose of determining whether an individual is an employee, it is not necessary to adhere strictly to the common law principles establishing an employer/employee relationship. The action was one for personal injuries involving an automobile collision in which the plaintiff sued B, a police sergeant, and the owner of the police vehicle, the city of Windsor. The action against B had already been dismissed as being statute-barred. The plaintiff was permitted to examine B as an employee of the defendant city, notwithstanding that B was employed by the Board of Commissioners of Police and not by the city, because he fell within the extended meaning of "employee" for the purpose of discovery. See further *Standen's Ltd. v. Pinkerton's of Canada Ltd.* (2001), 203 DLR (4th) 744 (Alta. QB) and *Alberta-Pacific Forest Industries Inc. v. Ingersoll-Rand Canada Inc.* (2002), 6 Alta. LR (4th) 186.

By contrast, in *Joseph Silaschi General Contractor v. City of Kitchener* (1986), 8 CPC (2d) 199 (Ont. HC), in a building dispute between the contractor and the owner (the city), the court refused to permit the examination of the owner's architect as an "officer or employee" of the city. It was common ground that the architect was a member of an architectural firm, which was a separate entity, and that neither he nor his firm had any connection with the city other than as its representative on the job. (There was no evidence that the architect acted as the city's agent.) While conceding that "officer or employee" could not be defined within rigid limits, but may be amplified or circumscribed by the circumstances of each individual case, the court held that the circumstances of this case did not justify amplification of the word "employee" to embrace a totally different entity, an independent contractor. The court noted that if information was withheld or was unavailable, recourse might be had to Ontario rule 31.10, which provides for the discovery of non-parties (see further below).

Which is the better approach to this problem: *Bell* and *Atherton* or the *City of Kitchener*? Given the existence of provisions for the examination of non-parties, at least in some jurisdictions—for example, see Ontario rule 31.10—does it matter which approach the court takes? How do proportionality rules impact these questions?

2. *Former officers and employees.* As we have seen, in Ontario, a party examining a corporation is entitled to only one examination of any "officer, director or employee," unless the

court orders otherwise, and no provision is made for the examination of *former* officers or employees. Compare Alberta rule 200(1).

Among the other provinces there are varying approaches to this question. In British Columbia (rule 27(4)), any person "who is or has been a director, officer, employee, agent or external auditor of a party" may be examined for discovery; however, once such a person has been examined, no other person may be examined except with leave of the court. In Manitoba (rule 31.03(3)) (Saskatchewan rule 223 is similar), any person who is or has been an officer, director, or employee of a corporation may be examined, but only one such person may be examined. In Alberta, rule 200(1) provides that "one or more other persons who are or were employed by the other party" may be examined. For a recent interpretation of this rule, see, for example, *Murphy Oil Co. v. Predator Corp.*, [2002] AJ No. 888 (QB). In Nova Scotia (rule 18.03), discovery is not limited to the parties and "any person" may be examined for discovery.

How do these provisions compare? Which is the better approach?

Typically, those jurisdictions that permit employees or former employees or officers to be examined for discovery place limits on the use of such examinations against the employer—that is, they may not be used against the employer at all, or only with leave of the court. See, for example, Alberta rule 214(1).

3. In Ontario, while there is no general right to examine former officers or employees, the courts have on occasion ordered the examination of such persons upon a showing that the officer or employee left the corporation in order to frustrate the opposite party's discovery (*Hamilton Harbour Commissioners v. J.D. Porter Co. Ltd.* (1978), 19 OR (2d) 66 (HC)), or where all the officers and directors of a corporation had resigned and there was reason to doubt that the resignations were *bona fide*: *Butler v. Dimitrieff* (1988), 66 OR (2d) 707 (Master). Where these unusual circumstances do not exist, the court will not be as inclined to order discovery of the former officer or employee. See, for example, *Sudbury Downs, a Division of MacRanald Enterprises Inc. v. Ontario Harness Horse Assn.*, [2002] OJ No. 5505 (SCJ), in which the court distinguished *Hamilton* and *Butler* on their facts, thereby refusing to allow discovery of a former officer.

3. Examination of Non-Parties

A basic policy choice facing rule makers is whether to make examination for discovery available against persons other than the parties. In the United States, discovery is typically not limited to the parties—any person may be examined for discovery (deposed). In Canada, the traditional position has been to restrict the availability of discovery to the parties (though, as we have seen, some provinces have extended this right to include former officers or employees of a party). With the nationwide reform movement of the past few decades, this situation has changed. For example, Newfoundland adopted the US model and permits the examination, without leave, of "any person." Other provinces have adopted more limited departures from the traditional position. British Columbia and Nova Scotia permit the examination of non-parties with leave of the court, subject to certain conditions. Ontario has adopted a similar approach: see Ontario rule 31.10, which permits the court to grant leave for the examination of a non-party, but subject to a stringent test. The Alberta rules did not generally provide for discovery of non-parties, except for limited exceptions regard-

ing employees or former employees of a party (see, for example, Alberta rule 200(1) discussed above), and some documentary production (see, for example, Alberta rule 209, also
discussed above). However, examination of certain kinds of non-parties will be made available if reforms currently proposed at the time of publication of this edition are implemented. (See Proposed Alberta Rules of Court 5.18 online at: http://www.law.ualberta.ca/alri/
docs/1.%20Appendix%20H%20-%20Proposed%20Rules%20of%20Court.pdf.)

What arguments can be made in favour of broadening discovery to non-parties? Are
there factors to suggest that the traditional restriction to parties is, on balance, preferable?
The following case illustrates the courts' interpretation of Ontario's approach to the issue
(see Ontario rule 31.10).

Carleton Condominium Corporation No. 25 v. Shenkman Corporation Ltd.
(1986), 9 CPC (2d) 233 (Ont. HC)

MASTER DONKIN: This is a motion by a defendant, Dineen Construction Limited, for
leave pursuant to R. 31.10 to examine a person who was not a party to this action.

The action involves a claim by the plaintiff, Condominium Corporation, for damages
with respect to the construction of a building and for damages for certain repair work
undertaken on that building. J.L. Richards & Associates Limited was the consulting engineer with respect to certain aspects of the original construction and was retained to
supervise certain repair work after the problems originally arose. The witness whom the
moving party seeks to examine is one John Hall McCalla who was at all material times
an employee of J.L. Richards & Associates Limited and charged with the responsibility
for that firm's involvement in the construction and the repairs. At some period following
the relevant time he ceased to be an employee. It is apparent that he would have information relevant to material issues in the action and no counsel has disputed this fact.

The third party, J.L. Richards & Associates Limited, opposes the motion on the basis
that the moving party has not satisfied the Court that the moving party has been unable
to obtain the information from other persons whom the moving party is entitled to examine for discovery. It is apparent that many questions have been asked of the representative
of J.L. Richards & Associates Limited on discovery to which he could not give an immediate answer, but undertakings were given and according to the affidavit of Kevin Murin
filed in opposition to the motion those undertakings are in the process of being fulfilled.
Many of the undertakings were given in response to requests to make inquiry of Mr.
McCalla, and the information which will be provided in response to the undertakings
will include the knowledge, information and belief of Mr. McCalla. That being the case I
am not satisfied that the moving party has been unable to obtain the information from
the person whom it is entitled to examine for discovery on behalf of J.L. Richards & Associates Limited. It is uncontested that Mr. McCalla's position is that he would prefer not
to discuss the matter with the solicitors for the other parties.

The question to be decided in this motion is whether the moving party is in fact
required to satisfy the Court that the information cannot be obtained from the person
whom the moving party is entitled to examine. Counsel for the moving party points out
that in this complex action it will be time-consuming to get the answers from a

representative of J.L. Richards & Associates Limited by way of questions, undertakings, the response to those undertakings, and possibly further questions arising from the response. It would be in his view far more practical and expeditious to get those answers directly from Mr. McCalla. He cites *Weiszman v. 491 Lawrence Ave. West Ltd.* (1985), 5 CPC (2d) 160 (Ont. HC) as authority for the proposition that the Court should grant leave in such circumstances. In the course of his reasons in that case his Lordship stated [at 163]:

> Unquestionably, it is a balance of convenience. Courts do not wish to unnecessarily or unreasonably ask non-parties to an action to attend for examination for discovery. They are required to attend at trial. But, in my view, when there are material facts suggested by the party seeking the examination for discovery, which are not sufficiently covered in the actual statements provided, then that party ought to have not merely some of the information but all of the information. I asked and was advised that the reasons that the non-parties refused to be interviewed by the defendant was that they had simply said we have given our statement and have nothing more to add. Laymen do not appreciate the niceties of the judicial system. They think their statements are sufficient but that is not necessarily the case. With respect to the lawyer for the plaintiff who questioned the witnesses, and there is no suggestion that he was hiding any information, he may not have asked all the questions that the defendants would like to ask.
>
> As counsel for the defendants put it, are the statements sufficient? He does not really know. He would like to have the same opportunity as the plaintiff has had to find out whether or not these witnesses have any more relevant information. They may not but at least then he would have conducted a complete investigation of the matter prior to going to trial or to negotiating the possibility of settlement.

He further stated:

> I should also add that r. 1.04(1) states:
>
> > 1.04(1) These rules shall be liberally construed to secure the just, most expeditious and least expensive determination of every civil proceeding on its merits.

I think that is very relevant to the interpretation of these rules. As a matter of fairness both parties should have access to the same witnesses in order to promote the most expeditious and least expensive determination of every civil proceeding on its merits. That goes not merely to the determination of issues at trial but to the possibility of resolving the matter before trial by way of settlement. Both parties should have all the information so that either party does not have to go to trial lacking information.

I have examined the documents filed in that case, including the affidavits and the factums filed by both parties before Potts J, and also those filed before Sirois J, who refused leave to appeal on September 12, 1985. That material includes the affidavit of Roger Shoreman who sets out what the issues are in the action and who states at para. 6 that

> neither the plaintiff nor the defendant had any knowledge of these two issues. The only information that we have is from the witness' statements on behalf of Mr. Frankin and Mr. Bower.

It was the submission of the moving party in that case that the statements spoken of were not sufficient to provide all the relevant information. From the affidavit material and from the factums it is apparent that the question of whether the information might be obtained from the person whom the moving party was entitled to examine was not addressed and it appears to have been assumed that the information could only be obtained directly from the two witnesses. That case therefore can be distinguished from the present case.

In addition there is the decision in *Rothwell v. Raes* (1986), 13 OAC 60 (Ont. HC). In that case the facts were that the moving party had not shown that it was unable to get the required information directly from the non-party because there was no evidence of requests to that non-party to remedy certain insufficiencies in information he had already given. In the course of his judgment Eberle J states [at 61]:

> We are primarily concerned with the provisions of subclause (a) above and with the question of whether or not the comma following the word "discovery," together with the word "or" which follows, have a disjunctive or a conjunctive effect. Must the applicant show both that he has been unable to obtain the information from parties to the action and as well from the person sought to be examined; or is it sufficient to show an inability to obtain the information either from parties to the action or alternatively from the person sought to be examined?

The learned local judge held as follows:

> I am not satisfied on the material before me that the moving party has been unable to obtain the information he seeks from the witness as required by Section (sic) 31.10(1)(a).

> In so saying, he impliedly held that both parts of the clause in question must be satisfied. I am in entire agreement.

[A]nd further:

> It is evident that the framers of the Rule, while granting a new remedy for the examination for discovery of a non-party, felt it proper to establish a number of conditions which must be satisfied before the new remedy may be resorted to. Otherwise the remedy could easily be subject to abuse. Accordingly, it is consistent with the overall thrust of the Rule to read the two parts of sub-clause (a) as cumulative and not alternative.

> In addition, it appears to me that to read sub-clause (a) disjunctively would have the effect of reading out of it one or other of the parts thereof. For example, if on examination for discovery a party were unable to give certain information, the examiner would be able to apply for discovery of the non-party even though the non-party might willingly give the information. That would not be the most expeditious and least expensive way to proceed: see rule 1.04(1). It is likely that in the vast majority of cases the application of rule 31.10 would arise in the manner outlined, i.e., from a failure to get information requested on an examination for discovery of an existing party.

> I am satisfied that it is the intent of the Rule as framed that "or" be treated conjunctively and further, that the opposite view would lead to absurd results.

Therefore, since I am not satisfied that the moving party cannot get the information from the representative of J.L. Richards & Associates Limited by way of questions, undertakings and replies to undertakings, the motion is dismissed.

The interpretation of r. 31.10 is probably not yet settled, and costs should be to J.L. Richards & Associates Limited in the cause as between it and Dineen Construction Limited.

Motion dismissed.

NOTES AND QUESTIONS

1. From a rules perspective, which is the better approach—that taken by the court in *Weiszman* or that taken in *Carleton Condominium*? From a policy perspective, which makes most sense?

2. In general, the Ontario courts have been strict in the interpretation of the requirements of rule 31.10 for the granting of leave, and the reported incidents of courts granting leave have been relatively few. Indeed, there are relatively few reported cases on *requests* for leave to examine non-parties. How might this be explained?

3. In another motion in the Ballard estate litigation (see the *Stavro* case, above), Ground J considered whether to grant leave to examine a non-party for discovery: *Ontario (Attorney General) v. Stavro* (1995), 44 CPC (3d) 98 (Gen. Div.). He decided as follows:

This is a motion brought by the defendants in the above action for an order pursuant to subrule 31.10(1) of the [Ontario] *Rules of Civil Procedure* granting leave to examine a non-party, Mr. David R. Peterson.

Mr. Peterson was, at times relevant to issues in this action, Chairman of the Board of the Toronto Raptors Basketball Club Inc. (the "Raptors"). An affidavit of Mr. Peterson filed by the plaintiffs on the motion for an injunction heard August 8, 9 and 10, 1994 referred to discussions between the Raptors and Maple Leaf Gardens Limited ("MLGL") regarding a proposed joint use facility, the interest of the Raptors in acquiring the shares of MLGL held by the Estate of Harold E. Ballard and the price which the Raptors would have been prepared to pay for such shares. In view of the fact that the affidavit was filed at the opening of the hearing of the injunction motion, there was no opportunity to cross-examine Mr. Peterson on his affidavit. The defendants now seek an order pursuant to subrule 31.10(1) to examine for discovery Mr. Peterson as a non-party. ...

It was conceded by counsel for the plaintiffs that the questions of whether the Executors received fair market value for their shares of MLGL and whether a higher price was obtainable elsewhere are material issues in this action. I find that there is good reason to believe that the information which Mr. Peterson has as to discussions between the Raptors and MLGL for a joint use facility, the interest of the Raptors in acquiring the Estate's shares of MLGL and the price which the Raptors [were] prepared to pay is information relevant to such issues and that any threshold test as to degree of relevance has been met.

Subrule 31.10(2) provides as follows:

An order under subrule (1) shall not be made unless the court is satisfied that,

(a) the moving party has been unable to obtain the information from other persons whom the moving party is entitled to examine for discovery, or from the person he or she seeks to examine;

(b) it would be unfair to require the moving party to proceed to trial without having the opportunity of examining the person; and

(c) the examination will not,

(i) unduly delay the commencement of the trial of the action,

(ii) entail unreasonable expense for other parties, or

(iii) result in unfairness to the person the moving party seeks to examine.

Counsel for the plaintiffs conceded that branch (c) of the test for granting leave has been met.

With respect to branch (a) of the test, I am satisfied on the evidence before me that the defendants have been unable to obtain the information from persons whom they are entitled to examine for discovery or from Mr. Peterson.

It remains to consider whether it would be unfair to require the defendants to move to trial without having the opportunity of examining Mr. Peterson.

It is evident from the reasons of Justice Lederman on the injunction motion that he placed considerable reliance upon the information contained in the affidavit of Mr. Peterson in granting the motion. It also appears to me that the evidence of Mr. Peterson as to the nature and the outcome of the discussions with Maple Leaf Gardens on the joint use facility, the extent of the interest of the Raptors in acquiring the Estate's shares of MLGL, as to why no offer was made to the Executors or no competing bid made at the time of the takeover bid and as to the price which the Raptors [were] prepared to pay for the shares and how that price was arrived at is very important evidence on questions which are central to one of the main issues in this action, that is whether the Executors were in breach of their fiduciary duties, and another of the main issues in this action, that is what the fair market value of the shares of MLGL was at the time that the Executors sold their shares. I conclude, therefore, that it would be most difficult for the defendants to adequately prepare for trial or to determine what evidence or witnesses they must call without having this information. This is particularly so in the circumstances of this case where obviously the plaintiffs have had an opportunity to question Mr. Peterson on all these issues in preparing his affidavit filed by the plaintiffs on the injunction motion. On any test of fairness, it seems to me that the defendants should have a similar opportunity to obtain information from Mr. Peterson prior to trial.

With respect to the submissions of Mr. McRae that the Intervenors be permitted to ask questions on the examination for discovery of Mr. Peterson, the Intervenors are not a moving party on this motion and it appears to me that the order to be made is an order granting the moving party the right to examine a non-party for discovery. As contemplated by subrule 31.10(3), other parties may attend on the discovery and are entitled to a transcript of the discovery but, in my view, are not entitled to ask questions.

Accordingly, an order will issue that the defendants are granted leave to examine for discovery Mr. David R. Peterson pursuant to rule 31.10 of the Rules of Civil Procedure.

See also *Lana International Ltd. v. Menasco Aerospace Ltd.* (2000), 195 DLR (4th) 497 (Ont. Master); aff'd. [2000] OJ No. 4798 (Div. Ct.). Further, how does the analysis in this decision of the fairness issue for granting leave to examine a non-party for discovery compare with the analysis in the decision from the *Stavro* case, excerpted earlier in this chapter, regarding leave to obtain documentary discovery from a non-party?

4. *Letters of request.* Parties to litigation may wish to obtain evidence by examining persons who are outside the province. Where the non-resident to be examined is a party, there is little problem because the court has jurisdiction over a party and can direct where and at whose expense the examination is to be conducted: see, for example, Ontario rule 34.07(1), Alberta rule 270, BC rule 38, and Nova Scotia rule 56. However, where the non-resident to be examined is a non-party, the situation is more complex because a court in jurisdiction A has no power to force a non-party in jurisdiction B to attend the examination. The party who seeks the examination must ask the court in jurisdiction A to issue "letters rogatory" or "letters of request" addressed to a court in jurisdiction B, seeking the latter court's assistance in securing the attendance of the person to be examined. For example, see Ontario rules 34.07(2) to (7). If the person to be examined will not voluntarily attend, then the examining party will request the jurisdiction B court to issue an order enforcing the letters rogatory. As Mr. Justice Blair noted in *Fecht v. Deloitte & Touche* (1996), 28 OR (3d) 188 (Gen. Div.),

> the circumstances in which an Ontario court will grant an order enforcing letters rogatory for purposes of pre-trial discovery of non-parties should not be any rarer, at least, than those in which a similar request might emanate from an Ontario court to a foreign jurisdiction. At the same time, the authorities support the proposition that the enforcement of letters rogatory by an Ontario court will not be limited to those in which an Ontario court would make an order for discovery of non-parties under rule 31.10. ... While I agree ... that the court need not confine the exercise of its discretion, in favour of enforcing letters rogatory where non-parties are the target of the request, to those circumstances in which the requirements of rule 31.10 have been met, I do not believe that those requirements need be disregarded entirely as useful guideposts.

In *Fecht*, the letters rogatory emanated from New York in a class action pending against Northern Telecom based on allegations that the company and some of its directors had made falsely optimistic public statements that artificially raised share prices and caused them later to fall dramatically when the company announced losses. Blair J described the US action, the positions of the parties on the letters rogatory and his conclusions as follows:

> Class actions of this sort are unknown to Canadian law but are not uncommon in the United States, although Congress has recently taken steps to attempt to limit their scope and frequency. They are known pejoratively, by those who oppose them, as "strike suits," apparently because the plaintiffs "strike" immediately upon the downturn of share values and before the makeup or membership of the class they purport to represent can even be known. In some quarters such actions themselves are thought to be "fishing expeditions" in substance, and that characterization plays an important role in the opposition to these letters rogatory by the respondents. ...
>
> Deloitte & Touche and Northern Telecom both vigorously oppose the granting of an order enforcing the letters rogatory. They submit that the US class action is by nature a "fishing expedition" in itself, and that an Ontario court ought not to countenance an extension of the fishing

waters into this jurisdiction—"fishing expeditions" being a well-recognized example of the kinds of circumstances in which courts will decline to enforce letters rogatory. They submit, as well, that the court should be very wary about enforcing letters rogatory for purposes of pre-trial discovery rather than for the purpose of providing testimony at trial, and ought particularly to be wary about doing so in a way that will expose Canadian professional firms who simply provide advice to companies that do business in the United States to the very extensive American deposition process. Finally, they raise various technical defences.

The applicants, on the other hand, argue that principles of international comity dictate a liberal approach to requests from foreign tribunals for judicial assistance. They contend that all necessary criteria for the enforcement of letters rogatory, as reflected in the letters rogatory themselves, have been met in the circumstances of this case, and that notwithstanding the pre-trial discovery flavour of the production and examination sought, the evidence gathered will be of great assistance for purposes of trial. In addition, they submit that the court should not embark on an adjudication of the merits of the foreign action, nor should it conduct a review of whether the letters rogatory ought to have been issued. ...

I am not inclined to exercise the court's discretion in the circumstances of this case to order enforcement of the letters rogatory because of the more general principles enunciated in these reasons. In my opinion the record does not justify a finding that the evidence and information sought could not be—or could not have been—otherwise obtained. The transcripts of the depositions to which I was referred do not bear out that Deloitte & Touche was involved in the matters which are at the heart of the US action in any fashion other than the normal connection between independent auditor and client. Without more, I am not prepared to sanction what is in essence the extension of the American pre-trial deposition practice to a non-party providing auditing services in Ontario in the circumstances of this case, particularly in view of the fact that the many senior witnesses from Northern Telecom who have already been deposed were not even asked what information they had provided to Deloitte & Touche and what information had been imparted to them by Deloitte & Touche on the specific areas of questioning now sought to be pursued.

On appeal (1997), 32 OR (3d) 417, the Ontario Court of Appeal upheld Blair J's use of the rule 31.10 requirements as guideposts on an application to examine non-party witnesses for a foreign proceeding. It held, however, that Ontario courts do have the power to narrow a request where this would permit the request to be granted.

To what extent do you agree with the suggestion that the letters rogatory in this case were part of a "fishing expedition"? To what extent could the breadth of the request be explained by the greater emphasis placed on discovery rather than on pleadings for notice giving and issue defining in litigation in the United States?

5. *Globalization.* Domestic legal rules continue to be developed and applied at the local level. However,

[a]s a result of the internationalization of cases and litigants before domestic courts—largely resulting from commercial globalization—the interpretation of domestic procedural laws in turn has become of increased interest and importance ... [including] extraterritorial discovery.

(Trevor C.W. Farrow, "Globalization, International Human Rights, and Civil Procedure" (2003), 41 *Alta L Rev.* 671, at 688 and 709.) What role does (and should) increase free trade and globalization play in the interpretation of domestic procedural rules—including discovery rules—in litigation involving issues, documents, and parties/non-parties from multiple jurisdictions? See further *In re Application Pursuant to 28 USC 1782 for an Order Permitting Bayer AG*, 146 F3d 188 (3d Cir. 1998); *VitaPharm Canada Ltd. v. F. Hoffmann-La Roche Ltd.* (2001), 11 CPR (4th) 230 (Ont. Sup. Ct.); aff'd. (2002), 18 CPR (4th) 267 (Ont. Div. Ct.), both cited in Farrow, above.

D. Scope of Examination for Discovery

The scope of examination for discovery is generally dealt with by the rules—for example, see Ontario rule 31.06, BC rule 27.22, Nova Scotia rule 18.09, and Alberta rule 200(1.2)— and whether a matter on which a party wishes to examine another party is discoverable is determined by reference to the pleadings (including any particulars). To understand the scope of permitted questioning, it is essential to keep in mind two primary purposes served by examination for discovery. These are, first, to obtain information about the case of the other party, and, second, to secure admissions of fact that can be used as evidence at the trial by the examining party either to advance his or her own case or to weaken or destroy that of his or her opponent (see above). Whether a question on examination for discovery seeks to achieve either or both of these objectives, it is the pleadings that disclose the case of the examining party or the case of the party examined, whichever is relevant. Thus, a question cannot be properly asked on examination for discovery unless it either relates to the pleadings in the sense of seeking an elucidation of the claim or defence raised in the pleadings, or is directed to establishing a fact, the existence or non-existence of which is shown by the pleadings to be in issue.

The traditional position (now departed from in several provinces, including Ontario) held that a party being examined need only state the facts on which he or she relies and not the evidence by which they are to be proved. The rule was easy to state but difficult to apply because the distinction between the facts that constitute the case of a party and the evidence to prove them was not always clear. Cases held that in the case of doubt, "resolution must be in favour of fact *disclosure*": *Rubinoff v. Newton*, [1967] 1 OR 402 (HC). The rationale for the rule restricting discovery to facts and not evidence is discussed and criticized in Williams, "Discovery of Civil Litigation Trial Preparation in Canada" (1980), 58 *Can. Bar Rev.* 1.

Some provinces have now expressly abrogated the rule restricting discovery of evidence or of witnesses' names or evidence. For example, see BC rule 27(22) and Ontario rule 31.06.

For further reform proposals, see, for example, the Canadian Bar Association, *Report of the Canadian Bar Association, Task Force on Systems of Civil Justice* (Ottawa: The Canadian Bar Association, 1996), recommending that "every jurisdiction (a) amend its rules of procedure to limit the scope and number of oral examinations for discovery and the time available for discovery" (recommendation 16). As discussed above in relation to documentary production, rule changes in Ontario, for example, will likely narrow the scope of examination for discovery and increase the onus on parties to cooperate in planning and completing examinations for discovery: Ontario Civil Justice Reform Project: Summary of Findings and Recommendations (Ontario: November 2007), online at: http://www.attorneygeneral.jus .gov.on.ca/english/about/pubs/cjrp/CJRP-Report_EN.pdf, pp. 64-67).

1. Relation to Pleadings

Forliti (Guardian ad litem of) v. Woolley
(2002), 21 CPC (5th) 246, 2002 BCSC 858

GARSON J: Three applications are before the court concerning the examinations for discovery of the plaintiff Mrs. Forliti, the defendant Dr. Woolley, and the defendant Dr. Kim Sing.

On all three examinations there were objections taken to the questions asked, or the form of the questions asked. The parties appear before me, as their case management judge, to request rulings on the objections taken at the three examinations for discovery.

I propose first to describe the facts alleged by the plaintiff to the extent that it is necessary to make determinations of relevancy, next to outline the legal principles that govern the conduct of examinations for discovery as those principles apply to these applications, and then to rule on each objection taken. Both counsel have requested that I rule on these objections despite the fact that neither counsel completed their oral submissions. Counsel have provided me with written briefs. I made rulings on some of the objections during the course of the oral hearing and I will not repeat those rulings in these Reasons.

Background Factual Allegations

Mrs. Forliti gave birth to Blue Forliti on October 18, 1997, at Burnaby Hospital. Blue Forliti was born by vaginal breech delivery.

The plaintiffs allege that the defendants were negligent in failing to apply reasonable skill in the provision of medical care, treatment and professional services, in failing to consider whether in all the circumstances a vaginal delivery was appropriate and in failing to intervene in a timely manner or at all to prevent injury to Blue Forliti.

The plaintiffs allege that as a result of the defendants' negligence Blue Forliti has suffered severe injuries associated with a lack of oxygen during birth. I will not detail the extensive list of injuries alleged.

It is important to note (for the purposes of the rulings I am requested to make) that at some time before Mrs. Forliti's labour began there was an attempt to reposition the baby in the womb, owing to the fact the baby was in a breech position. This procedure is called an "external version." This procedure was not performed by Dr. Woolley. I am told that one of the issues to be determined in this action relates to Dr. Woolley's knowledge of this earlier procedure. Some of the objections taken at the examination for discovery of Dr. Woolley relate to his knowledge of this earlier external version procedure.

Scope of Examination for Discovery

Examinations for discovery are governed by Rule 27 of the *Rules of Court*. Concerning the scope of the examination R. 27(22) states, in part:

Unless the court otherwise orders, a person being examined for discovery shall answer any question within his or her knowledge or means of knowledge regarding any matter, not privileged, relating to a matter in question in the action …

The following are principles, relevant to this application, which emerge from the case law concerning the conduct of examinations for discovery:

(a) The scope of an examination for discovery extends to any matter relating to a matter in question in the action and is in the nature of a cross-examination. The question need not be focused directly on a matter in question in the action but need only relate to such a matter. "Rigid limitations rigidly applied can destroy the right to a proper examination for discovery."

(*Cominco Ltd. v. Westinghouse Canada Ltd. (No. 4)* (1979), 11 BCLR 142 (CA))

(b) On an examination for discovery, questions are limited to relevant issues (relevance being broadly defined, in this context, by the judgment in *Cominco*) between the party conducting the discovery and the party being examined. In other words, questions may not be put which are relevant only to issues between the party conducting the discovery and another party (not being examined).

(*Nikal et al. v. Caira* (1993), 16 CPC (3d) 119 (BCSC))

(c) A witness need not answer questions soliciting an opinion on an examination for discovery. There is an exception to this rule where the party examined is asked questions regarding his or her professional conduct or competence where that conduct and/or competence is in issue in the action. Questions soliciting an opinion must pertain to the area of expertise of the individual being examined. The party being examined need not answer questions pertaining to the conduct of another defendant. For example in this case the doctor sued for professional negligence may properly be asked questions which solicit from him his professional opinion concerning his own treatment of Ms. Forliti during her labour and delivery, but he may not be asked questions which solicit from him an opinion as to the negligence of another doctor or a nurse.

Teachers' Investment & Housing Co-operative (Trustee of) Jennings Chong (Guardian ad litem of) v. Royal Columbian Hospital (1996), 2 CPC (4th) 242

Gelt Holdings Ltd. v. Pannell, (1997), 13 CPC (4th) 249 (BCSC)

Crocker v. MacDonald, (1992), 116 NSR (2d) 181 (NSSCTO)

(But see also *Beber v. Bloch*, [2000] OJ No. 3142 (QL) (Ont. SCJ)) in which the Ont. SCJ per Lamek J held that it was not "improper on discovery to seek the opinion of one defendant about the conduct of another.")

(d) Hypothetical questions may properly be put to a witness where the witness has expertise and when the hypothetical question is relevant to some issue in the case, provided the question is not overly broad or vague.

Motaharian v. Reid (1989), 39 CPC (2d) 141 (Ont. H Court)

(e) Counsel for the party being examined may object to the form of a question on the grounds that it is vague, confusing, unclear, overly broad or misleading. An example of a misleading question is the misstatement of earlier testimony. The proper conduct of counsel in this instance is to state the objection to the form of the question and the reasons for objection. It is not appropriate for counsel to make comments, suggestions, or criticisms.

McLachlin & Taylor (*British Columbia Practice*, 2d ed. (Butterworths: Markham, 2002) at p. 27-114-120) say in their commentary on Rule 27(24):

> The court will not order a question to be answered if the meaning of the question to be answered is not clear, or if it appears to involve questions of law: ... [citations omitted] The questions should be set out in concrete form and should not depend for their meaning on previous questions or answers. ...

(See also C.D. Cudmore, *Choate on Discovery*, 2d ed. (Carswell: Toronto, 2002) at 224; G. Harris, *Discovery Practice in British Columbia*, looseleaf, (CLE: Vancouver, 2002) at 3.658, 3:85; F.D. Cass et al., *Discovery Law, Practice and Procedure in Ontario* (Carswell: Toronto, 1993) at p. 279.)

Rulings on Examination for Discovery of Dr. Woolley

It serves no useful purpose to reproduce each portion of the transcript containing the questions objected to. In most cases the contentious questions, dialogue between counsel, and answers cover several pages. I therefore attach to these reasons, an appendix of the rulings I have made on the individual questions [appendix omitted].

Conclusion

At the hearing of this matter I indicated to plaintiff's counsel my views regarding certain intemperate comments which he made at the examinations for discovery when objections were made. I do not need to repeat my comments in these Reasons.

As mentioned above in *Cominco*, Mr. Justice Seaton said, at p. 151, "Rigid limitations rigidly applied can destroy the right to a proper examination for discovery." Counsel should endeavour to be restrained in their objections. An examination for discovery is not a three-way conversation. It is best to follow a more formalistic approach to objections. Although, in this examination for discovery, many questions posed did require clarification because they were ambiguous, misleading, or vague there were many other instances in which the objections or interjections were overly rigid.

Counsel should contact the registry to arrange a convenient time to hear the application with respect to the examination for discovery of the plaintiff, Mrs. Forliti.

NOTES AND QUESTIONS

1. *Forliti* sets out the typical scope of discovery in Canada. In Alberta, however, as a result of 1999 amendments to the rules (see rule 200(1.2)), the scope of discovery has been made somewhat more limited, requiring that only "relevant and material questions" be

answered. See, for example, the *750869 Alberta Ltd. v. Cambridge Shopping Centres Ltd.* (2001), 283 AR 391 (QB). Similarly, the scope of discovery either has been or is likely to be narrowed in Ontario, British Columbia, and Nova Scotia through rule amendments in those jurisdictions. See, for Ontario, O. Reg. 438/08; for British Columbia, rules 7-1 and 7-2 online at http://www.ag.gov.bc.ca/justice-reform-initiatives/publications/pdf/CivilRules07-07-09 .pdf; and for Nova Scotia, rule 14.01(1).

2. In *Forliti*, Garson J held, at para. 9(a), that "[t]he scope of an examination for discovery extends to any matter relating to a matter in question in the action … . The question need not be focused directly on a matter in question in the action but need only relate to such a matter. 'Rigid limitations rigidly applied can destroy the right to a proper examination for discovery.'" What are the outer bounds? If a question cannot be related to the pleadings, need it be answered? Should the pleadings form the boundaries of what is answerable? The new language in the Ontario rule will focus on information *relevant* to matters a issue—a test of simple relevance. How will this change the parameters of examination for discovery?

3. In *Milton Farms Ltd. v. Dow Chemical Canada* (1986), 13 CPC (2d) 174 (Sask. QB), an action for damages for breach of warranty and negligence arising from damage sustained to crops after using the defendant's herbicide, the defendant was required to produce complaints received from persons other than the plaintiffs respecting the product, as they were relevant to issues raised by the pleadings—that is, whether the defendant knew or ought to have known that the herbicide might be hazardous, and whether it was in fact hazardous. The defendant was also required to produce a report of a consultant to a complainant not a party to the action because it might lead to a train of inquiry enabling the plaintiffs to advance their case. The case also raised various questions as to the scope of examination for discovery. How should the court have dealt with the discoverability of the following: (1) The volume of sales of the herbicide? (2) The existence of other claims regarding the herbicide? (3) Evidence of the settlement of such claims? (4) Questions as to the dollar value of sales of the product? (5) Questions as to an application by the defendant for registration of a different herbicide for sale in the United States?

2. Answering from Knowledge, Information, and Belief

Typically, a person examined for discovery is required to answer to the best of his or her "knowledge, information and belief": for example, see Ontario rule 31.06(1). The nature and extent of this obligation is described in Holmested and Watson, *Ontario Civil Procedure*, 31 §15[4] as follows:

> "[A]n examination for discovery requires the witness to give not only his knowledge but his information and belief": *Rubinoff v. Newton*, [1967] 1 OR 402 (HC). Though not generally permitted at trial, hearsay evidence is permissible on discovery. "As a witness, the party must confine himself to his knowledge: on examination [for discovery] he not only may, but he must give his information": *Van Horn v. Verall* (1911), 3 OWN 439 (HC). … On the matter of "belief," the following passage from *Bray on Discovery*, p. 128 was quoted, with approval, in *Kirkpatrick v. CPR*, [1926] 3 DLR 542 (Sask. KB):

> As to facts not happening within his own knowledge … he must answer as to his information and belief and not his information merely without stating any belief either one way or the other; … as to the act of another which defendant does not certainly know he ought to say he thinks or believes it to be true or does not, and not say only that he has heard … He is also bound to state the grounds on which his belief is founded in order that the reality and value of his belief may be tested.

Not only must a party examined give his information, he must inform himself. In *Rubinoff v. Newton*, above, Haines J said: "I can think of no more simple and direct question than, 'On what facts do you rely?' The witness may not know those facts but he must be informed by his counsel. It must be kept in mind that on an examination for discovery a party must qualify himself to give an intelligent statement of his case." A party to an action is bound to inform himself as to the knowledge possessed by his servants, employees and agents: *Bondar v. Usinovitch*, [1918] 1 WWR 557 (Sask.); Holmested & Gale, *Ontario Judicature Act and Rules of Practice*, R. 342 §§ 35-36. As a general principle there is no obligation on a party to make inquiries of third parties over whom he has no control, in order to inform himself: see *Star Electric Fixtures Ltd. v. Sussex Fire Ins. Co.*, [1936] OWN 654; *Concept 80 Ltd. v. W.A. Const. Co.* (1975), 1 CPC 96 (Ont. HC) (no duty on party to inform himself from independent contractor).

The duty on the party to inform himself or herself is particularly important, and onerous, with regard to persons examined on behalf of a corporation. Such a person is typically under an obligation to inform himself or herself by making inquiries of the corporation and its officers and servants.

Moreover, the limitations stated above (there is no obligation on a party to make inquiries of third persons over whom he or she has no control in order to inform himself or herself) are disappearing. For example, *Gravlev v. Venturetek International Ltd.* (1979), 15 CPC 18 (Ont. HC) imposed an obligation to make inquiries from former officers and agents: "The test really is that the plaintiff is bound to obtain the information from such former agents or servants unless he can show that it would be unreasonable to require him to do so." To the same effect, see *Signcorp Investments Limited v. Cairns Homes Limited* (1988), 24 CPC (2d) 1 (Sask. QB). In *Quintette Co. Limited v. Bow Valley Resource Services Limited* (1988), 29 BCLR (2d) 109 (SC), the corporate defendant's key person in the execution of the project at issue in the litigation had died. The opposing party was left to examine for discovery someone who had no first-hand knowledge of the facts. It was held that, because the claim amounted to millions of dollars and in the light of the substantial issues involved, the defendant's representative had a duty to inform himself by making inquiries of independent corporations that had been subcontractors of the defendant. Each of the three corporations was outside of the jurisdiction, two in Alberta and one in France. The defendant had already had three consultations with one of the corporations in Edmonton and two with the French corporation, one in Montreal and one in Paris. Notwithstanding this, the defendant was required to make further inquiries with regard to questions that were clearly relevant to the issues in the action. What would happen if the subcontractors refused to answer the inquiries put to them by the defendant? In jurisdictions where a number of representatives can be discovered (see, for example, Alberta), does the same obligation apply? Should it?

3. Continuing Discovery Obligations

Should a party be required to disclose documents or information that come to light after discovery? What should happen where a party later finds that an answer given on oral examination for discovery was inaccurate? What sanctions are available? See, for example, Ontario rules 31.09 (examination for discovery) and 30.07 (concerning documents). See further, for example, BC rules 26(13)-(14).

While the matter is now specifically dealt with by the rules in some jurisdictions—for example, the Ontario rules just referred to—such rules essentially confirm doctrine developed in the case law: see *Ontario Bean Producers' Marketing Board v. W.G. Thompson & Sons Limited* (1982), 35 OR (2d) 711 (Div. Ct.), holding that there is a duty to update an affidavit of documents and a duty to give an undertaking to provide after-acquired information when requested.

E. Sanctions for Failure To Comply with Discovery Obligations

1. Spoliation

"Spoliation" involves the destruction of evidence. Intentional destruction of evidence can constitute an independent tort, although Canadian jurisprudence has generally addressed such conduct by imposing procedural and evidentiary sanctions within an existing action.

Spencer v. Quadco Equipment Inc.
2005 NBQB 2 (CanLII)

. . .

[17] The law concerning spoliation in Canada begins with the decision by the Supreme Court of Canada in *St. Louis v. R* (1895) SCR 649 which stands for the proposition that where one party destroys evidence there is a rebuttable presumption that the evidence destroyed would have been adverse to that party's interest.

[18] In more recent times, cases in British Columbia have concluded that only where it can be shown that the party which destroyed the evidence did so in bad faith or intentionally will an adverse inference be drawn and sanctions imposed. See *Dawes v. Jajcaj*, [1995] BCJ No. 2366 (SC) affirmed [1990] BCJ No. 845 (CA) and *Endean v. Canadian Red Cross Society*, 1998 CanLII 6489 (BC CA), (1998), 157 DLR (4th) 465 (CA).

[19] More recent cases in Ontario accept the proposition that a trial judge may apply appropriate evidentiary and procedural sanctions at trial for spoliation if the circumstances warrant (see *Cheung v. Toyota Canada Inc.*, [2003] OJ No. 411 (SC) and *Doust v. Schatz*, [2002] SJ No. 674 (CA) and *Spasic Estate v. Imperial Tobacco Ltd.*, 2000 CanLII 17170 (ON CA), (2000), 188 DLR (4th) 577 (Ont. CA).

[20] In the *Cheung* case, supra. the Court further observed, albeit as *obiter dicta*, at paragraph 23:

> As to whether any sanctions can be imposed for spoliation prior to trial in the absence of evidence of intentional destruction or alteration through bad faith, in reliance on the courts

inherent jurisdiction, it seems to me that in appropriate circumstances the Court should be able to impose sanctions.

NOTES AND QUESTIONS

1. Sanctions may be imposed in relation to destruction of physical property, as well as for destruction of digital data and records. For example, in *Western Tank & Lining Ltd. v. Skrobutan*, 2006 MBQB 205 (CanLII), Scurfield J concluded that the defendant employees had intentionally attempted to destroy evidence by erasing information from their computers after their employer requested that the computers be returned. The court concluded that this act of spoliation supported the drawing of a negative inference that the defendants had probably been involved in direct solicitation of the plaintiff employer's customers. The employees' attempted destruction of evidence also factored into the comparatively strenuous terms of the interlocutory injunction issued by the court. See also: *iTrade Finance Inc. v. Webworx Inc.*, 2005 CanLII 9196 (ON SC).

2. In *Dreco Energy Services Ltd. v. Wenzel*, 2005 ABCA 185 (CanLII), the defendants had been found in contempt of a court order relating to production and discovery, resulting in a $5,000 cost award being made against them. On appeal, the $5,000 cost sanction was found to be inadequate in light of new evidence that the defendants had erased computer records. In remitting the matter of sanction back to the case management judge for reconsideration, the Court of Appeal judge noted it was open to her to strike the defendants' pleadings and to draw adverse inferences against them. The Court of Appeal, at para. 12, identified seven factors for consideration in assessing the sanction for contempt: "(1) the role of counsel, including the extent to which the actions of the respondents' counsel might have contributed to the respondents' contempt; (2) the motivation for the destruction/ erasure of the computer records while the undertakings to produce them remained extant; (3) the consequences flowing from the destruction of those records and what redress should flow from that, including consideration of whether any adverse inferences should be drawn as a result thereof; (4) the entire context and history of the litigation; (5) the amount of reasonable thrown-away costs properly incurred; (6) the nature of the contempt; and (7) the degree of culpability of the contemnors."

2. Breach of Continuing Discovery Obligations

Burke v. Gauthier
(1987), 24 CPC (2d) 281 (Ont. HC)

CAMPBELL J:

The Issue. The case raises this question: should new evidence of a plaintiff's changed physical condition since discovery be admitted in a personal injury action when the new evidence favourable to the plaintiff differs significantly from the answers given on examination for discovery and the plaintiff has given no notice at all of the new evidence?

The Claim. Edward Burke claims damages for personal injuries resulting from a boat collision. Liability is admitted and the only issue is the quantum of damages.

Mr. Burke, a 53-year-old bus driver, is married with nine children. He lives in the isolated village of Killarney, about 75 miles from Sudbury. He is a credible witness and there is no reason to doubt his testimony.

The Accident. On July 1, 1984, Mr. Burke was standing on his 21-foot boat, idling at rest in Killarney Channel. The defendant's 14-foot aluminum boat collided suddenly. It struck so hard that its bow came out of the water and hit the plaintiff in the head, knocking him out and gashing his scalp badly.

The Initial Treatment. Bleeding heavily from the head wound, he was flown by rescue helicopter from Killarney to hospital in Sudbury. He had a laceration of the upper left scalp with heavy bleeding. His scalp was sewn up and he received blood transfusions. His skull was not fractured as the doctors initially suspected. He was reluctant to stay in hospital for any length of time and was released the next day. He had no neurological symptoms but did have a post-concussion syndrome which included headaches.

The Symptoms. His headaches continued as did some neck discomfort. The medical diagnosis was hyperextension injury—of a mild degree to the cervical spine.

He said that he felt rough all through the summer of 1984 and had severe headaches. They gradually improved but he still gets them, sometimes as often as twice a week, and they are sometimes strong. He had significant neck pain, described a year after the accident as moderate and radiating into his shoulder. It hurts particularly if he turns his head to the left. He has a scar from the crown of the head to a point about four inches above the bridge of his nose. The scar is noticeable but not badly disfiguring. He has no sensation in the area of the scar. The lack of sensation, caused by nerve damage from the laceration, is permanent. He finds the scar somewhat embarrassing and has to be careful in winter to guard against frostbite in the area where he has no sensation.

Effect on Earning Potential. He drives a bus with passengers and freight from Killarney to Sudbury and back, loading and unloading the parcels and freight by himself. He has worked since the accident (although he was off for some time during the summer of 1985 with an unrelated ankle injury) and had no trouble passing the regular medical examinations required for his bus driver's licence. He has some difficulty turning his neck but his bus is solid at the back and he used the side mirrors when backing up. The neck pain is worse after driving a lot.

He is worried that his neck might deteriorate and that he might be unable to drive any more, because he would have few other job opportunities. Dr. McMullen testified that X-rays in September 1984, show some degenerative change in the neck. The onset of symptoms was likely caused by the accident. He said it was possible that the plaintiff would become unable to drive because of neck pain brought on by further degenerative change, but that he was all right to drive now and there was no present indication that he would be unable to drive in the future. The evidence does not establish any compensable likelihood of future deterioration that would affect his job. I find no basis for compensation for any possible loss of future earnings or future earning potential.

Overall Prognosis. The plaintiff tendered evidence that his problems became more serious since the examination for discovery in August 1986. The plaintiff did not inform the defendants before trial that his condition or activities had changed.

The defendants objected to that evidence on the ground that they were taken completely by surprise and the plaintiff had taken no steps to inform them before trial of the changed nature of the case.

The plaintiff at the examination for discovery in August 1986, said that he had been able to resume his recreational and sporting activities since the accident, to the same extent as before the accident. His neck bothered him, but he still went fishing. He used his boat less than usually, but he was not thinking of selling it. He had no problems lifting heavy parcels at work.

At trial he tendered evidence that was quite different. He tendered evidence that the pain got worse in the Fall of 1986. After completing his day's work, he could not do much more. He could no longer snowmobile and sold his skidoo. He used to hunt a lot but only went hunting twice the previous year. It affected his bowling, fishing, woodcutting. It was hard to lift things. His wife and friends tendered evidence that he was not the same; he was quieter and "not such a fun loving guy," it was hard to get him to go out, he didn't skidoo or ice fish or dance or cut wood any more.

The plaintiff's answer on discovery that he had no trouble lifting and no diminution of his recreational or sporting activities except that he boated a little bit less, was no longer correct and complete at the time of trial. It had ceased to be correct and complete sometime in the six or nine months before trial.

The case he presented at the examination for discovery was a mild whiplash with no change in personality or lifestyle and no significant work problems. The case he presented at trial was quite different. It involved a loss of recreational activity, trouble lifting, and a change from a fun-loving personality.

Rule 31.09. Rule 31.09(1) puts a duty on the plaintiff to provide the defendant in writing with information that any answer given at the examination for discovery is no longer correct and complete.

Rule 31.09(3) provides that if the plaintiff does not provide the defendant in writing with such information, the information subsequently discovered if favourable to the plaintiff is inadmissible at trial except with leave of the Court.

The purpose of the provision is obvious. The parties prepare for trial on the basis of the evidence given at the discoveries. They assume that the answers given on discovery continue to be correct and complete, unless they are given information to the contrary. They figure out what they have to meet, decide how to prepare their own case, what investigations if any to undertake, what witness to call, what instructions to seek, and what kind of settlement might be reasonable, on the basis of the evidence given at the discoveries. If that evidence changes then there is a different case to meet. If the changes are not brought to the attention of the adverse party before trial he has no time or opportunity to investigate and prepare and consider the need for fresh medical examination and must meet a case different from the one that his opponent has led him to expect.

Unless there is some incentive to the plaintiff to disclose a change in the evidence, there is nothing to discourage trial by ambush and little to promote the objects of discovery which include the encouragement of settlement, the narrowing of issues, and the basic rule of fairness that a party should have reasonable knowledge of the case he must meet.

Rule 31.09, by enacting very explicitly a continuing duty of disclosure or discovery, is obviously designed to give these principles some teeth.

The new evidence in this case goes far beyond mere detail. It goes to the type of personal injury case the defendant has to meet, and it is the very kind of evidence designed to be governed by the rule. It is just about as relevant and material as any evidence can be in a personal injury case.

The difficulty in a personal injury case in deciding whether to grant leave under r. 31.09(3) to lead undisclosed evidence is this: the more significant the change in condition, the greater is the potential prejudice to the defendant in meeting a new case but also and correspondingly greater is the prejudice to the plaintiff in being unable to put favourable evidence before the Court.

In this case the plaintiff was obviously well aware of the change and therefore obviously aware of the new favourable evidence. He gave no reason for failing to provide the defendant with the new evidence favourable to the plaintiff's case. There was no application before trial for an adjournment in order to do so and the plaintiff put forward his case in the face of the rule without giving the defendants any knowledge of the new case they had to meet and no opportunity to investigate the new evidence, or to prepare to meet it or to consider their settlement position.

Had the plaintiff made any attempt to overcome the unfairness to the defendants by even mentioning it before trial or somehow trying to overcome the complete surprise, I might have been inclined to grant leave to introduce the evidence under r. 31.09(3), on terms under r. 53.08 unless the defendants showed some more concrete evidence of specific forms of prejudice.

But the plaintiff decided to move ahead into the teeth of the rule without trying to do anything to overcome the obvious unfairness and prejudice to the defendants at being met in the middle of the trial for the first time with a new case and I therefore see no basis to relieve against the clear consequences of the rule.

The evidence of the change in condition since the examination for discovery will therefore not be admitted.

Damages. On the evidence properly admissible at trial, Mr. Burke suffered a nasty head injury followed by considerable pain for a few months. He felt rough for a few months after the accident. He has some continuing and probably permanent discomfort to his neck. There is a mild permanent disability to his neck which does not affect his present or future earning capacity. He had severe headaches for some months and a temporary suspension of his normal activities for perhaps a year or more but less than two years. He still has some bad headaches.

He has a permanent scar on his head, quite obvious to sight but not badly disfiguring. The loss of sensation around the scar is troublesome for a man so used to being outdoors for long periods in the dead of winter and he has to take precautions against frostbite.

I assess his non-pecuniary damages at $14,000.

The plaintiff shall have judgment for $14,000 plus the subrogated OHIP claim of $1,690.94 plus Dr. Spegiel's account of $525 (US) which is not covered by OHIP, plus $3,200 for boat repairs, plus prejudgment interest.

If the parties cannot agree on the amount of prejudgment interest they may speak to me. The plaintiff shall have his costs unless the parties bring to my attention some reason to the contrary.

Judgment accordingly.

NOTES AND QUESTIONS

1. Was the judgment in this case fair to Mr. Burke? Whose fault was likely the cause of the non-disclosure? Where subsequent evidence does not amount to a different case at trial, see, for example, *Marchand (Litigation Guardian of) v. Public General Hospital Society of Chatham* (2000), 51 OR (3d) 97 (CA); leave to appeal to SCC refused, SCC Bulletin, 2001, p. 1685.

2. Contrast *Burke* to the decision in *Machado v. Berlet* (1986), 15 CPC (2d) 207 (Ont. HC). There, the plaintiff sued the defendants in negligence for personal injuries suffered in a motor vehicle accident. During cross-examination of the plaintiff at trial, the plaintiff denied that he could run, shovel snow, or scrape ice off windshields. As part of the defendants' case, counsel for the defendants sought to introduce surveillance films of the plaintiff doing those activities. The defendants had claimed privilege over the surveillance films and did not disclose them on production of documents. The plaintiff moved to exclude from evidence the surveillance films on the basis of Ontario rule 30.09 (which prohibits privileged documents from being introduced at trial except in certain circumstances). The motion was dismissed, subject to the right of the plaintiff to call reply evidence to explain the impeaching evidence. It was held that the surveillance films were admissible to impeach the testimony of the plaintiff, notwithstanding that the defendants claimed privilege over them. Rule 30.09 reflects a compromise between the obligation to disclose and the right not to disclose privileged documents. In this case, the defendants obviously intended to use the films to impeach the plaintiff's testimony that he was physically incapacitated by reason of the defendants' negligence.

Can the decision in *Machado* be reconciled with the decision in *Burke*?

3. Contrast the result in *Burke* to that in *MacDonald Construction* in chapter 6, Pleadings, where the defendants surprised the plaintiff at trial by presenting a different case from that which they had pleaded. There, the court adjourned to permit the defendants to amend their pleadings but ordered the defendants to pay the costs of and occasioned by the amendment including those thrown away for the hearing. Why do you think the court in *Burke* did not adopt the same approach?

CHAPTER EIGHT

Privilege and Deemed Undertakings

I. PRIVILEGE

A. Types and Sources of Privilege

We have seen that in the rules and principles governing modern discovery, there is an unmistakable trend toward more complete pretrial disclosure. Against this pressure is a countervailing one derived from recognition that there are certain interests that merit special protection and require that certain materials not be disclosed before trial. The law on privilege has traditionally been considered to be part of the law of evidence and is typically discussed at length in texts on that subject. In civil cases, the modern, broad discovery rules cause issues of privilege to be raised and resolved typically at the discovery stage, rather than at trial. Because privilege is *the* major limitation on the scope of discovery, in civil cases the law on privilege is to a considerable extent now being developed within the framework of policy debates, such as how broad discovery should be.

Material that is relevant to the case but that need not be disclosed is said to qualify for a claim of *privilege*. The effect of a rule of privilege is to prevent a party and a court from having relevant information. Inhibiting the search for the truth in a particular case is justified on the basis that more important interests are at stake.

McCormick, *Evidence*, 3rd ed. (1984), at 171 explains:

> Rules which serve to render accurate ascertainment of the truth more difficult, or in some instances impossible, may seem anomalous in a rational system of fact-finding. Nevertheless, rules of privilege are not without a rationale. Their warrant is the protection of interests and relationships which, rightly or wrongly, are regarded as of sufficient social importance to justify some sacrifice of availability of evidence relevant to the administration of justice.

There are many grounds for privilege that illustrate this point. The right against self-incrimination is an important aspect of criminal and constitutional law. Accused persons may often be the best source of the truth in a criminal case, yet interests of individual dignity and security are seen to prevail, and the accused person need not testify unless he or she chooses to do so. State privilege permits governments to shield information from disclosure on the theory that the public interest in maintaining certain state secrets should prevail over the interests of private litigants in having their disputes resolved correctly. Detailed study of these and other aspects of privilege must be left to a course in evidence. The focus here will be on those aspects of privilege that are related to the civil litigation process itself.

The general rule is that at a trial or other hearing, everyone is subject to being compelled to testify, and all relevant questions may be asked and must be answered. There are exceptions. Certain persons may not be required to testify—for example, an accused at his or her own criminal trial. Moreover, certain types of information need not be disclosed—for example, solicitor-and-client communications, material for which litigation privilege can be claimed, matters affecting the public interest (Crown privilege or state secrets), spousal communications, and the identity of police informers. We do not deal with the last three categories, as these arise more commonly in criminal cases. Analysis of the privilege regarding settlement discussion will be discussed in chapter 10, Managing the Process. Given that the purpose of a privilege not to answer certain questions is, in part, to stop information from being disclosed, privileged documents or privileged information need not be produced or disclosed during the discovery process in civil litigation.

The law does not recognize privilege for "confidential communications" generally—that is, for example, for statements made in confidence to doctors, journalists, priests, or between those involved in business. Consequently, notwithstanding the lofty language as to the sanctity of privilege, it is important to bring a critical eye to this subject and to note who benefits directly and indirectly from it. In civil litigation the important privileges are solicitor-and-client privilege, litigation privilege, settlement negotiation privilege, and (to a lesser extent) Crown privilege. These categories, and that of informer and marital privilege, are recognized as "class" privileges. Other claims to confidentiality are assessed on a "case-by-case" basis in Canadian law. The solicitor-and-client, litigation, and settlement negotiation privileges are framed in terms of being the *client's* privilege, but they also have the effect of cloaking a large amount of *lawyer's* work with the protection of privilege. Crown privilege, by definition, protects the Crown (that is, the government). One does not have to be too much of a cynic to realize that those who benefit substantially from the important privileges in civil litigation are also those who are regularly involved in the law-making process: lawyers and the government. Compare "Developments in the Law—Privileged Communications" (1985), 98 *Harvard Law Review* 1450 (attorney–client privilege is a political device for according special protection to a favoured elite). In this context it is worth noting A.A.S. Zuckerman's observation:

> Those who place legal professional privilege on the exalted and unassailable pedestal of fundamental justice may be reminded that there are other professions that provide invaluable services, such as medical practitioners and accountants, who seem to render perfectly good service to both individuals and the public without the benefit of immunity from disclosing what passes between themselves and their clients. "Legal Professional Privilege—the Cost of Absolutism" (1996), 112 LQR 535, at 539.

Below we discuss solicitor-and-client privilege and the litigation privilege. We begin with the philosophical underpinnings and development of solicitor-and-client privilege and trace its emergence from a rule of evidence to what the Supreme Court of Canada now calls "an important civil and legal right and a principle of fundamental justice in Canadian law": *Lavallee, Rackel & Heintz v. Canada*, [2002] 3 SCR 209, at para. 49. Solicitor-and-client privilege can be abrogated but only when "absolutely necessary." The Supreme Court of Canada recently stated that its "categorical jurisprudence" makes clear "[A]bsolute necessity is as restrictive a test as may be formulated short of an absolute prohibition": *Goodis v. Ontario (Ministry of Correctional Services)*, 2006 SCC 31, at para. 20. Recently, Canadian courts have opined on the distinct but related concept of "litigation privilege," and we provide cases to demonstrate its importance in the discovery process. Briefly, this claim protects the confidentiality of documents that are prepared by lawyers in the context of contemplated or actual litigation. Increasingly, litigation involves multiple parties and issues arise about whether sharing documents between parties (or even non-parties) with a similar interest in the proceedings constitutes a waiver of privilege on what would otherwise have been protected communications. We explain the notion of "common-interest" privilege, which has been created by courts to deal with these situations and still adequately safeguard the interests that privilege is designed to serve. "Ingathered" documents—that is, copies of documents that are placed in a lawyer's file—raise different concerns. We present recent commentary on that issue before turning to other aspects of privilege that are useful to keep in mind in deciding when it can be claimed to prevent disclosure during discovery.

We conclude this chapter by explaining the difference between "class" and "case-by-case" assessments of privilege mentioned earlier. Finally, we review the important Supreme Court of Canada decision *Juman v. Doucette*, 2008 SCC 8, which holds that parties in civil suits are bound by a "deemed undertaking" or "rule of confidentiality" with respect to information obtained in the discovery process.

B. Philosophy of Solicitor-and-Client Privilege

Communications between a solicitor and client for the purpose of giving or receiving legal advice are privileged. The rationale for protecting such communications is well known and generally accepted. If the client does not have the guarantee of confidence, candour will be inhibited and the client will be unable to obtain adequate legal advice. The rationale was well put by Jessel MR in *Anderson v. Bank of British Columbia* (1876), 2 Ch. D 644, at 649:

> The object and meaning of the rule is this: that is, by reason of the complexity and difficulty of our law, litigation can only be properly conducted by professional men; it is absolutely necessary that a man, in order to prosecute his rights or to defend himself from an improper claim, should have recourse to the assistance of professional lawyers, and it being so absolutely necessary, it is equally necessary, to use a vulgar phrase, that he should be able to make a clean breast of it to the gentleman whom he consults with a view to the prosecution of his claim, or substantiating his defense against the claim of others; that he should be able to place unrestricted and unbounded confidence in the professional agent, and that the communications he so makes to him should be kept secret, unless with his consent (for it is his privilege, and not the privilege of the confidential agent), that he should be enabled properly to conduct his litigation. That is the meaning of the rule.

The Supreme Court of Canada has consistently affirmed the above-quoted passage from *Anderson*, and explained in *R v. McClure*, [2001] 1 SCR 445, at para. 33:

> The law is complex. Lawyers have a unique role. Free and candid communication between the lawyer and client protects the legal rights of the citizen. It is essential for the lawyer to know all of the facts of the client's position. The existence of a fundamental right to privilege between the two encourages disclosure within the confines of the relationship. The danger in eroding solicitor–client privilege is the potential to stifle communication between the lawyer and the client. The need to protect the privilege determines its immunity from attack.

See also *Smith v. Jones*, [1999] 1 SCR 445, at para. 46, and *Canada (Privacy Commissioner) v. Blood Tribe Department of Health*, 2008 SCC 44, at para. 9. A powerful line of authorities emerged from Supreme Court of Canada decisions in the 1990s. These cases reflect a nearly absolutist regard for solicitor-and-client privilege. In *Foster Wheeler Power Co. v. Société Intermunicipale de gestion et d'élimination des déchets (SIGED) Inc.*, [2004] 1 SCR 456, at para. 34, LeBel J stated on behalf of a unanimous court: "The lawyer's obligation of confidentiality is necessary to preserve the fundamental relationship of trust between lawyers and clients. Protecting the integrity of this relationship is itself recognized as indispensable to the continued existence and effective operation of Canada's legal system."

To obtain the protection of solicitor-and-client privilege, certain conditions must be met. The criteria are relatively straightforward and must be applied to each separate document or matter at issue. In *Canada v. Solosky*, [1980] 1 SCR 821, at 837, the court stated these are (1) a communication between solicitor and client, (2) which entails the seeking of legal advice, and (3) which is intended to be confidential. Once these conditions are met, privilege exists, whether or not it has been claimed (*Lavallee*, above, at para. 39).

Solicitor-and-client privilege extends beyond the context of litigation and protects any communication made to a lawyer in a bona fide effort to obtain legal advice. The communication must have been made in confidence—for example, where the communication is oral it would not apply if people other than clients of the solicitor are present, nor does it apply to communications between solicitor and client other than those relating to obtaining legal advice—for example, to social conversations or the giving of business advice. Nor is there any protection for communications made in order to facilitate the commission of a crime or fraud (see *Solosky*, above, at 835). The privilege similarly extends to communications made by the solicitor to the client for the purpose of giving legal advice. The vast majority of cases where the privilege is invoked are standard situations where the client is clearly seeking or receiving legal advice. However, there are a number of issues that surround the solicitor-and-client privilege—for example, exactly when it arises, under what circumstances it may be waived or lost through inadvertent disclosure, and how it applies when the client is a corporation.

C. History of Solicitor-and-Client Privilege

The decision of the Supreme Court of Canada in *Canada v. Solosky*, above, provides a starting point for discussions of solicitor-and-client privilege. The appellant, Solosky, was a prisoner and sought a declaration that the director of Millhaven Institution could not open and read mail to and from his lawyer. In the course of deciding his case, the court explained the historical context for the protection of solicitor-and-client communications (at 834):

> [Privilege] stemmed from respect for the "oath and honour" of the lawyer, dutybound to guard closely the secrets of his client, and was restricted in operation to an exemption from testimonial compulsion. Thereafter, in stages, privilege was extended to include communications exchanged during other litigation, those made in contemplation of litigation, and finally, any consultation for legal advice, whether litigious or not.

In more recent case law, the Supreme Court of Canada recognized that the honour theory may be erroneous and the explanation for the privilege may be far less noble (*McClure*, above, at para. 21). More important is the conceptual shift in *Solosky* from privilege being regarded as a rule of evidence to it being treated as a substantive principle. As a rule of evidence, it merely prevents the privileged information from being tendered as evidence in a judicial proceeding by the legal adviser. That was not at issue in *Solosky* because there was no proceeding. In the later case of *Descôteaux v. Mierzwinski*, [1982] 1 SCR 860, at 875, Lamer J referred to *Solosky* and noted:

> It is quite apparent that the Court in that case applied a standard that has nothing to do with the rule of evidence, the privilege, since there was never any question of testimony before a tribunal or court. The Court in fact, in my view, applied a substantive rule, without actually formulating it, and, consequently, recognized implicitly that the right to confidentiality, which had long ago given rise to a rule of evidence, had also since given rise to a substantive rule.
>
> It would, I think, be useful for us to formulate this substantive rule, as the judges formerly did with the rule of evidence; it could, in my view, be stated as follows:
>
> 1. The confidentiality of communications between solicitor and client may be raised in any circumstances where such communications are likely to be disclosed without the client's consent.
>
> 2. Unless the law provides otherwise, when and to the extent that the legitimate exercise of a right would interfere with another person's right to have his communications with his lawyer kept confidential, the resulting conflict should be resolved in favour of protecting the confidentiality.
>
> 3. When the law gives someone the authority to do something which, in the circumstances of the case, might interfere with that confidentiality, the decision to do so and the choice of means of exercising that authority should be determined with a view to not interfering with it except to the extent absolutely necessary in order to achieve the ends sought by the enabling legislation.
>
> 4. Acts providing otherwise in situations under paragraph 2 and enabling legislation referred to in paragraph 3 must be interpreted restrictively.

This extraordinary regard for solicitor-and-client privilege is equally apparent in a series of criminal cases in which the Supreme Court of Canada struck down s. 488.1 of the *Criminal Code*. It set out a procedure for determining a claim of solicitor-and-client privilege in relation to documents seized from a law office under a warrant. The court found that s. 488.1 unjustifiably violated s. 8 of the *Canadian Charter of Human Rights and Freedoms*, which protects against unreasonable search and seizure. In *Lavallee* (above, at para. 36) the majority approved the powerful line of authority and added emphasis to the following passages from *McClure*, above, at paras. 34-36:

> *Despite its importance, solicitor–client privilege is not absolute.* It is subject to exceptions in certain circumstances. ...
>
> However, solicitor–client privilege must be as close to absolute as possible to ensure public confidence and retain relevance. As such, it will only yield in certain clearly defined circumstances, and does not involve a balancing of interests on a case-by-case basis.
>
> Indeed, solicitor–client privilege must remain as close to absolute as possible if it is to retain relevance. Accordingly, this Court is compelled in my view to adopt stringent norms to ensure its protection. Such protection is ensured by labeling as unreasonable any legislative provision that interferes with solicitor–client privilege more than is absolutely necessary.

The fatal weakness of the seizure law at issue was that it permitted privilege to be destroyed without the client's authorization. This offended the court, which opined (*Lavallee*, above, at para. 39): "[T]he privilege belongs to the client and can only be asserted or waived by the client or through his or her informed consent ... . Privilege does not come into being by an assertion of a privilege claim; it exists independently."

There are few exceptions to privilege. They arise more frequently in criminal cases and can be briefly noted. The "innocence-at-stake" exception arises where the disclosure is sought to prevent an innocent person from being unjustly convicted; see *R v. McClure*, above, and its elaboration in *R v. Brown*, [2002] 2 SCR 185. The public-safety exception was developed in *Smith v. Jones*, above. A psychiatrist sought a declaration that he was entitled to disclose solicitor-and-client communication that he had in his possession because he believed the client at issue to be a serious threat to the safety of prostitutes in the relevant area. A majority of the Supreme Court of Canada affirmed the order, which declared the psychiatrist entitled to disclose the information because the potential danger posed by the client was clear, serious, and imminent. The court stressed that the disclosure would have to be narrow and arise only in exceptional cases.

The following case from the Supreme Court of Canada allows us to appreciate how firmly entrenched solicitor-and-client privilege is, and also how it has been adapted to respond to changes in legal practice over time, from small offices of sole practitioners to large firms with many lawyers throughout the country, and many institutions with in-house counsel.

Pritchard v. Ontario (Human Rights Commission)
2004 SCC 31

MAJOR J:

I. Introduction

The appellant, Ms. Colleen Pritchard, filed a human rights complaint with the respondent Ontario Human Rights Commission, against her former employer Sears Canada Inc., alleging gender discrimination, sexual harassment and reprisal. The Commission decided, pursuant to s. 34(1)(b) of the Ontario *Human Rights Code*, RSO 1990, c. H.19, not to deal with her complaint. The appellant sought judicial review and brought a motion for production of all documents that were before the Commission when it made its decision, including a legal opinion provided to the Commission by in-house counsel.

The motions judge, MacFarland J of the Divisional Court, ordered production and a three-judge panel of that court later upheld that decision. The Ontario Court of Appeal overturned the decision, holding instead that the opinion was privileged. The appeal was dismissed with reasons to follow.

· · ·

V. Issues

The sole issue in this appeal is whether the Court of Appeal erred in overturning the decision of the motions judge ordering production of the legal opinion. The question is whether a legal opinion, prepared for the Ontario Human Rights Commission by its in-house counsel, is protected by solicitor–client privilege in the same way as it is privileged if prepared by outside counsel retained for that purpose.

VI. Analysis

A. Solicitor–Client Privilege Defined

· · ·

As stated in *R v. McClure*, [2001] 1 SCR 445, 2001 SCC 14, at para. 2:

> Solicitor–client privilege describes the privilege that exists between a client and his or her lawyer. This privilege is fundamental to the justice system in Canada. The law is a complex web of interests, relationships and rules. The integrity of the administration of justice depends upon the unique role of the solicitor who provides legal advice to clients within this complex system. At the heart of this privilege lies the concept that people must be able to speak candidly with their lawyers and so enable their interests to be fully represented.

The privilege is jealously guarded and should only be set aside in the most unusual circumstances, such as a genuine risk of wrongful conviction.

In *Lavallee, Rackel & Heintz v. Canada (Attorney General)*, [2002] 3 SCR 209, 2002 SCC 61, this Court confirmed that the privilege must be nearly absolute and that exceptions to it will be rare. Speaking for the Court on this point, Arbour J reiterated what was stated in *McClure, supra*:

> *... solicitor–client privilege must be as close to absolute as possible to ensure public confidence and retain relevance. As such, it will only yield in certain clearly defined circumstances and does not involve a balancing of interests on a case-by-case basis.* [Emphasis in original.]

(Arbour J in *Lavallee, supra*, at para. 36, citing Major J in *McClure, supra*, at para. 35.)

Solicitor–client privilege has been held to arise when in-house government lawyers provide legal advice to their client, a government agency: see *R v. Campbell*, [1999] 1 SCR 565, at para. 49. In *Campbell*, the appellant police officers sought access to the legal advice provided to the RCMP by the Department of Justice and on which the RCMP claimed to have placed good faith reliance. In identifying solicitor–client privilege as it applies to government lawyers, Binnie J compared the function of public lawyers in government agencies with corporate in-house counsel. He explained that where government lawyers give legal advice to a "client department" that traditionally would engage solicitor–client privilege, and the privilege would apply. However, like corporate lawyers who also may give advice in an executive or non-legal capacity, where government lawyers give policy advice outside the realm of their legal responsibilities, such advice is not protected by the privilege.

Owing to the nature of the work of in-house counsel, often having both legal and non-legal responsibilities, each situation must be assessed on a case-by-case basis to determine if the circumstances were such that the privilege arose. Whether or not the privilege will attach depends on the nature of the relationship, the subject matter of the advice, and the circumstances in which it is sought and rendered: *Campbell, supra*, at para. 50.

Where solicitor–client privilege is found, it applies to a broad range of communications between lawyer and client as outlined above. It will apply with equal force in the context of advice given to an administrative board by in-house counsel as it does to advice given in the realm of private law. If an in-house lawyer is conveying advice that would be characterized as privileged, the fact that he or she is "in-house" does not remove the privilege, or change its nature.

. . .

C. Application to the Case at Bar

As stated, the communication between the Commission and its in-house counsel was protected by solicitor–client privilege.

The opinion provided to the Commission by staff counsel was a *legal opinion*. It was provided to the Commission by in-house or "staff" counsel to be considered or not considered at their discretion. It is a communication that falls within the class of communications protected by solicitor–client privilege. The fact that it was provided by in-house counsel does not alter the nature of the communication or the privilege.

There is no applicable exception that can remove the communication from the privileged class. ...

. . .

Procedural fairness does not require the disclosure of a privileged legal opinion. Procedural fairness is required both in the trial process and in the administrative law context. In neither area does it affect solicitor–client privilege; both may coexist without being at the expense of the other. In addition, the appellant was aware of the case to be met without production of the legal opinion. The concept of fairness permeates all aspects of the justice system, and important to it is the principle of solicitor–client privilege.

Section 10 of the *Judicial Review Procedure Act*, RSO 1990, c. J.1, provides:

> 10. When notice of an application for judicial review of a decision made in the exercise or purported exercise of a statutory power of decision has been served on the person making the decision, such person shall forthwith file in the court for use on the application the record of the proceedings in which the decision was made.

Legislation purporting to limit or deny solicitor–client privilege will be interpreted restrictively: see *Lavallee, supra*, at para. 18. Solicitor–client privilege cannot be abrogated by inference. While administrative boards have the delegated authority to determine their own procedure, the exercise of that authority must be in accordance with natural justice and the common law.

Where the legislature has mandated that the record must be provided in whole to the parties in respect of a proceeding within its legislative competence and it specifies that the "whole of the record" includes opinions provided to the administrative board, then privilege will not arise as there is no expectation of confidentiality. Beyond that, whether solicitor–client privilege can be violated by the express intention of the legislature is a controversial matter that does not arise in this appeal.

Section 10 of the *Judicial Review Procedure Act*, in any event, does not clearly or unequivocally express an intention to abrogate solicitor–client privilege, nor does it stipulate that the "record" includes legal opinions. As such, "record of the proceedings" should not be read to include privileged communications from Commission counsel to the Commission.

VII. Disposition

The communication between the Ontario Human Rights Commission and its in-house counsel is protected by solicitor–client privilege. It was a communication from a professional legal advisor, the Commission's in-house counsel, in her capacity as such, made in confidence to her client, the Commission. Accordingly, this appeal is dismissed and the decision of the Ontario Court of Appeal is confirmed.

NOTES AND QUESTIONS

1. In *Canada (Privacy Commissioner) v. Blood Tribe Department of Health*, 2008 SCC 44, a dismissed employee filed a complaint with the privacy commissioner to gain access to her personal file from her former employer. The employer provided the commissioner with almost all of the records, but claimed that the remainder were covered by solicitor-and-client privilege. The commissioner subsequently ordered production of the privileged records, relying on her power in s. 12 of the *Personal Information Protection and Electronic Documents Act* (PIPEDA) to compel the production of any records "in the same manner and to the same extent as a superior court of record" and to "receive and accept any evidence and other information ... whether or not it is or would be admissible in a court of law." The Supreme Court of Canada rejected her argument, holding the solicitor-and-client privilege "cannot be abrogated by inference," and that "open-textured language governing production of documents will be read *not* to include solicitor–client documents." As a result, it was held that s. 12 of PIPEDA did not grant the commissioner power to review the documents because it lacked the "clear and explicit language" required to abrogate the solicitor-and-client privilege.

2. A challenge to a claim of privilege obviously requires a response and the decision maker must look at the documents to assess the validity of the claim. In *Foster Wheeler*, above, counsel argued that the adjudicator should not be able to look at privileged material in assessing the validity of the privilege claim. The Supreme Court of Canada rejected that argument in gentle but unambiguous language (at para. 47):

> The City's attitude is without doubt motivated by a cautious tactical strategy which seeks to avoid allowing the trial judge to be influenced by the content of documents the City alleges are inadmissible. These concerns, while common, are unjustified. We must remember that every day judges must rule on the admissibility of evidence that they must inspect or hear before excluding, and that this duty is an indispensable part of their role in the conduct of civil or criminal trials. Judges understand that they must disregard any evidence that they deem inadmissible and base their judgments solely on the evidence entered into the court record. Seen in this light, the appellant's argument would have us ask judges not to carry out one of their core functions in the consideration of evidence, based on the unverified and unverifiable statement of the appellant's counsel. I would very much like to take the appellant's counsel at their word and trust in their oath of office, but the courts do not even have at their disposal a sworn statement identifying the documents in dispute and giving a summary of the nature of their content and of the reasons for objecting to their production. In these circumstances, the City is asking the courts to abdicate their traditional role of ruling on the admissibility and relevance of evidence that is always accorded them, with certain exceptions, under the applicable law of evidence in Canada. The fate of these objections cannot be decided on the mere basis of one party's unilateral declaration. The judge must carry out the function of verifying these documents, as the Court of Appeal rightly decided (see *Champagne v. Scotia McLeod Inc.*, [1992] RDJ 247 (CA); *Lab Chrysotile Inc. v. Société Asbestos Ltée*, [1993] RDJ 641 (CA)). After examining the documents, the judge may rule on the admissibility of the request for access. It is also worth noting that the rules of practice in some provinces expressly recognizes this critical component of judges' duties (see rule 30.04(6), Ontario *Rules of Civil Procedure*, RRO 1990, Reg. 194; rule 31.04(4), *New Brunswick Rules of Court*).

In *Blood Tribe*, above, the Supreme Court of Canada further opined the privacy commissioner is an "administrative investigator not an adjudicator" (at para. 20). It held the court's power to review a privileged document in order to determine a disputed claim for privilege was derived from its power to adjudicate disputed claims over legal rights. As a result, administrative investigators, like the privacy commissioner in that case, were held not to have the power to review privileged documents.

3. *Blood Tribe* affirmed an earlier decision of the Supreme Court of Canada in *Foster Wheeler* [2004] 1 SCR 456, which held that an assertion of solicitor-and-client privilege in an affidavit regarding information between a client and lawyer gives rise to a rebuttable "presumption of fact" that the shared information is "*prima facie* confidential in nature" (*Blood Tribe*, para. 16). That presumption is accurate for most but not all communications between a lawyer and a client. Not everything a lawyer does for a client is actually legal in nature. The trick is figuring out how to tell, in the context of discovery, what is in and what is out. In *Foster Wheeler* the court articulated an approach to dealing with the claim to privilege in situations where the solicitor and client's relationship is more complicated than the traditional one (at paras. 37-38 and 40-42):

However, as important as professional secrecy may be, it does have its limits. Not every aspect of relations between a lawyer and a client is necessarily confidential. The exigencies of other values and concern for competing interests may sometimes necessitate the disclosure of confidential information, as provided for under s. 9 of the *Quebec Charter* (see *Smith v. Jones*, [1999] 1 SCR 455, at para. 51; *R v. McClure*, [2001] 1 SCR 445, 2001 SCC 14, at para. 34, per Major J).

This appeal does not require us to examine potential conflicts between the obligation of confidentiality and the exercise of competing rights. Apart from the collateral issue of waiver, the issues in dispute here are limited to identifying the content of the obligation of confidentiality and, above all, determining the methodology for defining and then giving effect to the immunity from judicial disclosure. Even with these limits, the issue remains a sensitive and complex one in practice. It would be inaccurate to reduce the content of the obligation of confidentiality to opinions, advice or counsel given by lawyers to their clients. While this is, on many occasions, the main goal in creating a professional relationship with a lawyer, it is often the case that this relationship can also entail some highly diverse activities, such as representing clients before various tribunals or administrative bodies, negotiating or drawing up contracts, preparing reports, filling out various forms and having discussions with members of governing bodies of public entities or private corporations. In the course of carrying out these mandates, lawyers receive and send out a wide range of information. Some of these activities, such as the filing of pleadings or representing a client in court, pose few difficulties because of their public nature. However, when the professional relationship arises out of a complex and prolonged mandate, as in the case at bar, the limits of the scope of application of the obligation of confidentiality can sometimes only be arrived at after the court has taken a close look at the relationship between the parties, including the nature and context of the professional services rendered.

It is unrealistic to expect that we could set absolutely clear and simple rules and tests that would leave trial courts with no margin of uncertainty or individual discretion in such matters. Solutions will vary and must be tailored to the circumstances of a case. In the case of an individual professional act, the person claiming professional secrecy would without doubt need only simple or summary evidence to show the confidentiality of the information sought and his or her right to immunity from disclosure. The burden of proof can thus be placed on the professional without compromising the exercise and integrity of the institution.

In the case of complicated and prolonged mandates, the obligation of justifying each case as one where confidentiality and, by extension, immunity from judicial disclosure apply is poorly adapted to the nature of professional relationships and the safeguards required to maintain secrecy in an effective manner. ...

In such cases, a different method would be preferable. It would be enough to have the party invoking professional secrecy establish that a general mandate had been given to a lawyer for the purpose of obtaining a range of services generally expected of a lawyer in his or her professional capacity. At this stage, there would be a presumption of fact, albeit a rebuttable one, to the effect that all communications between client and lawyer and the information they shared would be considered *prima facie* confidential in nature. Although the case concerned a different field of law, namely criminal procedure, this Court recommended an analogous method in the initial steps of the examination of difficulties arising out of potential conflicts between solicitor–client privilege in the common law and the need to protect the presumption of innocence (*McClure*, *supra*, at paras. 46-51). The opposing party would then have to give a specific indication of the nature of the information sought and show that it is subject neither to the obligation of confidentiality nor to immunity from disclosure, or that this is a case where the law authorizes disclosure notwithstanding professional secrecy. This method would have procedural consequences. The opposing party would be obliged to ask precise and limited questions about the information sought. This sort of question would better take into account the sensitive nature of any line of questioning regarding professional relationships between clients and lawyers and the need to minimize violations of professional secrecy. This would prevent "fishing expeditions" in which lawyers, through the files they handle and reports they prepare for their clients, are used as a source of information for building cases against their own clients. One would also hope that every effort would first be made to obtain the information from available sources other than lawyers. A sound judicial policy, mindful of the social importance of lawyers' professional secrecy and the need to protect it, should certainly not attempt to facilitate this sort of questioning, but rather restrain it as much as possible.

D. Scope of Solicitor-and-Client Privilege: Corporate Clients and Government

When the client is a corporation or the government, it is important to determine to *whom* the privilege applies. Excerpts from the Supreme Court of Canada in *R v. Campbell*—in which the government is the client—and *Ontario (Ministry of Environment) v. McCarthy Tétrault*—in which a corporation is the client—serve to illustrate how courts decide whether privilege attaches. In Sopinka, Lederman, and Bryant, *The Law of Evidence in Canada*, 3rd ed. (Toronto: LexisNexis, 2009), Alan W. Bryant, Sidney N. Lederman, and Michelle K. Fuerst introduce the issue by comparing Canada with the United States with respect to corporate clients. The contrast is illuminating: Canadian law is much simpler to both understand and apply. They explain (at 950-51) (internal citations omitted):

§14.108 Canadian courts have never been troubled with the question of identifying which individuals in the corporation are the client for the purpose of determining whose communications are protected by solicitor–client privilege. On the other hand, there has been considerable jurisprudence in the United States on this subject. At one time, only that small group of individuals who could be in a position to control or even to take a substantial part in a decision about any action which the corporation may take upon the advice of attorneys would have the protection of the privilege. Another test that gained some favour in the US was known as the "subject-matter test," which recognized that an employee outside of the control group would have his or her communications protected by legal privilege only if the communication was at the direction of his or her superiors and the subject-matter for which legal advice was sought fell within the performance by the employee of the duties of his or her employment. The US Supreme Court reviewed the issue of corporate privilege in *Upjohn v. United States* and rejected the control group test. It stressed that it was essential for counsel to be able to communicate with the lower levels of the company without fear of disclosure. Chief Justice Burger, in a separate judgment, put forth a test which has similar hallmarks to the subject-matter test, in that the communication of the employee must concern a matter within the scope of his or her employment and must be made at the bidding of a superior for the purpose of obtaining legal advice.

§14.109 In Canada, there has been broad protection for confidential communications emanating from an employee, regardless of the level of his or her position in the corporate hierarchy, provided the objective was to obtain legal advice. Moreover, as long as the statement was made generally in the course of his or her employment, no specific inquiry needed to be made of the subject-matter to ensure that it fell squarely within the scope of his or her duties. For the most part, the issue has been treated by Canadian courts as one coming within the agency theory of privilege; that is, any employee can be engaged by the corporate client to pass on information to solicitors for the purpose of receiving legal advice.

Ontario (Ministry of Environment) v. McCarthy Tétrault
(1992), 9 CELR (NS) 12 (Ont. Prov. Div.)

MacDONALD PROV. DIV. J: This is a ruling under s. 160(8) of the *Provincial Offences Act,* RSO 1990, c. P.33 with respect to whether a claim of solicitor–client privilege should be sustained in respect of a number of documents seized pursuant to a search warrant issued under s. 158(1) of the Act. Under the authority of the warrant, the documents were seized from the law firm of McCarthy Tétrault on April 14, 1992. In accordance with the provisions of s. 160(1) and (2) of the Act, the investigators who conducted the search did not examine or make copies of any documents, but rather permitted them to be placed in a sealed envelope which has been filed, unopened, with the clerk of this court. ...

Neil Rickey is an investigator with the Ontario Ministry of the Environment and the informant with respect to the search warrant which was issued in this case. The investigation which he has been conducting concerns alleged spills of wastes at the Lafarge Canada Inc. cement plant at Bath, Ontario. Donald Stafford is the Environmental and Process Quality Manager for Lafarge at the Bath facility. The law firm of McCarthy Tétrault was at all material times retained by Lafarge Canada Inc. to provide legal advice. The solicitor at McCarthy Tétrault who is responsible for advising Lafarge Canada Inc. with respect to environmental law matters is Douglas Thompson. The applicants— Lafarge Canada Inc., Donald Stafford, and McCarthy Tétrault—assert that the documents in issue are protected from seizure by solicitor–client privilege. That claim arises in the following circumstances.

On July 29 and 30, 1991, Mr. Thompson attended a meeting at the Bath facility. Mr. Stafford was present at the meeting, as was the Environmental Director for Lafarge Canada's American parent, and certain other senior managers of the Lafarge group of companies. According to the affidavit which Mr. Thompson filed in support of this application, "the purpose of the meeting was to receive confidential information and provide legal advice concerning the compliance of the Bath facility with applicable environmental statutes, regulations and policies." Mr. Thompson further deposed that during the course of the meeting confidential discussions also took place regarding a potential prosecution in relation to a coal storage settling pond at the Bath facility. The only notes of the meeting were taken by Thompson. He deposed "that the documents for which Lafarge claims privilege are notes and memoranda prepared by me of confidential communications between me and my client, and confidential communications from my client, which were prepared for the purpose of receiving information and providing or recording the provision of ... legal advice" in relation to the facility's compliance with the relevant legal requirements.

Mr. Thompson was cross-examined by Crown counsel on the assertions contained in his affidavit. He was confronted with a reminder notice, circulated by one of the participants prior to the July 29 and 30 meeting, which referred to the meeting as an "environmental audit," and which described Thompson's role as "serving as the recorder and keeper of the information developed." Mr. Thompson firmly insisted that regardless of what was said in that notice, the purpose of the meeting and the role he played was as described in his affidavit.

The claim of privilege made by the applicants is resisted by the Crown on the basis that while Mr. Thompson is a solicitor, and Lafarge Canada Inc. is his client, the purpose of the meeting on July 29 and 30 was not to obtain Mr. Thompson's "legal" advice, and any documents generated for use at this meeting or developed as a result of the meeting were not intended to be confidential. ...

The assertions made by Mr. Thompson in his affidavit and viva voce on this application constitute sworn evidence that all of the circumstances required to establish a solicitor–client privilege were present in relation to the communications between Mr. Thompson and his client concerning the meeting at the Bath facility. As stated above, the position of the Crown, advanced with force and ability by Mr. Berger, is that on the whole of the evidence it has not been shown either that the communications between Mr. Thompson and his client were for the purpose of obtaining legal advice or that they were intended to be confidential.

Underlying the specific dispute in this case concerning the communications between Mr. Thompson and his client is a wider controversy within the field of environmental law, namely the evidentiary status of information and documents generated as part of an exercise known as an "environmental audit." In his cross-examination of Mr. Thompson, Mr. Berger sought to characterize the meeting at Bath as such an exercise; Mr. Thompson vigilantly resisted those efforts; both were plainly alert to the implications which might be argued to flow from classifying the meeting in that way.

In a document entitled *Canadian Environmental Protection Act: Enforcement and Compliance Policy* (Minister of Supply and Services, May 1988), Cat. No. En 40-356/1988E), at p. 29, Environment Canada describes environmental audits as follows:

> Environmental audits are internal evaluations by companies and government agencies to verify their compliance with legal requirements as well as their own internal policies and standards. They are conducted by companies, government agencies and others on a voluntary basis, and are carried out by either outside consultants or employees of the company or facility from outside the work unit being audited. Audits can identify compliance problems, weaknesses in management systems, or areas of risk. The findings are documented in a written report.

The elasticity of the term "environmental audit" is well recognized. In "Confidentiality in Environmental Auditing," JELP 1, Paul Edwards states, at pp. 5-6:

> The objectives or purposes of an environmental audit will vary widely. In fundamental terms, the purposes of most audits will be those described by Environment Canada; that is,

to verify compliance with legal requirements and with the organization's own policies and standards. Some audits, however, will be for the sole purpose of assessing legislative compliance. Others may be designed to assist facility management in improving their performance, to assess risks, or to identify potential cost savings. ...

The term "environmental audit" is not a term of art, and somewhat loosely describes a spectrum of activities. Some corporations deliberately avoid using the term audit; others employ it deliberately in order to establish credibility with outside agencies. Other terms that are sometimes used to describe similar activities include: environmental site assessment, evaluation, survey and review.

With respect to the confidentiality of an audit report, Mr. Edwards states, at p. 20:

... [I]n order for the [solicitor–client] privilege to attach, the report must have been created for the purpose of obtaining legal advice or assistance. Whether or not the corporation takes the precaution of asking the consultant to address the report, and all other communications, to the lawyer, can it truly be said that most environmental audits are commissioned for the purpose of seeking legal advice? Even where a legal opinion is given based on the audit report, is not the audit report the document that is of the greatest interest to the client? *There may very well be cases in which the legal opinion really is the client's ultimate objective in having the environmental audit commissioned.* The "audit" in such a case, however, is a substantially different, and less useful, exercise than what is usually thought of an environmental audit. [Emphasis added.]

It is clear that characterizing an exercise as an environmental audit does not, in itself, answer the question of whether the information communicated to a solicitor as part of the exercise is privileged. Thus, the relevant inquiry in the case at bar is not whether the meeting on July 29 and 30 at the Bath facility should or should not be termed an environmental audit, but rather whether the exercise that was conducted at that meeting was truly conducted for the bona fide purpose of obtaining legal advice from Mr. Thompson.

The vigour with which the claim of privilege was challenged in this case was fuelled, at least in part, by a general concern that corporations wishing to conceal their environmental sins from the eyes of regulatory agencies might attempt to adorn environmental audits with the badges of solicitor–client communications in order to assert, disingenuously, that the purpose of the exercise was to obtain legal advice. The concern is not unreasonable. Edwards, supra, notes, at p. 21, that "it is not inconceivable that a court may in certain circumstances be made a little wary of a claim to privilege specifically because of the number of published writings which exhort corporations to have their environmental audits addressed to a lawyer for the express purpose of structuring a claim to privilege."

It is only reasonable that courts be cautious in assessing claims of privilege arising out of environmental self-assessments, however described. The concern must be placed in context, however. Assessing the bona fides of transactions, and the candour and credibility of those who testify about them, is not a novel exercise for the courts. A claim of privilege will not be established by merely asserting it: *R v. Morra* [(1991), 5 OR (3d) 255 (Gen. Div.)]. There must be evidence establishing all the required elements before the claim can be sustained. In most cases, that evidence will consist of the testimony of the solicitor that he or she believes that those elements exist in relation to the communications or documents in issue. The solicitor would be required to swear to a belief that a substantial and bona fide purpose of the communication was to obtain legal advice. Obviously, if the solicitor were aware that the obtaining of legal advice was a mere convenience to attract the protection of the privilege, he or she could not truthfully make that assertion. There is a very high duty on a solicitor who gives evidence to establish a claim of privilege to frankly disclose the existence of any other purpose for which, to the solicitor's knowledge, the communication was made, so that the court can fairly assess the claim. Further, a solicitor's evidence is not determinative of whether a claim of privilege should be sustained. The court is entitled to assess the credibility of that evidence in the same manner as any other evidence. Where the claim is made with respect to documents, as in the case at bar, the court will have the very important advantage of being able to examine the material for which privilege is claimed in order to form an independent opinion as to whether it supports the evidence of the solicitor. These are important practical safeguards, and, in light of them, a court is no more likely to be duped by a claim of privilege in relation to environmental audits than with respect to any other matter.

With respect to the particular circumstances of the case at bar, Mr. Berger submitted that the meeting at the Bath facility was an environmental audit, conducted for internal corporate purposes rather than an assessment of Lafarge's compliance with the law. He submitted that the information developed at such an audit would necessarily be intended to be shared widely, not only within the company but, if the company's written environmental policy is to be taken seriously, with persons outside of the company. He characterized Mr. Thompson's evidence as an ex post facto recasting of the purpose of the meeting in order to shelter the company behind a solicitor–client privilege.

There is little in the record before me to support those submissions. The strongest circumstance in the Crown's favour is the reminder notice sent in advance of the meeting to the apparent participants, including Mr. Thompson. It described the meeting as an environmental audit and Thompson's role as "the keeper and recorder of the information developed," and it made no reference to the obtaining of a legal opinion. However, Mr. Thompson was confronted with that document in cross-examination, and he was adamant that it did not reflect accurately the role which it was clearly understood that he was to play at the meeting. He testified that immediately following the meeting he prepared a written opinion which was circulated only to those who had attended. He testified that this document was contained in the sealed packet, available for the court's perusal.

Mr. Thompson was a credible witness. In addition, I have now had the opportunity of reviewing the document he prepared for his client as well as the related documents which were placed in the sealed envelope. In my opinion, they confirm Mr. Thompson's evidence as to the purpose of the meeting and his role in it. I accept his evidence. Whatever may be the legitimate general concerns of regulatory agencies with respect to the role of solicitors in environmental audits, there is no reason, on the facts of this case, not to take Mr. Thompson's evidence at face value.

As a practical matter, the rejection of the Crown's submission that the purpose of the meeting with Mr. Thompson was other than to obtain legal advice disposes of the Crown's related submission that the communications were not intended to be confidential. I find, based on the affidavit and viva voce evidence of Mr. Thompson that they were so intended. ...

For the foregoing reasons, I find that the claim of solicitor–client privilege, which has been made in relation to documents seized from the law firm of McCarthy Tétrault on April 14, 1992, has been established, and the claim is accordingly sustained.

In order to preserve the confidentiality of the documents while at the same time preserving the status quo pending any appeal from this ruling, I order that the documents remain sealed and in the possession of the clerk of this court pending further order of this court, or any other court having jurisdiction over these proceedings, on application brought by any of the parties.

Application allowed.

The next case affords an example of the claim of solicitor-and-client privilege for advice given between government departments—here, the Department of Justice and the Royal Canadian Mounted Police with respect to the likely constitutional validity of an undercover police operation.

R v. Campbell
[1999] 1 SCR 565

[As the result of an RCMP "reverse sting operation," the appellants were charged with conspiracy to traffic in cannabis resin and conspiracy to possess cannabis resin for that purpose. They were found guilty on both counts at trial. Before sentencing, the trial judge heard a motion from the appellants for a stay of any further steps in the proceeding. As part of their case for a stay, the appellants sought access to the legal advice provided to the police by the Department of Justice on which the police claimed to have relied in good faith. The Crown claimed that the legal advice was subject to solicitor-and-client privilege. Both lower courts denied the appellants access to the legal advice. On appeal to the Supreme Court of Canada, two issues with respect to the question of privilege were considered: (1) the solicitor-and-client privilege invoked by the RCMP, and (2) pre-trial disclosure of solicitor-and-client communications to which privilege had been waived. The excerpt below addresses the first question. The court's discussion of the second question is in the following section on waiver of privilege.]

BINNIE J: ... The solicitor–client privilege is based on the functional needs of the administration of justice. The legal system, complicated as it is, calls for professional expertise. Access to justice is compromised where legal advice is unavailable. It is of great importance, therefore, that the RCMP be able to obtain professional legal advice in connection with criminal investigations without the chilling effect of potential disclosure of their confidences in subsequent proceedings. ...

Cpl. Reynolds' consultation with Mr. Leising of the Department of Justice falls squarely within this functional definition, and the fact that Mr. Leising works for an "in-house" government legal service does not affect the creation or character of the privilege.

It is, of course, not everything done by a government (or other) lawyer that attracts solicitor–client privilege. While some of what government lawyers do is indistinguishable from the work of private practitioners, they may and frequently do have multiple responsibilities including, for example, participation in various operating committees of their respective departments. Government lawyers who have spent years with a particular client department may be called upon to offer policy advice that has nothing to do with their legal training or expertise, but draws on departmental know-how. Advice given by lawyers on matters outside the solicitor–client relationship is not protected. A comparable range of functions is exhibited by salaried corporate counsel employed by business organizations. Solicitor–client communications by corporate employees with in-house counsel enjoy the privilege, although (as in government) the corporate context creates special problems: see, for example, the in-house inquiry into "questionable payments" to foreign governments at issue in *Upjohn Co. v. United States*, 449 US 383 (1981), *per* Rehnquist J (as he then was), at pp. 394-95. In private practice some lawyers are valued as much (or more) for raw business sense as for legal acumen. No solicitor–client privilege attaches to advice on purely business matters even where it is provided by a lawyer. ...

Whether or not solicitor–client privilege attaches in any of these situations depends on the nature of the relationship, the subject matter of the advice and the circumstances in which it is sought and rendered. One thing is clear: the fact that Mr. Leising is a salaried employee did not prevent the formation of a solicitor–client relationship and the attendant duties, responsibilities and privileges. ...

In support of their assertion that no privilege exists in respect of communications between the police and Crown counsel in the course of a criminal investigation, the appellants rely upon *Re Girouard and the Queen* (1982), 68 CCC (2d) 261 (SCBC), and *R v. Ladouceur*, [1992] BCJ No. 2854 (QL) (SC). Girouard concerned the admissibility of the details of a conversation between Crown counsel and a police officer who was to be a Crown witness in the hallway outside the courtroom on the day of a preliminary inquiry. The conversation was overheard by defence counsel. The BC Supreme Court held, *inter alia*, that because the conversation had been overheard, any privilege that might have existed had been waived.

Girouard advocates the proposition that communications as to the question of identification between a police officer who is to be a Crown witness and Crown counsel are not protected by solicitor–client privilege. This seems to be based on the Court's view that because a police officer was not an agent of the Attorney General, no solicitor–client relationship could exist between a Crown counsel and a police officer. I disagree with this analysis. The existence of an agency relationship is not essential to the creation of solicitor–client privilege. In seeking advice from a lawyer about the exercise of his original authority that "cannot be exercised on the responsibility of any person but himself" [citation omitted], Cpl. Reynolds satisfied the conditions precedent "to the existence of the right of the lawyer's client to confidentiality" [citation omitted]. Subject to what is said below, when Mr. Leising of the Department of Justice initially advised Cpl. Reynolds about the legality of a reverse sting operation, these communications were protected by solicitor–client privilege.

NOTE

Misuse of privilege. Geoffrey Hazard ("An Historical Perspective on the Attorney–Client Privilege" (1978), 66 *California Law Review* 1061, at 1062) has suggested that solicitor-and-client privilege is often a device for covering up "legally dubious or dirty business." It now appears that the tobacco industry systematically used the device of routing third-party communications, including marketing and other research, through its lawyers in an attempt to attract privilege. See "Release of Tobacco Documents Ordered—Evidence Shows Companies Used Lawyers To Hide Data, State Judge Says," *The Wall Street Journal*, March 9, 1998, reporting that tobacco companies were ordered to produce 39,000 internal documents for which privilege had been claimed. Included were documents concerning research about nicotine addiction and brand preferences of children. Judge Kenneth Fitzpatrick of the Minnesota District Court said "the industry's lawyers misused the attorney–client privilege and deliberately misrepresented documents to hide evidence of crime and fraud from Minnesota's lawyers" in an action by the state to recover health care costs associated with smoking. One example cited by the judge was a study reviewing "apparently problematic research" conducted by "an outside marketing firm for a Canadian affiliate [of BAT Industries plc], Imperial Tobacco Co. The research, according to the review, contained 'multiple references to how very young smokers at first believe they cannot become addicted, only to discover later, to their regret, that they are.'" See also *Minnesota v. Philip Morris Inc.*, 1998 WL 257214 (Minn. Dist. Ct., March 7, 1998) and 1998 WL 154543 (Minn. Sup. Ct., March 27, 1998).

E. Limits on Solicitor-and-Client Privilege: Waiver

We have already noted that privilege belongs to the client, not the lawyer. Clients who choose to disclose information are said to have "waived" the privilege. *Campbell*, reproduced next on this point, is an example. Sopinka, Lederman, and Bryant, *The Law of Evidence in Canada*, 3rd ed., above, offer a concise account of the law on voluntary waiver (at 957-59) (internal citations omitted):

§14.121 It was once thought that certain requirements should be established in order for waiver of the privilege to be established; for example, the holder of the privilege must possess knowledge of the existence of the privilege which he or she is forgoing, have a clear intention of waiving the exercise of his or her right of privilege, and a complete awareness of the result. But, as will be pointed out, other considerations unique to the adversarial system, such as fairness to the opposite party and consistency of positions, have overtaken these factors.

§14.122 An obvious scenario of waiver is if the holder of the privilege makes a voluntary disclosure or consents to disclosure of any material part of a communication. Thus, the Court in *Frind v. Sheppard* [[1940] OWN 135 (Master)] held that a client had waived the privilege which attached to letters passing between himself and his solicitor because they had been read into the record in a previous proceeding. In other cases, waiver was said to have taken place when documents over which privilege was claimed had been disclosed in proceedings in another jurisdiction or were referred to in an Affidavit of Documents and had been inspected. Similarly, if a client testifies on his or her own behalf and gives evidence of a professional, confidential communication, he or she will have waived the privilege shielding all of the communications relating to the particular subject-matter. Moreover, if the privilege is waived, then production of all documents relating to the acts contained in the communication will be ordered.

§14.123 A party may voluntarily waive solicitor–client privilege on a limited basis to a particular defined subject matter unless the selective disclosure would be misleading or would be taking unfair advantage.

§14.124 If the communication is elicited in cross-examination of the client, it seems that unless it can be shown that the witness was misled or did not comprehend what was being asked of him or her, the assertion of the communication would amount to a waiver. Of course, if the client merely testifies as a witness to the facts in issue, that will not constitute a waiver of privilege. Nor would solicitor–client privilege be lost by a party merely because his or her memory was refreshed from notes made by him or her for counsel in preparation for trial. ...

§14.125 Where a party makes privileged documents available to the police for a limited purpose, namely, to assist in the conduct of a criminal investigation and then a criminal trial, such disclosure cannot be construed as a waiver of its privilege to which the party was entitled in the civil action for which the documents had been created. In *British Coal Corp. v. Dennis Rye Ltd. (No. 2)*, [[1988] 3 All ER 816 (CA)] it was held that, as the party had a duty to assist in the conduct of the criminal case, it would be contrary to public policy to construe disclosure of documents as an express or implied waiver of the privilege which had been accorded the documents in the civil action. ...

§14.127 It has also been said that clear intention is not in all cases an important factor. In some circumstances, waiver may occur even in the absence of any intention to waive the privilege. There may also be waiver by implication only.

R v. Campbell
[1999] 1 SCR 565

[See facts above. The following excerpt deals with the issue of whether pre-trial disclosure of solicitor-and-client communications to which privilege had been claimed constituted a waiver.]

BINNIE J:

· · ·

Waiver of Solicitor–Client Privilege

The record is clear that the RCMP put in issue Cpl. Reynolds' good faith belief in the legality of the reverse sting, and asserted its reliance upon his consultations with the Department of Justice to buttress that position. The RCMP factum in the Ontario Court of Appeal has already been quoted in para. 46. In my view, the RCMP waived the right to shelter behind solicitor–client privilege the contents of the advice thus exposed and relied upon. I characterize the RCMP rather than Cpl. Reynolds as the client in these circumstances because even though he was exercising the duties of his public office as a police officer, Cpl. Reynolds was seeking the legal advice in the course of his RCMP employment. The identification of "the client" is a question of fact. There is no conceptual conflict between the individual responsibilities of the police officer and characterizing the "client" as the RCMP. Despite the existence of the *Royal Canadian Mounted Police Act* and related legislation, I believe the relationship among individual policemen engaged in criminal investigations is accurately set out in *Halsbury's Laws of England* (4th ed. 1981), vol. 36, at p. 107:

> The history of the police is the history of the office of constable and, notwithstanding that present day police forces are the creation of statute and that the police have numerous statutory powers and duties, in essence a police force is neither more nor less than a number of individual constables, whose status derives from the common law, organized together in the interests of efficiency.

If Cpl. Reynolds himself were characterized as the client, it could be said that sharing the contents of that advice with his fellow officers would have breached the confidentiality and waived the privilege, which would be absurd. At the same time, if the legal advice were intentionally disclosed outside the RCMP, even to a department or agency of the federal government, such disclosure might waive the confidentiality, depending on the usual rules governing disclosure to third parties by a client of communications from its solicitor.

It is convenient to recall at this point that at the time of the original disclosure motions, the position of the appellants was clear, i.e., disclose the communications or forswear reliance upon them. Notwithstanding this caution, the RCMP and their legal counsel chose to rely upon the communications to support their argument of good faith reliance. In doing so, the privilege was waived.

In *Rogers v. Bank of Montreal*, [1985] 4 WWR 508 (BCCA), the bank put a defaulting customer into receivership, and the customer sued both the bank and the receiver, who then launched third party proceedings at each other. The bank said it had relied on the receiver's advice in putting the customer into receivership. The receiver denied detrimental reliance on its advice, and wanted to know what other professional advice the bank had received at the relevant time. In particular, the receiver wanted to know what legal advice the bank had received from its own lawyers, MacKimmie Matthews. The bank claimed solicitor–client privilege over this correspondence. In rejecting the bank's claim of privilege, the court, *per* Hutcheon JA, stated as follows, at p. 513:

> The issue in this case is not the knowledge of the bank. *The issue is whether the bank was induced to take certain steps in reliance upon the advice from the receiver on legal matters.* To take one instance, the receiver, according to the bank, advised the bank that it was not necessary to allow Abacus [the plaintiff debtor] time for payment before the appointment of the receiver. A significant legal decision had been rendered some months earlier to the opposite of that advice. *The extent to which the bank had been advised about that decision, not merely of its result, is important* in the resolution of the issue whether the bank relied upon the advice of the receiver. [Emphasis added.]

The Court goes on to adopt the reasoning of the United States District Court for the District of Columbia in *United States v. Exxon Corp.*, 94 FRD 246 (1981) as follows, at pp. 248-49:

> Most courts considering the matter have concluded that a party waives the protection of the
> attorney–client privilege when he voluntarily injects into the suit the question of his state of
> mind. For example, in *Anderson v. Nixon*, 444 F Supp. 1195, 1200 (DDC 1978), Judge Gesell
> stated that as a general principle "a client waives his attorney–client privilege when he brings
> suit or raises an affirmative defense that makes his intent and knowledge of the law relevant."
>
>   • • •
>
> Thus, the only way to assess the validity of Exxon's affirmative defenses, voluntarily in-
> jected into this dispute, is to investigate attorney–client communications where Exxon's
> interpretation of various DOE policies and directives was established and where Exxon
> expressed its intentions regarding compliance with those policies and directives.

It appears the court in *Rogers* found that any privilege with respect to correspondence
with the bank's solicitors had been waived as necessarily inconsistent with its pleading of
reliance, even though the bank itself had not referred to, much less relied upon, the existence of advice from its own solicitors.

The present case presents a stronger argument for waiver than *Rogers*. The Crown led
evidence from Cpl. Reynolds about his knowledge of the law with respect to reverse sting
operations—he testified that he had read the Superior Court decision in [*R v. Lore* (February 26, 1991), Que. Sup. Ct. doc. no. 500-01-013926-891] and was of the view that the
operation in question was legal. But Cpl. Reynolds also testified, in answer to the appellants' counsel, that he sought out the opinion of Mr. Leising of the Department of Justice
to verify the correctness of his own understanding. The appellants' counsel recognized
that this alone was not enough to waive the privilege. Cpl. Reynolds was simply responding to questions crafted by the appellants, as he was required to do. Appellants' counsel
accepted that he had no right at that point to access the communications. His comment
to the judge was simply that "I certainly don't want to hear the argument that 'Oh well,
the police acted in good faith because they acted on legal advice.'" The critical point is
that the Court *did* hear that precise argument from the Crown at a later date. The RCMP
and its legal advisers were explicit in their factum in the Court of Appeal, where it was
argued that "regard *must* be had to the following considerations ... (f) The RCMP ...
consulted with the Department of Justice with regard to any problems of illegality" (emphasis added). We understand that the same position was advanced to the trial judge. As
Rogers, supra, shows, it is not always necessary for the client actually to disclose part of
the contents of the advice in order to waive privilege to the relevant communications of
which it forms a part. It was sufficient in this case for the RCMP to support its good faith
argument by undisclosed advice from legal counsel in circumstances where, as here, the
existence or non-existence of the asserted good faith depended on the content of that legal
advice. The clear implication sought to be conveyed to the court by the RCMP was that
Mr. Leising's advice had assured the RCMP that the proposed reverse sting was legal.

Cpl. Reynolds was not required to pledge his belief in the legality of the reverse sting
operation (comparable to the bank's putting in issue its belief in the correctness of the
advice it was obtaining from the receiver in *Rogers, supra*). Nor was it necessary for the
RCMP to plead the existence of Mr. Leising's legal opinion as a factor weighing against
the imposition of a stay of proceedings (which went beyond what was done in *Rogers*).
The RCMP and the Crown having done so, however, I do not think disclosure of the advice in question could fairly be withheld.

NOTES AND QUESTIONS

1. The decision in *Campbell* rests on a concept of fundamental fairness. In essence, the court held that a client cannot have his or her cake and eat it too. Do you think the resolution is adequately protective of the solicitor-and-client relationship? Do you think that it matters that Campbell faced criminal charges rather than a civil claim, or does the court's reasoning belie any significance attaching to that distinction?

2. Professor Garry D. Watson in "Solicitor–Client Privilege in Litigation: Current Developments and Future Trends" (Canadian Bar Association—Ontario: Continuing Legal Education, October 19, 1991) has suggested that the law may move more toward increasing disclosure where a legal advice issue is legitimated in play in litigation:

> It seems reasonably clear that the "fairness" test has emerged as the relevant principle for determining when solicitor and client privilege is waived by conduct in the course of the litigation. While the courts have not yet clearly embraced the view that the unilateral assertion of an issue by one party can lead to compulsory disclosure of the adverse Party's solicitor–client communications, do not be surprised if the law moves in this direction; ultimately, the fairness test may be interpreted as meaning that solicitor–client privilege is waived whenever the communications between the solicitor and the client are legitimately brought in issue in the action.

3. In *Foster Wheeler*, above, a waiver of confidentiality arose because of the presence of a third party. The court overturned the Quebec Court of Appeal on this point (at paras. 48-49):

> Before I conclude, despite the rejection of the City's objections, I believe it would still be useful to comment on one of the reasons given by the Court of Appeal for allowing the questions about the December 2, 1995 meeting of the SIGED. The Court of Appeal's conclusions on this point could affect the conduct of the parties' examinations on discovery, if not the evidence at trial. The Court ruled that the mere presence of a professional facilitator hired for the purpose of chairing that meeting implied a waiver of professional secrecy, given that a third party attended the meeting in question.
>
> This conclusion is incorrect, given the circumstances of this case. The meeting was held with a view to maintaining confidentiality. The intensity of the political conflict within the municipal body prevented the chair from carrying out his duties. To maintain order at the meeting in every aspect, including with respect to the reports to be tabled by public servants or lawyers, the Régie had hired an independent person to moderate the proceedings as if she were the Chair. The presence of this facilitator was not only helpful but necessary. Under these conditions, the facilitator's presence did not imply a waiver of professional secrecy (*Pfieffer et Pfieffer Inc. v. Javicoli*, [1994] RJQ 1 (CA), at pp. 6 and 8) The facilitator was a temporary participant in the organization and its deliberations, performing a function necessary for its effective operation. The meeting still took place in camera, with a view to maintaining the confidentiality that was so critical to the participants' discussions, despite the presence of opposing factions within the organization and divergent views on the desirability and the execution of the project in question. The nature of the meeting and the discussions remained the same. In these circumstances, we cannot infer from this procedure an implied waiver of professional secrecy with regard to communications made by the lawyers who took part in the meeting in the capacity of legal advisers of the SIGED and the Régie.

4. What are the ethical responsibilities of a lawyer with regard to asserting and fighting a claim for privilege? Does a lawyer have a duty to make every possible claim of privilege to protect his or her client's interest? Or does a lawyer have a responsibility not to assert specious claims of privilege?

5. *Inadvertent disclosure.* A recurring nightmare for lawyers is the one in which they inadvertently disclose privileged material. The traditional approach to such mistakes is harsh—privilege is lost. Occasionally, the disclosure by the client, or the solicitor, is totally inadvertent, without any intention of waiver, deliberate or implied. The communication may have come into a third party's possession by accident or by stealth. Is the manner by which disclosure occurred significant? Or is the mere loss of confidentiality, whether accidental or by design, sufficient to constitute a loss of the privilege? The traditional common law has said it does not matter. In either circumstance, the privilege is gone and the communication is admissible. Recent cases, however, reflect a more sensitive analysis of the circumstances in which disclosure occurred (see *Airst v. Airst*, (1998), 37 OR (3d) 654 (Gen. Div.), and *R v. Chapelstone Developments Inc.* (2004), 191 CCC (3d) 152 (NBCA)). The following decision from the Manitoba Court of Appeal is indicative of this trend.

Metcalfe v. Metcalfe
(2001), Man. R. (2d) 207, 2001 MBCA 35

HELPER JA: ... In the course of opposing the motion to set aside default judgment, the respondents, through their solicitors, requested copies of all relevant documents which would have been on the file of the appellant's previous solicitors, D'Arcy & Deacon. Certain letters dated April 23, 1996, and July 17, 1996, written by the appellant's former solicitor to him were produced with sentences blacked out as containing solicitor–client privileged communications. At the cross-examination of the appellant on his affidavit, the appellant, through his present solicitor, agreed that some sentences in the blacked-out portions of the correspondence could be read into the record as being relevant to the issues before the court. Subsequently, through inadvertence on the part of the appellant's solicitor, copies of those same letters were sent to the respondents' solicitor without any of the solicitor–client privileged portions being blacked out.

• • •

... [W]here there is an inadvertent disclosure of a document covered by solicitor–client privilege, and it is clear that there is no intention of waiver, the case law has generally upheld the privilege over the document itself. However, the more complicated issue involves the question of whether copies of the privileged documents can be used.

In England, the traditional common law took the view that although an inadvertent disclosure of privileged materials leading to the loss of confidentiality will not waive the privilege over the materials themselves, the privilege could not protect against the use of copies: *Calcraft v. Guest*, [1898] 1 QB 759 (CA). In that case, some documents which were prepared in contemplation of litigation and protected by solicitor–client privilege were accidentally found by the opposing party, copied, and returned. The opposing party wished to use the copies in appealing the trial court decision which had gone against it.

The Court of Appeal determined that although the originals were still privileged, the copies were admissible in evidence, regardless of how the originals had been obtained.

The traditional common law was tempered somewhat by the equitable remedy of injunction. In *Ashburton (Lord) v. Pape*, [1913] 2 Ch. 469 (CA), Pape was a bankrupt and Lord Ashburton a creditor. By trickery, Pape obtained letters which had been written by Lord Ashburton to his solicitor and were therefore privileged. Pape had the letters copied and proposed to use the letters in his bankruptcy proceedings. Lord Ashburton brought an action for an injunction to enjoin Pape's use of the letters or the copies, and the court, at first instance, enjoined Pape's use of the originals, but not the copies. The Court of Appeal extended the injunction to include the copies as well.

The difference between the two cases appears to rest mainly upon the occasion when a party seeks to prevent the use of a privileged document in the hands of the opposing party. If the party seeks to prevent the use of the privileged document at trial, *Calcraft* would apply and there would be no investigation into the means by which the document came into the opposing party's hands. The document would be admissible. If the party wishing to prevent the use of the privileged document seeks an injunction prior to trial, however, then *Ashburton* would apply since the means by which the document came into the opposing party's hands could be investigated. Under the latter proposition, a pre-trial injunction could be granted at the very least in those situations where the document had been acquired wrongfully by the opposing party. See also *The Law of Evidence in Canada* at pp. 764-66, para. 14.119.

The dichotomy in English law was refined in *Goddard v. Nationwide Building Society*, [1986] 3 All ER 264 (CA). May LJ commented at p. 270:

> … I think that [*Ashburton*] and *Calcraft v. Guest* are good authority for the following proposition. If a litigant has in his possession copies of documents to which legal professional privilege attaches, he may nevertheless use such copies as secondary evidence in his litigation: however, if he has not yet used the documents in that way, the mere fact that he intends to do so is no answer to a claim against him by the person in whom the privilege is vested for delivery up of the copies or to restrain him from disclosing or making any use of any information contained in them.

Nourse LJ agreed with this proposition at p. 271 and went on to say at p. 272:

> … [O]nce it is established that a case is governed by *Lord Ashburton v. Pape*, there is no discretion in the court to refuse to exercise the equitable jurisdiction according to its view of the materiality of the communication, the justice of admitting or excluding it or the like. The injunction is granted in aid of the privilege which, unless and until it is waived, is absolute.

Similar comments were made in *English and American Insurance Co. Ltd. v. Herbert Smith & Co.* (1987), 137 NLJ 148, and in *Guinness Peat Properties Ltd. v. Fitzroy Robinson Partnership (a firm)*, [1987] 2 All ER 716 (CA).

In *Derby & Co. Ltd. v. Weldon (No. 8)*, [1990] 3 All ER 762 (Ch. D and CA), 14 documents subject to litigation privilege were inadvertently turned over by the plaintiff's solicitor to the defendant's solicitor during discovery. When the mistake came to the attention of the plaintiff's solicitor, he asked for an injunction restraining the use of the documents. The motions judge held that the defendant's solicitor should have realized that an obvious mistake had occurred with respect to 11 of the documents, which were clearly privileged on their face, and granted an injunction with relation to these 11 documents. However, because the three remaining documents did not appear on their face to be privileged, an obvious mistake would not be apparent. Thus, the use of these three documents was not restrained. The Court of Appeal, however, was satisfied that in keeping the documents which counsel knew had been received by mistake, the solicitor should be restrained from using not only the 11 documents, but the three remaining documents, even though they were not obviously privileged on their face. This case thus settled the law to be that if a lawyer for one party inadvertently turned over privileged documents to the other party, the other party could be restrained from taking any advantage of the inadvertent disclosure if it was clear that an obvious mistake had been made. This position of the law was affirmed in *Pizzey v. Ford Motor Co.*, [1993] EWJ No. 1023 (CA).

The Canadian position does not generally adhere to the English position. In Canada, generally, an opposing party is restrained from using inadvertently released privileged materials whether the mistake was obvious or not. Many of the Canadian cases start with the principle that the privilege belongs to the client and that an inadvertent release does not constitute a true waiver of privilege. In Canada, the inadvertent disclosure of privileged materials will be restrained on the basis "of the proper administration of justice" or "in the interests of justice," not merely on the basis of whether the mistake would have been obvious to the opposing side. See *McPherson v. Inst. of Chartered Accountants of B.C.*, [1989] 2 WWR 649 (BCCA), and *Double-E, Inc. v. Positive Action Tool Western Ltd.*, [1989] 1 FC 163 (TD).

In *Bernardo v. Deathe*, [1991] OJ No. 862 (Gen. Div.), a copy of a letter which the defendant wrote to his lawyers was inadvertently included in some documents attached to a motions record, and the plaintiff's lawyer sought to cross-examine the defendant on that letter. Granger J considered the principle that the client must clearly and conscientiously intend to waive privilege before waiver results. He stated at p. 3, quoting the following passage of McEachern CJSC (as he then was) in *Somerville Belkin Industries Ltd. v. Brocklesby Transport, a division of Kingsway Freightlines Ltd.* (1985), 5 CPC (2d) 239 at 244 (BCSC):

> ... Although there are some bizarre cases where privilege seems to have been lost through inadvertence, the modern law seems to be that privilege may be waived in civil cases only by the client, in this case the insurer or plaintiff, and then only when it is waived deliberately and knowingly and not inadvertently: [authority omitted].
>
> I regard this as a salutary rule because the consequences of inadvertence should be minimized. ...

Granger J concluded that unless some prejudice would result by allowing the solicitor and client privilege to be maintained, the trial judge should exercise his or her discretion in favour of upholding the privilege.

. . .

Thus, on the basis of *Descôteaux*, where a third party (to the solicitor and the client) wishes to introduce a confidential communication between the solicitor and his client into evidence, and privilege has not been waived (i.e., it has been inadvertently released), the party wishing to introduce the evidence will have the onus of satisfying the judge that the evidence is important to the issues in the case and that no other form of evidence is available which would serve the same purpose.

The cases which have affirmed this rule and, in fact, broadened it include *Vancouver Hockey Club Ltd. v. National Hockey League* (1987), 44 DLR (4th) 139 (BCSC), *Royal Bank v. Lee* (1992), 9 CPC (3d) 199 (Alta. CA), *Syncrude Canada Ltd. v. Babcock & Wilcox Canada Ltd.* (1992), 10 CPC (3d) 388 (Alta. CA), and *Cineplex Odeon Corp. v. Canada (Attorney General)* (1994), 26 CPC (3d) 109 (Ont. Gen. Div.). All of the above-noted cases confirm the principle that solicitor–client privilege should not be lost by inadvertence.

The above-noted review leads to the following conclusion—that there are two questions to be addressed on the issue of waiver. One is whether there has been an express or implied waiver. It is clear from the jurisprudence that the inadvertent disclosure of privileged information is not to be considered a waiver because the client who owns the privilege has not intentionally decided to forego the privilege. The second question is whether the information can nonetheless be used by a third party who has seen the privileged information, which has lost its confidentiality. In this regard, the jurisprudence has held that a court should protect the confidentiality of communications between a solicitor and client as much as possible. In the situation where a third party wishes to introduce such communications into evidence, the court must be satisfied that what is being sought to be proved by the communications is important to the outcome of the case and that there is no reasonable alternative form of evidence that can serve the same purpose.

[In this particular case, the court found that the communications clearly were confidential and subject to solicitor-and-client privilege. There had been no waiver of privilege, express or implied, as the letters had nothing to do with Metcalfe's state of mind or any attempt by him to delay proceedings. The letters were therefore excluded from the record.]

F. Litigation Privilege/Lawyer's Brief Rule

Notwithstanding that the litigation privilege is applied every day in Canada—that is, every time a lawyer or articling student prepares an affidavit of documents—and the privilege is fundamental to our procedural law, clear and articulate statements of the rationale for the privilege were rare in Anglo-Canadian case law. Courts and academics debated the relationship between solicitor-and-client privilege and "litigation privilege" and whether they are two branches of the same tree. Many thought they were. Recent authoritative case law holds otherwise. It is now clear that litigation privilege is a "distinct conceptual animal" with a different scope, purpose and rationale than solicitor-and-client. We begin with the excerpts from each of the three opinions in the ground-breaking decision of the Ontario Court of Appeal in *General Accident Assurance Company v. Chrusz* (1999), 45 OR (3d) 321 and then turn to the comprehensive survey of the jurisprudence and statement of the litigation privilege doctrine in the recent Supreme Court of Canada decision, *Blank v. Canada (Minister of Justice)*, 2006 SCC 39.

General Accident Assurance Co. v. Chrusz
(1999), 180 DLR (4th) 241; 45 OR (3d) 321 (CA) (footnotes omitted)

[The appellant Chrusz and others owned a hotel. The hotel was destroyed in a fire on November 15, 1994. The respondents, General Accident Assurance Co. (G Co.), were the principal fire insurers. G Co. hired a claims adjuster to investigate. On November 16 the claims adjuster (Bourret) reported that he suspected arson. The respondents retained a lawyer (Eryon) and on December 1, 1995, directed the claims adjuster to report directly to him. Following delivery of proof of loss in January 1995, the respondent company made partial payments on the claim. On May 23, 1995, a former employee (Pilotte) of the appellants' hotel, who had been dismissed from his job in January 1995, delivered a videotape and a "float sheet and additional time sheets" from the hotel, and made a statement under oath that the appellant had fraudulently inflated the insurance claim. The respondent's lawyer made a copy of the videotape and had a transcript prepared of the former employee's statement. On June 2, 1995, the videotape and a copy of the transcript were given to the former employee on the condition that they should be kept confidential. The respondent company commenced an action in fraud against the appellant and others. The appellant filed a counterclaim against the respondent, the claims adjuster, and the former employee and his wife. In those proceedings the defendants (appellants) sought production of documents over which the plaintiffs (respondents) claimed privilege.

On a motion for production of the documents, Kurisko J ruled that: (1) all communications between G Co. and the lawyer were privileged; (2) communications between the claims adjuster and G Co. or the lawyer before May 23, 1995 were not privileged; (3) communications between the claims adjuster or G Co. and third parties before May 23, 1995 were not privileged; (4) communications between the claims adjuster and G Co. or the lawyer after May 23, 1995 were privileged; (5) privilege in the dismissed employee's statement had been waived; and (6) the videotape was not privileged. The Divisional Court set aside the order of Kurisko J and ordered that privilege applied to everything except the videotape. The Ontario Court of Appeal, Doherty JA dissenting in part, allowed Chrusz's appeal. The majority's opinion on litigation privilege was authored by Carthy JA and concurred in by Rosenberg JA with a reservation on the question of "ingathered" documents.]

CARTHY JA:

Analysis [of Litigation Privilege]

. . .

The origins and character of litigation privilege are well described by Sopinka, Lederman and Bryant in *The Law of Evidence in Canada* (Toronto: Butterworths, 1992), at p. 653:

> As the principle of solicitor–client privilege developed, the breadth of protection took on different dimensions. It expanded beyond communications passing between the client and solicitor and their respective agents, to encompass communications between the client or his solicitor and third parties if made for the solicitor's information for the purpose of pend-

ing or contemplated litigation. Although this extension was spawned out of the traditional solicitor–client privilege, the policy justification for it differed markedly from its progenitor. It had nothing to do with clients' freedom to consult privately and openly with their solicitors; rather, it was founded upon our adversary system of litigation by which counsel control fact-presentation before the Court and decide for themselves which evidence and by what manner of proof they will adduce facts to establish their claim or defence, without any obligation to make prior disclosure of the material acquired in preparation of the case. Accordingly, it is somewhat of a misnomer to characterize this aspect of privilege under the rubric (solicitor–client privilege), which has peculiar reference to the professional relationship between the two individuals.

[Carthy JA cited extensively from an article by R.J. Sharpe, "Claiming Privilege in the Discovery Process," in LSUC Special Lectures, *Law in Transition: Evidence* (Toronto: De Boo, 1984), 163, at 164-65, and then continued his reasons.]

It can be seen from these excerpts, quoted without their underlying authorities, that there is nothing sacrosanct about this form of privilege. It is not rooted, as is solicitor–client privilege, in the necessity of confidentiality in a relationship. It is a practicable means of assuring counsel what Sharpe calls a "zone of privacy" and what is termed in the United States, protection of the solicitor's work product: see *Hickman v. Taylor*, 329 US 495 (1946).

The "zone of privacy" is an attractive description but does not define the outer reaches of protection or the legitimate intrusion of discovery to assure a trial on all of the relevant facts. The modern trend is in the direction of complete discovery and there is no apparent reason to inhibit that trend so long as counsel is left with sufficient flexibility to adequately serve the litigation client. In effect, litigation privilege is the area of privacy left to a solicitor after the current demands of discoverability have been met. There is a tension between them to the extent that when discovery is widened, the reasonable requirements of counsel to conduct litigation must be recognized.

Our modern rules certainly have truncated what would previously have been protected from disclosure. Under rule 31.06(1) information cannot be refused on discovery on the ground that what is sought is evidence. Under rule 31.06(2) the names and addresses of witnesses must be disclosed. A judicial ruling in *Dionisopoulous v. Provias* (1990), 71 OR (2d) 547, 45 CPC (2d) 116 (HCJ) compelled a party to reveal the substance of the evidence of a witness, demonstrating that it is not just the *Rules of Civil Procedure* that may intrude upon traditional preserves.

Rule 31.06(3) provides for discovery of the name and address and the findings, conclusions and opinions of an expert, unless the party undertakes not to call that expert at trial. This is an example of the Rules Committee recognizing the right to proceed in privacy to obtain opinions and to maintain their confidentiality if found to be unfavourable. The tactical room for the advocate to manoeuvre is preserved while the interests of a fair trial and early settlement are supported. The actual production of an expert's report is required under rule 53.03(1). Similar treatment is given to medical reports under rules 33.04 and 33.06.

In a very real sense, litigation privilege is being defined by the rules as they are amended from time to time. Judicial decisions should be consonant with those changes and should be driven more by the modern realities of the conduct of litigation and perceptions of discoverability than by historic precedents born in a very different context.

One historic precedent that in my view does have modern application but that has been given a varied reception in Ontario is the House of Lords' decision in *Waugh v. British Railways Board*, [1979] 2 All ER 1169, [1979] 3 WLR 150 (HL). That case concerned a railway inspector's routine accident report. It was prepared in part to further railway safety and in part for submission to the railway's solicitor for liability purposes. It was held that while the document was prepared in part for the purpose of obtaining legal advice in anticipated litigation, that was not its dominant purpose and thus it must be produced.

After considering authorities that had protected documents from production where one purpose of preparation was anticipated litigation, Lord Wilberforce concluded at pp. 1173-74:

> It is clear that the due administration of justice strongly requires disclosure and production of this report: it was contemporary; it contained statements by witnesses on the spot; it would be not merely relevant evidence but almost certainly the best evidence as to the cause of the accident. If one accepts that this important public interest can be overridden in order that the defendant may properly prepare his case, how close must the connection be between the preparation of the document and the anticipation of litigation? On principle I would think that the purpose of preparing for litigation ought to be either the sole purpose or at least the dominant purpose of it. …

> ⋯

> … It appears to me that unless the purpose of submission to the legal adviser in view of litigation is at least the dominant purpose for which the relevant document was prepared, the reasons which require privilege to be extended to it cannot apply. On the other hand to hold that the purpose, as above, must be the sole purpose, would, apart from difficulties of proof, in my opinion, be too strict a requirement, and would confine the privilege too narrowly. …

[Carthy JA noted that the appellate courts in Nova Scotia, New Brunswick, British Columbia, and Alberta have adopted the dominant purpose test.]

In Ontario, the predominant view of judges and masters hearing motions is that the substantial purpose test should be applied. This, of course, provides a broader protection against discovery than the dominant purpose test and, in my view, runs against the grain of contemporary trends in discovery. These authorities find their root in a decision of this court in *Blackstone v. Mutual Life Insurance Co. of New York*, [1944] OR 328, [1944] 3 DLR 147 where Robertson CJO said at p. 333:

> I agree with the proposition of the defendant's counsel that it is not essential to the validity of the claim of privilege that the document for which privilege is claimed should have been written, prepared or obtained solely for the purpose of, or in connection with, litigation then pending or anticipated. It is sufficient if that was the substantial, or one of the substantial, purposes then in view.

The real issue in that case was whether the reports in question were prepared in anticipation of litigation. Gillanders JA wrote concurring reasons with no mention of "substantial purpose," and similarly there was none in the dissenting reasons of Kellock JA. Even as an obiter remark by Robertson CJO it is not presented as a reasoned conclusion based upon a consideration of the authorities and does not match substantial purpose against dominant purpose. I do not consider the quoted statement binding on this court and, based upon policy considerations of encouraging discovery, would join with the other appellate authorities in adopting the dominant purpose test.

An important element of the dominant purpose test is the requirement that the document in question be created for the purposes of litigation, actual or contemplated. Does it apply to a document that simply appears in the course of investigative work? The concept of creation has been applied by some courts to include copying of public documents and protection of the copies in the lawyer's brief. In *Hodgkinson v. Simms* (1988), 55 DLR (4th) 577, 33 BCLR (2d) 129 the majority of the British Columbia Court of Appeal applied the dominant purpose test but then, relying principally on *Lyell v. Kennedy* (1884), 27 Ch. D 1 (CA), held that copies of public documents gathered by a solicitor's office attained the protection of litigation privilege. In *Lyell v. Kennedy* the protected copies were of tombstone inscriptions and Cotton LJ upheld the privilege, stating at p. 26:

> In my opinion it is contrary to the principle on which the Court acts with regard to protection on the ground of professional privilege that we should make an order for their production; they were obtained for the purpose of his defence, and it would be to deprive a solicitor of the means afforded for enabling him to fully investigate a case for the purpose of instructing counsel if we required documents, although perhaps *publici juris* in themselves, to be produced, because the very fact of the solicitor having got copies of certain burial certificates and other records, and having made copies of the inscriptions on certain tombstones, and obtained photographs of certain houses, might shew what his view was as to the case of his client as regards the claim made against him.

[Carthy JA reviewed the majority reasons of McEachern CJBC, in *Hodgkinson, supra*, who took the position that where a lawyer is exercising legal knowledge, judgment and industry to assemble a collection of relevant copy documents in anticipation of litigation, then those documents are protected. Craig JA had dissented on this point and Carthy JA referred to the following statement by Craig JA in *Hodgkinson*, at 594:]

> I fail to comprehend how original documents which are not privileged (because they are not prepared with the dominant purpose of actual or anticipated litigation) can become privileged simply because counsel makes photostatic copies of the documents and puts them in his "brief." This is contrary to the intent of the rules and to the modern approach to this problem. If a document relates to a matter in question, it should be produced for inspection.

· · ·

I agree with the tenor of Craig JA's reasons. The majority reasons reflect a traditional view of the entitlement to privacy in a lawyer's investigative pursuits. It is an instinctive reflex of any litigation counsel to collect evidence and to pounce at the most propitious moment. That's the fun in litigation! But the ground rules are changing in favour of early discovery. Litigation counsel must adjust to this new environment and I can see no reason to think that clients may suffer except by losing the surprise effect of the hidden missile.

Returning to the specific topic, if original documents enjoy no privilege, then copying is only in a technical sense a creation. Moreover, if the copies were in the possession of the client prior to the prospect of litigation they would not be protected from production. Why should copies of relevant documents obtained after contemplation of litigation be treated differently? Suppose counsel for one litigant finds an incriminating filing by the opposite party in the Security Commission's files. Could there be any justification for its retention until cross-examination at trial? Further, such copies, if relevant in their content, must be revealed in oral discovery under rule 31.06(1) which provides that questions must be answered even though the information sought is evidence.

The production of such documents in the discovery process does little to impinge upon the lawyer's freedom to prepare in privacy and weighs heavily in the scales supporting fairness in the pursuit of truth.

In disagreeing with the majority reasons in *Hodgkinson*, I am at the same time differing from the reasons and result in *Ottawa-Carleton (Regional Municipality) v. Consumers' Gas Co.* (1990), 74 OR (2d) 637, 74 DLR (4th) 742 where the Ontario Divisional Court held copies of public documents to be privileged. Montgomery J, the motions judge in that case, indicated a preference for the reasoning of Craig JA in *Hodgkinson*. The Divisional Court preferred to follow the majority. In the present case the Divisional Court appears to agree with my view, although without analysis of authorities.

This court does not easily turn aside authorities such as *Lyell v. Kennedy* that have stood as the law for many years. However, consistent with the theme of these reasons, deference must be given to modern perceptions of discoverability in preference to historic landmarks that no longer fit the dynamics of the conduct of litigation. The zone of privacy is thus restricted in aid of the pursuit of early exchange of relevant facts and the fair resolution of disputes.

Common Interest Privilege

In some circumstances litigation privilege may be preserved even though the information is shared with a third party. The circumstance giving rise to this issue on the present appeal is the provision to Pilotte by the solicitor for the insurer of a copy of Pilotte's signed statement.

While solicitor–client privilege stands against the world, litigation privilege is a protection only against the adversary, and only until termination of the litigation. It may not be inconsistent with litigation privilege vis-à-vis the adversary to communicate with an outsider, without creating a waiver, but a document in the hand of an outsider will only be protected by a privilege if there is a common interest in litigation or its prospect.

The general principle was first enunciated by Denning LJ in *Buttes Gas and Oil Co. v. Hammer (No. 3)*, [1980] 3 All ER 475 at pp. 483-84, [1981] QB 223 (CA):

> In case this be wrong, however, I must go on to consider the claim for legal professional privilege. The arguments became complicated beyond belief. Largely because a distinction was drawn between Buttes (who are the party to the litigation) and the ruler of Sharjah

(who is no party to it). Such as questions as to who held the originals and who held the copies and so forth. Countless cases were cited. Few were of any help.

I would sweep away all those distinctions. Although this litigation is between Buttes and Occidental, we must remember that standing alongside them in the selfsame interest are the rulers of Sharjah and UAQ respectively. McNeill J thought that this gave rise to special considerations, and I agree with him. There is a privilege which may be called a "common interest" privilege. That is a privilege in aid of anticipated litigation in which several persons have a common interest. It often happens in litigation that a plaintiff or defendant has other persons standing alongside him who have the selfsame interest as he and who have consulted lawyers on the selfsame points as he but who have not been made parties to the action. Maybe for economy or for simplicity or what you will. All exchange counsels' opinions. All collect information for the purpose of litigation. All make copies. All await the outcome with the same anxious anticipation because it affects each as much as it does the others. Instances come readily to mind. Owners of adjoining houses complain of a nuisance which affects them both equally. Both take legal advice. Both exchange relevant documents. But only one is a plaintiff. An author writes a book and gets it published. It is said to contain a libel or to be an infringement of copyright. Both author and publisher take legal advice. Both exchange documents. But only one is made a defendant.

In all such cases I think the courts should, for the purposes of discovery, treat all the persons interested as if they were partners in a single firm or departments in a single company. Each can avail himself of the privilege in aid of litigation. Each can collect information for the use of his or the other's legal adviser. Each can hold originals and each make copies. And so forth. All are the subject of the privilege in aid of anticipated litigation, even though it should transpire that, when the litigation is afterwards commenced, only one of them is made a party to it. No matter that one has the originals and the other has the copies. All are privileged.

In language more specifically directed to the issue on this appeal the US Court of Appeal put it this way in *United States of America v. American Telephone and Telegraph Company*, 642 F2d 1285 (1980 SCCA) at pp. 1299-1300:

> The *attorney–client privilege exists* to protect confidential communications, to assure the client that any statements he makes in seeking legal advice will be kept strictly confidential between him and his attorney; in effect, *to protect the attorney–client relationship*. Any voluntary disclosure by the holder of such a privilege is inconsistent with the confidential relationship and thus waives the privilege.
>
> By contrast, the *work product privilege* does not exist to protect a confidential relationship, but rather *to promote the adversary system by safeguarding the fruits of an attorney's trial preparations from the discovery attempts of the opponent*. The purpose of the work product doctrine is to protect information against opposing parties, rather than against all others outside a particular confidential relationship, in order to encourage effective trial preparation. In the leading case on the work product privilege, the Supreme Court stated: "Proper preparation of a client's case demands that he assemble information, sift what he considers to be the relevant from the irrelevant facts, prepare his legal theories and plan his strategy without undue and needless interference. A disclosure made in the pursuit of such trial preparation, and not inconsistent with maintaining secrecy against opponents, should be

allowed without waiver of the privilege. We conclude, then, that *while the mere showing of a voluntary disclosure to a third person will generally suffice to show waiver of the attorney-client privilege, it should not suffice in itself for waiver of the work product privilege.*

We do not endorse a reading of the GAF Corp. standard so broad as to allow confidential disclosure to *any* person without waiver of the work product privilege. The existence of common interests between transferor and transferee is relevant to deciding whether the disclosure is consistent with the nature of the work product privilege. But "common interests" should not be construed as narrowly limited to co-parties. So long as transferor and transferee anticipate litigation against a common adversary on the same issue or issues, they have strong common interests in sharing the fruit of the trial preparation efforts. Moreover, with common interests on a particular issue against a common adversary, the transferee is not at all likely to disclose the work product material to the adversary. When the transfer to a party with such common interests is conducted under a guarantee of confidentiality, the case against waiver is even stronger. [Emphasis in original.]

Although the subject of common interest has arisen in other contexts in Canadian cases, I am satisfied that the above two excerpts should be adopted as expressing both the applicable principle and the specific application of that principle to the issues on this appeal. Canadian authorities which have dealt with common interest privilege in different contexts include: ... .

Application of Principles to the Disputed Categories

I will depart somewhat from Kurisko J's categories of communication in order to relate them more directly to my legal analysis.

There is no question that all communications between Eryou and General Accident are protected by solicitor–client privilege, there being no indication of waiver.

The more contentious issue is whether communications between Bourret and Eryou or Bourret and General Accident are privileged.

In my view, an insurance company investigating a policy holder's fire is not, or should not be considered to be, in a state of anticipation of litigation. It may be that negotiations and even litigation will follow as to the extent of the loss but until something arises to give reality to litigation, the company should be seen as conducting itself in good faith in the service of the insured. The reality of anticipation of litigation arose in this case when arson was suspected and Eryou was retained. Chrusz was presumably a suspect if this was a case of arson and litigation privilege attached to communications between Bourret and Eryou or from Bourret through General Accident to Eryou so long as such litigation was contemplated. The dominant purpose test is satisfied.

However, I would not accord communications between Bourret and Eryou with the protection of solicitor–client privilege. Bourret was retained to perform the functions of investigating and reporting. He was expected to be honest in doing his job, and no special legal protection was necessary to ensure a candid report. I agree with the reasoning of Doherty JA on this subject.

Viewed from another perspective, when the end comes to contemplated litigation what purpose is served by protecting such information if relevant in other proceedings? The sanctity of the client's secrets which are shared with a lawyer is untouched. If the circumstances surrounding the fire are relevant in other litigation there may be no better evidence than Bourret's reports. Thus, the interest of the determination of truth is served by production without effect upon the fundamental protection afforded to solicitor–client communications.

The payments by General Accident to Chrusz between January and April 1995 are clear evidence that his involvement in arson was no longer a consideration. The parties had essentially returned to the original positions of insurer and insured negotiating over the value of the claim. Litigation was, as always, a possibility, but, so far as the evidence reveals it was not in contemplation.

At that point, in my view, the previous existing litigation privilege came to an end and documents that had once been protected on that account became compellable in any proceedings where they were relevant.

On May 23, 1995, a metamorphosis occurred. The revelations of Pilotte immediately brought new litigation into contemplation—the eventual claim by General Accident of fraud and misrepresentation by Chrusz following the fire. However, it was Pilotte's evidence that he was acting because his conscience bothered him. The lack of any assertion that he contemplated litigation prior to receiving the counterclaim, requires a separate analysis of whether documents in his hands must be produced, notwithstanding protection in the hands of Eryou by reason of the fresh litigation privilege.

Dealing first with Eryou, any communications or reports from Bourret after May 23, 1995, whose dominant purpose was directed to the litigation now before us are protected by litigation privilege, subject to the rules as to discovery of evidence and witnesses. Similarly, any contacts with third parties reported on by Bourret would be protected.

The Divisional Court refers to the "float book and additional time sheets" together with the video. It is unclear on the record before us what was delivered by Pilotte to Eryou but I will assume it was these three items, two of which were copies or originals of documents taken from the motel. None of these were created or prepared for the purpose of litigation and so, on the principles enunciated earlier in these reasons, they cannot qualify for any form of privilege in the hands of any of Eryou, General Accident, or Pilotte.

The statement taken by Eryou from Pilotte is protected by litigation privilege in the hands of Eryou, again subject to the discovery rules, but the copy delivered to Pilotte must be considered separately. It is clear that Pilotte did not at that time contemplate litigation. In my view, however, he was closely enough aligned with General Accident in seeing his evidence pressed forward against Chrusz to protect Eryou against a waiver of his client's litigation privilege: see, in this respect, *United States v. American Telephone*, *supra*. There was nothing inconsistent in giving a copy of a statement to this witness and maintaining privilege against the adversary. This was especially so when a promise of confidentiality was requested.

As closely as he was aligned in interest to General Accident, I do not consider that Pilotte acquired a common interest privilege. In all of the examples cited by Lord Denning in *Buttes*, there is an actual contemplation of litigation shared by individuals against a common adversary. Pilotte was merely a witness who was under no apparent threat of litigation. If events had proceeded in the normal course without a counterclaim and he was called as a witness at trial he would have no more reason to refuse production of the statement than any witness to a motor vehicle accident who has been provided with a written statement to refresh his or her memory before giving evidence. The cross-examiner would be entitled to its production and claims of litigation privilege would be hollow.

The fact that Pilotte became a party to the counterclaim did not change the status of this statement in his hands. It was not created for this litigation and is simply a relevant piece of factual information that came to counsel with the original brief.

• • •

DOHERTY JA (dissenting in part):

• • •

I agree with Carthy JA that the communications between Mr. Bourret and General Accident and Mr. Eryou before May 23, 1995 are not protected by litigation privilege and that the communications between those parties from that date forward are protected by litigation privilege assuming they are not subject to disclosure under the applicable *Rules of Civil Procedure*.

I also agree with much of my colleague's analysis of the litigation privilege claim. In particular, I agree with:

- his description of the different rationales underlying client–solicitor privilege and litigation privilege (paras. 22-24);
- his conclusion that litigation privilege exists to provide "a protected area to facilitate investigation and preparation of a case for trial by adversarial advocates" (para. 23);
- his assertion that the reach of litigation privilege must take cognizance of the broad rules of discovery which are aimed at full disclosure of relevant facts by all parties to the litigation (paras. 25-28);
- his adoption of the dominant purpose test as being consistent with contemporary notions of full pre-trial discovery (paras. 29-32);
- his conclusion that any litigation privilege General Accident may have had with respect to communications prior to May 23 disappeared when General Accident no longer suspected Chrusz of any involvement in arson (paras. 50-54); and
- his conclusion that communications from or to Mr. Bourret by General Accident and or Mr. Eryou after May 23 are subject to litigation privilege assuming they are not subject to disclosure under the applicable *Rules of Civil Procedure* (para. 56).

In the course of his analysis of the litigation privilege claim, Carthy JA holds that copies of non-privileged documents placed into a lawyer's brief in the course of preparation for litigation are never protected by litigation privilege (paras. 33-41). I do not concur in that part of his analysis. That issue does not arise directly on this appeal as there is no appeal from the holding of Kurisko J and the Divisional Court that the copies of the videotape and business records provided to Mr. Eryou by Mr. Pilotte are not privileged. My colleague has addressed the question, however, no doubt because of the Divisional Court's observation at p. 796 that:

> It is true that a copy of an original document incorporated by a solicitor into his litigation brief becomes privileged, but that privilege does not extend to the original.

Carthy JA, while acknowledging the line of authority which supports the position taken by the Divisional Court, prefers the view of Craig JA, in dissent, in *Hodgkinson v. Simms* (1988), 55 DLR (4th) 577 at p. 594, 33 BCLR (2d) 129, where Craig JA observed:

> I fail to comprehend how original documents which are not privileged (because they are not prepared with the dominant purpose of actual or anticipated litigation) can become privileged simply because counsel makes photostatic copies of the documents and puts them in his "brief."

I do not disagree with the observation of Craig JA. A non-privileged document should not become privileged merely because it is copied and placed in the lawyer's brief. I would not, however, go so far as to say that copies of non-privileged documents can never properly be the subject of litigation privilege. In *Nickmar Pty Ltd. v. Preservatrice Skandia Insurance Ltd.* (1985), 3 NSWLR 44 at pp. 61-62 (SC), Wood J opined:

> In my view, it is incorrect to state, as a general proposition, that a copy of an unprivileged document becomes privileged so long as it is obtained by a party, or its solicitor, for the sole purpose of advice or use in litigation. I think that the result in any such case depends on the manner in which the copy or extract is made or obtained. If it involves a selective copying or results from research or the exercise of skill and knowledge on the part of a solicitor, then I consider privilege should apply [*Lyell v. Kennedy* (No. 3) (1884), 27 Ch. D 1]. Otherwise, I see no reason, in principle, why disclosure should be refused of copies of documents which can be obtained elsewhere, and in respect of which no relationship of confidence, or legal profession privilege exists.

The review of the case law provided in Manes and Silver, *Solicitor–Client Privilege in Canadian Law*, *supra*, at 170-73 suggests to me that Wood J's analysis is the appropriate one: see also *Commissioner Australian Federal Police v. Propend Finance Pty Ltd.* (1997), 141 ALR 545 (HC). I would leave the question of when, if ever, copies of non-privileged documents can be protected by litigation privilege to a case where the issue is squarely raised and fully argued.

I turn now to General Accident's claim that it is not required to produce the transcript of Mr. Pilotte's statement of May 23 because it is protected by litigation privilege. Unlike Carthy JA, I would hold that the statement is not so protected.

There is no doubt that the statement meets the conditions precedent to the operation of litigation privilege in that it was prepared by counsel in contemplation of litigation and for the purpose of assisting him in that litigation. ...

I do not think, however, that every document which satisfies the condition precedent to the operation of litigation privilege should be protected from disclosure by that privilege. In my view, the privilege should be recognized as a qualified one which can be overridden where the harm to other societal interests in recognizing the privilege clearly outweighs any benefit to the interest fostered by applying the privilege in the particular circumstances. ...

· · ·

There is considerable academic support for the view that litigation privilege should be a qualified one which must, in some circumstances, give way to the interests served by full disclosure: see Manes and Silver, *Solicitor–Client Privilege in Canadian Law, supra*, at 21-22; Watson and Au, "Solicitor–Client Privilege and Litigation Privilege in Civil Litigation," *supra*, at 344-45; R. Sharpe, "Claiming Privilege in the Discovery Process," in *Law in Transition: Evidence, Law Society of Upper Canada Special Lectures* (Toronto: DeBoo, 1984), at 164-65. These authors point to the American experience where the lawyer's work product privilege against production has always been a qualified one: *Hickman v. Taylor*, 329 US 495 (1947) at 511. The statutory manifestation of that qualification is found in Rule 26(b)(iii) of the US *Rules of Federal Procedure* which permits production upon a showing by the party seeking production that there is "a substantial need" for the material and that the party is "unable without undue hardship to obtain the substantial equivalent of the material." This statutory language reflects some of the factors which, in my view, should be considered in determining whether a document should be produced even though it fulfills the conditions precedent to the operation of litigation privilege.

• • •

My review of the statement does not indicate that any of General Accident's legal strategy or the thoughts or opinions of its counsel will be revealed if the statement is ordered produced. The statement does not contain anything which comes within the ambit of what is usually referred to as "lawyers' work product." It is not like an expert's report, which may well reflect the theory of the case developed by counsel or reveal the weaknesses and strengths of the case as seen by counsel. This statement is purely informational and purports to be Mr. Pilotte's account of the relevant events. There can be no suggestion that it somehow reflects counsel's view of the case. Indeed, there was no case until this statement was made.

If the May 23 statement is produced, the basis upon which General Accident chose to deny coverage and sue Chrusz for fraud will be revealed. This can hardly be described as an invasion of counsel's "privacy zone." I do not think that the policies underlying General Accident's privacy interests in non-disclosure are in any way adversely affected by disclosure of this statement. As I see it, the real risk attendant upon disclosure of the statement in so far as General Accident is concerned is that Chrusz will manufacture or tailor evidence in an effort to respond to the very specific allegations of fraud found in the statement. As indicated above, I do not regard this concern as relevant to the determination of whether litigation privilege should be applied to protect the statement from disclosure.

In summary, production of Mr. Pilotte's May 23 statement will yield significant benefits to the fair and accurate determination of this litigation. It will not compromise counsel's ability to effectively prepare and present a case for General Accident. When the competing interests are identified and weighed in the context of the facts of this case, the scales tip clearly in favour of requiring production of the statement by General Accident.

I see no basis upon which Mr. Pilotte's privilege claim with respect to the copy of the statement could be maintained in the face of an order directing production of the statement by General Accident. In my view, the copy of the statement in the possession of Mr. Pilotte's lawyer should also be produced.

Conclusion

I would answer the three questions posed at the outset of these reasons as follows:

- Communications between Mr. Bourret and the insurers and/or Mr. Eryou made prior to May 23, 1995 are not protected by either client–solicitor privilege or litigation privilege. Communications between Mr. Bourret and General Accident and/or Mr. Eryou on or after May 23, 1995 are protected from disclosure by litigation privilege unless they are required to be produced under the *Rules of Civil Procedure*;
- The transcript of Mr. Pilotte's May 23 statement in the possession of the insurers is not protected against production by litigation privilege; and
- The copy of the transcript of Mr. Pilotte's May 23 statement in the possession of his lawyer is not protected against production by Mr. Pilotte by virtue of litigation privilege.

. . .

ROSENBERG JA (concurring): I agree with Carthy JA, subject to the following comments. Like him, I accept Doherty JA's analysis of solicitor–client privilege. I agree with Carthy JA's application of those principles to the facts of this case, subject to Doherty JA's reservation, which I share, concerning pre-May 23, 1995 communications between Mr. Eryou and General Accident.

I agree with Carthy JA's analysis of litigation privilege. The litigation privilege is well established, even if some of the nuances are not. In my view, the competing interests or balancing approach proposed by Doherty JA is more appropriate for dealing with emerging claims of privilege such as those claims dealt with in *Slavutych v. Baker*, [1976] 1 SCR 254 and *R v. Gruenke*, [1991] 3 SCR 263, 67 CCC (3d) 289. I am concerned that a balancing test would lead to unnecessary uncertainty and a proliferation of pre-trial motions in civil litigation.

That is not to say that litigation privilege is absolute. The Supreme Court of Canada has made it clear that all of the established privileges are subject to some exceptions. As Cory J said in *Smith v. Jones*, [1999] 1 SCR 455 at 474, 132 CCC (3d) 225 at 239:

> Both parties made their submissions on the basis that the psychiatrist's report was protected by solicitor–client privilege, and it should be considered on that basis. It is the highest privilege recognized by the courts. *By necessary implication, if a public safety exception applies to solicitor–client privilege, it applies to all classifications of privileges* and duties of confidentiality. It follows that, in these reasons, it is not necessary to consider any distinctions that may exist between a solicitor–client privilege and a litigation privilege. [Emphasis added.]

In my view, with established privileges like solicitor–client privilege and litigation privilege it is preferable that the general rule be stated with as much clarity as possible. Deviations from the rule should be dealt with as clearly defined exceptions rather than as a new balancing exercise each time a privilege claim is made: see *Smith v. Jones*, at p. 477 SCR, p. 242 CCC. Where, as in *Smith v. Jones*, a party seeks to set aside the privilege, the onus properly rests upon the party seeking to set aside the privilege: see *Smith v. Jones*, at pp. 474-75 SCR, p. 240 CCC.

It follows that I agree with Carthy JA's statement of the litigation privilege and its application to the facts of this case subject only to one reservation. As to copies of non-privileged documents, like Doherty JA, I find the reasons of Wood J in *Nickmar Pty Ltd. v. Preservatrice Skandia Insurance Ltd.* (1985), 3 NSWLR 44 (SC) persuasive. However, since that issue does not arise in this case, I would prefer to leave the question open.

In all other respects, I agree with the reasons of Carthy JA and with his disposition of the appeal.

NOTE ON COMMON INTEREST

We have noted that privilege can be waived. The case law on waiver is complex; litigation arises when one party is alleged to have either expressly or impliedly waived the right to keep the materials at issue confidential. This is usually a fact-sensitive inquiry, and an important development in the law in this regard is the idea of "common-interest" privilege. Essentially, it is a defence to a charge of waiver that arises whenever a document is in the hands of a third party. This issue arose in two of the cases reproduced above. Recall that in *Chrusz*, Carthy JA reviewed the case law on point and drew attention to the leading English decision of Lord Denning MR in *Buttes Gas and Oil*. Lord Denning explained that it "often happens in litigation that a plaintiff or defendant has other persons standing alongside him who have the selfsame interest as he and who have consulted lawyers on the selfsame points as he but who have not been made parties to the action." He developed the concept that we now call common-interest privilege: "In all such cases I think the courts should, for the purposes of discovery, treat all persons interested as if they were partners in a single firm or dependants in a single company" (cited in *Chrusz*, above, at para. 44). In *Chrusz*, the majority concluded that it did not apply because Pilotte (the dismissed former employee) was merely a witness "who was under no apparent threat of litigation" (at para. 59). Pilotte was later added as a party to a counterclaim, but, according to the court, this did not change his status as a witness. The statement he made in advance of being added as a party was not privileged.

It is clear that the conditions for establishing a common-interest exception are strict. In the *Pritchard* case, reproduced at the beginning of this chapter, solicitor-and-client privilege was claimed with respect to the legal work of in-house counsel to an administrative tribunal. The appellant in that case wanted access to the legal advice; she argued that the privilege did not apply as against her, because she had a common interest with the administrative tribunal, namely, whether or not the doctor violated the relevant human rights provisions as she alleged he did. The Supreme Court of Canada rejected her claim and probably foreclosed any further cases on this point in the following passages (*Pritchard*, above, at paras. 22-26):

> The appellant submitted that solicitor–client privilege does not attach to communications between a solicitor and client as against persons having a "joint interest" with the client in the subject-matter of the communication. This "common interest," or "joint interest" exception does not apply to the Commission because it does not share an interest with the parties before it. The Commission is a disinterested gatekeeper for human rights complaints and, by definition, does not have a stake in the outcome of any claim.

The common interest exception to solicitor–client privilege arose in the context of two parties jointly consulting one solicitor. See *R v. Dunbar and Logan* (1982), 138 DLR (3d) 221, *per* Martin JA at p. 245:

> The authorities are clear that where two or more persons, each having an interest in some matter, jointly consult a solicitor, their confidential communications with the solicitor, although known to each other, are privileged against the outside world. However, as between themselves, each party is expected to share in and be privy to all communications passing between each of them and their solicitor. Consequently, should any controversy or dispute arise between them, the privilege is inapplicable, and either party may demand disclosure of the communication. …

The common interest exception originated in the context of parties sharing a common goal or seeking a common outcome, a "selfsame interest" as Lord Denning MR described it in *Buttes Gas & Oil Co. v. Hammer (No. 3)*, [1980] 3 All ER 475 (CA), at p. 483. It has since been narrowly expanded to cover those situations in which a fiduciary or like duty has been found to exist between the parties so as to create common interest. These include trustee–beneficiary relations, fiduciary aspects of Crown–aboriginal relations and certain types of contractual or agency relations, none of which are at issue here.

The Commission neither has a trust relationship with, nor owes a fiduciary duty to, the parties appearing before it. The Commission is a statutory decision-maker. The cases relied on by the appellant related to trusts, fiduciary duty, and contractual obligations. These cases are readily distinguishable and do not support the position advanced by the appellant. The common interest exception does not apply to an administrative board with respect to the parties before it.

What do you think of the "common interest" privilege? Is it expanding privilege too much? Or is it a necessary correction to the law that, after all, emerged in the context of single-party litigation, which is no longer as common as it once was. Moreover, facts are not privileged and thus, to the extent that a third party has relevant information that is necessary to achieve a just outcome, this exception does not offer any cover for unfavourable evidence. Following our discussion of ingathered documents, we will deal briefly with this important distinction between communications and facts and how it operates to ensure that discovery is not hampered by claims to privilege beyond what is needed to preserve the administration of justice and the relationships required to sustain it.

Blank v. Canada (Minister of Justice)
[2006] 2 SCR 319, 2006 SCC 39

FISH J: This appeal requires the Court, for the first time, to distinguish between two related but conceptually distinct exemptions from compelled disclosure: the *solicitor–client privilege* and the *litigation privilege*. They often co-exist and one is sometimes mistakenly called by the other's name, but they are not coterminous in space, time or meaning.

More particularly, we are concerned in this case with the litigation privilege, with how it is born and when it must be laid to rest. And we need to consider that issue in the narrow context of the *Access to Information Act*, RSC 1985, c. A-1 ("*Access Act*"), but with prudent regard for its broader implications on the conduct of legal proceedings generally.

This case has proceeded throughout on the basis that "solicitor–client privilege" was intended, in s. 23 of the *Access Act*, to include the litigation privilege which is not elsewhere mentioned in the Act. Both parties and the judges below have all assumed that it does.

As a matter of statutory interpretation, I would proceed on the same basis. The *Act* was adopted nearly a quarter-century ago. It was not uncommon at the time to treat "solicitor–client privilege" as a compendious phrase that included both the legal advice privilege and litigation privilege. This best explains why the litigation privilege is not separately mentioned anywhere in the *Act*. And it explains as well why, despite the *Act's* silence in this regard, I agree with the parties and the courts below that the *Access Act* has not deprived the government of the protection previously afforded to it by the legal advice privilege *and* the litigation privilege: In interpreting and applying the *Act*, the phrase "solicitor–client privilege" in s. 23 should be taken as a reference to both privileges.

In short, we are not asked in this case to decide whether the government can invoke litigation privilege. Quite properly, the parties agree that it can. Our task, rather, is to examine the defining characteristics of that privilege and, more particularly, to determine its lifespan.

The Minister contends that the solicitor–client privilege has two "branches," one concerned with confidential communications between lawyers and their clients, the other relating to information and materials gathered or created in the litigation context. The first of these branches, as already indicated, is generally characterized as the "legal advice privilege"; the second, as the "litigation privilege."

Bearing in mind their different scope, purpose and rationale, it would be preferable, in my view, to recognize that we are dealing here with distinct conceptual animals and not with two branches of the same tree. Accordingly, I shall refer in these reasons to the solicitor–client privilege as if it includes only the legal advice privilege, and shall indeed use the two phrases—solicitor–client privilege and legal advice privilege—synonymously and interchangeably, except where otherwise indicated.

As a matter of substance and not mere terminology, the distinction between litigation privilege and the solicitor–client privilege is decisive in this case. The former, unlike the latter, is of temporary duration. It expires with the litigation of which it was born. Characterizing litigation privilege as a "branch" of the solicitor–client privilege, as the Minister would, does not envelop it in a shared cloak of permanency.

The Minister's claim of litigation privilege fails in this case because the privilege claimed, by whatever name, has expired: The files to which the respondent seeks access relate to penal proceedings that have long terminated. By seeking civil redress for the manner in which those proceedings were conducted, the respondent has given them neither fresh life nor a posthumous and parallel existence.

I would therefore dismiss the appeal.

The respondent is a self-represented litigant who, though not trained in the law, is no stranger to the courts. He has accumulated more than ten years of legal experience first-hand, initially as a defendant and then as a petitioner and plaintiff. In his resourceful and persistent quest for information and redress, he has personally instituted and conducted a plethora of related proceedings, at first instance and on appeal, in federal and provincial courts alike.

This saga began in July 1995, when the Crown laid 13 charges against the respondent and Gateway Industries Ltd. ("Gateway") for regulatory offences under the *Fisheries Act*, RSC 1985, c. F-14, and the *Pulp and Paper Effluent Regulations*, SOR/92-269. The respondent was a director of Gateway. Five of the charges alleged pollution of the Red River and another eight alleged breaches of reporting requirements.

The counts relating to reporting requirements were quashed in 1997 and the pollution charges were quashed in 2001. In 2002, the Crown laid new charges by way of indictment—and stayed them prior to trial. The respondent and Gateway then sued the federal government in damages for fraud, conspiracy, perjury and abuse of its prosecutorial powers.

This appeal concerns the respondent's repeated attempts to obtain documents from the government. He succeeded only in part. His requests for information in the penal proceedings and under the *Access Act* were denied by the government on various grounds, including "solicitor–client privilege." The issue before us now relates solely to the *Access Act* proceedings. We have not been asked to decide whether the Crown properly fulfilled, in the criminal proceedings, its disclosure obligations under *R v. Stinchcombe*, [1991] 3 SCR 326. And in the record before us, we would in any event be unable to do so.

In October 1997, and again in May 1999, the respondent requested from the Access to Information and Privacy Office of the Department of Justice all records pertaining to his prosecution and the prosecution of Gateway. Only some of the requested documents were furnished.

Additional materials were released after the respondent lodged a complaint with the Information Commissioner. The Director of Investigation found that the vast majority of the remaining documents were properly exempted from disclosure under the solicitor–client privilege.

The respondent pursued the matter further by way of an application for review pursuant to s. 41 of the *Access Act*. Although the appellant relied on various exemptions from disclosure in the *Access Act*, proceedings before the motions judge focused on the appellant's claims of solicitor–client privilege in reliance on s. 23 of the *Access Act*.

On the respondent's application, Campbell J held that documents excluded from disclosure pursuant to litigation privilege should be released if the litigation to which the record relates has ended (2003 CarswellNat 5040, 2003 FCT 462).

On appeal, the Federal Court of Appeal divided on the duration of the privilege. Pelletier JA, for the majority on this point, found that litigation privilege, unlike legal advice privilege, expires with the end of the litigation that gave rise to the privilege, "subject to the possibility of defining … litigation … broadly" ([2005] 1 FCR 403, 2004 FCA 287, at para. 89). He therefore held that s. 23 of the *Access Act* did not apply to the documents for which a claim of litigation privilege is made in this case because the criminal prosecution had ended.

Létourneau JA, dissenting on this point, found that the privilege did not necessarily end with the termination of the litigation that gave rise to it. He would have upheld the privilege in this case.

Section 23 of the *Access Act* provides:

> The head of a government institution may refuse to disclose any record requested under this
> Act that contains information that is subject to solicitor–client privilege.

The narrow issue before us is whether documents once subject to the litigation privilege remain privileged when the litigation ends.

According to the appellant, this Court has determined that litigation privilege is a branch of the solicitor–client privilege and benefits from the same near-absolute protection, including permanency. But none of the cases relied on by the Crown support this assertion. The Court has addressed the solicitor–client privilege on numerous occasions and repeatedly underlined its paramount significance, but never yet considered the nature, scope or duration of the litigation privilege.

Thus, the Court explained in *Descôteaux v. Mierzwinski*, [1982] 1 SCR 860, and has since then reiterated, that the solicitor–client privilege has over the years evolved from a rule of evidence to a rule of substantive law. And the Court has consistently emphasized the breadth and primacy of the solicitor–client privilege: see, for example, *Geffen v. Goodman Estate*, [1991] 2 SCR 353; *Smith v. Jones*, [1999] 1 SCR 455; *R v. McClure*, [2001] 1 SCR 445, 2001 SCC 14; *Lavallee, Rackel & Heintz v. Canada (Attorney General)*, [2002] 3 SCR 209, 2002 SCC 61; and *Goodis v. Ontario (Ministry of Correctional Services)*, 2006 SCC 31. In an oft-quoted passage, Major J speaking for the Court, stated in *McClure* that "solicitor–client privilege must be as close to absolute as possible to ensure public confidence and retain relevance" (para. 35).

It is evident from the text and the context of these decisions, however, that they relate only to the legal advice privilege, or solicitor–client privilege properly so called, and not to the litigation privilege as well.

Much has been said in these cases, and others, regarding the origin and rationale of the solicitor–client privilege. The solicitor–client privilege has been firmly entrenched for centuries. It recognizes that the justice system depends for its vitality on full, free and frank communication between those who need legal advice and those who are best able to provide it. Society has entrusted to lawyers the task of advancing their clients' cases with the skill and expertise available only to those who are trained in the law. They alone can discharge these duties effectively, but only if those who depend on them for counsel may consult with them in confidence. The resulting confidential relationship between solicitor and client is a necessary and essential condition of the effective administration of justice.

Litigation privilege, on the other hand, is not directed at, still less, restricted to, communications between solicitor and client. It contemplates, as well, communications between a solicitor and third parties or, in the case of an unrepresented litigant, between the litigant and third parties. Its object is to ensure the efficacy of the adversarial process and not to promote the solicitor–client relationship. And to achieve this purpose, parties to litigation, represented or not, must be left to prepare their contending positions in private, without adversarial interference and without fear of premature disclosure.

R.J. Sharpe (now Sharpe JA) has explained particularly well the differences between litigation privilege and solicitor–client privilege:

It is crucially important to distinguish litigation privilege from solicitor–client privilege. There are, I suggest, at least three important differences between the two. First, solicitor–client privilege applies only to confidential communications between the client and his solicitor. Litigation privilege, on the other hand, applies to communications of a non-confidential nature between the solicitor and third parties and even includes material of a non-communicative nature. Secondly, solicitor–client privilege exists any time a client seeks legal advice from his solicitor whether or not litigation is involved. Litigation privilege, on the other hand, applies only in the context of litigation itself. Thirdly, and most important, the rationale for solicitor–client privilege is very different from that which underlies litigation privilege. This difference merits close attention. The interest which underlies the protection accorded communications between a client and a solicitor from disclosure is the interest of all citizens to have full and ready access to legal advice. If an individual cannot confide in a solicitor knowing that what is said will not be revealed, it will be difficult, if not impossible, for that individual to obtain proper candid legal advice.

Litigation privilege, on the other hand, is geared directly to the process of litigation. Its purpose is not explained adequately by the protection afforded lawyer–client communications deemed necessary to allow clients to obtain legal advice, the interest protected by solicitor–client privilege. Its purpose is more particularly related to the needs of the adversarial trial process. Litigation privilege is based upon the need for a protected area to facilitate investigation and preparation of a case for trial by the adversarial advocate. In other words, litigation privilege aims to facilitate a process (namely, the adversary process), while solicitor–client privilege aims to protect a relationship (namely, the confidential relationship between a lawyer and a client).

R.J. Sharpe, "Claiming Privilege in the Discovery Process," in *Law in Transition: Evidence*, [1984] *Special Lect. LSUC* 163, at pp. 164-65.

With the exception of *Hodgkinson v. Simms* (1988), 33 BCLR (2d) 129, a decision of the British Columbia Court of Appeal, the decisions of appellate courts in this country have consistently found that litigation privilege is based on a different rationale than solicitor–client privilege: *Liquor Control Board of Ontario v. Lifford Wine Agencies Ltd.* (2005), 76 OR (3d) 401; *Ontario (Attorney General) v. Ontario (Information and Privacy Commission, Inquiry Officer)* (2002), 62 OR (3d) 167 ("*Big Canoe*"); *College of Physicians and Surgeons (British Columbia) v. British Columbia (Information and Privacy Commissioner)* (2002), 9 BCLR (4th) 1, 2002 BCCA 665; *Gower v. Tolko Manitoba Inc.* (2001), 196 DLR (4th) 716, 2001 MBCA 11; *Mitsui & Co. (Point Aconi) Ltd. v. Jones Power Co.* (2000), 188 NSR (2d) 173, 2000 NSCA 96; *General Accident Assurance Co. v. Chrusz* (1999), 45 OR (3d) 321.

American and English authorities are to the same effect: see *In re L. (A Minor)*, [1997] AC 16 (HL), and *Three Rivers District Council v. Governor and Company of the Bank of England (No. 6)*, [2004] QB 916, [2004] EWCA Civ 218, and *Hickman v. Taylor*, 329 US 495 (1947). In the United States communications with third parties and other materials prepared in anticipation of litigation are covered by the similar "attorney work product" doctrine. This "distinct rationale" theory is also supported by the majority of academics: Sharpe; J. Sopinka, S.N. Lederman and A.W. Bryant, *The Law of Evidence in Canada* (2nd ed. 1999), at pp. 745-46; D.M. Paciocco and L. Stuesser, *The Law of Evidence* (3rd ed.

2002), at pp. 197-98; J.-C. Royer, *La preuve civile* (3rd ed. 2003), at pp. 868-71; G.D. Watson and F. Au, "Solicitor–Client Privilege and Litigation Privilege in Civil Litigation" (1998), 77 *Can. Bar Rev.* 315. For the opposing view, see J.D. Wilson, "Privilege in Experts' Working Papers" (1997), 76 *Can. Bar Rev.* 346, and "Privilege: Watson & Au (1998), 77 *Can. Bar Rev.* 346: REJOINDER: "It's Elementary My Dear Watson" (1998), 77 *Can. Bar Rev.* 549.

Though conceptually distinct, litigation privilege and legal advice privilege serve a common cause: The secure and effective administration of justice according to law. And they are complementary and not competing in their operation. But treating litigation privilege and legal advice privilege as two branches of the same tree tends to obscure the true nature of both.

Unlike the solicitor–client privilege, the litigation privilege arises and operates *even in the absence of a solicitor–client relationship*, and it applies indiscriminately to all litigants, whether or not they are represented by counsel: see *Alberta (Treasury Branches) v. Ghermezian* (1999), 242 AR 326, 1999 ABQB 407. A self-represented litigant is no less in need of, and therefore entitled to, a "zone" or "chamber" of privacy. Another important distinction leads to the same conclusion. Confidentiality, the *sine qua non* of the solicitor–client privilege, is not an essential component of the litigation privilege. In preparing for trial, lawyers as a matter of course obtain information from third parties who have no need nor any expectation of confidentiality; yet the litigation privilege attaches nonetheless.

In short, the litigation privilege and the solicitor–client privilege are driven by different policy considerations and generate different legal consequences.

The purpose of the litigation privilege, I repeat, is to create a "zone of privacy" in relation to pending or apprehended litigation. Once the litigation has ended, the privilege to which it gave rise has lost its specific and concrete purpose—and therefore its justification. But to borrow a phrase, the litigation is not over until it is over: It cannot be said to have "terminated," in any meaningful sense of that term, where litigants or related parties remain locked in what is essentially the same legal combat.

Except where such related litigation persists, there is no need and no reason to protect from discovery anything that would have been subject to compellable disclosure but for the pending or apprehended proceedings which provided its shield. Where the litigation has indeed ended, there is little room for concern lest opposing counsel or their clients argue their case "on wits borrowed from the adversary," to use the language of the US Supreme Court in *Hickman*, at p. 516.

I therefore agree with the majority in the Federal Court of Appeal and others who share their view that the common law litigation privilege comes to an end, absent closely related proceedings, upon the termination of the litigation that gave rise to the privilege: *Lifford*; *Chrusz*; *Big Canoe*; *Boulianne v. Flynn*, [1970] 3 OR 84 (HCJ); *Wujda v. Smith* (1974), 49 DLR (3d) 476 (Man. QB); *Meaney v. Busby* (1977), 15 OR (2d) 71 (HCJ); *Canada Southern Petroleum Ltd. v. Amoco Canada Petroleum Co.* (1995), 176 AR 134 (QB). See also Sopinka, Lederman and Bryant; Paciocco and Stuesser.

Thus, the principle "once privileged, always privileged," so vital to the solicitor–client privilege, is foreign to the litigation privilege. The litigation privilege, unlike the solicitor–client privilege, is neither absolute in scope nor permanent in duration.

As mentioned earlier, however, the privilege may retain its purpose—and, therefore, its effect—where the litigation that gave rise to the privilege has ended, but related litigation remains pending or may reasonably be apprehended. In this regard, I agree with Pelletier JA regarding "the possibility of defining ... litigation more broadly than the particular proceeding which gave rise to the claim" (at para. 89): see *Ed Miller Sales & Rentals Ltd. v. Caterpillar Tractor Co.* (1988), 90 AR 323 (CA).

At a minimum, it seems to me, this enlarged definition of "litigation" includes separate proceedings that involve the same or related parties and arise from the same or a related cause of action (or "juridical source"). Proceedings that raise issues common to the initial action and share its essential purpose would in my view qualify as well.

As a matter of principle, the boundaries of this extended meaning of "litigation" are limited by the purpose for which litigation privilege is granted, namely, as mentioned, "the need for a protected area to facilitate investigation and preparation of a case for trial by the adversarial advocate" (Sharpe, p. 165). This purpose, in the context of s. 23 of the *Access Act* must take into account the nature of much government litigation. In the 1980s, for example, the federal government confronted litigation across Canada arising out of its urea formaldehyde insulation program. The parties were different and the specifics of each claim were different but the underlying liability issues were common across the country.

In such a situation, the advocate's "protected area" would extend to work related to those underlying liability issues even after some but not all of the individual claims had been disposed of. There were common issues and the causes of action, in terms of the advocate's work product, were closely related. When the claims belonging to that particular group of causes of action had all been dealt with, however, litigation privilege would have been exhausted, even if subsequent disclosure of the files would reveal aspects of government operations or general litigation strategies that the government would prefer to keep from its former adversaries or other requesters under the *Access Act*. Similar issues may arise in the private sector, for example in the case of a manufacturer dealing with related product liability claims. In each case, the duration and extent of the litigation privilege are circumscribed by its underlying purpose, namely the protection essential to the proper operation of the adversarial process.

In this case, the respondent claims damages from the federal government for fraud, conspiracy, perjury and abuse of prosecutorial powers. Pursuant to the *Access Act*, he demands the disclosure to him of all documents relating to the Crown's conduct of its proceedings against him. The source of those proceedings is the alleged pollution and breach of reporting requirements by the respondent and his company.

The Minister's claim of privilege thus concerns documents that were prepared for the dominant purpose of a criminal prosecution relating to environmental matters and reporting requirements. The respondent's action, on the other hand, seeks civil redress for the manner in which the government conducted that prosecution. It springs from a different juridical source and is in that sense unrelated to the litigation of which the privilege claimed was born.

The litigation privilege would not in any event protect from disclosure evidence of the claimant party's abuse of process or similar blameworthy conduct. It is not a black hole from which evidence of one's own misconduct can never be exposed to the light of day.

Even where the materials sought would otherwise be subject to litigation privilege, the party seeking their disclosure may be granted access to them upon a *prima facie* showing of actionable misconduct by the other party in relation to the proceedings with respect to which litigation privilege is claimed. Whether privilege is claimed in the originating or in related litigation, the court may review the materials to determine whether their disclosure should be ordered on this ground.

Finally, in the Court of Appeal, Létourneau JA, dissenting on the cross-appeal, found that the government's status as a "recurring litigant" could justify a litigation privilege that outlives its common law equivalent. In his view, the "[a]utomatic and uncontrolled access to the government lawyer's brief, once the first litigation is over, may impede the possibility of effectively adopting and implementing [general policies and strategies]" (para. 42).

I hesitate to characterize as "[a]utomatic and uncontrolled" access to the government lawyer's brief once the subject proceedings have ended. In my respectful view, access will in fact be neither automatic nor uncontrolled.

First, as mentioned earlier, it will not be automatic because all subsequent litigation will remain subject to a claim of privilege if it involves the same or related parties and the same or related source. It will fall within the protective orbit of the *same litigation defined broadly*.

Second, access will not be uncontrolled because many of the documents in the lawyer's brief will, in any event, remain exempt from disclosure by virtue of the legal advice privilege. In practice, a lawyer's brief normally includes materials covered by the solicitor–client privilege because of their evident connection to legal advice sought or given in the course of, or in relation to, the originating proceedings. The distinction between the solicitor–client privilege and the litigation privilege does not preclude their potential overlap in a litigation context.

Commensurate with its importance, the solicitor–client privilege has over the years been broadly interpreted by this Court. In that light, anything in a litigation file that falls within the solicitor–client privilege will remain clearly and forever privileged.

I hasten to add that the *Access Act* is a statutory scheme aimed at promoting the disclosure of information in the government's possession. Nothing in the Act suggests that Parliament intended by its adoption to extend the lifespan of the litigation privilege when a member of the public seeks access to government documents.

The language of s. 23 is, moreover, permissive. It provides that the Minister *may* invoke the privilege. This permissive language promotes disclosure by encouraging the Minister to refrain from invoking the privilege unless it is thought necessary to do so in the public interest. And it thus supports an interpretation that favours *more* government disclosure, not *less*.

The extended definition of litigation, as I indicated earlier, applies no less to the government than to private litigants. As a result of the *Access Act*, however, its protection may prove less effective in practice. The reason is this. Like private parties, the government may invoke the litigation privilege only when the original or extended proceedings are pending or apprehended. Unlike private parties, however, the government may be required under the terms of the *Access Act* to disclose information once the original proceedings have ended and related proceedings are neither pending nor apprehended. A mere hypothetical possibility that related proceedings may in the future be instituted does not suffice. Should that possibility materialize—should related proceedings in fact later be instituted—the government may well have been required in the interim, in virtue of the *Access Act*, to disclose information that would have otherwise been privileged under the extended definition of litigation. This is a matter of legislative choice and not judicial policy. It flows inexorably from Parliament's decision to adopt the *Access Act*. Other provisions of the *Access Act* suggest, moreover, that Parliament has in fact recognized this consequence of the Act on the government as litigator, potential litigant and guardian of personal safety and public security.

For example, pursuant to s. 16(1)(b) and (c), the government may refuse to disclose any record that contains information relating to investigative techniques or plans for specific lawful investigations or information the disclosure of which could reasonably be expected to be injurious to law enforcement or the conduct of lawful investigations. And, pursuant to s. 17, the government may refuse to disclose any information the disclosure of which could reasonably be expected to threaten the safety of individuals. The special status of the government as a "recurring litigant" is more properly addressed by these provisions and other legislated solutions. In addition, as mentioned earlier, the nature of government litigation may be relevant when determining the boundaries of related litigation where multiple proceedings involving the government relate to common issues with closely related causes of action. But a wholesale expansion of the litigation privilege is neither necessary nor desirable.

Finally, we should not disregard the origins of this dispute between the respondent and the Minister. It arose in the context of a criminal prosecution by the Crown against the respondent. In criminal proceedings, the accused's right to discovery is constitutionally guaranteed. The prosecution is obliged under *Stinchcombe* to make available to the accused all relevant information if there is a "reasonable possibility that the withholding of information will impair the right of the accused to make full answer and defence ..." (p. 340). This added burden of disclosure is placed on the Crown in light of its overwhelming advantage in resources and the corresponding risk that the accused might otherwise be unfairly disadvantaged.

I am not unmindful of the fact that *Stinchcombe* does not require the prosecution to disclose everything in its file, privileged or not. Materials that might in civil proceedings be covered by one privilege or another will nonetheless be subject, in the criminal context, to the "innocence at stake" exception—at the very least: see *McClure*. In criminal proceedings, as the Court noted in *Stinchcombe*:

> The trial judge might also, in certain circumstances, conclude that the recognition of an existing privilege does not constitute a reasonable limit on the constitutional right to make full answer and defence and thus require disclosure in spite of the law of privilege. [p. 340]

On any view of the matter, I would think it incongruous if the litigation privilege were found in civil proceedings to insulate the Crown from the disclosure it was bound but failed to provide in criminal proceedings that have ended.

The result in this case is dictated by a finding that the litigation privilege expires when the litigation ends. I wish nonetheless to add a few words regarding its birth.

652   Chapter 8   Privilege and Deemed Undertakings

The question has arisen whether the litigation privilege should attach to documents created for the substantial purpose of litigation, the dominant purpose of litigation or the sole purpose of litigation. The dominant purpose test was chosen from this spectrum by the House of Lords in *Waugh v. British Railways Board*, [1979] 2 All ER 1169. It has been adopted in this country as well: *Davies v. Harrington* (1980), 115 DLR (3d) 347 (NSCA); *Voth Bros. Construction (1974) Ltd. v. North Vancouver S. Dist. No. 44 Board of School Trustees* (1981), 29 BCLR 114 (CA); *McCaig v. Trentowsky* (1983), 148 DLR (3d) 724 (NBCA); *Nova, an Alberta Corporation v. Guelph Engineering Co.* (1984), 5 DLR (4th) 755 (Alta. CA); *Ed Miller Sales & Rentals*; *Chrusz*; *Lifford*; *Mitsui*; *College of Physicians*; *Gower*.

I see no reason to depart from the dominant purpose test. Though it provides narrower protection than would a substantial purpose test, the dominant purpose standard appears to me consistent with the notion that the litigation privilege should be viewed as a limited exception to the principle of full disclosure and not as an equal partner of the broadly interpreted solicitor–client privilege. The dominant purpose test is more compatible with the contemporary trend favouring increased disclosure. As Royer has noted, it is hardly surprising that modern legislation and case law

> [TRANSLATION] which increasingly attenuate the purely accusatory and adversarial nature of the civil trial, tend to limit the scope of this privilege [that is, the litigation privilege]. [para. 1139]

Or, as Carthy JA stated in *Chrusz*:

> The modern trend is in the direction of complete discovery and there is no apparent reason to inhibit that trend so long as counsel is left with sufficient flexibility to adequately serve the litigation client. [p. 331]

While the solicitor–client privilege has been strengthened, reaffirmed and elevated in recent years, the litigation privilege has had, on the contrary, to weather the trend toward mutual and reciprocal disclosure which is the hallmark of the judicial process. In this context, it would be incongruous to reverse that trend and revert to a substantial purpose test.

A related issue is whether the litigation privilege attaches to documents gathered or copied—but not *created*—for the purpose of litigation. This issue arose in *Hodgkinson*, where a majority of the British Columbia Court of Appeal, relying on *Lyell v. Kennedy* (1884), 27 Ch. D 1 (CA), concluded that copies of public documents gathered by a solicitor were privileged. McEachern CJBC stated:

> It is my conclusion that the law has always been, and in my view, should continue to be, that in circumstances such as these, where a lawyer exercising legal knowledge, skill, judgment and industry has assembled a collection of relevant copy documents for his brief for the purpose of advising on or conducting anticipated or pending litigation he is entitled, indeed required, unless the client consents, to claim privilege for such collection and to refuse production. [p. 142]

This approach was rejected by the majority of the Ontario Court of Appeal in *Chrusz*.

The conflict of appellate opinion on this issue should be left to be resolved in a case where it is explicitly raised and fully argued. Extending the privilege to the gathering of documents resulting from research or the exercise of skill and knowledge does appear to be more consistent with the rationale and purpose of the litigation privilege. That being said, I take care to mention that assigning such a broad scope to the litigation privilege is not intended to automatically exempt from disclosure anything that would have been subject to discovery if it had not been remitted to counsel or placed in one's own litigation files. Nor should it have that effect.

For all of these reasons, I would dismiss the appeal. The respondent shall be awarded his disbursements in this Court.

[Concurring reasons of Bastarache J, Charron J concurring, omitted.]

NOTES AND QUESTIONS

1. Ontario rules 31.06(3)(a) (disclosure of expert opinions on examination for discovery) and 33.04(2) (production of medical reports by a party to be medically examined) refer to expert opinions and reports as not having to be disclosed if they were prepared for contemplated or pending litigation and "*for no other purpose.*" Does this suggest that the rule makers envisaged a "sole purpose" test for the litigation privilege? In general, the language has gone unnoticed by the courts who have regularly applied the dominant-purpose test: see, however, *Grant v. St. Clair Region Conservation Authority* (1985), 5 CPC (2d) 281 (Ont. Div. Ct.), *Proctor and Redfern Limited v. Lakehead Region Conservation Authority* (1987), 21 CPC (2d) 163 (Ont. HC), and *2245647 Manitoba Ltd. v. Economical Mutual Insurance Co.* [1991] MJ No. 271.

2. When a claim for privilege succeeds, whether because it has gone unchallenged or because it was upheld, the party can "bury" the evidence. Often, this is why the privilege is asserted—to suppress unfavourable evidence. However, a party may not use the assertion of privilege to surprise the adversary at trial—by claiming privilege at the discovery stage, but abandoning it at trial and adducing the evidence. See, for example, Ontario rule 30.09. What is the justification for the "impeachment exception" in that rule?

3. *Ingathered Documents.* In *Blank*, above, the court expressly left to another day the issue of "ingathered documents." A decision of the New Brunswick Court of Appeal is precisely on this point and suggests a trend away from finding copying—when not combined with legal knowledge, skill or industry—to be adequate to protect material from disclosure on discovery. Counsel argued that copying non-privileged documents was adequate as long as the copying was done in anticipation of litigation. The court disagreed (*Edgar v. Auld*, [2000] NBJ No. 69, at paras. 12 and 15):

> Mr. Auld and his co-defendants in the appeal before us, argue that the trial judge was correct in rejecting the reasons of the majority in *Hodgkinson* as being contrary to the modern approach of disclosure. I am sympathetic to that view in relation to this appeal. There was no legal skill or industry involved in ordering records of hospital services and medical treatments accorded Mr. Edgar. They were not created nor brought into being for the dominant purpose of the litigation. I am persuaded to the view expressed in the decision of *Ventouris v. Mountain*,

[1991] 1 WLR 607 (CA) where Bingham LJ, held that our system of civil procedure is founded on the general rule that the interests of justice are best served if parties to litigation are obliged to disclose and produce for the other party's inspection all documents in their possession, custody or power relating to the issues in the action. This is not an absolute rule as is demonstrated by solicitor–client privilege and litigation privilege. At p. 621 para. C he held:

> … I can see no reason in principle why a pre-existing document obtained by a solicitor for purposes of litigation should be privileged from production and inspection …

and at 621-622, Bingham LJ criticized the argument that one should look to the purpose for which the document was obtained in order to determine privilege. He said that, instead, one should look to the purpose for which it was brought into existence.

· · ·

> In my view, there is no merit to extending litigation privilege to cover the hospital and medical reports obtained by Mr. Edgar's solicitor. I leave until another day the ingenuity of counsel in persuading a trial judge that the legal knowledge, skill and industry of counsel are sufficient, on a case-by-case basis, to attract the mantle of litigation privilege in the case then under review. The documents here must be available for inspection and be made available for copying by the respondents, Mr. Auld and his co-defendants. The same applies to the two statements, copies of which were obtained by Mr. Edgar's solicitor from the Section B coverage insurer.

The New Brunswick Court of Appeal in *Edgar v. Auld*, above, followed a case from England on this point. In *Ventouris v. Mountain*, [1990] 3 All ER 157, the English Queen's Bench Division held that privilege attached to the *originals* of documents that had not previously been in the possession of a party to actual or contemplated litigation and that had not come into existence for the purpose of that litigation, but that had been obtained by the solicitor of that party for that purpose. The court further held that privilege also attaches to *copies* taken by solicitors of documents held by third parties, where the copying is done for the purpose of actual or contemplated litigation. The lower court saw no reason to distinguish between copying documents for the purpose of litigation or ingathering the originals. On appeal in *Ventouris* ([1991] 3 All ER 472, at 484), the Court of Appeal reversed. Bingham LJ stated: "I can see no reason in principle why a pre-existing document obtained by a solicitor for the purpose of litigation should be privileged from production and inspection. … I find nothing in anything of the cases which suggests, let alone justifies, such a result. Such a rule would in my view pose a threat to the administration of justice."

G. Privilege on Grounds of Confidentiality

Traditionally, Canadian courts have been loath to recognize privilege beyond the accepted categories—for example, solicitor-and-client privilege, litigation privilege, without-prejudice communications, or Crown privilege. While solicitor-and-client privilege is based on the confidentiality of the communication, no general privilege has been extended to confidential communications—for example, with doctors or with spiritual advisers. Instead, the issue is considered on a case-by-case basis.

In *Slavutych v. Baker*, [1976] 1 SCR 254, the Supreme Court adopted the test propounded by Professor Wigmore that four fundamental conditions must be met before privilege is extended to any communication on the ground of confidentiality (*Wigmore on Evidence*, vol. 8 (McNaughton rev. 1961), sec. 2285). The conditions, quoted in *Slavutych*, at 260, are:

1. The communications must originate in a confidence that they will not be disclosed.

2. This element of confidentiality must be essential to the full and satisfactory maintenance of the relation between the parties.

3. The relation must be one which in the opinion of the community ought to be sedulously fostered.

4. The injury that would enure to the relation by the disclosure of the communications must be greater than the benefit thereby gained for the correct disposal of litigation.

Subsequently, in *R v. Gruenke*, [1991] 3 SCR 263, the Supreme Court of Canada (in analyzing statements made by the accused to a spiritual advisor) indicated that the approach it took in *Slavutych* is to be followed in any case involving a claim to confidentiality that does not fall under a class privilege. In *Gruenke*, Lamer CJC stated at 290:

This is not to say that the Wigmore criteria are now "carved in stone," but rather that these considerations provide a general framework within which policy considerations and the requirement of fact-finding can be weighed and balanced on the basis of their relative importance in the particular case before the Court. Nor does this preclude the identification of a new class on a principled basis.

A.M. v. Ryan
[1997] 1 SCR 157

McLACHLIN J: After having been sexually assaulted by the respondent Dr. Ryan, the appellant sought counselling from a psychiatrist. The question on this appeal is whether the psychiatrist's notes and records containing statements the appellant made in the course of treatment are protected from disclosure in a civil suit brought by the appellant against Dr. Ryan. Put in terms of principle, should a defendant's right to relevant material to the end of testing the plaintiff's case outweigh the plaintiff's expectation that communications between her and her psychiatrist will be kept in confidence?

I. The Facts and History of Proceedings

When the appellant was 17 years old, she underwent psychiatric treatment from Dr. Ryan. In the course of treatment, Dr. Ryan had sexual relations with her. He also committed acts of gross indecency in her presence. The appellant asserts that this conduct injured her and has sued Dr. Ryan for damages. Dr. Ryan does not deny that this sexual conduct occurred. He contends, however, that the appellant consented to the acts. He also takes the position that the conduct was not the cause of the injury for which the plaintiff sues.

The appellant alleges that the sexual assault and gross indecency caused her mental distress and anguish, loss of dignity and self-esteem, humiliation and embarrassment, difficulty in forming and maintaining relationships with other persons, lasting psychological and emotional trauma, continuing fear and anxiety, foregone career and educational opportunities, inability to verbalize emotions and recollections of the events, repeated suicide attempts, severe depression and post-traumatic stress disorder. In order to deal with these difficulties as well as other problems, the appellant sought psychiatric treatment from Dr. Parfitt.

The appellant was concerned that communications between her and Dr. Parfitt should remain confidential. Dr. Parfitt assured her that everything possible would be done to ensure that their discussions would remain confidential. At one point, the appellant's concerns led Dr. Parfitt to refrain from taking her usual notes.

The British Columbia Rules of Court permit each party to an action to examine the other for discovery and to obtain discovery of all documents in the possession of the other party that are relevant to the lawsuit and not protected from disclosure by privilege or some other legal exemption. If a party has not voluntarily produced a required document, the court may order that it be produced. The rules also provide for documents to be obtained from third parties. Failing voluntary production, an application for production may be brought under Rule 26(11).

During the examination for discovery of the appellant, counsel for Dr. Ryan requested production of Dr. Parfitt's records and notes. The appellant's counsel advised that they would not be produced without a court order. Accordingly, Dr. Ryan's counsel brought a motion to obtain disclosure. At the hearing before Master Bolton, Dr. Parfitt agreed to release her reports, but claimed privilege in relation to her notes. Counsel for the appellant was present. He supported Dr. Parfitt's objections to production, but did not assert a formal claim to privilege on behalf of the appellant.

The Master found that Dr. Parfitt had no privilege in the documents and ordered that they all be produced to Dr. Ryan. In his view, there is no blanket privilege for communications between patient and physician. The only basis upon which privilege could be asserted would be under the principles approved by this Court for case-by-case privilege, sometimes referred to as the "Wigmore test." The first branch of this test requires that the communications originate in confidence. The Master ruled that this was not the case here, since the appellant had been fearful throughout that the doctor's notes would be disclosed and Dr. Parfitt had assured her only that everything possible would be done to ensure that their discussions were kept private. The Master went on to consider whether the discretion granted by the Rules of Court permitted him to accede to Dr. Parfitt's claim for confidentiality. He found the notes to be relevant. The only remaining question was whether Dr. Parfitt's "embarrassment" at revealing the notes outweighed this probative value. It did not, in the Master's view. Although he acknowledged the legitimate interest of keeping patient–therapist discussions free-ranging and confidential, he held that this was not a factor that he could consider under the law as it stood.

Dr. Parfitt appealed to the Supreme Court of British Columbia. That appeal was dismissed ... . Vickers J agreed that the notes were not privileged, not on the ground that they had not been made in confidence as the Master had found, but on the ground that the public interest in the proper administration of justice outweighed confidentiality concerns where the appellant had placed the matters in issue by initiating the suit.

Dr. Parfitt appealed to the British Columbia Court of Appeal. The appeal was allowed in part … . Southin JA began by stating that she was only concerned with Dr. Parfitt's privilege and not the plaintiff's, since the plaintiff had not properly claimed privilege. A physician could only assert privilege if disclosure would harm the physician. Dr. Parfitt had not shown this to be the case. Therefore, no claim for privilege could be made by anyone, and the matter fell to be considered exclusively under the Rules of Court.

Under Rule 26(11), relevant or "material" documents should be produced unless the order is oppressive of the plaintiff or will have such an adverse effect on her that it would be unjust to order production, the Court of Appeal ruled. In applying this test, the court should consider whether the particular invasion of privacy is necessary to the proper administration of justice and, if so, whether terms are appropriate to limit that invasion. On the one hand, a plaintiff should not be "scared away" from suing by fear of disclosure. On the other hand, a defendant should not be deprived of an assessment of the true loss caused by the alleged wrong. There is no perfect balance to be struck, in the court's view.

Southin JA ordered disclosure of Dr. Parfitt's reporting letters and notes recording discussions between her and the appellant. Southin JA did not order disclosure of Dr. Parfitt's personal notes which she uses to make sense of what the patient is telling her. These notes were not disclosed because the appellant assured the court that Dr. Parfitt would not be called at trial and therefore her diagnosis was "of no moment" (p. 19 BCLR). The disclosure ordered was protected by four conditions: that inspection be confined to Dr. Ryan's solicitors and expert witnesses, and that Dr. Ryan himself could not see them; that any person who saw the documents should not disclose their contents to anyone not entitled to inspect them; that the documents could be used only for the purposes of the litigation; and that only one copy of the notes was to be made by Dr. Ryan's solicitors, to be passed on as necessary to Dr. Ryan's expert witnesses.

The appellant objects to this order for limited production and appeals to this Court.

II. The Legislation

British Columbia Supreme Court Rules, Rule 26(11):

Where a document is in the possession or control of a person who is not a party, the court, on notice to the person and all other parties, may order production and inspection of the document or preparation of a certified copy that may be used instead of the original. An order under Rule 41(16) in respect of an order under this subrule may be made if that order is endorsed with an acknowledgment by the person in possession or control of the document that the person has no objection to the terms of the proposed order.

III. Preliminary Issues

The findings of the courts below raise three preliminary issues. The first is whether the appellant's alleged failure to assert privilege in the records before the Master deprives her of the right to claim it. I respectfully dissent from the Court of Appeal's view that it did. If the appellant had privilege in the documents, it could be lost only by waiver. The appellant's conduct does not support a finding of waiver. …

A second preliminary issue concerns the relationship between the Rules of Court and the common law rule of privilege. In my view, the present appeal falls to be decided solely on the law of privilege. Where the doctrine of privilege applies, it displaces any residual discretion which might otherwise be thought to inhere in favour of the party claiming privilege. ...

A third preliminary issue concerns the distinction between absolute or blanket privilege, on the one hand, and partial privilege on the other. While the traditional common law categories conceived privilege as an absolute, all-or-nothing proposition, more recent jurisprudence recognizes the appropriateness in many situations of partial privilege. The degree of protection conferred by the privilege may be absolute or partial, depending on what is required to strike the proper balance between the interest in protecting the communication from disclosure and the interest in proper disposition of the litigation. Partial privilege may signify that only some of the documents in a given class must be produced. Documents should be considered individually or by sub-groups on a "case-by-case" basis.

IV. General Principles

The common law principles underlying the recognition of privilege from disclosure are simply stated. They proceed from the fundamental proposition that everyone owes a general duty to give evidence relevant to the matter before the court, so that the truth may be ascertained. To this fundamental duty, the law permits certain exceptions, known as privileges, where it can be shown that they are required by a "public good transcending the normally predominant principle of utilizing all rational means for ascertaining truth": *Trammel v. United States*, 445 US 40 (1980), at p. 50.

While the circumstances giving rise to a privilege were once thought to be fixed by categories defined in previous centuries—categories that do not include communications between a psychiatrist and her patient—it is now accepted that the common law permits privilege in new situations where reason, experience and application of the principles that underlie the traditional privileges so dictate: *Slavutych v. Baker*, [1976] 1 SCR 254; *R v. Gruenke*, [1991] 3 SCR 263, at p. 286. The applicable principles are derived from those set forth in Wigmore on Evidence, vol. 8 (McNaughton rev. 1961), sec. 2285. First, the communication must originate in a confidence. Second, the confidence must be essential to the relationship in which the communication arises. Third, the relationship must be one which should be "sedulously fostered" in the public good. Finally, if all these requirements are met, the court must consider whether the interests served by protecting the communications from disclosure outweigh the interest in getting at the truth and disposing correctly of the litigation.

It follows that the law of privilege may evolve to reflect the social and legal realities of our time. One such reality is the law's increasing concern with the wrongs perpetrated by sexual abuse and the serious effect such abuse has on the health and productivity of the many members of our society it victimizes. Another modern reality is the extension of medical assistance from treatment of its physical effects to treatment of its mental and emotional aftermath through techniques such as psychiatric counselling. Yet another development of recent vintage which may be considered in connection with new claims for privilege is the *Canadian Charter of Rights and Freedoms*, adopted in 1982: *RWDSU v. Dolphin Delivery Ltd.*, [1986] 2 SCR 573, at pp. 592-93; *Dagenais v. Canadian Broadcasting Corp.*, [1994] 3 SCR 835, at pp. 876-77; *Hill v. Church of Scientology of Toronto*, [1995] 2 SCR 1130, at para. 121.

I should pause here to note that in looking to the *Charter*, it is important to bear in mind the distinction drawn by this Court between actually *applying* the *Charter* to the common law, on the one hand, and ensuring that the common law *reflects Charter* values, on the other. As Cory J stated in *Hill, supra*, at paras. 93 and 95:

> ... The most that the private litigant can do is argue that the common law is inconsistent with Charter *values*. It is very important to draw this distinction between Charter rights and Charter values. Care must be taken not to expand the application of the Charter beyond that established by s. 32(1), either by creating new causes of action, or by subjecting all court orders to Charter scrutiny. Therefore, in the context of civil litigation involving only private parties, the Charter will "apply" to the common law only to the extent that the common law is found to be inconsistent with Charter values. [Emphasis in original.]

While the facts of *Hill* involved an attempt to mount a *Charter* challenge to the common law rules of defamation, I am of the view that Cory J's comments are equally applicable to the common law of privilege at issue in this case. In view of the purely private nature of the litigation at bar, the *Charter* does not "apply" *per se*. Nevertheless, ensuring that the common law of privilege develops in accordance with "*Charter* values" requires that the existing rules be scrutinized to ensure that they reflect the values the *Charter* enshrines. This does not mean that the rules of privilege can be abrogated entirely and replaced with a new form of discretion governing disclosure. Rather, it means that the basic structure of the common law privilege analysis must remain intact, even if particular rules which are applied within that structure must be modified and updated to reflect emerging social realities.

V. Privilege for Communications Between Psychiatrist and Patient

The first requirement for privilege is that the communications at issue have originated in a confidence that they will not be disclosed. The Master held that this condition was not met because both the appellant and Dr. Parfitt had concerns that notwithstanding their desire for confidentiality, the records might someday be ordered disclosed in the course of litigation. With respect, I do not agree. The communications were made in confidence. The appellant stipulated that they should remain confidential and Dr. Parfitt agreed that she would do everything possible to keep them confidential. The possibility that a court might order them disclosed at some future date over their objections does not change the fact that the communications were made in confidence. With the possible exception of communications falling in the traditional categories, there can never be an absolute guarantee of confidentiality; there is always the possibility that a court may order disclosure. Even for documents within the traditional categories, inadvertent disclosure is always a possibility. If the apprehended possibility of disclosure negated privilege, privilege would seldom if ever be found.

The second requirement—that the element of confidentiality be essential to the full and satisfactory maintenance of the relation between the parties to the communication—is clearly satisfied in the case at bar. It is not disputed that Dr. Parfitt's practice in general and her ability to help the appellant in particular required that she hold her discussions with the appellant in confidence. Dr. Parfitt's evidence establishes that confidentiality is essential to the continued existence and effectiveness of the therapeutic relations between a psychiatrist and a patient seeking treatment for the psychiatric harm resulting from sexual abuse. ...

The appellant too sees confidentiality as essential to her relationship with Dr. Parfitt. She insisted from the first that her communications to Dr. Parfitt be held in confidence, suggesting that this was a condition of her entering and continuing treatment. The fact that she and Dr. Parfitt feared the possibility of court-ordered disclosure at some future date does not negate the fact that confidentiality was essential "to the full and satisfactory maintenance" of their relationship.

The third requirement—that the relation must be one which in the opinion of the community ought to be sedulously fostered—is equally satisfied. Victims of sexual abuse often suffer serious trauma, which, left untreated, may mar their entire lives. It is widely accepted that it is in the interests of the victim and society that such help be obtained. The mental health of the citizenry, no less than its physical health, is a public good of great importance. Just as it is in the interest of the sexual abuse victim to be restored to full and healthy functioning, so is it in the interest of the public that she take her place as a healthy and productive member of society. ...

The fourth requirement is that the interests served by protecting the communications from disclosure outweigh the interest of pursuing the truth and disposing correctly of the litigation. This requires first an assessment of the interests served by protecting the communications from disclosure. These include injury to the appellant's ongoing relationship with Dr. Parfitt and her future treatment. They also include the effect that a finding of no privilege would have on the ability of other persons suffering from similar trauma to obtain needed treatment and of psychiatrists to provide it. The interests served by non-disclosure must extend to any effect on society of the failure of individuals to obtain treatment restoring them to healthy and contributing members of society. Finally, the interests served by protection from disclosure must include the privacy interest of the person claiming privilege and inequalities which may be perpetuated by the absence of protection.

As noted, the common law must develop in a way that reflects emerging *Charter* values. It follows that the factors balanced under the fourth part of the test for privilege should be updated to reflect relevant *Charter* values. One such value is the interest affirmed by s. 8 of the *Charter* of each person in privacy. Another is the right of every person embodied in s. 15 of the *Charter* to equal treatment and benefit of the law. A rule of privilege which fails to protect confidential doctor/patient communications in the context of an action arising out of sexual assault perpetuates the disadvantage felt by victims of sexual assault, often women. The intimate nature of sexual assault heightens the privacy concerns of the victim and may increase, if automatic disclosure is the rule, the difficulty of obtaining redress for the wrong. The victim of a sexual assault is thus placed in a disadvantaged position as compared with the victim of a different wrong. The result may be that the victim of sexual assault does not obtain the equal benefit of the law to which s. 15 of the *Charter* entitles her. She is doubly victimized, initially by the sexual assault and later by the price she must pay to claim redress—redress which in some cases may be part of her program of therapy. These are factors which may properly be considered in determining the interests served by an order for protection from disclosure of confidential patient–psychiatrist communications in sexual assault cases.

These criteria, applied to the case at bar, demonstrate a compelling interest in protecting the communications at issue from disclosure. More, however, is required to establish privilege. For privilege to exist, it must be shown that the benefit that inures from privilege, however great it may seem, in fact outweighs the interest in the correct disposal of the litigation.

At this stage, the court considering an application for privilege must balance one alternative against the other. The exercise is essentially one of common sense and good judgment. This said, it is important to establish the outer limits of acceptability. I for one cannot accept the proposition that "occasional injustice" should be accepted as the price of the privilege. It is true that the traditional categories of privilege, cast as they are in absolute all-or-nothing terms, necessarily run the risk of occasional injustice. But that does not mean that courts, in invoking new privileges, should lightly condone its extension. In the words of Scalia J (dissenting) in *Jaffee v. Redmond*, 116 S Ct. 1923 (1996), at p. 1941:

> It is no small matter to say that, in some cases, our federal courts will be the tools of injustice rather than unearth the truth where it is available to be found. The common law has identified a few instances where that is tolerable. Perhaps Congress may conclude that it is also tolerable ... . But that conclusion assuredly does not burst upon the mind with such clarity that a judgment in favor of suppressing the truth ought to be pronounced by this honorable Court.

It follows that if the court considering a claim for privilege determines that a particular document or class of documents must be produced to get at the truth and prevent an unjust verdict, it must permit production to the extent required to avoid that result. On the other hand, the need to get at the truth and avoid injustice does not automatically negate the possibility of protection from full disclosure. In some cases, the court may well decide that the truth permits of nothing less than full production. This said, I would venture to say that an order for partial privilege will more often be appropriate in civil cases where, as here, the privacy interest is compelling. Disclosure of a limited number of documents, editing by the court to remove non-essential material, and the imposition of conditions on who may see and copy the documents are techniques which may be used to ensure the highest degree of confidentiality and the least damage to the protected relationship, while guarding against the injustice of cloaking the truth. ...

It must be conceded that a test for privilege which permits the court to occasionally reject an otherwise well-founded claim for privilege in the interests of getting at the truth may not offer patients a guarantee that communications with their psychiatrists will never be disclosed. On the other hand, the assurance that disclosure will be ordered only where clearly necessary and then only to the extent necessary is likely to permit many to avail themselves of psychiatric counselling when certain disclosure might make them hesitate or decline. The facts in this case demonstrate as much. ...

The view that privilege may exist where the interest in protecting the privacy of the records is compelling and the threat to proper disposition of the litigation either is not apparent or can be offset by partial or conditional discovery is consistent with this Court's view in *R v. O'Connor*, [1995] 4 SCR 411. The majority there did not deny that privilege in psychotherapeutic records may exist in appropriate circumstances. Without referring directly to privilege, it developed a test for production of third party therapeutic and other records which balances the competing interests by reference to a number of factors including the right of the accused to full answer and defence and the right of the complainant to privacy. Just as justice requires that the accused in a criminal case be permitted to answer the Crown's case, so justice requires that a defendant in a civil suit be permitted to answer the plaintiff's case. In deciding whether he or she is entitled to production of confidential documents, this requirement must be balanced against the privacy interest of the complainant. This said, the interest in disclosure of a defendant in a civil suit may be less compelling than the parallel interest of an accused charged with a crime. The defendant in a civil suit stands to lose money and repute; the accused in a criminal proceeding stands to lose his or her very liberty. As a consequence, the balance between the interest in disclosure and the complainant's interest in privacy may be struck at a different level in the civil and criminal case; documents produced in a criminal case may not always be producible in a civil case, where the privacy interest of the complainant may more easily outweigh the defendant's interest in production.

My conclusion is that it is open to a judge to conclude that psychiatrist–patient records are privileged in appropriate circumstances. Once the first three requirements are met and a compelling prima facie case for protection is established, the focus will be on the balancing under the fourth head. A document relevant to a defence or claim may be required to be disclosed, notwithstanding the high interest of the plaintiff in keeping it confidential. On the other hand, documents of questionable relevance or which contain information available from other sources may be declared privileged. The result depends on the balance of the competing interests of disclosure and privacy in each case. It must be borne in mind that in most cases, the majority of the communications between a psychiatrist and her patient will have little or no bearing on the case at bar and can safely be excluded from production. Fishing expeditions are not appropriate where there is a compelling privacy interest at stake, even at the discovery stage. Finally, where justice requires that communications be disclosed, the court should consider qualifying the disclosure by imposing limits aimed at permitting the opponent to have the access justice requires while preserving the confidential nature of the documents to the greatest degree possible.

It remains to consider the argument that by commencing the proceedings against the respondent Dr. Ryan, the appellant has forfeited her right to confidentiality. I accept that a litigant must accept such intrusions upon her privacy as are necessary to enable the judge or jury to get to the truth and render a just verdict. But I do not accept that by claiming such damages as the law allows, a litigant grants her opponent a licence to delve into private aspects of her life which need not be probed for the proper disposition of the litigation.

VI. *Procedure for Ascertaining Privilege*

In order to determine whether privilege should be accorded to a particular document or class of documents and, if so, what conditions should attach, the judge must consider the circumstances of the privilege alleged, the documents, and the case. While it is not essential in a civil case such as this that the judge examine every document, the court may do so if necessary to the inquiry. On the other hand, a judge does not necessarily err by proceeding on affidavit material indicating the nature of the information and its expected relevance without inspecting each document individually. The requirement that the court minutely examine numerous or lengthy documents may prove time-consuming, expensive and delay the resolution of the litigation. Where necessary to the proper determination of the claim for privilege, it must be undertaken. But I would not lay down an absolute rule that as a matter of law, the judge must personally inspect every document at issue in every case. Where the judge is satisfied on reasonable grounds that the interests at stake can properly be balanced without individual examination of each document, failure to do so does not constitute error of law.

VII. Application to This Case

The Court of Appeal declined to order production of Dr. Parfitt's notes to herself on the ground that they were unnecessary given that she would not be called to testify. It ordered the production of notes and records of consultations with the appellant, but under stringent conditions. While the Court of Appeal did not proceed on the basis of privilege, its orders are supported by the principles relating to privilege that I have attempted to set forth.

The interest in preserving the confidentiality of the communications here at issue was, as discussed, compelling. On the other hand, the communications might be expected to bear on the critical issue of the extent to which the respondent Dr. Ryan's conduct caused the difficulties the appellant was experiencing. A court, in a case such as this, might well consider it best to inspect the records individually to the end of weeding out those which were irrelevant to this defence. However, the alternative chosen by the Court of Appeal in this case of refusing to order production of one group of documents and imposing stringent conditions on who could see the others and what use could be made of them cannot be said to be in error. In the end, the only persons to see the documents in question will be the lawyers for the respondent Dr. Ryan and his expert witnesses. Copies will not be made, and disclosure of the contents to other people will not be permitted. In short, the plaintiff's private disclosures to her psychiatrist will be disclosed only to a small group of trustworthy professionals, much in the fashion that confidential medical records may be disclosed in a hospital setting. I am not persuaded that the order of the Court of Appeal should be disturbed.

[Dissenting judgment of L'Heureux-Dubé J omitted.]

Ryan has been applied countless times to guide judicial decisions in the area of case-by-case privilege. The basic features of class and case-by-case privilege and their differences were helpfully summarized by Binder J in *R v. Trang*, [2002] AJ No. 119 (Alta. QB). While this is a criminal case, the summary is equally useful in civil contexts; it was noted with approval by the Manitoba Court of Appeal in the civil case *Gower v. Tolko Manitoba Inc.*, [2001] MJ No. 39 (Man. CA).

NOTES AND QUESTIONS

As indicated by the Supreme Court of Canada in *Ryan*, some courts have been willing to exercise their jurisdiction to limit public disclosure of the names of parties, as well as the content of documents required to be produced in litigation, even where the information sought to be protected does not qualify as privileged. In *CPC International Inc. v. Seaforth Creamery Inc.*, [1996] OJ No. 2059 (Gen. Div.); motion to stay dismissed [1996] OJ No. 3537 (CA), the court referred to its jurisdiction under ss. 136 and 137 of the *Courts of Justice Act*, RSO 1990, c. C.43, and granted a motion for a protective order sealing the court record and imposing a procedure to limit the copying of and access to documents produced on discovery. In that case, the plaintiff was concerned that the value of its trade secrets regarding mayonnaise production would be undermined in the discovery process. Orders of this nature are not infrequently issued "on consent" of all parties or, at least, with little or no opposition from other parties to the litigation. What competing interests are involved in the exercise of this discretion? When should the public interest in the openness of the judicial process trump other private considerations? Consider *Vickery v. Nova Scotia Supreme Court (Prothonotary)*, [1991] 1 SCR 671. See discussion of this point in *Juman v. Doucette*, below, at para. 23.

II. IMPLIED/DEEMED UNDERTAKINGS

What is the status of documents that would remain private, but for having been produced for other parties as part of discovery? Can a party for whom the documents are produced make them public or use them in another proceeding? Is there a rule of confidentiality? Should parties seeking to protect documents from other use or parties seeking to use documents bear the onus of persuading a court that they should be permitted to do so? The law on this topic is now clear and uniform across Canada. The most important case in which this was developed is *Juman v. Doucette*, below. Together with the Supreme Court of Canada decision in *Lac d'Amiante du Quebec*, [2001] 2 SCR 743, these authorities establish a common and civil law concept of confidentiality in discovery that will be enforced by courts on pain of contempt. For a recent example of a court doing just that, see *M. Paterson & Sons Ltd. v. St. Lawrence Seaway Management Corp.*, [2002] FCJ No. 1713, 2002 FCT 1247.

Juman v. Doucette
2008 SCC 8, [2008] 1 SCR 157

BINNIE J: [1] The principal issue raised on this appeal is the scope of the "implied undertaking rule" under which evidence compelled during pre-trial discovery from a party to civil litigation can be used by the parties only for the purpose of the litigation in which it was obtained. The issue arises in the context of alleged child abuse, a matter of great importance and concern in our society. The Attorney General of British Columbia rejects the existence of an implied undertaking rule in British Columbia (factum, at para. 4). Alternatively, if there is such a rule, he says it does not extend to *bona fide* disclosures of criminal activity. In his view the parties may, without court order, share with the police any discovery documents or oral testimony that tend to show criminal misconduct.

[2] In the further alternative, the Attorney General argues that the existence of an implied undertaking would not in any way inhibit the ability of the authorities, who are not parties to it, to obtain a subpoena *duces tecum* or to seize documents or a discovery transcript pursuant to a search warrant issued under s. 487 of the *Criminal Code*, RSC 1985, c. C-46.

[3] The British Columbia Court of Appeal held that the implied undertaking rule "does not extend to *bona fide* disclosure of criminal conduct" ((2006), 55 BCLR (4th) 66, 2006 BCCA 262, at para. 56). This ruling is stated too broadly, in my opinion. The rationale of the implied undertaking rule rests on the statutory compulsion that requires a party to make documentary and oral discovery regardless of privacy concerns and whether or not it tends to self-incriminate. The more serious the criminality, the greater would be the reluctance of a party to make disclosure fully and candidly, and the greater is the need for broad protection to facilitate his or her cooperation in civil litigation. It is true, as the chambers judge acknowledged, that there is an "immediate and serious danger" exception to the usual requirement for a court order prior to disclosure ((2005), 45 BCLR (4th) 108, 2005 BCSC 400, at paras. 28-29), but the exception is much narrower than is suggested by the *dictum* of the Court of Appeal, and it does not cover the facts of this case. In my view a party is not in general free to go without a court order to the police or any non-party with what it may view as "criminal conduct," which is a label that covers many shades of suspicion or rumour or belief about many different offences from the mundane to the most serious. The qualification added by the Court of Appeal, namely that the whistle blower must act *bona fides*, does not alleviate the difficulty. Many a tip to the police is tinged with self-interest. At what point does the hope of private advantage rob the communication of its *bona fides*? The lines need to be clear because, as the Court of Appeal itself noted, "non-*bona fide* disclosure of alleged criminal conduct would attract serious civil sanctions for contempt" (para. 56).

[4] Thus the rule is that both documentary and oral information obtained on discovery, including information thought by one of the parties to disclose some sort of criminal conduct, *is* subject to the implied undertaking. It is not to be used *by the other parties* except for the purpose of that litigation, unless and until the scope of the undertaking is varied by a court order or other judicial order or a situation of immediate and serious danger emerges.

[5] Here, because of the facts, much of the appellant's argument focused on her right to protection against self-incrimination, but the implied undertaking rule is broader than that. It includes the wrongdoing of persons other than the examinee and covers innocuous information that is neither confidential nor discloses any wrongdoing at all. Here, if the parents of the victim or other party wished to disclose the appellant's transcript to the police, he or she or they could have made an application to the BC Supreme Court for permission to make disclosure, but none of them did so, and none of them is party to the current proceeding. The applicants are the Vancouver Police Department and the Attorney General of British Columbia supported by the Attorney General of Canada. None of these authorities is party to the undertaking. They have available to them the usual remedies of subpoena *duces tecum* or a search warrant under the *Criminal Code*. If at this stage they do not have the grounds to obtain a search warrant, it is not open to them to build their case on the compelled testimony of the appellant. Further,

even if the authorities were thereby to obtain access to this compelled material, it would still be up to the court at the proceedings (if any) where it is sought to be introduced to determine its admissibility.

[6] I agree with the chambers judge that the balance of interests relevant to whether disclosure should be made by a party of alleged criminality is better evaluated by a court than by one of the litigants who will generally be self-interested. Discoveries (both oral and documentary) are likely to run more smoothly if none of the disputants are in a position to go without a court order to the police, or regulators or other authorities with their suspicions of wrongdoing, or to use the material obtained for any other purpose collateral or ulterior to the action in which the discovery is obtained. Of course the implied undertaking does not bind the Attorney General and the police (who are not parties to it) from seeking a search warrant in the ordinary way to obtain the discovery transcripts if they have the grounds to do so. Apparently, no such application has been made. At this stage the matter has proceeded only to the point of determining whether or not the implied undertaking permits "the *bona fide* disclosure of criminal conduct" without court order (BCCA, at para. 56). In my view it does not do so in the circumstances disclosed here. I would allow the appeal.

Facts

[7] The appellant, a childcare worker, provided day services in her home. A 16-month-old child, Jade Doucette, suffered a seizure while in the appellant's care. The child was later determined to have suffered a brain injury. She and her parents sued the owners and operators of the day-care centre for damages, alleging that Jade's injury resulted from its negligence and that of the appellant.

[8] The appellant's defence alleges, in part, that Jade suffered a number of serious mishaps, including a bicycle accident while riding as a passenger with her father, none of which involved the appellant, and none of which were disclosed to the appellant when the child was delivered into her care (Statement of Defence, at para. 3).

[9] The Vancouver Police have for several years been conducting an investigation, which is still ongoing. In May 2004, the Vancouver police arrested the appellant. She was questioned in the absence of her counsel (AR, at p. 179). She was later released. In August 2004, the appellant and her husband received notices that their private communications had been intercepted by the police pursuant to s. 196 of the *Criminal Code*. To date, no criminal charges have been laid. In furtherance of that investigation, the authorities seek access to the appellant's discovery transcript.

[10] In November 2004, the appellant brought an interlocutory motion to prohibit the parties to the civil proceeding from providing the transcripts of discovery (which had not yet been held) to the police. She also sought to prevent the release of information from the transcripts to the police or the Attorney General of British Columbia and a third motion to prohibit the Attorney General of British Columbia, the police and the RCMP from obtaining and using copies of the transcripts and solicitor's notes without further court order. She relied upon the implied undertaking rule.

[11] The Attorney General of British Columbia opposed the appellant's motions and brought his own cross-motion for an order (if necessary) varying the legal undertaking

to permit release of the transcripts to police. He also brought a second motion for an order permitting the police to apply for the transcripts by way of search warrant, subpoena or other investigative means in the usual way.

[12] The appellant was examined for discovery for four days between June 2005 and September 2006. She claimed the protection of the *Canada Evidence Act*, RSC 1985, c. C-5, the British Columbia *Evidence Act*, RSBC 1996, c. 124, and (though an explicit claim was not necessary) of the *Canadian Charter of Rights and Freedoms*, and says that she answered all the appropriate questions put to her. The transcripts are now in the possession of the parties and/or their counsel.

[13] In 2006, the underlying claim was settled. The appellant's discovery was never entered into evidence at a trial nor its contents disclosed in open court.

Judicial History

A. Supreme Court of British Columbia (Shaw J) (2005), 45 BCLR (4th) 108, 2005 BCSC 400

[14] The chambers judge observed that an examination for discovery is statutorily compelled testimony by rule 27 of the BC *Rules of Court*, BC Reg. 221/90. As a general rule, there exists in British Columbia an implied undertaking in civil actions that the parties and their lawyers will use discovery evidence strictly for the purposes of the court case. Discovery exists because getting at the truth in the pursuit of justice is an important social goal, but so (he held) is limiting the invasion of the examinee's privacy. Evidence taken on oral discovery comes within the scope of the undertaking. He noted that the court has the discretionary power to grant exemptions from or variations to the undertaking, and that in the exercise of that discretion courts must balance the need for disclosure against the right to privacy.

[15] The chambers judge rejected the contention that the implied undertaking does not apply to evidence of crimes. Considerations of practicality supported keeping evidence of crimes within the scope of the undertaking because such evidence could vary from mere suspicion to blatant admissions and from minor to the most serious offences. It was better to leave the discretionary power of relief to the courts.

[16] As to the various arguments asserted by the appellant under ss. 7, 11(c) and 13 of the *Charter*, the chambers judge concluded that "[t]he state is forbidden to use its investigatory powers to violate the confidentiality requirement of solicitor–client privilege; so too, in my view, should the state be forbidden to violate the confidentiality protected by discovery privilege" (para. 62). In his view, it was not open to the police to seize the transcript under a search warrant.

B. Court of Appeal for British Columbia (Newbury, Low and Kirkpatrick JJA) (2006), 55 BCLR (4th) 66, 2006 BCCA 262

[17] The Court of Appeal allowed the appeal. In its view, the parties were at liberty to disclose the appellant's discovery evidence to the police to assist in the criminal investigation. Further, the authorities could obtain the discovery evidence by lawful investigative means such as subpoenas and search warrants.

[18] Kirkpatrick JA, speaking for a unanimous court, noted the English law on the implied undertaking of confidentiality had been applied in British Columbia only in recent years. See *Hunt v. T & N plc* (1995), 4 BCLR (3d) 110. In that case, however, the British Columbia Court of Appeal had held that "[t]he obligation the law imposes is one of confidentiality from improper publication. It does not supersede all other legal, social or moral duties" (para. 65; quoted at para. 32). Thus, in Kirkpatrick JA's opinion, "the undertaking in the action cannot form a shield from the detection and prosecution of crimes in which the public has an overriding interest" (para. 48).

[19] Kirkpatrick JA then turned to the *Charter* issues in the case. She noted that no charges had been laid against the appellant and therefore that ss. 11(c) (which applies to persons "charged with an offence") and 13 (which provides use immunity) were not engaged. The appellant was not in any imminent danger of deprivation of her right to liberty or security, and therefore any s. 7 claim was premature. Kirkpatrick JA declared that an implied undertaking, being just a rule of civil procedure, should not be given "constitutional status. "Discovery material is not immune to search or seizure. The appeal was therefore allowed.

Analysis

[20] The root of the implied undertaking is the statutory compulsion to participate fully in pre-trial oral and documentary discovery. If the opposing party seeks information that is relevant and is not protected by privilege, it must be disclosed even if it tends to self-incrimination. See BC *Rules of Court*, rules 27(2), 44, 60(41), 60(42) and 64(1); *Ross v. Henriques*, [2007] BCJ No. 2023 (QL), 2007 BCSC 1381, at paras. 180-81. In Quebec, see *Lac d'Amiante du Québec Ltée v. 2858-0702 Québec Inc.*, [2001] 2 SCR 743, 2001 SCC 51, at para. 42. In Ontario, see *Stickney v. Trusz* (1973), 2 OR (2d) 469 (HCJ), aff'd. (1974), 3 OR (2d) 538 (Div. Ct.), at p. 539, aff'd. (1974), 3 OR (2d) 538 (p. 539) (CA), leave to appeal ref'd., [1974] SCR xii. The rule in common law jurisdictions was affirmed post-*Charter* in *Tricontinental Investments Co. v. Guarantee Co. of North America* (1982), 39 OR (2d) 614 (HCJ), and has been applied to public inquiries, *Phillips v. Nova Scotia (Commission of Inquiry into the Westray Mine Tragedy)*, [1995] 2 SCR 97.

[21] The Attorney General of British Columbia submits that *Lac d'Amiante*, which was based on the Quebec *Code of Civil Procedure*, RSQ, c. C-25, "was wrongly decided" (factum, at para. 16). An implied undertaking not to disclose pre-trial documentary and oral discovery for purposes other than the litigation in which it was obtained is, he argues, contrary to the "open court" principle stated in *Attorney General of Nova Scotia v. MacIntyre*, [1982] 1 SCR 175, and *Edmonton Journal v. Alberta (Attorney General)*, [1989] 2 SCR 1326 (factum, at para. 6). The Vancouver Police support this position (factum, at para. 48). The argument is based on a misconception. Pre-trial discovery does not take place in open court. The vast majority of civil cases never go to trial. Documents are inspected or exchanged by counsel at a place of their own choosing. In general, oral discovery is not conducted in front of a judge. The only point at which the "open court" principle is engaged is when, if at all, the case goes to trial and the discovered party's documents or answers from the discovery transcripts are introduced as part of the case at trial.

[22] In *Attorney General of Nova Scotia v. MacIntyre*, relied on by the Vancouver Police as well as by the Attorney General of British Columbia, the contents of the affidavit in support of the search warrant application were made public, but not until after the search warrant had been executed, and "the purposes of the policy of secrecy are largely, if not entirely, accomplished" (p. 188). At that point the need for public access and public scrutiny prevail. Here the action has been settled but the policies reflected in the implied undertaking (privacy and the efficient conduct of civil litigation generally) remain undiminished. Nor is *Edmonton Journal* helpful to the respondents. In that case the court struck down a "sweeping" Alberta prohibition against publication of matrimonial proceedings, including publication of the "comments of counsel and the presiding judge." In the face of such prohibition, the court asked, "how then is the community to know if judges conduct themselves properly" (p. 1341). No such questions of state accountability arise in pre-trial discoveries. The situations are simply not analogous.

A. The Rationale for the Implied Undertaking

[23] Quite apart from the cases of exceptional prejudice, as in disputes about trade secrets or intellectual property, which have traditionally given rise to express confidentiality orders, there are good reasons to support the existence of an implied (or, in reality, a court-imposed) undertaking.

[24] In the first place, pre-trial discovery is an invasion of a private right to be left alone with your thoughts and papers, however embarrassing, defamatory or scandalous. At least one side in every lawsuit is a reluctant participant. Yet a proper pre-trial discovery is essential to prevent surprise or "litigation by ambush," to encourage settlement once the facts are known, and to narrow issues even where settlement proves unachievable. Thus, rule 27(22) of the BC *Rules of Court* compels a litigant to answer all relevant questions posed on an examination for discovery. Failure to do so can result in punishment by way of imprisonment or fine pursuant to rules 56(1), 56(4) and 2(5). In some provinces, the rules of practice provide that individuals who are not even parties can be ordered to submit to examination for discovery on issues relevant to a dispute in which they may have no direct interest. It is not uncommon for plaintiff's counsel aggressively to "sue everyone in sight" not with any realistic hope of recovery but to "get discovery." Thus, for the out-of-pocket cost of issuing a statement of claim or other process, the gate is swung open to investigate the private information and perhaps highly confidential documents of the examinee in pursuit of allegations that might in the end be found to be without any merit at all.

[25] The public interest in getting at the truth in a civil action outweighs the examinee's privacy interest, but the latter is nevertheless entitled to a measure of protection. The answers and documents are compelled by statute solely for the purpose of the civil action and the law thus requires that the invasion of privacy should generally be limited to the level of disclosure necessary to satisfy that purpose and that purpose alone. Although the present case involves the issue of self-incrimination of the appellant, that element is not a necessary requirement for protection. Indeed, the disclosed information need not even satisfy the legal requirements of confidentiality set out in *Slavutych v. Baker*, [1976] 1 SCR 254. The general idea, metaphorically speaking, is that whatever is disclosed in the

discovery room stays in the discovery room unless eventually revealed in the courtroom or disclosed by judicial order.

[26] There is a second rationale supporting the existence of an implied undertaking. A litigant who has some assurance that the documents and answers will not be used for a purpose collateral or ulterior to the proceedings in which they are demanded will be encouraged to provide a more complete and candid discovery. This is of particular interest in an era where documentary production is of a magnitude ("litigation by avalanche") as often to preclude careful pre-screening by the individuals or corporations making production. See *Kyuquot Logging Ltd. v. British Columbia Forest Products Ltd.* (1986), 5 BCLR (2d) 1 (CA), *per* Esson JA dissenting, at pp. 10-11.

[27] For good reason, therefore, the law imposes on the parties to civil litigation an undertaking *to the court* not to use the documents or answers for any purpose other than securing justice in the civil proceedings in which the answers were compelled (whether or not such documents or answers were in their origin confidential or incriminatory in nature). See *Home Office v. Harman*, [1983] 1 AC 280 (HL); *Lac d'Amiante; Hunt v. T & N plc; Shaw Estate v. Oldroyd*, [2007] BCJ No. 1310 (QL), 2007 BCSC 866, at para. 21; *Rayman Investments and Management Inc. v. Canada Mortgage and Housing Corp.*, [2007] BCJ No. 628 (QL), 2007 BCSC 384, *Wilson v. McCoy* (2006), 59 BCLR (4th) 1, 2006 BCSC 1011; *Laxton Holdings Ltd. v. Madill*, [1987] 3 WWR 570 (Sask. CA); *Blake v. Hudson's Bay Co.*, [1988] 1 WWR 176 (Man. QB); *755568 Ontario Ltd. v. Linchris Homes Ltd.* (1990), 1 OR (3d) 649 (Gen. Div.); *Rocca Enterprises Ltd. v. University Press of New Brunswick Ltd.* (1989), 103 NBR (2d) 224 (QB); *Eli Lilly and Co. v. Interpharm Inc.* (1993), 161 NR 137 (FCA). A number of other decisions are helpfully referenced in W.A. Stevenson and J.E. Côté, *Civil Procedure Encyclopedia* (2003), Vol. 2, at pp. 42-36 *et seq.*; and C. Papile, "The Implied Undertaking Revisited" (2006), 32 *Adv. Q* 190, at pp. 194-96.

[28] The need to protect the privacy of the pre-trial discovery is recognized even in common law jurisdictions where there is no implied undertaking. See J.B. Laskin, "The Implied Undertaking" (a paper presented to the CBA—Ontario, CLE Conference on *Privilege and Confidential Information in Litigation—Current Developments and Future Trends*, October 19, 1991), at pp. 36-40. Rule 26(c) of the United States *Federal Rules of Civil Procedure* provides that a court may, upon a showing of "good cause," grant a protective order to maintain the confidentiality of information disclosed during discovery. The practical effect is that the courts routinely make confidentiality orders limited to pre-trial disclosure to protect a party or person being discovered "from annoyance, embarrassment, oppression, or undue burden or expense." See, e.g., *Cipollone v. Liggett Group, Inc.*, 785 F2d 1108 (3d Cir. 1986).

B. Remedies for Breach of the Implied Undertaking

[29] Breach of the undertaking may be remedied by a variety of means including a stay or dismissal of the proceeding, or striking a defence, or, in the absence of a less drastic remedy, contempt proceedings for breach of the undertaking owed to the court. See *Lac d'Amiante*, at para. 64, and *Goodman v. Rossi* (1995), 125 DLR (4th) 613 (Ont. CA), at p. 624.

C. *Exceptional Circumstances May Trump the Implied Undertaking*

[30] The undertaking is imposed in recognition of the examinee's privacy interest, and the public interest in the efficient conduct of civil litigation, but those values are not, of course, absolute. They may, in turn, be trumped by a more compelling public interest. Thus, where the party being discovered does not consent, a party bound by the undertaking may apply to the court for leave to use the information or documents otherwise than in the action, as described in *Lac d'Amiante*, at para. 77:

> Before using information, however, the party in question will have to apply for leave, specifying the purposes of using the information and the reasons why it is justified, and both sides will have to be heard on the application.

In such an application the judge would have access to the documents or transcripts at issue.

D. *Applications Should Be Dealt with Expeditiously*

[31] The injury to Jade Doucette occurred on November 19, 2001. The police investigation was launched shortly thereafter. Almost four years ago the appellant was (briefly) arrested. Three and a half years ago the present court applications were launched. Over two years ago the appellant was examined for discovery. It is apparent that in many of these cases delay will defeat the purpose of the application. It is important that they proceed expeditiously.

E. *Criteria on the Application for a Modification or Variance of the Implied Undertaking*

[32] An application to modify or relieve against an implied undertaking requires an applicant to demonstrate to the court on a balance of probabilities the existence of a public interest of greater weight than the values the implied undertaking is designed to protect, namely privacy and the efficient conduct of civil litigation. In a case like the present, of course, there weighs heavily in the balance the right of a suspect to remain silent in the face of a police investigation, and the right not to be compelled to incriminate herself. The chambers judge took the view (I think correctly) that in this case that factor was decisive. In other cases the mix of competing values may be different. What is important in each case is to recognize that unless an examinee is satisfied that the undertaking will only be modified or varied by the court in exceptional circumstances, the undertaking will not achieve its intended purpose.

[33] Reference was made to *Crest Homes plc v. Marks*, [1987] 2 All ER 1074, where Lord Oliver said, on behalf of the House of Lords, that the authorities "illustrate no general principle beyond this, that the court will not release or modify the implied undertaking given on discovery save in special circumstances and where the release or modification will not occasion injustice to the person giving discovery" (p. 1083). I would prefer to rest the discretion on a careful weighing of the public interest asserted by the applicant (here the prosecution of a serious crime) against the public interest in protecting the right against self-incrimination as well as upholding a litigant's privacy

and promoting an efficient civil justice process. What is important is the identification of the competing values, and the weighing of one in the light of the others, rather than setting up an absolute barrier to occasioning any "injustice to the person giving discovery." Prejudice, possibly amounting to injustice, to a particular litigant may exceptionally be held justified by a higher public interest, as in the case of the accused whose solicitor–client confidences were handed over to the police in *Smith v. Jones*, [1999] 1 SCR 455, a case referred to in the courts below, and discussed hereafter. Of course any perceived prejudice to the examinee is a factor that will always weigh heavily in the balance. It may be argued that disclosure to the police of the evil secrets of the psychopath at issue in *Smith v. Jones* may have been prejudicial to him but was not an "injustice" in the overall scheme of things, but such a gloss would have given cold comfort to an accused who made his disclosures in the expectation of confidentiality. If public safety trumps solicitor–client privilege despite a measure of injustice to the (unsympathetic) accused in *Smith v. Jones*, it can hardly be disputed in this jurisdiction that the implied undertaking rule would yield to such a higher public interest as well.

[34] Three Canadian provinces have enacted rules governing when relief should be given against such implied or "deemed" undertakings, (see *Queen's Bench Rules*, MR 553/88, r. 30.1 (Manitoba), *Rules of Civil Procedure*, RRO 1990, Reg. 194, r. 30.1 (Ontario), and *Rules of Civil Procedure*, r. 30.1 (Prince Edward Island)). I believe the test formulated therein (in identical terms) is apt as a reflection of the common law more generally, namely:

> If satisfied that the interest of justice outweighs any prejudice that would result to a party who disclosed evidence, the court may order that [the implied or "deemed" undertaking] does not apply to the evidence or to information obtained from it, and may impose such terms and give such direction as are just.

[35] The case law provides some guidance to the exercise of the court's discretion. For example, where discovery material in one action is sought to be used in another action with the same or similar parties and the same or similar issues, the prejudice to the examinee is virtually non-existent and leave will generally be granted. See *Lac Minerals Ltd. v. New Cinch Uranium Ltd.* (1985), 50 OR (2d) 260 (HCJ), at pp. 265-66; *Crest Homes*, at p. 1083; *Miller (Ed) Sales & Rentals Ltd. v. Caterpillar Tractor Co.* (1988), 90 AR 323 (CA); *Harris v. Sweet*, [2005] BCJ No. 1520 (QL), 2005 BCSC 998; *Scuzzy Creek Hydro & Power Inc. v. Tercon Contractors Ltd.* (1998), 27 CPC (4th) 252 (BCSC).

[36] On the other hand, courts have generally not favoured attempts to use the discovered material for an extraneous purpose, or for an action wholly unrelated to the purposes of the proceeding in which discovery was obtained in the absence of some compelling public interest. See, e.g., *Lubrizol Corp. v. Imperial Oil Ltd.* (1990), 33 CPR (3d) 49 (FCTD), at p. 51. In *Livent Inc. v. Drabinsky* (2001), 53 OR (3d) 126 (SCJ), the court held that a non-party to the implied undertaking could in unusual circumstances apply to have the undertaking varied, but that relief in such cases would virtually never be given (p. 130).

[37] Some applications have been refused on the basis that they demonstrate precisely the sort of mischief the implied undertaking rule was designed to avoid. In *755568 Ontario Ltd.*, for example, the plaintiff sought leave to send the defendant's discovery

transcripts to the police. The court concluded that the plaintiff's strategy was to enlist the aid of the police to discover further evidence in support of the plaintiff's claim and/or to pressure the defendant to settle (p. 655).

(i) The Balancing of Interests

[38] As stated, the onus in each case will be on the applicant to demonstrate a superior public interest in disclosure, and the court will be mindful that an undertaking should only be set aside in exceptional circumstances. In what follows I do not mean to suggest that the categories of superior public interest are fixed. My purpose is illustrative rather than exhaustive. However, to repeat, an undertaking designed in part to encourage open and generous discovery by assuring parties being discovered of confidentiality will not achieve its objective if the confidentiality is seen by reluctant litigants to be too readily set aside.

(ii) Statutory Exceptions

[39] The implied undertaking rule at common law, and in those jurisdictions which have enacted rules, more or less codifying the common law, is subject to legislative override. In the present case for example, the Attorney General of British Columbia and the Vancouver Police rely on s. 14 of the *Child, Family and Community Service Act*, RSBC 1996, c. 46, which provides that:

> (1) A person who has reason to believe that a child needs protection under section 13 must promptly report the matter to a director or a person designated by a director.
> (2) Subsection (1) applies even if the information on which the belief is based
>   (a) is privileged, except as a result of a solicitor–client relationship, or
>   (b) is confidential and its disclosure is prohibited under another Act.

It is apparent from the extensive police investigation to date and the appearance of the Attorneys General and the Vancouver Police in these proceedings that a report was made to the authorities. We do not know the details. Undoubtedly, a report could have been made without reference to anything said or produced at discovery. At this point the matter has proceeded beyond a mere "report" and involves the collection of evidence. This will require, in the ordinary way laid down by Parliament in s. 487 of the *Criminal Code*, the application for a search warrant or a subpoena *duces tecum* at trial, if there is a trial.

(iii) Public Safety Concerns

[40] One important public interest flagged by the chambers judge was the "public safety" issue raised by way of analogy to *Smith v. Jones*, a case dealing with solicitor–client privilege. While solicitor–client privilege constitutes an interest higher than the privacy interest at issue here, the chambers judge used the case to illustrate the relevant balancing of interests. There, a psychiatrist was retained by defence counsel to prepare an assessment of the accused for purposes of the defence generally, including potential submissions on sentencing in the event of a conviction. During his interview with the psychiatrist, the accused described in considerable detail his plan to kidnap, rape and kill prostitutes. The

psychiatrist concluded the accused was a dangerous individual who would, more likely than not, commit future offences unless he received immediate psychiatric treatment. The psychiatrist wished to take his concerns to the police and applied to the court for leave to do so notwithstanding that the psychiatrist's only access to the accused was under the umbrella of solicitor–client privilege. In such a case the accused/client would undoubtedly consider himself to be the victim of an injustice, but our Court held that the privilege yielded to "clear and imminent threat of serious bodily harm to an identifiable group … if this threat is made in such a manner that a sense of urgency is created" (para. 84). Further, in circumstances of "immediate and serious danger," the police may be contacted without leave of the court (paras. 96-97). If a comparable situation arose in the context of an implied undertaking, the proper procedure would be for the concerned party to make application to a chambers judge but if, as discussed in *Smith v. Jones* there existed a situation of "immediate and serious danger," the applicant would be justified in going directly to the police, in my opinion, without a court order.

(iv) Impeaching Inconsistent Testimony

[41] Another situation where the deponent's privacy interest will yield to a higher public interest is where the deponent has given contradictory testimony about the same matters in successive or different proceedings. If the contradiction is discovered, the implied undertaking rule would afford no shield to its use for purposes of impeachment. In provinces where the implied undertaking rule has been codified, there is a specific provision that the undertaking "does not prohibit the use of evidence obtained in one proceeding, or information obtained from such evidence, to impeach the testimony of a witness in another proceeding," see Manitoba r. 30.1(6), Ontario r. 30.1.01(6), Prince Edward Island r. 30.1.01(6). While statutory, this provision, in my view, also reflects the general common law in Canada. An undertaking implied by the court (or imposed by the legislature) to make civil litigation more effective should not permit a witness to play games with the administration of justice: *R v. Henry*, [2005] 3 SCR 609, 2005 SCC 76. Any other outcome would allow a person accused of an offence "[w]ith impunity [to] tailor his evidence to suit his needs in each particular proceeding" (*R v. Nedelcu* (2007), 41 CPC (6th) 357 (Ont. SCJ), at paras. 49-51).

(v) The Suggested "Crimes" Exception

[42] As stated, Kirkpatrick JA concluded that "the undertaking in the action cannot form a shield from the detection and prosecution of crimes in which the public has an overriding interest" (para. 48). In her view,

> a party obtaining production of documents or transcriptions of oral examination of discovery is under a general obligation, in most cases, to keep such document confidential. A party seeking to use the discovery evidence other than in the proceedings in which it is produced must obtain the permission of the disclosing party or leave of the court. However, the obligation of confidentiality does not extend to *bona fide* disclosure of criminal conduct. On the other hand, non-*bona fide* disclosure of alleged criminal conduct would attract serious civil sanctions for contempt. [para. 56]

[43] The chambers judge put his finger on one of the serious difficulties with such an exception. He wrote:

> … considerations of practicality support keeping evidence of crimes within the scope of the undertaking. In this regard, it should be understood that evidence relating to a crime may vary from mere suspicion to blatant admissions, from peripheral clues to direct evidence, from minor offences to the most heinous. There are also many shades and variations in between these extremes. [para. 27]

This difficulty is compounded by the fact that parties to civil litigation are often quick to see the supposed criminality in what their opponents are up to, or at least to appreciate the tactical advantage that threats to go to the police might achieve, and to pose questions to the examinee to lay the basis for such an approach: see *755568 Ontario Ltd.*, at p. 656. The rules of discovery were not intended to constitute litigants as private attorneys general.

[44] The chambers judge took the view that "leaving the discretionary power of exemption or variation with the courts is preferable to giving litigants the power to report to the police, without a court order, anything that might relate to a criminal offence" (para. 27). I agree. On such an application the court will be able to weigh against the examinee's privacy interest the seriousness of the offence alleged, the "evidence" or admissions said to be revealed in the discovery process, the use to which the applicant or police may put this material, whether there is evidence of malice or spite on the part of the applicant, and such other factors as appear to the court to be relevant to the exercise of its discretion. This will include recognition of the potential adverse effects if the protection of the implied undertaking is seen to be diluted or diminished.

[45] Kirkpatrick JA noted that in some circumstances

> neither party has an interest in or is willing to seek court ordered relief from the disclosure of information under the undertaking or otherwise. Nor does it [the chambers judge's approach] contemplate non-exigent circumstances of disclosed criminal conduct. It is easy to imagine a situation in which criminal conduct is disclosed in the discovery process, but no one apprehends that immediate harm is likely to result. [para. 55]

This is true, but it presupposes that the police are entitled to be handed a transcript of statutorily compelled answers which they themselves have no authority to compel, thereby using the civil discovery process to obtain indirectly what the police have no right to obtain directly. Such a rule, if accepted, would undermine the freedom of a suspect to cooperate or refuse to cooperate with the police, which is an important element of our criminal law.

[46] In reaching her decision, Kirkpatrick JA relied on *dicta* of the House of Lords in *Rank Film Distributors Ltd. v. Video Information Centre*, [1982] AC 380 (p. 425). Lord Fraser said:

> If a defendant's answers to interrogatories tend to show that he has been guilty of a serious offence I cannot think that there would be anything improper in his opponent reporting the matter to the criminal authorities with a view to prosecution, certainly if he had first obtained leave from the court which ordered the interrogatories, and probably without such leave… . [p. 447]

These observations, however, must be read in light of the fact that in England, unlike British Columbia, there existed at the time (since amended) "a privilege against compulsory self-incrimination by discovery or by answering interrogatories" (p. 446). There was thus absent from the English procedure the very foundation of the appellant's case, namely that she had *no* right to refuse to answer questions on discovery that might incriminate her, because she was obliged by statute to give the truth, the whole truth and nothing but the truth.

[47]   It is true that solicitor–client privilege includes a "crime" exception, but here again there is no proper analogy to an implied undertaking. In *Solosky v. The Queen*, [1980] 1 SCR 821, Dickson J observed at p. 835:

> ... if a client seeks guidance from a lawyer in order to facilitate the commission of a crime or a fraud, the communication will not be privileged and it is immaterial whether the lawyer is an unwitting dupe or knowing participant.

See also *R v. Campbell*, [1999] 1 SCR 565. Abuse of solicitor–client privilege to facilitate criminality is contrary to its purpose. Adoption of the implied undertaking to facilitate full disclosure on discovery *even by crooks* is of the very essence of its purpose. In England, the weight of authority now seems to favour requiring leave of the court where the protected material relates to alleged criminality. See *Attorney-General for Gibraltar v. May*, [1999] 1 WLR 998 (CA), at pp. 1007-8; *Bank of Crete S.A. v. Koskotas (No. 2)*, [1992] 1 WLR 919 (Ch. D), at p. 922; *Sybron Corp. v. Barclays Bank Plc.*, [1985] 1 Ch. 299, at p. 326. The same practice prevails in Australia: *Bailey v. Australian Broadcasting Corp.*, [1995] 1 Qd. R 476 (SC); *Commonwealth v. Temwood Holdings Pty Ltd.* (2001), 25 WAR 31, [2001] WASC 282.

[48]   In reaching her conclusion, Kirkpatrick JA rejected the view expressed in *755568 Ontario Ltd.* and *Perrin v. Beninger*, [2004] OJ No. 2353 (QL) (SCJ), that the public interest in investigating possible crimes is *not* in all cases sufficient to relieve against the undertaking. It is inherent in any balancing exercise that one interest will not always and in every circumstance prevail over other interests. It will depend on the facts. In *Tyler v. MNR*, [1991] 2 FC 68 (CA), in a somewhat analogous situation of statutory compulsion, the appellant was charged with narcotics offences. Revenue Canada, on reading about the charges in a newspaper, began to investigate the possibility that the appellant had not reported all of his income in earlier years. The Minister invoked his statutory powers to compel information from the appellant, who sought to prevent the Minister from communicating any information thereby obtained to the RCMP. Stone JA, speaking for an unanimous Federal Court of Appeal, agreed that the Minister should be permitted to continue using his compulsory audit for *Income Tax Act* purposes but prohibited the Minister from sharing the information compulsorily obtained from the appellant with the RCMP. Stone JA was of the view that the prosecution of crime did not necessarily trump a citizen's privacy interest in the disclosure of statutorily compelled information and I agree with him.

[49]   The BC Court of Appeal qualified its "crimes" exception by the requirement that the communication to the police be made in good faith. Aside from the difficulties in applying such a requirement, as previously mentioned, I do not see how a "good faith" requirement is consistent with the court's rationale for granting relief against the under-

taking. If, as the hypothesis requires, it is determined in a particular case that the public interest in investigating a crime and bringing the perpetrators to justice is paramount to the examinee's privacy interest, the good faith of the communication should no more be an issue here than in the case of any other informant. Informants are valued for what they can tell not for their worthy motives.

[50] Finally, Kirkpatrick JA feared that

> if an application to court is required before a party may disclose the alleged conduct, the perpetrator of the crime may be notified of the disclosure and afforded the opportunity to destroy or hide evidence or otherwise conceal his or her involvement in the alleged crime. [para. 55]

This concern is largely remedied by permitting the party wishing to be relieved of the obligation of confidentiality to apply to the court *ex parte*. It would be up to the chambers judge to determine whether the circumstances justify proceeding *ex parte*, or whether the deponent and other parties to the proceeding should be notified of the application.

F. Continuing Nature of the Implied Undertaking

[51] As mentioned earlier, the lawsuit against the appellant and others was settled in 2006. As a result the appellant was not required to give evidence at a civil trial; nor were her examination for discovery transcripts ever read into evidence. The transcripts remain in the hands of the parties and their lawyer. Nevertheless, the implied undertaking continues. The fact that the settlement has rendered the discovery moot does not mean the appellant's privacy interest is also moot. The undertaking continues to bind. When an adverse party incorporates the answers or documents obtained on discovery as part of the court record at trial the undertaking is spent, but not otherwise, except by consent or court order. See *Lac d'Amiante*, at paras. 70 and 76; *Shaw Estate v. Oldroyd*, at paras. 20-22. It follows that decisions to the contrary, such as the decision of the House of Lords in *Home Office v. Harman* (where a narrow majority held that the implied undertaking not to disclose documents obtained on discovery continued even after the documents in question had been read aloud in open court), should not be followed in this country. The effect of the *Harman* decision has been reversed by a rule change in its country of origin.

G. Who Is Entitled to Notice of an Application to Modify or Vary the Implied Undertaking

[52] While the issue of notice will be for the chambers judge to decide on the facts of any particular case, I do not think that in general the police are entitled to notice of such an application. Nor are the media. The only parties with a direct interest, other than the applicant, are the deponent and the other parties to the litigation.

H. Application to Modify or Vary an Implied Undertaking by Strangers to It

[53] I would not preclude an application to vary an undertaking by a non-party on the basis of standing, although I agree with *Livent Inc. v. Drabinsky* that success on such an application would be unusual. What has already been said provides some illustrations

of potential third party applicants. In this case the Attorney General of British Columbia, supported by the Vancouver Police, demonstrated a sufficient interest in the appellant's transcripts to be given standing to apply. Their objective was to obtain evidence that would help explain the events under investigation, and possibly to incriminate the appellant. I think it would be quite wrong for the police to be able to take advantage of statutorily compelled testimony in civil litigation to undermine the appellant's right to silence and the protection against self-incrimination afforded him by the criminal law. Accordingly, in my view, the present application was rightly dismissed by the chambers judge. On the other hand, a non-party engaged in *other* litigation with an examinee, who learns of potentially contradicting testimony by the examinee in a discovery to which that other person is not a party, would have standing to seek to obtain a modification of the implied undertaking and for the reasons given above may well succeed. Of course if the undertaking is respected by the parties to it, then non-parties will be unlikely to possess enough information to make an application for a variance in the first place that is other than a fishing expedition. But the possibility of third party applications exists, and where duly made the competing interests will have to be weighed, keeping in mind that an undertaking too readily set aside sends the message that such undertakings are unsafe to be relied upon, and will therefore not achieve their broader purpose.

I. Use Immunity

[54] Reference was earlier made to the fact that at her discovery the appellant claimed the benefit of s. 5 of the *Canada Evidence Act* which eliminates the right formerly enjoyed by a witness to refuse to answer "any question on the ground that the answer to the question may tend to criminate him, or may tend to establish his liability to a civil proceeding at the instance of the Crown or of any person" (s. 5(1)). Answers given under objection, however, "shall not be used or admissible in evidence against him in any criminal trial or other criminal proceeding against him thereafter taking place, other than a prosecution for perjury" (s. 5(2)). Similar protection is provided under s. 4 of the British Columbia *Evidence Act*. Section 13 of the *Charter* applies without need of objection. Derivative use immunity is a question for the criminal court at any trial that may be held: *R v. S. (R.J.)*, [1995] 1 SCR 451, at paras. 191-92 and 204. The appellant's statutory or *Charter* rights are not in peril in the present appeal and her claims to *Charter* relief at this stage were properly dismissed.

J. Implied Undertaking Is No Bar to Persons Not a Party to It

[55] None of the parties to the original civil litigation applied to vary the undertaking. Neither the Attorneys General nor the police are parties to the implied undertaking and they are not bound by its terms. If the police, as strangers to the undertaking, have grounds, they can apply for a search warrant under s. 487 of the *Criminal Code* in the ordinary way.

[56] The appellant's discovery transcript and documents, while protected by an implied undertaking of the parties to the court, are not themselves privileged, and are not exempt from seizure: *R v. Serendip Physiotherapy Clinic* (2004), 189 CCC (3d) 417 (Ont. CA), at para. 35. A search warrant, where available, only gives the police access to the

material. It does not authorize its use of the material in any proceedings that may be initiated.

[57] If criminal charges are brought, the prosecution may also compel a witness to produce a copy of the documents or transcripts in question from his or her possession by a subpoena *duces tecum*. The trial judge would then determine what, if any use could be made of the material, having regard to the appellant's *Charter* rights and any other relevant considerations. None of these issues arise for decision on the present appeal.

K. Disposition of the Present Appeal

[58] As stated, none of the parties bound by the implied undertaking made application to the court to be relieved from its obligations. The application is made solely by the Attorney General of British Columbia to permit

> any person in lawful possession of the transcript to provide a copy to the police or to the Attorney-General to assist in the investigation and/or prosecution of any criminal offence which may have occurred … . [BCSC, at para. 6]

While I would not deny the Attorney General standing to seek to vary an implied undertaking to which he is not a party, I agree with the chambers judge that his application should be rejected on the facts of this case. The purpose of the application was to sidestep the appellant's silence in the face of police investigation of her conduct. The authorities should not be able to obtain indirectly a transcript which they are unable to obtain directly through a search warrant in the ordinary way because they lack the grounds to justify it.

IV. Disposition

[59] I would allow the appeal with costs to the appellant both here and in the courts below.

NOTES

1. In the pre-*Juman* case of *Tanner v. Clark* (2003), 63 OR (3d) 508 (leave to appeal dismissed [2003] SCCA No. 192), the plaintiffs were injured in motor vehicle accidents and began arbitration proceedings with respect to accident benefits, and a tort action for damages. They were required to submit to medical examinations at the request of their insurer in the arbitration proceeding, and the defendants in the tort actions wanted production of those reports. The motions judge held that the plaintiffs' reports in the arbitration proceeding were protected from disclosure in the civil suits on the basis of the common law implied undertaking rule, but that the deemed undertaking under rule 30.1 (Ontario) did not apply because the arbitration proceeding was not a "proceeding" covered by the *Rules of Civil Procedure*. On appeal, the Divisional Court agreed that rule 30.1.01(3) did not apply to the accident benefits proceedings, but also held that the common law implied undertaking rule could not be used to prevent their production in the civil suits. The Court of Appeal agreed, and held the rules were intended to limit the ability of a party *receiving* documents produced under compulsion in one proceeding to use them in a subsequent proceeding, but

were not intended to limit the pursuit of truth by allowing a party who had *produced* a relevant document in a prior proceeding to avoid its production in a subsequent proceeding. The court reasoned:

> It is "used by the other party" and "use them to the detriment of the party who has produced them" that are the keynote phrases. Rule 30.1.01(1) speaks in the same voice—it is "evidence obtained" on discovery that shall not be "used." These verbs describe the acts of receiving and disseminating information; they do not label the evidence as sealed or privileged. The applicants in the AB proceedings submitted to medical examinations knowing that the information they impart will not be used by the two insurance companies except in those proceedings, and will not be communicated to others for their use in other proceedings. That has not happened here. The insurers in the tort proceedings are different companies and the information is sought, not from the insurers in the AB proceedings, but from the source of that information, the respective plaintiffs in the tort actions. Those plaintiffs are not constrained in any way from the use of their medical information for any purpose. What they argue for is not enforcement of an undertaking, but a protective shield against production of very relevant evidence.
>
> In my view, it would do no service to the implied undertaking rule to extend it in this fashion and would, indeed, be a considerable disservice. It would wrap a cloak of privilege around evidence given in any administrative tribunal hearing where a related issue arose in other proceedings. It would stand in the way of courts and tribunals having available the best evidence, or all of the evidence, bearing upon the issue in dispute.
>
> In sum, the rule should be as it has been—a party is encouraged to be candid with an opponent knowing that the opponent will not breach the confidence.
>
> The intervenor, Ontario Trial Lawyers Association, supported the appeals and urged the court to restrain production of the reports based upon access to justice concerns. As the argument goes, production would necessitate the plaintiffs hiring more medical experts to oppose those who had written, presumably critical reports, in the earlier proceedings. In other words, plaintiffs were being compelled to arm the defendants with ammunition and would have to hire new experts to fend against them. This overlooks the limit on the number of expert witnesses and, in any event cannot dictate limitations on discovery and detract from a trial on the merits.

2. As noted in *Juman*, one of the remedies for a breach is a stay of proceedings. For an example see: *Antoncic v. Wylie*, [2009] OJ No. 1277 (SCJ). One of the exceptions in *Juman* is that relief from a deemed undertaking can be ordered if litigation involves the same parties and/or issues. The logic of this exception is that deponents ought not be allowed to change their stories and "play games with the administration of justice" (at para. 41) under cover of the deemed undertaking rule. Left unclear is what a litigant must do to establish that grounds for relief: does there have to be an evidentiary basis for the claim of inconsistency? If so, is this fair? Where would such an evidentiary foundation come from if all parties are faithfully observing the undertaking? On the other hand, if no such a foundation is demanded, then the relief may be too easy to obtain, and be improperly in the service of fishing expeditions. It is likely courts will decide this based on the nexus between the parties and the issues in the different proceedings: see, for example: *Jomha v. Hicks Estate*, [2008] AJ No. 1073 (relief granted—no evidence required where the parties and issues are the same), *Biehl v. Strang*, [2009] BCJ No. 793 (relief denied—evidence of inconsistency required where party is the same but issues are different).

CHAPTER NINE

Pre-Trial Relief and Disposition Without Trial

I. INTRODUCTION

As we have seen, the system of civil procedure in Canada has as its primary goal the final disposition of the rights of the parties through either (1) the trial of an action before a judge or judge and jury, or (2) the hearing of an application or parallel procedure before a judge. Accordingly, the various pre-trial processes that we have considered concerning commencement of proceedings, pleadings, expansion of litigation, and mandatory mediation, to name a few, create a number of specific obligations on parties to litigation, or procedural rights and choices that must be fulfilled or exercised before the trial or hearing. Similarly, the system is built on the assumption that the final order of the court, and any remedy to the parties, will not be determined until after the trial or hearing is concluded.

In the course of the interval between the commencement of proceedings and any projected trial, there will inevitably be occasions when a party will want to raise a matter for consideration and decision by the court. These circumstances include:

1. where a party raises the issue of compliance or non-compliance of another party with procedural rules;
2. where a party seeks the permission of the court to take a procedural step where the court's authorization is required;

3. where a party wishes to raise an issue of legal or factual substance in the action or defence before trial; and
4. where a party wishes to obtain an interim remedy or relief in the action.

Generally, the process by which these kinds of questions are placed before the court for decision before trial is called a *motion* (see, for example, rule 37 in each of Ontario, Manitoba, PEI, and New Brunswick, and Alberta rule 384; in British Columbia, Newfoundland, and Nova Scotia, a motion is called an *interlocutory application* (see BC rule 44; Nova Scotia rule 37; and Newfoundland and Labrador rule 29)). Most motions are also *interlocutory motions*, in that they take place at an interim stage of the proceeding and do not result in the final disposition of the merits of the proceeding.

This section deals with the circumstances posed in (1) through (4) above, as well as those circumstances where the court's resolution of these issues may result in an *interlocutory order*—an order that affects only the process of the continuing action—or a *final order*—an order that finally disposes of all or part of the claims or defences in the action.

In addition, this chapter discusses:

1. the consequences of a party failing to respond to an originating process, and
2. the procedures available where a party wishes to unilaterally withdraw from an action.

II. MOTIONS

A. Resolution of Disputes Within a Proceeding

A motion involves a party applying to a court for the purpose of obtaining an order directing that some act be done in favour of the applicant, or otherwise ruling on some matter at the request of the applicant. As noted above, motions are generally brought within the framework of an existing proceeding or, exceptionally, in respect of a proceeding that will be commenced subsequently.

The procedure relating to motions and interlocutory applications is localized, both with respect to the applicable rules and the manner in which they are customarily applied—that is, local practice. There are, however, a number of basic elements that show how, in most cases, they work.

1. Initiating Documents

In each jurisdiction there is a prescribed form for the document used to initiate a motion, almost always called a *notice of motion*. This document specifies the date and place for the hearing of the motion; the nature of the order being sought; a summary of the reasons for seeking the order, including any applicable statutes or rules relied on, and a list of the evidence relied on in support of the motion.

2. Evidence

Unless the motion being brought is one in respect of which no evidence is permitted (such as a motion to strike a pleading or dismiss an action for failure to state a reasonable cause of action or defence, discussed below), evidence is required to prove any facts required for the court's decision.

On motions and interlocutory application, evidence is generally provided by affidavits, which are sworn, written statements in the first person by an individual who is called the deponent; any documents referred to by the deponent are annexed to the affidavit as exhibits. Affidavits in support of and in opposition to the motion are exchanged between the parties in advance of the motion and filed with the court for use on the hearing of the motion.

Given that the facts set out in any affidavits filed with a motion may be in conflict or subject to challenge, most provinces provide that a person swearing an affidavit for use on a motion may be cross-examined by the other parties. (In some provinces, such as British Columbia, there is no right of cross-examination on an affidavit, and leave of the court must be sought). Cross-examinations are generally conducted out of court and in advance of the hearing before a court reporter; a transcript of the questions and answers is produced for use at the hearing.

The effect of this process is that, in most cases, the evidence used on the hearing of a motion is entirely in writing. Oral testimony from witnesses at the hearing of a motion or interlocutory application is generally not permitted, or is permitted only in exceptional circumstances.

3. Notice

A motion must be made through service of notice and supporting materials on any party to the proceeding whose interests may be affected by the order sought. In exceptional cases, where notice is impracticable, or where the giving of notice may frustrate the purpose of the order (that is, by prompting the respondent to take action to defeat the remedy sought), the court may hear a motion without notice or *ex parte*.

Because a motion does not commence a proceeding, the rules respecting personal service generally do not apply. Local rules usually provide for service of motion materials flexibly on counsel or parties acting without counsel, through mail, fax, email, or other means.

4. The Hearing

The hearing of a motion proceeds by way of argument in court on the basis of the written notice of motion and evidence filed. In some provinces, for some motions, the parties are also required to file appellate-style memoranda of fact and law (factums) in advance of the hearing. Other provinces mandate lesser requirements, while others are silent on the question and leave the filing of written submissions on the motion to local practice and the choice of the parties.

While the tradition and general rule is that contested matters are argued by live attendance of counsel before the court, many jurisdictions now permit motions to proceed by telephone conference call or in writing without oral argument.

In Alberta and Ontario, certain motions and other proceedings may be heard by a judicial officer, called a master, who, to a degree, specializes in procedural disputes under the rules. Otherwise, motions and interlocutory applications are heard by judges.

B. Interim Substantive Relief

While the primary focus of this chapter relates to the resolution of procedural disputes and the disposition of proceedings without trial, motions that seek interim relief relating to the substantive remedy being sought in the lawsuit form an important part of the court's jurisdiction and caseload.

The ability of the court to grant interim substantive relief is governed by a combination of rules and statutory provisions in each Canadian jurisdiction. Generally, the ability to obtain an order that preserves the rights of a party pending the final trial or to obtain some other form of interim relief must be authorized by legislation. The most commonly encountered forms of interim substantive relief are summarized below.

1. Interlocutory Injunctions

In each Canadian jurisdiction, legislation empowers the court to grant an injunction or mandatory order (*mandamus*) "where it appears just and convenient." See, for example, the Ontario *Courts of Justice Act*, s. 101 and the BC *Law and Equity Act*, s. 39. The procedural rules make further provision for the hearing of a motion for an interlocutory injunction or mandatory order until trial or further order of the court: see Ontario rule 40 and BC rule 45.

An injunction is an order of the court that restrains a party from carrying out specified acts. There has been considerable judicial consideration of the test for the grant of an interlocutory injunction. Some of the issues involved in the grant of an interlocutory injunction are considered below.

2. Interim Preservation and Recovery of Property

All jurisdictions have statutory provisions or rules that give the court the power to make interim orders for the preservation, inspection, or custody of any personal property that is relevant to the subject matter of litigation. See, for example, Ontario rule 45. Further, where a plaintiff claims the recovery of personal property held by a defendant, the court may make an interim order for the recovery of that property on terms that often include posting security for the value of the property recovered. See, for example, Ontario *Courts of Justice Act*, s. 104 and Ontario rule 44. This latter remedy has historically been called *replevin* and is governed in some provinces by legislation or rules bearing that same name. See Alberta rule 427 and Saskatchewan rule 406.

3. Certificate of Pending Litigation Respecting Real Property

Parties claiming an interest in land may apply to the court for an order issuing a certificate of pending litigation, which may then be registered against the land title. The effect of this process is to provide formal public notice of the claim to the interest in the land. Anyone who subsequently deals with the property after the certificate is registered does so with notice of and potentially subject to the prior rights of the claim being asserted. This relief is also called *lis pendens*; it may be provided for under the relevant real property legislation rather than under procedural statutes and rules. Compare the Ontario *Courts of Justice Act*, s. 103 and Ontario rule 42 with the BC *Land Titles Act*, s. 213.

All forms of interim substantive relief reflect a tension between two goals—(1) the need to protect the rights of a party on an interim basis in circumstances where the inevitable time that must elapse before a case can be tried could result in serious prejudice to or loss of those rights; and (2) the desire not to make interim orders that unduly prejudge or affect the final substantive outcome. This has led courts in Canada to focus less on the merits of the claim and more on other procedural and equitable factors in determining motions and applications for interim substantive relief.

RJR-MacDonald Inc. v. Canada (Attorney General)
[1994] 1 SCR 311

[The applicant tobacco companies challenged the constitutional validity of the *Tobacco Products Control Act*, which regulated the advertisement of tobacco products and mandated health warnings on those products. The Court of Appeal found the legislation to be constitutional. Before a decision on applicants' leave applications in the action was made, the applicants applied to the Supreme Court of Canada for a stay from compliance with the new packaging and warning requirements.]

SOPINKA J: The primary issue to be decided on these motions is whether the applicants should be granted the interlocutory relief they seek. The applicants are only entitled to this relief if they can satisfy the test laid down in *Manitoba (Attorney General) v. Metropolitan Stores (MTS) Ltd.*, [[1987] 1 SCR 110]. If not, the applicants will have to comply with the new regulations, at least until such time as a decision is rendered in the main actions.

A. Interlocutory Injunctions, Stays of Proceedings and the Charter

. . .

Generally, the same principles should be applied by a court whether the remedy sought is an injunction or a stay. In *Metropolitan Stores*, at p. 127, Beetz J expressed the position in these words:

> A stay of proceedings and an interlocutory injunction are remedies of the same nature. In the absence of a different test prescribed by statute, they have sufficient characteristics in common to be governed by the same rules and the courts have rightly tended to apply to the

granting of interlocutory stay the principles which they follow with respect to interlocutory injunctions.

We would add only that here the applicants are requesting both interlocutory (pending disposition of the appeal) and interim (for a period of one year following such disposition) relief. We will use the broader term "interlocutory relief" to describe the hybrid nature of the relief sought. The same principles apply to both forms of relief.

Metropolitan Stores adopted a three-stage test for courts to apply when considering an application for either a stay or an interlocutory injunction. First, a preliminary assessment must be made of the merits of the case to ensure that there is a serious question to be tried. Secondly, it must be determined whether the applicant would suffer irreparable harm if the application were refused. Finally, an assessment must be made as to which of the parties would suffer greater harm from the granting or refusal of the remedy pending a decision on the merits. It may be helpful to consider each aspect of the test and then apply it to the facts presented in these cases.

B. The Strength of the Plaintiff's Case

Prior to the decision of the House of Lords in *American Cyanamid Co. v. Ethicon Ltd.*, [1975] AC 396, an applicant for interlocutory relief was required to demonstrate a "strong *prima facie* case" on the merits in order to satisfy the first test. In *American Cyanamid*, however, Lord Diplock stated that an applicant need no longer demonstrate a strong *prima facie* case. Rather it would suffice if he or she could satisfy the court that "the claim is not frivolous or vexatious; in other words, that there is a serious question to be tried." The *American Cyanamid* standard is now generally accepted by the Canadian courts, subject to the occasional reversion to a stricter standard: see Robert J. Sharpe, *Injunctions and Specific Performance* (2nd ed. 1992), at pp. 2-13 to 2-20.

In *Metropolitan Stores*, Beetz J advanced several reasons why the *American Cyanamid* test rather than any more stringent review of the merits is appropriate in Charter cases. These included the difficulties involved in deciding complex factual and legal issues based upon the limited evidence available in an interlocutory proceeding, the impracticality of undertaking a s. 1 analysis at that stage, and the risk that a tentative determination on the merits would be made in the absence of complete pleadings or prior to the notification of any Attorneys General.

· · ·

What then are the indicators of "a serious question to be tried"? There are no specific requirements which must be met in order to satisfy this test. The threshold is a low one. The judge on the application must make a preliminary assessment of the merits of the case. The decision of a lower court judge on the merits of the Charter claim is a relevant but not necessarily conclusive indication that the issues raised in an appeal are serious: see *Metropolitan Stores*, supra, at p. 150. Similarly, a decision by an appellate court to grant leave on the merits indicates that serious questions are raised, but a refusal of leave in a case which raises the same issues cannot automatically be taken as an indication of the lack of strength of the merits.

Once satisfied that the application is neither vexatious nor frivolous, the motions judge should proceed to consider the second and third tests, even if of the opinion that the plaintiff is unlikely to succeed at trial. A prolonged examination of the merits is generally neither necessary nor desirable.

Two exceptions apply to the general rule that a judge should not engage in an extensive review of the merits. The first arises when the result of the interlocutory motion will in effect amount to a final determination of the action. This will be the case either when the right which the applicant seeks to protect can only be exercised immediately or not at all, or when the result of the application will impose such hardship on one party as to remove any potential benefit from proceeding to trial. Indeed Lord Diplock modified the *American Cyanamid* principle in such a situation in *N.W.L. Ltd. v. Woods*, [1979] 1 WLR 1294, at p. 1307:

> Where, however, the grant or refusal of the interlocutory injunction will have the practical effect of putting an end to the action because the harm that will have been already caused to the losing party by its grant or its refusal is complete and of a kind for which money cannot constitute any worthwhile recompense, the degree of likelihood that the plaintiff would have succeeded in establishing his right to an injunction if the action had gone to trial is a factor to be brought into the balance by the judge in weighing the risks that injustice may result from his deciding the application one way rather than the other.
>
> • • •

The circumstances in which this exception will apply are rare. When it does, a more extensive review of the merits of the case must be undertaken. Then when the second and third stages of the test are considered and applied the anticipated result on the merits should be borne in mind.

The second exception to the *American Cyanamid* prohibition on an extensive review of the merits arises when the question of constitutionality presents itself as a simple question of law alone. This was recognized by Beetz J in *Metropolitan Stores*, at p. 133:

> There may be rare cases where the question of constitutionality will present itself as a simple question of law alone which can be finally settled by a motion judge. A theoretical example which comes to mind is one where Parliament or a legislature would purport to pass a law imposing the beliefs of a state religion. Such a law would violate s. 2(a) of the Canadian *Charter of Rights and Freedoms*, could not possibly be saved under s. 1 of the Charter and might perhaps be struck down right away; see *Attorney General of Quebec v. Quebec Association of Protestant School Boards*, [1984] 2 SCR 66, at p. 88. It is trite to say that these cases are exceptional.

A judge faced with an application which falls within the extremely narrow confines of this second exception need not consider the second or third tests since the existence of irreparable harm or the location of the balance of convenience are irrelevant inasmuch as the constitutional issue is finally determined and a stay is unnecessary.

The suggestion has been made in the private law context that a third exception to the *American Cyanamid* "serious question to be tried" standard should be recognized in cases where the factual record is largely settled prior to the application being made. Thus in *Dialadex Communications Inc. v. Crammond* (1987), 34 DLR (4th) 392 (Ont. HC), at p. 396, it was held that:

> Where the facts are not substantially in dispute, the plaintiffs must be able to establish a
> strong *prima facie* case and must show that they will suffer irreparable harm if the injunc-
> tion is not granted. If there are facts in dispute, a lesser standard must be met. In that case,
> the plaintiffs must show that their case is not a frivolous one and there is a substantial ques-
> tion to be tried, and that, on the balance of convenience, an injunction should be granted.

To the extent that this exception exists at all, it should not be applied in Charter cases.
Even if the facts upon which the Charter breach is alleged are not in dispute, all of the
evidence upon which the s. 1 issue must be decided may not be before the motions court.
Furthermore, at this stage an appellate court will not normally have the time to consider
even a complete factual record properly. It follows that a motions court should not attempt to undertake the careful analysis required for a consideration of s. 1 in an interlocutory proceeding.

C. Irreparable Harm

Beetz J determined in *Metropolitan Stores*, at p. 128, that "[t]he second test consists in
deciding whether the litigant who seeks the interlocutory injunction would, unless the
injunction is granted, suffer irreparable harm." The harm which might be suffered by the
respondent, should the relief sought be granted, has been considered by some courts at
this stage. We are of the opinion that this is more appropriately dealt with in the third
part of the analysis. Any alleged harm to the public interest should also be considered at
that stage.

At this stage the only issue to be decided is whether a refusal to grant relief could so
adversely affect the applicants' own interests that the harm could not be remedied if the
eventual decision on the merits does not accord with the result of the interlocutory
application.

"Irreparable" refers to the nature of the harm suffered rather than its magnitude. It is
harm which either cannot be quantified in monetary terms or which cannot be cured,
usually because one party cannot collect damages from the other. Examples of the former
include instances where one party will be put out of business by the court's decision (*R.L.
Crain Inc. v. Hendry* (1988), 48 DLR (4th) 228 (Sask. QB)); where one party will suffer
permanent market loss or irrevocable damage to its business reputation (*American Cyanamid*, *supra*); or where a permanent loss of natural resources will be the result when a
challenged activity is not enjoined (*MacMillan Bloedel Ltd. v. Mullin*, [1985] 3 WWR 577
(BCCA)). The fact that one party may be impecunious does not automatically determine
the application in favour of the other party who will not ultimately be able to collect
damages, although it may be a relevant consideration (*Hubbard v. Pitt*, [1976] QB
142 (CA)).

· · ·

D. The Balance of Inconvenience and Public Interest Considerations

The third test to be applied in an application for interlocutory relief was described by
Beetz J in *Metropolitan Stores* at p. 129 as: "a determination of which of the two parties
will suffer the greater harm from the granting or refusal of an interlocutory injunction,

pending a decision on the merits." In light of the relatively low threshold of the first test and the difficulties in applying the test of irreparable harm in Charter cases, many interlocutory proceedings will be determined at this stage.

The factors which must be considered in assessing the "balance of inconvenience" are numerous and will vary in each individual case. In *American Cyanamid*, Lord Diplock cautioned, at p. 408, that:

> [i]t would be unwise to attempt even to list all the various matters which may need to be taken into consideration in deciding where the balance lies, let alone to suggest the relative weight to be attached to them. These will vary from case to case.

He added, at p. 409, that "there may be many other special factors to be taken into consideration in the particular circumstances of individual cases."

The decision in *Metropolitan Stores*, at p. 149, made clear that in all constitutional cases the public interest is a "special factor" which must be considered in assessing where the balance of convenience lies and which must be "given the weight it should carry." This was the approach properly followed by Blair J of the General Division of the Ontario Court in *Ainsley Financial Corp. v. Ontario Securities Commission* (1993), 14 OR (3d) 280, at pp. 303-4:

> Interlocutory injunctions involving a challenge to the constitutional validity of legislation or to the authority of a law enforcement agency stand on a different footing than ordinary cases involving claims for such relief as between private litigants. The interests of the public, which the agency is created to protect, must be taken into account and weighed in the balance, along with the interests of the private litigants.

1. The Public Interest

Some general guidelines as to the methods to be used in assessing the balance of inconvenience were elaborated by Beetz J in *Metropolitan Stores*. A few additional points may be made. It is the "polycentric" nature of the Charter which requires a consideration of the public interest in determining the balance of convenience: see Jamie Cassels, "An Inconvenient Balance: The Injunction as a Charter Remedy," in J. Berryman, ed., *Remedies: Issues and Perspectives*, 1991, 271, at pp. 301-5. However, the government does not have a monopoly on the public interest. As Cassels points out at p. 303:

> While it is of utmost importance to consider the public interest in the balance of convenience, the public interest in Charter litigation is not unequivocal or asymmetrical in the way suggested in *Metropolitan Stores*. The Attorney General is not the exclusive representative of a monolithic "public" in Charter disputes, nor does the applicant always represent only an individualized claim. Most often, the applicant can also claim to represent one vision of the "public interest." Similarly, the public interest may not always gravitate in favour of enforcement of existing legislation.

It is, we think, appropriate that it be open to both parties in an interlocutory Charter proceeding to rely upon considerations of the public interest. Each party is entitled to make the court aware of the damage it might suffer prior to a decision on the merits. In addition, either the applicant or the respondent may tip the scales of convenience in its

favour by demonstrating to the court a compelling public interest in the granting or refusal of the relief sought. "Public interest" includes both the concerns of society generally
and the particular interests of identifiable groups.

We would therefore reject an approach which excludes consideration of any harm not
directly suffered by a party to the application. Such was the position taken by the trial
judge in *Morgentaler v. Ackroyd* (1983), 150 DLR (3d) 59 (Ont. HC), per Linden J, at
p. 66.

> The applicants rested their argument mainly on the irreparable loss to their potential
> women patients, who would be unable to secure abortions if the clinic is not allowed to
> perform them. Even if it were established that *these women* would suffer irreparable harm,
> such evidence would not indicate any irreparable harm to *these applicants*, which would
> warrant this court issuing an injunction at their behest. [Emphasis in original.]

When a private applicant alleges that the public interest is at risk that harm must be
demonstrated. This is since private applicants are normally presumed to be pursuing
their own interests rather than those of the public at large. In considering the balance of
convenience and the public interest, it does not assist an applicant to claim that a given
government authority does not represent the public interest. Rather, the applicant must
convince the court of the public interest benefits which will flow from the granting of the
relief sought.

· · ·

2. The Status Quo

In the course of discussing the balance of convenience in *American Cyanamid*, Lord
Diplock stated at p. 408 that when everything else is equal, "it is a counsel of prudence
to ... preserve the status quo." This approach would seem to be of limited value in private
law cases, and, although there may be exceptions, as a general rule it has no merit as such
in the face of the alleged violation of fundamental rights. One of the functions of the
Charter is to provide individuals with a tool to challenge the existing order of things or
status quo. The issues have to be balanced in the manner described in these reasons.

· · ·

VII. Application of the Principles to These Cases

A. A Serious Question To Be Tried

The applicants contend that these cases raise several serious issues to be tried. Among
these is the question of the application of the rational connection and the minimal impairment tests in order to justify the infringement upon freedom of expression occasioned by a blanket ban on tobacco advertising. On this issue, Chabot J of the Quebec
Superior Court and Brossard JA in dissent in the Court of Appeal held that the government had not satisfied these tests and that the ban could not be justified under s. 1 of the
Charter. The majority of the Court of Appeal held that the ban was justified. The conflict
in the reasons arises from different interpretations of the extent to which recent jurisprudence has relaxed the onus fixed upon the state in *R v. Oakes*, [1986] 1 SCR 103, to justify

its action in public welfare initiatives. This Court has granted leave to hear the appeals on the merits. When faced with separate motions for interlocutory relief pertaining to these cases, the Quebec Court of Appeal stated that "[w]hatever the outcome of these appeals, they clearly raise serious constitutional issues." This observation of the Quebec Court of Appeal and the decision to grant leaves to appeal clearly indicate that these cases raise serious questions of law.

B. Irreparable Harm

The applicants allege that if they are not granted interlocutory relief they will be forced to spend very large sums of money immediately in order to comply with the regulations. In the event that their appeals are allowed by this Court, the applicants contend that they will not be able either to recover their costs from the government or to revert to their current packaging practices without again incurring the same expense.

Monetary loss of this nature will not usually amount to irreparable harm in private law cases. Where the government is the unsuccessful party in a constitutional claim, however, a plaintiff will face a much more difficult task in establishing constitutional liability and obtaining monetary redress. The expenditures which the new regulations require will therefore impose irreparable harm on the applicants if these motions are denied but the main actions are successful on appeal.

C. Balance of Inconvenience

Among the factors which must be considered in order to determine whether the granting or withholding of interlocutory relief would occasion greater inconvenience are the nature of the relief sought and of the harm which the parties contend they will suffer, the nature of the legislation which is under attack, and where the public interest lies.

The losses which the applicants would suffer should relief be denied are strictly financial in nature. The required expenditure is significant and would undoubtedly impose considerable economic hardship on the two companies. Nonetheless, as pointed out by the respondent, the applicants are large and very successful corporations, each with annual earnings well in excess of $50,000,000. They have a greater capacity to absorb any loss than would many smaller enterprises. Secondarily, assuming that the demand for cigarettes is not solely a function of price, the companies may also be able to pass on some of their losses to their customers in the form of price increases. Therefore, although the harm suffered may be irreparable, it will not affect the long-term viability of the applicants.

Second, the applicants are two companies who seek to be exempted from compliance with the latest regulations published under the *Tobacco Products Control Act*. On the face of the matter, this case appears to be an "exemption case" as that phrase was used by Beetz J in *Metropolitan Stores*. However, since there are only three tobacco producing companies operating in Canada, the application really is in the nature of a "suspension case." The applicants admitted in argument that they were in effect seeking to suspend the application of the new regulations to all tobacco producing companies in Canada for a period of one year following the judgment of this Court on the merits. The result of these motions will therefore affect the whole of the Canadian tobacco producing industry.

Further, the impugned provisions are broad in nature. Thus it is appropriate to classify these applications as suspension cases and therefore ones in which "the public interest normally carries greater weight in favour of compliance with existing legislation" (p. 147).

The weight accorded to public interest concerns is partly a function of the nature of legislation generally, and partly a function of the purposes of the specific piece of legislation under attack. As Beetz J explained, at p. 135, in *Metropolitan Stores*:

> Whether or not they are ultimately held to be constitutional, the laws which litigants seek to suspend or from which they seek to be exempted by way of interlocutory injunctive relief have been enacted by democratically-elected legislatures and are generally passed for the common good, for instance: ... *the protection of public health* ... . It seems axiomatic that the granting of interlocutory injunctive relief in most suspension cases and, up to a point, as will be seen later, in quite a few exemption cases, is susceptible temporarily to frustrate the pursuit of the common good. [Emphasis added.]

The regulations under attack were adopted pursuant to s. 3 of the *Tobacco Products Control Act* which states:

> 3. The purpose of this Act is to provide a legislative response to a national public health problem of substantial and pressing concern and, in particular,
>
> (a) to protect the health of Canadians in the light of conclusive evidence implicating tobacco use in the incidence of numerous debilitating and fatal diseases;
>
> (b) to protect young persons and others, to the extent that is reasonable in a free and democratic society, from inducements to use tobacco products and consequent dependence on them; and
>
> (c) to enhance public awareness of the hazards of tobacco use by ensuring the effective communication of pertinent information to consumers of tobacco products.

The Regulatory Impact Analysis Statement, in the *Canada Gazette*, Part II, Vol. 127, No. 16, p. 3284, at p. 3285, which accompanied the regulations stated:

> The increased number and revised format of the health messages reflect the strong consensus of the public health community that the serious health hazards of using these products be more fully and effectively communicated to consumers. Support for these changes has been manifested by hundreds of letters and a number of submissions by public health groups highly critical of the initial regulatory requirements under this legislation as well as a number of Departmental studies indicating their need.

These are clear indications that the government passed the regulations with the intention of protecting public health and thereby furthering the public good. Further, both parties agree that past studies have shown that health warnings on tobacco product packages do have some effects in terms of increasing public awareness of the dangers of smoking and in reducing the overall incidence of smoking in our society. The applicants, however, argued strenuously that the government has not shown and cannot show that the specific requirements imposed by the impugned regulations have any positive public benefits. We do not think that such an argument assists the applicants at this interlocutory stage.

When the government declares that it is passing legislation in order to protect and promote public health and it is shown that the restraints which it seeks to place upon an industry are of the same nature as those which in the past have had positive public benefits, it is not for a court on an interlocutory motion to assess the actual benefits which will result from the specific terms of the legislation. That is particularly so in this case, where this very matter is one of the main issues to be resolved in the appeal. Rather, it is for the applicants to offset these public interest considerations by demonstrating a more compelling public interest in suspending the application of the legislation.

The applicants in these cases made no attempt to argue any public interest in the continued application of current packaging requirements rather than the new requirements. The only possible public interest is that of smokers' not having the price of a package of cigarettes increase. Such an increase is not likely to be excessive and is purely economic in nature. Therefore, any public interest in maintaining the current price of tobacco products cannot carry much weight. This is particularly so when it is balanced against the undeniable importance of the public interest in health and in the prevention of the widespread and serious medical problems directly attributable to smoking.

The balance of inconvenience weighs strongly in favour of the respondent and is not offset by the irreparable harm that the applicants may suffer if relief is denied. The public interest in health is of such compelling importance that the applications for a stay must be dismissed with costs to the successful party on the appeal.

NOTES AND QUESTIONS

1. The Supreme Court notes that the House of Lords decision in *American Cyanamid* explicitly changed the merits test for an interlocutory injunction from a "strong prima facie case" to a lesser "serious question to be tried." What is the possible rationale for *reducing* consideration of the merits of the case in interlocutory injunction cases? The explanation offered in *American Cyanamid v. Ethicon*, [1975] AC 396, at 407 was brief:

> The use of such expressions as "a probability," "a prima facie case," or "a strong prima facie case" in the context of a discretionary power to grant an interlocutory injunction leads to confusion as to the object to be achieved by this form of temporary relief. The court no doubt must be satisfied that the claim is not frivolous or vexatious; in other words, that there is a serious question to be tried.
>
> It is no part of the court's function at this stage of the litigation to try to resolve conflicts of evidence on affidavit as to facts on which the claims of either party may ultimately depend nor to decide difficult questions of law which call for detailed arguments and mature considerations. These are matters to be dealt with at trial. ... So unless the material available to the court at the hearing of the application for an interlocutory injunction fails to disclose that the plaintiff has any real prospect of succeeding in his claim for a permanent injunction at the trial, the court should go on to consider whether the balance of convenience lies in favour of granting or refusing the interlocutory relief that is sought.

2. It is clear from the emphasis placed by the courts on the balance of convenience, the status quo, and irreparable harm that a primary concern is to attempt to gauge whether the benefits of granting an injunction are outweighed by the potential detriments. One of the

ways that the courts attempt to mitigate the risk of possible error in granting an injunction is to require a successful applicant for an injunction to give an "undertaking as to damages." This is an undertaking (or promise) to the court that, if at trial, an injunction is not awarded and the interlocutory injunction is dissolved, the plaintiff will pay to the defendant any damages it has suffered in the interim as a consequence of being bound by the injunction. The undertaking requirement, which originated in the common law of injunctions practice, has also been codified in the rules of several provinces: see rule 40.03 in Ontario, Manitoba, and PEI; BC rule 45(6); and NB rule 40.04.

3. The law of interlocutory injunctions is both deep in complexity and wide in the number of issues raised: see, generally, Sharpe, *Injunctions and Specific Performance*, 3d ed. (2001); Berryman et al., *Remedies*, 4th ed. (2001), ch. 8.

4. The question of the balance between pre-trial examination of the merits and other factors in deciding motions for interlocutory injunctions is reflected in the tests for other forms of interim substantive relief. For example, on motions for the interim recovery of personal property (replevin), the court considers whether the applicant for the order has shown substantial grounds for the claim to ownership of the property and the balance of convenience favours the granting of the orders: see, for example, *Clark Door of Canada Ltd. v. Inline Fiberglass Ltd.* (1996), 45 CPC (3d) 244 (Ont. Gen. Div.).

III. DISPOSITION WITHOUT TRIAL—MERITS RELATED

A. Motions To Strike and Dismiss

As we saw in chapter 6 on pleadings, a first requirement of a pleading is that it disclose a legally valid cause of action or defence. This means that the plaintiff must make allegations that, if true, will amount to a valid legal claim. Similarly, a defendant must plead matters by way of defence that, if true, will as a matter of law amount to a defence to the plaintiff's claim.

The reason for the basic requirement that pleadings be substantively adequate and why this issue can be raised and determined at the outset of the litigation is an obvious one—protracted pre-trial proceedings and the trial itself are unnecessary if the plaintiff's pleading does not set out a claim that is legally recognized or if the defendant's statement of defence is, in law, no valid answer to the plaintiff's claim.

In this context, it is important to recall that pleadings are not expressed in terms of direct statements of law. Pleadings are required to contain a "concise statement of material facts upon which the party pleading relies." Such statements of fact, however, must invoke a recognized legal theory of claim or defence. We have seen that various jurisdictions may take different approaches to the question of what form pleadings must take; contrast the situation between pleading requirements in Canada and the United States. However, the requirement that pleadings be substantively adequate is basic to every common law procedural system. Similarly, each system provides machinery by which the substantive adequacy of a plaintiff's statement of claim or of the defendant's statement of defence may be challenged and the question determined at the outset or very early in the proceeding. The following provision (Ontario rule 21.01) is typical. (See also Alberta rules 129 and 220; BC rules

19(24) and 34; New Brunswick rule 23; Nova Scotia rules 14.25 and 25.01; PEI rules 14.25 and 25.01; and Saskatchewan rules 173 and 188-189.)

> 21.01(1) A party may move before a judge,
>
> (a) for the determination, before trial, of a question of law raised by a pleading in an action where the determination of the question may dispose of all or part of the action [and] substantially shorten the trial or result in a substantial saving of costs; or
>
> (b) to strike out a pleading on the ground that it discloses no reasonable cause of action or defence, and the judge may make an order or grant judgment accordingly.
>
> (2) No evidence is admissible on a motion,
>
> (a) under clause (1)(a), except with leave of a judge or on consent of the parties;
>
> (b) under clause (1)(b).

The provision is typical in providing for two methods of raising the question of substantive adequacy. How do paragraphs 21.01(1)(a) and (b) differ?

It is important to understand that, as a consequence of these devices for testing the substantive adequacy of a pleading, substantive and procedural law meet at the commencement of the action. Unless the party pleading is able to allege facts that in law invoke a recognized legal theory of recovery or defence, there is a strong possibility that the opposite party will move to have the offending pleading struck out. It is not surprising that there should be this intersection of substantive and procedural law at the pleading stage, for it is something that the lawyer must assess when his or her client asks, "Do I have a good case?"

The rules governing the form of the pleadings, in particular the requirement to plead all material facts, are obviously linked to the requirement of substantive adequacy. Unless you have set out in your pleading all facts material to the establishment of a legally recognizable cause of action or defence, your pleading is subject to attack by your opponent. For instance, in the *Jane Doe* litigation, assume that Jane Doe advances her claim in negligence. A possible line of attack on the plaintiff's pleading might be that the statement of claim fails to allege facts that, if true, would establish that the police owed a duty of care to Jane. In other words, the pleading fails to allege all facts material to the cause of action and is thus defective. Here one might argue either that the pleadings fail to disclose a reasonable cause of action or that the pleadings fail to comply with the requirement to plead all material facts. In essence, these are two ways of raising the same complaint. Here, in all likelihood, the plaintiff will be able to amend her claim to set out the necessary facts. Accordingly, the court may have three choices in deciding a motion to strike a pleading: first, find the pleading adequate and dismiss the motion; second, find the pleading defective, but determine that it may be remediable, and accordingly strike all or a portion of the pleading with leave to amend; and third, determine that the pleading is defective and incapable of being remedied, with the result that the pleading is struck without leave to amend. In the latter case, if the pleading being struck is the statement of claim, the court will dismiss the action.

In the following decision, the Court of Appeal for Ontario, on an appeal from a decision on a motion granting summary judgment under rule 20, had occasion to consider the scope of rule 21 as it applies to attacks on pleadings and to compare it to the next rule to be considered in this chapter, rule 20, dealing with summary judgment.

Dawson v. Rexcraft Storage and Warehouse Inc.
(1998), 164 DLR (4th) 257 (Ont. CA)

BORINS JA: ... In my view, a helpful way to discuss these issues [relating to summary judgment] is to compare the principal devices provided by the Rules of Civil Procedure for the pre-trial resolution of a claim or a defence. The first is a motion under rule 21.01(1)(b) to strike out a pleading on the ground that it discloses no reasonable cause of action or defence. The second is a motion for summary judgment under rule 20.01(1) or (3) on the ground, provided by rule 20.04(2), that there is no genuine issue for trial with respect to a claim or defence. Generically, each may be characterized as a device to challenge the merits of the plaintiff's claim, or the defendant's defence, before trial, with the goal of foreclosing the need for a trial to resolve all, or part, of the lawsuit. As background to this discussion, it is necessary to recognize the paramountcy of the due process requirements which apply to the resolution of disputes which have been incorporated in the Rules of Civil Procedure, notably pre-trial discovery and a plenary trial on the merits before a trial judge presiding alone, or with a jury. ...

Under rule 21.01(1)(b), a defendant may move to strike out a plaintiff's statement of claim on the ground that it does not disclose a reasonable cause of action. The essence of the defendant's motion is that the "wrong," described in the statement of claim, is not recognized as a violation of the plaintiff's legal rights, with the result that the court would be unable to grant a remedy, even if the plaintiff proved all the facts alleged. Thus, to permit the plaintiff to litigate the claim through discovery and trial would be a waste of both the parties' and the court's time.

Because the purpose of a rule 21.01(1)(b) motion is to test whether the plaintiff's allegations (assuming they can be proved) state a claim for which a court may grant relief, the only question posed by the motion is whether the statement of claim states a legally sufficient claim, i.e., whether it is substantively adequate. Consequently, the motions judge, as mandated by rule 21.01(2)(b), does not consider any evidence in deciding the motion. The motions judge addresses a purely legal question: whether, assuming the plaintiff can prove the allegations pleaded in the statement of claim, he or she will have established a cause of action entitling him or her to some form of relief from the defendant. Because dismissal of an action for failure to state a reasonable cause of action is a drastic measure, the court is required to give a generous reading to the statement of claim, construe it in the light most favourable to the plaintiff, and be satisfied that it is plain and obvious that the plaintiff cannot succeed. See *Hunt v. Carey Canada Inc.*, [1990] 2 SCR 959.

In some cases, a statement of claim will be vulnerable to dismissal under rule 21.01(1)(b) because the plaintiff has sought relief for acts that are not proscribed under the law. The typical textbook example is a statement of claim that alleges that the defendant made a face at the plaintiff, or that the defendant drove a car of an offensive colour. In other cases, however, the statement of claim may be defective because it has failed to allege the necessary elements of a claim that, if properly pleaded, would constitute a reasonable cause of action.

To illustrate the second situation, suppose, for example, that P sues D for damages for malicious prosecution. To recover for malicious prosecution, a plaintiff must establish these elements: institution of criminal proceedings by the defendant without reasonable and probable cause; an improper purpose in instituting the proceedings such as malice, or a primary purpose other than that of carrying the law into effect; termination of the criminal proceedings in favour of the plaintiff; and damages: J. Fleming, *The Law of Torts* (8th ed., 1992, The Law Book Co. Ltd.) at 610. If P fails to plead favourable termination of the criminal proceedings, D may move to strike out the statement of claim on the ground that P failed to allege a necessary element of the tort. P's failure to plead favourable termination may simply be an oversight. If so, the court should allow P to amend the statement of claim to add this allegation, and the lawsuit will proceed. See *AGF Canadian Equity Fund v. Transamerica Commercial Finance Corp. Canada* (1993), 14 OR (3d) 161 at 172-74 (Gen. Div.).

Although I have analyzed rule 21.01(1)(b) from the perspective of a defendant's motion to strike out a statement of claim on the ground that it is substantively inadequate, a similar analysis applies to a plaintiff's motion to strike out a statement of defence on the ground that it does not state a reasonable defence.

In contrast, a motion for summary judgment under Rule 20 permits the motions judge to consult not only the pleadings, but affidavits, cross-examination of the deponents, examinations for discovery, admissions and other evidence to determine whether there is a genuine factual dispute between the parties. No witnesses testify (unless, in exceptional circumstances, leave is granted under rule 39.03(4)). The essential purpose of summary judgment is to isolate, and then terminate, claims and defences that are factually unsupported. Because a motion for summary judgment is decided on the basis of documentary evidence, American commentators have described summary judgment as "a form of quick 'paper trial.'" See S.C. Yeazell, J.M. Landers and J.A. Martin, Civil Procedure, (3rd ed., 1992, Little, Brown & Co.) at 653. Rule 24.04(2), which is mandatory, provides that a motion for summary judgment is to be granted where the record shows "[t]here is no genuine issue for trial with respect to a claim or a defence," and the moving party is entitled to judgment as a matter of law. See *T1T2 Ltd. Partnership v. Canada* (1995), 23 OR (3d) 81 (Gen. Div.), aff'd. (1995), 24 OR (3d) 546 (CA). The second part of this requirement is essentially a replay of a rule 21.01(1)(b) motion. However, as most motions for summary judgment focus on the factual foundation of the claim, or defence, their legal sufficiency does not arise frequently on a motion for summary judgment. Even though there is no genuine issue for trial with respect to the facts, a plaintiff is not entitled to summary judgment if the facts do not establish a cause of action which entitles the plaintiff to some remedy from the defendant. However, as I will discuss, where the court determines that the material facts are not in dispute, and the only genuine issue is a question of law, the motions judge has the discretion under rule 24.04(4) to either determine the question and grant judgment accordingly, or to send the action on to trial.

Thus, while a rule 21.01(1)(b) motion focuses on the substantive adequacy of a claim, or a defence, it offers no assistance in weeding out cases where a substantively adequate claim, or defence, has been pleaded, but cannot be proved. This is the function of a motion for summary judgment. This can be illustrated by reference to the hypothetical action for malicious prosecution. Suppose that P has pleaded the essential elements of the tort, and D knows that the case was stayed by the court, rather than dismissed. If this disposition does not constitute "favourable termination," P cannot win his malicious prosecution action. Under Rule 20, D may challenge P's ability to prove favourable termination by moving for summary judgment, supported by evidence that provides proof that the case was stayed without a finding, and legal argument that a stay is insufficient to meet the "favourable termination" element of a malicious prosecution action.

NOTES AND QUESTIONS

1. Where a motion is brought to strike a pleading for failing to state a reasonable cause of action, should the court hearing the motion decide the underlying question of law if it has not been already resolved by an appellate court? Here the courts seem to be divided. This division is clearly demonstrated in *Nelles v. The Queen in Right of Ontario* (1989), 60 DLR (4th) 609 (SCC). The plaintiff, Susan Nelles, brought an action against the attorney general of Ontario and others in which she alleged that the defendants had maliciously prosecuted her. She had been charged with the death of four infant patients at the Hospital for Sick Children but was discharged after a preliminary hearing. The defendants challenged the pleading, alleging that the claim disclosed no reasonable cause of action and, in the alternative, asking for the determination of a question of law as to whether the attorney general enjoyed immunity from prosecution for malicious prosecution. MacIntyre J held that "before laying down any proposition to the effect that the Attorney General and his agents enjoy absolute immunity from civil suit, there must be a trial to permit a conclusion of the question of prosecutorial immunity and to furnish—in the event that it is decided that the immunity is not absolute—a factual basis for a determination of whether or not in this case the conduct of the prosecution was such that the appellant is entitled to a remedy."

Lamer J (Dickson CJC and Wilson and La Forest JJ concurring), while agreeing that the case ought not to be struck for the failure to disclose no reasonable cause of action, took a different view about the determination of the question of law raised by the pleading:

> I am of the opinion that the question of immunity should be addressed by this court in this case, and that nothing prevents the court from so doing. I set out the relevant rules of the Ontario Rules of Practice, RRO 1980, Reg. 540, as they were at the time of the case for ease of reference:
>
> > 124. Either party is entitled to raise by his pleadings any point of law, and by consent of the parties or by leave of a judge, the point of law may be set down for hearing at any time before the trial, otherwise it shall be disposed of at the trial. …
> >
> > 126. A judge may order any pleading to be struck out on the ground that it discloses no reasonable cause of action or answer, and in any such case, or in the case of the action or defence being shown to be frivolous or vexatious, may order the action to be stayed or dismissed, or judgment to be entered accordingly.
>
> A review of the cases dealing with the application of Rule 124 [rule 21.01(1)(a)] and Rule 126 [rule 21.01(1)(b)] reveals the following. The difference between the two rules lies in the summary nature of Rule 126 as opposed to the more detailed consideration of issues under Rule 124. A court should strike a pleading under Rule 126 only in plain and obvious cases where the pleading is bad beyond argument. Rule 124 is designed to provide a means of deter-

mining, without deciding the issues of fact raised by the pleadings, a question of law that goes to the root of the action. I would like to point out that what is at issue here is not whether malicious prosecution is a reasonable cause of action. A suit for malicious prosecution has been recognized at common law for centuries dating back to the reign of Edward I. What is at issue is whether the Crown, Attorney General and Crown Attorneys are absolutely immune from suit for the well-established tort of malicious prosecution. This particular issue has been given careful consideration both by the Court of Appeal and in argument before this court. The Court of Appeal for Ontario undertook a thorough review of authorities in the course of a lengthy discussion of arguments on both sides of the issue. As such it matters not in my view whether the matter was disposed of under Rule 124 or 126. To send this matter back for trial without resolving the issue of prosecutorial immunity would not be expeditious and would add both time and cost to an already lengthy case.

Furthermore, I am of the view that the rules of civil procedure should not act as obstacles to a just and expeditious resolution of a case. Rule 1.04(1) of the Rules of Civil Procedure in Ontario, O. Reg. 560/84, confirms this principle in stating that "[T]hese rules shall be liberally construed to secure the just, most expeditious and least expensive determination of every civil proceeding on its merits."

Lamer J then proceeded to conclude that the attorney general did not enjoy immunity from civil suit founded upon a claim of malicious prosecution. L'Heureux-Dubé J, in dissent, agreed with Lamer J that the court ought to determine the legal issue, but decided the issue in favour of the attorney general.

Which of these approaches do you prefer and why? While the rules clearly contemplate that a question of law can be determined at the outset, what do you think might underlie the reluctance of the court to do so?

The *Nelles* case also raises the issue of the effect of preliminary challenges on the litigation of novel claims. What impact is the unsuccessful challenge by the defendants to strike out the claim and the ruling of Lamer J likely to have on future settlement negotiations between the parties, and on the financial and emotional resources of the plaintiff? What is the possible impact of the delay of seven years from the commencement of the action to the decision of the Supreme Court of Canada? The *Nelles* case was ultimately settled. What, if anything, is lost when a case such as *Nelles* is not litigated to a final conclusion on the merits?

2. In *D.H.L. v. G.A.F.* (1987), 28 CPC 78 (Ont. HC), the plaintiff alleged that her mother, one of the defendants, was negligent in failing to protect her from the abuse of the plaintiff's father. The mother moved to strike out the action against her as disclosing no reasonable cause of action. The court dismissed the motion, noting that while the claim might have been novel, it was not a clear case where the plaintiff could not succeed at trial. This case demonstrates the difficulties encountered in attempting to expand the boundaries of causes of action. Until recently, claims for damages arising out of an incestuous relationship have been unknown to the courts. Many societal factors continue to discourage naming, blaming, and claiming in these situations. Obviously, one of the impediments is the conduct of litigation itself—limitation periods drafted without this in mind, the very public nature of trials, and the delay and expense that can be incurred in litigation, especially when it is challenged at the preliminary proceeding stage.

Jane Doe v. Board of Commissioners of Police for the Municipality of Metropolitan Toronto
(1990), 74 OR (2d) 225 (Div. Ct.)

[A motion to strike the claim as disclosing no reasonable cause of action was first heard by a master, who granted leave to the plaintiff to amend her statement of claim. Another motion was then brought before Henry J to strike the amended statement of claim at (1989), 58 DLR (4th) 396 (Ont. HC). Henry J dismissed the motion, again granting leave to the plaintiff to amend her pleading. The decision was appealed to the Ontario Divisional Court. The reasons of the court appear below. Again, the motion was dismissed. The defendants were denied leave to appeal to the Ontario Court of Appeal. Jane Doe was ultimately successful at trial: (1998), 39 OR (3d) 487.

The defendants in *Jane Doe* pursued two lines of attack under the "no reasonable cause of action" rubric. One line of attack was to claim that the law did not recognize such a claim and thus the pleadings disclosed no reasonable cause of action. The second line of attack was to claim that even if the law recognized such a cause of action, the pleading failed to disclose the facts necessary to make out such a claim. In other words, the pleading failed to disclose all material facts.]

MOLDAVER J:

Brief Summary of Case

On August 24, 1986 Jane Doe was confronted by an intruder. He had gained access to her second floor apartment by forcible entry through a locked balcony door. Ms. Doe was raped. The attacker fled. The police were called immediately.

Several months later, the attacker was captured. He ultimately pleaded guilty to a number of sexual assaults. These included the attack upon Ms. Doe and assaults upon several other women who had been previously violated in a manner similar to Ms. Doe. The accused was sentenced to 20 years' imprisonment.

All of the prior attacks had occurred within a one-year period in the vicinity of Church and Wellesley Streets, Toronto. They involved white, single women, living in second or third floor apartments. In each case, the attacker had gained entry through a balcony door.

Ms. Doe has now started a civil action against:

(1) Kim Derry and William Cameron, the investigating officers in charge of the case;
(2) Jack Marks, Chief of the Metropolitan Toronto Police Force at that time; and
(3) the Board of Commissioners of Police for the Municipality of Metropolitan Toronto.

She seeks damages for pain and suffering, inconvenience and loss of enjoyment of life. In addition, she has incurred expenses and lost income. She suffers from serious and prolonged bouts of depression and anxiety. This has led to psychiatric counselling and therapy.

Ms. Doe has raised two causes of action against each of the defendants. The first of these is framed in tort. The second seeks a declaration that her right to security of the person and her right to equal protection of the law under ss. 7 and 15(1) of the Canadian Charter of Rights and Freedoms respectively, have been violated. ...

Issues

There are three main issues to be determined by this court. They are:

(1) Do the pleadings support a cause of action against the defendants, or any of them, in tort?
(2) Do the pleadings support a cause of action against the defendants, or any of them, for violating the plaintiff's Charter rights?
(3) Have these causes of action been properly pleaded?

The History of the Action

The matter came to this court by way of appeal from the decision of Mr. Justice Henry, released March 31, 1989 [reported 58 DLR (4th) 396 (HC)]. Leave to appeal was granted by Madam Justice MacFarland on July 17, 1989.

All of the submissions presented to this court were thoroughly canvassed before Henry J in a hearing which lasted some five days. Henry J reserved judgment and later delivered thorough and extensive reasons. He concluded that the causes of action advanced by Ms. Doe were both legally founded and properly pleaded. However, he granted Ms. Doe leave to amend the pleadings, if counsel so advised, as follows:

(1) to specifically allege the necessary proximity of relationship between herself and the defendants; and
(2) to specifically allege that the defendants irresponsibly failed to exercise or improperly exercised their power to make policy decisions.

In his judgment, Mr. Justice Henry reviewed each and every argument advanced by the defendants. As well, he carefully and thoroughly considered the case law.

I do not intend to embark upon such a detailed analysis. For the reasons which follow, I am satisfied that Ms. Doe is entitled to proceed with her action against each of the defendants by way of tort. She is also entitled to continue her action against each of the defendants for a declaration that her s. 7 and s. 15(1) Charter rights have been violated. As well, I find that both causes of action have been properly pleaded.

General Principles Applicable to All Pleadings

Before considering the several causes of actions pleaded, it may be helpful to review some of the principles relating to statements of claim generally. The following factors are significant:

(1) The pleadings must disclose a cause of action founded in law. So long as this criterion is met, the novelty of the cause is of no concern. See *Johnson v. Adamson*

(1981), 34 OR (2d) 236, 128 DLR (3d) 470, 18 CCLT 282 (CA) [leave to appeal to SCC refused (1982), 35 OR (2d) 64n; 41 NR 447n].

(2) In determining whether a cause of action exists, the material facts pleaded are to be taken as proved. However, this principle does not apply where the alleged facts are based on assumptive or speculative conclusions which are incapable of proof. See *Operation Dismantle Inc. v. R*, [1985] 1 SCR 441, 13 CRR 287, 12 Admin. LR 16, 18 DLR (4th) 481, 59 NR 1.

(3) If the facts, taken as proved, disclose a reasonable cause of action, that is, one with some chance of success, then the action may proceed. See *Operation Dismantle Inc., supra*.

(4) The statement of claim must be read as generously as possible, with a view to accommodating any inadequacies in the form of the allegations due to drafting deficiencies. See *Operation Dismantle Inc., supra*.

With these principles in mind, I now turn to a consideration of issue one.

Issue One

Do the Pleadings Support a Legal Cause of Action Against the Defendants, or Any of Them, in Tort?

Under what circumstances will the police owe a private law duty of care to a member of the public?

Section 57 of the Police Act, RSO 1980, c. 381, reads as follows:

> 57. The members of police forces appointed under Part II except assistants and civilian employees, are charged with the duty of preserving the peace, preventing robberies and other crimes and offences, including offences against the by-laws of the municipality and apprehending offenders, and commencing proceedings before the proper tribunal, and prosecuting and aiding in the prosecuting of offenders, and have generally all of the powers and privileges and are liable to all the duties and responsibilities that belong to constables.

This section imposes certain duties upon the police. They include (1) preserving the peace; (2) preventing crimes; and (3) apprehending offenders. The police are charged with the duty of preserving law and order within our society, including the protection of the public from those who would commit or have committed crimes.

When a crime has been committed, society is best protected by the ultimate detection and apprehension of the offender. This holds especially true when the criminal is at large and likely to commit further offences.

For the most part, the police are free to go about their task of detecting and apprehending criminals without fear of being sued by individual members of society who have been victimized. The reason for this is simple. While the police owe certain duties to the public at large, they cannot be expected to owe a private law duty of care to every member of society who might be at risk.

Foreseeability of risk alone is not sufficient to impose a private law duty of care. See *Hill v. Chief Constable of West Yorkshire*, [1989] 1 AC 53, 11988] 2 All ER 238 (HL).

To establish a private law duty of care, foreseeability of risk must coexist with a special relationship of proximity. In the leading case of *Anns v. Merton (London Borough)*, [1978] AC 728, [1977] 2 All ER 492, 121 Sol. Jo. 377 (HL), Lord Wilberforce defined the requirements of this special relationship as follows at pp. 751-52 AC:

> First one has to ask whether, as between the alleged wrongdoer and the person who has suffered damage there is a sufficient relationship of proximity or neighbourhood such that, in the reasonable contemplation of the former, carelessness on his part may be likely to cause damage to the latter—in which case a prima facie duty of care arises.

This principle has been approved by the Supreme Court of Canada in *Kamloops (City) v. Nielsen*, [1984] 2 SCR 2, 66 BCLR 273, 29 CCLT 97, 8 CLR 1, 10 DLR (4th) 641, 26 MPLR 81, 54 NR 1, [1984] 5 WWR 1.

Do the Pleadings Support a Private Law Duty of Care by the Defendants in This Case?

The plaintiff alleges that the defendants knew of the existence of a serial rapist. It was eminently foreseeable that he would strike again and cause harm to yet another victim. The allegations therefore support foreseeability of risk.

The plaintiff further alleges that by the time she was raped, the defendants knew or ought to have known that she had become part of a narrow and distinct group of potential victims, sufficient to support a special relationship of proximity. According to the allegations, the defendants knew:

    (1) that the rapist confined his attacks to the Church-Wellesley area of Toronto;
    (2) that the victims all resided in second or third floor apartments;
    (3) that entry in each case was gained through a balcony door; and
    (4) that the victims were all white, single and female.

Accepting as I must the facts as pleaded, I agree with Henry J that they do support the requisite knowledge on the part of the police sufficient to establish a private law duty of care. The harm was foreseeable and a special relationship of proximity existed.

Do the Pleadings Support a Breach of the Private Law Duty of Care?

The law is clear that in certain circumstances, the police have a duty to warn citizens of foreseeable harm. See *Schact v. R*, [1973] 1 OR 221, 30 DLR (3d) 641 (CA), aff'd. *sub nom. O'Rourke v. Schact*, [1976] 1 SCR 53, 55 DLR (3d) 96, 3 NR 453, and *Beutler v. Beutler; Adams v. Beutler* (1983), 26 CCLT 229 (Ont. HCJ). The obvious purpose of the warning is to protect the citizens.

I would add to this by saying that in some circumstances where foreseeable harm and a special relationship of proximity exist, the police might reasonably conclude that a warning ought not to be given. For example, it might be decided that a warning would cause general and unnecessary panic on the part of the public which could lead to greater harm.

It would, however, be improper to suggest that a legitimate decision not to warn would excuse a failure to protect. The duty to protect would still remain. It would simply have to be accomplished by other means.

In this case the plaintiff claims, *inter alia*, that the duty owed to her by the defendants required (1) that she be warned of the impending danger; or (2) in the absence of such a warning, that she be adequately protected. It is alleged that the police did neither.

Instead, she claims they made a conscious decision to sacrifice her in order to apprehend the suspect. They decided to use her as "bait." They chose not to warn her due to a stereotypical belief that because she was a woman, she and others like her would become hysterical. This would have "scared off" the attacker, making his capture more difficult.

It should here be noted that the plaintiff cannot say which of the defendants made the decisions not to warn or adequately protect her. It is alleged that the investigating officers and the Chief of Police took part in this.

However, the pleadings also allege that both the Chief of Police and the Board of Commissioners were negligent in allowing or authorizing a decision which favoured apprehension of the suspect over the protection of his likely victims. Further, it is alleged that both the Chief of Police and the Board of Commissioners failed to provide adequate resources to investigate and apprehend the rapist, even though they knew or ought to have known that he would strike again against Ms. Doe or others like her. The failure to properly protect the plaintiff is implicit in this latter allegation.

Pleadings of this nature have been upheld by the Ontario Court of Appeal in the case of *Johnson v. Adamson, supra*.

Basis Upon Which the Police Chose Not To Warn

The defendants submitted that the decision not to warn was obviously one of policy. As such, it could not form the basis of a cause of action in tort so long as it was reasonably and responsibly made. Mere error in judgment, if such was the case here, would not support the claim.

This principle is well established. It has been recognized and approved by the Supreme Court of Canada. See *Kamloops (City) v. Nielsen, supra*. In that case, Madam Justice Wilson, speaking for the majority of the court, stated that even if a private law duty of care exists, policy decisions made by public officials will not attract liability in tort so long as they are reasonably and responsibly made. On the other hand, when it comes to the implementation of policy decisions, *i.e.*, the operational area, public officials who owe a private law duty of care will be exposed to the same liability as others if they fail to take reasonable care in discharging their duties.

While this distinction will undoubtedly be important at trial, in my opinion it does not affect the validity of these pleadings. Whether the decision not to warn was one of policy made in the operational context or an operational decision made in the context of some broader policy, the facts pleaded support a claim in either case.

If the decision not to warn was based on policy, the plaintiff implicitly alleges that it was made arbitrarily, unreasonably and irresponsibly. It stemmed from a conscious decision to use the plaintiff as "bait," combined with an unwarranted stereotypical belief that such warning would cause hysteria.

I would go further and suggest that even if the decision not to warn was one of policy and was responsibly made, it may have carried with it an enhanced duty to provide the necessary resources and personnel to protect the plaintiff and others like her. As already indicated, the plaintiff has alleged that the defendants failed to do this.

Causation

This leaves the question of causation. How can it be proved that if the police had discharged their private law duty of care to the plaintiff, she would not have been assaulted?

In my opinion, it is open to the plaintiff to show that had she been warned, she could have taken steps to prevent the attacker from entering her apartment. Alternatively, she could have moved, stayed with a friend or had someone stay with her. Many options would have been available to her, all of which she was denied as a result of the failure to warn.

Furthermore, the plaintiff pleads that in the absence of warning, if the police had properly protected her, she would not have been assaulted.

Where the negligent conduct alleged is the failure to take reasonable care to guard against the very happening which was foreseeable, the claim should not be dismissed for want of causal connection. See *Funk v. Clapp* (1986), 35 BCLR (2d) 222, 68 DLR (4th) 229 (CA).

For all of these reasons, the claim in tort against all defendants must be allowed to proceed.

Issue Two

Do the pleadings support a cause of action against the defendants, or any of them, for violating the plaintiff's Charter rights?

Do the pleadings support a violation of the plaintiff's rights under s. 15(1) of the Charter?

Section 15(1) reads as follows:

> 15(1) Every individual is equal before and under the law and has the right to equal protection and equal benefit of the law, without discrimination and, in particular, without discrimination based on race, national or ethnic origin, colour, religion, sex, age or mental or physical disability.

The plaintiff alleges that her s. 15(l) right to equal protection and benefit of the law, without discrimination, was violated. She states that the defendants had a legal duty to warn her of impending danger. They chose, or at least adopted a policy not to warn her because of a stereotypical and therefore discriminatory belief that as a woman, she and others like her would become hysterical and "scare off" the attacker. As a result, she was turned into "bait," without her knowledge or consent. A man would have been warned and perhaps given the choice of exposing himself to danger to help capture the criminal. She was denied this choice because she was a woman.

It is immediately apparent that the alleged violation of s. 15(1) does not relate to discriminatory legislation. Instead, it points to discriminatory conduct by state officials in the carrying out and enforcing of the law.

In my opinion, these pleadings do support a violation of the plaintiff's rights under s. 15(1) of the Charter.

Do the pleadings support a violation of the plaintiff's rights under
s. 7 of the Charter?

Section 7 reads as follows:

> 7. Everyone has the right to life, liberty and security of the person and the right not to be deprived thereof except in accordance with the principles of fundamental justice.

The plaintiff claims that she was deprived of her right to security of the person. The defendants chose, or at least adopted a policy which favoured the apprehension of the criminal over her protection as a targeted rape victim. By using Ms. Doe as "bait," without her knowledge or consent, the police knowingly placed her security interest at risk. This stemmed from the same stereotypical and therefore discriminatory belief already referred to.

According to the plaintiff, she was deprived of her right to security of the person in a manner which did not accord with the principles of fundamental justice. These principles, while entitled to broad and generous interpretation, especially in the area of law enforcement, could not be said to embrace a discretion exercised arbitrarily or for improper motives. See *R v. Bearer; R v. Higgins*, [1988] 2 SCR 387, 36 CRR 90, 45 CCC (3d) 57, 66 CR (3d) 97, 55 DLR (4th) 481, 88 NR 205, 71 Sask. R 1, [1989] 1 WWR 97.

As a result, the plaintiff claims that her rights under s. 7 of the Charter were violated. Again, in my opinion, these pleadings do support such a violation.

The Position of the Defendants

The defendants submit that the Charter has no application in this case for the following reasons:

(1) The purpose of the Charter is to limit state action. It does not guarantee certain minimal levels of government services. Here, there was no state action that caused injury to the plaintiff. The harm she suffered was caused by her attacker.

(2) Even if the failure to act on the part of the state could give rise to a Charter violation, such a claim should be narrowly limited to cases involving a special relationship between the state and the victim. This relationship can only exist when the victim is in the custody or control of the state.

(3) Mere negligence on the part of the state cannot support such a claim.

(4) The allegations of the plaintiff are conclusory. They fail to set out facts demonstrating a particularized pattern or series of constitutionally invalid acts.

(5) Even assuming that the plaintiff's Charter rights were violated, such violations were reasonably and demonstrably justified in a free and democratic society in accordance with s. 1 of the Charter.

(6) Section 15(1) of the Charter has no application here. The plaintiff asserts that the classes to be compared are men and women. Women are discriminated against because they are not afforded the equal protection of the law provided to men. But, since men are not subject to the material risk of sexual assault, no amount of police protection could achieve "equality" in these circumstances.

I will now deal with each of these arguments separately.

Argument 1

The proposition advanced is essentially derived from the thoughts expressed by Mr. Justice Dickson (as he then was) in the case of *Hunter v. Southam Inc.*, [1984] 2 SCR 145, 9 CRR 355, 33 Alta. LR (2d) 193, 55 AR 291, 27 BLR 297, 14 CCC (3d) 97, 2 CPR (3d) 1, 41 CR (3d) 97 *sub nom. Director of Investigation and Research, Combines Investigation Branch v. Southam Inc.*, 11 DLR (4th) 641, 84 DTC 6467, 55 NR 241, [1984] 6 WWR 577. At pp. 156-57 SCR, p. 365 CRR, p. 650 DLR, Dickson J stated:

> I begin with the obvious. The Canadian Charter of Rights and Freedoms is a purposive document. Its purpose is to guarantee and to protect, within the limits of reason, the enjoyment of the rights and freedoms it enshrines. It is intended to constrain governmental action inconsistent with those rights and freedoms; it is not in itself an authorization for governmental action.

The defendants further rely on the decision of the United States Supreme Court in *DeShaney v. Winnebago County Department of Social Services*, 109 SCt. 998 (1989). There, Chief Justice Rehnquist, speaking for the majority of the court, held that the due process clause of the Fourteenth Amendment to the Constitution imposed no duty on the state to provide members of the public with adequate protective services. The relevant portion of the Fourteenth Amendment reads as follows:

> … nor shall any State deprive any person of life, liberty or property, without due process of law; nor deny to any person within its jurisdiction the equal protection of the laws.

This clause was phrased as a limitation on the state's power to act, not a guarantee of certain minimal levels of safety and security. While it forbade the state itself from depriving individuals of life, liberty and property without due process of law, it did not impose an affirmative obligation on the state to ensure that those interests did not come to harm through other means.

I agree with these propositions. However, they have no bearing on this case.

This case involves the imposition by law of a positive duty upon the police to act. They are required by the Police Act to preserve the peace, prevent crimes and apprehend offenders. Their failure to perform a duty mandated by law for improper reasons may well amount to an infringement of the rights guaranteed by ss. 7 and 15(1) of the Charter. This was clearly recognized by Chief Justice Rehnquist in *DeShaney, supra*, where he said:

> If the due process clause does not require the state to provide its citizens with particular protective services, it follows that the state cannot be held liable under the clause for injuries that could have been averted had it chosen to provide them.

Having said this, Chief Justice Rehnquist immediately pointed out, by way of foot-note, the following:

> The state may not, of course, selectively deny its protective services to certain disfavoured minorities without violating this equal protection clause. But no such argument has been made here. See *Yick Wo v. Hopkins*, 118 US 356, 6 SCt. 1064, 30 LEd. 220 (1886).

Surely, that is exactly the situation alleged here.

Argument 2

The defendants rely again on *DeShaney, supra*, for the proposition that a special relation-ship can only exist when the state takes a person into custody and holds that person against his or her will. Only then does the Constitution impose a corresponding duty to assume some responsibility for the safety and general well-being of that individual. The affirmative duty to protect arises not from the state's knowledge of the individual's pre-dicament or from its expression of intent to help, but from the limitation which is im-posed on the individual's freedom to act.

Again, with respect, this has nothing to do with this case. The positive duty here which requires government officials to act arises under s. 57 of the Police Act. Whether a special relationship exists or not will depend on the circumstances of each case. I have already found that the allegations here support such a finding.

In any event, there is no suggestion on the part of Chief Justice Rehnquist that state denial of protective services *mandated by law* will only arise if persons entitled to protec-tion are in the custody of the state against their will. Such a proposition would make no sense.

It would be absurd to suggest that a police officer who observed a citizen under attack could simply walk away because the citizen was not involuntarily in the custody of the state. In my view, the police officer would have a duty to intervene in accordance with s. 57 of the Police Act. Furthermore, a special relationship of proximity would clearly exist. Finally, if the police officer chose not to intervene because of bias or prejudice against the victim, this would amount to a violation of the victim's s. 7 and s. 15(1) Char-ter rights.

Argument 3

It is not necessary to decide whether mere negligence on the part of the state is sufficient to support a violation of an individual's Charter rights.

The plaintiff here does not allege that her rights under s. 15(1) and s. 7 of the Charter were violated as a result of mere negligence. Instead, she alleges that the police chose, or at least adopted a policy not to warn her because of a stereotypical and therefore dis-criminatory belief that a warning to women would lead to hysteria.

Argument 4

This argument must fail for the reasons stated by Henry J at pp. 95-97 of his decision. In particular, I adopt the following passage at pp. 96-97 [at 445 DLR]:

In the case at bar, however, the plaintiff has asserted the nature of the alleged violations and has particularized to the extent known to the plaintiff the manner in which the defendants have done so. In the case of the Board and to some extent in the case of the chief, the allegation of default will concern functions in the policy field which because of their supervisory powers and duties, are of a different character from the powers and duties of the constables. In the case of all the defendants, however, the allegations even if conclusory may be made, as the Court of Appeal found in *Johnson v. Adamson*, and in my opinion are not incapable of proof, both as to the allegations of failure to adopt adequate policies, regulations and procedures to protect the plaintiff's Charter rights and to the causal connection.

Argument 5

In my opinion, s. 1 of the Charter can play no part in this application. This section may afford a defence at trial, if the trial judge finds that the plaintiff's Charter rights under either s. 7 or s. 15(1) have been violated.

Argument 6

As I perceive it, the defendants submit that it is impossible to find discrimination against women because men are not generally subject to this type of offence. Indeed, the plaintiff has so pleaded.

How then can the treatment of women be compared to the treatment of men in order to decide whether or not such treatment is discriminatory?

While superficially attractive, in my opinion this argument must fail.

The fact that men are generally not subject to this type of crime cannot be determinative. The discriminatory treatment alleged here stems not from the nature of the crime but from a stereotypical view of women held or adopted by the defendants.

The issue may be more clearly defined by altering the facts somewhat. Suppose instead of a serial rapist, a serial murderer who preyed upon men was at large. Assuming that a special relationship of proximity existed between the police and a certain definable group of men, would the police have warned the men? According to the plaintiff, the answer would be "*yes*" since the decision to warn would not have been clouded by the stereotypical presumption that men are prone to hysteria.

When considered this way, it is apparent that the position of the defendants cannot be sustained.

For all of these reasons, the plaintiff is entitled to pursue her action against all of the defendants on the basis that her s. 7 and s. 15(1) Charter rights have been violated.

Issue Three

Have the causes of action been properly pleaded?

In my opinion, having regard to the general principles that apply to all statements of claim, these pleadings are sufficient.

So far as the alleged failure on the part of the plaintiff to specifically plead a special proximate relationship between her and the police, I am satisfied that the facts alleged implicitly support this.

As regards the submission that in the area of policy, the plaintiff has failed to specifically plead that the discretion of the defendants or any of them was irresponsibly made, this too is implicit in the facts alleged.

In my view, these arguments go to form as opposed to substance. In accordance with the guidelines set out by Dickson J (as he then was) in *Operation Dismantle, supra*, the claim must be read as generously as possible, with a view to accommodating any inadequacies in the form of the allegations due to drafting deficiencies. With this principle in mind, I am satisfied that these pleadings may stand.

Conclusion

The plaintiff is entitled to proceed with both causes of action against each of the defendants. Furthermore, the pleadings need not be amended.

I wish to make it perfectly clear that this decision merely entitles the plaintiff to continue her action. It should not be taken as an indication that the allegations or any of them against the defendants are true or that the defendants are liable to the plaintiff. These are matters for trial.

Costs of this appeal to the plaintiff (respondent).

Appeal dismissed.

B. Summary Judgment

A motion to strike judgment on the basis of a failure to state a cause of action involves an attack on the substantive adequacy of the opponent's pleading. The moving party contends that, even if what has been alleged can be proven, as a matter of law the claim will fail. On such a motion only the substantive validity of the claim or defence is at issue; the facts alleged are assumed to be true and capable of proof. Consequently, on such a motion, affidavit evidence is generally not receivable.

But what if a party wishes to attack the opponent's case, not on the ground that the pleading lacks substantive validity but on the ground that the facts pleaded in the claim fail to disclose a genuine claim or defence, because, for instance, evidence necessary to establish a material fact cannot be proven or a material fact alleged is untrue? Historically, the answer was that such an objection could not be raised at the pleading stage; under the procedural system in common law jurisdictions, factual inquiries about the merits of claims and defences were a matter to be determined at trial. A party would not be permitted to precipitate a "trial by affidavit" by bringing a motion, supported by affidavit evidence, attacking the factual allegations of the opponent. While this approach is, *prima facie*, reasonable, it is not without its difficulties, for it is easy for an unscrupulous party to make it appear that there are genuine controverted issues of fact by making unsupportable allegations and denials in the pleadings. Since pleadings are statements, allegations, or contentions that are not sworn, an unscrupulous party may be tempted to make assertions known to be untrue. Given this state of affairs, civil procedure can become a device for harassment if the system clings steadfastly to the concept that controverted issues of fact can only be resolved at trial after lengthy and expensive pre-trial procedures.

1. The Initial Approach

Dissatisfaction with the motion to dismiss for failure to state a cause of action (or "demurrer" as it was then called) as the only way of avoiding a plenary trial emerged in the 19th century. One cause of this was the practice of people who were liable on bills of exchange of asserting spurious defences to delay collection of their debts. "In 1855 the [English] Parliament enacted legislation to enable the courts to 'pierce the pleadings' in such cases, in order to render prompt decisions without trial against deadbeats taking advantage of the law's delay to the injury of their honest creditors": Carrington and Babcock, *Civil Procedure* 744.

Since 1855, procedures for obtaining summary judgment have broadened gradually, though the scope of summary judgment varies from jurisdiction to jurisdiction. In some provinces it is available only to a plaintiff, but in others such as British Columbia, New Brunswick, Nova Scotia, and Ontario, it is also available to a defendant. In many provinces, it is now available in any type of case. The details of the procedure vary, but the essential element is the same in all jurisdictions—a motion for a final judgment in which the parties put forward affidavit evidence (with or without cross-examination thereon) with the moving party attempting to establish that there is no "triable issue" or no "genuine issue of fact requiring a trial" and that he or she is entitled to judgment as a matter of law. For the rules governing summary judgment in the various provinces, see Alberta rules 159-164; BC rule 18; Manitoba rule 20; New Brunswick rule 22; Nova Scotia and PEI rule 13; Newfoundland and Labrador rule 17; Ontario rule 20; and Saskatchewan rules 129-137. Before considering the following cases, read carefully the summary judgment rule in your jurisdiction. Consider how these cases would have been handled under those rules.

The current summary judgment rules in Ontario, and a number of other provinces, were enacted with the intent of broadening the scope of the summary judgment procedure, and were considered to be a major change from the earlier procedure. Initially the courts struggled with the powers under the rule and, in particular, with the scope of what constituted a "genuine issue for trial," in the absence of which the court could grant summary judgment.

Early cases that considered "the no genuine issue for trial test" evidenced a continuing debate between judges about the extent to which the evidence and ultimate merits of each party's case raised a genuine issue for trial. The majority of cases appeared to conclude that a "hard look" at the merits of the action was required. This approach was best captured in the frequently quoted reasons of Boland J in *Vaughan v. Warner Communications Inc.* (1986), 56 OR (2d) 242 (HC):

> The specific changes to the summary judgment rules and the spirit in which other rules are changed indicates in my respectful view that Rule 20 should not be eviscerated by the practice of deferring actions for trial at the mere suggestion that further evidence may be made available or that the law is in a state of confusion. The responding party has a positive responsibility to go beyond mere supposition and the court now has the duty to take a hard look at the merits of an action at this preliminary stage.

A more constrained approach to the "hard look" test was provided by Watt J in *Menash v. Robinson* (February 22, 1989) (Ont. HC) [unreported], who, borrowing from the approach taken in the area of a defendant discharging an evidential burden in the criminal trial context, opted for a test calling for the court to determine whether "the claim in respect of which summary judgment is sought has an air of reality in light of the evidence upon which reliance is placed on the motion." Watt J went on to state his suggested approach as follows:

> The critical issue, however, is whether, assuming the evidence in support of the claim to be true, it is sufficient to justify the consideration of the claim by the trier of fact. The evidence will be sufficient for such purpose where there is at least some evidence upon the basis of which a reasonable trier of fact, properly instructed, could find in favour of the responding party upon the issue at trial.
>
> In practical terms, the sufficiency of proof upon a particular issue by a party bearing the onus in respect of that issue can be but rarely adjudged on the basis of controverted affidavit material even with cross-examination. Indeed, it has been elsewhere said that when there are controverted facts relating to matters essential to a decision, such facts cannot be found by an assessment of the credibility of deponents who have been neither seen nor heard by the trier of fact. See *R v. Jetco Manufacturing Ltd. and Alexander* (1987), 31 CCC (3d) 171 (Ont. CA), at p. 176. It is nonetheless so where what is being determined is whether summary judgment should issue where the facts which underlie the claim or defence are controverted. As it would appear to me, it will be a comparatively rare case where controverted factual issues may be resolved upon a motion for summary judgment. If indeed they could be so as a matter of routine, one might be forgiven for wondering as to the purpose of a trial.

The constrained approach as exemplified in *Menash* and other similar decisions was expressly criticized by Henry J in *Pizza Pizza Ltd. v. Gillespie* (1990), 75 OR (2d) 225 (Gen. Div.) as an approach that "emasculates the developing concept of the new Rule 20." After a detailed review of the various approaches taken by Ontario courts in interpreting and applying the summary judgment rules to date, Henry J summarized the general approach as follows:

- Rule 20 contemplates a radically new attitude to motions for judgment; the objective is to screen out claims that in the opinion of the court, based on evidence furnished as directed by the rule, ought not to proceed to trial because they cannot survive the "good hard look."
- There is no arbitrary or fixed criterion that the motions judge must apply. It is a case by case decision to be made on the law and on the facts that he is able to find on the evidence submitted to him in support of the claim or defence, whether the plaintiff has laid a proper foundation in its affidavit and other evidence to sustain the claims made.
- It is not sufficient for the responding party to say that more and better evidence will (or may) be available at trial. The occasion is now. The respondent must set out specific facts and coherent evidence organized to show that there is a genuine issue for trial.
- Apparent factual conflict in evidence does not end the inquiry.
- The court may, on a common sense basis, draw inferences from the evidence.
- The court may look at the overall credibility of the plaintiff's action, i.e. does the plaintiff's case have the ring of truth about it such that it would justify consideration by the trier of fact?
- Matters of credibility requiring resolution in a case of conflicting evidence ought to go to trial; however, that depends upon the circumstances of the case; the court in taking the

"hard look" at the merits must decide if any conflict is more apparent than real, i.e. whether there is really an issue of credibility that must be resolved in order to adjudicate on the merits.

- Motions under Rule 20 must be made sparingly and judiciously; the court will control abuse of this process if necessary by its order for costs.

The approach adopted by Henry J in *Pizza Pizza*, which requires the court to take a critical and close look at the merits of each party's case on a motion for summary judgment, quickly became the dominant approach to the hearing of summary judgment motions.

2. *The Developing Approach*

Irving Ungerman Ltd. v. Galanis
(1991), 4 OR (3d) 545 (CA)

MORDEN ACJO: The appellants, Irving Ungerman Limited and Karl Ungerman Limited, appeal from a summary judgment against them granted by Sutherland J under R. 20 of the *Rules of Civil Procedure*. His reasons are reported at (1990), 13 RPR (2d) 102 (Ont. HC).

The only issue raised is whether the learned motions court judge erred in concluding that there was no "genuine issue for trial" (r. 20.04(2)). ...

Mr. Galanis, who is a defendant and plaintiff-by-counterclaim in this proceeding, brought his motion for summary judgment on the counterclaim following the exchange of pleadings. The appellants brought a countermotion for summary judgment on their claim in the action. The parties placed extensive evidence before the court on these motions, including affidavits of the parties or their representatives, affidavits of witnesses, transcripts of cross-examinations on these affidavits and of the examination for discovery of Mr. Galanis which was combined with his cross-examination. (I might mention that the appellants' countermotion was dismissed in light of the judge's conclusion on Mr. Galanis's motion. There is no appeal from this particular decision.)

Sutherland J reviewed the evidence in considerable detail and I shall not repeat what he has done. The appellants' contention was that Mr. Galanis had not validly exercised his option to buy the property because he had not presented to Mrs. Haut, within the requisite time (before midnight on October 21, 1988), an offer matching the appellants' offer accompanied by a deposit cheque for $10,000 payable to "Howard Ungerman in Trust." Howard Ungerman was Mrs. Haut's lawyer in the transaction with the appellants.

The appellants submitted to Sutherland J that there were several genuine issues of fact which required a trial. He ruled against each submission. In the argument before us, the appellants confined their submissions to two issues: (1) that Mr. Galanis had not presented Mrs. Haut with an offer matching that of the appellants; and (2) that he did not present her with the requisite deposit cheque for $10,000. Clearly, on the evidence, the second submission raises more difficulties than the first as far as Mr. Galanis is concerned.

Before considering the relevant law relating to the granting of summary judgment and its application to the evidence in this case, I shall refer to those passages in Sutherland J's reasons which indicate how he approached the issues before him.

He quoted the following passage from the judgment of Anderson J in *209991 Ontario Ltd. v. Canadian Imperial Bank of Commerce* (1988), 24 CPC (2d) 248, 8 PPSAC 135, 39 BLR 44 (Ont. HC) at 261 [CPC]:

> No doubt the extent to which it is appropriate for the Court on a motion such as this to investigate questions of fact, and the nature of the issues of fact which will comprise a "genuine issue for trial," will vary from case to case. ...

Sutherland J then said at pp. 134-135 [RPR]:

> I am respectfully and wholly in agreement with that statement. Anderson J continues, at p. 261, as follows:
>
> > As a matter of present impression, I see nothing in the language of the rule, or in the review of the law contained in Vaughan [*Vaughan v. Warner Communications Inc.* (1986), 56 OR (2d) 242 (H Ct.)], to suggest any clear or arbitrary limit, although it seems safe to say that, where there are contested issues of fact involving the credibility of witnesses, the only appropriate forum remains a trial Court. A lawyer ... schooled in the tradition that almost any substantial issue was to be determined at trial requires a material change in attitude to give appropriate effect to the rule.
>
> I am more comfortable with the last quoted sentence than with the sentence that precedes it. I note that the second last sentence is obiter for the reason that Anderson J as he stated, did not on the facts before him have to choose between contradictory factual allegations. My reservation about the penultimate quoted sentence is that it tends to give too much effect to what may be mere vehement and self-serving assertion. In my view the question of a genuine issue for trial means that, admittedly within narrow limits not often attainable, the Court can look at the whole of the evidence and consider the inherent probability or improbability of an assertion of fact, having regard to the number of other assertions by the same witness or witnesses that have subsequently been admitted to be or clearly shown to be incorrect. Regard should also be had to how self-serving or conclusory the factual assertion may be. The rule does not, in my opinion require an admission that a previously asserted fact is not or may not be the truth. In the absence of admission, the Court will properly proceed with great caution, requiring a very high level of probability, but in my view the Court must not be stopped in its tracks by a vehement and dogged assertion where the person's other evidence has been repeatedly, and often admittedly, shown to be incorrect and where the doggedly asserted fact is both inherently improbable and contrary to the evidence of witnesses, the body of whose evidence has not been shown to be significantly or inherently improbable. ...
>
> In this case I have reviewed the evidence with care—and at what I am confident many will agree to be tedious length—in order to satisfy myself that, and to demonstrate the reasons why, this is one of the rare and exceptional cases where in the face of controverted evidence as to a material matter there is no genuine issue for trial and the defendant Galanis is entitled to the order for specific performance that he seeks and to related declarations and relief to be referred to below.

Specifically, with respect to the issue of whether or not Mr. Galanis delivered a deposit cheque of $10,000 to Mrs. Haut on October 21, 1988, he concluded at p. 139 [RPR]:

> On all the evidence and despite Haut's persistent denials, I am satisfied that there is no genuine issue for trial on the question of whether on Friday, October 21 Galanis left with Haut along with the second Galanis offer an uncertified deposit cheque dated October 21, 1988, and payable to Howard Ungerman in trust in the amount of $10,000. That means that Galanis properly exercised his option on October 21, 1988 and I so find.

Rule 20, which came into force on January 1, 1985 as part of the *Rules of Civil Procedure*, O. Reg. 560/84, substantially expanded the potential scope of a litigant's right to move for summary judgment beyond that provided for in the former Rules of Practice, RRO 1980, Reg. 540, as amended. Under the former rules, only a plaintiff could move for summary judgment and only in actions where the writ of summons was specially endorsed (see former R. 33 and 58). Now, either party may so move (r. 20.01(1) and 20.01(3)).

Under the former rules, only the defendant had to support his or her position by affidavit (see former R. 42 and 58). The new rule contemplates both parties "delivering affidavit material or other evidence" (r. 20.01(1) and 20.01(3)). There are other distinctions between the former and the new rules which need not be mentioned.

The key provision in the new practice, as far as the present appeal is concerned, is r. 20.04(2), which reads:

> Where the court is satisfied that there is no genuine issue for trial with respect to a claim or defence, the court shall grant summary judgment accordingly.

The expression "genuine issue" was borrowed from the third sentence in R. 56(c) in the *Federal Rules of Civil Procedure* in the United States which were adopted in 1938. It reads:

> The judgment sought shall be rendered forthwith if the pleadings, depositions, answers to interrogatories, and admissions on file, together with the affidavits, if any, show that there is no genuine issue as to any material fact and that the moving party is entitled to a judgment as a matter of law.

Our rule does not contain, after "genuine issue," the additional words "as to any material fact." Such a requirement is implicit. If a fact is not material to an action, in the sense that the result of the proceeding does not turn on its existence or non-existence, then it cannot relate to a "genuine issue for trial." (See 10A Wright, Miller and Kane, *Federal Practice and Procedure*, 2d ed. (Saint Paul, Mn.: West Publishing Co., 1983) at 93-95.) Similar reasoning applies to the absence from our rule of the words "and the moving party is entitled to a judgment as a matter of law." This is implicit.

Because the term "genuine issue" is taken from R. 56(c), it is reasonable to think that some of the judicial experience with that provision would be of assistance in applying the term. In a relatively early United States decision concerned with R. 56(c), *Engl v. Aetna Life Insurance Co.*, 139 F2d 469 (1943), Judge Charles E. Clark, one of the drafters of the *Federal Rules of Civil Procedure*, said at p. 472:

But the matter is sufficiently important so that we should go beyond the bare words of the summary-judgment rule to the reasons behind it. The federal summary judgment proceeding is the most extensive of any jurisdiction in that it is equally available to plaintiffs and defendants and in all forms and kinds of civil actions. But the history of the development of this procedure shows that it is intended to permit "a party to pierce the allegations of fact in the pleadings and to obtain relief by summary judgment where facts set forth in detail in affidavits, depositions, and admissions on file show that there are no genuine issues of fact to be tried." 3 *Moore's Federal Practice* 3175.

I refer, in particular, to the intention of enabling "a party to pierce the allegations of fact in the [other party's] pleadings." This means that, in addition to having a right to move for early resolution of a question of law, as a means of avoiding a trial or shortening a proceeding as provided for in R. 21 and 22, it is now possible to avoid a trial or shorten the proceeding on satisfying a court that there is no need for a trial because there is no genuine issue of fact requiring one.

The summary judgment rule, properly applied, is one of several rules which enables the policy expressed in r. 1.04(1) to be given effect. It reads:

These rules shall be liberally construed to secure the just, most expeditious and least expensive determination of every civil proceeding on its merits.

A litigant's "day in court," in the sense of a trial, may have traditionally been regarded as the essence of procedural justice and its deprivation the mark of procedural injustice. There can, however, be proceedings in which, because they do not involve any genuine issue which requires a trial, the holding of a trial is unnecessary and, accordingly, represents a failure of procedural justice. In such proceedings, the successful party has been both unnecessarily delayed in the obtaining of substantive justice and been obliged to incur added expense. Rule 20 exists as a mechanism for avoiding these failures of procedural justice.

It would be convenient if the term "genuine issue" could be expressed in a precise formula for the ease of its application. Having regard, however, to the varied and unpredictable ways in which issues under R. 20 may arise, it cannot—and the experience with R. 56(c) in the United States has shown that it can be harmful to gloss the wording of the rule with expressions that fail to capture its meaning. (See 10A Wright, Miller and Kane, op. cit. at pp. 97-107 and 176-177.)

It is safe to say that "genuine" means "not spurious" and, more specifically, that the words "for trial" assist in showing meaning of the term. If the evidence on a motion for summary judgment satisfies the court that there is no issue of fact which requires a trial for its resolution, the requirements of the rule have been met. It must be clear that a trial is unnecessary. The burden is on the moving party to *satisfy* the court that the requirements of the rule have been met. Further, it is important to keep in mind that the court's function is not to resolve an issue of fact but to determine whether a genuine issue of fact exists. (See 6 James W. Moore, *Moore's Federal Practice*, 2d ed. (New York: Bender, Matthew & Co. Inc., 1989), p. 56-391; 10A Wright, Miller and Kane, op. cit., at pp. 574-575.)

At the heart of the proceeding before us is the issue of credibility. Mrs. Haut has steadfastly maintained in her evidence that she did not receive a deposit cheque for $10,000 on October 21, 1988. The evidence on behalf of the respondent is that a cheque for $10,000 was delivered to her in the evening of October 21, 1988.

It is a sensible general proposition that, if there is an issue of credibility, a trial is required and summary judgment should not be granted. This is reflected in the settled practice under R. 56(c) in the United States. In 6 *Moore's Federal Practice*, 2d ed. (1989) [supra], at p. 56-519 the following appears:

> The general and well settled rule is that the court should not resolve a genuine issue of credibility at the hearing on the motion for summary judgment, whether the case be a jury or court case; and if such an issue is present the motion should be denied and the issue resolved at trial by the appropriate trier of the facts, where, to the extent that witnesses are available, he will have the opportunity to observe their demeanor.

At pp. 56-521 to 56-522 the following appears in Moore with respect to whether an issue of credibility exists:

> Judge Hutcheson's statement as to the test to be applied in determining whether the materials favorable to the opposing party present an issue of credibility will bear repetition:
>
> To proceed to summary judgment it is not sufficient then that the judge may not credit testimony proffered on a tendered issue. It must appear that there is no substantial evidence on it, that is, either that the tendered evidence is in its nature too incredible to be accepted by reasonable minds, or that conceding its truth, it is without legal probative force. [*Whitaker v. Coleman* (1940), 115 F2d 305, 306]
>
> The test has been applied and often quoted. Evidence, then, that is too incredible to be accepted by reasonable minds does not raise an issue of credibility. Conversely, if the evidence is such that a jury would not be at liberty to disbelieve it no issue of credibility is present. Or, stated differently, a summary judgment may be granted on evidence that would compel the direction of a verdict; and should be denied when a directed verdict would be improper.

As the first passage indicates, the proposition that an issue of credibility precludes the granting of summary judgment applies only when what is said to be an issue of credibility is a genuine issue of credibility. In the present case, Sutherland J was satisfied that "this is one of the rare and exceptional cases where in the face of controverted evidence as to a material matter there is no genuine issue for trial ..." (p. 135 [RPR]).

With respect, I do not think that the evidence before the court reasonably justifies this conclusion.

Sutherland J formed the view, and it was open to him to do so on the evidence, that Mrs. Haut was an unsatisfactory witness. He also was impressed by the evidence of the witnesses who testified that the cheque had been presented to Mrs. Haut on October 21. This evidence was referred to by the respondent before us as undisputed objective evidence. With respect, I think that this puts the matter too highly. It would be open to a trier of fact to reject the evidence of Mr. Galanis and his son with respect to presenting the cheque. The acceptance of this evidence, ultimately, turns on the credibility of these witnesses and that of Mrs. Haut. ...

I shall refer to one further matter covered in the evidence. Both Mrs. Haut and Irving Ungerman gave evidence that on the evening of October 21, 1988, around 10:00 to

10:30 p.m., Mrs. Haut telephoned Mr. Ungerman and told him that no deal had been made with Mr. Galanis. No matching offer had been presented and Mr. Galanis had not brought a cheque. Mr. Ungerman was not clear on whether Mrs. Haut said "certified cheque" or simply "cheque." To match the terms of the Ungerman offer the cheque did not have to be certified. In any event, although this evidence might not ultimately prove anything in favour of the appellants it is evidence that tends to support them in that it reflects Mrs. Haut's position, on the very evening in question, that she had no agreement with Mr. Galanis. She would not appear to have had any reason to mislead Mr. Ungerman at that time.

As indicated, I think Sutherland J erred in concluding that there was no genuine issue for trial. No doubt there are contradictions in Mrs. Haut's evidence. There are also circumstantial features which support, perhaps strongly so, the probability that the $10,000 deposit cheque was presented to Mrs. Haut on October 21, 1988. The motions court judge obviously thought that the level of probability was such that Mrs. Haut's evidence could be rejected as incredible. With respect, on the basis of the evidence to which I have referred, including that of Mrs. Haut, I do not think that the materials before the court were such that the court could properly be "satisfied" that there was no genuine issue requiring a trial.

Appeal allowed.

NOTES AND QUESTIONS

1. *Genuine issue for trial.* The genuine issue for trial in *Ungerman*, according to the Court of Appeal, was whether the evidence of Mr. Galanis and his son should be preferred to the evidence of Mrs. Haut. Why is a trial a more appropriate place for such a determination to be made? Does this mean that any conflict in evidence on an essential point requires a trial, no matter how strange or implausible the story of one of the parties? Consider this situation. Someone yells, "Fire!" in a crowded theatre, provoking a stampede in which a number of people are injured. One person in the crowd is accused of negligently or deliberately making the statement and is sued as a result. Five people swear in affidavits on a motion for summary judgment that the defendant is the person who caused the stampede. The defendant files an affidavit in which he denies the allegation. Should a motion for summary judgment succeed? Would it matter if 50 people so identify the defendant?

2. *Onus on the responding party.* What approach should a respondent take to a summary judgment motion? It is clear that the onus lies on the moving party to show that there is no genuine issue for trial. However, many summary judgment rules specifically require that, in response to a summary judgment motion, "a party may not rely on the mere allegations or denials of the party's pleading, but must set out, in affidavit material or other evidence, specific facts showing that there is a genuine issue for trial." See Ontario rule 20.04(1); Manitoba rule 20.02(1); Northwest Territories rule 176(1); PEI rule 20.04(1); Saskatchewan rule 131(1); and federal rule 432.2(1). Why have this requirement? What is the practical impact of this on a respondent?

3. *The need for discovery to contest a motion for summary judgment.* How does summary judgment relate to discovery? In most provinces, a motion may be brought any time after

the delivery of the statement of defence and before discovery has taken place. Does this mean that a party has to be prepared to prove his or her case in possible response to a motion for summary judgment at the time pleadings are delivered? What of the case where the plaintiff alleges negligence but does not know the precise act of the defendant that constitutes negligence? Authority in Ontario has held that a party may not respond to a motion for summary judgment by stating that it requires discovery first or that more evidence may be available at trial: *645952 Ontario Inc. v. Guardian Insurance Co. of Canada* (1989), 69 OR (2d) 341 (HC). The US federal rules specifically permit such a response. Does this raise the risk that an early motion for summary judgment may unfairly eliminate valid claims or defences? Consider this in the light of the provisions of the rules relating to evidence on motions and the options available to a party to a summary judgment motion in obtaining evidence for the motion. Contrast the rule relating to evidence on motions and applications (rule 39) and the general ability to examine non-party witnesses out of court under that rule (rules 39.02 and 39.03) with the scope of oral examination for discovery (rule 31) and the limitations on the discovery of non-parties (rule 39.10). In short, does the summary judgment process itself offer the parties the equivalent of discovery; procedures that are broader than examination for discovery? Compare rules 39.03 and 31.10—which of these two rules is broader?

5. It can be said that while the decision in *Ungerman* sounded a note of caution in the aggressive use of the summary judgment procedure, similar cases that preceded and followed it seemed to encourage a more active use of the procedure by allowing the court to focus on and make judgments about the *genuineness* of the issue for trial. This resulted in a number of cases where the court found that an apparent conflict or testimony on a material issue did not preclude a court from taking a "hard look" at the evidence and the basis for the conflict to determine whether, in fact, there was a *genuine* issue for trial.

6. Following *Ungerman*, the Ontario Court of Appeal sounded a further cautionary note in two decisions released in 1998 that attempted to further clarify the role of the motions judge on a summary judgment motion. In *Aguonie v. Galion Solid Waste Material Inc.* (1998), 38 OR (3d) 161 (CA), Borins JA expounded further on the meaning of "genuine issue for trial," where he explained at paras. 32 and 35:

> [32] An issue of fact must relate to a material fact. As Morden ACJO pointed out in *Ungerman, supra*, at p. 550: "[I]f a fact is not material to an action, in the sense that the result of the proceeding does not turn on its existence or non-existence, then it cannot relate to a 'genuine issue for trial.'" In ruling on a motion for summary judgment, the court will never assess credibility, weigh the evidence, or find the facts. Instead, the court's role is narrowly limited to assessing the threshold issue of whether a genuine issue exists as to material facts requiring a trial. Evaluating credibility, weighing evidence, and drawing factual inferences are all functions reserved for the trier of fact. …
>
> [35] … Summary judgment, valuable as it is for striking through sham claims and defences which stand in the way to a direct approach to the truth of a case, was not intended to, nor can it, deprive a litigant of his or her right to a trial unless there is a clear demonstration that no genuine issue exists, material to the claim or defence, which is within the traditional province of a trial judge to resolve.

Subsequently, in *Dawson v. Rexcraft Storage and Warehouse Inc.* (1998), 164 DLR (4th) 257 (Ont. CA), Borins JA recommended to Ontario judges the approach that their US counterparts adopt in adjudicating motions for summary judgment (referring favourably to the analysis of summary judgment by Wright J in *(Paula) Jones v. (William) Clinton*, 990 F Supp. 657 (1998 US Dist. Ct., E Dist. Ark.)):

> In applying a test which focuses on whether the entire record could lead a rational trier of fact to find for the non-moving party, what the court is saying is that there is no evidence on which the plaintiff's claim, or the defendant's defence, can succeed. In a sense, the courts have come to equate "genuine issue for trial" with "genuine need for trial." However, at the end of the day, it is clear that the courts accord significant deference to the trial process as the final arbiter of the dispute which has brought the parties to litigation. If there is a genuine issue with respect to material facts then, no matter how weak, or how strong, may appear the claim, or the defence, which has been attacked by the moving party, the case must be sent to trial. It is not for the motions judge to resolve the issue.

Borins JA recommended the following analytical approach in deciding a motion for summary judgment. The elements of the plaintiff's claim need to be identified. The case law relating to the claim should be reviewed to determine the range of facts that courts have accepted as establishing the claim. Finally, the entire evidentiary record should be examined with a view to determining whether it discloses a genuine issue for trial with respect to a fact material to the proof of the claim. Does this make sense? Consider the approach in the following recent decision from the Supreme Court.

Canada (Attorney General) v. Lameman
[2008] 1 SCR 372, 2008 SCC 14

THE COURT: ... The plaintiffs bring this action on their own behalf and on behalf of all descendants of the Papaschase Indian Band No. 136. The facts are shrouded in the mists of time and some details are disputed, but the broad picture is the following.

In 1877, the Papaschase Indians adhered to Treaty No. 6 and were allotted a reserve in what is now southeast Edmonton. In 1886, Chief Papaschase and a number of other members of his Band—the Band's core leadership group—"took scrip." This meant that in exchange for a cash payment they surrendered their treaty rights and rights connected with the Reserve. These members left the Reserve. A few years later in 1889, the people whom government officials found to be remaining members of the Band—three men and their families—entered into an agreement to surrender their interest in the Reserve to the government with a view to its sale or lease, on condition that the proceeds be held in trust and paid to Band members and their descendants. It appears that these people ended up joining the Enoch Band. Over the years, the government paid monies from the sale of the Papaschase Reserve to the members of the Enoch Band, in accordance with an agreement signed in 1894 between the government and the two surviving Band members who had agreed to the Reserve's surrender.

In 2001, the plaintiffs, claiming to be descendants of Chief Papaschase and other Papaschase Band members, commenced an action against the Crown. Their claim alleged that the government had wrongfully allowed Papaschase Band members to take scrip without properly advising them of the consequences; that the government had wrongfully pressured the Band to surrender the Reserve under the influence of the Edmonton settlement's lobbying; and that the government had thereby caused the dissolution of the Band. The claim also alleged that the government did not follow the rules to obtain a legal surrender of the Reserve; that the government had not sold the Reserve land for market value; and that the government had mismanaged the sale proceeds, in particular by distributing them to the Enoch Band. Finally, the claim alleged that the government had breached its treaty obligations by not granting the Band all the land to which it was entitled under the Treaty; and by failing to provide the Band with farming implements, and food in times of famine. These allegations, it was said, gave rise to causes of action for breach of fiduciary duty, fraudulent and malicious behaviour, and treaty breach.

The government brought a motion for summary judgment, asking that the claim be dismissed on the ground that the allegations in the statement of claim raised no genuine issue for trial. The main issues on the motion were: (1) whether the facts alleged disclosed triable issues; (2) whether the plaintiffs had standing to raise these issues; and (3) whether the claims were barred by statutes of limitations or the equitable doctrines of laches and acquiescence.

The chambers judge, Slatter J, found that most of the claims lacked the factual basis necessary to qualify as genuine issues for trial: (2004), 43 Alta. LR (4th) 41, 2004 ABQB 655. However, he held that the statement of claim disclosed three triable issues: (1) whether the Reserve granted to the Papaschase Band was the proper size; (2) whether the government had properly disposed of the proceeds of the sale of the Reserve; and (3) whether the Crown had breached the Band's treaty rights to food.

The chambers judge went on to find against the plaintiffs on the remaining two issues. He found the plaintiffs lacked standing to bring the representative action; they were claiming collective rights of a Band that had ceased to exist, and did not meet the criteria for Band membership (i.e. showing their ancestors were Band members who had not taken up scrip or joined other bands, or by showing their ancestors were entitled to funds from the Reserve sale). And he found that the claims were barred by the *Limitation of Actions Act*, RSA 1980, c. L-15, with the exception of the claim for an accounting of any proceeds of sale the Crown might still have in its possession.

The majority of the Court of Appeal found that all or most of the issues raised were genuine, triable issues, with Côté JA dissenting and finding that the claims for malice, fraud and bad faith should be dismissed: (2006), 66 Alta. LR (4th) 243, 2006 ABCA 392. Unlike the Chambers Judge, the Court of Appeal found that whether the plaintiffs had standing to bring the action was a triable issue. It cited the circularity and unfairness of denying Band status for purposes of litigating the destruction of Band status; and held that the government bore the burden of proving that there were no persons in existence who could have standing. On the limitations issue, the Court of Appeal held that the evidence was mixed on whether the claim was discoverable in the 1970s and that this was a matter that should be resolved at trial.

The government appeals to this Court, asking us to dismiss the plaintiffs' action on the grounds that they have no standing and that their claims are statute-barred, and asking us to reinstate the order of the chambers judge. We note that no notice of a constitutional question was given, and that no constitutional challenges lie before the Court.

This appeal is from an application for summary judgment. The summary judgment rule serves an important purpose in the civil litigation system. It prevents claims or defences that have no chance of success from proceeding to trial. Trying unmeritorious claims imposes a heavy price in terms of time and cost on the parties to the litigation and on the justice system. It is essential to the proper operation of the justice system and beneficial to the parties that claims that have no chance of success be weeded out at an early stage. Conversely, it is essential to justice that claims disclosing real issues that may be successful proceed to trial.

For this reason, the bar on a motion for summary judgment is high. The defendant who seeks summary dismissal bears the evidentiary burden of showing that there is "no genuine issue of material fact requiring trial": *Guarantee Co. of North America v. Gordon Capital Corp.*, [1999] 3 SCR 423, at para. 27. The defendant must prove this; it cannot rely on mere allegations or the pleadings: *1061590 Ontario Ltd. v. Ontario Jockey Club* (1995), 21 OR (3d) 547 (CA); *Tucson Properties Ltd. v. Sentry Resources Ltd.* (1982), 22 Alta. LR (2d) 44 (QB (Master)), at pp. 46-47. If the defendant does prove this, the plaintiff must either refute or counter the defendant's evidence, or risk summary dismissal: *Murphy Oil Co. v. Predator Corp.* (2004), 365 AR 326, 2004 ABQB 688, at p. 331, aff'd. (2006), 55 Alta. LR (4th) 1, 2006 ABCA 69. Each side must "put its best foot forward" with respect to the existence or non-existence of material issues to be tried: *Transamerica Life Insurance Co. of Canada v. Canada Life Assurance Co.* (1996), 28 OR (3d) 423 (Gen. Div.), at p. 434; *Goudie v. Ottawa (City)*, [2003] 1 SCR 141, 2003 SCC 14, at para. 32. The chambers judge may make inferences of fact based on the undisputed facts before the court, as long as the inferences are strongly supported by the facts: *Guarantee Co. of North America*, at para. 30.

We are of the view that, assuming that the claims disclosed triable issues and that standing could be established, the claims are barred by operation of the *Limitation of Actions Act*. There is "no genuine issue" for trial. Were the action allowed to proceed to trial, it would surely fail on this ground. Accordingly, we agree with the chambers judge that it must be struck out, except for the claim for an accounting of the proceeds of sale, which is a continuing claim and not caught by the *Limitation of Actions Act*.

This Court emphasized in *Wewaykum Indian Band v. Canada*, [2002] 4 SCR 245, 2002 SCC 79, that the rules on limitation periods apply to Aboriginal claims. The policy behind limitation periods is to strike a balance between protecting the defendant's entitlement, after a time, to organize his affairs without fearing a suit, and treating the plaintiff fairly with regard to his circumstances. This policy applies as much to Aboriginal claims as to other claims, as stated at para. 121 of *Wewaykum*:

> Witnesses are no longer available, historical documents are lost and difficult to contextualize, and expectations of fair practices change. Evolving standards of conduct and new standards of liability eventually make it unfair to judge actions of the past by the standards of today.

Pursuant to s. 13 of the *Limitations Act*, SA 1996, c. L-15.1, Aboriginal claims are governed by the previous *Limitation of Actions Act*. The applicable limitation periods provision reads:

> 4(1) The following actions shall be commenced within and not after the time respectively hereinafter mentioned: ...
>
> (c) actions
>
> (i) for the recovery of money, other than a debt charged on land, whether recoverable as a debt or damages or otherwise, and whether on a recognizance, bond, covenant or other specialty or on a simple contract, express or implied, or
>
> (ii) for an account or for not accounting,
>
> within 6 years after the cause of action arose;
>
> • • •
>
> (e) actions grounded on accident, mistake or other equitable ground of relief not hereinbefore specifically dealt with, within 6 years from the discovery of the cause of action;
>
> • • •
>
> (g) any other action not in this Act or any other Act specifically provided for, within 6 years after the cause of action therein arose.

The issue becomes when the cause of action "arose" or, in the case of equitable claims, was actually "discovered."

The applicable definition of when a cause of action arises was articulated by this Court in *Central Trust Co. v. Rafuse*, [1986] 2 SCR 147, at p. 224:

> ... a cause of action arises for purposes of a limitation period when the material facts on which it is based *have been discovered* or *ought to have been discovered* by the plaintiff *by the exercise of reasonable diligence* ... [Emphasis added.]

It is argued that the causes of action here advanced were discoverable as early as the 1880s and 1890s. We do not find it necessary, however, to go back so far. The evidence filed by the government establishes that in the 1970s the causes of action now raised would have been clear to the plaintiffs, exercising due diligence. In the mid-1970s, an Edmonton lawyer, James C. Robb, sent letters of inquiry to the Department of Indian and Northern Affairs on behalf of unidentified Papaschase descendants. The ensuing correspondence reveals that in 1974, a group of Papaschase descendants intended to submit a land claim "in the near future." This suggests some actual knowledge of the relevant facts, but there is more. When the Department advised Mr. Robb that the Enoch Band had already submitted a claim regarding the surrender of the Papaschase Reserve, Mr. Robb responded that a joint claim would not be possible. Having been informed of the Enoch Band's claim, these Papaschase descendants knew that the Enoch Band had or was in the process of gathering the relevant information. Indeed, in 1979 the Enoch Band provided funding to Kenneth James Tyler to write a Master's thesis on the events surrounding the surrender of the Papaschase Reserve. The Tyler Thesis covers most if not all of the facts that form the basis of the claims in this action. Mr. Tyler interviewed several Enoch Band elders in the course of his research. It is thus clear that members of the

Enoch Band were aware of the facts on which this action was based in 1979. The chambers judge, on all the evidence, concluded that any interested party exercising due diligence could have uncovered the same facts Mr. Tyler did.

The plaintiffs filed no material in response to this evidence. They did not say whether or not, in the 1970s, they knew of the causes of action they now raise. There is no explanation for how, as members of the Papaschase Descendants Council, they could have been unaware of these matters, with due diligence, when some Papaschase descendants were aware of the Enoch Band's claim. On this state of the evidence, the only available inference is that these causes of action became discoverable within the meaning of the *Limitation of Actions Act* in the 1970s, and that the claims are now statute-barred.

We add this. In the Court of Appeal and here, the case for the plaintiffs was put forward, not only on the basis of evidence actually adduced on the summary judgment motion, but on suggestions of evidence that might be adduced, or amendments that might be made, if the matter were to go to trial. A summary judgment motion cannot be defeated by vague references to what may be adduced in the future, if the matter is allowed to proceed. To accept that proposition would be to undermine the rationale of the rule. A motion for summary judgment must be judged on the basis of the pleadings and materials actually before the judge, not on suppositions about what might be pleaded or proved in the future. This applies to Aboriginal claims as much as to any others.

For these reasons, we would allow the appeal and restore the order of the chambers judge.

NOTES AND QUESTIONS

1. What if the facts in this case had been slightly different? What if the plaintiffs had adduced some evidence that the cause of action could not have been discovered until a point in time that was not barred by the limitations legislation. Would this have been sufficient to demonstrate a genuine issue for trial?

2. If the court concludes that there is a "triable issue" but it suspects that the defence is likely to fail, there are other alternatives to simply allowing the defendant to defend in the normal course. The court may impose terms—for example, that the defendant pay the amount into court as a condition of being permitted to defend. Another alternative is for the court to order a speedy trial—that is, within a few weeks; see, for example, Ont. rule 20.05(1)(a). What objectives do such terms seek to achieve? These rules are, however, rarely invoked. Why is this so?

3. In *Guarantee Co. of North America v. Gordon Capital Corp.*, [1999] 3 SCR 423, at para. 27 (SCC), Iacobucci and Bastarache JJ very briefly discussed the legal principles that govern a motion for summary judgment, without discussing any of the case law:

> The appropriate test to be applied on a motion for summary judgment is satisfied when the applicant has shown that there is no genuine issue of material fact requiring trial, and therefore summary judgment is a proper question for consideration by the court. See *Hercules Managements Ltd. v. Ernst & Young*, [1997] 2 SCR 165, at para. 15; *Dawson v. Rexcraft Storage and Warehouse Inc.* (1998), 164 DLR (4th) 257 (Ont. CA), at pp. 267-68; *Irving Ungerman Ltd. v.*

Galanis (1991), 4 OR (3d) 545 (CA), at pp. 550-51. Once the moving party has made this showing, the respondent must then "establish his claim as being one with a real chance of success" (*Hercules*, *supra*, at para. 15).

Is this standard consistent with *Dawson* and/or *Ungerman*? Is this consistent with the *Lameman* decision, above?

4. *Comparing applications and motions for summary judgment.* Compare the procedure used on a motion for summary judgment and the test for summary judgment to that where the application procedure is used. Is a motion for summary judgment a mechanism that enables a defendant to convert an action to a *de facto* application? To what extent are the procedures similar or different?

5. *Costs of and on a motion for summary judgment.* How expensive is it to bring or defend a motion for summary judgment? A simple motion might cost each side about $15,000. However, a motion of any complexity can cost the parties $50,000 or more.

While summary judgment rules seek to address the concern that matters that need not go to trial be determined at a preliminary stage in the litigation process, the rules also attempt to address the situation where resort to summary judgment is used inappropriately. Note, for example, that Ontario rule 20.06(1) provides that where the moving party obtains no relief, "the court shall fix the opposite party's costs of the motion on a substantial indemnity basis … unless the court is satisfied that the making of the motion, although unsuccessful, was nevertheless reasonable." When can it be considered that a motion for summary judgment, though unsuccessful, was reasonably brought? What is the likely impact of this provision on the bringing of such motions?

3. The Current and Future Trend

Two complaints are perennially levelled at the litigation process: it takes too long and it costs too much. These two complaints are generally seen to be interrelated—that is, one of the reasons that litigation costs too much is that too much time is spent preparing the case for the ultimate trial. The current jurisprudence on summary judgment, as reflected in *Aguonie*, *Dawson* and *Ungerman*, above, clings to the traditional notion that due process in a civil context requires a trial wherever there are issues that require the assessment of credibility or the weighing of evidence.

Is this principle inviolate? Manitoba and British Columbia have attempted to come to grips with this problem with a different procedure. In British Columbia, in addition to a summary judgment procedure under rule 18, the *Supreme Court Rules* make separate provision for an application for judgment under rule 18A. Under this procedure, which has come to be called the "summary trial procedure," the court has an additional power to grant judgment on the merits without a trial. In Manitoba, a BC-style summary trial provision is blended with an Ontario summary judgment provision, as follows:

Where no genuine issue

20.03(1) Where the court is satisfied that there is no genuine issue for trial with respect to a claim or defence, the court shall grant summary judgment accordingly.

Only genuine issue is amount

20.03(2) Where the court is satisfied that the only genuine issue is the amount to which the moving party is entitled, the court may order a trial of that issue or grant judgment with a reference to determine the amount.

Only genuine issue is question of law

20.03(3) Where the court is satisfied that the only genuine issue is a question of law, the court may determine the question and grant judgment accordingly.

Trial on affidavit evidence

20.03(4) Where the court decides there is a genuine issue with respect to a claim or defence, a judge may nevertheless grant judgment in favour of any party, either upon an issue or generally, unless

(a) the judge is unable on the whole of the evidence before the court on the motion to find the facts necessary to decide the questions of fact or law; or

(b) it would be unjust to decide the issues on the motion.

Trial and expedited trial

20.03(5) Where a motion for summary judgment is dismissed, either in whole or in part, a judge may order the action, or the issues in the action not disposed of by summary judgment, to proceed to trial in the ordinary way, but upon the request of any party, the judge may order an expedited trial under rule 20.06.

No further motion without leave

20.03(6) Where a motion for summary judgment is dismissed, the moving party may not make a further motion under rule 20.01 without leave of the court.

20.04 A plaintiff who obtains judgment under rule 20.03 may proceed against the same defendant for any other relief and against any other defendant for the same or any other relief.

Most recently, effective January 2010, Ontario rule 20 has been amended to explicitly broaden the scope of the summary judgment rule. The test of "no genuine issue for trial" has been changed to "no genuine issue requiring a trial." Further the rules were amended to provide as follows:

In determining … whether there is a genuine issue requiring a trial, the court shall consider the evidence submitted by the parties and, if the determination is being made by a judge, the judge may exercise any of the following powers for the purpose, unless it is in the interest of justice for such powers to be exercised only at a trial:

1. Weighing the evidence.

2. Evaluating the credibility of a deponent.

3. Drawing any reasonable inference from the evidence.

What is the cumulative impact of these changes on the approaches in *Aguonie*, *Ungerman*, *Dawson*, and *Lameman*?

The following case, decided under the BC summary trial rule, illustrates the operation of these types of rules.

Inspiration Management Ltd. v. McDermid St. Lawrence Limited
(1989), 36 BCLR (2d) 202 (CA)

McEACHERN CJBC (Seaton, Esson, and Wallace JJA concurring):

I. The Nature of the Appeal

This appeal is against an order made in chambers dismissing the plaintiffs' (appellants') application for judgment under R. 18A in an action for restitution or damages for shares of the plaintiffs sold by the defendant broker.

The plaintiff Robert J. McGowan ("McGowan") is the principal and sole shareholder of both of the other plaintiffs, Inspiration Management Ltd. ("Inspiration") and Wabenung Resources Ltd. ("Wabenung"). McGowan is also the owner of a "control" block of shares in Dragoon Resources Ltd. ("Dragoon").

The defendant McDermid St. Lawrence Limited ("MSL") is a licensed security brokerage house and the defendant, John Wheeler ("Wheeler") is a registered representative in the employment of MSL.

Prior to the events in question in this action, the plaintiffs Inspiration and Wabenung had accounts with MSL. In Inspiration's account were a number of shares in Dragoon which were endorsed for transfer. It is the defendants' sale of Dragoon shares out of the accounts of Inspiration and Wabenung about which the plaintiffs complain in this action.

The chambers judge dismissed the plaintiff's motion for judgment under R. 18A because she considered the test for disposition of such an application was such that judgment should not be given "unless it is clear that a trial in the usual way could not possibly make any difference in the outcome."

We have convened this five-judge court for the purpose of pronouncing upon the proper application of R. 18A. In addition, of course, it is necessary properly to dispose of the plaintiff's appeal. These issues require an examination of the facts.

I propose first to state in an overview what I am able to discern from the material which was before the chambers judge, and secondly to examined the pleadings and affidavits.

II. Overview

Each of Inspiration and Wabenung opened an account with MSL pursuant to client account agreements which, amongst other things, permitted the broker to sell shares in any account which was in a debit position, but neither McGowan personally nor either of the companies guaranteed the debts of the others.

As of 1st October 1987 and at all material times Inspiration's account was long 197,580 shares in Dragoon and there was a small cash credit balance.

The account of Wabenung on the other hand was in a debit position but there were some securities in the account including 10,000 shares in Dragoon.

Early in October 1987 McGowan, who was desperate for money, arranged a one-week loan of $77,000 from the defendants or one of them (it does not matter which) for which he agreed to pay a fee of $3,000. These funds were paid by MSL or Wheeler into the account of Wabenung on 6th October 1987 on which date McGowan signed a letter addressed to Wheeler in the following terms:

October 6, 1987

John Wheeler,
McDermid St. Lawrence Limited,
601 West Hastings Street
Vancouver, BC

Dear John,

On October 14, 1987, I promise to repay $80,000.00 in return against the $77,000.00 loan of October 6, 1987.

Yours truly,

Robert J. McGowan,

Wabenung Resources Ltd.

McGowan says this letter was prepared by Wheeler's assistant. Wheeler says its terms were dictated by McGowan to his assistant at the time McGowan picked up the proceeds of the loan at the defendant's office. The loan proceeds were first paid into and then out of the account of Wabenung which thereby fell into a debit position.

There is a serious conflict of evidence about the collateral for this loan which became important when the market crashed during the one-week period of the loan and McGowan was unable to repay as promised.

McGowan says a "liquidation agreement" was reached after default in which he agreed to furnish a quantity of shares of Geostar Resources Ltd. ("Geostar") to Wabenung sufficient to significantly reduce its debt; that MSL would sell all Wabenung's securities except the Dragoon shares first; and that MSL would not sell any Dragoon shares without consultation.

Wabenung's ledger card shows the sale previously by McGowan of 21,000 shares of Geostar between 6th and 14th October at prices of between 61 and 65; the deposit of 150,000 Geostar shares into that account on 21st October 1987; and the sale of 169,000 Geostar shares between 23rd and 27th October at prices from 38 to 44.

Wheeler, on the other hand, starts the collateral narrative earlier. He says the loan of $77,000 was a personal loan to McGowan; that McGowan agreed that all the securities in all companies accounts were to be available as collateral for the loan; and that when McGowan failed to repay the loan more security was demanded which led McGowan to deposit 150,000 shares of Geostar; that he told McGowan that all the accounts had to be out of a debit position by the end of the month; that he never agreed not to sell Dragoon shares; that McGowan later promised further Geostar shares but he failed to deliver them, so at the month end Wheeler sold 10,000 shares of Dragoon out of the Wabenung account at 30 to 31 and 55,000 shares in Dragoon out of the Inspiration account at prices of 21 to 40.

McGowan did deposit an additional 19,000 shares in Geostar into Wabenung's account around the end of October. McGowan says the shares were deposited at 11:00 a.m.

on 30th October but Wheeler says they did not arrive until 2nd November after the Dragoon shares had already been sold. Wabenung's ledger card records the deposit on 30th October 1987 but it is not clear whether this was an accounting date or a transaction date.

McGowan says that at a later conversation Wheeler admitted he caused these sales to be made and that "he had made a mistake." Counsel for the plaintiffs point to this as an admission by Wheeler of absence of authority to sell shares from the Inspiration account. However, the defendants say that it can be understood merely as a statement by Wheeler that he did not know that the additional Geostar shares had been deposited.

There is a letter dated 29th October 1987 from Inspiration, signed by McGowan, to MSL authorizing payment of the $3,000 loan fee out of Inspiration's account. McGowan says he signed this in early November before he knew of the sale of any Dragoon shares and that he did this in appreciation for the cooperation he thought he was receiving from MSL. The plaintiffs say that this letter helps prove their case because, had Inspiration been liable on the $77,000 loan, the letter would have been unnecessary. The defendants say that the letter is entirely equivocal on that question.

There is also some correspondence between solicitors which I do not think is relevant to any issue of fact or law.

It is obvious that the terms of the loan agreement are crucial to the outcome of this case and that the defendants' authority for MSL or Wheeler to sell shares out of the Inspiration account, if any, could only arise by the agreement of McGowan as Inspiration's account was always in a credit position. This is the crucial issue in the case.

There is, however, a subsidiary issue and that is whether Wheeler sold more Dragoon shares than was necessary to liquidate the loan. In addition to other securities, Wheeler sold 10,000 shares in Dragoon out of the Wabenung account and 55,000 shares in Dragoon out of the Inspiration account, all at post-crash prices.

With the foregoing overview I shall now review the material which was before the chambers judge.

III. Pleadings and Affidavits

The chambers judge had to wrestle with the following disjointed volume of information.

There is no mention of the $77,000 loan in the statement of claim. It alleges that the Wabenung account was in a debit position in October 1987; that there was a debit repayment arrangement, one of the terms of which was that MSL would not unilaterally exercise any of its contractual rights to sell Dragoon shares; that McGowan would provide shares in Geostar Resources Ltd. as security; and that in no event would MSL sell any shares of Dragoon without first consulting with McGowan. This was alleged to be a "liquidation agreement." The statement of claim then goes on to allege that at all material times the Inspiration account remained in a credit position, and relief is claimed both for the unauthorized sale of Dragoon shares out of the Wabenung account and for the sale of any shares out of the Inspiration account.

The defence, filed 28th January 1988, is a pro forma, four line denial of all the allegations in the statement of claim. Pleading this way, which furnishes no answer to the statement of claim, is to be deplored. It was not filed by counsel appearing for the defendants on this appeal.

It is not therefore surprising that the plaintiffs on 23rd February brought a motion for summary judgment under R. 18A.

In his first affidavit sworn 23rd February 1988 McGowan does not mention the $77,000 loan or the words which passed between himself and Mr. Wheeler regarding security for or repayment of such loan. He merely verifies the allegations contained in the statement of claim (which did not mention the $77,000 loan), and he describes the state of the trading accounts of the two companies and verifies the separate existence of Inspiration, and the "unauthorized" sale of its shares in Dragoon.

In para. 30 of this affidavit McGowan says that between 19th December 1987 and 5th January 1988, in discussions with Wheeler about the sales of Dragoon shares from the Inspiration account, "Mr. Wheeler admitted to me that he had caused the said sales to be made, explaining that he had made 'a mistake.'"

On 23rd March McKenzie J made an order in chambers acceding to an application to adjourn the R. 18A motion and he ordered the defendants to provide to the solicitor for the plaintiffs draft copies of an amended statement of defence and the defendants' material to be filed in opposition to the R. 18A application, unexecuted, by 30th March 1988. This amended defence, although not filed until 28th April, recites the $77,000 loan and alleges in para. 2(c):

> (c) As security for the loan, Mr. McGowan was required to provide collateral of 150,000 shares in Geostar Mining Corp. and in addition, all of the shares in the accounts of Inspiration and Wabenung were to stand as security for the debt.

Mr. Wheeler's first affidavit sworn 7th April 1988 describes the $77,000 loan in the following terms:

> 4. THAT on or about October 5, 1987, Mr. McGowan approached me for a loan in the amount of $77,000.00 which he said he required within 24 hours in order to prevent the forfeiture of certain assets that he owned in respect of a mining company that he was involved with.
>
> 5. THAT Mr. McGowan advised me that a private placement for Dragoon had been completed and that he had money in an account in a London brokerage house or Bank but that he needed the loan as he was unable to get these monies transferred quickly enough.
>
> 6. THAT Mr. McGowan suggested and it was agreed that he would pay the funds within 7 days and would pay a fee of $3,000.00 in respect of the loan. Mr. McGowan further agreed that in order to collateralize the loan, he would deposit a further 150,000 shares of Geostar Mining Corp. *in addition to all shares on deposit at McDermid St. Lawrence in all of the Plaintiff's accounts* [my emphasis]. ...
>
> 10. THAT I started to commence selling the shares of Geostar Mining Corp. in order to realize upon the loan security. At this time, Mr. McGowan requested that I not sell his Dragoon shares. However, I did not at any time specifically agree that the Dragoon shares would not be sold. I told Mr. McGowan that the Plaintiff's accounts would be liquidated at month end.

Mr. McGowan swore his second affidavit on 5th April (filed 8th April 1988) but he had obviously seen the amended defence and Mr. Wheeler's first affidavit, in draft, because he purports to respond to them in this second affidavit. He describes the loan agreement as follows:

> (b) The description of the said loan agreement referred to in the Amended Statement of Defence and the Wheeler Affidavit is not true in any event. The said agreement actually transpired as set out herein below;
>
> (c) On or about October 6, 1987 I, for and on behalf of the Plaintiff Wabenung Resources Ltd. (hereinafter called "Wabenung"), arranged with Wheeler to borrow $77,000.00 from the Defendant McDermid St. Lawrence Limited (hereinafter called "MSL"). The said amount was to be repaid on October 14, 1987, together with interest in the amount of $3,000.00;
>
> (d) My said agreement with MSL was documented in a letter dated October 6, 1987 and signed by me for and on behalf of Wabenung. The said letter was prepared by Ms. Bernice Kosiur of MSL on Wheeler's instructions. At no time was Inspiration or any securities, or other property held by it, made a part of the said loan agreement.

Mr. Wheeler swore his second affidavit on 14th April 1988 which was filed the same day. He says:

> (a) the loan was made to Mr. McGowan personally by me personally and the agreement that I made with McGowan and the Plaintiffs was that the shares in the accounts of all of the Plaintiffs would stand as security for the loan made to McGowan. More specifically Mr. McGowan pleaded that I lend him money and that I should do so as I had all of the securities in the Plaintiffs [sic] accounts as collateral. He told me that I was the only person in Vancouver that he could turn to.
>
> (b) the monies were advanced to Mr. McGowan personally through the Wabenung Resources Ltd. account and the indebtedness was registered as a debit in the Wabenung Resources Ltd. account.
>
> (c) the letter of October 6, 1987 attached as Exhibit "C" to Mr. McGowan's affidavit recorded only the promise of Mr. McGowan to repay $80,000 on October 14, 1987. The purpose of this letter was to record only the promise to pay made by McGowan and did not refer to any of the security provisions granted by McGowan, Wabenung Resources Ltd., or Inspiration Management Ltd. The letter was dictated by Mr. McGowan to Bernice Kosiur in my absence as Mr. McGowan required the money immediately on that day and I was not in my office at that time.

Mr. McGowan's third affidavit was sworn 22nd April 1988 (filed 25th April 1988). It does not purport to answer Wheeler's allegations about the terms of the loan agreement. Presumably McGowan thought this had been done sufficiently in his second affidavit.

IV. Rule 18A

As I have said, the learned chambers judge dismissed the McGowan application for judgment under R. 18A because she considered the test to be applied under this rule precluded her from giving judgment unless it was "clear that a trial in the usual way could not possibly make any difference to the outcome."

Before us Mr. Campbell argued that the test described by the chambers judge was not the correct one. It is accordingly necessary as a first step in the determination of this appeal to settle this and other important questions concerning the operation of R. 18A.

The Rules of Court have prescribed a summary judgment procedure for many years. Until our present rules were adopted, this procedure was found in O. 14, R. 1 (MR 115) of the old rules which was limited to liquidated demands and a number of other special kinds of cases. This summary judgment procedure was carried forward into the present rules in 1976, particularly R. 18 which permits judgment to be given in any action on the ground that there is no defence to the whole or any part of the claim or any defence except as to amount (R. 18(1)). This rule understandably received a restricted construction having regard to its provisions. In *Golden Gate Seafood (Vancouver) Co. v. Osborn & Lange Inc.* (1986), 1 BCLR (2d) 145, 13 CPC (2d) 227, Lambert JA at p. 171 said:

> Rule 18 is entitled "Summary Judgment in Action." The ground of the application must be that there is no defence to the whole or a part of the claim or, if the application is made by the defendant, no merit in the whole or a part of the claim. The judge before whom the application is brought is not to decide questions of fact or law as on a trial; his function is restricted to determining whether there is a bona fide triable issue. If there is, he must dismiss the application. See *Hughes v. Sharp* (1969), 68 WWR 706, 5 DLR (3d) 760 (BC CA), and *Memphis Rogues Ltd. v. Skalbania* (1982), 38 BCLR 193, 29 CPC 105 (CA). If there is not, he may give judgment.

The problem with R. 18 of course is that artful pleaders are usually able to set up an arguable claim or defence and any affidavit that raises any contested question of fact or law is enough to defeat a motion for judgment. Rule 18 was often ineffective in avoiding unjust delay or in avoiding unnecessary expense in the determination of many cases.

As a consequence, R. 18A was added to the Rules of Court in 1983 in an attempt to expedite the early resolution of many cases by authorizing a judge in chambers to give judgment in any case where he can decide disputed questions of fact on affidavits or by any of the other proceedings authorized by R. 18A(5) unless it would be unjust to decide the issues in such a way.

I endeavoured to state the differences between applications under RR. 18 and 18A in *Soni v. Malik* (1985), 61 BCLR 36, 1 CPC (2d) 53 (SC), which was quoted with apparent approval by Taggart JA, speaking for this court in *Placer Dev. Ltd. v. Skyline Explor. Ltd.* (1985), 67 BCLR 366 at 377. At pp. 40-41 of *Soni* I said:

> There are substantial differences between an application under RR. 18 and 18A. Under the former, summary judgment should not be given if "there is a bona fide triable issue": *Memphis Rogues Ltd. v. Skalbania* (1982), 38 BCLR 193 at 202, 29 CPC 105 (CA).
>
> Under R. 18A, on the other hand, the court actually tries the issues raised by the pleadings on affidavits. The hearing of a R. 18A application has been called a summary trial: *Imbrook Properties Ltd. v. Bordignon Const. Ltd.* (1984), 51 BCLR 66 at 73, 7 DLR (4th) 602, 4 CLR 223 (CA).
>
> This is a useful way to illustrate the distinction between the two rules although I would have preferred to reserve the term summary trial for expedited proceedings under

R. 18A(5). For convenience I am content to describe the various proceedings under RR. 18, 18A and 18A(5) as summary judgment, summary trial and expedited trial respectively.

The important point, however, is that the raising of a triable issue or arguable defence will not always defeat an application under R. 18A, for the court is authorized under that rule to conduct a summary trial of that issue or defence. The court's function is described in R. 18A(3), which provides that on such an application the court "... may grant judgment ... unless (a) the court is unable on the whole of the evidence [that is, affidavits] ... to find the facts necessary to decide the issues of fact or law ..." or unless it is unjust to do so: *Royal Bank v. Vista Homes Ltd.* (1984), 54 BCLR 252 (SC).

While the court must always be careful in exercising this new jurisdiction, it is clearly the intention and expectation of the rule that cases will be decided summarily if the court is able to find the facts necessary for that purpose, even though there may be disputed issues of fact and law.

In *Placer Dev. Ltd. v. Skyline Explor. Ltd.* Taggart JA also referred to R. 1(5) which provides:

(5) The object of these rules is to secure the just, speedy and inexpensive determination of every proceeding on its merits.

Taggart JA then reviewed a number of authorities and said at pp. 385-86:

Clearly the opening language of subr. (3) of R. 18A contemplates the possibility of judgment being entered on one or more or all issues raised by the pleadings. But that contemplation is, for the judge hearing the application, tempered by the language of paras. (a) and (b) of subr. (3). They clothe the judge with a broad discretion to refuse to proceed with the application where he decides he cannot find the facts necessary to decide the issues of fact or law or if it would be unjust to decide the issues raised on the application. Although those two matters are stated in separate clauses of subr. (3), they will often have to be considered together. I can envisage circumstances where the judge will decide on the whole of the evidence that while it is possible to find the facts necessary to decide the issues of fact or law it would be unjust to decide those issues. On the other hand, I cannot think of a case where, notwithstanding his inability to find the necessary facts, the judge would be justified in proceeding with the application.

Having said that, however, I am far from saying that the judge is precluded from finding facts where he has before him affidavits which conflict. The ability of the judge to find the necessary facts and to decide if it is just to resolve the issues before him will to a large extent depend on the nature and quality of the material before him. I think the rule contemplates that the judge may make the necessary findings of fact on conflicting evidence. Here I think the judgment of the Chief Justice of the Supreme Court in the *Soni* case, the statement of Macdonald J in the *Anglo-Amer. Cedar Prod.* case, including his quotation from the judgment of the Privy Counsel in *Eng Mee Yong v. Letchumanan*, and the statements of principle by Leggatt Co. Ct. J in the *J.M. Stafford & Assoc.* case, may all have application.

In summary, the rule is a means whereby the general principles stated by R. 1(5) may be attained. The rule must, however, be applied only where it is possible to do justice between the parties in accordance with the requirements of the rule itself and in accordance with the general principles which govern judges in their daily task of ensuring that justice is done.

With respect, I think the foregoing accurately describes the proper practice to be followed by a judge hearing an application under R. 18A.

Notwithstanding this, R. 18A has not received a consistent application. In some cases judgment has been given in fairly complicated cases such as *Bank of BC v. Anglo-Amer. Cedar Prod. Ltd.* (1984), 57 BCLR 350, 47 CPC 89 (SC), and in *Soni Placer* and *Golden Gate*. Other decisions point out the usefulness of R. 18A such as *United Services Fund v. Ward* (1986), 1 BCLR (2d) 396 (CA); and *Wolf Mountain Coal Ltd. Partnership v. Netherlands Pac. Mining Co.* (1988), 31 BCLR (2d) 16 (SC). But other decisions have adopted an extremely cautious approach resulting in the development of the test adopted by the chambers judge in this case. Such cases include *Stuart v. Russell*, [1988] BCWLD 1649, CA, Vancouver No. CA006892, 2nd March 1988 (not yet reported), and *Lafleur v. Maryniuk* (1988), 23 BCLR (2d) 131, 28 CPC (2d) 67 (CA). In *Royal Bank v. Stonehocker* (1985), 61 BCLR 265 (CA), it was held that where there are conflicting affidavits it is not open to a judge hearing an application for judgment under R. 18A to prefer the affidavit of one party over that of the other and in such cases the proper course is to dismiss the motion for judgment and remit the matter to the trial list.

It is timely, in my view, for this court to settle the practice to be followed on applications brought under R. 18A keeping always in mind that the variable circumstances under which such applications may be made are unlimited and it may not be possible to foresee every eventuality which may arise.

In my judgment, it must be accepted that while every effort must be made to ensure a just result, the volumes of litigation presently before our courts, the urgency of some cases, and the cost of litigation do not always permit the luxury of a full trial with all traditional safeguards in every case, particularly if a just result can be achieved by a less expensive and more expeditious procedure. I agree with Hinkson JA when he said in *United Services Fund v. Ward* at p. 399:

> My concern is with respect to the intention of promulgating R. 18A. McEachern CJSC has referred to it as a summary trial proceeding, adopting a decision of this court in that respect. It seems to me that that was the intention in R. 18A, that it not be a full-blown trial with all the rights and safeguards that accompany such a trial, but indeed it involved short-cutting some of the normal processes that are involved in a trial and expedited the administration of justice.

In fact R. 18A substitutes other safeguards which are sufficient to ensure the proper attainment of justice. First, 14 days' notice of the application must be given (R. 18A(1.1)); secondly, the chambers judge cannot give judgment unless he can find the facts necessary to decide issues of fact or law (R. 18A(3)(a)); and thirdly, the chambers judge, even if he can decide the necessary factual and legal issues, may nevertheless decline to give judgment if he thinks it would be unjust to do so. The procedure prescribed by R. 18A may not furnish perfect justice in every case, but that elusive and unattainable goal cannot always be assured even after a conventional trial and I believe the safeguards furnished by the rule and the common sense of the chambers judge are sufficient for the attainment of justice in any case likely to be found suitable for this procedure. Chambers judges should be careful but not timid in using R. 18A for the purpose for which it was intended.

In deciding whether it will be unjust to give judgment the chambers judge is entitled to consider, *inter alia*, the amount involved, the complexity of the matter, its urgency, any prejudice likely to arise by reason of delay, the cost of taking the case forward to a conventional trial in relation to the amount involved, the course of the proceedings and any other matters which arise for consideration on this important question. ...

The test for R. 18A, in my view, is the same as on a trial. Upon the facts being found the chambers judge must apply the law and all appropriate legal principles. If then satisfied that the claim or defence has been established according to the appropriate onus of proof he must give judgment according to law unless he has the opinion that it will be unjust to give such judgment.

In deciding whether the case is an appropriate one for judgment under R. 18A, the chambers judge will always give full consideration to all of the evidence which counsel place before him but he will also consider whether the evidence is sufficient for adjudication. For example, the absence of an affidavit from a principal player in the piece, unless its absence is adequately explained, may cause the judge to conclude either that he cannot find the facts necessary to decide the issues, or that it would be unjust to do so. But even then, as the process is adversarial, the judge may be able fairly and justly to find the facts necessary to decide the issue.

Lastly, I do not agree, as suggested in *Royal Bank v. Stonehocker* that a chambers judge is obliged to remit a case to the trial list just because there are conflicting affidavits. In this connection I prefer the view expressed by Taggart JA in *Placer*, ... [at 212-13] of these reasons. Subject to what I am about to say, a judge should not decide an issue of fact or law solely on the basis of conflicting affidavits even if he prefers one version to the other. It may be, however, notwithstanding sworn affidavit evidence to the contrary, that other admissible evidence will make it possible to find the facts necessary for judgment to be given. For example, in an action on a cheque, the alleged maker might by affidavit deny his signature while other believable evidence may satisfy the court that he did indeed sign it. Again, the variety of different kinds of cases which will arise is unlimited. In such cases, absent other circumstances or defences, judgment should be given.

But even if there is a conflict of evidence which cannot easily be resolved on affidavits, as is often the case, the chambers judge is still not required to remit the case to the trial list. He could, for example, adjourn the application and order cross-examination on one or more affidavits, or he could order the deponents to appear to be cross-examined before him or another judge after which time it may be possible to find the facts necessary to give judgment. The chambers judge also has the option of employing any of the other procedures included in R. 18A(5) instead of remitting the case to the trial list.

I have no doubt that R. 18A is destined to play an increasingly important role in the efficient disposition of litigation, and experience has already shown that its use is not limited to simple or straightforward cases. Many complex cases properly prepared and argued can be resolved summarily without compromising justice in any way.

But it is necessary to recognize that it is essential on all applications under R. 18A for counsel to bring an appropriate measure of professional skill to the preparation of both the substance and the form of their material. It is unfair to scoop-shovel volumes of disjointed affidavits and exhibits upon the chambers judge and expect him or her to make an informed judgment. While I also have the view that many of these applications will in future be heard [i]n Chambers Division III which will inevitably be expanded, many of these applications will continue to be heard on a chambers list or by a referral judge where there is little or no opportunity for judicial preparation. Thus it is incumbent upon counsel to ensure, as the old pleaders used to say, that there is a proper joinder of issues on all questions on fact and law, and the practice of serial affidavits as in this case should be avoided.

It should not be good enough in such serious matters for counsel to throw up volumes of ill-considered affidavits and exhibits which do not squarely raise or answer the real issues in the case. The preparation of affidavits for an application or defence under R. 18A is a serious matter which requires the careful professional attention of counsel.

Fortunately, most counsel take great care in the preparation of their material. If they do not do this the chambers judge is entitled to send them away to put their material in proper order. Serial affidavits, as in this case, should be avoided if possible. One of counsel's objectives is to persuade, and they cannot expect to succeed in this endeavour if they permit confusion in the form of masses of disorganized fact and paper to intrude into the decisional process.

V. Judgment on This Appeal

In my view, the learned chambers judge applied the wrong test in this case. Instead of the test she applied (that a conventional trial could not possibly make any difference), she should have followed the process I have just discussed.

But even if the chambers judge had applied the proper test it is my view that she could not have found the facts with sufficient certainty to give judgment because the real question was whether McGowan agreed, as Wheeler alleges, that all of the shares in the accounts of all of the plaintiffs would stand as security for the loan made by the defendants. McGowan in his second affidavit denies this and says that the loan agreement is described in the brief letter of 6th October 1987 and he adds: "At no time was Inspiration or any securities or other property held by it made a part of the said loan agreement." His position is that the only security he gave for this loan was his personal covenant, the securities in the Wabenung account and of course, the debt owed by the company.

Notwithstanding the fact that the conflict between these two deponents could not be resolved on affidavits, the chambers judge was not required to dismiss the application and leave the action to be tried in the usual way. She could have required McGowan and Wheeler to be cross-examined on their affidavits because such cross-examination would put her in a position to decide this crucial question and all other questions which would dispose of the action, or she could have exercised any one or more of the other jurisdictions conferred by R. 18A(5) in an endeavour to bring this relatively straightforward litigation to an early and inexpensive disposition. The learned chambers judge did give leave to the plaintiff to bring a fresh application under R. 18A after examination for discovery. That was an option that was also open to her but it seems to me, with respect, that cross-examination before a judge would have been the preferable course to follow.

At the end of the day I am left with the view that the use of an improper test by the chambers judge may have led her to conclude that she had no choice but to dismiss the application.

Because of the urgency of this matter to the parties (a trial date was pending) the court, on 21st April 1989, allowed this appeal and authorized the plaintiffs, if they wished, to renew their application for judgment under R. 18A on the ground that, if Mr. McGowan and Mr. Wheeler were cross-examined on their affidavits before the judgment, either on an issue or generally, under R. 18A(3). These are my reasons for allowing this appeal to the extent just mentioned.

Appeal allowed.

NOTES AND QUESTIONS

1. This case was decided under the BC summary trial rule. Compare the application of that rule with the approach of the Ontario courts in the summary judgment decisions already considered. Is the BC approach fair? Is it justified as a form of "rough and ready" justice that is cheaper and faster? Should other provinces adopt a similar provision?

2. Note that in British Columbia, there is no right to cross-examine on affidavits filed with the court. Compare Ontario rule 39.02. How would the difference affect the hearing and disposition of a motion for summary judgment?

C. Special Case

Each jurisdiction allows for the determination of a point of law in a proceeding by way of a "special case" (often referred to as a "stated case"). The scope for such a procedure is relatively narrow, as it may only be used by mutual agreement of the parties, and expressly or implicitly requires an agreed statement of facts. See rule 22 in Ontario, Manitoba, and PEI; Manitoba rule 24; Nova Scotia rule 27; Saskatchewan rule 263; Alberta rule 232; and BC rule 33.

IV. DISPOSITION WITHOUT TRIAL—PROCESS-BASED

A. Default Proceedings

If the defendant fails to respond to the originating process within the time required, the plaintiff may use provisions in the rules—default proceedings—that allow the plaintiff to proceed to judgment. Note that in most jurisdictions, the defendant has the right to respond notwithstanding the expiry of the time for response, unless the plaintiff has taken steps toward default judgment that have the effect, under the rules, of preventing the defendant from filing a response.

Recall the warning to the defendant on the form of the originating process; it states in emphatic terms that if the defendant fails to respond in the specified time limit, judgment may be given without further notice to the defendant. While notice of proceedings to the defendant is a fundamental aspect of the procedural system and the basis of the requirement of personal service, once that notice is given and the defendant does not respond, there is no requirement that further notice be given to the defendant. Accordingly, the rules make specific provision that if a defendant properly served does not respond to the originating process as required, the defendant is generally not entitled to further notice of steps in the proceeding.

The precise path available to a plaintiff where the defendant does not respond is defined in the specific rules dealing with default proceedings (that is, Ontario rule 19; Nova Scotia rule 12; or BC rules 17 and 25). While the precise terminology may vary from province to province, the essential elements follow:

1. The time for response has expired.
2. The plaintiff files proof of service with the court, with a request that causes the court to cut off the ability of the defendant to file a response. (In Ontario, this is known as requisitioning the registrar to note the defendant in default.)
3. Where the default is in delivering a statement of defence, the rules deem the defendant to have admitted all allegations in the statement of claim.
4. The defendant is not entitled to notice of further steps in the action except in specified situations.

Following that, the manner in which the plaintiff proceeds to judgment following the defendant's default depends on the type of claim advanced. Consider the distinctions in the rules between, on the one hand, debts or liquidated claims and, on the other hand, other types of claims. There is a long judicial history considering when a claim is either a "debt or liquidated demand" or not, because this distinction was important for other reasons that predate the present rules. The definition generally accepted is as quoted by the master in *J. Cooke (Concrete Blocks) Ltd. v. Campbell*, [1947] OWN 713:

> A claim is liquidated "whenever the amount to which the plaintiff is entitled (if he is entitled to anything) can be ascertained by calculation or fixed by any scale of charges or other positive data."

What is the difference in procedure between the granting of default judgment in the case of debts or liquidated demands and other situations? What is the justification for the difference in treatment?

The first notice that a defendant will have that a default judgment has been granted will ordinarily be when the plaintiff takes steps to have the judgment enforced against the defendant. The rules give the court the power to set aside a default judgment (and, in jurisdictions that treat the noting in default as a separate step, a noting in default). When should the court exercise its power to set aside a default judgment and allow a defendant who has not responded to the originating process the opportunity to defend the lawsuit? Do you agree with the judge's exercise of discretion in the following decision?

Lenskis v. Roncaioli
(1992), 11 CPC (3d) 99 (Ont. Gen. Div.)

MACDONALD J (orally): ... This motion was brought by the defendants, Ibi Roncaioli and Joseph Roncaioli for an order setting aside the noting of pleadings closed, and the default judgment signed against the defendants on Monday, February 10, 1992, pursuant to r. 19.09(1) of the *Rules of Civil Procedure*.

The motion record discloses that default judgment was signed by the Honourable Mr. Justice Webb. The judgment ordered the defendants, the moving party in this motion, to pay to the plaintiff Raisa Lenskis ("Lenskis"), the responding party in this motion, the sum of $44,399.48. The judgment further ordered that the defendants would pay to the plaintiff Sonia Grimman ("Grimman") the sum of $13,513.36, and costs as assessed by the court.

The essential grounds for the motion brought by the defendants is that they now allege that they have a good defence to the plaintiffs' claim. In support of their position, the defendant Mrs. Roncaioli has sworn an affidavit dated March 11, 1992 deposing to a number of facts and circumstances. She was cross-examined on this affidavit and I was referred on several occasions during argument to the transcript of her cross-examination.

Without going into the background in detail, the statement of claim as initially issued, seeks repayment of moneys alleged to be owed by the defendants to the plaintiffs. It is alleged that during the course of the relationship between the parties, substantial amounts of money were lent by the plaintiffs to the defendants. There are allegations of illicit activities made by the defendant Ibi Roncaioli in her affidavit wherein she states that prior to the issuing of the statement of claim, the plaintiff Lenskis owned a variety store and sold illegal contraband cigarettes through her business. She states that at no time did she borrow money from Lenskis, but that Lenskis gave her money to buy cigarettes for Lenskis, and that she did so without making a profit.

The defendant Ibi Roncaioli was charged in Provincial Court for defrauding the plaintiffs of moneys exceeding $1,000. At the preliminary hearing before the Honourable Mr. Justice Crossland, the defendant Ibi Roncaioli was discharged. In her affidavit, the defendant Ibi Roncaioli relies on this discharge in support of her position that in these civil proceedings she now has a defence to the plaintiffs' action. The defendant Ibi Roncaioli acknowledges that she executed documents purporting to settle her claims with the plaintiffs in the office of Mr. David Sloan, the solicitor of record for the plaintiffs.

In her affidavit filed in support of this motion, the defendant Mrs. Roncaioli attempts to put a different interpretation on the settlement documents and suggests that they were merely documents that she described as "settlement agenda containing figures in a format for payment." She also argues that she was under extreme duress by reason of the following circumstances:

1. She was unrepresented by counsel.
2. She did not want her husband to find out what was going on, as the plaintiffs were actively pressuring her and threatening to expose their illegal enterprises to him.
3. She was under heavy medication at the time, including morphine, as a result of pain and discomfort associated with a serious complication that developed from a broken ankle that had left her partially disabled.
4. She thought if she repaid the plaintiffs' losses she would be able to prevent further trouble.

After having made two settlement agreements, both of which she defaulted on, the plaintiffs appeared to have decided not to pursue the matter, but the defendant, Ibi Roncaioli, did not take any steps to dismiss the plaintiffs' claim.

Things changed significantly when the defendant, Ibi Roncaioli, won $5 million dollars in the Lotto 649. She now states that she is a very wealthy woman and alleges that the plaintiffs who took no steps in the interim to pursue the matter are now attempting "a fast grab." The plaintiffs' motion record is comprised of two affidavits. One is sworn May 5, 1992 by Suzie Larado, who alleges that she is a former friend of the defendants and that she was involved with the defendants on a direct basis in her dealings with the plaintiffs in late 1985 and 1986. She states that the moving party told her that she owed the money to Ms. Lenskis and that she was agreeable to paying the money back.

As a result of her feeling that she owed the money and agreeing to paying it back, the defendant, Ibi Roncaioli, attended at the offices of J. David Sloan, the plaintiffs' solicitor, in January 1986, and in the presence of the deponent of the affidavit that I have just identified, the negotiations were carried out directly between Mr. Sloan and Mrs. Roncaioli.

These negotiations resulted in a settlement. I find that there was a settlement, although this settlement was referred to in argument before me as a purported settlement, I see nothing on the face of the documents before me that would suggest that it was not in fact a settlement. The word "purported" was used only to indicate that while a settlement had been reached it was purported in that Mrs. Roncaioli did not meet the obligations for repayment which [was] contemplated in the settlement.

In *Dealers Supply (Agriculture) Ltd. v. Tweed Farm & Garden Supplies Ltd.* (1987), 22 CPC (2d) 257 (Ont. Dist. Ct.), the Honourable Mr. Justice Miesener sets out three requirements that a moving party must meet in order to have judgment against him or her set aside. The requirements are as follows [at 262-63]:

1. The motion to set aside a default judgment should be made as soon as possible after the applicant becomes aware of the judgment.
2. More importantly, the moving party's affidavit must set out circumstances under which the default arose that give a plausible explanation for the default.
3. The moving party must set forth facts to support the conclusion that there is at least an arguable case to present on its merits.

In addition, Miesener DCJ commented that there is still a broad obligation to look at all the circumstances and to be satisfied that no injustice is done to the innocent party, the respondent to the motion, in any order that is finally made. Miesener DCJ cited with approval the decision of Urquhart J in *Nelligan v. Lindsay*, [1945] OWN 295 (HC), and while it is an older case, it is still good authority for the principles that are to be followed in a motion of this sort.

In *Nelligan v. Lindsay*, supra, the delay was short, and it occurred by reason of a misunderstanding between the solicitors for the parties, with the result that the pleadings were noted closed. The delay was negligible and the court found that there could be no prejudice caused to the plaintiff who was capable of being compensated for in costs. In addition, and most importantly, the defendant set out in his motion material circumstances which could afford a defence. Urquhart J quoted from *Klein v. Schile*, [1921] 2 WWR 78, 14 Sask. LR 220, 59 DLR 102 (CA), at p. 221 [Sask. LR] as follows:

> It is not sufficient to merely state that the defendant has a good defence upon the merits. The affidavits must show the nature of the defence and set forth facts which will enable the

Court or Judge to decide whether or not there was a matter which would afford a defence to the action.

Counsel for the moving party has drawn to my attention a recent decision of the Ontario Court of Appeal; *Earl v. Koloszar*, [1991] OJ 45, oral reasons released January 17, 1991 [(Doc. CA 506/89), Tarnopolsky, Finlayson and Galligan JJA]. Counsel on behalf of the moving party today, strenuously argued that the decision of the Court of Appeal in *Earl v. Koloszar* relaxes the tests and considerations which were set forth in *Nelligan v. Lindsay*, supra. The Court of Appeal made the following comments with respect to the setting aside a default judgment [at 1-2, unreported]:

> While the decision whether or not to set aside a default judgment is a matter of discretion, the exercise of that discretion is reviewable by an appellant court. The principles to be applied in such cases have been set out in numerous decisions. It is not necessary to make any review of authority because the factors and principles can vary depending on the circumstances. However, among the factors which always have to be considered and which apply in this case are the following:
>
> 1. the delay between the default and the noting pleadings closed;
>
> 2. the delay on the part of the defendant between learning of the default judgment and moving to set it aside;
>
> 3. the reasons for the delay;
>
> 4. the prejudice, if any, which either or both of those delays caused the plaintiff;
>
> 5. whether or not there was a matter disclosed which could afford a defence to the motion.

I do not agree with counsel that the Court of Appeal decision relaxes the tests or in any way departs from the principles which emerge from *Dealers Supply v. Tweed Farm*, … [(1987), 22 CPC (2d) 257 (Ont. Dist. Ct.)], and *Nelligan v. Lindsay*, supra.

In this case, I find Mrs. Roncaioli did move with relative speed and accordingly I do not find anything under this heading of the test which deprives her of her right to bring the motion. I do not find however that Mrs. Roncaioli has set out in her affidavit material, circumstances which are acceptable to this court that explain the reasons why the default arose. In addition, she has not set forth in the material filed, facts which support the conclusion that she would have an arguable case to present on the merits. In addition, I do not find anything that suggests to me that the moving party when she reached her settlement, was incapacitated and I am cognizant of the extensive medical material that was provided to me which suggests that this moving party had a history of medical problems. There is nothing in the material that convinces me that when she attended at Mr. Sloan's office, she was suffering in any way from any disability which made her unable to understand what she was attempting to do in achieving settlement.

On the material in this motion before me, I do not find facts that afford a valid defence. As I have indicated, I do not accept what appears to be some defence related to duress in respect of the settlement negotiations, nor do I find the fact that there was a discharge in the criminal proceedings … one which I should take as being compelling or conclusive in my considerations with respect to this civil matter. …

In view of the absence of a defence, or if the defendant has a valid defence, it is not adequately set out in the pleadings as mandated by the authorities. The motion to set aside the default judgment is dismissed accordingly.

Motion dismissed.

B. Dismissal for Delay and Non-Compliance with Rules

Belanger v. Southwestern Insulation Contractors Ltd.
(1993), 32 CPC (3d) 256, 16 OR (3d) 457 (Gen. Div.)

BORINS J: These are four motions brought by the defendant Lorcon Inc. ("Lorcon") and a fifth motion brought by the defendant Solar Conservation Services Ltd. ("Solar") in four related actions in which the plaintiffs are claiming damages from a number of defendants arising out of the installation of urea formaldehyde foam insulation ("UFFI") in their homes. At the relevant time Lorcon was a manufacturer and distributor of UFFI.

In *Belanger v. Southwestern Insulation Contractors Ltd.*, which was commenced in 1981, Lorcon and Solar seek an order under r. 24.01 dismissing the actions of Mr. & Mrs. Belanger and Mr. & Mrs. Spitzer for delay. In *Berlin v. Solar Conservation Services Ltd.* and *Hilton v. Total Insulation Services Ltd.* each of which was commenced in 1982, and in *Novielli v. Solar Conservation Services Ltd.*, which was commenced in 1983, Lorcon seeks judgment against the plaintiffs in the terms of an accepted offer to settle under r. 49.09 or, in the alternative, an order dismissing each of the actions for delay. Counsel for Reichhold Limited, a defendant in each action, attended but did not participate in the motions.

Background

Each of the actions was commenced at least 10 yeas ago. In each action damages are claimed arising out of the installation of UFFI in the home of the plaintiffs. In each action pleadings have been exchanged but examinations for discovery have not been conducted. As such, these actions represent only four of a larger number of similar actions ("the Ontario UFFI actions"). The law firm of Lyons, Arbus and Goodman represented the plaintiffs at the time these proceedings were commenced. At or about the same time as the Ontario UFFI actions were commenced a number of homeowners commenced similar actions claiming similar relief in the Quebec Superior Court ("the Quebec UFFI actions"). The trial of six of the Quebec UFFI actions commenced in September, 1983, and concluded in February, 1990. On December 13, 1991, a 1200 page judgment was released dismissing the plaintiffs' actions. The trial produced an 810 volume transcript and resulted in about 1850 exhibits being entered and about 100 individuals being qualified as expert witnesses. I am told that the plaintiffs have now perfected their appeal to the

Quebec Court of Appeal and that the defendants have until February, 1995, to perfect their appeal.

On April 16, 1986, Mr. C. Michael Harpur of Lyons, Arbus and Goodman, on behalf of the plaintiffs in the Ontario UFFI actions, wrote a letter to the lawyers acting on behalf of the defendants in these actions. Mr. R.A. Stradiotto of Borden & Elliot, who represents Lorcon, received a copy of this letter. In the letter Mr. Harpur reported that the plaintiffs in the Quebec UFFI actions had completed their case, that the defendants' case was to begin at the end of April and that it appeared that a judgment in the Quebec actions would be rendered sometime in 1989. The significant portion of Mr. Harpur's letter reads:

> Our clients have indicated their willingness to defer "reactivation" of their law suits in Ontario until judgment is rendered in Quebec provided this great delay is without prejudice. I would appreciate your confirmation in writing that the plaintiffs' failure to proceed until the rendering of the judgment in Quebec will be without prejudice.

Mr. Stradiotto replied to this letter on behalf of Lorcon on August 26, 1986 as follows:

> … I can confirm … that, for such time as we agree to defer the suits in Ontario pending the outcome of the action before the Quebec Superior Court, the deferral is to be without prejudice to either party. It is to be understood that this arrangement does not bind our respective clients to a deferment of this matter until a judgment of the Quebec Superior Court is rendered and our clients are at liberty to insist that one or other of the actions in question proceed upon written notice to this effect. …

He added that Lorcon's "agreement to this arrangement does not mean that we agree to be bound by what the Quebec Superior Court may decide."

• • •

With respect to the motions of Lorcon and Solar to dismiss the Belanger action for delay, on August 18, 1992 Mr. Stradiotto wrote to Ms. McPhadden to inquire whether she had as yet received instructions from the Belangers in respect to the dismissal of their action without costs. Mr. Glen Cohen replied on August 24, 1992 that he had been unable to locate his clients and, therefore, had no instructions from them and, in the circumstances, would be unable to respond to a motion to dismiss their action. In his letter of February 4, 1993 Mr. Maxwell Cohen advised Mr. Stradiotto: "We have not been able to locate or communicate with the Belangers for some time." However, the Belangers have now been located and, as I have indicated, Mrs. Belanger has provided an affidavit in response to the motions to dismiss her action.

Lorcon has presented no evidence of any prejudice which it has or will sustain in respect to the Belanger action other than the belief of a law clerk at Borden & Elliot that Lorcon "has been prejudiced due to the [Belangers'] delay in proceeding with this action." Mr. Peter Daley, who is a solicitor with the law firm representing Solar, swore in his affidavit that he believes "that the delay since the rendering of the decision in the Quebec Superior Court is inordinate and inexcusable and has created a substantial risk that a fair trial will not take place." He adds his belief that Solar has been greatly prejudiced due to the delay of the Belangers in setting their action down for trial.

· · ·

Should the Claims of the Belangers and the Spitzers Against Lorcon and Solar Be Dismissed for Delay?

It is the position of Lorcon and Solar that the actions brought against them by the Belangers and the Spitzers should be dismissed for delay as they were not set down for trial within six months after the close of pleadings: r. 24.01(c). The Belangers, Sgros and Spitzers commenced their action in 1981. As noted previously, the Sgros' action has been dismissed consequent to their acceptance of Lorcon's offer to settle. Counsel for the Belangers and the Spitzers submits that their actions should not be dismissed on the ground that counsel for the parties agreed in 1986 that they could defer proceeding with their actions until the completion of the Quebec UFFI actions, including any and all appeals from the trial judgment. He further submits that, in any event, the actions cannot be dismissed for delay as Lorcon and Solar have not established that they have been prejudiced by the plaintiffs' failure to set down their actions for trial. Although there is no cross-motion by the Belangers and the Spitzers, what they are really asking is that the court stay their actions pursuant to s. 106 of the *Courts of Justice Act*, RSO 1990, c. C.43 until the completion of all appeals in the Quebec UFFI actions.

In my view, Lorcon and Solar have established a *prima facie* case that the actions should be dismissed for delay under r. 24.01(c): cf., *Kowalczyk v. Scarborough General Hospital* (1985), 48 CPC 185 (Ont. HC). Although counsel for the plaintiffs takes the position that in his letter of April 16, 1986, Mr. Harpur, who was then the plaintiffs' counsel, sought and obtained the agreement of the defendants to a deferral of the Ontario UFFI actions pending a final determination of the Quebec litigation, this is not what Mr. Harpur's letter requested. As set out on page 5 [p. 261 *ante*] of these reasons, Mr. Harpur wrote: "Our clients have indicated their willingness to defer 'reactivation' of their law suits in Ontario until judgment is rendered in Quebec provided this great delay is without prejudice." In responding to this request Lorcon's lawyer made it clear that although Lorcon agreed to defer the Ontario UFFI actions "pending the outcome of the action before the Quebec Superior Court" the deferral was "without prejudice to either party" and did not bind either the plaintiffs or Lorcon "to a deferment of this matter until a judgment of the Quebec Superior Court is rendered." He expressly reserved the right on behalf of Lorcon to insist that any of the Ontario UFFI actions proceed upon written notice to this effect. Accordingly, I find that there was no agreement on the part of counsel that the plaintiffs were not required to proceed with their action until the appeal process in respect to the Quebec UFFI actions came to an end.

It is unnecessary to review the many cases which have discussed the factors to be considered by the court on a motion to dismiss an action for delay or for want of prosecution. Nor is it necessary to consider the relatively rare case where the plaintiff's delay was intentional and contumelious. In order to succeed on a motion to dismiss a plaintiff's claim for delay the defendant must establish that the delay has been unreasonable in the sense that it is inordinate and inexcusable and that there is a substantial risk that a fair trial will not be possible for the defendant at the time the action is tried if it is allowed to continue. The second part of this proposition is often expressed as the likelihood of prejudice to the defendant giving rise to a substantial risk that a fair trial will not be possible when the case is actually tried. Examples of prejudice are the death of a witness, the inability to locate a witness, the inability of a witness to recall important facts or the loss of important evidence. In determining whether the delay has been unreasonable the court should consider the issues raised by the case, the complexity of the issues, the explanation for the delay and all relevant surrounding circumstances. In considering whether the defendant has sustained prejudice the court should consider the availability of its witnesses, whether the evidence is largely documentary or based on the recollection of individuals, the efforts made by the defendant to preserve its evidence and any other relevant consideration. Prejudice to the defendant is to be considered relative to the time the case will likely be reached for trial if permitted to proceed. The court will then balance the right of the plaintiff to proceed to trial with the defendant's right to a fair trial and make its decision.

Viewed from the perspective of 1981 when the plaintiffs issued their writ of summons the delay of 12 years in proceeding with their actions may, on any standard, be said to be unreasonable. However, when one considers the explanation for the delay together with the defendants' concurrence in the reason for the delay it is difficult to conclude that it has been unreasonable. I will discuss the reason for the delay in more detail when I consider whether the plaintiffs' request for a stay of their action should be granted or whether I should dispose of the defendants' motion for dismissal for delay by extending the time for the plaintiffs to set down their action for trial. In considering the explanation for the delay, in my view the proper date for the commencement of the delay is December 13, 1991, when judgment was delivered in the Quebec UFFI actions as the parties had agreed to allow this action to wait until that event occurred subject to the right of the defendants to insist it proceed earlier. In any event, however, neither Lorcon nor Solar has produced any evidence that it has been prejudiced as that term has been considered by the authorities in the context of the dismissal for delay cases. It follows, therefore, that the Belanger and Spitzer actions should not be dismissed for delay.

The issue, therefore, becomes whether the court should require the Belangers and the Spitzers to set down their actions for trial within, say, one month of this order failing which Lorcon and Solar would be at liberty to move without notice for an order that the actions be dismissed for delay, or whether the court should accede to the plaintiffs' request that their actions be stayed until the completion of the appeal process in the Quebec UFFI actions. The resolution of this issue requires an examination of the explanation given by the plaintiffs for the course which their actions has taken until now.

When the plaintiffs learned that similar actions were underway in Quebec in which the plaintiffs' legal expenses were to be paid by the government of Quebec it made sense, both economically and jurisprudentially, to hold the Ontario UFFI actions in abeyance after pleadings had been exchanged pending the result of the Quebec UFFI actions. As the Quebec actions were to canvass the same issues which were raised in the Ontario actions, the plaintiffs in Ontario were hoping that a result favourable to the plaintiffs in Quebec would be persuasive in the resolution of their claims against the Ontario defendants. This is why they requested and obtained the defendants' agreement to a delay of the Ontario actions. The plaintiffs' concerns that the Ontario actions would be lengthy and costly were borne out by the seven years which were required to litigate the Quebec claims. Counsel for the plaintiffs submits that it would be unfair to them if they were required to proceed with their actions at this time as they would be unable to finance their litigation leading to the result that the defendants would ultimately succeed in their motion to dismiss the actions for delay. He argued that the defendants would not be prejudiced if they were required to wait until after all appeals, including a possible appeal to the Supreme Court of Canada, have been decided. As I indicated earlier, this could be after 2000. Counsel for the plaintiffs submitted that as most of the evidence is documentary it would not result in the risk of unfairness to the defendants if they were required to wait 20 years or more after their actions were commenced to proceed to trial. He stated that this approach would result in the most efficient use of public resources.

Counsel for Lorcon and Solar submit that the time has come when the Belangers and the Spitzers must decide whether or not they are going to proceed with their claims. Since the judgment in the Quebec UFFI actions they have taken no steps to move their actions forward and do not intend to do so in the foreseeable future. In effect, the defendants submit that fairness does not require that they be forced to wait until sometime in the next century for the plaintiffs to make a decision to go forward with their case. They say that they are entitled to have the action terminated or to an order requiring the plaintiffs to proceed with it. It is submitted that the plaintiffs cannot have it both ways. On the one hand they state that they are not bound by the result of the Quebec UFFI actions, while on the other hand they are hoping for a favourable appellate result and wish to reserve their right to litigate on the chance that such a result might occur and be persuasive in producing a settlement of their claims. However, there is no guarantee that even if a result is achieved which favours the plaintiffs in the Quebec UFFI actions that the defendants will agree to compensate the plaintiffs.

Mr. Stradiotto relies on two cases in which a plaintiff unsuccessfully attempted to obtain a stay of its own action. In *Manufacturers Life Insurance Co. v. Guarantee Co. of North America* (1987), 62 OR (2d) 147 (HC) the plaintiff commenced proceedings in two states in the United States and in Ontario and moved for a stay of the Ontario action. O'Driscoll J at p. 153 stated that he was referred to no authorities which permit a plaintiff to commence a lawsuit in a number of jurisdictions, including Ontario, and to obtain a stay of the Ontario action while it "tests the waters in other jurisdictions in search of a court and laws that favour the plaintiff's cause more than the laws of Ontario." In dismissing the plaintiff's motion he concluded at p. 153:

> 4. Assuming that a plaintiff is entitled to "forum shop," in my view, the plaintiff is not entitled to put the defendant "on hold" until the plaintiff has shopped the world.

> 5. The plaintiff has chosen to commence proceedings in Ontario; it cannot be heard to say that such a proceeding is vexatious or oppressive. If the plaintiff is of such a view, the action may be discontinued or dismissed with costs without any difficulties.

However, I see no reason why the Ontario action should be stayed until the plaintiff has played out all its potential options in other jurisdictions. The plaintiff must choose.

In my view, to allow the plaintiff's motion and grant a stay would not be in harmony with the objects of s. 119 of the *Courts of Justice Act, 1984*, but would be an order allowing the plaintiff to continue its forum shopping whims.

Although this case does not involve multiple actions brought by the plaintiffs in multiple jurisdictions, the situation in this case is analogous as the plaintiffs wish to stay this action until, they hope, a result which supports their case is achieved in the Quebec UFFI actions.

In *Great-West Life Assurance Co. v. Continental Insurance Co.* (1988), 30 CPC (2d) 128 (Ont. HC) the plaintiff had sued its two fidelity insurers in California. The first defendant attorned to the California jurisdiction. The second defendant, Guarantee, successfully challenged that jurisdiction and the plaintiff appealed from this decision. While its appeal was pending the plaintiff sued both defendants in Ontario to protect against a limitation period. Neither the plaintiff nor the first defendant wished to proceed in Ontario, but Guarantee insisted on the Ontario action proceeding. This resulted in the plaintiff's motion to stay the Ontario action pending the outcome of its appeal. Austin J considered that the plaintiff and Guarantee each had justifiable positions and at p. 131 stated: "The question posed by this motion is whether, both sides having entirely justifiable positions, which should prevail?"

In order to resolve this question Austin J was required to determine the onus to be satisfied by a plaintiff which moves to stay its own case. He concluded that a plaintiff must satisfy the same onus which rests on a defendant who wishes to obtain a stay of an action—which was the position also taken by O'Driscoll J in the *Manufacturers Life* case, *supra*. He concluded that the onus is on the applicant to show that there is something oppressive, vexatious or abusive in the continuance of the Ontario action. His reference to "the Ontario action" was based on the fact that all of the cases on which he relied involved an action in Ontario and a similar action in one or more other jurisdictions. Austin J was not persuaded that it would be any more just to grant the stay than to refuse it, so he dismissed the plaintiff's motion. At pp. 132-3 he stated:

> The plaintiff, having commenced an action here has, at least in one sense, chosen this jurisdiction. Having taken that step, for whatever reason, Guarantee is entitled to respond as provided by the rules. While the stay asked for by Great-West appears at this stage to be only momentary and while I am assured that the appeal is to be argued on October 13, 1988, and that the decision will be made that day or shortly thereafter, there is no real assurance either that it will be argued on that day or that the decision will be handed down quickly. There is no compelling reason why any risk of delay or extra expense should be borne by Guarantee.

As in the *Great-West Life* case, there is merit in the positions taken by the Belangers and the Spitzers and by Lorcon and Solar. The plaintiffs submit that it would be costly to proceed with this action without knowing the final result of the appeals from the dismissal of the Quebec UFFI actions. The defendants do not wish to have this action hanging over their heads for, perhaps, another decade and face the prospect of a trial more than 20 years after the plaintiffs' actions were commenced. In my view, the plaintiffs have not demonstrated that there is something oppressive, vexatious or abusive were they to be forced to continue their actions. They quite properly chose Ontario for their actions as they reside here. However, having chosen Ontario they are required to comply with its *Rules of Civil Procedure* and the defendants are entitled to rely on any procedural rights contained in the Rules. On the facts the Belangers and the Spitzers sought and obtained the defendants' indulgence to permit them to hold their actions in abeyance until the decision of the trial judge in the Quebec UFFI actions. Judgment was given just over two years ago. Fairness to the defendants requires that the plaintiffs now proceed with their actions. They will have 30 days from the date of this order to set their actions down for trial. If they fail to do so, Lorcon and Solar are at liberty to move without notice for an order dismissing the plaintiffs' actions for delay.

. . .

Motion to dismiss action for delay dismissed.

NOTES AND QUESTIONS

1. Each Canadian jurisdiction has rules that provide for the dismissal of an action for delay or for "want of prosecution": Alberta rule 244; BC rule 25(1); Newfoundland and Labrador rule 327; Nova Scotia rule 28.13; New Brunswick rule 26; and Manitoba rule 24.

2. Delay in legal proceedings, immortalized in 1853 by Charles Dickens in *Bleak House* ("Jarndyce and Jarndyce still drags its dreary length before the Court") has remained a perennial problem. Dismissal for delay is the court's ultimate weapon for dealing with the problem, at least in individual cases of excessive delay. But it is a Draconian remedy and one that must attempt to reconcile competing principles. "Courts do not like to deprive a plaintiff of the right to his day in court or of having his action tried but, at the same time, delays cannot be permitted to the prejudice of defendants who are entitled to have the issues disposed of promptly and in accordance with the rules": *Ross v. Crown Fuel Co.* (1962), 41 WWR 65, at 69 (Man. CA).

3. One difficulty with motions to dismiss for delay at the behest of the defendant is that they typically ask for too much (outright dismissal of a plaintiff's action), too late (long after the action should have been prodded along by somebody). Is it appropriate to rely on a party to enforce the timely prosecution of lawsuits?

4. Case management provides a different approach to the question of delay and, in theory at least, substitutes court monitoring of the progress of action and the imposition of schedules for completion of litigation steps. As case management expands, will there be need for rules such as Ontario rule 24?

5. The *Belanger* case raises two additional side issues: the "wait-and-see" plaintiff and the "forum-shopping" plaintiff. How did the court deal with the interaction between the Ontario litigation and the Quebec litigation? Should the court have taken a different approach if, for example, the Quebec litigation involved different plaintiffs and the Ontario plaintiffs genuinely wished to see the outcome of the Quebec litigation before proceeding with their claims? How are plaintiffs to deal with these issues in the context of the constraints of limitation periods, *res judicata* rules, and the pressures to prosecute actions in a timely manner?

6. *The role of the solicitor.* Additional concerns arise when it appears that the solicitor's inadvertence or negligence has played a role in the failure to prosecute a claim in a timely manner. This is discussed in the following decision by the Court of Appeal for Ontario.

Marché D'Alimentation Denis Thériault Ltée v. Giant Tiger Stores Ltd.
2007 ONCA 695

R.J. SHARPE JA: When should a litigant be permitted to revive an action that has been dismissed for delay?

The respondents commenced this action in October 1996, but by early 1998 the matter had stalled. The respondents did not answer undertakings on discovery and failed to deliver amended pleadings to comply with court orders. The respondents changed solicitors, but the new solicitor failed to file a Notice of Change of Solicitors. On March 4, 1999, the Registrar dismissed the action pursuant to rule 48.14 of the *Rules of Civil Procedure*, RRO 1990, Reg. 194 for failure to set the action down within the prescribed time. Because of the failure to file a Notice of Change of Solicitors, neither the respondents nor their new counsel were aware that the action had been dismissed. Nothing happened for over four years. The respondents' solicitor discovered in June 2003 that the action had been dismissed, but did not inform his client until October. The respondents' motion to set aside the Registrar's order dismissing the action was not brought until December 2003, and not heard until February 2005, almost six years after the order was made. The Master dismissed the motion, but the respondents successfully appealed that decision to a single judge of the Divisional Court who reinstated the action. The appellant appeals, with leave, to this court and asks that the Master's order be restored. For the following reasons, I would allow the appeal and restore the decision of the Master.

Facts

The respondents commenced this action in October 1996 for damages arising from the appellant's agreement to lease, with an option to purchase, a building owned by the corporate respondent. The appellant terminated the lease agreement prior to its commencement, alleging breaches by the corporate respondent. The respondents deny these breaches and allege that without the appellant's rental payments, they were unable to maintain the mortgage on the building. Upon the respondents' default, the mortgagee took possession and eventually sold the building to the appellant for $225,000 less than the appellant had agreed to pay the respondents in the option agreement. The respondents claimed $3 million for loss of rent, as well as damages for loss of reputation, pain and suffering, and mental distress. The appellant counterclaimed for $1.1 million.

By mid-March 1997, the respondents had retained a new solicitor, but she failed to file a Notice of Change of Solicitors. Denis Thériault was examined for discovery in his personal capacity and as a representative of Thériault Ltée on May 29, 1997. The respondents did not examine a representative of the appellant. The appellant successfully moved to strike the claim of Josée Thériault in its entirety, to strike the claims of Denis Thériault and his company for pain and suffering, loss of amenities of life, mental distress and loss of reputation, and to strike the allegation that the appellant attempted to intimidate the respondents by breaching the lease agreement. This left only the claim for loss of rent.

From June 1997 to January 1998, the appellant's solicitor made numerous requests for answers to undertakings given on discovery and for an amended statement of claim that would comply with the successful pleadings motion. A small number of undertakings were answered, but nothing further was heard from the respondents.

In February 1998, the respondents retained a third lawyer who served a Notice of Change of Solicitors along with a Trial Record. However, his assistant was unable to file these materials as the respondent's original solicitor, still on the record, could not be found and consequently could not be served. The assistant failed to inform the solicitor of this problem and no further attempt was made to file either the Notice of Change of Solicitors or the Trial Record.

The appellant continued to press for answers to undertakings on discovery and for a trial record that contained properly amended pleadings. The respondents' solicitor's sporadic responses to numerous letters from the appellant failed to satisfy those requests.

On March 4, 1999 the Registrar dismissed the respondents' action for failure to set the action down for trial in the time prescribed by rule 48.14. The respondents' solicitor, who had not filed a Notice of Change of Solicitors, did not receive the Notice of Status Hearing or the order dismissing the action. He made no attempt to move the matter forward for over four years and indeed remained unaware of the dismissal of the action. In late May 2003, the solicitor left his partnership and the respondents' file was transferred to another lawyer in the office. In mid-June 2003, the new lawyer discovered that the action had been dismissed.

Throughout, the respondents maintained regular contact with their solicitor. In 2001, the solicitor requested and received additional funds from them to prepare a motion to deal with outstanding issues concerning the pleadings in order to set the matter down for trial. That motion was never brought.

The respondents were not advised of the dismissal until October 2003 and their motion to set aside the order dismissing the action was not served until December 2003.

The limitation period for the respondents' cause of action expired in June 2002 and the appellant's Vice-President of Finance, the individual best able to substantiate the appellant's set-off and counterclaim, died in May 2000. In view of the dismissal of the action and the passage of time, the appellant's solicitors stripped their file, destroyed all their notes, and sent what was left in the file to storage. The appellant destroyed many of the documents relating to the litigation including a significant portion of its records relating to its set-off and counterclaim.

Master's Decision Refusing To Set Aside the Order Dismissing the Action

The Master applied the four-pronged test described in *Reid v. Dow Corning Corp.* (2001), 11 CPC (5th) 80 at para. 41 (Ont. SCJ), rev'd. on other grounds 48 CPC (5th) 93 (Ont. Div. Ct.):

(1) *Explanation of the Litigation Delay*: The plaintiff must adequately explain the delay in the progress of the litigation from the institution of the action until the deadline for setting the action down for trial as set out in the status notice. She must satisfy the court that steps were being taken to advance the litigation toward trial, or if such steps were not taken to explain why. ... If either the solicitor or the client made a deliberate decision not to advance the litigation toward trial then the motion to set aside the dismissal will fail.

(2) *Inadvertence in Missing the Deadline*: The plaintiff or her solicitor must lead satisfactory evidence to explain that they always intended to set the action down within the time limit set out in the status notice, or request a status hearing, but failed to do so through inadvertence. In other words the penultimate dismissal order was made as a result of inadvertence.

(3) *The Motion is Brought Promptly*: The plaintiff must demonstrate that she moved forthwith to set aside the dismissal order as soon as the order came to her attention.

(4) *No Prejudice to the Defendant*: The plaintiff must convince the court that the defendants have not demonstrated any significant prejudice in presenting their case at trial as a result of the plaintiff's delay or as a result of steps taken following the dismissal of the action.

· · ·

The contextual approach mandated by Scaini [*Scaini v. Prochnicki* (2007), 85 OR (3d) 179 (CA)] to determine what "is just in the circumstances of the particular case" invites the application of important underlying principles and values of the civil justice system that are inherent in the four *Reid* factors. As I read his reasons, the Master's interpretation of the four Reid factors implicitly embraced these principles and values.

On this appeal, three of the four elements from the *Reid* test are at issue, namely, explanation for the litigation delay, inadvertence in missing the deadline, and prejudice to the plaintiff.

Explanation for the Litigation Delay

The *Reid* test's requirement of an explanation for the litigation delay ties into a dominant theme in modern civil procedure: the discouragement of delay and the enhancement of an active judicial role to ensure timely justice. This action was dismissed by the Registrar under rule 48.14: a status notice was sent because the action had not been placed on the trial list within two years of the filing of a statement of defence, and the respondents failed to set the action down for trial within ninety days after receiving the status notice. Rule 48.14 is one of many rules of civil procedure designed to promote the timely resolution of disputes, to discourage delay in civil litigation, and to give the courts a significant role in reducing delays. Before the promulgation of Rule 48.14, parties had total control over when cases were placed on the trial list. Rule 48.14 "establishes a procedure which gives the court a degree of control over the speed at which litigation proceeds to a conclusion. ... In essence the rule provides for a very limited form of case management." Garry D. Watson & Craig Perkins, *Holmested and Watson: Ontario Civil Procedure*, vol. 4 Supplement (Toronto: Carswell, 1984) 48§15. The case management regime, for which rule 48.14 was a precursor, was introduced in part to reduce "unnecessary cost and delay in civil litigation": rule 77.02.

Dismissal for delay is not, of course, an invention of case management. Rule 24.01 allows a party to move to dismiss an action for delay where the plaintiff has failed to prosecute the action in a timely fashion in accordance with the rules. Moreover, courts may dismiss actions for delay even when the relevant rules do not mandate it. A court has inherent jurisdiction to control its own process, which "includes the discretionary power to dismiss an action for delay." *Housser v. Savin Canada Inc.* (2005), 77 OR (3d) 251 at para. 9 (SCJ). As the Manitoba Court of Appeal wrote, "The power of a superior court to strike a matter for want of prosecution does not hinge on the niceties of the wording of the rules, but rather flows from the inherent power of the court to prevent an abuse of its own process." *Kuhr v. Pearlman* (1991), 76 Man. R (2d) 67 at para. 16. ...

These rules and cases rest upon an important principle: there is a strong public interest in promoting the timely resolution of disputes. "The notion that justice delayed is justice denied reaches back to the mists of time. ... For centuries, those working with our legal system have recognized that unnecessary delay strikes against its core values and have done everything within their powers to combat it": *Blencoe v. British Columbia (Human Rights Commission)*, [2000] 2 SCR 307 at para. 146. The interest of litigants involved in the civil justice system in timely justice is obvious. Litigants are entitled to have their disputes resolved quickly so that they can get on with their lives. Delay multiplies costs and breeds frustration and unfairness.

In the light of the important principle of promoting the timely resolution of disputes, I see no reason on the record before us to disagree with the Master's finding that the respondents failed to satisfy the first step of the Reid test. The solicitor "had put the file in abeyance" and that his conduct indicated "a deliberate intention not to advance the litigation toward trial." As the Divisional Court judge found, the delay flowed from the solicitor's "intentional and stubborn refusal to proceed with the action." The respondents' solicitors failed to observe the rules relating to filing Notices of Change of Solicitor or to ensure adequate communication within their office when the assistant encountered difficulties in that regard. This failure meant that the solicitor did not receive the Registrar's Rule 48.14 Notice, but he nonetheless should have known that under the *Rules of Court*, failure to set the action down for trial within two years of the statement of defence would lead to the action being dismissed.

Inadvertence in Missing the Deadline

The Master and the Divisional Court disagreed as to whether the solicitor's conduct constituted "inadvertence" for the purposes of the second branch of the test. The Master, focusing on the conduct of the solicitor, held that it was not. The Divisional Court judge, focusing on the fact that the client believed that the action was proceeding to trial, held that the solicitor's neglect of the file should be considered inadvertent. I agree with the Master that, in light of the length of the delay and the fact that it was caused by the solicitor effectively abandoning the file, this is not a case where the failure to move the case along to trial can be considered as mere inadvertence.

One important consideration is that the plaintiff will not be left without a remedy. I recognize here the need to ensure that adequate remedies are afforded where a right has been infringed. The law will not ordinarily allow an innocent client to suffer the irrevocable loss of the right to proceed by reason of the inadvertence of his or her solicitor: see e.g. *Chiarelli v. Wiens* (2000), 46 OR (3d) 780, at para. 9 (CA).

However, this calculus implicitly assumes that the court is left with a stark choice between defeating the client's rights and forcing the opposite party to defend the case on its merits. That assumption is faulty where, as in this case, the solicitor's conduct is not mere inadvertence, but amounts to conduct very likely to expose the solicitor to liability to the client. When the solicitor is exposed in this way, the choice is different; refusing the client an indulgence for delay will not necessarily deny the client a legal remedy.

In these circumstances, and contrary to the view expressed by the Divisional Court judge, the Master properly distinguished inadvertence from negligence. Leaving the Registrar's order in place would not necessarily deprive the respondents of a remedy. It was appropriate on these facts for the Master to tell the respondents that they should "consider what other remedies are available to them."

A second consideration is that the nature of the delay and the solicitors' conduct in this case amount to more than that kind of lapse or inadvertent mistake that the legal system can countenance. We should opt for a resolution that discourages this type of conduct which undermines the important value of having disputes resolved in a timely fashion. The decision of the Master sends the right message and provides appropriate incentives to those involved in the civil justice system.

Moreover, excusing a delay of this magnitude and gravity risks undermining public confidence in the administration of justice. Lawyers who fail to serve their clients threaten public confidence in the administration of justice. The legal profession itself has recognized this danger: Commentary to rule 2.01 of the Law Society of Upper Canada's *Rules of Professional Conduct* states, "A lawyer who is incompetent does the client a disservice, brings discredit to the profession, and *may bring the administration of justice into disrepute.*" [Emphasis added.] There is a risk that the public would perceive disregarding the solicitor's conduct in the circumstances of this case as the legal system protecting its own. Excusing a delay of this kind would through into question the willingness of the courts to live up to the stated goal of timely justice.

Overall, reinstating this action would excuse a five-year delay after the dismissal of an action, explained only by the fact that a lawyer formed "a deliberate intention not to advance the litigation toward trial" and "put the file in abeyance." That would risk undermining the integrity and repute of the administration of justice.

Prejudice to the Plaintiff

The fourth step in the Reid test focuses on prejudice to the defendant and the goal of having disputes resolved on their merits. The *Rules of Civil Procedure* must be interpreted in a manner that recognizes that expeditious justice is only one value to be weighed against others and that delay may be excused where necessary to ensure complete justice. As Rule 1.04(1) states, the rules are to be "liberally construed to secure the just, most expeditious and least expensive determination or every civil proceeding *on its merits.*" [Emphasis added]. Expeditious justice must be balanced with the public interest in having disputes determined on their merits. Where, despite the delay, the defendant would not be unfairly prejudiced should the matter proceed for resolution on the merits, according the plaintiff an indulgence is generally favoured.

While I view the Master's finding that the appellant would not be prejudiced in presenting its case despite the delay to have been generous to the respondents, that finding was not challenged before us. This aspect of the fourth *Reid* factor and the underlying value of having disputes resolved on their merits favour the respondents. However, it is not enough for the respondents to show that the appellant could advance its case despite the delay if the matter were allowed to proceed to trial. There are four branches to the *Reid* test, and, according to *Scaini*, those four factors are not exhaustive.

Moreover, as the Master correctly observed, the jurisprudence from this court identifies as relevant to the fourth *Reid* factor the security of legal position gained by a litigant through a court order granted because of delay or default: see *Halton Community Credit Union Ltd. v. ICL Computers Canada Ltd.*, supra.

Finality, like the avoidance of unnecessary delay, is a central principle in the administration of justice. "The law rightly seeks a finality to litigation" and finality is "a compelling consideration": *Danyluk v. Ainsworth Technologies Inc.*, [2001] 2 SCR 460 at paras. 18 and 19.

When an action has been disposed of in favour of a party, that party's entitlement to rely on the finality principle grows stronger as the years pass. Even when the order dismissing the action was made for delay or default and not on the merits, and even when the party relying on the order could still defend itself despite the delay, it seems to me that at some point the interest in finality must trump the opposite party's plea for an indulgence. This is especially true where, as in the present case, the opposite party appears to have another remedy available.

The delay in this case was inordinate. From the appellant's perspective, the respondents did absolutely nothing to move this file forward for more than five years, and before that, the respondents had proceeded in what could only be described as a desultory fashion for two and one-half years after commencing the action.

I agree with the Master that, when viewed in the light of a delay of this magnitude, the security of the legal position obtained by the appellant becomes an important factor to consider. Five years after the action against it had been dismissed, the appellant was entitled to rest on the assurance that the judicial system had disposed of the respondents' claim once and for all.

Conclusion

I conclude that the Master's analysis is appropriate because it takes account of important principles and values of the civil justice system. The solicitor's behaviour resulted in an excessive delay. Delays of this kind are inimical to the important goal of timely justice. The legal system should not condone the solicitor's behaviour as to do so would fail to provide appropriate incentives to those engaged in the justice system and would risk harming the integrity and repute of the administration of justice. Reinstating the action at this point would undermine the finality principle while refusing the reinstate the action does not interfere with the need to ensure adequate remedies. ...

NOTES AND QUESTIONS

1. *Effect of non-compliance with rules.* The rules of each jurisdiction provide for the consequences of failure to comply with them. These rules generally provide that non-compliance with the rules does not render any act or proceeding void (or a nullity), but rather requires the court to treat the non-compliance as an irregularity with which the court

may deal by order to ensure compliance with the rules. See Alberta rule 43; Saskatchewan rule 5; BC, Manitoba, Ontario, New Brunswick, Nova Scotia, and Newfoundland and Labrador rule 2. The primary object of the reference to "void" and "nullity" was to eliminate the historical distinction drawn between nullities and irregularities. Procedural defects were said to fall into two categories—nullities and irregularities—the former were incapable of being relieved against, whereas the latter could be cured. The use of this distinction was particularly troublesome because it frequently led the court to deny relief by making an initial characterization that a non-compliance with the rules was a nullity—without the court ever directing its attention to the real issue—that is, whether it would be just and reasonable, in view of any potential prejudice to the other party, to permit the correction of the defect. Under the current rules, any non-compliance with the rules is to be treated as capable of being corrected or remedied, subject to the court's discretion.

2. Under the rules, the general approach to non-compliance is for the court to make the appropriate order that addresses the non-compliance and requires that it be fixed and, to use the BC rule as an example, may include orders that

(a) set aside a proceeding, either wholly or in part,

(b) set aside any step taken in the proceeding, or a document or order made in the proceeding,

(c) allow an amendment to be made under Rule 24,

(d) dismiss the proceeding or strike out the statement of defence and grant judgment, or

(e) make any other order it thinks just.

Other rules of court also have specific non-compliance provisions. In each case, the starting point for the court is to make an order requiring compliance with the rules, rather than using non-compliance with the rules as a means to short-circuit the prosecution or defence of an action.

3. Once the court makes an order requiring compliance with a procedural rule, failure to comply with the terms of the court's order becomes a more serious matter. Other procedural rules give the court specific powers to enforce compliance with its orders generally, and specifically in the case of Ontario rule 60.12, interlocutory orders (see also Manitoba rule 60.11 and BC rule 2(6)). Dismissal of a claim for failure to comply with procedural orders is a last resort, but one that the court will invoke in order to protect the integrity of its process. As Southin JA, speaking for the court in *Household Trust Co. v. Golden Horse Farms Inc.* (1992), 65 BCLR (2d) 355, at 361-62 (CA), said:

> In my opinion, the Supreme Court of British Columbia has an inherent jurisdiction and a corresponding duty to exercise that jurisdiction to protect a petitioner or plaintiff who seeks relief in that Court from proceedings by a defendant who is vexatiously abusing the process of the court. That it is a jurisdiction to be exercised with great caution, I have no doubt. But not to exercise it where there is no other way to bring reason into proceedings is, in effect, to deprive the plaintiff or petitioner of justice according to law.

4. In addition to the various rules relating to non-compliance, many jurisdictions have provisions authorizing the court to dispense with compliance with the rules "in special cir-

cumstances" (federal rule 55) or "where … necessary in the interests of justice" (Manitoba and Ontario rule 2.03). In what kinds of circumstances would it be appropriate for a court to completely waive compliance with a rule?

C. Discontinuance

Rules in each jurisdiction regulate the discontinuance of an action by a plaintiff. See Alberta rule 225; BC rule 36; Manitoba and Ontario rule 23; New Brunswick rule 25; Newfoundland and Labrador and Nova Scotia rule 40; and Saskatchewan rule 198.

While specifics for discontinuance by a plaintiff in each jurisdiction vary, all have the following common elements:

1. a period of time from the commencement of the lawsuit during which the plaintiff may unilaterally discontinue without leave or consent;
2. a requirement for court leave or defendant's consent to discontinue after that period of time; and
3. a requirement that a discontinuing plaintiff pay the costs of the defendants.

A discontinuance does not, absent agreement or a court order, prevent the plaintiff from commencing an action on the same facts again. Accordingly, it does not have the same effect as a dismissal of the action.

In many jurisdictions (that is, British Columbia, Manitoba, New Brunswick, Newfoundland, Nova Scotia, and Ontario), the rules respecting discontinuance also permit a defendant to withdraw all or part of the statement of defence with respect to any plaintiff at any time by delivering the appropriate notice to all parties. In some provinces leave is required after a certain point in the proceedings; in others, the ability to withdraw is unlimited except for circumstances where there is a counterclaim or third-party claim. Where a defendant withdraws the whole of the statement of defence, the defendant is either deemed to be noted in default or liable to have default proceedings taken against them.

Managing the Process

I. INTRODUCTION

There are a variety of lenses through which to view and consider civil litigation. One key approach to analyzing the adjudicative process focuses on civil litigation's role as a mechanism of dispute resolution. While litigation dominates society's conception of legal dispute resolution, it is important to remember that only a small percentage of all civil actions (somewhere in the neighbourhood of 1 to 3 percent) are actually determined by a trial. Rather, the vast majority of civil claims are ultimately resolved through a variety of related processes that have come to be grouped under the broad heading of "alternative dispute resolution" (ADR).

In Canada, as elsewhere, there has been a growing focus on the increasing burden imposed on the civil trial system by escalating rates of litigation. Mirroring this rise in the rates and complexity of commenced actions has been a steady increase in the financial and time commitment associated with bringing an action to trial. Gradually, policy shifts can be seen in response to these trends, and we are now witnessing a reaction in the way in which we manage disputes in this country. In an attempt to alleviate trial docket backlogs and to ensure improved access to justice, bodies charged with examining our provincial rules of civil procedure are implementing legislative changes that include various ADR processes.

We are witnessing in Canadian jurisdictions the application of a concept coined the "multidoor courthouse," wherein each dispute that is commenced undergoes an assessment according to a set of relevant criteria and is then managed (and hopefully resolved) through the application of the most appropriate process of resolution for that dispute. In some cases, this results in an action being rerouted through a mandatory mediation process. In other situations, where mandatory mediation is deemed inappropriate, a dispute would continue along the more traditional route to adjudication, although perhaps with added opportunities along the way to consider settlement of the action before trial.

Conceptually, there is an increasing belief that not every dispute, and not every disputant, is best solved or served by a judge imposing a decision on the parties in the traditional model. While some disputes require the conventional treatment of an adjudicator assessing the relevant facts within a context of legal rules and rights, we are acknowledging that there exist more appropriate means of solving many conflicts. Certain disputes have a greater chance of achieving a just and speedy resolution through processes recognizing that, often, party satisfaction is more about meeting interests and needs than it is about applying a rights-based, legal analysis of duties and entitlements.

Some of the reforms that have grown out of these shifts in focus and policy have resulted in processes that operate outside the civil litigation structure, with varying degrees of separation, while others have been integrated into the formal framework of the trial process. The common thread among these procedural reforms is that all of them entail an increasing *management* of the civil litigation process, be it management that is executed by judges or by those external to the adjudicative model. By looking at some of these processes, both internal and external, we can mark the development of a variety of policies surrounding dispute resolution practices that now, in part, drive our formal civil litigation processes in Canada. Additionally, by considering certain components of our civil litigation process, we are able to identify the expanding notion of dispute resolution within our existing institutional frameworks.

This chapter looks closely at three of these aspects of our current civil litigation process, each of which reflects the conceptual reforms discussed above. The first aspect that we consider is that which has come to be known as "case management," an approach that has been integrated into the traditional framework of civil procedure. Case management, at its most basic, is about imposing time standards and regularly reviewing the status of litigation matters. This section compares provincial case management regimes from several Canadian jurisdictions and also raises some questions about the appropriateness of certain aspects of case management. As will be seen, case management reforms have been connected to ADR in many Canadian jurisdictions, a link that is discussed below for its policy implications and motivations. After discussing case management in general, we turn our critical attention to the shifting role of judges, necessitated by the case management framework and its various component parts. From the perspective of social policy, we consider how appropriate it is that judges in our adversarial system perform this function.

The next major aspect of reform to be highlighted in this chapter is that of court-connected mediation. Court-connected mediation is rapidly becoming a mainstream, rather than an "alternative," application and it is having a significant impact on the trajectory of civil disputes in those jurisdictions in which it operates. The scholarly community continues to struggle to produce an acceptable definition of "mediation," because the label implies such a varied list of components and characteristics, depending on the context. Without a common definition, evaluating this process proves challenging. For the purposes of this discussion, we are going to look closely at the mandatory model currently being implemented in Ontario's Superior Court of Justice and discuss other models, mandatory and voluntary, operating in Saskatchewan, Alberta, and British Columbia. In this category, we discuss the value that mediation purports to bring to the table and we consider those contexts in which it may or may not be appropriate. No discussion surrounding mediation in the context of civil procedure would be complete without stepping back to consider the broader debate surrounding the concept of "informalism." Often, the descriptor "ADR" is used to identify a variety of dispute resolution mechanisms that are not court-based adjudication, but that still include a number of processes in which adjudication is preserved. This section includes some readings on ADR generally, and then turns to those mechanisms that have caught the imagination of reformers in Canada—the informal, non-adjudicatory methods of dispute resolution, of which mediation is a leading example. While this section illustrates some of the oft-cited arguments in support of informal, non-adjudicatory frameworks for dispute resolution, it also raises a number of weaknesses that critics claim defeat the objectives and outcomes of this processes.

In the chapter's final section, we take a closer look at the third aspect of reform, that of managing process in the context of the settlement of actions. As noted, a significant number of cases commenced are resolved through a settlement negotiated by the parties (with or without the assistance of a third party, as in the case of mediation) rather than through a trial. As such, settlement is an essential component of our system as it helps to maintain efficient levels of the number of actions that ultimately require adjudication. Settlement also illustrates the ideals of individual autonomy on which the adversarial system is founded, as reflected in party initiation and control of litigated actions. Settlement permits each party to negotiate and bargain for resolution of the dispute through a process driven by self-interest and evaluation of the comparative strengths and weaknesses of the respective positions. As we will see, processes intended to encourage pre-trial settlement are forming an increasingly significant component of our case management frameworks.

As we have already seen, costs are used as a regulatory device to encourage or discourage particular kinds of litigation or conduct by parties and their counsel. With the process of settlement, costs are used to encourage the acceptance of reasonable offers and, conversely, to reprimand recalcitrant litigants who refuse to consider appropriate offers of resolution. As we will review in greater detail, most Canadian jurisdictions have rules of practice that explicitly address these policy concerns. To reinforce the need for parties to consider reasonable offers toward the resolution of litigation, many jurisdictions also have rules of professional conduct that mandate lawyers to encourage settlement. (See, for example, Ontario's rule 3, commentary 5: "The lawyer should advise and encourage the client to compromise or settle a dispute whenever it is possible to do so on a reasonable basis." See also Ontario rule 10, commentary 6. Also, see British Columbia's *Professional Conduct Handbook*, chapter 1, rule 3(3); "Whenever the dispute will admit of fair settlement the client should be advised to avoid or to end the litigation." See also the Canadian Bar Association's *Code of Professional Conduct*, chapter IX, commentary 8: "Whenever the case can be settled fairly, the lawyer should advise and encourage the client to do so rather than commence or continue a legal proceeding.")

To further illustrate this emphasis on the encouragement of settlement, we will consider the role played by the doctrine of settlement privilege. While the broader category of privilege includes several examples that demonstrate the trend toward a wider and more complete disclosure, the notion of settlement privilege recognizes that the revelation of failed settlement negotiations might pose a threat to parties actively participating in such attempts at resolution. As such, the doctrine of settlement privilege, which protects these communications, has carved out another exception to the general move toward broader disclosure within the trial process.

NOTES

1. See, generally, Canadian Bar Association, *Report of the Canadian Bar Association Task Force on Systems of Civil Justice* (Ottawa: Canadian Bar Association, 1996), chapter 4.3, 34-40.

2. For a very brief summary of developments across the country in the area of litigation management, see Doris I. Wilson, "Managing Litigation in Canada" (Fall 2002), no. 5 *News & Views on Civil Justice Reform*, available online at Canadian Forum on Civil Justice: http://cfcj-fcjc.org/publications/newsviews-05/n5-dwilson.php.

II. CASE MANAGEMENT AND PRE-TRIAL CONFERENCES

A. Introduction

In various Canadian jurisdictions, caseflow management has been at the centre of many recent civil justice reforms. Notably, the very concept of shifting control over certain aspects of a litigated action from the parties (through their counsel) to the judiciary marks a significant shift from the traditional model. At its heart, case management is intended to further the fundamental goals of ADR processes—namely, to enhance access to justice for litigants through decreases in delays and costs. These objectives are illustrated through various aspects of case management regimes in Canada, including the case conference (in which the judge plays a role in screening cases for alternative processes), the settlement conference (in which a judge has a direct role in seeking a settlement of the dispute prior to trial), and in the mandatory mediation scheme (at least in Ontario), which compels parties and their counsel to consider settlement with the assistance of a mediator at a very early stage in the case-managed litigation.

From a policy perspective, the case management framework is clearly underpinned by a focus on judicial efficiency in managing cases and in achieving the settlement of those cases at an earlier, and more cost-effective, stage in the proceedings. In order to achieve this end, legislators in various Canadian jurisdictions have shifted away from strict reliance on the historical principle of party prosecution as illustrated by a purely adversarial model of adjudication that is entirely party-initiated and party-driven. In its place, rules of practice are implementing judge-managed litigation schedules and imposing consequences that are often quite significant for parties who fail to comply. On January 1, 2010, Ontario reverted to a more flexible, party-driven style of litigation (see rule 77.01(2)). Ontario's rule 77 has been merged with rule 78; the set timelines and track system are no longer active. The following is an excerpt from the first report of Ontario's Civil Justice Review project, rationalizing the implementation of a case management scheme in Ontario.

Ontario Civil Justice Review, "Management of Cases," *First Report*
(March 1995), chapter 13 (footnotes omitted)

The notion of case management entails a significant shift in the cultural mind set that has characterized the processing of civil cases in our courts for generations.

In that tradition it has been the role of the lawyers, together with their clients, to decide if and when a lawsuit would proceed, and when various steps would be taken. They have done so within the framework of the Rules of Civil Procedure, and the time parameters laid out in those Rules. With few exceptions, however, the prevailing attitude in Ontario has always been that those time parameters are to be honoured more in the breach than in the observance.

There is a growing recognition that this mode of operation is no longer appropriate. It has ceased to work effectively in delivering civil justice to the public. Given the rising costs and unacceptable delays in litigation and the similarly escalating demands on the administration and the judiciary, it is apparent to us that we no longer have the resources as a society to permit this laissez-faire approach to the processing of cases to continue.

Caseflow management involves the transfer of principle responsibility for management of the pace of litigation to the judiciary. *It also involves the establishment of reasonable, but firm, time limits and the adherence to those parameters.* In short, caseflow management entails a more active form of management and intervention by the court in the various phases of litigation. It does so with a view to promoting the earlier resolution of cases, to eliminating unacceptable delays, and, ultimately, to reducing costs and enhancing the quality of justice.

Ideally, this intervention occurs early and also with some frequency during the life of the case. We have heard constantly from lawyers, administrators, judges and members of the public that *early intervention by the judiciary is of critical importance* in the disposition of cases. This is true in all cases, but is particularly true in family law cases. It is often, and in our view accurately, said that the more times one can build into the system an occasion when counsel has to pick up his or her file and think about it, the more likely it is that there will be an earlier resolution of the case.

We think this emphasis is important.

Studies show that approximately 55% of cases commenced never proceed to the point where a statement of defence is filed. They are either resolved by way of a default judgment, settled outside of the courts before reaching that stage, or any interest in pursuing them simply dissipates. The remaining 45% of the case load proceeds through various additional stages of litigation, with the vast majority settling at some point between the pleading stage and the eve or morning of trial.

The reality is that 95% to 97% of all civil cases are never tried. They are settled. This seems to be the experience in Anglo-Canadian-American court systems wherever located and regardless of the structure which is in place to process the flow of cases through the system.

If this is the reality, then, it makes sense that the overall mechanism for the disposition of disputes should focus on dealing with the vast majority of cases that settle, *as well as* focusing on those that have to be tried. Historically in Ontario, however, the primary focus has been on the processing of cases in preparation for trial.

Caseflow management permits the necessary broadening of perspective and emphasis from this primary focus to a duality of focus—disposition where possible, and trial where necessary. It does so by building in the potential for early—and if appropriate, repeated—judicial or quasi-judicial intervention. This is accomplished by means of case conferences which are either prescribed at fixed points in the process by the rules, or called at the instance of the case management judge or counsel. The case conference can take the form of an early evaluation or screening exercise; it can be used as an occasion to discuss the diversion of the dispute into one or another of the ADR channels; it can take the form of a settlement conference; or, if the case cannot be settled and is bound for trial, the case conference can take the form of a trial management conference. These events each provide occasions where the file must be dealt with by counsel. Moreover, they provide opportunities where the judge or the judicial support officer can work out with counsel how the case is to proceed.

Caseflow management is a concept which in our opinion offers great potential for combining and co-ordinating the various disparate elements of the civil justice system and integrating them into a more effective whole. It is able to do this by facilitating a combination of the following features:

1. overall management of the case flow process by the judiciary;
2. early intervention in a case either by a judge or by a quasi-judicial officer;
3. the disposition of all interlocutory matters;
4. the deployment of ADR mechanisms and techniques;
5. the utilization of case conferences, settlement conferences and trial management conferences;
6. the utilization of registrars, case management officers and judicial support officers to perform the administrative and quasi-judicial tasks which do not require a "section 96" judge to perform, thus freeing up judges to concentrate their efforts on the truly "judicial" activities of trying cases and assisting the parties in settling their disputes.

NOTES

Following closely on the heels of the Civil Justice Review, *First Report* ("the CJR"), the Canadian Bar Association conducted the first national survey of case management in Canada and released the results of its task force in 1996 ("the CBA Report"). Building on the work of the CJR, the CBA Report became a key advocate for reform in Canada. In particular, the CBA Report recommended that all Canadian jurisdictions have a case management system "to provide for early court intervention in the definition of issues and for the supervision of the progress of cases."

As suggested above, there are a variety of "techniques," any combination of which may define a case management scheme in a given jurisdiction. Across the Canadian jurisdictions, we see a wide range of procedural provisions traditionally associated with case management systems, illustrating the diversity of this approach. Some jurisdictions can be described as having adopted a more comprehensive or "systemic" approach to case management (where cases are significantly managed throughout the litigation process), while others are better described as having adopted certain free-standing "tools" of case management in the absence of an integrated system.

In some jurisdictions, case management is reserved for extremely long or complex litigation, while others apply it across the board to all actions. Often, actions based on identified subject matters are excluded from case management schemes. For example, in Ontario's *Rules of Civil Procedure*, rule 77 governing case management does not apply to certain family law, construction lien, or bankruptcy matters. Similarly, in some jurisdictions, case management regimes include various tracks that provide different "routes" depending on the identified criteria. An action may be commenced on the "fast track" that employs significantly different timetabling from an action commenced on the "standard track."

Similarly, some case management regimes are highly directive in terms of the specific timetables and deadlines imposed for completing each stage, compelling, for example, that a statement of defence be delivered within 20 days or that discoveries be completed within 240 days. Other case management systems are less rigorous with regard to imposed timetables, allocating to judges or masters the discretion to set appropriate deadlines on a case-by-case basis. One might argue that this latter approach illustrates greater flexibility that could lead to better outcomes, rather than the rigid application of predetermined treatment to all actions, regardless of their unique circumstances.

1. Case Management in the Ontario Superior Court of Justice

Ontario first began its case management experiment in 1991, piloting certain schemes in several Ontario jurisdictions. While a central component of case management as early as 1991 was the active timetabling of civil disputes by the judiciary (and its agents), case management regimes have also been marked by an active focus on the promotion of dispute settlement, particularly through the "conference" and, in the case of Toronto, Ottawa, and Essex, early mandatory mediation sessions, of which more will be said below. The Civil Justice Review in Ontario led to the implementation of a new rule of practice before Ontario's Superior Court of Justice (the Ontario Court General Division, as it was then) in Toronto, Ottawa, and Essex, rule 77.

As stated in rule 77.02, the purpose of case management in Ontario is to reduce unnecessary cost and delay in civil litigation, to facilitate early and fair settlements, and to bring proceedings "expeditiously to a just determination while allowing sufficient time for the conduct of the proceeding." (Note: On January 1, 2010, the purpose of rule 77 was changed. The new purpose simply states that parties should manage litigation themselves and should only seek case management if needed (rule 77.01(1)). If the parties seek case management by the court, criteria are set out in rule 77.05(4) to determine whether, and to what extent, case management is needed.) In addition to imposing firm timetables for completing the progressive steps in the litigation of an action, rule 77 has now adopted a strong focus on the dispute resolution objective of case management. (Note: As previously stated, rule 77 was made more flexible on January 1, 2010; there are no longer firm deadlines set to apply to all cases; as a result, the differentiated "track" system is no longer in place either.) All cases falling under this regime are automatically referred to a three-hour, mandatory mediation session early in the action, pursuant to rule 24.1. This encourages parties to thoroughly canvass the possibility of settlement at a moment in the litigation before parties have devoted significant time and resources toward supporting their conflicting positions.

Central to the Ontario model is the notion of different "tracks," sometimes referred to as differential case management. This approach attempts to identify certain aspects of individual cases and to match those cases, on the basis of complexity, with appropriate time frames for completion. Closely monitored deadlines are imposed for the completion of specific milestones in the litigation; in some cases, the flexibility to depart from those time frames may be strictly limited, depending on the track being followed.

Additionally, rule 77 provides for the case management conference, during which the judge or case management master will seek to resolve any contested issues that remain in the litigation and to set a timetable for the proceeding. The case management conference is intended to be holistic in approach, helping parties either to resolve conflict or, failing that, to be well prepared for the upcoming trial.

As with some other Canadian jurisdictions, Ontario's courts have considered the appropriateness of ADR, generally, and mediation, specifically, as a means of resolving disputes that would otherwise be solved through the traditional adjudicative process.

O. (G.) v. H. (C.D.)
(2000), 50 OR (3d) 82 (SCJ)

KITELEY J: This is a motion brought by the defendant pursuant to rule 24.1.05 for an exemption from mandatory mediation. The plaintiff consented. ...

In her affidavit in support of the motion, the defendant deposed that after a brief courtship, she became engaged to the plaintiff in April 1998. They began living together in June 1998. As a result of alleged economic, emotional, psychological and physical abuse by the plaintiff, the defendant moved out of the plaintiff's residence in February 1999.

During the relationship, the defendant was employed by the plaintiff corporation. The plaintiff's claim was issued in September 1999 and includes allegations of conversion of funds belonging to the corporation and wrongful removal of furniture. The defendant filed a defence in which she denied the allegations. And she filed a counterclaim against G.O. in which she sought $200,000 as general damages for sexual assault, indecent assault, and other torts and $100,000 as punitive damages.

The defendant deposed to the effects of the alleged behaviour by the plaintiff G.O. And she said the following:

> 9. I am advised by my solicitor that this action is subject to mandatory mediation which requires my presence in the same room as the Plaintiff. I know that the Plaintiff will attempt to intimidate me and I am fearful of being in the same room as him.
>
> 10. I am now making some progress in getting over my psychological trauma but I am afraid that the experience of being in the same room with the Plaintiff will cause a setback.

11. My solicitor has advised me of the mediation process and I do not believe that I would be able to participate productively in a mediation with the plaintiff present.

Analysis

In Toronto, cases randomly selected for case management are also subject to Rule 24.1. The rule does not contain any category of cases which is automatically excluded. Nor does the subrule provide any guidance for when an exemption should be granted. Rule 24.1.05 states as follows:

> 24.1.05 The court may make an order on a party's motion exempting the action from this Rule.

On March 13, I indicated to counsel that I intended to make my own inquiries and research other authorities. Since Rule 24.1 forms the basis of a pilot project, there are statistics maintained on a regular basis by the Local Mediation Co-ordinators in Toronto and Ottawa. I inquired of the Toronto Mediation Co-ordinator if there were statistics as to the reasons for exemption. She reported that as of May 5, 2000, approximately 75 per cent of the 40 exemption orders were made in "related actions," i.e., where the case management action was a third or fourth party action in an existing non-case-managed action. Of the remaining exemptions, five or six were summarized as "unusual circumstances or complex factual/legal issues." There are at least 14 exemption orders arising from Ottawa cases. I attempted to locate the reasons for each of these exemption orders but I was successful in obtaining reasons in only three cases.

. . .

[I]t would appear that the following criteria are relevant to whether an exemption order should be granted:

- whether the parties have already engaged in a form of dispute resolution, and, in the interests of reducing cost and delay, they ought not to be required to repeat the effort [*Garneau v. Allstate Insurance Co.*, [1999] OJ No. 3756 (SCJ)];
- whether the issue involves a matter of public interest or importance which requires adjudication in order to establish an authority which will be persuasive if not binding on other cases [*Wilson v. Canada (Attorney General)*, [1998] OJ No. 1780 (Gen. Div.)];
- whether the issue involves a claim of a modest amount with little complexity which is amenable to a settlement conference presided over by a judicial officer without examination for discovery [*Riviera Properties Ltd. v. Royal Bank of Canada*, [1999] OJ No. 4282 (SCJ)];
- whether one of the litigants is out of the province and not readily available;
- whether the exemption for any other reason would be consistent with the stated objectives of reducing cost and delay in litigation and facilitating early and fair resolution. [*Garneau v. Allstate Insurance Co.*, [1999] OJ No. 3756 (SCJ)]

In his written submissions, Mr. Hickey referred to *Slater v. Amendola, supra,* and the passage to which reference was made above. He pointed out that mediation is not mandatory for family law matters due to the special handling that family law issues require.

Although this is not a family law case, he asserted that the defence and counterclaim raised issues similar to those heard in a family law case. For the same reasons that mediation was not made mandatory for family law cases, he urged that this case should be exempt from mandatory mediation.

The defendant's concern is that she would be forced to participate in the same room with the plaintiff G.O. and that as a result of his intimidating behaviour, she will regress from the gains which she has experienced. It is not essential to mandatory mediation that it occur in the presence of both the litigants simultaneously. Rule 24.1.02 is as follows:

> 24.1.02 In mediation, a neutral third party facilitates communication among the parties to a dispute, to assist them in reaching a mutually acceptable resolution.

Mediators, particularly those involved in family law disputes, are trained to identify needs associated with domestic abuse. In the Toronto Family Mediation Pilot Project, the roster mediators are required to devote at least 30 minutes per party, pre-screening them for issues such as abuse in the relationship. The mediator is required to be satisfied of the following:

- that abuse has not occurred that has rendered either party incapable of mediating;
- that no harm will come to either party as a result of mediating;
- that the parties' desire to mediate is voluntary;
- that any inequality in bargaining power can be managed so as to ensure that negotiations are balanced and procedurally fair;
- that parties are psychologically ready to mediate and have the capacity to do so;
- that the complexity of the case does not exceed the mediator's education, training and competence.

The Toronto Family Mediation Project is voluntary, as Mr. Hickey points out, and, consequently, the third point is not relevant to a case pursuant to Rule 24.1. However, I have listed all of the steps which the family law roster mediator is required to perform before beginning mediation. Roster mediators have agreed to participate for four hours at a cost of $300 per party. That is consistent with the time and the charges permitted for mediators on the roster for Rule 24.1.

Litigants are not required to accept the mediator assigned pursuant to Rule 24.1 by the Toronto local mediation co-ordinator. If the skills of the mediator who is assigned are not responsive to the needs of the case, an alternate mediator can be selected. In this case, those roster mediators involved with the Toronto Family Mediation Pilot Project are probably available.

The concerns of the defendant can be accommodated by (a) selecting a mediator with skills to address issues of violence; and (b) exploring with that mediator whether the mediation can proceed without the necessity of the plaintiff O. and the defendant being present in the same room. With those concerns accommodated, I see no reason to exempt this action from mandatory mediation. Indeed, I find that it is consistent with the objective of the mandatory mediation pilot project that the parties participate in mediation in order to give them an opportunity to explore an early and fair resolution.

I have taken into consideration the consent of the plaintiff. However, consent does not mandate the granting of the order requested. In the course of considering a request for an extension of time for mediation, Master Polika observed the following at para. 14 of *Rokicka v. Mechel* (January 26, 2000):

> The last reason deals with the consent of the parties. One of the reasons for the enactment of Rule 77 and Rule 24.1 were the concerns which were expressed by litigants about the manner in which their proceedings were being prosecuted by their own lawyers. Mere consent, by setting out a statement in the Form 77C certified by the moving parties' lawyer, in my view, is not enough for me to exercise my discretion to grant the extension. Lawyers, purportedly on behalf of their clients, cannot, without good real reason supported by the material filed in support of the motion, simply by consent justify the exercise of discretion to extend the time for holding mandatory mediation.

The same observation can be made with respect to consent to exempt.

2. Rule 78 in the Judicial Region of Toronto

Of particular interest has been the arrival of rule 78, originally a pilot project in the judicial region of Toronto in Ontario. In Toronto, it was found that automatic case management had the effect of *decreasing* rather than *increasing* efficiency in the processing of eligible cases. Lawyers were increasingly engaged in skirmishes before the case management masters and judges in Toronto, arguing over the application of various aspects of this regime.

In May 2005, rule 78 came into effect, applying to all actions commenced in the City of Toronto after December 31, 2004. Incorporating the key elements of the practice direction issued by Toronto's regional senior justice, rule 78 established a three-year pilot project whereby "parties will have greater responsibility for managing actions and moving them to trial or other resolution." That pilot has since achieved permanence as a feature of case management specific to Toronto. (Note: This model was expanded to all of Ontario on January 1, 2010 in the form of the new rule 77.)

Rule 78 is based on the view that case management, to be effective, should be targeted and should only be applied in those situations where the need for the court's intervention can be clearly demonstrated.

In practice, this means that "targeted case management" under rule 77 is only available:

1. on a party's motion; and
2. where there are complex factual or legal issues;
3. the litigation is a matter of public interest;
4. there are numerous parties or numerous related proceedings; or
5. there is a chronic and substantial obstruction to the timely disposition of the action.

NOTES

1. Arguably, the central element of any case management regime is the judicial conference. In more comprehensive schemes like that implemented by Ontario's rule 77 and others, we see the inclusion of discreet types of conferences, each with different characteristics and objectives. In Ontario's case, this functional distinction includes the case conference,

the settlement conference, and the trial management conference. At the other end of the range, we find jurisdictions that do not address case management through their rules in any substantial way. However, even in these provinces and territories where case management is not instituted comprehensively, we find rules providing for the convening of pre-trial conferences. As will be seen, the objectives of these conferences include the same goals of the distinct case management conferences found in the Ontario scheme, but without the division of function.

2. In Alberta, "at any time after an action has been commenced, the court, on application by any party to the action, or on its own initiative, may order" that a case should proceed by way of case management. See Court of Queen's Bench of Alberta, QB Civil Practice Note No. 1, "Case Management Practice Note," effective September 1, 2001, available online at: http://www.albertacourts.ab.ca/qb/practicenotes/civil/note1-casemgmt.pdf.

See also pre-trial conferences, as governed by Alberta rule 219 and Court of Queen's Bench of Alberta, QB Civil Practice Note No. 3, "Pretrial Conferences," effective April 1, 1998, available online at: http://www.albertacourts.ab.ca/qb/practicenotes/civil/practice_ notes.htm.

Further, in April 2004, the Alberta Court of Queen's Bench commenced a pilot project called Early Pre-Trial Conferences. The premise behind this "totally voluntary" project is "simple": "The civil justice system should be 'front-end loaded' with the resources focused on resolution since most cases settle and very few go to trial." These conferences will be directed to:

(1) determining the *real* issues;

(2) reaching agreement on as many items as possible which are not in dispute;

(3) canvassing whether some or all experts can be jointly retained and failing this, to agree on the experts who are truly required;

(4) agreeing on "will say statements" to avoid discoveries or reduce their length; [and]

(5) considering appropriate possible settlement, early JDR, private ADR, summary trial or other means to reduce the length and the cost of litigation.

See Allan H. Wachowich, Chief Justice, Court of Queen's Bench of Alberta, "Notice to the Profession: Early Pre-Trial Conferences (December 2, 2003)."

3. *Comprehensive Case Management Models*

British Columbia has implemented a comprehensive case management regime to be applied to "certain actions, the trial of which can be completed within two days." This "fast-track litigation," governed by rule 66 of the *Supreme Court Civil Rules*, is similar to Ontario's rule 77 in its scope and application, including the exclusion of family law proceedings from its application and its focus on expeditious timetabling of the various components in the trial process. While family law proceedings are excluded from rule 66, rule 60E(1) provides for family law judicial case conferences, which are similar to case management conferences: "Subject to subrule (2), a party to a family law proceeding commenced after July 1, 2002 must not deliver to another party a notice of motion or affidavit in support of an interlocutory application unless a judicial case conference has been conducted in relation to the proceeding." Rule 35 further provides a less specialized pre-trial conference that can be requested by any party to an action after having either delivered or received a notice of trial. Alternatively, a judge or master may request under this rule that a pre-trial conference, mini-trial, or settlement conference be convened. Although not mandated by the rules of court, British Columbia did amend its practice by Practice Direction 11/20/98, which mandated case management for all civil trials 20 days or more in length. By the same direction, those civil trials expected to be less than 20 days in length have access to case management only if a need can be shown for that intervention and supervision. Rule 68, akin to Ontario's Simplified Procedure rule 76, bars actions with claims for less than $100,000 from case management unless a party applies for case management after another party fails to comply with the timelines and Nova Scotia has included rule 26 for this purpose in the *Nova Scotia Civil Procedure Rules*. Under that rule, a judge may convene a case management conference that can also be used to determine issues, if the parties consent.

Through its rule 219.1, Alberta mandates systematic case management only for those actions deemed to be a "very long trial action" (anticipated to be in excess of 25 days). However, at any time after a regular action has been commenced, the court, on application by any party to the action, or on its own initiative, may order that a case should proceed by way of case management, provided that doing so would promote an efficient resolution of the matter.

For many other Canadian jurisdictions, case management objectives are implemented through the operation of the pretrial conference. The extent to which these jurisdictions explicitly state judicial efficiency objectives as underlying the operation of these conference provisions varies considerably.

4. Pre-Trial Conferences as Case Management

Rule 219 of Alberta's *Rules of Court* gives the court discretion, either on application by a party or on its own initiative, to direct a pretrial conference where a variety of matters can be considered, including amendments to pleadings, simplification of the issues, or the possibility of some degree of settlement through obtaining one or more admissions. How available the pretrial conference should be has been considered by Alberta courts; it has been held that rule 219 should not be used "routinely" to appoint case managers, absent the demonstration of a particular need. In *Tecon Investments Ltd. v. Ottawa Algonquin Travel Corp.* (2000), 269 AR 333, at 24 (QB), the court found:

> All counsel in this matter are experienced. There appears to be no particular stumbling block to the efficient disposition of all pre-trial process in these proceedings. The appointment of a case manager should not be done routinely: it imposes costly procedures on litigants and uses up some of the relatively meagre human resources of the court. Moreover, the appointment of a case manager tends to undermine the role and responsibility of lawyers in litigation. The appointment of a case manager should therefore not be routinely done.

Further, starting in April 2004, the Alberta Court of Queen's Bench commenced a pilot project, "Early Pre-Trial Conferences." This voluntary, opt-in project is based on a premise that investing resources early in a proceeding with the objective of resolving the litigation tends to avoid the greater expense associated with settling later in the process. Specifically, these pre-trial conferences are directed at:

1. determining the real issues;
2. reaching agreement on as many items as possible that are not in dispute;

3. canvassing whether some or all of the experts can be jointly retained and, failing this, agreeing on the experts who are truly required;

4. agreeing on "will say" statements either to avoid discoveries completely or at least to reduce their length; and

5. considering appropriate settlement—early judicial dispute resolution, private ADR, summary trial, or other means to reduce the costs and time associated with litigation.

Similar to the Alberta legislation, rules governing the availability of pre-trial conferences in Nova Scotia, New Brunswick, and Newfoundland also provide that they can be triggered by a party to the action or by the court on its own motion. (See *Nova Scotia Civil Procedure Rules*, rule 26.01, and *Rules of Court of New Brunswick*, rule 50.) While both the Nova Scotia and New Brunswick statutes list the various issues that the court might consider at such a conference, including a basket clause to provide full discretion to the court in determining appropriate subject matter, rule 50.01(1)(h) of the *Rules of Court of New Brunswick* is interesting in its comment that the court consider "any other matter that may assist in the just, least expensive and most expeditious disposition of the proceeding on its merits."

While, clearly, timely settlement is one of the central objectives behind provisions respecting pretrial conferences, both New Brunswick and Ontario (see Ontario *Rules of Civil Procedure*, rule 50.01), are notable in their explicit statement of this goal. In the case of Ontario, rule 50.01 provides for a party-initiated or court-initiated pretrial conference in any action or application, in addition to those actions that qualify for the case management scheme provided by rule 77.

Part XI of Manitoba's *Court of Queen's Bench Rules* governs pretrial procedures, including rules 48 and 50 that mandate a pretrial conference in all cases unless otherwise ordered by a judge. Rule 70 allows that a pretrial conference may be initiated at any time by either party or the court in family proceedings. As with the Alberta provisions, the Manitoba scheme enables a judge to convene a pretrial conference to consider myriad issues ranging from "housekeeping" tasks to be completed before trial to the narrowing of issues and settlement of the dispute. In Saskatchewan, rule 191 of the *Queen's Bench Rules* mandates that a pretrial conference must be held prior to an action being set down for trial. Rule 191(8) specifies the purpose of the pretrial conference to be "attempting to settle the proceeding" and then lists a number of other secondary objectives in the event that settlement is not possible. These range from narrowing issues in dispute to ascertaining trial readiness.

B. Critical Issues in Case Management

1. *Efficiency at What Cost to Justice?*

To achieve just ends, legal processes must strike an appropriate balance between efficiency of inputs and accuracy of outputs. Recent history across Canada and elsewhere reveals civil justice reform agendas dominated by streamlined procedures intended to deliver speedier and less costly dispute resolution. Responding to rapidly rising legal costs and delays, policy-makers have come to equate less process with greater access.

While empirical studies confirm that these reforms have created more efficient disputing frameworks and happier disputants, there has been scant data gathered to measure the other effects of such reforms. In particular, how have these tapered procedures affected the ability of our adversarial model to deliver accurate, legally correct outcomes?

In the excerpt that follows, Colleen Hanycz examines the potential danger resulting from reducing procedural safeguards without considering substantive impacts. It seems clear that efficiency reforms are bringing greater access, but what of greater justice?

Colleen M. Hanycz, "More Access to Less Justice: Efficiency, Proportionality and Costs in Canadian Civil Justice Reform"
(2008), 27 *Civil Justice Quarterly* 98 (footnotes omitted)

It is hard to imagine a time in history when achieving meaningful access to justice was a more pressing need. As our global boundaries shrink, giving way to greater transnational interaction, increasing numbers of disputes arise that require fair and timely resolution. This is an age characterised by shortcuts in legal process; a time when states promote, and citizens accept, less process in exchange for enhanced economies of time and money. Perhaps Lord Devlin was correct, almost 40 years ago, when he suggested that access to a less-than-perfect system is better than no access to a perfect system. What falls to procedural lawyers and scholars is to grapple with this balance between efficiency and accuracy and to ensure a model of justice that remains uncompromised by the erosion of its procedural safeguards.

While there are numerous frameworks within which to discuss "access" and "justice," this project considers the extent to which citizens are able to access existing systems of justice, most notably through our traditional institutions of dispute resolution—the courts. In particular, I focus on connections between access to justice and public policy reform in the context of civil justice models.

The past 25 years have witnessed rising concerns over the economic efficiency of civil trial models, resulting in the common knowledge that all but a small fraction of civil disputes are settled, often following significant expenditures of time and money. As lawyers' fees mount and trial dates are set further into the future, we continue to ask whether the average citizen has meaningful access to justice. In response, we have seen a growing policy focus on procedural and judicial efficiency in Canada, and elsewhere, culminating in significant civil justice reforms aimed solely at enhancing efficiency. The discourse that has developed around this issue has reinforced the tacit connections between judicial/procedural efficiency and meaningful access to civil justice. It is those assumed connections that form the heart of this project.

. . .

The Rise of Efficiency in Civil Justice Reform

While the vast majority of our civil cases settle before final adjudication, our culture of disputing locates these settlements very late in the litigation process. This practice has increased costs and delays as courts grapple with uncertain scheduling and significant backlogs. What we have seen of late is a series of civil justice reforms, aimed expressly at enhancing "efficiency" in our processes, where efficient procedures are narrowly defined as those that are faster and cheaper.

Faster and cheaper outcomes are only superior if they manage to retain those qualities that lend them credibility; namely, their accuracy and perceived justice. How can we regard ourselves as obligated by legitimate authority to comply with a judgment that we believe to be in error with respect to the substantive merits? In 1991, Professor Carrie Menkel-Meadow identified efficiency as the driving concern behind the American culture of settlement advocacy, yet marked this as a recent shift in that "the quality of justice proponents came first in very recent history."

What we have seen in Canada illustrates the full continuum of efficiency reforms, ranging from the establishment of court-connected ADR programmes through to shifting models of pre-trial discovery that consider efficiency a legitimate factor for limiting the scope of required productions and finally to the imposition of significant costs consequences for litigants who decline to settle litigation, only to lose at trial. As will be discussed later in this paper, perhaps the most troubling efficiency measure that we are witnessing in Canada is the growing willingness of courts to order the payment of interim or advance costs, between parties, in anticipation of litigation expenses. Given that this occurs in the absence of a full hearing on the merits of the respective positions, the opportunities for injustice are obvious.

How did "efficiency" come to be defined so narrowly in these policy conversations? Certainly, one obvious explanation comes from the field of law and economics. Borrowing from Richard Posner's theory of wealth maximisation, we see in recent rounds of civil justice reform a utilitarian approach of maximising economic welfare through regulation. Public Choice Theory offers a similar explanation of current reforms if we interpret these reforms as serving to advance the self-interests, ideological or otherwise, of policymakers participating in the reform process.

However, if these are indeed the ideologies that have shaped civil justice reform, we must also consider the accompanying critiques asserting the reductivist nature of law and economics that leads to distorted descriptions and prescriptions. If we are to operate within a policy environment framed by law and economics, must it not also include the measurement of productivity? In addition to reducing costs and delay, in what other ways does enhanced efficiency impact the accuracy and quality of accessible justice?

Clearly, one of the key criteria for measuring procedural fairness and utility is the extent to which legally correct outcomes can be achieved. While Solum suggests four sets of circumstances under which a departure from the requirement of substantive accuracy is justified, the costs of adjudication can only be used to justify such a departure if they are "excessive in relation to the interests at stake in the proceeding." Even Solum's proviso on systemic costs requires some inquiry into the nature of the interests at stake in the process, an inquiry that appears absent from the agenda of policy-reformers.

Among the most significant recent reforms in civil justice policy is the remodelling of the English system of civil procedure enacted following the Woolf Reports. In 1994, Lord Woolf was commissioned to review the current rules of court and civil procedure, with a view to reform. Central to his mandate were procedural revisions that would lead to reduced costs of litigation and, as a result, enhanced access to justice.

Lying at the heart of Woolf's mandate was the assumption, maintained to this day, that enhancing efficiency results in enhanced access to justice. It is this central, largely untested assumption that is most problematic. Certainly, providing less costly and time-consuming procedural mechanisms would seem logically connected to improving the access of citizens to that procedure. However, the bigger question remains as to whether that same procedure, in the light of its reduced processes, retains the ability to deliver just, accurate outcomes.

Unfortunately, this fundamental question seems to have been largely ignored not only in Lord Woolf's work, but in the body of scholarship that followed. Through his Interim and Final Reports, Lord Woolf voiced a number of key conclusions about the shape of civil justice in England and Wales. He enumerated several "prerequisites" for a system of civil justice to ensure acceptable access, including justice and fairness and a proportionality between the procedures provided, the costs incurred and the nature of the issues involved.

Lord Woolf's review led him to conclude that the existing system fell far short of these requirements for ensuring access to justice. In particular, he noted his concern with an "unrestrained adversarial culture" that was unduly complex and that failed to appropriately use resources.

Measuring the extent to which revised procedures enhance or reduce meaningful access to justice is empirically challenging. Alongside this ascendancy of efficiency has developed the justification that disputants are happier with "efficient" systems of justice. Since the advent of the most significant civil justice reforms promoting efficiency in Canada, there have been a number of empirical studies conducted that indicate an overall increase in satisfaction on the parts of participant stakeholders in civil justice.

While self-reported user-satisfaction is one measure of success for a given policy reform, is it appropriate to benchmark user-satisfaction as the central indicator of reform success? An evaluation based on user-satisfaction is significantly different from one that assesses efficiency reforms in terms of their productive, just and accurate outputs. If we hope to reform our civil justice systems in ways that produce positive systemic change, then we must include assessment standards that are located externally rather than impoverishing our inquiry by limiting it to internal standards driven by economic utility and user-satisfaction.

A failure to establish external instruments for measuring the impact of efficiency reforms threatens a diminished utilitarian conversation; namely, rational individuals will make decisions that seek to maximise personal happiness. If that means that litigants choose to settle their disputes voluntarily rather than proceeding to adjudication, then informal settlement is collectively better for society. Ignored, however, in such an analysis is the role of collective values. What of our fundamental belief in the promise of just procedures? What of our commitment to a procedural system that has the capacity to regularly deliver just, accurate outcomes? How is the nature of substantive justice, as a public good, impacted by less process, despite the convenience and access that less process brings? What value is more access if it is only to less justice?

Clearly, there are a variety of challenges that mitigate against an evaluation framework measuring indicators other than user-satisfaction and economic utility. Quite simply, if the procedural reforms allow the resulting system to deliver equal or better rates of "accuracy," then those reforms should be deemed successful. But how do we begin to agree on a definition for substantive accuracy in the context of adversarial outcomes? Absent a clear set of acceptable indicators of justice, we are paralysed from engaging in such an assessment. Instead, policy-makers seem to have accepted a causal relationship between enhanced efficiency and enhanced justice.

2. *The Reasonable Limits of Case Management*

Apart from concerns that case management pays too much attention to efficiency goals at the expense of justice goals, recent proposals for case management reforms in British Columbia have raised questions about the reasonable limits of case management. In particular these reform proposals challenge a fundamental foundation of an adversarial system of civil justice discussed earlier in the text—it is the parties and their lawyers who have responsibility for the conduct of a civil action. The argument is that giving too much responsibility to judges to case manage or plan a civil action's course usurps the lawyer and client's traditional roles. As you read a summary of these proposed reforms and their rationale, consider whether these proposed changes go too far. Do they unfairly or inappropriately take away the primary decision-making roles that lawyers and litigants have traditionally exercised in the conduct of a civil action? Do the BC reforms undermine the autonomy of the parties and their lawyers by vesting control and supervision in the hands of judges? Do the proposals exceed the reasonable limits of case management?

The following is summarized from several reports of the Civil Justice Reform Working Group created by the BC Justice Review Task Force. The full reports are online at http://www.bcjusticereview.org.

The Civil Justice Reform Working Group was formed to explore fundamental change to British Columbia's civil justice system from the time a legal problem develops through the entire Supreme Court litigation process. The overarching goal was to reform the civil justice system in a manner that assists citizens in obtaining just solutions to legal problems quickly and affordably.

The principles underlying the reforms were:

- *proportionality*: the amount of process used will be proportional to the value, complexity, and importance of the case;
- *flexibility and matching*: the process used will be designed to fit the needs of the case and the parties;
- *judicial intervention*: judges and masters will take a more active role in the management and resolution of cases;
- *expanded role for lawyers*: lawyers will use an expanded tool kit that reflects a multitude of process options to assist their clients in quickly arriving at just solutions; and
- *preservation of the rule of law*: the new system must support and be guided by the rule of law.

To achieve the desired reform, the working group not only recommended providing integrated information and services to those who wanted to resolve their legal problems on their own before entering the court system (a response to the growing problem of self-represented litigants) but also proposed significant changes to existing civil procedure.

A major and controversial change was an early case planning conference (CPC). Before the parties could go beyond the initial steps of initiating and responding to a claim, the parties and their lawyers must personally attend a CPC. The CPC would address a number of topics that would normally be a common part of case management-settlement possibilities and processes, narrowing of the issues, directions for discovery and experts, milestones to be accomplished, deadlines to be met and setting of the date and length of trial.

However, the proposed case planning conference had unique features that were based on the principle of increased judicial intervention with a corresponding limit to the autonomy of lawyers and their clients. First, the CPC would be an extensive conference where the CPC judge would facilitate a problem-solving discussion with respect not only to settlement and case management issues but also to case planning. Second, and related, prior to the conference the parties and their lawyers would have to develop a case plan for conducting the case and moving to resolution. Each case plan that would set out dispute resolution options, dates for the exchange of documents, the parameters of oral examinations for discovery, and information about the planned use of experts. If the parties cannot agree on a case plan, the court would order such a plan guided by proportionality principles. The working group foresaw an opportunity to help create a culture of collaboration between parties and their lawyers through jointly creating a proposed case plan prior to the CPC. Finally, one of the matters for discussion at the CPC would include consideration of the dispute resolution method best suited to the circumstances of the case. The CPC judge would have the power to move the focus from the "litigation track" and order mediation, neutral case evaluation, or other dispute resolution process.

The rationale for the CPC and required case plans was based on important research findings about civil litigation. Research revealed that while the vast majority of cases do not proceed to trial, civil cases do not always settle early, cost effectively, or to the satisfaction of the parties. Most settlements take place late in the proceedings after significant process and legal costs have been expended. Therefore, there was a need to streamline the litigation process through the early identification of issues and interests, ensuring the amount of process is proportional to the value, complexity, and importance of the case, and increased judicial intervention to establish and enforce timelines for completing major litigation events.

While the goals of making the civil justice system faster and less expensive were commonly held, it was the active judicial involvement that created controversy. The Civil Justice Reform Working Group identified a cultural barrier to achieving these goals that lay the responsibility squarely with lawyers:

> One obstacle is that many lawyers automatically take a familiar adversarial approach to litigation, which is not consistent with early resolution and which often results in unnecessary delay and costly to the parties. Current rules and legal training reinforce this obstacle and they will likely prevail if the conduct of the action is left entirely to the parties and their counsel. We concluded that a fundamental change is necessary in order to shift these ingrained cultural values and practices in any significant way. This change will require early and active judicial involvement in cases.

To support this reform, the working group also recommended a dramatic change in the manner in which civil proceedings are commenced. Rather than relying on the current pleading process, the working group recommended a new process requiring the parties to accurately and succinctly state the facts, certified by a sworn statement that the facts were true, and setting out the issues in dispute. The new commencing document, the Dispute Summary and Resolution Plan, would force the parties not only to be realistic about the facts (sworn to be true) but also force the parties to think about resolution options. The working group hoped this requirement would encourage an early dialogue between the parties about resolution. As mentioned, the working group anticipated that eventually the parties and their counsel would accomplish much of the collaborative planning process prior to the CPC and the CPC judge's role will be to affirm and facilitate that plan through appropriate consent orders.

In recommending the replacement of pleadings with a new case initiation process, the working group was responding to complaints that pleadings have long since ceased to function as a blueprint of a case and become too complex, convoluted, evasive, and boilerplate documents drafted strategically to leave as many avenues of attack or defence open to the parties as possible.

The British Columbia civil justice reform proposals have attracted much criticism particularly from trial lawyers despite the common observation that civil litigation is too slow and costly. Much of that criticism appears grounded in the expanded role that judges can play in case management and the observation that lawyers on their own are not likely to be able to improve the situation.

NOTES AND QUESTIONS

Do you see flaws in the reasoning behind these case management reforms? Does the concept of giving experienced judges, who have had long careers as lawyers in practice, more responsibility for helping the parties and their lawyers create case plans that would focus on early, affordable, and satisfactory resolution seem inconsistent with an adversarial system of civil justice?

New Supreme Court Civil Rules come into force in British Columbia on July 1, 2010. These rules reject the Dispute Summary and Resolution Plan as an appropriate document to commence civil proceedings and substitute traditional pleadings now called Notice of Claim and Response to Claim. The Case Planning Conference is retained, but now is optional if one party so requests. The focus of the conference is no longer specifically on early settlement with an emphasis on choosing the dispute resolution method best suited to the particular circumstances of the case, but on discovery, expert witness, witness list, and trial details. While the new rules do allow a judge to order a Case Planning Conference, the tenor of the new rules maintains case management primarily in the hands of the lawyers and their clients.

III. COURT-CONNECTED MEDIATION

One of the central aspects of developing case management regimes in North America is the availability of either compulsory or voluntary opportunities to attempt to resolve disputes through mediation. It is difficult to define with any clarity the elements of this court-connected "mediation," because it varies considerably among systems. Although court-connected mediation is growing in its use across Canada, it is by no means a novel function of case management systems. In fact, mediation has existed, some would argue, for hundreds of years and in countless forms.

At its most basic, mediation can be defined as "negotiation assisted by a third party." In its modern form, this is most commonly illustrated by the parties to a dispute sitting down with a neutral "outsider" whose objective it is to assist the parties in facilitating a resolution to the dispute. But even that most rudimentary definition raises controversy. Various legal anthropologists have studied the widespread and ancient use of mediation in "primitive" societies, only to discover that often the mediator is not a detached neutral, but may be an elder in the community who has a keen interest in the dispute's resolution. Certainly, in international disputes, we often see the emergence of a mediator who, while accepted by all parties to the dispute, is clearly not neutral and whose nation has some distinct interests in the terms of resolution of the given dispute.

Mediation advocates regard it as especially beneficial in situations where conflict arises within the context of an ongoing relationship. Proponents argue that the adversarial/adjudicative framework serves to inflict a number of harms on disputants who find themselves in a long-term relationship, be that personal or business-based. First, the adversarial model often engenders hostility, because it calls on each side to press its case to the fullest, without regard to the consequences suffered by one's opponent. Certainly, the longstanding professional responsibility of "zealous advocacy" among lawyers goes some way to explaining this resulting harm.

Adjudication necessarily entails a win–lose equation, as the adjudicator is called upon to select the "better case" following an application of accepted norms to the facts at hand. For disputants who find themselves in a continuing relationship, this binary approach to outcomes often makes it difficult to move forward in a positive way. While adjudication is often unable to answer the question of what is the "best" arrangement to guide the relationship of these parties into the future, mediation arguably possesses the philosophical and process components to assist parties in this way. While a one-sided adjudicative finding may hamper the ability of long-time partners in a commercial arrangement to continue their relationship, mediation arguably prioritizes this future connection by suggesting solutions that all parties can accept. In this way, future outcomes are enhanced rather than further harmed.

In Canada, we are witnessing a growing acceptance into our mainstream criminal justice systems of what are known as restorative justice processes (such as victim–offender reconciliation and sentencing circles). Rather than the traditional focus of criminal law on public retribution, the restorative justice approach recognizes the harm suffered by the entire community (victim, offender, and others) as a result of such unacceptable behaviour. A restorative justice lens adopts a focus based on healing the community rather than punishing the offender and basically ignoring everyone else. Again, this is not new. In fact, these mediation-based processes are the ones that have been practised for centuries by our First Nations communities and that are now gaining wider acceptance in modern legal systems. However, again, the way in which one might define "mediation" using a restorative justice lens may lead to a model that is totally unlike that which is being implemented as part of civil justice reforms. Clearly, there is no definitive model of mediation as practised either in Canada or elsewhere.

C. Menkel-Meadow, "The Many Ways of Mediation"
(1995), 11 *Negotiation Journal* 217, at 228-30
(reviewing D. Kolb, *When Talk Works* (San Francisco: Jossey-Bass, 1994))

Models of Mediation

The varieties of approaches to mediation described in *When Talk Works* help define several models of mediation that practitioners, rather than theorists, have developed for themselves. These models are instructive for demonstrating how simple practice routines must be altered depending on the context of the problem of the institution in which the dispute is situated. As the field has matured, we can see how varied the approaches are and how difficult it is to develop a single set of criteria for evaluation.

Once again, *When Talk Works* reveals greater variety, flexibility and plasticity of models. ...The profiles of the twelve mediators illustrate the following models or approaches to mediation which, in turn, may help us in the development of more focused analyses of how particular tactics or professional strategies need to be adapted to particular goals, contexts and situations. I have discerned the following variations ... :

1. In its "purest" form, mediation is facilitative—the third party neutral helps the parties to arrive at their own solutions. While this is the model most often articulated by mediators, the descriptions of mediation which appear in all three of the reviewed books demonstrate how rare it actually is for the mediator not to intrude somewhat in the process.

2. In its newest form, "evaluative" mediation is a hybrid of mediation and arbitration. ... Although the solution remains technically in the hands of the parties, the mediator may provide evaluative information on possible legal or legislative outcomes, offer financial data or advice or provide advocacy or negotiation training, as well as suggest possible outcomes or solutions.

3. ... [T]ransformative mediation seeks, on a number of different levels, to change either the dispute ... or the disputants (altering their appraisal of each other and their place in the world, which Bush and Folger call empowerment and recognition). The most ambitious mediators of all seek to transform their community through conflict resolution and the reduction of violence. ...

4. Bureaucratic mediations occur in court or other institutional settings...which control and limit both what processes may be used or what outcomes may be possible. In such mediation, the setting is the key influence on how mediation is conducted and greater rigidity, formalism and replicability may be evident. ...

5. Mediations can also be distinguished on the basis of how "open" or "closed" they are—by this I mean how much control the parties have over the process, rather than the outcome. Bush and Folger seek to describe a process in which the parties can choose what kinds of ground rules and other process choices they want. In other models, both bureaucratic mediators, as well as those in private practice, may have such set routines that, although they appear to give parties control over the solutions and agreements they reach, the process rules and routines of practice are in fact quite closed and dictated by the mediator.

NOTE

For our purposes, we are going to limit our scrutiny of mediation to those models that are directly connected to our courts in Canada. Borrowing from the First Report of Ontario's Civil Justice Review ("The Multi-Door Concept and Alternative Dispute Resolution," in Civil Justice Review, *First Report* (Toronto: Ontario Civil Justice Review, March 1995), 209, at 214-15 (footnotes omitted)), the following description of mediation was adopted:

> Mediation is a process in which a neutral person, agreeable to the disputing parties, acts as a facilitator to their negotiations and assists them in arriving at their own mutually acceptable solution. Mediation may occur before the litigation has commenced or at any time before trial. Generally, it is undertaken outside the court process, although judges will use mediating techniques in attempting to promote settlement discussions.

As we will examine, court-connected mediation across Canada, while still in its relative infancy, has taken on a variety of forms, the most notable distinguishing feature being whether it is mandatory. We begin our review of several Canadian models by considering the mandatory mediation scheme established in Ontario through the adoption of rule 24.1 of the *Rules of Civil Procedure*.

A. Rule 24.1 and the Ontario Mandatory Mediation Program

In 1994, Ontario established its Civil Justice Review, which was structured as a collaborative initiative of the Superior Court and the Ministry of the Attorney General. The review was established to respond to public complaints that our civil justice system was inaccessible for a variety of reasons. The Civil Justice Review, which ultimately led to the implementation of mandatory mediation in parts of Ontario, had the following mandate: "[T]o develop an overall strategy for the civil justice system in an effort to provide a *speedier, more streamlined and efficient structure to maximize the utilization of public resources allocated to civil justice*" (emphasis added).

In January 1999, following pilot projects in Toronto and Ottawa, rule 24.1 was introduced, mandating early mediation for all non-family, civil, case-managed cases filed in the Ontario Superior Court of Justice in Ottawa and Toronto. Following an evaluation of the pilot in 2001, rule 24.1 was deemed a success and added as a permanent rule of the *Rules of Civil Procedure*. The Ontario mandatory mediation program (OMMP) now applies to Toronto, Ottawa, and the County of Essex (Windsor area), with reputed expansion plans to govern all non-family, civil disputes brought across Ontario in the Superior Court.

Rule 24.1 operates to ensure that each eligible action is mediated within 180 days of filing the first statement of defence in that action (with a possible extension if all parties consent and notify the mediation coordinator). One of the historical criticisms of the Ontario model is that the former deadline of 90 days meant that mediation was often conducted before the examinations for discovery in the matter, serving to make early settlement virtually impossible, given the reluctance of many lawyers to recommend settlement without first having the benefit of discovery. One of the central rationales behind scheduling mediation so early in the trial process is to provide parties and lawyers with a genuine opportunity to settle the action before opposing positions are firmly entrenched and costs associated with the trial process (such as the costs of completing discoveries) have escalated to a point that makes compromise financially unattractive. How do we balance the financial objectives served by early mediation with the necessity of full disclosure as a prerequisite to meaningful settlement discussions?

Rundle v. Kruspe

[1998] OJ No. 2078 (Gen. Div.)

MASTER ROBERT BEAUDOIN: In this proceeding, the plaintiff brings a motion to strike paragraphs 17 and 18 of the Statement of Defence; for an order to postpone the mandatory mediation until after completion of examinations for discovery; and for an order requiring each defendant to produce a further and better affidavit of documents to include the student records and the Ontario student transcripts of each defendant. The motion also seeks alternative relief in the event that the defendants are successful in their own cross-motion.

Each of the defendants brings a separate motion to compel the plaintiff to provide a further and better affidavit of documents; specifically with regard to documents and records relating to an investigation conducted by the Ottawa School Board; an order requiring the plaintiff to deliver direction and authorization for documents and medical records and for an independent medical examination of the plaintiff.

The plaintiff was a former teacher with the Ottawa Board of Education. On June 2, 1997 she was suspended from her employment as a teacher at the Glebe Collegiate because of allegations of harassment and inappropriate behaviour. The Ottawa Board of Education conducted an investigation with respect to these allegations and subsequently decided to terminate the plaintiff's employment on October 7, 1997. In the course of this investigation, a social worker interviewed these defendants. The plaintiff has initiated these actions claiming that the words spoken by the defendants in the course of the investigation, were defamatory and damaged her reputation and were ultimately relied upon by the Ottawa Board of Education in terminating her employment. It was agreed by both counsel that the various issues raised in these three separate motions would be dealt as though it were one proceeding as the relief sought is similar in all three actions. It was also agreed that the court would deal with the matters raised in these respective motions on an issue by issue basis.

• • •

d) Mandatory Referral to Mediation

The plaintiff seeks to defer these proceedings from mandatory referral to mediation until such time as oral examinations for discovery are complete. In support of her position, her counsel submits that the plaintiff has yet to have an opportunity to tell her side of the story; that she has yet to be heard throughout this dispute. She also submits that the plaintiff cannot be forced to settle.

In this instance, the defendants submit that mediation is entirely appropriate; that the plaintiff has no real expectation of recovering any money from these defendants and that mediation ought to be attempted as a more cost effective means of resolving this dispute.

I agree. If the plaintiff is looking to confront the defendants and to give her version of what took place, this is precisely what can happen at a mediation. The contact is private; the atmosphere is less adversarial. It is hard to imagine that oral examinations for discovery will provide the plaintiff with a better opportunity to give her side of the story. A settlement is not the only successful outcome of a mediation. If the parties can narrow the issues in the dispute or, at the very least, come away with a better understanding of the other sides' position, the mediation can still be considered a success. There will no doubt be serious challenges to the mediator who will be asked to intervene in this matter and I accordingly encourage counsel to take great care in the selection of the mediator who will undertake this task.

Given the divided success on these motions, costs are in the cause.

Order accordingly.

Patrus v. Rosset
[2003] OJ No. 1302 (SCJ)

MASTER POLIKA: This case conference was convened by my order of February 11, 2003 at the request of counsel for the plaintiff for the purpose of addressing the issue of the mandatory mediation and to establish the balance of the timetable to ensure compliance with the provisions of Rule 77.14(2), (4), (5), and (6).

This action was commenced on May 17, 2002 and today is 307 days old. The first defence was filed on July 2, 2002. The parties failed to agree on a mediator within 30 days and a mediator was assigned from the roster. Plaintiff's counsel advises that the assigned mediator, Robert Kominar was not notified of the assignment and the parties were not contacted and the mediation was not held. The mediation, absent the parties' agreement to extend had to be held by September 30, 2002. Counsel did advise that in September and October, 2002 there was contact with the mediator and between counsel. The mediator took ill. Mr. Michelli was unwilling to go to mediation without particulars although his client's defence was delivered. All Counsel did nothing further concerning the mandatory mediation or to advance the action until plaintiff's counsel's letter of February 11, 2003.

The notices advising of the Trial Scheduling court went out to the parties on October 22, 2002 indicating that Trial Scheduling Court was fixed for March 5, 2003. Even that did little to trigger action by counsel. On the eve of Trial Scheduling Court counsel for the plaintiff wrote requesting a case conference purportedly to solely address the mandatory mediation issue. When I reviewed the case history I determined that the Trial Scheduling Court appearance was up coming and adjourned it to a date to be fixed today to avoid an unnecessary court appearance which would have been a waste of the court's time and the parties' money.

Patently it appears that all parties were in breach of the requirement to hold a mandatory mediation as required by Rule 24.1. Whether the mediator contacted them or not is immaterial. It is their obligation to ensure that the mediation takes place as required or the time for holding the mediation is extended by the court prior to its expiration. The parties and their counsel made no attempt to seek an order or ask for a case conference to address this issue until over 4 months after the time for holding the mandatory mediation went by. The parties failed in their obligation. I have no knowledge of whether this inaction was a result of the incompetence of counsel or counsel's decision to simply let the action lay fallow or at the specific direction of one or more of the parties. The parties had an obligation pursuant to Rule 24.1 to hold the mandatory mediation within 90 days of filing the first defence. It is the parties' obligation not that of the mediation co-ordinator or the mediator.

When the parties failed to choose a mediator it was their obligation to inquire of the mediation co-ordinator as to who the assigned mediator was and then to make arrangements with him to ensure the mediation was held within the time provided by Rule 24.1. The resulting delay by this breach by all the parties flies in the face of the purpose and object of Rule 24.1 and the purpose and object of Rule 77 as set out in Rule 77.02. Those coming to the court to use the processes of the court have an obligation to follow the rules of the court in the prosecution or defence of an action. The failure to follow the rules of the court should not be rewarded. After considering what transpired and the submissions of counsel on the breach it appears just that the parties each should bear their own costs of this case conference, the preparation for this case conference and all the costs of the mandatory mediation regardless of the result in the action.

I was advised that pleadings were closed and the affidavits of documents have been served. We then went on to set the timetable for both the mandatory mediation and the balance of this action up to and including Trial Scheduling Court.

After discussing the status of the proceedings and the matters set out aforesaid and hearing the submissions of counsel *IT IS ORDERED THAT*:

1. On any motions brought in this proceeding henceforth, whether before a judge or master, at trial scheduling court, at a settlement conference and at trial a copy of all Case Conference Memoranda—Orders made in this proceeding shall be included in the moving parties motion material or made available to the case management judge or case management master presiding to ensure that they are aware of what has transpired and been ordered in this proceeding at case conferences;

2. There shall be no costs to any party in any event of the cause of this case conference, the preparation for this case conference and the mandatory mediation;

3. The examinations for discovery shall be completed by on or before June 13, 2003 on the basis that they will be held one after the other in the order set out in the title of proceedings, unless counsel agree on some other order, without regard to undertakings or refusals until completed failing which a party is deemed to have waived the right to examine the party or parties adverse in interest;

4. Any undertakings given at the first round of examinations for discovery shall be answered on or before July 14, 2003;

5. Any motion seeking to compel answers to questions refused, taken under advisement or undertaken to be answered at the examinations for discovery or based upon Rule 30.10 shall be brought on and argued before me at any of my available weekly motion courts by no later than August 19, 2003 failing which a party is deemed to have waived the right to bring such a motion;

6. This order is effective without further formality and no formal order need be taken out to reflect the dispositions made by this Case Conference Memorandum—Order; and

7. The trial scheduling court appearance is adjourned to the first available date on or after August 27, 2003.

The times set out in the timetable are the *maximum* times within which the scheduled events are to be completed. *Counsel should immediately take steps to fix appointments for all events scheduled* in the timetable. Counsel are directed to have regard to the provisions of Rule 77.10 and in particular Rule 77.10(1)(b) and Rule 77.10(2)(a), (b) and (d) respecting the consequences of failure to meet the timetable as well as the provisions of Rule 77.14 and in particular Rule 77.14(2) and the time and content requirements for settlement briefs. *Counsel should make full use of requests to admit facts and authenticity of documents as soon as possible* particularly to assist in settlement and to reduce the time for examinations for discovery and trial.

Order accordingly.

B. Other Canadian Models of Court-Connected Mediation

1. Saskatchewan

Saskatchewan was the first Canadian jurisdiction to introduce mandatory court-annexed mediation, with its pilot program commencing in 1994. The program now applies to all but 20 percent of those cases brought in the Court of Queen's Bench in the judicial centres of Saskatoon, Regina, Prince Albert, and Swift Current. Pursuant to s. 42 of the *Queen's Bench Act, 1998*, the requirement to attend mediation is triggered by the filing of pleadings that respond to the statement of claim, most commonly the statement of defence.

There are some notable differences between the models implemented in Saskatchewan and Ontario including the fact that the Saskatchewan mediators are full-time or contract mediators provided by the Department of Justice, so that the first session of up to three hours is conducted at no additional cost to the parties. While rule 24.1 in Ontario requires that all parties attend mediation with their counsel, arguably another significant expense, the parallel legislation in Saskatchewan requires only that the parties themselves participate in mediation. Similarly, parties are not required to prepare in advance any additional statements for the mediator or each other. After the first session, parties can continue with the mediation or proceed towards trial or settle as they wish. Mediators are also given broad powers to strike the pleadings of a party who fails to attend the mandatory mediation, postpone mediation and exempt the appearance of any party without requiring judicial consent.

2. British Columbia

In British Columbia, a court-connected, quasi-mandatory mediation model has been implemented for almost all civil cases. Several types of proceedings are exempted as being unsuitable for mandatory mediation; notably, family law proceedings and claims for physical or sexual abuse are excluded.

Unlike the Ontario and Saskatchewan examples, which are clearly representative of the increased judicial case management discussed above, the BC models are distinctly party-driven and in keeping with the traditional party-prosecution aspect of the adversary system.

In British Columbia, any party to the dispute may initiate mediation by filing a notice to mediate with the other parties in the action and with the DRO. There are specific windows of opportunity when these notices may properly be delivered, but in all cases a mediation session is triggered.

Also of note in British Columbia is the mandatory settlement conference provided for by rule 7 of the *Small Claims Rules*. This conference is conducted by a provincial court judge and it must be held before setting down a matter for trial. Rule 7 provides that all parties must attend the conference and that each party is expected to bring with him or her all relevant documents to the action. The rule further provides that any party who attends the mandatory settlement conference "unprepared" may be ordered to pay the "reasonable expenses" of the other party. If all issues are not settled at the mandatory mediation session(s), a settlement conference will be scheduled. Of particular note is the description in rule 7(14) of what "happens" at this mandatory settlement conference:

7(14) What happens at a settlement conference

At a settlement conference, a judge may do one or more of the following:

(a) mediate any issues being disputed;

(b) decide on any issues that do not require evidence;

(c) make a payment order or other appropriate order in the terms agreed to by the parties;

(d) set a trial date, if a trial is necessary;

(e) discuss any evidence that will be required and the procedure that will be followed if a trial is necessary;

(f) order a party to produce any information at the settlement conference or anything as evidence at trial;

(g) order a party to

(i) give another party copies of documents and records by a set date, or

(ii) allow another party to inspect and copy documents and records by a set date;

(h) if damage to property is involved in the dispute, order a party to permit a person chosen by another party to examine the property damage;

(i) dismiss a claim, counterclaim, reply or third party notice if, after discussion with the parties and reviewing the filed documents, a judge determines that it

(i) is without reasonable grounds,

(ii) discloses no triable issue, or

(iii) is frivolous or an abuse of the court's process;

(j) before dismissing a claim, counterclaim, reply or third party notice, order a party to file an affidavit setting out further information;

(k) *Repealed.*

(l) make any other order for the just, speedy and inexpensive resolution of the claim.

While this British Columbia model has been called its "mandatory mediation" scheme, the definition of mediation as having a function independent from that of the trial process becomes more difficult to sustain. We must question the appropriateness of a judge presiding over one session at which the judge can supposedly mediate issues in dispute while also making a number of enumerated orders based on an assessment of the merits of the respective positions.

3. Alberta

The Alberta Court of Queen's Bench has been conducting a voluntary judicial dispute resolution (JDR) program for over 10 years. This program, while continually evolving, is becoming increasingly popular with practising members of Alberta's bar and bench. Depending on the judge and the judicial district considered, the processes employed typically include some form of mediation, mini-trial, or similar model. All cases commenced in Alberta's small claims court (the Alberta Provincial Court—Civil Division) are reviewed before being set down to trial. If considered suitable to be resolved through mediation, the case will be selected and directed to undergo mediation.

C. Critical Issues in Mediation

As suggested in the introduction to this chapter, case management, mediation, and settlement provisions all represent modern departures from the traditional party-driven adjudicative framework of civil litigation. Perhaps inappropriately, many of these non-adjudicative approaches to dispute resolution are gathered under the umbrella of alternative dispute resolution (ADR). As seen in the section above on mediation, one of the central problems in this field is the lack of a widely adopted definitional framework. When we talk about mediation, for example, some assume that to include the participation of a neutral third party while, in other contexts, to be credible, the mediator needs to adopt the position of an interested stakeholder.

For our purposes, in the context of civil litigation, we have limited our consideration of mediation to the process as it is being increasingly implemented in civil procedure schemes. What follows is a brief consideration of some critical issues central to any consideration of ADR in general and to various models of mediation in particular.

1. How Do We Measure Success?

Before we can determine whether civil justice reforms surrounding the introduction of mediation schemes into the litigation process have been successful, we need to return to the objectives of these reforms. In the case of Ontario's mandatory mediation program, as noted above, the key objectives stated in the Civil Justice Review were "to provide a *speedier, more streamlined and efficient structure to maximize the utilization of public resources allocated to civil justice.*" Has mediation accomplished this in Ontario? What follows is an excerpt from the executive summary of the independent evaluation of the mandatory mediation pilot project conducted between January 1999 and July 2001.

**R. Hann et al., *Evaluation of the Ontario Mandatory Mediation Program
(Rule 24.1): Executive Summary and Recommendations***
(Toronto: Queen's Printer, 2001), 1-2

The evaluation addresses a wide range of issues of interest to the Civil Rules Committee, to the judiciary, to governmental policy makers, to the general public—and to lawyers, mediators, court administrators, litigants and other stakeholders involved in the day to day operation of the court and litigation processes.

However, the focus of the evaluation was on the four major objectives of mandatory mediation under Rule 24.1, namely:

- Does Rule 24.1 improve the pace of litigation?
- Does Rule 24.1 reduce the costs to the participants in the litigation process?
- Does Rule 24.1 improve the quality of disposition outcomes?
- Does Rule 24.1 improve the operation of the mediation and litigation processes?

. . .

In light of its demonstrated positive impact on the pace, costs and outcomes of litigation, Rule 24.1 must be generally regarded as a successful addition to the case management and dispute resolution mechanisms available through the Ontario Superior Court of Justice in both Toronto and Ottawa. More specifically, the evaluation provides strong evidence that:

1. Mandatory mediation under the Rule has resulted in significant reductions in the time taken to dispose of cases.
2. Mandatory mediation has resulted in decreased costs to litigants.
3. Mandatory mediation has resulted in a high proportion of cases (roughly 40% overall) being completely settled earlier in the litigation process—with other benefits being noted in many of the other cases that do not completely settle.
4. In general, litigants and lawyers have expressed considerable satisfaction with the mediation process under Rule 24.1.
5. Although there were at times variations from one type of case to another, these positive findings applied generally to all case types—and to cases in both Ottawa and Toronto.

NOTES AND QUESTIONS

Are we comfortable using this measure of success? Some commentators have raised concerns about efficiency-based goals in our increasingly managerial civil trial process. As discussed above, another vehicle for achieving these goals, like mandatory mediation, is the compulsory settlement conference, a component of case management. In the following excerpt, Menkel-Meadow discusses the mandatory settlement conference and, in particular, the different conceptions of role that judges bring to such conferences. These conceptions, Menkel-Meadow argues, are tied to some of the competing value claims made by proponents of ADR.

C. Menkel-Meadow, "For and Against Settlement: Uses and Abuses of the Mandatory Settlement Conference"
(1985), 33 *UCLA Law Review* 485, at 486-511 (footnotes omitted)

One of the most fundamental disputes about non-adjudicatory dispute resolution concerns the values it is intended to promote. Some commentators contrast the quantitative, efficiency, process axis to the qualitative, justice, substance axis. Some extol mandatory settlement conferences, arbitration, and mediation programs because they decrease delay of case processing time and promote judicial efficiency. This claim is not supported by the empirical research at this stage. Others assert (and I am affiliated with this school) that the *quality* of dispute resolution is improved when models other than the formal adjudication model are used. Solutions to disputes can be tailored to the parties' polycentric needs and can achieve greater party satisfaction and enforcement reliability because they are not binary, win/lose results. Still others assert that quality solutions are more likely to emerge when the dispute resolution process is not privatized and individualized. This argument is characterized alternatively as the "cool efficiency/warm conciliation," "quantitative/qualitative," or "managerial/substantive" justifications for non-adjudicative dispute resolution.

A second dispute concerns the appropriate role of judges when they become involved in alternative dispute resolution or settlement conferences. The judges themselves characterize this issue as whether they should be "active" or "passive." Academics debate whether judges should be "managers" or "adjudicators."

A third dispute falls on the micro-macro axis of analysis. Is the appropriate unit of analysis the particular or individual disputes that are resolved and with which the parties and lawyers are satisfied or should the unit of analysis be the larger system as measured by judicial management statistics or by the quality of precedents produced? Owen Fiss has recently suggested that if too many cases are diverted from the courtroom into settlement, appellate judges will have an insufficient number and quality of cases from which to make the law. Fiss's prediction, if true, could have grave implications for the legitimacy of the entire legal system.

The three disputes outlined above raise issues that should affect significantly our assessment of the strengths and weaknesses of any dispute resolution device. In order to evaluate the arguments advanced in these disputes, we must explore the underlying values and the empirical claims made in support of these arguments.

· · ·

V. The Functions and Purposes of the Mandatory Settlement Conference: The How and Why of Settlement Practices

As greater numbers of judges and courts use settlement conferences, our information about particular practices increases. Our current sources of data include reports and articles written by judges and settlement officers, training materials written for new judges, some survey data collected by social scientists and court administrators, and descriptive and critical reports by academics. As we review this data, it is useful to think about how the manager of the settlement conference, whether judge or magistrate, views his or her role. What emerges from the data is a variety of role conceptions that parallel the various conceptions of the goals of settlement. For some, efficient case management is the primary role; for others, the primary role is the facilitation of substantive or procedural justice. For others still, the primary role is simple brokering of what would occur anyway in bilateral negotiations. Some judges avoid active settlement activity because they view adjudication as their primary role.

My concern with the settlement management role conception is twofold. First, role conception seems to have a direct effect on the choice of techniques used. In turn, the techniques may have a direct influence on the type of settlement reached. Second, without an open debate about the merits of particular technique choices, we may be unaware of both primary and secondary effects of making settlement conferences mandatory.

It is not surprising that the literature describing practices in settlement conferences reflects the full range of attitudes toward the appropriateness of judicial intervention. Those judges least comfortable with intervention in settlement describe the settlement process as a mere "by-product" of the mandatory pretrial conference. Such judges see themselves simply as facilitators of what the lawyers would do anyway, providing a meeting place for lawyers to get together and discuss their cases. In one well-documented case, the judge arranged several days of cocktail parties and country club dining to encourage a meeting of counsel in a complex case. Moving slightly closer to the activist line are those judges who maintain that the best intervention on behalf of settlement is the setting of a firm trial date, thereby expediting discovery, improving estimates of costs and predictions of trial outcomes, and setting firm deadlines for discovery and trial.

At the other extreme are the activist judges who see settlement of cases as one of their principal functions. In one of the more thoughtful judicial analyses of the advantages and disadvantages of judicial intervention, Judge Fox of the federal district court in western Michigan has analyzed both the quantitative efficiency, docket management arguments and the substantive values (results more closely related to the merits of the cases as the parties and their lawyers understand them) arguments in favor of intervention.

A. The Dangers of Efficiency-Seeking Settlement Techniques

For those who seek to use the settlement conference as a docket-clearing device, the conference becomes most problematic in terms of the substantive and process values (i.e., *quality* of solution) previously discussed. Judges see their role as simplifying the issues until the major issue separating the parties (usually described as money) is identified and the judge can attempt to "narrow the gap." In one study judges and lawyers were asked to report on judicial settlement activity. Seventy-two percent of the lawyers reported that they participated at least once in settlement conferences in which the judge requested the parties to "split the difference." The same study noted that when local rules require settlement conferences judges tend to be more assertive in their settlement techniques (using several techniques that some of the lawyers considered to be unethical). According to the study, jurisdictions with mandatory settlement conferences took more time in moving cases toward trial. This confirms the findings of earlier studies.

A much touted settlement technique is the use of the "Lloyds of London" formula: The settlement judge asks the parties to assess the probabilities of liability and damages and, if the figures are within reasonable range, to split the difference. The difficulty with such settlement techniques is that they tend to monetarize and compromise all the issues in the case. Although some cases are reducible to monetary issues, an approach to case evaluation on purely monetary grounds may decrease the likelihood of settlement by making fewer issues available for trade-offs. Furthermore, a wider definition of options may make compromise unnecessary. As the recent outpouring of popular and scholarly literature on negotiation illustrates, the greater the number of issues in controversy between the parties, the greater the likelihood of achieving a variety of solutions. Parties may place complementary values on different items. The irony is that settlement managers, who think they are making settlement easier by reducing the issues, may in fact be increasing the likelihood of deadlock by reducing the issues to one. Furthermore, as I have argued at length elsewhere, using money as a proxy for other interests the parties may have may thwart the possibilities for using party interests for mutual gain.

In addition to foreclosing a number of possible settlements, the efficiency-minded settlement officer seems prone to us[ing] coercive techniques such as suggesting a particular result, making threats about taking the case off the docket, directing meetings with clients or parties. Lawyers find these techniques problematic. Thus, the quest for efficiency may in fact be counterproductive.

B. The Search for Quality Solutions

Some recent data seem to indicate that greater satisfaction can be achieved with a different settlement management role—the facilitator of good settlements. Brazil's survey of lawyers practising in four federal districts reveals that lawyers favored intervention techniques that sought to produce the "best result." Lawyers favored such techniques because judges who analyzed the particular facts of the case (as opposed to those who used formulas like "Lloyds of London"), offered explicit suggestions and assessments of the parties' positions, occasionally spoke directly to recalcitrant clients, and expressed views about the unfairness of particular results. Brazil's data are interesting in that they point to variations in the desirability of particular settlement techniques, depending on size of case, case type, defense or plaintiff practice, and other demographic factors.

What emerges from Brazil's data is that lawyers want different things in different cases. Thus, a routinized settlement agenda is not likely to be successful in satisfying their desires. More significantly, the data show that lawyers do not perceive a judges' settlement role as significantly different from their adjudicative role when the judges employ the more favored settlement techniques. In alternative dispute resolution parlance, the lawyers of Brazil's study seek a hybrid of the adjudicator—the "med-arb" (mediator-arbitrator):

> They prefer that judges express opinions, offer suggestions, or analyze situations much more than they value judges asking the attorneys to make a presentation or conduct an analysis. Our respondents consistently give higher effective ratings to settlement conference procedures that revolve around inputs by judges than those that feature exposition by counsel. Thus, the lawyers' assessments of specific techniques reinforce the major theme that what litigators want most from judges in settlement conferences is *an expression of analytical opinion.*

The lawyers wanted help in achieving specific results through analysis and reasoned opinions, not formulaic compromises. Whether judges will deliver such help is another issue. If, as Resnik argues, there is a danger that judges will manipulate results to serve their own ends when the results do not have to be justified in print, we should view with distrust some of the techniques suggested here. But if judges (or magistrates) will serve as Howard Raiffa's "analytic mediators" (i.e., asking questions to explore the parties' interests and attempting to fashion tailor-made solutions from an "objective" outside-of-the-problem position, but with additional information), then judicial and magistrate settlement managers may be providing both better and more efficient (in the Pareto optimal sense) solutions to litigation problems.

Judges who perform these functions are not necessarily mediators, though they are frequently called that by themselves and others. Strictly speaking, a mediator facilitates communication between the parties and helps them to reach their own solution. As a mediator becomes more directly involved in suggesting the substantive solution, his or her role can change and he or she can become an arbitrator or adjudicator. It appears that the role judges and magistrates assume in many settlement conferences is this hybrid form of med-arb. Med-arb uses all the techniques associated with mediation and arbitration—caucusing (meeting with the parties separately), making suggestions to the parties, allowing closed or best-offer bidding, and meeting with principals (clients) who have authority to settle or to reconsider and reconceive the problem. As the med-arb process moves toward arbitration, "settlements" may closely resemble adjudication with rationalized, normative, or law-based solutions.

To the extent that settlement procedures are used to achieve substantive outcomes that are better than court-defined remedies, they have implications for how the settlement conference should be conducted and who should conduct it. First, those with knowledge about the larger implications of the litigation—the parties—should be present (this is the principle behind the mini-trial concept with business personnel in attendance) to offer or accept solutions that involve more than simple money settlements. Second, such conferences should be managed by someone other than the trial judge so that interests and considerations that might effect a settlement but would be inadmissible in court will not prejudice a later trial. Some argue for a separate "settlement officer" because the skills required for guiding negotiations are different from those required for trying cases. Third, some cases in which issues should not be traded off should not be subjected to the settlement process at all. For example, in employment discrimination cases, parties should not be asked to accept monetary settlements in lieu of a job for which they are qualified. Finally, a more traditional mediator's role may be more appropriate when the substantive process (i.e., direct communication between the parties) may be more important than the substantive outcome (i.e., employment disputes, some civil rights cases).

2. Protecting Confidentiality in Mediation

As we discuss in greater detail below in the context of settlement privilege, the promise of confidentiality has long been a traditional vehicle for encouraging candour, compromise, and, ultimately, settlement among parties to a dispute. As a result, we are seeing the infusion of confidentiality provisions into various case management components, including pre-trial conferences and mandatory mediation. The concern is to find a way of protecting the communications in those sessions from being revealed in the continued litigation of the action when settlement attempts prove unsuccessful. Yet is this protection not contrary to the fundamental principle of the trial process that encourages the disclosure of all relevant evidence in a dispute in order to ensure the integrity of the administration of justice?

Below, Watson Hamilton discusses the necessity for confidentiality in court-annexed mediation schemes, focusing on the models implemented in Ontario and Saskatchewan in her examination of this fundamental tension between mediation and adjudication.

J. Watson Hamilton, "Protecting Confidentiality in Mandatory Mediation: Lessons from Ontario and Saskatchewan"
(1999), 24 *Queen's Law Journal* 561, at 569-75 (footnotes omitted)

The Need for Legal Protection of Confidentiality

Almost all experts in the mediation field agree that some degree of legal protection for confidentiality is necessary. The necessity derives directly from the process of mediation itself. In the Ontario program, mediation is described as a process in which "a neutral third party *facilitates communication* among the parties to a dispute, to assist them in reaching a mutually acceptable resolution." The collaborative, integrative, problem-solving focus of mediation depends upon the participants disclosing their underlying interests and needs, rather than just their bargaining positions or demands. It is the identification of the substantive, procedural and psychological interests of the parties, and the education of each party about the others' interests, that is the key to this process. It is only after the parties' interests have been revealed and explored that the parties can begin a mutual search for solutions that will meet their needs.

A process that seeks to uncover the parties' substantive procedural and psychological interests and needs is a process that requires candour from its participants. The parties need that information in order to assess the strengths and weaknesses of the other side's case, as well as their own. They may need to admit facts adverse to their own case. An apology or acceptance of responsibility might be needed to satisfactorily settle a dispute. Mediation is also a process in which the information considered relevant to resolving a dispute includes information not considered *legally* relevant to the issues in the dispute. When a mediator encourages parties to discuss their motives, needs and psychological interests, the discussion may range far from the specific legal issues in dispute.

This need for candour among parties and between parties and the mediator is usually the first reason advanced for providing legal protection for confidentiality. Candour is facilitated by credible assurances of confidentiality and the consistent refusal to allow confidential communications to be used in subsequent legal proceedings. An oft-quoted passage from an older American case puts it thus:

> The guarantee of confidentiality permits and encourages [participants] to discuss matters in an uninhibited fashion … . If participants cannot rely on the confidential treatment of everything that transpires during these sessions then [they] of necessity will feel constrained to

conduct themselves in a cautious, tight-lipped, non-committal manner more suitable to a poker game than to adversaries attempting to arrive at a just resolution of a civil dispute.

[*Lake Utopia Paper Ltd. v. Connelly Containers Inc.*, 608 F2d 928, at 929-30 (2d Cir. 1979).]

Confidentiality, and its protection, is even more important in mandatory programs where mediation is annexed to a court or administrative proceeding. The parties may fear that if they do not reach agreement, anything they say may be reported back to the court or agency. This fear may be caused by the compulsory nature of mediation as by its placement as a step in legal proceedings. It may be further aggravated if the mandatory mediation program requires mediators to file some type of report with courts or administrative agencies to indicate compliance or non-compliance with the rule or statute mandating the mediation. Certificates of non-compliance, required by both the Ontario and Saskatchewan programs, do little more than indicate the name of the non-complying party. However, Ontario's program also requires a report on all mediations from all mediators under the program. In addition, if mediators cannot guarantee confidentiality for communications made during court-annexed mediation, or clearly and comprehensively describe the limits to confidentiality, the parties may be cautious about what they reveal. Caution, in this context, could render the mediation process a mere formality.

Closely related to the argument that confidentiality promotes candour, and this effective problem-solving in mediation, is an ethical argument based on the need for trust in mediation:

In normal, interpersonal relationships, trust is built upon past positive experiences. Conversely, in mediation, *two people who know from past experience they should not trust each other are thrust together against their will* and expected to give their most immediate enemy the tools needed to cause great emotional pain and financial damage. As a result, confidentiality facilitates mediation in the same way trust facilitates friendship. Confidentiality deprives the disputants of the ability to use the information they gain to the detriment of the other party.

This aspect of the candour argument is particularly *apropos* in the context of mandatory mediation. Parties who volunteer to meet with each other and a mediator to facilitate the negotiation and resolution of their dispute have already indicated some measure of trust. On the other hand, parties who appear for mediation under the Ontario and Saskatchewan programs are parties who have filed legal claims and defences. They are in an adversarial relationship. Confidentiality needs to be predictably and consistently protected to justify trusting that the others involved in the process will act benevolently and not harmfully.

The candour justification for protection and confidentiality rests on the dual basis of ensuring the integrity of the process and protecting the interests of the particular participants. Integrity of the mediation process is the sole basis of the second reason for protecting confidentiality in mediation: the need for the mediator to appear neutral and impartial. This appearance of neutrality is necessary to protect the integrity of the mediation process and is seen as essential to the effectiveness of mediation. Mediators have no authority to compel testimony or the production of documents. They cannot even require parties to remain at the bargaining table or to participate wholeheartedly. If a mediator were perceived to be partial toward one party, the requisite candour, trust and even participation in the process by the other party or parties would likely be jeopardized. If a mediator was perceived to be biased toward a particular resolution of the dispute, a party favouring another resolution would see no reason to remain in mediation.

The focus on this justification for protection of confidentiality is not on protecting mediators from the "burden" of testifying. Nor is it on the status or ability of any one mediator to attract and retain clients. Instead, the point of fostering the appearance of neutrality and impartiality is to promote the whole-hearted use of mediation, and especially court-annexed mediation, as an effective and fair method of dispute resolution. If mediators are witnesses in legal proceedings, and if production of their notes and records is compelled, then the evidence that they give is likely to favour one side over another. Then, no matter how impartial and neutral the mediator might have been in fact, he or she will be perceived or suspected of favouritism:

> A mediator's testimony, no matter how truthful or unbiased, is likely to be perceived as harmful by one or more of the parties. Since mediators generally make no formal record of the mediation, they will have difficulty testifying as to the specific statements made. Under such circumstances, the mediator's testimony is likely to be interpretive or evaluative, rather than descriptive, heightening the risk that the parties will view the mediator as biased after the fact. A party who viewed the mediator as neutral during the mediation is likely to alter her view if the testifying mediator reveals "damaging" mediation information.

The mediator neutrality justification for the protection of confidentiality is therefore a means to an end: the preservation of the effectiveness of the mediator in subsequent mediations, the program with which they are affiliated, and the mediation process itself for future disputes. This rationale is more persuasive in connection with mandatory mediation. Unlike most settlement negotiations and most confidential relationships, the facilitation of negotiation by a mediator and professional relationship with a mediator are not chosen by the parties. In any process forced upon parties, they must have confidence in the integrity of the process and those who have a major role in it. One of the results of requiring mediators to testify or produce documents may be a perception that the mediator, the program or the process itself does not keep confidences. While such a perception might normally cause parties to avoid mediation, they cannot do so where it is mandatory. They might, however, treat mediation as a mere formality.

Treating mediation as a formality would frustrate the goals of annexing it to the legal system. The goals of mandatory mediation include efficiency improvements for court systems and administrators by relieving case load pressures and reducing delay and cost for litigants, qualitative improvements for participants through more satisfying or more appropriate procedures and outcomes, relationship preservation and improvement and community and responsibility building. Indeed, if participation in mandatory mediation becomes merely an empty gesture, then the legal system will become less efficient, and the parties less satisfied rather than more.

These then are the most compelling reasons for protecting confidentiality in mediation. Just how compelling they are perceived to be, weighed against the need for all relevant evidence in legal proceedings to ensure the proper administration of justice, affects all decisions in this area.

NOTES

In the balance of her article, Watson Hamilton concludes that the mandatory mediation models implemented in both Ontario and Saskatchewan provide inadequate confidentiality protection of communications made during a mediation session. In the case of Ontario, she argues that rule 24.1 has essentially adopted the common law "without prejudice" exception rule of evidence and, as a result, retains the same significant flexibility of and exceptions to the common law doctrine. Her claim is that this flexibility leads to uncertainty and unpredictability in the application of the rule, permitting substantial judicial discretion in balancing the public interest in disclosure against the future credibility of the mandatory mediation process.

In Saskatchewan, confidentiality protection within the mandatory mediation model is provided through a blanket statutory privilege that, on its face, provides total protection from any disclosure of mediation communication. Again, Watson Hamilton claims that there exists room for exceptions to this privilege to be read in on a case-by-case basis, thereby removing from the statute an advantage it might have had, on its face, over Ontario's provision based in the common law.

The Ontario Court of Appeal considered this very issue in the context of an appeal from a contempt finding against a party to a mandatory mediation who subsequently published in a newspaper an article reporting on the mediation session.

Rogacki v. Belz
(2003), 67 OR (3d) 330 (CA)

[Reasons for judgment delivered by Borins JA (Armstrong JA concurring). Separate reasons delivered by Abella JA.]

BORINS JA: The appellant, Zbigniew Belz, appeals from an order of Brennan J holding him in contempt of court in respect of a breach of confidentiality arising from a mandatory mediation conducted pursuant to Rule 24.1 of the *Rules of Civil Procedure*. The mediation took place in the context of a libel action brought by the respondent concerning certain articles published in a Polish language newspaper known as Gazeta, of which the appellant was the editor and publisher. For the reasons that follow, I would allow the appeal.

The Facts

The mediation session took place on January 15, 2002. The mediator was William R. McMurtry. The parties and their lawyers were present. Prior to the commencement of the mediation, counsel for the parties signed what the court was told was a standard form mediation agreement. Clause 4 of the agreement reads as follows:

4. Confidentiality
The mediator will not disclose to anyone who is not a party to the mediation any information or documents submitted to the mediator, EXCEPT:

(a) to the lawyers, or any experts retained by the parties, as deemed appropriate by the mediator;

(b) where ordered to do so by judicial authority or where required to do so by law;

(c) with the written consent of all parties.

The parties agree that they will not require the mediator to testify in court, to submit any report for use in legal proceedings or otherwise to disclose any written or oral communication that has taken place during the mediation.

Mr. McMurtry explained to the parties that it was fundamental to the mediation process that discussions forming part of it be kept confidential. At the end of the mediation agreement he added in handwriting the following clause, which was signed by the parties:

The parties agree that everything that is said or done in the mediation is strictly confidential and privileged, and no reference will be made to anyone other than the parties or their solicitors of anything that is said during the process.

On January 16, 2002, the appellant wrote and published in Gazeta an article reporting on the mediation session which reads, in part, as follows [English translation]:

No reconciliation was reached in the action brought against Gazeta and its Editors Alicja Gettlich and Zbigniew Belz.

After a mediation session that lasted for a few hours last Tuesday, Ms. Elzbieta Rogacka, the Plaintiff (let us refresh our memory: a private action taken, corporate money used) rejected the Gazeta editors' proposal which might have served as a basis for reconciliation of the parties.

On January 28, 2002, the appellant was examined for discovery. Subsequently, he wrote and published a lengthy article in Gazeta in which he described his experience on being examined for discovery and recalled the content of some of the questions he was asked by the respondent's counsel. In addition, the appellant provided editorial comments concerning some of the questions.

The Contempt Motion

On the basis of the two articles, the respondent moved for the following orders:

1. An order that the defendant, Zbigniew Belz, be found in contempt of court for breach of Rule 24.1.14 of the *Rules of Civil Procedure* and the Confidentiality Agreement which guard the confidentiality of Mediations;

2. An order that the defendant, Zbigniew Belz, be found in contempt of court for breach of the deemed undertaking rule.

She gave as grounds for her motion, rules 24.1.14, 30.1.01, 60.05 and 60.11 of the Rules of Civil Procedure and the "Confidentiality Provision" that Mr. McMurtry added to the mediation agreement. Rule 30.1 is the deemed undertaking rule.

In his affidavit in response to the motion, the appellant discussed the two articles. In respect to the first article, he stated:

7. In the meantime a mediation was held on January 15, 2002, which lasted four hours. I was present, along with Mr. Czuma, Mrs. Gettlich, Mrs. Rogacki, two lawyers for Mrs. Rogacki and Mr. McMurtry, the mediator. A great deal was said during those four hours, some of it intemperate since the matters in issue provoked strong emotions on both sides. I did sign the Confidentiality Agreement, and whatever I did write, I did not include any details whatsoever about what was discussed, although a great deal was discussed, and the experience was a very emotional one for everyone concerned.

8. Gazeta is published five times a week, Monday to Thursday as a regular edition, and on Friday the weekly edition comes out, which includes a supplement. The mediation took place on January 15. The Article appeared in the next day's issue of Gazeta and consisted of a very brief report about the mediation, certainly nothing in terms of length with respect to details of what occurred. We were interested in settling the claim, and I was frustrated that it had not been settled. I do not believe that what I wrote is a contempt of court and was certainly never intended to be an insult to the court and, in my view, does not violate the Confidentiality Agreement.

In respect of the second article, the appellant stated:

11. Prior to writing the article, I was completely unaware that I was unable to report on this part of the court proceeding. There was no confidentiality agreement signed in advance and neither Mr. Bell, nor my own lawyer, told me that I could not write about my experiences on the Examination for Discovery. I found it an interesting experience, which I thought might interest my readers, who have been following the progress of this law suit in our pages. Had I known that I should not write about it, I certainly would not have written about it and I will never do so again. I did not intend any insult towards the court. As far as I was aware it was a court proceeding, and it could be made public. If there was any offence in what I did, I certainly apologize to the court, but it was entirely unintended. Perhaps Mr. Czuma would not suspect that I would write such an article, but he certainly did not tell me that I could not write such an article. Since he has told me, I have certainly not written any other articles about what happens at the discovery, or released any other confidential information.

The Motion Judge's Reasons

The motion judge found the appellant in contempt of court in respect to the first article, but not in respect to the second article.

In his endorsement, the motion judge wrote:

Motion granted. I find the defendant Belz in contempt of court in respect of his breach of the confidentiality of the mediation process. The importance of maintaining that confidentiality is demonstrated by the content of the Rule, elevating "all communications at a mediation session" to (*deemed*) without prejudice discussions. Further emphasis of that importance should have been apparent to Belz from the fact that the mediator insisted on the parties signing an express agreement on the matter.

I am not satisfied *that publication of information about his own examination for discovery* falls within the prohibition found now in Rule 30.1 and the deemed undertaking rule as I accept the submission made on his behalf that he consents to its use as Rule 30.1.01(4) provides. Even if some of the information published about his examination does not fall within such consent, I am not satisfied of his wilfulness in that regard, as contempt relief would require.

As suggested by counsel I am limiting my decision at this point to the finding that Belz's conduct amounts to contempt of court and requires that the court exercise some control of his conduct relating to the process of the court in the future [emphasis added].

In a subsequent endorsement, the motion judge imposed the following sanction on the appellant to "remedy" his contempt:

To remedy his contempt I order that Mr. Belz conform with the confidentiality provisions of the Rules of Civil Procedure and that he cause to be published on the front page of Gazeta the following text, without comment. The Polish version is to be provided by a translator mutually acceptable to counsel, in accordance with their agreement at the hearing before me on June 11, 2002.

> *Rogacki v. Belz, Gazeta and Gettlich:*
> Publisher Belz found to be in contempt of court.
>
> In the case of *Rogacki v. Belz, Gazeta and Gettlich* a motion was brought asking the court to find that Zbigniew Belz was in contempt of court. On May 29, 2002 the Superior Court of Justice granted the motion, finding that Mr. Belz was in contempt in allowing the publication of an article in Gazeta No. 11 on January 16, 2002 entitled "The case of the President of the National Council of the Canadian-Polish Congress v. Gazeta: No Reconciliation So Far." *The court found that publication of the story was a willful breach of confidentiality requirements of its Rules of Civil Procedure.*
>
> Mr. Belz has been ordered to conform *with the confidentiality provisions of the Rules of Civil Procedure* and to pay court costs in the amount of $11,700.00 plus GST and disbursements to indemnify the plaintiff in respect of her costs of the motion [emphasis added].

In addition, the motion judge ordered that the respondent be awarded costs on a substantial indemnity basis.

The following paragraphs of the formal judgment of the court are also relevant:

1. THIS COURT ORDERS that the defendant Zbigniew Belz is in contempt of court in respect of breach of confidentiality of the mediation process.

3. THIS COURT ORDERS that the defendant Zbigniew Belz pay costs in the amount of $11,700.00 plus GST in the amount of $819.00 plus disbursements in the amount of $380.34 for a total of $12,899.34 to the plaintiff forthwith and in any event of the cause.

4. THIS COURT ORDERS that the defendant Zbigniew Belz cause to be published on the front page of the weekend edition of Gazeta the text attached as Schedule A hereto as translated into Polish, without comment.

5. THIS COURT ORDERS that the defendant Zbigniew Belz conform with the confidentiality provisions of the Rules of Civil Procedure.

Relevant Rules of Civil Procedure

The following rules are relevant to this appeal:

Rule 24.1

24.1.14 All communications at a mediation session and the mediator's notes and records shall be deemed to be without prejudice settlement discussions.

Rule 30.1

30.1.01 (1) This Rule applies to,

    (a) evidence obtained under,

. . .

       (ii) Rule 31 (examination for discovery),

. . .

    (b) information obtained from evidence referred to in clause (a).

. . .

(3) All parties and their counsel are deemed to undertake not to use evidence or information to which this Rule applies for any purposes other than those of the proceeding in which the evidence was obtained.

(4) Subrule (3) does not prohibit a use to which the person who disclosed the evidence consents.

Rule 60

60.05 *An order requiring a person to do an act, other than the payment of money, or to abstain from doing an act,* may be enforced against the person refusing or neglecting to obey the order by a contempt order under rule 60.11.

60.11(1) A contempt order to *enforce an order requiring a person to do an act, other than the payment of money, or abstain from doing an act,* may be obtained only on motion to a judge *in the proceeding in which the order to be enforced was made.*

(5) In disposing of a motion under subrule (1) the judge may make such order as is just, and where a finding of contempt is made, the judge may order that the person in contempt,

    (a) be imprisoned for such period and on such terms as are just;

    (b) be imprisoned if he or she fails to comply with a term of the order;

    (c) pay a fine;

    (d) do or refrain from doing an act;

    (e) pay such costs as are just; and

    (f) comply with any other order that the judge considers necessary,

and may grant leave to issue a writ of sequestration under rule 60.09 against the person's property [emphasis added].

The Issues

In the respondent's notice of motion for the contempt order she relied on Rule 60 of the *Rules of Civil Procedure.* In my view, the respondent's reliance on Rule 60 raises the issue of the availability of the contempt power in the circumstances of this case, primarily because of the language of rules 60.05 and 60.11(1), which are parts of Rule 60, which is entitled "Enforcement of Orders." Rule 60.05 provides for the enforcement of "an order requiring a person to do an act ... or to abstain from doing an act ... by a contempt order under Rule 60.11." Rule 60.11(1) provides for a contempt order to enforce compliance with such an order "on a motion to a judge in the proceeding in which the order to be enforced was made." It is also apparent from the language of rule 60.11(5), which contains the sanctions that the court may impose where a finding of contempt is made, that the focus of the contempt power in Rule 60 is the failure of an individual to comply with an order made by the court. (Under Rule 1.03 "order" includes a judgment.) In this case, no order had been made that was enforceable under Rule 60.

In seeking the order under appeal, it was the respondent's position that in publishing the article reporting on the result of the mandatory mediation session the appellant was in contempt of court because he was in breach of both rule 24.1.14 and the "Confidentiality Provision" that was added to the mediation agreement. Thus, the first issue to be decided is whether either rule 24.1.14 or the "Confidentiality Provision" is an order within the meaning of Rule 60 and, therefore, capable of enforcement under that rule by a contempt order.

If, however, I am of the opinion that neither rule 24.1.14 nor the "Confidentiality Provision" is an order within the meaning of Rule 60, I think that the inherent jurisdiction of the court to invoke the contempt power should be considered if that jurisdiction forms a basis for the order under appeal, notwithstanding the fact that the respondent relied on Rule 60 and not on the inherent jurisdiction of the court. Although, as Morden JA pointed out in *Forrest v. Lacroix Estate* (2000), 48 OR (3d) 619 at para. 23 (CA), rule 60.11(1) "is intended to occupy the field in proceedings under the *Rules of Civil Procedure* relating to the enforcement of court orders which require an act to be done," the inherent jurisdiction of the court may be exercised to invoke the contempt power where the impugned conduct does not involve a failure to comply with a court order. See *R v. Bunn* (1994), 97 Man. R (2d) 20 (CA); *R v. Vermette*, [1987] 1 SCR 577. In the circumstances of this case, under the inherent jurisdiction of the court, the second issue then becomes whether the articles written and published by the appellant, or either of them, constitute a contempt of court as recognized by the Canadian authorities.

The Rule 60 Issue

In my opinion, Rule 60 was not available to the respondent as the foundation for a contempt order based on the article written and published by the appellant reporting on the result of the mandatory mediation session. Rule 60, and in particular rules 60.05 and 60.11(1), by their plain language provide for a contempt order to enforce a court order. There was no order of the court prohibiting the publication of the article. Indeed, in her notice of motion the respondent did not rely on the appellant's breach of a court order. The grounds for her motion were "breach of Rule 24.1.14 ... and the Confidentiality Agreement" signed by the parties at the outset of the mediation session. The respondent has provided no authority that the breach of a rule of court or a private agreement is equivalent to an order of the court within the meaning of Rule 60, and I have been unable to locate any such authority. The *Rules of Civil Procedure* contain many sanctions where a party has failed to comply with a rule of court. In the few instances where a contempt order is provided as a sanction for failing to comply with a rule, as in rules 34.15(2) and 69.14(9), such sanction is expressly provided. Had the Civil Rules Committee, in the exercise of its powers under s. 66(2)(s) of the *Courts of Justice Act*, RSO 1990, c. C.43, intended to provide that the contempt power may be used to enforce the obligations imposed on litigants under rule 24.1, it would have done so expressly.

In my respectful opinion, the motion judge not only misapprehended the contempt power contained in Rule 60, but he also misinterpreted rule 24.1.14. As I understand his reasons, as reflected in paragraph 1 of the formal order of the court, the motion judge appeared to interpret rule 24.1.14 as providing for the "confidentiality of the mediation process." (A similar misapprehension of rule 24.1.14 is reflected in paragraph 5 of the order which required the appellant to "conform with the confidentiality provisions of the *Rules of Civil Procedure*.") This is not what rule 24.1.14 states, nor is there any other subrule within Rule 24.1 that addresses the confidentiality of the mandatory mediation process. By deeming "all communications at a mediation session and the mediator's notes and records ... to be without prejudice settlement discussions," rule 24.1.14 codifies the principle that communications made without prejudice in an attempt to resolve a dispute are not admissible in evidence unless they result in a concluded resolution of the dispute. As such, rule 24.1.14 is a necessary ingredient of Rule 24.1 as it furthers the public interest in promoting free and frank settlement discussions by protecting communications for that purpose from compelled disclosure in subsequent proceedings involving the parties to the settlement discussions, such as discovery or trial, in circumstances where the mediation fails to resolve the litigation. In this regard, Clause 4 of the mediation agreement is consistent with the purpose of rule 24.1.14. Another rule, which serves a purpose similar to rule 24.1.14 is rule 50.03 which precludes disclosure of communications made at a pre-trial hearing at a subsequent trial or motion. See *Bell Canada v. Olympia & York Developments Ltd.* (1994), 17 OR (3d) 135 (CA).

The Inherent Jurisdiction Issue

Having found that a motion for a contempt order under Rule 60 was not available to the respondent in respect of the article published by the appellant reporting on the result of the mandatory mediation session, I turn to whether the inherent jurisdiction of the court may be exercised to sanction the appellant for publishing the article. I will include within my analysis the second article, in respect of which the respondent had unsuccessfully sought a contempt order under Rule 60 on the ground that its publication was in breach of Rule 30.1, the deemed undertaking rule. In this article, the appellant discussed his experience when he was examined for discovery. Although there is no cross-appeal from the dismissal of the contempt motion respecting this article, in her factum the respondent suggested that the publication of the article infringed Rule 30.1. In my view the motion judge was correct in dismissing the contempt motion for reasons that I will outline subsequently.

For the appellant to be found in contempt of court in respect of either article, the respondent was required to prove that the appellant did the relevant act (*actus reus*) with the necessary intent (*mens rea*). There is no doubt that the appellant published the articles. However, to complete the *actus reus* it was also necessary for the respondent to prove that the articles had some significant adverse effect on the administration of justice. If the respondent proved the *actus reus*, it would then be necessary for her to prove that the appellant published the articles with the necessary intent.

There are many forms of contempt of court. The publication of the two articles comes closest to that form of contempt embraced by the *sub judice* rule, which seeks to avoid prejudicing the fair trial of pending litigation by precluding the publication of material that would have that effect. As such, the *sub judice* rule represents the intersection of two principles of fundamental importance: freedom of expression, and the rule of law which precludes interference with the administration of justice. As stated by Jeffrey Miller in *The Law of Contempt in Canada* (Scarborough, Ont.: Carswell, 1997) at pp. 101-102, the leading case in Canada on this subject remains *Attorney General v. Times Newspapers Ltd.*, [1973] 3 All ER 54 (HL), from which the author extracted the following principles to be considered in assessing an impugned pre-trial publication:

(1) The issues must not be prejudged in a manner likely to affect the mind of the trier of fact.
(2) Contempt exists only if there is a real risk of prejudice as opposed to a mere possibility of interference with the due administration of justice.
(3) The rule applies even if the litigation is in a quiescent stage, such as during protracted settlement discussions.

Although civil contempts, as in this case, and criminal contempts take a variety of forms, it is important to emphasize that each involves an interference with the due administration of justice. Indeed, contempt of court, both civil and criminal, has existed for centuries. It is the mechanism used by the court to ensure compliance with its orders and to protect its process. As such, it is a sanction that serves the administration of justice in the public interest.

It is helpful to repeat what was said by Dickson CJC in *BCGEU v. British Columbia (Attorney General)*, [1988] 2 SCR 214 at 234:

> In some instances the phrase "contempt of court" may be thought to be unfortunate because, as in the present case, it does not posit any particular aversion, abhorrence or disdain of the judicial system. In a legal context the phrase is much broader than the common meaning of "contempt" might suggest and embraces "where a person, whether a party to a proceeding or not, does any act which may tend to hinder the course of justice or show disrespect to the court's authority," "interfering with the business of the court on the part of a person who has no right to do so," "obstructing or attempting to obstruct the officers of the Court on their way to their duties": see *Jowitt's Dictionary of English Law*, 2nd ed., vol. 1, at p. 441.

I find nothing in the record that would support a finding of contempt with respect to either article. As for the first article, it reported that a mandatory mediation session had taken place that did not result in a settlement of the respondent's claim. The second article was concerned with the appellant's perception of his examination for discovery interspersed with some comments critical of the questions that he had been asked. Although it would have been better in the circumstances of this hotly contested litigation had the appellant not published the articles, as I have explained, I find nothing in Rule 24.1 that precluded him from publishing the first article. Nor, as I will explain, did Rule 30.1 preclude him from publishing the second article. As he explained in his affidavit, in writing the articles he did not intend an insult to the court. In my view, each article has not been demonstrated to constitute a contempt of court. There is nothing in either article that was prejudicial to the respondent and that could have compromised a fair trial. Indeed, the respondent presented no evidence to that end.

Earlier I expressed agreement with the motion judge's dismissal of the contempt motion arising from the appellant's publication of the article about his own examination for discovery. However, in my view the motion judge was not correct in dismissing the motion on the application of rule 30.1.01(4) which, as I will explain, in the circumstances of this case does not apply.

This motion was brought on the ground that the article was in "breach of the deemed undertaking rule," which is Rule 30.1. The motion judge dismissed the motion because he was of the view "that the appellant's publication of information about his own examination for discovery" did not fall "within the prohibition found now in Rule 30.1 and the deemed undertaking rule." He was further of the view that because the appellant "consented" to the "use" of the information, rule 30.1(4) permitted its use for purposes other than those of the proceedings in which the information was obtained.

In my view, the motion judge was correct in concluding that the deemed undertaking provided by rule 30.1(3) did not apply in the circumstances of this case. The deemed, or implied, undertaking rule at common law was thoroughly discussed by Morden ACJO on behalf of this court in *Goodman v. Rossi* (1995), 24 OR (3d) 359 (CA). As explained in *Rossi*, there is an implied undertaking by the discovering party to a proceeding to whom testimony or documents are provided by the discovered party in the course of the discovery process that he or she will not use such information for purposes other than those of the proceeding in which the testimony or documents were obtained. Because the undertaking is to the court, its breach gives rise to direct sanctions that a court may impose, such as a finding of contempt of court, and can be relieved or modified by an order of the court. See, also, *Orfus Realty v. D.G. Jewellery of Canada Ltd.* (1995), 24 OR (3d) 379 (CA). Subsequent to the decision in *Rossi*, and based on it, the Civil Rules Committee introduced Rule 30.1.

The documents and testimony obtained from the discovered party are protected by the deemed undertaking from improper use by the discovering party. Under Rule 30.1 the discovered party is not constrained from any use of his testimony or the documents elicited by the discovering party. It is the discovering party's use of information obtained from the discovered party for a purpose other than that of the litigation in which it was obtained that is precluded by Rule 30.1. See *Tanner v. Clark* (2003), 63 OR (3d) 508 (CA). It follows, as the appellant was the discovered party, that in publishing the article recounting his experience on being examined for discovery he did not infringe Rule 30.1. In the circumstances, therefore, rule 30.1.01(4) has no application. Nevertheless, the motion judge correctly dismissed the contempt motion based on the publication of the discovery article.

I would apply the following passage from the reasons of Dubin JA in *R v. Kopyto* (1987), 62 OR (2d) 449 at 525-526 (CA) to the circumstances of this case:

It was essential for the Crown to prove that the statement made by the appellant was calculated to bring the administration of justice into disrepute. That is the *actus reus* of this offence. The mere fact that the words are capable of bringing the administration of justice into
disrepute does not suffice. What must be shown is that, by reason of the statement made by
the appellant, there was a serious risk that the administration of justice would be interfered
with. The risk of prejudice must be serious, real or substantial.

To this I would add the following passage written by Lord Reid in *Times Newspapers
Ltd.*, *supra*, at p. 60, quoted with approval by Dubin JA in *Kopyto* at p. 512:

> The law on this subject is and must be founded entirely on public policy. It is not there to
> protect the private rights of parties to a litigation or prosecution. It is there to prevent inter-
> ference with the administration of justice and it should in my judgment be limited to what
> is reasonably necessary for that purpose. Public policy generally requires a balancing of in-
> terests which may conflict. *Freedom of speech should not be limited to any greater extent than
> is necessary but it cannot be allowed where there would be real prejudice to the administration
> of justice* [emphasis added by Dubin JA].

I find nothing in either article that even suggests the risk of serious, real or substantial
prejudice to the administration of justice.

I conclude with the observation, found in many of the authorities, that it is a serious
matter for a person to be found in contempt of court. Even in a case of civil contempt
such as this, a contempt proceeding is punitive in nature with broad powers given to the
court including the power to order imprisonment. Because of the criminal nature of
contempt proceedings, the person who is its object has many of the safeguards accorded
a person accused of a criminal offence. The onus is on the applicant to prove its case
beyond a reasonable doubt. See *Bhatnager v. Canada (Minister of Employment and Immigration)*, [1990] 2 SCR 217. Given the gravity of a finding of contempt, the court's
contempt power should be exercised with scrupulous care and only when the circumstances are clear and beyond reasonable doubt.

Result

For the foregoing reasons, I would allow the appeal with costs, set aside paragraphs 1, 3,
4 and 5 of the order of the motion judge, and in their place make an order dismissing in
its entirety the respondent's motion for contempt with costs. The parties are to address
the costs of the motion and the appeal by way of written submissions. The appellant is to
provide the Senior Legal Officer with his submissions on costs and his bill of costs within
15 days from the release of these reasons. The respondent may file her submissions within 7 days after the receipt of the appellant's submissions. The appellant may respond
within 7 days thereafter.

ABELLA JA (concurring): I have had the benefit of reading the excellent reasons of
Borins JA. While I agree with his conclusions, I think this appeal raises important policy
questions about the mandatory mediation process.

Rule 24.1 compels parties to attend a mediation and to exchange information. Rule
24.1.14 provides that the settlement discussions are "without prejudice."

I agree with Borins JA that rule 24.1.14 does not create an enforceable guarantee of confidentiality, but that does not mean that there do not exist significant public policy reasons for keeping the mediation sessions confidential.

The purpose of protecting confidentiality in the mandatory mediation process is to further the public policy goal of encouraging settlement discussions. The particular significance of upholding confidentiality in mandatory mediation within the legal system is explained by Jonnette Watson Hamilton in her article, "Protecting Confidentiality in Mandatory Mediation: Lessons from Ontario and Saskatchewan" (1999) 24 *Queen's LJ* 561 at 574 as follows:

> In any process forced upon parties, they must have confidence in the integrity of the process and those who have a major role in it. One of the results of requiring mediators to testify or produce documents may be a perception that the mediator, the program or the process itself does not keep confidences. While such a perception might normally cause parties to avoid mediation, they cannot do so where it is mandatory. They might, however, treat mediation as a mere formality.
>
> Treating mediation as a formality would frustrate the goals of annexing it to the legal system. The goals of mandatory mediation include efficiency improvements for court systems and administrators by relieving case load pressures and reducing delay and cost for litigants, qualitative improvements for participants through more satisfying or more appropriate procedures and outcomes, relationship preservation and improvement and community and responsibility building. Indeed, if participation in mediation becomes merely an empty gesture, then the legal system will become less efficient, and the parties less satisfied rather than more. [citations omitted].

(See also *Canadian Broadcasting Corp. v. Paul* (2001), 198 DLR (4th) 633 at 643 (TD) per Sexton JA; *Owen v. Grey*, "Protecting the Confidentiality of Communications in Mediation" (1998) 36 *Osgoode Hall LJ* 667 at 677; David Vaver, "Without Prejudice Communications—Their Admissibility and Effect" (1974) 9 *UBCL Rev.* 85 at 94; and Lawrence Boulle and Kathleen Kelley, *Mediation: Principles, Process, Practice* (Markham: Butterworths, 1998)).

The failure to protect confidentiality could profoundly prejudice the effectiveness of mandatory mediation. It is difficult to see how anyone would agree to be open and frank in discussions designed to effect settlement—discussions they have no choice about participating in—when there is no protection for the confidentiality of the process.

A useful analogy can be made, it seems to me, with the implied undertaking found to be crucial to the integrity of the discovery process in *Goodman v. Rossi* (1995), 24 OR (3d) 359 (CA). This court held that much like an order, statutory rules for examinations for discovery require disclosure of relevant evidence, and as a result, the court can cite for contempt anyone who breaches an implied undertaking not to use discovery evidence for a collateral or ulterior purpose.

At p. 370 of *Goodman v. Rossi*, Morden ACJO explained the basis for the implied undertaking rule and the availability of contempt to sanction its breaches. Citing *Prudential Assurance Company v. Fountain Page Limited*, [1991] 1 WLR 756 at 764-65 (QB) per Hobhouse J, he said:

The rational basis for the rule is that where one party compels another, *either by the enforcement of a rule of court or a specific order of the court*, to disclose documents or information whether that other wishes to or not, the party obtaining the disclosure is given this power because the invasion of the other party's rights has to give way to the need to do justice between those parties in the pending litigation between them; it follows from this that the results of such compulsion should likewise be limited to the purpose for which the order was made, namely, the purposes of that litigation then before the court between those parties and not for any other litigation or matter or any collateral purpose: see, for example, per Lord Keith of Kinkel in *Home Office v. Harman* [1983] 1 AC 280, 308 [emphasis added].

Again referring to *Prudential, supra* at pp. 764-65, Morden ACJO aptly described the implied undertaking in connection with discoveries as follows at p. 370:

It is an obligation which arises from legal process and therefore is within the control of the court, gives rise to direct sanctions which the court may impose (*viz.* contempt of court) and can be relieved or modified by an order of the court.

Morden ACJO emphasized the necessity of having a contempt of court order available as a remedy to protect confidentiality during the discovery process at p. 371:

I think that there would be a serious gap in the range of possible sanctions for breach of the obligation not to make improper use of documents disclosed on discovery, if it were not associated with an implied undertaking to the court and, therefore, capable of giving rise to a contempt of court order.

This analysis is equally applicable to mandatory mediation, and, it seems to me, compels the same protection that the implied undertaking in discoveries affords. Just as parties to litigation are compelled by the discovery rules to disclose information they might not otherwise disclose, so too parties falling within the scope of Rule 24.1 are required to attend a mediation session and are required to submit certain information in the mediation process.

It is true that the purpose of mandatory mediation is to settle a dispute outside of the court's process, and, as in discovery, it is not conducted by a judge. But it is also true that aspects of mandatory mediation directly engage the court's process. First and foremost, the fact that mediation is mandated by the commencement of a proceeding under the rules, directly implicates the mediation in the court's process. Rule 24.1.09 provides that the mediation session shall take place within 90 days after the first defence has been filed. Rule 24.1.10 provides that at least seven days before the mediation, each party is to prepare a form that identifies the factual and legal issues in dispute, briefly sets out the position and interests of the party making the statement and, requires the "party making the statement [to] attach to it any documents that the party considers of central importance to the action."

In addition, Rule 24.1 sets out what conduct constitutes non-compliance: failure to provide a copy of a statement of issues to the mediator and the other parties; failure to provide a copy of the pleadings to the mediator and failure to attend within the first thirty minutes of the scheduled mediation session. Upon the occurrence of any of these events, a party files a certificate of non-compliance with the mediation co-ordinator, who then refers the matter to a case management master or judge who in turn can convene a case conference and make a number of orders pursuant to rule 24.1.13(2) such as an order striking pleadings, to pay costs, or "any other order that is just."

And while the mediation is mandatory, rule 24.1.05 provides that the court may make an order on a party's motion exempting its action from mandatory mediation, a course of conduct the courts have been rare to indulge. (See *O. (G.) v. H. (C.D.)* (2000), 50 OR (3d) 82 at 85 (SCJ)).

Mandatory mediation is a compulsory part of the court's process for resolving disputes in civil litigation. Wilful breaches of the confidentiality it relies on for its legitimacy, in my view, represent conduct that can create a serious risk to the full and frank disclosures the mandatory mediation process requires. It can significantly prejudice the administration of justice and, in particular, the laudable goal reflected in Rule 24.1 of attempting to resolve disputes effectively and fairly without the expense of a trial.

However, given the potential gravity of the consequences of a contempt finding, it should only be exercised, as Borins JA indicated, "when the circumstances are clear and beyond reasonable doubt." In the absence of a Rule or legislative provision explicitly declaring what most lawyers and participants to the mandatory mediation process likely assume, namely, that is confidential, no such clarity exists at this time sufficient to justify attracting so powerful a remedy.

I therefore agree with Borins JA that the appeal should be allowed.

NOTES AND QUESTIONS

In its consideration of the *Rogacki v. Belz* decision, the Ontario Superior Court of Justice in *Baker v. Zurich Canada* (2004), 68 OR (3d) 350 held that the existence of confidentiality as an implied term in mediation was a determination to be made contextually, on a case-by-case basis. While the court recognized the widely accepted importance of confidentiality as paramount to the mediation process, it was nevertheless unwilling to deem it an implied term unless the particular circumstances supported such a determination.

Most recently, the Ontario courts have considered the notion of a mediator's compulsion, notwithstanding norms of confidentiality, to provide evidence surrounding the terms of a settlement achieved through mediation. Could this line of reasoning lead to reduced candour in mediation, as parties and counsel face the possibility of a mediator becoming a witness to the mediation session itself and any settlement achieved?

In 2004, the case of *Rudd v. Trossacs Investments Inc.* (2006), 208 OAC 95, 79 OR (3d) 687, 265 DLR (4th) 718, 27 CPC (6th) 147, [2006] OJ No. 922 (SCJ) was heard by the Superior Court of Justice in Ontario. Justice Lederman notes as follows:

> On this motion, the plaintiffs seek an interim order requiring the mediator to give evidence as to what transpired at a mediation between the parties held on January 12 & 28, 2004, including the terms of the settlement reached. This is in aid of the plaintiffs' main motion which is in essence for rectification of the written minutes of settlement to correctly reflect the oral agreement arrived at in the mediation and for its enforcement. It is the position of the plaintiffs that the minutes of settlement, which were handwritten by the mediator with the input of counsel and executed at the mediation, inadvertently left out Morris Kaiser ("Kaiser") as a party to the settlement when, clearly, the intention was that he be made a party."

The defendants in the case denied that Mr. Kaiser was a party to the settlement, leaving Justice Lederman to consider the requirement of a mediator to give testimony about the contents of the mediation session that had led to the settlement. Referring to Justice Borins's decision in *Rogacki v. Belz*, Justice Lederman found that communications at a mediation session are not admissible "unless they result in a concluded resolution of the dispute." Therefore, given the settlement that had been achieved in the Rudd mediation, the mediator was ordered to be examined as a witness on the motion at bar.

On appeal to the Divisional Court (*Rudd v. Trossacs Investments Ltd.*, [2006] OJ No. 922), Justice Swinton delivered the decision after a careful analysis of the four conditions under which privilege can be attached to mediation communications, drawing on Wigmore's test. The court held that: (1) the communications made during the mediation originated in confidence, (2) confidentiality of communications in mediation is essential to its functioning, (3) there exists a significant public interest in protecting the confidentiality of mediation discussions, and (4) there was other evidence aside from the mediator's testimony to assist in determining the terms of the settlement. Using this reasoning, the Divisional Court allowed the appeal, denying the examination of the mediator as a witness. How do we begin to fairly balance the principles identified in Wigmore's test for attaching privilege to communications with the need for clarity when the terms of an agreed settlement are unclear?

3. Mediator Liability

J. Schulz, "Mediator Liability in Canada: An Examination of Emerging American and Canadian Jurisprudence"
(2001), 32 *Ottawa Law Review* 269 (footnotes omitted)

III. Mediator Liability in Canada

What are the circumstances in which Canadian mediators might be exposed to liability? As mentioned, mediators could attract civil liability for the unauthorized practice of law, breaching relevant statutes, breach of contract, or negligently performing their services.

A. Unauthorized Practice of Law

Drafting a mediation or settlement agreement may constitute the practice of law. If a mediator, in a purely facilitative fashion, captures the parties' own words of agreement in written form, the mediator is not practising law. The problem arises when mediators choose language and draft legally enforceable agreements themselves. "Once a facilitative mediator surpasses the secretarial role of memorializing the parties' agreement and makes editorial suggestions, the facilitative mediator is engaging in the practice of law." Therefore, if a non-lawyer mediator drafts a mediation agreement, it is quite likely that the non-lawyer mediator has crossed the line into the arena of legal practice, and could be held liable for the unauthorized practice of law.

What if a mediator who is also a lawyer drafts a mediation agreement? Lawyer-mediators who not only draft agreements, but also review them with an eye toward their legal sufficiency, have crossed the line and should be deemed to be practising law. In fact, because the participants to a mediation may expect such review from a lawyer-mediator, lawyer-mediators should exercise caution. All mediators should merely draft non-binding memoranda of understanding and allow counsel to use them as the bases for final, binding, mediation agreements.

In addition to drafting, advising can cause problems for mediators. If a non-lawyer-mediator provides legal advice during mediation it may constitute the unauthorized practice of law. "Laymen cannot practice evaluative mediation without practising law and, therefore, should not be permitted to do so." All mediators should ensure they do not dispense legal advice as that could be deemed the practice of law.

If a lawyer-mediator is deemed to be practising law instead of mediating, for example, by advising disputants, all of the standards of practice, codes of ethics, duties to clients, and legal and fiduciary duties of lawyers can then be imputed to that mediator. Most mediators, and certainly all facilitative mediators, do not wish to be held to the legal standards and duties of lawyers.

At least one American psychologist and one Canadian paralegal have been accused of the unauthorized practice of law for work done in their mediation practices. In *Werle v. Rhode Island Bar Association* [755 F2d 195 (1985)], the court examined divorce mediation and civil rights in the context of the unauthorized practice of law in the United States.

Dr Werle was a psychologist and professor of psychology experienced in family mediation working on Rhode Island. Dr Werle's business was called "Werle Consultants Family Mediation Center" and its services were described in a brochure. According to the brochure, the Center provided "'impartial mediation and arbitration service for divorcing couples,' assisting them in reaching agreement 'upon division of property, support and child custody.'" The Rhode Island Bar Association and members of its former Committee on Unauthorized Practice of Law agreed that the brochure and the practice described probably violated Rhode Island's laws. They sent Dr Werle a letter requesting that he discontinue his divorce mediation business on the grounds that it involved him in the unauthorized practice of law. After reading the letter the Committee sent to him, Dr Werle believed that the Committee on Unauthorised Practice of Law would recommend prosecution if he did not cease his practice. The Attorney General for Rhode Island refused to issue an opinion as to whether Werle's practice constituted the unauthorized practice of law. So, Dr Werle stopped mediating and sued the Rhode Island Bar Association and members of the Committee claiming they violated his First and Fourteenth Amendment rights to earn a living.

The court held that even if it was the threat of prosecution that stopped Dr Werle from offering divorce mediation services, allegedly in violation of laws prohibiting the unauthorized practice of law by non-lawyers, the Bar Association and its Committee were absolutely immune from damage liability under statute. The court found that the defendants' conduct "fell within the scope of the immunity, whether absolute or qualified, that they must have enjoyed if they were the state actors that Dr Werle claims they were." *Werle* demonstrates a clear intolerance in the United States for mediators who assist parties in tasks, such as division of property, traditionally done by lawyers.

The position in Canada is similar. In *R v. Boldt*, Ms Boldt, a paralegal working in Ontario, was accused of carrying on the unauthorized practice of law in contravention of the *Law Society Act*. The court found that there was enough evidence to suggest that she may have been practising law when she drafted a mediation agreement in a family dispute, and that it was proper to examine other alleged instances of her unauthorized practice of law to determine if a pattern existed.

> Now, it is completely appropriate for the crown [sic] to refer to other counts, where there may or may not have been convictions, to show a certain procedure being followed, to show a certain pattern, and say "Look, Ms Boldt did it this particular time and we encourage the court to find her guilty of this particular count because here is what she has done, here is her practice over the years, using pamphlets and so on and so forth without getting into the details." If it establishes a pattern, then the fact of course is relevant to shed some light on the situation which is currently before the court.

Thus, similar fact evidence was used for corroboration in a case wherein the unauthorized practice of law was alleged. This case demonstrates that if a mediator is accused of the unauthorized practice of law, Canadian courts can examine the mediator's past behaviour and brochures in order to reach a decision. If a pattern of similar behaviour exists, a conviction for the unauthorized practice of law is more likely.

In *Boldt*, a new trial was ordered to determine "whether or not the conduct alleged is indeed the practice of law or acting as a lawyer." As the decision of the court in the new trial is not yet known, Canadian non-lawyer mediators should operate under the assumption that drafting mediation agreements can constitute the unauthorized practice of law, which can lead to prosecution and liability.

B. Statutory Breach

One area of potential mediator liability that is rarely examined is statutory breach. While there are no reported complaints against Canadian mediators based upon statutory breach, there are provincial statutes, such as Ontario's *Business Practices Act*, that could be relevant to the practice of mediation. The *Business Practices Act* could be relevant because not only could a contravention of the Act lead to mediator liability, but breach of the *Business Practices Act* could be evidence of negligence.

The *Business Practices Act* states that an unconscionable consumer representation is an unfair practice, and that no person shall engage in an unfair practice. In order to determine whether a particular consumer representation is unconscionable, and therefore an unfair business practice, regard must be had to whether the person making the representation:

knows or ought to know,

    i. that the consumer is not reasonably able to protect his or her interests because of physical infirmity, ignorance, illiteracy, inability to understand the language of an agreement or similar factors,

. . .

v. that the proposed transaction is excessively one-sided in favour of someone other than the consumer,

vi. that the terms or conditions of the proposed transaction are so adverse to the consumer as to be inequitable,

vii. that he or she is making a misleading statement of opinion on which the consumer is likely to rely to his or her detriment,

viii. that he or she is subjecting the consumer to undue pressure to enter into the transaction.

Clearly, mediators could make unconscionable consumer representations and thereby engage in an unfair practice. For example, if a mediator knew that a disputant could not understand English, or ought to have known that the mediation agreement was one-sided, and that mediator concluded the mediation anyway, the mediator could be in breach of the *Business Practices Act*. If the transaction was inequitable, if the mediator made a misleading statement upon which the disputant relied, or if the mediator pressured a party to settle, that mediator could be liable to pay a large fine. "Every person who engages in an unfair practice ... knowing it to be an unfair practice is guilty of an offence and on conviction is liable to a fine of not more than $25,000 or to imprisonment for a term of not more than one year, or to both."

The *Business Practices Act* also addresses what happens to an agreement entered into by a consumer induced to enter the agreement by an unfair practice:

[A]ny agreement, whether written, oral or implied, entered into by a consumer after a consumer representation that is an unfair practice and that induced the consumer to enter into the agreement,

(a) may be rescinded by the consumer and the consumer is entitled to any remedy therefore that is at law available, including damages; or

(b) where rescission is not possible ... the consumer is entitled to recover the amount by which the amount paid under the agreement exceeds the fair value of the goods or services received under the agreement or damages, or both.

Thus, if a mediator facilitated a settlement between two parties, and it could be shown that one disputant settled due to reliance upon the mediator's opinion, that mediator would be in breach of the *Business Practices Act*, the settlement could be rescinded, and the disputant could receive damages. If a court of competent jurisdiction determined that the breach of statute also constituted evidence of negligence, the mediator could face tort liability as well. Clearly then, mediator liability for statutory breach, while yet untried, is an area worth further scholarly examination.

C. Breach of Contract

There have been no reported suits against Canadian or American mediators for breach of contract, despite the fact that "breach of contract claim has the best chances of success, but only if there is a contractual provision on point, and only if the plaintiff can show that the breach caused damage."

"[L]egally enforceable standards for practice can be established by contract between the mediator and the mediation participants," and therefore, if mediators wish to escape liability, they should be sure to adhere to all of the terms in their contracts to mediate. "The greatest concern should be to ensure that parties are not promised more than the process can deliver .... Risks as well as benefits to the process should be clearly outlined in the mediation agreement and promotional material." And, "[s]ince there can be no assurance that mediation will be better than the alternatives in any specific case, such representations should be avoided." Simply stated, if a mediator makes an express or implied promise about the process or results of mediation, the mediator could be contractually liable if the process or results differ from what was promised.

In addition to any promises mediators might make in their contracts to mediate, Canadian common law implies a term into all contracts that all services contracted for will be provided competently. Esquibel notes that "even if it is not an explicit term of any such contract [to mediate], neutrality and impartiality are such a fundamental aspect of what the parties seek that they should be considered a part of the contract. It is akin to courts implying terms of good faith and fair dealing in contracts." If a term to provide competent (or even impartial) service is implied in a contract to mediate, the mediator will be in breach of the contract if he or she fails to provide competent service. If a breach of a mediation contract occurs, the disputant, as always, is entitled to his or her provable damages.

Finally, some mediation contracts seek to exempt mediators from liability. For example, waivers are used to protect acts and omissions unless the act or omission is fraudulent. However, it remains to be seen how effective a waiver of responsibility in a mediation contract might be.

D. Negligence Liability

Mediators, like any other Canadian service providers, can be liable in negligence if their conduct creates an unreasonable, foreseeable risk of harm to those to whom they owe a duty of care. There are three main elements of the tort of negligence: a duty of care must exist between the parties; there must be a breach of the standard of care; and provable damages must result. Mediators are clearly in relationships of sufficient proximity to their disputants to ground a duty of care. There are also no policy reasons that would mitigate against establishing a duty upon mediators to take reasonable care not to injure disputants.

In fact, due to the reliance placed by disputants on mediators to help them, good policy strongly favours the establishment of a duty of care. However, due to the lack of uniform standards in the field, it is difficult to establish breach of the standard of care, as there is no agreement on what is the standard for proper mediation practice. Consequently, it can be difficult to prove a causal connection between breach of the standard of care and damages. To date, no Canadian or American mediator has been held liable in negligence.

Despite the difficulties of standard and of proof, it is theoretically possible to hold mediators liable for their negligent conduct. Tortious liability for mediators could stem from a negligent act or from a negligent misrepresentation that caused economic loss.

While tortious liability for mediator malpractice has yet to be successfully proved, grounding liability for mediator mistakes in negligence law is the best way to ensure quality of service and to compensate disputants for substandard mediator practice. Quite simply, civil liability may lead to improvements in mediation and in the quality of mediators.

The best method of assuring the quality of the neutrals and the ADR services they provide is to make the neutrals civilly liable for their actions and allow them the common law defences that already exist. The alternative of simply including neutrals under the umbrella of absolute judicial immunity only adds to the confusion.

Although American neutrals have been granted immunity for negligent conduct, the existence of immunity has not stopped allegations of mediator malpractice in the United States nor complaints against mediators in Canada.

4. Judicial Dispute Resolution (JDR)

Increasingly, judges are acting as mediators in settlement conferences and other case management settings. In fact, appointment processes for judges now often include consideration of the judge's previous experience as a lawyer in problem-solving/mediation. Is it a sound practice to have judges act as mediators to help disputants in a civil case negotiate solutions to their cases? Is there a problem with the development of judicial dispute resolution or JDR?

In the following extract from "Judges as Mediators: What's the Problem with Judicial Dispute Resolution in Canada?" the authors not only discuss the historical evolution of "managerial judges" but also raise the question of whether judges acting as mediators in a courthouse is a positive development from both practical and policy points of view. While it may be acceptable to amend the rules of court to encourage court connected mediation using mediators from private practice, should judges be acting as these mediators? Does the judicial function in a modern civil justice system include room for judges to be mediators? Are judges qualified to act as mediators or should judicial responsibilities be limited solely to adjudicative decision making? Do you agree with the authors' conclusion that "done uniquely well, JDR would surely not diminish the respect for the judiciary in the minds of (the public) but only enhance it.

**H. Landerkin and A. Pirie, "Judges as Mediators: What's the
Problem with Judicial Dispute Resolution in Canada?"**
(2003), 82 *Can. Bar Rev.* 249 (footnotes omitted)

Some Historical Reflections on Judging and Procedural Justice

An ancient proverb, perhaps known to many cultures, tells us that "to know the road ahead, ask those coming back." From another perspective, in order to understand where we are, it is often important to look at where we have come from. Some historical reflections on the changing faces of judging and procedural justice in North America reveal the longstanding interaction and mutual influence of formal and informal means of dispute resolution. The modern emergence of judges as mediators and judicial dispute resolution activities seem almost a natural evolution.

(a) Pre-Trial Conferences and Managerial Judges

While the full history of Anglo-American courts and their procedure is beyond the scope of this paper, a useful starting point for our purposes is Judith Resnik's article on the emergence of managerial judges. Twenty years ago, Resnik observes a profound change in the role of judges before adjudication. Rather than expressing attributes of disengagement, dispassion, and disinterest, judges were increasingly meeting with parties in chambers as case managers encouraging settlement, supervising case preparation, shepherding the case to completion, and playing a critical role in shaping litigation and influencing results. Judges had become, Resnik concludes, "mediators, negotiators, and planners—as well as adjudicators."

These managerial roles stood in stark contrast to the traditional juridical role that was part of the foundation of the adversarial tradition. In an adversarial system, as opposed to an inquisitorial system, party autonomy is very much paramount. The parties control case preparation, decide what witnesses to call and what submissions to make. The judge, on the other hand, is left with responsibilities for justice and contemporary depictions of justice point to the nature of the judge's role. The classical image of the goddess of justice, typically consisting of a large female figure, draped in Greco-Roman robes, carrying scales and a sword, her eyes covered with a blindfold, called for the judge to be even-handed and free from distractions that could bias or corrupt her, able to make decisions with authority and courage. The image did not capture reflections of a mediator; swordless, eyes wide open, helping the parties bargain in the shadow of the law.

Resnik posits a number of reasons for the emergence of managerial judges. First, early 20th century changes in procedural rules around discovery required judges to get more involved in pre-trial conflicts. This led judges to believe their presence at other times in a lawsuit's history would be beneficial. As Resnik states, "supervision of discovery became a conduit for judicial control over all phases of litigation." Second, increasing caseloads and the consequent delays and costs associated with litigation also moved judges and judicial administrators to find more ways for speedy resolutions and to encourage litigants to settle rather than go to court. Similar pressures for more activist judging also came from access to justice initiatives.

Galanter also describes a history of judicial interventions in the development of "settlement processes" in the courts through what was then called "adjustment," "compromise," and "conciliation." While most civil cases are settled out of court, he finds "in many instances the negotiations are encouraged, brokered, or actively mediated by the judge" and "this has become a respectable, even esteemed, feature of judicial work." This judicial involvement recognized a distinction between conciliation and the exercise of a trial court's "coercive power." Galanter views this interaction between the themes of conciliation and judicial administration to be at the very core of the subsequent debate, viz., judicial participation in settlement processes.

A major vehicle for this judicial involvement was the pretrial conference. From earlier beginnings, pretrial conferences in the United States became a distinct procedure by the late 30s. In 1944, the United States Federal Court Pre-Trial Committee acknowledged that settlement was a "byproduct of good pretrial procedure rather than a primary objective to be actively pursued by the judge," a restrained endorsement of this process. But, Galanter notes there were others who were ardent proponents of pre-trial, equating it with mediation as early as 1947:

> Pre-Trial seems to have developed a method of disposing of controversies, within the courts, with the aid of lawyers, but without the delay, expense and technicality that has cursed judicial process for years. It eliminates appeals. It commends itself to businessmen as a sensible and practical procedure. It provides a method by which disputes can be disposed of in a way that leaves all parties satisfied instead of one or both disgruntled and with a grievance against courts and law. It should increase the use of the courts.

Galanter identifies a serious shift—"the fading away of the preparation for trial rhetoric and the heightened emphasis on the judicial production of settlements"—as early as the 1960s. Citing a Federal Court judge from Pennsylvania, Galanter further documents this change in role:

> I feel it is incumbent upon every judge to use the pretrial as an aid in effectuating settlement ... the judge can be most effective in acting as the catalytic agent to bring the two parties together ... [I]n a great majority of the cases reasonable men, after all the facts are on the table, can arrive at an area of agreement.

By the 1970s, Galanter finds a new idealism existing in the Federal Court on this issue:

> In the words of one thoughtful federal district judge, settlement "produces results which are probably as close to the ideal of justice as we are capable of producing."

Thus, he asserts that if "settlements are good, it is also good that the judge actively participates in bringing them about. He should do this not only by management of the court ... but also by acting as a mediator." Another Federal District Court judge who spoke to a seminar for newly appointed judges in 1977, said:

> ... I urge that you see your role not only as a home plate umpire in the courtroom, calling balls and strikes. Even more important are your functions as mediator and judicial administrator.

• • •

Judicial involvement in settlement has been, for the most part, more modest in Canada. The pre-trial conference was a procedural innovation only in the 1960s, but as late as 1977 the goal of settlement in these conferences still seemed an add-on to more important objectives focused on improving the quality of the upcoming trial. As Watson notes:

> In essence, the pre-trial conference seeks to shorten the trial time by a clarification and reduction of the issues, by limiting the number of witnesses, by obtaining admissions of fact and of documents, and in other ways. The conference may seek to improve the quality of the trial by increasing the preparedness of counsel, by facilitating the avoidance of surprise and

by generally aiding the clear presentation of the case. In addition, the conference may obviate the necessity for a trial by encouraging a settlement of the case.

This is not to say that Canada did not have its share of judges who promoted settlement. Many Canadian lawyers will have memories of being called into the judge's chambers early in a trial and being "helped" to settle the case. This judicial intervention, often
would be given in a manner suggesting counsel proceed with the trial at their peril or accept the judge's recommendation. Other judges such as Chief Justice Andrews, and Justices Lieff, Gold, Linden, Chadwick, Williams, Moore, and others, were well known for
their leadership roles in judicial involvement in settlement. While some Canadian judges
called for more emphasis on co-operation and less attention to confrontation, this plea
was mostly directed to lawyers and their clients. Canadian judges certainly led many
procedural reforms but the settlement activism of their American counterparts was generally absent.

Only recently would it be fair to say that mediation has become a part of the judges'
role in Canada through rule changes permitting mediation-type activities in specific
cases or courts. For example, in British Columbia, the Provincial Court now conducts
mandatory settlement conferences in which the judge "may mediate any issues being
disputed." Judges order and hold settlement conferences in most Canadian jurisdictions.
For these conferences, the judge is generally given directions in the rules to "explore all
possibilities of settlement of the issues that are outstanding." Mediation training has been
provided to a limited number of judges. Anecdotal evidence suggests judges with back-
grounds or experience in mediation prior to their appointments will be the ones most
comfortable in assuming this role.

An explanation for differences in Canada–US approaches to the judge's role in settlement may be found in the following quote from the 1989 Canadian Bar Association Task
Force Report on Alternative Dispute Resolution:

> The reasons for this difference may be a more conservative concept of the role of the courts
> in Canada, a circuit court structure that limits individual case management, the absence of
> training in dispute resolution skills for judges and, finally, a court system that is, on average,
> functioning efficiently. This latter reason may be the most significant. Judicial initiatives in
> ADR in most cases have been in response to perceived problems with the effectiveness of
> court adjudication. As concerns with access to justice, administrative efficiency or the ap-
> propriateness of court adjudication for particular kinds of cases increase, there may be a
> greater motivation for the Canadian judiciary to assume more leadership in identifying and
> evaluating new or improved procedures both inside and outside the formal court
> structure.

[Having considered some of the historical evolution of judicial dispute resolution (JDR),
Landerkin and Pirie offer a critical assessment of its appropriateness in Canada, focusing
on three grounds: fundamental justice policy considerations, jurisdictional matters, and
whether judges are necessarily possessed of the requisite skill to practise JDR. The first
consideration, that of fundamental judicial policy, bears repeating here.]

Policy Considerations

At the policy level, is JDR a wise choice? Should judges be doing JDR? This is a complex inquiry since it invites a review of a host of related policy considerations falling under headings such as the administration of justice, access to justice, the role of the courts, the judicial function, the economics of justice, the rule of law, and indeed justice itself in a free and democratic society. The policy question—should judges be doing JDR?—at the very least involves a fundamental analysis of whether judicial dispute resolution creates incompatibilities with the myriad of justice system values and beliefs that are at the heart of the proper functioning of courts and the judicial role in Western societies. Insurmountable policy differences would be cause for concern.

From a practical perspective, the answer may be obvious. Judge-led JDR developments to date such as settlement conferences, mini-trials, case management, and the like seem to suggest the idea of judges appropriately helping parties settle their cases does not undermine the foundations of our formal justice system. In fact, the policy reasons behind the rapid developments in ADR and mediation generally appear to mirror the arguments for supporting JDR's integration into formal justice systems. Court congestion and long delays, staggering legal costs, and problems enforcing judicial orders can mean access to justice is compromised. As an essential element in the ordering of a democratic society pursuant to the rule of law, the court's adjudicative mechanisms have to be working and be seen to be working, particularly by those segments of society most in need of the court's protection. The courts cannot be viewed, as a 1996 report on the Canadian justice system found, as a system in which "many Canadians feel that they cannot exercise their rights effectively because using the civil justice system takes too long, is too expensive, or is too difficult to understand."

Alternative dispute resolution in the courts is an obvious antidote, the argument goes, to help cure the ailments that plague the adjudicative process. The challenge is to adopt a court-friendly definition of ADR—originally the antithesis to the courts—for use within the courts so common ADR benefits, such as saving time and money, reaching win–win results, making lasting arrangements, reducing recidivism, and increasing disputant satisfaction with the process and the result, would also accrue to parties who are using the courts to resolve their problems. Long-pursued justice policies seem a good fit with many ADR goals and practices. JDR can thus be viewed as complimenting, not conflicting with, the appropriate administration of justice.

This is not to say that the concerns raised by Resnik, Menkel-Meadow and others are diminished. But, in a way, these are much the same concerns that confronted the legal profession faced with the burgeoning interest in ADR in the 1980s and 1990s. With ADR recast as the way for the legal profession to better exercise problem-solving skills and techniques, questions about ADR's negative potential have not proved to be a barrier to ADR's rapid integration into legal practices. The policy challenge for the courts, meditatively reframed, seems to be similar. How can the positive features of ADR be incorporated into justice system structures and practices in a manner that does not undermine or destroy the essential values and beliefs that underpin the system? This challenge—how to dispute better—was the same one faced by the legal profession two decades ago when ADR proponents saw overall benefits in making lawyers more aware of and adept at using a wider range of dispute resolution options. The dark side of ADR—concerns about oppression, co-option, regression and injustice—cannot be ignored. But the formal justice system may be able to respond in the same way that the legal profession has managed with ADR.

However, the justice policies that ground the function of a judge may appear more troubling for JDR inroads. It may be a sound policy to amend the rules of court to provide for mandatory or quasi-mandatory mediation of most civil cases by rostered mediators before a trial can be held. It may be quite another thing altogether to have a sitting judge act as the mediator.

Are judges as mediators or judges practicing JDR compatible with our understanding of the modern judicial function? While some long-standing judicial tasks that conform to the JDR mould are historically traced [elsewhere], a closer look at the role of the judge appears to reveal further policy grounds supporting the judicial adoption of JDR.

The role of the judge is often inextricably connected to the adversarial system in Western society. An adversarial justice system, with its principles of party autonomy and party-led prosecution "limits the judge's function to disputes that have been presented to him" or her. Judges sit impassively above the dispute, hear the proofs and arguments presented by the parties, and render binding decisions at the conclusion of the case. This reactive function can be contrasted with the judge's role in an inquisitorial system where the judge directs fact finding, "constantly looking for the jugular—for the issue of law or fact that might dispose of the case. Free of constraints that arise from party presentation of evidence, the court investigates the dispute in the fashion most likely to narrow the ... particularly cogent lines of inquiry."

For the judge in the disputant-directed adversarial process, the benefit is that the integrity of the adjudicator is protected by demanding the litigants shoulder more responsibility for carriage of the action. Independence and impartiality are less likely to be compromised when the judge distances herself or himself from the manner in which the case is presented and defended. The hierarchical structure of the courts allows disputants to appeal decisions through several layers of judicial thinking, reinforcing the conclusion that the judge's role is primarily an arbiter of disputes.

However, two reasons suggest this adversarially-inspired and traditional role for the judge is incomplete. On policy grounds, there may be ample room for JDR. First, despite the obvious advantages of an adversary system, some suggest such a system is flawed. There are concerns this laissez-faire, individualistic system of justice, where parties fight it out to determine who is right and who is wrong, contributes to or causes unacceptable delays in getting disputes to trial, high legal costs, procedural and substantive complexities, breakdowns in continuing relationships, and other access to justice problems. The adversarial system may encourage certain beliefs and attitudes that not only obstruct fair and effective dispute resolution, but also legitimize socially undesirable behaviour.

Competitive aggression is encouraged over reciprocity and empathy; hostility trumps trust; selfishness supplants generosity; antipathy replaces care. At the extreme, there are tragic examples where the adversarial way of thinking about dispute resolution nurtures disrespect, disregard, violence, and even death.

A recent Canadian Bar Association Task Force Report on Systems of Civil Justice concluded: "the adversarial approach is central to the civil justice system, and should remain a key feature in the future" with the caveat that "a preoccupation with gaining advantage through an adversarial approach too often has the result of displacing substantive communication, common sense and a problem-solving orientation, all of which assist in resolving disputes."

Carrie Menkel-Meadow also calls attention to a related procedural problem with the adversarial system.

> [T]he grievant tells a story of felt or perceived wrong to a third party (the lawyer) and the lawyer transforms the dispute by imposing "categories" on "events and relationships" which re-define the subject matter of a dispute in ways "which make it amenable to conventional management procedures." This process of "narrowing" disputes occurs at various stages in lawyer–client interactions.

This legal reconstruction of the dispute may be required by the rules and procedures in order for the system's ultimate decision-maker, the judge sitting in court, to effectively adjudicate. However, the "narrowing" of the dispute may miss what is really at issue and thus hinder efforts to reach a reliable and lasting solution. The divorcing couple furiously fighting over who gets the silverware or business assets under division of property laws may have no trouble dealing with these essentially economic matters if the underlying cause of the conflict—the breach of trust that led to the relationship breakdown—is dealt with first. An apology may go a long way in repairing a damaged relationship. Unfortunately, this non-legal relationship issue and remedy are not usually included with the causes of action and relief common in family law pleadings.

A smoothly running adversarial system of justice might mean judges could be left with only their adjudicatory role. But in the same way that criticisms of adversary justice have led to reforms in lawyer roles and indeed in the adversarial system itself (a new emphasis on problem solving, consensus building, collaborative lawyering, transformative justice), so too can we envision corresponding changes to the judge's role. The role of judge primarily predicated on a seriously flawed, publicly maligned and changing adversarial approach to justice is surely not sustainable.

A second and more direct line of analysis also suggests the judicial function can be broader than that traditionally expected in an adversarial system of justice. While the role of judges in North America developed within an adversarial system, descriptions of the judicial function both in codes of judicial ethics and court decisions fit with judicial dispute resolution. Consider, for example, the ABA Model Code of Judicial Conduct (1990). While the preamble refers to the judge as "an arbiter of facts and law for the resolution of disputes," Canon 3(7)(d) states that as a part of the judge's judicial duties:

> A judge may, with the consent of the parties, confer separately with the parties and their lawyers in an effort to mediate or settle matters pending before the judge.

Additionally, the commentary on Canon 3(8) requiring a judge to "dispose of all judicial matters promptly, efficiently, and fairly" directs judges to "encourage and seek to facilitate settlement, but parties should not feel coerced into surrendering the right to have their controversy resolved by the courts." These provisions clarify concerns that judicial mediation may be prohibited as unauthorized *ex-parte* communications and also, more importantly, demonstrate the role of the judge as mediator requires a balancing of the rights of the parties to be heard with an early and satisfactory settlement.

In Canada, the ethical language is similar although not as direct. In the 1998 Canadian Judicial Council's Ethical Principles for Judges, "judges should devote their professional activity to judicial duties *broadly defined* which include not only presiding in court but other judicial tasks essential to the court's operation" so that "today, judicial duties include administrative and other out of court activities. Judges have important responsibilities, for example, in case management and pre-trial conferences."

The challenging ethical nature of the judicial function, beyond the boundaries suggested by the adversarial system, is perhaps best captured in the Honourable J.O. Wilson's ground-breaking "A Book for Judges." He referred to judges as "confronted each day with new and often fascinating problems, students forever, learning new things." He saw the practicalities of judicial conduct subject to an important principle governing all aspects of judicial behaviour: It is of fundamental importance that justice should not only be done, but should manifestly and undoubtedly be seen to be done.

When considered from an ethical perspective, the change in judicial function is very clear, moving from traditional adjudicative limits to carefully flexing the new judicial boundaries to settlement roles.

The courts themselves also have had to consider the nature of the judicial function. In a recent case, *Re Therrien*, [2001] 2 SCR 3, the Supreme Court of Canada discussed the function of a judge in deciding whether to support the revocation of Therrien's judicial commission for failing to disclose in the appointment process a criminal conviction, for which he had been pardoned. In this case, the Court was faced with competing policy considerations; the pardon as an act of forgiveness and selfless generosity, brotherhood and justice on the part of society which supported non-disclosure compared to the unique role embodied by the judge in that society, which meant the past was always relevant.

While a first year law student, the police charged Therrien in November 1970 under the *Public Order Regulations, 1970*, enacted under the *War Measures Act*, RSC 1952. It was alleged Therrien unlawfully assisted four members of the Front de Liberation du Québec (FLQ), an association declared unlawful by the regulations. This event occurred during a serious political crisis in Quebec. The Supreme Court of Canada described the appellant's role as "quite minor." He pleaded guilty and was sentenced to imprisonment for one year. After serving his sentence, he completed his legal studies, was called to the bar, practised law "in a competent and dignified manner, thus winning the respect of his colleagues and members of the bench." The Governor in Council granted him a pardon in 1987 under the *Criminal Records Act*, RSC 1970, c. 12. Pursuant to the legislation the pardon stated "that he was of good behaviour and that the conviction in respect of which it is granted should no longer reflect adversely on his character ... the pardon granted vacates the conviction and removes any disqualification to which the person so convicted is subject by virtue of any Act of the Parliament of Canada or a regulation made thereunder."

In 1996 he was interviewed for appointment as a judge and asked whether he had ever been in trouble with the law. He answered, "No." The Supreme Court of Canada described the values that underpin the "unique" function of a judge:

> Individual and institutional impartiality and independence are key elements in the function of a judge; they are inherent in the very definition of a judge and are an integral part of the constitutional structure of the parliamentary democracy of the United Kingdom, which we have inherited through the preamble to our Constitution.

Describing the role of the Judge as "A Place Apart," the Supreme Court of Canada said:

> The judicial function is absolutely unique. Our society assigns important powers and responsibilities to the members of its judiciary. Apart from the traditional role of an arbiter which settles disputes and adjudicates between the rights of the parties, judges are also responsible for preserving the balance of constitutional powers between the two levels of government in our federal state. Furthermore, following the enactment of the *Canadian Charter*, they have become one of the foremost defenders of individual freedoms and human rights and guardians of the values it embodies.

If we then look beyond the jurist to whom we assign responsibility for resolving conflicts between parties, judges also play a fundamental role in the eyes of the external observer of the judicial system. The judge is the pillar of our entire justice system, and of the rights and freedoms which that system is designed to promote and protect. Thus, to the public, judges not only swear by taking their oath to serve the ideals of Justice and Truth on which the rule of law in Canada and the foundations of our democracy are built, but they are asked to embody them.

The Supreme Court of Canada also quoted approvingly from *Ethical Principles for Judges* written for judges by the Canadian Judicial Council:

> Public confidence in and respect for the judiciary are essential to an effective judicial system and, ultimately, to democracy founded on the rule of law. Many factors, including unfair or uninformed criticism, or simple misunderstanding of the judicial role, can adversely influence public confidence in and respect for the judiciary. Another factor which is capable of undermining public respect and confidence is any conduct of judges, in and out of court, demonstrating a lack of integrity. Judges should, therefore, strive to conduct themselves in a way that will sustain and contribute to public respect and confidence in their integrity, impartiality, and good judgment.

and also from academic descriptions of the judicial role:

> The dictates of tradition require the greatest restraint, the greatest propriety and the greatest decorum from the members of our judiciary. We expect our judges to be almost superhuman in wisdom, in propriety, in decorum and in humanity. There must be no other group in society which must fulfil this standard of public expectation and, at the same time, accept numerous constraints. At any rate, there is no question that a certain loss of freedom accompanies the acceptance of an appointment to the judiciary.

The Court found the appellant's conduct in not disclosing his previous conviction during the appointment process when specifically asked whether he had been in trouble with the law "has sufficiently undermined public confidence, rendering him incapable of performing the duties of his office." While the Court acknowledged "this case represented, in a sense, an invitation to society to be ever more generous," due to the legal uncertainty surrounding the impact of a pardon the Court concluded:

> ... [W]e cannot ignore the unique role embodied by the judge in that society, and the extraordinary vulnerability of the individuals who appear before that judge seeking to have their rights determined, or when their lives or liberty are at stake. Above all, a person who appears before a judge is entitled to have justice done in his or her case, and that justice be *seen* to be done by the general public. That kind of generosity is not something that a person can be compelled to offer. In the specific circumstances of the case at bar, the values of forgiveness and selfless generosity must therefore yield to the values of justice and the all-important integrity of the justice system.

The language from the Supreme Court of Canada's reasoning used to describe a judge—*impartiality, independence, integrity, public respect and confidence, good judgment, a pillar of the process, serving ideals of Justice and Truth, irreproachable conduct, restraint, propriety, decorum, humanity, unique*—might easily describe the mediator. Indeed, the Court's vision of responsibilities for judges went beyond "the traditional role of arbiter," to the judge "having responsibility for resolving conflicts between parties." The Supreme Court of Canada's words are echoes of earlier ADR sentiments urging less emphasis on adjudication. Judges appropriately helping parties to settle disputes, apart from adjudication, is not excluded from their judicial function by the Supreme Court of Canada. Judges acting as judicial mediators are now part of the fabric of the judicial function.

What is essential to the judicial function from a policy perspective in the Supreme Court of Canada's reasoning is two-fold. First, impartiality, independence, and integrity must be maintained for they are the *sina qua non* of the essence of a judge's being. Second, public confidence in the judge can never be eroded. These qualities are sacrosanct in everything a judge does, even when applying to be a judge. These are also the hallmarks of good intervenors. The virtues of impartiality and integrity are specifically included in various codes of ethics promulgated for mediators. The other fundamental characteristic of the judicial function—public confidence—would be compromised if the judge as mediator was not qualified or skilled. We address concerns of competency below. However, subject to the adoption of appropriate procedures, goals and an overarching core meaning for judicial intervention, it is difficult to imagine that a reasonable, fair-minded and informed public would not endorse and support this continued evolution of the judicial function as a part of a similarly evolving adversarial system. Public confidence would not be eroded whether the judge is judging, mediating, opining, managing, writing, counselling a distraught witness, or otherwise dispensing justice. Done uniquely well, JDR would surely not diminish the respect for the judiciary in the minds of such persons but only enhance it.

5. Informalism: A Word from the Critics

The enthusiasm for mediation and other informal methods of dispute resolution, while widely shared among civil justice reformers, has not been universal. Indeed, there is a well-developed theoretical critique and, increasingly, an empirically based critique of many of the central claims advanced by mediation proponents.

> **Ian Morrison and Janet Mosher, "Barriers to Access to**
> **Civil Justice for Disadvantaged Groups"**
> in Ontario Law Reform Commission, *Rethinking Civil Justice:*
> *Research Studies for the Civil Justice Review* (Toronto: Ontario Law
> Reform Commission, 1996), 637, at 663-74 (footnotes omitted)
>
> ### 3. Models of Disputing and Their Relation to Disadvantage
>
> ... The claims made with respect to the strengths and benefits of ADR are equally expansive and frequently attributed to ADR in all of its manifestations as though it were a monolith. In what follows we focus on those processes and forums which are more likely to touch the lives of the "disadvantaged": few economically "disadvantaged persons" will be parties to rent-a-judge proceedings while many are likely to be affected by mediation and particularly by a move to mandatory mediation in the context of family law.
>
> As described by many of its proponents, mediation, as a process, offers a range of benefits: win/win solutions; creative outcomes fashioned in the shadow of the law but not constricted by formal legal rationality; direct participation which makes good on the promise of dignity (unlike due process which fails to do so because participation is usually so attenuated); improved communication paving the way for a better future relationship; harmony; low cost (less cumbersome and costly formal procedures); speed; flexibility; greater participant satisfaction; and more lasting results. Beyond these process benefits it is claimed that mediation (and similar processes) will relieve court congestion, enhance community involvement, and facilitate access to justice. Challenges to each of these claims have been fully developed and many, we might add, are extremely persuasive. But, given time and space constraints, we propose to address specifically the potential of mediation (and other informal processes). In particular we want to consider whether mediation is capable of adequately taking account of the dependency, the on-going nature of the relationship, or the inequalities of resources in disputes between individuals and the state, or between private individuals.
>
> The claim is frequently made that mediation is particularly well-suited to the resolution of disputes which arise in the context of an on-going relationship. Thus, disputes arising in families, in employment, in certain commercial contexts, and in housing (landlord and tenant) have often been identified as being well-suited for mediation. Other on-going relationships, such as those between welfare recipients and the state, have received relatively little attention in the ADR literature. With the exception of the commercial context, the relationships in each of these contexts are frequently marked by vast inequalities of resources and of power more generally. Coupled with these power imbalances are the ideologies of mediator "neutrality" and "harmony," both of

which actively work in favour of the more powerful party. The ideology of mediator "neutrality" presupposes that the role of the mediator is simply to facilitate the communication necessary for the parties to come to their own agreement. For many, neutrality put into practice mandates non-intervention in aid of one of the parties to the mediation. As many authors have observed, the failure to intervene in circumstances where one party is taking advantage of the other can hardly be characterized as neutral. To the contrary, non-intervention works to actively promote the interests of the more powerful party.

The "harmony" ideology of mediation has a number of problematic ramifications. It signals that one ought to make concessions—it's a process of give and take to reach an amicable settlement. This can be problematic in a context where one is seeking to have a legal right acknowledged and enforced. Why should this party be expected to make any concessions? While we do not mean to suggest that one can never voluntarily agree to concede a legal right, nor that parties ought not to be permitted to resolve their disputes other than in accordance with the normative parameters recognized by law, we do think it critical to attend to the notion of voluntariness. Voluntariness requires more than the absence of explicit or indeed, subtle coercion. Explicit coercion in this context frequently comes in the form of mandatory mediation, or the "strong arm" of the mediator. Subtle coercion may be pervasive within the mediation process because of the expectation of settlement and compromise. Voluntariness requires a *real* choice of options, adequate information about one's legal rights and entitlements, and mechanisms that in some manner redress the inequalities of power. We emphasize *real* choice here to signal the importance of attending to the social and economic context in which choices are exercised. For those with few economic resources no meaningful choice exists if one option is enormously expensive, the other inexpensive. This observation has led many to express the concern that the creation of institutionalized ADR will result in its substitution for the right of "disadvantaged groups" to litigate and would create a two tier justice system, "that dispenses informal 'justice' to poor people with 'small claims' and 'minor' disputes, who cannot afford legal services, and who are denied access to courts."

This leads us to a second implication of the harmony ideology. It positions lawyers or other advocates as antithetical to "good" outcomes because their adversarial tactics are seen to undermine the process. While in the context of family law mediation, review of mediated agreements by lawyers is encouraged, all other forms of participation by advocates is usually discouraged. In the context where one party is much better resourced in terms of knowledge about the law, and experience in negotiating, this raises concerns that legal rights may be conceded through ignorance of them or an inability to successfully negotiate their respect.

The informality of mediation may also work in favour of more powerful parties. This claim has been particularly well developed in the context of disputes involving racial minority persons. Delgado et al. argue, based upon theories of prejudice that suggest that much prejudice is environmental (people express it because the setting encourages or tolerates it), that the rules and structures of formal justice tend to suppress bias, whereas informality tends to increase it. They argue that two features of formal settings decrease opportunities for the expression of racial bias; aspects of the role of judges (freedom from political pressure, commitment to apply rules, *stare decisis*, and codes of conduct);

and several basic features of legal procedure (public trials, requirements of courts to give reasons, guaranteed opportunities to call and contest evidence, pre-trial discovery, and the rules of evidence). They conclude that formality and adversarial procedures counter-act bias among legal decision-makers and disputants. They also maintain that minority group members are more apt to participate in processes which they believe will respond to reasonable efforts and thus, that "it is not surprising that a favoured forum for redress of race-based wrongs has been the traditional adjudicatory setting. Minorities recognize that public institutions, with their defined rules and formal structure, are more subject to rational control than private or informal structures."

While acknowledging that informal processes may less effectively curb racial and other biases than formal processes (this is not of course to suggest that formal processes are free of bias against "out groups"), other commentators have suggested that *if* the intro-duction of state-sponsored alternative disputes resolution processes and forums result in an over-all increase in the capacity of the system to deal with disputes, and in the avail-ability of less costly alternatives (neither of which necessarily follows from the introduc-tion of institutionalized ADR), access to justice for the poor may be enhanced in the sense that access may be had to at least some form of dispute resolution where none was available before. But if these alternatives fail to take seriously systemic inequalities of power and if "disadvantaged persons" are routinely encouraged (if not coerced) to con-cede legal rights, there is good reason to doubt that greater numbers will have access to a forum for dispute resolution—who would seek out such forums? There is equally good reason to doubt that justice in any substantive sense would be enhanced for "disadvan-taged persons."

Many claim that mediation and other informal methods of dispute resolution are empowering, both for individuals and potentially for communities. At least for individ-uals, this is understood to be possible because disputants participate directly in the reso-lution of their own dispute. For many the experience may well be empowering. But it is unlikely to be for "disadvantaged persons" when pitted against powerful adversaries. The other piece of the empowerment claim is that because the disputants are not bound by the rational application of law, they are free to select the normative principles that will inform the resolution of the dispute. At the level of community, the claim has been made that community-based mediation (wherein the mediation is conducted by a panel of mediators from the community) offers the scope for the enunciation and development of community norms. This claim is one frequently made with respect to "neighbourhood justice centres." As Cohen notes, "in theory, neighbourhood programs allow prompt community resolution of disputes using community values instead of the rule of law ... . Applying shared values, [they] solve certain community problems more effectively than the court system. Nader appropriately questions this theory,

> ... Neighbourhood justice organizations, one outcropping of ADR reform, were set up on a Crown policy model: "Let's make believe that this is a self-contained community and let's make believe that within this community you can create your own organizations to increase access to justice." The community was a make-believe, the self-containment was a make-believe, and the idea that problems that they might take to justice were only between people who lived in the community was make-believe.

While we, like Nader, are wary about the claims regarding the application and evolution of community norms and values for the reasons she articulates, we do believe that there is at least one special case wherein community-based dispute resolution is genuinely *community*-based. Here we refer specifically to First Nations communities. While we discuss this in somewhat more detail *infra* we also want to emphasize that a mediation-style process, located within a culture respectful of the principle of harmony and based upon very different cultural traditions than those found in dominant Canadian society, is not subject to the whole of the critique of mediation which we have advanced above.

In sum, there seems to be no reason to believe that mediation, or other informal dispute resolution processes, hold out much promise for oppressed persons in terms of access to justice. The barriers to naming, blaming and claiming that impede access to a due process hearing also impede access to mediation. As a process of dispute resolution, mediation, while *potentially* less expensive, fares even less well than adversarial adjudication in addressing imbalances of power. It is hard to imagine that a person dependent upon the state (or abusive husband, or landlord) in an on-going way would be any more willing to take on conventional power through mediation, than through a due process hearing. It is not at all hard to imagine that such a person might fare less well if mediation is the process of dispute resolution.

Where does this leave us then in terms of dispute resolution processes? First, it is clear that simply creating opportunities for mediation will not improve access to justice for "disadvantaged groups"; nor indeed would simply creating additional opportunities for due process hearings. It seems to us that whatever the process, attention must be given to what would be the necessary pre-conditions for meaningful participation. As Tyler suggests in his research on small claims courts, "… disputants place great weight on having a dispute settled in a way which is perceived to be fair … one important element in perceiving the procedure to be fair relates to the opportunity to participate in the process … ." Both mediation and adversarial adjudication claim to value party participation yet both have been criticized for failing to respect it in practice; the former largely because of inequalities of bargaining power and the latter because of the attenuated form that participation usually takes. What are the pre-conditions for meaningful participation? At a very general level these include an understanding of the process(es); real choice about entering the process, or as between processes; adequate information about legal rights, entitlements, obligations and remedies; advocacy supports; a conceptualization of advocacy which respects client narratives (see discussion *infra* of advocacy services); an opportunity to tell one's story; and a decision-maker or mediator who is able to hear and respect that story and its teller (see discussion *infra* on personnel of the justice system). While both mediation and adjudication could be dramatically improved should these pre-conditions be satisfied, it nevertheless is imperative that persons not be required to mediate disputes. As we stated at the outset, quoting from Walker and Fricker, "[w]e both begin [and end] our consideration of the issues from a belief in the validity and centrality of a formal process of litigation and the right of citizens to have access to justice in its most institutionalized form." For all of the reasons we have just canvassed then, any move to make mediation mandatory in the context of family law (as the new government has promised) or in the context of landlord–tenant law (as the *First Report* suggests) will further impede access to justice for disadvantaged groups.

Owen M. Fiss, "Against Settlement"
(1984), 93 *Yale Law Journal* 1073, at 1075-90 (footnotes omitted)

The advocates of ADR are led to support [measures to encourage settlement] and to exalt the idea of settlement more generally because they view adjudication as a process to resolve disputes. They act as though courts arose to resolve quarrels between neighbors who had reached an impasse and turned to a stranger for help. Courts are seen as an institutionalization of the stranger and adjudication is viewed as the process by which the stranger exercises power. The very fact that the neighbors have turned to someone else to resolve their dispute signifies a breakdown in their social relations; the advocates of ADR acknowledge this, but nonetheless hope that the neighbors will be able to reach agreement before the stranger renders judgment. Settlement is that agreement. It is a truce more than a true reconciliation, but it seems preferable to judgment because it rests on the consent of both parties and avoids the cost of a lengthy trial.

In my view, however, this account of adjudication and the case for settlement rests on questionable premises. I do not believe that settlement as a generic practice is preferable to judgment or should be institutionalized on a wholesale and indiscriminate basis. It should be treated instead as a highly problematic technique for streamlining dockets. Settlement is for me the civil analogue of plea bargaining: Consent is often coerced; the bargain may be struck by someone without authority; the absence of a trial and judgment renders subsequent judicial involvement troublesome; and although dockets are trimmed, justice may not be done. Like plea bargaining, settlement is a capitulation to the conditions of mass society and should be neither encouraged nor praised.

By viewing the lawsuit as a quarrel between two neighbors, the dispute-resolution story that underlies ADR implicitly asks us to assume a rough equality between the contending parties. It treats settlement as the anticipation of the outcome of trial and assumes that the terms of settlement are simply a product of the parties' predictions of that outcome. In truth, however, settlement is also a function of the resources available to each party to finance the litigation, and those resources are frequently distributed unequally. Many lawsuits do not involve a property dispute between two neighbors, or between AT&T and the government (to update the story), but rather concern a struggle between a member of a racial minority and a municipal police department over alleged brutality, or a claim by a worker against a large corporation over work-related injuries. In these cases, the distribution of financial resources, or the ability of one party to pass along its costs, will invariably infect the bargaining process, and the settlement will be at odds with a conception of justice that seeks to make the wealth of the parties irrelevant.

The disparities in resources between the parties can influence the settlement in three ways. First, the poorer party may be less able to amass and analyze the information needed to predict the outcome of the litigation, and thus be disadvantaged in the bargaining process. Second, he may need the damages he seeks immediately and thus be induced to settle as a way of accelerating payment, even though he realizes he would get less now than he might if he awaited judgment. All plaintiffs want their damages immediately, but an indigent plaintiff may be exploited by a rich defendant because his need is so great that the defendant can force him to accept a sum that is less than the ordinary present value of the judgment. Third, the poorer party might be forced to settle because he does not have the resources to finance the litigation, to cover either his own projected expenses, such as his lawyer's time, or the expenses his opponent can impose through the manipulation of procedural mechanisms such as discovery. It might seem that settlement benefits the plaintiff by allowing him to avoid the costs of litigation, but this is not so. The defendant can anticipate the plaintiff's costs if the case were to be tried fully and decrease his offer by that amount. The indigent plaintiff is a victim of the costs of litigation even if he settles.

There are exceptions. Seemingly rich defendants may sometimes be subject to financial pressures that make them as anxious to settle as indigent plaintiffs. But I doubt that these circumstances occur with any great frequency. I also doubt that institutional arrangements such as contingent fees or the provision of legal services to the poor will in fact equalize resources between contending parties: The contingent fee does not equalize resources; it only makes an indigent plaintiff vulnerable to the willingness of the private bar to invest in his case. In effect, the ability to exploit the plaintiff's lack of resources has been transferred from rich defendants to lawyers who insist upon a hefty slice of the plaintiff's recovery as their fee. These lawyers, moreover, will only work for contingent fees in certain kinds of cases, such as personal-injury suits. And the contingent fee is of no avail when the defendant is the disadvantaged party. Governmental subsidies for legal services have a broader potential, but in the civil domain the battle for these subsidies was hard-fought, and they are in fact extremely limited, especially when it comes to cases that seek systemic reform of government practices.

Of course, imbalances of power can distort judgment as well: Resources influence the quality of presentation, which in turn has an important bearing on who wins and the terms of victory. We count, however, on the guiding presence of the judge, who can employ a number of measures to lessen the impact of distributional inequalities. He can, for example, supplement the parties' presentations by asking questions, calling his own witnesses, and inviting other persons and institutions to participate as amici. These measures are likely to make only a small contribution toward moderating the influence of distributional inequalities, but should not be ignored for that reason. Not even these small steps are possible with settlement. There is, moreover, a critical difference between a process like settlement, which is based on bargaining and accepts inequalities of wealth as an integral and legitimate component of the process, and a process like judgment, which knowingly struggles against those inequalities. Judgment aspires to an autonomy from distributional inequalities, and it gathers much of its appeal from this aspiration. ...

Justice Rather Than Peace

The dispute-resolution story makes settlement appear as a perfect substitute for judgment, as we just saw, by trivializing the remedial dimensions of a lawsuit, and also by reducing the social function of the lawsuit to one of resolving private disputes: In that story, settlement appears to achieve exactly the same purpose as judgment—peace between the parties—but at considerably less expense to society. The two quarreling neighbors turn to a court in order to resolve their dispute, and society makes courts available because it wants to aid in the achievement of their private ends or to secure the peace.

In my view, however, the purpose of adjudication should be understood in broader terms. Adjudication uses public resources, and employs not strangers chosen by the parties but public officials chosen by a process in which the public participates. These officials, like members of the legislative and executive branches, possess a power that has been defined and conferred by public law, not by private agreement. Their job is not to maximize the ends of private parties, nor simply to secure the peace, but to explicate and give force to the values embodied in authoritative texts such as the Constitution and statutes: to interpret those values and to bring reality into accord with them. This duty is not discharged when the parties settle.

In our political system, courts are reactive institutions. They do not search out interpretive occasions, but instead wait for others to bring matters to their attention. They also rely for the most part on others to investigate and present the law and facts. A settlement will thereby deprive a court of the occasion, and perhaps even the ability, to render an interpretation. A court cannot proceed (or not proceed very far) in the face of a settlement. To be against settlement is not to urge that parties be "forced" to litigate, since that would interfere with their autonomy and distort the adjudicative process; the parties will be inclined to make the court believe that their bargain is justice. To be against settlement is only to suggest that when the parties settle, society gets less than what appears, and for a price it does not know it is paying. Parties might settle while leaving justice undone. The settlement of a school suit might secure the peace, but not racial equality. Although the parties are prepared to live under the terms they bargained for, and although such peaceful coexistence may be a necessary precondition of justice, and itself a state of affairs to be valued, it is not justice itself. To settle for something means to accept less than some ideal.

I recognize that judges often announce settlements not with a sense of frustration or disappointment, as my account of adjudication might suggest, but with a sigh of relief. But this sigh should be seen for precisely what it is: It is not a recognition that a job is done, nor an acknowledgment that a job need not be done because justice has been secured. It is instead based on another sentiment altogether, namely, that another case has been "moved along," which is true whether or not justice has been done or even needs to be done. Or the sigh might be based on the fact that the agency of judgment has been avoided. ...

Someone like Bok sees adjudication in essentially private terms: The purpose of lawsuits and the civil courts is to resolve disputes, and the amount of litigation we encounter is evidence of the needlessly combative and quarrelsome character of Americans. Or as Bok put it, using a more diplomatic idiom: "At bottom, ours is a society built on individualism, competition, and success." I, on the other hand, see adjudication in more public terms: Civil litigation is an institutional arrangement for using state power to bring a recalcitrant reality closer to our chosen ideals. We turn to the courts because we need to, not because of some quirk in our personalities. We train our students in the tougher arts so that they may help secure all that the law promises, not because we want them to become gladiators or because we take a special pleasure in combat.

NOTES AND QUESTIONS

In her article considering the way in which mediation functions within our adversarial framework (C. Menkel-Meadow, "Pursuing Settlement in an Adversary Culture: A Tale of Innovation Co-opted or the Law of ADR?" (1991), 19 *Florida State University Law Review* 1),

Menkel-Meadow posits the following questions surrounding the interplay between ADR and the adjudicative system (at 4-5):

1. What are the values of settlement and adjudication?
2. When is a court not a court? What makes a court a "special" institution and what should it be doing? Related to these concerns are issues of legal authority for the variations on court adjudication—when can a court "order" someone to settle, require a juror to serve a non-juror function, or exclude the public from a proceeding?
3. What values should a court-institutionalized ADR device serve? Who should pay? Who should have access? What are the consequences of using ADR devices for the rest of the system? When should a "public system" subsidize "private agreements"?
4. What are the politics of ADR? Are there patterns of usage? Do particular kinds of clients choose different processes? Are there differences between big cases and small cases or in the choices of wealthy clients and poorer clients?
5. What should be the system or values implicated in case allocation—should it be a fair market? Should there be restrictions or regulations of case types? Should these programs be voluntary or mandatory?
6. How can we measure the effects of different allocations or assignments to particular processes? How should we measure the "quality" of justice?
7. What processes are appropriate within our system of dispute resolution? When is an adversarial model appropriate, and when is it not? What other processes can be used while preserving our long tradition of process-fairness and rights protection?
8. On what basis should cases be settled, decided, or tried—by considering only legal rules, personal needs, or economic expediency?

IV. SETTLEMENT: FORMAL OFFERS TO SETTLE AND SETTLEMENT PRIVILEGE

A. Formal Offers To Settle

1. *Statutory Regimes for Settlement*

Formal offers to settle play a strategic role in litigation. The rules surrounding formal offers to settle include the threat of paying a portion of the opposing party's legal costs if a litigant fails to accept a reasonable settlement offer. Costs in settlement are thus used as a regulatory device to encourage reasonable settlement behaviour among litigants. Although the details of the "offer to settle" rules vary among the Canadian jurisdictions, these particular costs rules share essential elements. Parties are, of course, encouraged at any time to negotiate their way to the resolution of a claim and are given various resources under the particular procedural regime to assist them in this regard (i.e., judicial case conferences, mediation). However, if one party is willing to compromise but the other steadfastly clings to a position, the party willing to terminate the proceeding on particular terms (usually the payment or acceptance of a specific sum of money) makes a formal written offer of settlement. If the opposite party accepts it, then the proceeding is ended. However, if the opposite party refuses to settle on those terms and if, at the end of the proceedings (often the trial), the opposite party either loses the case entirely or is awarded less than what was offered in the formal settlement, particular costs sanctions are usually applicable (unless the court makes a specific ruling to the contrary). Ontario's Rule 49.10 is an example of such a regime:

Cost Consequences of Failure to Accept

Plaintiff's Offer

49.10(1) Where an offer to settle,

(a) is made by a plaintiff at least seven days before the commencement of the hearing;

(b) is not withdrawn and does not expire before the commencement of the hearing; and

(c) is not accepted by the defendant,

and the plaintiff obtains a judgment as favourable as or more favourable than the terms of the offer to settle, the plaintiff is entitled to partial indemnity costs to the date the offer to settle was served and substantial indemnity costs from that date, unless the court orders otherwise.

Defendant's Offer

(2) Where an offer to settle,

(a) is made by a defendant at least seven days before the commencement of the hearing;

(b) is not withdrawn and does not expire before the commencement of the hearing; and

(c) is not accepted by the plaintiff,

and the plaintiff obtains a judgment as favourable as or less favourable than the terms of the offer to settle, the plaintiff is entitled to partial indemnity costs to the date the offer was served and the defendant is entitled to partial indemnity costs from that date, unless the court orders otherwise.

Thus, through this device, parties can be exposed to increased liability for the payment of legal costs if they refuse to participate in the pre-trial settlement process and to seriously consider a reasonable offer of settlement. The "reasonability" of such an offer is inferred by the fact that it was equal to or better than what that party ultimately achieved through the trial process. Note that, aside from rule 49 in Ontario, most Canadian jurisdictions include similar rules that operate to encourage parties, through the use of costs, to actively pursue the private settlement of disputes. See, for example, Alberta, *Rules of Court*, ss. 169 and 174; British Columbia, *Supreme Court Rules*, rule 37; Manitoba, *Court of Queen's Bench Rules*, rule 49; New Brunswick, *Rules of Court*, rule 49; Nova Scotia, *Civil Procedure Rules*, s. 41A; Newfoundland and Labrador, *Rules of the Supreme Court 1986*, s. 20A; Northwest Territories, *Supreme Court Rules*, rules 173-180; Prince Edward Island, *Rules of Civil Procedure*, rule 49; and Saskatchewan, *Queen's Bench Rules*, s. 178.

Many of the same issues that arise in respect of access to justice re-emerge in the context of settlement. The same barriers that prevent access to the litigation process may render a party incapable of pursuing the legal process through to its conclusion, the trial. An imbalance of factors such as economic wealth, expertise, and bargaining power may cause a party to accept a less-than-optimal settlement rather than proceeding with the litigation. Often, because of the threat of an adverse costs award for failure to settle, the practical choice in litigation is to accept a settlement offer that undervalues the position being asserted or to abandon the litigation entirely. Given this, to what extent should settlement "incentives" focus on the early stages of litigation rather than on costs awards at the end of the process?

2. Settlement Privilege

Settlement negotiations are privileged communications (for other types of privileged communications in the civil justice system, see chapter 8). Certainly, the public policy fostered by the development of the settlement privilege is the notion that parties should be supported in their attempts to resolve their disputes, short of relying on the courts to do so. As such, the common law has evolved to protect from disclosure those communications which are made with the specific objective of resolving a dispute. The reasoning is grounded in the assumption that, absent such protections, parties would be loathe to candidly participate in settlement negotiations, fearing that any concessions proffered as a settlement offer, but subsequently rejected, could be used to their detriment if disclosed in the trial process.

As noted above, with regards to formal offers to settle made after litigation is commenced and pursuant to rules relating to this subject, the rules of court typically attach specific privilege to such offers to settle. For example, see Ontario rules 49.05 and 49.06. However, note that while the various rules of court have served to codify to some extent the doctrine of settlement privilege, the common enunciation of this privilege is far broader and not limited to formal offers to settle under the rules of court. Settlement privilege has even been held to cover those actions and discussions with the objective of settlement, even when the dispute has not yet been formally commenced as an action in litigation.

It is worth noting the common practice of the party making an intended settlement communication is to claim that statement is being made "without prejudice." This practice is arguably misguided as the without-prejudice label carries no magic with it. If a statement is made that meets the conditions for inclusion as a settlement communication, the absence of the without-prejudice label will not operate to render admissible what would otherwise be inadmissible. Conversely, a party who attaches the label "without prejudice" to a communication that would not otherwise qualify for protection under the grounds of settlement privilege will not suddenly be granted immunity from disclosure.

Three conditions must generally be present for settlement privilege to be properly claimed by a party: (1) a litigious dispute must be in existence or within contemplation; (2) the communication must be made with the express or implied intention that it would not be disclosed to the court in the event negotiations failed; and (3) the purpose of the communication must be to attempt to effect a settlement. (See J. Sopinka, S. Lederman, and A. Bryant, *The Law of Evidence in Canada* (Toronto: Butterworths, 1992) at 722-25.)

B. Contents of the Offer To Settle

What constitutes a formal offer to settle?

The following case demonstrates some probative factors in determining whether or not a particular "offer" is a formal offer to settle to which the cost consequences of the particular statutory regime attach.

Clark Agri Service Inc. v. 705680 Ontario Ltd.
(1996), 2 CPC (4th) 78 (Ont. Ct. (Gen. Div.))

QUINN J:

I. Introduction

This motion is the result of two offers to settle and one tornado. At issue is whether either of two offers to settle served by the plaintiff had been withdrawn before being accepted by the defendants. The defendants move for judgment in the terms of the allegedly accepted offers. The plaintiff hopes for judicial intervention to undo what divine intervention hath wrought.

[The plaintiff had entered into an agreement to purchase land on which a grain elevator operated. The dealings became protracted during the sale and litigation ensued. On March 26, 1996, the plaintiff's lawyer made a formal Offer to Settle (the "First Offer"), which was never expressly withdrawn. On May 3rd, the plaintiff's lawyer sent a letter containing a settlement proposal (the "Second Offer") which was also never expressly withdrawn. On May 7th, the defendant's lawyer asked for an extension of the offer contained in the May 3rd letter, because the defendants could not be immediately contacted. On May 8th, the plaintiff's lawyer replied by letter, granting the extension.

The plaintiff never heard from the defendant as to whether the Second Offer was acceptable until May 13th, when the defendant's lawyer wrote to say that his clients' "position had not changed" and the "terms of your proposal did not reflect our earlier discussions." On May 20th, a tornado caused damage to a grain storage bin on the defendants' property. On June 17th, the defendants' lawyer wrote to accept the May 3rd settlement proposal. The plaintiff's lawyer wrote to ask if any property was damaged in the recent tornado.

On June 19, 1996, the defendants' lawyer replied by letter as follows: "Further to your letter of June 18, 1996, I confirm having advised you by telephone on the 18th day of June, 1996 that the damage to the Elevator caused by the recent storm has not been repaired. However, my client has accepted your offer dated the 3rd day of May, 1996 and we are prepared to close the transaction on the 28th day of June, 1996 based upon the price set out in the Letter of Intent dated the 8th day of February, 1996." This was followed by a letter days later from the defendants' lawyer, stating: "... should it be determined that there has been no acceptance of the [Second Offer] we hereby accept the [First Offer]."]

IV. Discussion of the Issues and the Law

1. Were Either or Both of the First Offer and the Second Offer Made Pursuant to Rule 49?

An offer to settle made pursuant to Rule 49 ("Rule 49 offer") has the following features:

(a) It must be in writing.
(b) It must be effectively delivered to the opposing party.

(c) It must be a proposal that can be construed as an offer to settle, open for acceptance and binding if accepted.
(d) It may be in Form 49A, but the use of that form is permissive.
(e) It may be communicated in correspondence between counsel.

If these features are present, an offer will be *presumed* to be a Rule 49 offer unless expressly stated otherwise or unless the offeror can demonstrate that he or she did not intend the offer to be a Rule 49 offer. The point was put this way by Blair J in *McDougall v. McDougall* (1992), 7 OR (3d) 732 (Gen. Div.), at p. 735:

> Rule 49 was a deliberate departure from the practice as it existed under the former rules and from the common law approach to settlement. Its purpose was to promote settlement and to encourage offers in this respect by using the carrot of cost advantages for the successful offerer and the stick of cost disadvantages for the reluctant offeree. If we are to give maximum effect to this change in procedure and policy, *parties should know that if an offer complies in substance with the requirements of rule 49.02 it will be treated as a Rule 49 offer unless it is expressly stated not to be such.* [Emphasis added.]

In the case at bar, the First Offer clearly was intended to be a Rule 49 offer because Form 49A was utilized. As well, it met the criteria for such an offer. The Second Offer was a "letter offer." However, since it complied with the essential features of a Rule 49 offer, and there being no evidence, express or otherwise, that it was intended to be a common law offer, it must be presumed to be a Rule 49 offer. The distinction is important to this motion because a prior counter-offer or rejection of an offer has the effect of terminating a common law offer, whereas a Rule 49 offer may be accepted notwithstanding a prior counter-offer or rejection.

2. Were Either or Both of the First Offer and the Second Offer Open for Acceptance When Purportedly Accepted?

Rule 49.04(3) provides as follows:

> (3) Where an offer to settle specifies a time within which it may be accepted and it is not accepted or withdrawn within that time, it shall be deemed to have been withdrawn when the time expires.

The Second Offer contains this sentence:

> May we please hear from you before the end of business on Tuesday, May 7, 1996.

Does this amount to a specification of time within which the offer may be accepted, as contemplated by Rule 49.04(3)? Certainly the solicitors for the defendants thought so because in their letter of May 7, 1996, we see these words:

> We would appreciate an extension of the offer until 5:00 p.m. on Thursday, May 9, 1996.

By letter dated May 8, 1996, the solicitors for the plaintiff granted the extension. The result is that, as of May 8, 1996, the Second Offer was a Rule 49 offer comprised of the letters of May 3rd, 7th and 8th, respectively.

May 9, 1996, came and went without an acceptance by the defendants.

By letter dated May 13, 1996, the solicitors for the defendant wrote to the solicitors for the plaintiff and *rejected* the Second Offer. However, it was not theirs to reject since it was deemed to have been withdrawn, pursuant to Rule 49.04(3), due to the expiration of the time specified for acceptance. Likewise, when the solicitors for the defendants purported to *accept* the Second Offer, in their letter of June 17, 1996, there was nothing to accept. The letter from the solicitors for the plaintiff dated June 18, 1996, does not alter the matter, since it clearly does not amount to an extension of, or an agreement to extend, the expired period for acceptance.

That brings us to the First Offer. What was its status on June 25, 1996, when it was purportedly (and conditionally) accepted by the defendants in the letter which reads:

> ... should it be determined that there has been no acceptance of the [Second Offer] we hereby accept the [First Offer]?

• • •

... I have before me a plaintiff who made an offer that is less favourable to that plaintiff than its earlier offer. Should I, therefore, lean to adopting the normal understanding of a litigant that the earlier offer is "a piece of history"? I answer that question in the affirmative. In the circumstances of this case, I see it as neither sensible nor fair to conclude that, when the Second Offer was made, the parties regarded the First Offer as still open for acceptance. Furthermore, the conduct of the parties (up until the date that the tornado struck) is consistent with this view ...

• • •

I take the *Financings Ltd.* case to stand for the very fair and rational proposition that in every offer, absent evidence to the contrary, there is an implied term that the object of the offer, as of the date of acceptance, will be in substantially the same condition as it was when the offer was made. I should also add that I do not see that Rule 49 has altered that piece of the common law.

In the case at bar, I have no hesitation in finding such an implied term and I am equally comfortable with the conclusion that, on the date of purported acceptance, the effect of the tornado of May 20, 1996, had substantially altered the condition of the defendants' business, as compared with its condition on the date of both the First Offer and Second Offer, such that there was no offer to be accepted.

• • •

Because I am inclined to view the actions of the defendants as an outrageous and unseemly attempt to visit upon the plaintiff the disastrous effects of the tornado (after all, what, other than the tornado, occurred between May 13, 1996, the date when the defendants purported to reject the Second Offer, and June 17, 1996, the date when the defendants purported to accept the Second Offer) I invite submissions as to the appropriateness of solicitor and client costs fixed and payable forthwith.

C. Strategic Settlement Options

Multiparty litigation often complicates the settlement dynamic. The involvement of multiple defendants in a case puts additional pressure on plaintiffs to settle reasonably or be subject to potential costs awards from more than one defendant if the plaintiff is unsuccessful. Similarly, there is additional pressure on co-defendants to either settle the case among themselves or with the plaintiff to avoid being saddled with legal costs of other co-defendants who were successful. The constantly mutable strategic context of multiparty litigation has led to the invention of two types of settlement options: Mary Carter agreements and Pierringer agreements. In the following two cases, think about the various strategic consequences at play between the plaintiffs and co-defendants.

1. Mary Carter Agreements

Pettey v. Avis Car Inc.
(1993), 13 OR (3d) 725 (Gen. Div.)

FERRIER J:

Reasons for Ruling on Mid-Trial Motion

The plaintiffs claim damages for injuries and losses arising out of a tragic motor vehicle accident which occurred on August 19, 1983, in the town of Barrhead, Alberta. There are five defendants. Soon after the commencement of the trial, the plaintiffs entered into a settlement agreement with two of the defendants, Avis Car and Douglas Pettey (the "contracting defendants"). The agreement was a "Mary Carter" type of agreement. The remaining defendants (the "non-contracting defendants") immediately moved for a stay of the action by the plaintiffs as against them, taking the position that the agreement was an abuse of process and void as against public policy. I dismissed the motion for reasons to be delivered in due course. Eventually, the entire action was settled, in the third week of trial, but because the issues raised in the motion brought by the non-contracting defendants are of general importance, I now deliver my reasons for the dismissal of the motion.

. . .

The Agreement

At the beginning of the second day of trial, counsel for the plaintiffs advised the court that an agreement had been reached which was in the process of being committed to writing. Counsel for the plaintiff advised the court of the complete terms of the agreement, but did not disclose the dollar amounts in the agreement. Counsel for the plaintiff was willing to disclose the dollar amounts but did not do so because counsel for the defendants Reuben Transport Ltd. and St. Yves objected to the amounts being disclosed. Up to this point, Avis Car and Douglas Pettey were represented by the same counsel. At this juncture, however, the court was advised that Avis Car's and Douglas Pettey's interests might diverge at this point on the choice of law questions. Accordingly, new counsel, from this point forward, acted for Avis Car separately. The court was also advised by Avis Car's new counsel that as between Avis and Pettey there was an outstanding insurance issue outside this action, and that Avis had undertaken in reference to Mr. Douglas Pettey that it would not make any claim against Douglas Pettey's assets in the event it achieved any form of judgment against Douglas Pettey.

· · ·

The effect of the agreement is that the plaintiffs are guaranteed a $3,000,000 recovery plus $300,000 in costs from the contracting defendants. In addition, the contracting defendants have capped their exposure to the plaintiffs in an amount certain. The plaintiffs are at liberty to continue their claims against the non-contracting defendants. The contracting defendants are at liberty to continue with their cross-claims for indemnity against the non-contracting defendants. The non-contracting defendants are no longer exposed to joint and several liability, but only to several liability. In addition, the contracting defendants have agreed to indemnify the plaintiffs for their reasonable fees and disbursements in prosecuting their claims beyond the date of the agreement.

The effect of para. 3 of the agreement needs close examination. An example of a possible result was tendered in argument by counsel for Barrhead. If the plaintiffs' damages were assessed by the court at $6,000,000 and the liability attributed 50% to the contracting defendants and 50% to the non-contracting defendants, then the result would be that the contracting defendants would achieve a return of $1,500,000 (leaving them having paid a net of $1,500,000) and the non-contracting defendants would be required to pay $3,000,000. In this example, while the plaintiffs would obtain judgment at trial for $6,000,000 damages, they would only, in fact, receive a net of $4,500,000. The balance of $1,500,000 would be recovered by the plaintiffs for the benefit of the contracting defendants.

The Motion

In the face of this agreement, the defendant Barrhead moved for an order that the main action be stayed and Reuben and St. Yves joined with Barrhead in seeking the same relief. In argument, the moving parties also sought a declaration that the agreement was null, void and unenforceable as against the non-contracting defendants. Alternatively the moving parties sought a declaration of a mistrial because the agreement was revealed only after the police officer had testified.

The Issues

The issues can be summarized as follows:

1. If such an agreement is entered into, when must it be disclosed?
2. Must the complete terms of the agreement, including the dollar amounts of the settlement, be disclosed to the court?
3. Does such an agreement amount to an abuse of process?

The Law

The expression "Mary Carter agreement" has its origins in the Florida case *Booth v. Mary Carter Paint Co.*, 202 So.2d 8 (Fla. Dist. Ct. App. 1967). Cases in the United States have indicated that a typical Mary Carter agreement contains the following features:

1. The contracting defendant guarantees the plaintiff a certain monetary recovery and the exposure of that defendant is "capped" at that amount.

2. The contracting defendant remains in the lawsuit.
3. The contracting defendant's liability is decreased in direct proportion to the increase in the non-contracting defendant's liability.
4. The agreement is kept secret.

· · ·

In reported decisions, the majority of the courts in the United States which have considered the validity of Mary Carter agreements have allowed them to stand provided the agreement is disclosed to the parties and to the court. ...

In Nevada and Texas, Mary Carter type of agreements have been declared void as against public policy. ...

· · ·

In *Elbaor v. Smith*, a 1992 decision, the Supreme Court of Texas considered the issues at length, at pp. 247 and following:

> The settling defendant, who remains a party, guarantees the plaintiff a minimum payment, which may be offset in whole or in part by an excess judgment recovered at trial ... This creates a tremendous incentive for the settling defendant to ensure that the plaintiff succeeds in obtaining a sizable recovery, and thus motivates the defendant to assist greatly in the plaintiff's presentation of the case (as occurred here). Indeed, Mary Carter agreements generally, but not always, contain a clause requiring the settling defendant to participate in the trial on the plaintiff's behalf.
>
> Given this Mary Carter scenario, it is difficult to surmise how these agreements promote settlement. Although the agreements do secure the partial settlement of a lawsuit, they nevertheless nearly always ensure a trial against the non-settling defendant ... .

· · ·

> In his concurring opinion in *Scurlock Oil Co. v. Smithwick*, 724 SW2d 1, 8 (Tex. 1986) (on motion for rehearing), Justice Spears pointed out that "Mary Carter agreements should be prohibited because they are inimical to the adversary system, and they do not promote settlement—their primary justification." The truth of this statement has been recognized by commentators and has been proven by the subsequent history regarding the use of Mary Carter agreements.

· · ·

> Many jurisdictions have decided to tolerate the ill effects of Mary Carter agreements, presumably because they believe that the agreements promote settlement.

· · ·

> Mary Carter agreements not only allow plaintiffs to buy support for their case, they also motivate more culpable defendants to "make a 'good deal' [and thus] end up paying little or nothing in damages." *Id.*; *cf. Slayton v. Ford Motor Co.*, 140 Vt. 27, 435 A.2d 946, 947 (1981) (jury may infer that non-settling defendant was the most culpable defendant because plaintiff did not settle with that defendant). Remedial measures cannot overcome nor sufficiently alleviate the malignant effects that Mary Carter agreements inflict upon our adversarial system. No persuasive public policy justifies them, and they are not legitimized simply because this practice may continue in the absence of these agreements. The Mary Carter agreement is simply an unwise and champertous device that has failed to achieve its intended purpose. See *Lum*, 488 P.2d at 351 (Mary Carter agreements essentially champertous because settling

defendant retains financial interest in plaintiff's success against non-settling defendant); *cf.*
Monjay v. Evergreen School Dist., 18 Wash.App. 654, 537 P.2d 825, 830 (1975).

· · ·

As a matter of public policy, this Court favours settlements, but we do not favor partial
settlements that promote rather than discourage further litigation. And we do not favor
settlement arrangements that skew the trial process, mislead the jury, promote unethical
collusion among nominal adversaries, and create the likelihood that a less culpable defendant will be hit with the full judgment. The bottom line is that our public policy favoring fair
trials outweighs our public policy favoring partial settlements.

This case typifies the kind of procedural and substantive damage Mary Carter agreements can inflict upon our adversarial system. Thus, we declare them void as violative of
sound public policy.

Justice Dogget in a strong dissent, supported by two other members of the court, said
this at p. 252 and following:

At the outset let it be clear that I am opposed to litigation agreements in any form that
"skew the trial process, mislead the jury" or endanger the public … . A lawsuit is more than
a battle of private contestants; it is conducted in a taxpayer-funded forum with the involvement of public employees and invested with a public interest. Careful scrutiny is appropriate
for agreements with a potential to distort the search for truth that lies at the heart of the litigation process, and public policy will sometimes require their disapproval. See, e.g., *Tom L.
Scott, Inc. v. McIlhany*, 798 SW 2d 556, 560 (Tex. 1990) (orig. proceeding) (invalidating a
private agreement permitting one party from purchasing control of an opponent's expert
witnesses). Just as litigants can no longer enter legally enforceable agreements to bar the
public's right to know about the dangers to health and safety lurking in discovery documents, see *Tex.R.Civ.P.* 76a, they should not be permitted to distort their relationship with
one another in the courtroom so as to subvert a fair trial. Usually before invalidating such
an agreement, however, we first ascertain whether the integrity of the judicial process can
be preserved through reasonable procedural safeguards. See *Cypress Creek Util. Serv. Co. v.
Muller*, 640 SW 2d 860, 866 (Tex. 1982) (noting that procedural modifications are preferable
to changes in the substantive law in protecting against potentially collusive trial tactics).
Here a procedural remedy was adequate; the trial judge handled this matter in a responsible
manner. The truth finding process was appropriately preserved, but, dissatisfied with the
truth determined, the majority once again overrules precedent to achieve a desired result.

· · ·

The chief problem associated with a Mary Carter agreement is that a hidden alteration of
the relationship of some of the parties will give the jury a misleading and incomplete basis
for evaluating the evidence. As is true in so many areas of jurisprudence, secrecy is the first
enemy of justice. To address this concern, trial judges have appropriately implemented several procedural safeguards that remove the veil of secrecy from such settlements. Accordingly, we have emphasized the importance of complete disclosure of these arrangements.

· · ·

Simply because jurors may initially expect the plaintiff to have interests adverse to all
defendants does not mean that they are incapable of understanding that certain defendants
have an incentive for the plaintiff to succeed. Indeed the same may occur in some multiparty litigation where no Mary Carter agreement is involved. The trial cannot be a "sham of

adversity" ... when the jury, as here, is fully aware of this shift in alliances. Nor does the trial become less adversarial merely because some of the parties have switched sides—the names may have changed but the struggle is left intact. So long as at least two parties with antagonistic interests remain, the likelihood that the truth will emerge is not diminished.

· · ·

Accordingly, most jurisdictions allow Mary Carter agreements when trial courts implement similar procedural safeguards to those adopted here. ... In rejecting the full disclosure approach, today's opinion embraces a decidedly minority view accepted in only "a couple of states" that have previously chosen to prohibit such agreements ... . Indeed, the majority cannot point to a single case in any jurisdiction that has ever approved today's prohibition of a named party from participating at trial because of a disclosed pretrial agreement.

· · ·

Texas has today become the first state in the nation to lock the courthouse door on a party solely because of a pretrial contract involving a partial settlement which the majority dislikes. The elitist view that ordinary people acting as jurors are incapable of determining the facts after full disclosure has once again prevailed ... .

In the Oklahoma case of *Cox v. Kelsey-Hayes Co.*, 594 P2d 354 (Okla. 1978) at 358, the Oklahoma Supreme Court said that the feature of the Mary Carter agreement whereby the contracting defendant's liability is decreased in direct proportion to the increase in the non-contracting defendant's liability, is the element that is unique to such agreements and creates the most unfair prejudice to the non-agreeing defendant and his right to a fair trial. ...

Apparently, Mary Carter agreements have become commonplace in the majority of states in the United States, and are increasingly in use in Canada. Although one Canadian decision (*J & M Chartrand Realty Ltd. v. Martin* (1981), 22 CPC 186 (Ont. HC)) expressly left open the question of the validity of such agreements, there is apparently no Canadian decision that has found them to be invalid. All judgments in cases in which a Mary Carter agreement had been entered into were unaffected by the existence of that agreement. In none of the reported Canadian decisions were the proceedings stayed by the court on its own initiative pursuant to its inherent right to control its process. ...

· · ·

Quite obviously any consideration of the issues and the principles to be applied must be made in the context of the terms of the agreement in question. The ruling I have made and the application of the principles must be considered only in the context of the agreement before the court and not as a blanket approval of all Mary Carter type agreements.

Further, it is trite that parties are free to contract and to settle lawsuits; the court will not lightly interfere with such settlements freely entered into by the parties.

Also, it is trite that this court encourages settlements of all issues and when that is not achieved encourages settlement of as many issues as possible.

1. When Must Such Agreements Be Disclosed?

The answer is obvious. The agreement must be disclosed to the parties and to the court as soon as the agreement is made. The non-contracting defendants must be advised immediately because the agreement may well have an impact on the strategy and line of cross-examination to be pursued and evidence to be led by them. The non-contracting

parties must also be aware of the agreement so that they can properly assess the steps being taken from that point forward by the plaintiff and the contracting defendants. In
short, procedural fairness requires immediate disclosure. Most importantly, the court
must be informed immediately so that it can properly fulfill its role in controlling its process in the interests of fairness and justice to all parties.

The non-contracting defendants argue that the agreement should have been disclosed
to the court before the commencement of the trial of the action. I would agree with that
proposition if the agreement had in fact been made before the trial commenced. Such
was not the case here. The agreement was not made until the morning of the second day
of trial and the court was immediately advised. I note that Commentary 4 to R. 10 of The
Rules of Professional Conduct contemplates the possibility that such an agreement
would be made after the commencement of a trial. The non-contracting defendants further argue that since the agreement was not made and the court advised until after evidence had been given by the plaintiffs' first witness, the non-contracting defendants were
prejudiced. I was unable to glean any resulting prejudice to the defendants in this case.
The witness in question was called on the issues of liability. All defendants cross-
examined the witness. All defendants, at that point, were exposed to the claims of the
plaintiffs ranging from zero to 100% liability.

2. Must the Complete Terms of the Agreement Including the Dollar Amounts of the Settlement Be Disclosed to the Court and to the Parties?

Excepting the dollar amounts, it is rather obvious that all of the terms of the agreement
must be disclosed, especially for the purpose of enabling the court to control its own
process. I agree with the statements in the Florida case of *Insurance Co. of North America
v. Sloan*, 432 So.2d 132 (Fla. App. 4 Dist. 1983) to the effect that gratuitous and self-serv-
ing language ought not to be part of the disclosure.

The disclosure of the dollar amounts is patently in the discretion of the court. In the
case at bar, as above noted, a copy of the full text of the agreement, including the dollar
amounts, was sealed and made an exhibit in the trial, so that full disclosure was entirely
within the court's control. I declined to be apprised of the dollar amounts, being of the
view that they would be of no assistance to me in controlling the process or in deciding
the issues. It is not for me to consider whether, in given circumstances, the court ought
to learn the dollar amounts. I note that in some jurisdictions in the United States, disclosure of the amounts to the jury is prohibited. See *Ratterree v. Bartlett*, supra. See also
Hatfield v. Continental Homes, 610 A2d 446 at 452 (Pa. 1992).

3. Does Such an Agreement Amount to an Abuse of Process?

The agreement here has not been kept secret. Accordingly, the court is able to control its
process with full knowledge of all relevant circumstances.

The contracting defendants remain in the lawsuit. They remain for the specific purpose of establishing their claims for contribution and indemnity against their co-
defendants. Such claims would have been vigorously pursued even in the absence of the
agreement. The agreement did not bring those cross-claims into existence, nor did it

prejudice the non-contracting defendants' position in defending the cross-claims. I see no reason why the agreement should prohibit the pursuit of those cross-claims.

The additional feature similar to a Mary Carter agreement is that the contracting defendants' exposure is decreased in direct proportion to the increase in the non-contracting defendant's exposure. This is so to a degree in the case at bar. With such an agreement, it is in the interests of the contracting defendants to pursue the non-contracting defendants on the issues of liability; but this would be so as well in the absence of an agreement. However, it is also in the interests of the contracting defendants, once having made the agreement, to have the plaintiffs' damages assessed as high as possible in the circumstances. The higher the assessment, the greater the return to the contracting defendants. I note what happened at trial in *Elbaor v. Smith* (at pp. 246-247):

> During the trial, the settling defendants' attorneys, who sat at the table with Dr. Elbaor's attorneys, vigorously assisted Ms. Smith in pointing the finger of culpability at Dr. Elbaor. This created some odd conflicts of interest and some questionable representations of fact. For example, although Ms. Smith's own experts testified that Dr. Syrquin committed malpractice, her attorney stated during *voir dire* and in her opening statement that Dr. Syrquin's conduct was "heroic" and that Dr. Elbaor's negligence caused Ms. Smith's damages. And during her closing argument, Ms. Smith's attorney urged the jury to find that Dr. Syrquin had not caused Ms. Smith's damages. This is hardly the kind of statement expected from a plaintiff's lawyer regarding a named defendant. ACH and Drs. Syrquin and Stephens had remained defendants of record, but their attorneys asserted during *voir dire* that Ms. Smith's damages were "devastating," "astoundingly high," and "astronomical." Furthermore, on cross-examination they elicited testimony from Ms. Smith favorable to her and requested recovery for pain and mental anguish. The settling defendants' attorneys also abandoned their pleadings on Ms. Smith's contributory negligence, argued that Ms. Smith should be awarded all of her alleged damages, and urged that Dr. Elbaor was 100 percent liable.

Without some procedural safeguards to prevent the kind of distortions which occurred in *Elbaor*, there would be a legitimate concern that the agreement resulted in an abuse of process.

Accordingly, I directed, when dismissing the motion for a stay, that the contracting defendants would not be permitted to cross-examine on issues related to the quantum of damages, except with leave of the court.

In these circumstances is the agreement an abuse of process? I think not. The court has been fully informed, to all necessary extent, of the terms of the agreement and has been able to control the process of the trial accordingly. The moving parties submit that in given circumstances the agreement would usurp the function of the court. I return to the $6 million example above referred to. In that example, if the court awarded $6 million and apportioned the question of liability as above indicated, the plaintiff would be obliged by the agreement to pay $1.5 million to the contracting defendants, leaving a net recovery to the plaintiff of only $4.5 million. This is the effect of the agreement. I see nothing wrong with that. Any plaintiff faces success risks in an action. An actual recovery of only $4.5 million is the trade-off for a guaranteed recovery of $3 million, in the example. I fail to see why a plaintiff cannot achieve a guaranteed minimum result by such an agreement, preserving its ability to continue against the other defendants in an attempt to better that result. Nor can I see why a defendant who wishes to settle is prohibited from so doing unless it gives up its right to proceed against its co-defendants.

The moving parties also submit that the agreement usurps the function of the court in another respect. A given judgment would result in joint and several liability against the non-contracting defendants, whereas the agreement restricts the right of the plaintiff to recover against the non-contracting defendants on the basis of several liability only. In my view, this argument hardly illustrates a prejudice to the non-contracting defendants and is something the parties ought to be free to contract.

· · ·

Champerty and Maintenance

The moving parties assert that the agreements constitute champerty and maintenance in two respects: first, the agreement makes the contracting defendants participants in the plaintiff's recovery; secondly, the indemnity for legal fees and disbursements for the balance of the proceeding is a financing by the contracting defendants of the plaintiffs pursuing their claims against the non-contracting defendants.

On the first point, on the questions of liability, the parties are in no different position following the agreement than they were prior to the agreement. The contracting defendants have sought contribution and indemnity from the non-contracting defendants. The contracting defendants have a legitimate interest in the pursuit of their claims against the non-contracting defendants. That has been the case from the commencement of the proceedings. The agreement does not alter that. If they are successful in their cross-claims, then that success enures to their benefit by potentially reducing the net exposure to the plaintiffs. There was no improper purpose. There was no "officious intermeddling with a law suit which in no way belongs to one, by assisting either party with money or otherwise to prosecute or defend a suit." See *Langtry v. Dumoulin* (1884), 7 OR 644 (Div. Ct.) at 661, aff'd. 13 SCR 258; *Newswander v. Giegerich* (1907), 39 SCR 354; and *Wiegand v. Huberman* (1979), 108 DLR (3d) 450 (BC SC).

In *Goodman v. R,* [1939] 4 DLR 361 at 364, [1939] SCR 446 at 449, Kerwin J (as he then was) adopted the definition of maintenance given to it by Lord Abinger in *Findon v. Parker*, [1843] 11 M. & W. 675 at 682, 152 ER 976 (Exch. Ct.) at 979:

> The law of maintenance, as I understand it upon the modern constructions, is confined to cases where a man improperly, and for the purpose of stirring up litigation and strife, encourages others either to bring actions, or to make defences which they have no right to make.

Such is not the case here.

Champerty is a particular kind of maintenance in which the maintainer stipulates for a portion of the proceeds of the litigation as his reward for the maintenance: *Re Trepca Mines Ltd.*, [1962] 3 All ER 351 (CA) at 359.

Such is not the case here.

· · ·

In reference to the second point, concerning the indemnity for the ongoing costs of the trial, I view that part of the agreement simply as one of the items of consideration paid by the contracting defendants in order to achieve an upper limit cap on their exposure to the plaintiffs. If such a provision were to be considered void or improper, then there would be a simple way around the problem. The contracting defendants would simply increase the amount of the recovery to be paid to the plaintiffs and include a provision that from that point forward the plaintiff was responsible for its own costs. The parties to the agreement here have not done that but rather have been forthright with the court in disclosing the full and accurate terms of their agreement.

Accordingly, as above noted, I dismissed the motion with the added proviso that the contracting defendants not cross-examine on the quantum of damages without leave of the court.

2. Pierringer Agreements

M. (J.) v. Bradley
(2004), 71 OR (3d) 171 (CA)

CRONK JA: The sole issue in these proceedings is whether the Superior Court of Justice has jurisdiction under s. 1 of the *Negligence Act*, RSO 1990, c. N.1 (the "Act") to apportion fault or neglect in a multi-party tort action against persons who were originally named as party defendants but who, as a result of pre-trial settlements, will not be parties to the action at the time of trial.

Twenty individual plaintiffs commenced this action in January 1997, claiming damages for historical sexual abuses and assaults that they allege were perpetrated upon fourteen of them, when they were children, by the defendants William Bradley and Earl McDonald. They also allege that there may be other victims of similar tortious conduct by these defendants, apart from any of the plaintiffs. As well, they claim that the remaining defendants breached duties owed to the plaintiffs by failing to take steps that would have prevented the alleged abusive and assaultive activities of Bradley and McDonald, or by permitting such activities to occur.

The incidents in question are alleged to have occurred between 1960 and 1991, thus spanning a period of about thirty-one years. As a result, several of the defendants are now elderly or in poor health.

After the commencement of the action, the following events transpired:

(i)   Bradley, McDonald, and one other defendant died;
(ii) the claims of several plaintiffs were discontinued or dismissed on consent;
(iii) some of the defendants defaulted in defending the action;
(iv) the defendant, Dr. Archibald Kerr, defended the action and cross-claimed against some of his co-defendants, seeking contribution and indemnity from them and reserving his right to cross-claim against other co-defendants following discoveries; and
(v)   third party claims were initiated by the defendant, The Governing Council of the Salvation Army, and Kerr against two individuals: the mother of some of the plaintiffs, who was married first to Bradley and subsequently to McDonald, and

a second individual who the plaintiffs assert was a witness to some of the abuse involving children other than the plaintiffs.

By September 2002, those plaintiffs who remained involved in the litigation had each entered into partial settlement agreements (the "Agreements") with all the defendants (the "Settling Defendants") save for Bradley, McDonald and Kerr (the "Non-Settling Defendants"). Under the Agreements, the plaintiffs settled their claims against the Settling Defendants and agreed to limit their claims against the Non-Settling Defendants.

On September 26, 2002, Métivier RSJ of the Superior Court of Justice granted an order approving the Agreements, to the extent that they affected the interests of minors, and dismissing the plaintiffs' action as against the Settling Defendants, without costs.

As a result of all these events, Kerr became the only remaining Non-Settling Defendant active in the action.

Prior to the dismissal order, Kerr and the Settling Defendants reserved their respective rights to bring cross-claims against each other at any time during the action. Although Kerr was aware that the plaintiffs were negotiating the Agreements, and was provided with copies of two of the Agreements after they were executed, he did not receive notice of the plaintiffs' dismissal motion before Métivier RSJ.

Given the terms of the Agreements and the granting of the dismissal order, Kerr was concerned that the judge who presided over the trial might lack jurisdiction to determine the degree, if any, in which the fault or neglect of the Settling Defendants caused or contributed to the plaintiffs' alleged injuries and damages. Kerr feared that, by virtue of the dismissal order, he could be deprived of his right to obtain such an apportionment of liability, if any, against the Settling Defendants.

Accordingly, Kerr moved to set aside the dismissal order and for leave to amend his pleading to assert cross-claims against the Settling Defendants.

In response to Kerr's motion, the Settling Defendants amended their statement of claim, on consent, to refer to the Agreements and some of their essential terms. They also agreed that, if requested by Kerr or the plaintiffs, they would consent to being examined for discovery.

To address the jurisdictional issue raised by Kerr and the ability of the court to give full effect to the terms of the Agreements at trial, the parties also agreed to adjourn parts of Kerr's motion and to submit a special case for the opinion of the court under rule 22 of the *Rules of Civil Procedure*, RRO 1990 Reg. 194. With the concurrence of all parties, the following question was posed for the opinion of the court:

> Does the Court have the jurisdiction to determine whether any fault or neglect of the Settling Defendants or any of them caused or contributed to the damages alleged by the plaintiffs, and the degree of any such contribution, if the Settling Defendants are not parties to the action at the time of trial, in circumstances where the Settling Defendants have entered into Partial Settlement Agreements with the plaintiffs, and consent to the Court so determining the fault or neglect of the Settling Defendants?

The special case was heard by Forget J of the Superior Court of Justice on February 18, 2003. By order dated March 17, 2003, he held that the Superior Court of Justice did not have jurisdiction to apportion fault or neglect at trial against the Settling Defendants who, by then, would not be parties to the action.

The plaintiffs and some of the Settling Defendants now jointly appeal from that decision. Although three separate appeals were initiated, the appeals were consolidated and heard together by this court. For ease of reference, I refer throughout the balance of these reasons to the plaintiffs as the appellants.

For the reasons that follow, I conclude that the Superior Court of Justice has jurisdiction, in the circumstances of this case, to determine whether and to what extent any fault or neglect of the Settling Defendants caused or contributed to the damages alleged by the appellants, although the Settling Defendants will not be parties to the action at trial. Accordingly, I would allow the appeals.

· · ·

By September 2002, all the appellants who continued as participants in the action had entered into Agreements with the Settling Defendants. The terms of the Agreements are identical and modelled on a type of settlement agreement known as a "Pierringer" agreement, as described in the Wisconsin case of *Pierringer v. Hoger*, 124 NW2d 106 (US Wis. SC 1963).

The parties indicated in the special case that the Agreements are intended, in part, "to permit the Settling Defendants to exit the action by settling their claims with the plaintiffs, and by attempting to eliminate any joint liability the Settling Defendants might be found to have with the remaining defendants."

The Agreements each provide:

(i)   that the settlement and payment contemplated thereunder are not to be taken as an admission of liability on the part of the Settling Defendants;

(ii) that the action will be dismissed as against the Settling Defendants, on consent and without costs;

(iii) that the appellants will use their best efforts to cause any cross-claims against the Settling Defendants to be similarly dismissed, without costs, "in order to fully and finally conclude all litigation arising from the matters pleaded" in the action against the Settling Defendants;

(iv) a full and final release by the appellants in favor of the Settling Defendants;

(v)   that the appellants will indemnify and hold harmless the Settling Defendants from any cross-claim or third party claim, and any other proceeding or claim arising from the issues and allegations in the action; and

(vi) for the disclosure of the Agreement, including the settlement amount provided thereunder, to the trial court, on certain conditions.

The indemnity provision contained in each of the Agreements states:

The [appellants] restrict their claim to whatever the non-settling defendants may be directly liable for and as such non-settling defendants cannot be jointly liable with the settling defendants. This clause means non-settling defendants have no basis to seek contribution, indemnity, relief over by way of equitable subrogation, declaratory relief or otherwise against the [Settling Defendants].

In February 2003, after the dismissal of the appellants' claims against the Settling Defendants, the appellants amended their statement of claim, on consent, to reflect the compromises of their claims detailed in the Agreements. The amended version of their pleading states:

> 89. The Plaintiffs have agreed with the Settling Defendants that they shall limit their claims against the Non-settling Defendants to claims for damages, costs and interest attributable only to the Non-settling Defendants' several share of liability to the Plaintiffs and joint liability to one another, if any, such that *the Plaintiffs' recovery shall be limited to recovering the damages, costs and interest attributable to the Non-settling Defendants' several share of liability, or joint share of liability among them, proven against them at trial.*
>
> 90. For greater certainty, the Plaintiffs shall have no claim directly or indirectly against the Settling Defendants and *the Plaintiffs shall limit their claims against the Non-settling Defendants so as to exclude any cross-claim or third party claim made against or which could be made against the Settling Defendants arising from the issues in this action.*
>
> 91. The Plaintiffs admit that the Court at any trial of this matter has and shall have full authority to adjudicate upon the apportionment of liability, if any, between all Defendants named in this Statement of Claim, including the Settling Defendants, whether or not the Settling Defendants remain as parties by cross-claim or third party claim in this action. [emphasis added]

The Non-Settling Defendants are defined in the appellants' amended pleading to mean Bradley, McDonald and Kerr.

All parties agree that the terms of the Agreements require that Kerr should have the opportunity and right, if so advised, to obtain an adjudication at trial as to whether the neglect or fault of one or more of the Settling Defendants caused or contributed to the damages alleged by the appellants. Indeed, it is common ground that the trial judge who presides over the trial of the action will be required to determine the degree to which the Settling Defendants are at fault or negligent in order to give effect to the Agreements.

The parties, including Kerr, also agree that if the appeals are allowed, the factual and legal issues in dispute will be reduced, costs savings for all parties will be realized, and no prejudice will be caused to any party.

Kerr, therefore, does not oppose the dismissal of the appellants' claims against the Settling Defendants so long as he is not deprived of his right to seek to limit his potential liability, if any, by having the Settling Defendants' share of liability adjudicated at trial. Kerr's proposed cross-claims against the Settling Defendants are intended to preserve his access to such an apportionment. However, if the Settling Defendants are required to remain in the action as defendants to cross-claims brought by Kerr, the substance of their settlement bargain with the appellants will be threatened and, potentially, lost entirely.

III. Motions Judge's Decision

In his reasons dated March 17, 2003, the motions judge implicitly acknowledged that the active parties to this action either agreed to, or did not oppose, the terms of settlement contained in the Agreements. He also recognized that the parties consented to the jurisdiction of the Superior Court of Justice to apportion liability at trial as against the Settling Defendants.

The motions judge held that the proposed apportionment of liability to the Settling Defendants, "[did] not pose a risk of prejudice to any of the persons involved in the present proceedings ... ."

However, the motions judge also reviewed the decision in *Martin v. Listowel Memorial Hospital* (2000), 51 OR (3d) 384 (Ont. CA), in which this court stated in *obiter* that a court could only apportion degrees of fault under s. 1 of the Act to a defendant who was a party to the applicable proceedings. Primarily on the basis of that case, the motions judge concluded that the Superior Court of Justice lacked the asserted jurisdiction to apportion fault or neglect to the Settling Defendants at trial.

IV. Analysis

(1) "Pierringer" Settlement Agreements

In recent years, "Pierringer" settlement agreements have been increasingly utilized in Canada in a variety of litigation settings. In *Amoco Canada Petroleum Co. v. Propak Systems Ltd.* (2001), 200 DLR (4th) 667 (Alta. CA), at 673-74, the Alberta Court of Appeal outlined the factors leading to their emergent use:

> Now past is the day when "settlement agreement" can be understood to refer solely to the final resolution of all outstanding issues between all parties to a lawsuit, effectively bringing the suit to an end. In the last several years, in response to increasingly complex and commensurately dilatory and costly litigation, a new generation of settlement agreements has been cautiously adopted by the litigation bar.
>
> The new settlement agreements, which include such exotically named species as the Mary Carter agreement and the Pierringer agreement, endeavour to attain a more limited objective: rather than trying to resolve all outstanding issues among all parties, a difficult task in complicated suits, they aim to manage proactively the risk associated with litigation. In short, contracting litigants prefer the certainty of settlement to the uncertainty and expense of a trial and the possibility of an undesirable outcome. This "risk-management" objective is accomplished by settling issues of liability between some but not all of the parties, thereby reducing the number of issues in dispute, simplifying the action, and expediting the suit. Ancillary benefits include a reduction in the financial and opportunity costs associated with complex, protracted litigation, as well as savings of court time and resources.

The court in *Amoco* described a "Pierringer" settlement agreement in this way (at p. 671):

> Such agreements permit some parties to withdraw from the litigation, leaving the remaining defendants responsible only for the loss they actually caused, with no joint liability. As the non-settling defendants are responsible only for their proportionate share of the loss, a Pierringer agreement can properly be characterized as a "proportionate share settlement agreement."

"Pierringer" agreements, however, are not free from settlement complications. As observed by the court in *Amoco* (at pp. 674-75):

> As a result of third party proceedings, settling defendants are almost always subject to claims for contribution and indemnity from non-settling defendants for the amount of the

plaintiff's loss alleged to be attributable to the fault of the settling defendants. Before the settling defendants can be released from the suit, some provision must be made to satisfy these claims.

This obstacle is overcome by including an indemnity clause in which the plaintiff covenants to indemnify the settling defendants for any portion of the damages that a court may determine to be attributable to their fault and for which the non-settling defendants would otherwise be liable due to the principle of joint and several liability. Alternatively, the plaintiff may covenant not to pursue the non-settling defendants for that portion of the liability that a court may determine to be attributable to the fault of the settling defendants. … [I]n either case the goal of the proportionate share settlement agreement is to limit the liability of the non-settling party to its several liability.

The Agreements in this case, as I have said, contain both an indemnity clause in favour of the Settling Defendants and an agreement by the appellants to restrict their claims against the Non-Settling Defendants to only those defendants' *several*, rather than *joint and several*, shares of liability. In respect of the Non-Settling Defendants, therefore, the Agreements effectively represent a contractual "opting-out" by the appellants of the joint liability provision set out in s. 1 of the Act, save for joint liability, if any, among the Non-Settling Defendants.

(2) Implementation of the Agreements in this Case

The parties who appeal from the motions judge's decision challenge it on three main grounds. First, they argue that there is nothing in the reasoning of this court in *Martin*, *supra*, or under the Act, that operates in the circumstances of this case to preclude the requested liability apportionment at trial against the Settling Defendants. Second, they maintain that the motions judge's decision is contrary to the decisions of other courts in Canada, which have endorsed the implementation of 'Pierringer' settlement agreements. Finally, they assert that the motions judge's decision is also contrary to the settled policy of Canadian courts to encourage settlement. I will address each of these submissions in turn.

(i) Lack of Legal Impediment to the Asserted Jurisdiction of the Superior Court

In Ontario, the implications of a Pierringer settlement agreement for the apportionment of liability at trial must be assessed in light of s. 1 of the Act. That section reads:

> 1. Where damages have been caused or contributed to by the fault or neglect of two or more persons, the court shall determine the degree in which each of such persons is at fault or negligent, and, where two or more persons are found at fault or negligent, they are jointly and severally liable to the person suffering loss or damage for such fault or negligence, but as between themselves, in the absence of any contract express or implied, each is liable to make contribution and indemnify each other in the degree in which they are respectively found to be at fault or negligent.

The terms of s. 1 of the Act are mandatory. They require the court, in a negligence action involving two or more tortfeasors, to "determine the degree in which *each of such persons* is at fault or negligent" [emphasis added]. In contrast to other sections of the Act, in which express reference is made to the "parties" to an action, s. 1 refers to the apportionment of fault or neglect among "persons" found to have caused or contributed to the damages established at a trial. Thus, Ontario courts have been required to determine whether the word "persons," as used in s. 1, includes persons who are not parties to the negligence action in which damages are proven.

• • •

The motions judge appears to have regarded *Martin* as dispositive of the jurisdictional question posed by the parties on the special case. I disagree. With respect, I am of the view that neither the reasoning in *Martin* nor the language of s. 1 of the Act precludes the apportionment of fault or neglect at trial to one or more of the Settling Defendants. I reach that conclusion for the following reasons.

First, the Superior Court of Justice enjoys a wide jurisdiction under s. 11 of the *Courts of Justice Act*, RSO 1990, c. C-43 that encompasses, "all the jurisdiction, power and authority historically exercised by courts of common law and equity in England and Ontario." This jurisdiction cannot be displaced absent clear and unequivocal statutory language: ... .

• • •

Second, the facts in *Martin* are markedly different from the facts in this case. In *Martin*, the nurse was never sued by the plaintiffs and, thus, had never been a party to the main action. Accordingly, she had no opportunity to respond directly to the plaintiffs' allegations of negligence against her, or to their claims for relief. As between the plaintiffs and the nurse, the nurse was a stranger to the action.

In contrast, in this case, the Settling Defendants were sued by the appellants and defended the action. They are aware of the allegations made by the appellants and had an opportunity to resist any potential findings of fault or negligence against them. Similarly, from the outset of the litigation, the appellants were aware of the involvement of the Settling Defendants and, knowing this, chose to voluntarily compromise their claims against them under the Agreements. In those important respects, the Settling Defendants are in a position analogous to that of the doctors, rather than to that of the nurse, in *Martin*.

• • •

Third, *Martin* is also distinguishable from this case on another fundamental factual basis. In *Martin*, the settlement agreements entered into by the defendant doctors were secret, and were not disclosed to the other defendants or to the courts. In contrast, the parties to the Agreements here have agreed to the disclosure of the Agreements to the trial court and copies of two of the Agreements have been provided to Kerr, the single remaining active defendant. Thus, consideration of the fairness of the settlement with the Settling Defendants, insofar as it relates to minors, was possible by the court prior to the approval of the settlement by Métivier RSJ and it is open to the judge at trial to assess the impact of the settlement on the Non-Settling Defendants and Settling Defendants alike.

Fourth, ... it is noteworthy, in this regard, that the court in *Martin* expressly agreed at para. 47 with the recommendation of the Ontario Law Reform Commission in its 1988 *Report on Contribution Among Wrongdoers and Contributory Negligence* (Toronto: Ministry of the Attorney General, 1988) at 187, that no degree of fault should be apportioned under s. 1 of the Act to an "absent concurrent wrongdoer." ...

There is no "absent" tortfeasor in this case. Rather, the Settling Defendants are "sued persons" in the appellants' action. Accordingly, although the Settling Defendants will not be participants at trial, a trial apportionment of liability against them is consistent with the reasoning in *Martin*.

Fifth, the decision in *Martin* is distinguishable on another, critical ground. The interpretive result in *Martin* was driven by important policy considerations that do not apply here. The court was concerned in *Martin* that a finding of a degree of fault in respect of a non-party could have significant consequences for other defendants under s. 1 of the Act. ...

This concern is met by the type of "Pierringer" settlement agreement employed by the appellants and Settling Defendants. By the terms of the Agreements and their amended pleading, the appellants have acknowledged and agreed that they will hold the Non-Settling Defendants accountable for their *several* liability only. As well, the Settling Defendants have agreed that the trial judge may apportion fault or negligence against them, although they will not take part in the trial.

By reason of these concessions, no risk of a "gap" in liability arises, in the sense described in *Martin*, from the potential apportionment of liability at trial to the Settling Defendants. As I have said, there is no absent or unknown tortfeasor in the case at bar, and the appellants have contractually limited their claims as against *both* the Settling Defendants and the Non-Settling Defendants. As a result, if the Agreements are given effect at trial, any Non-Settling Defendant against whom fault or neglect is found will not be exposed to the risk of an apportionment to them of a larger percentage of the appellants' total loss, based on joint liability with the Settling Defendants, than would otherwise occur, based on their own direct fault.

Finally, Kerr advances an additional compelling reason to support a liability apportionment at trial against the Settling Defendants. He asserts that there is a real risk that none of the Non-Settling Defendants, except himself, will have the financial means to satisfy any judgment granted against them. He therefore submits that he may be exposed under the operation of s. 1 of the Act to the risk of paying damages in excess of any several shares of damages that might be apportioned against him, because he will be jointly liable under s. 1 for the several liability of any impecunious Non-Settling Defendant. As a result, Kerr wishes to be free to take the position at trial that his exposure to any shortfall in the appellants' recovery of damages occasioned by the insolvency of another Non-Settling Defendant should be reduced by a proportion related to the fault of the Settling Defendants.

Assuming, without deciding, that this argument is available under Ontario law, Kerr will be unable to advance this submission at trial if the trial judge lacks the authority to determine the degree in which the Settling Defendants are at fault or negligent, if at all.

On the basis of all these factors, it is my view that the purpose of s. 1 of the Act is not undermined by the Agreements and no question of potential unfairness or prejudice to any of the parties will arise from the implementation of the part of the settlements that contemplates the apportionment of fault or neglect at trial to the Settling Defendants.

In my view, the reasoning in *Martin* does not mean that persons who have been sued by a plaintiff and who, therefore, are not strangers to the action, invariably cannot be subject to an apportionment of liability at trial under s. 1 of the Act if they become non-parties to the plaintiff's action by reason of a pre-trial settlement. To the contrary, in my opinion, when a named party defendant invokes the jurisdiction of the court by defending claims of negligence brought against it, and thereafter relinquishes its right to pursue its defence of those claims by voluntarily entering into a pre-trial settlement, that party is a "person" against whom an apportionment of liability may properly be made where, as here, no question of unfairness or prejudice will arise. Such an apportionment, in my opinion, comports with the interpretation of the substance of s. 1 of the Act that was articulated by this court in *Martin*. In this case, the absence of unfairness or prejudice is indicated by the fact that the parties active in the litigation consent to, or do not oppose, an apportionment at trial of fault or neglect, if any, to the Settling Defendants.

(ii) Experience in Other Provinces with "Pierringer" Agreements

The parties also argue that the motions judge's decision is contrary to the developed experience in other provinces concerning the implementation of "Pierringer" settlement agreements. They point out that the implementation of settlement agreements of the "Pierringer" type has been approved by the appellate courts of Alberta and British Columbia, even in the absence of the consent, or the non-opposition, of all parties: see *Amoco, supra*, and *British Columbia Ferry Corp. v. T & N plc* (1995), 27 CCLT (2d) 287 (BC CA). See also, concerning the assessment of fault against non-parties, *Wells v. McBrine* (1988), 33 BCLR (2d) 86 (BC CA) and the discussion regarding that case by this court in *Martin* at para. 43.

· · ·

In my view, however, the *Amoco* decision and similar cases are instructive in this respect: they essentially emphasize that the interests of the administration of justice are not facilitated by requiring the involvement at trial of a litigant for purely procedural purposes where this can be avoided without unfairness or prejudice to the parties. I endorse this proposition.

As observed by this court in *Martin* at para. 27:

> With litigation becoming more and more expensive and numerous initiatives being taken to reduce the cost of litigation, it would be counterproductive to interpret the *Negligence Act* as requiring the addition of unnecessary parties, purely for form, in order to obtain a fair and proper apportionment of fault.

This statement in *Martin* was concerned with the suggestion by the trial judge in that case, a suggestion rejected by this court, that persons for whom a defendant may be found to be vicariously liable must be added as third parties in order to support a finding of vicarious liability against the named defendant. Nonetheless, it underscores the desirability of avoiding the joinder or involvement in litigation, for purely procedural or technical purposes, of persons who are not otherwise necessary parties.

The conclusion that I have reached regarding the proper interpretation of s. 1 of the Act and the decision in *Martin* avoids this result. I again underscore, as argued by some of the Settling Defendants in these proceedings, that the "persons" against whom a finding of contributory fault or neglect is sought in this case (the Settling Defendants), are persons who had proper notice of the appellants' allegations and a full opportunity to respond to them. They voluntarily elected to terminate their involvement in the litigation on terms that contemplate that the Non-Settling Defendants will continue to have the right to seek a trial apportionment of the Settling Defendants' degree of contributory responsibility, if any, despite the absence of the Settling Defendants at trial. Moreover, they have agreed to be discovered, should discovery of them be sought by the appellants or Kerr. Thus, there is no suggestion in this case of potential procedural unfairness to the Non-Settling Defendants. Finally, all active parties to this litigation either consent, or do not object, to the apportionment of liability at trial as against the Settling Defendants. These factors obviate any need for the Settling Defendants to remain involved in the litigation as passive or active litigants.

(iii) Public Interest in Promoting Settlement

Finally, there is an additional, and powerful, reason to support the implementation of the Agreements in this case: the overriding public interest in encouraging the pre-trial settlement of civil cases. This laudatory objective has long been recognized by Canadian courts as fundamental to the proper administration of civil justice: ... . Furthermore, the promotion of settlement is especially salutary in complex, costly, multi-party litigation. As observed in *Amoco* at p. 677:

> In these days of spiralling litigation costs, increasingly complex cases and scarce judicial resources, settlement is critical to the administration of justice.

The negotiated settlement between the appellants and the Settling Defendants, as recorded in the Agreements and reflected in the appellants' amended pleading, is in the public interest and the interests of all active parties to the litigation. The implementation of the Agreements, which necessitates an apportionment of liability at trial against the Settling Defendants, will result in the participation of fewer parties at trial and will shorten the duration of the trial. This, in turn, will reduce the legal costs of the parties and permit the efficient use of judicial and court resources. As well, and importantly, the implementation of the Agreements is in the interests of all the defendants to the action. The interests of the Settling Defendants are furthered by the release contained in the Agreements and the potential liability of the Non-Settling Defendants is significantly limited under the bargain made by the appellants.

I conclude that "Pierringer" settlement agreements, of the type employed in this case, should be supported in circumstances where, as here, the fairness of the settlement is unchallenged and prejudice arising from the full implementation of the settlement has not been alleged or shown. Cases of this kind cannot be rendered "unsettleable," for all practical purposes, without just and substantive cause. Such cause does not arise in the case at bar.

(iv) Other Relevant Factors

I wish to comment upon two additional and related considerations arising in these proceedings. Kerr argued before this court that the trial judge in this action would be faced with a most difficult, if not impossible, task if required to determine the Non-Settling

Defendants' several share of liability without being in a position to make the same determination concerning the responsibility, if any, of the Settling Defendants for the appellants' losses. Correspondingly, he asserted that the determination of his share of liability without regard to the Settling Defendants' contributory responsibility would be manifestly unfair.

I agree with both of these submissions. The appellants' allegations, if proven, will make Kerr, the other Non-Settling Defendants and the Settling Defendants concurrent tortfeasors. The liability of the Non-Settling Defendants, however, will be limited to their several liability, and their joint liability with each other, in accordance with the contractual concessions made by the appellants in the Agreements. In these circumstances, it is difficult to conceive how the several liability of the Non-Settling Defendants could properly and justly be determined by the trial judge without regard to the proportionate fault or neglect of the Settling Defendants.

In some ways, this is analogous to the apportionment of vicarious liability addressed in *Martin*. In that case, as I have said, this court held that the hospital's total liability, including its vicarious liability, could not be justly determined without a determination of the degree of fault of the negligent nurse. Similarly, fairness requires that Kerr's several share of fault or neglect not be determined in a vacuum, without consideration of the several liability of all other proven tortfeasors. Were it otherwise, Kerr could be exposed at trial to the potential risk of being required to pay damages to the appellants for part of the Settling Defendants' several shares of liability, claims to which, as Kerr properly points out, have been compromised and released by the appellants under the Agreements.

D. Settlement Approval

In some settlement contexts, courts exercise their *parens patriae* jurisdiction to protect the vulnerable party. A common example is mandatory judicial settlement approval for those cases involving minors or parties under a disability (see, for example, Ontario rules 7.08 and 49.08). Another example is the judicial approval of class actions settlements (see chapter 11). Judicial settlement approval adds another procedural layer to the claim. Court approval is required to ensure that the settlement is in the best interests of the particular party who, on his or her own, is presently unable to look after his or her own rights (i.e., a minor, incapacitated party, or an entire class of plaintiffs in a class action). In the following case, how does the process of settlement approval become problematic, to operate against the interests of the very party it is designed to protect?

Wu Estate v. Zurich Insurance Co.
(2006), 27 CPC (6th) 207 (Ont. CA)

PER CURIAM: A party under disability died unexpectedly before the court approved the defendant's agreement to settle her accident benefits claim for a lump sum. The issue before us on this appeal is whether the estate of the party under disability can enforce the settlement.

Facts

Yuan Yuan Wu (known as "Rebecca Wu") was hit by an impaired driver as she crossed a street in downtown Toronto. She suffered serious physical injuries and brain injuries resulting in significant cognitive impairment. At the time of the accident, Rebecca Wu was twenty-eight years old. She was married and had one child.

Rebecca Wu, represented by her mother and litigation guardian, commenced an action claiming tort damages against the tortfeasor and claiming statutory accident benefits against Zurich Insurance Company and ING Insurance Company of Canada ("the respondents"), pursuant to the *Insurance Act*, RSO 1990, c. I.8 and the *Statutory Accident Benefits Schedule—Accidents After December 31, 1993 and Before November 1, 1996*, Reg. 776/93.

The respondents obtained comprehensive medical assessments of Rebecca Wu's injuries and future care costs. Despite her severe injuries, Rebecca Wu's life expectancy was estimated to be sixty-eight years. Her own experts estimated her claim for past and future income loss and future care costs at between $5.8 and $6.6 million. After mediation, the respondents agreed to settle her claim for $3.1 million. Because of Rebecca's mental disability, the settlement was "subject to necessary court approval." The tort claim remained outstanding but subject to ongoing settlement discussions.

Three months after the date of the settlement with the respondents, Rebecca died suddenly and unexpectedly. Pending resolution of the tort claim, Rebecca Wu's counsel had not presented the settlement of the accident benefits claim for court approval.

The settlement agreement was reduced to writing in the form of minutes of settlement.

Accident of Benefits of Rebecca Wu

Minutes of Settlement

In consideration of the amount $3,000,000 plus $90,000 for party and party costs and $10,000 for disbursements, Yuan Yuan Wu also known as Rebecca Wu, by her Guardian of Property, Zhi Chen and Zhi Chen and Xu-Qi Wu personally, hereby agree to settle with Zurich Insurance Company and ING Insurance Company of Canada and any successors, for all past, present and future accident benefit claims in connection with the motor vehicle accident of August 29, 1996.

All of the above is subject to necessary court approval to be obtained by counsel for the applicants.

Pending securing all necessary approval, Zurich/ING agree to pay all current AB Benefits to the time of securing necessary court approval. The total amount of accident benefits paid after February 3, 2003 and up to the date of court approval shall be paid back by the applicants to Zurich/ING out of the court approved settlement amount. The Full and Final Release and Disclosure Notice will be paid by counsel for the insurer and will be executed by the applicants after court approval [emphasis added].

Rebecca Wu's estate, her estate trustees, her spouse and her parents ("the appellants") brought an application to enforce the minutes of settlement. The application judge ruled that the requirement for court approval amounted to a "true condition precedent" that had to be satisfied in order to make the settlement agreement enforceable. He ruled that

Rebecca Wu's death made it impossible for the court to approve the settlement and, as her estate could not meet the condition precedent, there was no longer a binding agreement between the parties.

Issue

The sole issue on this appeal is whether the appellants can enforce the settlement of the accident benefits claim against the respondents.

Analysis

The starting point for analyzing the legal status of the settlement agreement is to consider the situation that existed immediately before Rebecca Wu's unexpected death. In *Smallman v. Smallman*, [1971] 3 All ER 717 (Eng. CA), at 720, Denning MR provided the following helpful statement of the legal status of a settlement agreement that is subject to court approval:

> In my opinion, if the parties have reached an agreement on all essential matters, then the clause "subject to the approval of the court" does not mean there is no agreement at all. There is an agreement, but the operation of it is suspended until the court approves it. It is the duty of one party or the other to bring the agreement before the court for approval. If the court approves, it is binding on the parties. If the court does not approve, it is not binding. But, pending the application to the court, it remains a binding agreement which neither party can disavow.

The requirement for court approval of settlements made on behalf of parties under disability is derived from the court's *parens patriae* jurisdiction. The *parens patriae* jurisdiction is of ancient origin and is "founded on necessity, namely the need to act for the protection of those who cannot care for themselves ... to be exercised in the 'best interest' of the protected person ... for his or her 'benefit' or 'welfare'": *Eve, Re*, [1986] 2 SCR 388 (SCC) at para. 73. The jurisdiction is "essentially protective" and "neither creates substantive rights nor changes the means by which claims are determined": *Tsaoussis (Litigation Guardian of) v. Baetz* (1998), 41 OR (3d) 257 (Ont. CA), at 268. The duty of the court is to examine the settlement and ensure that it is in the best interests of the party under disability: *Poulin v. Nadon*, [1950] OR 219 (Ont. CA). The purpose of court approval is plainly to protect the party under disability and to ensure that his or her legal rights are not compromised or surrendered without proper compensation.

The requirement for court approval of settlements involving parties under disability is codified in Ontario in rule 7.08(1):

> No settlement of a claim made by or against a person under disability, whether or not a proceeding has been commenced in respect of the claim, is binding on the person without the approval of a judge.

As explained by Garry D. Watson & Craig Perkins, *Holmested and Watson: Ontario Civil Procedure*, looseleaf (Toronto: Carswell, 1984) vol. 2 at 7-33

> Rule 7.08 ... merely codifies a rule established by case law that a party under disability is bound only by a settlement that is for his or her benefit ... it is designed to protect the party

under disability from mistakes of the litigation guardian. The settlement of a claim by or against a party under disability, whether or not a proceeding has been commenced, is not binding on the party under disability without the approval of a judge.

The wording of rule 7.08(1) may be contrasted with the language of the English "compromise rule" that provides that no settlement involving a party under disability shall "be valid without the approval of the court." This wording was considered by the House of Lords in *Dietz v. Lennig Chemicals Ltd.* (1967), [1969] 1 AC 170 to deprive a settlement that is subject to court approval of any legal effect and to allow either party to repudiate it unless and until it was approved by the court. The situation in Ontario is different: see *Richard v. Worth* (2004), 73 OR (3d) 154 (Ont. SCJ), holding that an insurer could not repudiate an infant settlement, yet to be approved by the court, on the ground that the law relating the insurer's liability had been changed by a subsequent Court of Appeal decision. The effect of rule 7.08(1) coincides with *Smallman v. Smallman, supra,* to this extent: the party under disability has an agreement from which the opposite party cannot resile and that will become fully operational once approved by the court.

We conclude from this analysis that immediately prior to Rebecca Wu's death there was in law an agreement, which the respondents could not disavow, to settle her claim on the terms recorded in the minutes of settlement, but that the operation of that agreement was suspended pending "necessary" court approval.

The crucial issue for us to decide is what effect did Rebecca Wu's death have on the status of the settlement agreement? The respondents make two central submissions. First, they say that the obligation to pay the settlement never arose because the requirement for court approval was never met. They say that the application judge correctly found that the requirement for court approval is a "true condition precedent" upon which the existence of any contractual obligation to pay depends and, as the settlement was not approved, it died with Rebecca Wu. Second, the respondents submit that it is an implicit term of the settlement that Rebecca Wu must be alive to permit the court to approve it. As her death makes court approval impossible, the respondents submit that the agreement must be treated as being void *ab initio.*

For the following reasons, we are unable to accept the respondents' submissions.

With respect to the respondent's first submission, we do not agree that that the settlement died with Rebecca Wu. Prior to her death, Rebecca Wu's claim for accident benefits had, by virtue of the settlement, become a contractual right to the agreed amount, contingent upon obtaining the court's approval of the settlement. That contractual right was a chose in action that, by operation of law, devolved to Rebecca Wu's estate upon her death: *Estates Administration Act,* RSO 1990, c. E.22, s. 2.; Carmen S. Thériault ed., *Widdifield on Executors and Trusts,* looseleaf (Toronto: Carswell, 2002) at p. 2-52: "The general principle is that a right of action in common law survives death and is transmissible automatically to the personal representative." By their terms, the minutes of settlement speak of "necessary" court approval. Once Rebecca Wu's contractual right passed to the estate, there was no longer a party under disability. Court approval was no longer necessary to protect the interest of the party seeking to enforce the settlement. As the need for court approval disappeared upon Rebecca Wu's death, the minutes of settlement became operational and her estate could enforce the obligation to pay.

This analysis is supported by a purposive interpretation of the need for court approval. The respondents' argument that the settlement in Rebecca Wu's favour should be nullified because it was not approved in her lifetime runs directly contrary to the protective purpose of *parens patriae* jurisdiction and of court approval of settlements involving parties under disability. The risk created by the enforced gap in time to allow the court to review the settlement to ensure it meets the plaintiff's interests should not be borne by the plaintiff and *parens patriae* jurisdiction should not be used to defeat the very interests it serves to protect. In this regard, we find persuasive the reasoning in *Reed v. United States*, 891 F2d 878 (US 11th Cir. Fla. 1990), at 881. The claim of an infant plaintiff was settled days prior to his death and "all that remained for final judgment to obtain was for the court to approve the settlement and enter judgment." The court ruled that as "[t]he statute requiring court approval is designed for the protection of minors" and as the defendant had agreed to settle the case, the only legitimate basis for refusing enforcement would be the failure of the agreement to protect the minor's interests. ...

· · ·

It is significant that rule 7.08(1) provides that the agreement is not binding on the party under disability unless the court approves the agreement, but says nothing to limit the binding effect of the agreement on the other party. This reflects the unilateral and protective purpose of court approval that is related to ensuring the fairness of the agreement itself, quite unlike the type of extraneous third-party decision at issue in *Zhilka v. Turney*. In our view, *Zhilka v. Turney* does not apply to the contract at issue here.

With respect to the respondent's second submission, even if we were to accept the respondents' submission that court approval is a "condition precedent" that must be satisfied to make the agreement enforceable by the appellant, we see no reason why court approval cannot be granted despite Rebecca Wu's death. The purposive interpretation of the *parens patriae* jurisdiction and rule 7.8(1) that we have already outlined suggests that authority to approve the settlement should survive the death of the party under disability to the benefit of that party's estate. There was an obvious risk that Rebecca Wu might die earlier than projected and the respondents must have taken into account her projected life expectancy as one of the many contingencies that influenced their assessment of the value of her claim: *White (Litigation Guardian of) v. Godin*, [1997] OJ No. 314 (Ont. CA) at para. 3: "In agreeing to the assessment of damages, the defendants knew that there was a risk that their evaluation of the life expectancy of the plaintiff ... might be proved wrong by future events." Parties under disability cannot re-open settled claims when unfavourable contingencies materialize: see *Tsaoussis (Litigation Guardian of) v. Baetz*, *supra*. Fairness requires similar treatment for insurers. The minutes of settlement could have provided that Rebecca Wu must be alive at the time of court approval but they do not. We do not agree that it would be just to imply a term that would, after the fact, materially alter the parties' allocation of the risk related to her life expectancy.

· · ·

The death of the plaintiff may eliminate the cost of future care and thereby diminish the value of the claim but, for the reasons already expressed, it does not create a new situation that should not have been contemplated by the parties. Life expectancy is but one of many contingencies that parties settling personal injury claims are bound to take into account when determining the worth of the claim, and the unexpected death of the plaintiff does not remove the entire foundation for the agreement.

· · ·

In the absence of any persuasive authority to the contrary, we hold that if it were necessary to do so, the settlement in favour of Rebecca Wu could be approved by the court after her death.

Finally, we note that the considerations of fairness and promoting settlements favour enforcement. We see nothing unfair to the respondents in enforcing this settlement. They agreed to pay the sum specified in the minutes of settlement to settle Rebecca Wu's accident benefits claim. When they decided to settle the claim for that amount, they were in possession of all the relevant facts respecting the claim and had ample opportunity to assess all contingencies. There are no grounds such as mistake or misrepresentation for refusing to enforce the settlement.

Conclusion

For these reasons, the appeal is allowed, the decision below is set aside, and in its place, there shall be judgment in the following terms:

1. A declaration that a valid settlement agreement was reached between Yuan Yuan Wu (also known as Rebecca Wu) by her guardian of property, Zhi Chen, Zhi Chen personally, Xu-Qi Wu, Zurich Insurance Company and ING insurance Company of Canada on February 3, 2003, on the following terms:

   (i) payment in the amount of $3,000,000.00, plus $90,000.00 for costs and $10,000.00 for disbursements from Zurich Insurance Company and/or ING Insurance Company of Canada to Rebecca Wu, Zhi Chen and Xu-Qi Wu; and

   (ii) settlement of all past, present and future accident benefit claims in connection with a motor vehicle accident that occurred on August 29, 1996.

2. An order and judgment requiring the respondents to pay the appellants the sum of $3,100,000.00.

3. Pre-judgment interest and post-judgment interest pursuant to the provisions of the *Courts of Justice Act*, RSO 1990, c. C.43, as amended.

The appellants are entitled to their costs of this appeal fixed at $20,000 inclusive of disbursements and GST. If the parties are unable to agree as to the costs before the application judge, we will receive brief written submissions in that regard.

E. Confidential Settlement Agreements

Many settlement agreements contain confidentiality clauses which require that the parties keep secret some or all aspects of the settlement. The parties may be required to keep confidential such information as the amount of the settlement, the admission of liability or fault, the identity of the parties, and sensitive trade and business information.

Erik S. Knutsen, "Secret Settlements in Canada"
(2009, forthcoming) (footnotes omitted)

A. Secret Settlements Revealed

This article discusses settlements in the civil justice system only. A secret settlement is a settlement of a civil dispute about which some aspect has been agreed upon by the parties to remain confidential. The legal vehicle for this is typically a settlement agreement with a clause where the parties promise to keep some or all of the settlement details secret. Secrecy could be about any aspect of the settlement. Most often, parties agree to keep one or more of the following a secret:

a) the identity of the parties;
b) the amount of the settlement;
c) the admission or denial of fault of one or more parties;
d) facts relating to the loss; or
e) sensitive financial or trade information.

The effective clause in the settlement agreement could be quite simple: "the terms of this settlement shall remain confidential." The clause may include exceptions to the agreed-upon secrecy. Such exceptions can exclude applicability of confidentiality for immediate family members, lawyers, accountants, the government, or for the purposes of obtaining therapy. The clause could also include certain conditions where secrecy is allowed to be broken such as if a court must review the agreement, or if other legal obligations come into being. Finally, the clause could detail the sanctions for breaking secrecy, such as whether or not the breach of secrecy constitutes a fundamental breach of the contract with the result being the contract is void. Alternatively, there may be liquidated damages clauses for breaches of secrecy that detail precisely how much is to be paid upon breach. Neither of these conditions appear to be common in standard settlement agreements at present.

B. Why Use Secret Settlements?

i. Defendants

Defendants use secret settlements in civil lawsuits to create value in the settlement. There is a "price" for secrecy. A defendant is often willing to pay more to a plaintiff if the plaintiff keeps some terms of the settlement confidential. Secret settlements are frequently used for products liability cases, medical negligence, employment cases, and cases involving abuse. Defendants use confidentiality as a bargaining chip to avoid two potentially negative outcomes: negative publicity and future lawsuits. If a defendant can suppress the information about the settlement, such information will not find its way into a public forum and the media. This is worth something to a defendant. The reasons could be varied. The obvious reason is to avoid dissemination of any information of potential fault or wrongdoing. Yet there is still a strong incentive to suppress information of the mere fact that the defendant was sued, regardless of fault or wrongdoing of the defendant. The presence of a lawsuit alone can often create aspersions of fault when no fault, in fact, exists. This can damage the defendant's reputation and client base.

The defendant will also usually want to keep confidential the facts about any payments to the plaintiff. There could be a multitude of reasons beyond admission of fault as to why a defendant might settle a lawsuit with a plaintiff. If, however, information about a payment or settlement is disseminated, the public can often make a deduction— rightly or wrongly—that there must have been some fault on the part of the defendant in order for the dispute to have settled. In reality, the dispute may have settled for reasons wholly unrelated to fault. The defendant, for example, could have decided it was less costly to settle the dispute than fight about the merits. Defendants may also use secret settlements to protect proprietary information, such as trade or business secrets discovered in the process of the litigation. Confidential settlement agreements avoid these negative, costly, and often incorrect, public exposures for defendants. To a defendant, the contractual opportunity to bargain for secrecy about some element of the dispute often has value. It is an important part of the dynamics of settlement.

ii. Plaintiffs

Plaintiffs also use confidential settlement agreements to create value in settlement negotiations. Plaintiffs can capitalize on the value of secrecy to defendants and increase available settlement options. A secret settlement is often worth more to a defendant than a settlement with no disclosure restrictions. A plaintiff will therefore have one more aspect of the case, beyond allegations of fault, with which to bargain.

Theoretically, in fact, it could be possible that a plaintiff's only bargaining chip in a dispute is secrecy. Imagine a case in which the plaintiff either has no substantiated information of a defendant's fault or, as would be more common, where it is too risky and expensive for a plaintiff to gamble on a trial with a defendant over a dispute where fault could be difficult for the plaintiff to prove. The plaintiff at least has the option to bargain for secrecy if a particular defendant values secrecy to any degree.

Plaintiffs also use confidential settlement agreements in a similar vein to defendants in that privacy can be paramount in certain disputes. Plaintiffs may want to keep their identities a secret. There could be sensitive reputational information at stake in a lawsuit, such as in a wrongful dismissal case. Plaintiffs could also be concerned about intimate privacy issues that were disclosed in the lawsuit, such as medical or family information. Victimization concerns could also be paramount where the dispute concerns alleged wrongdoings that are emotionally damaging to the plaintiff. A plaintiff may want to keep all details of such a dispute completely confidential.

Lastly, like defendants, plaintiffs may often want to keep the amount of the settlement a secret. If the amount of the settlement is large, plaintiffs may be concerned about the undue and unwanted attention that a sudden financial influx may bring. The long-lost uncles, twice removed, may suddenly appear, looking for a handout. Secret settlements avoid this problem. Conversely, if the amount of the settlement is not large, a plaintiff may be concerned that the public would view her settled dispute as a failure, frivolous, or unsuccessful (even if, in fact, it is not). The public has a skewed perception of settlement value and is unable to evaluate efficacies of civil settlements. There could be a multitude of reasons as to why the monetary amount of a settlement may not be large, yet the settlement is still a success to the plaintiff. The plaintiff may have bargained to implement organizational changes with the defendant. Perhaps the plaintiff's case was nearly impossible or too expensive to prove in court and some settlement amount was far better than a court-sanctioned cost award after a failed trial. The public is not exposed to the settlement dynamics that went into the agreement between the parties. To avoid public scorn in instances where the public's expected outcome differs from the plaintiff's actual monetary outcome, the plaintiff may wish to keep the settlement amount confidential.

Plaintiffs and defendants alike use confidential settlement agreements to achieve goals that the otherwise simplistic monetization of the dispute cannot solve. Secret settlements can be used as effective value-creation tools in certain circumstances, as discussed later. These tools benefit both plaintiffs and defendants. Removing such tools from the settlement negotiation toolbox therefore hampers parties' abilities to solve disputes using additional non-monetary ways. Secret settlements thus have the potential to engineer additional social outcomes which provide additional value to the settlement.

II. The Public and Private Views of Secret Settlements (and the Civil Justice System)

How anyone views the efficacy of secret settlements in the civil justice system depends upon how one views the role of the civil justice system. That same view also necessarily drives whether or not one argues to curb, ban, or foster secret settlements. There are two competing views as to how the civil justice system as a whole is operating and is meant to operate: the "public view" and the "private view." Unpacking these two views through the lens of secret settlements helps to explain the real debate behind how one sculpts a normative perspective of the civil justice system as a whole.

A. The Public View of Secret Settlements

The public view of the civil litigation system sees the system as a publicly funded, open system operating with transparency to engineer greater social good. Litigation and court decisions contribute to the public commons and enrich social debate through dispute resolution. Those who hold tight to the public view of civil litigation are either against the notion of confidential settlement agreements altogether or instead clamor for strict regulation of secret settlements.

The public view of civil litigation owes its genesis to those scholars who see the civil litigation system, and indeed dispute resolution, as capable of transforming society into something more. Courts mediate a social and political dialog which is performing an inherent service. Court decisions perpetuate an exploratory discussion about the boundaries of the law. This is a decidedly public law-inspired vision of the litigation system. The detriments of secret settlements as catalogued by scholars who espouse the public view of civil litigation therefore emphasize a balance toward public, not private, benefit. Secret settlements therefore hinder the values of the public litigation process.

B. *The Private View of Secret Settlements*

The private view of the civil litigation system sees the system as a party-driven mechanism for efficiently resolving private disputes between parties. Those who espouse the private view of civil litigation are often supportive of a disputing party's opportunity to bargain with secrecy. Secret settlements are a positive dynamic in the civil litigation system.

The private view of civil litigation rests on the idea of party autonomy in the adversary system. The parties within a dispute have complete control as to how the dispute is run. It is the disputing parties themselves who choose to bring a dispute into the public justice system in the first place. The parties decide what issues will comprise the dispute. The parties have complete control over settlement. The parties can also choose when to settle, and how to structure the settlement. Courts, by contrast, can take only the cases brought before them. Therefore, the "public" nature of any dispute in the civil justice system is a mere by-product or, as Arthur Miller puts it, "collateral" to the actual private dispute between the parties. Parties often do not even require interaction with the public justice system to solve their dispute. Instead, they bargain within the "shadow of the law," knowing that certain legal rules will apply if the case proceeds to trial. The shift of the civil justice system from one of trial as main event to pre-trial practices as main event has lead to a decreasing role for adjudication in civil litigation. Most cases settle. The strong arm of the law is not necessarily applied within the courtroom. With so little "public" in the public dispute resolution system, the public view of civil litigation seems to forget that much of what is driving the system are disputes about private law issues.

In fact, the public view may well be an uncomfortable fit with the down-and-dirty world of real-life litigation. The predominant majority of disputes in the civil litigation system are not broad-reaching societal watermarks exploring important public rights but are instead disputes involving injury or simple contract breach. The public view of civil litigation thus appears to be suitable more for a world where every second civil case is about school segregations or civil rights, instead of fender-benders and fence disputes between neighbors.

The private view's difficulty with the public view conception of civil settlements stems largely from the fact that civil disputes live, breathe, and die by the parties themselves. Private civil litigation is not being done for the benefit of the "public." Private litigants pay the costs and are saddled with the risks of litigation. Therefore, private litigants should be free to bargain with whatever tools are available, including their rights to disclose matters about their own case. Ask any litigant in the middle of a lawsuit why he or she sued in the first place. The answer will undoubtedly be: "I was hurt." The public view of civil litigation and secret settlements thus appears to be far removed from the individual litigants who are the actors in the litigation system and control it by their own decisions.

NOTES AND QUESTIONS

1. Does the "public" or "private" view of civil litigation fit better with what the Canadian civil justice's perspective on secret settlements ought to be?

2. Five common arguments against secret settlements, as espoused by the "public view" of civil litigation, include:

1. secret settlements deny systemic transparency in what should be an open and public justice system;
2. secret settlements do not contribute to the public good because no case precedents are created for other litigants and the public, which help to define the rule of law;
3. secret settlements perpetuate danger by keeping the identities of defective products and potential wrongdoers a secret;
4. secret settlements take advantage of the vulnerable litigant by pressuring him or her into agreeing to secrecy; and
5. government entities should not enter into secret settlements.

How might the "private" view of secret settlements see these criticisms differently?

3. Should confidential settlement agreements be partially or totally banned in Canada? If they are to be regulated, should it be:

1. by statute or regulation;
2. by judicial approval of settlements;
3. by lawyer conduct, as a requirement under rules for lawyers' professional conduct; or
4. left unregulated by the market and for the parties to decide?

4. When would you want a confidential settlement agreement for your client? When would you not want one?

5. For more discussion about confidential settlement agreements, see Erik S. Knutsen, "Keeping Settlements Secret" (2010), 37 *Florida State UL Rev.* (forthcoming) and Christopher R. Drahozal and Laura J. Hines, "Secret Settlement Restrictions and Unintended Consequences" (2006), 54 *Kansas L Rev.* 1457; Laurie Kratky Doré, "Secrecy by Consent: The Use and Limits of Confidentiality in the Pursuit of Settlement" (1999), 74 *Notre Dame L Rev.* 283; Carrie Menkel-Meadow, "Whose Dispute Is It Anyway?: A Philosophical and Democratic Defense of Settlement (In Some Cases)" (1995), 83 *Geo. LJ* 2663; Arthur R. Miller, "Confidentiality, Protective Orders, and Public Access to the Courts" (1991), 105 *Harv. L Rev.* 427; and David Luban, "Settlements and the Erosion of the Public Realm" (1995), 83 *Geo. LJ* 2619.

Class Proceedings

I. INTRODUCTION

The concept of class actions was introduced in chapter 5 as a device for joining similar claims in a single action so that they can be advanced by a representative plaintiff on behalf of a large number of other plaintiffs. This chapter explores the way in which class actions have developed in Canada in recent years.

> **Garry D. Watson, "Class Actions: The Canadian Experience"**
> (2001), 11 *Duke Journal of Comparative and International Law* 269
> (footnotes omitted)

... A foundational document in Canada on class actions is the Ontario Law Reform Commission's (OLRC) Report on Class Actions (1982) ... , [which] bases its recommendation of the introduction of class actions in Ontario on three underlying policy objectives.

The first, and most important objective, is to afford greater access to justice. Litigation has become so expensive that claims of modest amounts, and even those of significant amounts, are not economically feasible to pursue on an individual basis. In class action terminology, these are referred to as "individually non-viable claims." There are many more individually non-viable claims in Canada than in the United States for several reasons: (1) Canada has ceilings on damages for pain and suffering in personal injury cases, and relative to awards in the United States, these ceilings are very low; (2) Canadian courts rarely award punitive damages; (3) the vast majority of civil actions in Canada are tried by judges sitting alone rather than being tried by relatively uncontrolled juries as in the United States; and (4) Canada has a fee shifting rule (generally the losing party must pay a large part of the winning party's legal fees), which is a major deterrent to litigation.

The second policy objective is to improve judicial efficiency. Where the alternative to a class action is repetitive litigation relating to the same events, the result is judicial inefficiency. For example, when class action certification was refused for claims against Canada's blood system relating to transfusion-related AIDS transmission, more than eighty such cases were filed in Ontario alone. The filing of individual claims resulted in three very long trials without significant plaintiff-wide settlements. Such individual actions often cover the same ground time and again; they are not only inefficient, but can lead to inconsistent decisions. It is noteworthy that the judicial efficiency rationale really only comes into play where the claims asserted are individually viable; permitting class actions for individually non-viable claims brings about litigation which would, without class actions, never be brought. This may increase the judicial workload and thereby decrease judicial efficiency.

The third policy objective is to achieve behavioral modification. When manufacturers and other entities can inflict small amounts of damage on a large number of people who cannot afford to litigate individual claims, the deterrent function of the law, such as tort law, is lost. Hopefully, subjecting potential defendants to the risk of a class action will modify their behavior.

Canadian courts refer to the above social or policy objectives constantly when interpreting class action legislation. ...

The procedures provided by the legislation in each of the three provinces are structurally similar to those prescribed by Rule 23 of the US *Federal Rules of Civil Procedure* ... The claim must disclose a cause of action. There must be an identifiable class of two or more persons. The claims of the class must raise common issues. A class action must be the preferable procedure for resolving these common issues. The representative plaintiff must fairly and adequately represent the interests of the class, not have a conflict on the common issues with other class members, and have a workable plan for processing the action. ... The following are the other major features of the Canadian class action regime.

A. *Notice*—Notice to class members of certification and settlement is normal but not mandatory. The court may determine how it is to be given or dispensed with and who will bear the cost.

B. *Opt Out*—Once the proceeding is certified, members of the class are presumed to be in the proceeding and are bound by the court's determination, unless they take active steps to "opt out" within a time set by the court.

C. *Discovery*—At the certification and common issues phases, discovery is prima facie limited to the named parties. The defendant is given the right to examine for discovery (i.e., depose) only the class representative and not other individual class members; after deposing the class representative, the defendant may request leave from the court for discovery of other individual class members (this regime is consistent with the general approach in Canada to the availability of discovery).

D. *Settlements*—To ensure the protection of absent class members, the settlement of all actions commenced under the Class Proceedings Act, whether or not they are certified, must be approved by the court.

E. *Fee Shifting*—This has been an area of considerable difficulty for class actions in Canada. Unlike in the United States, the general rule in litigation in Canada is the so-called "English rule," that a losing party must usually pay the winning parties' legal fees, or a good portion thereof. The challenge has been synthesising this rule with class actions: if the class action fails, who is liable for the defendant's legal fees and other costs? For litigation in which the class does not prevail, each Province's class action statute stipulates that the representative plaintiff is the only class member liable for defendant's legal fees and other costs. When and to what extent the representative plaintiff is liable varies amongst the three provinces. British Columbia adopted the Ontario Law Reform Commission's recommendation, rendering the representative plaintiff virtually immune from paying costs— she is only liable if the action is "frivolous or vexatious" (merely losing is not enough). Quebec allows for costs against the representative plaintiff, but after one very large costs award the legislation changed, allowing only nominal costs to be paid (on the scale of the small claims court). Ontario is the most extreme. The legislation provides that costs can be awarded against a losing representative plaintiff, unless the court is of the view that the action was a "test case, raised a novel point of law or involved a matter of public interest." ... An Ontario Class Proceedings Fund exists primarily to relieve the representative plaintiff from liability for the defendant's costs. It works in the following way: when a plaintiff applies to, and receives assistance from, the Fund, the Fund becomes liable to pay any costs awarded to the defendant, and in such circumstances, the representative plaintiff is relieved of any liability for the defendant's costs. However, the Fund has been a failure in that, due to inadequate financing, it has given funding to very few class actions (approximately six to date). It started out with an initial capital of $500,000, to be "topped up" by a levy of ten percent of any settlement or judgment in any action it has funded. The Fund has been extremely cautious in funding class actions because one cost order could wipe it out. ...

F. *Class Counsels' Fees*—The court determines the fees for class counsel, typically using a combination of a multiplier test (i.e., hours worked multiplied by the hourly rate) and a percentage contingency fee. Usually these fees come out of the damages recovered by the class.

G. *National Classes*—Because the courts (particularly in Ontario) have permitted national classes (i.e., actions in which the class as defined is not limited to Ontario residents, but any Canadian resident), the effect has been to extend the class action regime even to those provinces that have not enacted class action legislation.

NOTES

1. *Class action legislation.* Nine provinces now have class action legislation—Quebec (1978), Ontario (1992), British Columbia (1996), Newfoundland and Labrador (2001), Saskatchewan (2002), Manitoba (2003), Alberta (2004), New Brunswick (2006), and Nova Scotia (2007). The *Federal Courts Rules* were amended to provide for class actions in 2002. This leaves just Prince Edward Island without a provincial statute. The Quebec legislation is unique. The BC legislation is based on the Ontario Act, but with a few differences. The other common law provinces have generally followed the BC model.

2. *Bibliography.* The leading sources on class actions in Canada are Ontario Law Reform Commission (OLRC), *Report on Class Actions*, 3 vols. (Toronto: Ministry of the Attorney General, 1982); M. Eizenga, M. Peerless, and C. Wright, *Class Actions Law and Practice* (Toronto: Butterworths) (looseleaf); Ward K. Branch, *Class Actions in Canada* (Vancouver: Western Legal Publications) (looseleaf); and Craig Jones, *Theory of Class Actions* (Toronto: Irwin Law, 2003). For a selected but extensive bibliography on class actions, see Holmested and Watson, *Ontario Civil Procedure*, rule 12.

3. In the following case, *Western Canadian Shopping Centres*, the first case in a trilogy of foundational cases decided by the Supreme Court of Canada, the court considered whether a class action could be pursued in Alberta even though at that time there was no legislation for class actions. The court reversed a 1983 decision and held that, in the absence of class action legislation, the courts must use their inherent power to settle the rules of practice and procedure and thus fill the gaps in the general representative action rules. The court also began its articulation of the standards to be applied at certification.

Western Canadian Shopping Centres Inc. v. Dutton
[2001] 2 SCR 534

McLACHLIN CJ: This appeal requires us to decide when a class action may be brought. While the class action has existed in one form or another for hundreds of years, its importance has increased of late. Particularly in complicated cases implicating the interests of many people, the class action may provide the best means of fair and efficient resolution. Yet absent legislative direction, there remains considerable uncertainty as to the conditions under which a court should permit a class action to be maintained.

The claimants wanted to immigrate to Canada. To qualify, they invested money in Western Canadian Shopping Centres Inc. ("WCSC"), under the Canadian government's Business Immigration Program. They lost money and brought a class action. The defendants (appellants) claim the class action is inappropriate and ask the Court to strike it out. For the following reasons, I conclude that the claimants may proceed as a class.

· · ·

A. The History and Functions of Class Actions

The class action originated in the English courts of equity in the late seventeenth and early eighteenth centuries. The courts of law focussed on individual questions between the plaintiff and the defendant. The courts of equity, by contrast, applied a rule of compulsory joinder, requiring all those interested in the subject matter of the dispute to be made parties. The aim of the courts of equity was to render "complete justice"—that is, to "arrang[e] all the rights, which the decision immediately affects." ... The compulsory-joinder rule "allowed the Court to examine every facet of the dispute and thereby ensure that no one was adversely affected by its decision without first having had an opportunity to be heard" ... . The rule possessed the additional advantage of preventing a multiplicity of duplicative proceedings.

The compulsory-joinder rule eventually proved inadequate ... where interested parties in such cases were too numerous to be joined. The courts of equity responded by relaxing the compulsory-joinder rule where strict adherence would work injustice. The result was the representative action. ... .

The representative or class action proved useful in pre-industrial English commercial litigation. ...The courts of equity applied a liberal and flexible approach to whether a class action could proceed. ... This flexible and generous approach to class actions prevailed until the fusion of law and equity under the *Supreme Court of Judicature Act, 1873* (UK), 36 & 37 Vict., c. 66, and the adoption of Rule 10 of the *Rules of Procedure*:

> 10. Where there are numerous parties having the same interest in one action, one or more of such parties may sue or be sued, or may be authorised by the Court to defend in such action, on behalf or for the benefit of all parties so interested.

While early cases under the new rules maintained a liberal approach to class actions ... later cases sometimes took a restrictive approach. ... This, combined with the widespread use of limited-liability companies, resulted in fewer class actions being brought.

The class action did not forever languish, however. Conditions emerged in the latter part of the twentieth century that once again invoked its utility. Mass production and consumption revived the problem that had motivated the development of the class action in the eighteenth century—the problem of many suitors with the same grievance. As in the eighteenth century, insistence on individual representation would often have precluded effective litigation. And, as in the eighteenth century, the class action provided the solution.

The class action plays an important role in today's world. The rise of mass production, the diversification of corporate ownership, the advent of the mega-corporation, and the recognition of environmental wrongs have all contributed to its growth. A faulty product may be sold to numerous consumers. Corporate mismanagement may bring loss to a large number of shareholders. Discriminatory policies may affect entire categories of employees. Environmental pollution may have consequences for citizens all over the country. Conflicts like these pit a large group of complainants against the alleged wrongdoer. Sometimes, the complainants are identically situated vis-à-vis the defendants. In other cases, an important aspect of their claim is common to all complainants. The class action offers a means of efficiently resolving such disputes in a manner that is fair to all parties.

Class actions offer three important advantages over a multiplicity of individual suits. First, by aggregating similar individual actions, class actions serve judicial economy by avoiding unnecessary duplication in fact-finding and legal analysis. The efficiencies thus generated free judicial resources that can be directed at resolving other conflicts, and can also reduce the costs of litigation both for plaintiffs (who can share litigation costs) and for defendants (who need litigate the disputed issue only once, rather than numerous times). ...

Second, by allowing fixed litigation costs to be divided over a large number of plaintiffs, class actions improve access to justice by making economical the prosecution of claims that would otherwise be too costly to prosecute individually. Without class actions, the doors of justice remain closed to some plaintiffs, however strong their legal claims. Sharing costs ensures that injuries are not left unremedied: ...

Third, class actions serve efficiency and justice by ensuring that actual and potential wrongdoers do not ignore their obligations to the public. Without class actions, those who cause widespread but individually minimal harm might not take into account the full costs of their conduct, because for any one plaintiff the expense of bringing suit would far exceed the likely recovery. Cost-sharing decreases the expense of pursuing legal recourse and accordingly deters potential defendants who might otherwise assume that minor wrongs would not result in litigation: ...

B. The Test for Class Actions

In recognition of the modern importance of representative litigation, many jurisdictions have enacted comprehensive class action legislation. In the United States, *Federal Rules of Civil Procedure*, 28 USCA para. 23 (introduced in 1938 and substantially amended in 1966) addressed aspects of class action practice, including certification of litigant classes, notice, and settlement. The English procedural rules of 1999 include detailed provisions governing "Group Litigation": United Kingdom, *Civil Procedure Rules 1998*, SI 1998/3132, rr. 19.10-19.15. And in Canada, the provinces of British Columbia, Ontario, and Quebec have enacted comprehensive statutory schemes to govern class action practice: see British Columbia *Class Proceedings Act*, RSBC 1996, c. 50; Ontario *Class Proceedings Act, 1992*, SO 1992, c. 6; Quebec *Code of Civil Procedure*, RSQ, c. C-25, Book IX. Yet other Canadian provinces, including Alberta and Manitoba, are considering enacting such legislation: see Manitoba Law Reform Commission, Report #100, *Class Proceedings* (January 1999); Alberta Law Reform Institute, Final Report No. 85, *Class Actions* (December 2000); see also R. Rogers, "A Uniform Class Actions Statute," Appendix O to the Proceedings of the 1995 Meeting of The Uniform Law Conference of Canada.

Absent comprehensive codes of class action procedure, provincial rules based on Rule 10, Schedule, of the English *Supreme Court of Judicature Act, 1873* govern. This is the case in Alberta, where class action practice is governed by Rule 42 of the *Alberta Rules of Court*:

> 42 Where numerous persons have a common interest in the subject of an intended action, one or more of those persons may sue or be sued or may be authorized by the Court to defend on behalf of or for the benefit of all.

The intention of the Alberta legislature is clear. Class actions may be brought. Details of class action practice, however, are largely left to the courts.

Alberta's Rule 42 does not specify what is meant by "numerous" or by "common interest." It does not say when discovery may be made of class members other than the representative. Nor does it specify how notice of the suit should be conveyed to potential class members, or how a court should deal with the possibility that some potential class members may desire to "opt out" of the class. And it does not provide for costs, or for the distribution of the fund should an action for money damages be successful.

Clearly, it would be advantageous if there existed a legislative framework addressing these issues. The absence of comprehensive legislation means that courts are forced to rely heavily on individual case management to structure class proceedings. This taxes judicial resources and denies the parties *ex ante* certainty as to their procedural rights. One of the main weaknesses of the current Alberta regime is the absence of a threshold "certification" provision. In British Columbia, Ontario, and Quebec, a class action may proceed only after the court certifies that the class and representative meet certain requirements. In Alberta, by contrast, courts effectively certify *ex post*, only after the opposing party files a motion to strike. It would be preferable if the appropriateness of the class action could be determined at the outset by certification.

Absent comprehensive legislation, the courts must fill the void under their inherent power to settle the rules of practice and procedure as to disputes brought before them. ... However desirable comprehensive legislation on class action practice may be, if such legislation has not been enacted, the courts must determine the availability of the class action and the mechanics of class action practice.

Alberta courts moved to fill the procedural vacuum in [*Korte v. Deloitte, Haskins & Sells* (1993), 8 Alta. LR (3d) 337]. *Korte* prescribed four conditions for a class action: (1) the class must be capable of clear and definite definition; (2) the principal issues of fact and law must be the same; (3) success for one of the plaintiffs must mean success for all; and (4) no individual assessment of the claims of individual plaintiffs need be made.

The *Korte* criteria loosely parallel the criteria applied in other Canadian jurisdictions in which comprehensive class-action legislation has yet to be enacted. ...

The *Korte* criteria also bear resemblance to the class-certification criteria in the British Columbia, Ontario, and Quebec class action statutes. ... While there are differences between the tests, four conditions emerge as necessary to a class action. First, the class must be capable of clear definition. Class definition is critical because it identifies the individuals entitled to notice, entitled to relief (if relief is awarded), and bound by the judgment. It is essential, therefore, that the class be defined clearly at the outset of the litigation. The definition should state objective criteria by which members of the class can be identified. While the criteria should bear a rational relationship to the common issues asserted by all class members, the criteria should not depend on the outcome of the litigation. It is not necessary that every class member be named or known. It is necessary, however, that any particular person's claim to membership in the class be determinable by stated, objective criteria. ...

Second, there must be issues of fact or law common to all class members. Commonality tests have been a source of confusion in the courts. The commonality question should be approached purposively. The underlying question is whether allowing the suit to proceed as a representative one will avoid duplication of fact-finding or legal analysis. Thus an issue will be "common" only where its resolution is necessary to the resolution of each class member's claim. It is not essential that the class members be identically situated vis-à-vis the opposing party. Nor is it necessary that common issues predominate over non-common issues or that the resolution of the common issues would be determinative of each class member's claim. However, the class members' claims must share a substantial common ingredient to justify a class action. Determining whether the common issues justify a class action may require the court to examine the significance of the common issues in relation to individual issues. In doing so, the court should remember that it may not always be possible for a representative party to plead the claims of each class member with the same particularity as would be required in an individual suit.

Third, with regard to the common issues, success for one class member must mean success for all. All members of the class must benefit from the successful prosecution of the action, although not necessarily to the same extent. A class action should not be allowed if class members have conflicting interests.

Fourth, the class representative must adequately represent the class. In assessing whether the proposed representative is adequate, the court may look to the motivation of the representative, the competence of the representative's counsel, and the capacity of the representative to bear any costs that may be incurred by the representative in particular (as opposed to by counsel or by the class members generally). The proposed representative need not be "typical" of the class, nor the "best" possible representative. The court should be satisfied, however, that the proposed representative will vigorously and capably prosecute the interests of the class. ...

While the four factors outlined must be met for a class action to proceed, their satisfaction does not mean that the court must allow the action to proceed. Other factors may weigh against allowing the action to proceed in representative form. The defendant may wish to raise different defences with respect to different groups of plaintiffs. It may be necessary to examine each class member in discovery. Class members may raise important issues not shared by all members of the class. Or the proposed class may be so small that joinder would be a better solution. Where such countervailing factors exist, the court has discretion to decide whether the class action should be permitted to proceed, notwithstanding that the essential conditions for the maintenance of a class action have been satisfied.

The class action codes that have been adopted by British Columbia and Ontario offer some guidance as to factors that would generally not constitute arguments against allowing an action to proceed as a representative one. Both state that certification should not be denied on the grounds that: (1) the relief claimed includes a demand for money damages that would require individual assessment after determination of the common issues; (2) the relief claimed relates to separate contracts involving different members of the class; (3) different class members seek different remedies; (4) the number of class members or the identity of every class member is unknown; or (5) the class includes subgroups that have claims or defences that raise common issues not shared by all members of the class: see Ontario *Class Proceedings Act, 1992*, s. 6; British Columbia *Class Proceedings Act*, s. 7; see also Alberta Law Reform Institute, *supra*, at pp. 75-76. Common sense suggests that these factors should no more bar a class action suit in Alberta than in Ontario or British Columbia.

Where the conditions for a class action are met, the court should exercise its discretion to disallow it for negative reasons in a liberal and flexible manner, like the courts of equity of old. The court should take into account the benefits the class action offers in the circumstances of the case as well as any unfairness that class proceedings may cause. In the end, the court must strike a balance between efficiency and fairness. ...

To summarize, class actions should be allowed to proceed under Alberta's Rule 42 where the following conditions are met: (1) the class is capable of clear definition; (2) there are issues of fact or law common to all class members; (3) success for one class member means success for all; and (4) the proposed representative adequately represents the interests of the class. If these conditions are met the court must also be satisfied, in the exercise of its discretion, that there are no countervailing considerations that outweigh the benefits of allowing the class action to proceed.

Other procedural issues may arise. One is notice. A judgment is binding on a class member only if the class member is notified of the suit and is given an opportunity to exclude himself or herself from the proceeding. This case does not raise the issue of what constitutes sufficient notice. However, prudence suggests that all potential class members be informed of the existence of the suit, of the common issues that the suit seeks to resolve, and of the right of each class member to opt out, and that this be done before any decision is made that purports to prejudice or otherwise affect the interests of class members.

Another procedural issue that may arise is how to deal with non-common issues. The court retains discretion to determine how the individual issues should be addressed, once common issues have been resolved: see Branch [W.K. Branch, *Class Actions in Canada* (1998)], at para. 18.10. Generally, individual issues will be resolved in individual proceedings. However, as under the legislation of British Columbia, Ontario, and Quebec, a court may specify special procedures that it considers necessary or useful. ...

The diversity of class actions makes it difficult to anticipate all of the procedural complexities that may arise. In the absence of comprehensive class-action legislation, courts must address procedural complexities on a case-by-case basis. Courts should approach these issues as they do the question of whether a class action should be allowed: in a flexible and liberal manner, seeking a balance between efficiency and fairness. ...

II. CERTIFICATION

The requirements for certification in most of the Canadian class actions statutes are similar to the requirements set out in the Ontario statute as follows:

Class Proceedings Act, 1992, SO 1992, c. 6

  5(1) The court shall certify a class proceeding on a motion under section 2, 3 or 4 if,

  (a) the pleadings or the notice of application discloses a cause of action;

  (b) there is an identifiable class of two or more persons that would be represented by the representative plaintiff or defendant;

  (c) the claims or defences of the class members raise common issues;

  (d) a class proceeding would be the preferable procedure for the resolution of the common issues; and

  (e) there is a representative plaintiff or defendant who,

    (i) would fairly and adequately represent the interests of the class,

(ii) has produced a plan for the proceeding that sets out a workable method of advancing the proceeding on behalf of the class and of notifying class members of the proceeding, and

(iii) does not have, on the common issues for the class, an interest in conflict with the interests of other class members.

6. The court shall not refuse to certify a proceeding as a class proceeding solely on any of the following grounds:

1. The relief claimed includes a claim for damages that would require individual assessment after determination of the common issues.
2. The relief claimed relates to separate contracts involving different class members.
3. Different remedies are sought for different class members.
4. The number of class members or the identity of each class member is not known.
5. The class includes a subclass whose members have claims or defences that raise common issues not shared by all class members.

The class actions statutes of many provinces also contain factors to be considered in determining whether a class action is the preferable procedure as follows:

Class Proceedings Act, RSBC 1996, c. 50

· · ·

4(2) In determining whether a class proceeding would be the preferable procedure for the fair and efficient resolution of the common issues, the court must consider all relevant matters including the following:

(a) whether questions of fact or law common to the members of the class predominate over any questions affecting only individual members;

(b) whether a significant number of the members of the class have a valid interest in individually controlling the prosecution of separate actions;

(c) whether the class proceeding would involve claims that are or have been the subject of any other proceedings;

(d) whether other means of resolving the claims are less practical or less efficient;

(e) whether the administration of the class proceeding would create greater difficulties than those likely to be experienced if relief were sought by other means.

Under these liberal statutory requirements for certification, many early certification applications in Ontario and British Columbia were sought—in product liability cases (defective heart pacemakers, breast implants, Hepatitis C-contaminated blood); in mass tort cases (a subway crash, mass infection of patients with Hepatitis B as a result of a doctor's negligence); and in consumer class actions (recovery of interest on condominium deposits, recovery of damages for misrepresentations in the sale of a housing development). It seemed that the plaintiff had merely to show that the pleadings disclose a cause of action, that the claims of the class members raised common, though not necessarily identical, issues, and that a class proceeding would be the preferable procedure for the resolution of the *common issues*. Pursuant to the legislation, at the certification stage there is no inquiry into the (factual) merits of the action. However, in *Hollick* and *Rumley*, the two other cases in the trilogy, the Supreme Court made it clear that the standards for certification are more demanding than might appear from a literal reading of the words of the statutes.

Hollick v. Toronto (City)
[2001] 3 SCR 158

McLACHLIN CJ: The question raised by this appeal is whether the appellant has satisfied the certification requirements of Ontario's *Class Proceedings Act, 1992*, SO 1992, c. 6, and whether the appellant should accordingly be allowed to pursue his action against the City of Toronto as the representative of some 30,000 other residents who live in the vicinity of a landfill owned and operated by the City. For the following reasons, I conclude that the appellant has not satisfied the certification requirements, and consequently that he may pursue this action only on his own behalf, and not on behalf of the stated class.

I. Facts

The appellant Hollick complains of noise and physical pollution from the Keele Valley landfill, which is owned and operated by the respondent City of Toronto. The appellant sought certification, under Ontario's *Class Proceedings Act, 1992*, to represent some 30,000 people who live in the vicinity of the landfill, in particular:

A. All persons who have owned or occupied property in the Regional Municipality of York, in the geographic area bounded by Rutherford Road on the south, Jane Street on the west, King-Vaughan Road on the north and Yonge Street on the east, at any time on or after February 3, 1991, or where such a person is deceased, the personal representative of the estate of the deceased person; and
B. All living parents, grandparents, children, grandchildren, siblings, and spouses (within the meaning of s. 61 of the *Family Law Act*) of persons who were owners and/or occupiers ... .

The merits of the dispute between the appellant and the respondent are not at issue on this appeal. The only question is whether the appellant should be allowed to pursue his action as representative of the stated class.

· · ·

The appellant's claim is that the Keele Valley landfill has unlawfully been emitting, onto his own lands and onto the lands of other class members:

(a) large quantities of methane, hydrogen sulphide, vinyl chloride and other toxic gases, obnoxious odours, fumes, smoke and airborne, bird-borne or air-blown sediment, particulates, dirt and litter (collectively referred to as "Physical Pollution"); and
(b) loud noises and strong vibrations (collectively referred to as "Noise Pollution").

The appellant filed a motion for certification on November 28, 1997. In support of his motion, the appellant pointed out that, in 1996, some 139 complaints were registered with the respondent's telephone complaint system. (Before this Court, the appellant submitted that "at least 500" complaints were made "to various governmental authorities between 1991 and 1996" (factum, at para. 7).) The appellant also noted that, in 1996, the respondent was fined by the Ministry of Environment in relation to the composting of grass clippings at a facility located just north of the Keele Valley landfill. In the appellant's view, the class members form a well-defined group with a common interest vis-à-vis the respondent, and the suit would be best prosecuted as a class action. The appellant seeks, on behalf of the class, injunctive relief, $500 million in compensatory damages and $100 million in punitive damages.

The respondent disputes the legitimacy of the appellant's complaints and disagrees that the suit should be permitted to proceed as a class action. The respondent claims that it has monitored air emissions from the Keele Valley site and the data confirm that "none of the air levels exceed Ministry of the Environment trigger levels." It notes that there are other possible sources for the pollution of which the appellant complains, including an active quarry, a private transfer station for waste, a plastics factory, and an asphalt plant. In addition, some farms in the area have private compost operations. The respondent also argues that the number of registered complaints—it says that 150 people complained over the six-year period covered in the motion record—is not high given the size of the class. Finally, it notes that, to date, no claims have been made against the Small Claims Trust Fund.

· · ·

... The issue is whether the appellant has satisfied the certification requirements set out in s. 5 of the Act. The respondent does not dispute that the appellant's statement of claim discloses a cause of action. The first question, therefore, is whether there is an identifiable class. In my view, there is. The appellant has defined the class by reference to objective criteria; a person is a member of the class if he or she owned or occupied property inside a specified area within a specified period of time. Whether a given person is a member of the class can be determined without reference to the merits of the action. While the appellant has not named every member of the class, it is clear that the class is bounded (that is, not unlimited). There is, therefore, an identifiable class within the meaning of s. 5(1)(b): ...

A more difficult question is whether "the claims ... of the class members raise common issues," as required by s. 5(1)(c) of the *Class Proceedings Act, 1992.* ...

In this case there is no doubt that, if each of the class members has a claim against the respondent, some aspect of the issue of liability is common ... The difficult question, however, is whether each of the putative class members does indeed have a claim—or at least what might be termed a "colourable claim"—against the respondent. To put it another way, the issue is whether there is a rational connection between the class as defined and the asserted common issues: ... In asserting that there is such a relationship, the appellant points to the numerous complaints against the Keele Valley landfill filed with the Ministry of Environment. In the appellant's view, the large number of complaints shows that many others in the putative class, if not all of them, are similarly situated vis-à-vis the respondent. For its part the respondent asserts that "150 people making complaints over a seven-year period does not make it likely that some 30,000 persons had their enjoyment of their property interfered with" (Divisional Court's judgment, at pp. 479-80). The respondent also quotes the Ontario Court of Appeal's judgment (at p. 264), which declined to find commonality on the grounds that

[i]n circumstances such as are described in the statement of claim one would expect to see evidence of the existence of a body of persons seeking recourse for their complaints, such

as, a history of "town meetings," demands, claims against the no fault fund, [and] applications to amend the certificate of approval ... .

The respondent is of course correct to state that implicit in the "identifiable class" requirement is the requirement that there be some rational relationship between the class and common issues. Little has been said about this requirement because, in the usual case, the relationship is clear from the facts. In a single-incident mass tort case (for example, an airplane crash), the scope of the appropriate class is not usually in dispute. The same is true in product liability actions (where the class is usually composed of those who purchased the product), or securities fraud actions (where the class is usually composed of those who owned the stock). In a case such as this, however, the appropriate scope of the class is not so obvious. It falls to the putative representative to show that the class is defined sufficiently narrowly.

The requirement is not an onerous one. The representative need not show that everyone in the class shares the same interest in the resolution of the asserted common issue. There must be some showing, however, that the class is not unnecessarily broad—that is, that the class could not be defined more narrowly without arbitrarily excluding some people who share the same interest in the resolution of the common issue. ...

... In my view the Advisory Committee's report appropriately requires the class representative to come forward with sufficient evidence to support certification, and appropriately allows the opposing party an opportunity to respond with evidence of its own.

This appears to be the existing practice of Ontario courts. ...

In my view the appellant has met his evidentiary burden here. ... I conclude, therefore, that the appellant has shown a sufficient basis in fact to satisfy the commonality requirement.

I cannot conclude, however, that "a class proceeding would be the preferable procedure for the resolution of the common issues," as required by s. 5(1)(d). The parties agree that, in the absence of legislative guidance, the preferability inquiry should be conducted through the lens of the three principal advantages of class actions—judicial economy, access to justice, and behaviour modification: see also *Abdool v. Anaheim Management Ltd.* (1995), 21 OR (2d) 453 (Div. Ct.); compare British Columbia *Class Proceedings Act*, s. 4(2) (listing factors that court must consider in assessing preferability). Beyond that, however, the appellant and respondent part ways. In oral argument before this Court, the appellant contended that the court must look to the common issues alone, and ask whether the common issues, taken in isolation, would be better resolved in a class action rather than in individual proceedings. In response, the respondent argued that the common issues must be viewed contextually, in light of all the issues—common and individual—raised by the case. The respondent also argued that the inquiry should take into account the availability of alternative avenues of redress.

• • •

The Act itself, of course, requires only that a class action be the preferable procedure for "the resolution of the *common issues*" (emphasis added), and not that a class action be the preferable procedure for the resolution of the class members' claims. I would not place undue weight, however, on the fact that the Act uses the phrase "resolution of the common issues" rather than "resolution of class members' claims." As one commentator writes:

> The [American] class action [rule] requires that the class action be the superior method to resolve the "controversy." The BC and Ontario Acts require that the class proceeding be the preferable procedure for the resolution of the "common issues" (as opposed to the entire controversy). [This] distinctio[n] can be seen as creating a lower threshold for certification in Ontario and BC than in the US. However, it is still important in BC and Ontario to assess the litigation as a whole, including the individual hearing stage, in order to determine whether the class action is the preferable means of resolving the common issues. In the abstract, common issues are always best resolved in a common proceeding. However, it is important to adopt a practical cost–benefit approach to this procedural issue, and to consider the impact of a class proceeding on class members, the defendants, and the court.

See Branch, *supra*, at para. 4.690. I would endorse that approach.

The question of preferability, then, must take into account the importance of the common issues in relation to the claims as a whole. It is true, of course, that the Act contemplates that class actions will be allowable even where there are substantial individual issues: see s. 5. It is also true that the drafters rejected a requirement, such as is contained in the American federal class action rule, that the common issues "predominate" over the individual issues: see *Federal Rules of Civil Procedure*, Rule 23(b)(3) (stating that class action maintainable only if "questions of law or fact common to the members of the class predominate over any questions affecting only individual members"); see also British Columbia *Class Proceedings Act*, s. 4(2)(a) (stating that, in determining whether a class action is the preferable procedure, the court must consider "whether questions of fact or law common to the members of the class predominate over any questions affecting only individual members"). I cannot conclude, however, that the drafters intended the preferability analysis to take place in a vacuum. There must be a consideration of the common issues in context. As the Chair of the Attorney General's Advisory Committee put it, the preferability requirement asks that the class representative "demonstrate that, *given all of the circumstances of the particular claim*, [a class action] would be preferable to other methods of resolving these claims and, in particular, that it would be preferable to the use of individual proceedings" (emphasis added): M.G. Cochrane, *Class Actions: A Guide to the Class Proceedings Act, 1992* (1993), at p. 27.

I think it clear, too, that the court cannot ignore the availability of avenues of redress apart from individual actions. As noted above, the preferability requirement was intended to capture the question of whether a class proceeding would be preferable "in the sense of preferable to other procedures such as joinder, test cases, consolidation and so on. ..." In my view, the preferability analysis requires the court to look to all reasonably available means of resolving the class members' claims, and not just at the possibility of individual actions.

I am not persuaded that the class action would be the preferable means of resolving the class members' claims. Turning first to the issue of judicial economy, I note that any common issue here is negligible in relation to the individual issues. While each of the class members must, in order to recover, establish that the Keele Valley landfill emitted physical or noise pollution, there is no reason to think that any pollution was distributed evenly across the geographical area or time period specified in the class definition. On the contrary, it is likely that some areas were affected more seriously than others, and that some areas were affected at one time while other areas were affected at other times. As the Divisional Court noted, "[e]ven if one considers only the 150 persons who made complaints—those complaints relate to different dates and different locations spread out over seven years and 16 square miles" (p. 480). Some class members are close to the site, some are further away. Some class members are close to other possible sources of pollution. Once the common issue is seen in the context of the entire claim, it becomes difficult to say that the resolution of the common issue will significantly advance the action.

Nor would allowing a class action here serve the interests of access to justice. The appellant posits that class members' claims may be so small that it would not be worthwhile for them to pursue relief individually. In many cases this is indeed a real danger. As noted above, one important benefit of class actions is that they divide fixed litigation costs over the entire class, making it economically feasible to prosecute claims that might otherwise not be brought at all. I am not fully convinced, however, that this is the situation here. The central problem with the appellant's argument is that, if it is in fact true that the claims are so small as to engage access to justice concerns, it would seem that the Small Claims Trust Fund would provide an ideal avenue of redress. Indeed, since the Small Claims Trust Fund establishes a no-fault scheme, it is likely to provide redress far more quickly than would the judicial system. If, on the other hand, the Small Claims Trust Fund is not sufficiently large to handle the class members' claims, one must question whether the access to justice concern is engaged at all. If class members have substantial claims, it is likely that they will find it worthwhile to bring individual actions. The fact that no claims have been made against the Small Claims Trust Fund may suggest that the class members claims are either so small as to be non-existent or so large as to provide sufficient incentive for individual action. In either case access to justice is not a serious concern. Of course, the existence of a compensatory scheme under which class members can pursue relief is not in itself grounds for denying a class action—even if the compensatory scheme promises to provide redress more quickly: see *Rumley v. British Columbia*, [2001] 3 SCR 184, 2001 SCC 69, at para. 38. The existence of such a scheme, however, provides one consideration that must be taken into account when assessing the seriousness of access-to-justice concerns.

For similar reasons I would reject the argument that behaviour modification is a significant concern in this case. Behavioural modification may be relevant to determining whether a class action should proceed. As noted in *Western Canadian Shopping Centres*, *supra*, at para. 29, "[w]ithout class actions, those who cause widespread but individually minimal harm might not take into account the full costs of their conduct, because for any one plaintiff the expense of bringing suit would far exceed the likely recovery." This concern is certainly no less pressing in the context of environmental litigation. Indeed, Ontario has enacted legislation that reflects a recognition that environmental harm is a cost that must be given due weight in both public and private decision-making: see *Environmental Bill of Rights, 1993*, SO 1993, c. 28, and *Environmental Protection Act*. I am not persuaded, however, that allowing a class action here would serve that end. If individual class members have substantial claims against the respondent, we should expect that they will be willing to prosecute those claims individually; on the other hand if their claims are small, they will be able to obtain compensation through the Small Claims Trust Fund. In either case, the respondent will be forced to internalize the costs of its conduct.

I would note, further, that Ontario's environmental legislation provides other avenues by which the complainant here could ensure that the respondent takes full account of the costs of its actions. While the existence of such legislation certainly does not foreclose the possibility of environmental class actions, it does go some way toward addressing legitimate concerns about behaviour modification. ...

I conclude that the action does not meet the requirements set out in s. 5(1) of Ontario's *Class Proceedings Act, 1992*. Even on the generous approach advocated above, the appellant has not shown that a class action is the preferable means of resolving the claims raised here.

I should make one note on the scope of the holding in this case. The appellant took pains to characterize this case as raising the issue of whether Ontario's *Class Proceedings Act, 1992* permits environmental class actions. I would not frame the issue so broadly. While the appellant has not met the certification requirements here, it does not follow that those requirements could never be met in an environmental tort case. The question of whether an action should be permitted to be prosecuted as a class action is necessarily one that turns on the facts of the case. In this case there were serious questions about preferability. Other environmental tort cases may not raise the same questions. Those cases should be decided on their facts.

The appeal is dismissed. There will be no costs to either party.

Rumley v. British Columbia
[2001] 3 SCR 184

McLACHLIN CJ: Like *Hollick v. Toronto (City)*, [2001] 3 SCR 158, 2001 SCC 68, this case raises the question of whether the plaintiffs below (respondents here) meet the certification requirements set out in provincial class action legislation. In this case the respondents seek to represent current and former students who were abused at the Jericho Hill School, a residential school for the deaf and blind operated by the province of British Columbia. At the end of the hearing, the Court concluded that the respondents had satisfied the certification requirements set out in s. 4 of the British Columbia *Class Proceedings Act*, RSBC 1996, c. 50, and dismissed the appeal, reasons to follow. These are those reasons. ...

From the early 1950s until 1992, Jericho Hill School ("JHS") operated as a residential school for deaf children. Until 1979, the school also enrolled blind children. Whereas most schools in British Columbia are managed by district school boards, JHS was a "provincial school" under British Columbia's governing legislation, currently the *School Act*, RSBC 1996, c. 412, and was operated and maintained by British Columbia's Ministry of Education. It is now clear that sexual and physical abuse of children took place at the school throughout its history. ...

In a ministerial statement made in June 1995, the Attorney General acknowledged the allegations of sexual abuse at the school, acknowledged that "[t]he province was responsible for the care and well-being of these people when they were children," and stated that "[t]o the extent that the province failed them, [it] must see that they are now compensated." The province also established the Jericho Individual Compensation Program (JICP), which is structured according to the recommendations of the Berger report. The program is open to students and former students who allege abuse as a result of attending or having attended the school, and provides for awards according to the three-tier system. As of March 31, 1998, the JICP had heard 49 claims.

The respondents commenced this action in January 1998. The suit seeks compensatory and punitive damages on behalf of a class consisting of:

- all current and former JHS students who have suffered abuse or who failed to receive a proper education while students of the school;
- all family members of current or former JHS students who suffered damage as a result of the abuse of a JHS student;
- all family members or others who were themselves abused by current or former JHS students as a result of the prior abuse of the JHS student.

The respondents asserted that the following issues are common to the class:

- whether the defendant breached the standard of care it owed to the plaintiffs between 1950 and 1992;
- whether the defendant made negligent, reckless and/or fraudulent misrepresentations regarding the school;
- whether the defendant's conduct justified an award of punitive damages and, if so, what amount of punitive damages is appropriate.

(Initially the respondents also asserted that vicarious liability constituted a common issue, but the respondents abandoned their vicarious liability argument early in the proceedings.)

The only issue on this appeal is whether the respondents have satisfied the class certification requirements set out in s. 4 of British Columbia's *Class Proceedings Act*.

• • •

... The issues in dispute are whether there are questions common to the class, as required by s. 4(1)(c), and whether a class proceeding would be the preferable procedure for the fair and efficient resolution of the common issues, as required by s. 4(1)(d).

In my view, both the commonality and preferability requirements are satisfied in this case. With regard to commonality, I agree with Mackenzie JA that all class members share an interest in the question of whether the appellant breached a duty of care. ...

The appellant concedes that none of the class members can prevail without showing that the appellant's conduct fell below an acceptable standard, but contends that the nature of the required showing is inescapably individualistic and not amenable to resolution in general terms applicable to all class members. The appellant does not dispute Mackenzie JA's statement that the "duty of the school to reasonably protect its students from sexual abuse is clear and immutable throughout the period that the school was in operation" (p. 8). However in the appellant's view, "[t]he result of this litigation depends not on the definition of the standard of care, but rather the *application* of that standard to the facts found in respect of the circumstances of each claimant" (appellant's factum, at para. 64 (emphasis in original)). The appellant argues that in this case "[l]iability turns not on the breach of a standard of care in the abstract, but on whether the standard of care was breached with respect to the school's supervision of the particular class member in a way that contributed materially to his/her abuse" (appellant's factum, at para. 64). The theory of the appellant is essentially that the Court of Appeal was able to find a common issue within the meaning of s. 4(1)(c) only by framing the commonality between the class members in overly general terms.

There is clearly something to the appellant's argument that a court should avoid framing commonality between class members in overly broad terms. As I discussed in *Western Canadian Shopping Centres, supra*, at para. 39, the guiding question should be the practical one of "whether allowing the suit to proceed as a representative one will avoid duplication of fact-finding or legal analysis." It would not serve the ends of either fairness or efficiency to certify an action on the basis of issues that are common only when stated in the most general terms. Inevitably such an action would ultimately break down into individual proceedings. That the suit had initially been certified as a class action could only make the proceeding less fair and less efficient.

I cannot agree, however, that such are the circumstances here. As Mackenzie JA noted, the respondents' argument is based on an allegation of "systemic" negligence—"the failure to have in place management and operations procedures that would reasonably have prevented the abuse" (pp. 8-9). The respondents assert, for example, that JHS did not have policies in place to deal with abuse, and that JHS acted negligently by placing all residential students in one dormitory in 1978. These are actions (or omissions) whose reasonability can be determined without reference to the circumstances of any individual class member. It is true that the respondents' election to limit their allegations to systemic negligence may make the individual component of the proceedings more difficult; clearly it would be easier for any given complainant to show causation if the established breach were that JHS had failed to address her own complaint of abuse (an individualized breach) than it would be if, for example, the established breach were that JHS had as a general matter failed to respond adequately to some complaints (a "systemic" breach). As Mackenzie JA wrote, however, the respondents "are entitled to restrict the grounds of negligence they wish to advance to make the case more amenable to class proceedings if they choose to do so" (p. 9).

In arguing that the necessary inquiry is inescapably individualistic, the appellant's principal contention is that the relevant standard of care, if framed at the appropriate level of specificity, would have varied over time. I am not persuaded that this should be an obstacle to the suit's proceeding as a class action. It is true that there has been a "dramatic ... evolution" in law relating to sexual abuse between 1950 and 1992 and it is quite possible that the nature of a school's obligations to its students has changed over time. However, courts have often allowed class actions to proceed in similar circumstances, ...

That the standard of care may have varied over the relevant time period simply means that the court may find it necessary to provide a nuanced answer to the common question. The structure of the Berger report, which explicitly divides the years between 1982 and 1991 into three discrete subperiods, suggests that such an approach would not be infeasible. I further note that the *Class Proceedings Act* contemplates the possibility of subclasses and that the court may amend the certification order at any time: see s. 6(1) (permitting court to recognize subclasses under certain conditions); s. 7(e) (stating that the court "must not refuse to certify a proceeding as a class proceeding merely because … the class includes a subclass whose members have claims that raise common issues not shared by all class members"); s. 8(3) (stating that "[t]he court, on the application of a party or class member, may at any time amend a certification order"); s. 10(1) (stating that "[w]ithout limiting section 8(3), at any time after a certification order is made … the court may amend the certification order"). In my view the *Class Proceedings Act* provides the court with ample flexibility to deal with limited differentiation amongst the class members as and if such differentiation becomes evident.

… In any event I question the extent to which differences between the class members should be taken into account at this stage. The British Columbia *Class Proceedings Act* explicitly states that the commonality requirement may be satisfied "whether or not [the] common issues predominate over issues affecting only individual members": s. 4(1)(c). (This distinguishes the British Columbia legislation from the corresponding Ontario legislation, which is silent as to whether predominance should be a factor in the commonality inquiry.) While the British Columbia *Class Proceedings Act* clearly contemplates that predominance will be a factor in the preferability inquiry (a point to which I will return below), it makes equally clear that predominance should not be a factor at the commonality stage. In my view the question at the commonality stage is, at least under the British Columbia *Class Proceedings Act*, quite narrow.

As noted above, Mackenzie JA certified as common not only the standard-of-care issue but also the punitive damages issues. Here, too, I agree with his reasoning. In this case resolving the primary common issue—whether JHS breached a duty of care or fiduciary duty to the complainants—will require the court to assess the knowledge and conduct of those in charge of JHS over a long period of time. This is exactly the kind of fact-finding that will be necessary to determine whether punitive damages are justified: see, e.g., *Endean, supra*, at para. 48 ("An award of punitive damages is founded on the conduct of the defendant, unrelated to its effect on the plaintiff."). Clearly, the appropriateness and amount of punitive damages will not always be amenable to determination as a common issue. Here, however, the respondents have limited the possible grounds of liability to systemic negligence—that is, negligence not specific to any one victim but rather to the class of victims as a group. In my view the appropriateness and amount of punitive damages is, in this case, a question amenable to resolution as a common issue: … .

The question remains whether a class action would be the preferable procedure. Here I would begin by incorporating my discussion in *Hollick* as to the meaning of preferability: see *Hollick, supra*, at paras. 28-31. While the legislative history of the British Columbia *Class Proceedings Act* is of course different from that of the corresponding Ontario legislation, in my view the preferability inquiry is, at least in general terms, the same under each statute. The inquiry is directed at two questions: first, "whether or not the class proceeding [would be] a fair, efficient and manageable method of advancing the claim," and second, whether the class proceedings would be preferable "in the sense of preferable to other procedures" (*Hollick*, at para. 28). I would note one difference, however, between the British Columbia *Class Proceedings Act* and the corresponding Ontario legislation. Like the British Columbia legislation, the Ontario legislation requires that a class action be "the preferable procedure" for the resolution of the common issues: see Ontario *Class Proceedings Act, 1992*, s. 5(1)(d); British Columbia *Class Proceedings Act*, s. 4(1)(d). Unlike the Ontario legislation, however, the British Columbia legislation provides express guidance as to how a court should approach the preferability question, listing five factors that the court must consider: see s. 4(2). I turn, now, to these factors.

The first factor is "whether questions of fact or law common to the members of the class predominate over any questions affecting only individual members": s. 4(2)(a). As I noted above, it seems likely that there will be relevant differences between class members here. It should be remembered, however, that as the respondents have limited their claims to claims of "systemic" negligence, the central issues in this suit will be the nature of the duty owed by JHS to the class members and whether that duty was breached. Those issues are amenable to resolution in a class proceeding. While the issues of injury and causation will have to be litigated in individual proceedings following resolution of the common issue (assuming the common issue is decided in favour of the class, or at least in favour of some segment of the class), in my view the individual issues will be a relatively minor aspect of this case. There is no dispute that abuse occurred at the school. The essential question is whether the school should have prevented the abuse or responded to it differently. I would conclude that the common issues predominate over those affecting only individual class members.

The second factor is "whether a significant number of the members of the class have a valid interest in individually controlling the prosecution of separate actions," and the third is "whether the class proceeding would involve claims that are or have been the subject of any other proceedings": ss. 4(2)(b), (c). On these factors I would note again that no class member will be able to prevail without making an individual showing of injury and causation. Thus it cannot be said that allowing this suit to proceed as a class action will force complainants into a passive role. Each class member will retain control over his or her individual action, and his or her ultimate recovery will be determined by the outcome of the individual proceedings on injury and causation (assuming, again, that the common issue is resolved in favour of the class). Further there is little evidence here to suggest that any significant number of class members would prefer to proceed individually.

I turn next to the fourth factor, which asks "whether other means of resolving the claims are less practical or less efficient": s. 4(2)(d). On this point I would agree with the Court of Appeal that individual actions would be less practical and less efficient than would be a class proceeding. As Mackenzie JA noted (at pp. 9-10), "[i]ssues related to policy and administration of the school, qualification and training of staff, dormitory conditions and so on are likely to have common elements." Further, "[t]he overall history and evolution of the school is likely to be important background for the claims generally and it would be needlessly expensive to require proof in separate individual cases" (p. 10). I would also agree with Mackenzie JA (and indeed with Kirkpatrick J) that the JICP does not provide an adequate alternative to a class action. Amongst other limitations, the JICP program limits the recovery of any one complainant to $60,000, and it does not permit complainants to be represented by counsel before the panel. The JICP simply cannot be said to be an adequate alternative to a class proceeding.

The final factor is "whether the administration of the class proceeding would create greater difficulties than those likely to be experienced if relief were sought by other means": s. 4(2)(e). On this point it is necessary to emphasize the particular vulnerability of the plaintiffs in this case. The individual class members are deaf or blind or both. Litigation is always a difficult process but I am convinced that it will be extraordinarily so for the class members here. Allowing the suit to proceed as a class action may go some way toward mitigating the difficulties that will be faced by the class members. I am in full agreement, therefore, with Mackenzie JA's conclusion that "[t]he communications barriers faced by the students both at the time of the assaults alleged and currently in the litigation process favour a common process to explain the significance of those barriers and to elicit relevant evidence." As he wrote, "[a] group action should assist in marshalling the expertise required to assist individual students in communicating their testimony effectively" (p. 9).

I conclude that the respondents have satisfied the certification requirements set out in s. 4 of the British Columbia *Class Proceedings Act*.

The appeal is dismissed. The respondents shall have costs throughout.

NOTES

1. The Supreme Court of Canada ruling in *Hollick* seemed to many to be at odds with its statement of principle that the legislation should be given a generous interpretation. The application of the certification criteria to the facts of the case were conservative and designed to give courts broad discretionary control over class action certification. In evaluating the common issues requirement, the court held that the issue must be a "substantial ingredient" of each class member's claim that advances the litigation to a significant degree. Further interpreting the criterion of "preferability," the court diverged from the language of the Act ("a class proceeding would be the preferable procedure for the resolution of the *common issues*") by holding that the preferability of the resolution of the common issues was to be determined in the *context of the claim as a whole*, effectively importing the US predomination test (common issues must predominate over individual issues). Further, the court explained, "The examination of preferability is to be conducted through the lens of the three principal policies underlying class actions: in assessing preferability, the court should weigh the existence of common versus individual issues; the court should first consider whether a class action would be a fair, efficient, and manageable method of advancing the litigation as a whole; and the court should assess whether a class proceeding is preferable to other procedures such as individual proceedings, test cases, and joinder."

2. *Judicial discretion on certification.* This approach to preferability seemed to give judges discretion to grant or deny certification based on their beliefs as to the social utility of the actions. Following these rulings, it was initially more difficult to obtain certification. For example, in *Pearson v. Inco Ltd.* (2002), 33 CPC (5th) 264 (Ont. SCJ); rev'd. (2005), 78 OR (3d) 641, 261 DLR (4th) 629 (CA), certification was denied in a case of environmental contamination claims relating to Inco's Port Colbourne refinery because many individual issues of causation and damages would have to be resolved after the resolution of the common issues of the defendant's duty of care and failure to warn in relation to its alleged release of contaminants into the atmosphere. However, such issues could have been considered at a later

time because the Ontario class action regime contemplates a bifurcated process. In addition, the court concluded that the combination of governmental enforcement mechanisms and voluntary remediation commitments were more suitable procedures than a class proceeding and there was little economy to be achieved from a determination of the common issues in the light of inherently individualistic allegations. On the issue of preferability, the court weighed the common issues against the amount of individual issues raised in the claim and held that the case did not enhance any of the three policy advantages. The objective of judicial economy would not be served because too many individual issues would have to be assessed before any liability could be established; nor would the objective of access to justice be served, because the class members all had invested over $50,000 and seemed to be in a financial position to proceed individually; and the objective of behaviour modification had already been served by penalties imposed by the Ontario Securities Commission.

In contrast, in *1176560 Ontario Ltd. v. Great Atlantic & Pacific Company of Canada* (2002), 62 OR (3d) 535 (SCJ), Winkler J certified a claim by a class of franchisees against the defendant franchisor A & P. The plaintiffs alleged that the franchisor withheld rebates and allowances that were stipulated in the franchise agreement, and they sought to recover the rebates for the plaintiff class. The court held that the pleadings disclosed a valid cause of action and that there was an identifiable class that consisted of 66 current and 4 former franchisees. Further, the court was satisfied that there were substantial common issues, the resolution of which would advance the litigation to a significant extent. The court also concluded that a class proceeding would be the preferable procedure to resolve the dispute because all three policy advantages of class actions would be satisfied in this instance. Specifically, a class action would reduce 70 potential trials into one action that would save judicial resources and provide consistency with respect to the decision of all class members. Further, the goals of access to justice and behaviour modification would be enhanced because the vulnerability of the franchisees supported the necessity of certification. Last, on the issue of adequate representation, the court concluded that the plaintiffs, with their financial independence, were precisely the type of plaintiffs required to prosecute this type of action. This illustrates that with the judicial discretion available, the courts may equally seize on the liberal flexible statements enunciated in the trilogy to grant certification.

3. *Evidence required or permitted on certification motions.* A key holding in *Hollick* was that "the class representative must show some basis in fact for each of the certification requirements set out in ... the Act, other than the requirement that the pleadings disclose a cause of action." As a result, voluminous evidentiary material is now filed on such motions. The potential extent or breadth of evidence required on a certification motion was made clear by the Ontario Court of Appeal in *Chadha v. Bayer Inc.* (2003), 63 OR (3d) 22 (CA), a case involving an alleged "pass on" to proposed class members of an illegal increase in the price of tinted bricks, where the court refused certification for want of sufficient evidence, and in *Kumar v. Mutual Life Assurance Co. of Canada* (2003), 226 DLR (4th) 112 (Ont. CA), a "vanishing premiums" case. In *Chadha*, the plaintiffs failed to adduce any evidence as to how they proposed to demonstrate at trial that the illegal price increase had indeed adversely affected the price paid by end-purchasers, evidence that was crucial to both "common issues" and "preferable procedure" determinations; and in *Kumar*, the plaintiffs failed to introduce any evidence to support their allegations that a uniform set of misrepresentations had been made to proposed class members and/or that the defendant had trained its

agents to make such a uniform set of misrepresentations. The defendant introduced evidence that strongly disputed the plaintiff's contentions. In light of the plaintiffs' failure to adduce sufficient evidence, the motions court, the Divisional Court and the Court of Appeal found that the plaintiffs had failed to satisfy the "common issues" requirement and that such a finding did not entail an improper weighing of the merits of the case.

Andersen v. St. Jude Medical Inc., [2003] OJ No. 4314 (SCJ) reaffirmed the principle that evidence touching on the merits is admissible on a certification motion, but may be used only for the limited purpose of determining whether a proposed class action satisfies the requisite certification criteria, and not for determining whether the pleadings disclose a cause of action. In *St. Jude*, a case involving allegedly defective mechanical heart valves, Cullity J rejected the defendant's argument that evidence that goes to the merits of the case ought to be ruled inadmissible on a certification motion. Instead, he held that such evidence may be admitted provided that it assists the court in determining whether the requisite criteria for certification are met. For more discussion of these issues, see Garry D. Watson and Derek McKay, "More on Certification in the post-*Hollick* World: Scope of Appellate Review of Certification Decisions and the Requirement and Use of Evidence on Certification" (2004), 4 *Class Action* 155.

A. Reasonable Cause of Action

The first requirement for the certification of a class action is that the pleadings disclose a reasonable cause of action. The standard for determining this was addressed in one of the first certification motions in Ontario in *Abdool v. Anaheim Management Ltd.* (1995), 21 OR (3d) 453 (Div. Ct.). The plaintiffs purchased condominium units as tax-sheltered investments on the basis of sales presentations that indicated that the units were tax shelters and that for a payment of $1,000 they would eventually acquire title to the units. The project was unsuccessful, and the plaintiffs were called on to meet the financial obligations they had undertaken. They sued on the basis of misrepresentation, negligence and breaches of statutory and fiduciary duties, damages, and rescission of contract. The motions court judge refused certification against the various defendants for various reasons, and in particular, in respect of the mortgage brokers and financiers that the pleadings failed to disclose any cause of action against them. On Appeal to the Divisional Court, Moldaver J held that the principles to be applied when considering whether pleadings support a legal cause of action were the same as for any action and, beyond this, the court will not consider the merits of the case in the certification motion. The principles are:

(a) All allegations of fact, unless patently ridiculous or incapable of proof, must be accepted as proved;

(b) The defendant, in order to succeed, must show that it is plain and obvious beyond doubt that the plaintiffs could not succeed;

(c) The novelty of the cause of action will not militate against the plaintiffs; and

(d) The statement of claim must be read as generously as possible, with a view to accommodating any inadequacies in the form of the allegations due to drafting deficiencies.

Similarly, in *Endean v. Canadian Red Cross Society* (1998), 157 DLR (4th) 465 (BCCA), the BC Court of Appeal held that the test for determining whether the pleadings disclosed a reasonable cause of action was the same as the test set out for individual litigation in *Hunt v. Carey Canada Inc.*, [1990] 2 SCR 959, at 980:

> Thus, the test in Canada governing the application of provisions like Rule 19(24)(a) of the BC *Rules of Court* is the same as in the one that governs an application under RSC O. 18, Rule 19: assuming that the facts as stated in the statement of claim can be proved, is it "plain and obvious" that the plaintiff's statement of claim discloses no reasonable cause of action? As in England, if there is a chance that the plaintiff might succeed, then the plaintiff should not be "driven from the judgment seat." Neither the length and complexity of the issues, the novelty of the cause of action, nor the potential for the defendant to present a strong defence, should prevent the plaintiff from proceeding with his or her case. Only if the action is certain to fail because it contains a radical defect ranking with the orders listed in Rule 19(24) of the BC *Rules of Court*, should the relevant provisions of the plaintiff's statement of claim be struck out under Rule 19(24)(a).

The BC Court of Appeal went on to explain that the question to be decided, then, is whether it is "plain and obvious" that the plaintiff's statement of claim discloses no reasonable cause of action. Is there some radical defect which would amount to an abuse of process of the court such that the claim should be struck? The fact that the point is a novel one would not prevent the issue proceeding to trial. The claim in *Endean* was for relief for the harm suffered as a result of "spoliation," or the destruction of documents. The court held that the destruction of documents raises a presumption that the documents were damaging to the case of the person who failed to safeguard them, but it is not an independent tort giving rise to recovery other than that available in the proceeding in which the documents might have been entered as evidence. As a result, a class action for damages based on spoliation could not be certified. Certification was therefore denied.

In the specialized field of securities litigation, the concern to prevent abusive claims led to a 2005 amendment to the Ontario *Securities Act* that imposes an additional merits-based test (the one originally proposed by the OLRC for inclusion in the *Class Proceedings Act*, but not adopted) as follows:

> 138.8(1) No proceeding may be commenced under section 138.3 without leave of the court granted upon motion with notice to each defendant. The court shall grant leave only where it is satisfied that,
>
> (a) the action is being brought in good faith; and
>
> (b) there is a reasonable possibility that the action will be resolved at trial in favour of the plaintiff.
>
> (2) Upon an application under this section, the plaintiff and each defendant shall serve and file one or more affidavits setting forth the material facts upon which each intends to rely.
>
> (3) The maker of such an affidavit may be examined on it in accordance with the rules of court.
>
> (4) A copy of the application for leave to proceed and any affidavits filed with the court shall be sent to the Commission when filed.

The requirement that the pleadings disclose a reasonable cause of action has also called into question whether a number of similar defendants' claims may be aggregated in a single suit. In other words, can there be "industry class actions" with the whole industry being sued? In such a case, does the plaintiff require a cause of action against each, or only one? In Ontario, the answer is that for every defendant there must be at least one representative plaintiff having a valid cause of action against it. The answer is the same in Quebec, but different in British Columbia and presumably in the other provinces who have legislation modelled on the BC Act.

In *Ragoonanan v. Imperial Tobacco Canada Ltd.* (2000), 51 OR (3d) 603 (SCJ), the plaintiff was able to argue a cause of action against the makers of his cigarette brand but not against two other defendant manufacturers. The court held that, without a representative plaintiff who had suffered at the hands of these defendants, the defendants must be released from the suit. The court reasoned that claims that could be made by putative class members, who cannot be considered parties until certification is granted by the court, would be merely speculative. This approach was endorsed by the Ontario Court of Appeal in *Hughes v. Sunbeam Corp.* (2002), 219 DLR (4th) 467 (CA), leave to appeal to SCC refused 224 DLR (4th) vii. In *Bouchard v. Agropur Co.*, [2006] RJQ 2349 (CA), the Quebec Court of Appeal confirmed that, in Quebec, there too must be a representative plaintiff with a cause of action against each defendant.

In contrast, the BC courts have consistently taken a more liberal position with respect to standing. The BC legislation, unlike Ontario's, permits a representative plaintiff to be someone other than a member of the class. In *MacKinnon v. National Money Mart* (2005), 33 BCLR (4th) 21 (CA), the Court of Appeal upheld a motion to certify despite the fact that the representative plaintiff did not have a cause of action against each defendant. The Act requires there to be a cause of action against each named defendant, but that cause of action may be held by members of the class other than the representative plaintiff. The question that remains with this approach is whether the representative plaintiff will adequately represent the interests of the class, or whether this approach might give rise to conflicts of interest within the class and between members of the class and its counsel.

The disparity between these approaches could also cause confusion when looking at the *res judicata* effect of class action decisions. For instance, if a Manitoba court certifies a national class against a number of defendants despite the fact that the plaintiff has a cause of action only against one of the defendants, would it be possible to commence a subsequent action in Ontario against those defendants against whom the original Manitoba plaintiff had no cause?

B. Identifiable Class—Class Definition

After the general requirement of demonstrating that there is a reasonable cause of action, the first requirement for certification that is specific to class actions is that there is an identifiable class of two or more persons that would be represented by the representative plaintiff or defendant. As Chief Justice McLachlin explained in *Western Canadian Shopping Centres* at para. 38:

Class definition is critical because it identifies the individuals entitled to notice, entitled to relief (if relief is awarded), and bound by the judgment. It is essential, therefore, that the class be defined clearly at the outset of the litigation. The definition should state objective criteria by which members of the class can be identified. While the criteria should bear a rational relationship to the common issues asserted by all class members, the criteria should not depend on the outcome of the litigation. It is not necessary that every class member be named or known. It is necessary, however, that any particular person's claim to membership in the class be determinable by stated, objective criteria.

In *Hollick* at para. 21, Chief Justice McLachlin went on to say:

> The requirement is not an onerous one. The representative need not show that everyone in the class shares the same interest in the resolution of the asserted common issue. There must be some showing, however, that the class is not unnecessarily broad—that is, that the class could not be defined more narrowly without arbitrarily excluding some people who share the same interest in the resolution of the common issue. Where the class could be defined more narrowly, the court should either disallow certification or allow certification on condition that the definition of the class be amended. ...

Despite the reassurance that the requirement is not an onerous one, it has been fraught with complexity. In the following decision in an early motion for certification of a class following a fire in the subway in Toronto, Justice Winkler, as he then was, was called upon to consider the relationship between the description of the class and the determination of whether particular members had, in fact, suffered damages.

Bywater v. Toronto Transit Commission
(1998), 27 CPC (4th) 172 (Ont. Ct. Gen. Div.)

WINKLER J: The second requirement of the test for certification is that there be an identifiable class of two or more persons. The plaintiff proposes a class defined as follows:

A. All persons other that TTC employees and emergency personnel, who were exposed to smoke and toxic gases in TTC vehicles or on TTC premises arising from a fire which commenced at approximately 7:15 p.m. on Wednesday, August 6, 1997 at or near the Donlands subway station or, where such a person died after the fire, the personal representative of the estate of the deceased person ... [referred to as the] Directly Affected Class Members; and

B. All living parents, grandparents, children, grandchildren, siblings, and spouses (within the meaning of s. 61 of the Family Law Act) of the Directly Affected Class Members, or where such a family member died after the fire, the personal representative of the estate of the deceased family member [referred to as the] Family Claimants.

The defendant contends that in the present circumstances there is no identifiable class. It states that the class description proposed by the plaintiff is imprecise with the result that the class members will be unascertainable. I disagree.

The purpose of the class definition is threefold: a) it identifies those persons who have a potential claim for relief against the defendant; b) it defines the parameters of the lawsuit so as to identify those persons who are bound by its result; and lastly, c) it describes who is entitled to notice pursuant to the Act. Thus for the mutual benefit of the plaintiff and the defendant the class definition ought not to be unduly narrow nor unduly broad.

In the instant proceeding the identities of many of the passengers who would come within the class definition are not presently known. This does not constitute a defect in the class definition. In *Anderson v. Wilson* (1998), 37 OR (3d) 235 (Div. Ct.), Campbell J adopted the words of the Ontario Law Reform Commission and stated at 248:

> ... a class definition that would enable the court to determine whether any person coming forward was or was not a class member would seem to be sufficient.

On this point, Newberg on Class Actions (3d ed. Looseleaf) (West Publishing) states at 6-61:

> Care should be taken to define the class in objective terms capable of membership ascertainment when appropriate, without regard to the merits of the claim or the seeking of particular relief. Such a definition in terms of objective characteristics of class members avoids problems of circular definitions which depend on the outcome of the litigation on the merits before class members may be ascertained. ...

The Manual for Complex Litigation, Third (1995, West Publishing) states at 217:

> Class definition is of critical importance because it identifies the persons (1) entitled to relief, (2) bound by a final judgment, and (3) entitled to notice in a [class] action. It is therefore necessary to arrive at a definition that is precise, objective, and presently ascertainable ... Definitions ... should avoid criteria that are subjective (e.g., a plaintiff s state of mind) or that depend upon the merits (e.g., persons who were discriminated against). Such definitions frustrate efforts to identify class members, contravene the policy against considering the merits of a claim in deciding whether to certify a class, and create potential problems of manageability.

The defendant urges, in the alternative, that the class definition should include a reference to damages resulting from smoke inhalation. This requirement, if adopted, would run contrary to the tenets set out above. It would unduly narrow the class and it anticipates entitlement. Moreover, it would eliminate persons with strictly property damage claims. The reference to damages impinges on the merits of the claim and, thus, goes beyond the purpose of class definition. The definition proposed by the plaintiff is approved with the deletion of words "and toxic gases."

NOTES

The requirements for determining the definition of the class for the purposes of deciding whether to certify the class presents a conundrum that was examined in greater detail in *Ragoonanan Estate v. Imperial Tobacco Canada Ltd.* (2005), 78 OR (3d) 98 (SCJ). In *Ragoonanan*, a motion for certification was brought in a claim against a manufacturer of a "fire safe cigarette" that was advertised as having "a reduced propensity for igniting upholstered furniture and mattress fires." The claim was brought on behalf of all persons, or their estates, who suffered damages as a result of upholstered furniture or a mattress catching fire from a cigarette manufactured by the defendant.

Certification was refused in that case in part because the action failed to satisfy both "preferable procedure" and "workable litigation plan" requirements. However, the decision revealed that the existing principles for determining whether the proposed class is adequately defined can be contradictory. These principles are that the class cannot be defined in terms of the merits of the action; that the class definition should be neither overinclusive nor underinclusive; and that the class must be defined in terms of "objective" as opposed to "subjective" criteria.

Ragoonanan Estate v. Imperial Tobacco Canada Ltd.
(2005), 78 OR (3d) 98 (SCJ)

CULLITY J: ... The proposed representative plaintiffs are the personal representatives of Jasmine and Philip Ragoonanan and Ranuka Baboolal who died as a result of a fire at a residential property in Brampton, Ontario in the early hours of January 18, 1998. ...

The claims are for damages for the alleged negligent manufacture and design of cigarettes produced by the defendant. It is pleaded that the defendant knew, or ought to have known: (a) that its cigarettes were dangerous because they were not "fire safe"; and (b) how to manufacture and sell a fire-safe cigarette.

• • •

In this jurisdiction defendants' counsel increasingly rely on supposed rules that, they submit, serve to distinguish between acceptable class definitions and those that cannot be accepted for certification. It is said that a class must neither be over-inclusive nor under-inclusive, that class criteria must not depend on the merits of the claims and that they must be "objective" rather than "subjective." Taken to their logical extreme, the suggested interpretation and effect of these rules often appear to lead inexorably to decisions that certification must be denied for want of an acceptable class. ...

• • •

It is argued that a proposed class that contains persons who will not have valid claims is unacceptably over-inclusive, while a class that "arbitrarily" excludes persons who have—or may have—valid claims is under-inclusive. I adhere to the view I have expressed in other cases that neither of the suggested restrictive rules is supported by the following passage from the reasons of the Chief Justice in *Hollick*, at paras. 20-1, that is commonly relied on as authority for each of them:

> It falls to the putative representative to show the class is defined sufficiently narrowly.
>
> The requirement is not an onerous one. The representative need not show that everyone in the class shares the same interest in the resolution of the asserted common issue. There must be some showing, however, that the class is not unnecessarily broad—that is, that the class could not be defined more narrowly without arbitrarily excluding some people who share the same interest in the resolution of the common issues. Where the class could be

defined more narrowly, the court should either disallow certification or allow certification on condition that the definition of the class be amended ...

I understand that passage to accept a concept of over-inclusiveness confined to cases where more narrow class definitions would be possible without arbitrarily excluding persons who share the same interest in the resolution of the common issues. I do not understand it to imply that a plaintiff cannot choose—arbitrarily or otherwise—the persons whom he, or she, wishes to represent, or that the only class proceedings permissible are those where the class contains everyone with the same interest. Rather than supporting either of the suggested rules of class definition, it seems to me that the Chief Justice was recognising that an "over-inclusive" class contemplated by the first of those rules is permitted if a more narrow definition would arbitrarily exclude persons whose claims the plaintiff wishes to enforce. A class may be over-inclusive if necessary but not necessarily over-inclusive.

The restrictive effects of the supposed rules relating to inclusiveness are buttressed by a insistence that membership in the class must be determined without reference to the "merits of the action." Such a rule makes perfect sense—and is obviously necessary—where the reference to the "merits" results in circularity. A class, for example, could not be defined meaningfully in terms of persons to whom the defendant was liable, or owed a duty of care, if liability, or the existence of a duty of care owed to class members, was a common issue. However, where the reference to the merits relates to disputed individual issues—rather than common issues—circularity, in this sense, is not necessarily involved.

When it is sometimes said that merits-based individual issues create circularity, what appears to be meant is that persons who will be bound by a judgment on the common issues cannot (logically?) be identifiable by criteria that will determine whether they will have valid claims. As section 27 (3) of the CPA provides that a judgment on common issues binds class members, it is thought to follow that the class must be ascertainable before, or at least at the end of, the trial of the common issues. This will be relevant only where the common issues are decided in favour of the defendant but, so the argument proceeds, the defendant must then be able to identify the class members. Moreover, because only members will be able to make claims in reliance on common-issues judgments that are favourable to the class, it is thought that it must be possible to identify them before proceeding to proof of loss and the resolution of any other individual issues that will determine liability. Where merits-based criteria beg questions that are individual issues, the result of a decision on the common issues in favour of a defendant would be that the identity of members of the class might, and often would, never be determined.

Such objections are, I believe, formal rather than substantive and certainly not logically compelling. Whatever class criteria are employed, class members will very often not have been identified when an action is dismissed as a result of a decision on the common issues favourable to a defendant. Where the plaintiffs are successful on the common issues, the actual composition of the class will very often not be determined until the individual issues have been decided, as it will only then have been determined whether claimants satisfy whatever class criteria are employed. Even then as, pursuant to section

25 of the CPA, claimants will usually be required to come forward within a stipulated period, there may be class members whose identity is never ascertained. In short, at the conclusion of a trial of common issues—and before any individual issues are addressed—it will often be possible to identify the members of a sizable class only in terms of the class criteria.

It follows that, a defendant wishing to rely on *res judicata*, or issue estoppel, arising from a decision on the common issues in a class proceeding, may never have the benefit of a prior judicial, or other binding, decision on whether the plaintiff in the subsequent case was a member of the class. In consequence, the defendant might have to prove that the criteria for the plaintiff's membership in the class was satisfied. This, however, would be so whether the criteria were, or were not, considered to be merits-based. As I will indicate, I believe that the implications for subsequent proceedings may require that some limits be placed on the use of criteria that are likely to be seriously in dispute, but I do not believe this would justify a rejection of "merits-based" criteria as such. Most fundamentally, no meaningful distinction can, I think, be drawn between criteria that require proof of material facts that constitute the cause of action and other "objective" criteria. The ability of a claimant to satisfy any class criteria might be challenged by a defendant as a ground for denying liability to such person and any such criteria will be included in the material facts that comprise the cause, or causes, of action pleaded in the proceeding.

. . .

An assumption, again, appears to be that it will be necessary to identify each class member before individual claims can be considered. What is not explained is why merits-based criteria—like other class criteria—cannot, and should not, be considered to raise individual issues like any others that will determine whether individual claims will be sustained, and that may also be relevant to the question whether a resolution of the common issues will sufficiently advance the proceedings.

. . .

In practical—as well as logical—terms, the problem created by the supposed over-inclusive rule and the prohibition on merits-based class definitions is that they operate in opposition to each other. While the former insists that only those with valid—or, in the words of the Chief Justice, "colourable"—claims are included in the class, the latter restricts the possibility of achieving this end. If they are applied strictly, their combined application will tend to exclude the possibility of any acceptable class definition.

. . .

… I have difficulty in appreciating the force of the objections to all merits-based criteria and, in particular, the argument that such criteria would permit the common issues to be relitigated subsequently. Difficulties that may be thought to arise from an inability to identify each member of a class who will be bound by a decision on the common issues are, I believe, likely to be more theoretical than practical. In particular, I do not understand the sense in which harm, or damage, as a criterion necessarily involves unacceptable circularity, or a violation of the statutory policy that the merits are not to be decided at the certification stage. "Circularity"—in the questionable sense that class membership is dependent on individual issues that will determine the defendant's liability—cannot be avoided and acceptance of a merits-based criterion would not, in itself, require any decision on the merits. On the other hand, by placing the focus on the only persons who could benefit from the proceedings, merits-based criteria may make it unnecessary to define classes that are hugely over-inclusive, and their acceptance would avoid the difficulty of distinguishing between objectionable and unobjectionable criteria in terms of merits.

. . .

The problems of class definition have, arguably, achieved too great a prominence in certification motions. The suggestion that they can all be avoided simply by inserting the words "who claim" before what would otherwise be merits-based criteria has obvious attractions. Acceptance of the possibility may reflect a silent recognition of the problems with the supposed rules I have mentioned. It appears to have had its source in the decision of the British Columbia Court of Appeal in *Rumley v. British Columbia* (1999), 180 DLR (4th) 639 (BC CA)—a decision that was upheld—without comment on this point—in the Supreme Court of Canada [(2001), 205 DLR (4th) 39 (SCC)]. The class was defined by the Court of Appeal as:

> Students at the Jericho Hill School between 1950 and 1992 who reside in British Columbia and claim to have suffered injury, loss or damage as a result of misconduct of a sexual nature occurring at the school.

The application for certification in Rumley defined the class in terms of those who suffered damage resulting from the operation and management of the school. The reasons of the Court of Appeal contain no explanation for the introduction of the words "and claim." ...

The view that accepts that "objective" class criteria can be framed in terms of a person's claim to have suffered injury or harm was, however, quite clearly adopted in *Wheadon v. Bayer Inc.*, [2004] NJ No. 147 (NL TD) and *Walls v. Bayer Inc.*, [2005] MJ No. 4 (Man. QB). In *Wheadon*, the class was defined in part as including:

> Persons resident in Newfoundland and Labrador who were prescribed and ingested Baycol and who claim personal injury as a result ...

Barry J stated:

> Bayer says the class proposed by the plaintiffs in this case suffers from the fundamental defect that members of the proposed class cannot be identified at the outset of the litigation by the application of objective criteria, since the proposed definition leaves it to each possible class member to decide, subjectively, and at the time of the person's choosing, whether he or she wishes to assert injury that he or she attributes to use of Baycol.
>
> ... But although there will obviously be a subjective reason for making a claim, whether or not one makes a claim can be objectively determined. It is not necessary that every class member be named or known at the outset but only that a "claim to membership in a class be determinable by stated, objective criteria.

. . .

If it were possible to define a class in terms of persons who claim that one, or more, individual issues should be decided in their favour, there would very likely be no members of the class—and no one bound by the decision—if the common issues were decided in favour of the defendant. Persons who made no such claim could, in subsequent proceedings, resist a defence of issue estoppel on that ground. In a class action for damages for breach of contract, for example, a decision at a trial of common issues, that there was no contract, could be ignored by putative class members who had never been called on to make a claim, and who subsequently commenced proceedings for restitutionary, or equitable, remedies that did not depend on proof of damages.

Accordingly, and despite the respect and deference due, and accorded, to the judges who have expressed inconsistent views in other jurisdictions, I do not consider that the problem of merits-based definitions can be avoided in this case by replacing causation as a fact with the fact that causation is claimed or asserted—at some unspecified time—by a potential class member.

I conclude that none of the proposed class definitions is acceptable and that certification must be denied on that ground. I do not believe this is a case where I should struggle to find a definition that would satisfy the reasoning in the authorities I have cited, or properly allow certification on condition that the definition of a class would be amended. An invitation to find an acceptable definition was rejected by Winkler J in *Caputo* (at para. 41) where, after referring to comments of McLachlin CJ in *Hollick* (at para. 21), he continued:

> As I read her reasons, the court may either reject certification where the class is not properly defined or otherwise grant a conditional certification on the basis that the plaintiffs will have to provide an acceptable definition to the court. In some circumstances, it may be appropriate for the court to alter or amend a class definition to be consistent with other findings made on a certification motion. That is not the case here. What the plaintiff suggests is akin to having the court perform the role of class counsel by making wholesale changes to arrive at a definition that the court itself would accept. That goes beyond a simple exercise of discretion and verges into the prohibited territory of descending "into the arena" with the parties to the motion.

I reach the same conclusion. Experienced counsel have given this question considerable thought and have been unable to provide a definition that is in accordance with my understanding of the authorities I must follow. I will add only that no such acceptable definition is readily apparent to me. Given the first of the proposed common issues—to which I will refer below—I am not persuaded that any non-merits-based definition that would not extend to everyone in Canada could be formulated.

NOTES

1. *Merits-based class definitions.* The fairness of merits-based class definitions have been considered in the United States as well. In *Intratex Gas Company v. Beeson*, 22 SW3d 398 (2000) (Texas), the ultimate appeals court in Texas struck down a class definition that was improperly based on the ultimate issue of alleged liability in the case. The court observed:

> A fail-safe class that is based on resolving the ultimate liability issue is bound only by a judgment favorable to plaintiffs but not by a judgment favorable to defendants ...

Certifying a fail-safe class inevitably creates one-sided results. If the defendant is found liable, class membership is then ascertainable and the litigation comes to an end. A determination that the defendant is not liable, however, obviates the class, thereby precluding the proposed class members from being bound by the judgment. We do not support such a result when "[r]ule [42] was never meant to be an exception to the rules of *res judicata* or to provide a risk-free method of litigation."

2. *Class definition and res judicata.* In the course of grappling with the use of merits-based criteria in defining a class, *Ragoonanan* brings out the important issue of how the class definition interacts with *res judicata.* One of the main benefits of class actions is judicial economy, which is created by the fact that matters decided in a class action are binding on all parties. Unless they opt-out, class members (other than the named representative plaintiffs) cannot relitigate a matter once it has been determined with finality as a class action. This becomes problematic when there are issues with the class definition, because that is the basis for determining who is bound by such decisions. As Rachel Mulheron has noted, class definitions that include criteria based on causation could be problematic because if a class member "fails to establish the causal link ... , it will follow that person is not a group member and, therefore, is not bound by the result of the proceeding. The person would be free to bring a later proceeding against the respondents or any of them." (See Rachael Mulheron, in *The Class Action in Common Law Systems: A Comparative Perspective* (Oxford: Hart Publishing, 2004), at 322-37). However, despite the concern expressed in *Ragoonanan,* it is only the definitions that include criteria based on *legal liability* that have the potential to create this concern, not those based on the factual merits of the claim. Accordingly, concerns with "merits-based" class definitions may have been overstated.

3. *Overinclusiveness versus merits-based class definition.* In the Vioxx product liability case of *Tiboni v. Merck Frosst Canada Ltd.*, [2008] CanLII 37911 (Ont. SCJ), paras. 64-82, Cullity J followed up on his discussion in *Ragoonanan* of the conflict between overinclusive class definitions and merits-based class definitions. Justice Cullity noted that defendants often rely on *Hollick* for the principle that the class definitions must not be "unnecessarily broad," which is especially true in product liability cases where many potential class members have not actually suffered injury from the product, but are still included in the proposed class definition. Counsel for the defendants relied on the fact that only a small percentage of individuals who took the drug would suffer harm; however, the allegedly overinclusive class definition included all individuals who took Vioxx during the class period.

To remove the spectre of overinclusive class definitions, Cullity J recognized that "claims limiters" are often introduced into class definitions (i.e., the class is defined as all consumers of the product *who claim to have been injured* by the product). This would, arguably, introduce an element of subjectivity into the class definition, which directly conflicts with the requirement that class definitions use objective criteria; however, Cullity J reasoned that the use of a claims limiter, by itself, would not transform the class description into an impermissible merits-based definition because it "achieves nothing more than to create an illusion that a class has been narrowed in a significant respect so that it can no longer be described as 'over-inclusive.'" Any decision on the common issues would still be binding on *all* potential class members. Those who claimed harm in the initial action would either vindicate their rights or would be unable to relitigate the claim and any class members who claimed harm after the decision would be unable to advance an action because of *res judicata* arising from issue estoppel. Not all class members will have claims against the defendant. While a strict interpretation of *Hollick* seems to suggest that the class should be as narrowly defined as possible, Cullity J held that such an argument is based on a "misreading of *Hollick*." Part of the *Hollick* test for a certifiable class definition lies in the existence of a "rational relationship between the class and the common issues." In *Attis v. Canada (Minister of Health)*, [2007] OJ No. 1744 (SCJ), Winkler J held that such a relationship exists whether or not proposed class members suffered harm:

> In consideration of an allegation that a given product is unsafe for use, it is difficult to accept the proposition that all users would not have some interest in the outcome of the litigation. Conversely, it is equally difficult to accept a proposition that the defendants subject to the allegation would not want to ensure that all potential claims are resolved and all potential claimants bound by the results, including those claims that may fail.

4. *The need for evidence.* In the following case, Justice Sharpe (as he then was) considers the sufficiency of supporting affidavit evidence of an identifiable class of persons that is required for certification.

Taub v. The Manufacturers Life Insurance Co.
(1998), 40 OR (3d) 379 (Gen. Div.)

SHARPE J: While a number of issues were argued on this certification motion, I find it necessary to deal with only one, namely, whether there is an adequate evidential basis before me to justify certification.

The only evidence is the affidavit of the representative plaintiff, Ellen Taub. She deposes that the action is based on the presence of a certain mould in the apartment building in which she resides. While she gives the name of the mould (stachybotrys atra), she does not provide any details as to the nature of the harm it is alleged to cause. Nor does she give any indication that the mould has been found in any place in the building other than in her own bathroom. She gives no indication that anyone else in the proposed class has found this mould, or complained of any harm or ill-effect from the mould. Indeed, it is admitted that she herself does not claim to have suffered illness, physical injury or harm from the mould, nor does she allege any property damage from the mould.

Counsel for the plaintiff submits that the allegations in the statement of claim provide the proper basis for assessing whether the action should be certified under s. 5 of the *Class Proceedings Act, 1992*, SO 1992, c. 6 ("CPA"). The allegations in the statement of claim, still sparse in detail, are somewhat broader than the sworn statements of Ms. Taub. The statement of claim refers to the mould having been found by the plaintiff "in various areas" of the building, and that:

> These air borne contaminants have substantially affected the class members' health and interfered with the class members' quality and enjoyment of life, as well as their enjoyment of their residential premises. It has exposed them to health risks and health problems. It had caused or will cause members of the class to incur moving and relocation expenses.

In my view, s. 5 of the CPA requires the representative plaintiff to provide a certain minimum evidential basis for a certification order. The CPA clearly does not contemplate a detailed assessment of the merits of the claim of the representative plaintiff or of the claims of the members of the proposed class. That is clear from s. 5(5). However, it is my view that in order to certify the proceeding, the judge must be satisfied of certain basic facts required by s. 5 of the CPA as the basis for a certification order. The matter comes before the court on motion. I fail to see why the moving party should be relieved of the normal burden of providing the court with a factual record sufficient to ground the relief sought. While the point raised here has not been the subject of judicial determination, other courts have spoken of the need for an evidential basis for the certification motion: see, e.g., *Caputo v. Imperial Tobacco Ltd.* (1997), 34 OR (3d) 314 at pp. 318-19, 148 DLR (4th) 566 (Gen. Div.). At a minimum, the court must be satisfied that there is a class of more than one person and that the issues raised by members of the class satisfy the requirement that they raise common issues, and that a class proceeding would be the preferable procedure for the resolution of the common issues. In most class proceedings, these factual matters may well be obvious and require little evidence. Most class proceedings arise from situations where the fact of wide-spread harm or complaint is inherent in the claim itself. Obvious examples are claims arising from mass disasters such as subway or air crashes or claims based on allegations of harm from wide-spread pollution. I do not say that there must be affidavits from members of the class or that there should be any assessment of the merits of the claims of other class members. I do say, however, that there must, at the very least, be some basis in fact for the court to conclude that at least one other claim exists and some basis in fact for the court to assess the nature of those claims that exist that will enable the court to determine whether the common issue and preferability requirements are satisfied.

In the case at bar, there is no evidence that the harm complained of by the representative plaintiff is the subject of concern on the part of anyone else. The nature of the harm disclosed by the plaintiff's affidavit is not of a kind that makes it at all obvious that it would have affected anyone else. It is by no means self-evident that the presence of mould in one bathroom in one apartment indicates that there will be a similar problem in other areas of the building. As noted, in her affidavit, Ms. Taub gives no indication of the nature of harm caused by the mould, no indication how it might spread to other parts of the building, and no indication that the mould has in fact been the subject of concern or complaint by anyone else other than herself. On the basis of such a record, I fail to see how I am in a position to make the determinations I am required to make before certifying this action as a class proceeding. Accordingly, I dismiss the motion on this ground and find it unnecessary to consider the other points that were argued.

NOTES

1. *Evidence of a litigious class.* For plaintiff class actions, a disputed question is whether the criteron of an identifiable class requires not only evidence of the existence of a class of persons with the same or similar interest in the outcome of the common issues (i.e., a class of persons having the same or similar claims against the defendant), but also evidence that members of the proposed class want their claims litigated. In *Bellaire v. Independent Order*

of Foresters, [2004] OJ No. 2242 (SCJ), Nordheimer J held that evidence of a litigious class is required. The action was brought on behalf of persons who purchased "fixed premium" insurance policies from the defendant insurer. The statement of claim alleged that the defendant breached its "fixed premium" promises, and/or in the alternative, that the defendant fraudulently or negligently misrepresented the nature of its "fixed premium" policies. The defendant's evidence showed that in a similar US class action, pursuant to the terms of settlement, the defendant had implemented a dispute resolution program for dealing with potential complaints of the type alleged in the Ontario action, mailing nearly 70,000 dispute resolution packages to its customers. Only 3 percent of the defendant's customers chose to participate in the program. On the basis of the low response rate and other evidence, the defendant argued that the plaintiff had failed to demonstrate that anyone other than the representative plaintiff wanted his or her potential claims litigated. The court agreed.

However, in *1176560 Ontario Ltd. v. The Great Atlantic & Pacific Company of Canada Ltd.*, [2002] OJ No. 4781 (SCJ), Winkler J explicitly rejected such a requirement:

> ... To adduce evidence from individual class members as to the desirability of a class proceeding is to assume, as an underlying proposition, that certification motions are somehow determined through a referendum of the class members. Such is not the case. The legislature has spoken with respect to class proceedings in this province. The provisions dealing with opt outs and de-certification show that it was clearly alive to the prospect that not all members of a proposed class would wish to participate in a class proceeding or, alternatively, that a sufficient number of defections from the class would render a class proceeding unnecessary. Conversely, there are no provisions that expressly or implicitly mandate, or even suggest, that the suitability of a class proceeding is to be determined by a polling of the class prior to the certification motion.

C. Common Issues

The third criterion for certifying a class action (the second criterion specific to class actions) is that the claims or the defences of the class members raise common issues. This would appear to be a threshold requirement—that is, whether the claims or defences raise common issues *at all*. The further question—whether the common issues that are raised warrant the certification of a class action—is addressed under the subsequent criterion of "preferability." Nevertheless, whether a claim raises common issues at all has been contentious in some cases.

As the Supreme Court of Canada observed in *Western Canadian Shopping Centres* at paras. 39-40:

> The commonality question should be approached purposively. The underlying question is whether allowing the suit to proceed as a representative one will avoid duplication of fact-finding or legal analysis. Thus an issue will be "common" only where its resolution is necessary to the resolution of each class member's claim. It is not essential that the class members be identically situated vis-à-vis the opposing party. Nor is it necessary that common issues predominate over non-common issues or that the resolution of the common issues would be determinative of each class member's claim. However, the class members' claims must share a

substantial common ingredient to justify a class action. Determining whether the common issues justify a class action may require the court to examine the significance of the common issues in relation to individual issues. In doing so, the court should remember that it may not always be possible for a representative party to plead the claims of each class member with the same particularity as would be required in an individual suit. ... [w]ith regard to the common issues, success for one class member must mean success for all.

Chief Justice McLachlin went on in *Hollick* at para. 18 to explain that

... an issue will not be "common" in the requisite sense unless the issue is a "substantial ... ingredient" of each of the class members' claims" and in *Rumley* at para. 29 that "the guiding question should be the practical one of "whether allowing the suit to proceed as a representative one will avoid duplication of fact-finding or legal analysis." It would not serve the ends of either fairness or efficiency to certify an action on the basis of issues that are common only when stated in the most general terms. Inevitably such an action would ultimately break down into individual proceedings.

In the following case, the plaintiffs sought certification of an action against tobacco manufacturers for personal injuries suffered by Ontario smokers and their families caused by allegedly inherently defective and dangerous products marketed with knowledge that they were addictive and harmful.

Caputo v. Imperial Tobacco Ltd.
(2004), 236 DLR (4th) 348 (Ont. SCJ)

WINKLER J: The third element in the test for certification is that the claims of the class members raise common issues. Although s. 5(1)(c) is silent as to the quality of the common issues that must be present, in *Hollick*, McLachlin CJ stated at para. 18 "an issue will not be common in the requisite sense unless the issue is a substantial ingredient of each of the class members' claims." Further, the common issues must be such that their resolution will "significantly advance the action." (*Hollick* at para. 32).

The plaintiffs and the defendants have diametrically opposed views with respect to whether common issues are raised by the claim pleaded. The plaintiffs submitted that there are seven substantial common issues which in turn give rise to over 60 incidental common issues. The defendants on the other hand state that none of the common issues submitted by the plaintiffs meet the *Hollick* threshold and thus should be rejected.

Having made the submission that the plaintiffs' common issues should be rejected, the defendants did not proffer any alternative common issues during the hearing. This is not surprising given the defendants contention that the action as framed is still inherently individualistic and unsuitable for certification as a class proceeding.

The substantial common issues advanced by the plaintiffs were set out at para. 80 of their factum as follows:

(a) are the defendants liable to members of the class for damages relating to addiction and/or other injuries, and death;

(b)   are members of the class entitled to

    i. a global assessment of damages in respect of monies expended by them on the purchases of defendants' cigarette products, from the defendants, from the date class members sought, but were unable, to cease using defendants' cigarette products;

    ii. a global assessment of damages in respect of monies expended by them on the defendants' health reassurance cigarette products marketed as "filtered," "light," "extra light," "ultra light," "ultra mild" and similarly described terms, from the defendants, from the date class members switched to such cigarette products;

    iii. a global assessment of punitive and exemplary damages in respect of the defendants' alleged intentional, wanton, reckless, and reprehensible conduct directed at the class as a whole;

    iv. equitable relief;

(c)   should the court impose sanctions or determine other relief in respect of evidence suppression and concealment; in respect of class claims; and

(d)   [have limitation periods] begun to run, or are there special circumstances that would toll its running in respect of class claims, given the defendants' past and ongoing tortious conduct?

In my view, the majority of the foregoing proposed common issues proceed on a theory of aggregation that is fundamentally misconceived. First, the claim for damages for addiction, other injuries and death cannot proceed as a common issue through to a determination of liability. Although deficient in other respects, the record before the court makes it apparent that, regardless of the common issues asserted and potentially resolved through a single trial, individual issues will remain to be decided before the liability of the defendants to individual class members can be ascertained. Regardless of the conduct of the defendants, they are entitled to a fair procedure, whether by way of a class proceeding or otherwise.

Moreover, the plaintiffs have not put any evidence before the court on this motion that indicates that that liability could be determined as a common issue. Cogent evidence of that fact would be a prerequisite to granting certification of the common issue asserted by the plaintiffs regarding liability to the class as a whole. This principle was enunciated by the Court of Appeal for Ontario in *Chadha v. Bayer Inc.* (2003), 63 OR (3d) 22 (CA) where Feldman JA stated at para. 52 "[i]n my view, the motions judge erred in finding that liability could be proved as a common issue in this case. The evidence presented by the appellants on the motion does not satisfy the requirement prescribed by the Supreme Court in Hollick of providing sufficient evidence to support certification."

The plaintiffs assertion that there are common issues regarding aggregate damages in respect of monies expended by the class are equally flawed. Section 24(1) of the CPA speaks to the requirements that must be met prior to an assessment of aggregate damages in a class proceeding. It provides:

    24.(1) The court may determine the aggregate or a part of a defendant's liability to class members and give judgment accordingly where,

(a) monetary relief is claimed on behalf of some or all class members;

(b) no questions of fact or law other than those relating to the assessment of monetary relief remain to be determined in order to establish the amount of the defendant's monetary liability; and

(c) the aggregate or a part of the defendant's liability to some or all class members can reasonably be determined without proof by individual class members.

The plaintiffs asserted common issues regarding monies expended by the class run afoul of both 24(1)(b) and 24(1)(c). There will be individual issues to be determined at the conclusion of a common issue trial. Further, the issues as framed contemplate the need for proof by individual class members. The plaintiffs also propose, in paras. 97-100 of their factum, to have the common issues trial judge determine whether an aggregate assessment of pecuniary damages for cigarette-related injuries including nicotine addiction, lung cancer, oral cancers, respiratory disease and cardiovascular disease can be made on the basis of epidemiological, economic and other expert evidence. This damages assessment would have to be based largely on statistical evidence.

This latter proposition contravenes both s. 24 and the procedures governed by the CPA. In *Bywater* this court rejected a claim for an aggregate assessment on the grounds that the action involved a claim for damages for personal injuries, property damage and FLA claims. These required proof by individual class members and proof of causation. In the final analysis, each claim was fact driven and idiosyncratic in nature. That case involved exposure to smoke in a subway fire. As stated at para. 19:

> All of the usual factors must be considered in assessing individual damage claims for personal injury, such as: the individual plaintiff's time of exposure to smoke; the extent of any resultant injury; general personal health and medical history; age; any unrelated illness; and other individual considerations … [t]he property damage claims of class members must be assessed individually as the underlying facts will vary from one class member to the next.

The circumstances there were starkly similar to those in the present case. This case is equally unsuited to an aggregate assessment concerning the damages claimed. There are numerous, and significant, individual issues pertinent to the issue of liability and damages that must be determined. As stated by Feldman JA in *Chadha* at para. 49:

> … s. 24 of the Class Proceedings Act is applicable only once liability has been established, and provides a method to assess the quantum of damages on a global basis, but not the fact of damage.

Moreover, the plaintiffs' contention that the common issues judge should identify the common issues is ill conceived. That task must be completed at the certification stage and not left for later. As the phrase implies, the judge presiding over the "common issues trial" is there in the role of arbiter of issues that have already been set out. That role is to make findings with respect to issues certified for trial, rather than to decide what issues are to be resolved. Setting the issues for trial is the role of the motions judge on certification.

Nonetheless, there are three issues proposed by the plaintiffs that appear, at first impression, to be amenable to resolution on a class wide basis in general terms. The issues identified in paragraph 54 above as (b)(iii) regarding punitive damages, (c) relating to conduct of the defendants and (d) with respect to limitation periods, are all resolvable after inquiry into the conduct of the defendants and without participation from the class members. This is particularly so with regard to punitive damages. As stated by McLachlin CJ in *Rumley* at para. 34:

> In this case, resolving the primary common issue will require the court to assess the knowledge and conduct of those in charge of JHS over a long period of time. This is exactly the kind of fact-finding that will be necessary to determine the whether punitive damages are justified … "an award of punitive damages is founded on the conduct of the defendant, unrelated to its effect on the plaintiff." (Internal citation omitted).

However, as McLachlin CJ went on to say, "[c]learly, the appropriateness and amount of punitive damages will not always be amenable to determination as a common issue." This is the situation in the present circumstances with respect to the remaining three issues. The proposition is that the assessment or determination of each will be made on a class wide basis. Obviously there must be an identifiable class in existence for whom the assessment or determination applies. Here there is no such class.

In short, for these reasons I reject the plaintiffs common issues.

In *Hollick* the Supreme Court of Canada stated at para. 20 that … "implicit in the 'identifiable class' requirement is the requirement that there be some rational relationship between the class and the common issues," and later in the same para. that, "it falls to the putative representative to show that the class is defined sufficiently narrowly." In the present case I have concluded that the plaintiffs have failed to meet this requirement of establishing an identifiable class as required by the Act and reinforced by the Supreme Court. Absent a properly defined class, it is not appropriate, nor is it feasible, for me to craft common issues. Any such attempt in these circumstances would be to engage in mere speculation. Accordingly, I decline to exercise my discretion to state common issues with respect to this proceeding.

D. Preferable Procedure

The fourth criterion for certifying a class action (the third criterion specific to class actions) is that a class proceeding would be the preferable procedure for the resolution of the common issues.

As was mentioned in the discussion earlier of *Hollick*, the Supreme Court imported the objectives (as described by the Ontario Law Reform Commission) of access to justice, judicial economy, and behaviour modification as criteria for evaluating this requirement in a motion for certification brought under the Ontario Act. In *Rumley*, however, the Supreme Court relied upon the criteria set out in the BC Act as follows:

> (a) whether questions of fact or law common to the members of the class predominate over any questions affecting only individual members;
> (b) whether a significant number of the members of the class have a valid interest in individually controlling the prosecution of separate actions;
> (c) whether the class proceeding would involve claims that are or have been the subject of any other proceedings;
> (d) whether other means of resolving the claims are less practical or less efficient;

(e) whether the administration of the class proceeding would create greater difficulties than those likely to be experienced if relief were sought by other means.

Despite this, courts throughout Canada, including in British Columbia, have routinely referred to the Ontario Law Reform Commission objectives in making determinations of preferability. This may be a response to the inherent need for qualitative factors in the certification determination. In its Report on Class Actions, the Ontario Law Reform Commission had proposed a "cost–benefit" analysis for certification motions, which was not ultimately adopted by the legislators. This is what the commission said about that analysis:

> Having concluded that there is a need for a superiority provision in the proposed *Class Actions Act*, it remains to be considered what form this requirement should take. The Commission is attracted by the superiority prerequisite contained in Rule 23(b)(3), but we are of the view that it requires some modification.
>
> Perhaps the most unsatisfactory feature of the superiority provision of Rule 23(b)(3), as it has been applied in the United States, is the discrepancy that has developed between the actual language of the Rule and the manner in which it has been interpreted by the courts. On its face, the Rule grants authority to courts to refuse to certify a class action on the ground that it is not superior only where there are "other available methods for the fair and efficient adjudication of the controversy." As has been noted earlier, however, some courts have refused to certify class actions in the name of superiority or manageability where they believe that the disadvantages resulting from the class proceedings outweigh their advantages, even where there is, in fact, no truly available alternative. This refusal to certify means that the class members, practically speaking, will obtain "no relief."
>
> There is much to be said for the proposition that courts should be allowed to refuse certification of class actions that are not in the public interest because the costs of such proceedings outweigh the benefits. Indeed, in light of the American courts' assumption of the right to make such determinations in defiance of what seems to be the clear language of Rule 23 it is questionable whether any statutory language could be drafted that could prevent the making of such determinations in situations where a court is of the view that it is imperative that a particular class action should not be allowed to proceed.
>
> If such a power is to be exercised, however, it would seem preferable that it be authorized and regulated by express statutory language, instead of developing erratically through the case law in a manner at odds with the language of the class action provision. This argument is reinforced by the fact that such a judicial power to refuse the enforcement of a valid cause of action, because of what are, in essence, pure policy considerations, is a major departure from the practice in individual suits, where courts are obliged to hear and dispose of such claims no matter how burdensome they may be for the courts or the public.
>
> We, therefore, recommend that these questions, which American courts have treated as intermingled with the superiority test under Rule 23(b)(3), should be analyzed separately through a two-step process that would be reflected in two distinct sections of the proposed Ontario Class Actions Act. The courts would be required first to make a true superiority analysis, comparing class actions with other practicable alternatives in terms of their relevant advantages and disadvantages. If there were a truly available alternative that was as good as or better than a class action, the court would be obliged to refuse certification on that ground alone, and matters would not go any further.

Where, on the other hand, there was no truly available alternative to a class action, or where class proceedings were superior to those that did exist, the court would be given a further power to refuse to certify an action if it was satisfied that the advantages of a class action to the courts, the class, and the public were outweighed by its costs. While theoretically possible, it seems unlikely that a court would refuse to certify a class action on these grounds where another practicable, but inferior, means of asserting the claims of class members existed. By definition, such a denial of certification would result in the assertion of separate actions with all their adverse effects. Therefore, denial of certification on "cost-benefit" grounds would usually take place only where no alternative means of obtaining relief exists.

Consider also the following comments of Edward H. Cooper under the heading of "Classes That Help Lawyers, Not Members?" in his article, "Class Action Advice in the Form of Questions" (2001), 11 *Duke J of Comp. and Int'l L* 215:

At least one part of popular culture in the United States believes that class actions are driven by the greed of attorneys, not the prospect of real benefit to class members. Attorney fees may exceed the tangible benefits to class members, and some "coupon" settlements may actually benefit defendants more than class members when the coupon is redeemed with a discounted purchase from the defendant. The perception, and the results that feed it, often are linked to class actions that arise from small-scale injuries to many consumers.

Attempts to address this concern have proved difficult. The proposed Civil Rule 23 amendments published for comment in 1996 included a new factor for determining whether to certify a (b)(3) class: "whether the probable relief to individual class members justifies the costs and burdens of class litigation." The draft Committee Note suggested a particular view of class actions: "The prospect of significant benefit to class members combines with the public values of enforcing legal norms to justify the costs, burdens, and coercive effects of class actions that otherwise satisfy Rule 23 requirements. If probable individual relief is slight, however, the core justification of class enforcement fails." Substitution of private enforcement for public enforcement is therefore not enough alone to justify resolution by a court. Adversary litigation requires meaningful individual injury and the prospect of meaningful individual relief. The spirit was captured in the phrase that came to characterize this draft as the "just ain't worth it" proposal. As was expected, the proposal drew heavy opposition. The "just ain't worth it" proposal has gone no further, and does not seem likely to be pressed in the near future. The proposal does, however, serve to frame a question that should be asked by every system developing a class action practice. Does our system of law really need to supplement public enforcement of public values by private enforcement? Always? No matter how trivial the injury and how uncertain the wrong? The Swedish proposal would provide for a class proceeding if it "is not otherwise considered to be inappropriate." Open-ended language like this might accomplish what the "just ain't worth it" proposal failed to achieve.

An answer to this question will turn in part on the motivations that drive private class action litigation. Some observers in the United States fear that much of this litigation is driven by a desire for attorney fees and nothing more. Not as much attention is directed to another possible concern that interest groups will pursue agendas that are against the public interest by taking advantage of vaguely worded laws that responsible public officials would not seek to enforce against the challenged conduct. Other countries may share this concern. Much will turn on the broad factors described above: what is the nature of the substantive law that may be enforced through a class action, and what are the interests of those who drive the litigation, whether they be lawyers or citizens with an agenda?

An alternative response to the fear that class litigation may not reflect any concern for class members would be to shift to an opt-in class. Intervention by class members demonstrates a genuine class interest; lack of intervention defeats class litigation. The difficulty with this approach is that it is likely to work—if at all—only on a generalized basis. It is difficult to identify in a rule the circumstances of suspect motivation that justify a choice to certify an opt-in class rather than an opt-out class. One approach would be to assume that individual class members do not care about very small monetary recoveries, relying on opt-in procedure to identify the class members who do care. This approach, however, could easily defeat many consumer class actions, without a clear justification for the assumption that class members do not care about the money or about vindicating the public interest.

Recall the finely balanced decisions in *Hollick* and *Rumley* over the preferability of class proceedings on behalf of persons who may have been exposed to harm, either by reason of living within a prescribed geographical area in which there was environmental damage, or by reason of having attended a school in which there was physical and sexual abuse. The following decisions of the Divisional Court and the Court of Appeal for Ontario in *Cloud v. Canada* reflect not only a thoughtful debate on the question of preferability, but also the strongly divergent views that have been taken in respect of the preferability requirement in some cases.

Cloud v. Canada (Attorney General)
(2003), 65 OR (3d) 492 (Div. Ct.)

VALIN J: ... In this action, the appellants claim ... for breach of fiduciary duty, negligence, assault, battery and breaches of aboriginal and treaty rights [was] described in detail in the statement of claim and was described by the motion judge as an alleged "sustained, systematic programme of physical, emotional, spiritual and cultural abuse."

The list of types of harm for which the appellants seek damages ... includes, but is not limited to, a loss of aboriginal language, culture and family roots, a loss of self-esteem, an inability to complete their education, reduced earning capacity, physical pain and suffering, and psychological disorders.

The claims are made for the period from 1922 to 1969 on behalf of all students who attended the Institute during that period. The appellants estimate there were approximately 1400 such students. In addition, two of the appellants advance claims for breach of fiduciary duty and for loss of care, guidance and companionship under the *Family Law Act*. Those two appellants seek to represent the parents, siblings, spouses and children of former students. The number of such person is estimated to be 4200. As far as the claims based on aboriginal rights are concerned, the appellants acknowledged that it might be necessary to divide the proposed composite class into subclasses.

· · ·

For the purposes of this appeal, I find it is necessary to address only the issue of whether a class proceeding would be the preferable procedure for the resolution of common issues (s. 5(1)(d)).

. . .

To a large extent the issue of preferability was canvassed by the motion judge in the context of his analysis of the common issues question. Ultimately, the court must consider whether the resolution of common issues will significantly advance the litigation. The motion judge found that there were numerous significant individual issues that would require trial beyond the resolution of any common issues. At paragraph 71 of his reasons he stated:

> Given the evidence of the many and varied challenges encountered by the students both before and after they attended the Mohawk Institute it would not be possible to determine which losses, if any, are attributable to the conduct of the defendants without conducting a separate inquiry for each student. Such an inquiry would also be required to establish the amount of damages for each claimant.

The motion judge found that individual proceedings were inevitable. He concluded that there were no common issues with respect to claims for negligence, assault and battery, cultural and spiritual loss and breach of aboriginal rights, and punitive damages. In addition, he found that there were no common issues with respect to defences based on limitation periods and the doctrine of laches.

In my view, any issues in common between the class members in this action are relatively general in nature. The motion judge correctly determined that the resolution of the common issues presented to him for consideration would do nothing to avoid or limit the length of the individual claims which will be inevitable given the diverse experiences of each student. Given the findings of the motion judge regarding the inevitability of the advancement of significant and numerous individual claims, I am not convinced that any attempt to identify or formulate common issues raised in the pleadings in terms of systemic negligence would usefully or significantly advance the litigation.

In *Hollick v. Toronto (City)*, [2001] 3 SCR 158 (SCC) at paras. 27, 28 and 30, McLachlin CJC identified the following factors to be considered when assessing the preferability of a class action:

1. whether certifying the class action serves the purposes of the Act which are (i) judicial economy, (ii) access to justice, and (iii) behaviour modification;
2. whether a class proceeding would constitute a fair, efficient and manageable method of advancing the claim, taking into account the relative importance of the common issues when compared with the claims as a whole; and
3. the availability and preferability of other avenues of redress, including individual actions.

Commenting further on the issue of preferability, McLachlin CJC stated at para. 30:

> The question of preferability, then, must take into account the importance of the common issues in relation to the claims as a whole ... There must be a consideration of the common issues in context ... [T]he preferability requirement asks that the class representative "demonstrate that, given all of the circumstances of the particular claim, [a class action] would be preferable to other methods of resolving these claims and, in particular, that it would be preferable to the use of individual proceedings" ... .

I agree with the conclusion of the motion judge that no judicial economy would be achieved by certifying this proceeding as a class action. This case is similar to the conclusion reached by the Supreme Court of Canada in *Hollick* in that, once the common issues are seen in the context of the entire claim, it becomes difficult to say that the resolution of the common issues will significantly advance the action. I repeat that, even if the common issues advanced in this case were reformulated in terms of systemic negligence, the result would not be altered; the common issues will not significantly advance the action.

When considering the question of common issues, the motion judge concluded that the nature of the claims advanced would by necessity result in a multitude of individual trials. I find no fault or error in that conclusion. This compels a conclusion similar to that reached in *Mouhteros v. DeVry Canada Inc.* (1998), 41 OR (3d) 63 where Winkler J stated at p. 73:

> In the instant case, however, what common issues there may be are completely subsumed by the plethora of individual issues, which would necessitate individual trials for virtually each class member. Each student's experience is idiosyncratic, and liability would be subject to numerous variables for each class member. Such a class action would be completely unmanageable …
>
> In my view, certification in this case will result in a multitude of individual trials, which will completely overwhelm any advantage to be derived from a trial of a few common issues …

The motion judge found that individual actions would be necessary to deal with different types of abuse, different perpetrators, different circumstances before and after attendance by the students at the Institute, different limitation periods and different damages. Those findings compel the conclusion that, if anything could be dealt with among the claimants in common, it would be at such a general level that it would not be helpful in advancing the claims in a legally material way.

The onus is on the appellants to prove that a class action will improve access to justice. There were no facts placed before the motion judge that persons who attended the Institute and who may have claims have experienced difficulty accessing justice.

In *Abdool v. Anaheim Management Ltd.* (1995), 21 OR (3d) 453 at 473 (Div. Ct.), this court stated:

> As a rule, certification should have as its root a number of individual claims which would otherwise be economically unfeasible to pursue. While not necessarily fatal to an order for certification, the absence of this important underpinning will certainly weigh in the balance against certification.

I adopt that statement. This case will require numerous individual determinations. That fact compels a conclusion that the procedure of certification will not result in any judicial economy.

There were no facts before the motion judge to suggest that individual claims were economically unfeasible to pursue.

The Institute was closed in 1969. Currently, there are no residential schools for First Nations students in operation anywhere in Canada. I agree with counsel for Canada that, in those circumstances, there is no need at this stage for behaviour modification or deterrence.

As noted earlier, the decision of the Supreme Court of Canada in *Hollick* requires the court hearing an application for certification to consider whether a class proceeding would constitute a fair, efficient and manageable method of advancing the claim, taking into account the relative importance of the common issues when compared with the claims as a whole. The motion judge adopted the reasons of Carthy JA in *Hollick v. Toronto (City)* (1999), 46 OR (3d) 257 at 266-267 (CA) to the effect that there was no economy in the proposed proceeding and that the trial would be unmanageable. I agree with that finding.

To be certified, a class action must be a fair method of proceeding, not only for the plaintiffs, but also for the defendants. In *Chadha v. Bayer* (2001), 200 DLR (4th) 309 at 333 (Ont. Div. Ct.), Somers J held that the rights of a defendant opposing certification are an essential factor to be considered in assessing whether a class proceeding would be preferable.

The facts of this case suggest that the possibility of a finding of liability against the Company is quite remote. In addition, the exposure of the Diocese to liability may well be restricted to specified periods of time which are significantly less than the period of time during which the Institute was operated as a residential school. In fairness, those defendants should only have to respond to claims that arose during the restricted periods of time during which they could possibly be found liable. Certification would compel them to respond to the claims of the entire class in circumstances where they might otherwise be found to have no exposure on liability issues during specified periods of time. In my opinion, such a result would defy any notion of fairness to those defendants.

The last factor to be considered under s. 5(1)(d) of the Act is the availability and preferability of other avenues of redress, including individual actions. Several former students of the Institute have already commenced individual actions claiming damages for sexual assault. Given the findings of the motion judge outlined in paragraph 71 of his reasons, which findings I accept, individual actions will be required for each student. In the circumstances, individual actions by former students are a feasible, reasonable and preferable alternative to a class action.

· · ·

With respect to the issue of whether a class proceeding would be the preferable procedure, there is no basis for concluding that the motion judge committed any error in principle in arriving at his decision. Regardless of the analytical route he followed, he correctly determined that a class action is not the preferable procedure because the underlying policy objectives of access to justice, judicial economy and behaviour modification would not be served by certifying the action as a class proceeding. ...

Cloud v. Canada (Attorney General)
(2004), 247 DLR (4th) 667 (Ont. CA)

GOUDGE JA ... In a case like this, set in the context of a residential school, the primary challenge is to determine if there are common issues and then, in light of the almost inevitable individual issues, to assess the relative importance of those common issues in relation to the claim as a whole. That question is centre stage in this appeal.

Cullity J decided in favour of certification. I agree with his conclusion and, in large measure, with his analysis. Thus, for the reasons that follow, I would allow the appeal and certify the action.

. . .

As explained by the Supreme Court of Canada in *Hollick*, … the preferability requirement has two concepts at its core. The first is whether or not the class action would be a fair, efficient and manageable method of advancing the claim. The second is whether the class action would be preferable to other reasonably available means of resolving the claims of class members. The analysis must keep in mind the three principal advantages of class actions, namely judicial economy, access to justice, and behaviour modification and must consider the degree to which each would be achieved by certification.

Hollick also decided that the determination of whether a proposed class action is a fair, efficient and manageable method of advancing the claim requires an examination of the common issues in their context. The inquiry must take into account the importance of the common issues in relation to the claim as a whole.

At para. 30 of that decision the Court also makes clear that the preferability requirement in s. 5(1)(d) of the CPA can be met even where there are substantial individual issues and that its drafters rejected the requirement that the common issues predominate over the individual issues in order for the class action to be the preferable procedure. This contrasts with the British Columbia legislation in which the preferability inquiry includes whether the common issues predominate over the individual cases.

In Ontario it is nonetheless essential to assess the importance of the common issues in relation to the claim as a whole. It will not be enough if the common issues are negligible in relation to the individual issues. The preferability finding in *Hollick* itself was just this and the requirement was therefore found not to be met. That decision tells us that the critical question is whether, viewing the common issues in the context of the entire claim, their resolution will significantly advance the action.

Neither the motion judge nor the majority of the Divisional Court properly addressed this vital aspect of the preferability inquiry and thus their conclusion cannot stand. As Cullity J said, the determination of whether, in the context of the entire claim, the resolution of the common issues will significantly advance the action can only be done in light of the particular common issues identified. Here the motion judge found none and therefore could not make this assessment. The majority of the Divisional Court did not address the common issues requirement but simply stated its conclusion that any attempt to formulate common issues in terms of systemic negligence would not significantly advance the litigation given the numerous individual claims. With respect, without an articulation of what the common issues are, any assessment of their relative importance in the context of the entire claim cannot be properly made. It would risk a conclusion based not on relative importance but simply on the existence of a large number of individual issues. It would also preclude any appellate review.

On the other hand, as I have outlined, Cullity J found that in the context of the entire claim the resolution of the common issues he found would significantly advance the action and that otherwise the preferability requirement was met. I agree with that conclusion.

As they did with the common issues, the respondents contest this finding in several different ways. Here too their primary attack is that the vast majority of issues require individual determination. They say that these issues involve individual acts of abuse, different perpetrators, unique individual circumstances both before and after attendance at the school widely varying impacts and damage claims, and an array of different limitations, triggers and discoverability issues. They argue that the common issues are negligible in comparison and that their resolution will not significantly advance the action.

I do not agree. An important part of the claims of all class members turns on the way the respondents ran the School over the time frame of this action. The factual assertion is both that the respondents had in place policies and practices, such as excessive physical discipline, and that they failed to have in place preventative policies and practices, such as reasonable hiring and supervision, which together resulted in the intimidation, brutality and abuse endured by the students at the School. It is said that the respondents sought to destroy the native language, culture and spirituality of all class members. The legal assertion is that by running the School in this way the respondents were in breach of the various legal obligations they owed to all class members. Together these assertions comprise the common issues that must be assessed in relation to the claim as a whole.

I agree with Cullity J that whether framed in negligence, fiduciary obligation or aboriginal rights the nature and extent of the legal duties owed by the respondents to the class members and whether those duties were breached will be of primary importance in the action as framed. If class members are to recover, they must first succeed on this issue. It is only at that point that individual issues of the kind raised by the respondents would arise. Save for those relating to limitations they are all aspects of harm and causation, both of which the appellants acknowledge they will have to establish individual by individual. The limitations questions are all individual defences, which the appellants also acknowledge will require individual adjudication.

The resolution of these common issues therefore takes the action framed in negligence, fiduciary duty and aboriginal rights up to the point where only harm, causation and individual defences such as limitations remain for determination. This moves the action a long way.

The common issues are fundamental to the action. They cannot be described as negligible in relation to the consequential individual issues nor to the claim as a whole. To resolve the debate about the existence of the legal duties on which the claim is founded and whether these duties were breached is to significantly advance the action.

This assessment is not quantitative so much as qualitative. It is not driven by the mere number of individual adjudications that may remain after the common trial. The finding in *Rumley* demonstrates this. The class there was defined as students at the residential school between 1950 and 1992 who reside in British Columbia and claimed to have suffered injury, loss, or damages as a result of misconduct of a sexual nature occurring at the school. The common issues were defined very similarly to those in this case. The Supreme Court recognized that following their resolution, adjudication of injury and causation would be required individual by individual. Although the number of individual adjudications appears to have been uncertain, the time frame of the action alone suggests that it might be relatively high. Yet the Court was able to conclude that the common issues predominated over those affecting only individual class members, which is a consideration required by the British Columbia legislation. This as an even higher standard than that set for preferability under the CPA, namely that viewed in the context of the entire claim, the resolution of the common issues must significantly advance the action. However, in both cases the assessment is a qualitative one, not a comparison of the number of common issues to the number of individual issues.

In this case that qualitative assessment derives from the reality that resolving the common issues will take the action a long way. That assessment is also informed in an important way by the considerations of judicial economy and access to justice. Because residential schools for native children are no longer part of the Canadian landscape, the third objective of class proceedings, namely behaviour modification, is of no moment here.

However, I think that a single trial of the common issues will achieve substantial judicial economy. Without a common trial, these issues would have to be dealt with in each individual action at an obvious cost in judicial time possibly resulting in inconsistent outcomes. As Cullity J said, a single trial would make it unnecessary to adduce more than once evidence of the history of the establishment and operation of the School and the involvement of each of the respondents.

Access to justice would also be greatly enhanced by a single trial of the common issues. I do not agree with the majority of the Divisional Court that there is nothing in the record to sustain this conclusion. The affidavit material makes clear that the appellants seek to represent many who are aging, very poor, and in some cases still very emotionally troubled by their experiences at the school. Cullity J put it this way at para. 46 of his reasons:

> While the goal of behavioural modification does not seem to be a value that would be achieved to any extent by certification, I am satisfied that the vulnerability of members of the class—as evidenced by the uncontradicted statements in the affidavits sworn by the representative plaintiffs—is such that the objective of providing access to justice would be served to an appreciable extent. Each of the representative plaintiffs referred to the poverty of many of the former students, their inability to afford the cost of individual actions and the effect such proceedings would have on the continuing emotional problems from which they suffer as a result of their experiences at the Mohawk Institute. These statements were not challenged on cross-examination and, unlike my colleagues, I see no reason to reject their truth or their significance.

In short, I think that the access to justice consideration strongly favours the conclusion that a class action is the preferable procedure. The language used by the Chief Justice in *Rumley* at para. 39 is equally apt to this case:

> Litigation is always a difficult process but I am convinced that it will be extraordinarily so for the class members here. Allowing the suit to proceed as a class action may go some way toward mitigating the difficulties that will be faced by the class members.

The respondents also attack Cullity J's preferability finding by saying that a class action would be unfair to them and would create an unmanageable proceeding. I do not agree. The common issues require resolution one way or the other. It is no less fair to the respondents to face them in a single trial than in many individual trials. Nor, at this stage, is there any reason to think that a single trial would be unmanageable. The common issues centre on the way the respondents ran the School and can probably be dealt with even more efficiently in one trial than in fourteen hundred.

That conclusion is not altered even if one takes into consideration the individual adjudications that would follow. The fact of a number of individual adjudications of harm and causation did not render the action in *Rumley* unmanageable and does not do so here. Moreover, the CPA provides for great flexibility in the process. For example, s. 10 allows for decertification if, as the action unfolds, it appears that the requirements of s. 5(1) cease to be met. In addition, s. 25 contemplates a variety of ways in which individual issues may be determined following the common issues trial other than by the presiding trial judge. Thus at this stage in the proceedings, when one views the common issues trial in the context of the action as whole, there is no reason to doubt the conclusion that the class action is a manageable method of advancing the claim.

Lastly, the respondents argue that Cullity J was wrong because the class action is not preferable to other means of resolving class members' claims. They support this position with fresh evidence filed in this court describing the alternative dispute resolution system that has been put in place by Canada to deal with claims of those who attended native residential schools.

Even if we were to admit this fresh evidence I do not agree that this ADR system displaces the conclusion that the class action is the preferable procedure. It is a system unilaterally created by one of the respondents in this action and could be unilaterally dismantled without the consent of the appellants. It deals only with physical and sexual abuse. It caps the amount of possible recovery and, most importantly in these circumstances, compared to the class action it shares the access to justice deficiencies of individual actions. It does not compare favourably with a common trial.

Thus I conclude that each of the respondents' attacks must fail and that Cullity J was correct to find that the appellants have met the preferability requirement.

NOTES

1. Goudge JA observed that the BC preferability test, which specifically requires consideration of predominance as a factor, is a higher standard than the Ontario preferability test (that the resolution of the common issues must significantly advance the action in the context of the claim). Do you agree? Has this ostensibly more stringent standard produced a more conservative approach to certification in British Columbia than in Ontario?

2. Goudge JA described the standard for certification as one of whether the resolution of the common issues viewed in the context of the entire claim would significantly advance the action. Is this consistent with the standard enunciated by Winkler J in *Caputo* (i.e., that the question of liability be determined as a common issue)?

3. *Defendant's ADR compensation scheme as preferable procedure.* In some cases, a class action defendant will, prior to certification, propose a dispute resolution procedure to compensate the proposed class members and argue at the certification hearing that this constitutes a "preferable procedure" within the meaning of the Act and should be the basis for denying certification. Such a practice raises a number of questions and concerns. Should the court consider out-of-court processes as potentially preferable alternative procedures to a class action? Or does the CPA contemplate only other options for litigation? Does the court have jurisdiction to impose an extra-judicial, defendant-designed ADR scheme on the class? What if the ADR scheme in question places limits on the types and/or quantum of

recovery that might otherwise be available by statute or at common law? If the court could require claimants to resort to such a scheme, what effect might this have on Ontario's or Canada's class action regime? How could the fairness of the scheme be ensured? Should a distinction be drawn between ADR schemes established before the commencement of litigation and those set up in response to litigation? See Garry Watson and Derek McKay, "Why the Defendant's Own Alternative Dispute Resolution Process Cannot Be a Preferable Procedure" (July 2005), 2 *Can. Class Action Rev.* 1.

4. There is a concern with some ADR schemes that they have been developed merely to avoid having to pay class counsel's fees. The defendant argues that its self-designed ADR scheme should preclude class action litigation notwithstanding the fact that the ADR scheme was created in direct response to the litigation. However, there may be other incentives to develop such "in-house" solutions. For example, from a public relations, customer relations, or investor relations perspective, it is much better to be perceived as having identified and voluntarily corrected a problem than to have been forced into accepting responsibility for one's wrongdoing; and in-house solutions are "private" provided that the denial of certification brings the litigation to an end and the defendant avoids having to disclose potentially damaging evidence at discovery (or disclosure of documents in furtherance of settlement negotiations) that could exacerbate the defendant's legal problems. In one case, where the defendant's ADR scheme was not accepted, the proposal became the basis for a negotiated settlement, including the payment of substantial fees to class counsel by the defendants: see *Corless v. KPMG LLP*, [2008] OJ No. 3092 (SCJ).

E. Representative Plaintiff

The final requirement for certifying a class action is that there must be a representative plaintiff or defendant who would fairly and adequately represent the interests of the class; and who has produced a plan for the proceeding that sets out a workable method of advancing the proceeding on behalf of the class and of notifying class members of the proceeding; and who does not have, on the common issues for the class, an interest in conflict with the interests of other class members.

In *Western Canadian Shopping Centres*, Chief Justice McLachlin noted that

> [t]he class representative must adequately represent the class. In assessing whether the proposed representative is adequate, the court may look to the motivation of the representative, the competence of the representative's counsel, and the capacity of the representative to bear any costs that may be incurred by the representative in particular (as opposed to by counsel or by the class members generally). The proposed representative need not be "typical" of the class, nor the "best" possible representative. The court should be satisfied, however, that the proposed representative will vigorously and capably prosecute the interests of the class.

Like some of the other requirements, the interpretation of this requirement reflects some of the more distinctive features of class proceedings. For example, while the tradition of party prosecution and our law on standing rely on the assumption that it is the aggrieved party who is in the best position to direct the litigation, this is patently a legal fiction in the case of class proceedings where the representative plaintiff serves more to provide a sound factual basis for the claim and class counsel seem more directly involved in the management

of the litigation. Accordingly, while the Act requires that the representative plaintiff or defendant be in a position to fairly and adequately represent the interests of the class and that
the representative produce a plan for the proceeding that sets out a workable method of advancing the proceeding on behalf of the class and of notifying class members of the proceeding, these considerations are, in fact, more probative of class counsel's ability to do so.

However, the third requirement for fair and adequate representation—that the representative have no interest in conflict with the other class members—is clearly referable to the
individual put forward as a representative. This requirement is consistent with the ability of
the representative to provide a strong factual basis for the claim, independent of any particular skill in directing the litigation, because it is important for the proper resolution of the
matter for all those involved to have a clear example of the situation of the class members,
the nature of the harm they are alleged to have suffered, and the nature of the relief that
might be appropriate. Any interest of the representative that is in conflict with that of the
members of the class will impair the ability of counsel and the court to arrive at an appropriate resolution of the claim.

The third requirement is considered in the following case. Note, too, a further unusual
feature of the awkward fit of class actions with the traditions of party prosecution. Despite
the fact that the requirement of fair and adequate representation is designed to protect the
interests of class members in the event of certification, because the motion for certification
is determined in a party prosecution format, it falls to the defendant seeking to resist certification to argue that the requirement has not been met and in this way, ironically, to advocate on behalf of the interests of putative class members. Interestingly, the Australian legislation provides that only a class member could bring such a motion.

1176560 Ontario Ltd. v. The Great Atlantic & Pacific Company of Canada Ltd.
(2002), 62 OR (3d) 535 (SCJ)

WINKLER J: ... The main arguments advanced by A&P in opposition to certification related to the preferable procedure and representative plaintiff elements of the certification
criteria. ...

In this case, A&P's contention that other procedures are preferable is inextricably
linked with its submissions as to the suitability of the plaintiffs as representatives of the
proposed class. In this respect, A&P highlights the admitted "independence" of the three
proposed representative plaintiffs. It is common ground that the plaintiffs are prosper-
ous, unencumbered by debt to A&P and not intimidated by A&P's counterclaim. Simply
put, A&P contends that these characteristics distinguish the plaintiffs from the putative
class members and, as such, not only renders them unsuitable as representatives, but
mandates a decision from the court that individual actions are a preferable method of
resolving the claims of the class.

Simply stating the foregoing proposition is sufficient to disclose its flaws. Nonetheless,
A&P adduced evidence in an attempt to overcome its inherent defects and salvage the
argument. That evidence took the form of two affidavits from members of the proposed
class who are current franchisees. The intended purpose of the evidence was to support

the proposition that the rank and file members of the proposed class were satisfied with the status quo and did not want a class proceeding brought on their behalf that would upset the existing relationship between them and A&P.

The first affiant, Steve Bartley, expressed concern that in taking the action forward as a class proceeding, the representative plaintiffs could "screw up the system that we have now. And that's what I see them doing." He did not see opting out as a solution. The second affiant, Steve Duggan, stated that if he has received less than he is entitled to by way of rebates as a matter of strict legal meaning of the contract, he has been the beneficiary beyond what the agreement requires in other ways. He concludes on this point that "I may stand to lose much more than I gain."

This evidence raises at least two points for consideration. The first is obvious from the evidence itself and is particularly apparent in the latter statement by Mr. Duggan that he "may stand to lose" more than he gains. This equivocal statement must be weighed in the context of the allegations by the plaintiffs that A&P has wrongfully retained Rebates owed to the class members. Mr. Duggan's admitted uncertainty as to whether A&P has paid him all the Rebates he was entitled to receive makes it clear that any opinion expressed by the franchisees as to the adequacy of alternative arrangements would, in current circumstances, be uninformed. ...

The second consideration regarding evidence from class members is more general in nature. To adduce evidence from individual class members as to the desirability of a class proceeding is to assume, as an underlying proposition, that certification motions are somehow determined through a referendum of the class members. Such is not the case. The legislature has spoken with respect to class proceedings in this province. The provisions dealing with opt outs and de-certification show that it was clearly alive to the prospect that not all members of a proposed class would wish to participate in a class proceeding or, alternatively, that a sufficient number of defections from the class would render a class proceeding unnecessary. Conversely, there are no provisions that expressly or implicitly mandate, or even suggest, that the suitability of a class proceeding is to be determined by a polling of the class prior to the certification motion.

In fact, the expressed vulnerability of Bartley and Duggan to A&P on an individual basis is evidence in favour of granting certification of the action as a class proceeding rather than supporting the position that it would be preferable to require each class member to bring an individual action to vindicate his or her rights. Vulnerable franchisees may not be in a position to bring individual actions. On the other hand, the opt out provision provides a suitable recourse for those franchisees such as the affiants who wish to retain the existing laissez faire approach in reliance on the goodwill and beneficence of A&P. By the incorporation of the opt out provision in the CPA, the legislature has expressed its intention that simple dissent by some members of the class should not be sufficient to veto any efforts by others to enforce their legal rights through a class proceeding.

In view of this, I find that evidence from class members regarding their opposition to a class proceeding is of no assistance in determining whether a class proceeding should be certified. In addition, the attempts to gather this type of evidence generally has the effect of shifting the locus of the arena of the dispute from the court to the class members. This point is addressed in more detail below in these reasons relating to the ancillary relief claimed by [the] plaintiffs.

The alternative arguments advanced by A&P in opposition to certification are similarly unpersuasive. For the most part, as far as the preferability requirement is concerned, these arguments asserted that there were numerous individual issues arising from the pleadings, including the existing counterclaims against the plaintiffs and the proposed counterclaims against the class members.

Although there are 70 Franchise Agreements at issue, each is [a] standard form contract, identical in all material respects to each other agreement. The claim relates to the obligations flowing from a particular paragraph of that standard form agreement. By virtue of that paragraph, A&P has an obligation to treat all franchisees in the same manner. Although A&P has asserted in this proceeding that each franchisee now has a different individual deal by virtue of the voluntary payments that A&P makes to each, there is no evidence before the court to support the assertion. Moreover, materially different treatment of one franchisee would appear to be a breach of A&P's agreement with every other franchisee and may in itself give rise to another common issue.

In any event, A&P has asserted that the franchisees have no claim in that they have received everything that they are entitled to receive under the Franchise Agreements. Accordingly, if A&P is successful in its defence of the common issues, it will terminate the litigation. On the other hand, if the plaintiffs are successful, the only remaining individual issues would relate strictly to a non-contentious accounting of the amount of withheld Rebates to which each class member is entitled. When the entire factual matrix is considered, the significance of the common issues overwhelms the individual issues.

Moreover, I am not persuaded that the prospect of A&P asserting a counterclaim against the plaintiffs, or if the action is certified, against each individual member of the class, is an impediment to certification. ... As a general principle, if such a device could be employed by defendants as a means of defeating certification, the efficacy of the CPA would be effectively negated.

I note as well that, in consideration of the evidence, the prospect of counterclaims appears to be even less of a concern in this particular case. Although A&P asserts that it will claim recovery of all of its alternative payments to the franchisees since the inception of the net billing practice in 1996, to be successful it will still have to establish that it paid more under this arrangement than it was required to do under the method expressly set out in the Franchise Agreement. Given A&P's evidence that it does not retain documentation relating to the Rebates for more than six months, it appears that A&P would have difficulty establishing the basis for its counterclaim for any longer period and certainly not back to 1996. While I understand that as the litigation goes forth, A&P may find that its initial view of the extent of its retained documentation was mistaken, the court must deal with the evidence at the time the certification motion is brought.

The presence of these counterclaims and possible retaliatory actions by A&P bear directly on its assertions that the plaintiffs are unsuitable representatives for the proposed class. I cannot accede to the submission that a financially independent plaintiff is disqualified as potential representative by the very fact of his independence. Indeed, such a plaintiff would appear to represent the paradigm when one considers the views of the Supreme Court of Canada as expressed in *Western Canadian Shopping Centres Inc. v. Bennett Jones Verchere*, [2001] 2 SCR 534, 201 DLR (4th) 385 at para. 41:

The proposed representative need not be "typical" of the class, nor the "best" possible representative. The court should be satisfied, however, that the proposed representative will vigorously and capably prosecute the interests of the class.

The three proposed representative plaintiffs before this court are equipped to "vigorously and capably prosecute" the lawsuit.

Further, these are exactly the type of plaintiffs that may be required to prosecute a class action lawsuit in the context of a franchise relationship, with the inherent vulnerability in the dependent ongoing nature of the relationship between franchisor and franchisee. This aspect of the commercial realities of franchise arrangements has been commented upon in the context of class proceedings. In recognizing that access to justice is a major impediment for franchisees, the Ontario Law Reform Commission, *Report on Class Actions*, Vol. 1 (Toronto: Ministry of the Attorney General, 1982) states at p. 128:

> Even small businesses may be reluctant to sue more powerful companies where, for example, in a franchisor–franchisee situation, they must deal continuously with such companies on a basis of dependence.

Similarly, Samuel Grange QC in the report to the Ontario Government of the committee entitled *Report of the Minister's Committee on Franchising* (Toronto: Department of Financial and Commercial Affairs, 1971) stated at p. 40:

> … the franchisee is constantly plagued with the threat of termination of the franchise. Almost all franchise contracts give to the franchisor either an unfettered right to terminate or a right to terminate upon breach of the agreement, and it is all too easy for the franchisee to be in such breach. … the franchisee has invariably invested time and money, and he knows that he will lose it all if the franchise comes to an end. Naturally, he is prepared to be servile, and if not, he is generally not long for the franchise family.

The evidence of the president of one of the representative plaintiffs, Gary Petterson, is reflective of the above concerns. …

I find no merit in the contention that the independence of the plaintiffs disqualifies them as representatives. The fact that their circumstances may be different from some or all of the balance of the class does not represent a conflict "on the common issues" as that term is used in s. 5(1)(e) of the CPA. Nor do their different circumstances mean that they cannot fairly and adequately represent the class. In fact, the evidence is to the contrary.

A&P also contended that there is a conflict because certification of the action would upset the existing arrangements with the franchisees and cause A&P to revisit each of these arrangements. In my view, this is effectively an argument that there should be no litigation at all rather than an attack on either the adequacy of the plaintiffs as representatives or the preferability of a class proceeding as opposed to individual actions. Through this argument, A&P implies that if the plaintiffs are successful, that success entails a risk for the other franchisees. However, as counsel for A&P candidly admitted, a successful individual action would have the same effect with respect to the existing arrangements. The purpose of class proceedings legislation is to make the justice system accessible. To this end, the court must consider alternative procedures. However, as noted in *Hollick* at para. 16, the certification analysis is concerned with the "form of the action." Arguments that no litigation is preferable to a class proceeding cannot be given effect. If there is any basis to this argument, it is subsumed in the cause of action element of the test for certification.

A&P made one further submission in its attack on the adequacy of the plaintiffs. It contended that the representative plaintiffs ought to be disqualified from acting because they cannot be counted on to advise class members fairly and accurately as to what it will mean for them to remain in the class if the action is certified. Specifically, A&P submitted that it is concerned that the counterclaim will not be drawn to the attention of class members so they can, based on the information set out there, decide whether or not to opt out. On any fair analysis, this is more of a complaint against the provisions of the statute generally than it is against the proposed representative plaintiffs. It could apply with equal force to any representative plaintiff in any class action.

More importantly, A&P's submission in this regard ignores both s. 17 of the CPA and the role of the court in the class proceeding process. Section 17 deals with the requirements of a notice to class members. A Notice of Certification, which must be given to all class members, shall, unless the court orders otherwise, inter alia, *"describe any counterclaim being asserted against the class including the relief sought in the counterclaim"* (emphasis added). Further, under s. 20 of the CPA, the court must approve every notice issued under s. 17. This requirement, together with the notice section itself, provides a complete answer to A&P's concern as to the adequacy of any information that might be provided to class members.

In concluding its submission on the representative plaintiff element, A&P submitted that the litigation plan proposed by the plaintiffs is inadequate, and that even if it is accepted, the action ought to be divided into three parts: the interpretation phase; the accounting phase; and, the defence and counterclaim phase. I find the plaintiffs' plan to be acceptable. Although the timelines are tight, they are not unrealistic or unachievable in a case managed action. The unusual approach proposed by A&P of trifurcating the proceeding lacks any justification. In my experience, dividing a trial into parts rarely produces efficiencies. In this case not only would this unnatural division not produce any efficiencies, it would do the opposite. It would protract the proceedings, be more costly, require repetition and cause inconvenience to the court and to the judge presiding over the common issues trial.

For all of the above reasons, a class proceeding is the preferable procedure for resolving the claims of the franchisees and the plaintiffs are suitable representatives for the class.

NOTES

1. *Connection with other certification requirements.* Recall Justice Winkler's observation of the close connection in this case between the requirements of adequate representation and preferability. In *Taub v. The Manufacturers Life Insurance Co.*, which was excerpted earlier under the discussion of the identifiable class requirement, Justice Sharpe noted the connection between that requirement and the adequacy of the representative. The overlap between the two requirements in *Taub* reflects the requirement that the representative's claim be typical of the class. While "typicality" is not a formal requirement of certification under the legislation in Canada, it is easy to see how the fact that a representative's claim is

atypical could have implications for whether there is an identifiable class and for whether the representative can fairly and adequately represent the interests of the class.

2. In the following decision, the court considers the purpose of the adequacy of representation in terms of the qualifications of the representative plaintiff and of class counsel.

Reid v. Ford Motor Co.
[2003] BCSC 1632

GEROW J: The plaintiff is applying to have her action certified as a class proceeding pursuant to the *Class Proceedings Act*, RSBC 1996, c. 50.

This is a products liability case involving the ignition systems in 1983-1995 model years Ford, Lincoln and Mercury motor vehicles equipped with distributor mounted thick film ignition modules (TFI modules) (collectively, the proposed class vehicles). The plaintiff alleges that the TFI modules are defective and the defect is dangerous because it causes the vehicles to stall without warning. She submits that because the cost to repair and/or replace the TFI modules is modest compared to the costs of litigation of this nature, the only practical means for the class members to prove their allegations against the defendants and to recover the expense of making their vehicles safe is to band together in this class proceeding. ...

Section 4(1)(e) of the *Class Proceedings Act* mandates that the representative plaintiff must be able to fairly and adequately represent the class, has developed a plan for proceeding and does not have a conflict with the interests of the class on common issues. The representative plaintiff must be prepared to vigorously represent the interests of the class. ...

The inquiry with respect to the issue of whether the representative plaintiff adequately and appropriately representing class members and potential conflicts of interest is focused on the proposed common issues. If differences between the representative plaintiff and the proposed class do not impact on the common issues then they do not affect the representative plaintiff's ability to adequately and fairly represent the class, nor do they create a conflict of interest. ...

There is no indication that Ms. Reid has any interest in conflict with the class members on the proposed common issues. If such a conflict were to arise, sub-classes are available to deal with differences. ...

The purpose of the plan for proceeding at the certification stage is to aid the court by providing a framework within which the case may proceed and to demonstrate that the representative plaintiff and class counsel have a clear grasp of the complexities involved in the case which are apparent at the time of certification and a plan to address them. The court does not scrutinize the plan at the certification hearing to ensure that it will be capable of carrying the case through to trial and resolution of the common issues without amendment. It is anticipated that plans will require amendments as the case proceeds and the nature of the individual issues are demonstrated by the class members. ...

In my view, the proposed litigation plan sufficiently addresses the requisite issues and demonstrates that the plaintiff and class counsel have thought through the process of the proceeding.

I conclude that the plaintiff's theory of the case does permit her to represent all class members since a common defect is alleged. The defendants' submission that some class members may wish to argue certain parts of the case differently because of differences across the vehicles, or that they may wish to focus on certain parts of the case that the representative plaintiff does not, assumes that individual actions are a viable alternative which class members can and will pursue. I agree with the plaintiff that the economic realities of this case are such the class members only prospect of recovery is to engage in a simplified claim with a common theory of the TFI defect. ...

For those class members who wish to control their own actions or develop special theories inconsistent with the theory being advanced by the plaintiff in this action remain free to do so after opting-out of the class proceedings.

NOTES

Adequacy of representation was once rarely invoked to defeat certification, but recently there have been two such cases: one turning on the adequacy of the representative plaintiff and the other dealing with the adequacy of class counsel.

In *Poulin v. Ford Motor Co. of Canada Ltd.*, [2006] OJ No. 4625 (SCJ), a product liability case involving allegedly defective door latch mechanisms, MacKenzie J refused certification on the grounds that the proposed class action failed to satisfy the requirements of preferable procedure, adequacy of representation, and a workable litigation plan. He held that representative plaintiffs cannot be mere nominal figureheads of the litigation, but must instead play an active and informed role in the prosecution of the action. Further, the role played by US counsel in the prosecution of a Canadian class action may be subject to court scrutiny. The defendants submit that the plaintiff was incapable of fairly or adequately representing the interests of the proposed class, contending that "he is an unwitting pawn in this action, which was contrived and commenced by plaintiff's counsel and his US colleagues." In support of such submission, the defendants point to the plaintiff's lack of involvement:

(1) He was unaware of the alleged safety defects until they were brought to his attention by a law firm in Sudbury, Ontario.
(2) Notwithstanding his knowledge of the alleged safety defects, he has not repaired the vehicle and continues to drive it.
(3) He was unaware of the role of the US law firm and the terms upon which that firm is providing "litigation support" to his Canadian counsel.
(4) He had not reviewed the amended Statement of Claim before his cross-examination and had not reviewed the affidavit of Mr. Jekel until the day before his cross-examination.
(5) He did not know what a litigation plan was and accordingly, had no review or input into the terms of such plan.
(6) He was unable to identify all the vehicles within the Affected Vehicles.

As a result of the representative plaintiff's general lack of understanding or awareness of the primary evidence, his unawareness of what constitutes a litigation plan or of what the financial arrangements are between his Canadian and his US counsel, the court had serious reservations as to whether the plaintiff had capacity to properly instruct counsel on behalf of the members of the putative class.

In *Defazio v. Ontario (Ministry of Labour)*, [2007] OJ No. 902 (SCJ), Hoy J refused certification partly on the grounds that class counsel lacked the minimum experience required to satisfy the requirement of adequate representation. The proposed class action sought damages for "stress and anxiety" on behalf of persons allegedly exposed to asbestos during construction of a Toronto subway. Hoy J observed that proposed class counsel, which included a recent call to the bar, had never sought certification of a class action before and had no experience with the relevant area of tort litigation. Citing the Supreme Court's decision in *Western Canadian Shopping Centres Inc. v. Dutton* (2001), 201 DLR (4th) 385 (SCC), Hoy J noted that "competence of the representative's counsel" is a factor relevant to a court's s. 5(1)(e) determination, but cautioned that this not be taken to suggest "that counsel without experience in a particular area of the law can never represent plaintiffs in a proposed class proceeding involving that area of the law."

III. MULTIJURISDICTION CLASS ACTIONS

One area of increasing importance in class actions in Canada arises from the fact that plaintiff classes rarely correspond in size and scope with the provinces in which their members reside. Although it seems generally desirable to decide the claims of all class members in a single action, questions arise as to the authority of a court in one province to adjudicate the claims of class members whose individual claims would otherwise be likely to be decided in another province. Corresponding questions arise as to whether a court in a province where the individual claims of class members would otherwise be decided should recognize the judgment of a court in another province in a class action that purports to preclude those claims from being relitigated.

Until recently, these questions were largely theoretical in that courts had not refused to exercise jurisdiction over the claims of class members who resided in other provinces, and courts had not refused to recognize the preclusive effect of a judgment of courts in other provinces over class members whose claims they might otherwise have been asked to determine. Nevertheless, in anticipation of such a situation, the Uniform Law Conference of Canada created a task force to consider the questions arising from the possibility of "national class actions" and to make recommendations on how they might be coordinated to avoid situations that could produce conflicting results.

Janet Walker, "Coordinating Multijurisdiction Class Actions Through Existing Certification Processes"
(2005), 41 CBLJ 112 (footnotes omitted)

I—Introduction. Canada now has legislative regimes for class actions in several provinces and common law regimes in the remaining jurisdictions. It is increasingly possible for persons to be presumptively included in more than one class action. These persons can become subject to conflicting determinations of their rights. Defendants and class counsel may also be confronted with situations in which they are uncertain of the actual size and composition of plaintiff classes in actions in which they are involved. Under the current law it is difficult to anticipate with certainty the impact of competing class actions on the resolutions of the disputes that are reached and to know which plaintiffs will be bound by which decisions. It is important, therefore, to develop a means to regulate the scope of the multijurisdiction class actions that may be commenced in the same or related matters in different Canadian jurisdictions. This comment outlines the means by which this can be achieved through existing certification processes.

Any proposal to resolve multiplicity in multijurisdiction class actions must address two kinds of questions. First, it must articulate clear standards and criteria for determining the appropriate scope of multijurisdiction classes in view of the potential for multiplicity. This is the substantive question. It will be discussed in the next section. There could be debate about these standards, and there will certainly be further development and refinement of our understanding of the criteria to be applied in individual cases. However, to the extent that the standards and criteria can be articulated, the discussion of how best to coordinate multijurisdiction class actions can then focus on the separate procedural question.

Second, to address the procedural question, the proposal must identify the institutional mechanisms that exist or need to be developed to make certification rulings that will prevent multiplicity. Several approaches might be considered. This comment will not consider mechanisms involving the Federal Court—either as a court that would exercise jurisdiction to decide multijurisdiction class actions, or as a court that would serve as an equivalent to the US Multidistrict Litigation Panel in regulating the definition of the plaintiff classes in actions that would then be assigned to the provincial superior courts. ... Although this comment seeks to develop a workable proposal that is minimally disruptive of existing institutional structures and court processes, its implementation may benefit from certain administrative innovations and informal initiatives for cooperation between courts. Some of these initiatives are immediately apparent, such as those involving informal cooperation between counsel in different provinces permitting a matter to go forward as a lead case in one province with the outcome being tendered for court approval in other provinces. Others innovations would become more apparent as experience is gained with the process of regulating multijurisdiction class actions.

II—The Substantive Question: Standards for Avoiding Multiplicity in Multijurisdiction Class Proceedings. The standards for resolving multiplicity in multijurisdiction class proceedings have not yet been articulated with precision. However, the basis for them may be discerned in the law of jurisdiction in Canada more generally. The Supreme Court of Canada has determined that the law of jurisdiction is subject to the constitutional requirements of the principles of order and fairness. The Supreme Court has also said that these principles are vaguely defined, serving primarily to inspire the interpretation of various private international law rules. ...

                                              . . .

Although those resisting the certification of multijurisdictional classes have focused on the question of whether a provincial superior court can exercise such jurisdiction, this is not the real question. The real question is whether other Canadian courts are obliged to grant preclusive effect to the judgment in respect of the claims described in the notice of certification. To the extent that the criteria used to define multijurisdiction classes for certification purposes are consistent with the constitutional principles of order and fairness, Canadian courts are obliged to treat the claims of members of classes defined in this way as finally decided in the class action, whether or not those class members reside in the forum. Accordingly, opt-in requirements for non-residents are not necessary to ensure that a decision in a class action binds non-resident plaintiffs. Further, opt-in requirements reduce access to justice for residents in multijurisdiction classes in the same way as opt-in requirements reduce access to justice for residents of the province. Provided that a plaintiff class is defined in a certification order in a way that ensures that there is a real and substantial connection between the claim and the forum, the many reasons for adopting an *opt-out* regime for residents of a province apply equally to multijurisdiction class actions.

... [O]pt-in requirements for non-residents are based on unfounded concerns about the recognition by other courts of judgments in class actions. They create unnecessary restrictions on the ordinary scope of plaintiff classes—restrictions that impair the capacity of multijurisdiction class actions to serve the objectives of class actions generally. All three main objectives of class actions—access to justice, judicial economy and behaviour modification—are best served by ensuring that as many claimants as possible who might be entitled to recovery in a given claim are included in the plaintiff class regardless of their residence. This is a simple extension to the multijurisdiction setting of the principles on which class actions are based. Increased certainty in the definition of the plaintiff class could be achieved by adding the proviso to the basic definition of the class as certified that persons falling within the definition of any previously certified class in another court and those who take steps to be included in classes certified elsewhere are presumptively excluded from the class. Harmonized legislation that omits reference to residency could further clarify the situation, but it may not be necessary to facilitate opt-out multijurisdiction class actions if the courts regard them as a product of the constitutional requirements of order and fairness.

... The Canadian jurisprudence on appropriate forum is among the most even-handed in the world. Canadian courts have demonstrated a strong commitment to ensuring that cases are determined in the forum that is most suitable based on the interests of all the parties and the ends of justice. In particular, Canadian courts have regularly given priority to factors affecting litigation convenience, taking into account the relative abilities of the parties to undertake the challenges of litigating in distant fora. They have also shown great confidence in the ability of other Canadian courts in alternative fora to take a balanced approach to resolving multiplicity and accordingly to be entitled to their deference in making determinations of appropriate forum in related cases.

Accordingly, the main challenge in any mechanism for resolving multiplicity in multijurisdiction class actions through existing certification processes is to identify the factors that are relevant to adjudicative efficacy and administrative efficiency in the class actions context. These factors are not new. They have already begun to receive careful consideration in the emerging jurisprudence relating to adequate representation, particularly in the determinations of carriage and venue motions. The analysis in these decisions serves to provide a general framework for the kinds of factors that are relevant to resolving multiplicity.

The evolving jurisprudence will clarify the special considerations that arise in multijurisdiction situations. For example, where a distinct or distant group of persons stands to benefit from representation by local counsel before a court in that province, there may be some benefit to defining a class certified elsewhere so as to exclude that group. This might occur in situations where a widely used product with a common defect causes harm to consumers in several provinces but where consumers in one province have been harmed by a discreet product line from a particular manufacturer. This may also be warranted where there the claims of one group of claimants will be resolved in a accordance with the law of a forum that is different from the law that will govern the claims of other groups. The extent to which the interests of class members are better served through co-ordinated proceedings than they would be served through sub-classes in a single proceeding is also a question that will be better understood as the jurisprudence develops. Moreover, even where there is no indication that the plaintiff class would be better served if the matter proceeded in two or more different fora, there may be situations in which one forum is clearly more appropriate than another. This would prompt a determination of appropriate forum along the traditional lines often undertaken in non-class litigation. The courts' considerable discretion to refuse to certify, to de-certify and to amend the definition of the class will continue to play an important cautionary role in encouraging appropriate proposals for the size and scope of plaintiff classes.

III—The Procedural Question.   Coordinating Multijurisdiction Class Proceedings: Which Court Decides?

a) Second Seized Principle—There seems to be little doubt that Canadian courts are well equipped to adapt the familiar principles of appropriate forum to the context of multi-jurisdiction class actions. However, there remains the need to establish a mechanism for deciding which of two or more courts seized with similar or related class claims should make such a determination. It might seem unlikely that independently administered courts could establish a workable method of resolving instances of multiplicity in multi-jurisdiction class actions. Indeed, the US Multidistrict Litigation Panel precedent suggests that this function could be served only by an independent body formed for the purpose. However, the strong core of common appreciation of the principles of order and fairness, and the considerable deference that Canadian courts have shown to one another suggest otherwise.

Adapting the model used within the European Union, in which the court first seized of a matter has jurisdiction to determine it, Canadian courts could operate in reverse. It could be presumed that the court first seized of a class action would have carriage of it subject to counsel in another Canadian forum persuading the court subsequently seized that some or all members of the plaintiff class would be better served by having the matter determined in the court in the latter jurisdiction. This approach would be unworkable in some federal or regional systems. However, Canadian courts have shown sufficient confidence in one another to suggest that it could work well within Canada. Indeed, in situations of parallel class proceedings Canadian courts have sought counsel's advice on the status of such proceedings in an informal attempt to avoid multiplicity. Further, recognizing the potential for a second seized court to make such a determination would have a cautionary effect on preemptive strikes by counsel seeking to secure their carriage of matters that might better be undertaken by others or in other fora.

b) Jurisprudential Developments/Institutional Mechanisms—This simple principle would need to be developed significantly in order for it to function well within the Canadian court system. First, procedures would need to be recognized for encouraging submissions in certification motions from counsel in class claims previously commenced in other jurisdictions, perhaps as interveners. This could include mandatory requirements for notice to counsel in related claims previously commenced. It could also include court-to-court communications based on the American Law Institute's *Transnational Insolvency Project Guidelines*, which have been endorsed by the Ontario and British Columbia courts for use in commercial cases. Second, in cases of parallel claims there may be more than two claims commenced, including more than one within a single jurisdiction. Sequencing protocols would need to be established for deciding which court would need to determine itself to be a more appropriate forum than which other court. For example, where actions were commenced in rapid succession, would a third seized court need to be persuaded that it was a better forum than both of the other courts? Third, to the extent that there could arise divergences of opinion from time to time between courts on the appropriate scope of classes certified in the same or similar claims, it would be necessary for the courts to develop standards for disagreeing with the results reached in other courts. Not only would it be helpful for courts to agree on the factors to be considered in determining appropriate forum (such as the similarity of claims and legal issues, the location of the events giving rise to the claim and the claimants, and the location of the counsel with the most effective litigation plan); it would also be helpful for courts to agree on the level of deference to be accorded to the decisions of other Canadian courts in related claims. None of this is to suggest that these important developments would constitute pre-conditions to adopting this approach. Rather, it seems likely that these developments would occur as a natural consequence of doing so.

The main institutional innovation required by this approach would be a centralized registry for originating notices and statements of claim issued in class actions that could permit these documents to be accessed promptly upon their issuance.

NOTES

1. This approach to coordinating multijurisdiction class proceedings was reflected in the recommendations made by the Uniform Law Conference of Canada in 2005 in its "Report of the Uniform Law Conference of Canada's Committee on the National Class and Related Interjurisdictional Issues: Background, Analysis, and Recommendations" (2005). That report recommended the establishment of a registry as follows:

> An on-line Canadian Class Proceedings Registry of all class action filings in each Canadian jurisdiction should be created and maintained for use by the public, counsel and courts. All current or proposed class proceedings legislation in all Canadian jurisdictions should require that all class action filings be directed to this registry. In addition or alternatively, courts in each jurisdiction should issue practice directions setting out the details of such filings.

The report also recommended that all current or proposed class proceedings legislation in all Canadian jurisdictions should:

- expressly permit the court to certify, on an opt-out basis, a class that includes class members residing or located outside the jurisdiction;

- require that a plaintiff seeking to certify a class proceeding give notice of such an application to plaintiffs in any class proceeding in Canada with the same or similar subject matter;
- permit plaintiffs from other jurisdictions served with such notice to make submissions at or before the certification application, including submissions that their action is the preferable procedure for all or part of the overlapping class;
- require the court, in certifying any class proceeding, to consider whether there are one or more class proceedings relating to the same or similar subject matter that have been commenced in one or more other Canadian jurisdictions and to consider whether such class proceedings may be a preferable procedure for the resolution of the claims of all or some of the class members;
- require the court, in assessing whether related class actions in other jurisdictions may be a preferable procedure for the resolution of the claims of all or some of the class members, to consider all relevant factors including:
  - the nature and the scope of the causes of actions advanced, including any variation in the cause of actions available in the various jurisdictions,
  - the theories offered by counsel in support of the claims,
  - the state of preparation of the various class actions,
  - the number and extent of involvement of the proposed representative plaintiffs,
  - the order in which the class actions were commenced,
  - the resources and experience of counsel,
  - the location of class members, defendants, and witnesses,
  - the location of any act underlying the cause of action;
- permit the court to make any order it deems just, including:
  - certifying a national or multijurisdictional opt-out class proceeding, if (1) all statutory criteria for certification have been met, and (2) the court determines that it is the appropriate venue for a national or multijurisdictional class proceeding,
  - refusing to certify an action on the basis that it should proceed in another jurisdiction as a national or multijurisdictional class proceeding,
  - refusing to certify that portion of the proposed class that includes class members who may be included within a pending or proposed class proceedings in another jurisdiction,
  - requiring that a subclass with separate counsel be certified within the certified class proceeding.

In the event that multiple class actions are certified in relation to the same issues, the courts hearing the action should adopt the *Guidelines Applicable to Court-to-Court Communications in Cross-Border Cases* that have been promulgated in the insolvency area by the American Law Institute and have been adopted by some Canadian courts.

2. A registry was established and, eventually, competing class actions were commenced. For a time, it was only the regimes in Ontario and Quebec that provided for multijurisdiction class proceedings on an opt-out basis and, as a result, they were the only courts likely to face the challenges of inconsistent certification orders. The British Columbia statute required class members from other provinces to opt in to the class, eliminating any doubt about whether they would be bound by a proceeding certified in another province. Eventu-

ally, however, Saskatchewan took steps to amend its legislation in accordance with the ULCC recommendations and, soon after, its courts certified a class action in the Vioxx litigation that conflicted directly with an action commenced some time earlier in Ontario. The inconsistency of the result was all the more pronounced because the class counsel seeking certification in Saskatchewan and previously lost a motion in Ontario for carriage of the multijurisdiction class action, which had been granted to a consortium of other lawyers.

In the meantime, competing class actions were beginning to emerge in Quebec and Ontario. In one such action, *Canada Post Corp. v. Lépine*, [2009] SCC 16, claims were brought in Quebec and Ontario against Canada Post for cancelling the lifetime Internet subscriptions Canada Post had been marketing. The Ontario court certified a class proceeding and approved a settlement agreement under which the purchasers would be refunded the purchase price of the CD-ROM and receive three months of free Internet access. The Ontario judgment purported to bind every Canadian resident who had purchased the service, except those in British Columbia. The next day, the Quebec Court authorized a class proceeding for residents of Quebec. Canada Post sought recognition (as *res judicata*) in Quebec of the Ontario judgment but this was denied because the notice of certification of the Ontario proceeding was inadequate in Quebec and created confusion with the class proceeding under way in Quebec, which constituted a contravention of the fundamental principles of procedure. The Quebec Court of Appeal added that, although the Ontario court had jurisdiction over the proceeding, it should have declined jurisdiction over Quebec residents by applying the doctrine of *forum non conveniens*. The two class proceedings gave rise to a situation of *lis pendens* because the Quebec proceeding had been commenced first.

In *Canada Post Corp. v. Lépine*, the Supreme Court rejected the notion that the Quebec court could deny recognition on the basis that the Ontario court should have exercised its discretion to decline jurisdiction. However, it upheld the appeal on the basis that the notice to Quebec residents was inadequate and that the Quebec class proceeding was under way from the moment it was instituted (i.e., before the Ontario action) and not only from the moment it is authorized as a class proceeding. On the question of notice, the court's reasoning was summarized as follows:

> In the context in which they were published, the notices provided for in the judgment of the Ontario Superior Court of Justice contravened the fundamental principles of procedure within the meaning of art. 3155, para. 3 CCQ. In a class action, it is important that the notice procedure be designed so as to make it likely that the information will reach the intended recipients. The wording of the notice must take account of the context in which it will be published and, in particular, the situation of the recipients. Compliance with these requirements constitutes an expression of the necessary comity between courts and a condition for preserving it within the Canadian legal space. In the instant case, the clarity of the notice was particularly important in a context in which, to the knowledge of all those involved, parallel class proceedings had been commenced in Quebec and in Ontario. The Ontario notice was likely to confuse its intended recipients, as it did not properly explain the impact of the judgment certifying the class proceeding on Quebec members of the national class established by the Ontario Superior Court of Justice. It could have led those who read it in Quebec to conclude that it simply did not concern them.

The Supreme Court did not address in detail the question of multijurisdiction class proceedings. It merely noted the problem:

In addition to its conclusions of law, the Quebec Court of Appeal seems to have had reservations or concerns about the creation of classes of claimants from two or more provinces. We need not consider this question in detail. However, the need to form such national classes does seem to arise occasionally. The formation of a national class can lead to the delicate problem of creating subclasses within it and determining what legal system will apply to them. In the context of such proceedings, the court hearing an application also has a duty to ensure that the conduct of the proceeding, the choice of remedies and the enforcement of the judgment effectively take account of each group's specific interests, and it must order them to ensure that clear information is provided.

As can be seen in this appeal, the creation of national classes also raises the issue of relations between equal but different superior courts in a federal system in which civil procedure and the administration of justice are under provincial jurisdiction. This case shows that the decisions made may sometimes cause friction between courts in different provinces. This of course often involves problems with communications or contacts between the courts and between the lawyers involved in such proceedings. However, the provincial legislatures should pay more attention to the framework for national class actions and the problems they present. More effective methods for managing jurisdictional disputes should be established in the spirit of mutual comity that is required between the courts of different provinces in the Canadian legal space. It is not this Court's role to define the necessary solutions. However, it is important to note the problems that sometimes seem to arise in conducting such actions.

The refusal to recognize a judgment of another province in a multijurisdiction class action re-ignited the debate about whether the superior courts of the provinces have jurisdiction under the Constitution to certify a class that includes persons resident in other provinces. On one view, class actions legislation is promulgated pursuant to the constitutional grant to the provinces of exclusive authority to make laws in relation to procedure in civil matters and this grant contains a limit on the extraterritorial operation of that authority. However, on another view, s. 92 provides for legislative authority, not judicial authority. The judicial jurisdiction of the superior courts of Canada is founded on the traditional authority of the courts of England and the provinces as reflected in s. 129 of the *Constitution Act, 1867* and it is informed by the principles of order and fairness. See J. Walker, *The Constitution of Canada and the Conflict of Laws* (2001). The following excerpt refocuses the debate over who should be presumed to be part of the class on the rights of class members who are unlikely to sue independently and discusses other options for coordinating multijurisdiction class actions.

Janet Walker, "Recognizing Multijurisdiction Class Action Judgments Within Canada: Key Questions—Suggested Answers"
(2008), 46 CBLJ 450 (footnotes omitted)

1. Introduction—With the advent of parallel multijurisdiction class actions in Canada, we need to develop a workable means of coordinating them. To do so we must establish standards for granting or denying preclusive effect to class action judgments and for exercising jurisdiction over them, and we must find ways to assess when parallel actions should be consolidated and to determine which courts should decide them.

• • •

Who is affected by recognizing class action judgments from other jurisdictions?—Those affected include named parties, class members who could seek compensation or redress independently and, most importantly, class members who could not.

• • •

What did Morguard really say about recognizing class action judgments?—The *Morguard* decision supplies the constitutional principles of order and fairness but we must develop jurisdictional standards and other procedures appropriate to the interests of all three groups affected by the recognition of class actions in order to develop a system consistent with the needs of the Canadian federation.

4. WHEN Have Courts Recognized Class Action Judgments (and When Have They Refused)?—It might surprise persons from outside Canada to learn that Canadian courts have seemed more willing to recognize foreign class action judgments than they have been to recognize class action judgments from other parts of Canada. Nevertheless, examining the situations in which the courts have recognized class action judgments and the situations in which they have refused to do so can shed light on the considerations underlying a workable system for the recognition of class action judgments.

In *Currie v. McDonald's Canada*, ... the Court of Appeal for Ontario held that a foreign class action judgment could have preclusive effect provided there was a real and substantial connection between the matter and the forum, the non-resident class members were adequately represented and they were accorded procedural fairness, including adequate notice and an opportunity to opt out. This reasoning was consistent with the previous decisions rendered in challenges to the jurisdiction of Ontario courts to certify multijurisdiction class actions: it addresses the interests of the first and second groups of persons described earlier—the named parties and those whose claims could be brought elsewhere. ... However, ... in *Lépine v. Canada Post*, ... class actions were commenced in Ontario and Québec ... (and) when the defendant brought a motion in Québec to have the Ontario decision recognized as precluding the Québec action, the Québec Court refused to do so because the duplicate notices received by the Québec residents caused them confusion. ...

• • •

5. WHERE Should Multijurisdiction Class Actions Be Decided in Canada?— ...

Several courts have recognized the merits of having common issues decided in a single proceeding despite the fact that these might involve the claims of persons arising in different provinces. While it stretches the logic of a "real and substantial connection" to say that the real and substantial connection test supports jurisdiction over those claims, Canadian courts have felt obliged to base their conclusion on that test. For example, in response to a challenge to its jurisdiction to determine on an opt-in basis claims that had arisen in other provinces, the British Columbia Supreme Court said the common issue could serve as a basis for jurisdiction because "it is that common issue which establishes the real and substantial connection necessary for jurisdiction." Similarly, in a recent Ontario decision, it was observed that the courts in Ontario accept "as a sufficiently real and substantial connection a commonality of interest between non-resident class members and those who are resident in the forum and whose causes of action have sufficiently real and substantial connections to it to ground jurisdiction over their claims against the defendants."

But this does not end the analysis. There may be no question of jurisdiction *simpliciter*, but there is certainly a question of appropriate forum. If there was only one court in Canada capable of determining class actions, we would find ways to ensure to the extent possible that the benefits of the class actions decided there were enjoyed in all the communities throughout the country where the cause of action arose. But now we have class actions in most Canadian jurisdictions and we must find ways to address the concerns arising from overlapping and competing class actions without losing the benefits to those communities that might be gained by local representation, local adjudication, and local awards. In this way it is not so much that the rules of jurisdiction and judgments need to be adapted to the multijurisdiction context as the procedures developed for contested carriage motions and settlement approval hearings need to be adapted to take into account the special concerns of multijurisdiction class actions. ... [For example, in a complex series of developments, in parallel class actions in the Vioxx litigation, the Saskatchewan Court of Queen's Bench and the Superior Court of Justice (Ontario) proceeded to certify competing class actions, thereby demonstrating the urgency of developing a means of resolving such questions.]

Where should multijurisdiction class actions be decided in Canada?—This is the key question that we face, but it is best answered in two parts, which will comprise the last two parts of this paper. First, we must develop a more nuanced approach to the choices between appropriate fora by considering the interests of the third group and why from their perspective it might be reasonable to recognize class actions judgments from other courts. Second, we must develop adjudicative mechanisms to enable the multilateral determination of the appropriate forum for class actions in Canada that can operate in a legal system comprised of independently administered courts.

6. *WHY Should Canadian Courts Recognize Class Action Judgments?*—All private law litigation serves the combined purposes of compensating persons for losses suffered and creating incentives to others to act responsibly so as to avoid causing such loss. One extraordinary feature of class actions that has only become clear with experience is that as the aggregation of claims increases the ability of private law litigation to serve these purposes, it also tends to drive a wedge between them.

Some class actions serve primarily the needs of persons who have suffered measurable losses that would go uncompensated but for their ability to join together to seek relief. Other class actions, involving nominal losses, serve primarily the needs of the broader public to be protected from misconduct by establishing effective sanctions to encourage more responsible conduct. It would be wrong to suggest that there is an absolute distinction between these two kinds of class actions, but much confusion has resulted from trying to develop principles and procedures for both without regard to the differences between them.

In class actions commenced primarily to promote access to justice for those who have suffered measurable losses, the pressing considerations in resolving the matter relate to the adequacy of the recovery. The extent of recovery will almost always amount to a compromise between what the claimants "should" receive and what is reasonably available. Claimants often receive far less than what they might receive in theory if they claimed individually, but this is an abstract consideration because, as a practical matter, their claims could not be brought independently and these claims have been aggregated to make them economically viable.

The question in the multijurisdiction context is whether the relief granted to these persons has been diminished by reason of the fact that it was granted by a court other than the court being asked to recognize the judgment. This could be as a result of differences in the legal principles that the recognizing court would itself apply, or as a result of some other jurisdiction-specific feature of the litigation. Of course, considerable care would need to be taken in conducting a review of this sort to ensure that the availability of review was not taken as an opportunity to re-open the litigation, or to argue why different counsel might have provided better representation and obtained a different result—other than for forum-specific reasons. And to the extent that review of this sort was available in principle, it would be likely that these issues would be anticipated and addressed directly in a judgment or settlement approval, perhaps one that benefited from interventions from those who might otherwise challenge the result.

Indeed, to the extent that review of the relief granted might always have an inherent tendency to undermine the finality of class action judgments it would be preferable to develop a means for addressing this concern as a matter of course, at the certification stage, as will be discussed in the next section. Where such concerns are justified, certainty would be enhanced by ensuring that the class of persons who might be prejudiced by being prevented access to the court to which they would otherwise resort are given appropriate relief as a sub-class or are presumptively excluded from the original class action.

Different considerations arise in class actions that involve nominal losses and that are commenced primarily to serve the needs of the broader public by establishing effective sanctions to encourage more responsible conduct. In these actions, the question is whether recognizing the judgment will provide adequate incentives to the defendant, and to others who might cause similar harm, to take steps to avoid causing such harm in the future not only in the jurisdiction where the judgment was issued but also in the jurisdiction in which recognition is sought.

In conducting this analysis there may be a tendency to assume that local measures are the best protection for the local public. But any regulatory measures, including class actions, involve public expense and so the benefits of an additional local action should be weighed against the likelihood that the judgment would provide adequate incentives to the defendant and to others similarly situated to improve their conduct in ways that would benefit not only the public in the forum where the judgment was issued but also in the forum where the judgment is recognized. This could explain the inclination to recognize the US judgment in the case against McDonald's discussed above. Nevertheless, where an award provides nominal or no compensation for class members and, instead, requires some contribution to the welfare of the broader community, courts will be concerned to ensure that the communities that benefit include those in the fora in which other class actions might be commenced. This could explain the disinclination to recognize the Ontario judgment in the case against Canada Post discussed above.

These are reasons for recognizing class action judgments from other courts, but they can also provide guidance in the processes of defining the class, measuring the adequacy of representation and the litigation plan, resolving contested carriage motions, and assessing the adequacy of the proposed relief in a settlement hearing.

In some cases, these considerations would be enough to determine where a multijurisdiction class action would best be decided, but in other cases, these requirements might be met in more than one jurisdiction. To assist in addressing these situations s. 6 of the Saskatchewan Class Actions Act now provides guidance to courts in determining when to certify a multijurisdiction class action in circumstances in which there is a competing multijurisdiction class action [and other criteria are also used by the Judicial Panel on Multidistrict Litigation in the US Federal Court]. ...

Why should Canadian courts recognize class action judgments?—They should do so because, where appropriate, the persons who might otherwise seek recovery from them are not prejudiced by having had their rights being determined in another forum, or because the incentives to defendants and others similarly situated to modify their behaviour will result in sufficient benefits to the community of the recognizing court to render a local class action unwarranted. Beyond this, the Canadian courts may be guided in further developing the rules for determining the appropriate forum or fora the litigation of a class action or related class actions by referring to the factors considered by the US MDL Panel.

7. HOW Should the Appropriate Forum Be Determined?—A discussion of the standards to be applied in determining the appropriate forum for multijurisdiction class actions is only of practical benefit if there is an adjudicative mechanism or body capable of making determinations binding on the parties in all the possible fora throughout Canada. It is becoming increasingly evident that there is a potential for this sort of determination, when made in the existing adjudicative structure of independently administered courts, to suffer from incomplete information or conflicts between the interests of counsel and the class. Even where the court has the benefit of argument concerning the merits of deferring to an existing competing multijurisdiction class action, there continues to be a risk of conflicting determinations. For example, in the decision by the Saskatchewan Court to certify a multijurisdiction class in *Wuttunee v. Merck Frosst Canada Ltd.* the court was not dissuaded from doing so by the fact that counsel seeking certification had previously failed to be awarded carriage of the same multijurisdiction class action in Ontario. Despite the urgency, establishing a mechanism or body to make a single determination within the structure of the Canadian judicial system with its independently administered courts requires considerable collective will and some ingenuity. ...

Ultimately, the Committee proposed a series of principles that could be applied by Canadian courts in the ordinary course of determining motions for certification. Though this option was less likely to be as effective as an authoritative multilateral body, there seemed no way to endow a multilateral body with the necessary authority. How could such a body decide on behalf of a superior court whether it should or should not exercise jurisdiction over a matter before it? And so it was hoped that a central registry granting ready access to the information on class actions commenced across the country, and a sense of the urgency of coordinating multijurisdiction class actions, would encourage the provincial superior courts operating independently to generate an informal system of cooperation.

Since the time the *Report* was adopted by the Uniform Law Conference, the need to develop an effective means of coordinating multijurisdiction class actions has become even more pressing, as is evident from the rulings discussed above. Further reflection suggests that it may be possible to develop a means of overcoming the hurdles of an independently administered court system to create a Canadian version of the MDL Panel, based on a model proposed by Chief Justice Winkler, which in Canada could be called a Multijurisdiction Class Proceedings Panel ("MCPP"). [Once a class action was commenced in one province and entered on the Registry, it would automatically be commenced in the other provinces by the Attorneys-General and stayed pending the deliberations of the Panel, comprised of judges designated by the Chief Justices of the provinces, who would be authorized by their Chief Justices to proceed with the action in their province or to stay it permanently, as determined by the Panel.]

How should the appropriate forum be determined?—The appropriate forum for multijurisdiction class actions in Canada should be determined by a Canadian equivalent to the US MDL Panel adapted to meet the needs of the Canadian federation.

IV. COSTS, SETTLEMENT, FEES, AND TRIAL

A. Costs: Fee Shifting and the "Downside Risk" in Class Action Litigation

One important question in the design of class proceedings is whether to expose the representative plaintiff to liability for costs. As the OLRC explained in its 1982 *Report on Class Actions* (at 647):

> In our view, the question of costs is the single most important issue this Commission has considered in designing an expanded class action procedure for Ontario. As we shall explain later, the matter of costs will not merely affect the efficacy of class actions, but in fact will determine whether this procedure will be utilized at all.

The OLRC argued that if the representative plaintiff remained personally exposed to the risk of having to pay the defendant's costs in an unsuccessful action, there was a very real likelihood that people would not come forward to act as representative plaintiffs. Why would persons be willing to risk the substantial costs of a class action when they stand to recover only their own individual damages? To this end, the OLRC recommended that where a case satisfied the rigorous certification criteria and it was certified, the action would proceed without any liability or risk on the part of representative plaintiffs for the costs of the action in the event that it was unsuccessful, except where there had been vexatious, frivolous, or abusive conduct on the part of any party.

This recommendation was not implemented in Ontario. Instead, the *Class Proceedings Act* provides that the court, in exercising its discretion with respect to costs, may consider whether the class proceeding "was a test case, raised a novel point of law, or involved a matter of public interest": s. 31(1). A representative plaintiff can, however, avoid exposure to adverse cost awards by making an application for financial assistance from the Class Proceedings Fund. If funding is approved, the Law Foundation will finance certain disbursements and pay any adverse costs award. But applications have been few and few have been successful.

In drafting its legislation (which has been followed in most of the other common law jurisdictions in Canada), British Columbia adopted the OLRC recommendation and the Act provides that no costs may be awarded to any party to a certification application or class proceeding or to an appeal arising from a class proceeding. However, the court retains a residual discretion to award costs if the court considers that

1. there has been vexatious, frivolous, or abusive conduct on the part of any party;
2. an improper or unnecessary application or other step has been made or taken for the purpose of delay or increasing costs or for any other improper purpose; or
3. there are exceptional circumstances that make it unjust to deprive the successful party of costs.

Notwithstanding the Ontario legislature's decision not to create a special costs regime for class actions along the lines of the OLRC's recommendations, the courts initially tended to shelter representative plaintiffs from the full burden of liability for costs. Where courts awarded party-and-party (partial indemnity) costs following resolution of the certification stage, they ordered greater costs against losing defendants than against losing representative plaintiffs; while unsuccessful plaintiffs were typically ordered to pay costs in the range of $5,000 to $15,000, unsuccessful defendants had been ordered to pay costs in the approximate range of $50,000 to $95,000.

There are now two key issues in this area (1) what quantum of costs will the courts order (particularly against plaintiffs) and (2) how are the three categories of protection against costs listed in CPA s. 31(1) to be applied? Recall that s. 31(1) of the Ontario Act provides: "In exercising its discretion with respect to costs under subsection 131 (1) of the *Courts of Justice Act*, the court may consider whether the class proceeding was a test case, raised a novel point of law or involved a matter of public interest."

In *Pearson v. Inco Ltd.* (2006), 79 OR (3d) 427 (CA), the plaintiff was ultimately successful in the Court of Appeal in certifying a class proceeding, but of a much narrower scope than originally sought. On conventional costs principles this success brought with it costs in the lower courts despite the reduced scope for the class proceeding.

In contrast, in *Ruffolo v. Sun Life Assurance Co. of Canada*, [2009] OJ No. 1322 (CA); aff'g. (2007), 56 CCLI (4th) 116 (SCJ) (trial) and (2008), 90 OR (3d) 59 (SCJ) (costs), the Ontario Court of Appeal upheld an award of $215,000 in costs to the defendant in a case that the parties agreed to proceed with as a test case rather than by way of a class action. The Class Proceedings Fund was liable for costs pursuant to the funding agreement with the plaintiff and the Fund argued that the presence of all three s. 31(1) criteria militated against any award of costs to the defendant. However, the Court of Appeal held that

> the general rule that costs follow the event applies in class proceedings in this province, just as it does in other forms of litigation. ... Even if the presence of one or more of the s. 31(1) criteria is found to exist, a court need not refrain from awarding costs to a successful defendant in a class action. Otherwise, the continuing application of the "costs follow the event" regime to class proceedings would be rendered meaningless. Whether a "no costs" order, or some adjustment to the costs as claimed, is appropriate to reflect the s. 31(1) factors will depend on the circumstances of each case.

Accordingly, it seems that costs determinations are not influenced by the fact that the Class Proceedings Fund is ultimately liable for costs awarded against a plaintiff. Would the courts in *Ruffolo* have made the same order if the plaintiff had been liable personally for costs?

In cases where the plaintiff may bear the burden of a costs award, the Supreme Court's decision upholding the costs award against the unsuccessful representative plaintiff in *Kerr v. Danier Leather Inc.*, [2007] SCJ No. 44 (SCC) (reproduced in chapter 2) could compound the chill on the willingness to serve as a representative plaintiff, particularly in view of the following statement:

> [P]rotracted litigation has become the sport of kings in the sense that only kings or equivalent can afford it. Those who inflict it on others in the hope of significant personal gain and fail can generally expect adverse cost consequences.

Nevertheless, the *Danier* costs decision may not have as wide an application as it seems. The *Danier* litigation was characterized by the court as "a commercial dispute between sophisticated commercial actors who are well resourced," in which the representative plaintiff had made a substantial gain of approximately $1.5 million on his investment but claimed that his profits would have been greater but for the defendant's failure to disclose an allegedly material change in business circumstances. Consistent with this, the above quote from the Supreme Court also emphasizes the fact that the litigation was brought "in the hope of significant personal gain." As the Supreme Court also stated:

> Nor do general concerns about access to justice warrant a departure from the usual cost consequences in this case. … [I]t should not be assumed that class proceedings invariably engage access to justice concerns to an extent sufficient to justify withholding costs from the successful party. … Success would have reaped substantial rewards for the representative plaintiff and his counsel. He put the representative respondents to enormous expense and I see no error in principle that would justify our intervention in the discretionary costs order made against him by the Court of Appeal.

These decisions suggest that, in *Danier*, the usual concerns about the denial of access to justice associated with financially non-viable individual claims did not arise. Indeed, both decisions appear premised on the respective courts' views that, by virtue of the quantum of individual damages sought and the financial resources of the representative plaintiff, the representative plaintiff's claim could have been advanced as a non-class action commercial suit to which the usual rule that the losing party is liable for costs would apply. Accordingly, it is questionable whether courts will adopt this reasoning in the usual circumstances where the financial costs and risks of individual litigation act as a barrier to access to justice and behaviour modification. However, the question remains whether this approach would encourage counsel to put forward impecunious representative plaintiffs.

A 2002 proposal to make the BC costs regime similar to the Ontario model was criticized by Ward Branch in "If it ain't broke, don't fix it!" available online at: http://www.branmac .com/go/download/civil_lit_conference.pdf as follows:

> The threat of significant adverse costs awards at each and every stage of the proceeding will greatly discourage potential plaintiffs from pursuing claims through the avenue of class actions, and will generally stifle access to justice. In other words, the Ministry's proposal would, if

effected, undermine the very purpose that the Act was meant to achieve. As the title of our paper suggests, we think that the "no costs" regime is functioning very well and no "fix" is necessary. ...

The message to potential representative plaintiffs that is found in the *Gariepy* and *Pearson* decisions is: "proceed at your own risk"—a warning that will likely compromise the access to justice purpose for which class proceedings were created. This would certainly be unfortunate, particularly when one considers the unsupported assumptions that underlie these two decisions:

1. It is proper for a defendant to expend vast resources to defeat a certification motion and escape the "enormous potential liability that attaches to such claims if the proceeding is certified";

2. Access to justice will not be hindered by levelling the playing field through the award of equivalent (and substantial) costs against the losing party, whether plaintiff or defendant;

3. Representative plaintiffs are simply fronts for class counsel, who constitute the real party bringing the lawsuit and the party who will (and presumably, should) be liable for any costs award. Class counsel are as well-funded as the corporate defendants they are facing and enjoy equal access to resources, both financial and evidentiary.

• • •

While it is true that it costs more to defend a class action than a handful of individual proceedings, one may ask whether it is acceptable for defendants to bury class counsel in paper, to deluge them with motions, and to outspend, outspend, outspend! Given the increasing cost of court time, we do not believe that the courts should sanction or support defence by attrition Nevertheless, it seems to us that this sort of behaviour may be encouraged by the decisions of the Court in *Gariepy* and *Pearson*. A similar strategy may be employed in a "no costs regime," but when the representative plaintiff must constantly worry about having to foot the bill for each of the procedural skirmishes, the incentive to action for defendants is definitely increased.

Despite this concern, the prediction of the OLRC—that if we have fee shifting, no one, properly advised, would ever agree to become a representative plaintiff in a class action—did not materialize. In practice, it seems that the representative plaintiff rarely becomes personally responsible for costs. In some cases, plaintiff's counsel choose judgment-proof representative plaintiffs for whom the downside risk of an adverse costs award is of little or no concern. Alternatively, class counsel either expressly or implicitly agree to indemnify and hold harmless representative plaintiffs with respect to adverse cost awards. In this situation, the person who is "on the hook" for costs in a class action is, in fact, class counsel. It can be argued this is a reasonable state of affairs, given that class actions under the lawyer-entrepreneur model we have adopted in Canada (and in the United States) are essentially the lawyer's litigation and not that of the representative plaintiff or the class; the lawyer (1) will typically have invented or devised the class action, and (2) will be funding the action personally through his or her firm; it is really class counsel's law suit. Under the Ontario costs regime, it is usually the lawyer who ends up bearing the liability for costs, and that is reasonable as a "cost of doing business" and it deters the bringing of meritless class actions. Furthermore, it is a better solution than the one that externalizes the costs by depriving a successful defendant of any cost indemnity.

Ontario's Class Proceedings Fund. The Ontario class proceedings legislative package established the Class Proceedings Fund. (See the *Law Society Amendment Act (Class Proceedings Funding), 1992*, SO 1992, c. 7 and a regulation made under the Act (O. Reg. 771/92). Where a plaintiff applies to and receives assistance from the Fund, the Fund becomes liable to pay any costs awarded to the defendant and, in such circumstances, the representative plaintiff is relieved of any liability for the defendant's costs. However, the low rate of applications to the Fund and inadequate financing has necessitated caution in undertaking to fund proceedings as one substantial cost order could wipe it out. Funding is rarely sought in the "big, successful" cases perhaps because a levy of 10 percent is thought to be too high an amount for the class to bear, although this would have placed the Fund in a very good position financially. In 2003, the Fund received $2 million plus from the settlement of a medical malpractice case increasing the balance in the Fund to $3.3 million. Should the Fund be funding more cases? What are the arguments pro and con? Quebec also has a *"Fonds."* Funding does not automatically relieve an unsuccessful representative plaintiff of liability for the defendant's costs. However, if the agreement entered into between the *Fonds* and the plaintiff so provides, the *Fonds* may assume liability for costs and disbursements that the plaintiff is ordered to pay a defendant. See *An Act Respecting the Class Action* (LRQ, c. R-2.1, s. 29.)

Possible changes to help the Fund meet its objectives. One approach might be to amend the legislation to reduce the levy from 10 percent to 1–2 percent and apply it to all class action recoveries, whether or not funded by the Fund. Alternatively, in light of the "failure" of the Class Proceedings Fund to adequately deal with the fee-shifting issue, it could be argued that Ontario should amend its Act, resort to the BC model, and virtually abandon fee shifting in class actions. What is class counsel's duty in terms of informing the representative plaintiff of his or her right to apply for funding? What are the likely consequences, if the plaintiff is ordered to pay costs, of the lawyer not having informed the representative plaintiff of this right or of advising against making an application? Are lawyers acting prudently in not advising their clients to apply to the Fund?

Financing class actions. This will always be an issue for plaintiffs' class counsel who act on a "no win–no pay" contingency basis. As counsel work on the case, unbilled lawyer time builds up (some of it for associates whose salaries need to be paid) and disbursements are incurred that may have to be paid long before the litigation ends. This raises the question about how the litigation is to be financed. In the fee determination decision in the breast implant litigation, *Serwaczek v. Medical Engineering Corp.* (1996), 3 CPC (4th) 386 (Ont. Gen. Div.), it was stated that the disbursements were financed by a bank loan on which the class counsel paid interest at the prime rate. As reported in *The Toronto Star*, February 22, 1998, in the heart pacemaker litigation, *Nantais v. Telectronics Proprietary (Can.) Ltd.* (in which the ultimate disbursements allowed were $800,000), a less conventional financing method was used. Class counsel Harvey Strosberg "convinced a handful of wealthy investors to … [invest] a total of $350,000 to help finance [the] class action." "If the heart patients won, the investors would be first in line to get their money back, plus 20 per cent annual interest. If not, they'd lose the entire amount." It is reported that Mr. Strosberg stated that this financing method "had the okay of the judge hearing the case." Had the *Nantais* action failed, could the defendants have argued that they were entitled to their costs against either Mr. Strosberg or his investors as persons who had promoted the action through champerty and maintenance? Or should it be accepted that, in order for the legislatively created class-action regime to work (one which unabashedly relies on lawyer-entrepreneurs for its operation), lawyers must be permitted to make such financing arrangements even if they appear to offend traditional notions of champerty and maintenance? What are the acceptable methods of financing? Should class actions be permitted to become investment vehicles and "maintenance" abolished? See Poonam Puri, "Financing of Lawsuits by Third-Party Investors: A Share of Justice?" (1998), 36 *Osgoode Hall LJ* 515, proposing that class actions be permitted to become investment vehicles.

B. Settlement

Like named-party litigation, most class proceedings are resolved by way of settlement. However, the concern for the fairness of the settlement of a class action differs from other civil suits. In named-party litigation, a settlement reached between the parties binds only the parties. Its legitimacy is based on their consent to it. In contrast, the settlement of a class action affects the rights of class members who are unlikely to have been involved in the proceeding. To protect the interests of "absent class members," class actions legislation provides that class proceedings may be settled only with court approval.

The settlement of class actions is different from settlement of other litigation also because the relationships between the participants—parties, counsel, and judges—does not readily provide the same means of protecting the interests of those affected as do the relationships in named-party litigation. There exists an inherent risk of collusion between class counsel and the defendant, and a risk of conflict of interest between class counsel and the class members. In an important empirical study in the United States, the Rand Group concluded that the "clientless litigation" represented by class actions has led to questionable practices in the US: settlements are arrived at without adequate investigation of facts and law, creating little value for class members or society, and class counsel fees are often disproportionate to the effort actually invested by counsel in the case. The plaintiffs' attorney, once seen as a public-regarding private attorney general, is now viewed as a profit-seeking entrepreneur, capable of opportunistic actions and often willing to subordinate the interests of class members to the attorney's own economic self-interest. The Ontario Law Reform Commission (OLRC) noted this concern in its 1982 *Report on Class Actions* and Professor John Coffee observed in his article "Class Wars: The Dilemma of the Mass Tort Class Action" (1995), 95 *Colum. L Rev.* 1343 that "[c]ollusion within the class action context essentially requires an agreement—actual or implicit—by which the defendants receive a 'cheaper' than arm's length settlement and the plaintiffs' attorneys receive in some form an above-market attorneys' fee. In return for this ... settlement, defendants either pay the plaintiffs' attorneys' fees themselves or agree not to contest the plaintiffs' attorneys' application for court-awarded fees."

The overarching problem with class action settlements is that the principals (the class members) cannot effectively monitor their agent (the class lawyer)—the monitoring role ordinarily played by clients in non-class actions is absent in class actions. The OLRC anticipated this problem and recommended judicial scrutiny (court monitoring in place of client monitoring) as the solution. The recommendation that class action settlements be subject to court approval was incorporated into the class proceedings legislation, but it remains an open question as to whether this is sufficient or if more needs to be done.

In *Cheryl Reynolds v. Beneficial National Bank*, the court overturned a settlement approval observing that "[w]e and other courts have gone so far as to term the district judge in the settlement phase of a class action suit a fiduciary of the class, who is subject therefore to the high duty of care that the law requires of fiduciaries." The court explained the phenomenon of a "reverse auction" as follows.

Cheryl Reynolds v. Beneficial National Bank
288 F3d 277 (7th Cir. 2002)

POSNER J: The various objectors to the settlement, primarily intervening or would-be intervening plaintiffs who have claims that the settlement will release, contend that the settlement agreement is the product of a "reverse auction," the practice whereby the defendant in a series of class actions picks the most ineffectual class lawyers to negotiate a settlement with in the hope that the district court will approve a weak settlement that will preclude other claims against the defendant. … The ineffectual lawyers are happy to sell out a class they anyway can't do much for in exchange for generous attorneys' fees, and the defendants are happy to pay generous attorneys' fees since all they care about is the bottom line—the sum of the settlement and the attorneys' fees—and not the allocation of money between the two categories of expense. The defendants agreed to pay attorneys' fees in this case, to the three solo practitioners and the law firm that negotiated the settlement, of up to $4.25 million.

Although there is no proof that the settlement was actually collusive in the reverse-auction sense, the circumstances demanded closer scrutiny than the district judge gave it. He painted with too broad a brush, substituting intuition for the evidence and careful analysis that a case of this magnitude, and a settlement proposal of such questionable antecedents and circumstances, required. …

A high degree of precision cannot be expected in valuing a litigation, especially regarding the estimation of the probability of particular outcomes. Still, much more could have been done here without (what is obviously to be avoided) turning the fairness hearing into a trial of the merits. …

All things considered, we conclude that the district judge abused his discretion in approving the settlement. Because of this conclusion, the other issues raised by the appeals need not be decided, but for guidance on remand we will address the principal ones, which concern attorneys' fees. To begin with, we disapprove the practice (a practice we had never heard of and can find no case law concerning) of encouraging or permitting the submission of fee applications in camera. In the unlikely event that some confidential information is contained in the applications, that information can be whited out. To conceal the applications and in particular their bottom line paralyzes objectors, even though inflated attorneys' fees are an endemic problem in class action litigation and the fee applications of such attorneys must therefore be given beady-eyed scrutiny by the district judge. … Second, class counsel's compensation must be proportioned to the incremental benefits they confer on the class, not the total benefits. …

Several lawyers, each representing a class member, appeared at the fairness hearing to object to various features of the proposed settlement, primarily the reversion which the judge later struck. They wanted a fee for having conferred a benefit on the class by arguing successfully against the reversion. The judge turned them down.

· · ·

The situation here is similar. The clients being content with the settlement, the only issue is whether their lawyers are entitled to a fee. They are in effect volunteer lawyers for the class asking that they receive a fee for their efforts. We think they can appeal without their clients' having intervened. Intervention would not only be a pointless formality. ... It would be a futile one. For the clients, being content with the settlement, could not appeal even if they were parties, because they seek no relief from us and standing must continue throughout the entire litigation. ... Unless the lawyers can appeal, there will be no appellate review of the district judge's decision not to award them fees.

It would be a different case if the claim for attorneys' fees rested on a fee-shifting statute, so that the money would come from the defendants and not diminish the $25 million fund. Then the objectors would have to intervene, because it is the litigants rather than the lawyers who hold the entitlement to awards under fee-shifting statutes. ... The objectors might be obliged by contract to pay these sums to their lawyers, but that would not make the lawyers parties. To be entitled to appeal, however, the objectors would have to become parties.

But in fact the lawyers are claiming fees in their own name, so that any fees awarded to them would come from the $25 million fund under the common-fund doctrine. When a lawyer lays claim to a portion of the kitty, he becomes a real party in interest; and should he therefore have to intervene—not only for purposes of taking an appeal himself but so that he will be an appellee if class members oppose the district court's award and want the money back? We do not see why a person who has received money by order of the district court at the expense of a party must be named as a party in order for the party harmed by the order to be able to appeal. After all, a defendant could appeal from a fee award to the plaintiff's lawyer that he thought excessive.

We need not pursue this interesting question ... any further, since the claim for attorneys' fees falls with the settlement. But assuming these lawyers can appeal, let us for the sake of guidance for the future consider the merits of their appeals.

The law generally does not allow good Samaritans to claim a legally enforceable reward for their deeds. ... But when professionals render valuable albeit not bargained-for services in circumstances in which high transaction costs prevent negotiation and voluntary agreement, the law does allow them to claim a reasonable professional fee from the recipient of their services. ... That is the situation of objectors to a class action settlement. It is desirable to have as broad a range of participants in the fairness hearing as possible because of the risk of collusion over attorneys' fees and the terms of settlement generally. This participation is encouraged by permitting lawyers who contribute materially to the proceeding to obtain a fee. ...

The principles of restitution that authorize such a result also require, however, that the objectors produce an improvement in the settlement worth more than the fee they are seeking; otherwise they have rendered no benefit to the class. ...

NOTES AND QUESTIONS

1. *The role of the court as settlement approver.* As can be seen in the *Reynolds* decision, a variety of issues and challenges are posed by class action settlements and the court's obligation under the Act is to scrutinize the settlements and to approve them only if they are fair and reasonable. Should the court itself take steps to precipitate an adversarial hearing with regard to the adequacy of the settlement? What should be the standard of scrutiny to be applied by the court in approving the settlement? Should the court be concerned if plaintiff's and defendant's counsel have simultaneously negotiated both a settlement for the class and class counsel's fees?

Judge Posner remarked that "[w]hen a lawyer lays claim to a portion of the kitty, he becomes a real party in interest." This underscores the differences between the lawyer–client relationship for plaintiff's counsel in the settlement of class actions from that in ordinary litigation. Are the concerns that this raises resolved "if the claim for attorneys' fees rested on a fee-shifting statute, so that the money would come from the defendants and not diminish" the settlement fund?

These are complex questions in the context of the adversary system. The legitimacy for court decisions resolving litigation—adjudication—comes from the reasoned decisions given by an independent judiciary following an adversarial presentation of the case. In contrast, the legitimacy of the resolution of cases through settlement comes from the willingness of those who are to be bound to dispense with this process. Under these circumstances we accept that the result is fair because it has been accepted as fair by the named parties— whether or not it might be regarded as fair by others. As Judith Resnik pointed out (in "Aggregation, Settlement, and Dismay" (1995), 80 *Cornell L Rev.* 918 and "Litigating and Settling Class Actions: The Prerequisites of Entry and Exit" (1997), 30 *University of California at Davis L Rev.* 835), for various reasons (one being judicial self-interest), we have elevated settlements to being the best form of resolution, preferable to adjudication, and the current judicial regime often pushes for them. This is summed up in the statement, attributed to some judges, "a bad settlement is better than a good trial." This is a problem in class actions because, as Resnik noted:

> With class actions the situation is quite different. Because the settlement will finally determine the rights of absent parties and consent of all class members is not possible, nor required, *courts are charged with the responsibility of passing on the adequacy and fairness of class action settlements.* This function must be taken seriously and class action settlements must be carefully scrutinized by judges—difficult as this task may be. This is a situation where the courts are dealing with "other people's money"—the rights of people who are not before the court. The settlement of a class action is not the same as the settlement of an individual action. ... This is not a task which should be characterized by "umpirial judging" (with its approach of "hands off" and impartiality); rather it is a task which calls for the assertiveness of "managerial judging" and a serious enquiry into the substantive merit of the proposed settlement.

2. *The Rand report.* In *Class Action Dilemmas: Pursuing Public Goals for Private Gain* (Santa Monica: Rand Institute for Civil Justice, 2000), the Rand Institute for Civil Justice published an empirical study and report, based in part on ten intensive case studies of recent class actions in the United States. The report suggests that the key to improving

outcomes and eliminating abuses in class action litigation over money damages is increased regulation of settlements and fee awards by judges equipped with the training, resources and determination to do the job. Judicial regulation of damage class actions has two key components: settlement approval and fee awards. Judges need to take more responsibility for the quality of settlements, and they need to reward class counsel only for achieving outcomes that are worthwhile to class members and society. For assistance in these tasks, they can sometimes turn to objectors and intervenors. But because intervenors and objectors often are also a part of the triangle of interests that impedes regulation of damage class actions, judges should also turn for help to neutral experts and to class members themselves. The report observed:

> We think it is judges who hold the key to improving the balance of good and ill consequences of damage class actions. It is what the judge requires of the attorneys, parties, and process that determines the outcome of a damage class action. And it is the outcome of one class action that determines whether another similar class action will be brought. If judges approve settlements that are not in class members' interest and then reward class counsel for obtaining such settlements, they sow the seeds for frivolous litigation—settlements that waste society's resources— and ultimately disrespect for the legal system. If more judges in more circumstances dismiss cases that have no legal merits, refuse to approve settlements whose benefits are illusory, and award fees to class counsel proportionate to what they *actually* accomplish, over the long run the balance between public good and private gain will improve. ...
>
> Judges do not always exercise their full authority to scrutinize proposed class action settlements, and they do not always closely examine the rationale for class counsel fee requests.

3. Despite the generally critical tenor of Posner J's judgment, note that on one crucial point he (like most US courts) is tolerant of defendant's negotiating with the plaintiff's counsel as to the latter's fees and the defendant paying such fees directly (rather than have such fees come out of the gross settlement in an amount determined by the court). In a study jointly funded by the plaintiffs' and defence bar, the RAND/ICJ took a more systematic look at where the money goes in class settlements. The study indicates that in state court consumer class action settlements (i.e., non-personal injury monetary relief cases), the class counsel frequently receives more money than all class members combined. Significantly, another study found that this phenomenon was not occurring in federal courts—"[i]n most [class actions handled by federal courts], net monetary distributions to the class exceeded attorneys' fees by substantial margins." The implication of these findings is not that plaintiffs' lawyers have no legitimate interest in compensation for work done on successful cases, or that all class action settlements are unfair. However, class action filings have increased disproportionately in some jurisdictions for the apparent reason that those jurisdictions are less likely to enforce class action rules and more likely to approve troublesome settlements, thereby hurting the interests of absent class members.

4. *Are Canadian courts doing a better job?* There has been no empirical assessment of this process in Canada. Early commentators suggested that we are doing a better job, but as class actions and settlements proliferate, there is cause for concern that settlements are being approved that benefit class counsel more than they do class members.

One difference seems to be that US courts regularly approve settlements where the defendant pays directly the fees of class counsel. In Canada, there has been concern that it is improper for counsel for the defendant and for the class to agree on how much of the "pie" should go to class counsel because it represents a conflict of interest with the class. In many cases, the parties have agreed on the amount of the settlement and left it to the court to determine what part of the class recovery should be paid to class counsel by way of fees. However, this may now be changing. Another difference relates to the approval of coupon settlements, discussed below, whereby the recovery takes the form of a discount or an incentive to purchase further products or services. This is not uncommon in the US, but it is relatively rare in Canada. Consider the following decision in *Gariepy v. Shell Oil Co.*

Gariepy v. Shell Oil Co.
(2002), 26 CPC (5th) 358 (Ont. SCJ)

NORDHEIMER J: Three representative plaintiffs … move to certify this action as a class proceeding and to approve a settlement. …

The claims asserted in this action arise out of alleged defects in two products, polybutylene plumbing pipe and acetal insert fittings. The plaintiffs allege that fittings made from acetal resin, supplied by the defendants, Hoechst Celanese Corporation and E.I. Du Pont De Nemours and Company, and pipe made from polybutylene resin, supplied by the defendant, Shell Oil Company, are unsuitable for use in potable water plumbing systems. The plaintiffs allege that if such fittings and piping are used in potable water plumbing systems, they will fail prematurely leading to leaks and damages consequent on such leaks. The plaintiffs assert causes of action including negligent design, failure to warn, misrepresentation and breach of warranty.

In the proposed settlement, DuPont agrees to make payments to Canadian homeowners with polybutylene plumbing and heating systems from a fund of up to $30 million. The terms and conditions are set out in a settlement agreement entered into between Class Counsel and DuPont on February 13, 2002 and amended on March 15, 2002. Pursuant to the proposed settlement, settlement class members will be deemed to have released DuPont from all claims against it arising from polybutylene plumbing and heating systems, but will retain their rights to pursue their claims against the non-settling defendants, Shell and Celanese. On the basis of "bar order" language agreed upon by Class Counsel and DuPont, cross-claims, third party claims and all claims for contribution and indemnity are to be barred against DuPont. As a consequence of the bar order, settlement class members will be restricted to making "several" claims only against Shell and Celanese.

The proposed settlement was reached after Class Counsel had conducted a significant amount of investigation. As part of the investigation, Class Counsel retained expert witnesses, interviewed dozens of installers and plumbers, examined the plumbing in many structures, arranged for scientific analysis on failed plumbing parts and interviewed hundreds of other witnesses and class members throughout Canada. In addition, Class Counsel reviewed hundreds of documents that were produced in the course of litigation which has been ongoing for many years in the United States over these issues.

Class counsel say that these investigations and research, including the plaintiffs' involvement earlier in these proceedings regarding motions brought by the defendants disputing the jurisdiction of this court, as well as the plaintiffs' preparation for the substantive litigation, enabled them to negotiate a Settlement Agreement that they are confident is fair, reasonable and in the best interests of the class. It is not disputed that the parties entered into the proposed settlement after months of arm's length negotiations. It should also be noted that the negotiation of the fees to be paid to Class Counsel took place after the other terms of the proposed settlement had already been agreed upon by Class Counsel and DuPont.

Class counsel advise that the settlement discussions were guided by many factors including: discussions with homeowners with PB plumbing and/or heating systems, an analysis of the facts and law applicable to the claims of the settlement class, a consideration of the burdens and expense of litigation, including the risks and uncertainties associated with certification, trials and appeals, a consideration of a fair and cost-effective method of resolving the claims of the settlement class and a consideration of other settlements in Canada and the United States.

While it is the plaintiffs' position that this litigation has merit, in evaluating settlement options, Class Counsel have understandably assessed the risks associated with the litigation. Those risks include various risks that are necessarily associated with this type of litigation including procedural risks related to certification, risks associated with complex scientific evidence and the assertion of some novel causes of action. In addition, there is the ever present reality that even if the plaintiffs are successful on each and every material issue in the litigation, appeals by the defendants could significantly delay a resolution for many years. In this case, the procedural risks relative to certification are obvious given my decision, at first instance, to deny certification against the other two defendants.

There are companion proposed class proceedings ongoing in British Columbia and Quebec. This proposed settlement applies to all three actions and requires the approval of the courts in all three Provinces. Hearings seeking approval of the proposed settlement are scheduled to take place in British Columbia on November 7, 2002 and in Quebec on November 19, 2002.

. . .

Pursuant to the proposed settlement, DuPont has agreed to the following:

(a) DuPont will pay 25% of the reasonable cost of a replumb of a polybutylene plumbing system with acetal insert fittings provided that such replumb has been completed within 15 years of the installation of the unit's polybutylene plumbing system;

(b) DuPont will pay 25% of the actual cost of repair of physical damage to tangible property caused by a leak in a polybutylene plumbing system with acetal insert fittings occurring within 15 years of its installation (to the extent not reimbursed by insurance), provided a replumb of the property unit has been completed;

(c) DuPont will pay $200 of the cost of repair of a polybutylene heating system with acetal insert fittings, provided that all acetal insert fittings in such system are replaced within 15 years of installation of the unit's polybutylene heating system; and

(d) DuPont will pay the expenses of maintaining a claims processing facility to administer the settlement.

· · ·

DuPont has also agreed to:

(a) Pay solicitors' fees and expenses to Class Counsel of $4.5 million, subject to Court approval, which fees and expenses are in addition to the other funding; and

(b) Fund a notice campaign informing prospective Class Members of the approval of the settlement, the claims process and their opt out rights.

· · ·

I am satisfied therefore that the action should be certified as a class proceeding for the purposes of settlement.

· · ·

By virtue of section 29(2) of the Act, class action settlements must be approved by the Court to be binding. Before turning to my consideration of the settlement itself, I wish to address an issue that arose in the approval hearing and that is the right, if any, of the non-settling defendants to make submissions regarding the adequacy of the settlement. In this regard I am not dealing with the issue of the proposed bar order. I will deal with that later as a separate issue and one on which there was no dispute that the non-settling defendants have a direct interest and a clear right to make submissions.

Counsel for Shell did not attempt to make any submissions beyond its concerns respecting the bar order but counsel for Celanese did …

Aside from the bar order, I do not see how Celanese is affected by the fact that the plaintiffs and DuPont wish to resolve the issues that are outstanding between them. …

Ultimately, the court can and must control its own process. The court ought to be wary of allowing parties, who are clearly adverse in interest to the plaintiffs, to weigh in on matters such as the settlement of claims involving other parties in the guise of "protecting" the plaintiff class. …

[N]on-settling defendants have no standing to make submissions, as Celanese sought to do here, against the approval of the settlement on the basis that the settlement class members were not receiving enough under the settlement or that the settlement class members were unlikely to take up the settlement in sufficient numbers. If the court has any concerns in those respects regarding a proposed settlement, then the answer is for the court to appoint independent counsel to review the settlement and advise on such issues. To conclude otherwise would permit non-settling defendants to take on a role which fits neither comfortably nor properly on their shoulders given that the non-settling defendants' fundamental position is, after all, that the plaintiffs have no legitimate claim to advance in the first place.

In determining whether to approve a settlement the Court will consider whether the settlement is fair, reasonable and in the best interests of the class as a whole. In the leading case on class action settlements, *Dabbs v. Sun Life, Assurance Company of Canada*, [1998] OJ No. 1598 (Gen. Div.) Mr. Justice Sharpe approved the following list of considerations for the approval of a proposed settlement:

1. Likelihood of recovery, or likelihood of success
2. Amount and nature of discovery evidence
3. Settlement terms and conditions
4. Recommendation and experience of counsel
5. Future expense and likely duration of litigation
6. Recommendation of neutral parties if any
7. Number of objectors and nature of objections
8. The presence of good faith and the absence of collusion

· · ·

It is not the function of the court in reviewing a settlement to reopen the settlement or to attempt to re-negotiate it in the hope of improving its terms. Simply put, the court must decide either to approve the settlement or to reject it. Similarly, in deciding whether to approve the settlement, the court must be wary of second-guessing the parties in terms of the settlement that they have reached. Just because the court might have approached the resolution from a different perspective, or might have reached a resolution on a different basis, is not a reason to reject the proposed settlement unless the court is of the view that the settlement is inadequate or unfair or unreasonable.

In this particular case, I questioned the absence of any provision in the settlement which would allow members of the settlement class to be reimbursed for repairs alone without the requirement of undertaking a replumb. One of the reasons for not including such a provision was the parties' wish to have finality and not to be faced with a series of claims by the same Settlement Class member. While that issue could have been addressed in another way, for the court to insist on such a provision as part of the approval of the settlement would be to engage in the "arm chair quarterbacking" of the settlement which the court ought not to do. I also note that if any member of the proposed settlement class finds the absence of that, or any other, provision troublesome, he or she may opt out of the settlement.

Matching the proposed settlement against the factors from Dabbs, I would make the following observations:

(a) This is a complicated action. The likelihood of recovery, or likelihood of success, is very much uncertain as, indeed, is the issue of whether certification itself is appropriate. This settlement provides a measure of certainty in the result for those members of the Settlement Class who wish to partake of it.

(b) While there has yet to be any discovery in this case, voluminous materials are available to class counsel because of the many years of litigation that have occurred in the United States. The factual basis for the claims are therefore very well known notwithstanding that this action itself has only just begun.

(c) I find the settlement terms and conditions to be balanced and proper for the resolution as proposed.

(d) The settlement is recommended by Class Counsel who are very experienced in the area of class proceedings.

(e) The prosecution of these claims will involve significant future expense and the litigation itself will likely take a considerable period of time to get to trial.

(f) While there are no recommendations from neutral parties, I would note in this regard that similar types of settlements have been approved in the United States.

(g) There are no objectors to the proposed settlement.

(h) The settlement was reached after prolonged arm's length negotiations involving very experienced counsel on both sides.

For all of these reasons, therefore, I am satisfied that the settlement is fair and reasonable and one which ought to be approved subject to the resolution of two remaining issues—the proposed bar order and the proposed fees payable to Class Counsel.

• • •

There is also a concern in this regard that the terms of the settlement appear to bind future owners of polybutylene systems. The court has no ability to bind individuals who are not currently before it. The only people who can be bound are those that are currently covered by the class and those who may become subject to it during the opt out period. Again, counsel for the plaintiffs say that is all that was intended.

• • •

I turn to the final issue and that is the approval of the fees which DuPont has agreed to pay Class Counsel as part of the settlement. I am able to separate my consideration of this aspect of the overall settlement from my approval of the basic settlement itself due to the fact that Mr. Eizenga advised me that he was prepared to separate the approval of the settlement proper from the approval of the fees so that the settlement could proceed. In other words, counsel were prepared to "take their chances" on the fees issue in order to allow the settlement itself to move forward. I wish to commend plaintiff's counsel for the manifest fairness they demonstrate in taking that position.

Class Counsel's fees were resolved through a process of negotiations between the parties. Ultimately it was agreed that DuPont would pay fees and disbursements to Class Counsel in the total amount of $4.5 million inclusive of taxes. This amount includes the anticipated costs associated with the continued work required of Class Counsel as the implementation of the settlement proceeds. It bears repeating that the amount of the fees which DuPont has agreed to pay is over and above the amount set aside to address the claims of settlement class members.

Class Counsel, at some earlier point, entered into retainer agreements with the representative plaintiffs which provide that Class Counsel would pay all expenses associated with the litigation and would only be paid legal fees and be reimbursed for disbursements and taxes in the event of success in the litigation. The agreements provided for payment on the basis of a contingency fee of 30% of the first $10 million, or any part thereof, of damages awarded; 20% of the second $10 million, or any part thereof; and 10% of all additional amounts, plus disbursements and taxes. These retainer agreements have not, as yet, been approved by the court as required by section 32(2) of the *Class Proceedings Act, 1992* which states:

> An agreement respecting fees and disbursements between a solicitor and a representative party is not enforceable unless approved by the court, on the motion of the solicitor.

If the court does not approve the retainer agreements, then the court is to determine the amount owing to the solicitors for fees and disbursements under section 32(4) of the Act. Co-counsel in British Columbia and Quebec were retained under comparable contingency terms.

In support of their request for approval of the amount to be paid under the settlement for fees and disbursements, Class Counsel point to the fact that the value of the Settlement Agreement would give rise, under the retainer agreements, to Class Counsel being entitled to legal fees of $6,050,000 plus disbursements and taxes. The $4,500,000 inclusive of disbursements and taxes which DuPont has agreed to pay is clearly below that amount. In fact, after taxes and disbursements, the fees that will be paid are $3,023,956 which is almost exactly one-half of the amount provided for in the retainer agreements.

Class Counsel also point to the fact that significant time has been expended by them in pursuing this litigation. To date, I am told that the time invested in the file by all co-counsel is approximately $3,098,928 including taxes valued at regular hourly rates. Further, Class Counsel funded all of the disbursements associated with advancing the claims and did not apply to the Class Proceedings Fund for assistance. I am told that disbursements in excess of $1,279,507 inclusive of taxes have been incurred to date.

Class Counsel also note that considerable work remains to be done by them respecting the settlement including:

(a) responding to questions from class members regarding the Settlement Agreement;
(b) assisting class members with the completion and submission of their claims;
(c) assisting class members with the appeals process where necessary;
(d) monitoring the quality of service of the CPCF;
(e) involvement in any other matters which may arise as the Settlement Agreement is implemented.

Finally, Class Counsel offer certain comparatives to justify the fees to be received. They say that the fees and disbursements and taxes to be paid amount to 14.75% of the total value of the settlement. Once disbursements and taxes are paid, the legal fees remaining will amount to only 9.5% of the total value of the settlement. Class Counsel are required to pay all disbursements before applying settlement monies to fees. In this case, as I noted above, after the payment of all disbursements and applicable taxes, approximately $3,023,956 of the $4,500,000 will remain to pay fees. This equates to a multiplier of approximately 1.04 on the total time expended to date on the litigation by Class Counsel (including co-counsel).

I raised with counsel at the hearing a few concerns. First, I questioned my jurisdiction to approve fees for solicitors outside the Province of Ontario. In other words, I am uncertain on what basis I would necessarily approve the fees of lawyers from British Columbia, Quebec and the United States. For one thing, assuming that I can claim some knowledge, as part of my experience in fixing the costs of proceedings generally in this court, regarding the prevailing rates for lawyers in Ontario as well as some general idea of the amount of time that certain matters consume in the process of being litigated in Ontario, I am clearly without that level of knowledge when it comes to other jurisdictions. I also question why this court is being asked to pass on the fees to be received by lawyers in British Columbia and Quebec when the courts of those Provinces must also give their approval to the settlement.

Second, even assuming that I should approve the fees of all counsel involved, I am being asked in this case to approve a lump sum or block fee which the various lawyers involved will subsequently divide up among themselves. I am not convinced that that is the appropriate approach. It seems to me that counsel ought to have decided already what each group of counsel involved is going to receive from the total fees so that I can, in turn, measure the amount which each counsel group is to receive against their contribution to the overall prosecution of the litigation.

Third, I also questioned the appropriateness of using time spent on the certification motion as a justification for the reasonableness of the fees to be received. DuPont did not participate in the certification motion. The certification motion only involved the non-settling defendants and it was unsuccessful—at least it was before me. Certification has not been argued in the other Provinces. I question whether the time spent in a losing endeavour can provide a justification for the fees arising from a separate settlement. I will leave that concern at this time, however, as I intend to return to the whole issue of the approval of the fees at a later date.

As may be apparent, I am not prepared to approve the fees sought at this time. I am therefore going to adjourn the motion insofar as it seeks the approval of the fees. That aspect of the motion may be brought back before me once counsel have addressed at least the second concern by agreeing on the distribution that is to be made among themselves of the fees which are sought to be approved. Before bringing the matter back, however, counsel ought to consider how to address the first concern. In that regard, counsel may wish to consider whether it is more appropriate to ask each of the courts, before whom approval must be sought, to only approve the fees for the lawyers in their specific Province. That route, however, raises other issues including which court should approve the fees being paid to US counsel and what happens to any "surplus" created if a court reduces the fees for a particular group of counsel. Another alternative which counsel may wish to consider is whether some form of joint hearing by all three courts has to be held to address these issues.

On a final point, I suggest that any issue about the costs arising from this motion be addressed when the matter is brought back before the court for the final approval of the settlement. I will leave it up to counsel to determine if that final approval should await the approval hearings in Quebec and British Columbia in case further issues arise with respect to the basic settlement.

NOTES AND QUESTIONS

1. One unusual factor in this case was that certification had previously been denied. Should the value of the settlement to the class members therefore be weighed as against a non-viable individual claim, worth virtually nothing?

2. The judge spoke of the settlement as a fund of $30 million and said that the fees were only 9.5 percent of that amount, but should the total value of the settlement not be calculated on the basis of the claims likely to be made? In this case, that would be those who were willing to replumb their homes in order to claim 25 percent of the value of doing so. In this

particular case, the take-up rate was not entirely a matter of speculation as a similar settlement had previously been approved in the United States. This case did not involve the establishment of a fund per se, and so it was proposed that the defendant pay plaintiffs' counsel's fees directly. Is that appropriate?

3. Note that Posner J in *Reynolds* sets out a methodology by which the court can get a handle on the "value of the case" and start to understand what might justify the settlement—that is, why are we at a settlement proposal of $10 million rather than the $60 million originally claimed? (See the paragraph beginning "A high degree of precision cannot be expected in valuing a litigation.") In *Gariepy*, did the court go through a similar exercise? (Most Canadian courts do not.) How else can the court determine that the settlement is "fair, reasonable and in the best interests of class members"?

4. Two problematic forms of settlements are "coupon settlements" and reversionary settlements. Of the latter, Rand said: "When defendants keep any dollars not collected by class members [fees awarded on the basis of the negotiated size of a settlement fund, without regard to how many class members come forward to claim shares of the fund], this gives class action attorneys and defendants an incentive to collude in negotiating settlements whose actual monetary value is less than their face value." See also Lester Brickman, "Anatomy of a Madison County (Illinois) Class Action: A Study of Pathology" (2002), vol. 6 *Civil Justice Report*, who said:

> One of the more pernicious fee-setting devices that courts have permitted is the basing of the class action fee as a percentage of an artificially inflated settlement value when the reality is that the actual payments to the class will be a small fraction of the announced settlement value. This is what frequently occurs in the reversionary settlement ... where, ... any funds unclaimed by the class revert to the defendant. This provides an incentive to class counsel and defendant to act collusively to raise the stated amount of the settlement; the fee, which is usually a percentage of that amount, is thereby increased, thus paying off class counsel.

Is *DuPont* the same as a reversionary settlement—that is, will DuPont just keep the money that is not claimed?

5. Was the judge wise to deny Celanese standing to object to the settlement with DuPont? What if Celanese wanted to introduce evidence that, under a similar settlement by DuPont in the United States (but one paying only 10 percent of the cost of a replumb, not 25 percent) and involving a similar form of "administered fund" of $120 million, the take-up rate of the settlement had been very low while plaintiff class counsel was awarded $8.4 million in fees? Do you think that in seeking to oppose the settlement in *Gariepy*, Celanese was motivated by altruism or by a desire to stop the plaintiff's counsel from obtaining a war chest of $4.5 million with which to pursue appeals against Celanese and Shell re the denial of certification in the actions against them?

6. *Possible solutions to the "settlement problem."* Can settlements be improved through increased transparency? Numerous suggestions in this direction have been made by Rand and others—for example, class action outcomes and the reasons for them should be made more readily available to the judiciary, the profession, the press, and the public; the resources available to judges overseeing class actions should be increased; judges must give reasons for their decisions and the decisions themselves must be reasoned ones; full settlement

agreements should be appended to the reasons; steps should be taken to get such judgments reported, at least on electronic systems.

Professor Coffee has no faith in the Rand proposals—he does not believe that US judges can be relied on to improve the settlement approval process and he believes that other solutions must be found: see John C. Coffee Jr., "Class Action Accountability: Reconciling Exit, Voice, and Loyalty in Representative Litigation" (2000), 100 *Columbia L Rev.* 370. Is this also true of Canadian judges? Do they simply believe that any settlement is a good thing?

Suggestions have been made that monitors should be appointed to sit in on the whole litigation or at least all settlement discussions. See Alon Klement, "Who Should Guard the Guardians? A New Approach for Monitoring Class Action Lawyers" (2002), 21 *Review of Litigation* 25. (Klement sets out the economic incentives driving class counsel to settle at a point before class members would do so provided they were given the opportunity.)

Professor Garry Watson has argued that a major problem with the present regime is the lack of any adversarial presentation at the fairness hearing/settlements approval hearing and this needs to be changed because our courts rely on adversarial presentation. See Cara Zwibel, "Settling for Less: Problems and Proposals in the Settlement of Class Actions" (2004), 1 *Can. Class Action Rev.* 2, at 165:

> One final model that merits attention has been put forth by Prof. Garry Watson. The key difference with the Watson model is that it combines the role of the guardian as a monitor with the need for a dissenting voice in a settlement approval hearing. Under this model the individual appointed as a monitor would be a senior counsel and would have rights to discovery of the parties. Ideally the monitor should not be a member of the class action bar, in order to avoid collusion and prevent class action lawyers from using the guardian position to scratch each other's backs. Prof. Watson's litigation guardian would make submissions to the court with regards to: the accepted settlement approval factors; what will happen to any surplus in a settlement fund; the likely take-up rate of claims (i.e. the number of claimants who will pursue their claim under the settlement); what has occurred in similar settlements elsewhere; and any side agreements made during the course of negotiations.
>
> While Prof. Watson's model is in its early stages of development, it has some obvious benefits as well as some shortcomings. The major benefit under the Watson model is that the guardian is not only monitoring class counsel and the actions of the defendant, but is also monitoring the court. The monitor ensures that the fairness hearing allows for adequate attention to key issues. Despite this important benefit, Prof. Watson has acknowledged the concerns that the monitor not be co-opted by class counsel.

Watson proposes that the fees of the litigation guardian should normally be borne by the settling parties (who are prepared to throw millions at the settlement or take millions in fees). If a settlement is ultimately approved, it may be appropriate to deduct the litigation guardian's fees from the common fund.

7. As we will see below, Rand suggested that counsel fees should be based on the value of benefits actually received by class members—that is, fees should reflect actual claims made and amounts recovered by class members, rather than being determined merely by reference to the alleged total value of the settlement? Is this a sensible suggestion?

In the following case, *Gilbert v. CIBC*, the court approved a settlement and a fee determination in a class action alleging that CIBC, on its VISA cards, had been using a wholesale foreign exchange rate and then applying a mark-up fee when VISA holders made a purchase in foreign currency. Gilbert alleged that the mark-up fee constituted an undisclosed and unauthorized fee. A settlement was reached whereby CIBC agreed to pay a lump sum to the cardholders, or others in lieu of the cardholders.

Gilbert v. Canadian Imperial Bank of Commerce
(2004), 3 CPC (6th) 35 (Ont. SCJ)

WINKLER J (endorsement): This is a motion for certification as a class proceeding, on consent, and approval of a settlement in that class proceeding. There is a companion motion for approval of the class counsel fee.

CIBC, a chartered bank, has issued credit cards known as VISA cards in three categories, classic, premier and corporate. These cardholders may use the cards to make purchases in a foreign currency and be charged in Canadian dollars.

The Canadian dollar amount charged to cardholders in respect of foreign currency transactions since 1987 has been calculated using a foreign exchange rate established by applying a percentage mark-up to wholesale foreign exchange rates which are available to VISA International.

The plaintiffs allege that the mark-up charged constitutes undisclosed and unauthorized fees or charges in respect of debits and credits on their CIBC VISA accounts in foreign currency. CIBC responds in numerous ways to these allegations.

The specific allegations and claims were set forth in the statement of claim issued on July 22, 1997, later amended, and CIBC delivered its statement of defence as amended on November 19, 1998. On January 22, 2003, the plaintiffs received stage 1 funding from the Class Proceedings Committee.

In October 2003 the parties entered into settlement discussions, with disclosure by CIBC of pertinent information, culminating in an agreement in principle and ultimately a Settlement Agreement on August 13, 2004.

The essence of the settlement is as follows:

- CIBC will pay $16.5 million in full and final settlement of the claims of the class including interest.
- Up to $13.85 million will be paid directly to class members.
- At least $1 million will be paid to the United Way on behalf of certain class members.
- $1.65 million will be paid to the Class Proceedings Fund.
- Details of the particulars and mechanics of the settlement are contained in paragraph 3 of the plaintiffs' factum.
- CIBC will pay $3 million to counsel for the plaintiffs in full satisfaction of all fees, disbursements and taxes.

I am satisfied that all of the elements necessary for certification as a class proceeding are present. Even where certification is on consent the court must be satisfied that the requirements of s. 5 of the *Class Proceedings Act, 1992*, SO 1992, c. 6 have been met. …

There is a presumption of fairness when a proposed class settlement negotiated at arms length by class counsel is presented to the court for approval. A court will only reject a proposed settlement when it finds that the settlement does not fall within a range of reasonableness.

The test to be applied is whether the settlement is fair and reasonable and in the best interests of the class as a whole. This allows for a range of possible results and there is no perfect settlement. Settlement is a product of compromise, which by definition, necessitates give and take. It is a question of weighing the settlement in comparison to the alternative of litigation with its inherent risks and associated costs.

There are a number of factors, not all to be given equal weight, which are to be considered in determining whether to approve a settlement. These include likelihood of success, degree of discovery, the terms of the settlement, recommendation of counsel, expense and duration of litigation, number of objectors, presence of arms length bargaining, extent of communications with the class and the dynamics of the bargaining. See: *Dabbs v. Sun Life Assurance Co. of Canada*, 40 OR (3d) 429; *Parsons v. The Canadian Red Cross* …

There is a risk in this proceeding that if the matter went to trial the plaintiffs could not establish liability against CIBC. CIBC raised numerous defences including no need to disclose, the mark-up was reasonable, was understood and accepted, it did not retain all of the mark-up and limitation periods. Most striking, however, is the defence that new cardholders after 1994 were on notice regarding the terms of such transactions and that in 1996 all cardholders were given specific notice to this effect. The bank states that litigation risk to it after 1994 is minimal.

Even if the bank did not succeed on all of these defences there is a distinct possibility that it could reduce the recovery. If the case went to trial it would in all likelihood be a lengthy trial.

CIBC disclosed adequate pertinent information to the plaintiffs and the court to evaluate the claims.

I have reviewed the distribution schedule for the settlement funds as set out in paragraph 3 of the plaintiffs' factum. I am satisfied that it is appropriate in all of the circumstances. The distribution does not purport to reflect the actual transactions of each cardholder. The amount of individual payments to class members ranges from 72 cents to $14.32. These amounts are arbitrary and minor in amount. They do not purport to compensate class members in terms of actual amounts owing nor do they compensate only class members with valid claims. The bank justifies this scheme by stating that records are not available for a significant portion of the period in question and for periods when records are available the transactional analysis would simply be too costly and time consuming given the number and size of transactions. The CPA anticipates such a problem in s. 24(2) and (3) which provide that the court may order that an award be applied so that individual class members share in an award on an average or proportional basis and that the court shall consider whether it would be impractical or inefficient to identify class members entitled to share in the award or exact shares in making such a determination. This is the case in the present circumstances. One might observe that a situation such as this could be addressed with a settlement that is entirely Cy pres. However, it is not the role of this court to substitute its settlement for that fashioned by the parties. Also, a disadvantage of settlement that is entirely Cy pres is that it does not compensate individual class members.

Past cardholders are not part of the distribution list. The payment to the United Way on their collective part is in lieu of this and is acceptable given the peregrinations involved in pursuing those claims. This approach is acceptable in the present circumstances given the impossibility of identifying such class members. The CPA specifically contemplates a Cy pres distribution in s. 26(6). ... Other omissions from the distribution lists are also acceptable.

Plaintiffs' class counsel recommend the settlement. I accept this recommendation. They are highly experienced in class action litigation and their opinions are accorded considerable weight by this court. ...

Here the practicalities are such that if this case were not settled the likelihood of lengthy and expensive litigation going forward many years is a virtual certainty if these claims were to be pursued to finality. The settlement is a marked preference over the alternative. The settlement is a sensible one, and it is fair and reasonable.

Objections are a consideration in approving a settlement. The role of the court, however, is not to alter or amend a settlement. The court's exercise of discretion in determining whether to approve or reject a settlement is limited to approving or rejecting the settlement. Here counsel for the objectors William Dermody has received only 14 written objections. Given the size of the class, millions, this number is miniscule. Of the 14, two are not, in essence, objections. The remaining group includes some who became cardholders during the period when cardholders were on notice of the mark-up. These claims are problematic. The claims of others relate to periods when no records are available to track the transactions. There are only three objectors, other than these categories, whose claims are essentially that the amounts of compensation do not track their individual accounts. This may be so. If their claims involve substantial amounts, such persons may opt out and pursue their claims individually. Mr. Rhodes was the only objector to appear at the hearing and make submissions to the court. He submitted that the small number of objectors impugned the effectiveness of the notice. I cannot accept this submission. The notice was posted on the bank's web page and media notice was extensive although they were not, as he suggested they should be, sent to each account holder personally. His second point went to the arbitrary nature of the settlement distribution. He stated that he did not know what he was giving up for the settlement. His point in this respect has validity, although not in my view, sufficient to deny approval of the settlement. Without tracking each account no one knows these amounts, except perhaps individual cardholders. It must be remembered that the test is not whether the settlement meets the approval of each class member. Rather it is whether the settlement is in the best interests of the class as a whole.

The complaint that the settlement is arbitrary is not correct insofar as the overall settlement is concerned. That was established taking into account the profits of the bank relating to these transactions. As for individual settlement amounts, although arbitrary, these reflect the fact that during the majority of the period when liability is strongest for the plaintiffs, data is non-existent to establish individual claim amounts. During the period when the data is still in existence, the liability of the bank is problematic given the notice given by it to cardholders. In light of these facts, the structure of the settlement is acceptable. One of the goals of the CPA is behavioral modification. This goal, often given short shrift, is meaningful. In cases such as this, behavioral modification will justify the result achieved by class counsel. The amounts paid by the bank are substantial.

Prior to the settlement counsel did not communicate with registered class members because of the vast size of the class. It was impracticable to do so. However, the representative plaintiffs support and recommend this settlement.

I am satisfied that this settlement is fair, reasonable and in the best interests of the class as a whole. Accordingly, the settlement is approved.

The fee agreement between class counsel and the representative plaintiffs provides for a fixed fee of 20% of the amount recovered plus GST and disbursements contingent upon success. This computes to $3,530,000 plus disbursements and GST. Class counsel succeeded in having CIBC agree to pay $3 million all-inclusive in full satisfaction of the fee. In considering a class counsel fee the court must consider the success achieved and the risk associated with pursuing the litigation. See: *Gagne v. Silcorp*, 41 OR (3d) 417 (Ont. CA). As for the appropriateness, of a percentage contingent fee unrelated to actual work done, see: *Crown Bay Hotel Ltd. Partnership v. Zurich Indemnity Company*, 40 OR (3d) 83. The fee asked for and agreed to be paid by CIBC is within the accepted range and is approved.

Counsel and the Class Proceedings Fund are in dispute as to the Funds entitlement to a 10% portion of the counsel fee. Counsel have agreed to segregate this amount from their fee until this issue has been resolved.

NOTES AND QUESTIONS

1. Note that there was no indication in the judgment as to the amount claimed, what the case might have been worth—that is, no "Posnerian" analysis (the type of analysis of what the case might have been worth as Posner J did in *Reynolds*).

2. The settlement provided for direct payment by the defendant of class counsels' fees, notwithstanding that the total value of the settlement was clearly ascertained.

3. Winkler J notes that the only objector to the CIBC settlement took issue with the effectiveness of the notice of settlement provided to class members. Should CIBC have been required to give personal notice to all current card holders by including a notice of the proposed settlement in each card holder's monthly statement? Do you think the CIBC would be happy to do that? Might it have been willing to pay to avoid having to do that? If so, who would it pay? Had it given personal notice, would there likely have been more objectors?

4. In *Cassano v. Toronto-Dominion Bank*, [2005] OJ No. 845; rev'd. (2007), 87 OR (3d) 401 (CA), Cullity J refused to certify a similar case where certification was contested on the grounds that the loss in this case cannot be established on a class-wide basis. The agreement between the bank and cardholders differs from other contractual agreements in that the bank has a right to determine what charges will be made without the agreement of the other contracting parties. Without individual assessment, it cannot be assumed that any of the

cardholders would have behaved any differently had the fees been disclosed. A class proceeding will not be preferable to individual proceedings to resolve claims that cannot be
managed efficiently on a class-wide basis. The Court of Appeal disagreed and the matter
eventually came back to Justice Cullity in a motion to approve a settlement, which is considered in the following judgment. Like the *Gilbert* case, the settlement in *Cassano* involved
a substantial portion that was to be distributed *cy pres*. Who should decide where that money goes? And on what basis? Consider the careful analysis in *Cassano* and see if you agree
that the award was "as near as may be" to its proper purpose.

Cassano v. Toronto-Dominion Bank
[2009] OJ No. 2922 (SCJ)

M.C. CULLITY J: The parties moved for approval of the settlement of this action commenced under the *Class Proceedings Act, 1992*, SO 1992, c. 6 ("CPA").

The claims advanced on behalf of the class concern allegedly undisclosed and unauthorised charges levied by the defendant (the "Bank") for foreign currency transactions conducted with Visa credit cards it had issued. The Bank asserts that these were
not fees but rather part of the exchange rates that it was authorized by the provisions of
the cardholder agreements to determine from time to time. ...

The Settlement

... in all cases, the court must weigh the benefits to be conferred on the class against the
risks of continuing the litigation.

From the inception of the proceeding, the Bank has denied that the charges were fees
rather than part of the exchange rates it was authorised to determine from time to time.
It has also asserted that the rates were reasonable and that the plaintiffs' interpretation of
the cardholder agreements was contrary to the intentions of the parties, as well as inconsistent with commercial realities and the competitive practices adopted by other financial
institutions. At the hearing of the motion, the Bank's counsel emphasised that it was the
economic considerations of proceeding to trial and not any acknowledgement of the
validity of the claims advanced by the plaintiffs that influenced its agreement to settle.
The Bank has not resiled from its position that the alleged charges were disclosed to
cardholders.

While strongly contesting the correctness of the Bank's characterisation of the charges, class counsel were conscious that, on the main issue, this was all-or-nothing litigation,
and that it would be vigorously defended. Even if the plaintiffs were successful in charac-
terising the charges as fees, there were still limitations defences that potentially affected
a significant number of the class members' claims. They were also concerned about the
length and future expense of the litigation if it proceeded to trial and the difficulty that
class members would have in proving their damages if individual determinations were
found to be required.

... class counsel had estimated that the maximum amount recoverable for the class
was approximately $161.5 million. After taking into account the risk that the Bank would

succeed at trial, class counsel targeted $50 million-$60 million as a reasonable range for settlement. ... The plaintiffs' subsequent acceptance of the Bank's offer to pay $55 million in settlement of the claims was recommended by the mediator. ... In this case, the most difficult questions relate not to the amount the Bank has agreed to contribute in settlement of the claims advanced by the plaintiffs but rather to the nature and extent of the distributions that are proposed.

... In view of the difficulty of identifying class members with potential claims and quantifying the harm each had suffered, the requirement that the procedure of the CPA must be manageable was given considerable weight in this court and in the Divisional Court. In *Markson*, the proceeding was held to be manageable because, it seems, of the Court of Appeal's conclusion that there was a reasonable likelihood that an aggregate assessment of damages would be possible. The question whether difficulties of distributing damages had any bearing on the issue of manageability was not discussed, ...

A similar conclusion that an aggregate assessment of damages might be available was reached by the Court of Appeal in this case ... the Chief Justice accepted that problems of distribution may have some relevance to the issue of manageability that is inherent in the requirement that a class proceeding is the preferable procedure. Paras. 67-68 of the reasons of the Court of Appeal read as follows:

> [67] The CPA also provides a range of options for distributing amounts awarded under ss. 24 or 25. For example, s. 26(2)(a) permits the court to require the defendant to distribute monetary relief directly to class members "by any means authorised by the court, including abatement and credit." I draw particular attention to s. 26(3), which states:
>
> > 26(3) In deciding whether to make an order under clause (2)(a), a court shall consider whether distribution by the defendant is the most practical way of distributing the award for any reason, *including the fact that the amount of monetary relief to which each class member is entitled can be determined from the records of the Bank.* (emphasis in the original).
>
> [68] Evidently, the CPA provides a procedural mechanism on which the trial judge could rely to distribute amounts awarded under either s. 24 or s. 25. Thus, in my view, the preferable procedure requirement is satisfied in this case regardless of whether the assessment and distribution of damages, if necessary, are to be conducted on an aggregate or individual basis.

In this context, I note that the learned Chief Justice attributed no significance to the Bank's evidence that "it would take 1500 people about one year to identify and record the foreign exchange transactions on the cardholder statements that are available only on microfiche and that this would cost about $48,500,000": para. 48. As in *Markson*, this "economic argument" was specifically rejected.

Despite the emphasis given to section 26(3) of the CPA, I do not understand the Chief Justice to have excluded the possibility that the trial judge might rely on other provisions of section 26, including section 26(4) and (6) that read as follows:

> 26(4) The court may order that all or a part of an award under section 24 that has not been distributed within a time set by the court be applied in any manner that may reason-

ably be expected to benefit class members, even though the order does not provide for monetary relief to individual class members, if the court is satisfied that a reasonable number of class members who would not otherwise receive monetary relief would benefit from the order.

26(6) The court may make an order under subsection (4) even if the order would benefit,
    (a) persons who are not class members; or
    (b) persons who may otherwise receive monetary relief as a result of the class proceeding.

These provisions contemplate what are often called cy pres orders by analogy to the cy pres jurisdiction that courts of equity have traditionally applied in cases involving charities and rules against remoteness. As was the case in *Gilbert*, such orders are commonly made in settlements approved by the court by a further analogy to the provisions of section 26. In *Gilbert*, the settlement that was approved by the court provided for a payment of $1 million out of the settlement amount of $16.5 million to the United Way in order to benefit past cardholders who could no longer be identified.

· · ·

Under the proposed settlement in this case, approximately $39,100,000 would be available for distribution for the benefit of class members after the payment of the counsel fees and disbursements requested, the levy payable to the Law Foundation and administrative expenses out of the settlement amount of $55 million. From the amount of $39,150,000, approximately $10,750,000 would be paid directly to cardholders whose cards were issued before certain dates included in the class definition, and who were in good standing and active as of June 1, 2009. The balance of approximately $28.4 million would be applied cy pres as, despite the Court of Appeal's reference to section 26(3) of the CPA, the parties are in agreement that it would be impracticable to attempt to identify more than a relatively small percentage of the class members who are potential claimants.

Before finalising their proposals for the division between direct and indirect benefits to class members, counsel devoted considerable time and energy in considering different alternatives. The task of identifying cardholders who had engaged in foreign currency transactions—as well as the amounts involved—was hampered by the absence of records including some that had been destroyed inadvertently during the course of the proceeding. The various alternatives were discussed at case conferences prior to the hearing before counsel agreed on a final proposal.

I am satisfied that, in the light of these difficulties and when compared with the other alternatives, the proposed division between direct and indirect benefits strikes a reasonable balance between reimbursing class members and applying funds cy pres and should be approved. Although, as a general rule, cy pres distributions should not be approved where direct compensation to class members is practicable, the allocation of $10.75 million to be paid directly to cardholders is on the generous side as proof that one subgroup of them engaged in foreign currency transactions—and, in consequence, were within the class definition—will not be required.

As a general rule, the court's jurisdiction on motions under section 29(2) of the CPA is limited to granting, or withholding, approval. Exceptionally in this case, the minutes of settlement provide that, as part of the approval process, the court may change the amount proposed to be applied cy pres, the cy pres recipients and the division of funds between them. This provision reflects the parties' understanding that, in view of the size of the cy pres amount and the nature of the claims in this case, outright payments to charitable or other non-profit organisations—the most common form of cy pres distributions—might not be appropriate. For this reason, it was proposed that special purpose gifts would be made in order to ensure that the purposes for which the funds would be applied bore a sufficient relation to the interests and claims of the class members to justify a conclusion that the distribution would be for their benefit.

The question of the most appropriate cy pres distributions was discussed in a number of case conferences. Proposals by the plaintiffs with respect to one half of the cy pres amount of $28.4 million, and by the Bank for the other half were considered.

Cy Pres: The Plaintiffs' Proposal

The plaintiffs' original proposal involved grants to Canadian common law law schools to be used to foster professionalism and ethical conduct among practising lawyers. The amounts each law school would receive would reflect the distribution of class members across the country. It was suggested that teaching law students to be more professional and ethical in their behaviour when practising law would benefit class members and the public. It was said that:

> Contracts such as those in issue in this action may be more carefully drafted, banks, commercial institutions and all clients may be better advised and, as a result, disputes such as in this action and others may be avoided.

Apart from the establishment of a committee of five to seven members of the legal profession, with volunteers from the judiciary, to receive proposals and to disburse the funds to the law schools, no method of supervising or controlling the expenditure of the funds by the recipients was suggested. It may have been contemplated that the use of the funds would be entirely within the discretion of the recipients subject only to a moral obligation to apply them for the approved purposes.

Without—I hope—being unduly cynical about the optics of the plaintiffs' proposal in the present context, I suggested that a preferable alternative would be to create a trust fund to be administered by the Law Foundation of Ontario for the purpose of advancing public access to justice in Canada. Although in a number of cases—including *Gilbert*—cy pres distributions that benefit class members together with other members of the public have been approved, the suggested alternative would confer benefits on the class more directly than the original proposal and would do so in a manner that is consistent with, and would advance, one of the objectives of the CPA. Access to justice was relied on heavily by the Court of Appeal in *Markson* and in this case as a ground for certifying the proceeding. Class members have benefited thereby and they and other members of the public would benefit from its enhancement in the future.

This suggestion was discussed with representatives of the Law Foundation—including the Chair of its Board of Trustees and they have indicated that it is acceptable in principle.

The proposal contemplates the creation of a special trust fund to be administered by the Trustees of the Foundation. Section 56(2) of the *Law Society Act*, RSO 1990, c. L.8 provides that the Trustees have power to accept gifts and donations on trust in further-ance of the objects of the foundation. The objects include "legal aid"—a term that, I am informed, has been construed broadly by the Trustees and has, correctly in my opinion, not been confined to financial aid provided to Legal Aid Ontario—a corporation that is incorporated pursuant to the *Legal Aid Services Act, 1998*, SO 1998, c. 26 for the purpose of providing access to justice for low-income individuals, and is referred to by name in section 55 of the *Law Society Act*.

There are, of course, special difficulties that can be encountered in establishing valid purpose trusts under the laws of Ontario. Such trusts are not valid unless they are exclu-sively charitable, or can be treated as powers of appointment pursuant to section 16 of the *Perpetuities Act*, RSO 1990, c. P.9. In my opinion, this limitation is as applicable to trusts created pursuant to an order of the court as it is to other trusts and, if that is not correct, it is still one that the court should respect.

Is the purpose of promoting and advancing access to justice a charitable purpose? Given the repeated endorsement by courts, as well as by the Law Reform Commission, of access to justice as a socially valuable objective of the CPA—and even ignoring some of the rather more dubiously valuable purposes that have been accepted as charitable over the years—it would, I believe, be extraordinary if it were held that it is not worthy of recognition as a possible object of a valid trust. ...

I do not think there is any doubt that a purpose of providing or promoting access to justice must be considered to be beneficial to the public. As the Law Reform Commission stated, at page 139 of its report:

> Quite clearly, effective access to justice is a precondition to the exercise of all other legal rights.

Access to justice is, in other words, an essential component of the rule of law which, in turn, is one of the constitutional underpinnings of our democratic constitutional sys-tem of government. ...

For these reasons, I am satisfied that the proposed establishment of a fund to promote access to justice would create a valid charitable trust. I am also satisfied that such a trust could properly be administered by the Law Foundation as falling within its corporate object of "legal aid." As I have mentioned, this is consistent with the information provid-ed by the Chair of the board of Trustees of the Foundation that the object has in the past been construed broadly and has not been confined to financial aid provided to Legal Aid Ontario.

For reasons of completeness, I note, also, that if, contrary to my opinion, a trust to promote and advance access to justice is not charitable, it could I believe be upheld as a specific non-charitable purpose trust that, pursuant to section 16 of the *Perpetuities Act*, is to be treated as a power of appointment over capital and income for a maximum per-iod of 21 years.

The precise terms of the trust will be included in the order approving the settlement but, subject to any further submissions of counsel, or representations of the Law Foundation, my present preference would be for the Trustees of the Foundation to have discretion as to the application of funds for the approved purpose subject only to the limitation that they are not to form part of the Class Proceedings Fund established pursuant to section 59.1 of the *Law Society Act*.

Cy Pres: The Bank's Proposal

The bank proposed that the other half of the cy pres amount should be used to improve the financial literacy of low-income and otherwise economically disadvantaged Canadians. For this purpose, the funds would be paid to, and administered and distributed by, a non-profit charitable organisation, Social and Enterprise Development Innovations ("SEDI"). ...

SEDI is registered as a charitable organisation within the meaning of the *Income Tax Act* (Canada). It complies with the annual reporting obligations under the statute. To date it has been funded largely through grants and donations from federal, provincial and municipal governments, banks and other financial institutions, and private charitable foundations.

The promotion of financial literacy has been one of SEDI's principal activities since its creation. To this end it has worked with governmental agencies and community organisations to develop courses, programmes and projects and to train personnel whose employment brings them in contact with unemployed, poor and otherwise disadvantaged Canadians. SEDI's activities are founded on a conviction that there are social, market and governmental pressures that limit the ability of such persons to make informed financial decisions that are essential to their well-being and their capacity to become economically self-sufficient. Accordingly, financial literacy, in the sense understood by SEDI, refers to the knowledge, skills and ability to understand, analyse and use information to make informed judgments about financial decisions. Such decisions range from simple budgeting skills, to understanding choices between banking and credit products, to understanding rights and obligations created by financial documents such as credit card agreements, to understanding how to effectively save for retirement, home-ownership, or post-secondary education.

SEDI is administered under the supervision of a nine-member board of directors who serve without remuneration. In 2008 it had ten permanent and four part-time employees.

By a resolution of the board of directors of October 9, 2008, SEDI's financial literacy activities were expanded and organised by the creation of a new internal division known as the "Canadian Centre for Financial Literacy" (the "Centre"). This is dedicated to assisting and training the staff of community organisations to deliver literacy counselling and supportive services to needy and otherwise disadvantaged groups in society.

The Bank's proposal is for 50 per cent of the cy pres amount to be paid to SEDI. $3.5 million of this would be used for the support of the Centre for a period of five years and the balance would be held as a fund (the "TD Financial Literacy Fund") that, over a period of six years, would be applied in making grants to non-profit organisations who work with economically disadvantaged groups—such grants to be used by the recipients to promote and support financial literacy among the members of such groups. All such grants would require the approval of SEDI's directors.

Counsel for the bank made submissions and filed extensive material in support of its proposals. This included a description of SEDI's activities during the past five years, the annual reports filed with Canada Revenue Agency, explanation of its financial reporting, and a legal opinion of SEDI's solicitor, Fasken Martineau, that the promotion of financial literacy is charitable in law as educational and for the relief of poverty, and is within the objects of SEDI. I share that opinion.

In addition, letters attesting to the valuable work performed by SEDI in promoting financial literacy among low-income Canadians were provided by five individuals who have either participated in SEDI's activities, or occupied positions with governmental organisations that have been involved with them.

On the basis of the submissions of counsel and the material filed, I am satisfied that the advancement of financial literacy is a worthy method of applying the cy pres amount for the benefit of the class members. I am also satisfied that SEDI is an appropriate entity to administer the funds for this purpose.

For the purpose of settling the terms of the approval order, counsel should consider whether it is necessary to have a trust agreement between the Bank and SEDI with respect to the administration of the funds. In view of the relatively simple and short-term obligations of SEDI, in may be possible to define those obligations adequately in the body of the order. It must, however, be made clear that the funds provided to the Centre for the support of its work are intended to enhance it and not simply to make available for SEDI's other purposes funds that would otherwise be used for the support of the Centre. Given the provisions of the *Law Society Act* that govern the administration of gifts received by the Trustees of the Law Foundation, a separate trust agreement with respect to the other half of the cy pres amount should not be necessary to complement the provisions of the order.

Subject to settling the terms of the order, the settlement will be approved. ...

NOTES AND QUESTIONS

1. Can a settlement where the class get nothing but the defendant pays class counsel fees ever be "fair and reasonable and in the best interests of the class"? In *K. Field Resources Ltd. v. Bell Canada International Inc.*, [2005] OJ No. 3935 (SCJ) (*"BCI"*), the court approved a settlement that provided for (1) dismissal of the plaintiff's action without costs, and (2) payment of $3 million to class counsel. The case involved an oppression claim brought on behalf of holders of a type of the defendant's debentures. The action had been certified on consent and the court approved the settlement because after reviewing the relevant facts and law, class counsel concluded and the court agreed that the action would fail at trial, despite the fact that class counsel worked intensively and extensively on the case, and put the "defendants' feet ... to the fire." Dismissal at trial would have exposed the representative plaintiffs to liability for an estimated $4 million in costs and the settlement would permit class members to recoup a "reasonable proportion" of their claims by participating in a distribution pursuant to the *Canada Business Corporations Act*. Finally, the proposed settlement had

been negotiated during mediation with "a very experienced mediator and a very knowledgeable commercial judge."

This settlement approval stands in contrast to the decision in *Epstein v. First Marathon Inc.*, [2000] OJ No. 452 (SCJ) in which the court dismissed the proposed class action without costs on the condition that there was to be "no payment of any monies" to class counsel. In *Epstein*, a minority shareholder oppression case, the representative plaintiff had sought approval of a settlement that provided for dismissal without costs and payment of $190,000 to class counsel. The court noted that the plaintiff had filed an amended statement of claim purporting to reconstitute the proceeding as an individual action in what His Honour deemed an apparent attempt to avoid court scrutiny of the settlement. In refusing to approve the proposed settlement payment to class counsel, the plaintiff's action was characterized as a "strike suit" and an "abuse of substance and procedure of the CPA."

2. Returning to the *BCI* case, is it true that the class members received nothing? "A dismissal at trial of the claim would have exposed the class representatives to substantial costs—estimated at $4 million. If anything, I would think this may be somewhat understated." Discontinuance of an action usually requires that the plaintiff pay the defendant's costs to date. Short of trial, these costs would likely have been less than $4 million, but after three years of litigation, they would have been substantial. Who would have been "on the hook" for these costs? Should representative plaintiffs be allowed to "save their own hide" by settling the claims of class members for nothing?

3. *Different standards for certification in contested matters and settlement approvals.* Before approving the settlement of a class action, the court will be asked by the parties to certify the action. It is now clear from the case law that courts are applying different standards for certification depending on whether the claim is opposed or whether certification is being sought as part of a proposed settlement. In a number of early class proceedings with respect to "vanishing premiums" or "premium offset" actions were certified pursuant to settlement agreements (that is, they were unopposed): see, for example, *Dabbs v. Sun Life Assurance Co. of Canada* (1998), 40 OR (3d) 429 (Gen. Div.); *McKrow v. Manufacturers Life Insurance Co.* (1998), 28 CPC (4th) 104 (Ont. Gen. Div.).

Later, in similar types of cases *where the defendant opposed certification*, certification was refused. In *Williams v. Mutual Life Assurance Co. of Canada* (2000), 51 OR (3d) 54 (SCJ), Cumming J held that in such a case the claims of the class members did not raise common issues as required by s. 5(1)(c) of the *Class Proceedings Act, 1992*. A similar result was reached in *Zicherman v. Equitable Life Insurance Company*, [2000] OJ No. 5144 (SCJ). Both decisions were affirmed on appeal (2001), 2001 CarswellOnt 4449; 152 OAC 344; [2002] ILR I-4052; [2001] OJ No. 4952 (Div. Ct.) *sub nom. Kumar v. Mutual Life Assurance Company*. However, Cumming J later certified two "vanishing premiums" or "premium offset" cases where settlement approval was sought (that is, certification was unopposed) without any reference to his decision in *Williams* (or that in *Zicherman*): *Gibbs v. Jarvis* (2001), 10 CPC (5th) 332 (SCJ); *Directright Cartage Ltd. v. London Life Insurance Co.*, 2001 CarswellOnt 3658; [2001] ILR I-4013; 34 CCLI (3d) 118 (Ont. SCJ). In both of these cases he held that the criteria for certification, including the presence of a common issue, were satisfied.

In *Gariepy v. Shell Oil Company*, [2002] OJ No. 2766 (SCJ), Nordheimer J refused certification of a class action, against Shell, regarding allegedly defective polybutelene plumbing pipes, the basic ingredient of which was manufactured by the Shell and others. The court held, *inter alia*, that the plaintiff had not satisfied the common issue requirement because of the abundance of individual issues left to be determined in assessing causation for the leaks in each plumbing system. However, shortly thereafter in *Gariepy v. Shell Oil Company*, [2002] OJ No. 4022, Nordheimer J certified for settlement the very same class action against a different defendant, DuPont. He stated:

> The first issue is whether this action should be certified as a class proceeding for the purposes of the proposed settlement. The requirements for certification in a settlement context are the same as they are in a litigation context and are set out in section 5 of the *Class Proceedings Act, 1992*. However, their application need not, in my view, be as rigorously applied in the settlement context as they should be in the litigation context, principally because the underlying concerns over the manageability of the ongoing proceeding are removed.

Is this application of different standards for certification, depending on whether or not it is opposed as part of a proposed settlement, a good or a bad thing? The US case law is to the contrary. In *Amchem Products, Inc. v. Windsor*, 521 US 591 (1997), the US Supreme Court held that the standard for certification does not change where certification is for the purpose of settlement (as opposed to situations where certification is contested). The court reasoned that with a lower standard of certification for settlement, plaintiff's counsel with no ability of going to trial would lack the bargaining power to get a proper settlement for the class. Can a good case be made for the Canadian approach along the following lines?

While the United States can live with "no lower standard for certification for settlement," Canada should not take this route; there is a significant difference between the dynamics of class actions in the two countries. In the United States, in many class actions (particularly mass tort cases) there is an alternative to a class action. That is, typically, the class members' claims are independently viable so the plaintiff class members do not necessarily go away empty-handed if the court refuses to lower the standard for certification in the face of a proposed class action settlement. They can simply bring their individual action; this was exactly the situation before the US courts embraced class actions for mass torts. (In *Amchem*, the underlying asbestos claims were clearly individually viable.) This is generally not the situation in Canada. Class actions in Canada have allowed the assertion of claims through the class action mechanism that otherwise would never have been litigated because the underlying claims are not individually viable. The major achievement of class actions in Canada is to afford access to justice for claims that otherwise would not be asserted. This means that if Canadian courts refuse to certify a settlement class they, in effect, turn the plaintiff class away empty handed—that is, if they hold that the certification criteria have not been met then they will turn away the case without even looking at (or ever reaching the question of) the adequacy of the settlement. Of course, this does not mean that Canadian courts should always approve a settlement, and certainly not where they feel the settlement is inadequate. As long as the court has not determined that the case cannot be certified— that is, the court approves certification—the court must hold a fairness hearing and can refuse to approve the settlement, in effect sending plaintiff's counsel and defence counsel back to the bargaining table. It is hoped, in these circumstances, that a better offer will be forthcoming from the defendant, one that the court can approve. The logic of this argument is that the court should always certify a class where there is an agreement as to certification by plaintiff's counsel and the defendant—and then move to the really important step, which is the fairness hearing. The case law discussed above suggests this is exactly what the courts are doing.

C. Fees: Remunerating Class Counsel

Under the class proceedings legislation, the court must approve fees for class counsel; the amount so approved becomes a first charge on any settlement funds or monetary award. The governing statutory provisions are often complex—for example, the Ontario Act provides:

Agreements Respecting Fees and Disbursements

32(1) An agreement respecting fees and disbursements between a solicitor and a representative party shall be in writing and shall,

(a) state the terms under which fees and disbursements shall be paid;

(b) give an estimate of the expected fee, whether contingent on success in the class proceeding or not; and

(c) state the method by which payment is to be made, whether by lump sum, salary or otherwise.

Court to approve agreements

(2) An agreement respecting fees and disbursements between a solicitor and a representative party is not enforceable unless approved by the court, on the motion of the solicitor.

Priority of amounts owed under approved agreement

(3) Amounts owing under an enforceable agreement are a first charge on any settlement funds or monetary award.

Determination of fees where agreement not approved

(4) If an agreement is not approved by the court, the court may,

(a) determine the amount owing to the solicitor in respect of fees and disbursements;

(b) direct a reference under the rules of court to determine the amount owing; or

(c) direct that the amount owing be determined in any other manner.

Agreements for Payment Only in the Event of Success

33(1) Despite the *Solicitors Act* and *An Act Respecting Champerty*, being chapter 327 of Revised Statutes of Ontario, 1897, a solicitor and a representative party may enter into a written agreement providing for payment of fees and disbursements only in the event of success in a class proceeding.

Interpretation: success in a proceeding

(2) For the purpose of subsection (1), success in a class proceeding includes,

(a) a judgment on common issues in favour of some or all class members; and

(b) a settlement that benefits one or more class members.

Definitions

(3) For the purposes of subsections (4) to (7),

"base fee" means the result of multiplying the total number of hours worked by an hourly rate;

"multiplier" means a multiple to be applied to a base fee.

Agreements to increase fees by a multiplier

(4) An agreement under subsection (1) may permit the solicitor to make a motion to the court to have his or her fees increased by a multiplier.

Motion to increase fee by a multiplier

(5) A motion under subsection (4) shall be heard by a judge who has,

(a) given judgment on common issues in favour of some or all class members; or

(b) approved a settlement that benefits any class member.

(6) Where the judge referred to in subsection (5) is unavailable for any reason, the regional senior judge shall assign another judge of the court for the purpose.

(7) On the motion of a solicitor who has entered into an agreement under subsection (4), the court,

(a) shall determine the amount of the solicitor's base fee;

(b) may apply a multiplier to the base fee that results in fair and reasonable compensation to the solicitor for the risk incurred in undertaking and continuing the proceeding under an agreement for payment only in the event of success; and

(c) shall determine the amount of disbursements to which the solicitor is entitled, including interest calculated on the disbursements incurred, as totalled at the end of each six-month period following the date of the agreement.

(8) In making a determination under clause (7)(a), the court shall allow only a reasonable fee.

(9) In making a determination under clause (7)(b), the court may consider the manner in which the solicitor conducted the proceeding.

In *Gagne v. Silcorp Limited* (1998), 41 OR (3d) 417 (CA), the Court of Appeal allowed an appeal by plaintiff's counsel against a refusal by the judge at first instance to approve their contingent fee with a multiplier of three of their base fee, and, instead, awarded a fee with a multiplier of two. In the course of its reasons the court made the following statements:

Risk Factors

The multiplier is in part a reward to the solicitor for bearing the risks of acting in the litigation. The court must determine whether these risks were sufficient that together with the other relevant considerations a multiplier is warranted. While this determination is made after the class proceeding has concluded successfully, it is the risks when the litigation commenced and as it continued that must be assessed.

· · ·

I recognize that the selection of the precise multiplier is an art, not a science. All the relevant factors must be weighed. Here, while the risk of an adverse finding on liability was minimal, there was a material risk of non-certification. As well, as I have outlined, there were significant elements of success in the manner in which the solicitors conducted the proceedings. Weighed against these success factors is the fact that following the April 17, 1997 settlement, individual class members had to incur further legal fees to finally realize on their claims.

In the end, three considerations must yield a multiplier that, in the words of s. 33(7)(b), results in fair and reasonable compensation to the solicitors. One yardstick by which this can be tested is the percentage of gross recovery that would be represented by the multiplied base fee. If the base fee as multiplied constitutes an excessive proportion of the total recovery, the multiplier might well be too high. A second way of testing whether the ultimate compensation is fair and reasonable is to see whether the multiplier is appropriately placed in a range that might run from slightly greater than one to three or four in the most deserving case. Thirdly, regard can be had to the retainer agreement in determining what is fair and reasonable. Finally, fair and reasonable compensation must be sufficient to provide a real economic incentive to solicitors in the future to take on this sort of case and to do it well.

Although the Ontario Act seems to assume that the court will determine fees based on the multiplier approach, in fact counsel may request a straight percentage contingency fee and courts may approve such a fee with only passing reference to the multiplier approach.

Parsons v. Canadian Red Cross (2000), 49 OR (3d) 281 (SCJ)—the Hepatitis C/tainted blood litigation—although unusual in both the size of the settlement and the amount of the fees approved, is fairly representative of the approach of the courts in fixing fees. The global amount of the settlement was $1.5 billion. Class counsel sought and obtained court approval of their fees in the amount of $52.5 million. The court observed that the appropriateness of a premium fee, whether as a lump sum, a percentage of the recovery, or a multiplier of the base fee must be assessed against the facts of each case. The adoption of any standard multiplier or percentage fee would undoubtedly result in fee awards that have little relation to the risk undertaken or the results achieved. For example, a fee based on 20 percent or more of the recovery would be clearly excessive and would represent a windfall for the counsel's groups. The court then turned to a series of "useful, corroborating tests for analyzing the fairness and reasonableness of the fee" set out by Goudge JA in *Gagne*—testing the fee as a percentage against recovery, as a multiple of base fees, and against the retainer agreement and whether, in the circumstances, the fee will provide sufficient incentive for counsel to take on difficult cases in the future.

First, viewing the requested fee as a percentage of class recovery, the fees sought in the transfused action represented 2.36 percent of the portion of the settlement apportionable to the Ontario national class victims; the work in the haemophiliac action was for the benefit of all haemophiliacs and the fees sought equated to 3.33 percent of the amount of the settlement apportionable to the haemophiliac class members. On this basis, Winkler J concluded that the fees, although large, were more than reasonable. Second, testing the fees as a multiple of the base fee docketed by class counsel the lump-sum fees constituted a multiple of 3.57 in the transfused action and 4.29 in the haemophiliac action (if certain "additional work" to finalize the settlement was excluded). When the fees for the additional work were included, however, the multipliers were 3.07 and 3.87, respectively. Third, the fees were measured by the expectation of the representative plaintiff as evidenced by the retainer agreement.

NOTES AND QUESTIONS

1. In *Tesluk v. Boots Pharmaceutical PLC* (2002), 21 CPC (5th) 196 (Ont. SCJ), the court held that a higher percentage fee is justified where the recovery is relatively low, and it approved a fee representing about 27.4 percent of the recovery of about $2.25 million. In *Alfresh Beverages Canada Corp. v. Hoechst* (2002), 16 CPC (5th) 301 (Ont. SCJ), the court approved a multiplier of 3 in a price-fixing claim; in *Ho-A-Shoo v. Canada (Attorney General)*, 2001 DTC 5589 (Ont. SCJ), the court approved a fee representing about 60 percent of the recovery; in *Delgrosso v. Paul* (2001), 10 CPC (5th) 317 (Ont. SCJ), the court approved a fee

of about 28.9 percent of the amount recovered, which was equivalent to a multiplier of about 3.5; and in *Directright Cartage Ltd. v. London Life Insurance Co.* (2001), 34 CCLI (3d) 118 (Ont. SCJ), the court approved a fee of $7.5 million in a "premium offset" life insurance case, although the fee was to be received partly based on the time spent and then upon the amount of the award actually distributed.

2. *Statutory provisions for agreement between the representative plaintiff and class counsel re fees.* Class action legislation typically provides for the representative plaintiff and class counsel to enter into an agreement on fees and for the court to approve or disapprove such an agreement. Given that frequently class counsel will have chosen the representative plaintiff, do such provisions make any sense? Why should a deal struck between class counsel and a friendly representative plaintiff be the basis for binding the proceeds of a class action, which belong not to the representative plaintiff, but to all the class members? What is the rationale for such statutory provisions?

3. *Non-adversarial hearings.* Typically, fee approval hearings are non-adversarial—no one appears to oppose the requested fees; according to the case law, the defendant, having agreed to pay the settlement amount, no longer has an interest in the disposition of the funds nor standing on the fees issue. Class counsel appears, unopposed, asking the court to give them a sizeable amount of the proceeds of the action, which belong to the class. At this stage class counsel is not representing the class, but is in a real sense directly opposed to the class. (Class members may appear as "objectors" to oppose the fee approval, but this occurs rarely.)

Are non-adversarial hearings likely to be effective, given that our judges are used to adversarial hearings where they hear the arguments pro and con the requested relief? If it is a problem, how might it be solved? (As we saw above, a similar problem arises with settlement approval hearings where invariably the plaintiff and defendant both support the settlement approval and there is no adversarial presentation.)

4. *Should fees be determined in relation to the actual benefits created by the lawsuit?* Often in class actions there may be a "low take-up rate"—that is, few class members actually come forward to make an individual claim. Should fees reflect actual claims made and amounts recovered by class members, rather than being determined merely by reference to the alleged total value of the settlement?

According to the Report of the Rand Institute for Civil Justice, *Class Action Dilemmas: Pursuing Public Goals for Private Gain* (Santa Monica, CA: Rand Institute for Civil Justice, 2000), available online at: http://www.rand.org/publications/MR/MR969/, fees should be determined in relation to the *actual* benefits created by the lawsuit. In awarding fees, the court should follow a general rule that fees not be calculated on the basis of some estimate of the value of the total settlement, but on the basis of claims actually made by class members. Moreover, fees should not be paid until claims are made by class members. This ensures two things: (1) that counsel is not being compensated out of proportion to the actual value of the class action to the class members, and (2) that an incentive is created (by postponing payment until claims are made) for plaintiff's counsel to follow through and maximize claims made by class members. The report recommended that judges should:

- award fees in the form of a percentage of the fund *actually disbursed* to class members or other beneficiaries of the litigation

- award fees based on the monetary value of settlement coupons *redeemed*, not coupons offered
- award less, proportionally, when the total actual value of the settlement is very large
- award less, proportionally, when settlements are disbursed to nonclass members—cy pres remedies—except in instances where direct compensation to class members is clearly impracticable
- use phased awards when projected payouts are uncertain and disbursements will be made over time.

Is Rand's argument sound? What are the competing arguments?

5. In this context, consider Nordheimer J's ultimate approval of class counsel's requested fee of $4.5 million in the *Gariepy/DuPont* litigation and his reasoning, [2003] OJ No. 2490:

> In considering each of the appropriate factors, I accept that class counsel have spent a great deal of time on this matter. Class counsel became involved in this matter six years ago. The action itself has been ongoing for four years. I also accept that the issues raised are complicated and that class counsel have assumed considerable responsibility in deciding to take on the task of prosecuting these claims. There is a significant monetary value to the claims as the settlement of $30 million dollars would aptly demonstrate. There is also no question as to the skill and competence of class counsel. The factors of the client's ability to pay and the expectation of the client regarding the amount of the fee do not really come into play in this case as the class is not paying the fees nor are the fees being taken out of what would otherwise be funds available to settle the class members' claims. However, insofar as the retainer agreements evidence the expectation of the representative plaintiffs regarding the fees to be paid to class counsel, the fees sought are well within the terms of those agreements.
>
> Where I have some difficulty in this case is with the factors regarding the importance of the matter to the client and the results achieved. At this stage, there is no information available as to the number of members of the class who will actually decide to take up the settlement offered. Without that information, it is difficult to fully evaluate the results achieved. It is also difficult to evaluate whether the resolution of the claims was truly important to the class members. Put another way, if very few of the members of the class wind up taking advantage of the settlement, that might be some evidence that the results of the settlement were less favourable than they might otherwise appear to be and/or that the issue itself is not one of great importance to the members of the class. It must be remembered in this regard that this action deals with allegedly defective products used in plastic plumbing systems. The plaintiffs allege that if such fittings and piping are used in potable water plumbing systems, they will fail prematurely leading to leaks and damages consequent on such leaks. Under the settlement, Du Pont has agreed to pay a portion, namely 25%, of the costs of repairs to the systems and of damages caused by failures of the systems. It is theoretically possible that class members may view problems with the systems, if any, as being too inconsequential to bother with the settlement or they may view the steps they have to take to participate in the settlement as overwhelming the gain to be achieved through the settlement.
>
> Class counsel responds to these concerns in two ways. First, they assert that it is unfair to require class counsel to wait for the settlement to be completed particularly in a case such as this where the time frame to take up the settlement may extend for a number of years. Second,

they assert that the court has already passed on these issues by approving the settlement in the first place.

I accept that there would be an unfairness in requiring class counsel to await the completion of the settlement in order to obtain their remuneration if that required no payment being approved to class counsel. However, it seems to me that it is open to the court to approve a base level of remuneration at this stage and consider a request for additional remuneration once the take-up rate in the settlement is known, if the take-up rate would demonstrate that additional recompense is justified. For example, payment only of the value of the time spent together with the disbursements could be approved (in this case this would amount to $3 million of the $4.5 million sought) and the balance could be considered at a later stage. Indeed, it appears that just such an approach was negotiated, and approved, in *Directright Cartage Ltd. v. London Life Insurance Co.*, [2001] OJ no. 4073 (SCJ).

6. What is objectionable about the defendant agreeing to pay class counsel's fees directly, over and above the settlement amount to be paid (or made available) to class members? A defendant who offers to settle for $10 million and $2 million for class counsel's fees is really offering to settle for $12 million; by agreeing to directly pay the $2 million fee, the defendant is the one "cutting the pie" (rather than leaving it to the court to do so). Do you think a $9 million/$3 million split might be more attractive to class counsel in terms of agreeing to settle? Recall Coffee's comment in "Class Wars: The Dilemma of the Mass Tort Class Action," above:

> Collusion within the class action context essentially requires an agreement—actual or implicit— by which the defendants receive a "cheaper" than arm's-length settlement and the plaintiffs' attorneys receive in some form an above-market attorneys' fee. In return for this ... settlement, defendants either pay the plaintiffs' attorneys' fees themselves or agree not to contest the plaintiffs' attorneys' application for court-awarded fees.

D. Trial

Class proceedings legislation envisages that the issues common to the class (for example, the defendant's liability) will be determined first and the individual issues, requiring the participation of individual class members (for example, damage assessments), will be resolved subsequently and individually. It is the common-issues hearing that provides the "judicial efficiency" aspect of class action—that is, the ability of the court to decide once, for all hundred or thousand class members, the common issues—for example, was the defendant's product defective? Generally, the court is given great flexibility and may make any order it considers appropriate respecting the conduct of a class proceeding to ensure its fair and expeditious determination.

Where liability has been determined in favour of a plaintiff class, the court is given discretion as to how damages are to be assessed. Provision is made for individual proof and assessment of the damages suffered by individual class members, on a case-by-case basis, where that is appropriate: see, for example, Ontario's *Class Proceedings Act*, s. 25. However, the court is also given the power to direct an aggregate assessment of damages (that is, to make a determination, as a common issue, of the total liability of the defendant to the class members without resort to individual trial proceedings), where the underlying facts permit this to be done with an acceptable degree of accuracy.

Although the legislation affords the court broad discretion to determine the procedures and rules for resolving remaining individual issues in a class action, what seems logical in theory has not played out so simply in practice.

In *Webb v. 3584747 Canada Inc.*, [2004] OJ No. 215 (CA), the Ontario Court of Appeal set limits on the broad discretionary powers afforded to determine the procedures and rules for resolving individual issues in a manner that could have profound implications for Ontario's class actions regime. The action involved a class of former Kmart Canada employees whose employment was terminated without cause or sufficient notice. Subsequent to certification of the action at the motions court level, the defendant agreed that employees terminated without cause were entitled to reasonable notice or pay in lieu thereof. The remaining individual issues principally concerned the extent of the notice period that was owed to individual class members and whether such notice was in fact provided. The motions judge ordered that these issues be determined for Ontario class members by way of "references" to retired ADR judges, a process that ultimately proved too expensive when weighed against the relatively modest claims of individual class members. Consequently, the plaintiffs successfully brought a motion to vary the process and were granted an order directing claims for less than $25,000 to be heard in Small Claims Court, with claims for more than $25,000 to be heard by judges or masters of the Ontario Superior Court of Justice.

The defendant successfully appealed the variation of order for disposition of individual issues on the ground that, pursuant to s. 14(1) of the *Courts of Justice Act*, RSO 1990, c. C.43, only the chief justice of the Ontario Superior Court of Justice has the power to "direct and supervise the sittings of the Superior Court of Justice and the assignment of its judicial duties." More importantly, the Court of Appeal held that the power of the Ontario *Class Proceedings Act*, s. 25(1)(b) to "appoint one or more persons to conduct a reference" does not override s. 14(1) of the *Courts of Justice Act*. As the court stated:

> Clearly, the "persons" referred to in s. 25(1)(b) may include judges or judicial officers and … it would be open to a court acting under s. 25(1)(b) to appoint such a person. However, given that such an appointment falls outside the responsibilities that have historically been exercised by judges or other judicial officers, and given the potentially enormous impact of such appointments upon the deployment of judicial resources, we are of the view that a court should not appoint a judge or judicial officer to conduct a reference under s. 25(1)(b) of the *Class Proceedings Act* without first complying with the requirements of s. 14(1) of the *Courts of Justice Act* by obtaining authorization of the Chief Justice or her designate.

At first blush, the Court of Appeal's reasons in *Webb* suggest that the need to obtain authorization of the Chief Justice merely imposes an additional procedural step in securing the use of the government-funded court system for the resolution of individual issues. However, in the light of the court's stated concerns over already stretched court resources, one wonders whether the *Webb* decision does not lay a foundation for future refusal of use of the court system for resolution of individual issues on the ground of scarcity of means. Should this prove to be the case, the Court of Appeal's decision in *Webb* raises the question whether Ontario's court system is equipped to handle the additional burden of class action litigation. Does such a conclusion not severely undercut the "access to justice" purposes of class proceedings legislation articulated by the Supreme Court in *Hollick v. Toronto (City)*, [2001] 3 SCR 158 and *Western Canadian Shopping Centres Inc. v. Dutton*, [2001] 2 SCR 34?

The decision in *Caputo v. Imperial Tobacco Ltd.* (2004), 236 DLR (4th) 348 (Ont. SCJ) may be seen in the same light. In refusing to certify this tobacco class action, Winkler J stated, as one of the reasons for so doing, the following:

> [E]ven if the defendants were to only contest a portion of the individual claims, and each dispute could be concluded in one day, simple mathematics indicate that such a process would require the equivalent of 1,000 years of litigation, if it were to be conducted sequentially.

Index